HEALTH PSYCHOLOGY

EIGHTH EDITION

SHELLEY E. TAYLOR
University of California, Los Angeles

The McGraw-Hill Companies

Mc Graw Hill
Connect
Learn
Succeed™

HEALTH PSYCHOLOGY, EIGHTH EDITION
International Edition 2012

Exclusive rights by McGraw-Hill Education (Asia), for manufacture and export. This book cannot be re-exported from the country to which it is sold by McGraw-Hill. This International Edition is not to be sold or purchased in North America and contains content that is different from its North American version.

Published by McGraw-Hill, an imprint of The McGraw-Hill Companies, Inc., 1221 Avenue of the Americas, New York, NY 10020. Copyright © 2012 by The McGraw-Hill Companies, Inc. All rights reserved. Previous editions © 2009, 2006, and 2003. No part of this publication may be reproduced or distributed in any form or by any means, or stored in a database or retrieval system, without the prior written consent of The McGraw-Hill Companies, Inc., including, but not limited to, in any network or other electronic storage or transmission, or broadcast for distance learning.
Some ancillaries, including electronic and print components, may not be available to customers outside the United States.

10 09 08 07 06 05 04 03 02 01
20 15 14 13 12 11
CTP SLP

All credits appearing on page or at the end of the book are considered to be an extension of the copyright page.

When ordering this title, use ISBN 978-007-108686-8 or MHID 007-108686-2

Printed in Singapore

www.mhhe.com

SHELLEY E. TAYLOR is Distinguished Professor of Psychology at the University of California, Los Angeles. She received her Ph.D. in social psychology from Yale University. After a visiting professorship at Yale and assistant and associate professorships at Harvard University, she joined the faculty of UCLA. Her research interests concern the psychological and social factors that promote or compromise mental and physical health across the lifespan. Professor Taylor is the recipient of a number of awards—most notably, the American Psychological Association's Distinguished Scientific Contribution to Psychology Award, a 10-year Research Scientist Development Award from the National Institute of Mental Health, an Outstanding Scientific Contribution Award in Health Psychology, and election to the Institute of Medicine and the National Academies of Science. She is the author of more than 300 publications in journals and books and is the author of *Social Cognition, Social Psychology, Positive Illusions,* and *The Tending Instinct.*

CONTENTS

PART ONE

INTRODUCTION TO HEALTH PSYCHOLOGY

PART TWO

HEALTH BEHAVIOR AND PRIMARY PREVENTION

CHAPTER 5
Health-Compromising Behaviors: Alcoholism and Smoking 112

PART THREE
STRESS AND COPING

CHAPTER 6
Stress 138

PART FIVE

MANAGEMENT OF CHRONIC AND TERMINAL ILLNESS

CHAPTER 11
Management of Chronic Illness 258

CHAPTER 12
Psychological Issues in Advancing and
Terminal Illness 285

PART SIX

TOWARD THE FUTURE

When I wrote the first edition of *Health Psychology* over 30 years ago, the task was much simpler than it is now. Health psychology was a new field and was relatively small. In recent decades, the field has grown steadily, and great research advances have been made. Chief among these developments has been the use and refinement of the biopsychosocial model: the study of health issues from the standpoint of biological, psychological, and social factors acting together. Increasingly, research has attempted to identify the biological pathways by which psychosocial factors such as stress may adversely affect health and potentially protective factors such as social support may buffer the impact of stress. My goal in the eighth edition of this text is to convey this increasing sophistication of the field in a manner that makes it accessible, comprehensible, and exciting to undergraduates.

Like any science, health psychology is cumulative, building on past research advances to develop new ones. Accordingly, I have tried to present not only the fundamental contributions to the field but also the current research on these issues. Because health psychology is developing and changing so rapidly, it is essential that a text be up-to-date. Therefore, I have not only reviewed the recent research in health psychology but also obtained information about research projects that will not be available in the research literature for several years. In so doing, I am presenting a text that is both current and pointed toward the future.

A second goal is to portray health psychology appropriately as being intimately involved with the problems of our times. The aging of the population and the shift in numbers toward the later years has created unprecedented health needs to which health psychology must respond. Such efforts include the need for health promotion with this aging cohort and an understanding of the psychosocial issues that arise in response to aging and its associated chronic disorders. Because AIDS is a leading cause of death worldwide, the need for health measures such as condom use is readily apparent if we are to halt the spread of this disease. Obesity is now one of the world's leading health problems, nowhere more so than in the United States. Reversing this dire trend which threatens to shorten life expectancy worldwide is an important current goal of health psychology. Increasingly, health psychology is an international undertaking, with researchers from around the world providing insights into the problems that affect both developing and developed countries. The eighth edition includes current research that reflects the international focus of both health problems and the health research community.

Health habits lie at the origin of our most prevalent disorders, and this fact underscores more than ever the importance of modifying problematic health behaviors such as smoking and alcohol consumption. Increasingly, research documents the importance of a healthy diet, regular exercise, and weight control among other positive health habits for maintaining good health. The at-risk role has taken on more importance in prevention, as breakthroughs in genetic research have made it possible to identify genetic risks for diseases long before disease is evident. How people cope with being at risk and what interventions are appropriate for them represent important tasks for health psychology research to address.

Health psychology is both an applied field and a basic research field. Accordingly, in highlighting the accomplishments of the field, I present both the scientific progress and its important applications. Chief among these are efforts by clinical psychologists to intervene with people to treat biopsychosocial disorders, such as post-traumatic stress disorder; to help people manage health habits that have become life threatening, such as eating disorders; and to develop clinical interventions that help people better manage their chronic illnesses.

Finding the right methods and venues for modifying health continues to be a critical issue. The chapters on health promotion put particular emphasis on the most promising methods for changing health behaviors. The chapters on chronic diseases highlight how knowledge of the psychosocial causes and consequences of these disorders may be used to intervene with people at risk—first, to reduce the likelihood that such disorders will develop, and second, to deal effectively with the psychosocial issues that arise following diagnosis.

The success of any text depends ultimately on its ability to communicate the content clearly to student readers and spark interest in the field. In this eighth edition, I strive to make the material interesting and relevant to the lives of student readers. Most chapters open with a case history reflecting the experiences of college students. Others highlight news stories related to health. In addition, the presentation of material has been tied to the needs and interests of young adults. For example, the topic of stress management is tied directly to how students might manage the stresses associated with college life. The topic of problem drinking includes sections on college students' alcohol consumption and its modification. Health habits relevant to this age group—tanning, exercise, and condom use, among others—are highlighted for their relevance to the student population. By providing students with anecdotes, case histories, and specific research examples that are relevant to their own lives, they learn how important this body of knowledge is to their lives as young adults.

Health psychology is a science, and consequently, it is important to communicate not only the research itself but also some understanding of how studies were designed and why they were designed that way. The explanations of particular research methods and the theories that have guided research appear throughout the book. Important studies are described in depth so that students have a sense of the methods researchers use to make decisions about how to gather the best data on a problem or how to intervene most effectively.

Throughout the book, I have made an effort to balance general coverage of psychological concepts with coverage of specific health issues. One method of doing so is by presenting groups of chapters, with the initial chapter offering general concepts and subsequent chapters applying those concepts to specific health issues. Thus, Chapter 3 discusses general strategies of health promotion, and Chapters 4 and 5 discuss those issues with specific reference to particular health habits such as exercise, smoking, accident prevention, and weight control. Chapters 11 and 12 discuss broad issues that arise in the context of managing chronic and terminal illness. In Chapters 13 and 14, these issues are addressed concretely, with reference to specific disorders such as heart disease, cancer, and AIDS.

Rather than adopt a particular theoretical emphasis throughout the book, I have attempted to maintain a flexibility in orientation. Because health psychology is taught within all areas of psychology (for example, clinical, social, cognitive, physiological, learning, and developmental), material from each of these areas is included in the text so that it can be accommodated to the orientation of each instructor. Consequently, not all material in the book is relevant for all courses. Successive chapters of the book build on each other but do not depend on each other. Chapter 2, for example, can be used as assigned reading, or it can act as a resource for students wishing to clarify their understanding of biological concepts or learn more about a particular biological system or illness. Thus, each instructor can accommodate the use of the text to his or her needs, giving some chapters more attention than others and omitting some chapters altogether, without undermining the integrity of the presentation.

■ NEW TO THIS EDITION

The eighth edition brings a complete update to all time sensitive information in the text, tables, and figures with the most current available statistics. In addition, 280 new studies, not previously covered, have coverage in this new edition. Details of the revision by chapter follow:

Chapter 1 A new section on the history of health psychology is included under the subsection "The Need for Health Psychology". This section describes how psychologists' observations of health and health behaviors evolved from an informal field into an essential factor of the American Psychological Association, with specific inclusion in their mission statement. This chapter includes a new section on the Role of Theory and how theories influence scientific research and conclusions, as well as a new section on how neuroscience is influencing research in health psychology.

Chapter 2 This chapter includes new sections on dementia and major disorders of the cardiovascular system including ischemia and addresses the controversy surrounding genetic counseling and its value in guiding health behavior.

Chapter 3 A revised focus illuminates the emotional factors that influence health habits including the effect of fear appeals in health education, self-determination theory, cognitive behavior therapy and meditation, and emerging low-cost treatment venues including the telephone and Internet.

Chapter 4 Sections on health behaviors such as exercise, sun safety, and diet have been updated with new research that covers the positive effects of exercise on cognitive function, factors that influence sunscreen use, and the positive effects of popular diets. New research on the effects of positive expectations, stress management, weight loss, and sleep and weight management are also included in this chapter.

Chapter 5 New information on the treatment of alcohol abuse includes research on stress management techniques that can aid drinking cessation. Additional research on smoking and social groups, including friends, families, and workplace situations, has been added to the section on "Why Do People Smoke". Research on telephone support and Internet education campaigns to help people stop smoking are also new to this chapter.

Chapter 6 New research can be seen in the section "Individual Differences in Stress Reactivity and the box Can Stress Affect Pregnancy"? The box on "Post Traumatic Stress Disorder" also includes new research and a contemporary example involving an Iraq war veteran. A new box "Can an Exciting Sports Event Kill You"? describes the possible effects of viewing an exciting sporting event on individuals with cardiovascular disorders, using the World Cup match as an example.

Chapter 7 The setting of Hurricane Katrina provides examples that introduce new research in negative affectivity and its effect on general health and mortality. The section on coping resources has been revised to include updated research on conscientiousness, optimism, and pessimism and their effects on physical health and mortality.

There is a new section on Sources of Resilience which covers restorative activities that may benefit health as well as habits and coping methods to lessen an individual's response to later stress. The Coping Style section now includes information on proactive coping, an emerging area of coping research, and describes lifestyle choices that can affect an individual's resilience. Also new to this chapter: Information on the influence of social support from family, friends, and community on biological responses, health habits, and access to heath resources, as well as information on self-affirmation theory.

Chapter 8 Statistics and research on the use of health services, especially as they pertain to college students, have been updated throughout the chapter.

Chapter 9 A new box, Language Barriers to Effective Communication, describes the complications in providing effective health care when a language barrier exists between provider and patient.

Chapter 10 This chapter describes new findings from the field of neuroscience and the potential applications of these findings on the charting of pain disorders and their treatment. A new box, Headache Drawings Reflect Stress and Disability, describes how a patient's drawing can help clinicians understand their experiences of pain. Other new information in this chapter includes the early-model gate-control theory of pain and the influence of pain on emotions and vice versa, including research on anger management and the pain experience.

Chapter 11 The section on Psychotherapic Interventions has been updated with a new example of the impact of culturally sensitive intervention. The section on patient education now includes information on the efficacy of an Internet-based intervention. Additional updates include information and research relating patients' feelings of control and involvement in their care management and their quality of life.

Chapter 12 Chapter 12 includes some new statistics on assisted suicide in Oregon, the first state to pass a law permitting the practice. The chapter also includes the results of recent research on grief and its effect on immunologic functioning.

Chapter 13 This chapter contains updated research on the relationship between individuals' stress, social standing, and cardiovascular problems. The physiological effects of treated and untreated depression are discussed and supported by new research. The results of new research specific to social and familial support on patients with heart disease are included, as well as new findings about stroke treatment and recovery.

The section on Type II diabetes now covers changing methodologies and effectiveness of treatments, especially treatments that target patients' mood and physical condition. The chapter concludes with some promising research regarding lifestyle interventions that target Type II diabetes and can effectively combat this major public health problem.

Chapter 14 The focus of this chapter has broadened to cover immune-related disorders beyond AIDS, cancer, and arthritis. The discussion of Type I (childhood) diabetes has moved to this chapter and covers the causes of the disease, ways it can be managed by the patient, factors that can influence treatment adherence, special problems of adolescent diabetics, and the role the health psychologist can play in managing the disease.

New research on the relationship between stress and immune functioning has been added, specifically studies of environmental and social stressors. HIV and AIDS statistics were updated using data from the Center for Disease Control and Prevention and the CDC's recommendations regarding HIV testing and education areas. The section on the Psychosocial Impact of HIV infection includes new research on HIV/AIDS and depression. The Cognitive-Behavioral Interventions section has been thoroughly updated to include new findings on social support and interventions that have shown to help HIV/AIDS patients adhere to disease management plans and cope with the disease. The importance of social contact and social support, including couple and group therapies, in the treatment of cancer has been added. Additionally, new research is included in the Stress and Cancer section, the Psychosocial Factors section, and the Course of Cancer section.

Chapter 15 This chapter includes new statistics demonstrating recent positive effects of health psychology alongside challenges that still require study. New challenges include health disparities across socioeconomic classes, controversies surrounding genetic testing and information disclosure, the ethical use of new technologies, and the evaluation of new interventions.

■ SUPPLEMENTS

For Instructors

Online Learning Center   On the book's website, instructors will find an Instructor's Manual, PowerPoints, a Test Bank and Computerized Test Bank, and an Image Gallery with figures from the book. These materials are available on the password-protected side of the Online Learning Center (www.mhhe.com/taylorhealth8e). Contact your McGraw-Hill sales representative for access to the instructor's side of the site.

For Students

Online Learning Center   Students will find a number of study tools on the book's website: www.mhhe.com/taylorhealth8e. These include learning objectives, chapter outlines, lab exercises, study questions, the book's glossary, related publications, and web links.

■ ACKNOWLEDGMENTS

My extensive gratitude goes to Ian Boggero, Whitney Brammer, and Joelle Broffman for the many hours they put in on the manuscript. I thank my editor at McGraw-Hill, Marley Magaziner, who devoted much time and help to the preparation of the book. I also wish to thank the following reviewers who commented on all or part of the book:

Richard Contrada, *Rutgers University*
John Lu, *Concordia University*
Theodore Robles, *UCLA*
Nicholas Schwab, *University of Northern Iowa*
Alexandra Stillman, *Saint Paul College*
Benjamin Toll, *Yale University*

Shelley E. Taylor

CourseSmart eTextbooks

CourseSmart
Learn Smart. Choose Smart.

This text is available as an eTextbook from CourseSmart, a new way for faculty to find and review eTextbooks. It's also a great option for students who are interested in accessing their course materials digitally and saving money. CourseSmart offers thousands of the most commonly adopted textbooks across hundreds of courses from a wide variety of higher education publishers. It is the only place for faculty to review and compare the full text of a textbook online, providing immediate access without the environmental impact of requesting a print exam copy. At CourseSmart, students can save up to 50% off the cost of a print book, reduce their impact on the environment, and gain access to powerful web tools for learning including full text search, notes and highlighting, and email tools for sharing notes between classmates. For further details contact your sales representative or go to www.coursesmart.com.

McGraw-Hill Create
www.mcgrawhillcreate.com

Craft your teaching resources to match the way you teach! With McGraw-Hill Create you can easily rearrange chapters, combine material from other content sources, and quickly upload content you have written like your course syllabus or teaching notes. Find the content you need in Create by searching through thousands of leading McGraw-Hill textbooks. Arrange your book to fit your teaching style. Create even allows you to personalize your book's appearance by selecting the cover and adding your name, school, and course information. Order a Create book and you'll receive a complimentary print review copy in 3–5 business days or a complimentary electronic review copy (eComp) via email in about one hour. Go to www.mcgrawhillcreate.com today and register. Experience how McGraw-Hill Create empowers you to teach *your* students *your* way.

PART 1

Introduction to Health Psychology

What Is Health Psychology?

"Heart disease is a killer you can help to control" (April 5, 2010)

"Hop on a treadmill at your desk: It works" (May 21, 2007)

"Pantry Raid: Diet Makeover Doesn't Have to Be Tough" (September 28, 2009)

"A day at the beach is packed with stress relief and overall rejuvenation" (May 28, 2007)

"A supporting role in breast cancer: An author who's been there offers straight talk for men on how to help the women they love . . ." (January 10, 2005)

"Life span may be as wide as your smile" (March 29, 2010)

Every day, we see headlines about health, such as these from the *Los Angeles Times*. We are told that smoking is bad for us, that we need to exercise more, and that we've grown obese. We learn about new treatments for diseases about which we are only dimly aware, or we hear that a particular herbal remedy may make us feel better about ourselves. We are told that meditation or optimistic beliefs can keep us healthy or help us to get well more quickly. How do we make sense of all these claims, and which ones are personally important? Health psychology addresses important questions like these.

■ DEFINITION OF HEALTH PSYCHOLOGY

Health psychology is an exciting and relatively new field devoted to understanding psychological influences on how people stay healthy, why they become ill, and how they respond when they do get ill. Health psychologists both study such issues and develop interventions to help people stay well or get over illness. For example, a health psychology researcher might be interested in why people continue to smoke even though they know that smoking increases their risk of cancer and heart disease. Understanding this poor health habit leads to interventions to help people stop smoking.

Fundamental to research and practice in health psychology is the definition of health. Decades ago, a forward-looking World Health Organization defined **health** as "a complete state of physical, mental, and social well-being and not merely the absence of disease or infirmity" (World Health Organization, 1948). This definition, which was very advanced for its time, is at the core of health psychologists' conception of health.

Rather than defining health as the absence of illness, health is recognized to be an achievement involving balance among physical, mental, and social well-being. Many use the term **wellness** to refer to this optimum state of health.

Health psychology is concerned with all aspects of health and illness across the life span. Health psychologists focus on *health promotion and maintenance,* which includes such issues as how to get children to develop good health habits, how to promote regular exercise, and how to design a media campaign to get people to improve their diets.

Health psychologists also study the psychological aspects of *the prevention and treatment of illness.* A health psychologist might teach people in a high-stress occupation how to manage stress effectively so that it will not adversely affect their health. A health psychologist might work with people who are already ill to help them adjust to their illness and follow their treatment regimen.

Health psychologists also focus on *the etiology and correlates of health, illness, and dysfunction.* **Etiology** refers to the origins or causes of illness. Health psychologists focus especially on the behavioral and social factors that contribute to health, illness, and dysfunction, such as alcohol consumption, smoking, exercise, the wearing of seat belts, and ways of coping with stress.

Finally, health psychologists analyze and attempt to improve *the health care system and the formulation of health policy.* They study the impact of health institutions and health professionals on people's behavior and develop recommendations for improving health care.

In summary, health psychology examines the psychological and social factors that lead to the enhancement of health, the prevention and treatment of illness, and the evaluation and modification of health policies that influence health care.

Why Did Health Psychology Develop?

To many people, health is simply a matter of staying well or getting over illnesses quickly, states to which psychological and social factors might seem to have little to contribute. But consider some of the following puzzles that cannot be understood without the input of health psychology:

- When people are exposed to a cold virus, some get colds whereas others do not. Why?

- Men who are married live longer than men who are not. Why?

- Throughout the world, life expectancy is increasing. But in countries going through dramatic social upheaval, life expectancy can plummet. Why?

- Women live longer than men in all countries except those in which they are denied access to health care. But women are more disabled, have more illnesses, and use health services more. Why?

- Wealthier nations generally have better health care. In the United States, which has a gross national income per capita of $46,970, people can expect to live to about 78 years of age. But in Costa Rica, where the gross national income per capita is $10,950, life expectancy is exactly the same (World Health Organization, 2010). Why?

- At the beginning of the previous century, infectious diseases such as tuberculosis, pneumonia, and influenza were the major causes of illness and death. Now chronic diseases such as heart disease, cancer, and diabetes are the main causes of disability and death. Why?

- Attending a church or synagogue, praying, or otherwise tending to spiritual needs is good for your health. Why?

In this chapter, we consider why knowledge about health and health care issues has given rise to the field of health psychology. To begin, we consider how philosophers have conceived of the **mind-body relationship** and why we now regard the mind and body as inextricable influences on health. Next, we consider the dominant clinical and research model in health psychology: the biopsychosocial model. Finally, we discuss the trends in medicine, psychology, and the health care system that have contributed to the emergence of health psychology.

■ THE MIND-BODY RELATIONSHIP: A BRIEF HISTORY

Historically, philosophers have vacillated between the view that the mind and body are part of the same system and the idea that they are two separate systems. When we look at ancient history, it becomes clear that we have come full circle in our beliefs about the mind-body relationship.

During human prehistory, most cultures regarded the mind and body as intertwined. Disease was thought to arise when evil spirits entered the body, and treatment consisted primarily of attempts to exorcise these spirits. Some skulls from the Stone Age have small, symmetrical holes that are believed to have been made intentionally with sharp tools to allow the evil spirit to leave the body while the shaman performed the treatment ritual.

The ancient Greeks were among the earliest civilizations to identify the role of bodily factors in health and illness. Rather than ascribing illness to evil spirits, they developed a humoral theory of illness. According to their viewpoint, disease resulted when the four humors or circulating fluids of the body—blood, black bile, yellow bile, and phlegm—were out of balance. The goal of treatment was to restore balance among the humors. The Greeks did assign a role for the mind, however. They described personality types associated with each of the four humors, with blood being associated with a passionate temperament, black bile with sadness, yellow bile with an angry disposition, and phlegm with a laid-back approach to life. The Greeks, then, attributed disease to bodily factors but believed that psychological factors could also have an effect.

By the Middle Ages, however, the pendulum had swung back toward supernatural explanations for illness. Disease was regarded as God's punishment for evildoing, and cure often consisted of driving out the evil forces by torturing the body. Later, this form of "therapy" was replaced by penance through prayer and good works. During this time, the Church was the guardian of medical knowledge, and as a result, medical practice assumed religious overtones. The functions of the physician were typically absorbed by priests, and so healing and the practice of religion became virtually indistinguishable.

Beginning in the Renaissance and continuing into the present day, great strides have been made in understanding the technical bases of medicine. These advances include the invention of the microscope in the 1600s and the development of the science of autopsy, which allowed medical practitioners to see the organs that were implicated in different diseases. As the science of cellular pathology progressed, the humoral theory of illness was finally put to rest. As a result of scientific advances such as these, medical practice drew increasingly on laboratory findings and looked to bodily factors rather than to the mind as bases for health and illness. In an effort to break with the superstitions of the past, practitioners resisted acknowledging any role for the mind in disease processes. Instead, they focused primarily on organic and cellular pathology as a basis for their diagnoses and treatment recommendations.

Sophisticated, though not always successful, techniques for the treatment of illness were developed during the Renaissance. This woodcut from the 1570s depicts a surgeon drilling a hole in a patient's skull, with the patient's family and pets looking on.

Psychoanalytic Contributions

This view began to change with the rise of modern psychology, particularly with Sigmund Freud's (1856–1939) early work on **conversion hysteria.** According to Freud, specific unconscious conflicts can produce particular physical disturbances that symbolize repressed psychological conflicts. In conversion hysteria, the patient converts the conflict into a symptom via the voluntary nervous system; he or she then becomes relatively free of the anxiety the conflict would otherwise produce. Problems—including sudden loss of speech, hearing, or sight; tremors; muscular paralysis; and eating disorders such as anorexia nervosa and bulimia—have also been interpreted as forms of conversion hysteria. True conversion responses are now rarely seen.

Psychosomatic Medicine

Nonetheless, the idea that specific illnesses are produced by individuals' internal conflicts was perpetuated in the work of Flanders Dunbar in the 1930s (Dunbar, 1943) and Franz Alexander in the 1940s (Alexander, 1950). Unlike Freud, these researchers linked patterns of personality, rather than a single specific conflict, to specific illnesses. For example, Alexander developed a profile of the ulcer-prone personality as someone whose disorder is caused primarily by excessive needs for dependency and love.

A more important departure from Freud concerned the physiological mechanism postulated to account for the link between conflict and disorder. Whereas Freud believed that conversion reactions occur without any necessary physiological changes, Dunbar and Alexander maintained that conflicts produce anxiety, which becomes unconscious and takes a physiological toll on the body via the autonomic nervous system. The continuous physiological changes eventually produce an actual organic disturbance. In the case of the ulcer patient, for example, repressed emotions resulting from frustrated dependency and love-seeking needs were said to increase the secretion of acid in the stomach, eventually eroding the stomach lining and producing ulcers (Alexander, 1950).

Dunbar's and Alexander's work helped shape the emerging field of **psychosomatic medicine** by offering profiles of particular disorders believed to be psychosomatic in origin, that is, caused by emotional conflicts. The psychosomatic movement cordoned off a particular set of diseases as caused by psychological factors, namely ulcers, hyperthyroidism, rheumatoid arthritis, essential hypertension, neurodermatitis (a skin disorder), colitis, and bronchial asthma. As such, the range of medical problems to which psychological and social factors were deemed to apply was restricted.

We now know that all illnesses raise psychological issues. Moreover, researchers now believe that a particular conflict or personality type is not sufficient to produce illness. Rather, the onset of disease requires the interaction of a variety of factors; these include a possible genetic weakness in the organism, the presence of environmental stressors, early learning experiences and conflicts, current ongoing learning and conflicts, and individual cognitions and coping efforts.

Despite criticisms of the early psychosomatic movement, it laid the groundwork for a profound change in beliefs about the relation of the mind and the body. The mind and the body cannot be meaningfully separated in matters of health and illness.

Current Mind-Body Perspective

The renewed interest in the mind-body relationship has also been fueled by several new developments. One is the increasing attention in Western medicine to traditional East Asian medical philosophies and practices. For example, the Chinese approach to health and illness focuses on the whole person and, rather than regarding a diseased organ in isolation, considers its relations to all the body's systems. By identifying symptoms and using other diagnostic technologies, the pattern of disharmony that has resulted in illness is identified. The goal of treatment is to restore balance, which is often accomplished through treatments such as herbal remedies, acupuncture, massage, exercise, and nutrition. These insights have been increasingly incorporated into Western medical care.

The field of neuroscience has developed powerful new tools that permit glimpses into the brain as well as burgeoning knowledge of the autonomic neuroendocrine and immune systems. These developments have made it possible to connect psychosocial conditions, such as social support and positive beliefs, to underlying biology in ways that make believers out of skeptics. Neuroscience holds several of the keys to understanding the mechanisms that link psychosocial phenomena to illness outcomes (Lane et al., 2009a). The knowledge and methods of neuroscience also shed light on such questions as, how do placebos work? Why are many people felled by functional disorders that seem to have no underlying biological causes? Why is chronic pain so intractable to treatment? These and other applications of neuroscience will help to address clinical puzzles that have mystified practitioners for decades (Lane et al., 2009b).

■ THE BIOPSYCHOSOCIAL MODEL IN HEALTH PSYCHOLOGY

The idea that the mind and the body together determine health and illness logically implies a model for studying these issues. This model is called the **biopsychosocial model.** Its fundamental assumption is that health and illness are consequences of the interplay of biological, psychological, and social factors.

The Biopsychosocial Model Versus the Biomedical Model

Perhaps the best way to understand the biopsychosocial model is to contrast it with the biomedical model. The **biomedical model,** which governed the thinking of most health practitioners for the past 300 years, maintains that all illness can be explained on the basis of aberrant somatic bodily processes, such as biochemical imbalances or neurophysiological abnormalities. The biomedical model assumes that psychological and social processes are largely irrelevant to the disease process.

Although the biomedical model has undeniable benefits for studying some diseases, it has several potential liabilities. First, it is a reductionistic single-factor model. That is, it reduces illness to low-level processes, such as disordered cells and chemical imbalances, rather than recognizing the importance of more general social and psychological processes. Second, the biomedical model implicitly assumes a mind-body dualism, namely that mind and body are separate entities. Third, the biomedical model clearly emphasizes illness over health. That is, it focuses on aberrations that lead to illness rather than on the conditions that might promote health. Finally, the biomedical model fails to address common puzzles regarding health and illness. Why, for example, if six people are exposed to measles, do only three develop the disease?

Advantages of the Biopsychosocial Model

How, then, does the biopsychosocial model of health and illness overcome the disadvantages of the biomedical model? The biopsychosocial model, as noted, maintains that biological, psychological, and social factors are all important determinants of health and illness. As such, both macrolevel processes (such as the existence of social support or the presence of depression) and microlevel processes (such as cellular disorders or chemical imbalances) interact to produce a state of health or illness.

The model further maintains that the mind and body cannot be distinguished in matters of health and illness. The biopsychosocial model emphasizes both health and illness rather than regarding illness as a deviation from some steady state. From this viewpoint, health becomes something that one achieves through attention to biological, psychological, and social needs rather than something that is taken for granted.

But how do biological, social, and psychological variables interact, particularly if biological factors are microlevel processes and psychological and social factors are macrolevel processes? To address this question, researchers have adopted a **systems theory** approach to health and illness. Systems theory maintains that all levels of organization are linked to each other hierarchically and that change in any one level will effect change in all the other levels. This means that the microlevel processes (such as cellular changes) are nested within the macrolevel processes (such as societal values) and that changes on the microlevel can have macrolevel effects (and vice versa).

Clinical Implications of the Biopsychosocial Model

The biopsychosocial model has proven to be useful for clinical practice with patients as well. First, the process of diagnosis should always consider the interacting role of biological, psychological, and social factors in assessing an individual's health or illness (Oken, 2000). Therefore, an interdisciplinary team approach may be the best way to make a diagnosis (Suls & Rothman, 2004).

Second, recommendations for treatment must also involve all three sets of factors. By doing this, it should be possible to target therapy uniquely to a particular individual, consider a person's health status in total, and make treatment recommendations that can deal with more than one problem simultaneously. Again, a team approach may be most appropriate.

Third, the biopsychosocial model makes explicit the significance of the relationship between patient and practitioner. An effective patient-practitioner relationship can improve a patient's use of services, the efficacy of treatment, and the rapidity with which illness is resolved.

Finally, the biopsychosocial model maintains that the achievement and maintenance of health and the practice of health habits involve the interaction of biological, psychological, and social factors as well.

The Biopsychosocial Model: The Case History of Nightmare Deaths

To see how completely the mind and body are intertwined in matters of health, consider a case study that intrigued medical researchers for nearly 15 years. It involved the bewildering "nightmare deaths" among Southeast Asian refugees to the United States.

Following the Vietnam War, in the 1970s, a wave of immigrants from Southeast Asia, especially Laos, Vietnam, and Cambodia, came to the United States. Around 1977, the Centers for Disease Control (CDC) in Atlanta became aware of a strange phenomenon: sudden, unexpected nocturnal deaths among male refugees from these groups. These sudden deaths showed several important similarities. For example, death often occurred in the first few hours of sleep. Relatives reported that the victim began to gurgle and move about in bed restlessly. Efforts to awaken him were unsuccessful, and shortly thereafter he died. Even more mysteriously, autopsies revealed no specific cause of death.

However, most of the victims appeared to have a rare, genetically based malfunction in the heart's pacemaker. The fact that only men of particular ethnic backgrounds were affected was consistent with the potential role of a genetic factor. Also, the fact that the deaths seemed to cluster within particular families was consistent with the genetic theory. But how and why would such a defect be triggered during sleep?

As the number of cases increased, it became evident that psychological and cultural, as well as biological, factors were involved. Interviews with victims' families provided some clues. Family members reported that the victim or another close relative had often experienced a dream foretelling the death. Among the Hmong of Laos, a refugee group that was especially plagued by these nightmare deaths, dreams are taken seriously as portending the future. Anxiety due to these dreams, then, may have played a role in the deaths (Adler, 1991).

Another vital set of clues came from a few men who were resuscitated by family members. Several of them said that they had been having a severe night terror, an intensely frightening dream. One man, for example, said that his room had suddenly grown darker, and a figure like a large black dog had come to his bed and sat on his chest. He had been unable to push the dog off his chest and had become quickly and dangerously short of breath (Tobin & Friedman, 1983). This was also an important clue because night terrors are known to produce abrupt and dramatic physiologic changes.

Interviews with the survivors revealed that many of the men had been watching violent TV shows shortly before retiring, and the content of the shows appeared to have made its way into some of the frightening dreams. In other cases, the fatal event occurred immediately after a family argument. None of the men who succumbed to nightmare death had been through any identifiably traumatic event. However, many of them were said by their families to have been exhausted from combining demanding full-time jobs with a second job or with night school classes to learn English. The pressures to support their families had been taking their toll.

All these clues suggest that the pressures of adjusting to life in the United States played a role in the deaths. The victims may have been overwhelmed by cultural differences, language barriers, and difficulties finding satisfactory employment. The combination of this chronic strain, a genetic susceptibility, and an immediate trigger provided by a family argument, violent television, or a frightening dream culminated in nightmare death (Lemoine & Mougne, 1983). This intriguing phenomenon helps us see that health and illness are complex, and that the biopsychosocial model provides a useful perspective.

■ THE NEED FOR HEALTH PSYCHOLOGY

A number of trends within medicine, psychology, and the health care system have combined to make the emergence of health psychology inevitable. It is safe to say that health psychology is one of the most important developments within the field of psychology in the past 50 years.

What factors led to the development of health psychology? Since the inception of the field of psychology in the early 20th century, psychologists have made important contributions to health, developing models that explore how and why some people get ill and others do not, how people adjust to their health conditions, and what factors lead people to practice health behaviors. In response to these trends, health psychology as a field formally began in the 1970s.

In 1973, the American Psychological Association (APA) created a task force to focus on psychology's potential role in health research. Participants included counseling, clinical, and rehabilitation psychologists, many of whom were already employed in health settings. At the same time, social psychologists, developmental psychologists, and community/environmental psychologists were developing conceptual approaches for exploring health issues (Friedman & Adler, 2007; Friedman & Silver, 2007). These two groups joined forces, and in 1978, the Division of Health Psychology was formed within APA. In 1979, the first handbook appeared (Stone, Cohen, & Adler, 1979).

From the 1980s forward, the field gained momentum, so much so that in 2001, the American Psychological Association added "promoting health" as an important element of its mission statement. This addition marked a formal acknowledgment that psychology's traditional focus on behavior and mental health had broadened to include physical health as well. What other factors have fueled the growing field of health psychology?

Changing Patterns of Illness

An important factor influencing the rise of health psychology has been the change in illness patterns that has occurred in the United States and other technologically advanced societies in recent decades. As Figure 1.1 shows, until the 20th century, the major causes of illness and death in the United States were **acute disorders**—especially tuberculosis, pneumonia, and other infectious diseases. Acute disorders are short-term illnesses, often the result of a viral or bacterial invader and usually amenable to cure. Now, however, **chronic illnesses**—especially heart disease, cancer, and diabetes—are the main contributors to disability and death, particularly in industrialized countries. Chronic illnesses are slowly developing diseases with which people live for many years and that, typically, cannot be cured but rather only managed by patient and health care providers. Table 1.1 lists the main diseases worldwide at the present time. Note how the causes are projected to change over the next decade or so.

Why have chronic illnesses helped spawn the field of health psychology? First, these are diseases in which psychological and social factors are implicated as causes. For example, personal health habits, such as diet and smoking, contribute to the development of heart disease and cancer, and sexual activity is critical to the likelihood of developing AIDS (acquired immune deficiency syndrome). Consequently, health psychology has evolved, in part, to explore these causes and to develop ways to modify them.

Second, because people may live with chronic diseases for many years, psychological issues arise in connection with them. Health psychologists help chronically ill people adjust psychologically and socially to

FIGURE 1.1 | Death Rates for the 10 Leading Causes of Death per 100,000 Population, United States, 1900 and 2006

(*Sources:* Murphy, 2000; Centers for Disease Control and Prevention, April 2009)

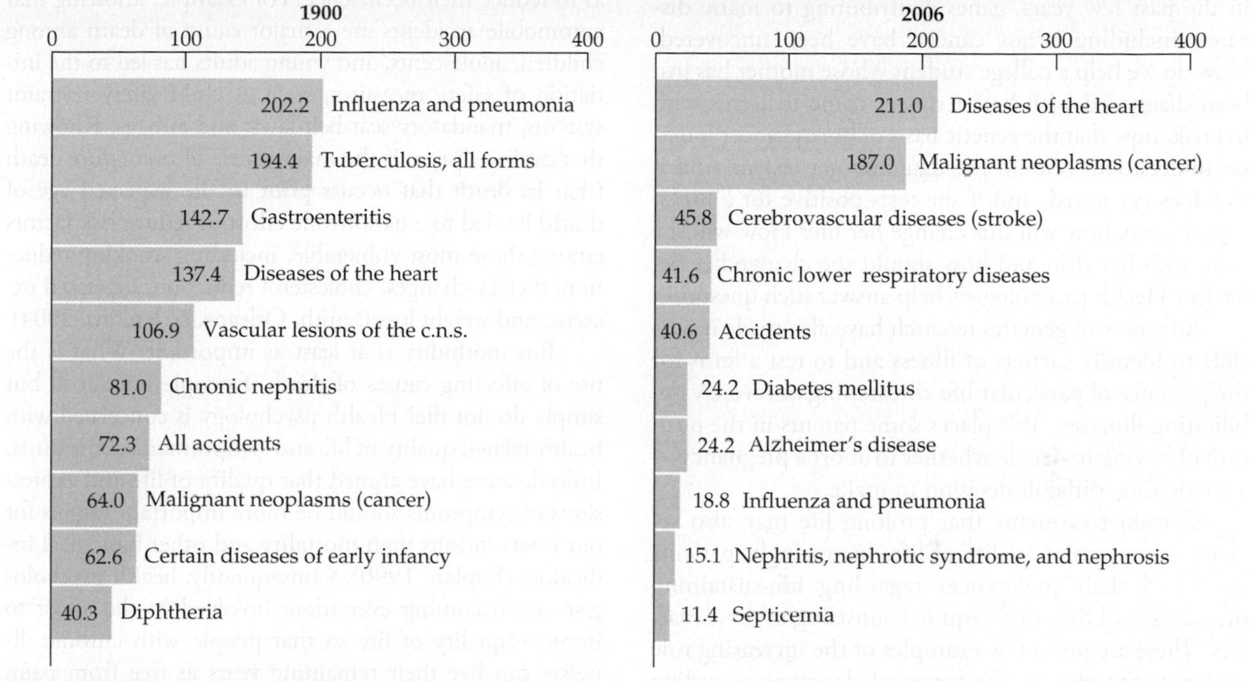

1900

Death Rate	Cause
202.2	Influenza and pneumonia
194.4	Tuberculosis, all forms
142.7	Gastroenteritis
137.4	Diseases of the heart
106.9	Vascular lesions of the c.n.s.
81.0	Chronic nephritis
72.3	All accidents
64.0	Malignant neoplasms (cancer)
62.6	Certain diseases of early infancy
40.3	Diphtheria

2006

Death Rate	Cause
211.0	Diseases of the heart
187.0	Malignant neoplasms (cancer)
45.8	Cerebrovascular diseases (stroke)
41.6	Chronic lower respiratory diseases
40.6	Accidents
24.2	Diabetes mellitus
24.2	Alzheimer's disease
18.8	Influenza and pneumonia
15.1	Nephritis, nephrotic syndrome, and nephrosis
11.4	Septicemia

their changing health state and treatment regimens, many of which involve self-care. Chronic illnesses affect family functioning, including relationships with a partner or children, and health psychologists help ease the problems in family functioning that may result.

Many people with chronic illnesses use unconventional therapies outside formal medicine. Understanding what leads people to seek unconventional treatments and evaluating their effectiveness are also issues on which health psychologists can shed light.

TABLE 1.1 | What Are the Worldwide Causes of Death?

The causes of death and disability are expected to change dramatically by the year 2020.

	1990		2020
Rank	**Disease or Injury**	**Projected Rank**	**Disease or Injury**
1	Lower respiratory infections	1	Ischemic heart disease
2	Diarrheal diseases	2	Unipolar major depression
3	Conditions arising during the perinatal period	3	Road traffic accidents
4	Unipolar major depression	4	Cerebrovascular disease
5	Ischemic heart disease	5	Chronic obstructive pulmonary disease
6	Cerebrovascular disease	6	Lower respiratory infections
7	Tuberculosis	7	Tuberculosis
8	Measles	8	War
9	Road traffic accidents	9	Diarrheal diseases
10	Congenital anomalies	10	HIV

Source: World Health Organization, 1996.

Advances in Technology and Research

The field of health psychology is also changing because of the rise of new technologies and scientific advances. Just in the past few years, genes contributing to many diseases, including breast cancer, have been uncovered. How do we help a college student whose mother has just been diagnosed with breast cancer come to terms with her risk, now that the genetic basis of breast cancer is better understood? Should the daughter get tested? And if she does get tested, and if she tests positive for a breast cancer gene, how will this change her life? How will she cope with her risk, and how should she change her behavior? Health psychologists help answer such questions.

Advances in genetics research have also made it possible to identify carriers of illness and to test a fetus for the presence of particular life-threatening or severely debilitating illnesses. This places some parents in the position of having to decide whether to abort a pregnancy—a wrenching, difficult decision to make.

Certain treatments that prolong life may also severely compromise quality of life. Increasingly, patients are asked their preferences regarding life-sustaining measures, and they may require counseling in these matters. These are just a few examples of the increasing role that patients play in fundamental decisions regarding their health and illness and its management, and of the help health psychologists can provide in this process.

The Role of Epidemiology in Health Psychology

Changing patterns of illness have been charted and followed by the field of epidemiology, a discipline closely related to health psychology in its goals and interests. **Epidemiology** is the study of the frequency, distribution, and causes of infectious and noninfectious disease in a population. For example, epidemiologists study not only who has what kind of cancer but also why some cancers are more prevalent than others in particular geographic areas or among particular groups of people.

In the context of epidemiologic statistics, we will see the frequent use of two important terms: "morbidity" and "mortality." **Morbidity** refers to the number of cases of a disease that exist at some given point in time. Morbidity may be expressed as the number of new cases (incidence) or as the total number of existing cases (prevalence). Morbidity statistics, then, tell us how many people are suffering from what kinds of illnesses at any given time. **Mortality** refers to numbers of deaths due to particular causes.

Morbidity and mortality statistics are essential to health psychologists. We need to know the major causes of disease, particularly the diseases that lead to early death, so as to reduce their occurrence. For example, knowing that automobile accidents are a major cause of death among children, adolescents, and young adults has led to the initiation of safety measures, such as child safety restraint systems, mandatory seat belt laws, and airbags. Knowing that cardiac disease is the major cause of premature death (that is, death that occurs prior to the expected age of death) has led to a nationwide effort to reduce risk factors among those most vulnerable, including smoking reduction, dietary changes, cholesterol reduction, increased exercise, and weight loss (Smith, Orleans, & Jenkins, 2004).

But morbidity is at least as important. What is the use of affecting causes of death if people remain ill but simply do not die? Health psychology is concerned with health-related quality of life and symptomatic complaints. Indeed, some have argued that quality of life and expressions of symptoms should be more important targets for our interventions than mortality and other biological indicators (Kaplan, 1990). Consequently, health psychologists are becoming ever more involved in the effort to improve quality of life so that people with chronic illnesses can live their remaining years as free from pain, disability, and lifestyle compromise as possible.

Expanded Health Care Services

Other factors contributing to the rise of health psychology involve the expansion of health care services. Health care is the largest service industry in the United States, and it is still growing rapidly. Americans spend more than $1.8 trillion annually on health care (National Center for Health Statistics, 2008). In recent years, the health care industry has come under increasing scrutiny, as massive increases in health care costs have not brought improvement in basic indicators of quality of health (Tovian, 2004).

Moreover, huge disparities exist in the United States such that some individuals enjoy the very best health care available in the world while others receive little health care except in emergencies. As of 2008, 46.3 million Americans had no health insurance at all (U.S. Census Bureau, 2009), with basic preventive care and treatment for common illnesses out of financial reach. These developments have fueled recent efforts to reform the health care system to provide all Americans with a basic health care package, similar to what already exists in most European countries.

Health psychology represents an important perspective on these issues for several reasons:

- Because containing health care costs is so important, health psychology's main emphasis on prevention—namely, modifying people's risky health behaviors before they become ill—can reduce the number of dollars devoted to the management of illness.

- Health psychologists know what makes people satisfied or dissatisfied with their health care (see Chapters 8 and 9), so they can help in the design of a user-friendly health care system.

- The health care industry employs millions of individuals in a variety of jobs. Nearly every individual in the country has direct contact with the health care system as a recipient of services. Consequently, its impact on people is enormous.

For all these reasons, then, health care delivery has a substantial social and psychological impact on people, an impact that is addressed by health psychologists.

Increased Medical Acceptance

Another reason for the development of health psychology is the increasing acceptance of health psychologists within the medical community. Although health psychologists have been employed in health settings for many years, their value is increasingly recognized by physicians and other health care professionals.

Health psychologists have developed a variety of short-term behavioral interventions to address a broad array of health-related problems, including managing pain, modifying bad health habits such as smoking, and managing the side effects of treatments. Techniques that may take a few hours to teach can produce years of benefit. Such interventions, particularly those that target risk factors such as diet or smoking, have contributed to the actual decline in the incidence of some diseases, especially coronary heart disease.

To take another example, psychologists learned many years ago that informing patients fully about the procedures and sensations involved in unpleasant medical procedures such as surgery improves their adjustment to those procedures (Janis, 1958; Johnson, 1984). As a consequence of these studies, many hospitals and other treatment centers now routinely prepare patients for such procedures. Ultimately, if a health-related discipline is to flourish, it must demonstrate a strong track record, not only as a research field but as a basis for interventions as well (Glasgow, 2008; King, Ahn, Atienza, & Kraemer, 2008). Health psychology is well on its way to fulfilling both tasks.

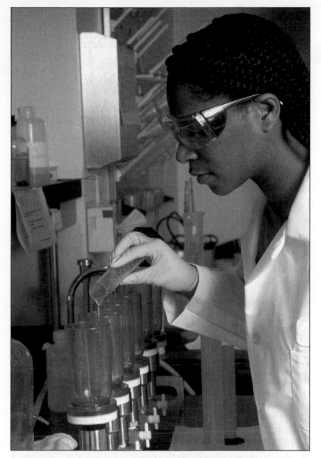

In the 19th and 20th centuries, great strides were made in the technical basis of medicine. As a result, physicians looked more and more to the medical laboratory and less to the mind as a way of understanding the onset and progression of illness.

Health Psychology Research

Health psychologists make important methodological contributions to the study of health and illness. Many issues that arise in medical settings demand rigorous research investigation. Although physicians and nurses receive some methodological and statistical education, their training is typically not sufficient to test complex, multi-level models of behavior or illness. Moreover, their practical orientation may ignore the potential that theory in health psychology has to offer. The health psychologist can be a valuable team member by providing the theoretical, methodological, and statistical expertise that is the hallmark of good training in psychology.

The Role of Theory   Although much research in health psychology is guided by practical problems, such as how to ease the transition from hospital to home care, about one-third of health psychology investigations are guided by theory (Painter, Borba, Hynes, Mays, & Glanz, 2008). A **theory** is a set of analytic statements that explain a set of phenomena, such as why people practice poor health behaviors. The best theories are simple and useful. Throughout this text, we will see references to many theories, such as the theory of planned behavior that predicts and explains when people change their health behaviors (Chapter 3) and the theory underlying cognitive behavior therapy that helps people to manage stress.

The advantages of a theory are several. Theories provide guidelines for how to do research and interventions. For example, the general principles of cognitive behavior therapy can tell one investigator what components should go into an intervention with breast cancer patients to help them cope with the aftermath of surgery, and these same principles can help a different investigator develop a weight loss intervention for obese patients. This is not to say that the two interventions would be identical, only that they would draw on the same theory for their development.

Theories generate specific predictions, and so they can be tested and modified as the evidence comes in. For example, testing theories of health behavior change revealed that people need to believe they can actually change their behavior, and so the importance of self-efficacy was incorporated into these theories. Theories help tie together loose ends. Everyone knows that smokers relapse, people go off their diets, and alcoholics have trouble remaining abstinent. A theory of relapse helps to unite these scattered observations into general principles of relapse prevention that can be incorporated into diverse interventions. A wise psychologist once said, "there is nothing so practical as a good theory" (Lewin, 1946), and we will see this wisdom borne out throughout the forthcoming chapters. We next turn to the methods by which research is conducted.

Experiments   Much research in health psychology is experimental. In an **experiment,** a researcher creates two or more conditions that differ from each other in exact and predetermined ways. People are then randomly assigned to experience these different conditions, and their reactions are measured. Experiments conducted by health care practitioners to evaluate treatments or interventions and their effectiveness over time are also called **randomized clinical trials.**

What kinds of experiments do health psychologists do? To determine if social support groups improve adjustment to cancer, cancer patients might be randomly assigned to participate in a support group or in a comparison condition, such as an educational intervention. The

patients could be evaluated at a subsequent time to pinpoint how the two groups differed in their adjustment.

Experiments have been the mainstay of science, because they typically provide more definitive answers to problems than other research methods. When we manipulate a variable and see its effects, we can establish a cause-effect relationship definitively. For this reason, experiments and randomized clinical trials have been the mainstays of health psychology research. However, sometimes it is impractical to study issues experimentally. People cannot, for example, be randomly assigned to diseases.

Correlational Studies   Other research in health psychology is **correlational research,** in which the health psychologist measures whether a change in one variable corresponds with changes in another variable. A correlational study, for example, might reveal that people who are higher in hostility have a higher risk for cardiovascular disease. The disadvantage of correlational studies is that it is usually impossible to determine the direction of causality unambiguously. For example, perhaps cardiovascular risk factors lead people to become more hostile. On the other hand, correlational studies often have advantages over experiments because they are more adaptable, enabling us to study issues when variables cannot be manipulated experimentally.

Prospective Designs   Some of the problems with correlational studies can be remedied by using a prospective design. **Prospective research** looks forward in time to see how a group of people change, or how a relationship between two variables changes over time. For example, if we were to find that hostility develops relatively early in life, but heart disease develops later, we might feel more confident that hostility is a risk factor for heart disease and recognize that the reverse direction of causality—namely, that heart disease causes hostility—is less likely.

Health psychologists conduct many prospective studies in order to understand the risk factors that relate to health conditions. We might, for example, intervene in the diet of one community and not in another and over time look at the difference in rates of heart disease. This would be an experimental prospective study. Alternatively, we might measure the diets that people create for themselves and look at changes in rates of heart disease, as determined by how good or poor the diet is. This would be an example of a correlational prospective study.

A particular type of prospective study is **longitudinal research,** in which the same people are observed over time. For example, if we wanted to know what factors are associated with early breast cancer in women at risk for it, we might follow a group of young women whose mothers developed breast cancer in an effort to identify which daughters developed breast cancer and whether there are any reliable factors associated with that development, such as diet, smoking, or alcohol consumption.

Retrospective Research   Investigators also use **retrospective research,** which looks backward in time, in an attempt to reconstruct the conditions that led to a current situation. Retrospective methods, for example, were critical in identifying the risk factors that led to the development of AIDS. Initially, researchers saw an abrupt increase in a rare cancer called Kaposi's sarcoma and observed that the men who developed this cancer often eventually died of general failure of the immune system. By taking extensive histories of the men who developed this disease, researchers were able to determine that the practice of anal-receptive sex without a condom is related to the development of the disorder. Because of retrospective studies, researchers knew some of the risk factors for AIDS even before they had identified the retrovirus.

■ WHAT IS HEALTH PSYCHOLOGY TRAINING FOR?

Students who are trained in health psychology on the undergraduate level go on to many different occupations (American Psychological Association Division 38, 2010).

Careers in Practice

Some students go into medicine, becoming physicians and nurses. Because of their experience in health psychology, they are often able to manage the social and psychological aspects of health problems better than if their education had included only training in traditional medicine. Thus, for example, they may realize that a self-care plan for a chronically ill person will be unsuccessful unless the family members are educated in the regimen. Some of these health care practitioners conduct research as well.

Other health psychology students go into the allied health professional fields, such as social work, occupational therapy, dietetics, physical therapy, or public health. Social workers in medical settings, for example, are often responsible for assessing where patients go after discharge, decisions that are informed by knowledge of the psychosocial needs of patients. A woman recovering from breast cancer surgery, for example, may need linkages to breast cancer support groups and contacts for obtaining a prosthesis. Occupational therapists are involved in the vocational and avocational retraining of the chronically ill and disabled to improve their occupational abilities and skills for daily living. Dietetics is an important field, as the role of diet in the development and management of chronic illnesses, such as cancer, heart disease, and diabetes, has become clear. Physical therapists help patients regain the use of limbs and functions that may have been compromised by illness and its treatment.

Careers in Research

Many students go on to conduct research in psychology, public health, and medicine. Public health researchers are involved in research and interventions that have the broad goal of improving the health of the general population. Public health researchers typically work in academic settings, public agencies (such as county health departments), the Centers for Disease Control, family planning clinics, the Occupational Safety and Health Administration and its state agencies, and air quality management district offices, as well as in hospitals, clinics, and other health care agencies.

In these settings, public health researchers can be responsible for a variety of tasks. They may be involved in developing educational interventions for the public to help people practice better health behaviors. They may formally evaluate programs for improving health-related practices that have already been implemented through the media and in communities. They may administer health agencies, such as clinics or health and safety offices. They may chart the progress of particular diseases, monitor health threats in the workplace and develop interventions to reduce these threats, and conduct research on health issues.

Many undergraduates in health psychology go on to graduate school in psychology, where they learn the research, teaching, and intervention skills necessary to practice health psychology. Some then become professors in university departments of psychology, where they conduct research and train new students; others work in medical schools; many are in independent practice, where they work with patients who have health-related disorders; others work in hospitals and other treatment settings; and others work in industrial or occupational health settings to promote health behavior, prevent accidents and other job-related morbidity, and control health care costs (Quick, 1999; Williams & Kohout, 1999).

The remainder of this book focuses on the kind of knowledge, training, research, and interventions that health psychologists undertake. In the last chapter, Chapter 15, information about how to pursue a career in health psychology is provided. At this point, it is useful to turn to the content of this exciting and growing field. ●

SUMMARY

1. Health psychology is devoted to understanding psychological influences on how people stay healthy, why they become ill, and how they respond when they do get ill. It focuses on health promotion and maintenance; prevention and treatment of illness; the etiology and correlates of health, illness, and dysfunction; and improvement of the health care system and the formulation of health policy.

2. The interaction of the mind and the body has concerned philosophers and scientists for centuries. Different models of the relationship have predominated at different times in history, but current emphasis is on the inextricable unity of the two.

3. The rise of health psychology can be tied to several factors, including the increase in chronic or lifestyle-related illnesses, the expanding role of health care in the economy, the realization that psychological and social factors contribute to health and illness, the demonstrated importance of psychological interventions to improving people's health, and the rigorous methodological contributions of researchers.

4. The biomedical model, which dominates medicine, is a reductionistic, single-factor model of illness that regards the mind and the body as separate entities and emphasizes illness concerns over health.

5. The biomedical model is currently being replaced by the biopsychosocial model, which regards any health or illness outcome as a complex interplay of biological, psychological, and social factors. The biopsychosocial model recognizes the importance of interacting macrolevel and microlevel processes in producing health and illness. Under this model, health is regarded as an active achievement.

6. The biopsychosocial model guides health psychologists in their research efforts to uncover factors that predict states of health and illness and in their clinical interventions with patients.

7. Health psychologists perform a variety of tasks. They develop theories, conduct research, and examine the interaction of biological, psychological, and social factors in producing health and illness. They help treat patients suffering from a variety of disorders and conduct counseling for the psychosocial problems that illness may create. They develop worksite interventions to improve employees' health habits and work in organizations as consultants to improve health and health care delivery.

KEY TERMS

acute disorders
biomedical model
biopsychosocial model
chronic illnesses
conversion hysteria
correlational research
epidemiology
etiology

experiment
health
health psychology
longitudinal research
mind-body relationship
morbidity
mortality
prospective research

psychosomatic medicine
randomized clinical trials
retrospective research
systems theory
theory
wellness

The Systems of the Body

CHAPTER OUTLINE

An understanding of health requires a working knowledge of human physiology. This knowledge makes it possible to understand such issues as how good health habits make illness less likely, how stress affects bodily functioning, how repeated stress can lead to hypertension or coronary artery disease, and how cell growth is radically altered by cancer.

Physiology is the study of the body's functioning. The body is made up of millions of cells that grouped together form tissues, which form organs whose functions overlap to produce the body's systems. In this chapter, we provide a brief overview of the major systems of the body, the ways in which each system functions normally, and some of the disorders to which the system may be vulnerable.

■ THE NERVOUS SYSTEM

Overview

The **nervous system** is a complex network of interconnected nerve fibers. Sensory nerve fibers provide input to the brain and spinal cord by carrying signals from sensory receptors; motor nerve fibers provide output from the brain or spinal cord to muscles and other organs, resulting in voluntary and involuntary movement. The nervous system is made up of the central nervous system, which consists of the brain and the spinal cord, and the peripheral nervous system, which consists of the rest of the nerves in the body, including those that connect to the brain and spinal cord.

The peripheral nervous system is, itself, made up of the somatic nervous system and the autonomic nervous system. The somatic, or voluntary, nervous system connects nerve fibers to voluntary muscles and provides the brain with feedback in the form of sensory information about voluntary movement. The autonomic, or involuntary, nervous system connects the central nervous system to all internal organs over which people do not customarily have control.

Regulation of the autonomic nervous system occurs via the sympathetic nervous system and the parasympathetic nervous system. As will be seen in Chapter 6, the **sympathetic nervous system** prepares the body to respond to emergencies, to strong emotions such as anger or fear, and to strenuous activity. As such, it plays an important role in reactions to stress. Because it is concerned with the mobilization and exertion of energy, it is called a catabolic system.

In contrast, the **parasympathetic nervous system** controls the activities of organs under normal circumstances and acts antagonistically to the sympathetic nervous system. When an emergency has passed, the parasympathetic nervous system helps to restore the body to a normal state. Because it is concerned with the conservation of body energy, it is called an anabolic system. The components of the nervous system are summarized in Figure 2.1. We now consider several of these components in greater detail.

FIGURE 2.1 | The Components of the Nervous System

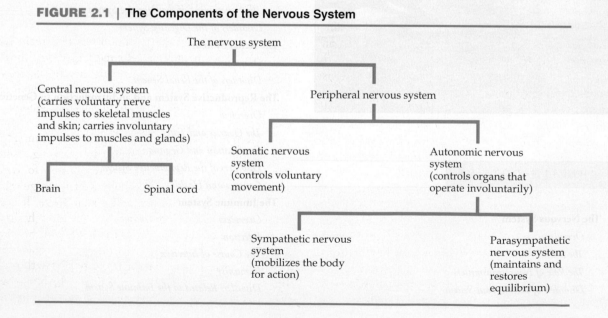

FIGURE 2.2 | The Brain

FIGURE 2.2 | The Brain

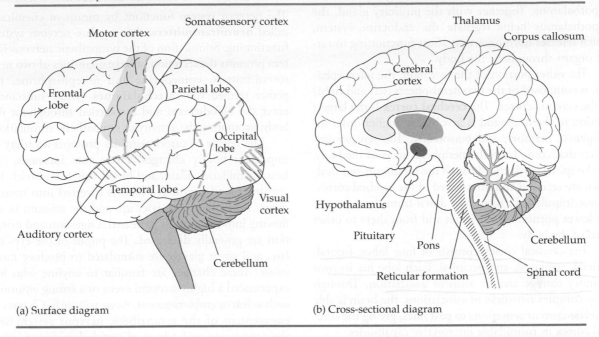

(a) Surface diagram

(b) Cross-sectional diagram

The Brain

The brain may be thought of as the command center of the body. It receives afferent (sensory) impulses from the peripheral nerve endings and sends efferent (motor) impulses to the extremities and to internal organs to carry out necessary movement. The parts of the brain are shown in Figure 2.2.

The Hindbrain and the Midbrain   The hindbrain has three main parts: the medulla, the pons, and the cerebellum. The **medulla,** located just above the point where the spinal cord enters the skull, is responsible for the regulation of heart rate, blood pressure, and respiration. The medulla receives information about the rate at which the heart is contracting and speeds up or slows down the heart rate as required. The medulla also receives sensory information about blood pressure and, based on this feedback, regulates constriction or dilation of the blood vessels. Sensory information about the levels of carbon dioxide and oxygen in the body also comes to the medulla, which, if necessary, sends motor impulses to respiratory muscles to alter the rate of breathing. The **pons** serves as a link between the hindbrain and the midbrain and also helps control respiration.

The **cerebellum** coordinates voluntary muscle movement, the maintenance of balance and equilibrium, and the maintenance of muscle tone and posture. Damage to this area makes it hard for a person to coordinate muscles; such damage can produce loss of muscle tone, tremors, and disturbances in posture or gait.

The midbrain is the major pathway for sensory and motor impulses moving between the forebrain and the hindbrain. It is also responsible for the coordination of visual and auditory reflexes.

The Forebrain   The forebrain has two main sections: the diencephalon and the telencephalon. The diencephalon is composed of the thalamus and the hypothalamus. The **thalamus** is involved in the recognition of sensory stimuli and the relay of sensory impulses to the cerebral cortex.

The **hypothalamus** helps regulate the centers in the medulla that control cardiac functioning, blood pressure, and respiration. It is also responsible for regulating water balance in the body and for regulating appetites, including hunger and sexual desire. It is an important transition center between the thoughts generated in the cerebral cortex of the brain and their impact on internal organs. For example, embarrassment can lead to blushing via the hypothalamus through the vasomotor center in the medulla to the blood vessels. Likewise, anxiety may result from secretion of hydrochloric acid in the stomach via signals from the hypothalamus. Together with the pituitary gland, the hypothalamus helps regulate the endocrine system, which releases hormones that affect functioning in target organs throughout the body.

The other portion of the forebrain, the telencephalon, is composed of the two hemispheres (left and right) of the cerebral cortex. The **cerebral cortex** is the largest portion of the brain and is involved in higher-order intelligence, memory, and personality. The sensory impulses that come from the peripheral areas of the body, up the spinal cord, and through the hindbrain and midbrain are received and interpreted in the cerebral cortex. Motor impulses, in turn, pass down from the cortex to the lower portions of the brain and from there to other parts of the body.

The cerebral cortex consists of four lobes: frontal, parietal, temporal, and occipital. Each lobe has its own memory storage area or areas of association. Through these complex networks of associations, the brain is able to relate current sensations to past ones, giving the cerebral cortex its formidable interpretive capabilities.

In addition to its role in associative memory, each lobe is generally associated with particular functions. The frontal lobe contains the motor cortex, which coordinates voluntary movement. The left part of the motor cortex controls activities of the voluntary muscles on the right side of the body, while the right part of the motor cortex controls voluntary activities on the left side of the body. The parietal lobe contains the somatosensory cortex, in which sensations of touch, pain, temperature, and pressure are registered and interpreted. The temporal lobe contains the cortical areas responsible for auditory and olfactory (smell) impulses, and the occipital lobe contains the visual cortex, which receives visual impulses. The basal ganglia—four round masses embedded deep in the cerebrum (the main portion of the brain)—help make muscle contractions orderly, smooth, and purposeful.

The Limbic System   The structures of the limbic system, which border the midline of the brain, play an important role in stress and emotional responses. The amygdala and the hippocampus are involved in the detection of threat and in emotionally charged memories, respectively. The cingulate gyrus, the septum, and areas in the hypothalamus are related to emotional functioning as well. The anterior portion of the thalamus and some nuclei within the hypothalamus are important for socially relevant behaviors.

The Role of Neurotransmitters

The nervous system functions by means of chemicals, called **neurotransmitters,** that regulate nervous system functioning. Stimulation of the sympathetic nervous system prompts the secretion of large quantities of two neurotransmitters, epinephrine and norepinephrine, together termed the **catecholamines.** These substances enter the bloodstream and are carried throughout the body, promoting the activity of sympathetic stimulation.

The release of catecholamines prompts a variety of important bodily changes. Heart rate increases, the heart's capillaries dilate, and blood vessels constrict, increasing blood pressure. Blood is diverted into muscle tissue. Respiration rate goes up, and the amount of air flowing into the lungs is increased. Digestion and urination are generally decreased. The pupils of the eyes dilate, and sweat glands are stimulated to produce more sweat. These changes are familiar to anyone who has experienced a highly stressful event or a strong emotion, such as fear or embarrassment. As we will see in Chapter 6, engagement of the sympathetic nervous system and the production and release of catecholamines are critically important in responses to stressful circumstances. Chronic or recurrent arousal of the sympathetic nervous system may have implications for the development of several chronic disorders, such as coronary artery disease and hypertension, which will be discussed in greater detail in Chapter 13.

Parasympathetic functioning is a counterregulatory system that helps restore homeostasis following sympathetic arousal. The heart rate decreases, the heart's capillaries constrict, blood vessels dilate, respiration rate decreases, and the metabolic system resumes its activities.

Disorders of the Nervous System

Approximately 25 million Americans have some disorder of the nervous system, which accounts for 20% of hospitalizations each year and 12% of deaths. The most common forms of neurological dysfunction are epilepsy and Parkinson's disease. Cerebral palsy, multiple sclerosis, and Huntington's disease also affect substantial numbers of people.

Epilepsy   A disease of the central nervous system affecting more than 3 million people in the United States (Epilepsy Foundation, 2009), epilepsy is often idiopathic, which means that no specific cause for the symptoms can be identified. Symptomatic epilepsy may be traced to injury during birth, severe injury to the head, infectious disease such as meningitis or encephalitis, or metabolic or nutritional disorders. Risk for epilepsy may also be inherited.

Epilepsy is marked by seizures, which range from barely noticeable staring or purposeless motor movements (such as chewing and lip smacking) to violent convulsions accompanied by irregular breathing, drooling, and loss of consciousness. Epilepsy cannot be cured, but it can often be controlled through medication and behavioral interventions designed to manage stress (see Chapters 7 and 11).

Cerebral Palsy

Currently, more than 764,000 people in the United States have or experience symptoms of cerebral palsy (United Cerebral Palsy, 2009). Cerebral palsy is a chronic, nonprogressive disorder marked by lack of muscle control. It stems from brain damage caused by an interruption in the brain's oxygen supply, usually during childbirth. In older children, a severe accident or physical abuse can produce the condition. Apart from being unable to control motor functions, sufferers may (but need not) also have seizures, spasms, mental retardation, difficulties of sensation and perception, and problems with sight, hearing, and/or speech.

Parkinson's Disease

Patients with Parkinson's disease have progressive degeneration of the basal ganglia, the group of nuclei that controls smooth motor coordination. The result of this deterioration is tremors, rigidity, and slowness of movement. As many as one million Americans suffer from Parkinson's disease, which primarily strikes people age 50 and older (Parkinson's Disease Foundation, 2009); men are more likely than women to develop the disease. Although the cause of Parkinson's is not fully known, depletion of the neurotransmitter dopamine may be involved. Parkinson's patients may be treated with medication, but massive doses, which can cause undesirable side effects, are often required for control of the symptoms.

Multiple Sclerosis

Approximately 400,000 Americans have multiple sclerosis, and every week about 200 more people are diagnosed (National Multiple Sclerosis Society, 2009). This degenerative disease of certain brain tissues can cause paralysis and, occasionally, blindness, deafness, and mental deterioration. Early symptoms include numbness, double vision, dragging of the feet, loss of bladder or bowel control, speech difficulties, and extreme fatigue. Symptoms

may appear and disappear over a period of years; after that, deterioration is continuous.

The effects of multiple sclerosis result from the disintegration of myelin, a fatty membrane that surrounds the nerve fibers and facilitates the conduction of nerve impulses. Multiple sclerosis is an autoimmune disorder, so-called because the immune system fails to recognize its own tissue and attacks the myelin sheath surrounding the nerves.

Huntington's Disease

A hereditary disorder of the central nervous system, Huntington's disease is characterized by chronic physical and mental deterioration. Symptoms include involuntary muscle spasms, loss of motor abilities, personality changes, and other signs of mental disintegration. Because some of the symptoms are similar to those of epilepsy, Huntington's disease is sometimes mistaken for epilepsy.

The disease affects 30,000 men and women in the United States (Huntington's Disease Society of America, 2009). The gene for Huntington's has been isolated, and a test is now available that indicates not only if one is a carrier of the gene but also at what age (roughly) one will succumb to the disease (Morell, 1993). As will be seen later in this chapter, genetic counseling with this group of at-risk individuals is important.

Polio

Poliomyelitis is a viral disease that attacks the spinal nerves and destroys the cell bodies of motor neurons so that motor impulses cannot be carried from the spinal cord outward to the peripheral nerves or muscles. Depending on the degree of damage that is done, the individual may be left with difficulties of walking and moving properly, ranging from shrunken and ineffective limbs to full paralysis. Once a scourge of childhood, polio is now on the verge of being conquered, although sufferers often experience complications late in life from polio contracted years earlier (called postpolio syndrome).

Paraplegia and Quadriplegia

Paraplegia is paralysis of the lower extremities of the body; it results from an injury to the lower portion of the spinal cord. Quadriplegia is paralysis of all four extremities and the trunk of the body; it occurs when the upper portion of the spinal cord is severed. Once the spinal cord has been severed, no motor impulses can descend to tissues below the cut, nor can sensory impulses from the tissues below the cut ascend to the brain. As a consequence, a person usually loses bladder and bowel control. Moreover, the muscles below the cut area may well lose their tone, becoming weak and flaccid.

Dementia   Dementia (meaning "deprived of mind") is a serious loss of cognitive ability beyond what might be expected from normal aging. It may be the result of a brain injury, or progressive, resulting in long-term decline due to damage or disease in the body. Although dementia is far more common in the geriatric population, it may occur at any stage of adulthood. First to be adversely affected in the process are higher mental functions, including memory, attention, language, and problem solving. The condition is normally present for at least 6 months before being diagnosed. Most such impairment cannot, at present, be reversed with treatment.

■ THE ENDOCRINE SYSTEM

Overview

The **endocrine system,** diagrammed in Figure 2.3, complements the nervous system in controlling bodily activities. The endocrine system is made up of a number of ductless glands, which secrete hormones into the blood, stimulating changes in target organs. The endocrine and nervous systems depend on each other, stimulating and inhibiting each other's activities. The nervous

FIGURE 2.3 | The Endocrine System
(*Source:* Lankford, 1979, p. 232)

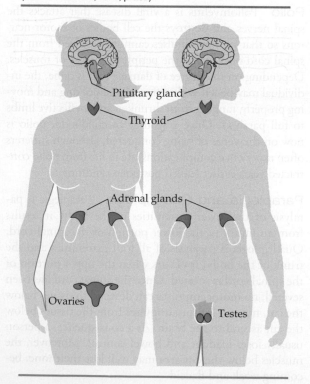

system is chiefly responsible for fast-acting, short-duration responses to changes in the body, whereas the endocrine system mainly governs slow-acting responses of long duration.

The endocrine system is regulated by the hypothalamus and the **pituitary gland.** Located at the base of the brain, the pituitary has two lobes. The posterior pituitary lobe produces oxytocin, which controls contractions during labor and lactation and may be involved in social affiliation, and vasopressin, or antidiuretic hormone (ADH), which controls the water-absorbing ability of the kidneys, among other functions. The anterior pituitary lobe of the pituitary gland secretes hormones responsible for growth: somatotropic hormone (STH), which regulates bone, muscle, and other organ development; gonadotropic hormones, which control the growth, development, and secretions of the gonads (testes and ovaries); thyrotropic hormone (TSH), which controls the growth, development, and secretion of the thyroid gland; and adrenocorticotropic hormone (ACTH), which controls the growth and secretions of the cortex region of the adrenal glands.

The Adrenal Glands

The **adrenal glands** are small glands located on top of each of the kidneys. Each adrenal gland consists of an adrenal medulla and an adrenal cortex. The hormones of the adrenal medulla are epinephrine and norepinephrine, which were described earlier.

The adrenal cortex is stimulated by adrenocorticotropic hormone (ACTH) from the anterior lobe of the pituitary, and it releases hormones called steroids, which include mineralocorticoids, glucocorticoids, androgens, and estrogens.

As Figure 2.4 implies, the adrenal glands are critically involved in physiological and neuroendocrine reactions to stress. Both catecholamines, secreted in conjunction with sympathetic arousal, and corticosteroids are implicated in biological responses to stress. We will consider these stress responses more fully in Chapter 6.

Disorders Involving the Endocrine System

Diabetes   Diabetes is a chronic endocrine disorder in which the body is not able to manufacture or properly use insulin. It is the third most common chronic illness in this country and one of the leading causes of death. Diabetes consists of two primary forms. Type I diabetes

FIGURE 2.4 | Adrenal Gland Activity in Response to Stress

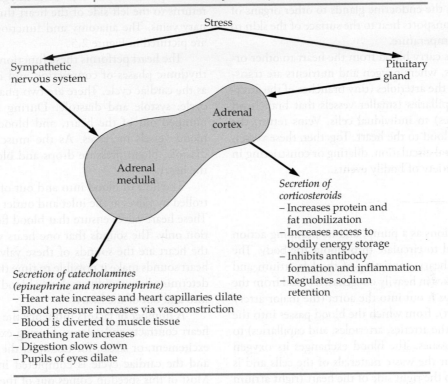

Stress

Sympathetic
nervous system

Pituitary
gland

Adrenal
cortex

Adrenal
medulla

*Secretion of
corticosteroids*
– Increases protein and
  fat mobilization
– Increases access to
  bodily energy storage
– Inhibits antibody
  formation and inflammation
– Regulates sodium
  retention

*Secretion of catecholamines
(epinephrine and norepinephrine)*
– Heart rate increases and heart capillaries dilate
– Blood pressure increases via vasoconstriction
– Blood is diverted to muscle tissue
– Breathing rate increases
– Digestion slows down
– Pupils of eyes dilate

(sometimes called insulin-dependent diabetes) is a severe disorder that typically arises in late childhood or early adolescence. At least partly genetic in origin, Type I diabetes is an autoimmune disorder, possibly precipitated by an earlier viral infection. The immune system falsely identifies cells in the islets of Langerhans in the pancreas as invaders and destroys those cells, compromising or eliminating their ability to produce insulin.

Type II diabetes, which typically occurs after age 40, is the more common form. In Type II diabetes, insulin may be produced by the body, but there may not be enough of it, or the body may not be sensitive to it. It is heavily a disease of lifestyle, involving a disturbance in glucose metabolism and the delicate balance between insulin production and insulin responsiveness. This balance appears to be dysregulated by such factors as obesity and stress, among others.

Diabetes is associated with a thickening of the arteries due to the buildup of wastes in the blood. As a consequence, diabetic patients show high rates of coronary heart disease. Diabetes is also the leading cause of blindness among adults, and it accounts for almost 50% of all the patients who require renal dialysis for kidney failure

(National Institute on Diabetes and Digestive and Kidney Diseases, 2007). Diabetes can also produce nervous system damage, leading to pain and loss of sensation. In severe cases, amputation of the extremities, such as toes and feet, is often required. As a consequence of these manifold complications, diabetics have a considerably shortened life expectancy. In later chapters, we will consider Type I (Chapter 14) and Type II (Chapter 13) diabetes, and the issues associated with their management more fully.

■ THE CARDIOVASCULAR SYSTEM

Overview

The **cardiovascular system** comprises the heart, blood vessels, and blood and acts as the transport system of the body. Blood carries oxygen from the lungs to the tissues and carbon dioxide, excreted as expired air, from the tissues to the lungs. Blood also carries nutrients from the digestive tract to the individual cells so that the cells may extract nutrients for growth and energy. The blood carries waste products from the cells to the kidneys, from which the waste is excreted in the urine. It also carries hormones from the endocrine glands to other organs of the body and transports heat to the surface of the skin to control body temperature.

The arteries carry blood from the heart to other organs and tissues, where oxygen and nutrients are transported through the arterioles (tiny branches of the arteries) and the capillaries (smaller vessels that branch off from the arteries) to individual cells. Veins return the deoxygenated blood to the heart. Together, these vessels control peripheral circulation, dilating or constricting in response to a variety of bodily events.

The Heart

The heart functions as a pump, and its pumping action causes the blood to circulate throughout the body. The left side of the heart, consisting of the left atrium and left ventricle, takes in heavily oxygenated blood from the lungs and pumps it out into the aorta (the major artery leaving the heart), from which the blood passes into the smaller vessels (the arteries, arterioles, and capillaries) to reach the cell tissues. The blood exchanges its oxygen and nutrients for the waste materials of the cells and is then returned to the right side of the heart (right atrium and right ventricle), which pumps it back to the lungs

via the pulmonary artery. Once oxygenated, the blood returns to the left side of the heart through the pulmonary veins. The anatomy and functioning of the heart are pictured in Figure 2.5.

The heart performs these functions through regular rhythmic phases of contraction and relaxation known as the cardiac cycle. There are two phases in the cardiac cycle: systole and diastole. During systole, blood is pumped out of the heart, and blood pressure in the blood vessels increases. As the muscle relaxes during diastole, blood pressure drops and blood is taken into the heart.

The flow of blood into and out of the heart is controlled by valves at the inlet and outlet of each ventricle. These heart valves ensure that blood flows in one direction only. The sounds that one hears when listening to the heart are the sounds of these valves closing. These heart sounds make it possible to time the cardiac cycle to determine how rapidly or slowly blood is being pumped into and out of the heart.

A number of factors influence the rate at which the heart contracts and relaxes. During exercise, emotional excitement, or stress, for example, the heart speeds up, and the cardiac cycle is completed in a shorter time. Most of this speedup comes out of the diastolic period, so that a chronically rapid heart rate reduces overall time

FIGURE 2.5 | The Heart

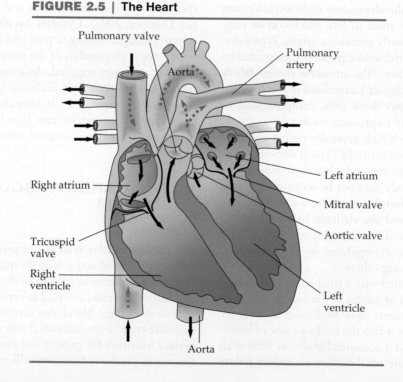

for rest. Consequently, a chronically or excessively rapid heart rate can decrease the heart's strength, which may reduce the volume of blood that is pumped.

Heart rate is also regulated by the amount of blood flowing into the veins. The larger the quantity of blood available, the harder the heart will have to pump. On the other hand, a lower supply of blood leads to a weaker and less frequent heartbeat.

Disorders of the Cardiovascular System

The cardiovascular system is subject to a number of disorders. Some of these are due to congenital defects—that is, defects present at birth—and others, to infection. By far, however, the major threats to the cardiovascular system are due to damage over the course of life that produces cumulative wear and tear. Lifestyle, in the form of diet, exercise, smoking, and stress exposure, among other factors, heavily affects the development of cardiovascular disease.

Atherosclerosis   The major cause of heart disease in this country is atherosclerosis, a problem that becomes worse with age. **Atherosclerosis** is caused by deposits of cholesterol and other substances on the arterial walls, which form plaques that narrow the arteries. The presence of atherosclerotic plaques reduces the flow of blood through the arteries and interferes with the passage of nutrients from the capillaries into the cells—a process that can lead to tissue damage. Damaged arterial walls are also potential sites for the formation of blood clots, which in themselves can completely obstruct a vessel and cut off the flow of blood.

Atherosclerosis is, in part, a disease of lifestyle, as we will see in Chapter 13. It is associated with a number of poor health habits, such as smoking and a high-fat diet. Moreover, it is a very common health problem. These two factors make it of paramount interest to health psychologists and explain the interest in changing these poor health behaviors.

Atherosclerosis is associated with several primary clinical manifestations:

- **Angina pectoris,** or chest pain, which occurs because the muscle tissue of the heart must continue its activity without a sufficient supply of oxygen or adequate removal of carbon dioxide and other waste products.
- **Myocardial infarction (MI),** which is most likely to occur when a clot has developed in a coronary

vessel and blocks the flow of blood to the heart. A myocardial infarction, also known as a heart attack, can cause death.

- Ischemia is a condition characterized by lack of blood flow and oxygen to the heart muscle. As many as 3 to 4 million Americans may have ischemic episodes without knowing it. These people have ischemia with no pain—silent ischemia—and they may consequently have a heart attack with no prior warning. People with angina also may have undiagnosed episodes of silent ischemia, as may people who have had previous heart attacks or those with diabetes.

Other major disorders of the cardiovascular system include the following.

- Congestive heart failure (CHF) occurs when the heart's delivery of oxygen rich blood to the body is inadequate to meet the body's need. Congestive heart failure can be caused by: diseases that weaken the heart muscle, diseases that cause stiffening of the heart muscles, or diseases that increase the oxygen demand beyond the capability of the heart to deliver.
- Arrhythmia refers to irregular beatings of the heart. Sudden arrhythmia death syndrome (SADS) is a disorder of the electrical system of the heart. The problem centers on the length of time it takes the electrical system to recharge following a heartbeat. This is known as the QT interval. People who have a long QT interval are more vulnerable to a very fast, abnormal heart rhythm. When this rhythm occurs, no blood is pumped out from the heart, and the brain quickly becomes deprived of blood, causing sudden loss of consciousness and sudden death.

Other vessel disorders include arteriosclerosis (or hardening of the arteries), aneurysms, phlebitis, and varicose veins. Arteriosclerosis results when calcium, salts, and scar tissue react with the elastic tissue of the arteries. The consequence is a decrease in the elasticity of the arteries, making them rigid and hard. Blood pressure then increases because the arteries cannot dilate and constrict to help blood move, and hypertension (high blood pressure) may result. An aneurysm is a bulge in a section of the wall of an artery or vein; it is the reaction of a weak region to pressure. When an aneurysm ruptures, it can produce instantaneous death from internal hemorrhaging and loss of blood pressure.

Phlebitis is an inflammation of a vein wall, often accompanied by water retention and pain. The condition typically results from an infection surrounding the vein, from varicose veins, from pregnancy-related bodily changes, or from the pressure of a tumor on the vein. The chief threat posed by phlebitis is that it can encourage the production of blood clots, which then block circulation.

Varicose veins are superficial veins that have become dilated or swollen. Typically, veins in the lower extremities of the body are most susceptible because they are subjected to great pressure from the force of gravity.

Rheumatic Fever

Rheumatic fever is a bacterial infection that originates in the connective tissue and can spread to the heart, potentially affecting the functioning of the heart valves. The flaps of the valves may be changed into rigid, thickened structures that interfere with the flow of blood between the atrium and the ventricle. People with rheumatic fever, or with congenital heart disease, are particularly vulnerable to endocarditis, the inflammation of the membrane that lines the cavities of the heart, which is caused by staphylococcus or streptococcus organisms.

Blood Pressure

Blood pressure is the force that blood exerts against the blood vessel walls. During systole, the force on the blood vessel walls is greatest; during diastole, it falls to its lowest point. The measurement of blood pressure is a ratio of these two pressures.

Blood pressure is influenced by several factors. The first is cardiac output—pressure against the arterial walls is greater as the volume of blood flow increases. A second factor influencing blood pressure is peripheral resistance, or the resistance to blood flow in the small arteries of the body (arterioles). Peripheral resistance is influenced by the viscosity (thickness) of the blood—specifically, the number of red blood cells and the amount of plasma the blood contains. Highly viscous blood produces higher blood pressure. In addition, blood pressure is influenced by the structure of the arterial walls: If the walls have been damaged, if they are clogged by deposits of waste, or if they have lost their elasticity, blood pressure will be higher. Chronically high blood pressure, called hypertension, is the consequence of too high a cardiac output or too high a peripheral resistance. We will consider the psychosocial issues involved in the management and treatment of hypertension in Chapter 13.

The Blood

An adult's body contains approximately 5 liters of blood, which consists of plasma and cells. Plasma, the fluid portion of blood, accounts for approximately 55% of the blood volume. The blood cells are suspended in the plasma, which contains plasma proteins and plasma electrolytes (salts) plus the substances that are being transported by the blood (oxygen and nutrients or carbon dioxide and waste materials). The remaining 45% of blood volume is made up of cells.

Blood cells are manufactured in the bone marrow, the substance in the hollow cavities of bones. Bone marrow contains five types of blood-forming cells: myeloblasts and monoblasts, both of which produce particular white blood cells; lymphoblasts, which produce lymphocytes; erythroblasts, which produce red blood cells; and megakaryocytes, which produce platelets. Each of these types of blood cells has an important function.

White blood cells play an important role in healing by absorbing and removing foreign substances from the body. They contain granules that secrete digestive enzymes, which engulf and act on bacteria and other foreign particles, turning them into a form conducive to excretion. An elevated white cell count suggests the presence of infection.

Lymphocytes also play an important role in combating foreign substances. They produce antibodies—agents that destroy foreign substances through the antigen-antibody reaction. Together, these groups of cells play an important role in fighting infection and disease. We will consider them more fully in our discussion of the immune system.

Red blood cells are important mainly because they contain hemoglobin, which is needed to carry oxygen and carbon dioxide throughout the body.

Platelets serve several important functions. They clump together to block small holes that develop in blood vessels, and they also play an important role in blood clotting. When an injury occurs and tissues are damaged, platelets help form thromboplastin, which, in turn, acts on a substance in the plasma known as fibrinogen, changing it to fibrin. The formation of fibrin produces clotting.

Blood flow is responsible for the regulation of body temperature. When body temperature is too high, skin blood vessels dilate and blood is sent to the skin, so that heat will be lost. When body temperature is too low, skin blood vessels constrict and blood is kept away from the skin so that heat will be conserved and body temperature maintained. Alterations in skin blood flow are caused partly by the direct action of heat on skin blood vessels and partly by the temperature-regulating mechanism located in the hypothalamus, which alters the sympathetic impact on the surface blood vessels. Blood flow to the skin is also regulated by the catecholamines—epinephrine and norepinephrine. Norepinephrine generally constricts blood vessels (vasoconstriction), whereas epinephrine constricts skin blood vessels while dilating muscle blood vessels. These changes, in turn, increase the force of the heart's contractions.

Disorders Related to White Cell Production

Some blood disorders affect the production of white blood cells; they include leukemia, leukopenia, and leukocytosis. Leukemia is a disease of the bone marrow, and it is a common form of cancer. It causes the production of an excessive number of white blood cells, thus overloading the blood plasma and reducing the number of red blood cells that can circulate in the plasma. In the short term, anemia (a shortage of red blood cells) will result. In the long term, if left untreated, leukemia will cause death.

Leukopenia is a deficiency of white blood cells; it may accompany such diseases as tuberculosis, measles, and viral pneumonia. Leukopenia leaves an individual susceptible to disease because it reduces the number of white blood cells available to combat infection.

Leukocytosis is an excessive number of white blood cells. It is a response to many infections, such as leukemia, appendicitis, and infectious mononucleosis. Infection stimulates the body to overproduce these infection-combating cells.

Disorders Related to Red Cell Production

Anemia is a condition in which the number of red blood cells or amount of hemoglobin is below normal. A temporary anemic condition experienced by many women is a consequence of menstruation; through loss of blood, much vital iron (essential for the production of hemoglobin) is lost. Iron supplements must sometimes be taken to offset this problem. Other forms of anemia, including aplastic anemia, may occur because the bone marrow is unable to produce a sufficient number of red blood cells. The result is a decrease in the blood's transport capabilities, causing tissues to receive too little oxygen and to be left with too much carbon dioxide. When it is not checked, anemia can cause permanent damage to the nervous system and produce chronic weakness.

Erythrocytosis is characterized by an excess of red blood cells. It may result from a lack of oxygen in the tissues or be a secondary manifestation of other diseases. Erythrocytosis increases the viscosity of the blood and reduces the rate of blood flow.

Sickle-cell anemia is another disease related to red blood cell production. Most common among Blacks, it is a genetically transmitted inability to produce normal red blood cells. These cells are sickle-shaped instead of flattened spheres, and they contain abnormal hemoglobin protein molecules. They are vulnerable to rupture, leaving the individual susceptible to anemia. The sickle cell appears to be a genetic adaptation promoting resistance to malaria among African Blacks. Unfortunately, although these cells are effective in the short term against malaria, the long-term implications are life threatening.

Clotting Disorders   A third group of blood disorders involves clotting dysfunctions. Hemophilia affects individuals who are unable to produce thromboplastin and fibrin. Therefore, their blood cannot clot naturally in response to injury, and they may bleed to death unless they receive medication.

As noted earlier, clots (or thromboses) may sometimes develop in the blood vessels. This is most likely to occur if arterial or venous walls have been damaged or roughened because of the buildup of cholesterol. Platelets then adhere to the roughened area, leading to the formation of a clot. A clot formed in this manner may have serious consequences if it occurs in the blood vessels leading to the heart (coronary thrombosis) or brain (cerebral thrombosis), because it will block the vital flow of blood to these organs. When a clot occurs in a vein, it may become detached and form an embolus, which may finally become lodged in the blood vessels to the lungs, causing pulmonary obstruction. Death is a likely consequence of these conditions.

■ THE RESPIRATORY SYSTEM

Overview

Respiration, or breathing, has three main functions: to take in oxygen, to excrete carbon dioxide, and to regulate the composition of the blood.

The body needs oxygen to metabolize food. During the process of metabolism, oxygen combines with carbon atoms in food, producing carbon dioxide (CO_2). The respiratory system brings in air, most notably oxygen, through inspiration; it eliminates carbon dioxide through expiration.

The Structure and Functions of the Respiratory System

The **respiratory system** involves a number of organs, including the nose, mouth, pharynx, trachea, diaphragm, abdominal muscles, and lungs. Air is inhaled through the nose and mouth and then passes through the pharynx and larynx to the trachea. The trachea, a muscular tube extending downward from the larynx, divides at its lower end into two branches called the primary bronchi. Each bronchus enters a lung, where it then subdivides into secondary bronchi, still-smaller bronchioles, and, finally, microscopic alveolar ducts, which contain many tiny, clustered sacs called alveoli. The alveoli and the capillaries are responsible for the exchange of oxygen and carbon dioxide. A diagram of the respiratory system appears in Figure 2.6.

The inspiration of air is an active process, brought about by the contraction of muscles. Inspiration causes the lungs to expand inside the thorax (the chest wall). Expiration, in contrast, is a passive function, brought about by the relaxation of the lungs, which reduces the volume of the lungs within the thorax. The lungs fill most of the space within the thorax, called the thoracic cavity, and are very elastic, depending on the thoracic walls for support. Therefore, if air gets into the space between the thoracic wall and the lungs, one or both lungs will collapse.

Respiratory movements are controlled by a respiratory center in the medulla of the brain. The functions of this center depend partly on the chemical composition of the blood. For example, if the blood's carbon dioxide level rises too high, the respiratory center will be stimulated and respiration will be increased. If the carbon dioxide level falls too low, the respiratory center will slow down until the carbon dioxide level is back to normal.

The respiratory system is also responsible for coughing. Dust and other foreign material is inhaled with every breath. Some of these substances are trapped in the mucus of the nose and the air passages and are then conducted back toward the throat, where they are swallowed. When a large amount of mucus collects in the large airways, it is removed by coughing (a forced expiratory effort).

Disorders of the Respiratory System

Hay Fever   Hay fever is a seasonal allergic reaction to foreign bodies—including pollens, dust, and other airborne allergens—that enter the lungs. These irritants prompt the body to produce substances called histamines, which cause the capillaries of the lungs to become inflamed and to release large amounts of fluid. The result is violent sneezing among other symptoms.

FIGURE 2.6 | The Respiratory System   (*Source:* Lankford, 1979, p. 467)

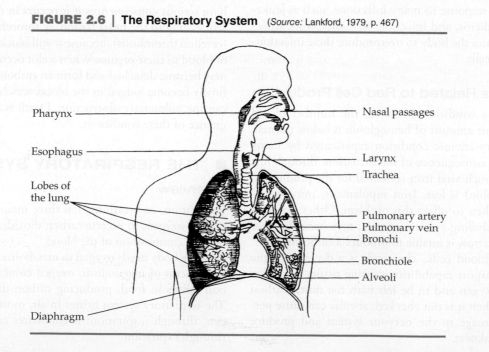

Pharynx

Esophagus

Lobes of the lung

Diaphragm

Nasal passages

Larynx

Trachea

Pulmonary artery
Pulmonary vein
Bronchi

Bronchiole

Alveoli

Asthma   Asthma is a more severe allergic reaction that can be caused by a variety of foreign substances, including dust, dog or cat dander, pollens, and fungi. An asthma attack can also be touched off by emotional stress or exercise (Kullowatz et al., 2008). These attacks may be so serious that they produce bronchial spasms and hyperventilation.

During an asthma attack, the muscles surrounding air tubes constrict, inflammation and swelling of the lining of the air tubes may occur, and increased mucus is produced, clogging the air tubes. The mucus secretion, in turn, may then obstruct the bronchioles, reducing the supply of oxygen and increasing the amount of carbon dioxide.

Statistics show a dramatic increase in the prevalence of allergic disorders, including asthma, in the past 20–30 years. Currently, approximately 300 million people worldwide have asthma, 34 million of them in the United States (World Health Organization, 2008). The numbers are increasing, especially in industrialized countries and in urban as opposed to rural areas. The reasons for these dramatic changes are not yet fully known. Children who have a lot of childhood infectious diseases are less likely to develop allergies, suggesting that exposure to infectious agents plays a protective role against developing allergies. Thus, paradoxically, the improved hygiene of industrialized countries may actually be contributing to the high rates of allergic disorders currently seen (Yazdanbakhsh, Kremsner, & van Ree, 2002).

Viral Infections   The respiratory system is vulnerable to a number of infections and chronic disorders. Perhaps the most familiar of these is the common cold, a viral infection of the upper and sometimes the lower respiratory tract. The infection that results causes discomfort, congestion, and excessive secretion of mucus. The incubation period for a cold—that is, the time between exposure to the virus and onset of symptoms—is 12–72 hours, and the typical duration of a cold is a few days. Secondary bacterial infections may complicate the illness. These occur because the primary viral infection causes inflammation of the mucous membranes, reducing their ability to prevent secondary infection.

A more serious viral infection of the respiratory system is influenza, which can occur in epidemic form. Flu viruses attack the lining of the respiratory tract, killing healthy cells. Fever and inflammation of the respiratory tract may result. A common complication is a secondary bacterial infection, such as pneumonia.

A third infection, bronchitis, is an inflammation of the mucosal membrane inside the bronchi of the lungs. Large amounts of mucus are produced in bronchitis, leading to persistent coughing.

Bacterial Infections   The respiratory system is also vulnerable to bacterial attack by, for example, strep throat, whooping cough, and diphtheria. Strep throat, an infection of the throat and soft palate, is characterized by edema (swelling) and reddening.

Whooping cough invades the upper respiratory tract and moves down to the trachea and bronchi. The associated bacterial growth leads to the production of a viscous fluid, which the body attempts to expel through violent coughing. Although diphtheria is an infection of the upper respiratory tract, its bacterial organisms secrete a toxic substance that is absorbed by the blood and is thus circulated throughout the body. Therefore, this disease can damage nerves, cardiac muscle, kidneys, and the adrenal cortex.

For the most part, strep throat, whooping cough, and diphtheria do not cause permanent damage to the upper respiratory tract. Their main danger is the possibility of secondary infection, which results from lowered resistance. However, these bacterial infections can cause permanent damage to other tissues, including heart tissue.

Chronic Obstructive Pulmonary Disease
Chronic obstructive pulmonary disease (COPD) is the fourth-leading killer of people in the United States. Some 16 million Americans have COPD (COPD International, 2008), and although lung cancer is deadlier, COPD is much more common and nearly as deadly (Lemonick, 2004). Chronic bronchitis and emphysema are two of the familiar disorders comprised in COPD.

Pulmonary emphysema involves a persistent obstruction of the flow of air. It occurs when the alveoli become dilated, atrophied, and thin, so that they lose their elasticity and cannot constrict during exhalation. As a result, exhalation becomes difficult and forced, so that carbon dioxide is not readily eliminated. Emphysema is caused by a variety of factors, including long-term smoking.

Although COPD is not curable, it is highly preventable. Its chief cause is smoking, which accounts for over 80% of all cases of COPD (COPD International, 2008). Specifically, exposure to toxic substances over a long period leads to inflammation and swelling of the cells lining the lungs. In COPD, this swelling is to a point that it restricts the flow of air, thus sapping energy (Lemonick, 2004).

Pneumonia

There are two main types of pneumonia. Lobar pneumonia is a primary infection of the entire lobe of a lung. The alveoli become inflamed, and the normal oxygen–carbon dioxide exchange between the blood and alveoli can be disrupted. Spread of infection to other organs is also likely.

Bronchial pneumonia, which is confined to the bronchi, is typically a secondary infection that may occur as a complication of other disorders, such as a severe cold or flu. It is not as serious as lobar pneumonia.

Tuberculosis and Pleurisy

Tuberculosis is an infectious disease caused by bacteria that invade lung tissue. When the invading bacilli are surrounded by macrophages (white blood cells of a particular type), they form a clump called a tubercle, which is the typical manifestation of this disease. Eventually, through a process called caseation, the center of the tubercle turns into a cheesy mass, which can produce cavities in the lung. Such cavities, in turn, can give rise to permanent scar tissue, causing chronic difficulties in oxygen and carbon dioxide exchange between the blood and the alveoli.

Pleurisy is an inflammation of the pleura, the membrane that surrounds the organs in the thoracic cavity. The inflammation, which produces a sticky fluid, is usually a consequence of pneumonia or tuberculosis and can be extremely painful.

Lung Cancer

Lung cancer is a disease of uncontrolled cell growth in tissues of the lung. The affected cells in the lungs begin to divide in a rapid and unrestricted manner, producing a tumor. Malignant cells grow faster than healthy cells. This growth may lead to metastasis, which is the invasion of adjacent tissue and infiltration beyond the lungs. The vast majority of primary lung cancers are carcinomas of the lung, derived from epithelial cells. The most common symptoms are shortness of breath, coughing (including coughing up blood), and weight loss.

The main types of lung cancer are small cell lung carcinoma and non-small cell lung carcinoma. This distinction is important because the treatment varies; non-small cell lung carcinoma is sometimes treated with surgery, while small cell lung carcinoma usually responds better to chemotherapy and radiation. The most common cause of lung cancer is long-term exposure to tobacco smoke. The occurrence of lung cancer in non-smokers, who account for as many as 15% of cases, can be attributed to a combination of genetic factors, radon gas, asbestos, and air pollution, including secondhand smoke and cancer-causing substances encountered in the workplace. Recognition of the underlying causes has led to changes (such as reduced rates of smoking and emissions legislation), and as a result, lung cancer is on the decline.

Dealing with Respiratory Disorders

A number of respiratory disorders are tied directly to health problems that can be addressed by health psychologists. For example, smoking is implicated in both pulmonary emphysema and lung cancer. The spread of tuberculosis can be reduced by encouraging people at risk to have regular chest X rays. Faulty methods of infection control, dangerous substances in the workplace, and air pollution are also factors that contribute to the incidence of respiratory problems.

As we will see in Chapters 3–5, health psychologists have conducted research on many of these problems and discussed the clinical issues they raise. Some respiratory disorders are chronic conditions with which an individual may live for some time. Consequently, issues of long-term physical, vocational, social, and psychological rehabilitation become crucial, and we will cover these issues in Chapters 11, 13, and 14.

■ THE DIGESTIVE SYSTEM AND THE METABOLISM OF FOOD

Overview

Food, essential for survival, is converted through the process of metabolism into heat and energy, and it supplies nutrients for growth and the repair of tissues. But before food can be used by cells, it must be changed into a form suitable for absorption into the blood. This conversion process is called digestion.

The Functioning of the Digestive System

Food is first lubricated by saliva in the mouth, where it forms a soft, rounded lump called a bolus. It passes through the esophagus by means of peristalsis, a unidirectional muscular movement toward the stomach. The stomach produces various gastric secretions, including pepsin and hydrochloric acid, to further the digestive process. The sight or even the thought of food starts the flow of gastric juices.

As food progresses from the stomach to the duodenum (the intersection of the stomach and lower intestine), the pancreas becomes involved in the digestive process. Pancreatic juices, which are secreted into the duodenum, contain several enzymes that break down proteins, carbohydrates, and fats. A critical function of the pancreas is the production of the hormone insulin, which facilitates the entry of glucose into the bodily tissues. The liver also plays an important role in metabolism by producing bile, which enters the duodenum and helps break down fats. Bile is stored in the gallbladder and is secreted into the duodenum as needed.

Most metabolic products are water soluble and can be easily transported in the blood. However, other substances are not soluble in water and so must be transported in the blood plasma as complex substances combined with plasma protein. Known as lipids, these substances include fats, cholesterol, and lecithin. An excess of lipids in the blood is called hyperlipidemia, a condition common in diabetes, some kidney diseases, hyperthyroidism, and alcoholism. It is also a causal factor in the development of heart disease (see Chapters 4 and 13).

The absorption of food takes place primarily in the small intestine, which produces enzymes that complete the breakdown of proteins to amino acids. The motility of the small intestine is under the control of the sympathetic and parasympathetic nervous systems, such that parasympathetic activity speeds up metabolism, whereas sympathetic nervous system activity reduces it.

Food then passes into the large intestine (whose successive segments are known as the cecum and the ascending, transverse, descending, and sigmoid colon), which acts largely as a storage organ for the accumulation of food residue and helps in the reabsorption of water. The entry of feces into the rectum then brings about the urge to defecate, or expel the solid waste from the body via the anus. The organs involved in the metabolism of food are pictured in Figure 2.7.

Disorders of the Digestive System

The digestive system is susceptible to a number of disorders, some of which are only mildly uncomfortable and temporary, and others of which are more serious and chronic.

Gastroesophageal reflux disease Gastroesophageal reflux disease (GERD), also known as gastric reflux disease or acid reflux disease, involves chronic symptoms or mucosal damage produced by the abnormal reflux in the esophagus. This is commonly due to changes in the barrier between the esophagus and the stomach. This can be due to incompetence of the lower esophageal sphincter, transient lower esophageal

FIGURE 2.7 | The Digestive System
(*Source:* Lankford, 1979, p. 523)

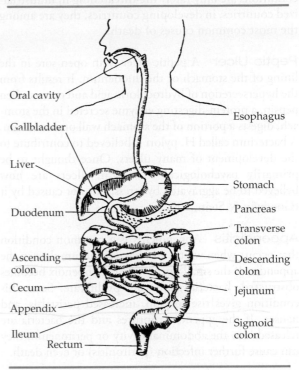

sphincter relaxation, impaired expulsion of gastric reflux from the esophagus, or a hiatal hernia. As much as one-third of the U.S. adult population experiences acid reflux at least occasionally (Locke, 2010).

Gastroenteritis, Diarrhea, and Dysentery

Gastroenteritis is an inflammation of the lining of the stomach and small intestine. It may be caused by such factors as excessive amounts of food or drink, contaminated food or water, or food poisoning. Symptoms appear approximately 2–4 hours after the ingestion of food; they include vomiting, diarrhea, abdominal cramps, and nausea.

Diarrhea, characterized by watery and frequent bowel movements, occurs when the lining of the small and large intestines cannot properly absorb water or digested food. Chronic diarrhea may result in serious disturbances of fluid and electrolyte (sodium, potassium, magnesium, calcium) balance.

Dysentery is similar to diarrhea except that mucus, pus, and blood are also excreted. It may be caused by a protozoan that attacks the large intestine (amoebic dysentery) or by a bacterial organism. Although these conditions are only rarely life threatening in industrialized countries, in developing countries, they are among the most common causes of death.

Peptic Ulcer

A peptic ulcer is an open sore in the lining of the stomach or the duodenum. It results from the hypersecretion of hydrochloric acid and occurs when pepsin, a protein-digesting enzyme secreted in the stomach, digests a portion of the stomach wall or duodenum. A bacterium called H. pylori is believed to contribute to the development of many ulcers. Once thought to be primarily psychological in origin, ulcers are now believed to be aggravated by stress, but not caused by it (Goodwin & Stein, 2002).

Appendicitis

Appendicitis is a common condition that occurs when wastes and bacteria accumulate in the appendix. If the small opening of the appendix becomes obstructed, bacteria can easily proliferate. Soon this condition gives rise to pain, increased peristalsis, and nausea. If the appendix ruptures and the bacteria are released into the abdominal cavity or peritoneum, they can cause further infection (peritonitis) or even death.

Hepatitis

A common, serious, contagious disease that attacks the liver is hepatitis. *Hepatitis* means "inflammation of the liver," and the disease produces swelling, tenderness, and sometimes permanent damage. When the liver is inflamed, bilirubin, a product of the breakdown of hemoglobin, cannot easily pass into the bile ducts. Consequently, it remains in the blood, causing a yellowing of the skin known as jaundice. Other common symptoms are fatigue, fever, muscle or joint aches, nausea, vomiting, loss of appetite, abdominal pain, and sometimes diarrhea.

There are several types of hepatitis, which differ in severity and mode of transmission. Hepatitis A, caused by viruses, is typically transmitted through food and water. It is often spread by poorly cooked seafood or through unsanitary preparation or storage of food. Hepatitis B is a more serious form, with more than 350 million carriers in the world and 1.25 million in the United States alone (Centers for Disease Control and Prevention, July 2008a). Also known as serum hepatitis, it is caused by a virus and is transmitted by the transfusion of infected blood, by improperly sterilized needles, through sexual contact, and through mother-to-infant contact. It is a special risk among intravenous drug users. Its symptoms are similar to those of hepatitis A but are far more serious. At present,

hepatitis B is a particular risk for people of Asian descent. They are 20–30 times more likely to be infected than any other group in the United States (Gottlieb & Yi, 2003, April 28). Overall, the prevalence of hepatitis A and B has begun to decline (McQuillan, Kruszon-Moran, Denniston, & Hirsch, 2010).

Hepatitis C, also spread via blood and needles, is most commonly caused by blood transfusions; more than 3 million people in the United States are infected (Centers for Disease Control and Prevention, June 2008a). Hepatitis D is found mainly in intravenous drug users who are also carriers of hepatitis B, necessary for the hepatitis D virus to spread. Finally, hepatitis E resembles hepatitis A but is caused by a different virus (Centers for Disease Control and Prevention, December 2006).

■ THE RENAL SYSTEM

Overview

The **renal system**—consisting of the kidneys, ureters, urinary bladder, and urethra—is also critically important in metabolism. The kidneys are chiefly responsible for the regulation of bodily fluids; their principal function is to produce urine. The ureters contain smooth muscle tissue, which contracts, causing peristaltic waves to move urine to the bladder, a muscular bag that acts as a reservoir for urine. The urethra then conducts urine from the bladder out of the body. The anatomy of the renal system is pictured in Figure 2.8.

FIGURE 2.8 | The Renal System
(*Source:* Lankford, 1979, p. 585)

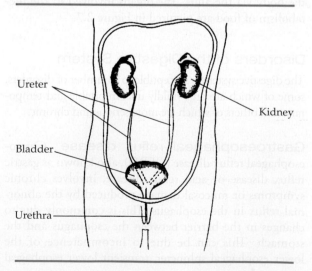

Urine contains surplus water, surplus electrolytes, waste products from the metabolism of food, and surplus acids or alkalis. By carrying these products out of the body, urine maintains water balance, electrolyte balance, and blood pH. Of the electrolytes, sodium and potassium are especially important because they are involved in the normal chemical reactions of the body, muscular contractions, and the conduction of nerve impulses. Thus, an important function of the kidneys is to maintain an adequate balance of sodium and potassium ions.

In the case of certain diseases, the urine also contains abnormal amounts of some constituents; therefore, urinalysis offers important diagnostic clues to many disorders. For example, an excess of glucose may indicate diabetes, and an excess of red blood cells may indicate a kidney disorder. This is one of the reasons that a medical checkup usually includes a urinalysis.

One of the chief functions of the kidneys is to control the water balance in the body. For example, on a hot day, when a person has been active and has perspired profusely, relatively little urine will be produced so that the body may retain more water. This is because much water has already been lost through the skin. On the other hand, on a cold day, when a person is relatively inactive or has consumed a good deal of liquid, urine output will be higher so as to prevent overhydration.

To summarize, the urinary system regulates bodily fluids by removing surplus water, surplus electrolytes, and the waste products generated by the metabolism of food.

Disorders of the Renal System *Kidneys*

The renal system is vulnerable to a number of disorders. Among the most common are urinary tract infections, to which women are especially vulnerable and which can result in considerable pain, especially on urination. If untreated, they can lead to more serious infection.

Nephrons are the basic structural and functional units of the kidneys. In many types of kidney disease, such as that associated with hypertension, large numbers of nephrons are destroyed or damaged so severely that the remaining nephrons cannot perform their normal functions.

Acute glomerular nephritis is a disease that results from an antigen-antibody reaction in which the glomeruli of the kidneys become markedly inflamed. These inflammatory reactions can cause total or partial blockage of a large number of glomeruli, which may lead to increased permeability of the glomerular membrane, allowing large amounts of protein to leak in. When

there is rupture of the membrane, large numbers of red blood cells may also pass into the glomerular filtrate. In severe cases, total renal shutdown occurs. Acute glomerular nephritis is usually a secondary response to a streptococcus infection. This infection usually subsides within 2 weeks.

Another common cause of acute renal shutdown is tubular necrosis, which involves destruction of the epithelial cells in the tubules of the kidneys. Poisons that destroy the tubular epithelial cells and severe circulatory shock are the most common causes of tubular necrosis.

Kidney failure is a severe disorder because the inability to produce an adequate amount of urine will cause the waste products of metabolism, as well as surplus inorganic salts and water, to be retained in the body. An artificial kidney, a kidney transplant, or **kidney dialysis** may be required in order to rid the body of its wastes. Although these technologies can cleanse the blood to remove the excess salts, water, and metabolites, they are highly stressful medical procedures. Kidney transplants carry many health risks, and kidney dialysis can be extremely uncomfortable for patients. Consequently, health psychologists have been involved in addressing the problems experienced by kidney patients.

■ THE REPRODUCTIVE SYSTEM AND AN INTRODUCTION TO GENETICS

Overview

The development of the reproductive system is controlled by the pituitary gland. The anterior pituitary lobe produces the gonadotropic hormones, which control development of the ovaries in females and the testes in males. A diagrammatic representation of the human reproductive system appears in Figure 2.9.

The Ovaries and Testes

The female has two ovaries located in the pelvis. Each month, one of the ovaries produces an ovum (egg), which is discharged at ovulation into the fallopian tubes. If the ovum is not fertilized (by sperm), it remains in the uterine cavity for about 14 days and is then flushed out of the system with the uterine endometrium and its blood vessels (during menstruation).

The ovaries also produce the hormones estrogen and progesterone. Estrogen leads to the development of secondary sex characteristics in the female, including breasts and the distribution of both body fat and body

FIGURE 2.9 | The Reproductive System *(Sources:* Green, 1978, p. 122; Lankford, 1979, p. 688)

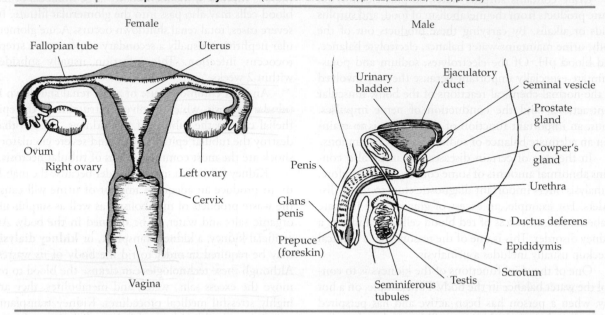

hair. Progesterone, which is produced during the second half of the menstrual cycle to prepare the body for pregnancy, declines if pregnancy fails to occur.

In males, testosterone is produced by the interstitial cells of the testes under the control of the anterior pituitary lobe. It brings about the production of sperm and the development of secondary sex characteristics, including growth of the beard, deepening of the voice, distribution of body hair, and both skeletal and muscular growth.

Fertilization and Gestation

When sexual intercourse takes place and ejaculation occurs, sperm are released into the vagina. These sperm, which have a high degree of motility, proceed upward through the uterus into the fallopian tubes, where one sperm may fertilize an ovum. The fertilized ovum then travels down the fallopian tube into the uterine cavity, where it embeds itself in the uterine wall and develops over the next 9 months into a human being.

Disorders of the Reproductive System

The reproductive system is vulnerable to a number of diseases and disorders. Among the most common and problematic are sexually transmitted diseases (STDs), which occur through sexual intercourse or other forms of sexually intimate activity. STDs include herpes,

gonorrhea, syphilis, genital warts, chlamydia, and, most seriously, AIDS.

For women, a risk of several STDs is chronic pelvic inflammatory disease (PID), which may produce a variety of unpleasant symptoms, including severe abdominal pain, and may lead to infections that may compromise fertility. Other gynecologic disorders to which women are vulnerable include vaginitis, endometriosis (in which pieces of the endometrial lining of the uterus move into the fallopian tubes or abdominal cavity, grow, and spread to other sites), cysts, and fibroids (nonmalignant growths in the uterus).

The reproductive system is also vulnerable to cancer, including testicular cancer in men (see Chapter 4) and gynecologic cancers in women. Every 6.4 minutes, or more than 80,000 times per year, a woman in the United States is diagnosed with a gynecologic cancer, including cancer of the cervix, uterus, and ovaries (American Cancer Society, 2007). Endometrial cancer is the most common female pelvic malignancy, while ovarian cancer is the most lethal.

Women are vulnerable to disorders of the menstrual cycle, including amenorrhea, which is the absence of menses, and oligomenorrhea, which is infrequent menstruation. These problems may originate in the hypothalamus, in the anterior pituitary, or in the ovaries or reproductive tract. Location of the cause is essential for correcting the problem, which may include hormone therapy or surgery.

Approximately 7% of U.S. couples experience fertility problems, defined as the inability to conceive a pregnancy after one year of regular sexual intercourse without contraception (National Center for Health Statistics, 2008). Although physicians once believed that infertility has emotional origins, researchers have now concluded that distress may complicate but does not cause infertility. Fortunately, over the past few decades, the technology for treating infertility has improved. A variety of drug treatments have been developed, as have more invasive technologies. In vitro fertilization (IVF) is the most widely used method of assistive reproductive technology, and the success rate for IVF is nearly 30% (American Society for Reproductive Medicine, 2004).

Menopause is not a disorder of the reproductive system; rather, it occurs when a woman's reproductive life ends. Because of a variety of unpleasant symptoms that can occur during the transition into menopause, including sleep disorders, hot flashes, joint pain, forgetfulness, and dizziness, some women choose to take hormone therapy (HT), which typically includes estrogen or a combination of estrogen and progesterone. HT was once thought not only to reduce the symptoms of menopause but also to protect against the development of coronary artery disease, osteoporosis, and even Alzheimer's disease, It is now believed that, rather than protecting against these disorders, HT may actually increase some of these risks (Hays et al., 2003; Hodis et al., 2003; Manson et al., 2003). HT also somewhat increases the risks of breast cancer. As a result of this new evidence, most women and their doctors are rethinking the use of HT, especially over the long term.

Genetics and Health

The fetus starts life as a single cell, which contains all the inherited information from both parents that will determine its characteristics. The genetic code regulates such factors as eye and hair color, as well as behavioral factors. Genetic material for inheritance lies in the nucleus of the cell in the form of 46 chromosomes, 23 from the mother and 23 from the father. Two of these 46 are sex chromosomes, which are an X from the mother and either an X or a Y from the father. If the father provides an X chromosome, a female child will result; if he provides a Y chromosome, a male child will result.

Genetic Studies   Genetic studies have provided valuable information about the inheritance of susceptibility to disease. Among several methods, scientists have

bred strains of rats, mice, and other laboratory animals that are sensitive or insensitive to the development of particular diseases and then used these strains to study other contributors to illness onset, the course of illness, and so on. For example, a strain of rats that is susceptible to cancer may be used to study the development of this disease and the cofactors that determine its appearance. The initial susceptibility of the rats ensures that many of them will develop malignancies when implanted with carcinogenic (cancer-causing) materials.

In humans, several types of research help demonstrate whether a characteristic is genetically acquired. Studies of families, for example, can reveal whether members of the same family are statistically more likely to develop a disorder, such as heart disease, than are unrelated individuals in a similar environment. If a factor is genetically determined, family members would be expected to show it more frequently than would unrelated individuals.

Twin research is another method for examining the genetic basis of a characteristic. If a characteristic is genetically transmitted, identical twins share it more commonly than do fraternal twins or other brothers and sisters. This is because identical twins share the same genetic makeup, whereas other brothers and sisters have only partially overlapping genetic makeup.

Examining the characteristics of twins reared together as opposed to twins reared apart is also informative regarding genetics. Attributes that emerge for twins reared apart are suspected to be genetically determined, especially if the rate of occurrence between twins reared together and those reared apart is the same.

Finally, studies of adopted children also help identify which characteristics are genetic and which are environmentally produced. Adopted children will not manifest genetically transmitted characteristics from their adoptive parents, but they will very likely manifest environmentally transmitted characteristics.

Consider, for example, obesity, which is a risk factor for a number of disorders, including coronary artery disease and diabetes. If twins reared apart show highly similar body weights, then we would suspect that body weight has a genetic component. If, on the other hand, weight within a family is highly related, and adopted children show the same weight as their parents and any natural offspring, then we would look to the family diet as a potential cause of obesity. For many attributes, including obesity, both environmental and genetic factors are involved.

Research like this has increasingly uncovered the genetic contribution to many health disorders and behavioral factors that may pose risks to health. Such diseases as asthma, Alzheimer's disease, cystic fibrosis, muscular dystrophy, Tay-Sachs disease, and Huntington's disease, as well as a number of chromosomal abnormalities, clearly have a genetic basis. There is also a genetic basis for coronary heart disease and for some forms of cancer, including some breast and colon cancers. This genetic basis does not preclude the important role of the environment, however.

Genetic contributions to obesity and alcoholism have emerged in recent years, and even some personality characteristics, such as optimism, which is believed to have protective health effects, appear to have genetic underpinnings (Plomin et al., 1992). Continuing advances in the field of genetics will undoubtedly yield much more information about the genetic contributions to behavioral factors that, in turn, contribute to health and illness (Facts of Life, June 2006).

Genetics and Health Psychology Health psychologists have important roles to play with respect to genetic contributions to health disorders (Shiloh, Gerad, & Goldman, 2006). One question concerns whether or not the public should be alerted to genetic risks (Smerecnik, Mesters, de Vries, & de Vries, 2009). Many people think that genetic risks are immutable and that any efforts they might undertake to affect their health would be fruitless if genes are implicated. Such erroneous beliefs may deter health behavior change and information seeking about one's risk (Marteau & Weinman, 2006). Genetic risk information may also evoke defensive processes whereby people downplay their risk (Shiloh, Drori, Orr-Urtreger, & Friedman, 2009). Accordingly, making the general public aware of genetic risk factors should be accompanied by educational information to offset these potential problems (Smerecnik et al., 2009).

Another role for health psychologists involves genetic counseling. Prenatal diagnostic tests are currently available that permit the detection of a variety of genetically based disorders, including Tay-Sachs disease, cystic fibrosis, muscular dystrophy, Huntington's disease, and breast cancer. Helping people decide whether to be screened and how to cope with genetic vulnerabilities if they test positive represents an important role for health psychologists (Van den Berg, Timmermans, et al., 2008).

In addition, people who have a family history of genetic disorders, those who have already given birth to a child with a genetic disorder, or those who have recurrent reproductive problems, such as multiple miscarriages, often seek such counseling (Van den Berg, Timmermans, et al., 2008). In some cases, technological advances have made it possible to treat some of these problems before birth. For example, drug therapy can treat some genetically transmitted metabolic defects, and surgery in utero has been performed to correct certain neural problems. However, when a prenatal diagnosis reveals that the fetus has an abnormal condition that cannot be corrected, the parents often must make the difficult decision of whether to abort the pregnancy.

In other cases, children, adolescents, or young adults may learn of a genetic risk to their health. Breast cancer, for example, runs in families, and among young women whose mothers, aunts, or sisters have developed breast cancer, vulnerability is higher. Families that share genetic risks may need special attention through family counseling (Mellon et al., 2009). Some of the genes that contribute to the development of breast cancer have been identified, and tests are now available to determine whether a genetic susceptibility is present. Although this type of cancer accounts for only 5% of breast cancer, women who carry these genetic susceptibilities are more likely to develop the disease at an earlier age; thus, these women are at high risk and need careful monitoring and assistance in making treatment-related decisions (Rini et al., 2009; Schwartz et al., 2009).

Many scientific investigations attest to both the immediate and the long-term distress that carriers of genetic risks may experience (Hamilton, Lobel, & Moyer, 2009; Timman, Roos, Maat-Kievit, & Tibben, 2004). In fact, reactions to this kind of bad news can be so problematic that some people concerned with ethical issues in medicine question the value of telling people about their genetic risks if nothing can be done to treat them. Growing evidence suggests, however, that people at risk for treatable disorders may benefit from genetic testing and not suffer long-term psychological distress (e.g., Beran et al., 2008; Hamilton et al., 2009). People who are chronically anxious, though, may require special attention and counseling (Rimes, Salkovskis, Jones, & Lucassen, 2006; Shiloh & Ilan, 2005).

In some cases, genetic risks can be offset by behavioral interventions to address the risk factor. For example, one study (Aspinwall, Leaf, Dola, Kohlmann, & Leachman, 2008) found that being informed that one had tested positive for a gene implicated in melanoma (a serious skin cancer) and receiving counseling led to better skin self-examination practices at a one-month follow-up. Health psychologists, thus, have an important role to play in research and counseling related to genetic risks, especially if they can help people modify their risk status. Knowledge of distress patterns (that is, who is most likely to be stressed and when) and coping styles can be helpful in counseling those who learn of their genetic risks (Dougall et al., 2009; Shiloh et al., 2006).

There are not only genetic bases of diseases but also genetic bases for fighting diseases. That is, certain genes may act as protective factors against development of a disease. For example, one gene appears to regulate whether the immune system can identify cancer (Carey, 2002, November 11). Just as attention to the genetic bases of disease will occupy research attention for decades to come, so the protective genetic factors that keep so many of us so healthy for so long may become better understood as well.

As yet, our ability to deal intelligently with such important psychological, social, and ethical issues has not kept pace with our scientific capacity to elucidate the role of genetics in illness and risk factors. For example, if prospective medical insurers or employers are allowed to conduct genetic screening, could a person's at-risk status be used to deny that person health insurance or employment? How might one avoid such abuses of the technology? An open discussion is essential if we are to make proper use of these valuable technologies. Suffice it to say here that the role of health psychologists in this debate is expanding and will evolve further in the coming decades.

■ THE IMMUNE SYSTEM

Overview

Disease can be caused by a variety of factors, including genetic defects, hormone imbalances, nutritional deficiencies, and infection. In this section, we are primarily concerned with the transmission of disease by infection—that is, the invasion of microbes and their growth in the body. The microbes that cause infection are transmitted to people in several ways:

- Direct transmission involves bodily contact, such as handshaking, kissing, and sexual intercourse. For example, genital herpes is generally contracted by direct transmission.

- Indirect transmission (or environmental transmission) occurs when microbes are passed to an individual via airborne particles, dust, water, soil, or food. Influenza is an example of an environmentally transmitted disease.

- Biological transmission occurs when a transmitting agent, such as a mosquito, picks up microbes, changes them into a form conducive to growth in the human body, and passes them on to the human. Yellow fever, for example, is transmitted by this method.

- Mechanical transmission is the passage of a microbe to an individual by means of a carrier that is not directly involved in the disease process. Dirty hands, bad water, rats, mice, and flies are methods of mechanical transmission. For example, hepatitis can be acquired through mechanical transmission. Box 2.1 tells about two people who were carriers of deadly diseases.

Infection

Once a microbe has reached the body, it penetrates into bodily tissue via any of several routes, including the skin, the throat and respiratory tract, the digestive tract, or the genitourinary system. Whether the invading microbes gain a foothold in the body and produce infection depends on three factors: the number of organisms, the virulence of the organisms, and the body's defensive capacities. The virulence of an organism is determined by its aggressiveness (that is, its ability to resist the body's defenses) and by its toxigenicity (that is, its ability to produce poisons, which invade other parts of the body).

The Course of Infection

Assuming that the invading organism does gain a foothold, the natural history of infection follows a specific course. First, there is an incubation period between the time the infection is contracted and the time the symptoms appear.

Next, there is a period of nonspecific symptoms, such as headaches and general discomfort, which precedes the onset of the disease. During this time, the microbes are actively colonizing and producing toxins. The next stage is the acute phase, when the disease and its symptoms are at their height. Unless the infection proves fatal, a period of decline follows the acute phase. During this period, the organisms are expelled from the mouth and nose in saliva and respiratory secretions, as well as through the digestive tract and the genitourinary system in feces and urine.

Infections may be localized, focal, or systemic. Localized infections remain at their original site and do not spread throughout the body. Although a focal infection

BOX 2.1

Portraits of Two Carriers

Carriers are people who transmit a disease to others without actually contracting that disease themselves. They are especially dangerous because they are not ill and so are not removed from society. Thus, it is possible for a carrier to infect dozens, hundreds, or even thousands of individuals while going about the business of everyday life.

"TYPHOID MARY"

Perhaps the most famous carrier in history was "Typhoid Mary," a young Swiss immigrant to the United States who infected thousands of people during her lifetime. During her ocean crossing, Mary was taught how to cook, and eventually, some 100 individuals aboard the ship died of typhoid, including the cook who trained her. Once Mary arrived in New York, she obtained a series of jobs as a cook, continually passing on the disease to those for whom she worked without contracting it herself.

Typhoid is precipitated by a Salmonella bacterium, which can be transmitted through water, food, and physical contact. Mary carried a virulent form of the infection in her body but was herself immune to the disease. It is believed that she was unaware that she was a carrier for many years. Toward the end of her life, however, she began to realize that she was responsible for the many deaths around her.

Mary's status as a carrier also became known to medical authorities, and she spent the latter part of her life in and out of institutions in a vain attempt to isolate her from others. In 1930, Mary died not of typhoid but of a brain hemorrhage (Federspiel, 1983).

"HELEN"

The CBS News program *60 Minutes* profiled an equally terrifying carrier: a prostitute, "Helen," who is a carrier of HIV, the virus that causes AIDS (acquired immune deficiency syndrome). Helen has never had AIDS, but her baby was born with the disease. As a prostitute and heroin addict, she is not only at risk for developing the illness herself but also poses a substantial threat to her clients and anyone with whom she shares a needle.

Helen represents a dilemma for medical and criminal authorities. She is a known carrier of AIDS, yet there is no legal basis for preventing her from coming into contact with others. Although she can be arrested for prostitution or drug dealing, such incarcerations are usually short-term and would have a negligible impact on her ability to spread the disease to others. For as yet incurable diseases such as AIDS, the carrier represents a nightmare. Although the carrier can augment the incidence of the disease, medical and legal authorities have been almost powerless to intervene (Moses, 1984).

---

is confined to a particular area, it sends toxins to other parts of the body, causing other disruptions. Systemic infections affect a number of areas or body systems.

The primary infection initiated by the microbe may also lead to secondary infections. These occur because the body's resistance is lowered from fighting the primary infection, leaving it susceptible to other invaders. In many cases, secondary infections, such as pneumonia, pose a greater risk than the primary one.

Immunity

Immunity is the body's resistance to harm from invading organisms. It may develop either naturally or artificially. Some natural immunity is passed from the mother to the child at birth and through breast-feeding, although this type of immunity is only temporary. Natural immunity is also acquired through disease. For example, if you have measles once, you are unlikely to develop it a second time; you will have built up an immunity to it.

Artificial immunity is acquired through vaccinations and inoculations. For example, most children and adolescents receive shots for a variety of diseases—among them, diphtheria, whooping cough, smallpox, poliomyelitis, and hepatitis—so that they will not contract them should they ever be exposed.

Nonspecific and Specific Immunity   How does immunity work? The body has a number of responses to invading organisms, some nonspecific and others specific. **Nonspecific immune mechanisms** are a general set of responses to any kind of infection or disorder; **specific immune mechanisms,** which are always acquired after birth, fight particular microorganisms and their toxins.

Nonspecific immunity is mediated in four main ways: through anatomical barriers, phagocytosis, antimicrobial substances, and inflammatory response. Anatomical barriers prevent the passage of microbes from one section of the body to another. For example, the skin functions as an extremely effective anatomical barrier to many infections, and the mucous membranes lining the nose and mouth (as well as other cavities that are open to the environment) also provide protection.

Phagocytosis is the process by which certain white blood cells (called phagocytes) ingest microbes. Phagocytes are usually overproduced when there is a bodily infection, so that sufficient numbers can be sent to the site of infection to ingest the foreign particles.

Antimicrobial substances are chemicals mobilized by the body to kill invading microorganisms. One that has received particular attention in cancer research is interferon, an antiviral protein secreted by cells exposed to a viral antigen to protect neighboring uninfected cells from invasion. Hydrochloric acid and enzymes such as lysozyme are other antimicrobial substances that help destroy invading microorganisms.

The inflammatory response is a local reaction to infection. At the site of infection, the blood capillaries first enlarge, and a chemical called histamine is released into the area. This chemical causes an increase in capillary permeability, allowing white blood cells and fluids to leave the capillaries and enter the tissues; consequently, the area becomes reddened and fluids accumulate. The white blood cells attack the microbes, resulting in the formation of pus. Temperature increases at the site of inflammation because of the increased flow of blood. Usually, a clot then forms around the inflamed area, isolating the microbes and keeping them from spreading to other parts of the body. Familiar examples of the inflammatory response are the reddening, swelling, discharge, and clotting that result when you accidentally lacerate your skin and the sneezing, runny nose, and teary eyes that result from an allergic response to pollen.

Specific immunity is acquired after birth and differs from nonspecific immunity in that it protects against particular microorganisms and their toxins. Specific immunity may be acquired by contracting a disease or through artificial means, such as vaccinations. It operates through the antigen-antibody reaction. Antigens are foreign substances whose presence stimulates the production of antibodies in the cell tissues. Antibodies are proteins produced in response to stimulation by antigens, which then combine chemically with the antigens to overcome their toxic effects.

Humoral and Cell-Mediated Immunity There are two basic immunologic reactions—humoral and cell mediated. **Humoral immunity** is mediated by B lymphocytes. The functions of B lymphocytes include providing protection against bacteria, neutralizing toxins produced by bacteria, and preventing viral reinfection. B cells confer immunity by the production and secretion of antibodies.

When B cells are activated, they differentiate into two types: mature, antibody-secreting plasma cells and resting, nondividing, memory B cells, which differentiate into antigen-specific plasma cells only when reexposed to the same antigen. Plasma cells produce antibodies or immunoglobulins, which are the basis of the antigen-specific reactions. Humoral immunity is particularly effective in defending against bacterial infections and against viral infections that have not yet invaded the cells.

Cell-mediated immunity, involving T lymphocytes from the thymus gland, is a slower-acting response. Rather than releasing antibodies into the blood, as humoral immunity does, cell-mediated immunity operates at the cellular level. When stimulated by the appropriate antigen, T cells secrete chemicals that kill invading organisms and infected cells.

There are two major types of T lymphocytes: cytotoxic T (T_C cells) and helper T (T_H cells). T_C cells respond to specific antigens and kill by producing toxic substances that destroy virally infected cells. T_H cells enhance the functioning of T_C cells, B cells, and macrophages by producing cytokines. T_H cells also serve a counterregulatory immune function, producing cytokines that suppress certain immune activities. Cell-mediated immunity is particularly effective in defending the body against fungi, viral infections that have invaded the cells, parasites, foreign tissue, and cancer.

What, then, does the integrated immune response look like? When a foreign antigen enters the body, the first line of defense involves mechanistic maneuvers, such as coughing or sneezing. Once the invader has penetrated the body's surface, the phagocytes, such as the macrophages, attempt to eliminate it by phagocytosis (engulfing and digesting the foreign invader). Macrophages also release interleukin-1 and display part of the antigen material on their surface as a signal to the T_H cells. These cells, in turn, secrete interleukin-2, which promotes the growth and differentiation of the T_C cells. Other types of T helper cells secrete substances that promote the development of antigen-specific B cells into antibody-producing plasma cells, which then assist in destroying the antigen. T_H cells also secrete gamma-interferon, which enhances the capacities of the macrophages. Macrophages and natural killer (NK) cells also secrete various types of interferon, which enhance the killing potential of the natural killer (NK) cells and inhibit viral reproduction in uninfected cells. In addition, macrophages, NK cells, and T_C cells directly kill infected cells. During this process, the T_H cells regulate and eventually turn off the immune response.

The Lymphatic System's Role in Immunity

The **lymphatic system,** which is a drainage system of the body, is involved in important ways in immune functioning. There is lymphatic tissue throughout the body, consisting of lymphatic capillaries, vessels, and nodes. Lymphatic capillaries drain water, proteins, microbes, and other foreign materials from spaces between the cells into lymph vessels. This material is then conducted in the lymph vessels to the lymph nodes, which filter out microbes and foreign materials for ingestion by lymphocytes. The lymphatic vessels then drain any remaining substances into the blood.

The spleen, tonsils, and thymus gland are important organs in the lymphatic system. The spleen aids in the production of B cells and T cells and removes old red blood cells from the body. The spleen also helps filter bacteria and is responsible for the storage and release of blood. Tonsils are patches of lymphoid tissue in the pharynx that filter out microorganisms that enter the respiratory tract. Finally, the thymus gland is responsible for helping T cells mature; it also produces a hormone, thymosin, which appears to stimulate T cells and lymph nodes to produce the plasma cells that, in turn, produce antibodies.

Additional discussion of immunity may be found in Chapter 14, where we consider the rapidly developing field of psychoneuroimmunology and the role of immunity in the development of AIDS. As we will see in that context, health psychologists are identifying the importance of stress and other psychological factors in the functioning of the immune system.

Disorders Related to the Immune System

The immune system and the tissues of the lymphatic system are subject to a number of disorders and diseases. One very important one is AIDS, which is a progressive impairment of immunity. Another is cancer, which is now believed to depend heavily on immunocompromise. We defer extended discussion of AIDS and cancer to Chapter 14.

Some diseases of the immune system result when bacteria are so virulent that the lymph node phagocytes are not able to ingest all the foreign matter. These diseases include lymphangitis, an inflammation of the lymphatic vessels that results from interference in the drainage of the lymph into the blood, and lymphadenitis, an inflammation of the lymph nodes associated with the phagocytes' efforts to destroy microbes.

A number of infections attack lymphatic tissue. For example, tonsillitis is an inflammation of the tonsils that interferes with their ability to filter out bacteria. Infectious mononucleosis is a viral disorder marked by an unusually large number of monocytes; it can cause enlargement of the spleen and lymph nodes, as well as fever, sore throat, and general lack of energy.

Lymphoma is a tumor of the lymphatic tissue. Hodgkin's disease, a malignant lymphoma, involves the progressive, chronic enlargement of the lymph nodes, spleen, and other lymphatic tissues. As a consequence, the nodes cannot effectively produce antibodies, and the phagocytic properties of the nodes are lost. If untreated, Hodgkin's disease can be fatal.

Infectious disorders were at one time thought to be acute problems that ended when their course had run. A major problem in developing countries, infectious disorders were thought to be largely under control in developed nations. Now, however, some important developments with respect to infectious diseases merit closer looks (Morens, Folkers, & Fauci, 2004). First, as noted in the discussion of asthma, the control of at least some infectious disorders through hygiene may have paradoxically increased the rates of allergic disorders. A second development is that some chronic diseases, once thought to be genetic in origin or unknown in origin, are now being traced back to infections. For example, Alzheimer's disease, multiple sclerosis, schizophrenia, and some cancers appear to have infectious triggers, at least in some cases (Zimmer, 2001). The fact that multiple sclerosis shows outbreaks in particular locations is strongly suggestive of an infectious pattern. Ulcers, once thought to be the result of stress, were traced in the 1980s to a microbe known as Helicobacter pylori; cases of ulcers and even gastric cancers that were once thought to be difficult to treat can now be cured through antibiotics (Zimmer, 2001). Increasingly, biologists are suggesting that pathogens cause or actively contribute to many if not most chronic diseases. Finally, of considerable concern is the development of bacterial strains that are increasingly resistant to treatment. The overuse of antibiotics is thought to be an active contributor to the development of increasingly lethal strains.

Infectious agents have also become an increasing cause for concern in the war on terrorism, as the possibility that smallpox and other infectious agents may be used as weapons becomes increasingly likely (Gruman, 2003).

The inflammatory response that is so protective against provocations ranging from mosquito bites and sunburn to gastritis in response to spoiled food is coming under increasing investigation as a contributor to chronic disease. The destructive potential of inflammatory responses has long been evident in diseases such as rheumatoid arthritis and multiple sclerosis, but researchers now know that inflammation underlies many other chronic diseases including atherosclerosis, diabetes, Alzheimer's disease, and osteoporosis. Inflammation is also implicated in asthma, cirrhosis of the liver, some bowel disorders, cystic fibrosis, heart disease, depression, and even some cancers (Duenwald, 2002, September 17) (Table 2.1).

The inflammatory response, like stress responses more generally, likely evolved in humans' early prehistory and was selected because it was adaptive. For example, among hunter-gatherer societies, natural selection would have favored people with vigorous inflammatory responses because life expectancy was fairly short. Few people would have experienced the long-term costs of vigorous or long-lasting inflamma-

TABLE 2.1 | Some Consequences of Chronic Low-Level Inflammation.

Inflammation is believed to play an important role in several diseases of aging. They include:

- Heart Disease
- Stroke
- Diabetes
- Alzheimer's Disease (and cognitive decline more generally)
- Cancer
- Osteoporosis
- Depression

tory responses, which now seem to play such an important role in the development of chronic diseases. Essentially, an adaptive pattern of earlier times has become maladaptive as life expectancy has lengthened (Duenwald, 2002, September 17).

Autoimmunity is a condition characterized by a specific humoral or cell-mediated immune response that attacks the body's own tissues. Autoimmunity is implicated in certain forms of arthritis, a condition characterized by inflammatory lesions in the joints that produce pain, heat, redness, and swelling. We will discuss arthritis more fully in Chapter 14. Multiple sclerosis is also an autoimmune disorder. One of the most severe autoimmune disorders is systemic lupus erythematosis, a generalized disorder of the connective tissue, which primarily affects women and which in its severe forms can lead to eventual heart or kidney failure, causing death.

In autoimmune disease, the body fails to recognize its own tissue, instead interpreting it as a foreign invader and producing antibodies to fight it. Approximately 50 million Americans suffer from autoimmune diseases. Women are more likely than men to be affected; some estimates are that 75% of those affected are women (American Autoimmune Related Diseases Association, 2008). Although the causes of autoimmune diseases are not fully known, researchers have discovered that a viral or bacterial infection often precedes the onset of an autoimmune disease.

Many of these viral and bacterial pathogens have, over time, developed the ability to fool the body into granting them access by mimicking basic protein sequences in the body. This process of molecular mimicry eventually fails but then leads the immune system to attack not only the invader but also the corresponding self-component. A person's genetic makeup may exacerbate this process, or it may confer protection against autoimmune diseases. Stress can aggravate autoimmune disease. ●

SUMMARY

1. The nervous system and the endocrine system act as the control systems of the body, mobilizing it in times of threat and otherwise maintaining equilibrium and normal functioning.

2. The nervous system operates primarily through the exchange of nerve impulses between the peripheral nerve endings and internal organs and the brain, thereby providing the integration necessary for voluntary and involuntary movement.

3. The endocrine system operates chemically via the release of hormones stimulated by centers in the brain. It controls growth and development and augments the functioning of the nervous system.

4. The cardiovascular system is the transport system of the body, carrying oxygen and nutrients to cell tissues and taking carbon dioxide and other wastes away from the tissues for expulsion from the body.

5. The heart acts as a pump to control circulation and is responsive to regulation via the nervous system and the endocrine system.

6. The cardiovascular system is implicated in stress, with cardiac output speeding up during times of stress and slowing down when threat has passed.

7. The heart, blood vessels, and blood are vulnerable to a number of problems—most notably, atherosclerosis—which makes diseases of the cardiovascular system the major cause of death in this country.

8. The respiratory system is responsible for taking in oxygen, expelling carbon dioxide, and controlling the chemical composition of the blood.

9. The digestive system is responsible for producing heat and energy, which—along with essential nutrients—are needed for the growth and repair of cells. Through digestion, food is broken down to be used by the cells for this process.

10. The renal system aids in metabolic processes by regulating water balance, electrolyte balance, and blood acidity-alkalinity. Water-soluble wastes are flushed out of the system in the urine.

11. The reproductive system, under the control of the endocrine system, leads to the development of primary and secondary sex characteristics. Through this system, the species is reproduced, and genetic material is transmitted from parents to their offspring.

12. With advances in genetic technology and the mapping of the genome has come increased understanding of genetic contributions to disease. Health psychologists play important research and counseling roles with respect to these issues.

13. The immune system is responsible for warding off infection from invasion by foreign substances. It does so through the production of infection-fighting cells and chemicals.

KEY TERMS

adrenal glands
angina pectoris
atherosclerosis
autoimmunity
blood pressure
cardiovascular system
catecholamines
cell-mediated immunity
cerebellum
cerebral cortex
endocrine system

humoral immunity
hypothalamus
immunity
kidney dialysis
lymphatic system
medulla
myocardial infarction (MI)
nervous system
neurotransmitters
nonspecific immune mechanisms
parasympathetic nervous system

phagocytosis
pituitary gland
platelets
pons
renal system
respiratory system
specific immune mechanisms
sympathetic nervous system
thalamus

PART 2

Health Behavior and Primary Prevention

Health Behaviors

Jill Morgan had just begun her sophomore year in college. Although her freshman year had been filled with required courses, sophomore year was looking more interesting, giving her the chance to really get into her major, biology. The professor whose work she had so admired had an opening in her lab for a research assistant and offered it to Jill. Jill's boyfriend, Jerry, had just transferred to her school, so instead of seeing each other only one or two weekends a month, they now met for lunch almost every day and studied together in the library at night. Life was looking very good.

Tuesday morning, Jill was awakened by the harsh ring of her telephone. Could she come home right away? Her mother had gone in for a routine mammogram and a malignant lump had been discovered. Surgery was necessary, her father explained, and Jill was needed at home to take care of her younger sister and brother. As soon as her mother was better, her father promised, Jill could go back to school, but she would have to postpone the beginning of her sophomore year for at least a semester.

Jill felt as if her world were falling apart. She had always been very close to her mother and could not imagine this cheerful, outgoing woman with an illness. Moreover, it was cancer. What if her mother died? Her mother's situation was too painful to think about, so Jill began to contemplate her own. She would not be able to take the courses she was currently enrolled in for another year, and she could forget about the research assistantship. And after all that effort so that she and Jerry could be together, now they would be apart again. Jill lay on her dorm room bed, knowing she needed to pack but unable to move.

"Breast cancer's hereditary, you know," Jill's roommate said. Jill looked at her in amazement, unable to speak. "If your mother has it, the chances are you'll get it too," the roommate went on, seemingly oblivious to the impact her words were having. Jill realized that she needed to get out of there quickly. As she walked, many thoughts came into her head. Would Jerry still want to date her, now that she might get breast cancer? Should she even think about having children anymore? What if she passed on the risk of breast cancer to her children? Without thinking, she headed for the biology building, which now felt like a second home to her. The professor who had offered her the lab job was standing in the hall as she went in. The professor could sense that something was wrong and invited Jill in for coffee. Jill told her what happened and broke down crying.

"Jill, you should know that breast cancer can now be treated, particularly when it's caught early. If they detected your mother's breast cancer through a mammogram, it probably means it's a pretty small lump. It's a good thing she was getting a regular mammogram. Cure rates are now 90% or better for early breast cancers. On the basis of what your dad has told you so far, your mother's situation looks pretty promising.

"Not only that, the surgeries they have for breast cancer now are often fairly minimal, just removal of the lump, so you and your father might find that her recovery will be a little quicker than it may look right now. Look, I'm not going to give this research assistantship away. Why don't you go home, find out how things are, and call me in a week or so?"

"My roommate says breast cancer's hereditary," Jill said.

"Heredity is only one of the factors that can contribute to breast cancer, and not all breast cancer is hereditary. The fact that your mother has it does mean you'll have to be aware of a possible risk and make sure you get screened on a regular basis. But it doesn't mean that you will necessarily get breast cancer. And even if you do, it won't be the end of the world. Early detection and quick treatment mean that most women survive and lead normal lives." The professor paused for a moment. "Jill, my mother had breast cancer, too, about 7 years ago. She's doing fine. I go in for regular checkups, and so far, everything has been okay. It's not knowledge I'm happy to be living with, but it hasn't changed my life. I have a husband, two great kids, and a wonderful career, and the possible risk of breast cancer is just something I know about. I'm sure that this feels like a tragedy right now, but I think you'll find that your greatest fears probably won't materialize."

"Thanks," said Jill. "I think I'd better go home and pack."

In Chapter 3, we take up the important issue of health behaviors and risk factors for illness. At the core of this chapter is the idea that good health is achievable through health habits that are practiced conscientiously. Health promotion means being aware both of health habits that pose risks for future disease and of already existing risks, such as the vulnerability to breast cancer that Jill and the biology professor may have. In the following pages, we consider health habits and risk factors with an eye toward their successful modification before they have a chance to lead to the development of illness.

■ HEALTH PROMOTION: AN OVERVIEW

Health promotion is a general philosophy that has at its core the idea that good health, or wellness, is a personal and collective achievement. For the individual, it involves developing a program of good health habits early in life and carrying them through adulthood and old age. For the medical practitioner, health promotion involves teaching people how to achieve a healthy lifestyle and helping people **at risk** for particular health problems offset or monitor those risks. For the health psychologist, health promotion involves the development of interventions to help people practice healthy behaviors and change poor ones. For community and national policy makers, health promotion involves a general emphasis on good health, the availability of information to help people develop healthy lifestyles, and the availability of resources to help people change poor health habits. The mass media can contribute to health promotion by educating people about health risks posed by certain behaviors, such as smoking or excessive alcohol consumption. Legislation can contribute to health promotion by mandating certain activities that may reduce risks, such as the use of child-restraining seats and seat belts.

The case for health promotion has grown clearer and more urgent with each decade. In the past, prevention efforts relied on early diagnosis of disease to achieve a healthy population, with only passing attention paid to promoting healthy lifestyles in the absence of disease. However, on grounds such as cost effectiveness, health promotion appears to be both more successful and less costly than disease prevention (Kaplan, 2000), making it increasingly evident that we must teach people the basics of a healthy lifestyle across the life span.

■ AN INTRODUCTION TO HEALTH BEHAVIORS

Role of Behavioral Factors in Disease and Disorder

In the past century, patterns of disease in the United States have changed substantially. The prevalence of acute infectious disorders, such as tuberculosis, influenza, measles, and poliomyelitis, has declined because of treatment innovations and changes in public health standards, such as improvements in waste control and sewage. Simultaneously, there has been an increase in what have been called the preventable disorders, including

TABLE 3.1 | Risk Factors for the Leading Causes of Death in the United States

Disease	Risk Factors
Heart disease	Tobacco, high cholesterol, high blood pressure, physical inactivity, obesity, diabetes, stress
Cancer	Smoking, unhealthy diet, environmental factors
Stroke	High blood pressure, tobacco, diabetes, high cholesterol, physical inactivity, obesity
Accidental injuries	On the road (failure to wear seat belts), in the home (falls, poison, fire)
Chronic lung disease	Tobacco, environmental factors (pollution, radon, asbestos)

Sources: American Cancer Society, 2009a; American Heart Association, 2009; Centers for Disease Control and Prevention, April 2009.

lung cancer, cardiovascular disease, alcohol and other drug abuse, and vehicular accidents.

The role of behavioral factors in the development of these disorders is clear (Table 3.1). It is estimated that nearly half the deaths in the United States are caused by preventable factors, with smoking, obesity, and drinking being the top three. This has been true for the past 15 years, the only change being that obesity and lack of exercise are about to overtake tobacco as the most preventable causes of death in the United States (Centers for Disease Control and Prevention, 2009a). Cancer deaths alone could be reduced by 50% simply by getting people to reduce smoking, eat more fruits and vegetables, boost their physical activity, and obtain early screening for breast and cervical cancer (Center for the Advancement of Health, April 2003).

Successful modification of health behaviors, then, will have several beneficial effects. First, it will reduce deaths due to lifestyle-related diseases. Second, it may delay time of death, thereby increasing general life expectancy. Third and most important, the practice of good health behaviors may expand the number of years during which a person may enjoy life free from the complications of chronic disease. Finally, modification of health behaviors may begin to make a dent in the more than $2.2 trillion that is spent yearly on health and illness (Centers for Medicare and Medicaid Services, 2008) (Table 3.2).

What Are Health Behaviors?

Health behaviors are behaviors undertaken by people to enhance or maintain their health. Poor health

TABLE 3.2 | Annual Cost of Unhealthy Lifestyles and Conditions, 2006

Condition/Lifestyle	Annual Cost in Billions
Heart disease and stroke	$403.1
Diabetes	151.6
Obesity	143.3
Smoking	206.4
Inactivity	188.2

Source: Health Promotion Advocates, 2008.

behaviors are important not only because they are implicated in illness but also because they may easily become poor health habits.

Health Habits   A **health habit** is a health-related behavior that is firmly established and often performed automatically, without awareness. These habits usually develop in childhood and begin to stabilize around age 11 or 12 (Cohen, Brownell, & Felix, 1990). Wearing a seat belt, brushing one's teeth, and eating a healthy diet are examples of these kinds of behaviors. Although a health habit may develop initially because it is reinforced by specific positive outcomes, such as parental approval, it eventually becomes independent of the reinforcement process and is maintained by the environmental factors with which it is customarily associated. As such, it can be highly resistant to change. Consequently, it is important to establish good health behaviors and to eliminate poor ones early in life.

A dramatic illustration of the importance of good health habits in maintaining good health is provided by a classic study of people living in Alameda County, California, conducted by Belloc and Breslow (1972). These scientists began by defining several important good health habits:

- Sleeping 7 to 8 hours a night
- Not smoking
- Eating breakfast each day
- Having no more than one or two alcoholic drinks each day
- Getting regular exercise
- Not eating between meals
- Being no more than 10% overweight

They then asked nearly 7,000 county residents to indicate which of these behaviors they practiced. Residents

were also asked how many illnesses they had had, which illnesses they had had, how much energy they had had, and how disabled they had been (for example, how many days of work they had missed) over the previous 6- to 12-month period. The researchers found that the more good health habits people practiced, the fewer illnesses they had had, the better they had felt, and the less disabled they had been.

A follow-up of these individuals 9–12 years later found that mortality rates were dramatically lower for people practicing the seven health habits. Specifically, men following these practices had a mortality rate only 28% that of the men following zero to three of the health practices, and women following the seven health habits had a mortality rate 43% that of the women following zero to three of the health practices (Breslow & Enstrom, 1980).

Primary Prevention   Instilling good health habits and changing poor ones is the task of **primary prevention.** This means taking measures to combat risk factors for illness before an illness has a chance to develop. There are two general strategies of primary prevention. The first and most common strategy has been to employ behavior-change methods to get people to alter their problematic health behaviors. Programs designed to help people lose weight are an example of this approach. The second, more recent approach is to keep people from developing poor health habits in the first place. Smoking prevention programs with young adolescents are an example of this approach, which we will consider in Chapter 5. Of the two types of primary prevention, it is obviously far preferable to keep people from developing problematic behaviors than to try to help them stop the behaviors once they are already in place.

Practicing and Changing Health Behaviors: An Overview

Who practices good health behaviors? What are the factors that lead one person to live a healthy life and another to compromise his or her health?

Demographic Factors   Health behaviors differ according to demographic factors. Younger, more affluent, better-educated people under low levels of stress with high levels of social support typically practice better health habits than people under higher levels of stress with fewer resources (Hanson & Chen, 2007; Gottlieb & Green, 1984).

Age   Health behaviors vary with age. Typically, health habits are good in childhood, deteriorate in adolescence and young adulthood, but improve again among older people (Leventhal, Prochaska, & Hirschman, 1985).

Values   Values heavily influence the practice of health habits. For example, exercise for women may be considered desirable in one culture but undesirable in another (Donovan, Jessor, & Costa, 1991). As a result, exercise patterns among women will differ between the two cultures (Guilamo-Ramos, Jaccard, Pena, & Goldberg, 2005).

Personal Control   Perceptions that one's health is under personal control also determine health habits. For example, the **health locus of control** scale (Table 3.3) (Wallston, Wallston, & DeVellis, 1978) measures the degree to which people perceive themselves to be in control of their health, perceive powerful others to be in control of their health, or regard chance as the major determinant of their health. People who are predisposed to see health as under personal control may be more likely to practice good health habits than those who regard their health as due to chance factors.

Social Influence   Family, friends, and workplace companions can all influence health-related behaviors—sometimes in a beneficial direction, other times in an adverse direction (Broman, 1993; Turbin et al., 2006). For example, peer pressure often leads to smoking in adolescence but may influence people to stop smoking in adulthood.

Personal Goals and Values   Health habits are heavily tied to personal goals (Eiser & Gentle, 1988). If personal fitness or athletic achievement is an important goal, the person will be more likely to exercise on a regular basis than if fitness is not a personal goal. When people have recently focused on their personal values, a process called **self-affirmation,** they show better health habits (Epton & Harris, 2008). Self-affirmation can also undermine defensive reactions to health threats (Harris, Mayle, Mabbott, & Napper, 2007; Van Koningsbruggen, Das, & Roskos-Ewoldsen, 2009).

Perceived Symptoms   Some health habits are controlled by perceived symptoms. For example, smokers may control their smoking on the basis of sensations in their throat. A smoker who wakes up with a smoker's cough and raspy throat may cut back in the belief that he or she is vulnerable to health problems at that time.

Access to the Health Care Delivery System   Access to the health care delivery system can also influence the practice of health behaviors. Using tuberculosis

TABLE 3.3 | Health Locus of Control

Health locus of control assesses whether you think you control your health or whether you believe it's controlled by health care professionals or by chance.

Each item below is a belief statement about your medical condition with which you may agree or disagree. Beside each statement is a scale that ranges from strongly disagree (1) to strongly agree (6). For each item, circle the number that represents the extent to which you agree or disagree with that statement.

1 = Strongly Disagree (SD)   4 = Slightly Agree (A)
2 = Moderately Disagree (MD)   5 = Moderately Agree (MA)
3 = Slightly Disagree (D)   6 = Strongly Agree (SA)

	SD	MD	D	A	MA	SA
1. If I get sick, it is my own behavior that determines how soon I get well again.	1	2	3	4	5	6
2. Most things that affect my health happen to me by accident.	1	2	3	4	5	6
3. Whenever I don't feel well, I should consult a medically trained professional.	1	2	3	4	5	6
4. I am in control of my health.	1	2	3	4	5	6
5. Health professionals control my health.	1	2	3	4	5	6
6. My good health is largely a matter of good fortune.	1	2	3	4	5	6
7. If I take the right actions, I can stay healthy.	1	2	3	4	5	6

Source: Wallston, Wallston, & DeVellis, 1978; see http://www.vanderbilt.edu/nursing/kwallston/mhlcscales.htm for the complete scale.

screening programs, obtaining a regular Pap smear, getting mammograms, and receiving immunizations for childhood diseases such as polio are examples of behaviors that are directly tied to the health care delivery system. Other behaviors, such as losing weight and stopping smoking, may be indirectly encouraged by the health care system because many people now often receive lifestyle advice from their physicians.

Cognitive Factors   Finally, the practice of health behaviors is tied to cognitive factors, such as knowledge and intelligence (Jaccard, Dodge, & Guilamo-Ramos, 2005). For example, the belief that certain health behaviors are beneficial or the sense that one may be vulnerable to an underlying illness if one does not practice a particular health behavior also predicts health behaviors.

Barriers to Modifying Poor Health Behaviors
Researchers know less than they would like about how and when poor health habits develop and exactly when and how one should intervene to change health habits (Center for the Advancement of Health, 2005). For example, young children usually get enough exercise, but as they get older, a sedentary lifestyle may set in. How and when should one intervene to offset this tendency? The process is gradual, and the decline in exercise is due more to changes in the environment, such as no longer having to take a compulsory physical education class in school, than to the motivation to get exercise.

Moreover, people often have little immediate incentive for practicing good health behaviors. Health habits develop during childhood and adolescence when most people are healthy. Smoking, drinking, poor nutrition, and lack of exercise have no apparent effect on health and physical functioning. The cumulative damage that these behaviors cause may not become apparent for years, and few children and adolescents are concerned about what their health will be like when they are 40 or 50 years old (Johnson, McCaul, & Klein, 2002). As a result, bad habits have a chance to make inroads.

Emotional Factors   Once bad habits are ingrained, people may not be motivated to change them. Unhealthy behaviors can be pleasurable, automatic, addictive, and resistant to change. Many people find it hard to change their health habits if their bad habits are enjoyable. Affective attitudes, namely emotional beliefs about a health habit, predict its practice, a factor that needs to be taken into account in trying to change health habits (Lawton, Conner, & McEachan, 2009).

Negative affect can undermine receptivity to health messages, and stressing benefits can undercut this source of resistance (Beckjord, Rutten, Arora, Moser, & Hesse, 2008).

Other emotional processes influencing health behavior change include defensive responses to threat. That is, health behavior messages often stress risk-related information that can be threatening to people, and so sometimes people deny their perceived risk or avoid processing risk-related messages, which undermines behavior change (Good & Abraham, 2007).

Instability of Health Behaviors   Health habits are only modestly related to each other. The person who exercises faithfully does not necessarily wear a seat belt, and the person who controls his or her weight may continue to smoke. Therefore, it can be difficult to teach people a concerted program of good health behavior, because health behaviors must often be tackled one at a time.

Another difficulty with modifying health habits is that they are unstable over time. A person may stop smoking for a year but take it up again during a period of high stress. A dieter may lose 50 pounds, only to regain them a few years later. Why are health habits relatively independent of each other and unstable?

First, different health habits are controlled by different factors. For example, smoking may be related to stress, whereas exercise may depend on ease of access to athletic facilities.

Second, different factors may control the same health behavior for different people. Thus, one person's overeating may be "social," and she may eat primarily in the presence of other people. In contrast, another individual's overeating may depend on levels of tension, and he may overeat only when under stress.

Third, factors controlling a health behavior may change over the history of the behavior (Costello, Dierker, Jones, & Rose, 2008). The initial instigating factors may no longer be significant, and new maintaining factors may develop to replace them. Although peer group pressure (social factors) is important in initiating the smoking habit, over time, smoking may be maintained because it reduces cravings and feelings of stress. One's peer group in adulthood may actually oppose smoking.

Fourth, factors controlling a health behavior may change across a person's lifetime. Regular exercise occurs in childhood because it is built into the school curriculum, but in adulthood, this automatic habit must be practiced consciously.

Fifth and finally, health behavior patterns, their developmental course, and the factors that change them across a lifetime will vary substantially between individuals (Leventhal, Prochaska, & Hirschman, 1985). Thus, one individual may have started smoking for social reasons but continue smoking to control stress; the reverse pattern may characterize the smoking of another individual.

In summary, health behaviors are elicited and maintained by different factors for different people, and these factors change over the lifetime as well as during the course of the health habit. Consequently, health habits are difficult to change. As a result, health habit interventions have focused heavily on those who may be helped the most—namely, the young.

Intervening with Children and Adolescents

Socialization   Health habits are strongly affected by early **socialization,** especially the influence of parents as both teachers and role models (Morrongiello, Corbett, & Bellissimo, 2008). Parents instill certain habits in their children (or not) that become automatic, such as wearing a seat belt, brushing teeth regularly, and eating breakfast every day. Nonetheless, in many families, even these basic health habits may not be taught, and even in families that conscientiously attempt to teach good health habits, there may be gaps. Especially in families in which parents are separated or there is familial distress, health habit guidance may slip through the cracks (Menning, 2006).

Moreover, as children move into adolescence, they sometimes backslide or ignore the early training they received from their parents. In addition, adolescents are vulnerable to an array of problematic health behaviors, including excessive alcohol consumption, smoking, drug use, and sexual risk taking, particularly if their parents aren't monitoring them very closely and their peers practice these behaviors (Andrews, Tildesley, Hops, & Li, 2002). Adolescents have an incomplete appreciation of the future risks they encounter through faulty habits such as smoking and drinking (Henson, Carey, Carey, & Maisto, 2006). Consequently, interventions with children and adolescents are a high priority.

Using the Teachable Moment   Health promotion efforts capitalize on educational opportunities to prevent poor health habits from developing. The concept of a **teachable moment** refers to the fact that certain times are better than others for teaching particular health practices.

Many teachable moments arise in early childhood. Parents have opportunities to teach their children basic safety behaviors, such as putting on a seat belt in the car or looking both ways before crossing the street, and basic health habits, such as drinking milk instead of soda with dinner (Peterson & Soldana, 1996).

Other teachable moments arise because they are built into the health care delivery system. For example, many infants in the United States are covered by well-baby care. Pediatricians often make use of these early visits to teach

The foundations for health promotion develop in early childhood, when children are taught to practice good health behaviors.

motivated new parents the basics of accident prevention and safety in the home. Dentists use a child's first visit to teach both the parents and the child the importance of correct brushing. Many school systems require a physical at the beginning of the school year or at least an annual visit to a physician. This procedure ensures that parents and children have regular contact with the health care delivery system so that information about health habits, such as weight control or accident prevention, can be communicated. Such visits also ensure that children receive their basic immunizations.

But what can children themselves really learn about health habits? Certainly, very young children have cognitive limitations that keep them from fully comprehending the concept of health promotion. Nevertheless, intervention programs with children clearly indicate that they can develop personal responsibility for aspects of their health. Such behaviors as choosing nutritionally sound foods, brushing teeth regularly, using car seats and seat belts, participating in exercise, crossing the street safely, and behaving appropriately in real or simulated emergencies (such as earthquake drills) are within the comprehension of children as young as age 3 or 4, as long as the behaviors are explained in concrete terms and the implications for actions are clear (Maddux, Roberts, Sledden, & Wright, 1986).

Teachable moments are not confined to childhood and adolescence. Pregnancy represents a teachable moment for several health habits, especially stopping smoking and improving diet (Levitsky, 2004; Solomon et al., 2006). Adults with newly diagnosed coronary artery disease may also be especially motivated to change their health habits, such as smoking and diet, due to the anxiety their recent diagnosis has caused. Emergency room visits, the primary source of medical care for many indigent people, can be a venue for inducing people to change their health behaviors, such as smoking (Boudreaux et al., 2008).

Identifying teachable moments—that is, the crucial point at which a person is ready to modify a health behavior—is a high priority for primary prevention.

Closing the Window of Vulnerability

Middle school appears to be a particularly important time for the development of several health-related habits. For example, food choices, snacking, and dieting all begin to crystallize around this time (Cohen et al., 1990). There is also a **window of vulnerability** for smoking and drug use that occurs in middle school, when students are first exposed to these habits among their peers and older siblings (D'Amico & Fromme, 1997). As we will see, interventions through the schools may help students avoid the temptations that lead to these health-compromising behaviors.

Adolescence is a window of vulnerability for many poor health habits. Consequently, intervening to prevent health habits from developing is a high priority for children in late elementary and middle school.

Adolescent Health Behaviors and Adult Health

A final reason for intervening with children and adolescents to modify health habits is that, increasingly, research shows that precautions taken in adolescence may affect disease risk after age 45 more than do adult health behaviors. This means that the health habits people practice as teenagers or college students may well determine which chronic diseases they develop and what they ultimately die of in adulthood.

For adults who decide to make changes in their lifestyle, it may already be too late. Research to date suggests that this is true for sun exposure and skin cancer and for calcium consumption for the prevention of osteoporosis. Diet, especially dietary fat intake and protein consumption in adolescence, may also predict adult cancers. Consequently, despite the sense of invulnerability that many adolescents have, adolescence may actually be a highly vulnerable time for several poor health behaviors that lay the groundwork for problems in adulthood.

Intervening with At-Risk People

I'm a walking time bomb.

—37-year-old woman at risk for breast cancer

Another vulnerable group is people who are at risk for particular health problems. For example, a pediatrician may work with obese parents to control the diet of their offspring in the hopes that obesity in the children can be avoided. If the dietary changes produce the additional consequence of reducing the parents' weight, so much the better. Daughters of women who have had breast cancer are a vulnerable population who need to monitor themselves for any changes in the breast tissue and obtain regular mammograms.

Benefits of Focusing on At-Risk People

There are several advantages to working with people who are at risk for health disorders. Early identification and intervention may prevent or eliminate the poor health habits that can exacerbate vulnerability. For example, helping men at risk for heart disease avoid smoking or getting them to stop at a young age may forestall a debilitating chronic illness (Schieken, 1988). Even if no intervention is available to reduce risk, knowledge of risk can provide people with information they need to monitor their situation (Swaveley, Silverman, & Falek, 1987). Women at risk for breast cancer are an example of such a group.

Working with at-risk populations represents an efficient and effective use of health promotion dollars.

When a risk factor has implications for only some people, there is little reason to implement a general health intervention for everyone. Instead, it makes sense to target those people for whom the risk factor is relevant.

Finally, focusing on at-risk populations makes it easier to identify other risk factors that may interact with the targeted factor to produce an undesirable outcome. For example, not everyone who has a family history of hypertension will develop hypertension, but by focusing on people who are at risk, other factors that contribute to its development may be identified.

Problems of Focusing on At-Risk People

Clearly, however, there are difficulties in working with populations at risk. People do not always perceive their risk correctly (Croyle et al., 2006; Rothman & Salovey, 1997). Generally, most people, even children, are unrealistically optimistic about their vulnerability to health risks (Albery & Messer, 2005; Weinstein & Klein, 1995). People tend to view their poor health behaviors as widely shared but their healthy behaviors as more distinctive. For example, smokers overestimate the number of other people who smoke. When people perceive that others are engaging in the same unhealthy practice, they may perceive a lower risk to their health (Suls, Wan, & Sanders, 1988).

Sometimes testing positive for a risk factor leads people into needless worry or hypervigilant and restrictive behavior (DiLorenzo et al., 2006; Elmore & Gigerenzer, 2005). For example, women at genetic risk for breast cancer appear to be more physiologically reactive to stressful events, raising the possibility that the chronic stress associated with this familial cancer risk may change psychobiological reactivity (Valdimarsdottir et al., 2002). People can also become defensive, minimize the significance of their risk factor, and avoid using appropriate services or monitoring their condition (Brewer, Weinstein, Cuite, & Herrington, 2004; Croyle, Sun, & Louie, 1993). Providing people with feedback about their genetic susceptibility to a disorder such as lung cancer can have immediate and strong effects on relevant behaviors, such as a reduction in smoking (Lerman et al., 1997). As yet, the conditions under which these problematic responses occur have not been fully identified.

Ethical Issues

There are important ethical issues in working with at-risk populations. At what point is it appropriate to alarm at-risk people if their personal risk may be low? Among people at risk for a particular disorder, only some will develop the problem and, in many cases, only many years later. For example, should adolescent daughters of breast cancer patients be alerted to their risk and alarmed at a time when they are attempting to come to terms with their emerging sexuality and needs for self-esteem? Psychological distress may be created in exchange for instilling risk reduction behaviors (Croyle et al., 1997).

Some people, such as those predisposed to depression, may react especially poorly to the prospect or results of genetic testing for health disorders (Vernon et al., 1997). These effects may occur primarily just after testing positive for a risk factor and may not be long term (Tibben, Timman, Bannick, & Duivenvoorden, 1997).

In many cases, there is no successful intervention for genetically based risk factors (Baum, Friedman, & Zakowski, 1997). For example, identifying boys at risk for coronary artery disease and teaching them how to manage stress effectively may be ineffective in changing their risk status.

For other disorders, we may not know what an effective intervention will be. For example, alcoholism is now believed to have a genetic component, particularly among men, and yet exactly how and when we should intervene with the offspring of adult alcoholics is not yet clear.

Finally, emphasizing risks that are inherited can raise complicated issues of family dynamics, potentially pitting parents and children against each other and raising the issue of who is to blame for the risk. Daughters of breast cancer patients may suffer stress and exhibit behavior problems, due in part to the enhanced recognition of their risk (Taylor, Lichtman, & Wood, 1984a). Intervening with at-risk populations remains a controversial issue.

Health Promotion and Older Adults

Frank Ford, 91, starts each morning with a brisk walk. After a light breakfast of whole wheat toast and orange juice, he gardens for an hour or two. Later, he joins a couple of friends for lunch, and if he can persuade them to join him, they fish during the early afternoon. Reading a daily paper and always having a good book to read keeps Frank mentally sharp. Asked how he maintains such a busy schedule, Frank says, "Exercise, friends, and mental challenge" are the keys to his long and healthy life.

Ford's lifestyle is right on target. One of the chief focuses of recent health promotion efforts has been older adults. At one time, prejudiced beliefs that health promotion efforts would be wasted in old age limited this emphasis. However, policy makers now recognize that a healthy older adult population is essential for controlling health care spending and ensuring that the nation

Among older adults, health habits are a major determinant of whether an individual will have a vigorous or an infirmed old age.

can sustain the increasingly older adults population that will develop over the next decades (Center for the Advancement of Health, March 2006).

Health promotion efforts with older adults have focused on several behaviors: maintaining a healthy, balanced diet; developing a regular exercise regimen; taking steps to reduce accidents; controlling alcohol consumption; eliminating smoking; reducing the inappropriate use of prescription drugs; and obtaining vaccinations against influenza (Kahana et al., 2002; Nichol et al., 2003).

Exercise is one of the most important health behaviors to target because exercise helps keep people mobile and able to care for themselves. Even merely keeping active has health benefits. Participating in social activities, running errands, and engaging in other normal activities that probably have little effect on overall fitness nonetheless reduce the risk of mortality, perhaps by providing social support or a general sense of self-efficacy (Glass, deLeon, Marottoli, & Berkman, 1999). Among the very old, exercise has particularly beneficial long-term benefits, substantially increasing the likelihood that older adults can maintain the basic activities of daily living (Kahana et al., 2002).

Controlling alcohol consumption is an important target for good health among older adults as well. Some older adults develop drinking problems in response to age-related issues, such as retirement or loneliness (Brennan & Moos, 1995). Others may try to maintain the drinking habits they had throughout their lives, which become more risky in old age. For example, metabolic changes related to age may reduce the capacity for alcohol. Moreover, many older people are on medications that may interact dangerously with alcohol. Alcohol consumption increases the risk of accidents, which, in conjunction with osteoporosis, can result in broken bones, which limit mobility, creating further health problems (Sheahan et al., 1995). Drunk driving among older adults represents a problem, inasmuch as diminished driving capacities may be further impaired by alcohol.

Middle-aged and older adults who are poor may cut back on their medications to save money. Unfortunately, those who do are more likely to experience health problems within the next few years (Reitman, 2004, June 28).

Vaccinations against influenza are important for several reasons. First, flu is a major cause of death among older adults. Moreover, it increases the risk of heart disease and stroke because it exacerbates other underlying disorders that older adults are more likely to have (Nichol et al., 2003). Finding ways to ensure that older adults get their flu vaccinations each fall, then, is an important health priority.

Older adults are at risk for depression, which also compromises health habits, leading to accelerated physical decline. Thus, addressing depression, commonly thought of as a mental health problem, can have effects on physical health as well (Wrosch, Schulz, & Heckhausen, 2002).

Many older adults fail to practice good health habits because they doubt their ability to do so. Consequently, enhancing self-efficacy generally and with respect to particular health habits, such as physical activity, can be an essential component of any intervention with older adults (Konopack et al., 2008).

The emphasis on health habits among older adults is well placed. By age 80, health habits are the major determinant of whether a person will have a vigorous or an infirmed old age (McClearn et al., 1997). Moreover, current evidence suggests that health habit changes are working. The health of our older adult population is improving (Lubitz, Cai, Kramarow, & Lentzner, 2003).

Ethnic and Gender Differences in Health Risks and Habits

There are ethnic and gender differences in vulnerability to particular health risks, and health promotion programs need to take these differences into account (Corral & Landrine, 2008; Facts of Life, February 2006). For example, African American and Hispanic women get less exercise than do Anglo women and are more likely to be overweight; Latinas acculturated to the mainstream culture do better than less acculturated Latinas (Pichon et al., 2007). Anglo and African American women are more likely to smoke than Hispanic women. Alcohol consumption is a substantially greater problem among men than women, and smoking is a somewhat greater problem for Anglo men than for other groups. We will return to these issues.

Health promotion programs for ethnic groups also need to take account of co-occurring risk factors. The combined effects of low socioeconomic status and a biologic predisposition to particular illnesses puts certain groups at substantially greater risk. Examples are diabetes among Hispanics and hypertension among African Americans, which we will consider in more detail in Chapter 13.

■ CHANGING HEALTH HABITS

Habit is habit, and not to be flung out of the window by any man, but coaxed downstairs a step at a time.

—Mark Twain

In the remainder of this chapter, we address the technology of changing poor health habits. First, we look at attitudinal approaches to health behavior change, which assume that, if we give people correct information about their poor health habits, they will be motivated to change those habits. As will be seen, attitude change campaigns may induce the desire to change behavior but may not be successful in teaching people exactly how to do so.

Attitude Change and Health Behavior

Educational Appeals   Educational appeals make the assumption that people will change their health habits if they have correct information. Research has provided the following suggestions of the best ways to persuade people through educational appeals:

- Communications should be colorful and vivid rather than steeped in statistics and jargon. If possible, they should also use case histories (Taylor &

Thompson, 1982). For example, a vivid account of the health benefits of regular exercise, coupled with a case history of someone who took up bicycling after a heart attack, may be persuasive to someone at risk for heart disease (de Wit, Das, & Vet, 2008).

- The communicator should be expert, prestigious, trustworthy, likable, and similar to the audience (McGuire, 1964). For example, a health message will be more persuasive if it comes from a respected, credible physician rather than from the proponent of the latest health fad.

- Strong arguments should be presented at the beginning and end of a message, not buried in the middle.

- Messages should be short, clear, and direct.

- Messages should state conclusions explicitly. For example, a communication extolling the virtues of a low-cholesterol diet should explicitly advise the individual to alter his or her diet to lower cholesterol.

- Extreme messages produce more attitude change, but only up to a point. Very extreme messages are discounted. For example, a message that urges people to exercise for at least half an hour 3 days a week will be more effective than one that recommends several hours of exercise a day.

- For illness detection behaviors (such as HIV testing or obtaining a mammogram), emphasizing the problems that may occur if the behaviors are not undertaken will be most effective (Banks et al., 1995; Kalichman & Coley, 1996). For health promotion behaviors (such as sunscreen use),

emphasizing the benefits to be gained may be more effective (Rothman & Salovey, 1997).

- If the audience is receptive to changing a health habit, then the communication should include only favorable points, but if the audience is not inclined to accept the message, the communication should discuss both sides of the issue. For example, messages to smokers ready to stop should emphasize the health risks of smoking. Smokers who have not yet decided to stop may be more persuaded by a communication that points out its risk while acknowledging and rebutting its pleasurable effects (Martinez, Ainsworth, & Elder, 2008).

- Interventions should be sensitive to the cultural norms of the community to which they are directed (Martinez et al., 2008). For example, family-directed interventions may be especially effective in Latino communities (Pantin et al., 2009).

Fear Appeals   Attitudinal approaches to changing health habits often make use of **fear appeals.** This approach assumes that if people are fearful that a particular habit is hurting their health, they will change their behavior to reduce their fear. Common sense suggests that the relationship between fear and behavior change should be direct: The more fearful an individual is, the more likely she or he will be to change the relevant behavior. However, research has found that this relationship does not always hold (Leventhal, 1970).

Persuasive messages that elicit too much fear may actually undermine health behavior change (Becker &

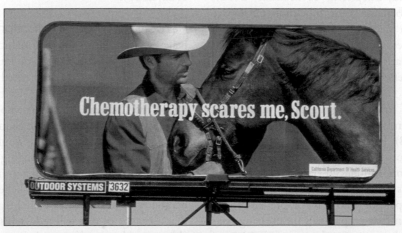

Fear appeals often alert people to a health problem but do not necessarily change behavior.

Janz, 1987). Moreover, research suggests that fear alone may not be sufficient to change behavior. Sometimes fear can affect intentions to change health habits (Sutton & Eiser, 1984), but it may not produce long-lasting changes in health habits unless it is coupled with recommendations for action or information about the efficacy of the health behavior (Self & Rogers, 1990).

Providing information does not ensure that people will perceive that information accurately. As noted, sometimes when people receive negative information about risks to their health, they process that information defensively (Millar & Millar, 1996). Instead of making appropriate health behavior changes, the person may come to view the problem as less serious or more common than he or she had previously believed (Croyle et al., 2006), particularly if he or she intends to continue the behavior (Gerrard, Gibbons, Benthin, & Hessling, 1996). Smokers, for example, know that they are at a greater risk for lung cancer than are nonsmokers, but they see lung cancer as less likely or problematic and smoking as more common than do nonsmokers. So fear appeals may increase awareness of risk but not necessarily change behavior.

Message Framing   Any health message can be phrased in positive or negative terms. For example, a reminder letter to get a flu immunization can stress the benefits of being immunized or, alternatively, stress the discomfort of the flu itself (Gerend & Shepherd, 2007). Which of these methods is more successful? Messages that emphasize potential problems seem to work better for behaviors that have uncertain outcomes or for health behaviors that need to be practiced only once, such as vaccinations (Gerend, Shepherd, & Monday, 2008); messages that stress benefits seem to be more persuasive for behaviors with certain outcomes (Apanovitch, McCarthy, & Salovey, 2003). As is the case with fear appeals, recommendations regarding exactly how to take the action increase effectiveness (McCaul, Johnson, & Rothman, 2002).

Which kind of message framing will most affect behavior also depends on people's own motivation (Latimer et al., 2008). People who have a promotion or approach orientation that emphasizes maximizing opportunities are more influenced by messages phrased in terms of benefits ("calcium will keep your bones healthy"), whereas people who have a prevention or avoidance orientation that emphasizes minimizing risks are more influenced by messages that stress the risks of not performing a health behavior ("low calcium intake

will increase bone loss") (Mann, Sherman, & Updegraff, 2005). On the whole, promotion-oriented messages may be somewhat more successful in getting people to initiate behavior change, and prevention focus may be more helpful in getting them to maintain behavior change over time (Fuglestad, Rothman, & Jeffery, 2008).

Health psychologists have developed approaches to health habit change that integrate educational and motivational factors into more general models for altering health behaviors (see Sturges & Rogers, 1996; Weinstein, 1993).

The Health Belief Model

The most influential attitude theory of why people practice health behaviors is the **health belief model** (Hochbaum, 1958; Rosenstock, 1966). According to this model, whether a person practices a particular health behavior depends on two factors: whether the person perceives a personal health threat, and whether the person believes that a particular health practice will be effective in reducing that threat.

Perceived Health Threat   The perception of a personal health threat is influenced by at least three factors: general health values, which include interest in and concern about health; specific beliefs about personal vulnerability to a particular disorder; and beliefs about the consequences of the disorder, such as whether they are serious. Thus, for example, people may change their diet to include low cholesterol foods if they value health, feel threatened by the possibility of heart disease, and perceive that the threat of heart disease is severe (Brewer et al., 2007).

Perceived Threat Reduction   Whether a person believes a health measure will reduce threat has two subcomponents: whether the individual thinks the health practice will be effective, and whether the cost of undertaking that measure exceeds its benefits (Rosenstock, 1974). For example, the man who feels vulnerable to a heart attack and is considering changing his diet may believe that dietary change alone would not reduce the risk of a heart attack and that changing his diet would interfere with his enjoyment of life too much to justify taking the action. Thus, although his belief in his personal vulnerability to heart disease may be great, if he lacks faith that a change of diet will reduce his risk, he would probably not make any changes. A diagram of the health belief model applied to smoking is presented in Figure 3.1.

FIGURE 3.1 | The Health Belief Model Applied to the Health Behavior of Stopping Smoking

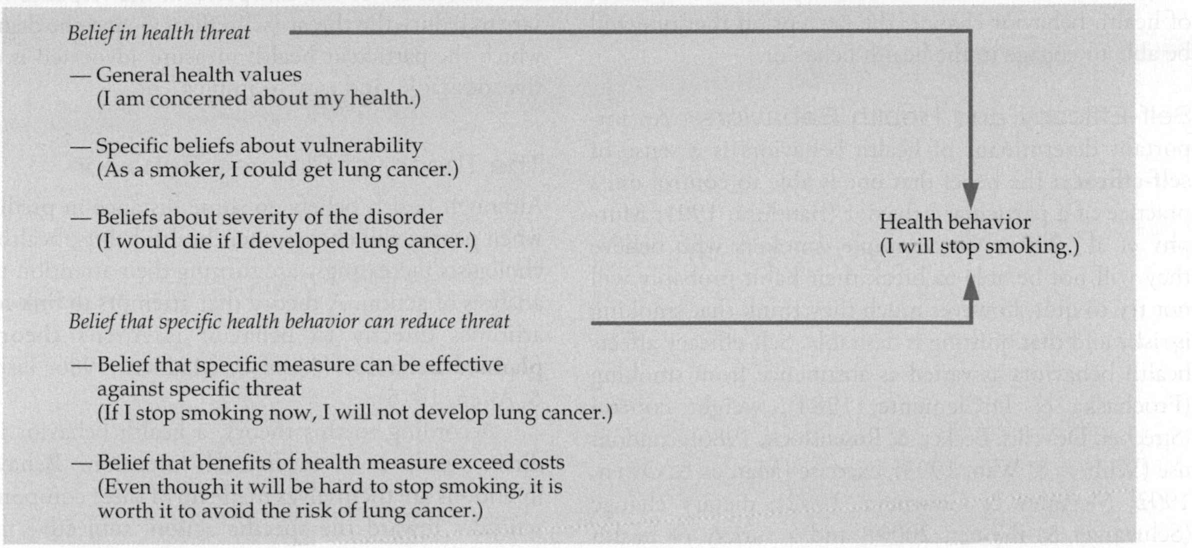

Belief in health threat

— General health values
(I am concerned about my health.)

— Specific beliefs about vulnerability
(As a smoker, I could get lung cancer.)

— Beliefs about severity of the disorder
(I would die if I developed lung cancer.)

Health behavior
(I will stop smoking.)

Belief that specific health behavior can reduce threat

— Belief that specific measure can be effective
against specific threat
(If I stop smoking now, I will not develop lung cancer.)

— Belief that benefits of health measure exceed costs
(Even though it will be hard to stop smoking, it is
worth it to avoid the risk of lung cancer.)

Support for the Health Belief Model The health belief model explains people's practice of health habits quite well. For example, it predicts preventive dental care (Ronis, 1992), breast self-examination (Champion, 1990), dieting for obesity (Uzark, Becker, Dielman, & Rocchini, 1987), AIDS risk-related behaviors (Aspinwall, Kemeny, Taylor, Schneider, & Dudley, 1991), participation in a broad array of health screening programs (Becker, Kaback, Rosenstock, & Ruth, 1975), and drinking and smoking intentions among adolescents (Goldberg, Halpern-Felsher, & Millstein, 2002). Typically, health beliefs are a modest determinant of intentions to take these health measures.

Using the Health Belief Model to Change Behavior The health belief model also predicts some of the circumstances under which people's health behaviors will change. A good illustration of this point comes from the experience of a student in my psychology class a few years ago. This student (call him Bob) was the only person in the class who smoked, and he was the object of some pressure from his fellow students to quit. He was familiar with the health risks of smoking. Although he knew that smoking contributes to lung cancer and heart disease, he believed the relationships are weak. Moreover, because he was in very good health and played a number of sports, his feelings of vulnerability were quite low.

Over Thanksgiving vacation, Bob went home to a large family gathering and discovered to his shock that his favorite uncle, a chain smoker all his adult life, had lung cancer and was not expected to live more than a few months. Suddenly, health became a more salient value for Bob. Bob's perceived susceptibility to the illness changed both because a member of his own family had been struck down and because the link between smoking and cancer had been graphically illustrated. Bob's perceptions of stopping smoking changed as well. He concluded that this step might suffice to ward off the threat of the disease and that the costs of quitting smoking were not as great as he had thought. When Bob returned from Thanksgiving vacation, he had stopped smoking.

Interventions that draw on the health belief model have generally supported its predictions. Highlighting perceived vulnerability and simultaneously increasing the perception that a particular health behavior will reduce the threat are somewhat successful in changing behavior, whether the behavior is smoking (Eiser, van der Plight, Raw, & Sutton, 1985), preventive dental measures (Ronis, 1992), or osteoporosis prevention measures (Klohn & Rogers, 1991).

However, the health belief model focuses heavily on beliefs about risk, rather than emotional responses to perceived risk, which also predict behavior (Lawton, Conner, & Parker, 2007; Peters, Slovic, Hibbard, &

Tusler, 2006; Weinstein et al., 2007). In addition, the health belief model leaves out an important component of health behavior change: the perception that one will be able to engage in the health behavior.

Self-Efficacy and Health Behaviors An important determinant of health behaviors is a sense of **self-efficacy:** the belief that one is able to control one's practice of a particular behavior (Bandura, 1991; Murphy et al., 2001). For example, smokers who believe they will not be able to break their habit probably will not try to quit, however much they think that smoking is risky and that quitting is desirable. Self-efficacy affects health behaviors as varied as abstinence from smoking (Prochaska & DiClemente, 1984), weight control (Strecher, DeVellis, Becker, & Rosenstock, 1986), condom use (Wulfert & Wan, 1993), exercise (Marcus & Owen, 1992; McAuley & Courneya, 1992), dietary change (Schwarzer & Renner, 2000), and a variety of health behaviors among older adults (Grembowski et al., 1993). Typically, research finds a strong relationship between perceptions of self-efficacy and both initial health behavior change and long-term maintenance of change.

To summarize, then, we can say that whether a person practices a particular health behavior depends on several beliefs: the magnitude of a health threat, the degree to which that person believes he or she is personally vulnerable to that threat, the degree to which that person believes he or she can perform the response necessary to reduce the threat (self-efficacy), and the degree to which the particular health measure advocated is effective, desirable, and easy to implement.

The Theory of Planned Behavior

Although health beliefs go some distance in predicting when people will change their health habits, health psychologists increasingly are turning their attention to the analysis of action. A theory that attempts to link health attitudes directly to behavior is Ajzen's **theory of planned behavior** (Ajzen & Madden, 1986; Fishbein & Ajzen, 1975).

According to this theory, a health behavior is the direct result of a behavioral intention. Behavioral intentions are themselves made up of three components: attitudes toward the specific action, subjective norms regarding the action, and perceived behavioral control (Figure 3.2). Attitudes toward the action are based on beliefs about the likely outcomes of the action and evaluations of those outcomes. Subjective norms are what a person believes *others* think that person should do (normative beliefs) and her or his motivation to comply with those normative beliefs. Perceived behavioral control is the perception that one is capable of performing the

FIGURE 3.2 | The Theory of Planned Behavior Applied to the Health Behavior of Dieting
(*Sources:* Ajzen & Fishbein, 1980; Ajzen & Madden, 1986)

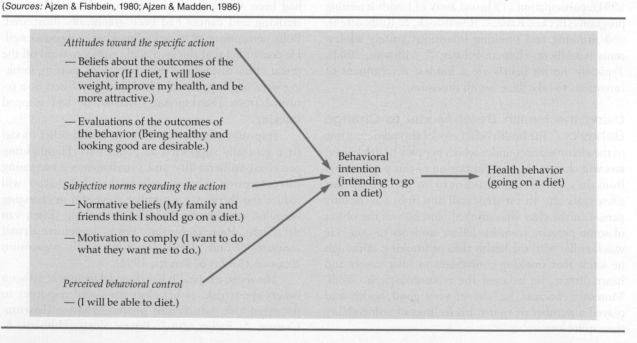

action and that the action undertaken will have the intended effect; this component of the model is very similar to self-efficacy. These factors combine to produce a behavioral intention and, ultimately, behavior change.

To take a simple example, smokers who believe that smoking causes serious health outcomes, who believe that other people think they should stop smoking, who are motivated to comply with those normative beliefs, who believe that they are capable of stopping smoking, and who form a specific intention to do so will be more likely to do so than people who do not hold these beliefs.

Benefits of the Theory of Planned Behavior
The theory of planned behavior is a useful addition to understanding health behavior change processes for two reasons. First, it provides a fine-grained picture of people's intentions with respect to a particular health habit. Second, it provides a model that links beliefs directly to behavior.

Evidence for the Theory of Planned Behavior
The theory of planned behavior predicts a broad array of health behaviors, including condom use among students (Sutton, McVey, & Glanz, 1999), sunbathing and sunscreen use (Hillhouse, Stair, & Adler, 1996), use of oral contraceptives (Doll & Orth, 1993), consumption of soft drinks among adolescents (Kassem & Lee, 2004), mammography participation (Montano & Taplin, 1991), testicular self-examination (Brubaker & Wickersham, 1990), exercise (Baker, Little, & Brownell, 2003), participation in cancer screening programs (DeVellis, Blalock, & Sandler, 1990), AIDS risk-related behaviors (Fisher, Fisher, & Rye, 1995), smoking (Van de Ven, Engles, Otten, & van den Eijnden, 2007), healthy eating (Baker et al., 2003), participation in health screening programs (Sheeran, Conner, & Norman, 2001), follow-up appointments for abnormal cervical screening results (Orbell & Hagger, 2006), and several daily health habits, including getting enough sleep and taking vitamins (Madden, Ellen, & Ajzen, 1992).

Implementation Intentions
In its own right, the intention to adopt or change a particular behavior at a particular time can influence health behavior practices (Armitage, 2009; Gollwitzer & Sheeran, 2006) and can be a simple but effective way to promote health behaviors (Martin, Sheeran, Slade, Wright, & Dibble, 2009). That is, forming a specific implementation intention (what, where, when) with respect to a health goal can help to bring it about (Sullivan & Rothman, 2008).

Self-Determination Theory
Because people are actively motivated to pursue their goals, interventions that build on these observations have been increasingly used in health behavior change efforts. Chief among these theoretical positions is **self-determination theory (SDT)** (Deci & Ryan, 1985; Ryan & Deci, 2000).

According to SDT, autonomous motivation and perceived competence are fundamental to behavior change. People are said to be autonomously motivated if they experience free will and choice when acting. From a health standpoint, then, behavior change is more likely when the change is personally important and tied to important values. The competence component is similar to self-efficacy.

Accordingly, if a woman changes her diet because her physician tells her to, she may not experience a sense of autonomy and instead may experience her actions as under another's control. The behavior change effort, according to the theory, would not have her wholehearted commitment under these circumstances. If experienced as autonomously chosen, however, she should be intrinsically motivated to persist. SDT has been used as a basis for interventions to reduce smoking (Williams, McGregor, Sharp, Levesque, et al., 2006) and alcohol and drug use in adolescents (Williams, Cox, Hedberg, & Deci, 2000), among other health behaviors.

Attitudes and Changing Health Behaviors: Some Caveats
Despite the success of theories that link beliefs to the modification of health habits, attitudinal approaches do not explain spontaneous behavior change very well, nor do they predict long-term behavior change very well (Kirscht, 1983). An additional complication is that communications designed to change people's attitudes about their health behaviors sometimes evoke defensive or irrational processes: People may perceive a health threat to be less relevant than it really is (Liberman & Chaiken, 1992), they may falsely see themselves as less vulnerable than others (Clarke, Lovegrove, Williams, & Macpherson, 2000), or they may see themselves as dissimilar to those who have succumbed to a particular health risk (Thornton, Gibbons, & Gerrard, 2002). Continued practice of a risky behavior may itself lead to changes in perception of a person's degree of risk, inducing a false sense of security (Halpern-Felsher et al., 2001).

Because health habits are often deeply ingrained and difficult to modify, attitude-change procedures may not go far enough by providing the informational base for altering health habits (Ogden, 2003). Attitude-change procedures may instill the motivation to change a health habit but not provide the preliminary steps or skills necessary to actually alter behavior and maintain behavior change (Bryan, Fisher, & Fisher, 2002). Consequently, health psychologists have also turned to therapeutic techniques.

■ COGNITIVE-BEHAVIORAL APPROACHES TO HEALTH BEHAVIOR CHANGE

Attitudinal approaches to the modification of health behaviors appear to be most useful for predicting when people will be motivated to change a health behavior. **Cognitive-behavior therapy (CBT)** approaches to health habit modification change the focus to the target behavior itself—the conditions that elicit and maintain it, and the factors that reinforce it (Dobson, 2010).

Cognitive-Behavior Therapy (CBT)

The most effective approach to health habit modification often comes from cognitive-behavior therapy (CBT). From an array of available techniques, a therapist selects several complementary methods to intervene in the modification of a target problem and its context.

The advantages of CBT for health behavior change are several. First, a carefully selected set of techniques can deal with all aspects of a problem: Self-observation and self-monitoring define the dimensions of a problem; stimulus control enables a person to modify antecedents of behavior; self-reinforcement controls the consequences of a behavior; and social skills training may be added to replace the maladaptive behavior once it has been brought under some degree of control. A combination of techniques can be more effective in dealing with all phases of a problem than one technique alone (van Kessel et al., 2008). We focus on each of these components in the next sections. An example of the application of this kind of therapy to the treatment of alcoholism appears in Box 3.1.

A second advantage is that the therapeutic plan can be tailored to each individual's problem. Each person's faulty health habit and personality are different, so, for example, the particular package identified for one obese client may not be the same as that developed for another obese client (Schwartz & Brownell, 1995). Third, the range of skills imparted by multimodal interventions

may enable people to modify several health habits simultaneously, such as diet and exercise, rather than one at a time (Persky, Spring, Vander Wal, Pagoto, & Hedeker, 2005; Prochaska & Sallis, 2004).

Cognitive-behavior therapy focuses especially heavily on the beliefs that people hold about their health habits. People often generate internal monologues that interfere with their ability to change their behavior. For example, a person who wishes to give up smoking may derail the quitting process by generating self-doubts ("I will never be able to give up smoking"). Unless these internal monologues are modified, the person will be unlikely to change a health habit and maintain that change over time.

Recognition that people's cognitions about their health habits are important in producing behavior change highlights another insight about the behavior change process: the importance of involving the patient as cotherapist in the behavior-change intervention. Clients monitor their own behaviors, and apply the techniques of cognitive-behavioral therapy to bring about change.

Self-Monitoring

Many programs of cognitive-behavioral modification use **self-monitoring** as the first step toward behavior change. The rationale is that a person must understand the dimensions of the target behavior before change can begin. Self-monitoring assesses the frequency of a target behavior and the antecedents and consequences of that behavior. This process also sets the stage for enlisting the patient's joint participation early in the effort to modify health behaviors.

The first step in self-monitoring is to learn to discriminate the target behavior. For some behaviors, this step is easy. A smoker obviously can tell whether he or she is smoking. However, other target behaviors or cognitions, such as the urge to smoke, may be less easily discriminated; therefore, an individual may be trained to monitor internal sensations closely so as to identify the target behavior more readily.

A second stage in self-monitoring is charting the behavior. Techniques range from very simple counters for recording the behavior each time it occurs to complex records documenting the circumstances under which the behavior was enacted as well as the feelings it aroused. For example, a smoker may be trained to keep a detailed behavioral record of all smoking events. She may record each time a cigarette is smoked, the time of day, the

BOX 3.1

Cognitive-Behavior Therapy in the Treatment of Alcoholism

Mary was a 32-year-old executive who came in for treatment, saying she thought she was an alcoholic. She had a demanding, challenging job, which she handled very conscientiously. Although her husband, Don, was supportive of her career, he felt it was important that evenings be spent in shared activities. They had had several arguments recently because Mary was drinking before coming home and had been hiding liquor around the house. Don was threatening to leave if she did not stop drinking altogether, and Mary was feeling alarmed by her behavior. Mary was seen over a 3-month period, with follow-up contact over the following year.

Mary's first week's assignment was to complete an autobiography of the history and development of her drinking problem—her parents' drinking behavior, her first drinking experience and first "drunk," the role of drinking in her adult life, her self-image, any problems associated with her drinking, and her attempts to control her drinking. She also self-monitored her drinking for 2 weeks, noting the exact amounts of alcohol consumed each day, the time, and the antecedents and consequences.

At the third session, the following patterns were identified. Mary started work at 8:30, typically had a rushed business lunch, and often did not leave work until 6:00, by which time she was tense and wound up. Because she knew Don did not approve of her drinking, she had begun to pick up a pint of vodka after work and to drink half of it during the 20-minute drive home, so that she could get relaxed for the evening. She had also begun stashing liquor away in the house just in case she wanted a drink. She realized that drinking while driving was dangerous, that she was drinking too much too quickly, and that she was feeling very guilty and out of control. Her husband's anger seemed to increase her urges to drink.

Mary agreed to abstain from any drinking during the third and fourth weeks of treatment. During this period, it became apparent that drinking was her only means of reducing the tension that had built up during the day and represented the one indulgence she allowed herself in a daily routine of obligations to external job demands and commitments to her husband and friends. A plan to modify her general lifestyle was worked out that included alternative ways of relaxing and indulging that were not destructive.

Mary joined a local health club and began going for a swim and a sauna every morning on the way to work. She also set aside 2 days a week to have lunch alone or with a friend. She learned a meditation technique, which she began using at the end of the day after getting home from work. She negotiated with Don to spend one evening a week doing separate activities so that she could resume her old hobby of painting.

Mary also decided that she wanted to continue drinking in a moderate way and that Don's support was essential so that she could drink openly. Don attended the sixth session with Mary, the treatment plan was explained to him, his feelings and concerns were explored, and he agreed to support Mary in her efforts to alter her lifestyle as well as to be more accepting of her drinking.

During the next few sessions, Mary learned a number of controlled drinking techniques, including setting limits for herself and pacing her drinking by alternating liquor with soft drinks. She also developed strategies for dealing with high-risk situations, which for her were primarily the buildup of tension at work and feelings of guilt or anger toward Don. She learned to become more aware of these situations as they were developing and began to practice more direct ways of communicating with Don. She also was instructed to use any urges to return to old drinking patterns as cues to pay attention to situational factors and use alternative responses rather than to interpret them as signs that she was an alcoholic.

The final two sessions were spent planning and rehearsing what to do if a relapse occurred. Strategies included the process of slowing herself down, cognitive restructuring, a decision-making exercise to review the consequences and relative merits and liabilities of drinking according to both the old and the new pattern, an analysis of the situation that led to the relapse, problem solving to come up with a better coping response to use next time, and the possibility of scheduling a booster session with her therapist.

At the final follow-up a year later, Mary reported that she was feeling better about herself and more in control, was drinking moderately on social occasions, and was communicating better with Don. She had had a couple of slips but had managed to retrieve the situation, in one case by being more assertive with a superior and in the other by simply deciding that she could accept some mistakes on her part without having to punish herself by continuing the mistake.

Source: Gordon & Marlatt, 1981, pp. 182–83. Reprinted by permission.

situation in which the smoking occurred, and the presence of other people (if any). She may also record the subjective feelings of craving that existed prior to lighting the cigarette, the emotional responses that preceded the lighting of the cigarette (such as anxiety or tension), and the feelings that were generated by the actual smoking of the cigarette. In this way, she can begin to get a sense of the circumstances in which she is most likely to smoke and can then initiate a structured behavior-change program that deals with these contingencies.

Although self-monitoring is usually only a beginning step in behavior change, it may itself produce behavior change (Quinn, Pascoe, Wood, & Neal, 2010). Simply attending to their own smoking may lead people to decrease the number of cigarettes they smoke. Typically, however, behavior change that is produced by self-monitoring is short-lived and needs to be coupled with other techniques (McCaul, Glasgow, & O'Neill, 1992).

Classical Conditioning

First described by Russian physiologist Ivan Pavlov in the early 20th century, **classical conditioning** was one of the earliest principles of behavior change identified by researchers. The essence of classical conditioning is the pairing of an unconditioned reflex with a new stimulus, producing a conditioned reflex. Classical conditioning is represented diagrammatically in Figure 3.3.

Classical conditioning was one of the first methods used for health behavior change. For example, consider its use in the treatment of alcoholism. Antabuse (unconditioned stimulus) is a drug that produces extreme nausea, gagging, and vomiting (unconditioned response) when taken in conjunction with alcohol. Over time, the alcohol will become associated with the nausea and vomiting caused by the Antabuse and elicit the same nausea, gagging, and vomiting response (conditioned response) without the Antabuse being present.

Classical conditioning approaches to health habit modification do work, but clients know why they work. Alcoholics, for example, know that if they do not take the drug they will not vomit when they consume alcohol. Thus, even if classical conditioning has successfully produced a conditioned response, it is heavily dependent on the client's willing participation. Procedures like these produce health risks as well, and as a result, they are no longer as widely used.

Operant Conditioning

In contrast to classical conditioning, which pairs an automatic response with a new stimulus, operant conditioning pairs a voluntary behavior with systematic

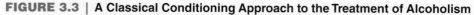

FIGURE 3.3 | A Classical Conditioning Approach to the Treatment of Alcoholism

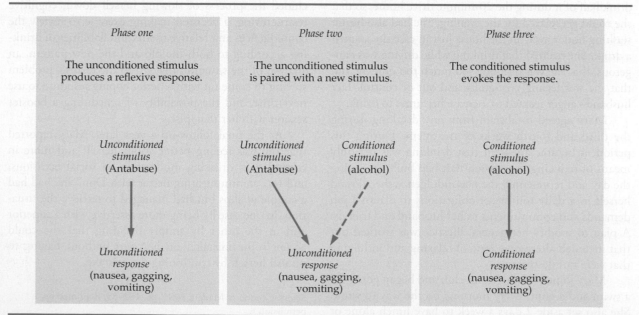

Phase one	Phase two	Phase three
The unconditioned stimulus produces a reflexive response.	The unconditioned stimulus is paired with a new stimulus.	The conditioned stimulus evokes the response.
Unconditioned stimulus (Antabuse)	Unconditioned stimulus (Antabuse) Conditioned stimulus (alcohol)	Conditioned stimulus (alcohol)
Unconditioned response (nausea, gagging, vomiting)	Unconditioned response (nausea, gagging, vomiting)	Conditioned response (nausea, gagging, vomiting)

consequences. The key to **operant conditioning** is reinforcement. When a person performs a behavior and that behavior is followed by positive reinforcement, the behavior is more likely to occur again. Similarly, if an individual performs a behavior and reinforcement is withdrawn or the behavior is punished, the behavior is less likely to be repeated. Over time, these contingencies build up those behaviors paired with positive reinforcement, while behaviors that are punished or not rewarded decline.

Many health habits can be thought of as operant responses. For example, drinking may be maintained because mood is improved by alcohol, or smoking may occur because peer companionship is associated with it. In both cases, reinforcement maintains the poor health behavior. Thus, using this principle to change behavior requires altering the reinforcement or its schedule.

An important feature of operant conditioning is the reinforcement schedule. A continuous reinforcement schedule means that a behavior is reinforced every time it occurs. However, continuous reinforcement is vulnerable to extinction: If the behavior is occasionally not paired with reinforcement, the individual may cease performing the behavior, having come to anticipate reinforcement each time. Psychologists have learned that behavior is often more resistant to extinction if it is maintained by a variable or an intermittent reinforcement schedule than a continuous reinforcement schedule.

Operant Conditioning to Change Health Behaviors

Operant conditioning is often used to modify health behaviors. At the outset, people typically will be positively reinforced for any action that moves them closer to their goal. As progress is made toward reducing or modifying the health habit, greater behavior change may be required for the same reinforcement. For example, suppose Mary smokes 20 cigarettes a day. She might first define a set of reinforcers that can be administered when particular smoking-reduction targets are met—reinforcements such as going out to dinner or seeing a movie. Mary may then set a particular reduction in her smoking behavior as a target (such as 15 cigarettes a day). When that target is reached, she would administer a reinforcement (the movie or dinner out). The next step might be reducing smoking to 10 cigarettes a day, at which time she would receive another reinforcement. The target then might be cut progressively to 5, 4, 3, 1, and none. Through this process, the target behavior of abstinence would eventually be reached.

Modeling

Modeling is learning that occurs by virtue of witnessing another person perform a behavior (Bandura, 1969). Observation and subsequent modeling can be effective approaches to changing health habits. For example, high school students who observed others donating blood were more likely to do so themselves (Sarason, Sarason, Pierce, Shearin, & Sayers, 1991).

Similarity is an important principle in modeling. To the extent that people perceive themselves as similar to the type of person who engages in a risky behavior, they are likely to do so themselves; to the extent that people see themselves as similar to the type of person who does not engage in a risky behavior, they may change their behavior (Gibbons & Gerrard, 1995). For example, a swimmer may decline a cigarette from a friend because she perceives that most great swimmers do not smoke.

Modeling can be an important long-term behavior-change technique. For example, the principle of modeling is implicit in some self-help programs that treat destructive health habits, such as alcoholism (Alcoholics Anonymous) and drug addiction. In these programs, a person who is newly committed to changing an addictive behavior joins people who have had the same problem and who have had at least some success in solving it. In meetings, people often share the methods that helped them overcome their health problem. By listening to these accounts, the new convert can learn how to do likewise and model effective techniques in his or her own rehabilitation.

Modeling can also be used as a technique for reducing the anxiety that can give rise to some bad habits or the fears that people may have when going through some preventive health behaviors, such as receiving inoculations. A person's fears can be reduced by observing the model engaging in the feared activity and coping with that fear effectively. For example, by observing a film of a person going through a noxious medical test and conquering his or her fears, one may better cope with the procedure when going through it oneself.

When modeling is used to reduce fear or anxiety, it is better to observe models who are also fearful but are able to control their distress rather than models who are demonstrating no fear in the situation. Because fearful models provide a realistic portrayal of the experience, the person trying to change his or her behavior may be better able to identify with them than with models who are unrealistically calm in the face of the threat. This identification process may enable the person to learn and model the coping techniques more successfully.

Stimulus Control

The successful modification of health behavior involves understanding the antecedents as well as the consequences of a target behavior. Individuals who practice poor health habits, such as smoking, drinking, and overeating, develop ties between those behaviors and stimuli in their environments. Each of these stimuli can come to act as a **discriminative stimulus** that is capable of eliciting the target behavior. For example, the sight and smell of food act as discriminative stimuli for eating. The sight of a pack of cigarettes or the smell of coffee may act as discriminative stimuli for smoking. The discriminative stimulus is important because it signals that a positive reinforcement will subsequently occur.

Stimulus-control interventions with patients who are attempting to alter their health habits take two approaches: ridding the environment of discriminative stimuli that evoke the problem behavior, and creating new discriminative stimuli, signaling that a new response will be reinforced.

How might stimulus control work in the treatment of a health problem? Eating is typically under the control of discriminative stimuli, including the presence of desirable foods and activities with which eating is frequently paired (such as watching television). As an early step in the treatment of obesity, individuals might be encouraged to reduce and eliminate these discriminative stimuli for eating. They would be urged to rid their home of rewarding and enjoyable fattening foods, to restrict their eating to a single place in the home, and to not eat while engaged in other activities, such as watching television. Other stimuli might be introduced in the environment to indicate that controlled eating will now be followed by reinforcement. For example, people might place signs in strategic locations around the home, reminding them of reinforcements to be obtained after successful behavior change.

The Self-Control of Behavior

As noted, cognitive-behavior therapy, including that used to modify health habits, emphasizes **self-control.** In this approach, the individual who is the target of the intervention acts as his or her own therapist and, together with outside guidance, learns to control the antecedents and consequences of the target behavior to be modified.

Self-control is not an unlimited resource, however. Successfully exerting self-control at one time or over one set of behaviors may deplete the ability to exhibit subsequent self-control (Hagger, Wood, Stiff, & Chatzisarantis,

2009; Shmueli & Prochaska, 2009). Breaks in exerting control and training in self-control can help to offset self-control depletion (Hagger et al., 2009).

Self-Reinforcement **Self-reinforcement** involves systematically rewarding oneself to increase or decrease the occurrence of a target behavior. Positive self-reward involves rewarding oneself with something desirable after successful modification of a target behavior. An example of positive self-reward is allowing oneself to go to a movie following successful weight loss. Negative self-reward involves removing an aversive factor in the environment after successful modification of the target behavior. An example of negative self-reward is taking the Miss Piggy poster off the refrigerator once regular controlled eating has been achieved.

An example of negative self-reward was used in a study to control obesity (Penick, Filion, Fox, & Stunkard, 1971). In this study, people who were overweight were instructed to keep large bags of suet (animal fat) in their refrigerators to remind themselves of their excess weight. Each time they succeeded in losing a certain amount of weight, they were permitted to remove a portion of the suet from the bag, thereby reducing this unattractive stimulus. Techniques such as these can be helpful for maintaining commitment to a behavior-change program.

Overall, self-reward has proven to be a useful technique in the modification of behavior. Moreover, self-reward techniques have intrinsic advantages in that no change agent, such as a therapist, is required to monitor and reinforce the behavior; the individual acts as her or his own therapist.

Like self-reward, self-punishment is of two types. Positive self-punishment involves the administration of an unpleasant stimulus to punish an undesirable behavior. For example, an individual might self-administer a mild electric shock each time he or she experiences a desire to smoke. Negative self-punishment consists of withdrawing a positive reinforcer in the environment each time an undesirable behavior is performed. For example, a smoker might rip up money each time he or she has a cigarette that exceeds a predetermined quota.

Studies that have evaluated the success of self-punishment suggest two conclusions: (1) Positive self-punishment works somewhat better than negative self-punishment, and (2) self-punishment works better if it is also coupled with self-rewarding techniques. Thus, a smoker is less likely to stop smoking if he rips up a dollar bill each time he smokes than if he self-administers electric shock; these principles are even more likely to reduce smoking if the smoker also rewards himself for not smoking—for example, by going to a movie.

Contingency Contracting

Self-punishment is effective only if people actually perform the punishing activities. When self-punishment becomes too aversive, people often abandon their efforts. However, one form of self-punishment that has been used in behavior modification is **contingency contracting.** In contingency contracting, an individual forms a contract with another person, such as a therapist, detailing what rewards or punishments are contingent on the performance or nonperformance of a behavior. For example, a person who wants to stop drinking might deposit a sum of money with a therapist and arrange to be fined each time he or she has a drink and to be rewarded each day that he or she abstained.

Cognitive Restructuring

As noted earlier, poor health habits and their modification are often accompanied by internal monologues, such as self-criticism or self-praise. **Cognitive restructuring** trains people to recognize and modify these internal monologues to promote health behavior change. Sometimes the modified cognitions are antecedents to a target behavior. For example, if a smoker's urge to smoke is preceded by an internal monologue that he is weak and unable to control his smoking urges, these beliefs are targeted for change. The smoker would be trained to develop antecedent cognitions that would help him stop smoking (for example, "I can do this" or "I'll be so much healthier").

Cognitions can also be the consequences of a target behavior. For example, an obese individual trying to lose weight might undermine her weight-loss program by reacting with hopelessness to every small dieting setback. She might be trained, instead, to engage in self-reinforcing cognitions following successful resistance to temptation and constructive self-criticism following setbacks ("Next time, I'll keep those tempting foods out of my refrigerator").

In a typical intervention, clients are first trained to monitor their monologues in stress-producing situations. In this way, they come to recognize what they say to themselves during times of stress. They are then taught to modify their self-instructions to include more constructive cognitions. For example, a client who wishes to stop smoking may learn to respond to smoking urges by thinking antismoking thoughts ("Smoking causes cancer") and thoughts that favor nonsmoking ("My food will taste better if I stop smoking"). To increase the frequency of these cognitions, the client may reinforce them with a rewarding activity, such as a favorite food.

Modeling can be used to train a client in cognitive restructuring. The therapist may first demonstrate adaptive cognitive restructuring. She may identify a target stress-producing situation and then self-administer positive instructions (such as "Relax, you're doing great"). The client then attempts to cope with the stress-producing situation, instructing himself out loud. Following this phase, self-instruction may become a whisper, and finally become internal.

Behavioral Assignments

A technique for increasing client involvement is **behavioral assignments,** home practice activities that support the goals of a therapeutic intervention. Behavioral assignments are designed to provide continuity in the treatment of a behavior problem, and typically, these assignments follow up points in the therapeutic session. For example, if an early therapy session with an obese client involved training in self-monitoring, the client would be encouraged to keep a log of his eating behavior, including the circumstances in which it occurred. This log could then be used by the therapist and the patient at the next session to plan future behavioral interventions. Figure 3.4 gives an example of the behavioral assignment technique.

FIGURE 3.4 | Example of a Systematic Behavioral Assignment for an Obese Client

(*Source:* Shelton & Levy, 1981, p. 6)

Homework for Tom [client]

Using the counter, count bites taken.

Record number of bites, time, location, and what you ate.

Record everything eaten for 1 week.

Call for an appointment.

Bring your record.

Homework for John [therapist]

Reread articles on obesity.

Note that it includes homework assignments for both client and therapist. This technique can ensure that both parties remain committed to the behavior-change process and that each is aware of the other's commitment. In addition, writing down homework assignments appears to work better than verbal agreements, in that it provides a clear record of what has been agreed to (Cox, Tisdelle, & Culbert, 1988).

In summary, the chief advantages of behavioral assignments are that (1) the client becomes involved in the treatment process, (2) the client produces an analysis of the behavior that is useful in planning further interventions, (3) the client becomes committed to the treatment process through a contractual agreement to discharge certain responsibilities, (4) responsibility for behavior change is gradually shifted to the client, and (5) the use of homework assignments increases the client's sense of self-control.

Social Skills Training   Some poor health habits develop in response to or are maintained by the anxiety people experience in social situations. For example, adolescents often begin to smoke in order to reduce their social anxiety by communicating a cool, sophisticated image. Drinking and overeating may also be responses to social anxiety. Social anxiety can then act as a cue for the maladaptive habit, necessitating an alternative way of coping with the anxiety.

A number of programs designed to alter health habits include either **social skills training** or **assertiveness training,** or both, as part of the intervention package. Individuals are trained in methods that will help them deal more effectively with social anxiety. The goals of social skills programs as an ancillary technique in a program of health behavior change are to reduce anxiety that occurs in social situations, to introduce new skills for dealing with situations that previously aroused anxiety, and to provide an alternative behavior for the poor health habit that arose in response to social anxiety.

Motivational Interviewing   Motivational interviewing (MI) is increasingly used in health promotion interventions. Originally developed to treat addiction, the techniques have been adapted to target smoking, dietary improvements, exercise, cancer screening, and sexual behavior among other habits (Miller & Rose, 2009).

In motivational interviewing, the interviewer is non-judgmental, nonconfrontational, encouraging, and supportive. The goal is to help the client express whatever positive or negative thoughts he or she has regarding the behavior in an atmosphere that is free of negative evaluation. Typically, clients talk at least as much as counselors during MI sessions.

Motivational interviewing is an amalgam of principles and techniques drawn from psychotherapy and behavior-change theory. It is a client-centered counseling style designed to get people to work through the ambivalence they may be experiencing about changing their health behaviors. It appears to be especially effective for those who are initially wary about whether to change their behaviors (Resnicow et al., 2002).

In motivational interviewing, there is no effort to dismantle the denial often associated with the practice of bad health behaviors or to confront irrational beliefs or even to persuade a client to stop drinking, quit smoking, or otherwise improve health. Rather, the goal is to get the client to think through and express some of his or her own reasons for and against change and for the interviewer to listen and provide encouragement in lieu of giving advice (Miller & Rose, 2009). Motivational interviewing has broadened the tools for addressing health promotion efforts, although, like any one-on-one therapeutic technique, it is limited in the number of people it reaches.

Meditation and Health Behavior Change   Recently, CBT interventions to change health habits have begun to include training in meditation techniques. This focus is based on the idea that stress can trigger many poor health behaviors, such as overeating, drinking, and smoking.

Mindfulness meditation teaches people to strive for a state of mind in which one is highly aware and focused on the present moment, accepting and acknowledging it without becoming distracted or distressed by stress. Thus, the goal of mindfulness meditation is to help people approach stressful situations mindfully rather than reacting to them automatically (Bishop, 2002).

Acceptance and commitment therapy (ACT) is a CBT technique that makes use of acceptance, mindfulness, and commitment to behavior change. Sometimes people need to be able to move away from difficult thoughts and feelings and simply accept them while still persisting in desired actions, such as controlling diet. The goal of ACT is to try to change the private experience and thereby maintain commitment. ACT does not challenge thoughts directly, but instead teaches people to notice their thoughts in a mindful manner and from a distance so as to be able to respond more flexibly to them (Lillis, Hayes, Bunting, & Masuda, 2009). Acceptance and mindfulness therapies can improve the quality of life while people are undertaking health habit change efforts (Lillis et al., 2009).

Relaxation Training   In 1958, psychologist Joseph Wolpe (1958) developed a procedure known as systematic desensitization for the treatment of anxiety. The procedure involved training clients to substitute relaxation in the presence of circumstances that usually produced anxiety. To induce relaxation, Wolpe taught patients how to engage in deep breathing and progressive muscle relaxation—that is, **relaxation training.** In deep breathing, a person takes deep, controlled breaths, which produce a number of physiological changes, such as decreased heart rate and blood pressure and increased oxygenation of the blood. People typically engage in this kind of breathing spontaneously when they are relaxed. In progressive muscle relaxation, an individual learns to relax all the muscles in the body to discharge tension or stress. As just noted, many deleterious health habits, such as smoking and drinking, represent ways of coping with social anxiety. Thus, in addition to social skills training or assertiveness training, people may learn relaxation procedures to cope more effectively with their anxiety.

CBT approaches to health behavior change have often achieved success when more limited programs have not, but such programs require intelligent application. Overzealous interventionists have sometimes assumed that more is better and have included as many components as possible, in the hope that at least a few of them would be successful. In fact, this approach can backfire (Brownell, Marlatt, Lichtenstein, & Wilson, 1986). Overly complex behavior-change programs may undermine commitment because of the sheer volume of activities they require. A multimodal program must be guided by an intelligent, well-informed, judicious selection of appropriate techniques geared to an individual problem. Moreover, much of the success of such programs comes from the presence of an enthusiastic, committed practitioner, not from the use of lots of techniques (Brownell et al., 1986).

Relapse

One of the biggest problems faced in health habit modification is the tendency for people to relapse to their previous behavior following initial successful behavior change (McCaul et al., 1992). This problem occurs both with people who make health habit changes on

their own and with those who join formal programs to alter their behavior. Relapse is a particular problem with the addictive disorders of alcoholism, smoking, drug addiction, and obesity (Brownell et al., 1986), which have relapse rates between 50 and 90% (Marlatt & Gordon, 1985).

What do we mean by "relapse"? A single cigarette smoked at a cocktail party or the consumption of a pint of ice cream on a lonely Saturday night does not necessarily lead to permanent relapse. However, over time, initial vigilance may fade and relapse may set in.

Reasons for Relapse   Many factors influence relapse. Genetic factors may be implicated in alcoholism, smoking, and obesity. Withdrawal effects occur in response to abstinence from alcohol and cigarettes and can prompt a relapse, especially shortly after efforts to change behavior. Conditioned associations between cues and physiological responses may lead to urges or cravings to engage in the habit (Marlatt, 1990). For example, people may find themselves in situations where they used to smoke, such as a party, and relapse at that vulnerable moment.

Relapse is more likely when the individual has low self-efficacy for performing the health behavior (e.g. abstinence from alcohol) and expects that the unwanted health behavior will be reinforcing (e.g., "A few drinks would relax me") rather than punishing (e.g., "I will have a hangover") (Witkiewitz & Marlatt, 2004). Relapse occurs when motivation flags or goals for maintaining the health behavior have not been established. Relapse is more likely if a person has little social support from family and friends to maintain the behavior change.

A potent catalyst for relapse is negative affect (Witkiewitz & Marlatt, 2004). Relapse is more likely when people are depressed, anxious, or under stress. For example, when people are breaking off a relationship or encountering difficulty at work, they are vulnerable to relapse. Peter Jennings, the national newscaster who announced his diagnosis of lung cancer in 2005, had relapsed back to smoking after the September 11, 2001 terrorist attacks on the United States.

A particular moment that makes people vulnerable to relapse is when they have one lapse in vigilance. For example, that one cigarette or that single pint of ice cream can produce what is called an **abstinence violation effect**—that is, a feeling of loss of control that results when a person has violated self-imposed rules. The result is a more serious relapse, as the person's resolve falters.

FIGURE 3.5 | A Cognitive-Behavioral Model of the Relapse Process

This figure shows what happens when a person is trying to change a poor health habit and faces a high-risk situation. With adequate coping responses, the person may be able to resist temptation, leading to a low likelihood of relapse. Without adequate coping responses, however, perceptions of self-efficacy may decline and perceptions of the rewarding effects of the substance may increase, leading to an increased likelihood of relapse.   (*Source:* Larimer, Palmer, & Marlatt, 1999)

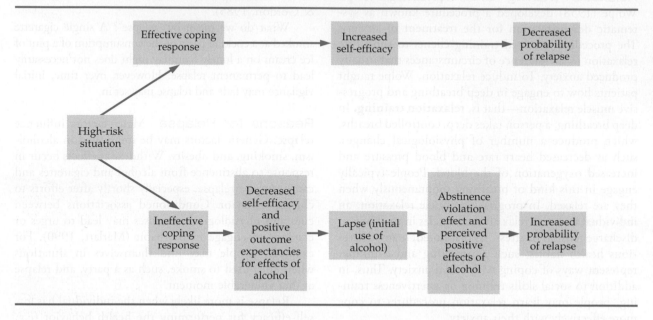

This is especially true for addictive behaviors because the person must also cope with the reinforcing impact of the substance itself. Figure 3.5 illustrates the relapse process.

Consequences of Relapse   What are the consequences of relapse? Clearly, relapse produces negative emotions, such as disappointment, frustration, unhappiness, or anger. Even a single lapse can lead a person to experience profound disappointment, a reduced sense of self-efficacy, and a shift in attributions for controlling the health behavior from the self to uncontrollable external forces. A relapse could also lead people to feel that they can never control the habit, that it is simply beyond their efforts. Relapse may be a deterrent to successful behavior change in other ways as well. For example, among the obese, repeated cycles of weight loss and regain make subsequent dieting more difficult (Brownell, Greenwood, Stellar, & Shrager, 1986).

In some cases, however, relapse may have paradoxical effects, leading people to perceive that they can control their habits, at least to a degree. With smoking, for example, multiple efforts to quit often take place before people succeed, suggesting that initial experiences with

stopping smoking may prepare people for later success. The person who relapses may nonetheless have acquired useful information about the habit and have learned ways to prevent relapse in the future.

Reducing Relapse   Because of the high risk of relapse, behavioral interventions build in techniques to try to reduce its likelihood. Typically, such interventions center on three techniques. Booster sessions following the termination of the initial treatment phase are one method. Several weeks or months after the end of a formal intervention, smokers may have an additional smoking-prevention session, or dieters may return to their group situation to be weighed in and to brush up on their weight-control techniques. Booster sessions are not always successful for preventing relapse, however (Brownell et al., 1986).

Another approach is to add more components to the behavioral intervention, such as relaxation therapy or assertiveness training. However, as noted earlier, the addition of components does not appear to increase adherence rates and, under some circumstances, may actually reduce them.

A third approach to relapse prevention is to consider abstinence a lifelong treatment process, as in such self-help programs as Alcoholics Anonymous. A drawback is that this philosophy can leave people feeling constantly vulnerable to relapse, potentially creating the expectation of relapse when vigilance wanes. Moreover, the approach implies that people are not in control of their habit, and research on health habit modification suggests that self-efficacy is an important component in initiating and maintaining behavior change.

Relapse Prevention   Researchers now believe that **relapse prevention** must be integrated into treatment programs from the outset. Enrolling people who are initially highly committed and motivated to change behavior reduces the risk of relapse and weeds out people who are not truly committed to behavior change and who are therefore vulnerable to relapse. This is a controversial measure. On the one hand, denying people access to a treatment program may be ethically dubious. On the other hand, including people who are likely to relapse may demoralize other participants in the behavior-change program, demoralize the practitioner, and ultimately make it more difficult for the relapser to change his or her behavior.

Relapse prevention techniques can also be built into the program itself. One strategy involves having people identify the situations that are likely to promote a relapse and develop coping skills that will enable them to manage that stressful event. This strategy draws on the fact that successful adherence promotes feelings of self-control. In addition, the mental rehearsal of coping responses in a high-risk situation can promote feelings of self-efficacy. For example, some programs train participants to engage in constructive **self-talk** that will enable them to talk themselves through tempting situations (Brownell et al., 1986). Because it is hard for people to anticipate how they will actually feel when temptation strikes (Nordgren, van der Pligt, & van Harreveld, 2008; Sayette, Loewenstein, Griffin, & Black, 2008), the closer people can get to experiencing these high-risk situations, the better.

Cue elimination involves restructuring the environment to avoid situations that evoke the target behavior (Bouton, 2000). For example, the alcoholic who drank exclusively in bars can avoid bars. For other habits, however, cue elimination is impossible. For example, smokers are usually unable to completely eliminate the circumstances in their lives that led them to smoke. Consequently, some relapse prevention programs deliberately expose people to the situations likely to evoke the old behavior to give them practice in using their coping skills (Marlatt, 1990). Such exposure can increase feelings of self-efficacy and decrease the positive expectations associated with the addictive behavior. Making sure that the new habit (such as exercise or alcohol abstinence) is practiced in as broad an array of new contexts as possible is important as well for ensuring that it endures (Bouton, 2000).

Lifestyle Rebalancing   Finally, long-term maintenance of behavior change can be promoted by leading the person to make other health-oriented changes in lifestyle, a technique termed **lifestyle rebalancing** (Marlatt & George, 1988). Lifestyle changes, such as adding an exercise program or using stress management techniques, may promote a healthy lifestyle more generally and help reduce the likelihood of relapse. Smoking or excessive alcohol consumption may come to feel inappropriate in the context of a generally healthier lifestyle.

The role of social support in maintaining behavior change is equivocal. At present, some studies suggest that enlisting the aid of family members in maintaining behavior change is helpful, but other studies suggest not (Brownell, Marlatt, et al., 1986). Possibly, research has not yet identified the exact ways in which social support may help maintain behavior change.

Overall, at present, relapse prevention seems to be most successful when people perceive their behavior change to be a long-term goal, develop coping techniques for managing high-risk situations, and integrate behavior change into a generally healthy lifestyle. In a meta-analysis of 26 studies with more than 9,000 participants treated for alcohol, tobacco, cocaine, and other substance use, Irvin and colleagues (1999) concluded that relapse prevention techniques were effective for reducing substance use and improving psychosocial functioning, and were particularly useful for people with alcohol problems.

■ THE TRANSTHEORETICAL MODEL OF BEHAVIOR CHANGE

Changing a bad health habit does not take place all at once. People go through stages while they are trying to change their health behaviors (Prochaska, 1994; Rothman, 2000).

Stages of Change

J. O. Prochaska and his associates (Prochaska, 1994; Prochaska, DiClemente, & Norcross, 1992) have developed the **transtheoretical model of behavior change,** a model that analyzes the stages and processes people go through in attempting to bring about a change in behavior and suggested treatment goals and interventions for each stage. Originally developed to treat addictive disorders, such as smoking, drug use, and alcohol addiction, the stage model has now been applied to a broad range of health habits, such as exercising and sun protection behaviors (Adams, Norman, Hovell, Sallis, & Patrick, 2009; Hellsten et al., 2008).

Precontemplation   The precontemplation stage occurs when a person has no intention of changing his or her behavior. Many individuals in this stage are not even aware that they have a problem, although families, friends, neighbors, or coworkers may well be. An example is the problem drinker who is largely oblivious to the problems he creates for his family. Sometimes people in the precontemplative phase seek treatment, but typically, they do so only if they have been pressured by others and feel themselves coerced into changing their behavior. Not surprisingly, these people often revert to their old behaviors and so make poor targets for intervention.

Contemplation   Contemplation is the stage in which people are aware that a problem exists and are thinking about it but have not yet made a commitment to take action. Many people remain in the contemplation stage for years. People in the contemplation stage are typically still weighing the pros and cons of changing their behavior, continuing to find the positive aspects of the behavior enjoyable. Increasing receptivity to the idea of an intervention can be helpful at this stage (Albarracín, Durantini, Earl, Gunnoe, & Leeper, 2008).

Preparation   In the preparation stage, people intend to change their behavior but may not yet have begun to do so. They may have been unsuccessful in the past, or they may simply be delaying action until they can get through a certain event or stressful period of time. In some cases, individuals in the preparation stage have already modified the target behavior somewhat, such as smoking fewer cigarettes than usual, but have not yet made the commitment to eliminate the behavior altogether.

Action   The action stage is the one in which individuals modify their behavior to overcome the problem. Action requires the commitment of time and energy to making real behavior change. It includes stopping the behavior and modifying one's lifestyle and environment to rid one's life of cues associated with the behavior.

Maintenance   Maintenance is the stage in which people work to prevent relapse and to consolidate the gains they have made. Typically, if a person is able to remain free of the addictive behavior for more than

Readiness to change a health habit is an important prerequisite to health habit change.

FIGURE 3.6 | A Spiral Model of the Stages of Change   (*Source:* Prochaska et al., 1992)

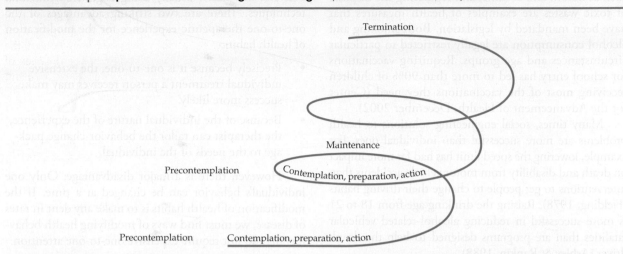

6 months, he or she is assumed to be in the maintenance stage (Wing, 2000).

Because relapse is the rule rather than the exception with addictive behaviors, this stage model is conceptualized as a spiral. As Figure 3.6 indicates, individuals may take action, attempt maintenance, relapse, return to the precontemplation phase, cycle through the subsequent stages to action, repeat the cycle again, and do so several times until they have eliminated the behavior (Prochaska et al., 1992).

Using the Stage Model of Change

The stage model of health behavior change is helpful because it suggests that particular interventions may be more valuable during one stage than another. For example, a smoker in the action phase is not going to be helped by information about the importance of not smoking, but information about the importance of controlling alcohol consumption may be valuable to a person who is just beginning to contemplate that he or she has a drinking problem.

At each stage, then, particular types of interventions may be warranted. Specifically, providing individuals in the precontemplation stage with information about their problem may move them to the contemplation phase. To move people from the contemplation phase into preparation, an appropriate intervention may induce them to assess how they feel and think about the problem and how stopping it will change them. Interventions designed to get people to make explicit commitments as to when and how they will change their behaviors may

bridge the gap between preparation and action. Interventions that emphasize providing self-reinforcement, social support, stimulus control, and coping skills should be most successful with individuals already moving through the action phase into long-term maintenance.

The stage model of health behavior change deserves to be true, but so far its applications have shown mixed success. The model has been used with many different health behaviors (Prochaska et al., 1992). In some cases, interventions matched to the particular stage a person is in have been successful (Lippke, Ziegelmann, Schwarzer, & Velicer, 2009; Park et al., 2003); in other cases, not (Armitage & Arden, 2008; Herzog, 2008; Lamb & Joshi, 1996; Weinstein, Rothman, & Sutton, 1998).

■ CHANGING HEALTH BEHAVIORS THROUGH SOCIAL ENGINEERING

Much behavior change occurs not through behavior-change programs but through social engineering. **Social engineering** involves modifying the environment in ways that affect people's ability to practice a particular health behavior. These measures are called passive because they do not require an individual to take personal action. For example, wearing seat belts is an active measure that an individual must take to control possible injury from an automobile accident, whereas airbags, which inflate automatically on impact, represent a passive measure.

Many health behaviors are already determined by social engineering. Banning the use of certain drugs, such as heroin and cocaine, and regulating the disposal of toxic wastes are examples of health measures that have been mandated by legislation. Both smoking and alcohol consumption are legally restricted to particular circumstances and age groups. Requiring vaccinations for school entry has led to more than 90% of children receiving most of the vaccinations they need (Center for the Advancement of Health, December 2002).

Many times, social engineering solutions to health problems are more successful than individual ones. For example, lowering the speed limit has had far more impact on death and disability from motor vehicle accidents than interventions to get people to change their driving habits (Fielding, 1978). Raising the drinking age from 18 to 21 is more successful in reducing alcohol-related vehicular fatalities than are programs designed to help the drunk driver (Ashley & Rankin, 1988).

The prospects for continued use of social engineering to change health habits are great. Controlling what is contained in vending machines at schools, putting a surcharge on foods high in fat and low in nutritional value, and controlling advertising of high-fat and high-cholesterol products, particularly those directed to children, can help combat the enormous rise in obesity that has occurred in recent decades (Jacobson & Brownell, 2000). Indeed, as the contributions of diet and obesity to poor health and early death become increasingly evident, such social engineering solutions may well be adopted.

There are limits to social engineering solutions. Even though smoking has been banned in many public areas, it is still not illegal to smoke; if this were to occur, most smokers and a substantial number of nonsmokers would find such mandatory measures unacceptable interference with civil liberties. Even when the health benefits of social engineering can be dramatically illustrated, the sacrifice in personal liberty may be considered too great. Thus, many health habits will remain at the discretion of the individual. It is to such behaviors that psychological interventions speak most persuasively.

■ VENUES FOR HEALTH-HABIT MODIFICATION

What is the best venue for changing health habits? There are several possibilities:

The Private Therapist's Office

Some health-habit modification is conducted by psychologists, psychiatrists, and other clinicians privately on a one-to-one basis, usually using cognitive-behavioral techniques. There are two striking advantages of the one-to-one therapeutic experience for the modification of health habits:

- Precisely because it is one-to-one, the extensive individual treatment a person receives may make success more likely.

- Because of the individual nature of the experience, the therapist can tailor the behavior-change package to the needs of the individual.

However, there is a major disadvantage: Only one individual's behavior can be changed at a time. If the modification of health habits is to make any dent in rates of disease, we must find ways of modifying health behaviors that do not require expensive one-to-one attention.

The Health Practitioner's Office

Many people have regular contact with a physician or other health care professional who knows their medical history and can help them modify their health habits. Among the advantages of intervening in the physician's office is that physicians are highly credible sources for instituting health habit change, and their recommendations have the force of their expertise behind them. Latinos in particular appear to be better served by health habit interventions that include face-to-face contact as compared with printed information (Elder et al., 2005). Nonetheless, as in the case of private therapy, the one-to-one approach is expensive and reduces only one person's risk status at a time.

The Family

Increasingly, health practitioners are intervening with the family to improve health (Fisher et al., 1998). The health-promoting aspects of family life are evident in the fact that married men have far better health habits than single men, in part because wives often run the home life that builds in these healthy habits (Hampson, Andrews, Barckley, Lichtenstein, & Lee, 2000). Children learn their health habits from their parents, so making sure the entire family is committed to a healthy lifestyle gives children the best chance at a healthy start in life.

Families typically have more organized, routinized lifestyles than single people do, so family life can be suited to building in healthy behaviors, such as getting three meals a day, sleeping 8 hours, brushing teeth, and using seat belts.

A stable family life is health promoting and, increasingly, interventions are being targeted to families rather than individuals to ensure the greatest likelihood of behavior change.

Another reason for intervening with families is that multiple family members are affected by any one member's health habits. A clear example is secondhand smoke, which harms not only the smoker but those around him or her.

Finally, and most importantly, if behavior change is introduced at the family level, all family members are on board, ensuring greater commitment to the behavior-change program and providing social support for the person whose behavior is the target (Wilson & Ampey-Thornhill, 2001).

Family interventions may be especially helpful in cultures that place a strong emphasis on family. Latino, Black, Asian, or southern European cultures may be more persuaded to engage in behavior change when the good of the family is at stake (Han & Shavitt, 1994; Klonoff & Landrine, 1999).

Managed Care Facilities

Increasingly, many of us get our health care from large medical groups, rather than from individual private physicians, and these groups provide opportunities for general preventive health education that reach many people at the same time. Clinics to help smokers stop

smoking, dietary interventions that provide information and recipes for changing diet, and programs for new parents that teach home safety are among the many interventions that can be implemented in these larger settings.

Self-Help Groups

An estimated 8–10 million people in the United States alone attempt to modify their health habits through self-help groups. Self-help groups bring together people with the same health habit problem, and, often with the help of a counselor, they attempt to solve their problem collectively. Some prominent self-help groups include Overeaters Anonymous and TOPS (Take Off Pounds Sensibly) for obesity, Alcoholics Anonymous for alcoholics, and Smokenders for smokers. Many group leaders employ cognitive-behavioral principles in their programs. The social support and understanding of mutual sufferers are also important factors in producing successful outcomes. At the present time, self-help groups constitute the major venue for health-habit modification in this country.

Schools

Interventions to encourage health behaviors can be implemented through the school system (Facts of Life, November 2003). Most children go to school, and therefore, virtually the entire population can be reached, at least in their early years. The school population is young. Consequently, we can intervene before children have developed poor health habits. Schools have a natural intervention vehicle—namely, classes of approximately an hour's duration; many health interventions can fit into this format. Moreover, certain sanctions can be used in the school environment to promote healthy behaviors, such as requiring inoculations in order to attend school. Finally, a school's social climate influences how likely students are to abuse drugs or alcohol (Eitle & Eitle, 2004), and so changing the norms about health habits may influence a large number of students simultaneously.

Workplace Interventions

Approximately 70% of the adult population is employed, and consequently, the workplace can reach much of this population (Haynes, Odenkirchen, & Heimendinger, 1990).

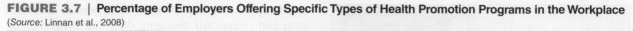

FIGURE 3.7 | Percentage of Employers Offering Specific Types of Health Promotion Programs in the Workplace
(*Source:* Linnan et al., 2008)

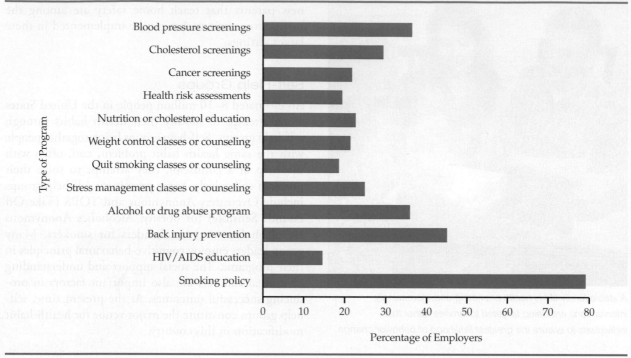

Workplace interventions include on-the-job health promotion programs that help employees stop smoking, reduce stress, change their diet, exercise regularly, lose weight, control hypertension, and limit drinking, among other problems (Linnan et al., 2002; Theorell, Emdad, Arnetz, & Weingarten, 2001) (Figure 3.7).

The workplace can also structure the environment to help people engage in healthy activities. Many companies ban smoking in the workplace. Others provide health clubs for employee use or restaurant facilities that serve healthier meals. Some companies provide special incentives, such as reduced insurance premiums for individuals who successfully modify their health habits (for example, individuals who stop smoking).

How successful are workplace interventions? Many such programs have not been formally evaluated. Those that have appear to achieve modest success (Abraham & Graham-Rowe, 2009), with some caveats. The enrollment rate can be low, at 20% or less (Winett, 2003). Interventions often reach those with jobs of higher rather than lower occupational prestige (Dobbins, Simpson, Oldenburg, Owen, & Harris, 1998); more efforts need to be made to recruit those in less prestigious occupations and positions. In any case, formal evaluation and high rates of success will be critical in the continuation of such programs. If corporations see reductions in absenteeism, insurance costs, accidents, and other indicators that these programs are successful, they will be more likely to adopt or continue them.

Community-Based Interventions

There are many kinds of community interventions. A community-based intervention could be a door-to-door campaign informing people of the availability of a breast cancer screening program, a media blitz alerting people to the risks of smoking, a grassroots community program to encourage exercise (Estabrooks, Bradshaw, Dzewaltowski, & Smith-Ray, 2008), a diet modification program that recruits through community institutions, or a mixed intervention involving both media and interventions directed to high-risk community members.

There are several potential advantages of community-based interventions. First, such interventions reach more people than individually based interventions or interventions in limited environments, such as a single workplace or classroom. Second, community-based interventions can build on social support for reinforcing adherence to recommended health changes. For example, if all your neighbors have agreed to switch to a low-cholesterol diet, you are more likely to do so as well. Third, community-based interventions can potentially address the problem of behavior-change maintenance. If the community environment is restructured so that the cues and reinforcements for previous risky behaviors are replaced by cues and reinforcements for healthy behaviors, relapse may be less likely (Cohen, Stunkard, & Felix, 1986). Finally, much evidence already shows that neighborhoods can have profound effects on health practices, especially those of adolescents. Monitoring of behavior within neighborhoods has been tied to a lower rate of smoking and alcohol abuse among adolescents, for example (Chuang, Ennett, Bauman, & Foshee, 2005).

Several community-based interventions have been implemented to help people reduce risk factors associated with heart disease. But community interventions have also been controversial. Despite some successes, some policymakers believe that these interventions are too expensive for the modest changes they bring about (Leventhal et al., 2008). Moreover, behavior change may not be maintained over time (Klepp, Kelder, & Perry, 1995).

One approach that may solve some of these problems is to partner interventions with existing community organizations, such as health maintenance organizations (HMOs), design and implement interventions with their help and cooperation, and build in follow-through steps with the partnering organizations to help sustain behavior change (Bogart & Uyeda, 2009). Such partnering arrangements may be especially effective in minority communities, because they ensure access and may facilitate culturally sensitive interventions.

The Mass Media

One of the goals of health promotion efforts is to reach as many people as possible, and consequently, the mass media have great potential. However, evaluations of the effectiveness of health appeals in the mass media suggest some qualifications regarding their success (Lau, Kane, Berry, Ware, & Roy, 1980). Generally, mass media campaigns bring about modest attitude change but less long-term behavior change. Nonetheless, the mass media can alert people to health risks that they would not otherwise know about (Lau et al., 1980).

The mass media can affect health behaviors in other ways than by simply providing health-relevant messages. Characters in soap operas, dramas, and comedies all often engage in health behaviors, such as eating, exercise, and smoking, and as such, can act as role models (Wilkin et al., 2007). For example, adolescents who see smoking in movies are more likely to start smoking themselves, and so eliminating smoking in movies may help prevent adolescents from starting to smoke (Heatherton & Sargent, 2009; Wills et al., 2007).

By presenting a consistent media message over time, the mass media can also have a cumulative effect in

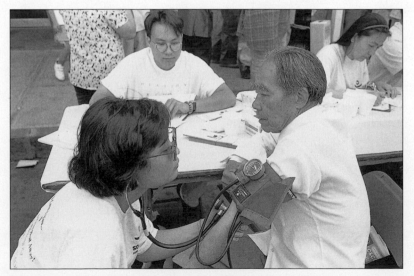

To reach the largest number of people most effectively, researchers are increasingly designing interventions to be implemented on a community basis through existing community resources.

changing the values associated with health practices. For example, the cumulative effects of antismoking mass media messages on social norms about smoking have been substantial.

Telephone

As cost containment pressures have mounted, researchers have increasingly sought low-cost effective treatment venues, and using the telephone to implement interventions is one such effort. CBT has been implemented with success via telephone to address fatigue and lack of activity in chronically ill populations, dietary change, and HIV risk-related behaviors (Lawler et al., 2010; Madlensky et al., 2008; Marcus et al., 2007; Mohr, Hart, & Vella, 2007; Picciano, Roffman, Kalichman, & Walker, 2007). Even automated telephone interventions can increase some health behaviors (King et al., 2007). Personalized text messages have been shown to help young smokers quit (Rodgers et al., 2005), and so texting represents another potentially effective low-cost intervention.

The Internet

The Internet provides low-cost access to health messages for millions of people who can benefit from the information, suggestions, and techniques offered on websites. These have included websites for smoking cessation (Wang & Etter, 2004) and learning sensible drinking habits (Linke, Murray, Butler, & Wallace, 2007), among many others.

The Internet can also be used to augment the effectiveness of other interventions, such as school-based smoking cessation programs (Norman, Maley, Skinner, & Li, 2008) or interventions with patients (Williams, Lynch, & Glasgow, 2007). One reason for their success may be that they increase people's perceptions of autonomy (Williams et al., 2007). More ambitious undertakings have included Internet-delivered, computer-tailored lifestyle interventions targeting multiple risk factors simultaneously, for example, diet, exercise, and smoking (Oenema, Brug, Dijkstra, de Weerdt, & de Vries, 2008).

Cognitive behavioral interventions for health habit modification delivered via the Internet may be as promising as face-to-face interventions; they have advantages of low cost, saving therapists' time, reducing waitlist and travel time, and accessibility to people who might not seek out a therapist on their own (Cuijpers, van Straten, & Andersson, 2008). The Internet also enables researchers to recruit a large number of participants for studies at relatively low cost, thus enabling data collection related to health habits (Lenert & Skoczen, 2002).

In conclusion, the choice of venue for health-habit change is an important issue. Understanding the particular strengths and disadvantages of each venue helps to identify interventions that reach the most people for the least expense. ●

SUMMARY

1. Health promotion is the process of enabling people to increase control over and improve their health. It involves the practice of good health behaviors and the avoidance of health-compromising ones.

2. Health habits are determined by demographic factors, social factors (such as early socialization in the family), values and cultural background, perceived symptoms, access to medical care, and cognitive factors (such as health beliefs). Health habits are only modestly related to each other and are highly unstable over time.

3. Health-promotion efforts target children and adolescents before bad health habits are in place. They also focus on individuals and groups at risk for particular disorders to prevent those disorders from occurring. An increasing focus on health promotion among older adults may help contain the soaring costs of health care at the end of life.

4. Attitudinal approaches to health behavior change can instill knowledge and motivation. But approaches such as fear appeals and information appeals have limited effects on behavior change.

5. Research using the health belief model, the self-efficacy principle, and the theory of planned behavior has identified attitudes related to health-habit modification: the belief that a threat to health is severe, that one is personally vulnerable to the threat, that one is able to perform the response needed to reduce the threat (self-efficacy), that the response will be effective in overcoming the threat (response efficacy), and that social norms support one's practice of the behavior. Behavioral intentions are also important determinants of behavior.

6. Cognitive-behavioral approaches to health-habit change use principles of self-monitoring, classical conditioning, operant conditioning, modeling, and stimulus control to modify the antecedents and consequences of a target behavior. Cognitive-behavior therapy brings patients into the treatment process by teaching them principles of self-control and self-reinforcement.

7. Social skills training and relaxation training methods are often incorporated into cognitive-behavioral interventions to deal with the anxiety or social deficits that underlie some health problems.

8. Increasingly, interventions focus on relapse prevention. Learning coping techniques for high-risk-for-relapse situations is a major component of such interventions.

9. Successful modification of health habits does not occur all at once. Individuals go through stages, which they may cycle through several times. When interventions are targeted to the stage an individual is in, they may be more successful.

10. Some health habits are best changed through social engineering, such as mandated childhood immunizations or smoking bans in the workplace.

11. The venue for intervening in health habits is changing. Expensive methods that reach one individual at a time are giving way to group methods that may be cheaper, including self-help groups, and school and workplace interventions. The mass media can reinforce health campaigns by alerting people to health risks. Telephone interventions, Internet interventions, and texting all show promise as health behavior change venues.

KEY TERMS

abstinence violation effect
assertiveness training
at risk
behavioral assignments
classical conditioning
cognitive-behavior therapy
    (CBT)
cognitive restructuring
contingency contracting
discriminative stimulus
fear appeals
health behaviors
health belief model

health habit
health locus of control
health promotion
lifestyle rebalancing
modeling
operant conditioning
primary prevention
relapse prevention
relaxation training
self-affirmation
self-control
self-determination theory (SDT)
self-efficacy

self-monitoring
self-reinforcement
self-talk
social engineering
socialization
social skills training
stimulus-control interventions
teachable moment
theory of planned behavior
transtheoretical model of behavior
    change
window of vulnerability

Specific Health-Related Behaviors

Every New Year's morning, Juanita sat down and took stock of what she wanted to accomplish during the next year. This year's list was like many other New Years' lists. It began with "lose 5 pounds" and included "get exercise every day" and "eat better (cut out junk food and soda)." After making the list, Juanita promptly went out running and returned 45 minutes later with a plan to consume a healthy lunch of steamed vegetables.

The phone rang. It was a friend inviting her to a last-minute New Year's Day brunch. The brunch sounded like a lot more fun than what Juanita had in mind, so off she went. Several hours later, after eggs Benedict and an afternoon of televised football, soda, and chips, Juanita had already broken her New Year's resolve.

Juanita is like most of us. We know what we should do to preserve and maintain our health, and we want to do it. Given a moment of private reflection, most of us would make decisions similar to Juanita's. In fact, surveys show that the most common New Year's resolutions, in addition to saving money, are losing weight and getting exercise. Although most of us manage to pursue our New Year's resolutions longer than the few hours that Juanita lasted, rarely do we get more than a few weeks into the new year before we lapse back to our more sedentary, less healthy lifestyle. Yet these health habits are important, and changing or maintaining our behavior in the direction of good health habits should be a high priority.

Chapter 4 examines how the attitudinal and behavioral principles identified in Chapter 3 apply to several self-enhancing behaviors, including exercise, accident prevention, cancer prevention, weight control, and healthy diet. These behaviors are important because each has been systematically related to at least one major cause of illness, disability, and death in industrialized countries. As people in third-world countries adopt the lifestyle of people in industrialized nations, these health habits will assume increasing importance throughout the world.

■ EXERCISE

In recent years, health psychologists have examined the role of aerobic exercise in maintaining mental and physical health. **Aerobic exercise** is sustained exercise that stimulates and strengthens the heart and lungs, improving the body's utilization of oxygen. All aerobic exercise is marked by its high intensity, long duration, and requisite high endurance. Among the forms of exercise that meet these criteria are jogging, bicycling, rope jumping,

and swimming. Other forms of exercise—such as iso-kinetic exercises (weight lifting, for example) or high-intensity, short-duration, low-endurance exercises (such as sprinting)—may be satisfying and may build up specific parts of the body but have less effect on overall fitness because they draw on short-term stores of glycogen rather than on the long-term energy conversion system associated with aerobics.

Benefits of Exercise

The health benefits of aerobic exercise are substantial (Table 4.1). A mere 30 minutes of exercise a day can decrease the risk of several chronic diseases including heart disease and some cancers including breast cancer (Facts of Life, March 2004). Exercise, coupled with dietary change, can cut the risk of Type II diabetes in high-risk adults. Other health benefits of exercise include increased efficiency of the cardiorespiratory system, improved physical work capacity, optimization of body weight, improvement or maintenance of muscle tone and strength, increases in soft tissue and joint flexibility, reduction or control of hypertension, lower levels of inflammation, improved cholesterol level, improved glucose tolerance, improved tolerance of stress, and reduction in poor health habits, including cigarette smoking, alcohol consumption, and poor diet (Center for the Advancement of Health, 2000a; Hamer & Steptoe, 2007). Exercise accelerates wound healing in those with injuries

TABLE 4.1 | Health Benefits of Regular Exercise

- Increases maximum oxygen consumption
- Decreases resting heart rate
- Decreases blood pressure (in some)
- Increases strength and efficiency of heart (pumps more blood per beat)
- Decreases use of energy sources, such as glutamine
- Increases slow-wave sleep
- Increases HDL cholesterol
- Decreases risk of cardiovascular disease
- Decreases obesity
- Increases longevity
- Decreases menstrual cycle length, decreases estrogen and progesterone
- Decreases risk of some cancers
- Improves immune system functions
- Decreases negative mood
- Promotes the growth of new neurons in the brain (Pereira et al., 2007)

(Emery, Kiecolt-Glaser, Glaser, Malarkey, & Frid, 2005). Exercise can be critical to recovery from certain disorders, such as hip fracture (Resnick et al., 2007).

However, over two-thirds of American adults do not achieve the recommended levels of physical activity, and about 40% of American adults do not engage in any leisure-time physical activity (National Center for Health Statistics, 2008). Physical inactivity is more common among women than men, among African-Americans and Hispanics than Whites, among older than younger adults, and among those with lower versus higher incomes (National Center for Health Statistics, 2008). Sixty-seven percent of men and 71% of women do not have any regular leisure-time source of physical activity, and over two-thirds of older adults are not as active as they should be (National Center for Health Statistics, 2008). Typically, people report lack of time, stress, interference with daily activities, and fatigue as barriers to obtaining exercise (Kowal & Fortier, 2007).

Perhaps more surprising is the fact that health practitioners do not uniformly recommend physical exercise, even to their patients who could especially benefit from it, such as their elderly patients (Center for the Advancement of Health, 2000g; Leveille et al., 1998). Yet studies show that a physician recommendation is one of the factors that lead people to increase their exercise (Calfas et al., 1997).

The effects of exercise translate directly into increased longevity and delayed mortality, particularly that due to cardiovascular disease and cancer (Facts of Life, May 2006). One study estimated that by age 80 the amount of additional life attributable to aerobic exercise is between 1 and 2 years (Paffenbarger, Hyde, Wing, & Hsieh, 1986). It is also true that, to achieve these extra 2 years of life, a person will have devoted the entire 2 years to exercise over his or her lifetime (Jacoby, 1986). Consequently, the quality of the exercise experience is also an important factor.

How Much Exercise?   The typical exercise prescription for a normal adult is 30 minutes or more of moderate-intensity activity on most, if not all, days of the week or 20 minutes or more of vigorous activity at least 3 days a week (U.S. Department of Health and Human Services, 2009). A person with low cardiopulmonary fitness may derive benefits with even less exercise each week. Women who have recently given birth are at particular risk of becoming physically inactive and so interventions may profitably be directed to this population as well (Fjeldsoe, Miller, & Marshall, 2010). Even

short walks, often recommended for older individuals or those with some infirmities, may have physical and psychological benefits (Ekkekakis, Hall, VanLanduyt, & Petruzzello, 2000; Schechtman, Ory, & the FICSIT group, 2001). Because it is difficult to get sedentary adults to commit to a full-fledged exercise program, a lifestyle intervention aimed at increasing physical activity may represent a good start for aging sedentary adults (Conn, Valentine, & Cooper, 2002) and for the obese (Levine et al., 2005). Lifestyle interventions may eventually lead to a commitment to exercise as well (Heesch, Mâsse, Dunn, Frankowski, & Mullen, 2003).

Effects on Psychological Health   Regular exercise improves mood and feelings of well-being immediately after a workout; there may also be some improvement in general mood and well-being as a result of long-term participation in an exercise program (Stathopoulou, Powers, Berry, Smits, & Otto, 2006). Sedentary behavior may even be a risk factor for depression (Teychenne, Ball, & Salmon, 2010).

At least some of the positive effects of exercise on mood may stem from factors associated with exercise, such as social activity and a feeling of involvement with others. For example, bicycling with friends, swimming with a companion, and running with a group may improve mood in part because of the companionship the exercise provides (Duncan, Duncan, & Strycker, 2005). Social support during exercise also increases the likelihood that people will maintain their exercise programs.

An improved sense of self-efficacy can also underlie some of the mood effects of exercise (McAuley et al., 2008). In one study (McAuley, Talbot, & Martinez, 1999), researchers recruited participants for an exercise group and manipulated the experience of self-efficacy during the program by providing contrived feedback to the participants about how well or poorly they were doing. Results indicated that, compared with a control group, people in the efficacy condition had significantly higher levels of perceived self-efficacy, and these perceptions were associated with improvements in mood and psychological well-being (Motl, Dishman, et al., 2005; Rhodes & Plotnikoff, 2006).

Because of its beneficial effects on mood and self-esteem, exercise has been used as a treatment for depression (Herman et al., 2002). One study assigned depressed women to an exercise condition, a drug treatment session, or a combined treatment. The exercise group improved their mood significantly and as much as those who received only the drug or the combined treatment. More importantly, once treatment was discontinued, those who continued to exercise were less likely to become depressed again when compared with those who had been on the drug treatment (Babyak et al., 2000). Indeed one of the risks of stopping exercise is an increase in symptoms of depression (Berlin, Kop, & Deuster, 2006).

The impact of exercise on well-being should not be overstated, however. The effects are often small, and the expectation that exercise has positive effects on mood may be one reason that people so widely report the experience. Despite these cautions, the positive effect of exercise on well-being is now quite well established (Paxton, Motl, Aylward, & Nigg, 2010).

Recently, health psychologists have studied the impact of exercise on cognitive functioning and found beneficial effects, especially on executive functioning involved in planning and higher-order reasoning (Smith

Regular aerobic exercise produces many physical and emotional benefits, including reduced risk for cardiovascular disease.

et al., 2010). Exercise also appears to promote memory and healthy cognitive aging (Pereira et al., 2007). Researchers believe that exercise beneficially affects executive control in older adults and that aerobic fitness is not essential for these beneficial cognitive effects to occur. This means that one need not engage in strenuous physical activity to get the cognitive benefits of exercise.

Exercise as Stress Management Exercise improves self-concept and well-being (Dishman et al., 2006; Marsh, Papaioannou, & Theodorakis, 2006). The fact that exercise improves well-being suggests that it might be an effective way of managing stress. Research suggests that this intuition is well placed. Brown and Siegel (1988) conducted a longitudinal study to see if adolescents who exercised were better able to cope with stress and avoid illness than those who did not. Results indicated that the negative impact of stressful life events on health declined as exercise levels increased. Thus, exercise may be a useful resource for combating the adverse health effects of stress (Castro, Wilcox, O'Sullivan, Baumann, & King, 2002).

One possible mechanism whereby exercise may buffer certain adverse health effects of stress involves its beneficial impact on immune functioning (Fiatarone et al., 1988). An increase in endogenous opioids (natural pain inhibitors; see Chapter 10) stimulated by exercise may affect immune activity during periods of psychological stress.

Exercise may offer economic benefits as well. A review of employee fitness programs, which are now a part of more than 50,000 U.S. businesses, suggests that such programs can reduce absenteeism, increase job satisfaction, and reduce health care costs, especially among women employees (see Rodin & Plante, 1989, for a review).

Determinants of Regular Exercise

Although the physical and mental health benefits of exercise are well established, most people's participation in exercise programs is erratic. Many children get regular exercise through required physical education classes in school. However, by adolescence, the practice of regular exercise has declined substantially, especially among girls (Davison, Schmalz, & Downs, 2010) and among boys not involved in formal athletics (Crosnoe, 2002). Smoking, being overweight, and teen pregnancy also account for some of the decline in physical activity (Kimm et al., 2002). Adults cite lack of time and other stressors in their lives as factors that undermine their good intentions (Kowal & Fortier, 2007). As humorist Erma Bombeck noted, "The only reason I would take up jogging is so that I could hear heavy breathing again."

Many people seem to share this attitude toward exercise. Evaluations of exercise programs indicate that 6-month participation levels range from 11% to 87%, averaging about 50% (Dishman, 1982). This statistic means that, on average, only half of those people who initiate a voluntary exercise program are still participating in that program after 6 months. People may begin an exercise program but find it difficult to make exercise a regular activity. Paradoxically, although exercise seems to be a stress buster, stress itself is one of the most common reasons that people fail to adhere to their exercise regimens (Kowal & Fortier, 2007). Accordingly, research has attempted to identify the factors that lead people to participate in exercise programs over the long term (Marcus et al., 2000).

Individual Characteristics   Who is most likely to exercise? People who come from families in which exercise is practiced, who have positive attitudes toward physical activity, who have a strong sense of self-efficacy for exercising (Marquez & McAuley, 2006), who perceive themselves as athletic or as the type of person who exercises (Salmon, Owen, Crawford, Bauman, & Sallis, 2003), who have social support from friends to exercise (Marquez & McAuley, 2006), who enjoy their form of exercise (Kiviniemi, Voss-Humke, & Seifert, 2007), and who believe that people should take responsibility for their health are more likely to get involved in exercise programs initially than people who do not have these attitudes.

Overweight people are less likely to participate in exercise programs than are those who are not overweight. It may be that exercise is harder for the overweight or that leaner people who had more active lifestyles before getting involved in exercise are better able to incorporate exercise into their activities (Dishman, 1982).

As noted, social support predicts exercise. Among people who participate in group exercise programs such as jogging or walking, a sense of support and group cohesion contributes to participation (Floyd & Moyer, 2010). This kind of support may be especially important for exercise participation among Hispanics (Marquez & McAuley, 2006). In fact, just viewing others engaging in exercise around one's neighborhood or on a jogging path can improve the practice of exercise (Kowal & Fortier, 2007).

The effects of health status on participation in exercise programs are still unclear. Individuals at risk for cardiovascular disease do show greater adherence to exercise programs than do those who are not (Dishman,

1982). However, outside of the cardiovascular area, there is no general relationship between health status and adherence to exercise programs (Dishman, 1982).

Beliefs about self-control are important to exercise as well. People who are high in self-efficacy with respect to exercise (that is, believing that they will be able to perform exercise regularly) are more likely to practice it and more likely to perceive that they are benefiting from it than are people low in self-efficacy (Marquez & McAuley, 2006). And interventions that enhance exercise self-efficacy can achieve good results (Hu, Motl, McAuley, & Konopack, 2007). The converse is also true: Those who do not exercise regularly may have little confidence in their ability to exercise and may regard exercise as entailing nearly as many costs as benefits (Marquez & McAuley, 2006). Consequently, interventions aimed at modifying exercise goals and self-efficacy might help increase exercise in older adults (Hall et al., 2010).

Characteristics of the Setting   Convenient and easily accessible exercise settings lead to higher rates of adherence (Humpel, Marshall, Leslie, Bauman, & Owen, 2004). If your exercise program consists of vigorous walking that can be undertaken near your home, you are more likely to do it than if your program is an aerobics workout in a crowded health club 5 miles from your home. Lack of resources for physical activity may be a particular barrier for regular exercise among those low in socioeconomic status (SES) (Estabrooks, Lee, & Gyurcsik, 2003; Feldman & Steptoe, 2004).

Improving environmental options for exercise, such as walking trails and recreational facilities, increases rates of exercise, and when neighborhoods have these facilities available, the likelihood of being overweight in the community is reduced (Dowda, Dishman, Porter, Saunders, & Pate, 2009; Wilson, Ainsworth, & Bowles, 2007). When people perceive their neighborhoods as safe, when they are not socially isolated, and when they know about what exercise opportunities are available to them in their area, they are more likely to engage in physical activity (Cerin, Vandelanotte, Leslie, & Merom, 2008; Hawkley, Thisted, & Cacioppo, 2009; Sallis, King, Sirard, & Albright, 2007).

Perhaps the best predictor of regular exercise is regular exercise. Long-term practice of regular exercise is heavily determined by habit (McAuley, 1992). The first 3–6 months appear to be critical. People who will drop out usually do so in that time period; those who have adhered for 3–6 months are more likely to continue to exercise (Dishman, 1982). Developing a regular exercise program, embedding it firmly in regular activities, and practicing it regularly for a period of time means that it begins to become automatic and habitual. However, habit has its limits. Unlike such habitual behaviors as wearing a seat belt or not lighting a cigarette, exercise takes willpower, the recognition that hard work is involved, and a belief in personal responsibility in order to be enacted on a regular basis (Valois, Desharnais, & Godin, 1988).

Characteristics of Interventions

Several studies confirm the usefulness of the transtheoretical model of behavioral change (that is, the stages of change model) in producing higher levels of physical activity. Interventions designed to increase physical activity that are matched to the stage of readiness of the sample are more successful than interventions that do not have this focus (Blissmer & McAuley, 2002; Litt, Kleppinger, & Judge, 2002; Marshall et al., 2003).

Interventions that incorporate principles of self-control (enhancing beliefs in personal efficacy) and that muster motivational efforts (enhancing a sense of perceived behavioral control and inducing people to form behavioral intentions) can be successful in changing exercise habits (Conroy, Hyde, Doerksen, & Riebeiro, 2010). Coupling self-monitoring with an enhanced sense of control appears to be especially effective (Michie, Abraham, Whittington, McAteer, & Gupta, 2009). Adding a motivational component is also helpful (van Stralen, De Vries, Mudde, Bolman, & Lechner, 2009).

As is true with other health behaviors, factors that predict the adoption of physical exercise are not necessarily the same as those that predict long-term maintenance of an exercise program. Perceived importance and concern about physical activity predicts initiation of an exercise program, whereas control over deterrents, both environmental and personal, such as low self-efficacy or poor availability of places to get exercise, predicts maintenance (Rhodes, Plotnikoff, & Courneya, 2008). Family-based interventions designed to get all family members to be more active have shown some success (Rhodes, Naylor, & McKay, 2010). Worksite interventions to promote exercise have small but positive effects on increased physical activity (Abraham & Graham-Rowe, 2009).

Even minimal interventions to promote exercise are showing some success. In an intervention that consisted of stage-targeted mailers encouraging physical exercise among older adults, those who reported receiving and reading the intervention materials were significantly more likely to be exercising 6 months later. The advantage of such an intervention, of course, is its low cost

and ease of implementation (Marshall et al., 2003). Text messaging has had success in promoting exercise such as brisk walking (Prestwich, Perugini, & Hurling, 2010).

Relapse prevention techniques have been used to increase long-term adherence to exercise programs. Such techniques include increasing awareness of the obstacles to obtaining regular exercise and helping people develop ways to cope with temptations not to exercise (Belisle, Roskies, & Levesque, 1987). With older adults, even simple telephone or mail reminders may help maintain adherence to a physical activity program (Castro, King, & Brassington, 2001; Facts of Life, May 2006).

Incorporating exercise into a more general program of healthy lifestyle change can be beneficial as well. Motivation to engage in one health behavior can spill over into another (Mata et al., 2009). For example, among adults at risk for coronary heart disease, brief behavioral counseling matched to stage of readiness helped them maintain physical activity, as well as reduce smoking and fat intake (Steptoe, Kerry, Rink, & Hilton, 2001). Although interventions targeted to multiple behaviors are sometimes less easy to undertake because of their complexity, linking health habits to each other in a concerted effort to address risk can work, as this intervention study showed. Targeting barriers to obtaining regular exercise, such as stress, fatigue, and a hectic schedule, may improve adherence (Blanchard et al., 2007). Behavioral intentions increased adherence to a physical exercise program (Scholz, Keller, & Perren, 2009; Schwarzer, Luszczynska, Ziegelmann, Scholz, & Lippke, 2008).

Exercise interventions may promote more general lifestyle changes. This issue was studied in an intriguing manner with 60 Hispanic and Anglo families, half of whom had participated in a 1-year intervention program of dietary modification and exercise. All the families were taken to the San Diego Zoo as a reward for participating in the program, and while they were there, their food intake and amount of walking were recorded. The results indicated that the families that had participated in the intervention consumed fewer calories, ate less sodium, and walked more than the families in the control condition, suggesting that the intervention had been integrated into their lifestyle (Patterson et al., 1988). The family-based approach of this intervention may have contributed to its success as well (Martinez, Ainsworth, & Elder, 2008).

If people participate in activities that they like, that are convenient, that they are motivated to pursue, and for which they can develop goals, exercise adherence will be greater (Dishman, 1982). Ensuring that people have realistic but positive expectations for their exercise programs may also improve long-term adherence (Dunton & Vaughan, 2008).

There may be unintended negative effects of interventions to increase exercise that need to be guarded against in the design of any intervention program. For example, one study (Zabinski, Calfas, Gehrman, Wilfley, & Sallis, 2001) found that an intervention program directed to college men and women inadvertently promoted an increase in the desire to be thin, despite warnings about dieting. Such pressures can promote eating disorders. Otherwise, exercise interventions do not appear to have negative side effects.

Physical activity websites would seem to hold promise for inducing people to participate in regular exercise (Napolitano et al., 2003). Of course, if one is on the Internet, one is by definition not exercising. Indeed, thus far, there is little evidence that physical activity websites provide the kind of individually tailored program that is needed to get people to participate on a regular basis (Doshi, Patrick, Sallis, & Calfas, 2003). To date, then, the Internet has demonstrated mixed success modifying physical activity levels.

Despite the problems health psychologists have encountered in getting people to exercise and to do so faithfully, the exercise level in the U.S. population has increased substantially in recent decades. In 1979, the surgeon general articulated a set of goals for the health of the American public, one of which included exercise. This goal has turned out to be the one on which the greatest progress has been made (McGinnis, Richmond, Brandt, Windom, & Mason, 1992). The number of people who participate in regular exercise has increased by more than 50% in the past few decades. Increasingly, it is not just sedentary healthy adults who are becoming involved in exercise but also the elderly and patient populations (Courneya & Friedenreich, 2001). This suggests that, although the population may be aging, it may be doing so in a healthier way than in any previous generation (McAuley et al., 2007).

■ ACCIDENT PREVENTION

No wonder that so many cars collide;
Their drivers are accident prone,
When one hand is holding a coffee cup,
And the other a cellular phone.

—Art Buck

Despite the jocular nature of this bit of doggerel, it captures an important point. Accidents represent one of the major causes of preventable death in this country. Worldwide, nearly 1.3 million people die as a result of road traffic injuries, and the estimated economic cost of accidents is $518 billion per year (World Health Organization, 2009). Of particular concern is traffic accidents, which represent one of the largest causes of death among children, adolescents, and young adults. Bicycle accidents cause more than 700 deaths per year, prompt more than 500,000 emergency room visits, and constitute the major cause of head injury, thereby making helmet use an important issue (National Safety Council, 2009). Several million people are poisoned each year in the United States, over half of whom are children under 6 years old (Centers for Disease Control and Prevention, February 2009). Occupational accidents and their resulting disability are a particular health risk for working men. Overall, home accidents are estimated to cost $217 billion in lost productivity and quality of life (Facts of Life, February 2005). Consequently, strategies to reduce accidents have increasingly been a focus of health psychology research and interventions.

Home and Workplace Accidents

Accidents in the home, such as accidental poisonings and falls, are the most common causes of death and disability among children under age 5 (Barton & Schwebel, 2007). Interventions to reduce home accidents are typically conducted with parents because they have control over the child's environment. Parents are most likely to undertake injury prevention activities if they believe that the recommended steps really will avoid injuries, if they feel knowledgeable and competent to teach safety skills to their children, and if they have a realistic sense of how much time will actually be involved in doing so (Peterson, Farmer, & Kashani, 1990).

Increasingly, pediatricians are incorporating such training into their interactions with new parents (Roberts & Turner, 1984). Parenting classes can be used to teach parents to identify the most common poisons in their household and to keep these safeguarded or out of reach of young children. A study evaluating training on how to childproof a home indicated that such interventions can be successful (Matthews, Friman, Barone, Ross, & Christophersen, 1987).

Statistics suggest that, overall, accidents in the workplace have declined since the 1930s (Figure 4.1).

FIGURE 4.1 | Accidental Deaths in the United States, 1930–2007
(*Source*: National Safety Council, 2009)

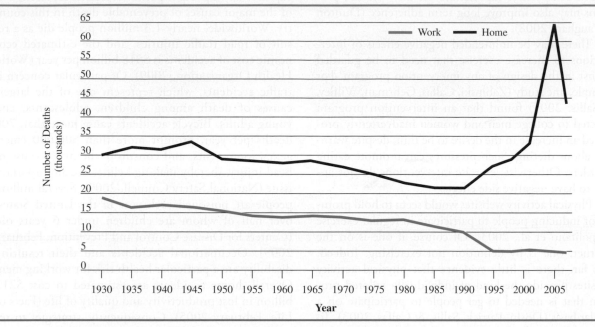

This decline may be due, in part, to better safety precautions by employers. However, accidents at home have actually increased. Social engineering solutions, such as safety caps on medications and required smoke detectors in the home, have mitigated the increase, but the trend is worrisome.

Among one group—namely, the elderly—falls remain a significant problem that is likely to increase as the demographics of the population change. More than $20 billion are spent each year as a result of fall-related injuries, with the largest cost the repair of hip fracture. More than 12,800 older adults die each year of fall-related injuries, and many more are disabled. At least 25% of older adults may remain hospitalized for at least a year due to injuries from a fall (Facts of Life, March 2006).

Several factors can reduce this risk. First, since dietary deficiencies are associated with osteoporosis, dietary and medication intervention to reduce bone loss is one possibility. Physical activity involving balance, mobility, and gait training reduces the risk of falls. Teaching older adults to make small changes in their homes that may reduce trip hazards can help, including nonslip bathmats in the bath or shower, grab bars and hand rails on both sides of stairs, and better lighting (Facts of Life, March 2006). The evidence suggests that fall prevention programs can reduce

mortality and disability substantially (Facts of Life, March 2006).

Motorcycle and Automobile Accidents

> You know what I call a motorcyclist who doesn't wear a helmet? An organ donor.
>
> —Emergency room physician

The single greatest cause of accidental death is motorcycle and automobile accidents (Centers for Disease Control and Prevention, August 2009a). To date, little psychological research has gone into helping people avoid vehicular traffic accidents. Instead, efforts have concentrated on such factors as the maintenance of roadways, the volume of travel, and safety standards in automobiles. However, psychological research can address factors associated with accidents, including the way people drive, the speed at which they drive, and the use of preventive measures to increase safety.

Safety measures such as reducing highway driving speed to 55 miles per hour, requiring seat belts, and placing young children in safety restraint seats have reduced the number of severe injuries and vehicular fatalities (Facts of Life, May 2004). Among bicycle and motorcycle riders, making themselves visible through reflective or fluorescent clothing and using helmets has

Automobile accidents represent a major cause of death, especially among the young. Legislation requiring child safety restraint devices has reduced fatalities dramatically.

reduced the severity of accidents by a substantial degree, especially serious head injury (Facts of Life, May 2004; Wells et al., 2004).

However, getting people to follow these safety measures is difficult. Although people often correctly perceive the risks of automobile accidents, their risk perceptions appear to have little impact on their driving (McKenna & Horswill, 2006). For example, many Americans still do not use seat belts, a problem especially common among adolescents, which helps account for their high rate of fatal accidents (Facts of Life, May 2004). To promote the use of seat belts, a combination of social engineering, health education, and psychological intervention may be most appropriate. For example, most states now require that infants and toddlers up to age 3 or 4 be restrained in safety seats. This requirement can lay the groundwork for proper safety behavior in automobiles, making people more likely to use seat belts in adolescence and adulthood.

Communitywide health education programs aimed at increasing seat belt usage and infant restraint devices can be successful. One such program increased the use from 24% to 41%, leveling off at 36% over a 6-month follow-up period (Gemming, Runyan, Hunter, & Campbell, 1984). On the whole, though, legal solutions may be more effective. Seat belt use is more prevalent in states with laws that mandate their use, and states that enforce helmet laws for motorcycle riders show reduced deaths and lower

health care costs related to disability due to motorcycle accidents (*Wall Street Journal,* 2005, August 9).

■ CANCER-RELATED HEALTH BEHAVIORS

Mammograms

The recent decrease in breast cancer mortality has been linked in part to better screening through mammograms. Although the number of women who are screened is increasing, many women still do not get screened (Champion et al., 2002). For women over age 50 and for at-risk women over age 40, national health guidelines recommend a mammogram every year. (For women not at particular risk between ages 40 and 50, the value of a yearly mammogram is less clear.) (U.S. Preventive Services Task Force, 2009)

Why is screening through mammography so important for older and high-risk women? The reasons are several:

- The prevalence of breast cancer in this country remains high.
- The majority of breast cancers continue to be detected in women over age 40, so screening this age group is cost effective.
- Early detection, as through mammograms, can improve survival rates.

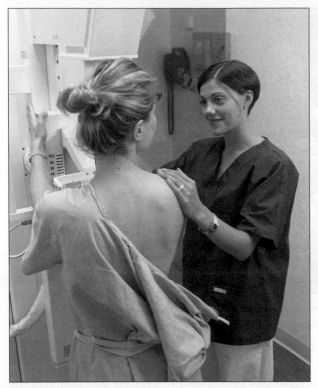

Mammograms are an important way of detecting breast cancer in women over 50. Finding ways to reach older women to ensure that they obtain mammograms is a high priority for health scientists.

Getting Women to Obtain Mammograms

Unfortunately, compliance with mammography recommendations is low. Surveys suggest that only 59% of women are screened for breast cancer over a 2-year period, and only 27% have had the age-appropriate number of repeat screening mammograms (Clark, Rakowski, & Bonacore, 2003). Unfortunately too, the use of mammograms declines with age, even though the risk of breast cancer increases with age (Ruchlin, 1997). Fear of radiation, embarrassment over the procedure, anticipated pain, anxiety, fear of cancer (Gurevich et al., 2004; Schwartz, Taylor, & Willard, 2003), and, most importantly, especially among poorer women, concern over costs act as deterrents to getting regular mammograms (Lantz, Weigers, & House, 1997). Lack of awareness, time, incentive, and availability are also important.

Changing attitudes toward mammography may increase the likelihood of obtaining a mammogram. In particular, the health belief model has been associated with a greater likelihood of obtaining a mammogram (Champion & Springston, 1999; McCaul, Branstetter, Schroeder, &

Glasgow, 1996). The theory of planned behavior also predicts the likelihood of obtaining regular mammograms: Women who have positive attitudes regarding mammography and who perceive social norms as favoring their obtaining a mammogram are more likely to participate in a mammography program (Montano & Taplin, 1991). Social support predicts use of mammograms and may be especially important for low-income and older women (Messina et al., 2004). Prochaska's transtheoretical model of behavior change (see Chapter 3) also predicts decisions about mammography, with interventions more successful if they are geared to the stage of readiness of prospective participants (Champion & Springston, 1999; Lauver, Henriques, Settersten, & Bumann, 2003).

Interventions need to be directed to health professionals as well to ensure that physicians routinely refer their older women patients to mammography centers, and health care delivery services need to be established so that mammography is cheaper and more accessible to older and low-income women (Messina, Lane, & Grimson, 2002). Mammograms have not been well integrated into standard care for older women. Instead of receiving all necessary diagnostic tests and checkups from one physician, as adult men do, many women must make at least three appointments—one with a general practitioner, one with a gynecologist, and one with a mammography center. Minority and older women especially fall through the cracks, because often they do not have a regular source of health care (Champion & Springston, 1999; National Cancer Institute Breast Cancer Screening Consortium, 1990).

Colorectal Cancer Screening

In Western countries, colorectal cancer is the second-leading cause of cancer deaths. In recent years, medical guidelines have increasingly recommended routine colorectal screening for older adults (Wardle, Williamson, McCaffery, et al., 2003). Colorectal screening is distinctive for the fact that people often learn that they have polyps (a benign condition that can increase risk for colorectal cancer) but not malignancies. To date, the evidence suggests that colorectal cancer screening does not unduly raise anxiety among either those who have polyps detected or those who are vulnerable to cancer (Wardle, Williamson, Sutton, et al., 2003).

Factors that predict the practice of other health behaviors also predict participation in colorectal cancer screening, including self-efficacy, perceived benefits of the procedure, a physician's recommendation to participate, social norms favoring participation, and low perceived barriers to taking advantage of the screening program (Hays et al., 2003; Manne et al., 2002; Sieverding, Matterne, & Ciccarello, 2010). As is true of many health behaviors, beliefs predict the intention to participate in colorectal screening, whereas issues related to life difficulties (low SES, poor health status) are better predictors of actions than intentions, with better life situation associated with more use of screening programs (Power et al., 2008).

Community-based programs that employ such strategies as mass media, community-based education, social networks, interventions through churches, health care provider recommendations, and reminder notices promote participation in cancer screening programs, including those for colorectal cancer, and indicate that community-based interventions can attract older populations to engage in appropriate screening behaviors (Campbell et al., 2004; Curbow et al., 2004). Siblings of people who have been diagnosed with colorectal cancer are at particular risk and therefore need to be targeted through interventions that are tailored to their risk (Manne et al., 2009). An intervention aimed at older adults that provided reassuring information regarding colorectal screening was effective in modifying initially negative attitudes and increasing rates of screening attendance (Wardle, Williamson, McCaffery, et al., 2003; see also Honda & Gorin, 2005). As Hispanics are at particular risk for colorectal cancer, it is especially important to reach them (Gorin, 2005).

Sun Safety Practices

The past 30 years have seen a nearly fourfold increase in the incidence of skin cancer in the United States. Over 50,000 new cases of skin cancer will be diagnosed this year alone. Although common basal cell and squamous cell carcinomas do not typically kill, malignant melanoma takes over 8,000 lives each year (Centers for Disease Control and Prevention, March 2009). In the past two decades, melanoma incidence has risen by 155%. Moreover, these cancers are among the most preventable. The chief risk factor for skin cancer is well known: excessive exposure to ultraviolet (UV) radiation. Living or vacationing in southern latitudes, participating in outdoor activities, and using tanning salons all contribute to dangerous sun exposure (Jones & Leary, 1994). Sun-protective behaviors are practiced consistently by less than one-third of American children, and more than three-quarters of American teens get at least one sunburn each summer (Facts of Life, July 2002).

As a result, health psychologists have increased their efforts to promote safe sun practices. Typically, these efforts have included educational interventions designed to alert people to the risks of skin cancer and to the effectiveness of sunscreen use for reducing risk (Katz & Jernigan, 1991; Lewis et al., 2005). Recently, scientists have explored Internet-based strategies as a vehicle for distributing sun safety materials. Responses have thus far been weak, suggesting that more personal approaches may be needed (Buller, Buller, & Kane, 2005). Moreover, based on what we know about

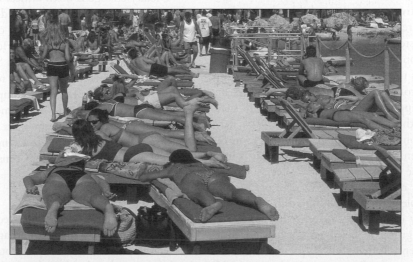

Despite the risks of exposure to the sun, millions of people each year continue to sunbathe.

attitudinal interventions with other health habits, education alone is unlikely to be entirely successful (Jones & Leary, 1994). Problems with getting people to engage in safe sun practices stem from the fact that tans are still perceived to be attractive (Cafri, Thompson, Jacobsen, & Hillhouse, 2009; Cox et al., 2009), and many people are oblivious to the long-term consequences of tanning (Orbell & Kyriakaki, 2008).

Many of us use sunscreens with an inadequate sun protection factor (SPF), and few of us apply sunscreen as often as we should during outdoor activities (Wichstrom, 1994). Effective sunscreen use is influenced by a number of factors, including knowledge about skin cancer, perceived need for sunscreen, perceived efficacy of sunscreen as protection against skin cancer, and social norms regarding sunscreen use (Stapleton, Turrisi, Hillhouse, Robinson, & Abar, 2010; Turrisi, Hillhouse, Gebert, & Grimes, 1999). Reducing perceived barriers to sunscreen use and increasing perceived self-efficacy for sun safe behavior appear to be important as well (Reynolds, Buller, Yaroch, Maloy, & Cutter, 2006). The type of skin one has—burn only, burn then tan, or tan without burning—is the strongest influence on the likelihood of using sun protection (Clarke, Williams, & Arthey, 1997), suggesting that people are beginning to develop some understanding of their risk. Health communications that enhance all these perceptions may be helpful in increasing sun safety behaviors (Jackson & Aiken, 2000).

Parents play an important role in ensuring that children reduce sun exposure (Turrisi, Hillhouse, Robinson, & Stapleton, 2007). Parents' own sun protection habits predict their attentiveness to their children's practices and to what children subsequently do on their own (Turner & Mermelstein, 2005).

Communications to adolescents and young adults that stress the gains that sunscreen use will bring them, such as freedom from concern about skin cancers or improvements in appearance, appear to be more successful than those that emphasize the risks (Detweiler, Bedell, Salovey, Pronin, & Rothman, 1999; Jackson & Aiken, 2006). When the risks are emphasized, it is important to stress the immediate adverse effects of poor health habits rather than the long-term risks of chronic illness, because adolescents and young adults are especially influenced by immediate concerns. In one clever investigation, one group of beachgoers experienced a photo-aging intervention that showed premature wrinkling and age spots; a second group received a novel UV photo intervention that made negative consequences of

UV exposure very salient; a third group received both interventions; and a fourth group was assigned to a control condition. Those beachgoers who received the UV photo information engaged in more protective behaviors for incidental sun exposure, and the combination of the UV photo with the photo-aging information led to substantially less sunbathing over the long-term (Mahler, Kulik, Gibbons, Gerrard, & Harrell, 2003; Mahler, Kulik, Gerrard, & Gibbons, 2007). Similar interventions appear to be effective in reducing the use of tanning salons (Gibbons, Gerrard, Lane, Mahler, & Kulik, 2005). Communication drawing on the stages-of-change model, which aims to move people who tan from a precontemplative to a contemplative stage and subsequently to implementation of sun-protective behaviors, may also work (Pagoto, McChargue, & Fuqua, 2003).

■ DEVELOPING A HEALTHY DIET

Developing and maintaining a healthy diet should be a goal for everyone. The dramatic rise in obesity in the United States has added urgency to this recommendation. Diet is an important and controllable risk factor for many of the leading causes of death and contributes substantially to risk factors for disease as well. However, only 14% of adults get the recommended servings of fruits and vegetables each day (Table 4.2). Experts estimate that unhealthful eating contributes to more than 400,000 deaths per year (Centers for Disease Control and Prevention, 2009b; Mokdad, Marks, Stroup, & Gerberding, 2004).

Dietary change is often critical for people at risk for or already diagnosed with chronic diseases such as coronary artery disease, hypertension, diabetes, and cancer (Center for the Advancement of Health, 2000f). These are diseases for which people low in SES are more at risk, and diet may explain some of the relation between low SES and these disorders. For example, supermarkets in high-SES neighborhoods carry more health-oriented food products than do supermarkets in low-income areas. Thus, even if the motivation to change one's diet is there, the food products may not be (Conis, 2003, August 4).

Why Is Diet Important?

Dietary factors have been implicated in a broad array of diseases and risks for disease. Perhaps the best known is the relation of dietary factors to total serum cholesterol levels in general and to low-density lipid proteins in particular (McCaffery et al., 2001). Although diet is only

TABLE 4.2 | Current USDA Recommendations for a Balanced Diet

The United States Agriculture Department currently recommends a 2,000-calorie-a-day diet made up of the following components:

–Dairy (3 cups)

–Fruits (2 cups)

–Vegetables (2.5 cups)

–Grain (3 oz)

–Meat (6 oz)

–Oil (6 tsp)

one determinant of a person's lipid profile, it can be an important one because it is controllable. Of dietary recommendations, switching from trans fats (as are used for fried and fast foods) and saturated fats (from meat and dairy products) to polyunsaturated fats and monounsaturated fats is one of the most widely recommended courses of action (Marsh, 2002, September 10). Reducing the consumption of red meat and fatty foods and increasing the consumption of fruit and vegetables is a primary way of achieving this goal (Nollen et al., 2008).

Dietary habits have been implicated in the development of several cancers, including colon, stomach, pancreas, and breast (Steinmetz, Kushi, Bostick, Folsom, & Potter, 1994). Dietary modification is also important for polyp prevention among individuals at risk for colorectal cancers—specifically, a low-fat, high-fiber diet (Corle et al., 2001). Overall, diet may contribute to 30% of all cancers (Key, Allen, Spencer, & Travis, 2002). An unhealthy diet can work together with stress and negative emotions to promote inflammation, a risk factor for several chronic health disorders (Kiecolt-Glaser, 2010).

The good news is that changing one's diet can improve health. For example, a diet high in fiber may protect against obesity and cardiovascular disease by lowering insulin levels (Ludwig et al., 1999). A diet high in fruits, vegetables, whole grains, peas and beans, poultry, and fish and low in refined grains, potatoes, and red and processed meats lowers the risk of CHD (Fung, Willett, Stampfer, Manson, & Hu, 2001).

Several diets, in addition to low-fat diets, have health benefits. Mediterranean diets are rich in vegetables and low in red meat and high in poultry and fish. Low-carbohydrate diets involve choosing vegetarian sources of fat and protein and reducing consumption of breads and other high-carbohydrate foods. The popular Atkins diet involves substantial reduction in carbohydrates, while consuming more sources of protein and fat as alternative sources of energy. Mediterranean and low-carbohydrate diets can be effective alternatives to low-fat diets, in part because they appear to have higher adherence rates and they have beneficial effects on lipids (low-carbohydrate diet) and on glycemic control (Mediterranean diet) (Shai et al., 2008).

Modifications in diet can lower blood cholesterol levels (Carmody, Matarazzo, & Istvan, 1987), and these modifications may, in turn, reduce the risk for atherosclerosis. A class of drugs, called statins, substantially reduces cholesterol in conjunction with dietary modification. Together, diet modification and a statin regimen appear to lower cholesterol levels significantly.

A controversial issue that will occupy scientific attention over the next decade concerns reduced-calorie diets (Spinney, 2006, June 15). In several animal species, caloric restriction, or a reduced-calorie diet, has increased life span (Antebi, 2007). It is not yet known if caloric restriction increases life span in humans, but experiments with primates suggests that it may. There is already evidence that caloric restriction is associated with biomarkers that predict longevity in humans (Roth et al., 2002). Thus, in addition to changing specific patterns of food consumption in the future, we may also all be urged to reduce our caloric intake overall (Lee & Ruvkun, 2002).

Resistance to Modifying Diet

It is difficult to get people to modify their diet, even when they are at high risk for CHD or when their physician recommends it. Indeed, the typical reason that people switch to a diet low in cholesterol, fats, calories, and additives and high in fiber, fruits, and vegetables is to improve appearance, not to improve health. Even so, fewer than half of U.S. adults meet the dietary recommendations for reducing fat and sodium levels and for increasing fiber, fruit, and vegetable consumption (Kumanyika et al., 2000).

Rates of adherence to a new diet may be high at first but fall off over time. One reason is the factors that plague all efforts to change poor health habits: insufficient attention to the need for long-term monitoring and for relapse prevention techniques. Some dietary recommendations are restrictive, monotonous, expensive, and hard to implement. Drastic changes in shopping, meal planning, cooking methods, and eating habits may be required. In addition, tastes are hard to alter. So-called comfort foods, many of which are high in fat and sugars, may help to turn off stress hormones, such as cortisol, thus contributing to eating things that are not good for us (Dallman et al., 2003). Preferences for high-fat foods are so well established that people will consume more of a food they have been told is high in fat, even when that information is false (Bowen, Tomoyasu, Anderson, Carney, & Kristal, 1992). A low sense of self-efficacy, a preference for meat, a lack of health consciousness, a limited interest in exploring new foods, and low awareness of the link between eating habits and illness are all associated with poor dietary habits (Hollis, Carmody, Connor, Fey, & Matarazzo, 1986).

Stress has a direct effect on eating, especially in adolescence. Increased stress is tied to the consumption of more fatty foods and less fruit and vegetables and to a lower likelihood of eating breakfast, with more snacking between meals (O'Conner, Jones, Ferguson, Conner, & McMillan, 2008). A lower-status job, high workload, and lack of control at work are also associated with less healthful diets (Devine, Connors, Sobal, & Bisogni, 2003). It may be that these factors enhance stress and that an unhealthful diet marked by comfort foods reduces it. Eating is often disinhibited when a person is under stress, distracted, or otherwise not paying attention to what he or she is eating. There are several external factors that reliably influence people's eating (such as the presence of desirable food or the amount of food eaten by a companion), but people are generally unaware that these external influences affect how much food they eat (Vartanian, Herman, & Wansink, 2008). Thus, the sheer cognitive burden of daily life can disinhibit our ability to control our food consumption by preventing us from monitoring the consequences of our eating (Ward & Mann, 2000). People who are high in conscientiousness and intelligence seem to do a better job of adhering to a cholesterol-lowering diet. A strong sense of self-efficacy, knowledge about dietary issues, family support, and the perception that dietary change has important health benefits are also critical to making dietary change (Anderson, Winett, & Wojcik, 2000; Campbell et al., 2008; Steptoe, Doherty, Kerry, Rink, & Hilton, 2000). People who are high in depression or anxiety or who are poorly informed about diet are less likely to make healthy dietary changes (Stilley, Sereika, Muldoon, Ryan, & Dunbar-Jacob, 2004).

Interventions to Modify Diet

Many efforts to modify diet are made on an individual basis in response to a specific health problem or health risk. Physicians, nurses, dietitians, and other experts work with patients to modify a diet-responsive risk, such as obesity, diabetes, CHD, or hypertension. As with any health habit change, the motivation to pursue dietary change and the commitment to long-term health are essential ingredients for success (Kearney, Rosal, Ockene, & Churchill, 2002).

Any effort to change diet needs to begin with education and self-monitoring training, because many people have little idea of the importance of particular nutrients, let alone how much of them their diet actually includes; estimation of fat intake appears to be poor, for example (O'Brien, Fries, & Bowen, 2000).

Much dietary change has been implemented through cognitive-behavioral interventions. These include self-monitoring, stimulus control, and contingency contracting, coupled with relapse prevention techniques for high-risk-for-relapse situations, such as parties. Obtaining social support for making a dietary change and increasing one's sense of self-efficacy are two critical factors for improving diet (Steptoe, Perkins-Porras, Rink, Hilton, & Cappuccio, 2004). For example, an intervention targeted to African-American adolescents' sense of self-efficacy found an increase in fruit and vegetable intake among those who experienced positive shifts in self-efficacy (Wilson, Kliewer, Teasley, Plybon, & Sica, 2002). Motivational interviewing is also helpful in getting people to increase their fruit and vegetable intake and otherwise improve their diets (Ahluwalia et al., 2007; Carels et al., 2007). Training in self-regulation can improve dietary adherence, including planning skills and formation of explicit behavioral intentions (Stadler, Oettingen, & Gollwitzer, 2010).

The stages of change model can be useful for identifying when people will be able to change their diets. People already contemplating dietary change are more likely to enroll in an intervention than those at the stage of precontemplation (McCann et al., 1996). The theory of planned behavior, especially implementation intentions, is also useful for identifying who may be most successful in making diet changes (Armitage, 2004).

Recently, efforts to intervene in the dietary habits of high-risk individuals have focused on the family group. When all family members are committed to and participate in dietary change, it is easier for the target family member to do so as well (Wilson & Ampey-Thornhill, 2001). Moreover, different aspects of diet are influenced by different family members. Whereas wives still usually do the shopping and food preparation, husbands' food preferences are often a more powerful determinant of what the family eats (Weidner, Archer, Healy, & Matarazzo, 1985). In family interventions, family members typically meet with a dietary counselor to discuss ways to change the family diet. Such family interventions have been effective in modifying diet (Epstein, Paluch, Roemmich, & Beecher, 2007). Families that have dinner together can not only achieve beneficial effects on each other's eating habits, but this process of sharing meals appears to promote better health habits and coping more generally. Eating together as a family, then, in the early years, may have multiple health benefits in later years (Franko, Thompson, Affenito, Barton, & Striegel-Moore, 2008).

Community interventions aimed at dietary change have also been undertaken. Nutrition education campaigns mounted in supermarkets have shown some success. In one study, a computerized, interactive nutritional information system placed in supermarkets significantly decreased high-fat purchases and somewhat increased high-fiber purchases (Jeffery, Pirie, Rosenthal, Gerber, & Murray, 1982; Winett et al., 1991). Even telephone counseling can achieve beneficial effects (Madlensky et al., 2008).

A more recent approach to modifying diet involves targeting particular groups for which dietary change may be especially important. Tailoring dietary interventions to ethnic identity and making them culturally and linguistically appropriate may achieve particularly high rates of success (Eakin et al., 2007; Martinez et al., 2008; Resnicow, Davis, et al., 2008). In Latino populations, face-to-face contact with a health advisor who goes through the steps

for successful diet modification may be especially important, due to the emphasis on personal contact in Latino culture and communities (Elder et al., 2005).

Researchers are also moving toward interventions that are cost-effective to alter behavior related to diet and exercise, rather than large-scale CBT interventions. For example, computer-tailored dietary fat intake interventions can be effective both with adults and with adolescents (Haerens et al., 2007). Such interventions also have the capability of reaching large groups of people at relatively low cost.

Change may come from social engineering as well. When children have access to school snack bars that include sodas, candy, and other unhealthy foods, it undermines their consumption of healthier foods (Cullen & Zakeri, 2004). Banning snack foods from schools, making school lunch programs more nutritious, making snack foods more expensive and healthy foods less so, and taxing products high in sugar or fats (Brownell & Frieden, 2009) will make some inroads into promoting healthy food choices (Horgen & Brownell, 2002). With respect to the schools, social engineering solutions may be most successful.

■ WEIGHT CONTROL AND OBESITY

Maintaining a proper diet and getting enough exercise jointly contribute to weight control, the issue to which we now turn. This issue has become especially urgent in recent years because of soaring levels of obesity. Consequently, our discussion will begin to cross the line into the area of health-compromising behaviors, as we will look at interventions both for normal, healthy adults to practice weight control and for the obese, who may need to modify their weight to promote their health.

The Regulation of Eating

All animals, including humans, have sensitive and complex systems for regulating food. Taste has been called the chemical gatekeeper of eating. It is an ancient sensory system and plays an important role in selecting certain foods and rejecting others.

A number of hormones control eating. Leptin and insulin, in particular, circulate in the blood in concentrations that are proportionate to body fat mass. They decrease appetite by inhibiting neurons that produce the molecules neuropeptide Y (NPY) and agouti-related peptide (AgRP), peptides that would otherwise stimulate eating. They also stimulate melacortin-producing neurons in the hypothalamus, which inhibit eating.

TABLE 4.3 | Body Mass Index Table

BMI	Normal						Overweight					Obese					
	19	20	21	22	23	24	25	26	27	28	29	30	31	32	33	34	35
Height (inches)	Body Weight (pounds)																
58	91	96	100	105	110	115	119	124	129	134	138	143	148	153	158	162	167
59	94	99	104	109	114	119	124	128	133	138	143	148	153	158	163	168	173
60	97	102	107	112	118	123	128	133	138	143	148	153	158	163	168	174	179
61	100	106	111	116	122	127	132	137	143	148	153	158	164	169	174	180	185
62	104	109	115	120	126	131	136	142	147	153	158	164	169	175	180	186	191
63	107	113	118	124	130	135	141	146	152	158	163	169	175	180	186	191	197
64	110	116	122	128	134	140	145	151	157	163	169	174	180	186	192	197	204
65	114	120	126	132	138	144	150	156	162	168	174	180	186	192	198	204	210
66	118	124	130	136	142	148	155	161	167	173	179	186	192	198	204	210	216
67	121	127	134	140	146	153	159	166	172	178	185	191	198	204	211	217	223
68	125	131	138	144	151	158	164	171	177	184	190	197	203	210	216	223	230
69	128	135	142	149	155	162	169	176	182	189	196	203	209	216	223	230	236
70	132	139	146	153	160	167	174	181	188	195	202	209	216	222	229	236	243
71	136	143	150	157	165	172	179	186	193	200	208	215	222	229	236	243	250
72	140	147	154	162	169	177	184	191	199	206	213	221	228	235	242	250	258
73	144	151	159	166	174	182	189	197	204	212	219	227	235	242	250	257	265
74	148	155	163	171	179	186	194	202	210	218	225	233	241	249	256	264	272
75	152	160	168	176	184	192	200	208	216	224	232	240	248	256	264	272	279
76	156	164	172	180	189	197	205	213	221	230	238	246	254	263	271	279	287

Source: National Heart, Lung & Blood Institute, 2004.

As may be evident, an important player in weight control is the protein leptin, which is secreted by fat cells. Leptin appears to signal the neurons of the hypothalamus as to whether the body has sufficient energy stores of fat or whether it needs additional energy. The brain's eating control center reacts to the signals sent from the hypothalamus to increase or decrease appetite. As noted, leptin inhibits the neurons that stimulate appetite and activates those that suppress appetite. These effects of leptin have made scientists optimistic about the use of leptin as a weight control agent, although thus far the promise of leptin as a pharmacological method of weight control has remained elusive (Morton, Cummings, Baskin, Barsh, & Schwartz, 2006).

Ghrelin may also play an important role in why dieters who lose weight often gain it back so quickly. Ghrelin is secreted by specialized cells in the stomach, spiking just before meals and dropping afterward. When people are given ghrelin injections, they feel extremely hungry. Therefore, blocking ghrelin levels or the action of ghrelin may help people lose weight and keep it off (Grady, 2002, May 23).

Why Is Obesity a Health Risk?

What is obesity? **Obesity** is an excessive accumulation of body fat. Generally, fat should constitute about 20–27% of body tissue in women and about 15–22% in men. Table 4.3 presents guidelines from the National Institutes of Health for calculating your body mass index and determining whether you are overweight or obese.

The World Health Organization estimates that 400 million people worldwide are obese and a further 1.6 billion are overweight, including 20 million children under age 5 (World Health Organization, 2006). Obesity is now so common that it has replaced malnutrition as the most prevalent dietary contributor to poor health worldwide (Kopelman, 2000) and will soon account for more diseases and deaths in the United States than smoking. The global epidemic of obesity stems from a combination of genetic susceptibility, the increasing availability of high-fat and high-energy foods, and low levels of physical activity (Kopelman, 2000).

Obesity is a worldwide problem, but nowhere is it more serious than in the United States. Americans are the fattest people in the world (Critser, 2003). At

Obese				Extreme Obesity														
36	37	38	39	40	41	42	43	44	45	46	47	48	49	50	51	52	53	54
Body Weight (pounds)																		
172	177	181	186	191	196	201	205	210	215	220	224	229	234	239	244	248	253	258
178	183	188	193	198	203	208	212	217	222	227	232	237	242	247	252	257	262	267
184	189	194	199	204	209	215	220	225	230	235	240	245	250	255	261	266	271	276
190	195	201	206	211	217	222	227	232	238	243	248	254	259	264	269	275	280	285
196	202	207	213	218	224	229	235	240	246	251	256	262	267	273	278	284	289	295
203	208	214	220	225	231	237	242	248	254	259	265	270	278	282	287	293	299	304
209	215	221	227	232	238	244	250	256	262	267	273	279	285	291	296	302	308	314
216	222	228	234	240	246	252	258	264	270	276	282	288	294	300	306	312	318	324
223	229	235	241	247	253	260	266	272	278	284	291	297	303	309	315	322	328	334
230	236	242	249	255	261	268	274	280	287	293	299	306	312	319	325	331	338	344
236	243	249	256	262	269	276	282	289	295	302	308	315	322	328	335	341	348	354
243	250	257	263	270	277	284	291	297	304	311	318	324	331	338	345	351	358	365
250	257	264	271	278	285	292	299	306	313	320	327	334	341	348	355	362	369	376
257	265	272	279	286	293	301	308	315	322	329	338	343	351	358	365	372	379	386
265	272	279	287	294	302	309	316	324	331	338	346	353	361	368	375	383	390	397
272	280	288	295	302	310	318	325	333	340	348	355	363	371	378	386	393	401	408
280	287	295	303	311	319	326	334	342	350	358	365	373	381	389	396	404	412	420
287	295	303	311	319	327	335	343	351	359	367	375	383	391	399	407	415	423	431
295	304	312	320	328	336	344	353	361	369	377	385	394	402	410	418	426	435	443

present, 67% of the adult U.S. population is overweight, and about 34% is obese (National Center for Health Statistics, 2008), with women somewhat less likely to be overweight or obese than men (Figure 4.2). Although obesity levels have begun to level off, the trend has not yet reversed (Stein, 2010, January 14).

There is no mystery as to why people in the United States have become so heavy. The food industry spends approximately $33 billion per year on ads and promotions for food. Portion sizes have increased, and healthful foods are often not available. The average American's food intake rose from 1,826 calories a day in the 1970s to more than 2,000 by the mid-1990s (O'Connor, 2004, February 6). Soda consumption has skyrocketed from 22.2 gallons to 56 gallons per person per year. Portion sizes at meals have increased substantially over the past 20 years (Nielsen & Popkin, 2003). So-called supersize portions are very high in calories. For example, whereas the original French fries order at McDonald's was 200 calories, today's supersize serving has 610 calories. Muffins that weighed 1.5 ounces in 1957 now average half a pound each (Raeburn, Forster, Foust, &

Brady, 2002, October 21). Even people who are not dieting for obesity should be attentive to portion sizes, and among those practicing weight control, this concern is critical (Nielsen & Popkin, 2003).

Risks of Obesity   Obesity is a risk factor for many disorders, both in its own right and because it affects other risk factors, such as blood pressure and plasma cholesterol level (Kopelman, 2000). Increased body weight contributes to increased death rates for all cancers combined and for the specific cancers of the colon, rectum, liver, gallbladder, pancreas, kidney, and esophagus, as well as non-Hodgkin's lymphoma and multiple myeloma. Estimates are that overweight and obesity may account for 14% of all deaths from cancer in men and 20% of all deaths from cancer in women (Calle, Rodriguez, Walker-Thurmond, & Thun, 2003). Most of these are due to obesity-related cancers that include cancers of the colon, breast, esophagus, uterus, ovary, kidney, and pancreas (Flegal, Graubard, Williamson, & Gail, 2007). Obesity also contributes substantially to deaths from cardiovascular disease (Flegal et al., 2009). Obesity has

FIGURE 4.2 | Percentage of Population Overweight and Obese   Overweight is BMI over 25 and obese is BMI over 30. (*Source:* National Center for Health Statistics, 2008)

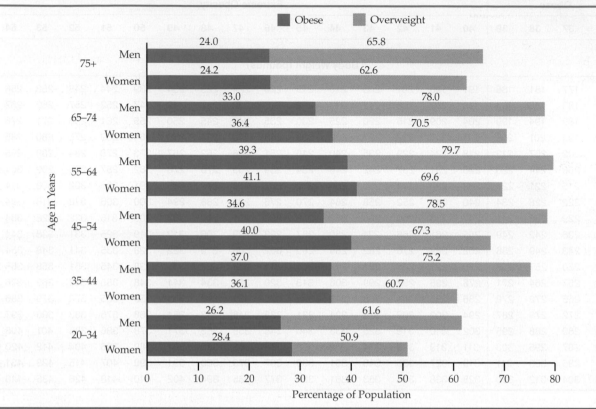

been associated with atherosclerosis, hypertension, diabetes, gallbladder disease, arthritis, and heart failure (Kenchaiah et al., 2002). Obesity also increases risks in surgery, anesthesia administration, and childbearing (Brownell & Wadden, 1992). One study found that women who were 30% overweight were more than three times as likely to develop heart disease as women who were of normal or slightly under normal weight (Manson et al., 1990). This risk increased to five times that of normal-weight women among the overweight women who were also smokers (Manson et al., 1990).

Obesity is also one of the chief causes of disability, and rates have soared in the past 15 years. The number of people age 30–49 who cannot care for themselves or perform routine household tasks has jumped by 50%. Moreover, this marker bodes poorly for the future. People who are disabled in their 30s and 40s are much more likely to have health care expenses and to need nursing home care in older age if they live that long (Richardson, 2004, January 9). Being obese reduces the likelihood that a person will exercise, and lack of exercise increases

the risk that people will become obese; yet obesity and lack of exercise appear to exert independent adverse effects on health, leading to greater risks than either risk factor alone (Hu et al., 2004).

As a consequence of its links to chronic disease (especially cardiovascular disease, kidney disease, and diabetes), obesity is associated with early mortality (Adams et al., 2006). As a ballpark statistic, people who are overweight at age 40 are likely to die 3 years earlier than those who are thin (Peeters et al., 2003). Even mildly overweight women are at an increased risk for heart disease and heart attack compared with women who are underweight (Manson et al., 1990) (Table 4.4). Abdominally localized fat, as opposed to excessive fat in the hips, buttocks, or thighs, is an especially potent risk factor for cardiovascular disease, diabetes, hypertension, cancer, and decline in cognitive function (Dore, Elias, Robbins, Budge, & Elias, 2008). Sometimes called "stress weight," abdominal fat increases in response to stress (Rebuffe-Scrive, Walsh, McEwen, & Rodin, 1992). People with excessive central weight (sometimes called "apples," in contrast to "pears," who carry their weight on their hips) are more psychologically reactive to stress and also show greater cardiovascular reactivity (Davis, Twamley, Hamilton, & Swan, 1999) and neuroendocrine reactivity to stress (Epel et al., 2000). This reactivity to stress may be the link between centrally deposited fat and increased risk for diseases. Fat tissue is a strong producer of

proinflammatory cytokines, which may exacerbate diseases related to inflammatory processes (see Chapter 2).

In addition, many of the treatments for overweight that people undertake on their own, such as use of diet pills and other medications, fad diets, fasting, and anorexia nervosa or bulimia, create risks of their own.

Often ignored among the risks of obesity is the psychological distress that can result. Although there is a robust stereotype of overweight people as more "jolly," studies suggest that the obese are more likely to have or develop personality disorders and psychiatric conditions, especially depression (Boutelle, Hannan, Fulkerson, Crow, & Stice, 2010; Mather, Cox, Enns, & Sareen, 2008; Petry, Barry, Pietrzak, & Wagner, 2008), and problems of self-regulation, such as low conscientiousness and impulsivity (Terracciano et al., 2009). Depression may be maintained by the recognition that the world is not designed for overweight people. One may have to pay for two seats on an airplane, have little luck finding clothes, endure derision and rude comments, and experience other reminders that the obese, quite literally, do not fit. The obese are subject to pernicious stereotypes and stigmas, which may further reduce psychological health (Carr & Friedman, 2005) (see Box 4.1).

As just noted, obesity increases the risk for a number of disorders, yet the obese often avoid the trips to the physician that might help them. For example, getting in

TABLE 4.4 | Even Moderate Overweight Can Increase Risk of Death

For women, being even mildly overweight can greatly increase risk of cancer and heart disease. This table, using the example of a woman who is 5 ft. 5 in. tall, shows the risk for death among women age 30–55 who were followed in this study for 16 years. To put these data into perspective, however, the same woman would have to gain more than 100 pounds to equal the health risks of smoking two packs of cigarettes a day.

Weight in Pounds	Risk
Less than 120	Lowest risk
120–149	+20%
150–160	+30%
161–175	+60%
176–195	+110%
Greater than 195	+120%

Source: Manson et al., 1995.

More than one-third of the adult population in the United States is overweight, putting them at risk for heart disease, kidney disease, hypertension, diabetes, and other health problems.

BOX 4.1

The Stigma of Obesity: Comments on the Obese

Obese people are often the target of insensitive comments about their weight. They are teased by their peers as children and called names such as "whale" or "fatty." The teasing endures into adulthood, where, while in public, they encounter people staring at them, whispering behind their backs, and calling them names.

Family life for obese people can be difficult as well. Receiving criticism and comments about their weight from loved ones can irreparably damage family relationships. Lack of family acceptance can remove the home as a buffer against peer cruelty. Some parents push their overweight children to lose weight, using techniques that shame their children into weight loss, such as withdrawing affection.

The resulting effect of repeated exposure to others' judgments about their weight can be social alienation and low self-esteem. From a young age, overweight children may recognize that they are different from other children. Childhood activities such as swimming and athletics, when children must wear a swimsuit or change in a locker room, may involve uncomfortable exposure that leads to more teasing. Unfortunately, obese children learn from a young age to avoid interaction with their peers and may thereby compromise their ability to develop close relationships. Obese adolescents show lower academic achievement, especially in schools with low average body weight and high rates of romantic activity, presumably because negative evaluations from others lower self-esteem and consequent academic achievement (Crosnoe & Muller, 2004).

Obese people are one of very few disabled groups to endure public criticism for their disability. Obesity is stigmatized as a disability whose fault lies with obese people (Carr & Friedman, 2005; Puhl, Schwartz, & Brownell, 2005; Wang, Houshyar, & Prinstein, 2006). This stigma fuels public sentiments that obese people are responsible for being obese, that they are lazy or gluttonous. Even health care providers may hold these stereotypes. One woman reported that her physician told her "I was too fat for a proper exam and to come back when I'd lost 50 pounds" (Center for the Advancement of Health, 2008).

Coping with views of their weight is difficult for obese people as well. To address teasing directly, especially when the comments are simply a stated fact, such as, "That person is fat," is to admit that being fat is a bad thing. Increasingly, our society will need to accommodate not only the physical needs of obese people but their emotional needs as well.

and out of a car and in and out of a doctor's office present challenges for the morbidly obese. The obese may not fit in standard chairs or in standard wheelchairs. X rays may not penetrate far enough to give accurate readings, blood pressure cuffs are not big enough, and hospital gowns do not cover them (Pérez-Peña & Glickson, 2003, November 29). If an obese person increasingly withdraws into a reclusive life, by the time he or she seeks treatment, the complications of diabetes, heart disease, and other disorders may be out of control.

Obesity in Childhood

In the United States, approximately 37% of children are overweight or obese, but other countries are gaining; the figure is 20% in Europe and 10% in China (Nash, 2003, August 25). Being overweight in childhood must now be considered a major health problem rather than merely a problem in appearance (Dietz, 2004). Specifically, 60% of overweight children and adolescents are already showing risk factors for cardiovascular disease, such as elevated blood pressure, elevated lipid levels, or hyperinsulemia (Sinha et al., 2002), and being overweight in childhood predicts risk for coronary heart disease in adulthood (Baker, Olsen, & Sørensen, 2007). African American

and Hispanic children and adolescents are at particular risk. For the first time in over 200 years, the current generation of children has a shorter life expectancy due to high rates of obesity than their parents (Belluck, 2005).

What is leading to childhood obesity? Genes contribute to risk of obesity (Herbert et al., 2006). Another important factor is increasingly sedentary lifestyles among children and adolescents, involving television, video games, and the Internet (Dietz & Gortmaker, 2001). Exercise and obesity are clearly related. Children are less likely to be obese if they participate in organized sports or physical activity, if they enjoy physical education, and if their family supports physical activity (Anderson, Hughes, & Fuemmeler, 2009; Epstein, Kilanowski, Consalvi, & Paluch, 1999; Sallis, Prochaska, Taylor, Hill, & Geraci, 1999). Early eating habits also contribute to obesity: Children who are encouraged to overeat in infancy and childhood are more likely to become obese adults (Berkowitz, Agras, Korner, Kraemer, & Zeanah, 1985). Figure 4.3 illustrates the high rates of obesity among children.

Lifestyle interventions involving encouragement and reinforcements to avoid sedentary activities like television watching, inducements to engage in sports and other physical activities, and steps to encourage

FIGURE 4.3 | Percentage of Young People Who Are Overweight   Overweight is defined as greater than or equal to the 95th percentile of the age- and sex-specific BMI.   (*Source:* National Center for Health Statistics, 2008)

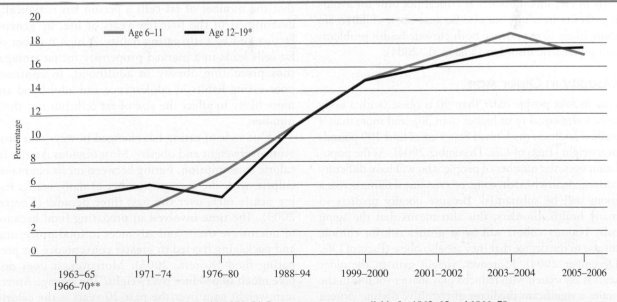

*Excludes pregnant women starting with 1971–74. Pregnancy status not available for 1963–65 and 1966–70.

**Data for 1963–65 are for children 6–11 years of age; data for 1966–70 are for adolescents 12–17 years of age, not 12–19 years.

Obesity in childhood is one of the fastest growing health concerns in the United States.

healthier eating practices represent a successful approach to this problem (Wilfley et al., 2007). Television viewing may itself contribute to obesity via another route; when children are exposed to food advertising, their consumption of food increases, in one study by 45% (Harris, Bargh, & Brownell, 2009).

School-based interventions directed to making healthy foods available and modifying sedentary behavior may help (Dietz & Gortmaker, 2001). Intervening early in childhood obesity is critical not only for avoiding obesity in adults but also because obese children are more likely to experience both chronic health problems and psychiatric disorders (Vila et al., 2004).

Obesity in Older Age

One in four people older than 50 is obese (with a body mass index equal to or higher than 30), and more than 9 million adults in the United States are at least 100 pounds overweight (Facts of Life, December 2004). As the population ages, the number of people who will have difficulty bathing themselves, dressing, or even just walking across a room will be substantial. Because obesity predicts so many health disorders, this also means that the aging baby boomer cohort will be at greater risk for chronic disease to the degree that they are also obese (Facts of Life, December 2004). Moreover, weight gain in the older years is associated with reduced gray matter volume in the brain, a significant predictor of cognitive decline (Soreca et al., 2009). Consequently, counseling older adults to adopt a healthy diet and increase their exercise is essential.

Factors Associated with Obesity

Obesity depends on both the number and the size of an individual's fat cells. Among moderately obese people, fat cells are typically large, but there is not an unusual number of them. Among the severely obese, there is a large number of fat cells, and the fat cells themselves are exceptionally large (Brownell, 1982).

Childhood constitutes a window of vulnerability for obesity for a number of reasons. One reason is that the number of fat cells a person has is typically determined in the first few years of life, by genetic factors and by early eating habits. A high number of fat cells leads to a marked propensity for fat storage, thus promoting obesity in adulthood. In contrast, poor eating habits in adolescence and adulthood are more likely to affect the size of fat cells but not their number.

Our style of eating has changed in ways that promote overweight and obesity. Most obvious is a rise in calorie consumption. Eating between meals is a major culprit, with the average number of daily snacks rising nearly 60% over the past three decades (Koretz, 2003). The time involved in preparing food because of microwave ovens and advances in food processing and packaging has led to greater convenience for preparing food (Koretz, 2003). Moreover, it does not take much to produce overweight. The average American weight gain over the past 20 years is the caloric equivalent of just three Oreo cookies or one can of soda a day (Koretz, 2003).

Family History and Obesity   Family history is clearly implicated in obesity. Overweight parents are more likely to have overweight children than are normal-weight parents. This relationship appears to be due to both genetic and dietary factors (Meyer & Stunkard, 1994). Evidence for genetic factors comes from twin studies: Twins reared apart show a tendency toward obesity when both natural parents were obese, even when the twins' environments are very different (Stunkard, 1988).

The impact of genetics on weight may be exerted, in part, through feeding style. In a study of healthy infants observed from birth to 2 years, Agras and his associates (Agras, Kraemer, Berkowitz, Korner, & Hammer, 1987) found that children who were later to become obese were distinguished by a vigorous feeding style, consisting of sucking more rapidly, more intensely, and longer, with shorter bursts between sucking. This style produced a higher caloric intake and greater overweight. The fact that the feeding style emerged very early suggests its role as a genetically-based predisposition to obesity. There also appear to be genetically based tendencies to store energy as either fat or lean tissue (Bouchard et al., 1990). Understanding the role of genetics in obesity is important because it helps identify individuals for whom weight management interventions are especially important.

But a family history of obesity does not necessarily implicate genetics. For example, one study found that 44% of the dogs of obese people were obese, compared with only 25% of the dogs of people with normal weight (Mason, 1970). Many factors in a home, such as the type of diet consumed, the size of portions, and exercise patterns, contribute to the obesity that runs in families (Klesges, Eck, Hanson, Haddock, & Klesges, 1990).

SES, Culture, and Obesity   Additional risk factors for obesity include social class and culture. In the United States, women of low socioeconomic status are heavier than high-SES women, and African American women, in particular, are vulnerable to obesity (Facts of Life, September 2005). Although SES differences in weight have previously been attributed to high-carbohydrate diets early in life, this does not explain why SES is not associated with obesity in men and children. One factor may be the simple fact that diets high in fats and sweets cost less than those high in vegetables, fish, and fruit (Drewnowski, Darmon, & Briend, 2004).

Obesity seems to spread through social networks, almost like an epidemic. A person's chances of becoming obese increases substantially when he or she has a friend, sibling, or partner who has become obese.

Exactly why this is the case is unknown, but it may be that obesity in one person changes the social norms associated with obesity, making it more acceptable to become obese (Christakis & Fowler, 2007).

Values also are implicated in obesity. Thinness is valued in women from high-SES levels and from developed countries, which in turn leads to a cultural emphasis on dieting and on physical activity (Wardle et al., 2004). These social norms prompt most women, not just those who are obese, to be discontented with their bodies (Foster, Wadden, & Vogt, 1997).

Obesity and Dieting as Risk Factors for Obesity   Paradoxically, obesity is also a risk factor for obesity. Many obese individuals have a high basal insulin level, which promotes overeating due to increased hunger. Moreover, the obese have large fat cells, which have a greater capacity for producing and storing fat than do small fat cells. Thus, the obese are at risk to become even more so.

Dieting contributes to the propensity for obesity. Successive cycles of dieting and weight gain, so-called **yo-yo dieting,** enhance the efficiency of food use and lower the metabolic rate (Bouchard, 2002). When dieters begin to eat normally again, their metabolic rate may stay low, and it can become easier for them to put on weight again even though they eat less food. Unfortunately, too, these decreases in metabolic rate may be more problematic with successive diets. Between one-third and two-thirds of dieters regain more weight than they lose, leading some researchers to question whether dieting is the answer to the obesity problem (Mann et al., 2007). Moreover, there may be health risks tied to restrained eating (Kiefer, Lin, Blackburn, & Epel, 2008).

There may be a selective preference for foods high in fat following weight loss (Gerardo-Gettens et al., 1991). Thus, yo-yo dieters may actually increase their chances of becoming obese (Brownell & Rodin, 1996). If these risks weren't enough, yo-yo dieters act as role models, inadvertently increasing their children's likelihood of engaging in the same behaviors and augmenting their risk for obesity (*New York Times,* 2000a).

Set Point Theory of Weight   In recent years, evidence has accumulated for a **set point theory of weight:** the idea that each individual has an ideal biological weight, which cannot be greatly modified (Garner & Wooley, 1991). According to the theory, the set point acts like a thermostat regulating heat in a home. A person eats if his or her weight gets too low and stops eating as the weight reaches its ideal point. Some individuals simply have a higher set point than others, leading them to be obese (Brownell, 1982). The theory argues that efforts to lose weight may be compensated for by adjustments of energy expenditure, as the body actively attempts to return to its original weight. Psychological changes such as depression or irritability can accompany these processes as well (Klem, Wing, McGuire, Seagle, & Hill, 1998).

Stress and Eating

Stress affects eating, although in different ways for different people. About half of people eat more when they are under stress, and half eat less (Willenbring, Levine, & Morley, 1986). For nondieting and nonobese normal eaters, the experience of stress or anxiety may suppress physiological cues suggesting hunger, leading to lower consumption of food. Stress and anxiety, however, can disinhibit the dieter, removing the self-control that usually guards against eating, thus leading to an increase in food intake among both dieters and the obese (Heatherton, Herman, & Polivy, 1991, 1992). Whereas men tend to eat less in stressful circumstances, many women eat more (Grunberg & Straub, 1992).

Stress also influences what food is consumed. People who eat in response to stress usually consume more low-calorie and salty foods, although when not under stress, stress eaters show a preference for high-calorie foods (Willenbring et al., 1986).

Anxiety and depression appear to figure into **stress eating** as well. One study found that stress eaters experience greater fluctuations in anxiety and depression than do nonstress eaters. Overweight individuals also have greater fluctuations in anxiety, hostility, and depression than do normal individuals (Lingsweiler, Crowther, & Stephens, 1987). Those who eat in response to negative emotions show a preference for sweet and high-fat foods (Oliver, Wardle, & Gibson, 2000).

Weight Control and Obesity

More people are treated for obesity in the United States than for all other health habits or conditions combined. More than half a million people attend weight-loss clinics, and Amazon.com currently lists more than 30,000 book titles that refer to diet or dieting. However, obesity is a very difficult condition to treat (Brownell & Wadden, 1992). Even initially successful weight-loss programs show a high rate of relapse. In this section, we review the most common approaches to treatment of obesity.

Dieting   Treating obesity through dieting has historically been the most common approach, and most weight-loss programs still begin with dietary treatment. People are trained to restrict their caloric and/or carbohydrate intake. In some cases, food may be provided to the dieters to ensure that the appropriate foods are being consumed. Providing structured meal plans and grocery lists may improve weight loss (Surwit et al., 1997; Wing et al., 1996), but it can do so at the expense of well-being. Dieting is a stressor that increases cortisol secretion and thus may itself produce health risks (Tomiyama et al., 2010).

Generally, weight loss produced through dietary methods is small and rarely maintained for long (Agras et al., 1996). Weight loss achieved through dieting rarely matches the expectations of clients, whose disappointment may contribute to regaining the lost weight (Foster, Wadden, Vogt, & Brewer, 1997). Very low-carbohydrate or low-fat diets do the best job in helping people lose weight initially, but these diets are the hardest to maintain, and people commonly revert to their old habits. Reducing caloric intake, increasing exercise, and sticking with an eating plan over the long term are the only factors reliably related to staying slim.

Surgery   Surgical procedures, especially gastric surgeries, represent a radical way of controlling extreme obesity. In the most common surgical procedure, the stomach is literally stapled up to reduce its capacity to hold food, so that the overweight individual must restrict his or her intake. As with all surgeries, there is some risk, and side effects such as gastric and intestinal distress are common. Consequently, this procedure is usually reserved for people who are at least 100% overweight, who have failed repeatedly to lose weight through other methods, and who have complicating health problems that make weight loss urgent. Despite its drastic nature, use of this surgical treatment for obesity has more than doubled in recent years, attesting again to how common and serious a problem obesity is (Steinbrook, 2004b). Unfortunately, because of obesity's increasing prevalence, many insurance companies are now phasing out coverage for surgery to treat the condition (Costello, 2004).

Cognitive Behavior Therapy (CBT)

Many current interventions with the obese use CBT to combat maladaptive eating behavior.

Screening   Some programs begin by screening applicants for their readiness to lose weight and their motivation to do so. Unsuccessful prior dieting attempts, weight lost and regained, high body dissatisfaction, and low self-esteem are all associated with less weight loss for behavioral weight-reduction programs, and these criteria can be used to screen individuals or to provide a better match between a particular treatment program and a client (Teixeira et al., 2002).

Self-Monitoring   Obese clients are trained in self-monitoring and are taught to keep careful records of what they eat, when they eat it, how much they eat, where they eat it, and other dimensions of eating. This record keeping simultaneously defines the behavior and makes clients more aware of their eating patterns (Baker & Kirschenbaum, 1998). Many patients are surprised to discover what, when, and how much they actually eat. Monitoring is always important for weight loss, but it becomes especially so at high-risk times, such as during the holidays, when weight gain reliably occurs (Boutelle, Kirschenbaum, Baker, & Mitchell, 1999).

Behavioral analysis next focuses on influencing the antecedents of the target behavior—namely, the stimuli that affect eating. Clients are trained to modify the stimuli in their environment that have previously elicited and maintained overeating. Such steps include purchasing low-calorie foods (such as raw vegetables), facilitating access to them, and limiting the high-calorie foods kept in the house. Behavioral-control techniques are also used to train patients to change the circumstances of eating. Clients are taught to confine eating to one place at particular times of day. They may also be trained to develop new discriminative stimuli that will be associated with eating. For example, they may be encouraged to use a particular place setting, such as a special placemat or napkin, and to eat only when those stimuli are present. Individualized feedback about specific weight problems and their management appears to be especially helpful to success in losing weight (Kreuter, Bull, Clark, & Oswald, 1999).

Controlling Eating   The next step is to train clients to gain control over the eating process itself. For example, clients may be urged to count each mouthful of food, each chew, or each swallow. They may be told to put down eating utensils after every few mouthfuls until the food in their mouths is chewed and swallowed. Longer and longer delays are introduced between mouthfuls so as to encourage slow eating (which tends to reduce intake). Such delays are first introduced at the end of the meal, when the client is already satiated, and progressively moved closer to the beginning of the meal. Finally, clients are urged to savor their food—to make a conscious effort to appreciate it while they are eating. The goal is to teach the obese person to eat less and enjoy it more (Stunkard, 1979).

Clients are also trained to gain control over the consequences of the target behavior and to reward themselves for activities they carry out successfully. For example, keeping records, counting chews, pausing between bites, or eating only in a specific place might be reinforced by a tangible positive reinforcement, such as going to a movie or making a long-distance phone call to a friend. Developing a sense of self-control over eating is an important part of behavioral treatments of obesity and can help people overcome temptations.

Adding Exercise   Exercise is a critical component of any weight-loss program. In fact, as people age, increasing exercise is essential just to maintain weight, let alone avoid gaining it (Jameson, 2004). High levels of physical activity are associated with initial weight loss and with the maintenance of that weight loss among both adults and children (Epstein et al., 1995; Jeffery & Wing, 1995).

Controlling Self-Talk
Cognitive restructuring is an important part of weight-reduction programs. As noted in Chapter 3, poor health habits can be maintained through dysfunctional monologues ("I'll never lose weight—I've tried before and

Approximately 500,000 Americans participate in organized weight-reduction programs. Many of these programs now include exercise.

failed so many times"). Participants in weight-loss programs are urged to identify the maladaptive thoughts they have regarding weight loss and to substitute positive self-instruction.

Positive expectations, the formation of explicit implementation intensions (Luszczynska, Sobczyk, & Abraham, 2007), and satisfaction with one's treatment outcome are both tied to weight loss (Finch et al., 2005). A strong sense of self-efficacy—that is, the belief that one will be able to lose weight—also predicts weight loss (Warziski, Sereika, Styn, Music, & Burke, 2008). The goal of these elements of interventions is to increase a sense of self-determination, which can enhance intrinsic motivation to continue weight loss and dietary efforts (Mata et al., 2009). For those who are unable to maintain motivation through self-help programs, the stepped up, more intensive motivation may bring them up to the same level of weight loss as that obtained by people who are able to lose weight through self-help programs (Carels et al., 2009).

Stress Management   Dieting and other efforts to lose weight can be stressful (Tomiyama et al., 2010), and so interventions designed to reduce the stressfulness of the weight loss process can be helpful. Among the techniques that have been used to this end are mindfulness training and acceptance and commitment theory (ACT).

Social Support   Because clients with high degrees of social support are more successful than those with little social support, most multimodal programs include training in eliciting effective support from families, friends, and coworkers (Brownell & Kramer, 1989; Brownell & Stunkard, 1981). Even supportive messages from a behavioral therapist over the Internet seem to help people lose weight (Oleck, 2001).

Relapse Prevention   Relapse prevention techniques are incorporated into many treatment programs. As noted earlier, initial relapse prevention begins with effective screening of applicants to weight-loss programs. Other relapse prevention techniques include matching treatments to the eating problems of particular clients, restructuring the environment to remove temptation, rehearsing high-risk situations for relapse (such as holidays), and developing coping strategies to deal with high-risk situations.

Relapse prevention is important not only for diet control but also for the self-recrimination that occurs when people are unsuccessful. Such negative consequences may fall more heavily on women than men.

When their diets fail, women tend to blame their own lack of self-discipline, whereas men tend to blame external factors such as work (*New York Times,* 2000b). Sometimes weight-loss efforts fail simply because the process of maintaining the behaviors needed for weight control is so arduous and the long-term rewards for so doing are limited (Jeffery, Kelly, Rothman, Sherwood, & Boutelle, 2004). Weight loss may also fail because attractive food triggers motivation and disinhibits the goal of dieting (Papies, Stroebe, & Aarts, 2008). Some people may feel that the benefits of weight loss are simply not worth the effort.

Where Are Weight-Loss Programs Implemented?

Workplace Weight-Loss Interventions   Weight-loss programs have been initiated through the workplace, and a technique that has proven effective has been competition between work groups to see which group can lose the most weight and keep it off (Brownell, Cohen, Stunkard, Felix, & Cooley, 1984; Brownell, Stunkard, & McKeon, 1985). Exactly why team competitions are successful is unknown. It may be that they draw effectively on social support or that the arousal produced by a competitive spirit motivates people to work harder to maintain weight loss. However, whether weight loss engaged through such team competitions can be maintained over time remains unknown (Brownell & Felix, 1987; Stunkard, Cohen, & Felix, 1989).

Commercial Weight-Loss Programs   Each year $30 billion goes to commercial weight-loss programs and specialized foods for these programs (American Obesity Association, 2005). More than 500,000 people each week are exposed to behavioral methods of controlling obesity through commercial clinics such as TOPS (Take Off Pounds Sensibly), Weight Watchers, and Jenny Craig. Many of these programs incorporate the behavior-change principles just described. Because of the sheer number of people affected by these programs, formal evaluation of their effectiveness is important; yet rarely have such organizations opened their doors to formal program evaluation.

Evaluation of Cognitive-Behavioral Weight-Loss Techniques

How successful are weight loss programs? Cognitive-behavioral programs typically produce better modest success, with weight loss of nearly 2 pounds a week for up to 20 weeks and long-term maintenance over 2 years (Brownell & Kramer, 1989). Programs that are longer lasting and that emphasize self-direction and exercise and include relapse prevention techniques are particularly successful (Baum, Clark, & Sandler, 1991; Brownell & Kramer, 1989; Jeffery, Hennrikus, Lando, Murray, & Liu, 2000).

An analysis of 66 lifestyle interventions that focused on diet, exercise, and other behaviors related to weight evaluated how effective each type of intervention was in modifying weight for children and adolescents. The results indicated that these interventions can be effective for children and adolescents under a wide range of conditions, with even better results achieved when parents are involved (Kitzmann et al., 2010).

Nonetheless, responses to weight loss programs are variable. Some people lose weight and are successful in keeping it off, whereas others put the weight back on almost immediately. Thus, effective techniques to enhance adherence to behavior change are critical (Williamson et al., 2010). Moreover, such programs may not be

aggressive enough to help the truly obese, who may require the more extreme measures of fasting and surgery.

We might expect that the stages-of-change model, by which interventions are tailored to a recipient's stage of readiness, would be successful in managing weight. As yet, however, the success of such efforts is equivocal (Jeffery, French, & Rothman, 1999). Table 4.5 describes some of the promising leads that current research suggests for enhancing long-term weight loss in cognitive-behavioral programs.

Taking a Public Health Approach

The high prevalence of obesity leads to enormous costs to the economy. For example, the state of California estimates $28.7 billion annually in lost productivity and health care expenses due to weight-control problems (Girion, 2005). The increasing prevalence of obesity makes it evident that a public health model that emphasizes prevention will be essential for combating this problem (Mello, Studdert, & Brennan, 2006). Although

TABLE 4.5 | Weight-Management Tips

Increasing Awareness	Exercise
Keep track of what you eat. Keep track of your weight. Write down when you eat and why.	Track your exercise progress: What do you enjoy doing? Incorporate exercise into your lifestyle—become more active in all areas of life.
While You're Eating	**Attitudes**
Pace yourself—eat slowly. Pay attention to your eating process. Pay attention to how full you are. Eat at the same place and at the same time. Eat one portion, and serve yourself before beginning the meal.	Think about your weight-loss goals—make them realistic. Remember that any progress is beneficial and that not reaching your goal does not mean you failed. Think about your desire for foods—manage and work through cravings.
Shopping for Food	**Working with Others**
Structure your shopping so that you know what you are buying beforehand. Limit the number of already prepared items. Don't shop when you are hungry.	Incorporate friends and family into your goals and your new lifestyle, including meal preparation and exercise routines. Communicate to them what they can do to help you reach your goals.
The Eating Environment	**Nutrition**
Make healthy foods more available than unhealthy ones. Do your best to stick to your eating routine when dining out. Think about the limitations and possible adjustments to your eating routine before dining out or eating with other people.	Be informed about nutrition. Know your recommended daily intake of calories, vitamins, and minerals. Know which foods are good sources of vitamins, minerals, proteins, carbohydrates, and healthy fats. Eat a balanced diet. Prepare foods that both are healthy and taste good.

BOX 4.2

The Barbie Beauty Battle

Many health psychologists have criticized the media and the products they popularize for perpetuating false images of feminine beauty (Anschutz, van Strien, & Engels, 2008). The Barbie doll has come under particular criticism because researchers believe that its widespread popularity with young girls may contribute to excessive dieting and the development of eating disorders. Using hip measurement as a constant, researchers have made calculations to determine the changes that would be necessary for a young, healthy woman to attain the same body proportions as the Barbie doll. She would have to increase her bust by 5 inches, her neck length by more than 3 inches, and her height by more than 2 feet while decreasing her waist by 6 inches (Brownell & Napolitano, 1995). This clearly unattainable standard may contribute to the false expectations that girls and women develop for their bodies. Nevertheless, Barbie remains the most popular doll worldwide.

cognitive-behavioral methods are helping at least some people lose weight, weight-loss programs are not a sufficient attack on the problems.

Prevention with families at risk for having obese children is one important strategy. If parents can be trained early to adopt sensible meal-planning and eating habits that they can convey to their children, the incidence of obesity may ultimately decline. Although obesity has proven to be very difficult to modify with adults, it is easier to teach children healthy eating and activity habits. Programs that increase activity levels through reinforcements for exercise are an important component of weight-control programs with children (Epstein, Saelens, Myers, & Vito, 1997). Interventions that reduce TV watching can also reduce weight in children (Robinson, 1999).

The Institute of Medicine and the National Academy of Sciences have criticized the food industry for marketing high-calorie, low-nutrient junk foods to children (Nestle, 2006), which is likely to prompt additional intervention by the government to control health risks for children. Whether treatment of childhood obesity will have long-term effects on adult weight remains to be seen (Wilson, 1994).

Weight-gain prevention programs for normal-weight adults is another possible approach. If exercise can be increased, diet altered in a healthy direction, and good eating habits developed, the weight gains that often accompany the aging process may be prevented (Epstein, Valoski, Wing, & McCurley, 1994). This approach may be particularly effective with women during menopause, as weight gain is common during this time (Simkin-Silverman, Wing, Boraz, & Kuller, 2003).

Like many health habits, social engineering strategies may become part of the attack on this growing problem. The World Health Organization has argued for several changes, including food labels that contain more nutrition and serving size information, a special tax on foods that are high in sugar and fat (the so-called junk food tax), and restriction of advertising to children or required health warnings (Arnst, 2004).

Some individuals have even gone so far as to sue fast-food restaurants and food companies. Although these suits may be found to lack merit, the pressure they bring on the industry to engage in responsible food marketing practices and scrutiny of their products may ultimately be of benefit (Nestle, 2003).

■ EATING DISORDERS

In pursuit of the elusive perfect body (Box 4.2), many women and an increasing number of men chronically restrict their diet and engage in other weight-loss efforts,

BOX 4.3

You Can Be Too Thin

In one study conducted in a high school (Lowry, Galuska, Fulton, Wechsler, & Kann, 2002), 56% of the girls and 25% of the boys reported being on diets. Virtually all these students were already of normal weight. Athletes often diet to get ready for events. For example, high school wrestlers may feel the need to "cut weight" for matches.

Research, however, suggests that these cycles of weight gain and loss may have adverse health consequences. One result is a lowered metabolic rate, which can lead to a general propensity to gain weight. There may also be changes in fat distribution and risk factors

for cardiovascular disease. For example, weight loss is associated with decreased blood pressure and weight gain with increased blood pressure, and successive gains appear also to produce successive gains in blood pressure. Consequently, these bouts of weight loss and regain may have an adverse long-term effect on blood pressure. Among female athletes who maintain a low body weight overall (such as gymnasts and figure skaters), the low percentage of fat distribution may lead to amenorrhea (cessation of menstrual periods) and problems with fertility (Brownell, Steen, & Wilmore, 1987; Steen, Oppliger, & Brownell, 1988).

---

such as laxative use, cigarette smoking, and chronic use of diet pills (Facts of Life, November 2002). Women ages 15–24 are most likely to practice these behaviors, but cases of eating disorders have been documented in people as young as 7 and as old as their mid-80s (Facts of Life, November 2002). (Box 4.3.)

The epidemic of eating disorders suggests that the pursuit of thinness is a public health threat of major proportions. Eating disorders have some of the highest disability and mortality rates of all behavioral disorders (Park, 2007). Recent years have seen an increase in the incidence of eating disorders, especially in the adolescent female population of Western countries (Hudson, Hiripi, Pope, & Kessler, 2007). Chief among these are anorexia nervosa and bulimia. Eating disorders result in death for about 6% of those who have them (Facts of Life, November 2002).

Anorexia Nervosa

One of my most jarring memories is of driving down a street on my university campus during Christmas vacation and seeing a young woman clearly suffering from anorexia nervosa about to cross the street. She had obviously just been exercising. The wind blew her sweatpants around the thin sticks that had once been normal legs. The skin on her face was stretched so tight that the bones showed through, and I could make out her skeleton under what passed for flesh. I realized that I was face-to-face with someone who was shortly going to die. I looked for a place to pull over, but by the time I had found a parking space, she had disappeared into one of the dormitories, and I did not know which one. Nor do I know what I would have said if I had caught up with her.

Anorexia nervosa is an obsessive disorder amounting to self-starvation, in which an individual diets and exercises to the point that body weight is grossly below optimum level, threatening health and potentially leading to death. Most sufferers are young women, but gay men and bisexual men are also at risk (Ackard, Fedio, Neumark-Sztainer, & Britt, 2008).

Developing Anorexia Nervosa   Genetic factors are clearly implicated, especially genes involving the serotonin, dopamine, and estrogen systems. These systems have been implicated in both anxiety and food intake, and accordingly, these systems seem to be disrupted in eating disorders (Klump & Culbert, 2007; Striegel-Moore & Bulik, 2007). Interactions between genetic factors and risks in the environment, such as early exposure to stress, may also play a role (Striegel-Moore & Bulik, 2007). Hypothalamic abnormalities may be involved in both anorexia and bulimia, especially a hyperactive HPA axis (Gluck, Geliebter, Hung, & Yahav, 2004), and evidence is mounting that both anorexia and bulimia may be tied to autoimmunity problems (*The Economist,* 2005). Researchers are increasingly thinking about eating disorders as particular behavioral manifestations of efforts to cope with stress (Rojo, Conesa, Bermudez, & Livianos, 2006). Both women who have eating disorders and those who have tendencies toward eating disorders show abnormalities in heart rate and blood pressure, probably prognostic for serious illness (Ishizawa, Yoshiuchi, Takimoto, Yamamoto, & Akabayashi, 2008). In addition, women with eating disorders or tendencies toward them are more likely to be depressed, anxious, and low in self-esteem and to have a poor sense of mastery. Suicide attempts are not uncommon

(Bulik et al., 2008). The fact that this profile is seen in women with eating disorder tendencies, as well as those women with full-blown eating disorders, suggests that they may be precipitating factors rather than consequences of eating disorders (Koo-Loeb, Costello, Light, & Girdler, 2000).

Personality characteristics and family interaction patterns may play as causal factors in anorexia. Anorexic girls are said to feel a lack of control coupled with a need for approval and to exhibit conscientious, perfectionistic behavior. Body image distortions are also common among anorexic girls, although it is not clear whether this distortion is a consequence or a cause of the disorder. For example, these girls see themselves as still overweight when they have long since dropped below their ideal weight (Hewig et al., 2008). A family temperament involving striving for perfectionism, a need for order, and sensitivity to praise and reward appears to be implicated, and may be partly genetic in origin (Wade et al., 2008).

Anorexic girls can come from families in which psychopathology or alcoholism is found or from families that are extremely close but have poor skills for communicating emotion or dealing with conflict (Garfinkel & Garner, 1983; Rakoff, 1983). Mothers of daughters with eating disorders appear to be more dissatisfied with their families, more dissatisfied with their daughters' appearance, and more vulnerable to eating disorders themselves (Pike & Rodin, 1991). Mothers who are preoccupied with their own weight and eating behaviors place their daughters at risk for developing eating problems (Francis & Birch, 2005). More generally, eating disorders have been tied to insecure attachment in relationships, that is, to the expectation of criticism or rejection from others (Troisi et al., 2006).

Recent evidence points to extremely high rates of comorbidity of eating disorders with other psychiatric problems including depression, post-traumatic stress disorder, psychosis, and obsessive-compulsive disorders, serving to complicate treatment further (Blinder, Cumella, & Sanathara, 2006). An insecure style of attachment is implicated in eating disorders as well (Troisi et al., 2006).

Treating Anorexia Initially, the chief target of therapy is to bring the patient's weight back up to a safe level, a goal that often must be undertaken in a residential treatment setting, such as a hospital. To achieve weight gain, most therapies use cognitive-behavioral approaches. Motivational issues are especially important.

That is, inducing the anorexic to want to change her behavior and to adapt an active, collaborative approach to regaining weight and changing behavior is essential (Wilson, Grilo, & Vitousek, 2007). Often, cognitive-behavioral interventions with anorexics must be maintained over a long period of time—as much as 1–2 years of individual therapy for those especially low in body weight (Wilson, Grilo, & Vitousek, 2007).

Family therapy may help families learn positive methods of communicating emotion and conflict. An approach known as the Maudsley Model involves 10–20 sessions with family members over a period of 6–12 months. During the early phases of treatment, parents are urged to assume complete control over the anorexic family member's eating, but as the anorexic family member begins to gain weight and comply with parental authority, he or she (usually she) begins to assume more control over eating (Wilson, Grilo, & Vitousek, 2007).

Because of the health risks of anorexia nervosa, research has increasingly moved toward prevention. Some interventions address social norms regarding thinness directly (Neumark-Sztainer, Wall, Story, & Perry, 2003). For example, one study gave women information about other women's weight and body type, on the grounds that women with eating disorders often wrongly believe that other women are smaller and thinner than they actually are (Sanderson, Darley, & Messinger, 2002). The intervention succeeded in increasing women's estimates of their actual and ideal weight (Mutterperl & Sanderson, 2002).

But the factors that may prevent new cases from arising may be quite different from those that lead students who already have symptoms to seek out treatment (Mann et al., 1997). An eating disorder prevention program aimed at college freshmen presented the students with classmates who had recovered from an eating disorder, described their experience, and provided information. To the researchers' dismay, following the intervention, the participants had slightly more symptoms of eating disorders than those who had not participated. The program may have been ineffective because, by reducing the stigma of these disorders, it inadvertently normalized the problem. Consequently, as Mann and her colleagues (1997) concluded, ideal strategies for prevention may require stressing the health risks of eating disorders, whereas the strategies for inducing symptomatic women to seek treatment may involve normalizing the behavior and urging them to accept treatment.

Bulimia

Bulimia is characterized by alternating cycles of binge eating and purging through such techniques as vomiting, laxative abuse, extreme dieting or fasting, and drug or alcohol abuse (Hamilton, Gelwick, & Meade, 1984). Bingeing appears to be caused at least in part by dieting. A related eating disorder, termed binge eating disorder, characterizes the many individuals who engage in recurrent binge eating but do not engage in the compensatory purging behavior to avoid weight gain (Spitzer et al., 1993). Binge eating usually occurs when the individual is alone; bingeing may be triggered by negative emotions produced by stressful experiences (Telch & Agras, 1996). The dieter begins to eat and then cannot stop, and although the bingeing is unpleasant, the binger feels out of control, unable to stop it. About half the people diagnosed with anorexia are also bulimic. Bulimia affects 1–3% of women (Wisniewski, Epstein, Marcus, & Kaye, 1997) although up to 10% of people may have episodes.

Developing Bulimia   Whereas many anorexics are thin, bulimics are typically of normal weight or overweight, especially through the hips. In bulimia, as in anorexia, bingeing and purging may be a reaction to issues of control. The binge phase has been interpreted as an out-of-control reaction of the body to restore weight, and the purge phase as an effort to regain control over weight. When a person goes on a diet, the association between physiological cues of hunger and eating break down. Dropping below the set point for her personal weight, the person reacts as if she may starve: Metabolism slows, and she begins to respond to external food cues. Eating shifts from reactions to internal sensations to decisions about when and what to eat, which is a cognitively based regulatory system.

Women prone to bulimia, especially binge eating, appear to have an altered HPA axis (Ludescher et al., 2009). This means that cortisol levels, especially in response to stress, may be elevated, helping to promote eating (Gluck et al., 2004). Food can become a constant thought. Restrained eating, then, sets the stage for a binge. This regulatory system is easily disrupted by stress or distraction, and when it is, the dieter is vulnerable to bingeing (Polivy & Herman, 1985).

People with binge eating disorders are characterized by an excessive concern with body and weight; a preoccupation with dieting; a history of depression, psychopathology, and alcohol or drug abuse; and difficulties with managing work and social settings (Spitzer et al., 1993). Overvaluing body appearance, a larger body mass than is desired, dieting, and symptoms of depression appear to be especially implicated in triggering binge episodes (Stice, Presnell, & Spangler, 2002).

Families that place a high value on thinness and appearance are especially likely to have bulimic daughters (Boskind-White & White, 1983). Bulimia may have a genetic basis, inasmuch as eating disorders cluster in families, and twin studies show a high concordance rate for binge eating (Wade, Bulik, Sullivan, Neale, & Kendler, 2000). Bulimics may suffer from low self-esteem and eat impulsively to control their negative emotions.

Stress, especially conflict with others, is implicated in the onset of binge-purge cycles, because the cues that normally restrain eating are less salient in times of stress. One study of women in college found that their bulimia worsened in response to stress or to any experience that led to a feeling of being unattractive, overweight, or ineffectual (Striegel-Moore, Silberstein, Frensch, & Rodin, 1989). Their disordered eating symptoms grew worse over the course of the school year, presumably because their level of stress also increased.

Physiological theories of bulimia focus on hormonal dysfunction (Monteleone et al., 2001), decreased leptin functioning (Jimerson, Mantzoros, Wolfe, & Metzger, 2000), hypothalamic dysfunction, food allergies or disordered taste responsivity (Wisniewski et al., 1997), disorder of the endogenous opioid system (Mitchell, Laine, Morley, & Levine, 1986), neurological disorder, and a combination of these. Bulimia, in turn, disrupts hormonal functioning among those with more chronic and severe diseases, and the production of leptin (a hormone that controls eating) is decreased, perhaps because malnutrition characterizes bulimia (Monteleone, Martiadis, Colurcio, & Maj, 2002).

Treating Bulimia   A barrier to treating bulimia is that many women do not seek treatment. Either they do not believe that their problem is a serious one, or they do not believe that a medical intervention will overcome it. Accordingly, one of the first steps in treatment is to convince bulimics that the disorder threatens their health and that interventions can help them overcome the disorder (Smalec & Klingle, 2000).

A combination of medication and cognitive-behavioral therapy appears to be the most effective therapy (Wilson, Grilo, et al., 2007). Typically, this treatment begins by instructing the patient to keep a diary of eating habits, including time, place, type of food consumed, and emotions experienced. Simple self-monitoring can produce decreases in binge-purge behavior.

Most therapies combine monitoring with an individualized program to bring eating under control (Wilson, Grilo, et al., 2007). Specific techniques include increasing the regularity of meals, eating a greater variety of foods, delaying the impulse to purge as long as possible, and eating favorite foods in new settings not previously associated with binges. All these techniques help women break down patterns that maintained bulimia and learn better eating habits (Kirkley, Schneider, Agras, & Bachman, 1985). Perceptions of self-efficacy facilitate the success of cognitive-behavioral interventions (Schneider, O'Leary, & Agras, 1987). Overall, CBT has been moderately successful in treating bulimia (Mitchell, Agras, & Wonderlich, 2007).

Relapse prevention techniques are often added to therapeutic programs. These include learning to identify situations that trigger binge eating and developing coping skills to avoid them. Relaxation and stress management skills are often added to these programs as well. When bulimia becomes compulsive, outright prevention of the behavior may be required, with the patient placed in a treatment facility.

The increasing prevalence of eating disorders, coupled with the difficulty of treating them effectively, suggests that health psychologists must think about ways to prevent eating disorders rather than exclusively treating them after they occur (Battle & Brownell, 1996). In one eating disorder prevention study, an intervention titled "Food, Mood, and Attitude" (FMA) used a CD-ROM prevention program targeted to women at risk for eating disorders. The intervention showed some success in reducing reported overeating and excessive exercise (Franko et al., 2005).

■ SLEEP

Michael Foster, a trucker who carried produce, was behind in his truck payments. To catch up, he needed to increase the number of runs he made each week. He could not shave any miles off his trips, so the only way he could make the extra money was to increase the number of trips and reduce his sleep each night. He began cutting back from 6 hours of sleep a night to 3 or 4, stretches that he grabbed in his truck between jobs. On an early-morning run between Fresno and Los Angeles, he fell asleep at the wheel and his truck went out of control, hitting a car and killing a family.

What Is Sleep?

Sleep is a health practice all of us engage in, but many of us abuse our sleep. There are two broad types of sleep: non–rapid eye movement (NREM) and rapid eye movement (REM). NREM sleep consists of four stages. Stage 1, the lightest and earliest stage of sleep, is marked by theta waves, when we begin to tune out the sounds around us, although we are easily awakened by any loud sound. In stage 2, breathing and heart rates even out, body temperature drops, and brain waves alternate between short bursts called sleep spindles and large K-complex waves. Stages 3 and 4, deep sleep, are marked by delta waves. These are the phases most important for restoring energy, strengthening the immune system, and prompting the body to release growth hormone. During REM sleep, eyes dart back and forth, breathing and heart rates flutter, and we often dream vividly. This stage of sleep is marked by beta waves, and it is believed to be important for consolidating memories, solving problems from the previous day, and turning knowledge into long-term memories (Weintraub, 2004). All of these phases of sleep are essential.

Sleep and Health

At least 40 million Americans, most over age 40, have chronic sleep disorders—most commonly, insomnia (National Institute of Neurological Disorders and Stroke, 2006). Many other people, such as college students, choose to deprive themselves of sleep in order to keep up with all the demands on their time. But sleep is an important restorative activity, and people may be doing themselves more harm than they realize.

Thirty-nine percent of adults sleep less than 7 hours a night on weeknights, one-third of adults experience sleep problems (Stein, Belik, Jacobi, & Sareen, 2008), and 54% of people over age 55 report insomnia at least once a week (Weintraub, 2004). For women, sleep disorders may be tied to hormonal levels related to menopause (Manber, Kuo, Cataldo, & Colrain, 2003).

It has long been known that insufficient sleep (less than 7 hours a night) affects cognitive functioning, mood, work performance, and quality of life (Pressman & Orr, 1997). Any of us who has spent a sleepless night tossing and turning over some problem knows how unpleasant the following day can be. Poor sleep can be a particular problem in certain high-risk occupations, with nightmares being one of the most common symptoms. This is especially true for occupations such as police work, in which police officers are exposed to traumatic events (Neylan et al., 2002).

Increasingly, scientists are also recognizing the health risks of inadequate sleep (Leger, Scheuermaier, Phillip, Paillard, & Guilleminault, 2001). Chronic insomnia can compromise the ability to secrete and respond to insulin (suggesting a link between sleep and diabetes), it can increase the risk of developing coronary heart disease (Ekstedt, Åkerstedt, & Söderström, 2004), it can affect weight gain (Motivala, Tomiyama, Ziegler, Khandrika, & Irwin, 2009), it can reduce the efficacy of flu shots, and it is tied to chronic inflammation (Motivala & Irwin, 2007). More than 70,000 of the nation's annual automobile crashes are accounted for by sleepy drivers, and 1,550 of these are fatal each year. In one study of healthy older adults, sleep disturbances predicted all-cause mortality over the next 4–19 years of follow-up (Dew et al., 2003). Even just six nights of poor sleep in a row can impair metabolic and hormonal function, and over time, chronic sleep loss can reduce pain tolerance (Kundermann, Spernal, Huber, Krieg, & Lautenbacher, 2004) and aggravate the severity of hypertension and Type II diabetes (Murphy, 2000); by contrast, good sleep quality can act as a stress buffer (Hamilton, Catley, & Karlson, 2007). Children who do not get enough sleep may show behavioral problems (Pesonen et al., 2009).

In addition to the mental and physical health costs of poor sleep, sleep disturbance has other liabilities. As noted, sleep is one way in which people consolidate their memories with resulting learning, and when sleep quality is compromised, consolidation of memory may be as well (Backhaus et al., 2006). In addition, sleep problems compromise role functioning, so that people do not perform their life roles, such as worker or parent, as effectively as do people with better sleep. Sleep may

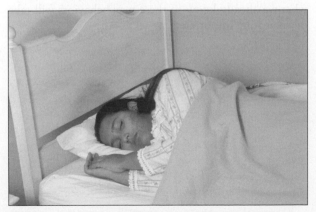

Scientists have begun to identify the health risks associated with little or poor-quality sleep.

have particular significance for those low in SES. Low SES is linked to poor subjective and objective sleep quality (Friedman et al., 2007; Mezick et al., 2008). Poor sleep also makes it harder to reduce calorie intake, thus contributing indirectly to obesity (Spiegel, Tasali, Penev, & Van Cauter, 2004).

People who are going through major stressful life events, who are suffering from major depression, who are experiencing stress at work (Burgard & Ailshire, 2009), or who have high levels of hostility or arousal (Fernández-Mendoza et al., 2010; Granö, Vahtera, Virtanen, Keltikangas-Järvinen, & Kivimäki, 2008) report sleep disturbances (Hall et al., 2000). When stressful events have been appraised as uncontrollable, insomnia may be the result (Morin, Rodrigue, & Ivers, 2003). People who deal with stressful events by ruminating or focusing on them are more prone to insomnia than are those who deal with stressful events by blunting their impact or via distraction (Voss, Kolling, & Heidenreich, 2006; Zoccola, Dickerson, & Lam, 2009). Chronic negative affect and resulting elevation of stress hormones are implicated in poor sleep as well (Wrosch, Miller, Lupien, & Pruessner, 2008). Changes in heart rate due to acute stress may be another way that stress disturbs sleep (Hall et al., 2004). Abuse of alcohol is also related to poor sleep quality (Irwin, Cole, & Nicassio, 2006). Older adults often experience sleep disturbances related to problems of unhealthy aging (Reynolds et al., 2010; Vitiello, 2009).

Although the health risks of insufficient sleep are now well known, less well known is the fact that people who habitually sleep more than 7 hours every night, other than children and adolescents, also incur health risks (van den Berg et al., 2008). Long sleepers, like short sleepers, have more symptoms of psychopathology, including chronic worrying, as well (Fichten, Libman, Creti, Balles, & Sabourin, 2004; Grandner & Kripke, 2004).

A number of behavioral interventions have been undertaken for the treatment of insomnia, including relaxation therapy, control of sleep-related behaviors, and cognitive-behavioral interventions. All three types of treatments show success in treating insomnia (Irwin et al., 2006).

Sleep Apnea

Recently, researchers have recognized that sleep apnea, an air pipe blockage that disrupts sleep, can compromise health. Each time that apnea occurs, the sleeper stops breathing, sometimes for as long as 3 minutes, until he or she suddenly wakes up, gasping for air. Some people are awakened dozens, even hundreds, of times each night without realizing it. Researchers now believe that sleep apnea triggers thousands of nighttime deaths, including heart attacks. Sleep apnea also contributes to high rates of accidents in the workplace and on the road and to irritability, anxiety, and depression. Sleep apnea is difficult to diagnose because the symptoms, such as grouchiness, are so diffuse, but fitful, harsh snoring is one signal that a person may be experiencing apnea.

The next years promise to enlighten us more fully as to the health benefits of sleep and liabilities of disordered sleeping. For those with persistent sleep problems, a variety of cognitive-behavioral interventions are available that typically make use of relaxation therapies (Perlis et al., 2000; Perlis, Sharpe, Smith, Greenblatt, & Giles, 2001). Such programs also recommend better sleep habits, many of which can be undertaken on one's own (Gorman, 1999; Murphy, 2000). How can we sleep better? See Table 4.6.

■ REST, RENEWAL, SAVORING

An important set of health behaviors that is only beginning to be understood involves relaxation and renewal, the restorative activities that help people reduce stress and restore their emotional balance. The ability to savor the positive aspects of life also has health benefits (Pressman et al., 2009). Health psychologists know, for example, that not taking a vacation can be a risk factor for heart attack among people with heart disease (Gump & Matthews, 1998; Steptoe, Roy, & Evans, 1996). Participation on a regular basis in enjoyable leisure time activities, such as hobbies, sports, socializing, or spending time in nature, is tied to lower blood pressure, lower cortisol, lower weight, and perceptions of better physical

TABLE 4.6 | A Good Night's Sleep

- Get regular exercise, at least three times a week.
- Keep the bedroom cool at night.
- Sleep in a comfortable bed that is big enough.
- Establish a regular schedule for awakening and going to bed.
- Develop nightly rituals that can get you ready for bed, such as taking a shower.
- Use a fan or other noise generator to mask background sound.
- Don't consume too much alcohol or smoke.
- Don't eat too much or too little at night.
- Don't have strong smells in the room, such as from incense, candles, or lotions.
- Don't nap after 3 P.M.
- Cut back on caffeine, especially in the afternoon or evening.
- If awakened, get up and read quietly in another place, to associate the bed with sleep, not sleeplessness.

Sources: Gorman, 1999; S. L. Murphy, 2000.

functioning. We also know that participation in leisure activities improves cognitive functioning among the elderly (Singh-Manoux, Richards, & Marmot, 2003). Unfortunately, little other than intuition currently guides our thinking about restorative processes. Nonetheless, health psychologists suspect that rest, renewal, and savoring—involving activities such as going home for the holidays, relaxing after exams, and enjoying a hiking path or a sunset—have health benefits.

This point underscores the fact that an understanding of health-enhancing behaviors is a work in progress. As new health risks are uncovered or the benefits of particular behaviors become known, the application of what we already know to these new behaviors will take on increasing importance. ●

SUMMARY

1. Health-enhancing behaviors are practiced by asymptomatic individuals to improve or enhance their current or future health and functioning. Such behaviors include exercise, accident prevention measures, cancer detection processes, weight control, consumption of a healthy diet, 7–8 hours of sleep each night, and opportunities for rest and renewal.

2. Aerobic exercise reduces risk for heart attack and improves other aspects of bodily functioning. Exercise also improves mood and reduces stress.

3. Few people adhere regularly to the standard exercise prescription of aerobic exercise for at least 30 minutes at least three times a week. People are more likely to exercise when the form of exercise is convenient and they like it. If their attitudes favor exercise and they come from families in which exercise is practiced, they are also more likely to exercise.

4. Cognitive-behavioral interventions, including relapse prevention components, have been at least somewhat successful in helping people adhere to regular exercise programs.

5. Accidents are a major cause of preventable death, especially among children and adolescents. Recent years have seen increases in the use of accident prevention measures, especially car safety restraint devices for children. These changes have been credited to publicity from the mass media, legislation promoting accident prevention measures, and training of parents by physicians and through interventions to promote safety measures for children.

6. Mammograms are recommended for women over age 50, yet few women, especially minority and older women, obtain them because of lack of information, unrealistic fears, and, most importantly, the cost and lack of availability of mammograms. Colorectal screening is also an important cancer-related health behavior.

7. Dietary interventions involving reductions in cholesterol, fats, calories, and additives and increases in fiber, fruits, and vegetables are widely recommended. Yet long-term adherence to such diets is limited for many reasons: Recommended diets are often boring; the relation of dietary change to improvement in health is uncertain; tastes are hard to change; attitudes may not favor dietary change; and behavior change often falls off over time.

8. Dietary interventions through the mass media and community resources have promise. Intervening with the family unit also appears to be helpful in promoting and maintaining dietary change.

9. Obesity is a health risk that has been linked to cardiovascular disease, kidney disease, diabetes, some cancers, and other chronic conditions.

10. Factors associated with obesity include genetic predisposition, early diet, a family history of obesity, low SES, little exercise, and cultural values. Ironically, dieting may contribute to the propensity for obesity.

11. Weight may also be regulated by an ideal set point and by prior caloric consumption. Some individuals eat in response to stress, and stress eating may exacerbate existing weight problems.

12. Obesity has been treated through diets, surgical procedures, drugs, and cognitive-behavioral (CBT) approaches. CBT includes monitoring eating behavior, modifying the environmental stimuli that control eating, gaining control over the eating process, and reinforcing new eating habits. Relapse prevention skills training helps in long-term maintenance.

13. Some weight loss has been achieved in the workplace using work group competition techniques and in commercial weight-loss programs that employ cognitive-behavioral techniques. Such programs can produce weight losses of 2 pounds a week for up to 20 weeks, maintained over a 2-year period.

14. Increasingly, interventions are focusing on weight-gain prevention with children in obese families and with high-risk adults. The role of unrealistic standards of thinness in the causes and perpetuation of eating disorders is receiving increasing attention.

KEY TERMS

aerobic exercise
anorexia nervosa
bulimia

obesity
set point theory of weight

stress eating
yo-yo dieting

CHAPTER 5

Health-Compromising Behaviors: Alcoholism and Smoking

Several decades ago, my father went for his annual physical, and his doctor told him, as the doctor did each year, that he had to stop smoking. As usual, my father told his doctor that he would stop when he was ready. He had already tried several times and had been unsuccessful. My father had begun smoking at age 14, long before the health risks of smoking were known, and it was now an integrated part of his lifestyle, which included a couple of cocktails before a dinner high in fat and cholesterol and a hectic life that provided few opportunities for regular exercise. Smoking was part of who he was. His doctor then said, "Let me put it this way. If you expect to see your daughter graduate from college, stop smoking *now.*"

That warning did the trick. My father threw his cigarettes in the wastebasket and never had another one. Over the years, as he read more about health, he began to change his lifestyle in other ways. He began to swim regularly for exercise, and he pared down his diet to one of mostly fish, chicken, vegetables, fruit, and cereal. Despite the fact that he once had many of the risk factors for early heart disease, he lived to age 83.

In this chapter, we turn our attention to health-compromising behaviors—behaviors practiced by people that undermine or harm their current or future health. My father's problems with stopping smoking illustrate several important points about these behaviors. Many health-compromising behaviors are habitual, and several, including smoking, are addictive, making them very difficult habits to break. On the other hand, with proper incentive and help, even the most intractable health habit can be modified. When a person succeeds in changing a health behavior for the better, often he or she will make other lifestyle changes in the direction of a healthier way of living. The end result is that risk declines, and a disease-free middle and old age becomes a possibility.

■ CHARACTERISTICS OF HEALTH-COMPROMISING BEHAVIORS

Many health-compromising behaviors share several additional important characteristics. First, there is a window of vulnerability in adolescence. Behaviors such as drinking to excess, smoking, taking illicit drugs, practicing unsafe sex, and taking risks that can lead to accidents or early death all begin in early adolescence and sometimes cluster together as part of a problem behavior syndrome (Donovan & Jessor, 1985; Lam, Stewart, & Ho, 2001).

This is not to suggest that all health-compromising behaviors evolve and are firmly implanted during adolescence. Several health problems, such as obesity, begin early in childhood, and others, such as alcoholism, may be special risks for older adults. These exceptions notwithstanding, there is an unnerving similarity in the factors that elicit and maintain many health-compromising behaviors.

Many of these behaviors are heavily tied to the peer culture, as children learn from and imitate their peers, especially the male peers they like and admire (Bricker et al., 2009; Gaughan, 2006). Wanting to be attractive to others becomes very important in adolescence, and this factor is significant in the development of eating disorders, alcohol consumption, tobacco and drug use, tanning, unsafe sexual encounters, and vulnerability to injury (Shadel, Niaura, & Abrams, 2004).

Several health-compromising behaviors are also intimately bound up in the self-presentation process—that is, in the adolescent's efforts to appear sophisticated, cool, tough, or savvy in his or her social environment (Evans, Powers, Hersey, & Renaud, 2006). The image conveyed by these behaviors, then, is another characteristic that must be considered in their modification.

A third similarity is that many of these behaviors are pleasurable, enhancing the adolescent's ability to cope with stressful situations, and some represent thrill seeking, which can be rewarding in its own right. However, each of these behaviors is also highly dangerous. Each has been tied to at least one major cause of death in this country, and several, especially smoking, are risk factors for more than one major chronic disease.

Fourth, development of all these behaviors occurs gradually, as the individual is exposed to the behavior, experiments with it, and later engages in it regularly. As such, these health-compromising behaviors are acquired through a process that may make different interventions important at the different stages of vulnerability, experimentation, and regular use.

Fifth, substance abuse of all kinds, whether cigarettes, alcohol, or drugs, as well as potentially health-compromising sexual behavior, can be predicted by some of the same factors (Peltzer, 2010). Adolescents who get involved in such risky behaviors often have high levels of conflict with their parents and poor self-control, suggesting that their risky behaviors may be coping mechanisms to manage a stressful life (Cooper, Wood, Orcutt, & Albino, 2003; Repetti, Taylor, & Seeman, 2002). Adolescents with a penchant for deviant behavior and with low self-esteem also show these behaviors

(Duncan, Duncan, Strycker, & Chaumeton, 2002; Lam et al., 2001). Adolescents who try to combine long hours of employment with school have an increased risk of alcohol, cigarette, and marijuana abuse (Johnson, 2004). Adolescents who abuse substances typically do poorly in school; family problems, deviance, and low self-esteem appear to explain this relationship (Andrews & Duncan, 1997). Reaching puberty early (van Jaarsveld, Fidler, Simon, & Wardle, 2007), and having low IQ, a difficult temperament, and deviance-tolerant attitudes are related to peer and adolescent use of tobacco, alcohol, and marijuana (Repetti et al., 2002).

Finally, problem behaviors are related to the larger social structure in which they occur (Latkin, Williams, Wang, & Curry, 2005; Pahl, Brook, Morojele, & Brook, 2010). Problem behaviors are more common in the lower social classes (Businelle et al., 2010). Class differences occur because of greater exposure to the problem behavior, and in other cases, lower social class is linked to more stressful circumstances with which the adolescent may need to cope (Novak, Ahlgren, & Hammarstrom, 2007). Practice of these health-compromising behaviors is thought to be one reason that social class is so strongly related to most causes of disease and death (Adler & Stewart, 2010).

In this chapter, we examine two of the most common health-compromising behaviors—alcohol abuse and smoking. Many of the points raised, however, will be relevant to other health-compromising behaviors, such as illicit drug use.

■ WHAT IS SUBSTANCE DEPENDENCE?

A person is said to be dependent on a substance when he or she has repeatedly self-administered it resulting in tolerance, withdrawal, and compulsive behavior (American Psychiatric Association, 2000). Substance dependence can include **physical dependence,** when the body has adjusted to the substance and incorporates the use of that substance into the normal functioning of the body's tissues. Physical dependence often involves **tolerance,** the process by which the body increasingly adapts to the use of a substance, requiring larger and larger doses of it to obtain the same effects, and eventually reaching a plateau. **Craving** is a strong desire to engage in a behavior or consume a substance. It results from physical dependence and from a conditioning process: As the substance is paired with various environmental cues, the presence of those cues triggers an intense desire for the substance.

Addiction occurs when a person has become physically or psychologically dependent on a substance following repeated use over time. **Withdrawal** refers to the unpleasant symptoms, both physical and psychological, that people experience when they stop using a substance on which they have become dependent. Although the symptoms vary, they include anxiety, irritability, intense cravings for the substance, nausea, headaches, tremors, and hallucinations. All these characteristics are common to addiction to smoking, alcohol, and drugs.

■ ALCOHOLISM AND PROBLEM DRINKING

The Scope of the Problem

Alcohol is responsible for approximately 79,000 deaths each year, making it the third-leading cause of preventable death after tobacco and improper diet and exercise. More than 20% of Americans drink at levels that exceed government recommendations (Centers for Disease Control and Prevention, September 2008). Originally characterized as a social ill, alcoholism was officially recognized as a disease by the American Medical Association in 1957.

As a health issue, alcohol consumption has been linked to high blood pressure, stroke, cirrhosis of the liver, some forms of cancer, and fetal alcohol syndrome, a condition of retardation and physiological abnormalities that can arise in the offspring of heavy-drinking mothers (Higgins-Biddle, Babor, Mullahyl, Daniels, & McRee, 1997). Alcoholics can have sleep disorders, which, in turn, may contribute to immune alterations that elevate risk for infection (Redwine, Dang, Hall, & Irwin, 2003).

According to data from 2008, approximately 32% of the 36,790 traffic-related deaths have been related to alcohol, and it is estimated that one in every two Americans will be in an alcohol-related accident during his or her lifetime (National Highway Traffic Safety Administration, 2008).

Economically, the costs of alcohol abuse and alcoholism are estimated to be approximately $184.6 billion per year and include the following:

- About $134.2 billion due to lost earnings, which includes approximately $87.6 billion due to lost productivity caused by alcohol-related illness

- At least $26.3 billion in treatment costs for alcohol misuse and related disorders, which includes about $18.9 billion in medical expenditures to treat the medical consequences of alcohol abuse and alcoholism

- About $24 billion in other costs, including motor vehicle accidents, fires, and crime (National Institute on Alcohol Abuse and Alcoholism [NIAAA], 2000)

An estimated 15% of the national health bill goes to the treatment of alcoholism (Dorgan & Editue, 1995). About 17.6 million American adults meet criteria for alcohol abuse and dependence (Grant et al., 2004). In addition to the direct costs of alcoholism through illness, accidents, and economic costs, alcohol abuse contributes to other problems. Alcohol disinhibits aggression, so a substantial percentage of homicides, suicides, and assaults occur under the influence of alcohol. Alcohol can also facilitate other risky behaviors. For example, among sexually active adults, alcohol leads to more impulsive sexuality (Weinhardt, Carey, Carey, Maisto, & Gordon, 2001) and poorer skills for negotiating condom use (Gordon, Carey, & Carey, 1997). Excessive alcohol consumption has also been tied to brain atrophy and consequent deteriorating cognitive function (Anstey et al., 2006).

Overall, though, it has been difficult to define the scope of alcoholism. Many problem drinkers keep their problem successfully hidden, at least for a time. By drinking at particular times of day or at particular places, and by restricting contacts with other people during these times, the alcoholic may be able to drink without noticeable disruption in his or her daily activities.

What Are Alcoholism and Problem Drinking?

Problem drinking and **alcoholism** encompass a variety of specific patterns (Jellinek, 1960; Wanburg & Horn, 1983). The term *alcoholic* is usually reserved for someone who is physically addicted to alcohol. Alcoholics show withdrawal symptoms when they stop drinking, they have a high tolerance for alcohol, and they have little ability to control their drinking. Problem drinkers may not have these symptoms, but they may have substantial social, psychological, and medical problems resulting from alcohol.

Problem drinking and alcoholism have been defined by a variety of specific behaviors. These patterns include the need for daily use of alcohol, the inability to cut down on drinking, repeated efforts to control drinking through temporary abstinence or restriction of alcohol to certain times of the day, binge drinking, occasional consumption of large quantities of alcohol, loss of memory while intoxicated, continued drinking despite known health problems, and drinking of nonbeverage alcohol, such as cough syrup.

Physiological dependence can be manifested in stereotypic drinking patterns (particular types of alcohol in particular quantities at particular times of day), drinking that maintains blood alcohol at a particular level, the ability to function at a level that would incapacitate less tolerant drinkers, increased frequency and severity of withdrawal, early-in-the-day and middle-of-the-night drinking, a sense of loss of control over drinking, and a subjective craving for alcohol (Straus, 1988).

Symptoms of alcohol abuse include difficulty in performing one's job because of alcohol consumption, inability to function well socially without alcohol, and legal difficulties encountered while drinking, such as drunk driving convictions (American Psychiatric Association, 1980).

Origins of Alcoholism and Problem Drinking

The origins of alcoholism and problem drinking are complex. Based on twin studies and on the frequency of alcoholism in sons of alcoholic fathers, genetic factors appear to be implicated (Hutchison, McGeary, Smolen, Bryan, & Swift, 2002). Modeling a parent's drinking is also implicated (van der Zwaluw et al., 2008). Men have traditionally been at greater risk for alcoholism than women (Robbins & Martin, 1993), although younger women and women employed outside the home are beginning to catch up (Christie-Mizell & Peralta, 2009; Williams, 2002). Sociodemographic factors, such as low income, also predict alcoholism. Overall, however, these factors account for relatively little alcoholism. Instead, a gradual process involving physiological, behavioral, and sociocultural variables appears to be implicated (Zucker & Gomberg, 1986).

Drinking and Stress   Drinking clearly occurs, in part, as an effort to buffer the impact of stress. People who face a lot of negative life events, experience chronic stressors, and have little social support are more likely to become problem drinkers than people without these problems (Brennan & Moos, 1990; Sadava & Pak, 1994). For example, alcohol abuse rises among people who have been laid off from their jobs (Catalano, Dooley, Wilson, & Hough, 1993); alienation from work, low job autonomy, underuse of one's abilities, and lack of participation in decision making at work are associated with heavy drinking (Greenberg & Grunberg, 1995); financial strain, especially if it produces depression, leads to drinking (Peirce, Frone, Russell, & Cooper, 1994); and a sense of powerlessness in one's life has also been related to alcohol use and abuse (Seeman et al., 1988).

Many people begin drinking to enhance positive emotions and reduce negative ones (Repetto, Caldwell, & Zimmerman, 2005), and alcohol does reliably lower anxiety and depression and improve self-esteem, at least temporarily (Steele & Josephs, 1990). Thus, there can be psychological rewards to drinking.

Social Origins of Drinking

Alcoholism is tied to the social and cultural environment of the drinker. Parents and peers influence adolescent drinking by shaping attitudes toward alcohol and by acting as role models (van der Zwaluw et al., 2008). Many people who eventually become problem drinkers or alcoholics learn early in life to associate drinking with pleasant social occasions. They may develop a social life centered on drinking, such as going to bars or attending parties where alcohol consumption is prominent (Wanburg & Horn, 1983). Even watching drinking on television and in the movies can act as a social influence on drinking (Cin et al., 2009). In contrast, people who marry and become parents reduce their risk of developing alcohol-related disorders (Chilcoat & Breslau, 1996).

There are two windows of vulnerability for alcohol use and abuse. The first, when chemical dependence generally starts, is between the ages of 12 and 21 (DuPont,

1988). The other window of vulnerability is in late middle age, in which problem drinking may act as a coping method for managing stress (Brennan & Moos, 1990). Late-onset problem drinkers are more likely to control their drinking on their own or be successfully treated, compared with people who have more long-term drinking problems (Moos, Brennan, & Moos, 1991).

Depression and alcoholism are linked. Alcoholism may represent untreated symptoms of depression, or depression may act as an impetus for drinking in an effort to improve mood. Accordingly, in some cases, symptoms of both disorders must be treated simultaneously (Oslin et al., 2003). Social isolation and lack of employment can exacerbate these problems. Poor psychological well-being may particularly contribute to increased alcohol use among women (Green, Freeborn, & Polen, 2001) and older problem drinkers. Drinking among older adults may be confounded by the fact that tolerance for alcohol reliably decreases with age, leaving the older person vulnerable to alcohol-related accidents such as falls.

Treatment of Alcohol Abuse

For years, alcohol abuse was regarded as an intractable problem, but substantial evidence now indicates that it can be modified. As many as half of all alcoholics stop or reduce their drinking on their own (Cunningham, Lin, Ross, & Walsh, 2000). This "maturing out" of alcoholism

Adolescence and young adulthood represent a window of vulnerability to problem drinking and alcoholism. Successful intervention with this age group may reduce the scope of the alcoholism problem.

BOX 5.1

After the Fall of the Berlin Wall

When the Berlin Wall came down in 1989, there were celebrations worldwide. In the midst of the jubilation, few fully anticipated the problems that might arise in its wake. Hundreds of thousands of East Germans, who had lived for decades under a totalitarian regime with a relatively poor standard of living, were now free to stream across the border into West Germany, which enjoyed prosperity, high employment rates, and a high standard of living. But for many people, the promise of new opportunities failed to materialize. Employment was less plentiful than had been assumed, and the East Germans were less qualified for the jobs that did exist. Discrimination and hostility toward the East Germans was greater than expected, and many migrating East Germans found themselves unemployed.

Unemployment is a severe stressor that has pervasive negative implications for one's entire life. It produces chronic tension, anxiety, and discouragement. Because alcohol reduces tension and anxiety and can stimulate a good mood, the potential for drinking to alleviate stress among the unemployed is high (Catalano et al., 1993). But not everyone responds to the stress of unemployment by drinking.

Two German researchers, Mittag and Schwarzer (1993), examined alcohol consumption among men who had found employment in West Germany and those who had remained unemployed. In addition, they measured self-efficacy with respect to coping with life's problems through such items as "When I am in trouble, I can rely on my ability to deal with the problem effectively." Presumably, individuals who have high feelings of self-efficacy are less vulnerable to stress, and so they may be less likely to consume alcohol under stressful circumstances than are those with a low sense of self-efficacy.

The researchers found that the men with a high sense of self-efficacy were less likely to consume high levels of alcohol. Self-efficacy appeared to be especially important in responding to the stress of unemployment. Those men who were unemployed and had a low sense of self-efficacy were drinking more than any other group. Thus, being male, being unemployed for a long time, and not having a sense of personal agency led to heavy drinking.

Although health psychologists cannot provide jobs to the unemployed, perhaps they can empower individuals to develop more positive self-beliefs. If one believes that one can control one's behavior, cope effectively with life, and solve one's problems, one may be better able to deal effectively with setbacks (Mittag & Schwarzer, 1993).

---

is especially likely in the later years of life (Stall & Biernacki, 1986). In addition, alcoholism can be successfully treated through cognitive-behavioral modification programs. Nonetheless, as many as 60% of the people treated through such programs may return to alcohol abuse. This high rate of recidivism may occur, in part, because the people most likely to seek treatment for alcohol abuse are those with the most severe drinking problems (Finney & Moos, 1995).

Earlier, we noted that alcohol consumption is heavily dependent on the social environment, and this fact is prominent in understanding the recovery process as well. Alcoholics who have high socioeconomic status (SES) and who are in highly socially stable environments (that is, who have regular jobs, intact families, and a circle of friends) do very well in treatment programs, achieving success rates as high as 68%. In contrast, alcoholics of low SES with low social stability often have success rates of 18% or less. Without employment and social support, the prospects for recovery are dim (MedicineNet.com, 2002). Box 5.1 presents an example of these problems.

Treatment Programs

For hard-core alcoholics, the first phase of treatment is **detoxification.** Because this can produce severe symptoms and health problems, detoxification is typically conducted in a carefully supervised and monitored medical setting. Once the alcoholic has at least partly dried out, therapy is initiated. The typical program begins with a short-term, intensive inpatient treatment followed by a period of continuing treatment on an outpatient basis (NIAAA, 2000a). Typically, inpatient programs last 10–60 days, with an average of approximately 28 days (Fuller & Hiller-Strumhöfel, 1999). After discharge, some patients attend follow-up sessions, while others are discharged to supervised living arrangements.

Approximately 720,000 people in the United States receive treatment for alcoholism on any given day (National Institute on Drug Abuse, 2008). A self-help group, especially Alcoholics Anonymous (AA), is the most commonly sought source of help for alcohol-related problems (NIAAA, 2000a) (Box 5.2).

BOX 5.2

A Profile of Alcoholics Anonymous

No one knows exactly when Alcoholics Anonymous (AA) began, but it is believed that the organization was formed around 1935 in Akron, Ohio. The first meetings were attended by a few acquaintances who discovered that they could remain sober by attending the services of a local religious group and sharing with other alcoholics their problems and efforts to remain sober. By 1936, weekly AA meetings were taking place around the country.

Currently, its membership is estimated to be more than 2 million individuals worldwide (*Columbia Encyclopedia*, 2004). The sole requirement for participation in AA is a desire to stop drinking. Originally, the organization attracted hardened drinkers who turned to it as a last resort; more recently, however, it has attracted many people who are experiencing drinking problems but whose lives are otherwise intact. Members come from all walks of life, including all socioeconomic levels, races, cultures, sexual preferences, and ages.

The philosophy of AA is a commitment to the concept of self-help. Members believe that the person who is best able to reach an alcoholic is a recovered alcoholic. In addition, members are encouraged to immerse themselves in the culture of AA—to attend "90 meetings in 90 days." At these meetings, AA members speak about the drinking experiences that prompted them to seek out AA and what sobriety has meant to them. Time is set aside for prospective new members to talk informally with longtime members so that they can learn and imitate the coping techniques that recovered alcoholics have used. Some meetings include only regular AA members and cover issues of problem drinking.

AA has a firm policy regarding alcohol consumption. It maintains that alcoholism is a disease that can be managed but never cured. Recovery means that an individual must acknowledge that he or she has a disease, that it is incurable, and that alcohol can play no part in future life. Recovery depends completely on staying sober.

Is AA successful in getting people to stop drinking? AA's dropout rate is unknown, and success over the long term has not been carefully chronicled. Moreover, because the organization keeps no membership lists (it is anonymous), it is difficult to evaluate its success. However, AA itself maintains that two out of three individuals who wish to stop drinking have been able to do so through its program, and one authorized study reported a 75% success rate for a New York AA chapter.

Evaluations of alcohol treatment programs have found that people do better if they attend AA meetings while also participating in a medically based formal treatment program, rather than only in the formal treatment program (Timko, Finney, Moos, & Moos, 1995). A study that compared AA participation with more formal treatment found comparable effects, a striking finding because the AA attendees had lower incomes and less education initially and thus had somewhat worse prospects for improving. Not incidentally, the treatment costs for the AA group were 45% lower than for the outpatient treatment program, translating into substantial savings per person.

AA programs are effective for several reasons. Participation in AA is like a religious conversion experience in which an individual adopts a totally new way of life; such experiences can be powerful in bringing about behavior change. Also, the member who shares his or her experiences develops a commitment to other members. The process of giving up alcohol contributes to a sense of emotional maturity and responsibility, helping the alcoholic accept responsibility for his or her life. AA may also provide a sense of meaning and purpose in the individual's life—most chapters have a strong spiritual or religious bent and urge members to commit themselves to a power greater than themselves. In addition, the group can provide affection and satisfying personal relationships and thus help people overcome the isolation that many alcoholics experience. Too, the members provide social reinforcement for each other's abstinence.

AA is significant as an organization for several reasons. First, it was one of the earliest self-help programs for individuals suffering from a health problem; therefore, it has provided a model for self-help organizations whose members have other addictive problems, such as Overeaters Anonymous and Gamblers Anonymous, among others. Second, in having successfully treated alcoholics for decades, AA has demonstrated that the problem of alcoholism is not as intractable as had been widely assumed.

Cognitive-Behavioral Treatments   Treatment programs for alcoholism and problem drinking typically use cognitive-behavioral therapy to treat the biological and environmental factors involved in alcoholism simultaneously (NIAAA, 2000b). The goals of the approach are to decrease the reinforcing properties of alcohol, to teach people new behaviors inconsistent with alcohol abuse, and to modify the environment to include reinforcements for activities that do not involve alcohol. These approaches teach coping techniques for dealing with stress and relapse prevention methods to enhance long-term maintenance.

Many programs begin with a self-monitoring phase, in which the alcoholic or problem drinker charts situations that give rise to drinking. Contingency contracting may be employed, in which the person agrees to a psychologically or financially costly outcome in the event of failure. Motivational enhancement procedures are often included because the responsibility and the capacity to change rely entirely on the client. Consequently, working to provide individualized feedback about the patient's drinking and the effectiveness of his or her efforts can get the client motivated and on board to continue a program of treatment that may be more resistant to the inevitable temptations to relapse (NIAAA, 2000a).

Some programs include medications for blocking the alcohol-brain interactions that may contribute to alcoholism. One such drug is naltrexone, which is used to help prevent relapse among alcoholics. It blocks the opioid receptors in the brain, thereby weakening the rewarding effects of alcohol. Another drug, acamprosate (Campral), has also shown effectiveness in treating alcoholism and may help alcoholics maintain abstinence by preventing relapse. It seems to achieve its effects by modifying the action of GABA, a neurotransmitter (Elchisak, 2001). Other drugs are being evaluated as well. Although drugs have shown some success, in conjunction with cognitive-behavioral interventions, in reducing alcohol consumption, successful maintenance requires patients to continue taking the drugs on their own. If they choose not to do so, they reduce the effectiveness of the chemical treatment.

Many treatment programs include stress management techniques that can be substituted for drinking because, as noted earlier, alcohol is sometimes used as a means of coping with stress. Because the occurrence of a major stressful event within the first 90 days after treatment can trigger relapse among apparently recovered alcoholics (Marlatt & Gordon, 1980), stress management techniques can help the alcoholic get through these events. For example, relaxation training, assertiveness training, and training in social skills (Maisto, Ewart, Connors, Funderburk, & Krenek, 2009) help the alcoholic or problem drinker deal with problem situations without resorting to alcohol. Forming specific implementation interventions about reducing drinking helps as well (Armitage, 2009). In some cases, family therapy and group counseling are added. The advantage of family counseling is that it eases the alcoholic's or problem drinker's transition back into his or her family (NIAAA, 2000a).

Relapse Prevention   A meta-analysis of past alcohol treatment outcome studies estimates that more than 50% of treated patients relapse within the first 3 months after treatment (NIAAA, 2000a). Accordingly, relapse prevention techniques are essential. Practicing coping skills or social skills in high-risk-for-relapse situations is a mainstay of relapse prevention interventions. In addition, the recognition that people often stop and restart an addictive behavior several times before they are successful has led to the development of techniques for managing relapses. Understanding that an occasional relapse is normal helps the problem drinker realize that any given lapse does not signify failure. Drink refusal skills and the substitution of nonalcoholic beverages in high-risk social situations are also important components of relapse prevention skills. Interventions with heavy-drinking college students have made use of these approaches (Box 5.3).

Evaluation of Alcohol Treatment Programs

Surveys of alcohol treatment programs suggest several factors that are consistently associated with success: identifying factors in the environment that control drinking and modifying those factors or instilling coping skills to manage them, ensuring a moderate length of participation (about 6–8 weeks), providing outpatient aftercare, and actively involving relatives and employers in the treatment process. Interventions that include these components produce up to a 40% treatment success rate (Center for the Advancement of Health, 2000d).

Minimal Interventions   Even minimal interventions can make a dent in drinking-related problems. In one study (Oslin et al., 2003), military veterans with

BOX **5.3**

The Drinking College Student

Most U.S. college students drink alcohol, and as many as 40% of them are heavy drinkers (O'Malley & Johnston, 2002). If anything, these statistics are increasing, as college women begin to drink as heavily as college men (*New York Times,* 2002, March 25). About 45% of college students overall appear to be involved in occasional binge drinking (Wechsler, Seibring, Liu, & Ahl, 2004). Moreover, if you are a college student who drinks, the odds are 7 in 10 that you have engaged in binge drinking (Wechsler et al., 2004). At one time, attending a women's college was protective for women against binge drinking, but binge drinking has increased in women's institutions as well (Wechsler et al., 2004) (Table 5.1).

Many colleges have tried to deal with the heavy-drinking problem by providing educational materials about the harmful effects of alcohol. However, dogmatic alcohol prevention messages may actually increase intentions to drink (Bensley & Wu, 1991). Moreover, the information conflicts markedly with the personal experiences of many college students who find drinking in a party situation to be enjoyable. For example, heavy drinking has been associated with active participation in a fraternity or sorority (Bartholow, Sher, & Krull, 2003). Many college students do not see drinking as a problem, and those who do may mistakenly assume that they are alone in their discomfort

(Suls & Green, 2003). Those students who would normally be a target for interventions may regard their drinking as a natural outgrowth of their social environment. Consequently, motivating students even to attend alcohol abuse programs, much less to follow their recommendations, is difficult.

Some of the more successful efforts to modify college students' drinking have encouraged students to gain self-control over drinking rather than explicitly trying to get them to reduce or eliminate alcohol consumption altogether. Some programs begin by giving heavy-drinking students information about how much other people do and do not drink. This kind of normative feedback can itself reduce drinking and adverse drinking-related consequences (Neighbors, Lewis, Bergstrom, & Larimer, 2006).

A program developed by Lang and Marlatt (Baer et al., 1991; Lang & Marlatt, 1982) incorporates techniques derived from cognitive-behavioral therapy in a total program to help college students gain such control. This program typically begins by getting students to monitor their drinking and to understand what blood alcohol levels mean and what their effects are. Often, merely monitoring drinking and recording the circumstances in which it occurs leads to a reduction in drinking. The program includes information about the risks of alcohol consumption, the acquisition of skills to moderate alcohol consumption, the use of drinking limits, relaxation training and lifestyle rebalancing, nutritional information, aerobic exercise, relapse prevention skills designed to help students cope with high-risk situations, assertiveness training, and drink-refusal training.

The consumption of alcohol among students is heavily determined by peer influence and the need to

TABLE 5.1 | Patterns of College Student Binge Drinking

	1999	2001
All students	44.5%	44.4%
Men	50.2	48.6
Women	39.4	40.9
Live in dormitory	44.5	45.3
Live in fraternity/sorority house	80.3	75.4

Source: Wechsler et al., 2002.

BOX 5.3

The Drinking College Student (*continued*)

relax in social situations (Murphy, Pagano, & Marlatt, 1986). Thus, many intervention programs include social skills training designed to get students to find alternative ways to relax and have fun in social situations without abusing alcohol (Kivlahan, Marlatt, Fromme, Coppel, & Williams, 1990). What are some of these skills?

To gain personal control over drinking, students are taught to identify the circumstances in which they drink, especially to excess. Then they are taught **controlled drinking** skills so that they can moderate their alcohol consumption. For example, one technique for controlling alcohol consumption in high-risk situations, such as a party, is **placebo drinking.** This involves either the consumption of nonalcoholic beverages while others are drinking or the alternation of an alcoholic with a nonalcoholic beverage to reduce the total volume of alcohol consumed.

Students are also encouraged to engage in lifestyle rebalancing (Marlatt & George, 1988). This involves developing a healthier diet, engaging in aerobic exercise, and making other positive health changes, such as stopping smoking. As the student comes to think of him- or herself as health oriented, excessive alcohol consumption becomes incompatible with other aspects of the new lifestyle.

Evaluations of 8-week training programs with college students involving these components have shown a fair degree of success. Students reported significant reductions in their drinking compared with a group that received only educational materials about the adverse effects of excessive drinking. Moreover, these

gains persisted over a yearlong follow-up period (Marlatt & George, 1988).

Despite the success of such programs, interest has shifted from treatment to prevention, because so many students get into a heavy-drinking lifestyle. Marlatt and colleagues (Marlatt et al., 1998) enrolled 348 students in an intervention during their senior year of high school and, in their freshman year of college, randomly assigned half to a brief motivational intervention and half to a no-treatment control condition. The intervention guided the students through their drinking patterns and risks and assessed their knowledge about alcohol's effects. Their rates of drinking were compared with college averages, and effects on grades, blackouts, and accidents were identified (Table 5.2). Points on which students lacked information about alcohol were also identified.

The interviewers were careful not to confront the students but did ask them questions such as "What do you make of this?" and "Are you surprised?" Each student was urged, but not forced, to come up with specific goals that might lead them to change their behavior, an intentional low-key effort to place responsibility for this change on the student. Over a 2-year follow-up period, students in the intervention showed significant reductions in both their drinking rates and the harmful consequences that frequently accompany heavy drinking (Table 5.3). Interventions such as these emphasize the importance of coming up with effective prevention strategies before problems have a chance to take root (Baer et al., 1991, 1992).

TABLE 5.2 | Alcohol-Related Problems of College Students Who Had a Drink in the Past Year

Alcohol-Related Problem	Drinkers Who Reported Problems
Had a hangover	51.7%
Missed class	27.3
Did something you regret	32.7
Forgot where you were or what you did	24.8
Engaged in unplanned sexual activity	19.5
Got hurt or injured	9.3

Source: Wechsler et al., 2002.

TABLE 5.3 | Alcohol Use by U.S. College Students Age 18–24

Alcohol-Related Incidents per Year

Deaths: 1,700

Injuries: 599,000

Assaults: 696,000 students assaulted by student who had been drinking

Sexual abuses: 97,000 victims of alcohol-related sexual assault or date-rape

Sex: 100,000 said they were too drunk to know if they had consented to having sex

Driving: 2.1 million drove under the influence of alcohol

Source: NIAAA, 2009.

depression or at risk for problem drinking received either usual care or a telephone alcoholism and depression management program in which a behavioral health specialist provided information and support over a 4-month period. Compared with usual care, the telephone-implemented intervention produced beneficial changes, suggesting a viable, low-cost approach to this problem (Oslin et al., 2003).

The biggest problem facing treatment for alcoholism is that most alcoholics (approximately 85%) do not receive any formal treatment. In response, many health psychologists have suggested that social engineering represents the best approach to the problem. Banning alcohol advertising, raising the legal drinking age, and strictly enforcing the penalties for drunk driving may be the best methods for reaching this untreated majority.

Can Recovered Alcoholics Ever Drink Again?

A controversial issue in the treatment of alcohol abuse is whether alcoholics and problem drinkers can learn to drink in moderation. For decades, researchers and self-help treatment programs for alcoholism, such as Alcoholics Anonymous, have argued that the alcoholic is an alcoholic for life and must abstain from all drinking.

It does appear that a small group of problem drinkers may be able to drink in moderation—namely, those who are young and employed, who have not been drinking long, and who live in a supportive environment (Marlatt, Larimer, Baer, & Quigley, 1993). Drinking in moderation has some advantages for these problem drinkers. First, moderate drinking represents a realistic social behavior for the environments that a recovered problem drinker may encounter. Second, traditional therapeutic programs that emphasize total abstinence often have high dropout rates. Programs for problem drinkers that emphasize moderation may be better able to hold onto these participants.

Preventive Approaches to Alcohol Abuse

Because alcoholism is a serious health problem, many researchers believe that a prudent approach is to appeal to adolescents to avoid drinking altogether or to control their drinking before the problems of alcohol abuse set in. Social influence programs in middle schools are typically designed to teach young adolescents drink-refusal techniques and coping methods for dealing with high-risk situations.

Research suggests some success with these programs, which appears to be due to several factors. First, such programs enhance adolescents' self-efficacy, which, in turn, may enable them to resist the passive social pressure that comes from seeing peers drink (Donaldson, Graham, Piccinin, & Hansen, 1995). Second, these programs can change social norms that typically foster adolescents' motivation to begin using alcohol, replacing them with norms stressing abstinence or controlled alcohol consumption (Donaldson, Graham, & Hansen, 1994). Third, these programs can be low-cost options for low-income areas, which have traditionally been the most difficult to reach.

Social engineering solutions for managing alcohol use and abuse include increasing taxes on alcohol, restricting alcohol advertising and promotions that especially target young people, cracking down on misleading health claims for alcohol, and strengthening the federal government's focus on alcohol as a major youth problem. As long as alcohol remains the substance of choice for abuse among young people, its prevention will be a high priority (Center for the Advancement of Health, 2001).

Drinking and Driving

Thousands of vehicular fatalities each year result from drunk driving. This aspect of alcohol consumption is probably the one that most mobilizes the general public against alcohol abuse. Programs such as MADD (Mothers Against Drunk Driving) have been founded and staffed by the families and friends of those killed by drunk drivers. Increasingly, the political impact of these and related groups is being felt, as they pressure state and local governments for tougher alcohol control measures and stiffer penalties for convicted drunk drivers.

Moreover, hosts and hostesses are now pressured to assume responsibility for the alcohol consumption of their guests, and people are urged to intervene when they recognize that their friends are too drunk to drive. But this can be a difficult task to undertake. How do you know when to tell a friend that he or she is too drunk to drive and intervene so that she won't? Knowing the driver well, perceiving that he or she really needs help, feeling able to intervene, and having had conversations in the past that encouraged intervention all enhance the likelihood that an individual will intervene in a situation when a peer is drunk (Newcomb, Rabow, Monto, & Hernandez, 1991). However, the norms to control others' drinking, though growing stronger, still fly in the face of beliefs in individual liberty and personal responsibility. Consequently, many drunk drivers remain on the road.

When drunk drivers are arrested and brought to court, they are typically referred to drinking programs not unlike those we have just discussed. How successful are these referral programs? A review (McGuire, 1982) examining these programs suggested that light drinkers did well in most of them. Unfortunately, heavy drinkers typically did poorly. As yet, it seems there is no good rehabilitation program for the heavy-drinking driver, other than getting him or her off the road through stiffer penalties.

With increased media attention on the problem of drunk driving, drinkers seem to be developing self-regulatory techniques to avoid driving while drunk. Such techniques involve limiting drinking to a prescribed number, arranging for a designated driver, getting a taxi, or delaying or avoiding driving after consuming alcohol (Brown, 1997). Thus, although prevention in the form of eliminating drinking altogether is unlikely to occur, the rising popularity of self-regulation to avoid drunk driving may help reduce this serious problem.

Is Modest Alcohol Consumption a Health Behavior?

Paradoxically, modest alcohol intake may contribute to a longer life. Moderate alcohol intake (approximately one to two drinks a day) may reduce risk of coronary artery disease. The benefits for women may occur at even lower levels of alcohol intake (Facts of Life, December 2003). Moderate drinking is associated with reduced risk of a heart attack, lower blood pressure, lower risk of dying after a heart attack, decreased risk of heart failure, less thickening of the arteries with age, an increase in high-density lipoprotein (HDL) cholesterol (the so-called good cholesterol), and fewer strokes among the elderly (Britton & Marmot, 2004; Facts of Life, December 2003). These benefits may be especially true for older adults and senior citizens. Moderate drinking in younger populations may actually enhance risk of death, probably through alcohol-related injuries (Facts of Life, December 2003). Although many health care practitioners fall short of recommending that people have a drink or two each day, the evidence is mounting that modest drinking may actually reduce the risk for some major causes of death. Nonetheless, this remains an area of controversy, and the jury is still out.

If there are benefits, they occur at fairly low levels, and they may be offset by other risks. For example,

women who drink an average of half a drink a day reduce their risk for high blood pressure, but those who have more than one and a half drinks a day can actually raise it as much as 20% (Facts of Life, December 2003). The World Health Organization has warned that the message that moderate drinking promotes health may encourage people to continue or increase alcohol consumption to dangerous levels. Overall, the number of deaths attributable to alcohol consumption continues to increase worldwide (Pearson, 2004).

■ SMOKING

Smoking is the single greatest cause of preventable death. By itself and in interaction with other risk factors, it remains the chief cause of death in developed countries. In the United States, smoking accounts for at least 443,000 deaths each year—approximately 1 in every 5, with the largest portion of these deaths attributed to cancer (Centers for Disease Control and Prevention, 2008). Smoking also accounts for at least 30% of all cardiovascular-related deaths (Centers for Disease Control and Prevention, July 2005) (Table 5.4). In addition to the risks for heart disease and lung cancer, smoking increases the risk for chronic bronchitis, emphysema, respiratory disorders, some additional cancers, damage and injuries due to fires and accidents, lower birth weight in offspring, and retarded fetal development (Center for the Advancement of Health, 2000h; Waller, McCaffery, Forrest, & Wardle, 2004). Smoking also increases risk of erectile dysfunction by 50% (Bacon et al., 2006).

Cigarette smokers are generally less health conscious (Castro, Newcomb, McCreary, & Baezconde-Garbanati, 1989), less educated, and less intelligent than nonsmokers (Hemmingsson, Kriebel, Melin, Allebeck, & Lundberg, 2008). Smoking and drinking often

TABLE 5.4 | **U.S. Cigarette Smoking-Related Mortality**

Disease	Deaths
Lung cancer	128,900
Heart disease	126,000
Chronic lung disease	92,900
Other cancers	35,300
Strokes	15,900
Other diagnoses	44,000

Source: Centers for Disease Control and Prevention, 2010.

The risks of smoking are not confined to the smoker. Coworkers, spouses, and other family members of smokers are at risk for many smoking-related disorders.

go together, and drinking seems to cue smoking, making it more difficult to give up smoking (Shiffman et al., 1994). Smokers are more impulsive, have more accidents and injuries at work, take off more sick time, and use more health benefits than nonsmokers, thereby representing substantial costs to employers (Flory & Manuck, 2009; Ryan, Zwerling, & Orav, 1992). Smoking appears to serve as an entry-level drug in childhood and adolescence for subsequent substance use and abuse. Trying cigarettes makes one significantly more likely to use other drugs in the future (Fleming, Leventhal, Glynn, & Ershler, 1989).

The dangers of smoking are not confined to the smoker. Studies of secondhand smoke reveal that spouses, family members, and coworkers are at risk for a variety of health disorders (Marshall, 1986). Parental cigarette smoking may lower cognitive performance in adolescents by reducing blood oxygen capacity and increasing carbon monoxide levels (Bauman, Koch, & Fisher, 1989).

Synergistic Effects of Smoking

Smoking enhances the detrimental effects of other risk factors. For example, smoking and cholesterol interact to produce higher rates of morbidity and mortality due to heart disease than would be expected from simply adding together their individual risks (Perkins, 1985).

Stress and smoking can also interact in dangerous ways. For men, nicotine can increase the magnitude of heart rate reactivity to stress. For women, smoking can reduce heart rate but increase blood pressure responses, also an adverse reactivity pattern (Girdler, Jamner, Jarvik, Soles, & Shapiro, 1997). The stimulating effects of nicotine on the cardiovascular system may put smokers at risk for a sudden cardiac crisis, and the long-term effects on reactivity may aggravate coronary heart disease (CHD) risk factors. Smoking acts synergistically with low SES as well: Smoking inflicts greater harm among disadvantaged groups than among more advantaged groups, perhaps because of the stress disadvantage creates (Pampel & Rogers, 2004).

Weight and smoking can interact to increase mortality. Cigarette smokers who are thin may be at increased risk of mortality, compared with average-weight smokers (Sidney, Friedman, & Siegelaub, 1987). Thinness is not associated with increased mortality in those people who had never smoked or among former smokers.

Smoking also appears to interact with exercise. Smokers engage in less physical activity as long as they continue smoking, but when they quit, their activity level increases (Perkins et al., 1993). Because physical exercise is so important to a variety of health outcomes, the fact that smoking reduces its likelihood represents a further indirect contribution of smoking to ill health.

Smoking is related to a fourfold increase in women's risk of developing breast cancer after menopause. Women who smoke and who carry genes that interfere with their ability to break down certain chemicals in cigarette smoke carry more of those chemicals in their bloodstream, which may trigger the growth of tumors (Ambrosone et al., 1996).

Smoking is more likely among people who are depressed (Pratt & Brody, 2010; Prinstein & La Greca, 2009), and smoking interacts synergistically with depression such that a depressed person who smokes is at substantially greater risk for cancer. Immune alterations associated with major depression interact with smoking to elevate white blood cell count and to produce a decline in natural killer cell activity. (Natural killer cells are thought to serve a surveillance function in detecting and responding to early cancers (Jung & Irwin, 1999).) Smoking is now considered to be a potential cause of depression, especially in young people (Goodman & Capitman, 2000), which makes the concern about the synergistic impact of smoking and depression on health even more alarming. Smoking is also related to an increased anxiety in adolescence; whether smoking and anxiety have a synergistic effect on health disorders is not yet known, but the chances of panic attacks and other anxiety disorders are increased (Johnson et al., 2000).

The synergistic health risks of smoking are extremely important and may be responsible for a substantial percentage of smoking-related deaths; however, research suggests that the public is largely unaware of the synergistic adverse effects of smoking (Hermand, Mullet, & Lavieville, 1997). But even the direct effects of smoking on poor health, especially for CHD and lung cancer, are well established, and well known. These risks are lowered by stopping smoking, which makes smoking the most important health-compromising behavior in existence.

A Brief History of the Smoking Problem

For years, smoking was considered to be a sophisticated and manly habit. Characterizations of 19th- and 20th-century gentry, for example, often depicted men retiring to the drawing room after dinner for cigars and brandy. Cigarette advertisements of the early 20th century built on this image, and by 1955, 53% of the adult male population in the United States was smoking. Women did not begin to smoke in large numbers until the 1940s, but once they did, advertisers began to bill cigarette smoking as a symbol of feminine sophistication as well (Pampel, 2001).

In 1964, the first surgeon general's report on smoking came out (U.S. Department of Health, Education, and Welfare and U.S. Public Health Service,

1964), accompanied by an extensive publicity campaign to highlight the dangers of smoking. The good news is that, in the United States, the number of adults who smoke has fallen dramatically to 20%. In recent years, however, smoking has increased slightly, and it continues to be a major health problem.

Critics argue that the tobacco industry has disproportionately targeted minority group members and teens for smoking, and indeed, the rates among certain low-SES minority groups, such as Hispanic men, are especially high (Navarro, 1996). These differences may be due in part to differences in cultural attitudes regarding smoking (Johnsen, Spring, Pingitore, Sommerfeld, & MacKirnan, 2002). At present, 22% of high school students smoke (Centers for Disease Control and Prevention, 2008). Table 5.5 presents current figures on the prevalence of smoking, and Figure 5.1 shows the relation of smoking prevalence to smoking-related historical events.

As pressures to reduce smoking among children and adolescents have mounted, tobacco companies have increasingly turned their marketing efforts overseas. In developing countries, smoking represents a growing health problem. For example, smoking has reached epidemic proportions in China and is expected to continue to grow. It is estimated that a third of all young Chinese men will die from the effects of tobacco, more than 3 million deaths each year by 2050 (Reaney, 1998).

Why Do People Smoke?

Nearly 3 decades of research on smoking have revealed how difficult smoking is to modify. Smoking runs in families. Smoking spreads through social ties, such that groups of interconnected people are more likely to smoke; groups of interconnected people also tend to stop smoking around the same time (Christakis & Fowler, 2008). There appear to be genetic influences on

TABLE 5.5 | Smoking Prevalence by Age and Sex

	Percentage of Population	
Age	**Males**	**Females**
18–24	28.5%	19.3%
25–34	27.4	21.5
35–44	24.8	20.6
45–64	24.5	19.3
65+	12.6	8.3

Source: National Center for Health Statistics, 2008.

FIGURE 5.1 | Adult per Capita Cigarette Consumption (Thousands per Year) and Major Smoking and Health Events, United States, 1900 to 2005 (*Source:* U.S. Department of Agriculture, 2006)

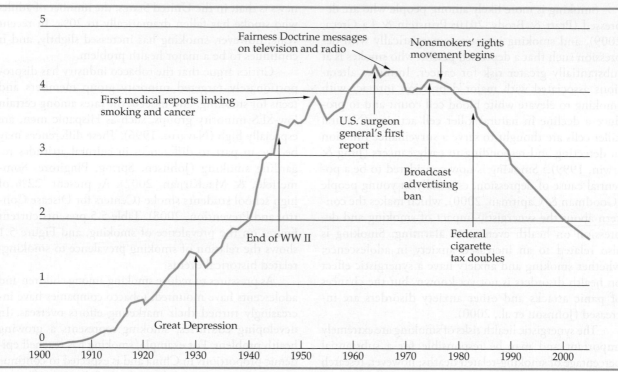

smoking (Piasecki, 2006). Genes that regulate dopamine functioning are likely candidates for heritable influences on cigarette smoking (Timberlake et al., 2006), particularly whether people are able to stop smoking and resist relapse during the treatment phase (Lerman et al., 2003). Should smokers be told if they have a genetic risk for smoking? This feedback may heighten a sense of vulnerability and promote distress, and it does not appear to enhance quitting in most smokers. Consequently, the value of providing such information is questionable.

Factors Associated with Smoking in Adolescents   The Centers for Disease Control and Prevention (May, 2006) indicate that 22% of high school students already smoke cigarettes regularly and consider themselves to be smokers; if anything, these statistics underestimate the adolescent smoking rate. However, smoking does not start all at once. There is a period of initial experimentation, during which the adolescent tries out cigarettes, experiences peer pressure to smoke, and develops attitudes about what a smoker is like. Following experimentation, only some adolescents

go on to become heavy smokers (Maggi, Hertzman, & Vaillancourt, 2007).

Peer and Family Influences   Starting to smoke results from a social contagion process, whereby nonsmokers have contact with others who are trying out smoking or with regular smokers and then try smoking themselves (Presti, Ary, & Lichtenstein, 1992). More than 70% of all cigarettes smoked by adolescents are smoked in the presence of a peer (Biglan, McConnell, Severson, Bavry, & Ary, 1984). Once they begin smoking, adolescents are more likely to prefer the company of peers who smoke (Simons-Morton, Chen, Abroms, & Haynie, 2004). The company of peers and family members who smoke can reduce the perception that smoking is harmful and thus encourage smoking (Rodriguez, Romer, & Audrain-McGovern, 2007; Mercken, Candel, Willems, & de Vries, 2009).

Adolescents are also more likely to start smoking if their parents smoke, if their parents smoked early and often (Chassin et al., 2008), if they are from a lower social class, if they feel social pressure to smoke, and if there has been a major stressor in the family, such as

FIGURE 5.2 | Percentage of High School Students Who Smoke (*Source:* National Center for Health Statistics, 2008)

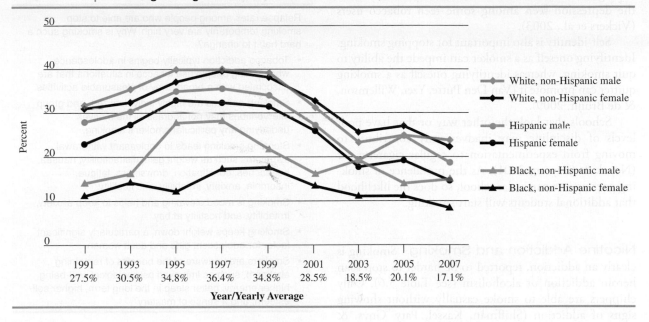

parental separation or job loss (Swaim, Oetting, & Casas, 1996; Unger, Hamilton, & Sussman, 2004). These effects are partly due to the increase in stress and depression that may result (Kirby, 2002; Unger et al., 2004). Even watching people smoke in movies and on television contributes to high rates of adolescent smoking (Sargent & Heatherton, 2009) (Figure 5.2).

Among adults, social influences are also important, and either sustain people's smoking or encourage them to quit. Smoking clusters in social networks, almost as an infectious disease might (Christakis & Fowler, 2008). Although smoking has declined overall, clusters of smokers who know each other increase the likelihood that a friend or relative will continue to smoke. The good news is that these geographic clusters also appear to spread quitting. The likelihood that someone will stop smoking increases by two-thirds if their spouse has stopped smoking, by 25% if a sibling has, and by 36% if a friend has. Even smoking cessation by a co-worker decreases the likelihood that one will continue to smoke by 34%. So smoking behavior, like so many other behaviors, spreads through social ties (Christakis & Fowler, 2008).

Still, there are "chippers," a term used to describe light smokers. These low-rate smokers consume only a few (less than five) cigarettes a day and seem to do so without moving on to heavy smoking. Researchers have been interested in what distinguishes them from people

who go on to be addicted heavy smokers. Chippers appear to share several risk factors with heavy smokers, including tolerance for deviance, and attitudes and health beliefs that match those of smokers. But they also have more protective factors such as high value placed on academic success, supportive relationships at home, less drug use, and little smoking among peers and parents. Somewhat surprisingly, the number of chippers has increased in recent decades. Chippers may be informative regarding tobacco control efforts generally and regarding theories of addiction as well (Zhu, Sun, Hawkins, Pierce, & Cummins, 2003).

Self-Identity and Smoking   The image of the smoker is a significant factor in beginning smoking. Teenagers whose ideal self-image is close to that of a typical smoker are most likely to smoke (Barton, Chassin, Presson, & Sherman, 1982). Low self-esteem, dependency, feelings of powerlessness, and social isolation all increase the tendency to imitate others' behavior (Ennett & Bauman, 1993). Smoking among adolescents is also tied to aggressive tendencies and depression (Repetto, Caldwell, & Zimmerman, 2005; Rodriguez, Moss, & Audrain-McGovern, 2005). Feelings of being hassled, angry, or sad increase the likelihood of smoking (Whalen, Jamner, Henker, & Delfino, 2001; Wills, Sandy, & Yaeger, 2002). Maladaptive coping styles, especially those that involve withdrawal or repressive coping, and lower levels of exercise may contribute to the depression seen among some teen tobacco users (Vickers et al., 2003).

Self-identity is also important for stopping smoking. Identifying oneself as a smoker can impede the ability to quit smoking, whereas identifying oneself as a smoking quitter can promote it (Van Den Putte, Yzer, Willemson, & de Bruijn, 2009).

Schools that look the other way or that have poor levels of discipline may inadvertently contribute to moving from experimentation to regular cigarette use (Novak & Clayton, 2001). As the prevalence of smoking goes up at a particular school, so does the likelihood that additional students will start smoking.

Nicotine Addiction and Smoking   Smoking is clearly an addiction, reported to be harder to stop than heroin addiction or alcoholism (see Table 5.6). Only chippers are able to smoke casually without showing signs of addiction (Shiffman, Kassel, Paty, Gnys, & Zettler-Segal, 1994). However, the exact mechanisms underlying nicotine addiction are unknown (Grunberg & Acri, 1991).

People smoke to maintain blood levels of nicotine and to prevent withdrawal symptoms. In essence, smoking regulates the level of nicotine in the body, and when plasma levels of nicotine depart from the ideal levels, smoking occurs.

Nicotine alters levels of active neuroregulators, including acetylcholine, norepinephrine, dopamine, endogenous opioids, and vasopressin. Nicotine may be used by smokers to engage these neuroregulators because they produce temporary improvements in performance or affect. Specifically, acetylcholine, norepinephrine, and vasopressin appear to enhance memory; acetylcholine and beta endorphins can reduce anxiety and tension. Alterations in dopamine, norepinephrine, and opioids improve mood, and people find that their performance of basic tasks can be improved when levels of acetylcholine and norepinephrine are high. Consequently, smoking among habitual smokers improves concentration, recall, alertness, arousal, psychomotor performance, and the ability to screen out irrelevant stimuli.

Consistent with this point, habitual smokers who stop smoking report that their concentration is reduced; their attention becomes unfocused; they show memory impairments; and they experience increases in anxiety, tension, irritability, craving, and moodiness.

TABLE 5.6 | Why Is Smoking So Hard to Change?

Relapse rates among people who are able to stop smoking temporarily are very high. Why is smoking such a hard habit to change?

- Tobacco addiction typically begins in adolescence, when young people use tobacco in situations that are associated with a broad array of pleasurable activities.
- Smoking patterns are highly individualized, and group interventions may not address all the motives underlying any particular smoker's smoking.
- Stopping smoking leads to unpleasant withdrawal symptoms such as weight gain, distractibility, nausea, headaches, constipation, drowsiness, fatigue, insomnia, anxiety, irritability, and hostility.
- Smoking is mood elevating and helps to keep anxiety, irritability, and hostility at bay.
- Smoking keeps weight down, a particularly significant factor for adolescent girls and adult women.
- Smokers are unaware of the benefits of remaining abstinent, such as improved psychological well-being, higher energy, better sleep in the long term, higher self-esteem, and a sense of mastery.

Sources: Stewart, King, Killen, & Ritter, 1995; Hertel et al., 2008.

However, this is not a complete picture. In studies that alter nicotine level in the bloodstream, smokers do not alter their smoking behavior enough to compensate for these manipulations. Moreover, smoking is responsive to rapidly changing forces in the environment long before such forces can affect blood plasma levels of nicotine. Finally, high rates of relapse are found among smokers long after plasma nicotine levels are at zero. Thus, the role of nicotine in addiction may be more complex.

Interventions to Reduce Smoking

Changing Attitudes Toward Smoking   Following the release of the surgeon general's report in 1964, the mass media engaged in a campaign to warn the public about the hazards of smoking. In a short time, the American public came to acknowledge these risks, and attitudes toward smoking changed substantially. Even adolescents now view smoking as addictive and as having negative social consequences (Chassin, Presson, Sherman, & Kim, 2003). Antismoking messages in the media have been largely effective in discouraging adults and adolescents from beginning to smoke as well (Hersey et al., 2005), although among existing smokers, the ads may actually increase the resolve to smoke (Rhodes, Roskos-Ewoldsen, Edison, & Bradford, 2008).

It Looks Just As Stupid When You Do It.

Smoking has been represented by the tobacco industry as a glamorous habit, and one task of interventions has been to change attitudes about smoking.

Anti-smoking messages in the media may also have contributed to increased worry about smoking. Although attitudes toward quitting go some distance in explaining the desire to quit, worrying about smoking, that is, the feelings one has about continuing to smoke, may move people closer to intending to quit (Köblitz et al., 2009; Magnan, Köblitz, Zielke, & McCaul, 2009). However, negative affect can also give rise to smoking, and smoking in turn reduces negative affect (Kendzor et al., 2009).

The Therapeutic Approach to the Smoking Problem Attitude-change campaigns alone do not help smokers stop smoking, so psychologists have increasingly adopted a therapeutic approach to the smoking problem, typically involving principles of CBT (Webb, de Ybarra, Baker, Reis, & Carey, 2010).

Nicotine Replacement Therapy Many therapies begin with some form of nicotine replacement. Therapeutic efforts have made use of transdermal nicotine patches, which release nicotine in steady doses into the bloodstream. Evaluations show that nicotine replacement therapy significantly improves smoking cessation (Cepeda-Benito, 1993; Hughes, 1993).

Interventions An important first step in intervening with smokers to get them to stop is developing techniques to enhance and encourage motivation.

Many smoking intervention programs have used the stage model of change as a basis for intervening. Interventions to move people from the precontemplation to the contemplation stage center on attitudes, empha-

sizing the adverse health consequences of smoking and the negative social attitudes that most people hold about smoking. Motivating a readiness to quit may, in turn, increase a sense of self-efficacy that one will be able to do so, contributing further to readiness to quit (Baldwin et al., 2006). Moving people from contemplation to action requires that the smoker develop implementation intentions to quit, including a timetable for quitting, a program for how to quit, and an awareness of the difficulties associated with quitting (Armitage, 2008). Moving people to the action phase employs many of the cognitive-behavioral techniques that have been used to modify other health habits.

As this account suggests, smoking would seem to be a good example of how the stage model might be applied. However, interventions matched to the stage of smoking are inconsistent in their effects (Quinlan & McCaul, 2000; Segan, Borland, & Greenwood, 2004; Stotts, DiClemente, Carbonari, & Mullen, 2000).

Social Support and Stress Management As is true for other health habit interventions, would-be ex-smokers are more likely to be successful over the short term if they have a supportive partner and if they have nonsmoking supportive friends. Social support from a partner appears to be more helpful for men attempting to stop smoking than for women (Westmaas, Wild, & Ferrence, 2002). The presence of smokers in one's social network is a hindrance to maintenance and a significant predictor of relapse (Mermelstein, Cohen, Lichtenstein, Baer, & Kamarck, 1986), as is a poor quality of social support (Lawhon, Humfleet, Hall, Reus, & Muñoz, 2009).

Because smoking is relaxing for so many people, teaching smokers how to relax in situations in which they might be tempted to smoke provides an alternative method for coping with stress or anxiety (Manning, Catley, Harris, Mayo, & Ahluwalia, 2005). Lifestyle rebalancing through changes in diet and exercise also helps people cut down on smoking or maintain abstinence after quitting. Overall, stress management training is helpful for successful quitting (Yong & Borland, 2008).

Earlier, we noted how important the image of the cool, sophisticated smoker is in getting teenagers to start smoking in the first place. Image is also important in helping people stop. Specifically, people who have a strong sense of themselves as nonsmokers may do better in treatment than those who have a strong sense of themselves as smokers (Gibbons & Eggleston, 1996; Shadel & Mermelstein, 1996).

Interventions with Adolescents Although adult smokers may be well served by cognitive behavioral interventions, these approaches may be less successful with adolescents. What may be needed instead are inexpensive, efficient, short-term interventions (McVea, 2006). Programs that include a motivation enhancement component, cognitive-behavioral techniques, a focus on self-efficacy, and social influence approaches appear to be successful and can be delivered in school clinics and classrooms (Sussman, Sun, & Dent, 2006; Van Zundert, Ferguson, Shiffman, & Engels, 2010).

Several interventions to induce adolescents to stop smoking have made use of self-determination theory. Because adolescents often begin smoking to shore up their self-image with a sense of autonomy and control, self-determination theory targets those same cognitions—namely, autonomy and self-control—but from the opposite vantage point; that is, they target the behavior of stopping smoking instead (Williams et al., 2006). Interventions that draw on these concepts have been successful with both adolescents (Williams, Cox, Kouides, & Deci, 1999) and both White and African American adults (Webb, 2008; Williams et al., 2006).

Maintenance To bridge the transition from action to maintenance, relapse prevention techniques are typically incorporated into smoking cessation programs (Piasecki, 2006). Relapse prevention is important because the ability to remain abstinent shows a steady month-by-month decline, such that, within 2 years after

smoking cessation, even the best programs do not exceed a 50% abstinence rate (Piasecki, 2006).

Like most addictive health habits, smoking shows an abstinence violation effect, whereby a single lapse reduces perceptions of self-efficacy, increases negative mood, and reduces beliefs that one will be successful in stopping smoking. Stress-triggered lapses appear to lead to relapse more quickly than do other kinds (Shiffman et al., 1996). Consequently, smokers are urged to remind themselves that a single lapse is not necessarily worrisome, because many people lapse on the road to quitting. Increasing a sense of self-efficacy, especially among adolescents, may help prevent a lapse from turning into a relapse (Van Zundert et al., 2010). Sometimes, buddy systems or telephone counseling procedures are made available to help quitters avoid turning a single lapse or temptation into a full-blown relapse (Lichtenstein, Glasgow, Lando, Ossip-Klein, & Boles, 1996).

Relapse Prevention Relapse prevention techniques begin by preparing people for the management of withdrawal, including cardiovascular changes, increases in appetite, variations in the urge to smoke, and increases in coughing and discharge of phlegm. These problems may occur intermittently during the first 7–11 days. In addition, relapse prevention focuses on the long-term, high-risk situations that lead to a craving for cigarettes, such as drinking coffee or alcohol (Piasecki, 2006) and on coping techniques for dealing with stressful interpersonal situations.

Some relapse prevention approaches include contingency contracting, in which the smoker pays a sum of money that is returned only on the condition of cutting down or abstaining. Relapse is least likely when smoking interventions are intensive, when pharmacotherapy is used, and when telephone counseling is available. However, such interventions are expensive and thus reach only some smokers (Ockene et al., 2000). Over the long term, simply remaining vigilant about not smoking best predicts abstinence.

Evaluation of Interventions How successful have smoking interventions been? Virtually every imaginable combination of therapies for getting people to stop has been tested. Typically, these programs show high initial success rates for quitting, followed by high rates of return to smoking, sometimes as high as 90%. Those who relapse are more likely to be young, and to have a high degree of nicotine dependence, a low sense of self-efficacy, greater concerns about gaining weight after stopping smoking, more previous quit attempts, and more slips (occasions when they used one or more cigarettes) (Lopez, Drobes, Thompson, & Brandon, 2008; Ockene et al., 2000).

Linking stopping smoking to other health behaviors can help reinforce the concept of an overall healthy lifestyle and may ultimately aid in preventing relapse as well. Thus, treating coexisting risk factors such as a high-fat diet or sun exposure, for example, can help in changing multiple habits simultaneously and does not undermine smoking cessation efforts (Prochaska, Velicer, Prochaska, Delucchi, & Hall, 2006).

Although the rates of relapse suggest some pessimism with respect to smoking, it is important to consider the cumulative effects of smoking cessation programs, not just each program in isolation. Any given effort to stop smoking may yield only a 20% success rate, but with multiple efforts to quit, eventually the smoker may indeed become an ex-smoker (Lichtenstein & Cohen, 1990). Over time, people may amass enough techniques and the motivation to persist. People who quit on their own have good self-control skills, self-confidence in their ability to stop, and a perception that the health benefits of stopping are substantial (McBride et al., 2001). In fact, hundreds of thousands of smokers have quit, albeit not necessarily the first time they tried. Factors that predict the ability to maintain abstinence include being well-educated, contemplating quitting smoking, being ready to quit at the beginning of an intervention, and having a sense of self-efficacy (Rosal et al., 1998). Stopping on one's own is easier if one has a supportive social network that does not smoke, if one is able to distance oneself from the typical smoker and identify with nonsmokers instead (Gerrard, Gibbons, Lane, & Stock, 2005), and if one was a light rather than a heavy smoker (S. Cohen et al., 1989). Stopping is also more likely to occur during or following an acute or chronic health event, especially among middle-aged smokers (Falba, 2005). A list of guidelines for people who wish to stop on their own appears in Table 5.7.

Brief Interventions   Brief interventions by physicians and other health care practitioners can help in bringing about smoking cessation and controlling relapse (Vogt, Hall, Hankins, & Marteau, 2009), but at present, advice about stopping smoking is only rarely given by health care practitioners (Ockene et al., 2000). Nonetheless, it can help people stop smoking, espe-

TABLE 5.7 | Quitting Smoking

Here are some steps to help you prepare for your Quit Day:

- Pick the date and mark it on your calendar.
- Tell friends and family about your Quit Day.
- Stock up on oral substitutes—sugarless gum, carrot sticks, and/or hard candy.
- Decide on a plan. Will you use nicotine replacement therapy? Will you attend a class? If so, sign up now.
- Set up a support system. This could be a group class, Nicotine Anonymous, or a friend who has successfully quit and is willing to help you.

On your Quit Day, follow these suggestions:

- Do not smoke.
- Get rid of all cigarettes, lighters, ashtrays, and any other items related to smoking.
- Keep active—try walking, exercising, or doing other activities or hobbies.
- Drink lots of water and juice.
- Begin using nicotine replacement if that is your choice.
- Attend a stop-smoking class or follow a self-help plan.
- Avoid situations where the urge to smoke is strong.
- Reduce or avoid alcohol.
- Use the four "A's" (avoid, alter, alternatives, activities) to deal with tough situations (described in more detail later).

Source: American Cancer Society, 2001

cially when combined with nicotine replacement therapy (Facts of Life, July 2005). However, managed care organizations have not yet developed tobacco use cessation guidelines that can be implemented easily during patient visits (Taylor & Curry, 2004). This step alone could improve the quit rate (Williams, Gagne, Ryan, & Deci, 2002). One health maintenance organization targeted the adult smokers in their program with a telephone counseling and newsletter approach to smoking; the program achieved its goal of reducing the smoking, and, most notably, it appeared to reach smokers that otherwise do not participate in cessation programs (Glasgow et al., 2008). The state of Massachusetts began offering free stop smoking treatment to poor residents in 2006 and achieved a decline in smoking from 38% to 28%, suggesting that incorporating brief interventions into Medicaid programs can be successful (Goodnough, 2009, December 17).

Workplace   Initially, workplace interventions were thought to hold promise in smoking cessation efforts.

To date, however, workplace interventions do not seem to be substantially more effective than other intervention programs (Facts of Life, July 2005), nor does quitting smoking appear to be sustained in workplaces over time (Sorensen et al., 1998). However, when workplace environments are entirely smoke free, employees smoke much less (Facts of Life, July 2005).

Commercial Programs and Self-Help Commercial stop-smoking clinics, which make use of cognitive-behavioral techniques, enjoy fairly wide attendance. Although cure rates are often advertised to be high, these assessments may be based on misleading statistics about the short-, but not long-, term, effects. Continued evaluation of these popular programs is essential.

A variety of **self-help aids** and programs have been developed for smokers to quit on their own. These include nicotine patches, as well as more intensive self-help programs. Cable television programs designed to help people stop initially and to maintain their resolution have been broadcast in some cities. Although it is difficult to evaluate self-help programs formally, studies suggest that initial quit rates are lower but that long-term maintenance rates are just as high as with more intensive behavioral interventions. Because self-help programs are less expensive, they represent an important attack on the smoking problem for both adults and adolescents (Curry, 1993; Lipkus, McBride, Pollak, Schwartz-Bloom, Tilson, & Bloom, 2004).

Quitlines provide telephone counseling to help people stop smoking and are quite successful (Lichtenstein, Zhu, & Tedeschi, 2010). People can call in when they want to get help for quitting or if they are worried about relapse. Most such programs are based on principles derived from CBT. Both adults and younger smokers can benefit from this kind of telephone counseling (Rabius, McAlister, Geiger, Huang, & Todd, 2004). Telephone counseling to quit smoking appears to work best if smokers receive several calls around the time they are attempting to quit (Facts of Life, July 2005).

The Public Health Approach Public health approaches to reducing smoking have included community interventions combining media blitzes with behavioral interventions directed especially at high-risk people, such as those who have other risk factors for CHD. As noted earlier in the discussion of community-focused interventions, such interventions are often expensive, and long-term follow-ups suggest limited long-term effects (Facts of Life, July 2005). Ultimately, banning cigarette smoking from workplaces and public settings has proven to be most successful in achieving health benefits (Orbell et al., 2009).

Increasingly, public education campaigns to help people stop smoking have been provided over the Internet. Internet intervention programs have several advantages: People can seek them out when they are ready to, and without regard to location. They can deal with urges to smoke by getting instant feedback from an Internet service. In a randomized control trial sponsored by the American Cancer Society, an Internet program for smoking cessation was found to be significantly more helpful to smokers trying to quit than a control condition. Moreover, the effects lasted longer than a year, suggesting the long-term efficacy of Internet interventions for smoking cessation (Seidman et al., 2010).

Smoking Prevention Programs

Because smoking is so resistant to intervention, the war on smoking has shifted from getting smokers to stop to keeping potential smokers from starting. These **smoking prevention programs** aim to catch potential smokers early and attack the underlying motivations that lead people to smoke (Ary et al., 1990).

Advantages of Smoking Prevention Programs The advantages of smoking prevention programs are several. They represent a potentially effective and cost-effective assault on the smoking problem that avoids the many factors that make it so difficult for habitual smokers to stop. Smoking prevention programs can be easily implemented through the school system. Little class time is needed, and no training of school personnel is required. How do these programs prevent smoking before it starts?

Social Influence Interventions Two theoretical principles have been central to the design of **social influence intervention.** The first is modeling. When people observe models who are apparently enjoying a risky behavior, fears of negative consequences are reduced. Thus, a successful intervention program with adolescents must include the potential for modeling high-status nonsmokers.

A second theoretical principle on which the social influence intervention is based is the concept of behavioral inoculation developed by W. J. McGuire (1964, 1973). **Behavioral inoculation** is similar in rationale to inoculation against disease. If one can expose individuals to a weak version of a persuasive message, they may develop counterarguments against that message, so that they can successfully resist it if they encounter it in a stronger form.

The following are the central components of the social influence intervention program:

- Information about the negative effects of smoking is carefully constructed so as to appeal to adolescents.

- Materials are developed to convey a positive image of the nonsmoker (rather than the smoker) as an independent, self-reliant individual.

- The peer group is used to facilitate not smoking rather than smoking.

Evaluation of Social Influence Programs

Do these programs work? Overall, social influence programs can reduce smoking rates (Resnicow, Reddy, et al., 2008) for as long as 4 years (Murray, Davis-Hearn, Goldman, Pirie, & Luepker, 1988). However, experimental smoking may be affected more than regular smoking, and experimental smokers may stop on their own (Flay et al., 1992). What is needed are programs that will reach the child destined to become a regular smoker, and as yet, we know less about the factors that are most helpful in keeping these youngsters from starting to smoke.

The Life-Skills-Training Approach Another effort to prevent smoking in adolescents is the **life-skills-training approach** (Botvin et al., 1992). Interestingly, this approach to smoking prevention deals with cigarette smoking per se in only a small way. The rationale for the intervention is that, if adolescents are trained in self-esteem and coping enhancement as well as social skills, they will not feel as much need to smoke to bolster their self-image. The skills will enhance their sense of being an efficacious person. The results of these programs to date appear to be as encouraging as the smoking prevention programs based on social influence processes. These

programs also show some success in the reduction of smoking onset over time (Botvin et al., 1992).

Social Engineering and Smoking

> Since smoking might injure your health, let's be careful not to smoke too much.
>
> —Warning label on cigarette packages in Japan
> (*Time,* June 25, 2001)

Ultimately, smoking may be more successfully modified by social engineering than by techniques of behavioral change. Although it is unlikely that cigarettes will be outlawed altogether, a number of social engineering alternatives may force people to reduce their smoking. Liability litigation is generally considered to be one of the most potentially effective means for the long-term control of the sale and use of tobacco (Kelder & Daynard, 1997). Transferring the costs of smoking to the tobacco industry via lawsuits would raise the price of cigarettes, lowering consumption. Second, access to tobacco may come to be regulated as a drug by the Food and Drug Administration (Kaplan, Orleans, Perkins, & Pierce, 1995).

Heavy taxation is a third possibility. Most smokers report that they would reduce their smoking if it became prohibitively expensive (Walsh & Gordon, 1986). Such actions are most likely to influence smoking among teenagers and young adults with little disposable income.

Smoking can be controlled by restricting it to particular places (Jacobson, Wasserman, & Anderson, 1997). The rationale for such interventions is the known harm that can be done to nonsmokers by secondhand smoke (Box 5.4). Thus, not permitting smoking in public buildings, confining smokers to particular places, and otherwise protecting the rights of nonsmokers have been increasingly utilized legislative options. Some business organizations have developed smoking cessation programs for their employees, others restrict on-the-job smoking to particular times or places, and still others have banned smoking. No doubt, social engineering interventions to restrict smoking will increase in the coming years. ●

BOX **5.4**

The Perils of Secondhand Smoke

Norma Broyne was a flight attendant with American Airlines for 21 years. She had never smoked a cigarette, and yet, in 1989, she was diagnosed with lung cancer, and part of a lung had to be removed. Broyne became the center of a class-action suit brought against the tobacco industry, seeking $5 billion on behalf of 60,000 current and former nonsmoking flight attendants for the adverse health effects of the smoke they inhaled while performing their job responsibilities prior to 1990, when smoking was legal on most flights (Collins, 1997, May 30).

Until recently, scientists and lawmakers had assumed that smokers hurt only themselves. However, increasing evidence suggests that people exposed to smokers' smoke are also harmed. This so-called **passive smoking,** or **secondhand smoke,** which involves inhaling smoke and smoky air produced by smokers, has been tied to higher levels of carbon monoxide in the blood, reduced pulmonary functioning, higher rates of lung cancer, and an increased risk of depression (Bandiera et al., 2010). Secondhand smoke is the third-leading cause of preventable death in the United States, killing up to 65,000 nonsmokers every year (Table 5.8). It is estimated to cause about 3,000 cases of lung cancer annually, as many as 62,000 heart disease deaths, and exacerbation of asthma in 1 million children (California Environmental Protection Agency, 2005). In addition, babies with prenatal exposure to secondhand smoke have a 7% reduction in birth weight (Environmental Health Perspectives, 2004).

In a dramatic confirmation of the problems associated with workplace smoking, the state of Montana imposed a ban on public and workplace smoking in June 2002 and then overturned it 6 months later. Two physicians charted the number of heart attacks that occurred before the ban, during it, and afterward. They reported that heart attack admissions dropped 40% when the workplace ban on smoking was in place but immediately bounced back when smoking resumed. Because secondhand smoke causes heart rates to rise, blood vessels to dilate less easily, and blood components to be more sticky, secondhand smoke raises the risk of heart attacks. What is remarkable about the Montana study is its demonstration of its immediate impact on a major health outcome—heart attacks—in such a short time (Glantz, 2004).

Two groups that may be at particular risk are the children and spouses of smokers. A study of 32,000 nonsmoking women (Collins, 1997) found that exposure to secondhand cigarette smoke almost doubled their risk of heart disease. A study conducted in Japan (Hirayama, 1981) found that the wives of heavy smokers had a higher rate of lung cancer than did the wives of husbands who smoked little or not at all. Moreover, these women's risk of dying from lung cancer was between a third and a half of what they would have faced had they been smokers

TABLE 5.8 | The Toll of Secondhand Smoke

Disease	Annual Consequences
Lung cancer	3,000 deaths
Heart disease	35,000–62,000 deaths
Sudden infant death syndrome	1,900–2,700 deaths
Low-birth-weight babies	9,700–18,600 cases
Asthma in children	Increases in the number and severity of asthma attacks in about 400,000–1 million children
Lower respiratory infection	150,000–300,000

Source: California Environmental Protection Agency, 2005.

BOX 5.4

The Perils of Secondhand Smoke (*continued*)

themselves. Young children of smokers are more vulnerable to ear infections, asthma, bronchitis, and pneumonia than those not exposed to secondhand smoke (Emmons et al., 2001). Nearly 40% of U.S. children are exposed to smoke in the home, and children exposed to secondhand smoke score lower on standardized tests than those not exposed to smoke (*Time*, January 2005). Even dogs whose owners smoke are at 50% greater risk of developing lung cancer than are dogs whose owners are nonsmokers (Reif, Dunn, Ogilvie, & Harris, 1992).

One intervention put nicotine monitors into the homes of smokers to show parents the actual effects smoking has on the air around them. Parents were informed that the monitors in their homes showed nico-

tine levels comparable to the ones in the bar down the street. In response to this feedback, many of the smokers reported that they would shift their smoking to outside their home or at least away from their children's rooms (Matt et al., 2004). Even with these measures, however, secondhand smoke poses a risk (Emmons et al., 2001).

The fact that secondhand smoking is harmful to health adds teeth to the idea that nonsmokers have rights vis-à-vis smokers. Increasingly, we are likely to see the effects of passive smoking used as a basis for legislative action against smoking. Norma Broyne finally saw her day in court. The tobacco companies that she and other flight attendants sued agreed to pay $300 million to set up a research foundation on cancer.

SUMMARY

1. Health-compromising behaviors are those that threaten or undermine good health. Many of these behaviors cluster and first emerge in adolescence.

2. Alcoholism accounts for thousands of deaths each year through cirrhosis, cancer, fetal alcohol syndrome, and accidents connected with drunk driving.

3. Alcoholism and problem drinking encompass a wide range of specific behavior problems with associated physiological and psychological needs.

4. Alcoholism has a genetic component and is tied to sociodemographic factors such as low SES. Drinking also arises in an effort to buffer the impact of stress and appears to peak between ages 18 and 25.

5. Most treatment programs for alcoholism use broad-spectrum cognitive-behavioral approaches. Many begin with an inpatient "drying out" period, followed by the use of cognitive-behavioral change methods including relapse prevention.

6. The best predictor of success is the patient. Alcoholics with mild drinking problems, little abuse of other drugs, and a supportive, financially secure environment do better than those without such supports.

7. Smoking accounts for more than 443,000 deaths annually in the United States due to heart disease, cancer, and lung disorders. Smoking adds to and may even exacerbate other risk factors associated with CHD.

8. Several theories have attempted to explain the addictive nature of smoking, including theories of nicotine regulation and those that emphasize nicotine's role as a neuroregulator.

9. In the past few decades, attitudes toward smoking have changed dramatically for the negative, largely due to the mass media. Attitude change has kept some people from beginning smoking, motivated many to try to stop, and kept some former smokers from relapsing.

10. Many programs for stopping smoking begin with some form of nicotine replacement, such as transdermal nicotine patches. Many multimodal programs include social skills training programs or relaxation therapies. Relapse prevention is an important component of these programs.

11. No particular venue for changing smoking behavior appears to be especially effective. However, physicians working directly with patients at risk may achieve greater success than do other change agents.

12. Smoking is highly resistant to change. Even after successfully stopping for a short time, most people relapse. Factors that contribute to relapse include addiction, lack of effective coping techniques for dealing with social situations, and weight gain.

13. Smoking prevention programs have been developed to keep youngsters from beginning to smoke. Many of these programs use a social influence approach and teach youngsters how to resist peer pressure to smoke. Others help adolescents improve their coping skills and self-image.

14. Social engineering approaches to control smoking have also been employed, because secondhand smoke harms others in the smoker's environment.

KEY TERMS

addiction
alcoholism
behavioral inoculation
controlled drinking
craving
detoxification

life-skills-training approach
passive smoking
physical dependence
placebo drinking
problem drinking
secondhand smoke

self-help aids
smoking prevention programs
social influence intervention
tolerance
withdrawal

Stress and Coping

Stress

The night before her biology final, Lisa confidently set her alarm and went to sleep. A power outage occurred during the night, and her alarm, along with most of the others in the dorm, failed to go off. At 8:45, Lisa was abruptly awakened by a friend banging on the door to tell her that her final started in 15 minutes. Lisa threw on some clothes, grabbed a muffin and a cup of coffee from the machines in her dorm, and raced to the exam room. Ten minutes late, she spent the first half hour frantically searching through the multiple-choice questions, trying to find ones she knew the answers to, as her heart continued to race.

■ WHAT IS STRESS?

Most of us have more firsthand experience with stress than we care to remember. Stress is being stopped by a police officer after accidentally running a red light. It is waiting to take a test when we are not sure that we have prepared well enough or studied the right material. It is missing a bus on a rainy day full of important appointments.

Psychologists have been studying stress and its impact on psychological and physical health for decades. **Stress** is a negative emotional experience accompanied by predictable biochemical, physiological, cognitive, and behavioral changes that are directed either toward altering the stressful event or accommodating to its effects (see Baum, 1990).

What Is a Stressor?

Initially, researchers focused on stressful events themselves, called **stressors.** In the United States, for example, people report money, the economy, work, family health problems, and family responsibilities as their top five stressors (American Psychological Association, 2008). The study of stressors has helped define some conditions that are more likely to produce stress than others.

But a focus on stressful events cannot fully explain the experience of stress. An experience may be stressful to some people but not to others. If the "noise" is the latest rock music playing on your radio, then it will probably not be stressful to you, although it may be to your neighbor. Whereas one person might find the loss of a job highly stressful, another might see it as an opportunity to try a new field, as a challenge rather than a threat. How a potential stressor is appraised determines whether it will be experienced as stressful.

Person–Environment Fit

Stress is the consequence of a person's appraisal processes: the assessment of whether personal resources are sufficient to meet the demands of the environment. Stress, then, is determined by **person–environment fit** (Lazarus & Folkman, 1984b; Lazarus & Launier, 1978).

When a person's resources are more than adequate to deal with a difficult situation, he or she may feel little stress and experience a sense of challenge instead. When the person perceives that his or her resources will probably be sufficient to deal with the event but only at the cost of great effort, he or she may feel a moderate amount of stress. When the person perceives that his or her resources will probably not suffice to meet an environmental stressor, he or she may experience a great deal of stress.

Stress, then, results from the process of appraising events (as harmful, threatening, or challenging), of assessing potential responses, and of responding to those events. To see how stress researchers have arrived at our current understanding of stress, it is useful to consider some of the early contributions to the field.

■ THEORETICAL CONTRIBUTIONS TO THE STUDY OF STRESS

Fight or Flight

One of the earliest contributions to stress research was Walter Cannon's (1932) description of the **fight-or-flight response.** Cannon proposed that when an organism perceives a threat the body is rapidly aroused and motivated via the sympathetic nervous system and the endocrine system. This concerted physiological response mobilizes the organism to attack the threat or to flee; hence, it is called the fight-or-flight response.

At one time, fight or flight literally referred to fighting or fleeing in response to stressful events such as attack by a predator. Now, more commonly, *fight* refers to aggressive responses to stress, such as getting angry or taking action, whereas *flight* may be seen in social withdrawal or withdrawal through substance use or distracting activities. On the one hand, the fight-or-flight response is adaptive because it enables the organism to respond quickly to threat. On the other hand, it can be harmful because stress disrupts emotional and physiological functioning, and when stress continues unabated, it lays the groundwork for health problems.

Selye's General Adaptation Syndrome

Another important early contribution to stress was Hans Selye's (1956, 1976) work on the **general adaptation syndrome.** Although Selye initially intended to explore the effects of sex hormones on physiological functioning, he became interested in the stressful impact his interventions seemed to have. Accordingly, he exposed rats to a variety of stressors, such as extreme cold and fatigue, and observed their physiological responses. To his surprise, all stressors, regardless of type, produced essentially the same pattern of physiological changes. They all led to an enlarged adrenal cortex, shrinking of the thymus and lymph glands, and ulceration of the stomach and duodenum.

From these observations, Selye (1956) developed his concept of the general adaptation syndrome. He argued that when an organism confronts a stressor it mobilizes itself for action. The response itself is nonspecific with respect to the stressor; that is, regardless of the cause of the threat, the individual will respond with the same physiological pattern of reactions. (As will be seen, this particular conclusion has now been challenged.) Over time, with repeated or prolonged exposure to stress, there will be wear and tear on the system.

The general adaptation syndrome consists of three phases. In the first phase, *alarm,* the organism becomes mobilized to meet the threat. In the second phase, *resistance,* the organism makes efforts to cope with the threat, as through confrontation. The third phase, *exhaustion,* occurs if the organism fails to overcome the threat and depletes its physiological resources in the process of trying. These phases are pictured in Figure 6.1.

Selye's model continues to have an impact on stress research. One reason is that it offers a general theory of reactions to a wide variety of stressors over time. As such, it provides a way of thinking about the interplay of physiological and environmental factors. Second, it posits a physiological mechanism for the

FIGURE 6.1 | The Three Phases of Selye's General Adaptation Syndrome

Hans Selye, a pioneering stress researcher, formulated the General Adaptation Syndrome. He proposed that people go through three phases in response to stress. The first is the alarm phase, in which the body reacts to a stressor with diminished resistance. In the second stage, the stage of resistance that follows continued exposure to a stressor, stress responses rise above normal. The third phase, exhaustion, results from long-term exposure to the stressor, and at this point, resistance will fall below normal.

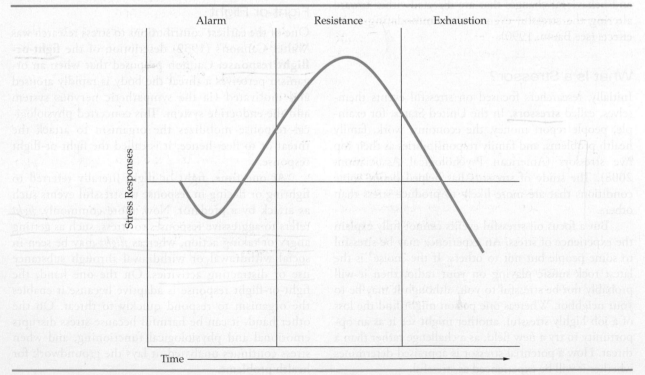

stress-illness relationship. Specifically, Selye believed that repeated or prolonged exhaustion of resources, the third phase of the syndrome, is responsible for the physiological damage that lays the groundwork for disease.

Criticisms of the General Adaptation Syndrome Selye's model has also been criticized on several grounds. First, it assigns a very limited role to psychological factors, and researchers now believe that the psychological appraisal of events is critical to experiencing stress (Lazarus & Folkman, 1984b). A second criticism concerns the assumption that responses to stress are the same. Not all stressors produce the same endocrinological responses (Kemeny, 2003). How people respond to stress is substantially influenced by their personalities, emotions, and biological constitutions (e.g., Moons, Eisenberger, & Taylor, 2010). A third criticism concerns whether it is the exhaustion of physiological resources or their chronic activation that is most implicated in stress; research suggests that continued activation (the second phase) may be most important for accumulating damage to physiological systems. A fourth criticism concerns the fact that Selye assessed stress as an outcome, that is, the endpoint of the general adaptation syndrome. In fact, people experience many debilitating effects of stress while a stressful event is going on and even in anticipation of its occurrence. Despite these limitations and reservations, Selye's model remains a cornerstone in the field.

Tend-and-Befriend

Animals, whether nonhuman or human, do not merely fight, flee, and grow exhausted in response to stress. They also affiliate with each other, whether it is the herding behavior of antelope in response to stress, the huddling one sees among female rats, or the coordinated responses to a stressor that a community shows when it is under the threat of flood, tornado, or other natural disaster.

To address this issue, S. E. Taylor and colleagues (Taylor, Klein, et al., 2000) developed a theory of responses to stress termed **tend-and-befriend.** The theory maintains that, in addition to fight or flight, humans respond to stress with social affiliation and nurturant behavior toward offspring. These responses may be especially true of women.

During the time that responses to stress evolved, men and women faced somewhat different adaptive challenges. Whereas men were responsible for hunting and protection, women were responsible for foraging and child care. These activities were largely sex segregated, with the result that women's responses to stress would have evolved so as to protect not only the self but offspring as well. These responses are not distinctive to humans. The offspring of most species are immature and would be unable to survive were it not for the attention of adults. In most species, that attention is provided by the mother.

Like the fight-or-flight mechanism, tend-and-befriend may depend on underlying biological mechanisms—in particular, the hormone oxytocin. Oxytocin is a stress hormone, rapidly released in response to at least some stressful events, and its effects are especially influenced by estrogen, suggesting a particularly important role in the responses of women to stress (Taylor, Gonzaga, et al., 2006). Oxytocin acts as an impetus for affiliation in both animals and humans; oxytocin increases affiliative behaviors of all kinds, especially mothering (Taylor, 2002). In addition, animals and humans with high levels of oxytocin are calmer and more relaxed, which may contribute to their social and nurturant behavior (McCarthy, 1995). Opioids may also contribute to affiliative responses to stress in females (Taylor, Klein, et al., 2000).

In support of the theory, women are indeed more likely than men to respond to stress by turning to others (Luckow, Reifman, & McIntosh, 1998; Tamres, Janicki, & Helgeson, 2002). Mothers' responses to offspring during times of stress also appear to be different from those of fathers in ways encompassed by the tend-and-befriend theory. Nonetheless, men, too, show social responses to stress, and so elements of the theory appear to apply to men as well. The tend-and-befriend theory brings social behavior into stress processes. We are affiliative creatures who respond to stress collectively, as well as individually, and these responses are characteristic of men as well as women (Taylor, Klein, et al., 2000).

Psychological Appraisal and the Experience of Stress

In humans, psychological appraisals are important determinants of whether an event is responded to as stressful.

Primary Appraisal Processes   R. S. Lazarus and S. Folkman, the chief proponents of the psychological view of stress (Lazarus & Folkman, 1984b), maintained that when individuals confront a new or changing environment they engage in a process of **primary appraisal** to determine the meaning of the event (Figure 6.2).

Events may be appraised as positive, neutral, or negative in their consequences. Negative or potentially negative events are further appraised for their possible harm, threat, or challenge. *Harm* is the assessment of the damage that has already been done by an event. Thus, for example, a man who has just been fired from his job may perceive harm in terms of his own loss of self-esteem and his embarrassment as his coworkers silently watch him pack up his desk.

Threat is the assessment of possible future damage that may be brought about by the event. Thus, the man who has just lost his job may anticipate the problems that loss of income will create for him and his family in the future. Primary appraisals of events as threats have important effects on physiological responses to stress. For example, blood pressure is higher when threat is higher or when threat is high and challenge is low (Maier, Waldstein, & Synowski, 2003).

Finally, events may be appraised in terms of their *challenge*, the potential to overcome and even profit from the event. For example, the man who has lost his job may perceive that a certain amount of harm and threat exists, but he may also see his unemployment as an opportunity to try something new. Challenge appraisals are associated with more confident expectations of the ability to cope with the stressful event, more favorable emotional reactions to the event, and lower blood pressure, among other benefits (Maier et al., 2003; Skinner & Brewer, 2002).

The importance of primary appraisal in the experience of stress is illustrated in a classic study of stress by J. Speisman and colleagues (Speisman, Lazarus, Mordkoff, & Davidson, 1964). College students viewed a gruesome film depicting unpleasant tribal initiation rites that included genital mutilation. Before viewing the film, they were exposed to one of four experimental conditions. One group listened to an anthropological account about the meaning of the rites. Another group heard a lecture that deemphasized the pain the initiates were experiencing and emphasized their excitement over the events. A third group heard a description that emphasized the pain and trauma that the initiates were undergoing. A fourth group was given no introductory information, and the film they viewed had no sound track. Measures of autonomic arousal (skin conductance, heart rate) and self-reports suggested that the first two groups experienced considerably less stress than did the group whose attention was focused on the trauma and pain. Thus, stress not only was intrinsic to the gruesome film itself but also depended on the viewer's appraisal of it.

Secondary Appraisal Processes   At the same time that primary appraisals of stressful circumstances are occurring, secondary appraisal is initiated. **Secondary appraisal** is the assessment of one's coping abilities and resources: whether they will be sufficient to meet the harm, threat, and challenge of the event. Ultimately, the subjective experience of stress is a balance between primary and secondary appraisals. When harm and threat are high and coping ability is low, substantial stress is felt. When coping ability is high, stress may be minimal.

Potential responses to stress are many and include physiological, cognitive, emotional, and behavioral

FIGURE 6.2 | The Experience of Stress

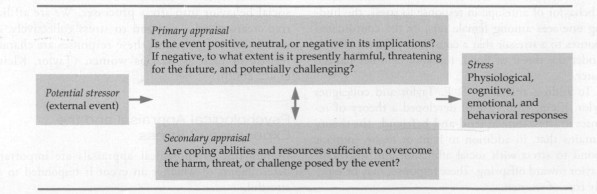

Primary appraisal
Is the event positive, neutral, or negative in its implications? If negative, to what extent is it presently harmful, threatening for the future, and potentially challenging?

Potential stressor
(external event)

Secondary appraisal
Are coping abilities and resources sufficient to overcome the harm, threat, or challenge posed by the event?

Stress
Physiological, cognitive, emotional, and behavioral responses

consequences. Some of these responses are involuntary reactions to stress, whereas others are voluntarily initiated in a conscious effort to cope.

Cognitive responses to stress include beliefs about the harm or threat an event poses and beliefs about its causes or controllability. They also include involuntary responses such as distractability and inability to concentrate, disruptions on cognitive tasks, and intrusive, repetitive, or morbid thoughts. Cognitive responses are also involved in the initiation of coping activities, as we will see in Chapter 7.

Potential emotional reactions to stress range widely; they include fear, anxiety, excitement, embarrassment, anger, depression, and even stoicism or denial. Emotional responses can be quite insistent, prompting rumination over a stressful event, which, in turn, may keep biological stress responses elevated (Glynn, Christenfeld, & Gerin, 2002).

Potential behavioral responses are virtually limitless, depending on the nature of the stressful event. Confrontative action against the stressor ("fight") and withdrawal from the threatening event ("flight") constitute two general categories of behavioral responses. We will examine others in the course of our discussion.

The Physiology of Stress

Stress is important, both because it causes psychological distress and because it leads to changes in the body that may have short- and long-term consequences for health. Two interrelated systems are heavily involved in the stress response. They are the sympathetic-adrenomedullary (SAM) system and the hypothalamic-pituitary-adrenocortical (HPA) axis. These components of the stress response are illustrated in Figure 6.3.

Sympathetic Activation When events are encountered that are perceived as harmful or threatening, they are labeled as such by the cerebral cortex, which, in turn, sets off a chain of reactions mediated by these appraisals. Information from the cortex is transmitted to the hypothalamus, which initiates one of the earliest responses to stress—namely, sympathetic nervous system arousal, or the fight-or-flight response first described by Walter Cannon. Sympathetic arousal stimulates the medulla of the adrenal glands, which, in turn, secrete the catecholamines epinephrine (EP) and norepinephrine (NE). These effects result in the cranked-up feeling we usually experience in response to stress. Sympathetic arousal leads to increased blood

FIGURE 6.3 | The Body's Stress Systems

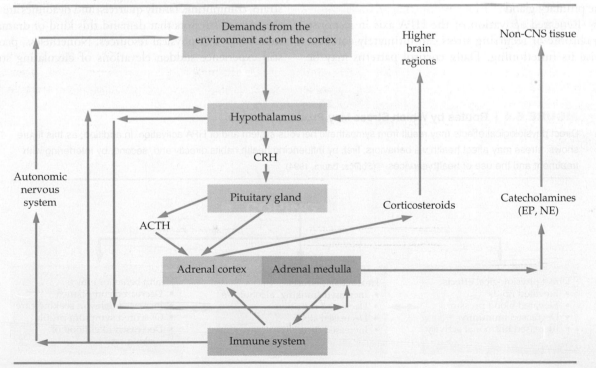

pressure, increased heart rate, increased sweating, and constriction of peripheral blood vessels, among other changes. As can be seen in Figure 6.3, the catecholamines have effects on a variety of tissues and modulate the immune system as well.

Parasympathetic functioning may also become dysregulated in response to stress. For example, stress can affect heart rate variability, including variability during sleep. Parasympathetic modulation is an important restorative aspect of sleep, and thus, changes in heart rate variability may both represent a pathway to disturbed sleep and help to explain the relation of stress to illness and increased risk for mortality (Hall, Vasko, et al., 2004).

HPA Activation   In addition to the activation of the sympathetic nervous system, the HPA axis is activated in response to stress. The hypothalamus releases corticotrophin-releasing hormone (CRH), which stimulates the pituitary gland to secrete adrenocorticotropic hormone (ACTH), which, in turn, stimulates the adrenal cortex to release glucocorticoids. Of these, cortisol is especially significant. It acts to conserve stores of carbohydrates and helps reduce inflammation in the case of an injury. It also helps the body return to its steady state following stress. In addition, HPA activation produces elevations in growth hormone and prolactin, secreted by the pituitary gland.

Repeated activation of the HPA axis in response to chronic or recurring stress can ultimately compromise its functioning. Daily cortisol patterns may be altered. That is, normally, cortisol levels are high upon waking in the morning, but decrease during the day (although peaking following lunch) until they flatten out at low levels in the afternoon. People under chronic stress, however, can show any of several deviant patterns: elevated cortisol levels long into the afternoon or evening (Powell et al., 2002), a general flattening of the diurnal rhythms, an exaggerated cortisol response to a challenge, a protracted cortisol response following a stressor, or, alternatively, no response at all (McEwen, 1998). Any of these patterns is suggestive of compromised ability of the HPA axis to respond to and recover from stress (McEwen, 1998; Pruessner, Hellhammer, Pruessner, & Lupien, 2003). When researchers study physiological and neuroendocrine stress responses, they look for signs such as these (Figure 6.4).

Effects of Long-Term Stress   We just examined some of the major physiological changes that occur in response to the perception of stress. What do these changes mean? Although the short-term mobilization that occurs in response to stress prepared humans to fight or flee in prehistoric times, only rarely do our current stressful events require these kinds of adjustments. That is, fighting or fleeing would be appropriate responses to a predator, a natural disaster, or attack, but job strain, commuting, family quarrels, and deadlines are not the sorts of stressors that demand this kind of dramatic mobilization of physical resources. Nonetheless, people still experience sudden elevations of circulating stress

FIGURE 6.4 | Routes by Which Stress May Produce Disease
Direct physiological effects may result from sympathetic nervous system and/or HPA activation. In addition, as this figure shows, stress may affect health via behaviors, first, by influencing health habits directly and, second, by interfering with treatment and the use of health services.   (*Source:* Baum, 1994)

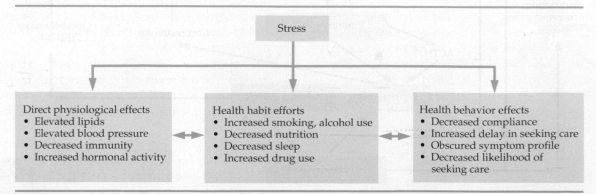

hormones in response to current-day stressors that, in certain respects, do not serve the purpose for which they were originally intended.

Over the long term, excessive discharge of epinephrine and norepinephrine can lead to suppression of cellular immune function; produce hemodynamic changes such as increased blood pressure and heart rate; provoke variations in normal heart rhythms, such as ventricular arrhythmias, which may be a precursor to sudden death; and produce neurochemical imbalances that may contribute to the development of psychiatric disorders. The catecholamines may also have effects on lipid levels and free fatty acids, all of which may be important in the development of atherosclerosis, as was seen in Chapter 2.

Corticosteroids have immunosuppressive effects, which can compromise the functioning of the immune system. Prolonged cortisol secretion has also been related to the destruction of neurons in the hippocampus. This destruction can lead to problems with verbal functioning, memory, and concentration (Starkman, Giordani, Brenent, Schork, & Schteingart, 2001) and may be one of the mechanisms leading to senility. Pronounced HPA activation is common in depression, with episodes of cortisol secretion being more frequent and of longer duration among depressed than nondepressed people. Another long-term consequence of the endocrine abnormalities that result from chronic HPA activation is the storage of fat in central visceral areas (i.e., belly fat), rather than in the hips. This accumulation leads to a high waist-to-hip ratio, which is used by some researchers as a marker for chronic stress (Bjorntorp, 1996).

Which of these responses to stress have implications for disease? Several researchers (Dientsbier, 1989; Frankenhaeuser, 1991) have suggested that the health consequences of HPA axis activation are more significant than those of sympathetic activation. Sympathetic arousal in response to stress may not be a pathway for disease; HPA activation may be required as well. Some researchers have suggested that this reasoning explains why exercise, which produces sympathetic arousal but not HPA activation, is protective for health rather than health compromising. Another possibility, however, is that, unlike exercise, stressors can be experienced long after an actual stressful event has terminated, as cardiovascular activation may persist for hours, days, weeks, or even years after an initial stressful event has occurred (Pieper & Brosschot, 2005). With such wear and tear on the cardiovascular system, disease states may be fostered.

Stress may also impair the immune system's capacity to respond to hormonal signals that terminate inflammation. One study compared 50 healthy adults, half of whom were parents of children with cancer and half of whom were parents of healthy children. Childhood cancer is known to be one of the most stressful events that parents encounter. The parents of the cancer patients reported more stress and had flatter daily slopes of cortisol secretion than was true for the parents of the healthy children. Moreover, the ability to suppress production of a proinflammatory cytokine called IL-6 was diminished among parents of the cancer patients. Because chronic inflammation is implicated in many diseases including coronary artery disease (see Chapter 2), these findings suggest that the impaired ability to terminate inflammation may be an important pathway by which stress affects illness outcomes (Miller, Cohen, & Ritchey, 2002).

Researchers are increasingly focusing on poor sleep quality as both an indicator of chronic stress and a consequence of chronic stress. It has long been suspected that chronic insomnia can result from stressful events. Evidence suggests that the combination of emotional arousal and neuroendocrine activation due to chronic stress underlies chronic insomnia (Shaver, Johnston, Lentz, & Landis, 2002). Because sleep represents a vital restorative activity, this mechanism, too, may represent an important pathway to disease (Edwards, Hucklebridge, Clow, & Evans, 2003).

Individual Differences in Stress Reactivity

People vary in their reactivity to stress. **Reactivity** is the degree of change that occurs in autonomic, neuroendocrine, and/or immune responses as a result of stress. Some people appear to be predisposed by their genetic makeup, prenatal experiences, and/or early life experiences to be more reactive to stress than others. These people, research suggests, may be especially vulnerable to stress-related health consequences, both on the short term and the long term (Boyce et al., 1995; Jacobs et al., 2006).

Reactivity to stress can affect vulnerability to illness. For example, in one study, a group of children ranging in age from 3 to 5 years old were tested for their cardiovascular reactivity (change in heart rate and blood pressure) or their immune response to a vaccine following a stressful task. Parents were then asked to report on the number of family stressors during a 12-week period, and illness rates were charted during this period. The results indicated that stress was associated with increased rates

Stressful events such as being struck in traffic produce agitation and physiological arousal.

of illness only among the children who had previously shown strong immune or cardiovascular reactions. The less reactive children did not experience any change in illness rates under stressful circumstances (Boyce, Alkon, Tschann, Chesney, & Alpert, 1995).

Do changes like this actually lead to illness? S. Cohen and colleagues (2002) found that people who reacted to laboratory stressors with high cortisol responses and who also had a high level of negative life events were especially vulnerable to upper respiratory infections when exposed to a virus. People who reacted to laboratory stressors with low immune responses were especially vulnerable to upper respiratory infection only if they were also under high stress. High immune reactors, in contrast, did not show differences in upper respiratory illness as a function of the stress they experienced, perhaps because their immune systems were quick to respond to the threat that a potential infection posed (see also Cohen, Janicki-Deverts, & Miller, 2007).

Studies like these suggest that psychobiological reactivity to stress is an important factor that influences the effects that stress has on the body and the likelihood that it will contribute to distress or disease. As will be seen in Chapter 13, differences in reactivity are believed to contribute to the development of hypertension and coronary artery disease.

Physiological Recovery Recovery following stress is also important in the physiology of the stress response (Rutledge, Linden, & Paul, 2000). In particular, the inability to recover quickly from a stressful event may be a marker for the cumulative damage that stress has caused. Researchers have paid special attention to the cortisol response—particularly, prolonged cortisol responses that occur under conditions of high stress.

In one intriguing study (Perna & McDowell, 1995), elite athletes were divided into groups that were experiencing a high versus a low amount of stress in their lives, and their cortisol response was measured following vigorous training. Those athletes under more stress went a longer time before their cortisol levels returned to normal. Because elevated cortisol affects the immune system, the researchers suggested that stress may widen the window of susceptibility for illness and injury among competitive athletes by virtue of its impact on cortisol recovery.

As the research on recovery processes implies, the long-term effects of stress on the body are of great importance in understanding the mechanisms by which physiological changes in response to stress may promote illness.

Allostatic Load As Selye noted, the initial response of the body to stressful circumstances may be arousal, excessive reactivity, and exhaustion, leading to cumulative damage to the organism. Building on these ideas, researchers developed the concept of **allostatic load** (McEwen & Stellar, 1993). This concept refers to the fact that physiological systems within the body fluctuate to meet demands from stress, a state called allostasis. Over time, allostatic load builds up, which is defined as the physiological costs of chronic exposure to fluctuating or heightened neural or neuroendocrine response to multiple physiological systems that results from repeated or chronic stress (Glei, Goldman, Chuang, & Weinstein, 2007).

This buildup of allostatic load—that is, the long-term costs of chronic or repeated stress—can be assessed by a number of indicators (Seeman, Singer, Horwitz, & McEwen, 1997). These include decreases in cell-mediated immunity, the inability to shut off cortisol in response to stress, lowered heart rate variability, elevated epinephrine levels, a high waist-to-hip ratio (reflecting abdominal fat), hippocampal volume (which can decrease with repeated stimulation of the HPA), problems with memory (an indirect measure of hippocampal functioning), high plasma fibrinogen, and elevated blood pressure. Many of these changes occur normally with age, so to the extent that they occur early, accumulating allostatic load may be thought of as accelerated aging in response to stress. Over time, this kind of wear and tear can lead to illness and increased risk of death (Karlamangla, Singer, & Seeman, 2006). The damage due to chronic or repeated stress is made worse if people also cope with stress via a higher-fat diet, less frequent

BOX 6.1

Can Stress Affect Pregnancy?

Common wisdom has long held that pregnant women should be treated especially well and avoid major stressors in their lives. Research now supports that wisdom by showing that stress can actually endanger the course of pregnancy and childbirth.

Stress affects the immune and endocrine systems in ways that directly affect the growing fetus. These changes are potentially dangerous because they can lead to preterm birth and low birth weight, among other adverse outcomes (Glynn, Dunkel-Schetter, Hobel, & Sandman, 2008; Khashan et al., 2008; Lobel et al., 2008; Tegethoff, Greene, Olsen, Meyer, & Meinlschmidt, 2010). African American women and acculturated Mexican American women appear to be especially vulnerable, due in large part to the stress they experience (Dominguez, Dunkel-Schetter, Glynn, Hobel, & Sandman, 2008; Hilmert et al., 2008).

Although a number of theories have been proposed to explain these relations, one that appears to have broad support is the idea that the mother's elevated cortisol levels in response to stress act as a signal to the fetus that it is time to be born (Diego et al., 2006; Hobel, Dunkel-Schetter, & Roesch, 1998; Mancuso, Dunkel-Schetter, Rini, Roesch, & Hobel, 2004).

Are there any factors that can protect against adverse birth outcomes due to stress? Social support, especially from a partner, has a protective effect against potential adverse birth outcomes (Feldman, Dunkel-Schetter, Sandman, & Wadhwa, 2000). Psychosocial resources such as mastery, self-esteem, and optimism may also help guard against adverse birth outcomes such as low birth weight (Rini, Dunkel-Schetter, Wadhwa, & Sandman, 1999) or vulnerability to neurological disorders (Li et al., 2009). The anxiety that can accompany stress and the prenatal period exacerbates the risk of elevated cortisol levels and increases the likelihood of an adverse birth outcome, and so interventions to reduce anxiety may be helpful as well (Mancuso et al., 2004; Orr, Reiter, Blazer, & James, 2007).

But the old adage about taking it easy during pregnancy and the more dire warnings about adverse birth outcomes in disadvantaged groups make it clear that pregnancy is an important time to avoid stress and to make use of psychosocial resources.

---

exercise, and smoking, all of which stress can encourage (Ng & Jeffery, 2003).

The physiology of stress and, in particular, the recent research on the cumulative adverse effects of stress are important because they suggest the pathways by which stress exerts adverse effects on the body, ultimately contributing to the likelihood of disease. The relationship of stress, both short and long term, to both acute disorders, such as infection, and chronic diseases, such as heart disease, is now so well established that stress is implicated in most diseases, either in their etiology, their course, or both. We explore these processes more fully when we address different diseases such as heart disease and hypertension in Chapter 13 and cancer and arthritis in Chapter 14. Stress can even affect the course of pregnancy, as Box 6.1 shows.

■ WHAT MAKES EVENTS STRESSFUL?

Assessing Stress

Given that stress can produce a variety of responses, what is the best way to measure it? Researchers have used many indicators of stress. These include self-reports of perceived stress, life change, and emotional distress; behavioral measures, such as task performance under stress; physiological measures of arousal, such as heart rate and blood pressure; and biochemical markers (or indicators), especially elevated catecholamines and alterations in the diurnal rhythm of cortisol or cortisol responses to stress. In each case, these measures have proven to be useful indicators.

However, each type of measurement has its own associated problems. For example, catecholamine secretion is enhanced by a number of factors other than stress. Self-report measures are subject to a variety of biases, because individuals may want to present themselves in as desirable a light as possible. Behavioral measures are subject to multiple interpretations. For example, performance declines can be due to declining motivation, fatigue, cognitive strain, or other factors. Consequently, stress researchers typically use multiple measures. With several measures, the possibility of obtaining a good model of the stress experience is increased.

Dimensions of Stressful Events

As just noted, most events themselves are not inherently stressful. Rather, whether they are stressful depends on how they are appraised by an individual. What are some characteristics of potential stressors that make them more likely to be appraised as stressful?

Negative Events   Negative events produce more stress than do positive events. Many events have the potential to be stressful because they present people with extra work or special problems that may tax or exceed their resources. Shopping for the holidays, planning a party, coping with an unexpected job promotion, and getting married are all positive events that draw off time and energy. Nonetheless, these positive experiences are less likely to be reported as stressful than are negative or undesirable events, such as getting a traffic ticket, trying to find a job, coping with a death in the family, or getting divorced.

Negative events show a stronger relationship to both psychological distress and physical symptoms than do positive ones (Sarason, Johnson, & Siegel, 1978). This may be because negative stressful events have implications for the self-concept, producing loss of self-esteem or erosion of a sense of mastery or identity.

There is one exception to this pattern. Among people who hold negative views of themselves, positive life events can have a detrimental effect on health, whereas for people with high self-esteem, positive life events are linked to better health (Brown & McGill, 1989).

Uncontrollable Events   Uncontrollable or unpredictable events are more stressful than controllable or predictable ones. When people feel that they can predict, modify, or terminate an aversive event or feel they have access to someone who can influence it, they experience it as less stressful, even if they actually can do nothing about it (Thompson, 1981). Unexpected uncontrollable stressors may take a special toll (Cankaya, Chapman, Talbot, Moynihan, & Duberstein, 2009).

Feelings of control not only mute the subjective experience of stress but also influence biochemical reactions to it. Believing that one can control a stressor is associated with lower catecholamine levels than is believing that one has no control over the stressor. Uncontrollable stress has been tied to immunosuppressive effects as well (Brosschot et al., 1998; Peters et al., 1999).

Ambiguous Events   Ambiguous events are typically perceived as more stressful than are clear-cut events. When a potential stressor is ambiguous, a person cannot take action. He or she must instead devote energy to trying to understand the stressor, which can be a time-consuming, resource-sapping task. Clear-cut stressors, on the other hand, let the person get on with the job of finding solutions and do not leave him or her stuck at the problem definition stage. The ability to take confrontative action is usually associated with less distress and better coping (Billings & Moos, 1984).

Overload   Overloaded people are more stressed than are people with fewer tasks to perform (Cohen, 1978; Cohen & Williamson, 1988). People who have too many tasks in their lives report higher levels of stress than do those who have fewer tasks. For example, one of the main sources of work-related stress is job overload, the perception that one is responsible for doing too much in too short a time.

Which Stressors?   People may be more vulnerable to stress in central life domains than in peripheral ones because important aspects of the self are overly invested in central life domains (Swindle & Moos, 1992). For example, one study of working women for whom parental identity was very salient found that role strains associated with the parent role, such as feeling that their children did not get the attention they needed, took a toll (Simon, 1992). Hammen and colleagues (Hammen, Marks, Mayol, & DeMayo, 1985) found that negative life events affecting personal relationships were stronger predictors of depression among women for whom relationships were paramount, whereas setbacks in the achievement domain made women whose values focused on achievement more vulnerable to depression.

To summarize, then, events that are negative, uncontrollable, ambiguous, or overwhelming or that involve central life goals are perceived as more stressful than are events that are positive, controllable, clear-cut, or manageable or that involve peripheral life tasks.

Must Stress Be Perceived as Such to Be Stressful?

As the preceding discussion suggests, stress is both a subjective and an objective experience. In fact, both of these aspects of stress affect the likelihood of resulting health problems. For example, in a study of air traffic controllers, Repetti (1993b) assessed their subjective perceptions of stress on various days and also gathered objective measures of daily stress, including the weather conditions and the amount of air traffic. She found that both subjective and objective measures of stress independently predicted psychological distress and health complaints.

Similarly, Cohen, Tyrrell, and Smith (1993) recruited 394 healthy people for a study of the common cold. Participants completed questionnaires designed to obtain objective information about the stressful life events they had encountered, and they also completed a measure of perceived stress. The researchers then exposed participants to a common cold virus and found that both objectively assessed stressful life events and perceived stress predicted whether the people developed a cold.

These kinds of studies suggest that, although the perception of stress is important to the physical and psychological symptoms it causes, objectively defined stress also shows a relation to adverse psychological and physiological changes.

Can People Adapt to Stress?

If a stressful event becomes a permanent or chronic part of their environment, will people eventually habituate to it, or will they develop **chronic strain?** Will it no longer cause them distress, drain psychological resources, or lead to symptoms of illness? The answer to this question depends on the type of stressor, the subjective experience of stress, and the indicator of stress.

Psychological Adaptation Most people are able to adapt psychologically to moderate or predictable stressors. At first, any novel, threatening situation can produce

stress, but such reactions often subside over time. For example, research on the effects of environmental noise (Nivison & Endresen, 1993) and crowding (Cohen, Glass, & Phillip, 1978) indicates few or no long-term adverse health or psychological effects, suggesting that most people simply adapt to chronic stressors.

However, particularly vulnerable populations, especially children, the elderly, and the poor, do seem to be adversely affected by chronic stressors (Cohen et al., 1978); they may show signs of helplessness and difficulty in performing tasks. One reason is that these groups already experience little control over their environments and, accordingly, may already be at high levels of stress; the addition of an environmental stressor, such as noise or crowding, may push their resources to the limits. Consistent with this argument, K. A. Matthews and colleagues (Matthews, Gump, Block, & Allen, 1997) found that children and adolescents who had recurrent or ongoing stressors in their lives exhibited larger diastolic blood pressure responses to acute laboratory stress tasks, as compared with children and adolescents who had less background stress in their lives.

Thus, the answer to the question of whether people can adapt to chronic stress might best be summarized as follows: People (and animals) show signs of long-term strain but also long-term habituation to chronically stressful events. Most people can adapt moderately well to mildly stressful events; however, it may be difficult or

Events such as crowding are experienced as stressful only to the extent that they are appraised that way. Some situations of crowding make people feel happy, whereas other crowding situations are experienced as adverse.

impossible for them to adapt to highly stressful events, and already-stressed people may be unable to adapt to even moderate stressors. Moreover, even when psychological adaptation may have occurred, physiological changes in response to stress may persist.

Physiological Adaptation   In terms of physiological adaptation, animal models of stress suggest evidence for both habituation and chronic strain. For example, rats exposed to relatively low-level stressors tend to show initial physiological responsiveness followed by habituation. When the stimuli that induce stress are intense, however, the animal may show no habituation (Pitman, Ottenweller, & Natelson, 1988; Thompson & Glanzman, 1976). Physiological evidence from studies of humans also suggests evidence for both habituation and chronic strain. Low-level stress may produce habituation in most people, but with more intense stress, damage from chronic stress can accumulate across multiple organ systems, as the allostatic load model suggests. Habituation is more likely for HPA responses to stress than for sympathetic responses to stress (Schommer, Hellhammer, & Kirschbaum, 2003). But chronic stress can also impair cardiovascular, neuroendocrine, and immune system recovery from stressors and, through such effects, contribute to an increased risk for diseases such as cardiovascular disorders (Matthews, Gump, & Owens, 2001).

Must a Stressor Be Ongoing to Be Stressful?

One of the wonders and curses of human beings' symbolic capacities is the ability to anticipate things before they materialize. We owe our abilities to plan, invent, and reason abstractly to this skill, but we also get from it our ability to worry. Unlike lower animals, human beings do not have to be exposed to a stressor to suffer stress.

Anticipating Stress   The anticipation of a stressor can be as stressful as its actual occurrence, and sometimes more so (Wirtz et al., 2006). Consider the strain of anticipating a confrontation with a boyfriend or girlfriend or worrying about an upcoming test. Sleepless nights and days of distracting anxiety attest to the human being's capacity for anticipatory distress.

One study that illustrates the importance of anticipatory stress made use of ambulatory blood pressure monitors to assess natural fluctuations in blood pressure during daily activities. In this study, medical students wore the pressure monitors on an unstressful lecture day, on the day before an important examination, and during the examination itself. Although the lecture day was characterized by stable patterns of cardiovascular activity, cardiovascular activity on the preexamination day, when the students were worrying about the exam, was as high as that seen during the examination (Sausen, Lovallo, Pincomb, & Wilson, 1992). Thus, in this instance, the anticipation of the stressful event taxed the cardiovascular system as much as the stressful event itself.

Aftereffects of Stress   Adverse **aftereffects of stress,** such as decreases in performance and attention span, often persist long after the stressful event itself is no longer present. Aftereffects of stress have been observed in response to a wide range of stressors, including noise, high task load, electric shock, bureaucratic stress, crowding, and laboratory-induced stress (Cohen, 1980). Box 6.2 profiles a particular kind of aftereffect of stress, post-traumatic stress disorder.

Stressors can produce deleterious aftereffects on social behavior as well as on cognitive tasks. For example, when people are exposed to avoidable stress, such as noise or crowding, they are less likely to help someone in distress when the stressor is over. In one study, people shopped in a shopping center that was either crowded or uncrowded and were required to purchase a large or a small number of items in a short time. Later, all the shoppers encountered a woman who pretended to have lost a contact lens and who requested help finding it. The people who had had to purchase lots of items in a short time or who had been more crowded were less likely to help the woman than were the people who had had few things to buy and more time to shop or who had shopped in less crowded conditions (Cohen & Spacapan, 1978).

In response to many stressful events, there may be prolonged activation of physiological stress responses. That is, instead of returning to baseline when a stressor has ended, physiological responses such as cardiovascular activation may persist over the long term. One possible reason is that psychological processes, such as worry or rumination and even unconscious processing of a stressor, keep cardiovascular activation at high levels (Pieper & Brosschot, 2005). This type of prolonged activation may contribute to, and even account for, the relations between stress exposure and disease (see Box 6.3).

BOX 6.2

Post-Traumatic Stress Disorder

An Iraq War veteran and his wife headed out to the movies one summer night. As they took their seats, the veteran scanned the rows for moviegoers who might be wired with explosives. A man who appeared to be Middle Eastern, wearing a long coat with bulging pockets, sat down in the same row. The Iraq War veteran instructed his wife to get low to the ground. Moments later, he heard a metal jangling as the man reached into his pocket, and he lunged at the man, sure that he was a suicide bomber about to strike. As he jerked away, the man dropped the deadly weapon—a can of Coke (Streisand, 2006, October 9).

When a person has been the victim of a highly stressful event, symptoms of the stress experience may persist long after the event is over. As we have seen, the aftereffects of stress can include physiological arousal, distractability, and other negative side effects that can last for hours. In the case of major traumas, these stressful aftereffects may go on intermittently for months or years.

Such long-term reactions are especially likely in the wake of wars, such as occurred in Vietnam and Iraq. But they may also occur in response to assault, rape, domestic abuse, a violent encounter with nature (such as an earthquake or flood) (Ironson et al., 1997), a disaster (such as 9/11) (Fagan, Galea, Ahern, Bonner, & Vlahov, 2003), being a hostage (Vila, Porche, & Mouren-Simeoni, 1999), and having a child with a life-threatening disease (Cabizuca, Marques-Portella, Mendlowicz, Coutinho, & Figueria, 2009). Particular occupations such as working as an urban police officer (D. Mohr et al., 2003) or

having responsibility for clearing up remains following war, disaster, or mass death (McCarroll, Ursano, Fullerton, Liu, & Lundy, 2002) increase the risk of trauma, and even major diseases and their aggressive treatments can produce effects like these (Wikman, Bhattacharyya, Perkins-Porras, & Steptoe, 2008).

The term **post-traumatic stress disorder (PTSD)** has been developed to explain these effects. The person suffering from PTSD has typically undergone a stressor of extreme magnitude (Lamprecht & Sack, 2002). One response to this stressful event is a psychic numbing, that may include reduced interest in once-enjoyable activities, detachment from friends, or constriction in emotions. In addition, the person often relives aspects of the trauma, as the Iraq War veteran did. Other symptoms include excessive vigilance, sleep disturbances, feelings of guilt, impaired memory or concentration, avoidance of the experience, an exaggerated startle response to loud noise (D. Mohr et al., 2003), and even suicidal behavior (Sareen et al., 2007).

PTSD can produce temporary and permanent changes in stress regulatory systems as well. People with PTSD may experience permanent changes in the brain involving the amygdala and the hypothalamic-pituitary-adrenal (HPA) axis (Nemeroff et al., 2006). Those suffering from PTSD show substantial variability in cortisol patterns (Mason et al., 2002) as well as higher levels of norepinephrine, epinephrine, and testosterone. These hormonal alterations can last a long time (Lindauer et al., 2006; O'Donnell, Creamer, Elliott, & Bryant, 2007). Studies have also reported alterations in immune functioning following a natural disaster (Hurricane Andrew) (Ironson et al., 1997) and among those with combat-related PTSD (Boscarino & Chang, 1999). Women are more likely than men to experience such long-term reactions (Holbrook, Hoyt, Stein, & Sieber, 2002).

PTSD predicts poor health, especially cardiovascular and lung disorders (Goodwin, Fischer, & Goldberg, 2007; Kubzansky, Koenen, Jones, & Eaton, 2009; Spitzer et al., 2009), and early mortality, especially from heart disease (Boscarino, 2008; Dedert, Calhoun, Watkins, Sherwood, & Beckham, 2010). It also is tied to poor habits such as problem drinking (Kaysen et al., 2008), and worsening symptoms of existing disorders (Dirkzwager, van der Velden, Grievink, & Yzermans, 2007). For example, PTSD resulting from the September 11, 2001, attacks on the World Trade Center contributed to severe

BOX 6.2

Post-Traumatic Stress Disorder (*continued*)

symptoms and use of urgent health care services among asthmatics in New York (Fagan et al., 2003). It contributes to the higher levels of medical illness in women than men and may contribute to particularly high illness rates among women with depression (Frayne et al., 2004). Poor health habits and substance abuse are among the factors that link PTSD to poor health (Flood, McDevitt-Murphy, Weathers, Eakin, & Benson, 2009).

Nearly half of adults in the United States experience at least one traumatic event in their lifetime, but only 10% of women and 5% of men develop PTSD (Ozer & Weiss, 2004). Who is most likely to develop PTSD? Poor cognitive skills (Gilbertson et al., 2006), catastrophic thinking about stress (Bryant & Guthrie, 2005), a preexisting emotional disorder or vulnerability (Keane & Wolfe, 1990), use of avoidant coping, low levels of social support, a history of chronic stress, preexisting heightened reactivity to trauma-related stimuli (Suendermann, Ehlers, Boellinghaus, Gamer, & Glucksman, 2010), and general negativity all predict who will develop PTSD in the wake of a traumatic stressor (Gil & Caspi, 2006; Widows, Jacobsen, & Fields, 2000). Soldiers who had combat experience, who observed atrocities, and who actually participated in atrocities were most likely to experience PTSD (Breslau & Davis, 1987). The more traumas one is exposed to, the greater the risk of PTSD, and the greater the health risk that may result (Sledjeski, Speisman, & Dierker, 2008).

Can PTSD be alleviated? Cognitive-behavioral therapies are often used to treat PTSD (Harvey, Bryant, & Tarrier, 2003; Nemeroff et al., 2006), and they appear to be successful with a broad array of people who have PTSD, including military veterans (Monson et al., 2006), children (Feeny, Foa, Treadwell, & March, 2004), and women who had been sexually abused as children (McDonagh et al., 2005). Perhaps counterintuitively, repeated exposure to the trauma through imagined exposure, homework assignments involving listening to therapy sessions, and discussion of thoughts and feelings related to the trauma seem to reduce symptoms of PTSD and enhance emotional processing of the traumatic event (Schnurr et al., 2007).

The goals of repeated exposure involve isolating the trauma as a discrete event, habituating to it and reducing overwhelming distress, providing new interpretive information about the event and its implications, and reducing anxiety and building a sense of mastery (Harvey et al., 2003). Once habituation is achieved, cognitive restructuring is added to integrate the trauma into the client's self-view and worldview, and anxiety management training is often included so that the patient can recognize and deal with intrusive traumatic memories (Harvey et al., 2003). With increases in social support and a shift toward problem-focused coping, symptoms of PTSD can also be reduced (Solomon, Mikulincer, & Avitzur, 1988).

■ HOW HAS STRESS BEEN STUDIED?

We now turn to methods that health psychologists have used for measuring stress and assessing its effects on psychological and physical health.

Studying Stress in the Laboratory

A common current way of studying stress is to bring people into the laboratory, expose them to short-term stressful events, and then observe the impact of that stress on their physiological, neuroendocrine, and psychological responses. This **acute stress paradigm** consistently finds that when people perform stressful tasks (such as counting backwards quickly by 7s or delivering an impromptu speech to an unresponsive audience) they show both psychological distress and strong indications of sympathetic

activity and neuroendocrine responses (Kirschbaum, Klauer, Filipp, & Hellhammer, 1995; Ritz & Steptoe, 2000).

Use of the acute stress paradigm has proven invaluable for understanding what kinds of events produce stress and how reactions to stress are influenced by factors such as personality, social support, and the presence of chronic stress in a person's life. For example, responses to acute stress among those who are also chronically stressed tend to be more exaggerated than among those not going through chronic stress as well (Pike et al., 1997), potentially identifying risky profiles prognostic for heart disease (Gregg, Matyas, & James, 2005; Strike et al., 2004).

The acute stress paradigm has also elucidated how individual differences contribute to stress. For example, people who are high in hostility show heightened blood pressure and cardiovascular responsiveness to laboratory stress, compared with people who are not as hostile

BOX 6.3

Can an Exciting Sports Event Kill You? Cardiovascular Events During World Cup Soccer

Everyone knows that fans get worked up during exciting sports matches. Near misses by one's own team, questionable calls by referees, and dirty plays can all rouse fans to fever pitch. But do these events actually have health effects? To examine this question, Wilbert-Lampen and colleagues (2008) studied acute cardiovascular events in 4,279 Germans when the German national team played in World Cup soccer events. On days of matches involving the German team, cardiac emergencies were nearly three times as likely as on days when they did not play. Nearly half of these people, mostly men, had previously been diagnosed with coronary heart disease.

The study concluded, then, that viewing a stressful soccer match, or indeed any other exciting sports event, may more than double the risk of an acute cardiovascular event. This increased risk falls especially hard on people who have already been diagnosed with heart

disease. So if someone you care about has a cardiovascular disorder and is a sports fan, that person may want to rethink whether exciting matches are worth the risk!

(Davis, Matthews, & McGrath, 2000). As we will see in Chapter 13, hostile individuals' tendency to respond to interpersonal stressors in a hostile manner and with strong sympathetic responses may contribute to their higher incidence of coronary heart disease.

The acute stress paradigm has also been proven helpful for showing what kinds of factors ameliorate the experience of stress. For example, when people go through these acute laboratory stressors in the presence of a supportive other person, such as their partner or even a stranger, their stress responses may be reduced (Ditzen et al., 2007; Stoney & Finney, 2000). We will explore social support more fully in Chapter 7.

Overall, the acute stress paradigm has proven to be very useful in identifying how biological, psychological, and social factors change and influence each other in situations of short-term stress.

Inducing Disease

A relatively recent way of studying the effects of stress on disease processes has involved intentionally exposing people to viruses and then assessing whether they get ill and how ill they get. For example, S. Cohen and colleagues (1999) measured levels of stress in a group of adults, infected them with an influenza virus by swabbing their nose with cotton soaked in a viral culture, and

measured their respiratory symptoms, the amount of mucus they produced, and interleukin-6 (IL-6), a proinflammatory cytokine that may link stress through the immune system to illness. They found that psychological stress led to more symptoms of illness and to increased production of IL-6 in response to the viral challenge than was true of people exposed to the virus whose lives were less stressful. This approach has been useful not only for studying the relation between stress and the likelihood of illness, but also for studying the factors that make some people undergoing stress more vulnerable to illness outcomes than others, such as personality factors or social support from others (e.g., Cohen et al., 2008).

Stressful Life Events

Another line of stress research has focused more heavily on the subjective experience of stress, such as **stressful life events**. These range from cataclysmic events, such as the death of one's spouse or being fired from a job, to more mundane but still problematic events, such as moving to a new home.

Two pioneers in stress research, T. H. Holmes and R. H. Rahe (1967) argued that, when a person must make a substantial adjustment to the environment, the likelihood of stress is high. They developed an inventory of stressful life events (Table 6.1) by ranking potentially

TABLE 6.1 | The Social Readjustment Rating Scale

Rank	Life Event	Mean Value
1	Death of spouse	100
2	Divorce	73
3	Marital separation from mate	65
4	Detention in jail or other institution	63
5	Death of a close family member	63
6	Major personal injury or illness	53
7	Marriage	50
8	Being fired at work	47
9	Marital reconciliation with mate	45
10	Retirement from work	45
11	Major change in the health or behavior of a family member	44
12	Pregnancy	40
13	Sexual difficulties	39
14	Gaining a new family member (e.g., through birth, adoption, oldster moving in)	39
15	Major business readjustment (e.g., merger, reorganization, bankruptcy)	39
16	Major change in financial state (e.g., a lot worse off or a lot better off than usual)	38
17	Death of a close friend	37
18	Changing to a different line of work	36
19	Major change in the number of arguments with spouse (e.g., either a lot more or a lot less than usual regarding child rearing, personal habits)	35
20	Taking out a mortgage or loan for a major purchase (e.g., for a home, business)	31
21	Foreclosure on a mortgage or loan	30
22	Major change in responsibilities at work (e.g., promotion, demotion, lateral transfer)	29
23	Son or daughter leaving home (e.g., marriage, attending college)	29
24	Trouble with in-laws	29
25	Outstanding personal achievement	28
26	Wife beginning or ceasing work outside the home	26
27	Beginning or ceasing formal schooling	26
28	Major change in living conditions (e.g., building a new home, remodeling, deterioration of home or neighborhood)	25
29	Revision of personal habits (e.g., dress, manners, associations)	24
30	Trouble with the boss	23
31	Major change in working hours or conditions	20
32	Change in residence	20
33	Changing to a new school	20
34	Major change in usual type and/or amount of recreation	19
35	Major change in church activities (e.g., a lot more or a lot less than usual)	19
36	Major change in social activities (e.g., clubs, dancing, movies, visiting)	18
37	Taking out a mortgage or loan for a lesser purchase (e.g., for a car, television, freezer)	17
38	Major change in sleeping habits (e.g., a lot more or a lot less sleep, or change in part of day when asleep)	16
39	Major change in number of family get-togethers (e.g., a lot more or a lot less than usual)	15
40	Major change in eating habits (e.g., a lot more or a lot less food intake, or very different meal hours or surroundings)	15
41	Vacation	13
42	Christmas	12
43	Minor violations of the law (e.g., traffic tickets, jaywalking, disturbing the peace)	11

Source: T. H. Holmes & Rahe, 1967.

stressful events that force people to make the most changes in their lives. Thus, for example, if one's spouse dies, virtually every aspect of life is disrupted. On the other hand, getting a traffic ticket may be annoying but is unlikely to produce much change in one's life. To obtain a stress score, one totals up the point values associated with the events one has experienced over the past year. Although all people experience at least some stressful events, some will experience a lot, and it is this group, according to Holmes and Rahe, that is most vulnerable to illness.

Studies show that stressful life events (SLE) predict illness. R. H. Rahe and colleagues (1970), for example, obtained SLE scores on sailors who were about to depart on 6-month cruises. They were able to predict with some success who would get sick and for how long.

Although life event inventories have been reliably tied both to the onset of acute illness and to the exacerbation of chronic diseases, the relation between the SLE scales and illness is quite modest. What are some of the problems of using an SLE inventory? First, some of the items on the list are vague; for example, "personal injury or illness" could mean anything from the flu to a heart attack. Second, because events have preassigned point values, individual differences in the way events are experienced are not taken into account (Schroeder & Costa, 1984). For example, a divorce may mean welcome freedom to one partner but a collapse in living standard or self-esteem to the other.

Third, inventories usually include both positive and negative events. They also include events that individuals choose, such as getting married, and events that simply happen, such as the death of a close friend. As we have seen, sudden, negative, unexpected, and uncontrollable events are reliably more stressful. Fourth, researchers typically do not assess whether stressful events have been successfully resolved (Thoits, 1994), which do not produce as many adverse effects (Turner & Avison, 1992).

Assessing specific stressful events may also tap ongoing life strain, that is, chronic stress that is part of everyday life. Chronic strain may also produce psychological distress and physical illness, but it needs to be measured separately from specific life events. Additional concerns are that some people may simply be prone to report more stress in their lives or to experience it more intensely (Epstein & Katz, 1992). Thus, more life events may be checked off by people with a propensity to react strongly to life's stresses and strains. SLE measures may be unreliable as well because people forget what stressful events they have experienced, especially if

the events occurred more than a few weeks earlier (Kessler & Wethington, 1991). Many people have theories about what kinds of events cause illness, so they may distort their reports of stress and reports of illness to correspond with each other.

A final difficulty concerns the time between stress and illness. Usually, stress over a 1-year period is related to the most recent 6 months of illness bouts. Yet, is it reasonable to assume that January's crisis caused June's cold or that last month's financial problems produced a malignancy detected this month? After all, malignancies can grow undetected for 10–20 years. Obviously, these cases are extreme, but they illustrate some of the problems in studying the stress-illness relationship over time. For all these reasons, SLE inventories are no longer used as much. Some researchers, as a result, have turned to perceived stress to assess the degree of stress people experience (Box 6.4).

Daily Stress

In addition to major stressful life events and past stressors, researchers have studied minor stressful events, or **daily hassles,** and their cumulative impact on health and illness. Such hassles include being stuck in a traffic jam, waiting in a line, doing household chores, and having difficulty making small decisions. Daily minor problems produce psychological distress, reports of physical symptoms, and enhanced use of health care services (Bolger, DeLongis, Kessler, & Schilling, 1989; Brantley et al., 2005).

R. S. Lazarus and his associates (Kanner, Coyne, Schaeffer, & Lazarus, 1981) developed a measure of minor stressful life events termed the "hassles scale."

Work strains, like the argument between these coworkers, are common sources of stress that compromise well-being and physical health.

A Measure of Perceived Stress

Because people vary so much in what they consider to be stressful, many researchers feel that **perceived stress** is a better measure of stress than are instruments that measure whether people have been exposed to particular events. To address this issue, S. Cohen and his colleagues (1983) developed a measure of perceived stress, some items of which follow. Note the differences between this measure of stress and the items on the social readjustment rating scale in Table 6.1. Research suggests that perceived stress predicts a broad array of health outcomes (Kojima et al., 2005; Young, He, Genkinger, Sapun, Mabry, & Jehn, 2004).

ITEMS AND INSTRUCTIONS FOR THE PERCEIVED STRESS SCALE

The questions in this scale ask you about your feelings and thoughts during the last month. In each case, you will be asked to indicate how often you felt or thought a certain way. Although some of the questions are similar, there are differences between them, and you should treat each one as a separate question. The best approach is to answer each question fairly quickly. That is, don't try to count up the number of times you felt a particular way, but, rather, indicate the alternative that seems like a reasonable estimate.

For each question, choose from the following alternatives:

0   Never
1   Almost never
2   Sometimes
3   Fairly often
4   Very often

1. In the last month, how often have you been upset because of something that happened unexpectedly?
2. In the last month, how often have you felt nervous and "stressed"?
3. In the last month, how often have you found that you could not cope with all the things that you had to do?
4. In the last month, how often have you been angered because of things that happened that were outside your control?
5. In the last month, how often have you found yourself thinking about things that you had to accomplish?
6. In the last month, how often have you felt difficulties were piling up so high that you could not overcome them?

If your score is high, you may want to think about whether there are ways you might reduce the stress in your life.

Research has tied daily hassles to declines in physical health (DeLongis, Coyne, Dakof, Folkman, & Lazarus, 1982) and to a worsening of symptoms in those already suffering from illnesses (Peralta-Ramírez, Jiménez-Alonso, Godoy-García, & Pérez-García, 2004). An example of how daily hassles can be measured is shown in Box 6.5.

Minor hassles can produce stress and aggravate physical and psychological health in several ways. First, the cumulative impact of small stressors may wear down an individual, predisposing him or her to become ill. Second, such events may interact with major life events to produce distress or illnesses. For example, daily hassles exacerbate psychological distress and physiological responses to stress when they occur in conjunction with chronic stress (Marin, Martin, Blackwell, Stetler, & Miller, 2007; Serido, Almeida, & Wethington, 2004).

Unfortunately, the measurement of daily hassles is subject to some of the same problems as the measurement of major stressful life events. In particular, people who report a lot of hassles may be high in anxiety and report more psychological distress.

■ SOURCES OF CHRONIC STRESS

Earlier, we posed the question of whether people can adapt to chronically stressful events. The answer is that people can adapt to a degree but continue to show signs of stress in response to severe chronic strains in their lives. Increasingly, stress researchers are coming to the conclusion that the chronic stressors may be more important than major life events in the development of illness.

BOX 6.5

The Measurement of Daily Strain

Psychologists have examined the role of minor stresses and strains in the development of illness. The following are some examples of how psychologists measure these stresses and strains.

INSTRUCTIONS

Each day, we can experience minor annoyances as well as major problems or difficulties. Listed are a number of irritations that can produce daily strain. Indicate how much of a strain each of these annoyances has been for you in the past month.

Severity

0   Did not occur

1   Mild strain

2   Somewhat of a strain

3   Moderate strain

4   Extreme strain

Hassles

1. A quarrel or problems with a neighbor	0	1	2	3	4
2. Traffic congestion	0	1	2	3	4
3. Thoughts of poor health	0	1	2	3	4
4. An argument with a romantic partner	0	1	2	3	4
5. Concerns about money	0	1	2	3	4
6. A parking ticket	0	1	2	3	4
7. Preparation of meals	0	1	2	3	4

Effects of Early Stressful Life Experiences

Recent research has focused on the health effects of early childhood stressors. Early adversity in the family can affect not only health risks in childhood (e.g., Marin, Chen, Munch, & Miller, 2009), but also health across the lifespan into adulthood and old age (Repetti, Taylor, & Seeman, 2002). Some of this work has been prompted by the allostatic load view of stress, which argues that major, chronic, or recurrent stress dysregulates stress systems, which, over time, can produce accumulating risk for disease.

Chronic physical or sexual abuse in childhood or adulthood has long been known to increase health risks (Midei, Matthews, & Bromberger, 2010). A likely reason is because abuse results in intense, chronic stress that taxes physiological systems (Baker, Norris, Jones, & Murphy, 2009; Talbot et al., 2009; Wegman & Stetler, 2009). It is now clear that even more modest family stress can increase risk for disease as well (Almeida et al., 2010; Buchman et al., 2010). Repetti and colleagues (2002) reported that "risky families"—that is, families that are high in conflict or abuse and low in warmth and nurturance—produce offspring with problems in stress regulatory systems. Some of these problems show up as difficulties in emotion regulation strategies and social skills. That is, children who grow up in these harsh families do not learn how to recognize other people's emotions and respond to them appropriately or regulate their own emotional responses to situations. As a result, they may overreact in many circumstances.

Not surprisingly, these tendencies have adverse effects on social relationships as well. Children who grow up in harsh families have more difficulty forming positive social relationships. These deficits in emotion regulation and social skills may persist across the lifespan long into adulthood, compromising the ways in which people from risky families cope with stress (Repetti et al., 2002; Taylor, Eisenberger, Saxbe, Lehman, & Lieberman, 2006). By virtue of having to cope with a chronically stressful family environment, children from such families may also develop heightened sympathetic reactivity to stressors and exaggerated cortisol responses. For example, merely experiencing parental divorce predicts earlier mortality (Tucker et al., 1997). Moreover, by virtue of exposure to chronic stress early in life, the developing stress systems themselves may become dysregulated, such that physiological and neuroendocrine stress responses across the life span are affected by these early experiences. Because these stress systems and their dysfunctions are implicated in a broad array of diseases, early stress can produce damage that is not apparent until much later in life.

The evidence for this position is quite substantial (Dube et al., 2009; Luecken, Rodriguez, & Appelhans, 2005; Repetti et al., 2002; Scott et al., 2008; Wickrama,

Conger, Wallace, & Elder, 2003). For example, in a retrospective study, V. J. Felitti and colleagues (1998) asked adults to complete a questionnaire regarding their early family environment that asked, among other things, how warm and supportive the environment was versus how cold, critical, hostile, or conflict-ridden it was. The more negative characteristics these adults reported from their childhood, the more vulnerable they were in adulthood to an array of disorders, including depression, lung disease, cancer, heart disease, and diabetes. At least some of the risk may have occurred not only because of stress-related biological dysregulations but also because of poor health habits, such as smoking, poor diet, and lack of exercise that these early stressful environments fostered.

Chronic Stressful Conditions

Sometimes, chronic stress is of the long-term, grinding kind, such as living in poverty, being in a bad relationship, or remaining in a high-stress job. Chronic stress is also an important contributor to psychological distress and physical illness (Kahn & Pearlin, 2006) (Figure 6.5).

In an early community study of 2,300 people, L. I. Pearlin and C. Schooler (1978) found that people who reported chronic stress in marriage, parenting, household functioning, or their jobs were more likely to be psychologically distressed. Chronic strains lasting for more than 2 years have been implicated in the development of depression (Brown & Harris, 1978), and uncontrollable stressors may be particularly virulent in this regard (McGonagle & Kessler, 1990). Even something as mundane as commuting can have an affect on daily cortisol levels and perceived stress. Because over 100 million Americans commute to work every weekday, this is a stressor that affects many people (Evans & Wener, 2006).

Chronic strain may influence the relationship between specific stressors and adverse physical or psychological effects. J. Pike and her colleagues (1997) found that people who were undergoing chronic life stress showed exaggerated sympathetic reactivity and decrements in natural killer cell activity in response to acute stress in the laboratory, as compared with people who had fewer background stressors.

FIGURE 6.5 | Stress and Mental and Physical Health
This figure shows some of the routes by which these effects may occur.   (*Source:* After Cohen, Kessler, & Gordon, 1995)

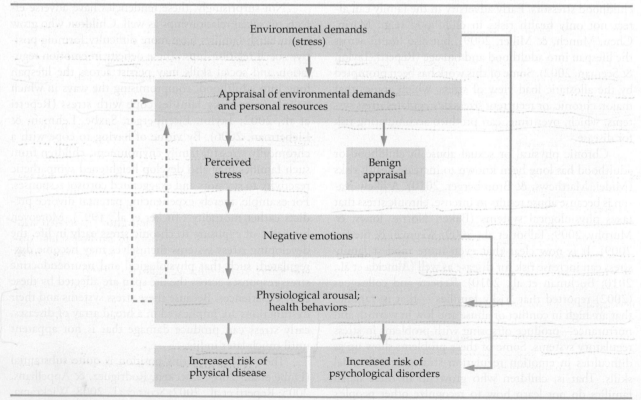

Chronic Stress and Health

Research relating chronic stress to mental and physical health outcomes is difficult to conduct, because it is often hard to show that a particular chronic stressor is the factor contributing to illness. A second problem concerns the measurement of chronic stress. Unlike life events, which can often be assessed objectively, chronic stress can be more difficult to measure objectively, because it is hard to tell whether particular chronic strains are actually going on. Third, as in the measurement of life events, inventories that attempt to assess chronic strain may also tap psychological distress and neuroticism rather than the objective existence of stressful conditions. Nonetheless, the evidence indicates that chronic stress is related to illness (Matthews, Gallo, & Taylor, 2010). Box 6.6 focuses on a particular type of chronic stress, namely, racism, and its relation to poor health.

Research showing social class differences in death from all causes and in rates of specific diseases, such as most cancers and cardiovascular disease, also attests to the relationship between chronic stress and health (Grzywacz, Almeida, Neupert, & Ettner, 2004). Poverty, exposure to crime, neighborhood stress, and other chronic stressors vary with SES and are all tied to poor health (Adler, Boyce, Chesney, Folkman, & Syme, 1993; Lantz, House, Mero, & Williams, 2005; Matthews & Yang, 2010). Even children from families with low SES experience greater health risks than those from families with more resources (Chen, Matthews, & Boyce, 2002), due to such stressors as family discord, violence exposure, and other SES-related stressors (e.g., Suglia, Ryan, Laden, Dockery, & Wright, 2008). In addition, many psychological disorders, such as depression, show the same pattern (Turner & Lloyd, 1999).

People who are low in SES typically have low-prestige occupations, which may expose them to greater interpersonal conflict and arousal at work; the consequences can include psychological distress and adverse changes in cardiovascular symptoms, among other stress-related outcomes (Matthews et al., 2000). Chronic SES-related stress has also been related to alterations in cortisol patterns, catecholamines, and inflammation (Friedman & Herd, 2010; Janicki-Deverts et al., 2007; Kumari et al., 2010) and the likelihood of developing coronary artery disease (see Chapter 13). At least some of the health risks tied to financial disadvantage may be reversible if circumstances improve (Steptoe, Brydon, & Kunz-Ebrecht, 2005).

Stress in the Workplace

Studies of stress in the workplace are important for several reasons:

- They help identify some of the most common stressors of everyday life.
- They provide additional evidence for the stress-illness relationship.
- Work stress may be one of our preventable stressors and so provide possibilities for intervention (Sauter, Murphy, & Hurrell, 1990).
- Economics matter: Stress-related physical and mental health disorders account for an enormous and growing percentage of disability and social security payments to workers.

Work and Sedentary Lifestyle The most common work that people undertook before the Industrial Revolution involved agricultural production, in which they engaged in physical activity as they went about their work. As people have moved into office jobs or other work contexts that require very little output of physical energy, the amount of exercise they get in their work lives has declined substantially (House & Smith, 1985). Even jobs that require high levels of physical exertion, such as construction work and firefighting, may include so much stress that the potential benefits of exercise are eliminated. Because activity level is related to health, this change in the nature of work creates the possibility of vulnerability to illness.

Overload Work overload is a chief factor producing high levels of occupational stress. Workers who feel required to work too long and too hard at too many tasks feel more stressed, practice poorer health habits, and sustain more health risks than do workers not suffering from overload (Repetti, 1993a). The chronic neuroendocrine activation and cardiovascular activation associated with overcommitment can contribute to cardiovascular disease (Steptoe, Siegrist, Kirschbaum, & Marmot, 2004; Von Känel, Bellingrath, & Kudielka, 2009).

An old rock song states, "Monday, Monday, can't trust that day." Increasingly, research suggests that Monday may indeed be one of the most stressful days of the week. Weekdays are generally associated with more worry and chronic work overload than weekends, resulting in altered cortisol levels that may be risky for health (Schlotz, Hellhammer, Schulz, & Stone, 2004). Unfortunately, many

BOX 6.6

Can Racism Kill You?

A young African American father pulled up in front of a house in a largely white neighborhood to pick up his daughter from a birthday party. Because he was early and the party had not ended, he sat waiting in the car. Within 8 minutes, a security car had pulled up behind him; two officers approached him and asked him to exit his vehicle. Neighbors had reported seeing a suspicious-looking African American man casing their neighborhood.

Stressful events of all kinds can erode health, and recently, researchers have explored the effects of prejudice and racism on health. It has long been known that African Americans experience greater health risks than the rest of the population. Life expectancy for African American men is 6 years less than for White men and life expectancy for African American women is 4.1 years less than for White women. African American men and women die of cardiovascular disease at nearly one and a half times the rate for White men and women. Heart disease has declined dramatically over the past few decades, but that decline has been slower among African Americans (Zheng, Croft, Labarthe, Williams, & Mensah, 2001). African Americans are more vulnerable to AIDS and far more likely to die of AIDS than Whites.

Many of these differences can be traced to differences in SES (Myers, 2009). Poverty, lower educational attainment, and unemployment are prevalent in many Black communities (Browning & Cagney, 2003). The day-in, day-out grinding discrimination associated with poor housing, little available employment, poor schools, and poor neighborhoods also contributes to stress through chronic exposure to violence and an enduring sense of danger or trouble to come (Ross & Mirowsky, 2001). Medical services in minority areas are often inadequate, with the result that African Americans are less likely to receive preventive services and more likely to suffer the consequences of delayed medical attention (Institute of Medicine, 2002). Racism and racial discrimination also contribute to disease risk, especially risk of cardiovascular disease (Brondolo, ver Halen, Pencille, Beatty, & Contrada, 2009; Williams & Mohammed, 2009). One may be treated badly by a store clerk or stopped by the police for no reason (driving while black).

Perceived racism coupled with inhibited angry responses to it is related to higher blood pressure, suggesting that the perception of racism contributes to the high incidence of hypertension seen among African Americans (Brondolo, Rieppi, Kelly, & Gerin, 2003; Richman, Bennett, Pek, Siegler, & Williams, 2007). Blood pressure usually falls when a person goes to sleep, but in some people, it remains elevated, or nondipping. Nondipping is an indicator of stress exposure, and African Americans experience it more often, especially if they have been exposed to violence (Tomfohr, Cooper, Mills, Nelesen, & Dimsdale, 2010; Wilson, Kliewer, Teasley, Plybon, & Sica, 2002). Racism may also help to explain the high levels of depression (Turner & Avison, 2003) and back pain (Edwards, 2008) in the African American population. Exposure to racism has been tied to problem drinking and to poor sleep quality in African Americans as well (Martin, Tuch, & Roman, 2003; Thomas, Bardwell, Ancoli-Israel, & Dimsdale, 2006).

Racism is not the only form of prejudice and discrimination that affects health. Sexism in the work environment predicts poor physical and emotional health among women (Ryff, Keyes, & Hughes, 2003). For example, women have the best health in states in which their earnings, employment, autonomy, and political participation are highest and the worst health in those states in which they score lowest on these indices of women's status (Jun, Subramanian, Gortmaker, & Kawachi, 2004). Discrimination against mothers is particularly rampant and difficult to combat (Biernat, Crosby, & Williams, 2004).

Suicide rates among ethnic immigrant groups have been tied to the amount of hate speech directed toward those groups (Mullen & Smyth, 2004). Perceived discrimination has been linked to substance abuse among Native American children (Whitbeck, Hoyt, McMorris, Chen, & Stubben, 2001) and to depression among Native American adults (Whitbeck, McMorris, Hoyt, Stubben, & LaFromboise, 2002). Converging evidence like this indicates clearly that the stressors associated with discrimination, racism, and sexism can adversely affect health.

people, particularly in the United States, don't use their weekends to recover and instead either work through the weekend or find that they are unable to relax and rest. Incomplete recovery from work contributes to death from cardiovascular disease (Kivimäki et al., 2006).

So well established is the relation between work overload and poor health that in Japan, a country notorious for its long working hours, long work weeks, little sleep, and lack of vacations, there is a term, *karoshi*, that refers to death from overwork. One study found that men who worked more than 61 hours a week experienced twice the risk of a heart attack as those working 40 hours or less; sleeping 5 hours or less at least 2 days a week increased this risk by two to three times (Liu & Tanaka, 2002). Under Japanese law, families are entitled to compensation if they can prove that the breadwinner died of *karoshi* (*Los Angeles Times,* March 1993). As a result, work hours have declined in Japan over the past 20 years.

Work overload is a subjective as well as an objective experience. The sheer amount of work that a person does—that is, how many hours he or she works each week—is not consistently related to poor health and compromised psychological well-being (Herzog, House, & Morgan, 1991). The *perception* of work overload shows a stronger relationship to physical problems and psychological distress.

Ambiguity and Role Conflict

Role conflict and role ambiguity are associated with stress. Role ambiguity occurs when a person has few clear ideas of what is to be

Research shows that workers with high levels of job strain and low levels of control over their work are under great stress and may be at risk for coronary heart disease.

done and no idea of the standards used for evaluating work. **Role conflict** occurs when a person receives conflicting information about work tasks or standards from different individuals. For example, if a college professor is told by one colleague to publish more articles, is advised by another colleague to publish fewer papers but of higher quality, and is told by a third to improve teaching ratings, the professor may experience role ambiguity and conflict. Chronically high blood pressure and elevated heart rate, as well as other illness precursors, have been tied to role conflict and role ambiguity (French & Caplan, 1973). When people receive clear feedback about the nature of their performance, they report lower levels of stress (Cohen & Williamson, 1988).

Social Relationships

The inability to develop satisfying social relationships at work has been tied to job stress (House, 1981), to psychological distress at work (Buunk, Doosje, Jans, & Hopstaken, 1993), and to poor physical and mental health (Landsbergis, Schnall, Deitz, Friedman, & Pickering, 1992; Repetti, 1993a).

Having a poor relationship with one's supervisor is especially related to job distress and may also increase a worker's risk for coronary heart disease (Davis, Matthews, Meilahn, & Kiss, 1995; Repetti, 1993a). Conversely, men and women who are able to develop socially supportive relationships at work have enhanced well-being (Loscocco & Spitze, 1990).

To a degree, having an amicable social environment at work depends on being an amicable coworker. A study of air traffic controllers found that individuals who were not particularly well liked by their coworkers and who consequently did not have much social contact were significantly more likely to become ill and to experience an accidental injury than were individuals who enjoyed and contributed to a more satisfying social climate (Niemcryk, Jenkins, Rose, & Hurst, 1987).

Social relationships may not only be important in combating stress in their own right; they may also buffer other job stressors. Social support may act as a buffer against low control over work or anger at co-workers (Fitzgerald, Haythornthwaite, Suchday, & Ewart, 2003). For example, one study of New York City traffic enforcement agents found that social support from coworkers and supervisors was associated with lower blood pressure, especially during stressful work conditions (Karlin, Brondolo, & Schwartz, 2003).

Control

Lack of control over work has been related to stress and illness indicators, including heightened catecholamine secretion, job dissatisfaction, absentee-ism, and the development of coronary artery disease (Bosma et al., 1997), as well as the risk of death from all causes (Amick et al., 2002). Paralleling these findings, the experience of job control can act as a coping resource for managing stressful events at work (Shimazu, de Jonge, & Irimajiri, 2008). Changes in job control can lead to corresponding changes in health as well (Smith, Frank, Bondy, & Mustard, 2008).

R. Karasek and his associates (1981) developed a model of job strain that is based on the relation between the worker and the job environment. They hypothesized that high psychological demands on the job with little decision latitude (such as low job control) causes job strain, which, in turn, can lead to the development of coronary artery disease. Research generally supports this idea (Cesana et al., 2003; Hintsanen et al., 2005; Kivimäki et al., 2006). The chronic anger that can result from these jobs may further contribute to coronary ar-tery disease risk (Fitzgerald et al., 2003). When high demands and low control are combined with little social support at work, in what has been termed as the demand-control-support model, risk for coronary artery disease may be even greater (Hintsanen et al., 2007; Muhonen & Torkelson, 2003).

The exact mechanisms whereby work stress contrib-utes to coronary heart disease are unknown, but poten-tially, a broad array of processes are implicated. High levels of work stress can lead to impaired fibrolytic capac-ity, which may be a result of the impact of chronic stress on insulin resistance (Steptoe et al., 2003). Overinvolve-ment in work is associated with higher cortisol levels in the morning and across the workday, as well as higher blood pressure (Steptoe et al., 2004). Long-term work stress has also been tied to higher lipid activity (Stoney, Niaura, Bausserman, & Matacin, 1999). Increases in blood pressure prognostic for cardiovascular disease have also been linked to work stress (Ming et al., 2004). Job insecurity and high or low psychological demands pro-mote weight gain, especially among those already high in body mass index, providing another potential route to heart disease (Hannerz, Albertsen, Nielsen, Tüchsen, & Burr, 2004). Chronic work stress may also contribute to cardiovascular disease by increasing acute inflammatory responsiveness (Hamer et al., 2006).

Unemployment

A final source of stress related to work concerns the impact of unemployment. Unem-ployment can produce a variety of adverse outcomes, including psychological distress (Burgard, Brand, &

House, 2007), physical symptoms, physical illness (Hamilton, Broman, Hoffman, & Renner, 1990), alco-hol abuse (Catalano, Dooley, Wilson, & Hough, 1993), difficulty achieving sexual arousal, low birth weight of offspring (Catalano, Hansen, & Hartig, 1999), elevated inflammation (Janicki-Deverts, Cohen, Matthews, & Cullen, 2008), and compromised immune functioning (Cohen et al., 2007; Segerstrom & Miller, 2004).

In a community study of high unemployment areas in Michigan, R. C. Kessler and associates (1988) found that unemployment was associated with high rates of depression, anxiety, symptom expression, and self-reported physical illness. These effects appear to be accounted for largely by financial strain produced by unemployment and the enhanced vulnerability to other life events that unemployment creates. Reemployment can largely reverse the adverse effects of unemployment (Cohen et al., 2007; Kessler, Turner, & House, 1987).

Uncertainty over one's continuing employment and unstable employment have also been tied to physical ill-ness (Heaney, Israel, & House, 1994). For example, a study found that men who had held a series of unrelated jobs were at greater risk of dying over a follow-up period than were men who had remained in the same job or in the same type of job over a longer time (Pavalko, Elder, & Clipp, 1993). Being stably employed is protective of health (Rushing, Ritter, & Burton, 1992).

Other Occupational Outcomes

Stress also shows up in ways other than illness that may be ex-tremely costly to an organization. Some of these factors may represent workers' efforts to control or to offset stress before it ever gets to the point of causing illness. For example, workers who cannot participate actively in decisions about their jobs show higher rates of absentee-ism, job turnover, tardiness, job dissatisfaction, sabo-tage, and poor performance on the job. Moreover, this problem may be getting worse. Workers take matters into their own hands and reduce stress by not working as long, as hard, or as well as their employers apparently expect (Kivimäki, Vahtera, Ellovainio, Lillrank, & Kevin, 2002).

Some Solutions to Workplace Stressors

CBT is not particularly effective in reducing work-related stress (De Vente, Kamphuis, Emmelkamp, & Blonk, 2008). Genuine changes in the workplace and work-based interventions that teach stress management skills and build on social support are more successful.

TABLE 6.2 | Reducing Stress at Work

Because work is such an important and time-consuming part of life, it can contribute to the joy but also to the stress that people experience each day. How can stress on the job be reduced?

1. Physical work stressors, such as noise, harsh lighting, crowding, or temperature extremes, should be reduced as much as possible.

2. Minimize unpredictability and ambiguity in expected tasks and standards of performance. When workers know what they are expected to do and at what level, they are less distressed.

3. Involve workers as much as possible in the decisions that affect their work.

4. Make jobs as interesting as possible.

5. Provide workers with opportunities to develop or promote meaningful social relationships.

6. Reward workers for good work, rather than focusing on punishment for poor work.

7. Look for signs of stress before stress has an opportunity to do significant damage. Supervisors can watch for negative affect, such as boredom, apathy, and hostility, among workers because these affective reactions often precede more severe reactions to stress, such as poor health or absenteeism.

A blueprint for change has been offered by several organizational stress researchers (for example, Kahn, 1981) (Table 6.2). A workplace intervention that addresses work stress was conducted by R. H. Rahe and colleagues (2002). They randomly assigned 500 participants to one of three groups: an intervention that included assessment for stress-related problems, personalized feedback, and six small-group, face-to-face counseling sessions; a self-help group that received personalized feedback and assessment by mail; and a wait-list control group. Although all three groups experienced less stress and anxiety over the course of the study, the participants in the first intervention showed a more rapid reduction in their stress responses, fewer days of illness, and a large reduction in their health care utilization, suggesting that even a relatively short-term intervention that includes stress management and social support can reduce workplace stress. Other factors include high control, reasonable demands, social support, and creative work (Mirowsky & Ross, 2007).

Combining Work and Family Roles

So far, our discussion of chronic stress has considered only factors related to employment. But much of the stress that people experience results not from one role in their lives but from the combination of several roles. As adults, most of us will be workers, partners, and parents, and each of these roles entails heavy obligations. Accordingly, recent research has focused on the stress that can result when one is attempting to combine multiple roles (Nylén, Melin, & Laflamme, 2007).

Women and Multiple Roles   These problems have been particularly acute for women. In the American workforce, the number of mothers with young children is large, with estimates that more than half of married women with young children are employed (Department for Professional Employees, April 2006).

The task of managing multiple roles is greatest when both work and family responsibilities are heavy (Emmons, Biernat, Teidje, Lang, & Wortman, 1990). Because concessions to working parents are rarely made at work and because mothers in the workforce usually bear a disproportionate load of household and child care tasks (Emmons et al., 1990), home and work responsibilities may conflict with each other, increasing stress. Studies of neuroendocrine responses to stress support this conclusion as well, with working women who have children at home showing higher levels of cortisol, higher cardiovascular reactivity, and more home strain than those without children at home (Frankenhaeuser et al., 1989; Luecken et al., 1997). Single women raising children on their own are most at risk for health problems (Hughes & Waite, 2002), whereas women who are happily married are less likely to show these effects (Saxbe, Repetti, & Nishina, 2008).

Protective Effects of Multiple Roles   Despite the potential for women to suffer role conflict and role overload by combining work and homemaker roles, there appear to be positive effects of combining home and work responsibilities (Waldron, Weiss, & Hughes, 1998). On the one hand, juggling heavy responsibilities at work with heavy responsibilities at home reduces the enjoyment of both sets of tasks and may leave women vulnerable to depression (Williams, Suls, Alliger, Learner, & Wan, 1991). However, combining motherhood with employment can be beneficial for women's well-being, improving self-esteem, feelings of self-efficacy, and life satisfaction (Verbrugge, 1983). Combining employment with the family role has also been tied to better health, including lower levels of coronary risk factors (Weidner, Boughal, Connor, Pieper, & Mendell, 1997).

Many women hold multiple roles, such as worker, homemaker, and parent. Although these multiple roles can provide much satisfaction, they also make women vulnerable to role conflict and role overload.

As we will see in Chapter 7, whether the effects of combining employment and child rearing are positive or negative can depend heavily on resources that are available. Having control and flexibility over one's work environment (Lennon & Rosenfield, 1992), having a good income (Rosenfield, 1992), having someone to help with the housework (Krause & Markides, 1985), having adequate child care (Ross & Mirowsky, 1988), having a partner (Ali & Avison, 1997), and having a supportive, helpful partner (Klumb, Hoppmann, & Staats, 2006; Rosenfield, 1992; Tobe et al., 2005, 2007) can all reduce the likelihood that multiple role demands will lead to stress and its psychological and physical costs.

Men and Multiple Roles   Men experience stress as they attempt to combine multiple roles as well. Evidence

suggests that men are more distressed by financial strain and work stress, whereas women are more distressed by adverse changes in the home (Barnett, Raudenbush, Brennan, Pleck, & Marshall, 1995). Satisfaction in the parent role is also important to men's well-being (Barnett & Marshall, 1993).

Combining employment and marriage is protective for men with respect to health and mental health (Burton, 1998), just as it seems to be for women who have enough help. But multiple roles can take their toll on men, too. R. L. Repetti (1989) studied workload and interpersonal strain and how they affected fathers' interactions with the family at the end of the day. She found that after a demanding day at work (high workload strain) fathers were more withdrawn in their interactions with their children. After stressful interpersonal events at work (high interpersonal strain), conflict with children increased. Employed, unmarried fathers may be especially at risk for psychological distress (Simon, 1998).

For both men and women, the research on multiple roles is converging on the idea that stress is lower when one finds meaning in one's life. The protective effects of employment, marriage, and parenting on psychological distress and the beneficial effects of social support on health are all testimony to the salutary effects of social roles (Burton, 1998). When these sources of meaning and pleasure in life are challenged, as through a demanding and unrewarding work life or stressful interpersonal relationships, the effects on health can be devastating (Stansfeld, Bosma, Hemingway, & Marmot, 1998).

Children   Children and adolescents have their own sources of stress that can make home life stressful. One study found that social and academic failure experiences at school, such as being rejected by a peer or having difficulty with schoolwork, significantly increased a child's demanding and aversive behavior at home—specifically, acting out and making demands for attention (Repetti & Pollina, 1994). Not surprisingly, children are affected by their parents' work and family stressors as well, and the strains their parents are under have consequences for both the children's academic achievement and the likelihood that they will act out their problems in adolescence (Menaghan, Kowaleski-Jones, & Mott, 1997). Such findings make it clear that to fully understand the impact of multiple roles it is important to study not just working parents but also children. ●

SUMMARY

1. Events are perceived as stressful when people believe that their resources (such as time, money, and energy) may not be sufficient to meet the harm, threat, or challenge of the environment. Stress produces many changes, including adverse emotional reactions, cognitive responses, physiological changes, and performance decrements.

2. Early research on stress examined how an organism mobilizes its resources to fight or flee from threatening stimuli (the fight-or-flight response). Building on this model, Selye proposed the general adaptation syndrome, arguing that reactions to stress go through three phases: alarm, resistance, and exhaustion. Recent efforts have focused on social responses to stress—that is, the ways in which people tend-and-befriend others in times of stress.

3. The physiology of stress implicates the sympathetic adrenomedullary (SAM) system and the hypothalamic-pituitary-adrenocortical (HPA) axis. Over the long term, repeated activation of these systems can lead to cumulative damage, termed allostatic load, which represents the premature physiological aging that stress produces.

4. Whether an event is stressful depends on how it is appraised. Events that are negative, uncontrollable or unpredictable, ambiguous, overwhelming, and threatening to central life tasks are especially likely to be perceived as stressful.

5. Usually, people can adapt to mild stressors, but severe stressors may cause chronic problems for health and mental health. Stress can have disruptive aftereffects, including persistent physiological arousal, psychological distress, poor task performance, and, over time, declines in cognitive capabilities. Vulnerable populations—such as children, the elderly, and the poor—may be particularly adversely affected by stress.

6. Research on stressful life events indicates that any event that forces a person to make a change increases stress and the likelihood of illness. The daily hassles of life can also affect health adversely, as can chronic exposure to stress.

7. Studies of occupational stress suggest that work hazards, work overload, work pressure, role conflict and ambiguity, inability to develop satisfying job relationships, inability to exert control in one's job, and unemployment can lead to increased illness, job dissatisfaction, absenteeism, tardiness, and turnover. Some of these job stresses can be prevented or offset through intervention.

8. Combining multiple roles, such as those related to work and home life, can create role conflict and role overload, producing psychological distress and poor health. On the other hand, such role combinations may enhance self-esteem and well-being. Which of these effects occurs depends, in large part, on available resources, such as time, money, social support, and help.

KEY TERMS

acute stress paradigm
aftereffects of stress
allostatic load
chronic strain
daily hassles
fight-or-flight response
general adaptation syndrome

perceived stress
person–environment fit
post-traumatic stress disorder (PTSD)
primary appraisal
reactivity
role conflict

secondary appraisal
stress
stressful life events
stressors
tend-and-befriend

Moderators of the Stress Experience

In August 2005, Hurricane Katrina struck the city of New Orleans. For several weeks, the city was flooded, and many people lost their houses and personal property. Those who survived were left with deep-seated insecurities about their families, friends, and their futures. Despite these extreme circumstances, not everyone was affected the same way.

Consider four families, all of whom lost the better part of their homes and possessions to the devastation. Despite apparent commonalities in their circumstances, each responded to the stressful experience in a different way. One family, newly arrived from Mexico, who had not yet found friends or employment, lost everything. They were devastated psychologically, peering out from the folds of a relief tent, uncertain what to do next. An older man with a heart condition succumbed to a heart attack, leaving his infirmed wife behind. A third family, who had financial resources and relatives in the area, were quickly cared for and moved out of the city while they looked for another home. A young couple, wiped out by the experience, responded with resilience, determined to make a new start in a new city.

The personal accounts that followed on the heels of this event revealed the diversity of individual experiences that people had. What the accounts illustrate, albeit in extreme form, is the degree to which stress is moderated by individual and circumstantial factors. People with many resources, such as money or social support, may find a stressful experience to be less so. Others, without resources or coping skills, may cope very poorly.

We term these factors **stress moderators** because they modify how stress is experienced and the effects it has. Moderators of the stress experience may have an impact on stress itself, on the relation between stress and psychological responses, on the relation between stress and illness, and on the degree to which a stressful experience intrudes into other aspects of life.

■ COPING WITH STRESS

People respond very differently to stress. We all know people who throw up their hands in despair when the slightest thing goes wrong with their plans, yet we know others who seem able to meet setbacks and challenges with equanimity, bringing their personal and social resources to bear on the problem at hand. The impact of any potentially stressful event is substantially influenced by how a person appraises it. **Coping** is therefore defined as the thoughts and behaviors used to manage the internal and external demands of situations that are appraised as stressful (Folkman & Moskowitz, 2004; Taylor & Stanton, 2007).

Coping has several important characteristics. First, the relationship between coping and a stressful event is a dynamic process. Coping is a series of transactions between a person who has a set of resources, values, and commitments and a particular environment with its own resources, demands, and constraints (Folkman & Moskovitz, 2004). Thus, coping is not a one-time action that someone takes but rather a set of responses, occurring over time, by which the environment and the person influence each other. For example, the impending breakup of a romantic relationship can produce a variety of reactions, ranging from emotional responses, such as sadness or indignation, to actions, such as efforts at reconciliation or attempts to find engrossing, distracting activities. These coping efforts will, in turn, be influenced by the way the partner in the relationship responds. With encouragement from the partner may come renewed efforts at reconciliation, whereas anger or rejection may drive a person further away.

A second important aspect of the definition of coping is its breadth. The definition clearly encompasses a great many actions and reactions to stressful circumstances. According to this definition, then, emotional reactions, including anger or depression, are part of the coping process, as are actions that are voluntarily undertaken to confront the event. In turn, coping efforts are moderated by the resources available to the individual. Figure 7.1 presents a diagram of the coping process.

Personality and Coping

The personality that each individual brings to a stressful event influences how he or she will cope with that event. These characteristics come both from genes (Kozak, Strelau, & Miles, 2005) and from environmental factors (Repetti, Taylor, & Seeman, 2002). Some personality characteristics make stressful situations worse, whereas others improve them.

Negativity, Stress, and Illness   Some people experience stressful events especially strongly, which may, in turn, increase their psychological distress, their physical symptoms, and/or their likelihood of illness. Research has especially focused on **negative affectivity** (Watson & Clark, 1984), a pervasive negative mood marked by anxiety, depression, and hostility.

FIGURE 7.1 | The Coping Process   (*Sources:* Cohen & Lazarus, 1979; Hamburg & Adams, 1967; Lazarus & Folkman, 1984b; Moos, 1988; Taylor, 1983)

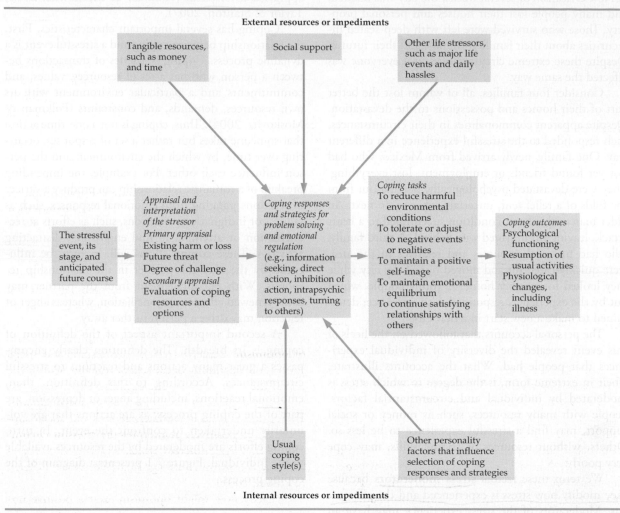

People high in negative affectivity (or neuroticism) express distress, discomfort, and dissatisfaction across a wide range of situations (Gunthert, Cohen, & Armeli, 1999). They are also more prone to drink heavily (Frances, Franklin, & Flavin, 1986), to be depressed (Francis, Fyer, & Clarkin, 1986), and to engage in suicidal gestures or even suicide (Cross & Hirschfeld, 1986). A related concept, the type D personality, is characterized by the experience of negative emotions coupled with the inhibition of expressing these emotions in social contexts. These two components, distress and social inhibition, are thought to be toxic with respect to mental and physical health (Ferguson et al., 2009; Kupper, Gidron, Winter, & Denollet, 2009; Mommersteeg et al., 2010).

Neuroticism is related to poor health. Studies have found increased risk for arthritis, diabetes, kidney or liver disease, stomach or gallbladder problems, ulcers, asthma, arthritis, headaches, and coronary artery disease (Friedman & Booth-Kewley, 1987; Goodwin, Cox, & Clara, 2006; Shipley, Weiss, Der, Taylor, & Deary, 2007). Neuroticism may play a particularly important role in disorders related to pain (Charles, Gatz, Kato, & Pedersen, 2008). Taken together, this research suggests that psychological distress involving depression, anger, hostility, and anxiety may form the core of a "disease-prone personality" that predisposes certain people to these disorders. Overall, negative affectivity is related to all-cause mortality (Grossardt, Bower, Geda, Colligan, & Rocca, 2009) and to higher risk of mortality in old age as well (Wilson et al., 2005). Negative affectivity is associated with elevated cortisol secretion (Polk, Cohen, Doyle, Skoner, & Kirschbaum, 2005), with elevated heart rate (Daly, Delaney, Doran, Harmon, & MacLachlan, 2010), and with risk factors for coronary heart disease (Midei & Matthews, 2009); these may be significant pathways linking negative affectivity to adverse health outcomes. Negative affectivity can also affect adjustment to treatment. One study (Duits, Boeke, Taams, Passchier, & Erdman, 1997) found that people who were very anxious or depressed prior to coronary artery bypass graft surgery were more likely to adjust badly during surgical recovery (see also P. G. Williams et al., 2002).

Although negativity can compromise health, it is also clear that negativity can sometimes create a false impression of poor health when none exists. People who are high in negative affectivity report more distressing physical symptoms, such as headaches, stomachaches, and other pains, especially under stress (Watson & Pennebaker, 1989). One reason may be that negative affect leads people to worry, be more aware of their symptoms, and attribute their symptoms to a new or existing health condition (Mora, Halm, Leventhal, & Ceric, 2007). But in other cases, there is no evidence of an underlying physical disorder (Diefenbach, Leventhal, Leventhal, & Patrick-Miller, 1996). For example, S. Cohen and associates (Cohen, Doyle, Turner, Alper, & Skoner, 2003) obtained both subjective complaints (runny nose and congestion) and objective measures (for example, mucus secretion) of illness from people who had been exposed to a respiratory virus. People high in negative affectivity had more complaints but their symptoms were no worse. People high in negative affectivity are more likely to use health services during stressful times than are people low in negative affectivity (Cohen & Williamson, 1991). Thus, people who are chronically high in negative affect may be more likely to get sick, but they also show distress, physical symptoms, and illness behavior even when they are not getting sick.

Coping Resources

Positive Emotional States Just as chronic negative affect/neuroticism has been shown to adversely affect health, so positive emotional states are associated with better mental and physical health (Cohen & Pressman, 2006; Pressman & Cohen, 2005; Richman et al., 2005) and longevity (Chida & Steptoe, 2008; Xu &

Roberts, 2010). A positive emotional style has been tied to lower cortisol levels (Polk et al., 2005), better responses to vaccinations (Marsland, Cohen, Rabin, & Manuck, 2006), resistance to illness following exposure to a flu virus (Cohen, Alper, Doyle, Treanor, & Turner, 2006), lower levels of CHD-related risk factors (Tsenkova, Love, Singer, & Ryff, 2008), and lower risk of some causes of death (Moskowitz, Epel, & Acree, 2008), among other beneficial outcomes. In addition to general well-being, there are specific positive psychological resources that contribute to coping and, in turn, to mental and physical health.

Optimism An optimistic nature can lead people to cope more effectively with stress and thereby reduce their risk for illness (Scheier, Carver, & Bridges, 1994). M. F. Scheier and colleagues developed a measure of dispositional optimism aimed at identifying generalized expectations that outcomes will be positive. Box 7.1 lists the items on this measure, the Life Orientation Test (LOT). As can be seen from the items, some measure optimism, whereas others assess pessimism.

In one study, college students completed measures of optimism, perceived stress, depression, and social stress at the beginning of the school year and again at the end of the first semester. The optimists experienced less stress and depression and enjoyed more social support. The optimists were more likely to seek out social support and to positively reinterpret the stressful circumstances they encountered, which was why they coped with the transition to college better (Brissette, Scheier, & Carver, 2002).

Exactly how might optimism exert a positive impact on symptom expression, psychological adjustment, and health outcomes? Optimists have a more positive mood, which can beneficially affect immunity (Segerstrom & Sephton, 2010). For example, the tendency to experience positive emotional states has been tied to greater resistance to the common cold (Cohen et al., 2003). Optimism also promotes more active and persistent coping efforts, which may improve long-term prospects for psychological adjustment and health (Segerstrom, Castañeda, & Spencer, 2003). Optimism may foster a sense of personal control, which has beneficial effects on physical functioning (Ruthig & Chipperfield, 2006). Optimists use more problem-focused coping and social support seeking, and they emphasize the positive aspects of stressful situations (Scheier, Weintraub, & Carver, 1986). In a study with coronary artery bypass patients (Scheier et al., 1989), optimists used more problem-focused coping

BOX **7.1**

The Measurement of Optimism: The LOT-R

People vary in whether they are fundamentally optimistic or pessimistic about life. M. F. Scheier, C. S. Carver, and M. W. Bridges (1994) developed a scale of dispositional optimism to measure this pervasive individual difference. Items from the Life Orientation Test are as follows. (For each item, answer "true" or "false.")

1. In uncertain times, I usually expect the best.
2. It's easy for me to relax.
3. If something can go wrong for me, it will.
4. I'm always optimistic about my future.
5. I enjoy my friends a lot.
6. It's important for me to keep busy.
7. I hardly ever expect things to go my way.
8. I don't get upset too easily.
9. I rarely count on good things happening to me.
10. Overall, I expect more good things to happen to me than bad.

Scoring
Sum how many "trues" you indicated for items 1, 4, and 10 and how many "falses" you indicated for items 3, 7, and 9 to obtain an overall score. Items 2, 5, 6, and 8 are filler items only.

and made less use of denial. They had a faster rate of recovery during hospitalization and a faster rate of returning to normal life activities after discharge. There was also a strong relationship between optimism and postsurgical quality of life 6 months later, with optimists doing better.

Optimism has health benefits (Segerstrom, 2006b). To begin with, optimists and pessimists differ in their physiological functioning. Pessimistic and anxious adults not only feel more negative but also have higher blood pressures than more optimistic adults (Räikkönen, Matthews, Flory, Owens, & Gump, 1999). Pessimists have higher levels of inflammation, explained in part by their enhanced risk for obesity, hypertension, and diabetes (Roy et al., 2010). An optimistic style, by contrast, is protective against the risk of coronary heart disease in older men (Kubzansky, Sparrow, Vokonas, & Kawachi, 2001), side effects of cancer treatments (de Moor et al., 2006), pain following surgery (Rosenberger, Kerns, Jokl, & Ickovics, 2009), cancer mortality among the elderly (Schulz, Bookwala, Knapp, Scheier, & Williamson, 1996), pain (Geers, Wellman, Helfer, Fowler, & France, 2008), loss of pulmonary function (Kubzansky et al., 2002), and illness-related disruption of social and recreational activities among breast cancer patients (Carver, Lehman, & Antoni, 2003). Optimism also makes people more attentive to personally relevant risk information (Geers, Wellman, Seligman, Wuyek, & Neff, 2010).

Optimism is not always beneficial, however. Because they are more persistent in pursuing goals, optimists sometimes experience short-term physiological costs (Segerstrom, 2001). When optimists' expectations are not met, as when they try to cope with especially difficult stressors, they may experience stress and compromised immune functioning as a result of their persistent unsuccessful efforts to cope (Segerstrom, 2006a). Overall, though, optimism is a potent and valuable resource. It helps people deal with stressful events by getting them to deploy their personal resources and coping skills more effectively (Segerstrom, 2006b).

Psychological Control The belief that one can exert control over stressful events has long been known to help people cope with stress (Taylor, Helgeson, Reed, & Skokan, 1991; Thompson, 1981). **Psychological control** is the belief that one can determine one's own behavior, influence one's environment, and bring about desired outcomes. Perceived control is closely related to self-efficacy, which is a more narrow perception that one can take the necessary actions to obtain a specific outcome in a specific situation (Bandura, 1977). Both types of beliefs help people cope with a wide variety of stressful events (Wrosch, Schulz, Miller, Lupien, & Dunne, 2007). For example, as we noted in Chapter 5, East German migrants to West Germany who found themselves unemployed often turned to alcohol for solace unless they had high feelings of self-efficacy; those migrants with high feelings of self-efficacy, which appeared to buffer them against the stress of unemployment, did not abuse alcohol.

Perceptions of control in one's work life and in the general tasks of living may protect against a risky lifestyle that involves health-compromising behaviors (Wickrama, Conger, & Lorenz, 1995). Across a wide variety of investigations, the belief that one can control stressful events has been related to emotional well-being, successful coping with a stressful event, good health behaviors (Gale, Batty, & Deary, 2008), good performance on cognitive tasks, and good health (Thompson & Spacapan, 1991). For example, among adolescents with asthma, beliefs in personal control are associated with better immune responses related to their disease (Chen, Fisher, Bacharier, & Strunk, 2003). A sense of control or mastery has also been linked to a lower risk for mortality, primarily that due to cardiovascular disease (Surtees, Wainwright, Luben, Khaw, & Day, 2006), and lower levels of cardiovascular risk factors (Mausbach et al., 2008; Paquet, Dubé, Gauvin, Kestens, & Daniel, 2010). Control may be especially important for vulnerable people, such as medical patients, children, and the elderly, who are at risk for health problems (Wrosch et al., 2007). Because control may be problematic for people who already have little opportunity to exercise control (Thompson & Spacapan, 1991), anything that enhances perceptions of control may benefit such individuals.

So powerful are the effects of psychological control that they have been used extensively in interventions to promote good health habits and to help people cope with stressful events such as surgery and noxious medical procedures. In Chapters 4 and 5, we saw how self-efficacy influences a wide variety of health behaviors, including exercising and stopping smoking. When people perceive events in their environment as controllable or regard their coping efforts as likely to succeed, the stress they experience is lessened, their distress is lower, and their physiological responses to stress are reduced.

Stressful Medical Procedures and Control-Enhancing Interventions
As an example, the principle of control has been used to intervene with people who are anticipating unpleasant medical procedures, such as gastroendoscopic examinations (Johnson & Leventhal, 1974), childbirth (Leventhal, Leventhal, Schacham, & Easterling, 1989), chemotherapy (Burish & Lyles, 1979), hysterectomies (Johnson, Christman, & Stitt, 1985), radiation therapy (Johnson, Lauver, & Nail, 1989), and cardiac catheterization (Kendall et al.,

1979), among many others. Reviewing a large number of studies, R. Ludwick-Rosenthal and R. W. J. Neufeld (1988) concluded that **control-enhancing interventions** that make use of information, relaxation, and cognitive-behavioral techniques, such as learning to think differently about the unpleasant sensations of a procedure, are all successful in reducing anxiety, improving coping, and enabling people to overcome the adverse effects of medical procedures more quickly.

Like optimism, control is not a panacea for all aversive situations. People who have a high desire for control may especially benefit from control-based interventions (Thompson, Cheek, & Graham, 1988). But control may actually be aversive if it gives people more responsibility than they want (Chipperfield & Perry, 2006). Too much control, as through too much information or too many choices, may be stressful, exacerbating distress over medical decisions (see, for example, Mills & Krantz, 1979; Thompson et al., 1988). Nonetheless, the benefits of control, especially in treatment settings, are clear.

Additional Coping Resources

High **self-esteem** improves coping. In one study of students facing exams, those with high self-esteem were less likely to become upset in response to stress (Shimizu & Pelham, 2004). However, self-esteem seems to be most protective at low levels of stress; at higher levels of stress, the stressful events themselves can overwhelm the benefits of self-esteem (Whisman & Kwon, 1993). High self-esteem can be associated with lower levels of HPA axis activity (Seeman et al., 1995), which may be the route whereby self-esteem affects illness.

Interventions designed to enhance a sense of self have been found to improve responses to stressful events. In an experimental study, for example, J. D. Creswell and associates (2005) assigned some people to focus on and write about their important values, and others about less important values. All participants then went through laboratory stressors, including doing mental arithmetic and delivering a speech to an unresponsive audience. The results revealed that people who had affirmed their important personal values showed lower biological responses to stress and, among those with high self-esteem, experienced less psychological stress as well.

Related to self-esteem is a cluster of personal qualities called ego strength—dependability, trust, and lack of impulsivity—that appear to have health benefits (Deary, Batty, Pattie, & Gale, 2008). In a longitudinal investigation (Friedman et al., 1995), researchers studied children who had first been interviewed in 1947. Some had impulsive and undercontrolled personalities, whereas others showed signs of ego strength. Those who were high in ego strength as children lived longer as adults. One reason was that they were somewhat less likely to smoke and use alcohol to excess (see also Temcheff et al., 2010).

Conscientiousness is associated with longevity (Kern, Friedman, Martin, Reynolds, & Luong, 2009; Taylor et al., 2009). One study (Friedman et al., 1993) looked at ratings of personality for youngsters in 1921 and 1922 to see if differences in personality would predict who lived longer. The researchers found that those children who were highly conscientious were more likely to live to an old age (Friedman et al., 1995). It may be that conscientious people are more successful in avoiding situations that could harm them, and they may also practice good health habits more reliably (O'Cleirigh, Ironson, Weiss, & Costa, 2007; O'Connor, Conner, Jones, McMillan, & Ferguson, 2009).

Being self-confident and having an easygoing disposition also mute the likelihood that stressful events will lead to psychological distress (Holahan & Moos, 1990, 1991), perhaps because self-confident, easygoing individuals cope with stressful events more actively (Holahan & Moos, 1990). Nonetheless, cheerful people die somewhat sooner than people who are not cheerful (Friedman et al., 1993). It may be that cheerful people grow up being more careless about their health and, as a result, encounter health risks (Martin et al., 2002).

Being smart is good for you as well. More intelligent people live longer (Deary et al., 2008). Emotional stability also predicts longevity (Terracciano, Löckenhoff, Zonderman, Ferrucci, & Costa, 2008; Weiss, Gale, Batty, & Deary, 2009).

To summarize, coping resources are important because they help people to manage the demands of a job, neighborhood stress, financial strain, and daily stressful events with less emotional distress, fewer health risks, and a higher quality of life (Steptoe & Marmot, 2003). Thus, just as some people appear to have an illness-prone personality, other people possess a health-prone personality, characterized by optimism, a sense of control, conscientiousness, self-esteem, and resilience.

Sources of Resilience

Coping resources and effective coping are sources of resilience against stress. Positive life events, positive emotions, and opportunities for rest, relaxation, and renewal

may help people cope more effectively with life stressors and/or prevent stressful events from taking a toll on health (Ong, Bergeman, Bisconti, & Wallace, 2006; Ryff & Singer, 2000). Experiencing positive events and having the opportunity to describe them or celebrate them with others affects both immediate mood and long-term well-being (Langston, 1994).

Exactly what restorative activities benefit health is not yet fully known. One restful event, however—taking a vacation—is now known to be beneficial for the health of one group—middle-aged men at risk for heart disease (Gump & Matthews, 2000). Whether similar positive experiences are beneficial for other people remains to be seen.

Resilience also reflects individual differences in how people cope with stressful events (Mancini & Bonanno, 2009). Some people seem to recover from stressful events quickly, whereas others do not. Psychological resilience is characterized by the ability to bounce back from negative emotional experiences and to adapt flexibly to the changing demands of stressful experiences (Fredrickson, Tugade, Waugh, & Larkin, 2003). Being able to experience positive emotions, even in the context of otherwise intensely stressful events, appears to be one way of coping that resilient people draw on (Tugade & Fredrickson, 2004). For example, being able to experience positive emotions, such as gratitude or love, following the 9/11 attacks enabled many people to cope with these distressing events and to experience post-traumatic growth.

A sense of coherence about one's life (Jorgensen, Frankowski, & Carey, 1999), a sense of purpose or meaning in one's life (Visotsky, Hamburg, Goss, & Lebovitz, 1961), a sense of humor (Cousins, 1979), trust in others (Barefoot et al., 1998), a sense that life is worth living (Sone et al., 2008), and religious beliefs (Folkman & Moskowitz, 2004) (Box 7.2) are all resources that promote effective coping.

Coping Style

Coping style is a propensity to deal with stressful events in a particular way. As an example, we all know people who deal with stress by talking a lot about it, whereas other people keep their problems to themselves. Coping styles have their origins in both genes and personal experience. Coping styles, then, are similar to personality traits in that they characterize a person's way of behaving in a general fashion, but they are more specific than personality traits because they come into play primarily when events become stressful.

BOX 7.2

Religion, Coping, and Well-Being

I just prayed and prayed and God stopped that thing just before it would have hit us.

—Tornado survivor

Long before researchers were studying coping, people going through stressful or traumatic events were encouraged by their family, friends, and religious counselors to turn to their faith and to God for solace, comfort, and insight. Surveys (Gallup Poll, 2009) indicate that the majority of people in the United States believe in God (80%), report attending church services at least once a month (55%), and say that religion is important in their personal lives (80%). Religion, then, appears to be an important part of American life. It may be especially so for women and some minority groups, such as African Americans (Holt, Clark, Kreuter, & Rubio, 2003).

Religion (or spirituality, independent of organized religion) can promote a sense of psychological well-being. People with strong spiritual beliefs report greater life satisfaction, greater personal happiness, and fewer negative consequences of traumatic life events in comparison with people who are not spiritual (George, Ellison, & Larson, 2002; Romero et al., 2006). Many people report that spiritual beliefs are helpful to them when they must cope with a stressful event. Surveys find that nearly half the population in the United States uses prayer to deal with health problems (Zimmerman, 2005, March 15), and it seems to work. For example, surgery patients with stronger religious beliefs experienced fewer complications and had shorter hospital stays than those with less strong religious beliefs (Contrada et al., 2004).

Religion (or spirituality) may be helpful for coping for several reasons. First, it provides a belief system and a way of thinking about stressful events that lessens distress and enables people to find meaning in the stressful events they encounter (Laubmeier, Zakowski, & Blair, 2004). Second, it provides a source of social support. Organized religion often confers a sense of group identity for people because it provides a network of supportive individuals who share their beliefs (George et al., 2002). For example,

in a study of parents who had lost an infant to sudden infant death syndrome, both components of religion—its importance as a belief system and active participation in a church— helped parents cope with their loss (McIntosh, Silver, & Wortman, 1993). Religion may also be associated with a healthier life style (Park, Edmondson, Hale-Smith, & Blank, 2009). Prayer itself, however, does not appear to have health benefits (Masters & Spielmans, 2007; Nicholson, Rose, & Martin, 2010).

Spiritual beliefs can lead to better health practices (Hill, Ellison, Burdette, & Musick, 2007), better health (Krause, Ingersoll-Dayton, Liang, & Sugisawa, 1999), and longer life (Koenig & Vaillant, 2009; McCullough, Friedman, Enders, & Martin, 2009; Schnall et al., 2008). Religious attendance protects against high blood pressure (Gillum & Ingram, 2006), complications from surgery (Ai, Wink, Tice, Bolling, & Shearer, 2009), and headache (Wachholtz & Pargament, 2008) among other disorders and symptoms (Berntson, Norman, Hawkley, & Cacioppo, 2008), perhaps because of its promotion of a health lifestyle (Musick, House, & Williams, 2004). However, religious beliefs do not appear to retard the progression of cancer or speed recovery from acute illness (Powell, Shahabi, & Thoresen, 2003). The benefits of religion for health may be due to the lesser cardiovascular, neuroendocrine, and immune function responses to stressful events that occur when religion is used for coping (Maselko, Kubzansky, Kawachi, Seeman, & Berkman, 2007; Seeman, Dubin, & Seeman, 2003).

Religious beliefs are not always an unmitigated blessing, however. If people see their health disorders as punishments from God, or if their health problems lead them to struggle with their faith, they may experience more psychological and physical distress (Gall, Kristjansson, Charbonneau, & Florack, 2009; Sherman, Plante, Simonton, Latif, & Anaissie, 2009). Nonetheless, typically religion is not only a meaningful part of life but can offer mental and physical health benefits (George et al., 2002; Powell et al., 2003).

Religion promotes psychological well-being, and those people with religious faith may be better able to cope with aversive events.

Much coping is proactive, that is, people anticipate potential stressors and act in advance, either to prevent them or to reduce their impact (Aspinwall & Taylor, 1997; Aspinwall, 2011). Proactive coping thus requires a set of important skills involving, first, the abilities to anticipate or detect potential stressors; second, coping skills for managing them; and third, self-regulatory skills, which are the processes through which people control, direct, and correct their actions as they move toward or away from various goals.

Proactive coping has been understudied because, by definition, if stressors are headed off in advance or reduced, they are less likely to occur or be experienced as intensely stressful, and therefore the proactive skills that led to such beneficial outcomes may remain unknown. Clearly though, heading off a stressor is preferable to coping with it when it hits full force, and so this aspect of coping merits additional attention by coping researchers (Aspinwall, 2011).

Approach Versus Avoidance   Some people cope with a threatening event by using an **avoidant (minimizing) coping style,** whereas others use an **approach (confrontative, vigilant) coping style,** by gathering information or taking direct action. Although each style can have advantages, on the whole, approach-related coping is more successful than avoidant coping and is tied to better mental and physical health outcomes. Approach-related coping is especially helpful if one can focus on the information present in the situation rather than on one's emotions and if specific actions can be taken to reduce the stressor (Taylor & Stanton, 2007).

People who cope with threatening events through approach-related methods may engage in the cognitive and emotional efforts needed to deal with long-term threats. In the short term, however, they may pay a price in anxiety and physiological reactivity (Smith, Ruiz, & Uchino, 2000). Thus, the avoider or minimizer may cope well with a trip to the dentist but poorly with on-going job stress. In contrast, the vigilant coper may fret over the visit to the dentist but take active efforts to reduce stress on the job.

Whether avoidant or approach-related coping is successful also depends on how long-term the stressor is. People who cope with stress by minimizing or avoiding threatening events may deal effectively with short-term threats (Wong & Kaloupek, 1986). However, if the stress persists over time, avoidance is not as successful. For example, much of the U.S. population reported high levels of post-traumatic stress disorder symptoms following the 9/11 attacks. Those who coped through avoidant coping strategies fared worse psychologically over the long term compared with those who used more active coping strategies (Silver, Holman, McIntosh, Poulin, & Gil-Rivas, 2002). The reason may be that people who cope using avoidance may not make enough cognitive and emotional efforts to anticipate and manage long-term problems (Suls & Fletcher, 1985; Taylor & Stanton, 2007).

Studies of short-term threats may have underestimated how unsuccessful avoidant coping strategies are. Substantial evidence now indicates that approach coping is generally associated with beneficial outcomes, such as less psychological distress and lower stress-related biological responses, whereas avoidance is associated with poor psychological and health outcomes (Wolf & Mori, 2009; see Taylor & Stanton, 2007, for a review).

Problem-Focused and Emotion-Focused Coping

Another useful distinction is between problem-focused and emotion-focused coping (cf. Folkman, Schaefer, & Lazarus, 1979; Leventhal & Nerenz, 1982; Pearlin & Schooler, 1978). **Problem-focused coping** involves attempts to do something constructive about the stressful conditions that are harming, threatening, or challenging an individual. **Emotion-focused coping** involves efforts to regulate emotions experienced because of the stressful event. Problem-focused coping skills appear to emerge during childhood; emotion-focused coping skills develop somewhat later, in late childhood or early adolescence (Compas, Barnez, Malcarne, & Worsham, 1991). Typically people use both problem-focused and emotion-focused coping during stressful events, suggesting that both types of coping are useful (Folkman & Lazarus, 1980).

However, the nature of the event also contributes to what coping strategies will be used (Vitaliano et al., 1990). For example, work-related problems lead people most commonly to use problem-focused coping, such as taking direct action or seeking help from others. Health problems, in contrast, lead to more emotion-focused coping, perhaps because health threats often must be tolerated but may not be amenable to direct action. When health problems are amenable to active coping, however, problem-focused coping is beneficial (Penley, Tomaka, & Wiebe, 2002). These findings suggest that situations in which something constructive can be done will favor problem-focused coping, whereas those situations that simply must be accepted favor emotion-focused coping (Zakowski, Hall, Klein, & Baum, 2001).

Emotion-focused coping includes coping of two kinds. One involves emotional distress, as may be experienced in rumination. Ruminating, that is, negative recurrent thoughts focused on a stressor, is detrimental to health (Thomsen et al., 2004).

The other type of emotion-focused coping is **emotional-approach coping**, which involves clarifying, focusing on, and working through the emotions experienced in conjunction with a stressor (Stanton, 2010). This type of coping is beneficial. Emotional-approach coping improves adjustment to many chronic conditions,

Coping researchers have found that direct action often leads to better adjustment to a stressful event than do coping efforts aimed at avoidance of the issue or denial.

including chronic pain (Smith, Lumley, & Longo, 2002), and medical conditions such as pregnancy (Huizink, Robles de Medina, Mulder, Visser, & Buitelaar, 2002) and breast cancer (Stanton, Kirk, Cameron, & Danoff-Burg, 2000). Even managing the stressors of daily life can benefit from emotional-approach coping (Stanton et al., 2000). For example, both emotional-approach coping and problem-focused coping predicted well-being in medical school in a study of medical students (Park & Adler, 2003). Coping via emotional approach appears to be especially beneficial for women (Stanton et al., 2000).

There are several reasons why emotional approach coping may be so successful. One is that it may be soothing and beneficially affect stress regulatory systems (Epstein, Sloan, & Marx, 2005). Another possibility is that it leads people to affirm important aspects of their identity, which leads to health benefits (Creswell et al., 2007; Low, Stanton, & Danoff-Burg, 2006).

Specific Coping Strategies

A seriously ill cancer patient was asked how she managed to cope with her disease so well. She responded, "I try to have cracked crab and raspberries every week." Although her particular choice of coping strategy may be somewhat unusual, her answer illustrates the importance of personal coping strategies for dealing with stressful events.

Research has focused on these more specific coping strategies as well as general coping strategies. This shift has occurred in part because general coping styles measured at the trait level do not always predict how people behave in specific situations (Schwartz, Neale, Marco, Shiffman, & Stone, 1999). Such an approach also provides a more fine-grained analysis of exactly how people manage the myriad stressful events they confront each day. C. S. Carver and colleagues (Carver, Scheier, & Weintraub, 1989) developed a measure called the COPE to assess the specific coping strategies people employ to deal with stressful events. Examples from this widely used instrument appear in Box 7.3.

Some researchers prefer to look at coping in an even more microscopic fashion. A. A. Stone and J. M. Neale (1984) developed a measure of daily coping designed to chart how changes in coping on a day-to-day basis influence psychological and health outcomes (Stone, Kennedy-Moore, & Neale, 1995). Examples of the coping strategies used to combat the threat of AIDS appear in Box 7.4.

People who are able to shift their coping strategies to meet the demands of a situation cope better with stress than those who do not. This point is, of course, suggested by the fact that the problem-solving and emotional approaches may work better for different stressors. Overall, research suggests that people who are flexible copers may cope especially well with stress (Cheng, 2003).

■ COPING AND EXTERNAL RESOURCES

Coping is influenced not only by the internal resources, such as coping resources and styles, but also by external resources. These include time, money, education, a decent job, friends, family, standard of living, the presence of positive life events, and the absence of other life stressors.

Individuals with greater resources typically cope with stressful events better because time, money, friends, and other resources simply provide more ways of dealing with a stressful event. For example, divorce is typically a very stressful experience. However, men and women with higher income, higher educational achievement, and a greater number of close friends experience less distress (Booth & Amato, 1991). In Chapter 6, we saw another example of the moderation of stress by resources. Relative to nonworking women, working women who had adequate child care and whose husbands shared in homemaking tasks benefited psychologically from their work, whereas women without these resources showed higher levels of distress.

One of the most potent external resources with respect to health is socioeconomic status (SES). People who are high in SES have fewer medical and psychiatric disorders of all kinds, and they show lower mortality from all causes of death. So strong is this relationship that, even in animals, higher-status animals are less vulnerable to infection than lower-status animals are (Cohen, Doyle, Skoner, Rabin, & Gwaltney, 1997). Figure 7.2 illustrates the relation between social class and mortality (see Adler, Boyce, Chesney, Folkman, & Syme, 1993).

The presence of other life stressors also moderates coping responses, acting, in essence, as a resource depleter. People who must simultaneously deal with several sources of stress in their lives—such as a failing marriage, financial difficulties, or health problems—have fewer resources left to use for coping with a new stressor than will people who do not have to deal with other life stressors (Cohen & Lazarus, 1979).

BOX **7.3**

The Brief COPE

The Brief COPE assesses commonly used coping styles for managing stressful events. People rate how they are coping with a stressful event by answering items on a scale from 0 ("I haven't been doing this at all") to 3 ("I've been doing this a lot"). Think of a stressful event that you are currently going through (a problem with your family, a roommate difficulty, problems in a course), and see which coping methods you use.

1. Active coping

    I've been concentrating my efforts on doing something about the situation I'm in.
    I've been taking action to try to make the situation better.

2. Planning

    I've been trying to come up with a strategy about what to do.
    I've been thinking hard about what steps to take.

3. Positive reframing

    I've been trying to see it in a different light, to make it seem more positive.
    I've been looking for something good in what is happening.

4. Acceptance

    I've been accepting the reality of the fact that it has happened.
    I've been learning to live with it.

5. Humor

    I've been making jokes about it.
    I've been making fun of the situation.

6. Religion

    I've been trying to find comfort in my religion or spiritual beliefs.
    I've been praying or meditating.

7. Using emotional support

    I've been getting emotional support from others.
    I've been getting comfort and understanding from someone.

8. Using instrumental support

    I've been trying to get advice or help from other people about what to do.
    I've been getting help and advice from other people.

9. Self-distraction

    I've been turning to work or other activities to take my mind off things.
    I've been doing something to think about it less, such as going to movies, watching TV, reading, daydreaming, sleeping, or shopping.

10. Denial

    I've been saying to myself "this isn't real."
    I've been refusing to believe that it has happened.

11. Venting

    I've been saying things to let my unpleasant feelings escape.
    I've been expressing my negative feelings.

12. Substance use

    I've been using alcohol or other drugs to make myself feel better.
    I've been using alcohol or other drugs to help me get through it.

13. Behavioral disengagement

    I've been giving up trying to deal with it.
    I've been giving up the attempt to cope.

14. Self-blame

    I've been criticizing myself.
    I've been blaming myself for things that happened.

Source: Carver, 1997.

■ COPING OUTCOMES

Throughout our discussion, we have referred to successful coping. What constitutes successful coping? Coping efforts center on several main tasks (Cohen & Lazarus, 1979):

- Reducing harmful environmental conditions
- Tolerating or adjusting to negative events or realities
- Maintaining a positive self-image
- Maintaining emotional equilibrium
- Continuing satisfying relationships with others
- Enhancing the prospects of recovery, if relevant

To the extent that these tasks are successfully addressed, a person may be said to have coped successfully.

BOX 7.4

Coping with AIDS

AIDS (acquired immune deficiency syndrome) has killed millions of people worldwide, and thousands more live, sometimes for years, with the knowledge that they have the disease. Such a threat requires and elicits many forms of coping, some of which are illustrated in the following excerpts from interviews with AIDS patients. These are valuable insights for people not struggling with a potentially fatal disease as well.

SOCIAL SUPPORT OR SEEKING INFORMATION

A key point in my program is that I have a really good support network of people who are willing to take the time, who will go the extra mile for me. I have spent years cultivating these friendships.

My family has been extremely supportive, and my lover has been extremely supportive, but it really wasn't quite enough. They weren't helping me in the right ways. That's when I went and got a therapist. Basically, she is the one who has helped me cope with [AIDS] and understand it.

DIRECT ACTION

My main concern is making it through another day without getting any disorder. I would really like to completely beat it.

My first concern was that, as promiscuous as I have been, I could not accept giving this to anyone. So I have been changing my lifestyle completely, putting everything else on the back burner.

The main thing I did was to get all my paperwork in order. I was good at it before, but when AIDS hit, I made sure everything was spelled out perfectly, and I figure that makes it easier for my lover left behind. He will go through grief, but he will not have to be sorting through all my junk.

STRATEGIES OF DISTRACTION, ESCAPE, OR AVOIDANCE

I used to depend on drugs a lot to change my mood. Once in a while, I still find that if I can't feel better any other way, I will take a puff of grass or have a glass of wine, or I use music. There are certain recordings that can really change my mood drastically. I play it loud and I dance around and try to clear my head.

There's an old disco song that says, "Keep out of my mind what's out of my hands." I try to do that, to not fret over things I really don't have control over.

It was important to me to focus on something besides AIDS, and my job is the most logical thing. I'm very good at what I do. I have a supervisory position, so I deal with other people's problems, which is good for me, because I take their problems and solve them and I forget about mine. I think that's a real constructive distraction for me. I drive. I feel so much more at peace when I am driving down the road in a car, listening to music, having my dog next to me. It is wonderful.

EMOTIONAL REGULATION/VENTILATION

When you're sad, you cry. That's what I've done a lot lately, over silly, well, not silly things, but over small things, and over reminders of a life that's probably cut short, the expectations of things that you were going to do and planned on doing and don't seem possible now.

I try to be like Spock on *Star Trek*. So this is an emotion. So that's what it makes you feel like. I try to analyze it and look as a third party would, like I am an observer from the fiftieth century.

Sometimes I will allow myself to have darker feelings, and then I grab myself by the bootstraps and say, okay, that is fine, you are allowed to have these feelings but they are not going to run your life.

PERSONAL GROWTH

In the beginning, AIDS made me feel like a poisoned dart, like I was a diseased person and I had no self-esteem and no self-confidence. That's what I have been really working on, is to get the self-confidence and the self-esteem back. I don't know if I will ever be there, but I feel very close to being there, to feeling like my old self.

I've made sure everybody knows how I feel about them. I have given away some of my precious things, some back to the people who gave them to me. I make sure that everyone has something from my past, everyone who's been important in my life, and for the most part, I've sent them all letters too. Not that it was always received well . . .

When something like this happens to you, you can either melt and disappear or you can come out stronger than you did before. It has made me a much stronger person. I literally feel like I can cope with anything. Nothing scares me, nothing. If I was on a 747 and they

BOX 7.4

Coping with AIDS (*continued*)

said we were going down, I would probably reach for a magazine.

POSITIVE THINKING AND RESTRUCTURING

Everyone dies sooner or later. I have been appreciating how beautiful the Earth is, flowers, and the things I like. I used to go around ignoring all those things. Now I stop to try and smell the roses more often, and just do pleasurable things.

I have been spending a lot of time lately on having a more positive attitude. I force myself to become aware every time I say something negative during a day, and I go, "Oops," and I change it and I rephrase it. So I say, "Wonderful," about 42,000 times a day. Sometimes I don't mean it, but I am convincing myself that I do. The last chapter has not been written. The fat lady has not sung. I'm still here.

Source: Reed, 1989.

FIGURE 7.2 | **Mortality Rate Ratios by Socioeconomic Status** (*Source:* Steenland, Hu, & Walker, 2004)

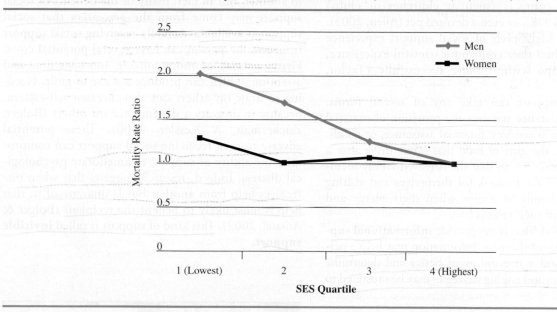

In addition, to assess successful coping, researchers have looked at a variety of specific outcomes. One set of **coping outcomes** has included measures of physiological and biochemical functioning. Coping efforts are generally judged to be more successful if they reduce arousal (and its indicators, such as heart rate, pulse, and skin conductivity) or keep blood or urine levels of catecholamines and corticosteroids at low levels.

A second criterion of successful coping is whether and how quickly people can return to their prestress activities. Many stressors—especially severe ones, such as the death of a spouse, or chronic ones, such as excessive noise—interfere with daily life activities. If

people's coping efforts enable them to resume usual activities, coping may be judged to be successful. In some cases, however, life is actually improved following a stressful event. Thus, in these cases, priorities may be reevaluated, and a person may seek to live a better and different life.

Third, and most commonly, researchers judge coping effectiveness as reducing psychological distress. When a person's anxiety or depression is reduced, the coping response is judged to be successful. Finally, coping can be judged in terms of whether it terminates, lessens, or shortens the duration of the stressful event itself (Harnish, Aseltine, & Gore, 2000).

■ SOCIAL SUPPORT

The most vital of all protective psychosocial resources is social support. Social ties and relationships with others have long been regarded as emotionally satisfying aspects of life. They can also mute the effects of stress, help people cope with stressful events, and reduce the likelihood that stress will lead to poor health.

What Is Social Support?

Social support is defined as information from others that one is loved and cared for, esteemed and valued, and part of a network of communication and mutual obligations. Social support can come from parents, a spouse or lover, other relatives, friends, social and community contacts (such as churches or clubs) (Rietschlin, 1998), or even a devoted pet (Allen, 2003). People with high levels of social support experience less stress when they confront a stressful experience, and they cope with it more successfully (Taylor, 2010).

Social support can take any of several forms. **Tangible assistance** involves the provision of material support, such as services, financial assistance, or goods. For example, the gifts of food that often arrive after a death in a family mean that the bereaved family members will not have to cook for themselves and visiting friends and family at a time when their energy and enthusiasm for such tasks is low.

Family and friends can provide **informational support** about stressful events. Information may help a person understand a stressful event better and determine what resources and coping strategies may be mustered to deal with it. For example, if an individual is facing an uncomfortable medical procedure, a friend who went through the same thing could provide information about the exact steps involved, the potential discomfort involved, and how long it takes.

During times of stress, people may experience bouts of depression, sadness, anxiety, and low self-esteem. Supportive friends and family can provide **emotional support** by reassuring the person that he or she is a valuable individual who is cared for. The warmth and nurturance provided by other people can enable a person under stress to approach it with greater assurance (Box 7.5).

The types of social support just discussed involve the actual provision of help and solace by one person to another. But in fact, many of the benefits of social support may come from the *perception* that social support is available. Actually receiving social support from another person can have several potential costs. First, one may be monopolizing another's time and attention, which can produce a sense of guilt. Needing to draw on others can also threaten self-esteem, because it suggests a dependence on others (Bolger, Zuckerman, & Kessler, 2000). These potential adverse costs of receiving social support can compromise the ability of support to ameliorate psychological distress. Indeed, research suggests that when one receives help from another but is unaware of it, that help is most likely to benefit the recipient (Bolger & Amarel, 2007). This kind of support is called **invisible support.**

Humor has long been thought to be an effective defense against stress.

In addition to being an enjoyable aspect of life, social support from family and friends helps keep people healthy and may help them recover faster when they are ill.

BOX 7.5

Is Social Companionship an Important Part of Your Life?

How would you describe your life? Take a few moments to write down a few paragraphs about how your life has progressed so far. What have been the major events of your life? What has been important to you? Now go back to see how often you mention other people in those paragraphs.

Two psychologists, Sarah Pressman and Sheldon Cohen (2007), did precisely this. They looked at the autobiographies of 96 psychologists and 220 literary writers and counted how often the authors mentioned social relationships. Pressman and Cohen then related the number of mentions of relationships to how long the writer lived.

They found that the number of social words used in these autobiographies predicted an increased life span for both the psychologists and the writers. Why would this be the case? Pressman and Cohen reasoned that social words used in autobiographies provide an indirect measure of the social relationships with which these people were engaged. As we have seen, good social relationships are associated with longer life.

So, to the extent that you mentioned important social relationships in your autobiography, it reflects positively on your ability to experience social support and ultimately to enjoy good health and a long life.

Effects of Social Support on Psychological Distress

Not having social support in times of need can itself be very stressful. For example, the elderly, the recently widowed, and victims of sudden, severe, uncontrollable life events may need support but have difficulty getting it (Sorkin, Rook, & Lu, 2002). In addition, people who have difficulty with social relationships, such as those who are chronically shy (Naliboff et al., 2004) or who anticipate rejection by others (Cole, Kemeny, Fahey, Zack, & Naliboff, 2003), are at risk for isolating themselves socially, with the result that they experience more psychological distress and are at greater risk for health problems. Loneliness leads to health risks, in large part because lonely people appear to have more trouble sleeping and show more cardiovascular activation (Cacioppo et al., 2002; Hawkley, Burleson, Berntson, & Cacioppo, 2003).

Simply believing that support is available (Smith, Ruiz, & Uchino, 2004) or contemplating the sources of support one typically has in life (Broadwell & Light, 1999) can yield these beneficial effects. Even a supportive video playing in the background while a person is going through a stressful event can have these beneficial effects (Thorsteinsson, James, & Gregg, 1998).

These calming effects are greater when support comes from a friend than from a stranger (Christenfeld, 1997). Both men and women seem to benefit somewhat more when the support provider is female rather than male (Glynn, Christenfeld, & Gerin, 1999). In fact, when women perform stressful tasks in the presence of a male partner, they sometimes are more stressed than when they complete such tasks alone (Kirschbaum,

Klauer, Filipp, & Hellhammer, 1995), unless their partner is actively supportive (Ditzen et al., 2007).

Going through a stressful event in the presence of a pet can keep heart rate and blood pressure lower (Allen, Blascovich, & Mendes, 2002). Dogs are somewhat better at providing social support than other pets. Even a short encounter with a friendly dog has been found to increase opioid functioning and to decrease levels of stress-related hormones such as cortisol; interestingly, the dogs experience many of these benefits as well (Odendaal & Meintjes, 2002). On the whole, the research suggests that interactions with pets typically lead to beneficial effects for both mental and physical health (Beck & Meyers, 1996).

Effects of Social Support on Illness and Health Habits

Social support can lower the likelihood of illness, speed recovery from illness or treatment (Krohne & Slangen, 2005), and reduce the risk of mortality due to serious disease (House, Landis, & Umberson, 1988; Rutledge, Matthews, Lui, Stone, & Cauley, 2003). Studies that control for initial health status show that people who have a high quantity and sometimes a high quality of social relationships have lower mortality rates (Berkman, 1985; House et al., 1988). Social isolation is a major risk factor for death for both humans and animals (House et al., 1988). Thus, the evidence linking social support to a reduced risk of mortality is substantial.

Social support may achieve health benefits, in part, by affecting inflammation (Penwell & Larkin, 2010). In a study of the common cold, healthy volunteers reported their social ties, such as whether they had a spouse, living parents, friends, or workmates, and whether they were members of social groups, such as clubs. The volunteers were then given nasal drops containing one of two viruses and observed for the development of the common cold. Those people with larger social networks were less likely to develop colds, and those who did had less severe colds (S. Cohen et al., 1997). Social support appears to help people hold off or minimize complications from more serious medical conditions and disorders as well.

In addition, people with good social support have fewer complications during pregnancy and childbirth (Collins, Dunkel-Schetter, Lobel, & Scrimshaw, 1993), report less pain (Brown, Sheffield, Leary, & Robinson, 2003), have a reduced risk of stroke (Rutledge et al., 2008), are less susceptible to herpes attacks (Vander-Plate, Aral, & Magder, 1988), have fewer new brain lesions if they have multiple sclerosis (Mohr, Goodkin, Nelson, Cox, & Weiner, 2002), are less likely to show age-related cognitive decline (Seeman, Lusignolo, Albert, & Berkman, 2001), are less likely to show early symptoms of cardiovascular disease (Midei & Matthews, 2009), and show better adjustment to coronary artery disease (Holahan, Moos, Holahan, & Brennan, 1997). They are less likely to develop diabetes, lung disease, cardiac disease, arthritis, and cancer (Penninx et al., 1998; Stone, Mezzacappa, Donatone, & Gonder, 1999). Not surprisingly, the advantages of social support during times of stress can be cumulative. One study reported that the cumulative effect of positive social experiences reduces risks for many chronic illnesses later in life (Seeman, Singer, Ryff, Love, & Levy-Storms, 2002).

Biopsychosocial Pathways

The challenge for social support research is to identify the biopsychosocial pathways by which social contacts exert beneficial or health-compromising effects. Studies suggest that social support has beneficial effects on the cardiovascular, endocrine, and immune systems (Taylor, 2010). Social support can reduce physiological and neuroendocrine responses to stress. Psychologists often study these effects using the acute stress paradigm—that is, by taking people into the laboratory, putting them through stressful tasks (such as counting backwards quickly by 13s or giving an impromptu speech to an unresponsive audience), and then measuring their sympathetic and HPA axis responses. Fairly consistently, these biological responses to stress are more subdued when a supportive companion is present than when no

companion is present (Christenfeld et al., 1997; Smith, Loving, Crockett, & Campbell, 2009). One reason may be that warm social contact can release oxytocin, which has been tied to lower stress responses (Holt-Lunstad, Birmingham, & Light, 2008; Taylor, 2010).

Studies have found that social support is associated with reduced cortisol responses to stress, which can have beneficial effects on a broad array of diseases, including heart disease and cancer (Turner-Cobb, Sephton, Koopman, Blake-Mortimer, & Spiegel, 2000). Generally, social support is associated with better immune functioning (Herbert & Cohen, 1993) and with a reduced likelihood of responses prognostic for heart disease (Midei & Matthews, 2009; Wirtz, Redwine, Ehlert, & von Känel, 2009).

These biopsychosocial pathways, then, provide the links between illness and social support. These links are important because they play critical roles in the leading causes of death—namely, cardiovascular disease, cancer, and respiratory illness.

Genetic Bases of Social Support?   Researchers have questioned exactly why social support is so helpful during times of stress. Certainly, some of these effects are due to benefits that one's close friends, family, and community ties can provide, but there are also advantages to perceiving that social support is available. Research using twin study methodology has discovered genetic underpinnings in the ability either to construe social support as available or to establish supportive networks (Kessler, Kendler, Heath, Neale, & Eaves, 1992).

Animals enjoy the benefits of social support just as humans do. For example, female horses who form relationships with other, unrelated females are more likely to give birth to foals that survive over the long term (Cameron, Setsaas, & Linklater, 2009).

During periods of high stress, genetic predispositions to draw on social support networks may be activated, leading to the perception that support will be available to mute stress.

Moderation of Stress by Social Support

What is the role of social support in moderating the effects of stress? Two possibilities have been explored. One hypothesis, the **direct effects hypothesis,** maintains that social support is generally beneficial during nonstressful as well as stressful times. The other hypothesis, known as the **buffering hypothesis,** maintains that the physical and mental health benefits of social support are chiefly evident during periods of high stress; when there is little stress, social support may offer few such benefits. According to this hypothesis, social support acts as a reserve and resource that blunts the effects of stress or enables the individual to cope with stress more effectively when it is at high levels.

Evidence suggests both direct and buffering effects of social support (Cohen & Hoberman, 1983; Cohen & McKay, 1984; Penninx et al., 1998; Wills, 1984). Generally, when researchers have looked at social support in social integration terms, such as the number of people one identifies as friends or the number of organizations one belongs to, direct effects of social support on health have been found. When social support has been assessed more qualitatively, such as the degree to which a person feels that there are other people available who will provide help if it is needed, buffering effects of social support have been found (House et al., 1988).

Extracting Support The effectiveness of social support depends on how an individual uses a social support network. Some people are better than others at extracting the support they need. To examine this hypothesis, S. Cohen and colleagues (Cohen, Sherrod, & Clark, 1986) assessed incoming college freshmen as to their social competence, social anxiety, and self-disclosure skills. The researchers wanted to see if these skills influenced whether the students were able to develop and use social support effectively and whether the same skills could account for the positive effects of social support in combating stress. Those students with greater social competence, lower social anxiety, and better self-disclosure skills did develop more effective social support networks, especially emotional support, and were more likely to form friendships. This finding lends credence to the idea that the use of social support as a coping technique reflects, in part, a difference in personality, social skills, or competence, rather than an external resource.

What Kinds of Support Are Most Effective?

Not all aspects of social support are equally protective against stress. For example, having a confidant (such as a spouse or partner or close friend) may be the most effective social support (Umberson, 1987). Social relationships that provide daily contact may be most effective (Stetler & Miller, 2008).

Marriage, especially a satisfying marriage, is one of the best protectors against stress (Ditzen, Hoppmann, & Klumb, 2008). On average, men's health benefits substantially from marriage (e.g., Sbarra, 2009), whereas women's health benefits only slightly from marriage. The quality of the marital relationship is especially important, as marital satisfaction and support received account for its health benefits (Holt-Lunstad, Birmingham, & Jones, 2008). Exiting a marriage, being unmarried, or being in an unsatisfying marriage all bring health risks, especially for women (Kiecolt-Glaser & Newton, 2001; Liu & Umberson, 2008; Sbarra & Nietert, 2009). Marital strain, fighting, and separation and divorce have powerful adverse effects on health (Nealey-Moore, Smith, Uchino, Hawkins, & Olson-Cerney, 2007).

Support from family is important as well. Receiving social support from one's parents in early life and living in a stable and supportive environment as a child have long-term effects on coping and on health (Repetti et al., 2002). A long-term study of undergraduate men at Harvard revealed that those men who perceived themselves to have had warm, close relationships with their parents were healthier 35 years later (Russek & Schwartz, 1997). Those men who did not report a warm relationship with their parents in childhood were more likely to be diagnosed in midlife with coronary artery disease, hypertension, ulcers, and alcoholism. Experiencing the divorce of one's parents in childhood predicts premature death in midlife (Friedman, Tucker, Schwartz, et al., 1995).

Support from one's community has long been known to beneficially affect health, but the mechanisms have not been particularly well-established. One investigation in Indonesia found that mothers who were active in the community obtained resources and information about health care for their children, resources that would otherwise have been inaccessible (Nobles & Frankenberg, 2009). Thus, one mechanism may be that active community participation increases knowledge of resources. High social status in a community may enhance a person's control over their environment and may also influence how community ties affect health (Beck, 2007).

Matching Support to the Stressor Different kinds of stressful events create different needs, and social support is most effective when it meets those needs. The hypothesis that social support has beneficial effects when there is a match between what one needs and what one receives from others in one's social network is called the **matching hypothesis** (Cohen & McKay, 1984; Cohen & Wills, 1985). For example, if a person has someone he or she can talk to about problems but actually needs only to borrow a car, the presence of a confidant is useless. But if a person is upset about how a relationship is going and needs to talk it through with a friend, then the availability of a confidant is a very helpful resource. In short, support that is responsive to a person's needs is most beneficial (Maisel & Gable, 2009).

Support from Whom? Providing effective social support is not always easy for the support network. It requires skill. When it is provided by the wrong person, support may be unhelpful or even rejected, as when a stranger tries to comfort a lost child.

Social support may also be ineffective if the type of support provided is not the kind that is needed. Emotional support is most important when it comes from intimate others, whereas information and advice may be more valuable coming from experts. Thus, a person who desires solace from a family member but receives advice instead may find that, rather than being supportive, the family member actually makes the stressful situation worse (Dakof & Taylor, 1990).

Social influences may adversely affect some health habits, as when one's peer group smokes, drinks heavily, or takes drugs (Wills & Vaughan, 1989) or when a lot of social contact is coupled with high levels of stress; under these circumstances, risk of minor illnesses such as colds or flus may actually increase (Hamrick, Cohen, & Rodriguez, 2002). However, typically social influences affect health habits beneficially (Cohen & Lemay, 2007). People with high levels of social support are more adherent to their medical regimens (DiMatteo, 2004), and they are more likely to use health services, especially when the support network is

Social support can come not only from family and friends but also from a loved pet. Research suggests that dogs are better at providing social support than cats or other animals.

positively inclined toward those services (Wallston, Alagna, DeVellis, & DeVellis, 1983).

Threats to Social Support Stressful events can interfere with the ability to use potential social support effectively. People who are under extreme stress may continually express distress to others and drive those others away, thus making a bad situation even worse (Alferi, Carver, Antoni, Weiss, & Duran, 2001).

Sometimes, would-be support providers fail to provide the support that is needed and, instead, react in an unsupportive manner that actually aggravates the negative event. Negative interactions may have a more adverse effect on well-being than positive social interactions may have on improving it (Newsom, Mahan, Rook, & Krause, 2008).

Too much or overly intrusive social contact may actually make stress worse. When social support is controlling or directive, it may have some benefits for health behaviors but produce psychological distress (Lewis & Rook, 1999). People who belong to "dense" social networks (friendship or family groups that are highly interactive and in which everyone knows everyone else) may find themselves besieged by advice and interference in times of stress. As comedian George Burns once noted, "Happiness is having a large, loving, caring, close-knit family in another city."

Effects of Stress on Support Providers

When a close friend, family member, or partner is going through a stressful event, the event also has an impact on close family members, who may also have needs for social support that go unmet. If family members and friends are adversely affected by the stressful event, they may be less able to provide social support to the person in greatest need (Melamed & Brenner, 1990). On the whole, though, giving social support to others, at least at moderate levels, has beneficial effects on mental and physical health (Li & Ferraro, 2005; Piliavin & Siegl, 2007). For example, one study assessed giving and receiving social support among older married people and related both to mortality rates over a 5-year period (Brown, Nesse, Vinokur, & Smith, 2003). Death was significantly less likely for those people who reported providing instrumental support to friends, relatives, and neighbors and to those who reported providing emotional support to their spouses. Receiving support did not affect mortality. This study, then, provides important evidence that the giving of support can promote health and retard illness progression.

These findings are especially important because social support and helping have long been thought to benefit the recipient of the help while taxing the resources of those that provide it. The fact that helping, altruism, and support lead to physical and mental health benefits for both giver and receiver make social support that much more important.

Enhancing Social Support

Health psychologists view social support as an important resource in primary prevention. Increasing numbers of people are living alone for long periods during their lives, either because they have never married, are divorced, or have lost a spouse to death (U.S. Census Bureau, 2000). Social isolation is a major risk factor for illness and death (Cornwell & Waite, 2009; Meisinger, Kandler, & Ladwig, 2009). Americans report that they have fewer close friends now than has ever been the case in the past. Yet as of early 2011, Facebook and other social networking websites have more than 500 million active users, 50% of whom log on at least once every day (Hulbert, 2006, July 16; McPherson, Smith-Lovin, & Brashears, 2006; Facebook, September, 2009). Clearly, patterns of social support are shifting. Finding ways to increase the effectiveness of existing or potential support from family, friends, and even Internet buddies should be a high research priority. In addition, social support groups (Taylor, 2010) and Internet-based social support interventions (Haemmerli, Znoj, & Berger, 2010) show promise for enhancing access to socially supportive resources. These interventions are covered more fully in Chapter 11.

■ COPING INTERVENTIONS

Not everyone is able to cope with stress successfully on their own, and so a variety of interventions for coping with stress have been developed.

Mindfulness Training

Mindfulness-based stress reduction (MBSR) refers to systematic training in meditation to enable people to self-regulate their reactions to stress and the negative emotions that may result (Brown & Ryan, 2003). Studies suggest that MBSR may be effective in reducing stress, anxiety, and distress (Carmody & Baer, 2008; Roth & Robbins, 2004). One study (Roth & Robbins, 2004) explored whether an 8-week MBSR program could improve health in a low-income Latino and Anglo inner-city community. The researchers found that reported health and quality of life improved among participants, suggesting that MBSR may have beneficial health effects as well as coping benefits. Neuroscience research has identified one reason why MBSR has these beneficial effects. Mindfulness engages the prefrontal cortical regions of the brain, which regulate affect and downregulate activity in limbic areas related to anxiety and other negative emotions (Creswell, Way, Eisenberger, & Lieberman, 2007).

Expressive Writing

The disclosure of emotional experiences can have beneficial effects on health. For many years, researchers suspected that when people undergo traumatic events and cannot or do not communicate about them, those events may fester inside them, producing obsessive thoughts for years and even decades. This inhibition of traumatic events involves physiological work, and the more people are forced to inhibit their thoughts, emotions, and behaviors, the more their physiological activity may increase (Pennebaker, 1997). Consequently, the ability to confide in others or to consciously confront one's feelings may eliminate the need to obsess about and inhibit the event, which may, in turn, reduce the physiological activity associated with the event (Stanton, 2010). These insights have been explored largely through an intervention called expressive writing.

J. W. Pennebaker and S. Beall (1986) had 46 undergraduates write either about the most traumatic and stressful event ever in their lives or about trivial topics. Although the individuals writing about traumas were more upset immediately after they wrote their essays (see also Pennebaker, Colder, & Sharp, 1990), they were less likely to visit the student health center for illness during the following 6 months.

A subsequent study (Pennebaker, Hughes, & O'Heeron, 1987) found that when people talked about traumatic events, their skin conductance, heart rate, and systolic and diastolic blood pressure all decreased. Emotional disclosure can also have beneficial long-term effects on immune functioning (Christensen et al., 1996; Petrie, Booth, Pennebaker, Davison, & Thomas, 1995). One risk of writing interventions is that they sometimes increase distress on the short-term. Possibly writing about perceived benefits from traumatic events may provide a less upsetting but nonetheless still effective way to benefit from writing interventions, rather than focusing directly on a traumatic experience itself (King & Miner, 2000).

Drawing on the value of this method, interventions have employed expressive writing to encourage emotional approach coping (Stanton, 2010). Such interventions have led to improved health among AIDS patients (Petrie, Fontanilla, Thomas, Booth, & Pennebaker, 2004), breast cancer patients (Stanton et al., 2002), people with asthma or arthritis (Smyth, Stone, Hurewitz, & Kaell, 1999), and headache patients (D'Souza, Lumley, Kraft, & Dooley, 2008), among other disorders. Even writing about emotional topics via email has been found to promote health (Sheese, Brown, & Graziano, 2004). Writing may also help people cope with debilitating treatments. For example, in one study, guided writing led to a more beneficial postoperative course in surgery patients (Solano, Donati, Pecci, Persichetti, & Colaci, 2003); those who wrote about their experience, on average, left the hospital several days earlier, with lower psychological distress. Expressive writing does not affect all medical conditions (Harris, Thoresen, Humphreys, & Faul, 2005), but its benefits suggest that it is a useful intervention for many patient groups.

There are many reasons why talking or writing about a stressful event or confiding in others may be useful for coping. Talking with others allows one to gain information about the event or about effective coping; it may also elicit positive reinforcement and emotional support from others. There may be beneficial cognitive effects associated with talking about or writing about a traumatic event, such as organizing one's thoughts and being able to find meaning in the experience (Lepore, Ragan, & Jones, 2000). These interventions may lead people to change their focus of attention from negative to positive aspects of this situation (Vedhara et al., 2010). Talking or writing about traumatic or stressful events provides an opportunity for emotional-approach coping (Lepore & Smyth, 2002) and for affirming one's personal values (Creswell, Way, Eisenberger, & Lieberman, 2007; Langens & Schüler, 2007). Alexithymia, which is difficulty identifying and expressing one's emotions, has been tied to health risks (e.g., Tolmunen, Lehto, Heliste, Kurl, & Kauhanen, 2010), and interventions such as expressive writing may reduce the risk.

Coping Effectiveness Training

Interventions directed toward teaching people effective coping techniques have considerable promise. Most of these interventions draw on cognitive-behavioral stress management (Antoni et al., 2006; Helgeson, Cohen, Schulz, & Yasko, 2000; Manne, Ostroff, Winkel, Grana, & Fox, 2005). Coping effectiveness training typically begins by teaching people how to appraise stressful events in order to disaggregate the stressors into specific tasks. The person learns to distinguish those aspects of a global stressor that may be changeable from those that are not. Specific coping strategies are then developed and practiced to deal with these more specific stressors. Encouraging people to maintain their social support is also an important aspect of coping effectiveness training (Folkman et al., 1991). We will discuss several coping effectiveness interventions in the chapters on chronic diseases. Here, we highlight the application of coping effectiveness training to managing the stress of college life.

Stress Management

Many people have difficulty managing stress themselves. Accordingly, health psychologists have increasingly turned their attention to developing techniques of **stress management.** Who participates in stress management programs? Some people obtain help in stress management through private therapists in a one-to-one psychotherapeutic experience. More commonly, stress management is taught through workshops, sometimes in the workplace. The financial impact of stress in the workplace may be as high as $68 billion in lost productivity each year, because stress leads to absences, claims against companies, and increased health care costs (Institute for Clinical Systems Improvement, 2004). Consequently, organizations have been motivated to help their workers identify and cope with the stressful events that they experience both on the job and in their lives more generally. Basic techniques of stress management can also help people reduce their risk of illness ranging from tension headaches to heart disease (Kirby, Williams, Hocking, Lane, & Williams, 2006).

Basic Techniques of Stress Management

Stress management programs typically involve three phases. In the first phase, participants learn what stress is and how to identify the stressors in their own lives. In the second phase, they acquire and practice skills for coping with stress. In the final phase, they practice these stress management techniques in targeted stressful situations and monitor their effectiveness (Meichenbaum & Jaremko, 1983).

There are many stressful aspects of college life, such as speaking in front of large groups. Stress management programs can help students master these experiences.

As an example, college can be an extremely stressful experience for many new students. For some, it is their first time away from home, and they must cope with living in a dormitory surrounded by strangers. They may have to share a room with another person from a very different background and with very different personal habits. High noise levels, communal bathrooms, institutional food, and rigorous academic schedules may all be trying experiences for new students. Academic life may prove to be more difficult than they had expected. And if they see little prospect for improvement, they may become increasingly anxious, find that the college environment is too stressful, and drop out. Recognizing that these pressures exist, college administrators have increasingly made stress management programs available to their students.

A Stress Management Program

An example of a program, called Combat Stress Now (CSN), makes use of these various phases of education, skill acquisition, and practice.

Identifying Stressors   In the first phase of the CSN program, participants learn what stress is and how it creates physical wear and tear. In sharing their personal experiences of stress, many students find reassurance in the fact that so many other students have experiences similar to their own. They learn that stress is a process of psychological appraisal rather than a factor inherent in events themselves. Thus, college life is not inherently stressful but is a consequence of the individual's perceptions of it. Through these messages, the students begin to see that, if they are armed with appropriate stress management techniques, they will come to experience currently stressful events as less stressful.

Monitoring Stress   In the self-monitoring phase of the CSN program, students are trained to observe their own behavior closely and to record the circumstances that they find most stressful. In addition, they record their physical, emotional, and behavioral reactions to those stresses as they experience them. Students also record their own maladaptive efforts to cope with these stressful events, including excessive sleeping or eating, television watching, and alcohol consumption.

Identifying Stress Antecedents   Once students learn to chart their stress responses, they are encouraged to examine the antecedents of these experiences. They learn to focus on what events happen just before they experience feelings of stress. For example, one student may feel overwhelmed with academic life only when contemplating having to speak out in class, whereas another student may experience stress primarily when thinking about having to use the computer in a particularly demanding course. Thus, by pinpointing exactly those circumstances that initiate feelings of stress, students can more precisely identify their own trouble spots.

Avoiding Negative Self-Talk   Students are next trained to recognize and eliminate the negative self-talk they go through when they face stressful events. Negative self-talk can contribute to irrational feelings that perpetuate stress (Meichenbaum, 1975). For example, the student who fears speaking out in class may recognize how self-statements contribute to this process: "I hate asking questions," "I always get tongue-tied," and "I'll probably forget what I want to say."

Completing Take-Home Assignments   In addition to in-class exercises, students have take-home assignments. They keep a stress diary in which they record what events they find stressful and how they respond to them. As they become proficient in identifying stressful incidents, they are encouraged to record the negative self-statements or irrational thoughts that accompany the stressful experience (see Ellis, 1962).

Acquiring Skills   The next stage of stress management involves skill acquisition and practice. These skills include cognitive-behavioral management techniques, time management skills, and other stress-reducing interventions, such as exercise. Some of these techniques are designed to eliminate the stressful event; others are geared toward reducing the experience of stress without necessarily modifying the event itself.

Setting New Goals   Students next begin to attack their stressful events by setting goals, engaging in positive self-talk, and using self-instruction. Each student first sets several specific goals that he or she wants to meet to reduce the experience of college stress. For one student, the goal may be learning to speak in class without suffering overwhelming anxiety. For another, it may be going to see a particular professor about a problem.

Once the goals have been set, the next challenge is to identify specific behaviors that will meet those goals. In some cases, an appropriate response may be leaving the stressful event altogether. For example, the student who is having difficulty in a rigorous physics course may need to modify his goal of becoming a physicist. Alternatively, students may be encouraged to turn a stressor into a challenge. Thus, the student who fears speaking up in class may come to realize that she must not only master this fearful event but actually come to enjoy it if she is to realize her long-term goal of becoming a trial lawyer.

In other cases, students may have to put up with a stressful event but simply learn to manage it more effectively. If a particular English course is highly stressful but is required for graduation, the student must learn to cope with the course in the best way possible.

Thus, goal setting is important in effective stress management, for two reasons. First, it forces the person to distinguish among stressful events to be avoided, tolerated, or overcome. Second, it forces her or him to be specific and concrete about exactly which events need to be tackled and what is to be done.

Engaging in Positive Self-Talk and Self-Instruction   Once students have set some realistic goals and identified some target behaviors for reaching their goals, they learn how to engage in self-instruction and positive self-talk, two skills that can help in achieving those goals. Self-instruction involves reminding oneself of the specific steps that are required to achieve the goal. Positive self-talk involves providing the self with specific encouragement. For example, students desiring to overcome a fear of oral presentations might remind themselves of all the occasions in which they have spoken successfully in public. Once some proficiency in public speaking is achieved, students might encourage themselves by highlighting the positive aspects of the experience (for example, holding the attention of the audience, making some points, and winning over a few converts to their positions).

Using Other Cognitive-Behavioral Techniques   In some stress management programs, contingency contracting (see Chapter 3) is encouraged. For example, students who have trouble getting motivated to make changes are encouraged to make a contract with the self. The student who fears making oral presentations may define a specific goal, such as asking three questions in class in a week, which is to be followed by a particular reward, such as tickets to a concert.

To summarize, this program for controlling stress involves a wide array of cognitive-behavior therapy techniques: self-monitoring, the modification of internal dialogues, goal setting, homework assignments, positive self-talk, self-instruction, and contingency contracting. Most stress management programs include a varied array of techniques so that people have a broad set of skills from which to choose. People can discover the skills that work best for them. In these ways, people can "inoculate" themselves against stress (Meichenbaum & Turk, 1982), helping them to confront stressful events with a clear plan and an array of potential measures that they can take before the stressful event becomes overwhelming.

Self-Affirmation   Earlier in this chapter we noted how important self-related resources, such as self-esteem, can be for helping people mobilize themselves to cope with stress. A technique that makes use of this insight is called self-affirmation. Self-affirmation theory (Steele, 1988) maintains that when people positively affirm values and other personal qualities that are important to them, they may experience beneficial physiological and psychological responses (see Sherman & Cohen, 2006, for a review). Self-affirmation may be one of the reasons why writing about or otherwise disclosing one's stressors is beneficial to health. That is, if during the writing process people are able to affirm their values and personal qualities, they may enhance the value of the writing intervention (Cresswell et al., 2007). Based on observations such as these, researchers are now using self-affirmation as an intervention to help people cope with stress. In one study (Sherman, Bunyan, Creswell, & Jaremka, 2009), students wrote about an important personal value just before taking a stressful exam. Heart rate and blood pressure responses to the stressor were attenuated by this self-affirmation, suggesting that affirmations can ameliorate the experience of stress.

Relaxation Training and Stress Management

Whereas the techniques we have discussed so far give a person cognitive insights into the nature and control of stress, another set of techniques—relaxation training—affects the physiological experience of stress by reducing arousal.

Relaxation training therapies include progressive muscle relaxation training, guided imagery, transcendental meditation, and other forms of meditation, including yoga and hypnosis. What are the benefits? These techniques can reduce heart rate, muscle tension, blood pressure, inflammatory processes, lipid levels, self-reports of anxiety, and tension among other physical and psychological benefits (Barnes, Davis, Murzynowski, & Treiber, 2004; Lutgendorf, Anderson, Sorosky, Buller, & Lubaroff, 2000; Scheufele, 2000; Speca, Carlson, Goodey, & Angen, 2000).

Because of the value of relaxation for physical and mental health, most stress management interventions include relaxation therapy. First, people learn how to control their breathing, taking no more than six to eight breaths per minute. They learn to relax the muscles in each part of the body progressively, until they experience no tension (progressive muscle relaxation). They learn to identify the particular spots that tense up during times of stress, such as a jaw that clamps shut or fists that tighten up. By becoming aware of these reactions, they can relax these parts of the body as well. Thus, for example, when students find that the stress of college life is overwhelming them, they can take a 5- or 10-minute break in which they breathe deeply and relax completely. They can then return to their tasks free of some of their previous tension.

Related techniques such as yoga may also have health benefits. For example, one study found that people who regularly practiced yoga experienced more positive emotions and showed lower inflammatory responses to stress than those who were new to the practice of yoga. Yoga, then, may ameliorate the burden that stress places on an individual (Kiecolt-Glaser et al., 2010). Even joyful music can be a stress buster (Miller, Mangano, Beach, Kop, & Vogel, 2010).

Supplementary Stress Management Skills

In addition to the basic cognitive and relaxation skills of stress management, many programs include supplementary skills. In many cases, the experience of stress depends on feeling that one has too much to do in too little time. Consequently, many stress management programs include training in **time management** and planning. CSN helps students set specific work goals for each day, establish priorities, avoid time wasters, and learn what to ignore altogether. Thus, a student may learn to set aside 2 hours for a particularly important task, such as studying for a test. In this way, the student has a particular goal and particular period in which to pursue it, and so is less subject to interruption. Simple "how to" manuals effectively illustrate the time management approach to stress management.

Many stress management programs emphasize good health habits and social skills as additional techniques for the control of stress. These include good eating habits, exercise, assertiveness in social situations, and use of social support. Stress often affects eating habits adversely: People under stress consume too many stimulants (such as coffee), too much sugar, and too much junk food. By learning to control dietary habits effectively and by eating three balanced meals a day, the student can ameliorate physiological reactions to stress. Likewise, regular exercise reduces stress. At least 20–30 minutes of sustained exercise at least three times a week is widely encouraged for all participants in the CSN program.

Assertiveness training is sometimes incorporated into stress management. Often, people experience stress because they are unable to confront the people who contribute to their stress. For example, in the CSN program, students who have identified other individuals in their environment as causing them special stress—called **stress carriers**—help one another practice dealing with these individuals. One student may practice approaching a professor with whom he is having difficulty communicating; another student may practice dealing tactfully with a roommate who constantly brags about how well she is doing in her classes.

As we have seen, social support can buffer the adverse effects of stress. Unfortunately, people under stress sometimes alienate rather than engage those people who might provide social support. For example, a harried worker snaps at his wife and children, or a student facing a big exam angrily rejects a friend's well-intentioned advice. Students in the CSN program are trained to recognize the important functions that social support can serve in helping them combat stress. They are urged to confide in close friends, to seek advice from people who can help them, and to use time with other people for relaxation and positive reinforcement after meeting their goals.

In the final stage of the CSN program, stress management techniques are put into effect. If some techniques fail to work, the trainees are urged to figure out why. Students take their experiences of stress management back to the group situation, where successes and failures can be analyzed. If initial efforts to cope with a stressful event are unsuccessful, the student may need to practice the technique or shift to a different technique. Overall, stress management training imparts valuable skills for living in a world with many sources of stress, and it improves mental and physical health as well. ●

SUMMARY

1. Coping is the process of managing demands that tax or exceed a person's resources. Coping is influenced by primary appraisals ("Is the event harmful, threatening, or challenging?") and by secondary appraisals ("What are my coping resources, and how adequate are they?").

2. Coping efforts are guided by internal and external resources. Internal resources include preferred coping style and coping resources such as optimism, personal control, and self-esteem. External resources include time, money, the absence of simultaneous life stressors, and social support.

3. Coping styles consist of predispositions to cope with stressful situations in particular ways. An important distinction is between approach-related coping styles and avoidance-related coping styles. Although avoidance may be successful in the short run, on the whole, approach-related coping styles are more successful.

4. Coping efforts may be directed to solving problems or to regulating emotions. Most stressful events evoke both types of coping, as well as more specific strategies.

5. Coping efforts are judged to be successful when they reduce physiological indicators of arousal, enable the person to resume desired activities, and free the individual from psychological distress.

6. Social support can be an effective resource in times of stress. It reduces psychological distress and the likelihood of illness. However, some events can undermine or threaten social support resources.

7. The tasks toward which coping efforts are typically directed include reducing harmful environmental conditions and enhancing the adjustment process, tolerating and adjusting to negative events and realities, maintaining a positive self-image, maintaining emotional equilibrium, continuing satisfying relations with others, and recovering from illness, if relevant.

8. Coping effectiveness training, which draws on the principles of cognitive-behavioral therapy, can communicate effective coping skills. Emotional disclosure and expressive writing about stressful events are also effective coping techniques.

9. Stress management programs exist for those who need help in developing their coping skills. These programs teach people to identify sources of stress in their lives, to develop coping skills to deal with those stressors, and to practice employing stress management skills and monitoring their effectiveness.

KEY TERMS

approach (confrontative, vigilant) coping style
avoidant (minimizing) coping style
buffering hypothesis
control-enhancing interventions
coping
coping outcomes
coping style
direct effects hypothesis

emotion-focused coping
emotional-approach coping
emotional support
informational support
invisible support
matching hypothesis
negative affectivity
problem-focused coping
psychological control

self-esteem
social support
stress carriers
stress management
stress moderators
tangible assistance
time management

PART 4

The Patient in the Treatment Setting

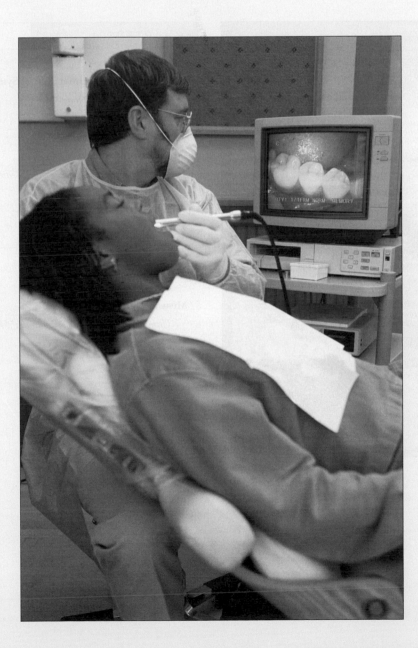

Using Health Services

Some years ago, the creative puppeteer Jim Henson died abruptly in his mid-50s from an apparent cold or flu that coursed rapidly through his system. Henson had been working long hours and was run down from heavy business and travel commitments, and although he knew he should see a doctor—his symptoms were getting worse—he put it off. When he finally did check into a hospital, the infection had spread so far that doctors could not save him. Generations of children and parents who had grown up with *Sesame Street* and who had come to love Kermit the Frog, Oscar the Grouch, Big Bird, and the other endearing inventions of Henson's mind were stunned, not only by the abrupt ending to his outstanding career but by the form it took.

A few days later, my young son developed a cold and low-grade fever that proved to be surprisingly intractable to my medication. I took him to the medical center and was informed by the overworked but patient physician that my son was just fine, the infection was viral in origin, and there was nothing to do but keep him at home, give him lots of rest and fluids, and continue to administer medication on a regular basis. I felt silly and told the doctor that I had probably been a bit overzealous in coming to see him because the Jim Henson account had alarmed me so much. He smiled wearily and said, "Dr. Taylor, you are probably the 30th 'Jim Henson' mother we have seen here this week."

On the surface, the questions of who uses health services and why would seem to be a medical issue. The obvious answer is that people use services when they are sick. But as the preceding anecdote illustrates, this issue can also be psychological: When and how does a person decide that he or she is sick? When are symptoms dismissed as inconsequential? When does a person decide that a symptom requires treatment by a professional, and when do chicken soup, fluids, and bed rest seem to be all that is needed?

■ RECOGNITION AND INTERPRETATION OF SYMPTOMS

Although people have some awareness of what is going on in their bodies, that awareness may be limited. This limitation leaves a great deal of room for social and psychological factors to operate in the recognition and interpretation of illness (Petrie & Weinman, 1997).

Recognition of Symptoms

> I have a tumor in my head the size of a basketball. I can feel it when I blink.
>
> —Woody Allen, *Hannah and Her Sisters*

Common observation reveals that some individuals maintain their normal activities in the face of what would seem to be debilitating symptoms, whereas others take to their beds the moment they detect any minor bodily disturbance.

Individual Differences   Some people are more likely to notice a symptom than are other people. Hypochondriacs, like many characters that Woody Allen has played, are convinced that normal bodily symptoms are indicators of illness. Although hypochondriacs represent only 4–5% of the population, because they make such extensive use of medical services, understanding who experiences symptoms more intensely is an important goal of health psychologists (Lecci & Cohen, 2002).

The most frequent symptoms that show up among patients who convert their distress into physical symptoms are back pain, joint pain, pain in the extremities, headache, abdominal symptoms such as bloating, "allergies" to particular foods, and cardiovascular symptoms such as palpitations (Carmin, Weigartz, Hoff, & Kondos, 2003; Rief, Hessel, & Braehler, 2001). Contrary to stereotypes, women are not more likely than men to report these symptoms. But there are pronounced age effects, with older people reporting more symptoms than young people.

Neuroticism also affects the perception of symptoms. As we saw in Chapter 7, neuroticism is a pervasive negative way of viewing the world marked by negative emotions, self-consciousness, and a concern with bodily processes. People who are high in neuroticism recognize their symptoms quickly and report their symptoms quickly (Feldman, Cohen, Doyle, Skoner, & Gwaltney, 1999), and they often erroneously believe they have serious diseases. Perhaps neurotic, anxious people exaggerate their symptoms, or they may simply be more attentive to real symptoms (Gramling, Clawson, & McDonald, 1996; Howren, Suls, & Martin, 2009; Ward & Leventhal, 1993).

Cultural Differences   There are reliable cultural differences in how quickly and what kind of symptoms are detected (Kirmayer & Young, 1998). For example, a comparative study of Anglos and Mexicans

(Burnam, Timbers, & Hough, 1984) found that Anglos reported symptoms that occurred infrequently (such as a new pain), but Mexicans reported symptoms that occurred frequently (such as diarrhea). Cultural differences in symptom experience and reporting have been recognized for decades (Zola, 1966), but as yet, the reasons underlying cultural differences are not fully understood.

Attentional Differences

Attentional differences influence the experience of symptoms. People who are focused on themselves (their bodies, their emotions, and their reactions in general) are quicker to notice symptoms than are people who are focused externally, on their environment and activities (Pennebaker, 1983). So, people who hold boring jobs, who are socially isolated, who keep house for a living, or who live alone report more physical symptoms than do people who have interesting jobs, who have active social lives, who work outside the home, or who live with others. One reason is that these latter people experience more distractions and attend less to themselves than do those people who have little activity in their lives (Pennebaker, 1983).

Situational Factors

Situational factors influence whether a person will recognize a symptom. A boring situation makes people more attentive to symptoms than does an interesting situation. For example, people are more likely to notice itching or tickling in their throats and to cough in response to the sensations during boring parts of movies than during interesting parts (Pennebaker, 1980). A symptom is more likely to be perceived on a day when a person is at home than on a day full of frenzied activity. Intense physical activity takes attention away from symptoms, whereas quiescence increases the likelihood of their recognition.

Any situational factor that makes illness or symptoms especially salient promotes their recognition. For example, a common phenomenon in medical school is **medical students' disease.** As they study each illness, many medical students imagine that they have it. Studying the symptoms leads the students to focus on their own fatigue and other internal states; as a consequence, symptoms consistent with the illness under study seem to emerge (Mechanic, 1972).

Stress

Stress can precipitate or aggravate the experience of symptoms. People who are under stress may believe that they are more vulnerable to illness and so attend more closely to their bodies. Financial strain,

disruptions in personal relationships, and other stressors lead people to believe that they are ill (Alonso & Coe, 2001; Angel, Frisco, Angel, & Chiriboga, 2003), perhaps because they experience stress-related physiological changes, such as accelerated heartbeat or breathing, and interpret these changes as symptoms of illness (Cameron, Leventhal, & Leventhal, 1995).

Mood

Mood influences self-appraised health. People who are in a good mood rate themselves as more healthy, report fewer illness-related memories, and report fewer symptoms. People in a bad mood, however, report more symptoms, are more pessimistic that any actions they might take will relieve their symptoms, and perceive themselves as more vulnerable to future illness (Leventhal, Hansell, Diefenbach, Leventhal, & Glass, 1996). Even people who have diagnosed illnesses report fewer or less serious symptoms when they are in a good mood (Gil et al., 2004).

In summary, then, when attention is directed outward, as by vigorous physical activity or a highly distracting environment, symptoms are less likely to be noticed. But when attention is directed toward the body, as by cues that suggest illness, stress, or neuroticism, symptoms are more likely to be detected.

Interpretation of Symptoms

The interpretation of symptoms is also a heavily psychological process. Consider the following incident. At a large metropolitan hospital, a man in his late 20s came to the emergency room with the sole symptom of a sore throat. He brought with him six of his relatives: his mother, father, sister, aunt, and two cousins. Because patients usually go to an emergency room with only one other person, and because a sore throat is virtually never seen in the emergency room, the staff were understandably curious about the reason for his visit. There was much chuckling about how Italian families stick together and how they panic at any sign of a disturbance in health. But one particularly sensitive medical student reasoned that something more must have caused the man to come to the emergency room with his entire family in tow, so he probed cautiously but persistently during the intake interview with the patient. Gradually, it emerged that the young man's brother had died a year earlier of Hodgkin's disease, a form of cancer that involves the progressive infection and enlargement of the lymph nodes. The brother's first symptom had been a sore throat, which he and the family had allowed to go untreated.

BOX 8.1

Can Expectations Influence Sensations?
The Case of Premenstrual Symptoms

Many women experience unpleasant physical and psychological symptoms just before the onset of menstruation, including swollen breasts, cramping, irritability, and depression. These symptoms clearly have a physiological basis, but research indicates that psychological factors may contribute as well. Specifically, it may be that women experience these symptoms more intensely because they *expect* to experience them (McFarland, Ross, & DeCourville, 1989; Ruble, 1972).

To test this idea, D. N. Ruble (1972) recruited a number of women to participate in a study. She told them she was using a new scientific technique that would predict their date of menstruation. She then randomly told participants that the technique indicated either that their period was due within the next day or two (premenstrual group) or that their period was not due for 7–10 days (intermenstrual group). In fact, all the women were approximately a week from their periods. All the women were then asked to complete a questionnaire indicating the extent to which they were experiencing symptoms typically associated with the premenstrual state.

The women who were led to believe that their period was due within the next day or two reported more of the psychological and physiological symptoms of premenstruation than did women who were told their periods were not due for 7–10 days.

Of course, the results of this study do not mean that premenstrual symptoms have no physical basis. Indeed, the prevalence and seriousness of premenstrual syndrome (PMS) bears testimony to the debilitating effect that premenstrual bodily changes can have on physiological functioning and behavior (Kendler et al., 1992; Klebanov & Jemmott, 1992). Rather, the results suggest that women who believe themselves to be premenstrual may be more attentive to and reinterpret naturally fluctuating bodily states as consistent with the premenstrual state. These findings also illustrate the significance of psychological factors in the experience of symptoms more generally.

This poignant incident illustrates how important social and psychological factors can be in understanding people's interpretations of their symptoms and their decisions to seek treatment (Frostholm et al., 2005a).

Prior Experience

As the preceding incident attests, the interpretation of symptoms is heavily influenced by prior experience. People who have experience with a medical condition estimate the prevalence of their symptoms to be greater and often regard the condition as less serious than do people with no history of the condition (Jemmott, Croyle, & Ditto, 1988). A symptom's meaning is also influenced by how common it is within a person's circle of acquaintances or culture (Croyle & Hunt, 1991). Highly prevalent risk factors and disorders are generally regarded as less serious than are rare or distinctive risk factors and disorders (Croyle & Ditto, 1990).

Expectations

Expectations influence the interpretation of symptoms. People may ignore symptoms they are not expecting and amplify symptoms they do expect (Leventhal, Nerenz, & Strauss, 1982). An example is described in Box 8.1.

Seriousness of the Symptoms

Symptoms that affect highly valued parts of the body are usually interpreted as more serious and as more likely to require attention than are symptoms that affect less valued organs. For example, people are especially anxious when their eyes or face are affected, but less so if the symptom involves part of the trunk. A symptom will prompt the seeking of treatment if it limits mobility or if it affects a highly valued organ, such as chest discomfort thought to be indicative of heart disease (Eifert, Hodson, Tracey, Seville, & Gunawardane, 1996). Above all, if a symptom causes pain, it will lead a person to seek treatment more promptly than if it does not cause pain.

Cognitive Representations of Illness

The **commonsense model of illness** argues that people hold implicit commonsense beliefs about their symptoms and illnesses that result in organized **illness representations** or schemas (Leventhal, Meyer, & Nerenz, 1980; Leventhal, Weinman, Leventhal, & Phillips, 2008). These coherent conceptions of illness are acquired through the media, through personal experience, and from family and friends who have had experience with similar disorders.

These commonsense models range from being quite sketchy and inaccurate to being extensive, technical, and complete. Their importance stems from the fact that they lend coherence to a person's comprehension of the illness experience (Hall, Weinman, & Marteau, 2004). As such, they can influence people's preventive health behaviors, their reactions when they experience symptoms or are diagnosed with illness, their adherence to treatment recommendations, and their expectations for their future health (Leventhal et al., 2008).

Commonsense models include basic information about an illness (Leventhal et al., 2008). The *identity*, or label, for an illness is its name; its *causes* are the factors that the person believes gave rise to the illness; its *consequences* are its symptoms, the treatments that result, and their implications for quality of life; *time line* refers to the length of time the illness is expected to last; and *control/cure* identifies whether the person believes the illness can be managed or cured through appropriate actions and treatments. *Coherence* refers to how well these beliefs hang together in a cogent representation of the disorder.

Most people have at least three models of illness (Leventhal et al., 2008):

- *Acute illness* is believed to be caused by specific viral or bacterial agents and is short in duration, with no long-term consequences. An example is the flu.

- *Chronic illness* is believed to be caused by multiple factors, including health habits, and is long in duration, often with severe consequences. An example is heart disease.

- *Cyclic illness* is marked by alternating periods during which there are either no symptoms or many symptoms. An example is herpes.

People's illness schemas vary, and their schema can greatly influence behavior related to that disease. For example, diabetes may be seen by one individual as an acute condition caused by a diet high in sugar, whereas another person with the same disease may see it as a lifelong condition, with potentially catastrophic consequences. Not surprisingly, these people will treat their disorders differently, maintain different levels of vigilance toward symptoms, and show different patterns of seeking treatment (Lange & Piette, 2006; Weinman, Petrie, Moss-Morris, & Horne, 1996). People's conceptions of disease give them a basis for interpreting new information, influence their treatment-seeking decisions, lead

them to alter or fail to adhere to their medication regimens (Coutu, Dupuis, D'Antono, & Rochon-Goyer, 2003), and influence expectations about future health (Leventhal et al., 2008).

Lay Referral Network

The meaning of a symptom ultimately blends into diagnosis, a process that begins not in the physician's office but in an individual's conversations with friends, neighbors, and relatives. Sociologists have written at length about the **lay referral network,** an informal network of family and friends who offer their own interpretations of symptoms well before any medical treatment is sought (Freidson, 1961). The patient may mention the symptoms to a family member or coworker, who may then respond with personal views of what the symptom is likely to mean ("George had that, and it turned out to be nothing at all") (Croyle & Hunt, 1991). The friend or relative may offer advice about the advisability of seeking medical treatment ("All he got for going to see the doctor was a big bill") and recommendations for various home remedies ("Lemon and tequila will clear that right up").

In many communities, the lay referral network is the preferred mode of treatment. A powerful lay figure, such as an older woman who has had many children, may act as a lay practitioner; because of her years of experience, she is assumed to have personal wisdom in medical matters (Freidson, 1961; Hayes-Bautista, 1976). Within ethnic communities, the lay referral network will sometimes incorporate beliefs about the causes and cures of disease that would be regarded as supernatural or superstitious by traditional medicine. In addition, these lay referral networks often recommend home remedies regarded as more appropriate or more effective than traditional medicine.

Complementary and Alternative Medicine

The use of complementary and alternative medicine (CAM), which builds on this tradition, is on the rise worldwide. As a consequence, the United Nation's World Health Organization (WHO) has recently begun evaluating the efficacy of these treatments (McNeil, 2002, May 17). For example, the Chinese herb *ma huang* helps breathing problems but can cause heart attacks and stroke in some individuals. *Ginkgo biloba* stimulates circulation but can also enhance bleeding, which is risky during surgery. The goal of the WHO is to catalogue all CAM remedies to identify those that are successful and not risky and to reduce or eliminate use of those that are unsuccessful or risky.

As many as one in three American adults may use an alternative or complementary therapy during the course of a year, producing an estimated 354 million visits to providers of these therapies and approximately $33.9 billion in costs (National Center for Complementary and Alternative Medicine, 2009). What therapies are people using? Complementary and alternative therapies include relaxation techniques, chiropracty, massage, imagery, spiritual healing, diets, herbal medicines, megavitamin therapy, self-help groups, energy healing, biofeedback, hypnosis, homeopathy, and acupuncture. Not all of these therapies are used as alternatives to formal treatment; many are used in conjunction with conventional therapy. But health care providers are often unaware that their patients are supplementing their care with complementary therapies, which can be risky.

Some CAM remedies do work, of course, and simple rest or relaxation can allow an illness to run its course as well. These cures help to perpetuate the use of CAM, and consequently, much illness is never formally treated within the medical community. At any given time, 70–90% of the population has a medical condition that could be diagnosed and treated by a health care provider, but 66–75% of those people choose not to consult one.

The Internet

The Internet constitutes a lay referral network of its own. On a typical day, more than 6 million Americans will look for health care information online (Center for the Advancement of Health, December 2002). The amount of health information on the Internet has mushroomed in recent years, with more than 100,000 health-related websites currently in existence (Center for the Advancement of Health, June 2002). Seeking health information online is one of the most common Internet activities. Sixty-one percent of Internet users report that they have used the Internet to find health information—more than those who shop, get sports scores, or buy stocks. Moreover, more than half the people who have gone online to find health information say it improved the way they took care of themselves (Dias et al., 2002).

Are these trends worrisome? According to a recent study of physicians, 96% said they believe that the Internet will affect health care positively, and many turn to the Internet themselves for the most up-to-date information on illnesses, treatments, and the processing of insurance claims. Nonetheless, some of what is on the Internet is not accurate (Kalichman et al., 2006), and people who use the Web to get information about their illness sometimes get worse (Gupta, 2004, October 24). Some health-related Internet sites simply want users to fill a shopping cart with their products. One excellent source of health-related issues is the Center for Advancing Health website (www.cfah.org). It is evident that the Internet is playing an increasingly major role in providing the information that people get about symptoms, illnesses, and potential cures.

■ WHO USES HEALTH SERVICES?

Just as illness is not evenly distributed across the population, neither is the use of health services.

Age

The very young and the elderly use health services most frequently (Meara, White, & Cutler, 2004). Young children develop a number of infectious childhood diseases as they are acquiring their immunities; therefore, they frequently require the care of a pediatrician. Both illness frequency and the use of services decline in adolescence and throughout young adulthood. Use of health services increases again in late adulthood, when people begin to develop chronic conditions and diseases of aging.

Gender

Women use medical services more than do men (Fuller, Edwards, Sermsri, & Vorakitphokatorn, 1993). Pregnancy and childbirth account for much of this gender difference in use, but not all. Various explanations have been offered, including, for example, the fact that women have better homeostatic mechanisms than men do: They report pain earlier, experience temperature changes more rapidly, and detect new smells faster. Thus, they may also be more sensitive to bodily disruptions, especially minor ones (Leventhal, Diefenbach, & Leventhal, 1992).

Another possible explanation stems from social norms. Men are expected to project a tough, macho image, which involves being able to ignore pain and not give in to illness, whereas women are not subject to these same pressures (Klonoff & Landrine, 1992).

Economic factors may also be important. Because more women are part-time workers and nonworkers, they may not lose income when they are ill. Consequently, women may use health services more because seeking treatment for illness disrupts their lives less and costs them less (Marcus & Siegel, 1982). However, the same factors—namely, that women are less likely to be employed, are more likely to work part-time, and are more likely to experience more economic hardship—also contribute to women's poorer health (Ross & Bird, 1994).

Women also use health care services more often because their medical care is more fragmented. Medical care for most men involves a trip to a general practitioner for a physical examination that includes all-preventive care. But women may visit a general practitioner or internist for a general physical, a gynecologist for Pap tests, and a breast cancer specialist or mammography service for breast examinations and mammograms. Thus, women may use services more than men in part because

Women use medical services more than men, they may be sick more than men, and their routine care requires more visits than men's. It is often easier for women to use services, and they require services for such gender-related needs as maternity care.

the medical care system is not particularly well structured to meet their basic needs.

Social Class and Culture

The lower social classes use medical services less than do the more affluent social classes (Adler & Stewart, 2010), in part because the poorer classes have less money to spend on health services. However, with Medicare for the elderly, Medicaid for the poor, and other inexpensive health services, the gap between medical service use by the rich and by the poor has narrowed somewhat.

Cost is one factor that discourages use of service among low SES people. Also, there simply are not as many high-quality medical services available to the poor, and what services there are, are often inadequate and understaffed (Kirby & Kaneda, 2005). Consequently, many poor people receive no regular medical care at all and see physicians only in the emergency room. These social-class differences are problematic because not only are the poor sick more often and for longer periods than are the well-to-do, but they die earlier (Adler, Boyce, Chesney, Folkman, & Syme, 1993). The biggest gap between the rich and the poor is in the use of preventive health services, such as inoculations against disease and screening for treatable disorders, which lays the groundwork for poorer health across the life span.

Social Psychological Factors

Social psychological factors—that is, an individual's attitude toward and beliefs about symptoms and health services—influence who uses health services. As we saw in Chapter 3, the health belief model maintains that whether a person seeks treatment for a symptom can be predicted from two factors: whether the person perceives a threat to health and whether he or she believes that a particular health measure will be effective in reducing that threat. The health belief model explains people's use of services quite well. But the model does a better job of explainig the treatment-seeking behavior of people who have money and access to health care services than of people who do not.

The use of health care services is influenced by socialization—chiefly, by the actions of one's parents. Just as children and adolescents learn other behaviors from their parents, they also learn when and how to use health care services.

Other factors that lead people to seek treatment involve relationships. For example, if one member of a couple is always tired, the partner eventually will become annoyed and insist that the other do something about the constant fatigue. Social interference is also a trigger for seeking help. When valued activities or social demands, such as a job or vacation, are threatened by a symptom, a person is more likely to seek prompt treatment than if no such threat is posed. Finally, social sanctioning, as when an employer applies pressure on a symptomatic individual to seek treatment or return to work, can lead to using health services.

Health services, then, are used by people who have the need, time, money, prior experience, beliefs that favor the use of services, and access to services.

■ MISUSING HEALTH SERVICES

Jerry rolled over when the alarm went off and realized that it was time to get ready to go to work. He'd been up late the night before playing cards with some friends, and as a result, he'd had only about 4 hours of sleep. As he thought about his assembly line job, the prospect of getting dressed and going to work on time seemed less and less attractive. As he swallowed, he noticed some tingling sensations in his throat. It could have been too many cigarettes, or maybe he was coming down with a cold. He thought, "If I call in sick today and get a note from the health clinic, I'll be in better shape for the rest of the week." Having rationalized his situation, Jerry went back to bed.

Health services may be abused as well as used. In this section, we consider several types of abuse. Some abuse is mild, such as Jerry's decision to get the health clinic to justify his sleeping off a late night instead of going to work. But in other cases, abuse is more serious. One type of abuse occurs when people seek out health services for problems that are not medically significant, overloading the medical system. Another type of abuse involves delay, when people should seek health care for a problem but do not.

Using Health Services for Emotional Disturbances

Physicians estimate that as much as half to two-thirds of their time is taken up by patients whose complaints are psychological rather than medical (Katon et al., 1990). This problem is more common for general practitioners than for specialists, although no branch of medicine is immune. (College health services periodically experience a version of this phenomenon during exam time; see Box 8.2.) These nonmedical complaints often stem from anxiety and depression, both of which, unfortunately, are widespread (Franko et al., 2005; Kubzansky,

Martin, & Buka, 2009). Patients who come to the emergency room with chest pain or who visit their physicians with cardiac symptoms are especially likely to have complicating anxiety and depressive disorders, with 23% estimated to have a co-occurring psychiatric disorder (Srinivasan & Joseph, 2004). Unfortunately, symptoms such as these can lead physicians to intervene with medical treatments that are inappropriate (Salmon, Humphris, Ring, Davies, & Dowrick, 2007).

Why do people seek a physician's care when their complaints should be addressed by a mental health specialist? There are several reasons (Henningsen, Zimmermann, & Sattel, 2003; Rief, Martin, Klaiberg, & Brähler, 2005). Stress and the emotional responses to it create a number of physical symptoms, and so, during stressful times, people use health services more. Anxiety, worry, depression, and other psychological disorders are accompanied by a number of physical symptoms (Pieper, Brosschot, van der Leeden, & Thayer, 2007). Anxiety can produce diarrhea, upset stomach, sweaty hands, shortness of breath (sometimes mistaken for asthma symptoms), difficulty in sleeping, poor concentration, and general agitation. Panic attacks can mimic the symptoms of a heart attack. Depression can lead to fatigue, difficulty in performing everyday activities, listlessness, loss of appetite, and sleep disturbances. People may mistake the symptoms of their mood disorder for a physical health problem and thus seek a physician's care (Vamos, Mucsi, Keszei, Kopp, & Novak, 2009). Psychopathology may not only influence the likelihood of seeking contact initially but also lead to multiple visits, slow recovery, and prolonged hospital stays as well (De Jonge, Latour, & Huyse, 2003; Rubin, Cleare, & Hotopf, 2004).

Who are these people? One group is the **worried well.** These people are concerned about physical and mental health, inclined to perceive minor symptoms as serious, and believe that they should take care of their own health. Paradoxically, their commitment to self-care actually leads them to use health services more (Wagner & Curran, 1984). The emphasis in our culture on living a healthy lifestyle, as well as media attention to new health problems and technologies, may inadvertently have increased the number of worried well people who use health services inappropriately (Filipkowski et al., 2009; Petrie & Wessely, 2002).

Another group of inappropriate users are **somaticizers**—that is, individuals who express distress and conflict through bodily symptoms (Escobar & Gureje, 2007; Verkuil, Brosschot, & Thayer, 2007). When they have experienced a threat to self-esteem, such individuals are

BOX 8.2

College Students' Disease

Visit the health service of any college or university just before exams begin, and you will see a unit bracing itself for an onslaught. Admissions to health services can double or even triple as papers become due and exams begin. Why does this influx occur?

Some of the increase in health service visits is due to an actual increase in illness. Students who are under academic pressure work long hours and eat and sleep poorly. As they run themselves down, their vulnerability to many common disorders can increase. Moreover, any one individual who develops an infectious disorder can give it to others who live in close proximity.

Some students may not actually be sick but think they are. Stressors such as upcoming exams can produce symptoms—such as inability to concentrate, sleeplessness, and upset stomach—which may be mistaken for illness. Moreover, exam time may preclude other activities that would provide distraction, so students may be more aware of these symptoms than they would otherwise be. In addition, the "symptoms" may make it hard for students to study, and disruption in important activities often acts as an impetus for seeking treatment.

Finally, there is the chronic procrastinator with four papers due but enough time to complete only two of them. What better excuse than illness for failure to meet one's obligations? Illness can legitimize procrastination, lack of motivation, lack of activity, and a host of other personal failures.

---

especially likely to somaticize, convince themselves they are physically ill, and seek treatment. This issue is so problematic that a study in the *Annals of Internal Medicine* suggested that physicians begin all their patient interviews with the direct questions "Are you currently sad or depressed" and "Are the things that previously brought you pleasure no longer bringing you pleasure?" Positive answers to questions such as these would suggest that the patient may need treatment for depression as well as, or even instead of, medical treatment (Means-Christensen, Arnau, Tonidandel, Bramson, & Meagher, 2005; Pignone et al., 2002; Rhee, Holditch-Davis, & Miles, 2005). Screening for traumatic life events has likewise been recommended for many of the same reasons (Holman, Silver, & Waitzkin, 2000). Unfortunately, psychiatric disorders continue to be underrecognized and undertreated in primary care (Jackson, Passamonti, & Kroenke, 2007).

Often, patients present with multiple physical symptoms that are chronic, unresponsive to treatment, and unexplained by any medical diagnosis; these patients have multisomatoform disorders (Jackson & Kroenke, 2008). Three or more unexplained symptoms may be a clue for identifying psychopathology in medical settings (Interian et al., 2004). Although a number of psychosocial interventions have been attempted with this group, so far, these interventions have not proven to be especially successful (Jackson & Kroenke, 2008).

Somaticization and related hypochondriasis may be more of an interpersonal disorder than vigilance regarding or misinterpretation of low-level symptoms. That is, hypochondriasis may be associated with insecure attachment that gives rise to the act of seeking care from others. Thus, people with interpersonal problems may seek reassurance by gaining medical attention (Noyes et al., 2003).

Another reason that people use health services for psychological complaints is that medical disorders are perceived as more legitimate than psychological ones. For example, a man who is depressed by his job and who stays home to avoid it will find that his behavior is more acceptable to both his employer and his wife if he says he is ill than if he admits he is depressed. Many people still believe that it is shameful to see a mental health specialist or to have mental problems.

Illness brings benefits, termed **secondary gains,** including the ability to rest, to be freed from unpleasant tasks, to be cared for by others, and to take time off from work. These reinforcements can interfere with the process of returning to good health. (Some of these factors may have played a role in one famous case of hysterical contagion; see Box 8.3.)

Finally, the inappropriate use of health services can represent true malingering. A person who does not want to go to work may know all too well that the only acceptable excuse that will prevent dismissal for absenteeism is illness. Moreover, workers may be required to document their absences in order to collect wages or disability payments and may thus have to keep looking until they find a physician who is willing to "treat" the "disorder."

Unfortunately, it can be hard to distinguish the worried well and those who seek treatment for psychological symptoms or needs from patients with legitimate medical complaints (Bombardier, Gorayeb, Jordan, Brooks, & Divine, 1991). Sometimes, patients are put

BOX 8.3

The June Bug Disease: A Case of Hysterical Contagion

One summer, a mysterious epidemic broke out in the dressmaking department of a southern textile plant, affecting 62 workers. The symptoms varied but usually included nausea, numbness, dizziness, and occasionally vomiting. Some of the ill required hospitalization, but most were simply excused from work for several days.

Almost all the affected workers reported having been bitten by a gnat or mite immediately before they experienced the symptoms. Several employees who were not afflicted said they had seen their fellow workers bitten before they came down with the disease. However, local, state, and federal health officials who were called in to investigate could obtain no reliable description of the suspected insect. Furthermore, careful inspection of the textile plant by entomologists and exterminators turned up only a small variety of insects—beetles, gnats, flies, an ant, and a mite—none of which could have caused the reported symptoms.

Company physicians and experts from the U.S. Public Health Service Communicable Disease Center began to suspect that the epidemic might be a case of hysterical contagion. They hypothesized that, although some of the afflicted individuals may have been bitten by an insect, anxiety or nervousness was more likely responsible for the onset of the symptoms. On hearing this conclusion, employees insisted that the "disease" was caused by a bite from an insect that was in a shipment of material recently received from England.

In shifting from a medical to a social explanation, health experts highlighted several points. First, the entire incident, from the first to the last reported case, lasted a period of 11 days, and 50 of the 62 cases (80%)

occurred on 2 consecutive days after the news media had sensationalized earlier incidents. Second, most of the afflicted individuals worked at the same time and place in the plant. Of the 62 afflicted employees, 59 worked on the first shift, and 58 worked in one large work area. Third, the 58 working at the same time and place were all women; one other woman worked on a different shift, two male victims worked on a different shift, and one man worked in a different department. Moreover, most of these women were married and had children; they were accordingly trying to combine employment and motherhood—often an exhausting arrangement.

The epidemic occurred at a busy time in the plant—June being a crucial month in the production of fall fashions—and there were strong incentives for employees to put in overtime and to work at a high pace. The plant was relatively new, and personnel and production management were not well organized. Thus, the climate was ripe for high anxiety among the employees.

Who, then, got "bitten" by the "June bug," and why? Workers with the most stress in their lives (married women with children) who were trying to cope with the further demands of increased productivity and overtime were most vulnerable. Job anxieties, coupled with the physical manifestations of fatigue (such as dizziness), created a set of symptoms that, given appropriate circumstances, could be labeled as illness. The rumor of a suspicious bug and the presence of ill coworkers apparently provided the appropriate circumstances, legitimizing the illness and leading to the epidemic that resulted.

Source: Kerckhoff & Back, 1968.

---

through many tests and evaluations before it is concluded that there may be a psychological rather than physical basis for their discomfort.

But errors can be made in the opposite direction as well: People with legitimate medical problems may be falsely assumed to be psychologically disturbed. Physicians are more likely to reach this conclusion about their female patients than their male patients (Redman, Webb, Hennrikus, Gordon, & Sanson-Fisher, 1991), even when objective measures suggest equivalent rates of psychological disturbance. Discriminating the truly physically ill from those who use health services to meet other needs can be a tricky business, complicated by physician bias as well as patient misuse of the system.

Delay Behavior

One morning, while Monica was taking a shower, she discovered a small lump in her left breast. She felt it a couple of times to make sure she wasn't just imagining it, but it was definitely there. A shudder of alarm passed through her, and she thought, "I should go in and get this checked." After she dried herself off and got dressed, she realized that this week would be a busy one and next week was no better. She had exams the following week, so she couldn't find any time in the next 2–3 weeks when she could get to the doctor to have it checked out.

"I'll have to wait until next month," she thought, "when things settle down a bit."

A very different misuse of health services occurs when an individual should seek treatment for a symptom but puts off doing so. A lump, chronic shortness of breath, blackouts, skin discoloration, radiating chest pain, seizures, and severe stomach pains are serious symptoms for which people should seek treatment promptly. Unfortunately, a person may live with one or more of these potentially serious symptoms for months without seeking care. This is called **delay behavior.** For example, a factor contributing to the high rate of death and disability from heart attacks is that patients often delay seeking treatment for its symptoms, instead normalizing them as gastric distress, muscle pain, and other, less severe disorders.

Delay is defined as the time between when a person recognizes a symptom and when the person obtains treatment. Delay is composed of several periods, diagrammed in Figure 8.1: **appraisal delay,** which is the time it takes an individual to decide that a symptom is serious; **illness delay,** which is the time between the recognition that a symptom implies an illness and the decision to seek treatment; **behavioral delay,** which is the time between deciding to seek treatment and actually doing so (Safer, Tharps, Jackson, & Leventhal, 1979); and **medical delay** (scheduling and treatment), which is the time that elapses between the person's calling for an appointment and his or her receiving appropriate medical care. Obviously, delay in seeking treatment for some symptoms is appropriate. For example, a runny nose or a mild sore throat usually will clear up on its own. However, in other cases, symptoms may be debilitating for weeks or months, and to delay seeking treatment is inappropriate.

Who Delays?   The reasons for delay have been extensively explored. Not surprisingly, the portrait of the delayer generally bears strong similarities to the portrait of the nonuser of services. A major factor in delay is the expense of treatment. When money is not readily available, people may persuade themselves that the symptoms are not serious enough to justify the expense (Safer et al., 1979). The elderly delay less than middle-aged individuals, particularly if they experience symptoms they think are serious (Leventhal, Easterling, Leventhal, & Cameron, 1995). Delay is common among people with no regular contact with a physician, because such people have the extra burden of finding someone from whom to seek treatment. Delay, like nonuse of services in general, is also more common among people who seek treatment primarily in response to pain or social pressure. People who are fearful of doctors, examinations, surgery, and medical facilities generally delay lon-

ger than do people who are not fearful. People with generally good medical habits are less likely to delay.

Because the delayer looks so much like the nonuser of services, one might expect the health belief model to predict delay behavior. In fact, it does. For example, people who fail to seek treatment for symptoms that may indicate cancer are more likely to believe that treatments will be extremely painful (high perceived costs of treatment) and to believe that nothing can be done to cure cancer (low perceived efficacy of treatment).

Symptoms and Delaying   Another factor that predicts delay is the nature of the symptoms. When a symptom is similar to one that previously turned out to be minor, the individual will seek treatment less quickly than if the symptom is new (see, for example, Safer et al., 1979). For example, women with a history of benign breast lumps may be less likely to have a new suspicious lump checked out than are women with no such history. Symptoms that do not hurt, symptoms that do not change quickly, and symptoms that are not incapacitating are less likely than their opposites to prompt a person to seek medical treatment (Safer et al., 1979).

Anytime a symptom is easily accommodated and does not provoke alarm, treatment may be delayed. For example, in the case of melanoma (Cassileth et al., 1988), people have trouble distinguishing between ordinary moles and melanomas and therefore delay seeking treatment, yet delay can be fatal. Similarly, if the primary symptom is a breast problem or a lump suggestive of breast cancer, women are more likely to be treated promptly than if the primary symptom is atypical (Meechan, Collins, & Petrie, 2003).

Treatment Delay   Surprisingly, delay does not end with the first treatment visit. Even after a consultation, up to 25% of patients delay taking recommended treatments, put off getting tests, or postpone acting on referrals. In some cases, patients have had their curiosity satisfied by the first visit and no longer feel any urgency about their condition. In other cases, patients become truly alarmed by the symptoms and, to avoid thinking about them, take no further action.

Provider Delay   Delay on the part of the health care practitioner is also a significant factor, accounting for at least 15% of all delay behavior (Cassileth et al., 1988). Medical delay occurs when an appropriate test or treatment is not undertaken with a patient until some time after it was needed. In most cases, health

FIGURE 8.1 | Stages of Delay in Seeking Treatment for Symptoms   (*Source:* Reprinted with permission from B. L. Anderson, J. T. Cacioppo, & D. C. Roberts, Delay in seeking a cancer diagnosis: Delay stages and psychophysiological comparison processes. *British Journal of Social Psychology* (1995) 34, 33–52. Fig.1, p. 35. © The British Psychological Society.)

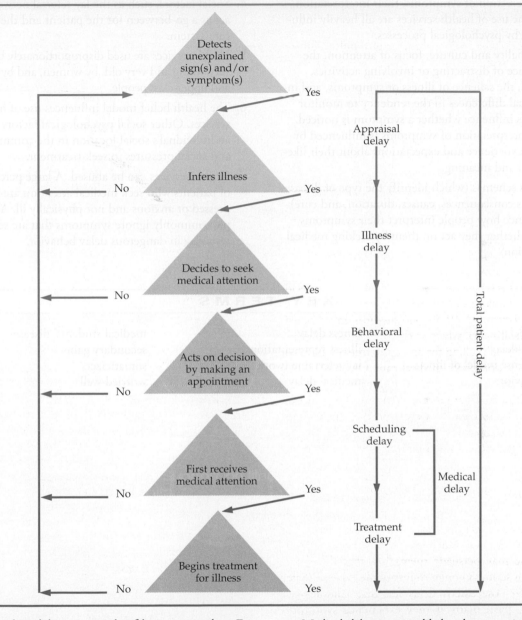

care providers delay as a result of honest mistakes. For example, blackouts can indicate any of many disorders ranging from heat prostration or overzealous dieting to diabetes or a brain tumor. A provider may choose to rule out the more common causes of the symptom before proceeding to the more invasive or expensive tests needed to rule out a less probable cause. Thus, when the more serious diagnosis is found to apply, the appearance of unwarranted delay exists.

Medical delay is more likely when a patient deviates from the profile of the average person with a given disease. For example, because breast cancer is most common among women age 45 or older, a 25-year-old woman with a breast lump might be sent home with a diagnosis of fibrocystic disease (a noncancerous condition) without being given a biopsy to test for possible malignancy. When a symptom indicates more than one possible diagnosis, the time before a proper diagnosis is reached may be increased. ●

SUMMARY

1. The detection of symptoms, their interpretation, and the use of health services are all heavily influenced by psychological processes.

2. Personality and culture, focus of attention, the presence of distracting or involving activities, mood, the salience of illness or symptoms, and individual differences in the tendency to monitor threats influence whether a symptom is noticed. The interpretation of symptoms is influenced by prior experience and expectations about their likelihood and meaning.

3. Illness schemas (which identify the type of disease and its consequences, causes, duration, and cure) influence how people interpret their symptoms and whether they act on them by seeking medical attention.

4. Social factors, such as the lay referral network, can act as a go-between for the patient and the medical care system.

5. Health services are used disproportionately by the very young and very old, by women, and by middle- and upper-class people.

6. The health belief model influences use of health services. Other social psychological factors include an individual's social location in the community and social pressures to seek treatment.

7. Health services can be abused. A large percentage of patients who seek medical attention are depressed or anxious and not physically ill. Also, people commonly ignore symptoms that are serious, resulting in dangerous delay behavior.

KEY TERMS

appraisal delay
behavioral delay
commonsense model of illness
delay behavior

illness delay
illness representations
lay referral network
medical delay

medical students' disease
secondary gains
somaticizers
worried well

Patient-Provider Relations

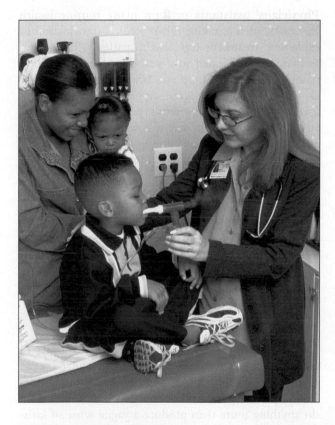

"I've had this cold for 2 weeks, so finally I went to the Student Health Services to get something for it. I waited more than an hour! And when I finally saw a doctor, he spent a whole 5 minutes with me, told me what I had was viral, not bacterial, and that he couldn't do anything for it. He sent me home and told me to get a lot of rest, drink fluids, and take over-the-counter medications for the stuffiness and the pain. Why did I even bother?!" (Student account of a trip to the health services)

Nearly everyone has a horror story about a visit to a physician. Long waits, insensitivity, apparently faulty diagnoses, and treatments that have no effect are the themes of these stories (Pescosolido, Tuch, & Martin, 2001). But in the same breath, the storyteller may expound on the virtues of his or her latest physician with an enthusiasm bordering on worship. To what do we attribute this seemingly contradictory attitude toward health care practitioners?

Health ranks among the values we hold dearest. Good health is a prerequisite to nearly every other activity, and poor health can interfere with nearly all one's activities. Moreover, illness is usually uncomfortable, so people want to be treated quickly and successfully. Perhaps, then, it is no wonder that physicians and other health care professionals are alternately praised and vilified: Their craft is fundamental to the enjoyment of life. In this chapter, we take up the complex issue of patient-provider interaction.

■ WHAT IS A HEALTH CARE PROVIDER?

Although physicians continue to be the main providers of health care, Americans are increasingly receiving much of their primary care from individuals other than physicians.

Nurses as Providers

Advanced-practice nursing is an umbrella term given to registered nurses who have gone beyond the typical 2–4 years of basic nursing education and who have multiple responsibilities for patients. For example, many **nurse-practitioners** are affiliated with physicians in private practice; they see their own patients, provide all routine medical care, prescribe treatment, monitor the progress of chronically ill patients, and see walk-in patients with a variety of disorders. As a consequence, they explain disorders and their origins, diagnoses, prognoses, and treatments. Even in medical practices that do not employ nurse-practitioners, much patient education falls to nurses. Nurses frequently give treatment instructions or screen patients before they are seen by a physician.

Other advanced-practice nurses include certified nurse midwives, who are responsible for some obstetrical care and births; clinical nurse specialists, who are experts in a specialty, such as cardiac or cancer care; and certified registered nurse anesthetists, who administer anesthesia. Given increasing demands on the medical system, an expanded role for nurses in primary health care is likely.

Physicians' Assistants as Providers

Physicians' assistants perform many routine health care tasks, such as taking down medical information or explaining treatment regimens to patients. Physicians' assistants are educated in 2-year programs in medical schools and teaching hospitals, as well as throughout the armed forces. Such programs typically require at least 2 years of college and previous experience in health care. In many instances, physicians' assistants take the same classes as medical students during the first year, and the second year is spent in clinical rotation, with direct patient contact.

As medical practice has become increasingly complex, other professionals, such as biofeedback technicians and psychologists, have also become involved in specialized care. Consequently, issues of communication—especially poor communication—that arise in medical settings are not the exclusive concern of the physician.

■ THE NATURE OF PATIENT-PROVIDER COMMUNICATION

Criticisms of providers usually center on volumes of jargon, lack of feedback, and depersonalized care. Clearly, the quality of communication with a provider is important to patients, but does good communication do anything more than produce a vague sense of satisfaction or dissatisfaction in the patient's mind? The answer is yes. Poor patient-provider communication has been tied to outcomes as problematic as nonadherence to treatment recommendations and the initiation of malpractice litigation.

Judging Quality of Care

People often judge the adequacy of their care by criteria that are irrelevant to its technical quality (Yarnold, Michelson, Thompson, & Adams, 1998). Most of us are insufficiently knowledgeable about medicine and standards of practice to know whether we have been treated well. Consequently, we often judge technical quality on the basis of the manner in which care is delivered. A warm, confident, friendly provider is judged to be both nice and competent, whereas a cool, aloof provider may be judged as both unfriendly and incompetent (Bogart, 2001). In reality, the technical quality of care and the manner in which care is delivered are unrelated.

Patient Consumerism

Whereas at one time the physician's authority was accepted without question or complaint, patients increasingly have adopted consumerist attitudes toward their health care (Steinbrook, 2006). This change is due to several factors.

First, to induce a patient to follow a treatment regimen, one must have the patient's full cooperation and participation in the treatment plan. Encouraging the patient to accept a role in the development and enactment of the plan can help ensure such commitment. Moreover, as we have seen, lifestyle is a major cause of disability and illness. Modifying lifestyle factors such as diet, smoking, and alcohol consumption must be done

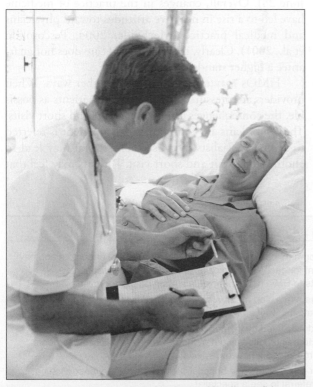

When physicians treat patients in a warm, friendly, confident manner, they are judged to be competent as well as nice.

with the patient's full cooperation if change is to be achieved (Lynch et al., 1992).

Patients often have expertise about their illness, especially if it is a recurring or chronic problem. A patient will do better if this expertise is tapped and integrated into the treatment program. For example, a study of pediatric asthma patients (Deaton, 1985) found that parents' modifications of a child's asthma regimen on the basis of severity of the disease, seasonal changes, symptoms, and side effects produced better asthma control than strict adherence to the prescribed medical regimen. Clearly, then, the relationship between patient and provider is changing in ways that make good communication essential. Nonetheless, many factors can erode communication.

Setting

In many ways, the medical office is an unlikely setting for effective communication. The average visit lasts only 12–15 minutes, and when you are trying to explain your symptoms, the physician will, on average, interrupt you before you get 23 seconds into your comments (Simon, 2003). Moreover, if you are ill, you must communicate that fact to another person, often a stranger; you must respond to specific and direct questions and then be content to be poked and prodded through the diagnostic process. At the very least, it is difficult to present your complaints effectively when you are in pain or have a fever, and your ability to be articulate may be reduced further by anxiety or embarrassment about the symptoms or the examination.

The provider, in turn, has the task of extracting significant information as quickly as possible from the patient. The provider is often on a tight schedule, with other patients backing up in the waiting room. The difficulties presented by the patient may have been made more complex by the use of various over-the-counter remedies, which can mask and distort the symptoms. Further, the patient's ideas of which symptoms are important may not correspond to the provider's knowledge, and so important signs may be overlooked. With the patient seeking solace and the provider trying to maximize the effective use of time, there clearly are many potential sources of strain.

Structure of the Health Care Delivery System

Until a few decades ago, the majority of Americans received their health care from private physicians, whom they paid directly on a visit-by-visit basis, in what was termed **private, fee-for-service care.** Each visit was followed by a bill, which the patient typically paid out of his or her own pocket.

That picture has changed. More than 69 million Americans now receive their health care through a prepaid financing and delivery system, termed a **health maintenance organization (HMO)** (National Center for Health Statistics, 2008). In this arrangement, an employer or employee pays an agreed-on monthly rate, and the employee is then entitled to use services at no additional (or a greatly reduced) cost. This arrangement is called **managed care.** In some cases, HMOs have their own staff, from which enrollees must seek treatment. In **preferred-provider organizations (PPOs),** a network of affiliated practitioners have agreed to charge preestablished rates for particular services, and enrollees in the PPO must choose from these practitioners when seeking treatment. Table 9.1 describes the differences among types of health care plans.

Patient Dissatisfaction in Managed Care

The changing structure of the health care delivery system can undermine patient-provider communication. Prepaid plans often operate on a referral basis, so that the provider who first sees the patient determines what is wrong and then recommends specialists to follow up with treatment. Because providers are often paid according to the number of cases they see, referrals are desirable. Therefore, a **colleague orientation,** rather than a client or patient orientation, can develop (Mechanic, 1975). Because the patient no longer pays directly for service, and because the provider's income is not directly affected by whether the patient is pleased with the service, the provider may not be overly concerned with

patient satisfaction. The provider is, however, concerned with what his or her colleagues think, because it is on their recommendations that he or she receives additional cases. In theory, such a system can produce high technical quality of care because providers who make errors receive fewer referrals; however, there is less incentive to offer emotionally satisfying care.

HMOs and Patient Care   In recent years, the question of whether HMOs offer a higher technical quality of care has come into question. As efficiency and cost-cutting pressures have assumed increasing importance, and as physicians have been urged to avoid expensive tests and shorten hospital stays, evidence suggests that quality of care has eroded. One study found that the ill elderly and poor fared especially poorly in HMOs, compared with people in fee-for-service practices. Because fee-for-service insurance allows patients a much broader choice of doctors and places fewer restrictions on services, their care is better, the study reported (Ware, Bayliss, Rogers, & Kosinski, 1996). An extensive evaluation of HMOs by an independent organization showed that quality of care ranged from barely satisfactory to excellent, depending on the facility (Spragins, 1996, June 24). Overall, changes in the practice of medicine have led to a rise in negative attitudes toward physicians and medical practice (Mechanic, 2004; Pescosolido et al., 2001). Clearly, then, managed care does not guarantee a higher standard of care.

HMOs may undermine care in other ways. When providers are pressured to see as many patients as possible, the consequences can be long waits and short visits. These problems are compounded if a patient is referred to several specialists, because each referral may lead to another long wait and short visit. Patients may feel that

TABLE 9.1 | Types of Health Care Plans

Name	How It Works
Health maintenance organization (HMO)	Members select a primary-care physician from the HMO's pool of doctors and pay a small fixed amount for each visit. Typically, any trips to specialists and nonemergency visits to HMO network hospitals must be preapproved.
Preferred-provider organization (PPO)	A network of doctors offers plan members a discounted rate. They usually don't need prior authorization to visit an in-network specialist.
Point-of-service plan (POS)	These are plans, administered by insurance companies or HMOs, that let members go to doctors and hospitals out of the network—for a price. Members usually need a referral to see a network specialist.
Traditional indemnity plan	Patients select their own doctors and hospitals and pay on a fee-for-service basis. They don't need a referral to see a specialist.

Sources: American Association of Health Plans, 2001; National Committee for Quality Assurance, 2001.

FIGURE 9.1 | Percentage of Physicians in Various Forms of Practice
(*Sources:* Bianco & Schine, 1997, March 24; Bureau of Labor Statistics, 2004)

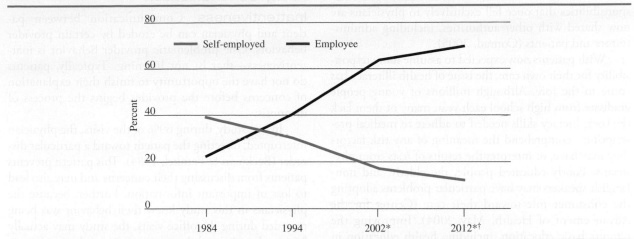

*Physicians & surgeons †Projected

they are being shunted from provider to provider with no continuity in their care and no opportunity to build up a personal relationship with any one individual. Increasingly, as Figure 9.1 suggests, third-party payment systems adopt cost-saving strategies that may inadvertently restrict clients' choices of when and how they can receive medical services. Because patients value choice, these restrictions contribute to dissatisfaction.

Precisely because problems have developed, some HMOs have taken steps to reduce long waits, to allow for personal choice, and to make sure a patient sees the same provider at each visit. However, the changing structure of medical practice generally may undermine emotional satisfaction and does not guarantee a high standard of care.

DRGs and Patient Care   One cost-containment effort involves the creation of **diagnostic-related groups (DRGs),** a patient classification scheme that determines the typical nature and length of treatment for particular disorders. Patients in a DRG category (for example, hernia surgery candidates) are assumed to be a homogeneous group that is clinically similar and that should require approximately the same types and amounts of treatments, length of hospitalization, and cost. DRGs define what are called trim points; these are the boundaries that define unusually long or short lengths of stay.

If patient care falls within the classification scheme, reimbursement for care will be forthcoming from the third party, whether the federal or state government or an insurance company. In the case of an outlier (for ex-

ample, a patient who stays in the hospital longer than the DRG specifies), the case is typically subject to review, and the extra costs may not be paid. This scheme thus puts pressure on medical facilities to limit patient stays and treatment costs.

Proponents maintain that DRGs can produce more efficient patient care, thereby reducing costs. The effects of DRGs on medical care are several. The DRG system implicitly rewards institutions for the detection and treatment of complications or co-occurring medically problematic conditions, so it provides an impetus for diagnostic vigilance. However, DRGs implicitly adopt biomedical criteria for how and how long a disease should be treated, often ignoring psychosocial issues. As a result, DRGs are quite poor predictors of patients' need for services and length of hospitalization. Finally, DRGs can contribute to a tendency to discharge patients before the DRGs' boundaries for length of stay are exceeded. Thus, although the presence of DRGs can have some positive effects on quality of care (such as attentiveness to the diagnostic process), they may also compromise care.

Changes in the Philosophy of Health Care Delivery

Changes in the philosophy of health care are altering delivery. Most importantly, the physician's role is changing. The newer organizational systems for delivering services, such as HMOs, and the rising numbers of women in the medical profession have changed what was once a physician role characterized by dominance and authority (Hartley, 1999; Warren, Weitz, & Kulis, 1998). Responsibilities that once fell exclusively to physicians are now shared with other authorities, including administrators and patients (Conrad, 2005).

With patients now expected to assume more responsibility for their own care, the issue of health illiteracy has come to the fore. Although millions of young people graduate from high school each year, many of them lack the basic literacy skills needed to adhere to medical prescriptions, comprehend the meaning of any risk factors they may have, or interpret the results of tests from physicians. Poorly educated people, the elderly, and non-English speakers may have particular problems adopting the consumer role toward their care (Center for the Advancement of Health, May 2004). Improving the nation's basic education, including health education in the early years, may help reduce this problem (Center for the Advancement of Health, May 2004).

The Holistic Health Movement and Health Care

Western medicine is increasingly incorporating Eastern approaches to medicine and nontraditional therapies, such as meditation and biofeedback. The philosophy of **holistic health,** the idea that health is a positive state to be actively achieved, not merely the absence of disease, has gained a strong foothold in Western medicine (Stewart, Brown, Weston, Mcwhinney, & McWilliam, 2003). This viewpoint acknowledges psychological and spiritual influences on achieving health, and it gives patients responsibility for both achieving health and curing illness through their behaviors, attitudes, and spiritual beliefs. Holistic health emphasizes health education, self-help, and self-healing. Natural, low-technology interventions and non-Western techniques of medical practice may be substituted for traditional care and include herbal medicine, acupuncture, acupressure, massage, psychic diagnosis, spiritual healing, the laying on of hands, and dance therapy (National Center for Complementary and Alternative Medicine, 2004).

These changes alter the relationship between provider and patient, making it more open, equal, and reciprocal and potentially bringing emotional contact into the relationship (McGregor, 2006). Even some physicians who do not subscribe to holistic health beliefs are trying to structure more egalitarian relationships with their patients and recognize that there may be less intrusive alternatives to traditional medical management that can achieve the same outcomes.

Provider Behaviors That Contribute to Faulty Communication

Inattentiveness   Communication between patient and physician can be eroded by certain provider behaviors. One problematic provider behavior is inattentiveness—that is, not listening. Typically, patients do not have the opportunity to finish their explanation of concerns before the provider begins the process of diagnosis.

In one study, during 69% of the visits, the physician interrupted, directing the patient toward a particular disorder (Beckman & Frankel, 1984). This pattern prevents patients from discussing their concerns and may also lead to loss of important information. Further, because the physicians in this study knew their behavior was being recorded during the office visits, the study may actually have underestimated the extent of this problem.

Physicians are often interrupted when they are with their patients, by a nurse, another doctor, the laboratory, a pharmacy, or a telephone call (Parikh, 2009, September 29). This is frustrating to patients and can undermine communication further.

Use of Jargon   Studies reveal that patients understand relatively few of the complex terms that providers often use. Why do providers use complex, hard-to-understand language? In some cases, jargon-filled explanations may be used to keep the patient from asking too many questions or from discovering that the provider actually is not certain what the patient's problem is.

Physicians have long used medical jargon to impress patients. As far back as the 13th century, the medieval physician Arnold of Villanova urged colleagues to seek refuge behind impressive-sounding language when they could not explain a patient's ailment. "Say that he has an obstruction of the liver," Arnold wrote, "and particularly use the word obstruction because patients do not understand what it means" (*Time,* 1970, p. 35). One physician explained, with great amusement, that if the term *itis* (meaning "inflammation of") was connected to whatever organ was troubled (for example, "stomachitis"), this would usually forestall any additional questions from the patient.

More commonly, however, providers' use of jargon may be a carryover from their technical training. Providers learn a complex vocabulary for understanding illnesses and communicating about them to other professionals; they often find it hard to remember that patients do not share this expertise. The use of jargon may also stem from an inability to gauge what the patient will understand.

Baby Talk   Because practitioners may underestimate what their patients will understand about an illness and its treatment, they may resort to baby talk and simplistic explanations. One woman, who is both a cancer researcher and a cancer patient, reports that when she goes to see her cancer specialist, he talks to her in a very complex and technical manner until the examination starts. Once she is on the examining table, he shifts to very simple sentences and explanations. She is now a patient and no longer a colleague.

Overly simple explanations coupled with infantilizing baby talk can make the patient feel like a helpless child. Moreover, such behavior can forestall questions. Having received a useless explanation, the patient may not know how to begin to ask for solid information. The tendency to lapse into simple explanations with a patient may become almost automatic.

The truth about what patients can understand lies somewhere between the extremes of technical jargon and baby talk. Typically, providers underestimate the ability of patients to understand information about the origins, diagnosis, prognosis, and treatment of their disorders (Waitzkin, 1985).

Nonperson Treatment   Depersonalization of the patient is another problem that impairs the quality of the patient-provider relationship (Kaufman, 1970). This nonperson treatment may be employed intentionally to try to keep the patient quiet while an examination, a procedure, or a test is being conducted, or it may be used unintentionally because the patient (as object) has become the focus of the provider's attention. One patient—a psychologist—reports:

> When I was being given emergency treatment for an eye laceration, the resident surgeon abruptly terminated his conversation with me as soon as I lay down on the operating table. Although I had had no sedative, or anesthesia, he acted as if I were no longer conscious, directing all his questions to a friend of mine—questions such as, "What's his name? What occupation is he in? Is he a real doctor?" etc. As I lay there, these two men were speaking about me as if I were not there at all. The moment I got off the table and was no longer a cut to be stitched, the surgeon resumed his conversation with me, and existence was conferred upon me again. (Zimbardo, 1969, p. 298)

To understand the phenomenon of nonperson treatment, consider what a nuisance it can be for a provider to have the patient actually there during a treatment—fussing, giving unhelpful suggestions, asking questions, and so on. If the patients could drop their bodies off, as they do their cars, and pick them up later, it would save both the provider and the patient a lot of trouble and anxiety. As it is, the provider is like an auto mechanic who has the misfortune of having the car's owner following him or her around, creating trouble, while he or she is trying to fix the car (Goffman, 1961). Erving Goffman suggests that providers cope with their bad luck by pretending that the patient is not there: "The patient is greeted with what passes for civility, and said farewell to in the same fashion, with everything in between going on as if the patient weren't there as a social person at all, but only as a possession someone has left behind" (pp. 341–342).

Nonperson treatment may be employed at particularly stressful moments to keep the patient quiet and to enable the practitioner to concentrate. In that way, it may serve a valuable medical function. But patient depersonalization can also have adverse medical effects. Medical staff making hospital rounds often use either highly technical or euphemistic terms when discussing cases with their colleagues. Unfortunately, these terms may confuse or alarm the nonparticipating but physically present patient, an effect to which the provider may be oblivious.

Patient depersonalization also provides emotional protection for the provider. It is difficult for a provider to work in a continual state of awareness that his or her every action influences someone's state of health and happiness (L. Cohen et al., 2003). Moreover, every provider has tragedies—as when a patient dies or is left incapacitated by a treatment—but the provider must find a way to continue to practice. Depersonalization helps provide such a way.

The emotion and empathy communicated by a provider in interaction with a patient can affect patient's attitude toward the provider, the visit, and his or her condition (Neumann et al., 2009). One study, for example, found that women getting their mammogram results from a seemingly worried physician recalled less information, perceived their situation to be more severe, showed higher levels of anxiety, and had significantly higher pulse rates than women receiving mammogram results from a nonworried physician (Shapiro, Boggs, Melamed, & Graham-Pole, 1992).

Generally speaking, when there is a mismatch between patient expectations regarding sharing of information, involvement in treatment, and socioemotional support, satisfaction with care is lower (Cvengros, Christensen, Cunningham, Hillis, & Kaboli, 2009).

BOX 9.1

What Did You Say?: Language Barriers to Effective Communication

Approximately 19% of the U.S. population speaks a language other than English at home, and more than 22 million people have limited English proficiency. Consequently, language barriers are a formidable problem. Often there are not interpreters available who can address this problem, and physicians' cultural competency, that is, their ability and comfort with dealing with patients from other backgrounds, may be low (Lucas, Michalopoulou, Falzarano, Menon, & Cunningham, 2008). Patients who experience language problems are less adherent to treatment, less likely to have a regular source of care, and more likely to leave the hospital against medical advice, among other problems (Flores, 2006).

Increasingly, language barriers contribute to communication problems (Fox, 2005). Consider the experiences of a 12-year-old Latino boy and his mother attempting to communicate what was wrong:

"La semana pasada a él le dio mucho mareo y no tenía fiebre ni nada, y la familia por parte de papá todos padecen de diabetes." (Last week, he had a lot of dizziness, and he didn't have fever or anything, and his dad's family all suffer from diabetes.) "Uh hum," replied the physician. The mother went on. *"A mí me da miedo porque él lo que estaba mareado, mareado, mareado y no tenía fiebre ni nada."* (I'm scared because he's dizzy, dizzy, dizzy, and he didn't have fever or anything.) Turning to Raul, the physician asked, "OK, so she's saying you look kind of yellow, is that what she's saying?" Raul interpreted for his mother: *"Es que se me vi amarillo?"* (Is it that I looked yellow?) *"Estaba como mareado, como pálido"* (You were dizzy, like pale), his mother replied. Raul turned back to the doctor. "Like I was like paralyzed, something like that," he said. (Flores, 2006, p. 229).

Stereotypes of Patients Communication may be eroded when physicians encounter patients or diseases that they would prefer not to treat. Negative stereotypes of patients may contribute to poor communication and subsequent treatment. Research shows that physicians give less information, are less supportive, and demonstrate less proficient clinical performance with Black and Hispanic patients and patients of lower socioeconomic class than is true for more advantaged patients, even in the same health care settings (van Ryn & Fu, 2003) (see Box 9.1). When a person is seen by a physician of the same race or ethnicity, satisfaction with treatment tends to be higher, underscoring the importance of increasing the number of minority physicians (Laveist & Nuru-Jeter, 2002).

Many physicians have negative perceptions of the elderly (Haug & Ory, 1987). Older patients may also be less likely to be resuscitated in emergency rooms or given active treatment protocols for life-threatening diseases (Haug & Ory, 1987; Morgan, 1985). The negative attitudes of physicians seem to be reciprocated in the elderly, in that among people age 65 and over, only 54% express high confidence in physicians.

Sexism is a problem in medical practice as well. For example, in experimental studies that attributed reported chest pain and stress to either a male or a female

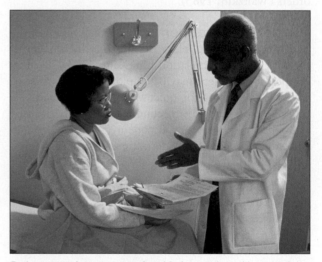

Patients are often most comfortable interacting with a physician who is similar to themselves.

patient, medical intervention was perceived to be less important for the female patient (Martin & Lemos, 2002). Male physicians and female patients do not always communicate well with each other.

Research suggests that in comparison with male physicians, female physicians generally conduct longer visits, ask more questions, make more positive comments during a visit, and show more nonverbal support, such as smiling and nodding (Hall, Irish, Roter, Ehrlich, & Miller, 1994). The matching of gender between patient and practitioner appears to foster more rapport and disclosure (Levinson, McCollum, & Kutner, 1984; Weisman & Teitelbaum, 1985). However, physicians of both genders still prefer male patients (Hall, Epstein, DeCiantis, & McNeil, 1993).

Patients who are regarded as seeking treatment largely for depression, anxiety, or other forms of psychological disorder also evoke negative reactions from physicians. With these patients, physician attention may be especially cursory (Epstein et al., 2006). Physicians also prefer healthier patients to sicker ones (Hall et al., 1993), and they prefer acutely ill to chronically ill patients; chronic illness poses uncertainties and raises questions about prognosis, which acute diseases do not (Butler, 1978). Chronic illness can also increase stress and distress over having to give bad news (L. Cohen et al., 2003).

Patients' Contributions to Faulty Communication

Within a few minutes of having discussed their illness with a provider, as many as one third of patients cannot repeat their diagnosis, and up to one half do not understand important details about the illness or treatment (Golden & Johnston, 1970). Some of these problems stem from faulty communication, but some also stem from patients themselves. Whereas dissatisfied patients complain about the incomplete or overly technical explanations they receive from providers, dissatisfied providers complain that even when they give clear, careful explanations to patients, the explanation goes in one ear and out the other.

Patient Characteristics   Several patient characteristics contribute to poor patient-provider communications. Neurotic patients often present an exaggerated picture of their symptoms (Ellington & Wiebe, 1999), compromising a physician's ability to effectively gauge the seriousness of a patient's condition. When patients are anxious, their learning can be impaired (Graugaard & Finset, 2000). Anxiety makes it difficult to focus attention and process incoming information and retain it (Graugaard & Finset, 2000).

Patient Knowledge   Some patients are unable to understand even simple information about their case (Galesic, Garcia-Retamero, & Gigerenzer, 2009; Link,

Phelan, Miech, & Westin, 2008), much less grasp the often bewildering health statistics with which they are confronted (Gigerenzer, Gaissmaier, Kurz-Milcke, Schwartz, & Woloshin, 2007). With patients now expected to assume more responsibility and increased decision making with respect to their care, lack of medical knowledge clearly interferes with their ability to play a consumer role effectively.

Patients for whom the illness is new and who have little prior information about the disorder show the greatest distortion in their explanations (DiMatteo & DiNicola, 1982). Cognitive deficits in memory and attention predict nonadherence and, as cognitive functioning can be quickly and easily assessed, measures of cognitive functioning may help to identify patients at particular risk for poor adherence (Stilley, Bender, Dunbar-Jacob, Sereika, & Ryan, 2010). Disorganized families with no regular routines have poorer adherence (Schreier & Chen, 2010). Low IQ, that is, low intelligence, is associated with a higher risk of early mortality (Hall, Dubin, Crossley, Holmqvist, & D'Arcy, 2009; Jokela, Elovainio, Singh-Manoux, & Kivimäki, 2009), in part because of low IQ's association with poor adherence, and so consequently, treatment recommendations must be very simple and very clear to offset risks.

Physicians are usually upper middle class and often White and male, whereas their patients may be of a lower social class, a different ethnicity, and a different sex. Consequently, there may also be class-based, sociolinguistic factors that contribute to poor communication (Waitzkin, 1985).

As people age, their number of medical problems usually increases, but their abilities to present their complaints effectively and to follow treatment guidelines can decrease. About 40% of patients over age 50 have difficulty understanding their prescription instructions. Extra time and care may be needed to communicate this vital information to older patients.

Patient Attitudes Toward Symptoms   Patients respond to different cues about their illness than do practitioners (Greer & Halgin, 2006). Patients place considerable emphasis on pain and on symptoms that interfere with their activities. But providers are more concerned with the underlying illness, its severity, and treatment. Patients may misunderstand the provider's emphasis on factors that they consider to be incidental, they may pay little attention, or they may believe that the provider has made an incorrect diagnosis.

Patients sometimes give providers misleading information about their medical history or their current concerns. Patients may be embarrassed about their health history (such as having had an abortion) or their health practices (such as being a smoker), and they may not report these important pieces of information to the physician (Smith, Adler, & Tschann, 1999).

Interactive Aspects of the Communication Problem

Qualities of the interaction between practitioner and patient can perpetuate faulty communication. A major problem is that the patient-provider interaction does not provide the opportunity for feedback to the provider. The provider sees the patient, the patient is diagnosed, treatment is recommended, and the patient leaves. When the patient does not return, any number of things may have happened: The treatment may have cured the disorder; the patient may have gotten worse and decided to seek treatment elsewhere; the treatment may have failed, but the disorder may have cleared up anyway; or the patient may have died. Not knowing which of these alternatives has actually occurred, the provider does not know the impact and success rate of the advice given. Obviously, it is to the provider's psychological advantage to believe that the diagnosis was correct, that the patient followed the advice, and that the patient's disorder was cured by the recommended treatment. However, the provider may never find out for certain.

The provider may also find it hard to know when a satisfactory personal relationship has been established with a patient. Many patients are relatively cautious with providers. If they are dissatisfied, rather than complain about it directly, they may simply change providers. The provider who finds that a patient has stopped coming does not know if the patient has moved out of the area or switched to another practice. When providers do get feedback, it is more likely to be negative than positive: Patients whose treatments have failed are more likely to go back than are patients whose treatments are successful (Rachman & Phillips, 1978).

Two points are important here. First, learning is fostered more by positive than by negative feedback; positive feedback tells one what one is doing right, whereas negative feedback may tell one what to stop doing but not necessarily what to do instead. Because providers get more negative than positive feedback, this situation is not conducive to learning. Second, learning occurs only with feedback, but in the provider's case,

lack of feedback is the rule. Clearly, it is hard for the provider to know whether communication is adequate and, if not, how to change it. It is no wonder, then, that when social scientists display their statistics on poor patient-provider communication, each provider can say with confidence, "Not me," because he or she indeed has no basis for self-recrimination.

■ RESULTS OF POOR PATIENT-PROVIDER COMMUNICATION

The patient-provider communication problems would be little more than an unfortunate casualty of medical treatment were it not for the toll they take on health. Dissatisfied patients are less likely to comply with treatment recommendations or to use medical services in the future; they are more likely to turn to alternative services that satisfy emotional rather than medical needs (Eisenberg et al., 1993); they are less likely to obtain medical checkups; and they are more likely to change doctors and to file formal complaints (Hayes-Bautista, 1976; Ware, Davies-Avery, & Stewart, 1978).

Nonadherence to Treatment Regimens

A 17th-century French playwright, Molière, aptly described the relationship that physicians and patients often have with respect to treatment recommendations:

> **THE KING:** You have a physician. What does he do?
> **MOLIÈRE:** Sire, we converse. He gives me advice which I do not follow and I get better. (Treue, 1958, as cited in Koltun & Stone, 1986).

Chapters 3, 4, and 5 examined **adherence** to treatment regimens in the context of health behaviors and noted how difficult it can be to modify or eliminate poor health habits, such as smoking, or to achieve a healthy lifestyle. In this section, we examine the role of health institutions, and particularly the role of the provider, in promoting adherence.

Rates of Nonadherence   When patients do not adopt the behaviors and treatments their providers recommend, the result is **nonadherence** or noncompliance (DiMatteo, 2004). Estimates of nonadherence vary from a low of 15% to a staggering high of 93%. Averaging across all treatment regimens, nonadherence to treatment recommendations is about 26% (DiMatteo, Giordani, Lepper, & Croghan, 2002).

BOX 9.2

Reducing Error in Adherence

The Center for the Advancement of Health is a non-profit organization whose goal is to promote greater recognition of the many ways that psychological, social, behavioral, economic, and environmental factors influence health and illness (Center for the Advancement of Health, 2009).

Among its concerns have been low levels of patient adherence to treatment. Included in the recommendations the center has proposed for treating this formidable problem are the following:

1. Make adult literacy a national priority.
2. Require that all prescriptions be typed on a keyboard.
3. Make commonplace a secure electronic medical record for each individual that documents his or her

complete medication history and that is accessible to both patients and their physicians.

4. Enforce requirements that pharmacists provide clear instructions and counseling along with prescription medication.
5. Develop checklists for both patients and doctors, so they can ask and answer the right questions before a prescription is written.

Recommendations such as these can empower patients and can even help mitigate racial and ethnic disparities in treatment (Maly, Stein, Umezawa, Leake, & Anglin, 2008).

But adherence rates vary dramatically, depending on the treatment recommendations. For short-term antibiotic regimens, one of the most common prescriptions, about one third of patients fail to comply adequately (see Rapoff & Christophersen, 1982). Between 50 and 60% of patients do not keep appointments for modifying preventive health behaviors (DiMatteo & DiNicola, 1982). More than 80% of patients who receive behavior-change recommendations from their doctors, such as stopping smoking or following a restrictive diet, fail to follow through. Even heart patients, who should be motivated to adhere, such as patients in cardiac rehabilitation, show an adherence rate of only 66–75% (Facts of Life, March 2003).

Overall, about 85% of patients fail to adhere completely to prescribed medications (O'Connor, 2006). Adherence is typically so poor that researchers believe that the benefits of many medications cannot be realized at the levels of adherence that most patients achieve (Haynes, McKibbon, & Kanani, 1996). Adherence is highest for treatments for HIV, arthritis, gastrointestinal disorders, and cancer, and lowest among patients with pulmonary disease, diabetes, and sleep disorders (DiMatteo et al., 2002).

Measuring Adherence Obtaining reliable indications of adherence is not an easy matter (Ingersoll & Cohen, 2008). One classic study that assessed use of the drug theophylline for patients suffering from chronic obstructive pulmonary disease (COPD) found that physicians reported that 78% of their COPD patients were on the medication, chart audit revealed that 62% of the

patients were on the medication, videotaped observation of patient visits produced an estimate of 69%, and only 59% of the patients reported they were on the drug (Gerbert, Stone, Stulbarg, Gullion, & Greenfield, 1988). And the study did not even assess whether theophylline was administered correctly, only if it was used at all.

Asking patients about their adherence yields artificially high estimates (Kaplan & Simon, 1990; Turk & Meichenbaum, 1991). As a consequence, researchers draw on indirect measures of adherence, such as the number of follow-up or referral appointments kept, but even these measures can be biased. Overall, the research statistics probably underestimate the amount of nonadherence that is actually going on.

Good Communication

Good communication fosters adherence (Gauchet, Tarquinio, & Fischer, 2007). Much nonadherence occurs because the patient does not understand what the treatment regimen is (Hauenstein, Schiller, & Hurley, 1987). Adherence is highest when the patient receives a clear, jargon-free explanation of the etiology, diagnosis, and treatment recommendations. Adherence is also enhanced by factors that promote good learning: Adherence is higher if the patient has been asked to repeat the instructions, if the instructions are written down, if unclear recommendations are pointed out and clarified, and if the instructions are repeated more than once (DiMatteo & DiNicola, 1982). Box 9.2 addresses some ways in which adherence errors may be reduced.

BOX 9.3

Protease Inhibitors (HAART): An Adherence Nightmare?

People living with AIDS who once believed they were at death's doorstep now have a life-prolonging treatment available to them in the form of protease inhibitors. Protease is an HIV enzyme that is required for HIV replication. Protease inhibitors, usually referred to as Highly Active Anti-Retroviral Therapy (HAART), prevent the protease enzyme from cleaving the virus complex into pathogenic virions (the infective form of a virus). Taken regularly, not only do protease inhibitors stop the spread of HIV, but in some cases, following treatment, people once diagnosed with AIDS show no trace of the virus in their bloodstreams.

But taking protease inhibitors regularly is the trick. Protease inhibitors have several qualities that make adherence problematic. First, many protease inhibitors must be taken four times a day. Most people can barely remember to take one tablet a day. Usually, a skipped date does not mean failure, whereas with protease inhibitors, missing even one dose may make the medication permanently unsuccessful. Many protease inhibitors require refrigeration, and consequently, the patient must remain close to the refrigerated drug throughout the day so as to take the medication on time. This factor is impractical for some people with AIDS.

For middle-class people with stable lives, regular employment, and socially supportive networks, adherence may be likely. However, for the poor, the homeless, and the unemployed, who may lack even a refrigerator for keeping protease inhibitors cold, much less the stable

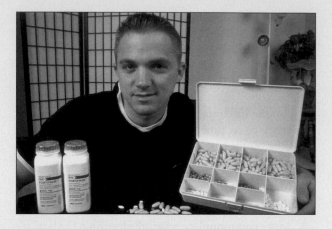

life that promotes their regular use, adherence is a difficult task. Moreover, drug use, chronic anxiety, and other affective or psychotic disorders interfere with the ability to use the drugs properly, and these states characterize some of the people who are eligible for protease inhibitors. Protease inhibitors also have unpleasant side effects, including diarrhea and nausea, which can lead to nonadherence.

In short, although protease inhibitors represent a life-saving discovery, they have many features that make their faithful use problematic. Integrating medication into busy, often chaotic and changing lives is difficult. But adherence holds the key to survival, so psychologists will be heavily involved in the effort to help people with AIDS adhere faithfully to the medication regimen.

Satisfaction with the patient-provider relationship predicts adherence (Gauchet et al., 2007). When patients perceive the provider as warm and caring, they are more compliant. Providers who answer patients' questions have more adherent patients (DiMatteo et al., 1993). Providers who show anger or impatience toward their patients, or who just seem busy, have more nonadherent patients (Sherbourne, Hays, Ordway, DiMatteo, & Kravitz, 1992).

The final step in adherence, one that is frequently overlooked, involves the patient's decision to adhere to a prescribed medical regimen. Many providers simply assume that patients will follow their advice, without realizing that the patients must decide to do so.

Treatment Regimen Qualities of the treatment regimen also influence the degree of adherence a patient

will exhibit (Ingersoll & Cohen, 2008). Treatment regimens that must be followed over a long time, that are highly complex, that require frequent dosage, and that interfere with other desirable behaviors in a person's life all show low levels of adherence (Ingersoll & Cohen, 2008; Turk & Meichenbaum, 1991). Unfortunately, as Box 9.3 illustrates, sometimes these can be the very treatment regimens on which survival depends. Keeping first appointments and obtaining medical tests are associated with high adherence rates (Alpert, 1964; for a review, see DiMatteo & DiNicola, 1982). Adherence is high (about 90%) when the advice is perceived as "medical" (for example, taking medication) but lower (76%) if the advice is vocational (for example, taking time off from work) and lower still (66%) if the advice is social or psychological (for example, avoiding stressful social situations) (Turk & Meichenbaum, 1991).

Complex self-care regimens show the lowest level of overall adherence (Blumenthal & Emery, 1988). Some people who have diabetes, for example, must take injections of insulin, monitor their blood glucose fluctuations, strictly control their dietary intake, and, in some cases, engage in prescribed exercise and stress management programs. Even with the best of intentions, it is difficult to engage in all the required behaviors, which take up several hours a day. Avoidant coping strategies are associated with poor adherence to treatment recommendations (Sherbourne et al., 1992). Consistent with the analysis of avoidant coping in Chapter 7, it may be that patients who cope with stressful events via avoidance are less attentive or responsive to information about threatening events, such as health problems.

Nonadherent patients also cite lack of time, no money, or distracting problems at home, such as instability and conflict, as impediments to adherence. Increasingly, people are cutting back on their prescriptions to save money (Heisler, Wagner, & Piette, 2005).

People who enjoy the activities in their lives are more motivated to adhere to treatment. Adherence is substantially higher with patients who live in cohesive families but lower with patients whose families are in conflict (DiMatteo, 2004). Likewise, people who are depressed show poor adherence to treatment medication (DiMatteo, Lepper, & Croghan, 2000).

Creative Nonadherence   One especially interesting form of nonadherence is termed **creative nonadherence,** or intelligent nonadherence, because it involves modifying and supplementing a prescribed treatment regimen. For example, a poor patient may change the dosage level of required medication to make the medicine last as long as possible or may keep some medication in reserve in case another family member comes down with the same disorder. One study of nonadherence among the elderly estimated that 73% of nonadherence was intentional rather than accidental (Cooper, Love, & Raffoul, 1982).

Creative nonadherence can also result from personal theories about a disorder and its treatment (Wroe, 2001). For example, patients may decide that particular symptoms that merit treatment were ignored by the provider; they may then supplement the treatment regimen with over-the-counter preparations or home remedies that interact with prescribed drugs in unpredictable, even dangerous ways. Alternatively, the patient may alter the dosage requirement, reasoning, for example, that

if four pills a day for 10 days will clear up the problem, eight pills a day for 5 days will do it twice as quickly. Nonadherence, then, is a widespread and complex behavior.

Malpractice Litigation

Once rare, the number of malpractice suits has exploded in recent decades. Some of this malpractice litigation can be tied to increases in the technical complexity of medicine. The overuse of new and complex machinery can lead to patient harm, either because the treatment is not necessary or because the side effects of the technology are not known. A 1999 report by the Institute of Medicine estimated that between 48,000 and 98,000 errors occur every year and that most of these are medication errors, such as prescribing the wrong drug or wrong dosage (Institute of Medicine, 1999). Malpractice litigation has also been tied to the administrative complexity of the health care system. Patients may be unwilling to sue an individual physician, but if they can sue an institution and convince themselves that the settlement money will never be missed, they are more likely to sue (Halberstam, 1971, February 14).

Although the most common grounds for a malpractice suit continue to be incompetence and negligence, patients are increasingly citing factors related to poor communication as a basis for their suits, such as not being fully informed about a treatment. Studies designed to unearth the causes of discretionary malpractice litigation confirm the importance of communication factors. The research found that more suits were initiated against physicians who were fearful of patients, insecure with them, or derogatory toward them.

When patients felt that their medical complaints had been ignored or rudely dismissed, they were more likely to file suit, perhaps as retaliation. According to a health care negotiator, patients are seeking three things when a medical mistake has occurred:

1. They want to find out what happened.
2. They want an apology from the doctor or hospital.
3. They want to know that the mistake will not happen again (Reitman, 2003, March 24).

An explanation, apology, and reassurance can go some way in muting the effects of malpractice. In a study designed to test this point, 958 members of an HMO were given a fictitious situation involving a doctor who made a mistake with varying consequences and then disclosed it with varying degrees of candor. For example, in one case, the doctor prescribed a drug without asking the patient whether he or she had allergies, and the patient suffered an adverse reaction as a result. In another case, the doctor prescribed a drug to an elderly patient that affected balance, and the patient subsequently fell. In some cases, the doctor apologized unreservedly ("This was my mistake, and I feel terrible"), whereas in other cases, the doctor was more evasive ("It is an unfortunate thing that happens every now and then"). Patients were then asked what they thought they would do in response to such a circumstance—stay with the doctor, change doctors, or talk with an attorney. On the whole, the physician was viewed more favorably when he admitted to making the mistake (Mazor et al., 2004).

The long-term fallout from the escalating frequency and costs of malpractice suits is that many physicians have had to change the way they conduct their practices, and some have had to leave medicine altogether. For example, malpractice premiums are so high for obstetricians that some have decided to move to other specialties where malpractice insurance is lower (Eisenberg & Sieger, 2003, June 9).

■ IMPROVING PATIENT-PROVIDER COMMUNICATION AND REDUCING NONADHERENCE

The fact that poor patient-provider communication appears to be so widespread and tied to problematic outcomes suggests that improving the communication process should be a high priority. One approach to the problem involves teaching providers how to communicate more effectively (Frostholm et al., 2005b).

Teaching Providers How to Communicate

Providers have known for some time that the course of medical treatment can be affected by communication (see, for example, Shattuck, 1907), yet many may see communication as a skill or knack that some people have and others do not. However, it is now known that anyone, given the desire, has the potential to be an effective communicator.

Training Providers   Any communication program should teach skills that can be learned easily, that can be incorporated in medical routines easily. Many commu-

nication failures in medical settings stem from violations of simple rules of courtesy: greeting patients, addressing them by name, telling them where they can hang up their clothes if an examination is necessary, explaining the purpose of a procedure while it is going on, saying goodbye, and, again, using the patient's name. Such simple behaviors add a few seconds at most to a visit, yet they are seen as warm and supportive (DiMatteo & DiNicola, 1982).

Communication needs to be practiced in situations in which the skills will be used. Training that uses direct, supervised contact with patients and gives students immediate feedback after a patient interview works well for training both medical and nursing students (Leigh & Reiser, 1986). Even experienced physicians profit from this kind of training (Haskard et al., 2008). Videotaping the student's interactions with patients makes it possible for good and bad points in the interview to be pointed out (Levenkron, Greenland, & Bowlby, 1987). Specially made tapes that illustrate common problems can be used so that students can see both the right and the wrong ways to

When physicians present concrete advice about lifestyle change, patients are more likely to adhere.

BOX 9.4

Improving Adherence to Treatment

Nonadherence to treatment is a formidable medical problem. More than 85% of patients are at least occasionally nonadherent to treatment (O'Connor, 2006). Many of the reasons for nonadherence can be traced directly to poor communication between provider and patient. The following are some guidelines generated by research findings that can help providers improve adherence:

1. Listen to the patient.
2. Ask the patient to repeat what has to be done.
3. Keep the prescription as simple as possible.
4. Give clear instructions on the exact treatment regimen, preferably in writing.
5. Make use of special reminder pill containers and calendars.
6. Call the patient if an appointment is missed.
7. Prescribe a self-care regimen in concert with the patient's daily schedule.
8. Emphasize at each visit the importance of adherence.
9. Gear the frequency of visits to adherence needs.
10. Acknowledge at each visit the patient's efforts to adhere.
11. Involve the patient's spouse or other partner.

12. Whenever possible, provide the patient with instructions and advice at the start of the information to be presented.
13. When providing the patient with instructions and advice, stress how important they are.
14. Use short words and short sentences.
15. Use explicit categorization where possible. (For example, divide information clearly into categories of etiology, treatment, or prognosis.)
16. Repeat things, where feasible.
17. When giving advice, make it as specific, detailed, and concrete as possible.
18. Find out what the patient's worries are. Do not confine yourself merely to gathering objective medical information.
19. Find out what the patient's expectations are. If they cannot be met, explain why.
20. Provide information about the diagnosis and the cause of the illness.
21. Adopt a friendly rather than a businesslike attitude.
22. Avoid medical jargon.
23. Spend some time in conversation about nonmedical topics.

Source: Based on DiMatteo, 2004.

---

handle issues (see, for example, Kagan, 1974). Increasingly, cultural competence—that is, developing knowledge and skills for communicating with a multicultural patient constituency—is emphasized (Fox, 2005).

Nonverbal communication can create an atmosphere of warmth or coldness. A forward lean and direct eye contact, for example, can reinforce an atmosphere of supportiveness, whereas a backward lean, little eye contact, and a postural orientation away from the patient can undercut verbal efforts at warmth by suggesting distance or discomfort (DiMatteo, Friedman, & Taranta, 1979). The ability to understand what patients' nonverbal behaviors may mean can also be associated with better communication and adherence (DiMatteo, Hays, & Prince, 1986) (see Box 9.4).

More complex material may be introduced into courses, such as how to draw out a reticent patient, how to deal with a patient's guilt or shame over particular

symptoms, how to learn what a symptom means to the patient, and how to communicate bad news (Ptacek & McIntosh, 2009). Patient-centered communication is one way to improve the patient-provider dialogue. This type of communication enlists the patient directly in decisions about medical care: Providers try to see the disorder and the treatment as the patient does, and in so doing enlist the patient's cooperation in the diagnostic and treatment process. This approach seems to be especially effective with "difficult" patients, such as those who are anxious (Neumann et al., 2009; Stewart et al., 2003). Evaluations of these methods indicate that communication training with physicians can improve patient satisfaction with care (Frostholm et al., 2005b).

Training Patients Interventions to improve patient-provider interaction include teaching patients skills for eliciting information from physicians (Greenfield, Kaplan,

Ware, Yano, & Frank, 1988). For example, a study by S. C. Thompson and colleagues (Thompson, Nanni, & Schwankovsky, 1990) instructed women to list three questions they wanted to ask their physician during their visit. Compared with a control group, women who listed questions in advance asked more questions during the visit and were less anxious. In a second study, Thompson and her colleagues added a third condition: Some women received a message from their physician encouraging question asking. These women, too, asked more of the questions they wanted to, had greater feelings of personal control, and were more satisfied with the office visit. This pair of studies suggests that either thinking up one's own questions ahead of time or perceiving that the physician is open to questions improves communication during office visits, leading to greater patient satisfaction.

Probing for Barriers to Adherence   Patients are remarkably good at predicting how compliant they will be with treatment regimens (Kaplan & Simon, 1990). By making use of this personal knowledge, the provider may discover what some of the barriers to adherence will be. For example, if the patient has been told to avoid stressful situations but anticipates several high-pressure meetings the following week at work, the patient and provider together might consider how to resolve this dilemma—one option may be to have a coworker take the patient's place at some of the meetings.

For the vocational and social advice for which non-adherence rates are known to be high, special measures are needed. The health care provider can begin by explaining why these seemingly nonmedical aspects of the treatment regimen are, in fact, important to health.

Because of the face-to-face nature of patient-provider interaction, the provider may be in a good position to extract a commitment from the patient—that is, a promise that the recommendations will be undertaken and followed through. Such verbal commitments are associated with increased adherence (Kulik & Carlino, 1987).

Breaking advice down into manageable subgoals that can be monitored by the provider is another way to increase adherence. For example, if patients have been told to alter their diet and lose weight, intermediate weight-loss goals that can be checked at successive appointments might be established ("Try to lose 3 pounds this week").

The importance of the physician's recommendation should not be underestimated. When lifestyle change programs are "prescribed" for patients by physicians, patients show higher rates of adherence than if they are simply urged to make use of them (Kabat-Zinn & Chapman-Waldrop, 1988). Reasons why the health provider can change patient's health behaviors are listed in Table 9.2.

Overall, perhaps the best way to think about adherence is as an effective combination of information, motivation, and behavioral skills (Figure 9.2).

Health Care Institution Interventions

Several interventions at the institutional level can foster adherence. Postcards or phone calls to patients reminding them to return can reduce high rates of no-shows (Friman, Finney, Glasscock, Weigel, & Christopherson, 1986). Reducing the amount of time a patient must wait before receiving service also improves the rate of follow-through on appointments (Mullen & Green, 1985).

FIGURE 9.2 | The Information-Motivation-Behavioral Skills Model of Health Behavior   The information-motivation-behavioral skills (IMB) model makes it evident that, to practice good health behaviors and adhere to treatment, one needs the right information, the motivation to adhere, and the skills to perform the behavior. Adapted from a model of AIDS risk-related behaviors, the IMB has applicability more generally to issues of adherence and health behavior change. (*Sources:* From Fisher & Fisher, 1992; Fisher, Fisher, Amico, & Harman, 2006; Fisher, Fisher, & Harman, 2003)

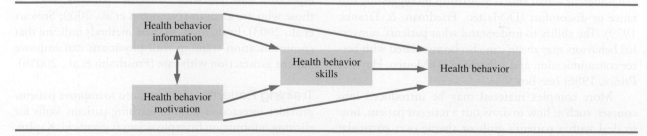

TABLE 9.2 | Why the Health Practitioner Can Be an Effective Agent of Behavior Change

- The health practitioner is a highly credible source with knowledge of medical issues.
- The health practitioner can make health messages simple and tailor them to the individual needs and vulnerabilities of each patient.
- The practitioner can help the patient decide to adhere by highlighting the advantages of treatment and the disadvantages of nonadherence.
- The private, face-to-face nature of the interaction provides an effective setting for holding attention, repeating and clarifying instructions, extracting commitments from a patient, and assessing sources of resistance to adherence.
- The personal nature of the interaction enables a practitioner to establish referent power by communicating warmth and caring.
- The health practitioner can enlist the cooperation of other family members in promoting adherence.
- The health practitioner has the patient under at least partial surveillance and can monitor progress during subsequent visits.

■ THE PATIENT IN THE HOSPITAL SETTING

More than 35 million people are admitted yearly to the nearly 6,000 hospitals in this country (American Hospital Association, 2009a). As recently as 60 or 70 years ago, hospitals were thought of primarily as places where people went to die (Noyes et al., 2000). Now, however, the hospital serves many treatment functions. As a consequence, the average length of a hospital stay has decreased, as Figure 9.3 illustrates. This has occurred largely because outpatient visits have increased, climbing to approximately 600 million in 2007 (American Hospital Association, 2009a). The hospital has always fascinated social scientists because its functions are so many and varied: It is a custodial unit, a treatment center, a teaching institution, a research center, and a laboratory. Because of the diversity of treatment needs, many kinds of skills are needed in hospitals.

Structure of the Hospital

To understand the psychological impact of hospitalization, it is useful to have a working knowledge of the hospital's structure and functions. The structure of

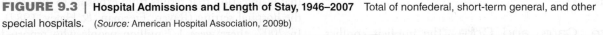

FIGURE 9.3 | Hospital Admissions and Length of Stay, 1946–2007   Total of nonfederal, short-term general, and other special hospitals.   (*Source*: American Hospital Association, 2009b)

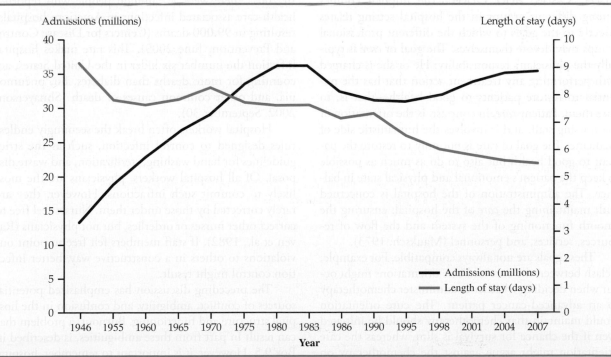

hospitals depends on the health program under which care is delivered. For example, some health maintenance organizations (HMOs) and other prepaid health care systems have their own hospitals and employ their own physicians. Consequently, the hospital structure is organized very much like any other hierarchical bureaucracy, with administration at the top and physicians, nurses, and technicians as employees.

In the case of the private hospital, a more unusual structure typically exists. There are two lines of authority—a medical line, which is based on technical skill and expertise, and an administrative line, which runs the business of the hospital. Physicians are at the top of the medical line of authority and are accorded high status because they are chiefly responsible for the treatment of patients. Typically, however, they are not directly employed by the hospital but, rather, admit their patients in exchange for laboratories, custodial services, equipment, and teaching facilities that the hospital can provide. Because physicians are not directly under the administrative line of authority, the two lines of authority can sometimes be at odds. Nurses are part of both lines of authority. Employed by the hospital, they also assist the physician and are thus subject to both lines of authority, which can create conflicting requirements and needs.

Cure, Care, and Core   The implicit conflict among different groups in the hospital setting relates directly to the goals to which the different professional groups may devote themselves. The goal of *cure* is typically the physician's responsibility: He or she is charged with performing any treatment action that has the potential to restore patients to good health—that is, to cure them. Patient *care,* in contrast, is the orientation of the nursing staff, and it involves the humanistic side of medicine. The goal of care is not only to restore the patient to good health but also to do as much as possible to keep the patient's emotional and physical state in balance. The administration of the hospital is concerned with maintaining the *core* of the hospital: ensuring the smooth functioning of the system and the flow of resources, services, and personnel (Mauksch, 1973).

These goals are not always compatible. For example, a clash between the cure and care orientations might occur when deciding whether to administer chemotherapy to an advanced-cancer patient. The cure orientation would maintain that chemotherapy should be initiated even if the chance for survival is slim, whereas the care orientation might argue against the chemotherapy on

the grounds that it causes patients great physical and emotional distress. In short, then, the different professional goals in a hospital treatment setting can create conflicting demands on the resources and personnel of the hospital.

Functioning of the Hospital

Conditions change rapidly in the hospital, which means that patient care often involves abrupt changes in roles and activities. That is, although each person involved in patient care has general responsibilities, under conditions of emergency, each must remain flexible to respond effectively to the changing situation.

The different goals of different professionals in the hospital setting are reflected in hospital workers' communication patterns. Occupational segregation is high: Nurses talk to other nurses, physicians to other physicians, and administrators to other administrators. Physicians have access to some information that nurses may not see, whereas nurses interact with patients daily and know a great deal about their day-to-day progress, yet often their notes on charts go unread by physicians.

An example of the problems associated with lack of communication is provided by nosocomial infection—that is, infection that results from exposure to disease in the hospital setting (Raven, Freeman, & Haley, 1982). In 2007, there were 1.7 million people who reported health-care associated infections in American hospitals, resulting in 99,000 deaths (Centers for Disease Control and Prevention, June 2009). This rate makes hospital infection the number six killer in the United States, accounting for more deaths than diabetes, flu, pneumonia, and other common causes of death (Shnayerson, 2002, September 30).

Hospital workers often break the seemingly endless rules designed to control infection, such as the strict guidelines for hand washing, sterilization, and waste disposal. Of all hospital workers, physicians are the most likely to commit such infractions. However, they are rarely corrected by those under them. Nurses feel free to correct other nurses or orderlies, but not physicians (Raven et al., 1982). If staff members felt free to point out violations to others in a constructive way, better infection control might result.

The preceding discussion has emphasized potential sources of conflict, ambiguity, and confusion in the hospital structure and functioning. Burnout, a problem that can result in part from these ambiguities, is described in Box 9.5. However, it is important to remember, hospital

Burnout Among Health Care Professionals

Burnout is an occupational risk for anyone who works with needy people (Maslach, 2003). It is a particular stress-related problem for physicians, nurses, and other medical personnel who work with sick and dying people (Rutledge et al., 2009). Burnout is marked by three components: emotional exhaustion, cynicism, and a low sense of efficacy in one's job. Staff members suffering from burnout show a cynical and seemingly callous attitude toward those whom they serve. Their view of clients is negative, and they often treat clients in detached ways (Maslach, 2003).

The effects of burnout are manifold. Burnout has been linked to absenteeism, high job turnover, lengthy breaks during working hours, and even suicide (Schernhammer, 2005). When burned-out workers go home, they are often irritable with their families. They are more likely to suffer from insomnia as well as drug and alcohol abuse, and they have a higher rate of psychosomatic disorders. Thus, burnout has substantial costs for both the institution and the individual (Parker & Kulik, 1995).

Why does burnout develop? Burnout may develop when a person is required to provide services for highly needy people who may not be helped by those services: The problems may be just too severe, as with patients who will not recover. Moreover, such jobs often require the staff member to be consistently empathic, an unrealistic expectation. Often, caregivers perceive that they give much more than they get back from their patients, and this imbalance aggravates burnout as well (Van Yperen, Buunk, & Schaufelli, 1992). Too much time spent with clients, little feedback, little sense of control or autonomy, little perception of success, role conflict, and role ambiguity are job factors that all aggravate burnout (Maslach, 1979).

High rates of burnout are found among nurses who work in stressful environments, such as intensive care, emergency rooms, or terminal care (Mallett, Price, Jurs, & Slenker, 1991; Moos & Schaefer, 1987). Many nurses find it difficult to protect themselves from the pain they feel from watching their patients suffer or die. The stress of the work environment, including the hectic pace of the hospital and the hurried, anxious behavior of coworkers, also contributes to burnout (Parker & Kulik, 1995).

Not surprisingly, because burnout results from stress, it is tied to neuroendocrine functioning. Burnout leads to elevated stress hormones (Pruessner, Hellhammer, & Kirschbaum, 1999) and disturbances in cortisol rhythms (Mommersteeg, Keijsers, Heijnen, Verbraak, & van Doornen, 2006; Zanstra, Schellekens, Schaap, & Kooistra, 2006). Burnout has also been tied to changes

in immune functioning (Lerman et al., 1999) and to poor health (Langelaan, Bakker, Schaufeli, van Rhenen, & van Doornen, 2007).

How can burnout be avoided? Group interventions can be helpful in reducing not only the distress of burnout but also the cortisol dysregulation that can accompany it (Mommersteeg et al., 2006). A support group can provide workers with an opportunity to meet informally with others to deal with the problems they face. These groups can give workers the opportunity to obtain emotional support, reduce their feelings of being alone, share feelings of emotional pain about death and dying, and vent emotions in a supportive atmosphere. In so doing, they may ultimately improve client care (Duxbury, Armstrong, Dren, & Henley, 1984). Interventions that enroll hospital workers in job stress management programs can help them control current feelings of burnout, as well as head off future episodes (Rowe, 1999). For example, seeing what other people do to avoid burnout can provide a useful model for one's own situation. People who are able to avoid burnout have higher self-esteem, a strong sense of personal control, and optimism about the future (Browning, Ryan, Greenberg, & Rolniak, 2006). They are also more likely to turn to others for help. Institutionalizing this kind of supportive buffer may be a way to control burnout (Moos & Schaefer, 1987; Shinn, Rosario, Morch, & Chestnut, 1984).

functioning is remarkably effective, given the changing realities to which it must accommodate. Thus, the ambiguities in structure, potential conflicts in goals, and problems of communication occur within a system that generally functions quite well.

Recent Changes in Hospitalization

In recent years, alternatives to traditional hospital treatment have emerged that patients use for many disorders. Walk-in clinics deal with less serious complaints and routine surgeries that used to require hospitalization. Clinics handle a large proportion of the smaller emergencies that historically have filled the hospital emergency room. Home help services and hospices provide care for the chronically and terminally ill who require primarily palliative and custodial care rather than active medical intervention. A consequence of removing these bread-and-butter cases from acute care hospitals has been to increase the proportion of resources devoted to the severely ill, whose care tends to be expensive and labor-intensive. With these pressures toward increasing costs, many hospitals may be unable to survive.

Cost-Cutting Pressures   In recent years, there have been increasing pressures to contain spiraling health care costs. With the institution of diagnostic-related groups (DRGs), hospitals have gone from being overcrowded to being underused, with vacancy rates as high as 70%. This situation, in turn, creates economic pressures to admit more patients to the hospital (Wholey & Burns, 1991), albeit for shorter stays. Increasingly, insurance companies and other third-party providers designate the particular hospital or treatment facility that a patient must use in order to be reimbursed for services. Patients who wish to go elsewhere have to pay the additional costs themselves. The consequence has been to keep treatment costs lower than they might otherwise be.

Hospitals are experiencing a variety of other changes as well. Approximately 48% of U.S. hospitals are currently part of a multihospital system (American Hospital Association, 2009b). This means that hospitals are no longer as independent as they once were and instead may be subject to rules and regulations established by a higher level of authority.

The Role of Psychologists   The number of psychologists in hospital settings has more than doubled over the past 10 years, and their roles have expanded. Psychologists participate in the diagnosis of patients, particularly through the use of personality, intelligence, and neuropsychological tests. Psychologists also determine patients' general level of functioning, as well as their strengths and weaknesses, which can help form the basis for therapeutic intervention. Psychologists are also involved in pre- and postsurgery preparation, pain control, interventions to increase medication and treatment compliance, and behavioral programs to teach appropriate self-care following discharge (Enright, Resnick, DeLeon, Sciara, & Tanney, 1990). In addition, they diagnose and treat psychological problems that can complicate patient care. As our country's medical care system evolves over the next decades, the role of psychologists in the hospital will continue to change.

The Impact of Hospitalization on the Patient

> The patient comes unbidden to a large organization which awes and irritates him, even as it also nurtures and cares. As he strips off his clothing so he strips off, too, his favored costume of social roles, his favored style, his customary identity in the world. He becomes subject to a time schedule and a pattern of activity not of his own making. (Wilson, 1963, p. 70)

Patients arrive at the hospital anxious about their disorder, anxious and confused over the prospect of hospitalization, and concerned with all the role obligations they must leave behind unfulfilled. The hospital does little, if anything, to calm anxiety and in many cases exacerbates it. The admission is often conducted by a clerk, who asks about scheduling, insurance, and money. The patient is then ushered into a strange room, given strange clothes, provided with an unfamiliar roommate, and subjected to peculiar tests. The patient must entrust him- or herself completely to strangers in an uncertain environment in which all procedures are new.

Hospital patients can show problematic psychological symptoms, especially anxiety and depression. Nervousness over tests or surgery and their results can produce insomnia, nightmares, and a general inability to concentrate. Procedures that isolate or immobilize patients are particularly likely to result in psychological distress. Hospital care can be fragmented, with as many as 30 different staff passing through a patient's room each day, conducting tests, taking blood, bringing food, or cleaning up. Often, the staff members have little time to spend with the patient beyond exchanging greetings, which can be alienating for the patient.

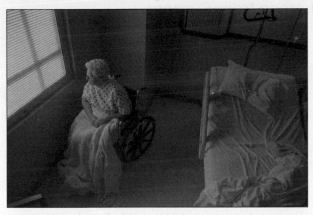

The hospital can be a lonely and frightening place for many patients, leading to feelings of helplessness, anxiety, or depression.

At one time, patients complained bitterly about the lack of communication they had about their disorders and their treatments. In part, precisely because of these concerns, hospitals have now undertaken efforts to ameliorate this problem. Patients are now typically given a road map of what procedures they can expect and what they may experience as a result.

■ INTERVENTIONS TO INCREASE INFORMATION IN HOSPITAL SETTINGS

In part because of the issues just noted, many hospitals now provide interventions that help prepare patients generally for hospitalization and for the procedures that they will undergo.

In 1958, psychologist Irving Janis conducted a landmark study that would forever change how patients are prepared for surgery. Janis was asked by a hospital to study its surgery patients to see if something could be done to reduce the stress that many of them experienced both before and after operations. One of Janis's earliest observations was that, without some anticipatory worry, patients were not able to cope well with surgery. He termed this the "work of worrying," reasoning that patients must work through the fear and loss of control that are raised by surgery before they are able to adjust to it.

To get a clearer idea of the relationship between worry and adjustment, Janis first grouped the patients according to the level of fear they experienced before the operation (high, medium, and low). Then he studied how well they understood and used the information the hospital staff gave them to help them cope with the aftereffects of surgery. Highly fearful patients generally remained fearful and anxious after surgery and showed many negative side effects, such as vomiting, pain, urinary retention, and inability to eat (see also Montgomery & Bovbjerg, 2004). Patients who initially had little fear also showed unfavorable reactions after surgery, becoming angry or upset or complaining. Of the three groups, the moderately fearful patients coped with postoperative stress most effectively as determined by both interviews and staff reports.

In interpreting these results, Janis reasoned that highly fearful patients had been too absorbed with their own fears preoperatively to process the preparatory information adequately and that patients with little fear were insufficiently vigilant to understand and process the information effectively. Patients with moderate levels of fear, in contrast, were vigilant enough but not overwhelmed by their fears, so they were able to develop realistic expectations of what their postsurgery reactions would be; when they later encountered these sensations and reactions, they expected them and were ready to deal with them.

Subsequent studies have borne out some but not all of Janis's observations. Whereas Janis believed that fear and the work of worrying are essential ingredients in processing information about surgery, most researchers now believe that the effect is primarily determined by the informational value of the preparatory communication itself (Johnson, Lauver, & Nail, 1989). That is, patients who are carefully prepared for surgery and its aftereffects will show good postoperative adjustment; patients who are not well prepared for the aftereffects of surgery will show poor postoperative adjustment.

In one study (Mahler & Kulik, 1998), patients awaiting coronary artery bypass graft (CABG) were exposed to one of three preparatory videotapes or to no preparation. One videotape conveyed information via a health care expert; the second featured the health care expert but also included clips of interviews with patients who reported on their progress; and the third presented information from a health care expert plus interviews with patients who reported that their recovery consisted of "ups and downs."

Compared to patients who did not receive videotaped preparation, patients who saw a videotape—any videotape—felt significantly better prepared for the recovery period, reported higher self-efficacy during the recovery period, were more adherent to recommended dietary and exercise changes during their recovery, and were released sooner from the hospital.

BOX 9.6

Social Support and Distress from Surgery

Patients who are hospitalized for serious illnesses or surgery often experience anxiety. From the earlier discussion of social support (see Chapter 7), we know that emotional support from others can reduce distress when people are undergoing stressful events. Researchers have made use of these observations in developing interventions for hospitalized patients. James Kulik and Heike Mahler (1987) developed a social support intervention for patients about to undergo cardiac surgery. Some of the patients were assigned a roommate who was also waiting for surgery (preoperative condition), whereas others were assigned a roommate who had already had surgery (postoperative condition). In addition, patients were placed with a roommate undergoing a surgery that was either similar or dissimilar to their own.

The researchers found that patients who had a postoperative roommate profited from this contact (see also Kulik, Moore, & Mahler, 1993). Patients with a postoperative roommate were less anxious before surgery, were more ambulatory after surgery, and were released more quickly from the hospital than were patients who had been paired with a roommate who was also awaiting surgery. Whether the type of surgery was similar or dissimilar made no difference, only whether the roommate's surgery had already taken place.

Why exactly did rooming with a postoperative surgical patient improve the adjustment of those awaiting surgery? It may be that postoperative patients were able to provide relevant information to patients about the postoperative period by telling them how they felt and what the patient might expect (Thoits, Harvey, Hohmann, & Fletcher, 2000). Postoperative roommates may also have acted as role models for how one might feel and react postoperatively. Alternatively, those awaiting surgery may simply have been relieved to see that somebody who had undergone surgery had come out all right.

Whatever the specific explanation, the social contact produced by the presence of the postoperative roommate clearly had a positive impact on the pre- and postoperative adjustment of these surgery patients. These results have intriguing implications and may well be used to design future interventions to improve the adjustment of those awaiting unpleasant medical procedures, such as surgery (Kulik & Mahler, 1993; Kulik et al., 1993).

Similar interventions have been employed successfully for patients awaiting other medical procedures (Auerbach, Penberthy, & Kiesler, 2004).

Research on the role of preparatory information in adjustment to surgery overwhelmingly shows that such preparation has beneficial effects on hospital patients. Patients who have been prepared are typically less emotionally distressed, regain their functioning more quickly, and are often able to leave the hospital sooner. One study (Kulik & Mahler, 1989) even found that the person who becomes your postoperative roommate can influence how you cope with the aftermath of surgery (Box 9.6). Preparation for patients is so beneficial that many hospitals show videotapes to patients to prepare them for upcoming procedures.

■ THE HOSPITALIZED CHILD

Were you ever hospitalized as a child? If so, think back over the experience. Was it frightening and disorienting? Did you feel alone and uncared for? Or was it a more positive experience? Perhaps your parents were able to room in with you, or other children were around to talk to. You may have had either of these experiences because procedures for managing children in the hospital have changed dramatically over the past few decades.

Although it is generally acknowledged that people should be hospitalized only when it is absolutely necessary, this caution is particularly important in the care of the ill child. Some hospitalized children show adverse reactions, ranging from regressive, dependent behavior, such as social withdrawal, bed-wetting, and extreme fear, to rebelliousness and temper tantrums. And some problematic responses to hospitalization often do not become evident until the child returns home.

Anxiety

It is hard for a child to be separated from family and home. Some children may not understand why they have been taken away from their families and mistakenly infer that they are being punished for some misdeed. The hospital environment can be lonely and isolating. Physical confinement in bed or confinement due to casts or traction keeps children from discharging energy through physical activity. The dependency that is fostered by bed

Recent changes in hospitalization procedures for children have made hospitals less frightening places to be. Increasingly, medical personnel have recognized children's needs for play and have provided opportunities for play in hospital settings.

rest and reliance on staff can lead to regression. Children, especially those just entering puberty, can be embarrassed or ashamed by having to expose themselves to strangers. The child may also be subject to confusing or painful tests and procedures.

Recent changes in hospitalization procedures for children have made hospitals less frightening places to be. Increasingly, medical personnel have recognized children's needs for play and have provided opportunities for play and contact with a caregiver in hospital settings.

Preparing Children for Medical Interventions

Children face many noxious procedures for which psychological preparation is valuable. Under some circumstances, distraction may be effective for managing pain or discomfort (Dahlquist, Pendley, Landthrip, Jones, & Steuber, 2002). In Chapter 7, we considered how principles of psychological control have been used to create interventions for adult patients. These principles have also been used with children, and control-based interventions can reduce distress (Jay, Elliott, Woody, & Siegel, 1991; Manne et al., 1990). In one study (Melamed & Siegel, 1975), children about to undergo surgery were shown either a film of another child being hospitalized and receiving surgery or an unrelated film. Those children exposed to the relevant film showed less pre- and postoperative distress than did children exposed to the irrelevant film. Moreover, parents of the children exposed to the modeling film reported fewer problem behaviors after hospitalization than did parents of children who saw the control film.

Coping skills preparation is helpful with children (Cohen, Cohen, Blount, Schaen, & Zaff, 1999). For example, T. R. Zastowny and colleagues (Zastowny, Kirschenbaum, & Meng, 1986) gave children and their parents information describing typical hospitalization and surgery experiences, relaxation training to reduce anxiety, or a coping skills intervention to teach children constructive self-talk. Both the anxiety reduction and the coping skills interventions reduced children's fearfulness and parents' distress. Overall, the children exposed to the coping skills intervention exhibited the fewest maladaptive behaviors during hospitalization, less problem behavior in the week before admission, and fewer problems after discharge.

Preparation of children often focuses not only on the hospitalization experience but also on the illness itself and its treatment (O'Byrne, Peterson, & Saldana, 1997). When a child understands what the illness is, what it feels like, and how soon he or she will get better, anxiety may be reduced. Researchers now believe that even very young children should be told something about their illness and treatment and encouraged to express their emotions and to ask questions.

Different forms of preparation may be needed for children who face multiple medical procedures. For example, children with cancer undergo numerous invasive medical procedures, many of which are repeated. Whereas preparation may be important initially, sometimes distraction from the painful procedures is preferable on subsequent occasions (Manne, Bakeman, Jacobsen, Gorfinkle, & Redd, 1994).

Some preparation can be undertaken by parents. If a parent prepares a child for admission several days before hospitalization—explaining why it is necessary, what it will be like, who will be there, how often the parent will visit, and so on—this preparation may ease the transition. During admission procedures, a parent or another familiar adult can remain with the child until the child is settled into the new room and engaged in some activity.

The presence of parents during stressful medical procedures is not an unmitigated benefit. Parents do not always help reduce children's fears, pain, and discomfort (Jacobsen et al., 1990; Lumley, Abeles, Melamed, Pistone, & Johnson, 1990; Manne et al., 1992). When present during invasive medical procedures, some parents can become distressed and exacerbate the child's own anxiety (Wolff et al., 2009). Nonetheless, parental support is important, and most hospitals now provide opportunities for extended parental visits, including 24-hour parental visitation rights. Despite some qualifications, the benefits of preparing children for hospitalization are now so widely acknowledged that it is more the rule than the exception. ●

SUMMARY

1. Patients evaluate their health care based more on the quality of the interaction they have with the provider than on the technical quality of care.

2. Many factors impede effective patient-provider communication. The office setting and the structure of the health care delivery system are often designed for efficient rather than supportive health care. The movement toward more humane health care is fueled by the philosophies of holism and wellness.

3. Providers contribute to poor communication by not listening, using jargon-filled explanations, alternating between overly technical explanations and infantilizing baby talk, communicating negative expectations, and depersonalizing the patient.

4. Patients contribute to poor communications by failing to learn details of their disorder and treatment, failing to give providers correct information, and failing to follow through on treatment recommendations. Patient anxiety, lack of education, lack of experience with the disorder, and incomplete information about symptoms interfere with effective communication as well.

5. Because the provider usually receives little feedback about whether the patient followed instructions or the treatments were successful, it is difficult to identify and correct problems in communication.

6. Poor communication leads to nonadherence to treatment and the initiation of malpractice litigation.

7. Adherence is lower when recommendations do not seem medical, when lifestyle modification is needed,

when complex self-care regimens are required, and when patients have personal and conflicting theories about the nature of their illness or treatment.

8. Adherence is increased when patients have decided to adhere, when they feel the provider cares about them, when they understand what to do, and when they have received clear written instructions.

9. Efforts to improve communication have included training in communication skills and taking advantage of the provider's potent professional role. Patient-centered communication improves adherence. Face-to-face communication with a physician can enhance adherence to treatment because of the personalized relationship that exists.

10. The hospital is a complex organizational system buffeted by changing medical, organizational, and financial climates. Different groups in the hospital have different goals, such as cure, care, or core, which may occasionally conflict. Such problems are exacerbated by communication barriers.

11. Hospitalization can be a frightening and depersonalizing experience for patients. The adverse reactions of children in hospitals have received particular attention.

12. Information and control-enhancing interventions improve adjustment to hospitalization and to stressful medical procedures in both adults and children. The benefits of information, relaxation training, and coping skills training are well documented.

KEY TERMS

adherence
colleague orientation
creative nonadherence
diagnostic-related group (DRG)
health maintenance organization (HMO)

holistic health
managed care
nonadherence
nurse-practitioners

physicians' assistants
preferred provider organization (PPO)
private, fee-for-service care

The Management of Pain and Discomfort

Jesse woke up to the sun streaming in through the windows of his new home. It was his first apartment, and with a sigh of contentment, he reveled in the experience of finally being on his own. Yesterday had been a busy day. He and several of his friends had moved all the stuff he had accumulated from college up two flights of narrow stairs to his small but cozy new place. It had been a lot of work, but it had been fun. They'd had a few beers and some pizza afterward, and everyone went home tired and sore but contented.

As Jesse rolled over to admire his apartment, he experienced a sharp pain. Muttering a curse, he realized that his back had gone out on him. It must have been from carrying all those boxes. Slowly and carefully, he eased himself into first a sitting and then a standing position. He was definitely stiff, probably having aggravated injuries he had acquired during years of football.

Pain is a valuable cue that tissue damage has occurred and activities must be curtailed.

It was not the first time he had had this experience, and he knew that taking over-the-counter painkillers and moving around would help him feel better as long as he did not exert himself too much that day.

Jesse is fortunate because he is young and his pain is only short term in response to the exertion of carrying boxes and using muscles not accustomed to regular use. For many people, though, the kind of experience that Jesse has is a chronic one—that is, long term, painful, and difficult to treat. In fact, chronic back pain is the most common cause of disability in this country, and large numbers of middle-aged and older Americans deal with back pain on a daily or intermittent basis. Even his short-term experience led Jesse to realize that he had to moderate his physical activity the following day.

Chronic pain lasting at least 6 months or longer affects 30–50 million people in the United States. Costs in disability and lost productivity add up to more than $100 billion annually (Lozito, 2004). Indeed, pain typically leads people to change their activity level and other aspects of their behavior. As this chapter explains, such pain behaviors are an important component of the pain experience. Jesse was annoyed with himself for not taking basic precautions in lifting and carrying that might have spared him this agony. For people who experience chronic pain, the emotional reactions are more likely to be anxiety and depression, and emotional reactions to pain are also integral to the pain experience.

■ THE SIGNIFICANCE OF PAIN

On the surface, the significance of pain would seem to be obvious. Pain hurts, and it can be so insistent that it overwhelms other, basic needs. But the significance of pain goes far beyond the disruption it produces. Although we normally think of pain as an unusual occurrence, we actually live with minor pains all the time. These pains are critical for survival because they provide low-level feedback about the functioning of our bodily systems, feedback that we then use, often unconsciously, as a basis for making minor adjustments, such as shifting our posture, rolling over while asleep, or crossing and uncrossing our legs.

Pain also has important medical consequences. It is the symptom most likely to lead a person to seek treatment (see Chapter 8). It can complicate illnesses and hamper recovery from medical procedures (McGuire et al., 2006). Complaints of pain often accompany other mental and physical disorders, and this comorbidity further complicates diagnosis and treatment (Berna et al., 2010; Kalaydjian & Merikangas, 2008). Unfortunately, the relationship between pain and the severity of an underlying problem can be weak. For example, a cancerous lump rarely produces pain, at least in its early stages, yet it is of great medical importance.

Pain is also medically significant because it can be a source of misunderstanding between a patient and the medical provider. From the patient's standpoint, pain is the problem. To the provider, in contrast, pain is a byproduct of a disorder. In fact, pain is often considered by practitioners to be so unimportant that many medical schools have little systematic coverage of pain in their curriculum. One student, reporting on his medical school experience, stated that pain had been mentioned exactly four times in the entire 4-year curriculum, and only one lecture had even a portion of its content devoted to pain management. Until recently, pain management was considered to be somewhat incidental to the management of illness, and for some groups, such as very young infants, pain was thought not to be experienced at all, a misperception that often led to painful interventions without anesthesia (Slater et al., 2006).

Although the practitioner focuses attention on symptoms, which, from a medical standpoint, may be more meaningful, the patient may feel that an important problem is not getting sufficient attention. As we saw in Chapter 9, patients may choose not to comply with their physician's recommendations if they think they have been misdiagnosed or if their chief symptoms have been ignored.

Pain has psychological as well as medical significance (Keefe et al., 2002). For example, depression, anxiety, and anger worsen the experience of pain (Berna et al., 2010; Bruehl et al., 2007; Vowles, Zvolensky, Gross, & Sperry, 2004). When patients are asked what they fear most about illness and its treatment, the common response is pain. The dread of not being able to reduce one's own suffering arouses more anxiety than the prospect of surgery, the loss of a limb, or even death. In fact, inadequate relief from pain is the most common reason for patients' requests for euthanasia or assisted suicide (Cherny, 1996).

No introduction to pain would be complete without a consideration of its prevalence and cost. Seventy to 85% of people in the United States suffer from back pain at some time in their life, 40 million people suffer from daily arthritis pain, 45 million have chronic headaches, and the majority of patients in intermediate or advanced stages of cancer suffer moderate to severe pain (New York Presbyterian Hospital, 2007). Nearly 25% of people who live in nursing homes have chronic pain (Sengupta, Bercovitz, & Harris-Kojetin, 2010). At least $532 million is spent every year on over-the-counter drugs (ABC News, 2004). The worldwide pain management prescription drug market totaled approximately $24 billion in 2002, reaching $29 billion in 2007 (Global Information Inc., 2007). The pain business is big business, reflecting the suffering, both chronic and temporary, that millions of people experience.

At least $532 million is spent annually in the United States on over-the-counter remedies to reduce the temporary pain of minor disorders.

BOX 10.1

A Cross-Cultural Perspective on Pain: The Childbirth Experience

Although babies are born in every society, the childbirth experience varies dramatically from culture to culture, and so does the experience of pain associated with it. Among Mexican women, for example, the word for labor (*dolor*) means sorrow or pain, and the expectation of giving birth can produce a great deal of fear. This fear and the anticipation of pain can lead to a more painful experience with more complications than is true for women who do not bring these fears and expectations to the birthing experience (Scrimshaw, Engle, & Zambrana, 1983).

In stark contrast is the culture of Yap in the South Pacific, where childbirth is treated as an everyday occurrence. Women in Yap perform their normal activities until they begin labor, at which time they retire to a childbirth hut to give birth with the aid of perhaps one or two other women. Following the birth, there is a brief period of rest, after which the woman resumes her activities. Problematic labors and complications during pregnancy are reported to be low (Kroeber, 1948).

There is no simple and direct relationship between expectations about pain and the childbirth experience, but expectations do play an important role in how labor

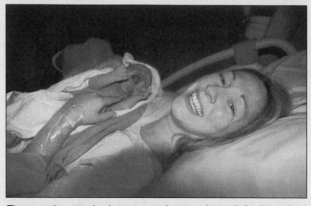

The meaning attached to an experience substantially determines whether it is perceived as painful. For many women, the joy of childbirth can mute the pain associated with the experience.

is experienced. Cultural lore and customs are a significant source of these expectations.

The meaning attached to an experience substantially determines whether it is perceived as painful. For many women, the joy of childbirth can mute the pain associated with the experience.

■ THE ELUSIVE NATURE OF PAIN

Pain is one of the more mysterious and elusive aspects of illness and its treatment. It is fundamentally a psychological experience, and the degree to which it is felt and how incapacitating it is depend in large part on how it is interpreted. Howard Beecher (1959), a physician, was one of the first to recognize this. During World War II, Beecher served in the medical corps, where he observed many wartime injuries. In treating soldiers, he noticed a curious fact: Only one quarter of them requested morphine (a widely used painkiller) for what were often severe and very likely painful wounds. When Beecher returned to his Boston civilian practice, he often treated patients who sustained comparable injuries from surgery. However, in contrast to the soldiers, 80% of the civilians appeared to be in substantial pain and demanded painkillers. To make sense of this apparent discrepancy, Beecher concluded that the meaning attached to pain substantially determines how it is experienced. For the soldier, an injury meant that he was alive and was likely to

be sent home. For the civilian, the injury represented an unwelcome interruption of valued activities.

Pain is also heavily influenced by the context in which it is experienced. Sports lore is full of accounts of athletes who injured themselves on the playing field but stayed in the game, apparently oblivious to their pain. Such action may be possible because sympathetic arousal, as occurs in response to vigorous sports, seems to diminish pain sensitivity (Fillingham & Maixner, 1996; Zillman, de Wied, King-Jablonski, & Jenzowsky, 1996). In contrast, stress and psychological distress can aggravate the experience of pain (Strigo, Simmons, Matthews, Craig, & Paulus, 2008).

Pain has a substantial cultural component. Although there are no ethnic differences in the ability to discriminate painful stimuli, members from some cultures report pain sooner and react more intensely to it than individuals from other cultures (Hernandez & Sachs-Ericsson, 2006). These cultural differences come from differences in norms regarding the expression of pain and in some cases from different pain mechanisms (Mechlin, Maixner, Light, Fisher, & Girdler, 2005; Sheffield, Biles, Orom, Maixner, & Sheps, 2000). An example of these kinds of cultural differences appears in Box 10.1. There are gender differences in the experience of pain as well, with women typically showing greater sensitivity to pain (Burns, Elfant, & Quartana, 2010).

Measuring Pain

One barrier to the treatment of pain is the difficulty people have in describing it objectively. If you have a lump, you can point to it; if a bone is broken, it can be seen in an X-ray. But pain does not have these objective referents.

Verbal Reports

One solution to measuring pain is to draw on the large, informal vocabulary that people use for describing pain. Medical practitioners usually use this information to understand patients' complaints. A throbbing pain, for example, has different implications than does a shooting pain or a constant, dull ache.

Researchers have developed pain questionnaires (Osman, Breitenstein, Barrios, Gutierrez, & Kopper, 2002) (Figure 10.1). Such measures typically ask about the nature of pain, such as whether it is throbbing or shooting, as well as its intensity (Dar, Leventhal, & Leventhal, 1993; Fernandez & Turk, 1992). Measures also address the psychosocial components of pain, such as the fear it causes or the degree to which it has been catastrophized, that is, become an exaggerated part of life (Osman et al., 2000). Measures like these can help practitioners get a full picture of the patient's pain. A novel effort to assess pain appears in Box 10.2.

Methodological tools from neuroscience have yielded some surprising insights about pain. Patients with chronic pain disorders show significant loss of gray matter in the brain regions involved in the processing of pain, specifically the prefrontal, cingular, and insular cortex (Valet et al., 2009). These structural markers not only provide objective neural information about changes in the brain due to pain, but may also be useful for charting functional pain disorders, such as fibromyalgia, in which no clear tissue damage is present, and for charting changes that may occur in response to successful treatment.

Pain Behavior

Other assessments of pain have focused on **pain behaviors**—behaviors that arise as manifestations of chronic pain, such as distortions in posture or gait, facial and audible expressions of distress, and avoidance of activity (Turk, Wack, & Kerns, 1995). Pain behaviors provide a basis for assessing how pain has disrupted the life of particular patients or groups of patients, distinguishing, for example, between how people manage low back pain versus chronic headaches. Because pain behavior is observable and measurable, the focus on pain behaviors has helped define the characteristics of different kinds of pain syndromes.

The Physiology of Pain

The view of pain as having psychological, behavioral, and sensory components is useful for making sense of the manifold pathways and receptors involved in the pain experience. Originally, these ideas were developed in the **gate-control theory of pain** (Melzack & Wall, 1982). Although our knowledge of the physiology of pain has now progressed beyond that early model, it was central to the progress that has been made in recent decades. Many of its insights are reflected in our current knowledge of the physiology of pain.

Pain and emotions

Emotional factors are greatly intertwined with the experience of pain. Negative emotions exacerbate pain, and pain exacerbates negative emotions. In particular, researchers have focused on efforts to suppress anger, the catastrophic expression of pain, depression, and efforts to suppress pain as emotionally-related factors that augment the pain experience (Gilliam et al., 2010). As will be seen, these emotions often need to be targeted alongside the management of pain itself.

Overview

The experience of pain is a protective mechanism to bring tissue damage into conscious awareness. At the time of the pain experience, however, it is unlikely to feel very protective. Unlike other bodily sensations, the experience of pain is accompanied by motivational and behavioral responses, such as withdrawal, and intense emotional reactions, such as crying or fear. These experiences are an integral part of the pain experience and are important to diagnosis and treatment.

Scientists have distinguished among three kinds of pain perception. The first is mechanical **nociception**—pain perception—that results from mechanical damage to the tissues of the body. The second is thermal damage, or the experience of pain due to temperature exposure. The third is referred to as polymodal nociception, a general category referring to pain that triggers chemical reactions from tissue damage.

FIGURE 10.1 | The McGill Pain Questionnaire

Patient's name _____   Date _____   Time _____   A.M./P.M.

1 Flickering ___ Quivering ___ Pulsing ___ Throbbing ___ Beating ___ Pounding ___ **2** Jumping ___ Flashing ___ Shooting ___ **3** Pricking ___ Boring ___ Drilling ___ Stabbing ___ Lancinating ___ **4** Sharp ___ Cutting ___ Lacerating ___ **5** Pinching ___ Pressing ___ Gnawing ___ Cramping ___ Crushing ___ **6** Tugging ___ Pulling ___ Wrenching ___ **7** Hot ___ Burning ___ Scalding ___ Searing ___ **8** Tingling ___ Itchy ___ Smarting ___ Stinging ___ **9** Dull ___ Sore ___ Hurting ___ Aching ___ Heavy ___ **10** Tender ___ Taut ___ Rasping ___ Splitting ___	**11** Tiring ___ Exhausting ___ **12** Sickening ___ Suffocating ___ **13** Fearful ___ Frightful ___ Terrifying ___ **14** Punishing ___ Grueling ___ Cruel ___ Vicious ___ Killing ___ **15** Wretched ___ Blinding ___ **16** Annoying ___ Troublesome ___ Miserable ___ Intense ___ Unbearable ___ **17** Spreading ___ Radiating ___ Penetrating ___ Piercing ___ **18** Tight ___ Numb ___ Drawing ___ Squeezing ___ Tearing ___ **19** Cool ___ Cold ___ Freezing ___ **20** Nagging ___ Nauseating ___ Agonizing ___ Dreadful ___ Torturing ___ **PPI** **0** No pain ___ **1** Mild ___ **2** Discomforting ___ **3** Distressing ___ **4** Horrible ___ **5** Excruciating ___

Brief ___ Momentary ___ Transient ___	Rhythmic ___ Periodic ___ Intermittent ___	Continuous ___ Steady ___ Constant ___

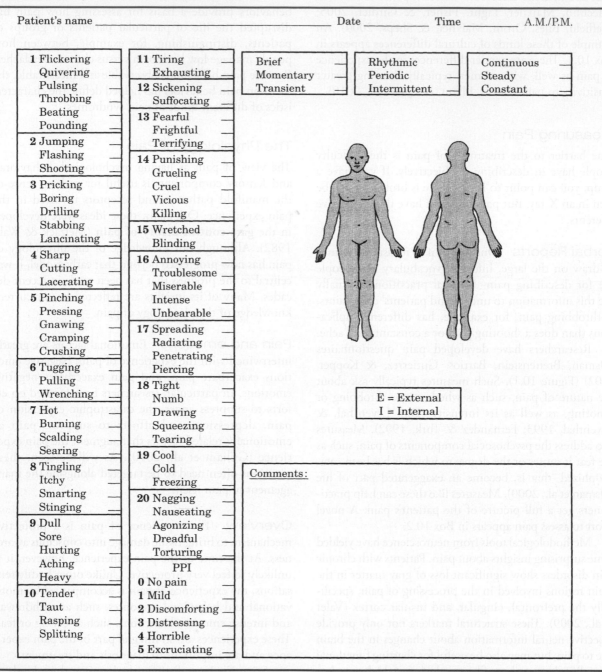

E = External
I = Internal

Comments:

Nociceptors in the peripheral nerves first sense injury and, in response, release chemical messengers, which are conducted to the spinal cord, where they are passed directly to the reticular formation and thalamus and into the cerebral cortex. These regions of the brain, in turn, identify the site of the injury and send messages back down the spinal cord, which lead to muscle contractions, which can help block the pain, and changes in other bodily functions, such as breathing.

Headache Drawings Reflect Distress and Disability

A recent way that psychologists have come to understand people's experiences with pain is through their drawings. In a recent study, students who experienced persistent headaches were asked to draw a picture of how their headaches affected them. The psychologists (Broadbent, Niederhoffer, Hague, Corter, & Reynolds, 2009) analyzed these drawings for their size, darkness, and content.

They found that darker drawings were associated with greater emotional distress and larger drawings were associated with perceptions of worse consequences and symptoms, more pain, and greater sadness. Drawings, then, offer a novel way to assess people's experiences of their headaches and appear to reliably reflect illness perceptions and distress. These may be a useful way for practicing clinicians to better understand their patients' experiences of pain.

Source: Broadbent, Niederhoffer, Hague, Corter, & Reynolds, 2009.

Two major types of peripheral nerve fibers are involved in nociception, as the gate-control theory of pain originally maintained. A-delta fibers are small, myelinated fibers that transmit sharp pain. They respond especially to mechanical or thermal pain, transmitting sharp, brief pains rapidly. C-fibers are unmyelinated nerve fibers, involved in polymodal pain, that transmit dull, aching pain. (Myelination increases the speed of transmission, so sudden, intense pain is more rapidly conducted to the cerebral cortex than is the slower, dull, aching pain of the C-fibers.)

Peripheral nerve fibers enter the spinal column at the dorsal horn. Sensory aspects of pain are heavily determined by activity in the A-delta fibers, which project onto areas in the thalamus and the sensory areas of the cerebral cortex. The motivational and affective elements of pain appear to be influenced more strongly by the C-fibers, which project onto different thalamic, hypothalamic, and cortical areas. The experience of pain, then, is determined by the balance of activity in these nerve fibers, which reflects the pattern and intensity of stimulation.

Several other regions of the brain are involved in the modulation of pain. The periductal gray, a structure in the midbrain, has been tied to pain relief when it is stimulated. Neurons in the periductal gray connect to the reticular formation in the medulla, which makes connections with the neurons in the substantia gelatinosa of the dorsal horn of the spinal cord. Sensations are modulated by the dorsal horn in the spinal column and by downward pathways from the brain that interpret the pain experience. Inflammation that originally occurs in peripheral tissue may be amplified, as pain-related information is conveyed to the dorsal horn (Ikeda et al., 2006).

Pain sensation, intensity, and duration interact to influence pain, its perceived unpleasantness, and related emotions through a central network of pathways in the limbic structures and the thalamus, which direct their inputs to the cortex. In the cortical regions of the brain, nociceptive input is integrated with contextual information about the painful experience. Processes in the cerebral cortex are involved in cognitive judgments about pain, including the evaluation of its meaning, which contributes to the strong emotions often experienced during pain and which can themselves exacerbate pain (Meagher, Arnau, & Rhudy, 2001). The overall experience of pain, then, is a complex outcome of the interaction of these elements of the pain experience (Figure 10.2). An example of just how complex pain and its management can be is provided in Box 10.3.

Neurochemical Bases of Pain and Its Inhibition

The brain controls the amount of pain an individual experiences by transmitting messages down the spinal cord to block the transmission of pain signals. One landmark study that confirmed this hypothesis was conducted by D. V. Reynolds (1969). He demonstrated that, by electrically stimulating a portion of a rat brain, one could produce such a high level of analgesia that the animal would not feel the pain of abdominal surgery, a phenomenon termed stimulation-produced analgesia (SPA). Reynolds's findings prompted researchers to

look for the neurochemical basis of this effect, and in 1972, H. Akil, D. J. Mayer, and J. C. Liebeskind (1972, 1976) uncovered the existence of endogenous opioid peptides.

What are **endogenous opioid peptides**? Opiates, including heroin and morphine, are pain control drugs manufactured from plants. Opioids are opiate-like substances, produced within the body, that constitute a neurochemically based, internal pain regulation system. Opioids are produced in many parts of the brain and glands of the body, and they project onto specific receptor sites in various parts of the body.

Endogenous opioid peptides are important because they are the natural pain suppression system of the body. Clearly, however, this pain suppression system is not always in operation. Particular factors must

FIGURE 10.2 | The Experience of Pain

The signal goes to the spinal cord, where it passes immediately to a motor nerve ① connected to a muscle, in this case, in the arm. This causes a reflex action that does not involve the brain. But the signal also goes up the spinal cord to the thalamus ②, where the pain is perceived.

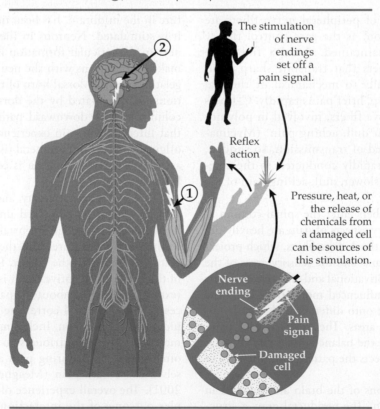

The stimulation of nerve endings set off a pain signal.

Reflex action

Pressure, heat, or the release of chemicals from a damaged cell can be sources of this stimulation.

Nerve ending

Pain signal

Damaged cell

BOX 10.3

Phantom Limb Pain: A Case History

Nerve injury of the shoulder is becoming increasingly common because motorcycles are widely accessible and, all too often, their power is greater than the skill of their riders. On hitting an obstruction, the rider is catapulted forward and hits the road at about the speed the bike was traveling. In the most severe of these injuries, the spinal roots are avulsed—that is, ripped out of the spinal cord—and no repair is possible.

C. A., age 25, an Air Force pilot, suffered such an accident. After 8 months, he had completely recovered from the cuts, bruises, and fractures of his accident. There had been no head injury, and he was alert, intelligent, and busy as a student shaping a new career for himself. His right arm was completely paralyzed from the shoulder down, and the muscles of his arm were thin. In addition, the limp arm was totally anesthetic so that he had no sensation of any stimuli applied to it. On being questioned, he stated that he could sense very clearly an entire arm, but it had no relationship to his real arm. This "phantom" arm seemed to him to be placed across his chest, while the real, paralyzed arm hung at his side. The phantom never moved and the fingers were tightly clenched in a cramped fist, with the nails digging into the palm. The entire arm felt "as though it was on fire." Nothing has helped his condition, and he finds that he can control the pain only by absorbing himself in his work.

Source: Melzack & Wall, 1982, pp. 21–22.

---

trigger its arousal. Research on animals suggests that stress is one such factor. Acute stress reduces sensitivity to pain, a phenomenon termed stress-induced analgesia (SIA), and research demonstrates that SIA can be accompanied by an increase in brain endogenous opioid peptides (Lewis, Terman, Shavit, Nelson, & Liebeskind, 1984). The release of endogenous opioid peptides may also be one of the mechanisms underlying various techniques of pain control (Bolles & Fanselow, 1982).

■ CLINICAL ISSUES IN PAIN MANAGEMENT

Historically, pain has been managed by physicians and other health care workers. Traditional pain management methods include pharmacological, surgical, and sensory techniques. Increasingly, psychologists have become involved in pain management, and as a result, techniques that include a heavily psychological component have been used to combat pain. These techniques include biofeedback, relaxation, hypnosis, acupuncture, distraction, and guided imagery. As these methods have gained prominence in the treatment of pain, the importance of patients' self-management, involving responsibility for and commitment to the course of pain treatment, has assumed centrality in the management of chronic pain (Glenn & Burns, 2003).

Acute and Chronic Pain

There are two main kinds of clinical pain: acute and chronic. **Acute pain** typically results from a specific injury that produces tissue damage, such as a wound or broken limb. As such, it is self-limiting and typically disappears when the tissue damage is repaired. Jesse's pain, from moving into his new apartment, is an example of acute pain. Acute pain is usually short in duration and is defined as pain that goes on for 6 months or less. While it is going on, it can produce substantial anxiety and prompt its sufferer to engage in an urgent search for relief. The pain decreases and anxiety dissipates once painkillers are administered or the injury begins to heal.

Types of Chronic Pain

Chronic pain typically begins with an acute episode, but unlike acute pain, it does not decrease with treatment and the passage of time. There are several different kinds of chronic pain. **Chronic benign pain** typically persists for 6 months or longer and is relatively unresponsive to treatment. The pain varies in severity and may involve any of a number of muscle groups. Chronic low back pain and myofascial pain syndrome are examples.

Recurrent acute pain involves a series of intermittent episodes of pain that are acute in character but chronic inasmuch as the condition recurs for more than 6 months. Migraine headaches, temporomandibular disorder (involving the jaw), and trigeminal neuralgia (involving spasms of the facial muscles) are examples.

Chronic progressive pain persists longer than 6 months and increases in severity over time. Typically, it is associated with malignancies or degenerative disorders, such as cancer or rheumatoid arthritis. More than 130 million Americans suffer from chronic pain at any given time (American Occupational Therapy Association, 2002), with back pain being the most common (Table 10.1). Chronic pain is not necessarily present every moment, but the fact that it is chronic virtually forces sufferers to organize their lives around it.

Acute Versus Chronic Pain   The distinction between acute and chronic pain is important in clinical management for several reasons. First, acute and chronic pain present different psychological profiles. Chronic pain often carries an overlay of psychological distress, which complicates diagnosis and treatment. The realization that pain is interfering with desired activities and the perception that one has little control over that fact produce psychological distress in pain patients (Maxwell, Gatchel, & Mayer, 1998). Depression, anxiety, and anger are common and may exacerbate pain and pain-related behaviors (Burns et al., 2008; Bair, Wu, Damush, Sutherland, & Kroenke, 2008). One study found that pain is present in two-thirds of patients who seek care from physicians with primary symptoms of depression (Bair et al., 2004). Thus, pain and depression appear to be especially heavily intertwined.

Some chronic pain patients develop maladaptive coping strategies, such as catastrophizing their illness,

engaging in wishful thinking, or withdrawing socially, which can further complicate treatment and lead to more care seeking (Severeijns, Vlaeyen, van der Hout, & Picavet, 2004). When patients have endured their pain for long periods of time without any apparent relief, it is easy to imagine that the pain will only get worse and be a constant part of the rest of their life—beliefs that magnify the distress of chronic pain and feed back into the pain itself (Tennen, Affleck, & Zautra, 2006; Vowles, McCracken, & Eccleston, 2008). When these psychological issues are effectively treated, this fact may in itself reduce chronic pain (Fishbain, Cutler, Rosomoff, & Rosomoff, 1998). The sheer duration of chronic pain can account for the fact that many chronic pain patients become nearly completely disabled over the course of their pain treatment (Groth-Marnat & Fletcher, 2000).

A second reason to distinguish between acute and chronic pain is that most of the pain control techniques presented in this chapter work well to control acute pain but are less successful with chronic pain, which requires multiple individualized techniques for its management.

Third, chronic pain involves the complex interaction of physiological, psychological, social, and behavioral components, more than is the case with acute pain. For example, chronic pain patients often experience social rewards from the attention they receive from family members, friends, or even employers; these social rewards, or secondary gains, of pain can help maintain pain behaviors (McClelland & McCubbin, 2008).

The psychological and social components of pain are important in part because they are an integral aspect of the pain experience and influence the likelihood of success (Burns, 2000). As such, chronic pain management is complicated and must be thought of not as merely addressing a particular pain that simply goes on for a long time but as an unfolding physiological, psychological, and behavioral experience that evolves over time into a syndrome (Flor, Birbaumer, & Turk, 1990).

Who Becomes a Chronic Pain Patient?   Of course, all chronic pain patients were once acute pain patients. What determines who makes the transition to chronic pain? Chronic pain may result from a predisposition to react to a bodily insult with a specific bodily response, such as tensing one's jaw or altering one's posture (Glombiewski, Tersek, & Rief, 2008). This

---

TABLE 10.1 | Common Sources of Chronic Pain

- Back pain—70–85% of Americans have back trouble at some point in their lives.
- Headaches—approximately 45 million Americans have chronic recurrent headaches.
- Cancer pain—the majority of advanced cancer patients suffer moderate to severe pain.
- Arthritis pain—arthritis affects 40 million Americans.
- Neurogenic pain—pain resulting from damage to peripheral nerves or the central nervous system.
- Psychogenic pain—pain not due to a physical cause.

Source: National Institute of Neurological Disorders and Stroke, 2007.

response can be exacerbated by stress or even by efforts to suppress pain (Quartana, Burns, & Lofland, 2007). One might assume that pain intensity is implicated in the transition into chronic pain, but, in fact, functional disability appears to play a more important role. Chronic pain patients may experience pain especially strongly because of high sensitivity to noxious stimulation, impairment in pain regulatory systems, and an overlay of psychological distress (Sherman et al., 2004). Patients for whom pain interferes with life activities make the transition into the chronic pain experience (Epping-Jordan et al., 1998).

Unlike acute pain, chronic pain usually has been treated through a variety of methods, used both by patients themselves and by physicians. Chronic pain may be exacerbated by inappropriate prior treatments, by misdiagnosis, and/or by inappropriate prescriptions of medications (Kouyanou, Pither, & Wessely, 1997).

More than 90 million Americans, many of them elderly, suffer from chronic pain.

The Lifestyle of Chronic Pain By the time a pain patient is adequately treated, this complex, dynamic interaction of physiological, psychological, social, and behavioral components is often tightly integrated, making it difficult to modify (Flor et al., 1990). The following case history suggests the disruption and agony that can be experienced by the chronic pain sufferer:

> A little over a year ago, George Zessi, 54, a New York furrier, suddenly began to have excruciating migraine headaches. The attacks occurred every day and quickly turned Zessi into a pain cripple. "I felt like I was suffering a hangover each morning without even having touched a drop. I was seasick without going near a boat," he says. Because of the nausea that often accompanies migraines, Zessi lost fifty pounds. At his workshop, Zessi found himself so sensitive that he could not bear the ringing of a telephone. "I was incapacitated. It was difficult to talk to anyone. On weekends, I couldn't get out of bed," he says. A neurologist conducted a thorough examination and told Zessi he was suffering from tension. He took several kinds of drugs, but they did not dull his daily headaches. (Clark, 1977, p. 58)

As this case history suggests, chronic pain can entirely disrupt a person's life. Many such sufferers have left their jobs, abandoned their leisure activities, withdrawn from their families and friends, and developed an entire lifestyle around pain. Typically, chronic pain sufferers have little social or recreational life and may even have difficulty performing simple tasks of self-care. Because their income is often reduced, their standard of living may decline, and they may need public assistance. Their lifestyle becomes oriented around the experience of pain and its treatment. A good night's sleep is often elusive for months or years at a time (Currie, Wilson, & Curran, 2002). Work-related aspirations and personal goals may be set aside because life has become dominated by chronic pain (Karoly & Ruehlman, 1996). The loss of self-esteem that is experienced by these patients can be substantial.

Some patients receive compensation for their pain because it has resulted from an injury, such as an automobile accident. Compensation can actually increase the perceived severity of pain, the amount of disability experienced, the degree to which pain interferes with life activities, and the amount of distress that is reported (Ciccone, Just, & Bandilla, 1999; Groth-Marnat & Fletcher, 2000) because it provides an incentive for being in pain.

The Toll of Pain on Relationships Chronic pain can take a toll on marriage and other family relationships. Chronic pain patients often do not communicate well with their families, and sexual relationships almost always deteriorate. Ironically, among those chronic pain patients whose spouses remain supportive, such positive attention may inadvertently maintain the pain and disability (Ciccone, Just, & Bandilla, 1999; Turk, Kerns, & Rosenberg, 1992).

Other social relationships also can be threatened by chronic pain. The resulting loss of social contact that pain patients experience may lead them to turn inward and become self-absorbed. Neurotic behavior, including preoccupation with physical and emotional symptoms, can result. Pain patients often have to deal with negative stereotypes that physicians and other providers hold about chronic pain patients, and this experience, too, may make psychological responses to pain worse (Marbach, Lennon, Link, & Dohrenwend, 1990). Many chronic pain patients are clinically depressed; a large number have also contemplated or attempted suicide.

Chronic Pain Behaviors Chronic pain leads to a variety of pain-related behaviors that can also maintain the pain experience. For example, sufferers may avoid loud noises and bright lights, reduce physical activity, and shun social contacts. These alterations in lifestyle then become part of the pain problem and may persist and interfere with successful treatment (Philips, 1983). Understanding what pain behaviors an individual engages in and knowing whether they persist after the treatment of pain are important factors in treating the total pain experience.

Pain and Personality

Because psychological factors are so clearly implicated in the experience of pain, and because at least some pain serves functions for the chronic pain sufferer, researchers have examined whether there is a **pain-prone personality**—a constellation of personality traits that predispose a person to experience chronic pain.

This hypothesis is too simplistic. First, pain itself can produce alterations in personality that are consequences, not causes, of the pain experience. Second, individual experiences of pain are far too varied and complex to be explained by a single personality profile. Nonetheless, certain personality correlates are reliably associated with chronic pain, including neuroticism, introversion, and the use of passive coping strategies (Ramirez-Maestre, Lopez-Martinez, & Zarazaga, 2004).

Pain Profiles Developing psychological profiles of different groups of pain patients has proven to be helpful for treatment. Although these profiles are not thought of as pain-prone personalities, they are useful in specifying problems that patients with particular types of pain have or may develop.

To develop profiles, researchers have drawn on personality instruments, such as the Minnesota Multiphasic Personality Inventory (MMPI) (Johansson & Lindberg, 2000). Chronic pain patients typically show elevated scores on three MMPI subscales: hypochondriasis, hysteria, and depression. This constellation of traits is commonly referred to as the "neurotic triad."

Depression reflects the feelings of despair or hopelessness that can accompany long-term experience with unsuccessfully treated pain. Pain does not appear to be a sufficient condition for the development of depression, but rather leads to a reduction in activity level and in perceptions of personal control or mastery, which, in turn, can lead to depression (Nicassio, Radojevic, Schoenfeld-Smith, & Dwyer, 1995). Depression itself increases perceptions of pain (Dickens, McGowan, & Dale, 2003), and so it can feed back into the total pain experience, increasing the likelihood of pain behaviors such as leaving work (Linton & Buer, 1995). Interventions with depressed pain patients must address both depression and the pain itself (Ingram, Atkinson, Slater, Saccuzzo, & Garfin, 1990).

Recently, anger and how it is managed has been tied to the pain experience. People who suppress their anger may experience pain more strongly than people who manage anger more effectively or people who do not experience as much anger (Burns, Quartana, & Bruehl, 2008; Quartana, Bounds, Yoon, Goodin, & Burns, 2010). These effects may be due to a dysfunction in the opioid system that controls pain or to psychological processes involving hypervigilance (Bruehl, Burns, Chung, & Quartana, 2008).

Chronic pain is also associated with other forms of psychopathology including anxiety disorders, substance use disorders, and other psychiatric problems (Nash, Williams, Nicholson, & Trask, 2006; Vowles, Zvolensky, Gross, & Sperry, 2004). The overlay of depression and anxiety makes pain worse (Bair et al., 2008). The reason chronic pain and psychopathology are so frequently associated is not fully known. One possibility is that chronic pain activates a latent psychological vulnerability that was not previously recognized (Dersh, Polatin, & Gatchel, 2002).

■ PAIN CONTROL TECHNIQUES

What exactly is pain control? **Pain control** can mean that a patient no longer feels anything in an area that once hurt. It can mean that the person feels sensation but not pain. It can mean that he or she feels pain but is no longer concerned about it. Or it can mean that he or she is still hurting but is now able to tolerate it.

Some pain control techniques work because they eliminate feeling altogether (for example, spinal blocking agents), whereas others succeed because they reduce pain to sensation (such as sensory control techniques), and still others succeed because they enable patients to tolerate pain more successfully (such as more psychological approaches). It will be useful to bear these distinctions in mind as we evaluate the success of specific pain control techniques.

Pharmacological Control of Pain

The traditional and most common method of controlling pain is through the administration of drugs. Morphine (named after Morpheus, the Greek god of sleep) has been the most popular painkiller for decades (Melzack & Wall, 1982). A highly effective painkiller, morphine has the disadvantage of addiction, and patients may build up a tolerance to it. Nonetheless, it is a mainstay of pain control, especially in the case of severe pain.

About 30-50 million people in the United States experience chronic pain that requires treatment.

Any drug that can influence neural transmission is a candidate for pain relief. Some drugs, such as local anesthetics, can influence the transmission of pain impulses from the peripheral receptors to the spinal cord. The application of an analgesic to a wound is an example of this approach. The injection of drugs, such as spinal blocking agents, is another method.

Pharmacological relief from pain may also be provided by drugs that act directly on higher brain regions. Antidepressants, for example, combat pain not only by reducing anxiety and improving mood but also by affecting the downward pathways from the brain that modulate pain. As such, antidepressant administration is often a successful pain reduction technique for depressed pain patients, as well as for pain patients not showing clinical signs of depression.

Sometimes pharmacological treatments make the pain worse rather than better. Patients may consume large quantities of painkillers that are only partially effective and that have a variety of undesirable side effects, including inability to concentrate and addiction. Nerve-blocking agents may be administered to reduce pain, but these can also produce side effects, including anesthesia, limb paralysis, and loss of bladder control; moreover, even when they are successful, the pain will usually return within a short time.

The main concern practitioners have about the pharmacological control of pain is addiction, but their concern seems to be exaggerated. In three studies involving 25,000 patients treated with opioids who had no history of drug abuse, only seven cases of addiction were reported (Brody, 2002, January 22). (Box 10.4 pursues this issue further.) Even long-term use of prescription pain drugs for such conditions as arthritis appears to produce very low rates of addiction. But the misguided concern over addiction leads to undermedication. One estimate is that about 15% of patients with cancer-related pain and as many as 80% with noncancer chronic pain do not receive sufficient pain medication, leading to a cycle of stress, distress, and disability (Chapman & Gavrin, 1999).

Surgical Control of Pain

The surgical control of pain also has a long history. Surgical treatment involves cutting or creating lesions in the so-called pain fibers at various points in the body so that pain sensations can no longer be conducted. Some surgical techniques attempt to disrupt the conduct of pain from the periphery to the spinal cord; others are

BOX 10.4

Managing Pain . . . or Not

Many physicians and other medical providers fear that if patients receive too much medication during their hospitalizations, they will become addicted to painkillers. However, consider the following letters to the editor of *Time* magazine following an article on precisely this problem:

> My father died in 1994 after a long illness. In the end, his heart simply wore out, and morphine was the wonderful drug that allowed him to relax and breathe easily. My father wasn't "snowed under" but, rather, was kept comfortable with small doses as needed. He no longer worried about dying (as he had for years), because he felt good mentally, emotionally, and physically. And when his time came, he died in peace.

When I had an operation several years ago, I asked my surgeon to start giving me pain killers while I was still in surgery, since I had read that this procedure would help curb post-operative pain. Not only did he do so, but he also gave me a morphine pump so I could administer my own pain medication. But most important, I was controlling a part of my recuperation. I didn't end up a drug addict and was out of the hospital sooner than expected.

Reports such as these are not unusual, and increasingly, medical providers are finding that proper medication for pain is not the risky venture it was once thought to be. Patients can participate actively and responsibly in controlling the amount of medication they receive.

---

designed to interrupt the flow of pain sensations from the spinal cord upward to the brain.

Although these surgical techniques are sometimes successful in reducing pain temporarily, the effects are often short-lived. Therefore, many pain patients who have submitted to operations to reduce pain may gain only short-term benefits, at substantial cost: the risks, possible side effects, and tremendous expense of surgery. It is now believed that the nervous system has substantial regenerative powers and that blocked pain impulses find their way to the brain via different neural pathways.

Moreover, surgery can worsen the problem because it damages the nervous system, and this damage can itself be a chief cause of chronic pain. Hence, whereas surgical treatment for pain was once relatively common, researchers and practitioners are increasingly doubtful of its value, even as a treatment of last resort.

Sensory Control of Pain

One of the oldest known techniques of pain control is **counterirritation**. Counterirritation involves inhibiting pain in one part of the body by stimulating or mildly irritating another area. The next time you hurt yourself, you can demonstrate this technique on your own (and may have done so already) by pinching or scratching an area of your body near the part that hurts. Typically, the counterirritation produced when you do this will suppress the pain to some extent.

This common observation has been increasingly incorporated into the pain treatment process. An example of a pain control technique that uses this principle is spinal cord stimulation (North et al., 2005). A set of small electrodes is placed or implanted near the point at which the nerve fibers from the painful area enter the spinal cord. When the patient experiences pain, he or she activates a radio signal, which delivers a mild electrical stimulus to that area of the spine, thus inhibiting pain. Sensory control techniques have had some success in reducing the experience of pain. However, their effects are often only short-lived, and they may therefore be appropriate primarily for temporary relief from acute pain or as part of a general regimen for chronic pain.

In recent years, pain management experts have turned increasingly to exercise and other ways of increasing mobility to help the chronic pain patient. At one time, it was felt that the less activity, the better, so that healing could take place. In recent years, however, exactly the opposite philosophy has held sway, with patients urged to stay active to maintain their functioning. This approach has been especially successful with older adults managing the discomfort of musculoskeletal disorders (Avlund, Osler, Damsgaard, Christensen, & Schroll, 2000).

We now turn to psychological techniques for the management of pain. Unlike the pharmacological, surgical, and sensory pain management techniques considered so far, these more psychological techniques require active participation and learning on the part of the patient. Therefore, they are more effective for managing slow-rising pains, which can be anticipated and prepared for, than sudden, intense, or unexpected pains.

Biofeedback

Biofeedback, a method of achieving control over a bodily process, has been used to treat a variety of health problems, including stress (see Chapter 6) and hypertension (see Chapter 13). It has also been used as a pain control technique.

What Is Biofeedback?   Biofeedback involves providing biophysiological feedback to a patient about some bodily process of which the patient is usually unaware. Biofeedback training can be thought of as an operant learning process. First, the target function to be brought under control, such as blood pressure or heart rate, is identified. This function is then tracked by a machine, which provides information to the patient. For example, heart rate might be converted into a tone, so the patient can hear how quickly or slowly his or her heart is beating. The patient then attempts to change the bodily process. Through trial and error and continuous feedback from the machine, the patient learns what thoughts or behaviors will modify the bodily function.

Thus, for example, a patient might learn that blocking out all sounds, concentrating, and breathing slowly help reduce heart rate. Although it is not always clear to the patient exactly what he or she is doing that achieves success, the patient may still become proficient at controlling the bodily function. Once patients are able to bring a process under bodily control with feedback from the machine, they can usually make the same changes on their own, without the need for the machine.

Biofeedback has been used to treat a number of chronic disorders, including headaches (Hermann & Blanchard, 2002), Raynaud's disease (a disorder in which the small arteries in the extremities constrict, limiting blood flow and producing a cold, numb aching), temporomandibular joint pain (Glaros & Burton, 2004), hypertension (see Chapter 13), and pelvic pain (Clemens et al., 2000).

Does Biofeedback Work?   How successful is biofeedback in treating pain patients? Despite widely touted claims for its efficacy, there is only modest evidence that it is effective in reducing pain (White & Tursky, 1982). Even when biofeedback is effective, it may be no more so than less expensive, more easily used techniques, such as relaxation (Blanchard, Andrasik, & Silver, 1980; Bush, Ditto, & Feuerstein, 1985).

In addition, when biofeedback training is successful, it is not clear exactly why. There is little evidence that success at controlling a target process and corresponding reduction of pain are related, which raises the possibility that the beneficial effects of biofeedback result from something other than modification of the target process—perhaps relaxation, suggestion, an enhanced sense of control, or even a placebo effect.

Relaxation Techniques

Relaxation training has been employed with pain patients extensively, either alone or in concert with other pain control techniques. One rationale for teaching pain patients relaxation techniques, then, is that it enables them to cope more successfully with stress and anxiety, which may also ameliorate pain. Relaxation may also affect pain directly. For example, the reduction of muscle tension or the diversion of blood flow induced by relaxation may reduce pains that are tied to these physiological processes.

What Is Relaxation?   In relaxation, an individual shifts his or her body into a state of low arousal by progressively relaxing different parts of the body. Controlled

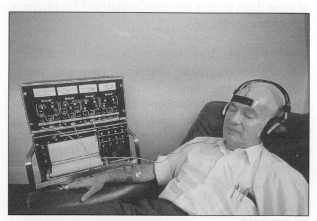

Biofeedback has been used successfully to treat muscle-tension headaches, migraine headaches, and Raynaud's disease. However, evidence to date suggests that other, less expensive relaxation techniques may be equally successful.

BOX 10.5

Using Relaxation to Combat Pain

The following are case histories of patients treated with relaxation to reduce pain that, in some instances, proved resistant to other pain control methods.

CASE 1

A 65-year-old ex-steeplejack was hospitalized for evaluation of increasingly severe intermittent chest pain which had been present for over 10 years. An extensive workup revealed esophagitis (inflammation of the esophagus). The patient used relaxation exercises frequently both for general relaxation and for relief of moderate pain. "I get into it and just sort of forget all about the pain." Over a period of six months, he found the method very useful. "If I catch the pain early enough, I can stop it before it gets too bad." He typically used the method for 10 to 15 minutes, following which he went directly to sleep.

CASE 2

A dramatic response was seen in a 22-year-old man who was hospitalized following extensive bullet wounds in the abdomen and hip. During the three months of hospitalization, he suffered severe pain, which responded partially to surgery. He was anxious, depressed, irritable, and occasionally panicky due to the continual pain. He ate poorly and steadily lost weight. Using relaxation, he was able to sleep if the pain was not severe. He stated, "I stay there as long as I can—maybe 30 minutes. The trouble is, I go to sleep." There was a marked improvement in his general mood and he began eating well.

Source: French & Tupin, 1974, pp. 283, 285.

---

breathing is added, in which breathing shifts from relatively short, shallow breaths to deeper, longer breaths. Anyone who has been trained in prepared childbirth techniques will recognize that these procedures are used for pain management during early labor. Box 10.5 gives two examples of the use of relaxation in pain control.

Zen meditation and mindfulness also reduce pain sensitivity and can produce analgesic effects, possibly through a combination of relaxation and strong self-regulatory skills (Grant & Rainville, 2009). Spiritual meditation tied to religious beliefs can aid in the control of some pains such as migraine headaches (Wachholtz & Pargament, 2008).

Does Relaxation Work? Relaxation is modestly successful for controlling some acute pains and may be useful in treating chronic pain when used with other methods of pain control. Some of the beneficial physiological effects of relaxation training may be due to the release of endogenous opioid mechanisms, and there seem to be some beneficial effects of relaxation on immune system functioning as well (McGrady et al., 1992; Van Rood, Bogaards, Goulmy, & von Houwelingen, 1993).

Hypnosis

Hypnosis is one of the oldest techniques for managing pain, and it is one of the most misunderstood. Its mere mention conjures up visions of Svengali-like power seekers forcing others to do their bidding by inducing a hypnotic trance. In one of his most difficult cases, Sherlock Holmes was nearly assassinated by a young man ordered to kill him while under the hypnotic control of a bewitching woman.

In fact, there are strict limitations on what a hypnotized person will do while in a trance. Although such people may perform some minor feats that they do not customarily perform, they typically cannot be induced to do injury to themselves or others. So much for mythology.

That hypnosis can help control pain has been noted for centuries. Old medical textbooks and anthropological accounts of healing rituals provide anecdotal evidence of such extreme interventions as surgery conducted with no apparent pain while the patient was under a hypnotic trance:

In 1829, prior to the discovery of anesthetic drugs, a French surgeon, Dr. Cloquet, performed a remarkable operation on a sixty-four-year-old woman who suffered from cancer of the right breast. After making an incision from the armpit to the inner side of the breast, he removed both the malignant tumor and also several enlarged glands in the armpit. What makes this operation remarkable is that, during the surgical procedure, the patient, who had not received any drugs, conversed quietly with the physician and showed no signs of experiencing pain. During the surgery, her respiration and pulse rate appeared stable and there were no notice-able changes in her facial expression. The ability of this patient to tolerate the painful procedures was attributed to the fact that she had been mesmerized immediately prior to the operation. (cited in Chaves & Barber, 1976, p. 443)

Cloquet's case is one of the first reports of painless surgery with mesmerism or, as it was later called, hypnosis.

How Does Hypnosis Work?

As an intervention, hypnosis relies on several pain reduction techniques. First, a state of relaxation is brought about so that the trance can be induced; relaxation alone can, of course, help reduce pain. Next, the patient is explicitly told that the hypnosis will reduce pain; the suggestion that pain will decline is also sufficient to reduce pain. Hypnosis is itself a distraction from the pain experience, and distraction can reduce the experience of pain.

In the hypnotic trance, the patient is usually instructed to think about the pain differently, and the meaning attached to pain influences its occurrence. And finally, the patient undergoing the painful procedure with hypnosis is often given painkillers. The beneficial effects of hypnosis in reducing pain are due at least in part to the composite effects of relaxation, reinterpretation, distraction, and drugs. Debate has centered on whether hypnosis is merely the sum of these other methods or whether it adds an altered state of consciousness to the experience. This issue has not yet been resolved.

How Effective Is Hypnosis?

In a study that made use of hypnotherapy, 28 patients with irritable bowl syndrome were randomly assigned to receive either hypnotherapy directed to modifying gastric experiences or a supportive verbal therapy as a control group. The hypnotherapy was found to reduce discomfort associated with the gastric, colonic response to their syndrome, suggesting that hypnotherapy may have clinical benefits for this patient group (Simrén, Ringströrm, Björnsson, & Abrahamsson, 2004). Hypnosis also helps children and adolescents cope with the pain of noxious medical procedures (Accardi & Milling, 2009), and cancer patients cope with the pain of metastatic cancer (Butler et al., 2009).

Regardless of the exact mechanism by which it works, the efficacy of hypnosis for the management of some acute pains is now established (Jensen & Patterson, 2006). It has been used successfully to control acute pain due to childbirth, dental procedures, burns, head-aches, and medical procedures (Liossi, White, & Hatira, 2006; Lutgendorf et al., 2007). It has also been used with success in the treatment of chronic pain, such as that due to cancer (Kogon et al., 1997), and may be especially successful in conjunction with other pain control techniques (Allison & Faith, 1996). The hypnotic treatment of chronic pain produces better pain control, in some cases, than medication management, physical therapy, and education or advice. The effects of self-hypnosis on chronic pain are roughly comparable to those of progressive muscle relaxation and similar relaxation therapies (Jensen & Patterson, 2006).

Acupuncture

Acupuncture has been in existence in China for more than 2,000 years. In acupuncture treatment, long, thin needles are inserted into designated areas of the body that theoretically influence the areas in which a patient is experiencing a disorder. Although the main goal of acupuncture is to cure illness, it is also used in pain management because it appears to have an analgesic effect. In China, a substantial percentage of patients are able to undergo surgery with only the analgesia of acupuncture. During surgery, these patients are typically conscious, fully alert, and able to converse while the procedures are going on.

How Does Acupuncture Work?

How acupuncture controls pain is not fully known. Acupuncture may function partly as a counterirritation technique. Moreover, patients believe that acupuncture will work, and acupuncture also induces a state of relaxation.

Before acupuncture begins, patients are usually fully prepared for it and are told what the sensations of the needles will be and how to tolerate them. Such informed preparation often reduces fear and increases tolerance of pain (see Chapter 9). Acupuncture needles and the process of inserting them are distracting; accordingly, attention may be directed away from pain. Patients undergoing acupuncture often receive analgesic drugs of various kinds, which also reduce the pain experience.

Finally, it is possible that acupuncture triggers the release of endorphins, thus reducing the experience of pain. When naloxone (an opiate antagonist that suppresses the effects of endorphins) is administered to acupuncture patients, the success of acupuncture in reducing pain is reduced (Mayer, Price, Barber, & Rafii, 1976).

Is Acupuncture Effective?

Acupuncture can help reduce some short-term pain, but it is not as effective for chronic pain. An evaluation of the effectiveness of acupuncture is also limited by its relatively uncommon use in the United States and by a lack of formal studies of the technique (Lee, 2000).

Distraction

People who are involved in intense activities, such as sports or military maneuvers, can be oblivious to painful injuries. These are extreme examples of a commonly employed pain technique: **distraction.** By focusing attention on an irrelevant and attention-getting stimulus or by distracting oneself with a high level of activity, one can turn attention away from pain (Dahlquist et al., 2007).

How Does Distraction Work?

There are two quite different mental strategies for controlling discomfort. One is to distract oneself by focusing on another activity. For instance, an 11-year-old boy described how he reduced pain by distracting himself while in the dentist's chair:

> When the dentist says, "Open," I have to say the Pledge of Allegiance to the flag backwards three times before I am even allowed to think about the drill. Once he got all finished before I did (Bandura, 1991).

The other kind of mental strategy for controlling stressful events is to focus directly on the events but to reinterpret the experience. The following is a description from an 8-year-old boy who confronted a painful event directly:

> As soon as I get in the dentist's chair, I pretend he's the enemy and I'm a secret agent, and he's torturing me to get secrets, and if I make one sound, I'm telling him secret information, so I never do. I'm going to be a secret agent when I grow up, so this is good practice.

According to Albert Bandura (1991), who reported these stories, occasionally, the boy "got carried away with his fantasy role-playing. One time the dentist asked him to rinse his mouth. Much to the child's own surprise, he snarled, 'I won't tell you a damned thing,' which momentarily stunned the dentist."

Is Distraction Effective?

Distraction is a useful technique of pain control, especially with acute pain (Dahlquist et al., 2007). In one study, 38 dental patients were exposed to one of three conditions. One third of the group heard music during the dental procedure; one third heard the music coupled with a suggestion that the music might help them reduce stress; and the third group heard no music. Patients in both music groups reported experiencing less discomfort than did patients in the no-treatment group (Anderson, Baron, & Logan, 1991).

Distraction appears to be most effective for coping with low-level pain. Its practical significance for chronic pain is limited by the fact that such patients cannot distract themselves indefinitely. Moreover, distraction by itself lacks analgesic properties (McCaul, Monson, & Maki, 1992). Thus, while effective, distraction may be most useful when used in conjunction with other pain control techniques.

Coping Techniques

Coping skills training has been used for helping chronic pain patients manage pain. For example, one study with burn patients found that brief training in cognitive coping skills, including distraction and focusing on the sensory aspects of pain instead of its painful qualities, led to reduced reported pain, increased satisfaction with pain control, and better pain coping skills (Haythornthwaite, Lawrence, & Fauerbach, 2001). Active coping skills have been found to reduce pain in patients with a variety of chronic pains (Mercado, Carroll, Cassidy, & Cote, 2000; Bishop & Warr, 2003), and passive coping has been tied to poor pain control (Walker, Smith, Garber, & Claar, 2005). The effects of coping are likely due to activity in pain processing and pain modulating circuits in the brain (Edwards, Campbell, Jamison, & Wiech, 2009).

Do Coping Techniques Work?

Is any particular coping technique effective for managing pain? The answers depend on how long patients have had their pain. In a study of 30 chronic pain patients and 30 recent-onset pain patients, researchers found that those with recent-onset pain experienced less anxiety and depression and less pain when employing avoidant coping strategies rather than attentional strategies. Because the pain was short term, putting it out of mind worked (Mullen & Suls, 1982).

In contrast, for chronic pain patients, attending directly to the pain, rather than avoiding it, was more adaptive, enabling these patients to mobilize their resources for reducing or controlling the pain (Holmes & Stevenson, 1990). Such studies suggest that pain patients might be trained in different coping strategies, avoidant versus attentive, depending on the actual or expected duration of their pain (Holmes & Stevenson, 1990).

Patients' assessments of their coping abilities may be useful for planning interventions with chronic pain patients (Walker et al., 2005). A study found that patients who appraised their problem-solving abilities as poor suffered increased pain, depression, and disability whereas those with a more favorable assessment of their problem-solving competence did better (Kerns, Rosenberg, & Otis, 2002).

Guided Imagery

Guided imagery has been used to control some acute pain and discomfort. In **guided imagery,** a patient is instructed to conjure up a picture that he or she holds in mind during the painful experience.

Some practitioners of guided imagery use it primarily to induce relaxation. The patient is encouraged to visualize a peaceful, relatively unchanging scene; to hold it in mind; and to focus on it fully. This process brings on a relaxed state, concentrates attention, and distracts the patient from the pain or discomfort—all techniques that have been shown to reduce pain.

The use of guided imagery to induce relaxation can control slow-rising pains, which can be anticipated and prepared for, or it can be used to control the discomfort of a painful medical procedure. As an example of the former use, advocates of prepared childbirth encourage a woman in labor to develop a focal point—a real or an imagined picture that she can focus on fully when labor pains begin. An example of using guided imagery to control the discomfort of a medical procedure is provided by a patient undergoing radiation therapy:

> When I was taking the radiation treatment, I imagined I was looking out my window and watching the trees and seeing the leaves go back and forth in the wind. Or, I would think of the ocean and watch the waves come in over and over again, and I would hope, "Maybe this will take it all away."

A very different kind of visualization technique may be used by patients trying to take a more personally aggressive stance toward pain. Instead of using imagery to calm and soothe themselves, these patients use it to rouse themselves into a confrontive stance by imagining a combative, action-filled scene. The following examples are from patients who used aggressive imagery in conjunction with their chemotherapy treatment:

> I happened to see something my husband was watching on TV. It was on World War II and the Nazis were in it. They were ruthless. They killed everything. I visualized my white blood cells were the German Army, and that helped me get through chemotherapy.

> I imagined that the cancer was this large dragon and the chemotherapy was a cannon, and when I was taking the chemotherapy, I would imagine it blasting the dragon, piece by piece.

The use of aggressive imagery may help those coping with the uncomfortable effects of illness or treatment. When the body is in a state of excitement or arousal, pain can be inhibited. Moreover, aggressive imagery can serve as a distraction to pain, and it gives the patient something to focus on.

Although relaxation imagery is more often used to combat pain than is aggressive imagery, aggressive imagery may work too. In fact, one chemotherapy patient apparently profited from the use of both:

> It was kind of a game with me, depending on my mood. If I was peaceful and wanted to be peaceful, I would image a beautiful scene, or if I wanted to do battle with the enemy, I would mock up a battle and have my defenses ready.

It is interesting to note that these two virtually opposite forms of imagery may actually achieve some beneficial effects in controlling pain through the same means. Both may induce a positive mood state (relaxation or excitement), which contributes to the reduction of pain. Further, both focus attention and provide a distraction from pain—one by concentrating attention on a single, unchanging or repetitive stimulus, the other by diverting attention to the drama of an active scene.

Does Guided Imagery Work?

How effective is guided imagery in controlling pain? Guided imagery is typically used in conjunction with other pain control techniques, so its unique contribution to pain reduction, if any, is as yet unknown. If it does add to the control of pain, it will likely be in the treatment of acute, slow-rising pain.

Additional Cognitive Techniques to Control Pain

In recent years, psychologists have included techniques from cognitive-behavioral therapy to control pain. These additions have several objectives. First, they encourage patients to reconceptualize the problem from overwhelming to manageable. The rationale is that the pain problem must be seen as modifiable for cognitive and behavioral methods to have any impact.

Second, clients must be convinced that the skills necessary to control the pain can and will be taught to them, thereby enhancing their expectations that the outcome of this training will be successful (Gil et al., 1996).

Third, clients are encouraged to reconceptualize their own role in the pain management process, from being passive recipients of pain to being active, resourceful, and competent individuals who can aid in the control of pain. These cognitions are important in the pain experience and may promote feelings of self-efficacy.

Fourth, clients learn how to monitor their thoughts, feelings, and behaviors to break up maladaptive cognitions that may have resulted in response to pain. As we noted in Chapter 3, patients often inadvertently undermine behavior change by engaging in discouraging self-talk. Leading pain patients to develop more upbeat monologues increases the likelihood that cognitive-behavioral techniques will be successful.

Fifth, patients are taught how and when to employ overt and covert behaviors in order to make adaptive responses to the pain problem. This skills-training component of the intervention may include biofeedback training or relaxation.

Sixth, clients are encouraged to attribute their success to their own efforts. By making internal attributions for success, patients come to see themselves as efficacious agents of change and may be in a better position to monitor subsequent changes in the pain and bring about successful pain modification.

Seventh, just as relapse prevention is an important part of health habit change, it is important in pain control as well. Patients may be taught to identify situations likely to give rise to their pain and to develop alternative ways of coping with the pain rather than engaging in the usual pain behaviors they have used in the past, such as withdrawing from social contact.

Finally, patients are often trained in therapies that can help them control their emotional responses to pain. Acceptance and commitment therapy, which involves a mindful distancing from the pain experience, as well as therapies for depression or anger implicated in the pain experience can be helpful (McCracken & Vowles, 2008).

Do Cognitive-Behavioral Interventions Work?   Evaluation of cognitive-behavioral interventions suggests that these techniques can be successful

(Keefe, Dunsmore, & Burnett, 1992). For example, back pain is the most common chronic pain in the United States, affecting 30% of the population annually. Cognitive-behavioral self-regulatory treatments are consistently helpful in managing this pain (Hoffman, Papas, Chatkoff, & Kerns, 2007). Techniques that enhance perceptions of self-efficacy may be especially so. Self-efficacy is important, both because it leads patients to undertake steps to control their pain and because perceptions of efficacy may offset the potential for depression that is so often seen in chronic pain patients.

■ MANAGEMENT OF CHRONIC PAIN: PAIN MANAGEMENT PROGRAMS

Only a half century ago, the patient who suffered from chronic pain had few treatment avenues available, except for the possibilities of addiction to morphine or other painkillers and rounds of only temporarily successful surgeries. Now, however, a coordinated form of treatment has developed to treat chronic pain.

These interventions are termed **pain management programs,** and they make available to patients all that is known about pain control. The first pain management program was founded in Seattle at the University of Washington by John Bonica, MD, in 1960. The earliest pain treatment programs were inpatient, multiweek endeavors designed to decrease use of pain medication and restore daily living skills. Presently, however, most chronic pain management efforts are outpatient programs, both because they can be successful and are less costly.

Typically, these programs are interdisciplinary efforts, bringing together neurological, cognitive, behavioral, and psychological expertise concerning pain (e.g., Turner-Stokes et al., 2003). As such, they involve the expertise of physicians, clinical psychologists or psychiatrists, and physical therapists, with consultation from specialists in neurology, rheumatology, orthopedic surgery, internal medicine, and physical medicine.

Initial Evaluation

Initially, patients are evaluated with respect to their pain and pain behaviors. Typically, such evaluation begins with a qualitative and quantitative assessment of the pain, including its location, sensory qualities, severity, and duration, as well as its onset and history. Functional status is then assessed, with patients providing information about the degree to which their work and family lives have been impaired. Exploring how the patient has coped with the pain in the past helps establish treatment goals for the future. For example, patients who withdraw from social activities in response to their pain may need to increase their participation in social activities or their family life. Often, withdrawal and avoidance of activities results from exaggerated fears over the pain that may result (Samwel, Kraaimaat, Crul, & Evers, 2007). Chronic pain patients appear to be deficient in self-regulatory skills, such as self-control, the ability to cognitively reappraise situations, and coping methods that draw on other "executive" functions, which may prolong and aggravate the chronic pain experience (Nes, Roach, & Segerstrom, 2009).

Many patients are very distressed and may suffer significant disruption in their lives (Arnow et al., 2006; Edwards et al., 2007). Formal evaluation of psychological distress, illness behavior, and psychosocial impairment is often a part of this phase of pain management, as failure to attend to emotional distress can undermine patients' self-management (Damush, Wu, Bair, Sutherland, & Kroenke, 2008; Osman et al., 2005; Rains et al., 1992; Roelofs et al., 2004). Patients may be assessed for their stage of readiness to assume a self-management approach to pain, which is ultimately critical for success (Glenn & Burns, 2003).

Individualized Treatment

Individualized programs of pain management are next developed. Such programs are typically structured and time limited. They provide concrete aims, rules, and endpoints so that the patient has specific goals to achieve.

Typically, these goals include reducing the intensity of the pain, increasing physical activity, decreasing reliance on medications, improving psychosocial functioning, reducing perception of disability, returning to full work status, and reducing the need to use health care services (Vendrig, 1999). An overarching goal has been to get patients to adopt a self-management approach for dealing with their pain (Glenn & Burns, 2003). For patients high in self-efficacy, involving them in choices regarding pain management techniques may be especially helpful (Rokke, Fleming-Ficek, Siemens, & Hegstad, 2004).

Components of Programs

Pain management programs include several common features. The first is patient education. Often conducted in a group setting, the educational component of the intervention may include discussions of medications; assertiveness or social skills training; ways of dealing with sleep disturbance; depression as a consequence of pain; nonpharmacological measures for pain control, such as relaxation skills and distraction; posture, weight management, and nutrition; and other topics related to the day-to-day management of pain.

Most patients are then trained in a variety of measures to reduce pain, such as relaxation training and exercise. The program may include components tailored to specific pains, such as temperature biofeedback for muscle contraction headaches or stretching exercises for back pain patients.

Because many pain patients are emotionally distressed, group therapy is often conducted to help them gain control of their emotional responses, especially catastrophic thinking. Catastrophic thinking enhances the pain experienced, possibly by its effects on muscle tension and blood pressure reactivity (Shelby et al., 2009; Wolff et al., 2008). Interventions are aimed at the distorted negative perceptions patients hold about their pain and their ability to overcome and live with it. For example, writing interventions have been undertaken with pain patients to get them to express their anger and make meaning in the experience; reductions in both distress and pain have been found (Graham, Lobel, Glass, & Lokshina, 2008). Likewise, depression complicates the treatment of pain, and so accompanying pain treatment with treatment for depression can both improve mental health and ameliorate the chronic pain experience (Teh, Zasylavsky, Reynolds, & Cleary, 2010). Increasingly, pain management programs try to tailor treatments to patients' methods of coping as well (Rokke & Al Absi, 1992).

Involvement of Family

Many pain management programs include family therapy. On the one hand, chronic pain patients often withdraw from their families; on the other hand, efforts by the family to be supportive can sometimes inadvertently reinforce pain behaviors. Working with the family to reduce such counterproductive behaviors may be necessary. Helping family members develop more positive perceptions of each other is also a goal of family therapy, as families can often be frustrated and annoyed by the pain patient's complaining and inactivity (Williamson, Walters, & Shaffer, 2002).

Relapse Prevention

Finally, relapse prevention is included so that patients will not backslide once they are discharged from the program. The incidence of relapse following initially successful treatment of persistent pain appears to range from about 30% to 60% (Turk & Rudy, 1991), and for at least some pains, relapse apparently is directly related to nonadherence to treatment. Consequently, the use of relapse prevention techniques may provide valuable assistance in the maintenance of posttreatment pain reduction (Turk & Rudy, 1991).

Evaluation of Programs

Pain management programs appear to be successful in helping control chronic pain. Studies that have evaluated behavioral interventions in comparison with nontreatment have found reductions in pain, disability, and psychological distress (Center for the Advancement of Health, 2000c; Haythornthwaite et al., 2001; Keefe et al., 1992). These interventions can improve social functioning as well (Stevens, Peterson, & Maruta, 1988).

Originally directed largely to the alleviation of pain itself, programs designed to manage chronic pain now acknowledge the complex interplay of physiological, psychological, behavioral, and social factors, representing a truly biopsychosocial approach to pain management.

■ THE PLACEBO AS A HEALER

Consider the following:

- Inhaling a useless drug improved lung function in children with asthma by 33%.

- People exposed to fake poison ivy develop rashes.

- Forty-two percent of balding men taking a placebo maintained or increased their hair growth.

- Sham knee surgery reduces pain as much as real surgery (Blakeslee, 1998, October 13).

All of these surprising facts are due to one effect—the placebo.

Historical Perspective

In the early days of medicine, few drugs or treatments gave any real physical benefit. As a consequence, patients were treated with a variety of bizarre, largely ineffective therapies. Egyptian patients were medicated with "lizard's blood, crocodile dung, the teeth of a swine, the hoof of an ass, putrid meat, and fly specks" (Findley, 1953),

concoctions that were not only ineffective but dangerous. If the patient did not succumb to the disease, he or she had a good chance of dying from the treatment. Medical treatments of the Middle Ages were somewhat less lethal, but not much more effective. These European patients were treated with ground-up "unicorn's horn" (actually, ground ivory), bezoar stones (supposedly a "crystallized tear from the eye of a deer bitten by a snake" but actually an animal gallstone or other intestinal piece), theriac (made from ground-up snake and between 37 and 63 equally exotic ingredients), and, for healing wounds, powdered Egyptian mummy (Shapiro, 1960).

In some cases, a clear, if somewhat naïve, logic was present in these treatments. For example, consumption (tuberculosis of the lung, which is marked by short-windedness) was treated with ground-up fox lung because the fox is a long-winded animal. As late as the 17th and 18th centuries, patients were subjected to bloodletting, freezing, and repeatedly induced vomiting to bring about a cure (Shapiro, 1960).

Such accounts make it seem miraculous that anyone survived these early medical treatments. But people did; moreover, they often seemed to get relief from these peculiar and largely ineffective remedies. Physicians have for centuries been objects of great veneration and respect, and this was no less true when few

This 16th-century woodcut shows the preparation of theriac, a supposed antidote to poison. If theriac was a successful treatment, it was entirely due to the placebo effect.

BOX 10.6

Cancer and the Placebo Effect

A dramatic example of the efficacy of the placebo effect is provided by the case history of a cancer patient, Mr. Wright. The patient thought he was being given injections of a controversial drug, Krebiozen, about which his physician was highly enthusiastic. In fact, knowing that Krebiozen was not an effective treatment, the physician gave Mr. Wright daily injections of nothing but fresh water. The effects were astonishing:

> Tumor masses melted. Chest fluid vanished. He became ambulatory and even went back to flying again. At this time he was certainly the picture of health. The water

injections were continued since they worked such wonders. He then remained symptom-free for over two months. At this time the final AMA announcement appeared in the press—"Nationwide Tests Show Krebiozen to Be a Worthless Drug in Treatment of Cancer."

Within a few days of this report, Mr. Wright was readmitted to the hospital in extremis; his faith was now gone, his last hope vanished, and he succumbed in less than 2 days.

Source: Klopfer, 1959, p. 339.

---

remedies were actually effective. To what can one attribute the success that these treatments provided? The most likely answer is that these treatments are examples of the **placebo effect.**

What Is a Placebo?

A **placebo** is "any medical procedure that produces an effect in a patient because of its therapeutic intent and not its specific nature, whether chemical or physical" (Liberman, 1962, p. 761). The word comes originally from Latin, meaning "I will please." Any medical procedure, ranging from drugs to surgery to psychotherapy, can have a placebo effect. Many patients who ingest useless substances or who undergo useless procedures find that, as a result, their symptoms disappear and their good health returns.

Moreover, placebo effects extend well beyond the beneficial results of ineffective substances (Stewart-Williams, 2004; Webb, Simmons, & Brandon, 2005). Much of the effectiveness of active treatments that produce real cures on their own include a placebo component. For example, in one study (Beecher, 1959), patients complaining of pain were injected with either morphine or a placebo. Although morphine was substantially more effective in reducing pain than was the placebo, the placebo was a successful painkiller in 35% of the cases. Another study demonstrated that morphine lost as much as 25% of its effectiveness when patients did not know they had been injected with a painkiller. In summarizing placebo effects, A. K. Shapiro (1964) stated:

> Placebos can be more powerful than, and reverse the action of, potent active drugs. . . . The incidence of placebo reactions approaches 100% in some studies. Placebos can have profound effects on organic illnesses,

> including incurable malignancies. . . . Placebos can mimic the effects usually thought to be the exclusive property of active drugs. (p. 74)

How does a placebo work? The placebo effect is not purely psychological, as stereotypes would have us believe. That is, people do not get better only because they _think_ they are going to get better, although expectations play an important role (Webb, Hendricks, & Brandon, 2007). The placebo response is a complex, psychologically mediated chain of events that often has physiological effects. For example, if the placebo reduces a negative mood, then activation of stress systems may be reduced (Aslaksen & Flaten, 2008). Placebos may also work in part by stimulating the release of opioids, the body's natural painkillers (Levine, Gordon, & Fields, 1978).

Research that examines brain activity using fMRI (functional magnetic resonance imaging) technology reveals that when patients report reduced pain after taking a placebo, they also show decreased activity in pain-sensitive regions of the brain (Wager et al., 2004). Evidence like this suggests that placebos may work via some of the same biological pathways as "real" treatments (Lieberman et al., 2004; Petrovic, Kalso, Peterson, & Ingvar, 2002). Box 10.6 describes a case of a successful placebo effect with a cancer patient. What factors determine when placebos are most effective?

Provider Behavior and Placebo Effects

The effectiveness of a placebo varies depending on how a provider treats the patient and how much the provider seems to believe in the curative powers of the treatment (Kelley et al., 2009). Providers who exude warmth, confidence, and empathy get stronger placebo effects than do more remote and formal providers. Placebo effects are strengthened when the provider radiates competence and provides reassurance to the patient that the condition will improve. Taking time with patients and not rushing them also strengthens placebo effects (Liberman, 1962; Shapiro, 1964).

Signs of doubt or skepticism may be communicated subtly, even nonverbally, to a patient, and these signs will reduce the effect. Even clearly effective drugs lose much of their effectiveness when providers express doubts over their effectiveness.

Patient Characteristics and Placebo Effects

Although there is no placebo-prone personality, some types of patients show stronger placebo effects than others. People who have a high need for approval or low self-esteem and who are persuasible in other contexts show stronger placebo effects. Anxious people experience stronger placebo effects. This effect seems to result less from personality than from the fact that anxiety produces physical symptoms, including distractibility, racing heart, sweaty palms, nervousness, and difficulty sleeping. When a placebo is administered, anxiety may be reduced, and this overlay of anxiety-related symptoms may disappear (Sharpe, Smith, & Barbre, 1985).

Patient-Provider Communication and Placebo Effects

As noted in Chapter 9, good communication between provider and patient is essential if patients are to follow through on their prescribed treatment regimens. This point is no less true for placebo responses. For patients to show a placebo response, they must understand what the treatment is supposed to do and what they need to do.

The benefit of the placebo is the symbolic value it may have for the patient. When patients seek medical treatment, they want an expert to tell them what is wrong and what to do about it. When a disorder is diagnosed and a treatment regimen is prescribed, however ineffective, the patient has tangible evidence that the provider knows what is wrong and has done something about it (Shapiro, 1964).

Situational Determinants of Placebo Effects

A setting that has the trappings of medical formality (medications, machines, uniformed personnel) will induce stronger placebo effects than will a less formal

setting. If all the staff radiate as much faith in the treatment as the physician, placebo effects will be heightened.

The shape, size, color, taste, and quantity of the placebo also influences its effectiveness: The more a drug seems like medicine, the more effective it will be (Shapiro, 1964). Treatment regimens that seem medical and include precise instructions, medications, and the like will produce stronger placebo effects than will regimens that do not seem very medical. Thus, for example, foul-tasting, peculiar-looking little pills that are taken in precise dosages ("take two" as opposed to "take two or three") and at prescribed intervals will show stronger placebo effects than will good-tasting, candylike pills with dosage levels and intervals that are only roughly indicated ("take one anytime you feel discomfort"). Exercise prescriptions and dietary restrictions show weaker placebo effects than do pills and other medications.

Social Norms and Placebo Effects

The placebo effect is facilitated by norms that surround treatment regimens—that is, the expected way in which treatment will be enacted. Drug taking is clearly a normative behavior (see Sharpe et al., 1985). In the United States, people spend approximately $216 billion each year on prescription drugs (National Center for Health Statistics, 2008), and an additional $532 million on over-the-counter drugs. About 40% of Americans use at least one prescription medication regularly, and 12% use three or more (National Center for Health Statistics, 2008) (Figure 10.3).

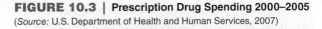

FIGURE 10.3 | Prescription Drug Spending 2000–2005
(*Source:* U.S. Department of Health and Human Services, 2007)

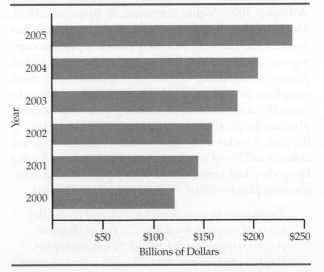

A large number of people are killed or seriously injured each year by overzealous drug taking. There are more than 2 million adverse side effects or disabilities in the United States each year (Center for Drug Evaluation and Research, 2002), which cost hospitals at least $1.5 billion in longer hospital stays and other complications. The more general cost to society of adverse drug reactions is estimated to be $47 billion a year (Bales et al., 1997). However, the drug-taking epidemic continues unabated. Clearly, there is enormous faith in medications, and the psychological if not the physical benefits can be quite substantial. Thus, placebos are effective in part because people believe that drugs work and because they have a great deal of experience in drug taking.

Equally important is the fact that most people have no experience that disconfirms their drug taking. If one is ill, takes a drug, and subsequently gets better, as most of us do most of the time, one does not in reality know exactly what caused this result. A drug may be responsible; the disease may have run its course; or one's mood may have picked up, altering the body's physiological balance and making it no longer receptive to an invader. Probably a combination of factors is at work. Regardless of the actual cause of success, the patient acting as his or her own naïve physician will probably attribute success to whatever drug he or she took, however erroneous that conclusion may be.

Generalizability of Placebo Effects

As noted earlier, virtually any medical procedure can have placebo effects (Miller, 1989). For example, many surgical patients show improvement simply as a function of having had surgery and not as a result of the actual procedure employed (Stolberg, 1999, April 25). Psychiatry and clinical psychology also show placebo effects; some patients feel better simply knowing that a psychiatrist or psychologist has found a cause for their

problems, even if this cause is not the real one. Adherence to a placebo can even be associated with lower death rates due to illness (Irvine, Baker, et al., 1999).

The placebo effect should not be thought of as either a medical trick or a purely psychological response on the part of the patient. Placebo effects merit respect. The placebo achieves success in the absence of truly effective therapy (Roberts, Kewman, Mercier, & Hovell, 1993). It increases the efficacy of a therapy that has only modest effects of its own, and it reduces substantial pain and discomfort. It is the foundation of most of early medicine's effectiveness, and it continues to account for many of medicine's effects today. Its continued success should be encouraged.

The Placebo as a Methodological Tool

The placebo response is so powerful that no drug can be marketed in the United States unless it has been evaluated against a placebo. The standard method for so doing is termed a **double-blind experiment.** In such a test, a researcher gives half a group of patients a drug that is supposed to cure a disease or alleviate symptoms; the other half receives a placebo. The procedure is called double-blind because neither the researcher nor the patient knows whether the patient received the drug or the placebo; both are "blind" to the procedure. Once the effectiveness of the treatment has been measured, the researcher looks in the coded records to see which treatment each patient received. The difference between the effectiveness of the drug and the effectiveness of the placebo is considered to be a measure of the drug's effectiveness (America & Milling, 2008). Comparison of a drug against a placebo is essential for accurate measurement of a drug's effect. Drugs may look four or five times more successful than they really are if there is no effort to evaluate them against a placebo (Miller, 1989; Shapiro, 1964). ●

SUMMARY

1. Pain is the symptom of primary concern to patients and leads them to seek medical attention. However, pain is often considered of secondary importance to practitioners.

2. Pain is intensely subjective and, consequently, has been difficult to study. It is heavily influenced by the context in which it is experienced. To objectify the experience of pain, pain researchers have developed questionnaires to assess its dimensions and methods to assess pain behaviors.

3. A-delta fibers conduct fast, sharp, localized pain; C-fibers conduct slow, aching, burning, and long-lasting pain; higher-order brain processes influence the experience of pain through the central control mechanism.

4. Neurochemical advances in the understanding of pain center around endogenous opioid peptides, which regulate the pain experience.

5. Acute pain is short term and specific to a particular injury or disease, whereas chronic pain does not decrease with treatment and time. As many as 130 million Americans suffer from chronic pain, which may lead them to disrupt their entire lives in an effort to cure it. Chronic pain is difficult to treat because it has a functional and psychological overlay.

6. Efforts to find a pain-prone personality have been largely unsuccessful. Nonetheless, personality profiles based on the MMPI do suggest that chronic pain patients have elevated scores on the neurotic triad.

7. Pharmacologic (for example, morphine), surgical, and sensory stimulation techniques were once the mainstays of pain control, but increasingly, treatments with psychological components, including biofeedback, relaxation, hypnosis, acupuncture, distraction, and guided imagery, have been added to the pain control arsenal.

8. Most recently, cognitive-behavioral techniques that help instill a sense of self-efficacy have been used successfully in the treatment of pain.

9. Chronic pain is often treated through coordinated pain management programs oriented toward managing the pain, extinguishing pain behavior, and reestablishing a viable lifestyle. These programs employ a mix of technologies in an effort to develop an individualized treatment program for each patient—a truly biopsychosocial approach to pain.

10. A placebo is any medical procedure that produces an effect in a patient because of its therapeutic intent and not its actual nature. Virtually every medical treatment shows some degree of placebo effect.

11. Placebo effects are enhanced when the physician shows faith in a treatment, the patient is predisposed to believe it will work, these expectations are successfully communicated, and the trappings of medical treatment are in place.

12. Placebos are also a useful methodological tool in evaluating drugs and other treatments.

KEY TERMS

acupuncture
acute pain
biofeedback
chronic benign pain
chronic pain
chronic progressive pain
counterirritation

distraction
double-blind experiment
endogenous opioid peptides
gate-control theory of pain
guided imagery
hypnosis
nociception

pain behaviors
pain control
pain management programs
pain-prone personality
placebo
placebo effect
recurrent acute pain

Management of Chronic and Terminal Illness

Management of Chronic Illness

During a race at a high school track meet, a young runner stumbled and fell to the ground, caught in the grips of an asthma attack. As her mother frantically clawed through her backpack, looking for the inhaler, three other girls on the track team offered theirs. As this account implies, asthma rates have skyrocketed in recent years, particularly among children and adolescents. Nearly 6 million children have asthma, and more than a third of those children require treatment in a hospital emergency room for an asthma attack each year (National Heart, Lung, and Blood Institute, 2008). Scientists are not entirely sure why asthma is on the increase, but the complications that it creates for young adults are evident. Caution, medication, and inhalers become a part of daily life. Psychosocial factors are clearly an important part of this adjustment, helping us answer such questions as "What factors precipitate an asthma attack?" and "What does it mean to have a chronic disease so early in life?"

At any given time, 50% of the population has a chronic condition. Taken together, the medical management of these chronic disorders accounts for three-quarters of the nation's health spending (Centers for Disease Control and Prevention, 2009c), not including nursing home care. The chronically ill account for 90% of home care visits, 83% of prescription drug use, 80% of the days spent in hospitals, 66% of doctor visits, and 55% of visits to hospital emergency rooms. In the United States, 1.7 million people die from heart disease, stroke, cancer, and other chronic diseases every year (Centers for Disease Control and Prevention, October 2009). And as the opening example implies, these conditions are not confined to the elderly (see Figure 11.1). More than one third of young adults age 18–44 have at least one chronic condition (Strong, Mathers, Leeder, & Beaglehole, 2005).

Chronic conditions range from moderate ones, such as partial hearing loss (Dillon, Gu, Hoffman, & Ko, 2010), to severe and life-threatening disorders, such as cancer, coronary artery disease, and diabetes. For example, in the United States, arthritis in its various forms afflicts 46 million people (Centers for Disease Control and Prevention, 2004a); 10.7 million people have had cancer (American Cancer Society, 2008); diabetes afflicts 23.6 million people (American Diabetes Association, 2009); more than 6 million people have sustained a stroke; 16.8 million people have a history of heart attack and/or chest pain (American Heart Association, 2009b); and 73.6 million people have diagnosed hypertension (American Heart Association, 2009b). In fact, most of us will eventually develop at least one chronic disability or disease, which may ultimately be the cause of our death. Thus,

FIGURE 11.1 | The Prevalence of Physical Limitations Increases with Age   (*Source*: Holmes, Powell-Griner, Lethbridge-Cejku, & Heyman, 2009)

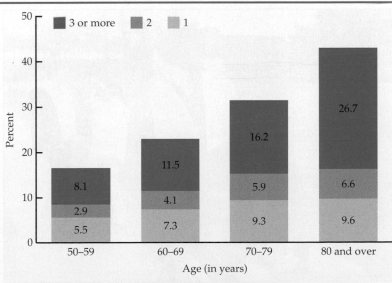

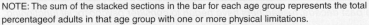

NOTE: The sum of the stacked sections in the bar for each age group represents the total percentage of adults in that age group with one or more physical limitations.

there is every likelihood that, at some time, each of us will hear a physician say that our condition is chronic and cannot be cured; it can only be managed.

■ QUALITY OF LIFE

Until recently, **quality of life** was not considered an issue of medical importance, except in terms of length of survival and signs of presence of disease. There was virtually no consideration of the psychosocial consequences of illness and treatments (Taylor & Aspinwall, 1990).

However, medical measures are only weakly related to patients' or relatives' assessments of quality of life. In fact, one classic study of hypertension (Jachuck, Brierley, Jachuck, & Willcox, 1982) found that although 100% of the physicians reported that their patients' quality of life had improved with the regular use of hypertensive medication, only half the patients agreed and virtually none of the relatives did. Moreover, some illnesses and treatments are perceived by patients to be "fates worse than death" because they threaten valued life activities so completely (Ditto, Druley, Moore, Danks, & Smucker, 1996).

Perhaps the most important impetus for evaluating quality of life stems from the psychological distress chronically ill patients often experience. The chronically ill are more likely to suffer from depression, anxiety, and generalized distress (De Graaf & Bijl, 2002; Mittermaier et al., 2004). In many cases, these are pre-existing mental health conditions; for example, depression is a risk factor for coronary heart disease. In other cases, these mental health conditions may result from the chronic physical health condition. In either case, depression, psychological distress, and neuroticism contribute to increased risks for mortality from chronic conditions (Christensen, Moran, Wiebe, Ehlers, & Lawton, 2002). Stress exacerbates the symptoms and course of many chronic illnesses, and because depression and anxiety are common consequences of stress, reducing stress levels and managing those stressors that cannot be eliminated are paramount for the management of chronic illness. Moreover, psychiatric and medical problems coupled with disease-related worries predict health-related quality of life better than the underlying course of the disease itself (Häuser, Zimmer, Schiedermaier, & Grandt, 2004).

What Is Quality of Life?

Because of findings like these, quality of life is now given attention in the management of chronic illness. Quality of life has several components—specifically, physical functioning, psychological status, social functioning, and disease- or treatment-related symptomatology (Kahn & Juster, 2002; Katz, Ford, Moskowitz, Jackson, & Jaffee, 1983; Power, Bullinger, Harper, & the World Health Organization Quality of Life Group, 1999). Researchers focus on how much the disease and its treatment interfere with the activities of daily living, such as sleeping, eating, going to work, and engaging in

In the past decade, researchers have begun to consider psychosocial functioning as an important aspect of quality of life among the chronically ill and disabled.

recreational activities. For patients with more advanced diseases, such assessments include whether the patient is able to bathe, dress, use the toilet, be mobile, be continent, and eat without assistance. Essentially, then, quality-of-life assessments gauge the extent to which a patient's normal life activities have been compromised by disease and treatment. A broad array of measures is now available for evaluating quality of life in both adults (see, for example, Hazuda, Gerety, Lee, Mulrow, & Lichtenstein, 2002; Logsdon, Gibbons, McCurry, & Teri, 2002) and children (Varni, Burwinkle, Rapoff, Kamps, & Olson, 2004).

Why Study Quality of Life?

Why should we study quality of life among the chronically ill?

- Documentation of exactly how illness affects vocational, social, and personal activities, as well as the general activities of daily living, provides an important basis for interventions designed to improve quality of life.

- Quality-of-life measures can help pinpoint exactly which problems are likely to emerge for patients with diseases. Such a measure, for example, might indicate that sexual functioning is a problem for patients with certain kinds of cancer but that depression is a more common problem for patients with other kinds of cancer.

- Quality-of-life measures assess the impact of treatments. For example, if a cancer treatment has

disappointing survival rates and produces adverse side effects, the treatment may be more harmful than the disease itself.

- Quality-of-life information can be used to compare therapies. For example, if two therapies produce approximately equivalent survival rates but one lowers quality of life substantially, the treatments that keep quality of life high would be preferable (Taylor & Aspinwall, 1990).

- Quality-of-life information can inform decision makers about care that will maximize long-term survival with the highest quality of life possible (Kaplan, 2003).

An important aspect of quality of life concerns people's perceptions of their own health. Often studies ask people to make self-ratings of their health, and these ratings have been found to predict morbidity and mortality over and above other medical and psychological knowledge (Frankenberg & Jones, 2004; McCullough & Laurenceau, 2004). As yet, medical practitioners and health psychologists do not know exactly what information people have about their own health that is not picked up by other assessments, but clearly, self-rated health is a distinctively important aspect of self-perceived quality of life.

Attention to quality-of-life issues has been useful in pinpointing some of the areas that require particular attention and interventions following the diagnosis of a chronic disease (Table 11.1), to which we now turn.

TABLE 11.1 | Quality of Life Scores for U.S. Population and Several Groups of Chronically Ill Individuals

A look at the typical score for the U.S. population indicates how each of several chronic conditions affects functioning in each area. For example, pain and vitality are most problematic for migraine sufferers, osteoarthritis compromises physical activities related to roles, diabetes undermines general health, and so on. An important point is that compared with the debilitating effects of clinical depression, which is an emotional disorder, the chronically ill generally fare quite well on quality of life, with the exception of areas directly affected by their diseases.

	Physical Functioning	Role— Physical	Bodily Pain	General Health	Vitality	Social Functioning	Role— Emotional	Mental Health
U.S. Population*	**92.1**	**92.2**	**84.7**	**81.4**	**66.5**	**90.5**	**92.1**	**81.0**
Clinical depression	81.8	62.8	73.6	63.6	49.0	68.5	47.8	53.8
Migraine	83.2	54.0	51.3	70.1	50.9	71.1	66.5	66.4
Hypertension	89.5	79.0	83.8	72.6	67.2	92.1	79.6	77.3
Osteoarthritis	81.9	66.5	69.7	70.4	57.0	90.1	85.5	76.5
Type II diabetes	86.6	76.8	82.8	66.9	61.4	89.4	80.7	76.6

*U.S. population estimates are for those reporting no chronic conditions. Scores take into account other chronic conditions, age, gender.

Source: Based on Ware, 1994.

■ EMOTIONAL RESPONSES TO CHRONIC ILLNESS

Many chronic diseases affect all aspects of a patient's life. As in acute diseases, there is a temporary first phase when all life activities are disrupted. Chronic disease, however, may also carry the need to make intermittent or permanent changes in physical, vocational, and social activities. In addition, people with chronic illnesses must integrate the patient role into their lives psychologically if they are to adapt to their disorders.

Immediately after a chronic disease is diagnosed, a patient can be in a state of crisis marked by physical, social, and psychological disequilibrium. If the patient's usual coping efforts fail to resolve these problems, the result can be an exaggeration of symptoms and their meaning, indiscriminate efforts to cope, an increasingly neurotic attitude, and worsening health may result (Cheng, Hui, & Lam, 1999; Drossman et al., 2000; Epker & Gatchel, 2000). Anxiety, fear, and depression may temporarily take over. These psychological changes are important, not only because they compromise quality of life, but because they predict adherence (Bruce, Hancock, Arnett, & Lynch, 2010) as well as course of disease and even mortality.

Eventually, the crisis phase of chronic illness passes, and patients begin to develop a sense of how the chronic illness will alter their lives. At this point, more long-term difficulties that require ongoing rehabilitative attention may set in.

Denial

Denial is a defense mechanism by which people avoid the implications of an illness. It is a common reaction to chronic illness (Krantz & Deckel, 1983; Meyerowitz, 1983). Patients may act as if the illness is not severe, as if it will shortly go away, or as if it will have few long-term implications. However, immediately after the diagnosis of illness, denial can serve a protective function by keeping the patient from having to come to terms with the full range of problems posed by the illness at a time when he or she may be least able to do so (Hackett & Cassem, 1973; Lazarus, 1983). One study of patients with myocardial infarction (MI) found that high initial denial was associated with fewer days in intensive care and fewer signs of cardiac dysfunction (Levine et al., 1988). Denial can also reduce the experience of unpleasant symptoms and side effects of treatment (Ward, Leventhal, & Love, 1988).

During the rehabilitative phase of illness, denial may have adverse effects if it interferes with the ability to take in necessary information that will be part of the patient's treatment or **self-management** program. For example, in the study that found initial benefits of denial among MI patients (Levine et al., 1988), high deniers showed poorer adaptation to disease in the year following discharge. They were less adherent to their treatment regimen and required more days of rehospitalization, suggesting that denial was interfering with successfully adopting a comanagement role in the illness.

Anxiety

Following the diagnosis of a chronic illness, anxiety is common. Many patients become overwhelmed by the potential changes in their lives and, in some cases, by the prospect of death. Every twinge of chest pain may raise concern over another heart attack for the patient recuperating from MI. Many cancer patients are constantly vigilant to changes in their physical condition, and each minor ache or pain may prompt fear of a possible recurrence. Anxiety levels are especially high when people are waiting for test results, receiving diagnoses, awaiting invasive medical procedures, and anticipating or experiencing adverse side effects of treatment (Rabin, Ward, Leventhal, & Schmitz, 2001). They are also high when people expect substantial lifestyle changes to result from an illness or its treatment, when they feel dependent on health professionals, and when they lack information about the nature of the illness and its treatment (Marks, Sliwinski, & Gordon, 1993).

Anxiety is a problem not only because it is intrinsically distressing but also because it can interfere with symptoms and treatment. For example, anxious patients can cope more poorly with surgery (Mertens, Roukema, Scholtes, & De Vries, 2010); anxious diabetic patients have poor glucose control and increased symptoms (Lustman, 1988); anxiety can increase the frequency of attacks of Raynaud's disease (Brown, Middaugh, Haythornthwaite, & Bielory, 2001); anxiety can lead to hyperreactivity in the gut for patients suffering from irritable bowel syndrome (Blomhoff, Spetalen, Jacobsen, & Malt, 2001); anxiety exacerbates sickle cell disease (Levenson et al., 2008) and multiple sclerosis (Kehler & Hadjistavropoulos, 2009); and anxious MI patients are less likely to return to work on schedule (Maeland & Havik, 1987). Anxiety is especially prevalent among people with asthma and pulmonary disorders and, not surprisingly, compromises quality of life

(Katon, Richardson, Lozano, & McCauley, 2004). Symptoms of anxiety may also be mistaken for symptoms of the underlying disease and thus interfere with assessments of the disease and its treatment (Chen, Hermann, Rodgers, Oliver-Welker, & Strunk, 2006).

Although anxiety directly attributable to the disease may decrease over time, anxiety about possible complications, the disease's implications for the future, and its impact on work and leisure-time activities may actually increase with time (Christman et al., 1988). Catastrophic thinking, that is, imagining and exaggerating how much worse things will get, can aggravate symptoms and complicate treatment (De Peuter, Lemaigre, Van Diest, & Van den Bergh, 2008).

Depression

Depression is a common and often debilitating reaction to chronic illness. Up to one third of all medical inpatients with chronic disease report at least moderate symptoms of depression, and up to one quarter suffer from severe depression (Moody, McCormick, & Williams, 1990). Although depression may occur somewhat later in the adjustment process than does denial or severe anxiety, it can also occur intermittently. Depression is especially common among stroke patients, cancer patients, and heart disease patients, as well as among those people experiencing more than one chronic disorder (Egede, 2005; see Taylor & Aspinwall, 1990, for a review).

At one time, depression was regarded as an unfortunate psychological consequence of chronic illness, but its medical significance is increasingly being recognized. Depression can be a sign of impending physical decline, especially among elderly men (Anstey & Luszcz, 2002). Depression exacerbates the risk and course of several chronic disorders, most notably coronary heart disease. Depression complicates treatment adherence and medical decision making. It interferes with patients adopting a comanagerial role, and it may confer enhanced risk of mortality from several chronic diseases (Anstey & Luszcz, 2002). For all these reasons, the assessment and management of depression in chronic illness has become of paramount importance to health care providers and health psychologists.

Depression is sometimes a delayed reaction to chronic illness, because it often takes time for patients to understand the full implications of their condition. For example, a stroke patient comments on his discharge from the hospital:

That was a glorious day. I started planning all the things I could do with the incredible amount of free time I was going to have, chores I had put off, museums and galleries to visit, friends I had wanted to meet for lunch. It was not until several days later that I realized I simply couldn't do them. I didn't have the mental or physical strength, and I sank into a depression. (Dahlberg, 1977, p. 121)

The Significance of Depression Depression is important not only for the distress it produces but also because of its impact on symptoms and prospects for recovery (Lieshout, Bienenstock, & MacQueen, 2009). Depressed stroke patients have longer hospital stays and are more often discharged from the hospital to nursing homes than are other patients (Cushman, 1986). They show less motivation to undergo rehabilitation (Thompson, Sobolew-Shubin, Graham, & Janigian, 1989) and are less likely to maintain gains during rehabilitation (Sinyor et al., 1986) or to restore their quality of life to pre-disease levels (Niemi, Laaksonen, Kotila, & Waltimo, 1988). Their overall quality of life can be low (Howren, Christensen, Karnell, & Funk, 2010). Depressed rheumatoid arthritis patients are more likely to catastrophize, overgeneralize, and negatively interpret their situation (Smith, Peck, Milano, & Ward, 1988). MI patients who are depressed while in the hospital are less likely to be back at work a year later and are more likely to be rehospitalized than are patients who were not depressed (Stern, Pascale, & Ackerman, 1977). Depression predicts mortality as well (e.g., Kinder et al., 2008).

Depression over illness and treatment has also been linked to suicide among the chronically ill (Goodwin, Kroenke, Hoven, & Spitzer, 2003; Rollman & Shear, 2003). For example, one out of every six long-term dialysis patients over age 60 stops treatment, resulting in death (Neu & Kjellstrand, 1986). The rate of suicide among cancer patients is approximately one-and-a-half times greater than that among adults who are not ill (Marshall, Burnett, & Brasure, 1983), and the rate of suicide among men with AIDS is higher than the national rate for their age group. Perhaps most importantly, depression is a potent risk factor for death among the chronically ill (Herrmann et al., 1998; Wulsin, Vaillant, & Wells, 1999).

Unlike anxiety, which ebbs and flows during the course of a chronic illness, depression can be a long-term reaction, lasting a year or more following onset of the disorder (Lustman, Griffith, & Clouse, 1988; Meyerowitz, 1980; Robinson & Price, 1982).

Assessing Depression   Assessing depression in the chronically ill can be problematic. Many of the physical signs of depression, such as fatigue, sleeplessness, and weight loss, can also be symptoms of disease or side effects of a treatment. If depressive symptoms are attributed to aspects of illness or treatment, their significance may be less apparent, and, consequently, depression may go untreated (Ziegelstein et al., 2005). These issues are especially problematic for illnesses that can affect brain functioning, such as cancer, stroke, diabetes, AIDS, and epilepsy. Depressed patients may make extreme decisions about their care, such as withdrawal of dialysis among end-stage renal disease patients (McDade-Montez, Christensen, Cvengros, & Lawton, 2006). Depression is so prevalent among chronically ill patients that experts recommend routine screening for these symptoms during medical visits (Löwe et al., 2003).

Who Gets Depressed?   Depression increases with the severity of the illness (Cassileth et al., 1985; Moody, McCormick, & Williams, 1990). The experiences of pain and disability, in particular, lead to depression (Turner & Noh, 1988; Wulsin et al., 1999), which, in turn, increases pain and disability. These problems are aggravated in those who are experiencing other negative life events, social stress, and lack of social support (Bukberg, Penman, & Holland, 1984; Thompson et al., 1989).

Physical limitations may predict depression somewhat better earlier in chronic illness, whereas psychological factors may better explain depression later on. For example, one study of stroke patients found that the location of stroke damage predicted depression in the first 6 months, whereas later on, cognitive impairment, physical disability, social support, changes in body image and self-esteem, and the adverse mood effects of therapeutic drugs were stronger determinants of depression (Morris & Raphael, 1987).

In recent years, effective cognitive behavioral interventions have been developed to deal with the depression that so frequently accompanies chronic illness (Center for the Advancement of Health, 2000d). Even telephone-administered cognitive behavioral therapy can improve depression (Beckner, Howard, Vella, & Mohr, 2010). Treatment for depression may not only alleviate psychological distress but also reduce symptoms associated with the illness (Mohr, Hart, & Goldberg, 2003).

■ PERSONAL ISSUES IN CHRONIC DISEASE

To fully understand changes in response to chronic illness requires a consideration of the self, its sources of resilience, and its vulnerabilities. The self is one of the central concepts in psychology. Psychologists refer to the **self-concept** as a stable set of beliefs about one's qualities and attributes. Self-esteem refers to the evaluation of the self-concept—namely, whether one feels good or bad about one's personal qualities and attributes.

A chronic illness can produce drastic changes in self-concept and self-esteem. Many of these changes will be temporary, but some may be permanent, such as the mental deterioration that is associated with certain diseases (Box 11.1). The self-concept is a composite of self-evaluations regarding many aspects of life, which include body image, achievement, social functioning, and the private self.

The Physical Self

Body image is the perception and evaluation of one's physical functioning and appearance. Body image plummets during illness. Not only is the affected part of the body evaluated negatively, the whole body image may take on a negative aura. For acutely ill patients, changes in body image are short-lived; however, for the chronically ill, negative evaluations may last. For example, when illness threatens sexual functioning—as it does for stroke, paralysis, some cancers, and heart conditions—body image may be affected.

These changes in body image are important. First, a poor body image is related to low self-esteem and an increased likelihood of depression and anxiety. Second, body image may influence how adherent a person is to the course of treatment and how willing he or she is to adopt a comanagement role. Finally, body image is important because it can be improved through psychological and educational interventions (Wenninger, Weiss, Wahn, & Staab, 2003), although it may take time (Wenninger et al., 2003).

Two exceptions are patients with facial disfigurements or with extensive burns (Hagedoorn & Molleman, 2006). An example of the potent impact of facial disfigurement is the case of Mrs. Dover:

> Before her disfigurement (amputation of half of her nose), Mrs. Dover, who lived with one of her two married daughters, had been an independent, warm, and friendly woman who enjoyed traveling, shopping,

BOX 11.1

A Future of Fear

Mollie Kaplan can remember half a century ago when she was 12 and met her husband, Samuel, at a Halloween party in the Bronx. What she can't remember is whether she had breakfast, so sometimes she eats it twice. She doesn't cook much anymore because if the recipe calls for salt, she can't remember whether she added it. "It's so frustrating," she said. "I can't read a book anymore, because if I stop and put a bookmark where I leave off, when I pick the book up again, I don't know what I have read."

If nothing else, Mollie Kaplan retains a disarming sense of humor. When asked about anything in the recent past, she often replies, "Who remembers? You are talking with an Alzheimer's." It isn't much of a humorous matter to Sam, now 64, who still loves the woman he met half a century ago but wearily confesses: "You don't know what this is like until you get there. I never thought this would happen to me. People say to me, 'Join a support group.' I say, 'Fine, but what is Mollie supposed to do while I'm at the group?'" (Larsen, 1990, pp. E1, E8).

Mollie Kaplan has Alzheimer's disease. Alzheimer's is the fourth leading cause of death among adults, behind heart disease, cancer, and strokes. Alzheimer's accounted for at least 72,314 deaths in 2006, and 5.3 million Amer-

icans currently have the disease, with numbers projected to rise to 7.7 million by 2030 (Alzheimer's Association, 2009). Typical symptoms of Alzheimer's (named after Dr. Alois Alzheimer, who described it in 1906) include gradual progression of memory loss or other cognitive losses (language problems, motor skills), personality change, and eventually loss of function (Mattson, 2004). Increasing frailty may foreshadow the onset of the disorder (Buchman, Boyle, Wilson, Tang, & Bennett, 2007). Personality changes include hostility, withdrawal, inappropriate laughing, agitation, and paranoia.

The strain of Alzheimer's disease on both the patient and the caregiver can be great. For the patient, the distress of being increasingly unable to do simple, routine tasks or to remember an activity just completed is frustrating and depressing. For caregivers, the emotional toll is substantial, and the effect on family finances can be huge. Often, the family is left with little alternative but to place the loved one in a nursing home. Despite this grim picture, many treatments for Alzheimer's are in development, and many are currently being tested or are generally available (Cowley, 2002, June 24). As neuroscientists learn more about the cellular and molecular changes that lead to neurodegeneration, progress in prevention and treatment will be made.

---

and visiting her many relatives. The disfigurement of her face, however, resulted in a definite alteration in her way of living. The first two or three years she seldom left her daughter's home, preferring to remain in her room or to sit in the backyard. "I was heartsick," she said; "the door had been shut on my life." (Goffman, 1963, p. 12)

Body image can be improved by stressing other aspects of appearance and health. Researchers have sometimes noted spontaneous increases in physical exercise and improvement of other aspects of physical appearance or health as a reaction to illness (Taylor, Wood, & Lichtman, 1983). In addition, feelings of social self-efficacy may mitigate the effects of disfigurement on social isolation (Hagedoorn & Molleman, 2006).

The Achieving Self

Achievement through vocational and avocational activities is also an important aspect of self-esteem and self-concept. Many people derive their primary satisfaction

from their job or career; others take great pleasure in their hobbies and leisure activities. If chronic illness threatens these valued aspects of the self, the self-concept may be damaged. The converse is also true: When work and hobbies are not threatened or curtailed by illness, the patient has these sources of satisfaction from which to derive self-esteem, and they can come to take on new meaning. Relatedly, maintaining cognitive function is important in adjusting to chronic illness, as it may contribute not only to the ability to pursue one's valued activities, but may also predict survival (Hall, Crossley, & D'Arcy, 2010).

The Social Self

Rebuilding the social self is an important aspect of readjustment after chronic illness. Interactions with family and friends can be a critical source of self-esteem. Social resources provide chronically ill patients with badly needed information, help, and emotional support. A breakdown in the support system has implications for

Chronic disease or disability can interfere with some life activities, but a sense of self that is based on broader interests and abilities will sustain self-esteem.

all aspects of life. Perhaps for these reasons, fears about withdrawal of support are among the most common worries of chronically ill patients. Consequently, family participation in the rehabilitation process is widely encouraged. Providing all family members, even young children, with at least some information about the disorder, its course, and its treatment can offset the potential for confusion and miscommunication (P. D. Williams et al., 2002).

The Private Self

The residual core of a patient's identity—ambitions, goals, and desires for the future—are also affected by chronic illness. Occasionally, adjustment to chronic illness may be impeded because the patient has an unrealized secret dream, which is now out of reach, or at least appears to be. For example, the dream of retiring to a cabin on a lake in the mountains may not be viable if the management of a chronic condition requires living near

a major medical center. Encouraging the patient to discuss this difficulty may reveal alternative paths to fulfillment and awaken the ability to establish new ambitions, goals, and plans for the future.

Positive self-perceptions are important not only because they contribute to a higher quality of life but because they can influence longevity. One study reported that older adults with more positive self-perceptions of aging lived on average several years longer than those with less positive perceptions of aging, and this effect remained even after health, age, gender, socioeconomic status, and social support were controlled (Levy, Slade, Kunkel, & Kasl, 2002). Feeling good about yourself, then, affects both mental and physical health outcomes.

■ COPING WITH CHRONIC ILLNESS

Despite the fact that most patients with chronic illness suffer at least some adverse psychological reactions as a result of the disease, most do not seek formal or informal psychological treatment for their symptoms. Instead, they draw on their internal and social resources for solving problems and alleviating psychological distress. How do they cope so well?

Coping Strategies and Chronic Illness

The appraisal of a chronic disease as threatening or challenging leads to the initiation of coping efforts (see Chapter 7) (Lazarus & Folkman, 1984a, 1984b). Relatively few investigations have looked systematically at coping strategies among chronically ill patient groups.

In one of the few such studies (Dunkel-Schetter, Feinstein, Taylor, & Falke, 1992), cancer patients were asked to identify the aspect of their cancer they found to be the most stressful. The results indicated that fear and uncertainty about the future were most common (41%), followed by limitations in physical abilities, appearance, and lifestyle (24%), and then pain management (12%). Patients were then asked to indicate the coping strategies they had used to deal with these problems. The five identified strategies were social support/direct problem solving ("I talked to someone to find out more about the situation"), distancing ("I didn't let it get to me"), positive focus ("I came out of the experience better than I went in"), cognitive escape/avoidance ("I wished that the situation would go away"), and behavioral escape/avoidance (efforts to avoid the situation by eating, drinking, or sleeping).

The strategies identified in this investigation are not substantially different from those employed to deal with other stressful events (see Chapter 7). One notable difference, though, is that the chronically ill report fewer active coping methods, such as planning, problem solving, and confrontative coping, and more passive coping strategies, such as positive focus and escape/avoidant strategies. This discrepancy may reflect the fact that some chronic diseases raise uncontrollable concerns that active coping strategies cannot directly address. But in the aftermath of a heart attack, confrontative coping and problem solving may emerge, as people attempt to modify their health habits and lifestyle, with the hope of reducing subsequent risk.

Which Coping Strategies Work?

Do any particular coping strategies facilitate psychological adjustment among the chronically ill? As is true for coping with other stressful events, the use of avoidant coping is associated with increased psychological distress and is a risk factor for adverse responses to illness (Heim, Valach, & Schaffner, 1997). It may also exacerbate the disease process itself. For example, avoidant coping has been related to poor glycemic control among insulin-dependent diabetics (Frenzel, McCaul, Glasgow, & Schafer, 1988).

Active coping predicts good adjustment to several disorders. Research has found lower distress among patients who cope using positive, confrontative responses to stress; solicit health-related information about their condition (Christensen, Ehlers, Raichle, Bertolatus, & Lawton, 2000); have a high internal locus of control (Burgess, Morris, & Pettingale, 1988); and believe that they can personally direct control over an illness (Affleck, Tennen, Pfeiffer, & Fifield, 1987; Taylor, Helgeson, Reed, & Skokan, 1991).

Because of the diversity of problems that chronic diseases pose, people who are flexible copers may cope better than do people who engage in a predominant coping style. Flexible coping strategies may be most effective when they are matched to the particular problem for which they are most useful (Cheng, Hui, & Lam, 2004).

Patients' Beliefs About Chronic Illness

Virtually all chronic illnesses require some alteration in activities and some degree of management. For example, diabetic patients must control their diet and perhaps take daily injections of insulin. Both stroke and heart patients must make alterations in their daily activities if they have impairments.

Patients who do not incorporate chronic illness into their self-concept may fail to follow their treatment regimen. They may be improperly attuned to possible signs of recurrent or worsening disease. They may engage in foolhardy behaviors that pose a risk to their health, or they may fail to practice important health behaviors that could reduce the possibility of recurrence or other complicating illnesses. Thus, developing a realistic sense of one's illness, the restrictions it imposes, and the regimen that is required is an important process of coping with chronic illness.

Beliefs About the Nature of the Illness   In Chapter 8, we described the commonsense model of illness and the fact that patients develop coherent beliefs about their illnesses, including its identity, causes, consequences, timeline, and controllability (Hekler et al., 2008). One of the problems that often arises in adjustment to chronic illness is that patients adopt an inappropriate model for their disorder—most notably, the acute model (see Chapter 8). For example, hypertensive patients may believe incorrectly that, if they feel all right, they no longer need to take medication because their hypertension must be under control; accordingly, they may fail to monitor their condition closely (Hekler et al., 2008). Thus, it is often important for health care providers to probe patients' beliefs about their illness to check for significant gaps and misunderstandings in their knowledge that may interfere with self-management (Stafford, Jackson, & Berk, 2008).

Beliefs About the Cause of the Illness   People with chronic illnesses often develop theories about where their illness came from (Costanzo, Lutgendorf, Bradley, Rose, & Anderson, 2005). These theories include stress, physical injury, disease-causing bacteria, and God's will. Of perhaps greater significance is where patients ultimately place the blame for their illness. Do they blame themselves, another person, the environment, or a quirk of fate?

Self-blame for chronic illness is widespread. Patients frequently perceive themselves as having brought on their illness through their own actions. In some cases, these perceptions are to some extent correct. Poor health habits, such as smoking, improper diet, or lack of exercise, can produce heart disease, stroke, or cancer. But in many cases, the patient's self-blame is ill placed.

What are the consequences of self-blame? Unfortunately, a definitive answer to this question is not available. Some researchers have found that self-blame can lead to guilt, self-recrimination, or depression (Bennett, Compas, Beckjord, & Glinder, 2005; Friedman et al., 2007), but perceiving the cause of one's illness as self-generated may represent an effort to assume control over the disorder; such feelings can be adaptive in coping with and coming to terms with the disorder. It may be that self-blame is adaptive under certain conditions but not others (Schulz & Decker, 1985; Taylor et al., 1984a).

Research uniformly suggests that blaming another person for one's disorder is maladaptive (Affleck et al., 1987; Taylor et al., 1984a). For example, some patients believe that their disorder was brought about by stress caused by family members, ex-spouses, or colleagues at work. Blame of this other person or persons may be tied to unresolved hostility, which can interfere with adjustment to the disease. Forgiveness, by contrast, is tied to fewer health complaints (Lawler et al., 2005) and better psychological well-being (Worthington, Witvliet, Pietrini, & Miller, 2007).

Beliefs About the Controllability of the Illness   Researchers have also examined whether patients who believe they can control their illness are better off than those who do not see their illness as under their control. Patients develop a number of control-related beliefs. They may believe, as do many cancer patients, that they can prevent a recurrence of the disease through good health habits or even sheer force of will. They may believe that by complying with treatments and physicians' recommendations, they achieve vicarious control over their illness. They may believe that they have direct control over the illness through self-administration of a treatment regimen. These control-related beliefs may or may not be accurate. For example, if patients do maintain a treatment regimen, they may very well be exercising real control over the possibility of recurrence or exacerbation of their illness. On the other hand, the belief that one's illness can be controlled through a positive attitude may or may not be correct.

Belief in control and a sense of self-efficacy are generally adaptive. For example, cancer patients who believed that they had control over their illness were better adjusted than were patients without such beliefs (Taylor et al., 1984a; Thompson, Nanni, & Levine, 1994). A sense of control or self-efficacy can lead to improved adjustment among people with asthma (Lavoie et al., 2008), sickle-cell disease (Edwards, Telfair, Cecil, & Lenoci, 2001), chronic obstructive pulmonary disease (Kohler, Fish, & Greene, 2002), AIDS (Taylor et al., 1991), ovarian cancer (Norton et al., 2005), spinal cord

injuries (Schulz & Decker, 1985), and functional disability in old age (Wrosch, Miller, & Schulz, 2009). Children also benefit from perceived control. M. J. Griffin and E. Chen (2006), for example, found that high perceived control was associated with better asthma control. Even among patients who are physically or psychosocially badly off, adjustment is facilitated by high perceptions of control (McQuillen, Licht, & Licht, 2003).

The experience of control or self-efficacy may prolong life. A study of patients with chronic obstructive pulmonary disease found that those with high self-efficacy expectations lived longer than those without such expectations (Kaplan, Ries, Prewitt, & Eakin, 1994). Box 11.2 describes a study that further addresses these issues. Not all studies find that feelings of control are adaptive in adjusting to chronic conditions. When the level of real control is low, efforts to induce it or exert it may be unsuccessful and even backfire (Burish et al., 1984; Tennen et al., 1992; Toshima, Kaplan, & Ries, 1992).

■ COMANAGEMENT OF CHRONIC ILLNESS

Chronic illness raises specific problem-solving tasks including physical problems, vocational problems, problems with social relationships, and personal issues. Some of these problems become so severe that they can be handled only through institutionalization, but more commonly, these problems are comanaged by patients and practitioners through short-term residential or outpatient treatment programs. Chronic illness depends critically on patient comanagement of the disorder because chronically ill patients have personal knowledge of its development, symptoms, and course over time (Goldring, Taylor, Kemeny, & Anton, 2002). We next turn to these issues.

Physical Problems Associated with Chronic Illness

Chronic disability can lead to anxiety, depression, and even thoughts of suicide. Some physical problems are produced by the disease itself. They include physical pain, such as the chest pain experienced by heart patients; the discomfort associated with cancer; and the chronic pain of rheumatoid arthritis (van Lankveld, Naring, van der Staak, van't Pad Bosch, & van de Putte, 1993). Breathlessness associated with respiratory disorders, metabolic changes associated with diabetes and

BOX 11.2

Causal Attributions, Feelings of Control, and Recovery from Myocardial Infarction

Causal attributions for an illness and feelings of control over it affect adjustment and the course of recovery. A study by Daniel Bar-On (1986, 1987) with patients recovering from myocardial infarction (MI) illustrates these points graphically. The patients were asked why they thought they had had a heart attack and what health measures they planned to take as a result of the attack. Several months later, their work and social functioning were measured.

Patients who attributed the cause of their MI to modifiable factors under their personal control (such as stress or smoking) were more likely to have made active plans for their recovery (for example, changing jobs or starting exercise) and to have returned to work and resumed other activities. In contrast, patients who attributed the MI to external factors beyond their personal control (bad luck or fate, for instance) had typically not generated active plans for recovery or returned to work; they were also less likely to have resumed other activities.

Bar-On also looked at the attributions that spouses made for the heart attack. Under most circumstances, when spouses made the same attributions for the heart attack as their mates, short-term rehabilitation progressed well. However, if the patient's attributions were to external, uncontrollable factors or if the patient denied that the heart attack even occurred, long-term rehabilitation progressed better when the spouse's attribution was incongruent with the patient's attributions. The spouse's attribution to internal and controllable factors may have counteracted the patient's tendency toward denial, nudging him or her in the direction of becoming more aware of the things he or she could do to reduce the risk for a second heart attack (Bar-On & Dreman, 1987).

These results suggest that when an illness is perceived as being modifiable and under one's personal control the process of recovery from chronic disease is enhanced (cf. Affleck et al., 1987). Moreover, these kinds of perceptions may be even more important predictors of successful rehabilitation than more traditional physical indicators used by physicians in predicting rehabilitation (Bar-On, 1986, 1987).

A sense of control can be enhanced by involving decision-making processes. When patients feel they have been involved in the decisions concerning their treatment and follow-up care, they show better long-term quality of life (Andersen, Bowen, Morea, Stein, & Baker, 2009).

---

cancer, and motor difficulties produced by spinal cord injuries are also important physical problems. Cognitive impairments may occur, such as the language, memory, and learning deficits associated with stroke. In many cases, then, the physical consequences of a chronic disorder place severe restrictions on an individual's life (see Box 11.3). Any measures that can improve activity level, physical independence, and the ability to manage the tasks of daily living will have positive effects, not only on daily functioning but also on psychosocial adjustment (Zautra, Maxwell, & Reich, 1989). Training in self-management of rehabilitation activities can also improve quality of life (Korstjens et al., 2008).

Goals of Physical Rehabilitation **Physical rehabilitation** involves several goals: to learn how to use one's body as much as possible, to learn how to sense changes in the environment in order to make the appropriate physical accommodations, to learn new physical management skills, to learn a necessary treatment regimen, and to learn how to control the expenditure of energy.

Patients must develop the capacity to read bodily signs that signal the onset of a crisis, know how to respond to that crisis, and maintain whatever treatment regimen is required. Even general exercise goes a long way in reducing the symptoms of many chronic disorders (van der Ploeg et al., 2008). For heart patients, exercise is a critical component of recovery programs. Clearly, good working relationships with staff who implement these interventions is critical for their success (Burns & Evon, 2007).

Many patients who require physical rehabilitation have problems resulting from prior injuries or participation in athletic activities earlier in life, including knee problems, shoulder injuries, and the like. Most such problems worsen with age. Functional decline in the frail elderly who live alone is a particular problem (Gill, Baker, Gottschalk, Peduzzi, Allore, & Byers, 2002). Physical therapy can ameliorate these age-related aches and pains and can also help patients recover from treatments designed to alleviate them, such as surgery (Stephens, Druley, & Zautra, 2002). Group cognitive-behavioral

Chronic Fatigue Syndrome and Other Functional Disorders

In recent years, health psychologists have become increasingly interested in **functional somatic syndromes.** These syndromes are marked by the symptoms, suffering, and disability, but not by any demonstrable tissue abnormality. In short, we don't know why people have these disorders.

Functional somatic syndromes include chronic fatigue syndrome, irritable bowel syndrome, and fibromyalgia, as well as chemical sensitivity, sick building syndrome, repetitive stress injury, complications from silicone breast implants, Gulf War syndrome, and chronic whiplash.

Chronic fatigue syndrome (CFS), one of the most common, is marked by debilitating fatigue present for at least 6 months. In addition, people with CFS show slowed thinking, reduced attention, and impairments in memory (Majer et al., 2008). For many years, no biological cause for CFS could be found. Recently, however, a viral agent and resulting inflammatory activity have been implicated as potential causes (Lombardi et al., 2009; Maugh, 2009, October 9; The Economist, 2007, July 1). Chronic fatigue syndrome has also been tied to higher levels of allostatic load, suggesting a likely vulnerability to other chronic disorders (Maloney, Boneva, Nater, & Reeves, 2009).

Fibromyalgia is an arthritic syndrome involving widespread pain with tenderness in multiple sites. About 6 million individuals suffer from this disorder. The origins of fibromyalgia are currently unclear and the symptoms are varied, but the disorder is associated with sleep disturbance, disability, and high levels of psychological distress (Finan, Zautra, & Davis, 2009; Zautra et al., 2005). Stress hormones related to sympathetic functioning and the HPA axis may also be altered (Buske-Kirschbaum et al., 2003; Riva, Mork, Westgaard, Rø, & Lundberg, 2010).

Functional disorders have proven to be extremely difficult to treat inasmuch as their etiology is not well understood. Because of their insidious way of eroding quality of life, the functional syndromes are typically accompanied by a great deal of psychological distress, including depression, and the symptoms of the illness have sometimes been misdiagnosed as depression (Mittermaier et al., 2004; Skapinakis, Lewis, and Mavreas, 2004).

Who develops functional somatic disorders? Functional somatic syndromes are more common in women than men, and people who have a prior psychiatric history of emotional disorders, especially anxiety and depression (Bornschein, Hausteiner, Konrad, Förstl, & Zilker, 2006; Nater et al., 2009). People who have low SES, who are unemployed, and who are members of minority groups have a somewhat elevated likelihood of developing chronic fatigue (Taylor, Jason, & Jahn, 2003). Twin studies of chronic fatigue syndrome suggest that there may be genetic underpinnings of these disorders (Buchwald et al., 2001). A history of childhood maltreatment and abuse or childhood trauma may also be implicated (Creed et al., 2005; Heim et al., 2009).

Substantial overlap exists among the functional syndromes in terms of symptoms and consequences (Kanaan, Lepine, & Wessely, 2007). Many of the disorders are marked by abdominal distention, headache, fatigue, and disturbances in the HPA axis (Di Giorgio, Hudson, Jerjes, & Cleare, 2005; Gaab et al., 2002). Among the common factors implicated in their development are a preexisting viral or bacterial infection and a high number of stressful life events (Fink, Toft, Hansen, Ornbol, & Olesen, 2007; Theorell, Blomkvist, Lindh, & Evengard, 1999).

The similarity among the functional symptoms should not be interpreted to mean that these disorders are psychiatric in origin or that the care of these patients should be shifted exclusively to psychology and psychiatry. For example, the placebo response in the treatment of chronic fatigue syndrome is very modest (Cho, Hotopf, & Wessely, 2005). Accordingly, the similarity among the syndromes suggests that breakthroughs in understanding the etiology and treatment of these disorders may be made by pooling knowledge from all these syndromes, rather than by treating them as separate disorders (Fink et al., 2007). Although each disorder has distinctive features (Moss-Morris & Spence, 2006), the core symptoms of fatigue, pain, sick-role behavior, and negative affect are all associated with chronic, low-level inflammation, and possibly this sustained or recurrent immune response is what ties these disorders together.

What helps people cope with these debilitating disorders? Although social support is helpful to those with functional somatic syndromes, particularly solicitous behavior from significant others may aggravate the disorder by increasing sick-role behavior (Romano, Jensen, Schmaling, Hops, & Buchwald, 2009). Positive reinterpretation and a sense of self-efficacy predict good psychological adjustment, whereas avoidant coping and

BOX 11.3

Chronic Fatigue Syndrome and Other Functional Disorders (*continued*)

emotional venting are associated with greater disability and poorer psychological well-being (Findley, Kerns, Weinberg, & Rosenberg, 1998; Moss-Morris, Petrie, & Weinman, 1996).

How are these disorders treated? Generally, medical practitioners combine pharmacological interventions for such symptoms as sleep deprivation and pain with behavioral interventions, including exercise and cognitive-behavioral therapy, efforts that appear to achieve some success (Rossy et al., 1999). Coping interventions such as written emotional expression can produce health benefits as well (Broderick, Junghaenel, & Schwartz, 2005). The specific treatment recommended for func-

tional disorders varies, of course, with the particular nature of the problem (Hamilton, Karoly, & Zautra, 2005). Those whose chronic fatigue developed in the wake of an infectious disorder may require different treatments than those whose chronic fatigue is unrelated to a prior infection; the latter group may require more psychological counseling (Masuda, Munemoto, Yamanaka, Takei, & Tei, 2002).

Overall, functional somatic syndromes are common, persistent, disabling, costly, and still fairly mysterious. Simultaneous attention to the medical symptoms and the psychosocial distress generated by these disorders is essential for successful treatment.

---

interventions may get people to adhere to physical activity more than individual interventions (Rejeski et al., 2003). Robots are increasingly being used to help disabled people maximize their functioning (Broadbent, Stafford, & McDonald, 2009). Physical activity can, in turn, pave the way for more general changes in self-efficacy (Motl & Snook, 2008).

Developing a Comprehensive Rehabilitation Program Comprehensive physical rehabilitation must take into account all illness and treatment-related factors. Patients may need a pain management program for the alleviation of discomfort. They may require prosthetic devices, such as an artificial limb after amputation related to diabetes. They may need training in the use of adaptive devices; for example, a patient with multiple sclerosis or a spinal cord injury may need to learn how to use a wheelchair. Certain cancer patients may elect cosmetic surgery, such as breast reconstruction after a mastectomy or the insertion of a synthetic jaw after head and neck surgery. Disorders such as stroke, diabetes, and high blood pressure may compromise cognitive functioning, requiring active intervention (Zelinski, Crimmins, Reynolds, & Seeman, 1998). Exercise is a vital part of any physical rehabilitation program, as it can improve quality of life, reduce pain, reduce fatigue, and enhance self-efficacy (Motl & McAuley, 2009). Because stress exacerbates so many chronic disorders, stress management programs are increasingly incorporated into the physical treatment regimens as well.

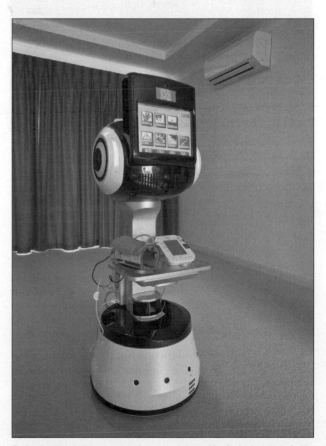

Robots, like the one seen here, are increasingly being used to help disabled people maximize their functioning.

Physical rehabilitation concentrates on enabling people to use their bodies as much as possible, to learn new physical management skills if necessary, and to pursue an integrated treatment regimen.

The Impact on Sexuality Many chronic illnesses—including heart disease, stroke, and cancer—lead to a decrease in sexual activity. In some cases, the condition itself prompts temporary restrictions on sexual activity; more commonly, however, the decline can be traced to psychological factors (such as loss of desire, fears about aggravating the chronic condition, or impotence). The ability to continue physically intimate relations can be protective of mental health and relationship satisfaction among the chronically ill, and attention to issues of physical intimacy can improve emotional functioning (Perez, Skinner, & Meyerowitz, 2002).

Adherence Physical rehabilitation must also tackle the problem of adherence to a long-term medical regimen. Cognitive and behavioral interventions may be needed to help a patient adhere to a medication regimen. For example, diabetic patients may be trained in how to recognize and treat symptoms as they change. Unfortunately, the features that characterize the treatment regimens of chronically ill patients are those typically associated with high levels of nonadherence. As will be recalled from Chapter 9, treatment regimens that must be followed over a long time, that are complex, that interfere with other desirable life activities, and that involve lifestyle change show very low levels of adherence (Turk & Meichenbaum, 1991).

Side effects of treatment also contribute to high rates of nonadherence. This problem is seen particularly with hypertensive medication (Love, Leventhal, Easterling, & Nerenz, 1989) but is also apparent with chemotherapy (Richardson et al., 1987; Taylor, Lichtman, & Wood, 1984b). However, the inclination to not follow an unpleasant treatment regimen can be offset by the recognition that it represents a potentially lifesaving measure.

An important first step in ensuring adherence to a treatment regimen is education. Some patients fail to realize that aspects of their treatment regimen are important to their functioning. Self-efficacy beliefs importantly affect adherence to treatment regimens among the chronically ill (Strecher, DeVillis, Becker, & Rosenstock, 1986). For example, high expectations for controlling one's health, coupled with knowledge of the treatment regimen, predict adherence among hypertensives (Stanton, 1987), diabetics (Grossman, Brink, & Hauser, 1987), and end-stage renal disease patients (Schneider, Friend, Whitaker, & Wadhwa, 1991).

Although patients' physical rehabilitative needs do receive some attention in the recovery process, an organized, comanaged, concerted effort is rare. Perhaps more important is the fact that the crucial educational, behavioral, and cognitive training efforts that enlist the patient's cooperative comanagement are even more rare. Comprehensive physical rehabilitation is a goal toward which we are currently striving. The health psychologist is a key figure in this emerging effort.

Vocational Issues in Chronic Illness

Many chronic illnesses create problems for patients' vocational activities and work status. Some patients may need to restrict or change their work activities. For example, a salesman who previously conducted his work from his car but is now newly diagnosed as an epileptic may need to switch to a job in which he can use the

BOX 11.4

Epilepsy and the Need for a Job Redesign

In infancy, Colin S. developed spinal meningitis, and although he survived, the physician expressed some concern that permanent brain damage might have occurred. Colin was a normal student in school until approximately age 11, when he began to have spells of blanking out. At first, his parents interpreted these as a form of acting out, the beginnings of adolescence. However, as it became clear that Colin had no recollection of these periods and became angry when questioned about them, they took him to a physician for evaluation. After a lengthy workup, the doctor concluded that Colin was suffering from epilepsy.

Shortly thereafter, Colin's blanking out (known as petit mal seizures) became more severe and frequent; soon after that, he began to have grand mal seizures, involving severe and frightening convulsions. The doctors tried several medications before finding one that controlled the seizures. Indeed, so successful was the medication that Colin eventually was able to obtain a driver's license, having gone 5 years without a seizure. After he completed high school and college, Colin chose social work as his career and became a caseworker. His livelihood depended on his ability to drive because his schedule involved visiting many clients for in-home evaluations. Moreover, Colin was married, and he and his wife were supporting two young children.

In his early 30s, Colin began to experience seizures again. At first, he and his wife tried to pretend that nothing was wrong, but they quickly recognized that the epilepsy was no longer under control. Colin's epilepsy represented a major threat to the family's income because Colin could no longer do his job as a caseworker. Moreover, his ability to find reemployment was compromised by the revocation of his driver's license. With considerable anxiety, Colin went to see his employer, the director of the social services unit.

After consultation, Colin's supervisor determined that he had been a valuable worker and they did not want to lose him. They therefore redesigned his position so that he could have a desk job that did not require the use of a car. By having his responsibilities shifted away from the monitoring to the evaluation of cases, and by being given an office instead of a set of addresses to visit, Colin was able to use in very similar ways the skills he had worked so hard to develop. In this case, then, Colin's employer responded sympathetically and effectively to the compromises that needed to be made in Colin's job responsibilities. Unfortunately, not all people with epilepsy or other chronic diseases are as fortunate as Colin (Mostofsky, 1998).

---

telephone instead. Patients with spinal cord injuries who previously held positions that required physical activity will need to acquire skills that will let them work from a seated position. This kind of creative job change is illustrated in Box 11.4.

Discrimination Against the Chronically Ill

Many chronically ill patients, such as heart patients, cancer patients, and AIDS patients, face job discrimination (Heckman, 2003). One survey, reported in *Time,* indicated that employees with cancer are fired or laid off five times as often as other workers. When these patients return to their jobs, they may be moved into less demanding positions, and they may be promoted less quickly because the organization believes that they have a poor prognosis and are not worth the investment of the time and resources required to train them for more advanced work (*Time,* 1996, October 7).

Because of these potential problems, any job difficulties that the patient may encounter should be assessed early in the recovery process. Job counseling, retraining programs, and advice on how to avoid or combat discrimination can then be initiated promptly. Box 11.5 focuses on some health care professionals who deal with such problems.

The Financial Impact of Chronic Illness Chronic illness can have an enormous impact on the patient and the family. Many people are not covered by insurance sufficient to meet their needs. Patients who must cut back on their work or stop working altogether may lose their insurance coverage, adding a huge financial burden. Thus, many chronically ill people are hit by a double whammy: The capacity to earn income may be reduced, and simultaneously, the benefits that would have helped shoulder the costs of care may be cut back. The United States is the only developed country in which this problem still exists.

Who Works with the Chronically Ill?

A variety of professionals are involved in the rehabilitation of the chronically ill. Many of these professionals are physicians, nurses, and psychologists. However, other people with technical training in particular aspects of rehabilitation also work with the chronically ill.

PHYSICAL THERAPISTS

Physical therapists typically receive their training at the college undergraduate level or in a master's program, which leads to required licensure. About 173,000 people work as licensed physical therapists in hospitals, nursing homes, rehabilitation centers, and schools for disabled children (U.S. Department of Labor, 2009). Physical therapists help people with muscle, nerve, joint, or bone diseases or injuries to overcome their disabilities. They work primarily with accident victims, disabled children, and older people. Physical therapists are responsible for the administration and interpretation of tests of muscle strength, motor development, functional capacity, and respiratory and circulatory efficiency. On the basis of these tests, they then develop individualized treatment programs, the goals of which are to increase strength, endurance, coordination, and range of motion. Physical therapists are also responsible for the ongoing evaluation and modification of these programs in light of treatment goals. In addition, they help patients learn to use adaptive devices and become accustomed to new ways of performing old tasks. They may use heat, cold, light, water, electricity, or massage to relieve pain and improve muscle function.

OCCUPATIONAL THERAPISTS

Occupational therapists work with individuals who are emotionally and physically disabled to determine skills, abilities, and limitations. They evaluate the existing capacities of patients, help them set goals, and plan a therapy program with other members of a rehabilitation team to try to build on and expand these skills. They help patients regain physical, mental, or emotional stability; relearn daily routines, such as eating, dressing, writing, or using a telephone; and prepare for employment. They plan and direct educational, vocational, and recreational activities to help patients become more self-sufficient.

Patients who are seen by occupational therapists range from children involved in crafts programs to adults who must learn new skills, such as typing or using power tools. In addition, occupational therapists teach creative tasks, such as painting, weaving, and other craft activities, that help relax patients, provide a creative outlet, and offer some variety to those who are institutionalized. Occupational therapists usually obtain their training through one of the occupational therapy training programs located in universities and colleges around the country, and, like physical therapists, they must be formally licensed.

DIETITIANS

Many of the country's 57,000 dietitians are involved in management of the chronically ill (U.S. Department of Labor, 2009). Although many **dietitians** are administrators who apply the principles of nutrition and food management to meal planning for hospitals, universities, schools, and other institutions, others work directly with the chronically ill to help plan and manage special diets. These clinical dietitians assess the dietetic needs of patients, supervise the service of meals, instruct patients in the requirements and importance of their diets, and suggest ways of maintaining adherence to diets after discharge. Many dietitians work with diabetics and with patients who have disorders related to obesity, because both groups need to control their caloric intake and types of foods. Dietitians are formally licensed and must complete a 4-year degree program and clinically supervised training to be registered with the American Dietetic Association.

SOCIAL WORKERS

Social workers help people and their families with social problems that can develop during illness and recovery by providing therapy, making referrals to other services, and engaging in general social planning. These social workers work in hospitals, clinics, community mental health centers, rehabilitation centers, and nursing homes.

A medical social worker might help a patient understand his or her illness more fully and deal with emotional responses to illness, such as depression or anxiety, through therapy. A social worker can also help a desperate patient and family find the resources they need to solve their problems. For example, if the patient has been a homemaker—responsible for cooking, cleaning, and coordinating family activities—the social worker might help the family find temporary help to fulfill these tasks. If the patient will need vocational retraining after a chronic illness, the social worker can help find or

BOX 11.5

Who Works with the Chronically Ill? (*continued*)

even develop the facilities to make this possible. If the patient needs to transfer from the hospital into a special facility, such as a nursing home or rehabilitation center, the social worker is often the one who will make these arrangements.

In 2006, approximately 595,000 individuals were employed as social workers; one-third worked for the local or state government (U.S. Department of Labor, 2009). The minimum qualification for social work is a bachelor's degree, but for many positions a master's degree (MSW) is required. About 458 colleges nationwide offer accredited undergraduate programs in social work, and about 181 colleges and universities offer graduate programs (U.S. Department of Labor, 2009).

Social Interaction Problems in Chronic Illness

The development of a chronic illness can create problems of social interaction for the patient. After diagnosis, patients may have trouble reestablishing normal social relations. They may complain about others' pity or rejection but behave in ways that inadvertently elicit these behaviors. They may withdraw from other people altogether or thrust themselves into social activities before they are ready.

Negative Responses from Others Acquaintances, friends, and relatives may have problems of their own adjusting to the patient's altered condition. Many people hold pejorative stereotypes about certain groups of chronically ill patients, including those with cancer or AIDS (Fife & Wright, 2000).

People with disabilities may elicit ambivalence. Friends and acquaintances may give verbal signs of warmth and affection while nonverbally conveying revulsion or rejection through their gestures, contacts, and postures. Distant relationships with friends and acquaintances appear to be more adversely affected in these ways than intimate relations (Dakof & Taylor, 1990). The newly disabled patient has difficulty interpreting and reacting to these behaviors.

Chronically ill patients may need to think through whether they want to disclose the fact of their illness to those outside their immediate family. If they decide to do so, they may need to consider the best approach because certain illnesses—particularly cancer, AIDS, and epilepsy—may elicit negative responses from others.

Working through problems with family members often helps patients lay the groundwork for reestablishing other social contacts. By developing effective ways of dealing with family members and friends, the patient simultaneously builds skills for dealing with other people in a variety of social situations.

The Impact on the Family Individuals do not develop chronic diseases; families do. The family is a social system, and disruption in the life of one family member invariably affects the lives of others (P. D. Williams et al., 2002). One of the chief changes brought about by chronic illness is an increased dependency of the chronically ill individual on other family members. If the patient is married, the illness inevitably places increased responsibilities on the spouse.

Intimate others may be distressed by the loved one's condition (Stein, Gordon, Hibbard, & Sliwinski, 1992) or may be worn down by the constant pain, disability, and dependency of the partner (Manne & Zautra, 1990). Moreover, they may be ineffective in providing support because their own support needs are unmet (Horwitz, Reinhard, & Howell-White, 1996).

New responsibilities may fall on children and other family members living at home. Consequently, the patient's family may feel that their lives have gone out of control as well (Compas, Worsham, Ey, & Howell, 1996). Role strains can emerge as family members find themselves assuming new tasks and simultaneously realize that their time to pursue recreational and other leisure-time activities has declined (Pavalko & Woodbury, 2000; Quittner et al., 1998; Williamson, Shaffer, & Schulz, 1998).

If family members' resources are already stretched to the limit, accommodating new tasks is very difficult. The wife of one stroke patient suggested some of the burdens such patients can create for their families:

> In the first few weeks, Clay not only needed meals brought to him, but countless items he wanted to use, to look at, and so forth. He was not aware of how much Jim [the patient's son] and I developed our leg muscles in fetching and carrying. When he was on the third floor I would say "I am going downstairs. Is there anything you want?" No, he couldn't think of a thing. When I returned he remembered something, but only one thing at a time. There are advantages to a home with stairs, but not with a stroke victim in the family. (Dahlberg, 1977, p. 124)

Children and adolescents who are suddenly forced into taking on more responsibilities than would normally be expected for their age group may react by rebelling or acting out. Problem behaviors may include regression (such as bed-wetting), difficulties at school, truancy, sexual activity, drug use, and antagonism toward other family members.

Despite the clear sources of strain that develop when a family member has a chronic illness, there is no evidence that such strains are catastrophic, and indeed, friends and family can provide each other with support (Rini et al., 2008). The divorce rate among families with a chronic illness is no higher, nor do such families show less cohesion. Moreover, some families actually become closer as a consequence of chronic illness.

The Caregiving Role Nonetheless, strains may fall on family members, and in no case is this strain more evident than in the case of the primary caregiver.

Care for the chronically ill is notoriously irregular. Few facilities provide the custodial care that is often required for chronically ill patients. Consequently, the burden often falls on a family member. Both men and women may be involved in caregiving, although on the whole, the role more commonly falls to women. The typical caregiver is a woman in her 60s caring for an elderly spouse, but caregivers also provide help for their own parents and for disabled children.

Caregiving may be intermittent or supplementary in the case of patients who can contribute actively to their own disease management; many cancer patients and heart patients fall into this category. In other cases, it may be intense for a period until recovery progresses; some stroke patients fall into this category. In still other cases, caregiving needs increase as the disease progresses to the point where the caregiver has responsibility for virtually every activity the patient must undertake, including brushing their teeth, feeding them, and cleaning them; progressive cancers, Alzheimer's disease, Parkinson's disease, and advanced multiple sclerosis are among the illnesses that may create this need for intense caregiving. Caregiving, especially by a loved one, can substantially improve the quality of life of a chronically ill patient. When a caregiver exudes confidence, the patient's recovery may be fostered (Molloy et al., 2008a).

However, family members who provide caregiving are at risk for distress, depression, and declining health (Mausbach, Patterson, Rabinowitz, Grant, & Schulz, 2007). To begin with, caregivers are often elderly, and, consequently, their own health may be threatened when caregiving begins. The process of caregiving may further erode health (Gallagher, Phillips, Drayson, & Carroll, 2009; von Kaenel, Dimsdale, Patterson, & Grant, 2003). Many studies attest to the risks that caregiving poses to immune functioning (Li et al., 2007; Redwine, Mills, Sada, Dimsdale, Patterson, & Grant, 2004), endocrine functioning (Mausbach et al., 2005), risk for depression (Mintzer et al., 1992), poor quality of sleep (Brummett et al., 2006), long-term changes in stress responses (Grant et al., 2002), cardiovascular diseases (Mausbach et al., 2007), an increased risk of infectious disease, and even death (Schulz & Beach, 1999). Caregivers who are experiencing other stressors in their lives or whose caregiving burden is especially great are at particular risk for mental and physical health declines (Brummett et al., 2005; Kim, Knight, & Longmire, 2007).

Caregiving can also strain the relationship between patient and caregiver (Martire, Stephens, Druley, & Wojno, 2002). Patients are not always appreciative of the help they receive and resent the fact that they need help. Their expression of resentment can contribute to the depression and distress so often seen in caregivers (Newsom & Schulz, 1998). The anxiety and depression that can result from caregiving may, in turn, feed back into the health of the caregiver (Shewchuk, Richards, & Elliott, 1998). Caregivers fare better when they have a high sense of personal mastery and active coping skills (Aschbacher et al., 2005).

Caregivers themselves may be in need of interventions (Ussher, Perz, Hawkings, & Brack, 2009), especially those involving social support, because the demands of caregiving may tie them to the home and give them little free time. Recently, the possibility that the Internet can be used to provide support to caregivers has been explored. One study (Czaja & Rubert, 2002) found that caregivers who were able to communicate online with other family members, a therapist, and an online discussion group found the services to be extremely valuable, suggesting that this intervention has promise. Interventions to help caregivers accept and find meaning in the caregiving experience can also reduce psychological distress (Kim, Schulz, & Carver, 2007).

Gender and the Impact of Chronic Illness

Chronically ill women appear to experience more deficits in social support than do chronically ill men. One study found that disabled women receive less social support because they are less likely to be married or get married than disabled men (Kutner, 1987; see also Bramwell, 1986). In another study, women who had sustained heart attacks were less likely to get married, and, if they were married, their prognosis was worse after the myocardial infarction than was true for men (Stern, Pascale, & Ackerman, 1977). Because ill and/or elderly women may experience reduced quality of life for other reasons as well, such as low income and high levels of disability (Haug & Folmar, 1986), problems in social support may exacerbate these already existing differences.

Even when chronically ill women are married, they are more likely to be institutionalized for their illnesses than are husbands. Married men spend fewer days in nursing homes than do married women (Freedman, 1993). It may be that husbands feel less capable providing care than wives, or, because husbands are older than wives, they may be more disabled earlier than are wives of chronically ill husbands.

Following the diagnosis of a chronic illness, women may nevertheless continue to carry a disproportionate burden of household responsibilities and activities, a burden that may pose a threat for progressive illness (Rose, Chassin, Presson, & Sherman, 1996). Gender differences in the availability and effects of social support among the chronically ill clearly merit concern.

Positive Changes in Response to Chronic Illness

At the beginning of this chapter, we considered quality of life, and throughout the chapter, we have focused on many of the adverse changes that chronic illness creates and what can be done to ameliorate them. This focus tends to obscure an important point, however—namely, that human beings are fundamentally resilient (Taylor, 1983; Zautra, 2009; Zautra, Hall, & Murray, 2008). As people strive to overcome the challenges posed by illness, they find that chronic illness can confer positive as well as negative outcomes (Taylor, 1983, 1989). Many people experience positive reactions (Ryff & Singer, 1996), such as joy (Levy, Lee, Bagley, & Lippman, 1988), optimism (Cordova, Cunningham, Carlson, & Andrykowski, 2001; Scheier, Weintraub, & Carver, 1986), and benefit finding (Low, Bower, Kwan, & Seldon, 2008). These reactions may occur because chronically ill people perceive that they have narrowly escaped death or because they have reordered their priorities in a more satisfying way. They may also find meaning in the daily activities of life in response to the illness (McFarland & Alvaro, 2000), or in their revised worldviews (Thombre, Sherman, & Simonton, 2010).

In one study (Collins, Taylor, & Skokan, 1990), more than 90% of cancer patients reported at least some beneficial changes in their lives as a result of the cancer, including an increased ability to appreciate each day and the inspiration to do things now rather than postponing them. These patients said that they were putting more effort into their relationships and believed they had acquired more awareness of others' feelings and more empathy and compassion for others. They reported feeling stronger and more self-assured as well. Benefit finding has now been identified for several different disorders and has been tied not only to psychological adjustment but to better social functioning and health as well (Aspinwall & MacNamara, 2005; Danoff-Burg & Revenson, 2005; Low, Stanton, & Danoff-Burg, 2006).

Studies comparing the quality of life experienced by cancer patients with that of a normal sample free of chronic disease find that the quality of life experienced by the cancer sample is higher than that of the non-ill sample (Danoff, Kramer, Irwin, & Gottlieb, 1983; Lacey et al., 2008; Tempelaar et al., 1989).

The ability to reappraise one's situation positively has been tied to a more positive mood (Pakenham, 2005) and to posttraumatic growth in women with breast cancer (Manne et al., 2004; Sears, Stanton, & Danoff-Burg, 2003), especially among people with more advanced disease. Finding meaning in a chronic illness and coping through religion can also improve adjustment to chronic illness (Schanowitz & Nicassio, 2006; Simonelli, Fowler, Maxwell, & Andersen, 2008).

How do people with chronic disease so often manage to achieve such a high quality of life? Many people perceive control over what happens to them, hold positive expectations about the future, and have a positive view of themselves. These kinds of beliefs are adaptive for mental and physical health much of the time (Taylor, 1983) but they become especially important when a person faces a chronic illness. In a recent investigation, V. S. Helgeson (2003) examined these beliefs in men and women treated for coronary artery disease with an angioplasty and then followed them over 4 years. These beliefs not only predicted positive adjustment to disease but also were associated with a reduced likelihood of sustaining a repeat cardiac event.

FIGURE 11.2 | **Positive Life Changes Experienced by MI Patients and Cancer Patients in Response to Their Illness**   Most of the benefits reported by MI patients involve lifestyle changes, perhaps reflecting the fact that the course of heart disease is amenable to changes in personal health habits. Cancer patients, in contrast, report more changes in their social relationships and meaning attached to life, perhaps because cancer may not be as directly influenced by health habits as heart disease but may be amenable to finding greater purpose or meaning in other life activities.   (*Source:* Petrie, Buick, Weinman, & Booth, 1999)

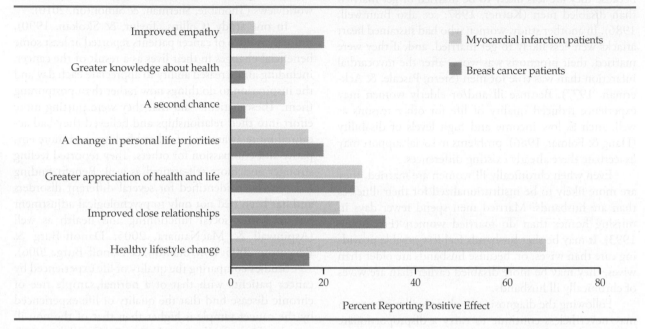

Regardless of why they occur, these positive reactions usually serve a beneficial function in recovery from illness, and health psychologists should be attentive to this fact (O'Carroll, Ayling, O'Reilly, & North, 2003) (see Figure 11.2).

When the Chronically Ill Patient Is a Child

Chronic illness can be especially problematic when the chronically ill patient is a child. First, children may not fully understand the nature of their diagnosis and treatment and thus experience confusion as they try to cope with illness and treatment (Strube, Smith, Rothbaum, & Sotelo, 1991). Second, because chronically ill children often cannot follow their treatment regimen by themselves, the family must participate in the illness and treatment process even more than is the case with a chronically ill adult (Gross, Eudy, & Drabman, 1982). Accordingly, there can be a close relationship between family adjustment and children's symptoms (Kaugars, Klinnert, Robinson, & Ho, 2008). Such interdependence can also lead to tension between parent and child (Manne, Jacobsen, Gorfinkle, Gerstein, & Redd, 1993).

Sometimes, children must be exposed to isolating and terrifying procedures to treat their condition (Kellerman, Rigler, & Siegel, 1979). All these factors can create problems of adjustment for both children and parents (Silver, Bauman, & Ireys, 1995).

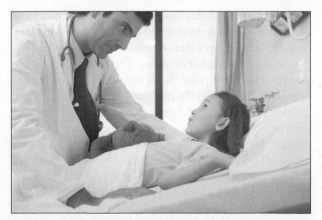

Children's needs to be informed about their illness and to exert control over illness-related activities and over their lives have prompted interventions to involve children in their own care.

Although many children adjust to these radical changes in their lives, some do not. Children suffering from chronic illness exhibit a variety of behavioral problems, including rebellion and withdrawal (Alati et al., 2005). They may suffer low self-esteem, either because they believe that the chronic illness is a punishment for bad behavior or because they feel cheated because their peers are healthy. Nonadherence to treatment, underachievement in school, and regressive behavior, such as bed-wetting or temper tantrums, are not uncommon. These problems can be aggravated if families do not have adequate styles of communicating with each other and of resolving conflict (Manne et al., 1993). In addition, chronically ill children may develop maladaptive coping styles involving repression, which may interfere with their understanding of and ability to comanage their disorders (Phipps & Steele, 2002). Like other chronic diseases, childhood chronic diseases can be exacerbated by stress. For example, among children with asthma, number of hospitalizations was associated with family conflict and strain and with the strain experienced by caregivers as well (Chen, Bloomberg, Fisher, & Strunk, 2003).

Improving Coping   Several factors can improve a chronically ill child's ability to cope. Parents with realistic attitudes toward the disorder and its treatment can soothe the child emotionally and provide an informed basis for care. If the parents are free of depression, have a sense of mastery over the child's illness, and can avoid expressing distress, especially during treatments (DuHamel et al., 2004), this may also aid adjustment (Timko, Stovel, Moos, & Miller, 1992). If children are encouraged to engage in self-care as much as possible, and only realistic restrictions are placed on their lives, adjustment will be better. Encouraging regular school attendance and reasonable physical activities is particularly beneficial. If the parents can learn to remain calm in crisis situations, maintain emotional control, and become familiar with the child's illness, these factors can contribute positively to the child's functioning.

When families are unable to provide help for their chronically ill child and develop ineffective communication patterns, interventions may be needed. Providing family therapy and training the family in the treatment regimen can improve family functioning. Alternatively, interventions may need to be directed separately to parents and to children. Children's and parents' views of illness are not necessarily the same (Strube et al., 1991), so interventions directed to either parents or children to the exclusion of the other may be limited in their effec-

tiveness. Thus, different but complementary interventions may be required for parents and children.

■ PSYCHOLOGICAL INTERVENTIONS AND CHRONIC ILLNESS

As we have seen, the majority of chronically ill patients appear to achieve a relatively high quality of life after diagnosis and treatment for their illness. However, as we have also seen, there are reliable adverse effects of chronic disease. Consequently, health psychologists have increasingly focused on ways to ameliorate these problems.

The fact that levels of anxiety and depression are intermittently high among chronically ill patients suggests that evaluation for these problems should be a standard part of chronic care. Patients who have a history of depression or other mental illness prior to the onset of their chronic illness are at particular risk and so should be evaluated early for potential interventions (Goldberg, 1981; Morris & Raphael, 1987). Various interventions have been developed to deal with these and other problems associated with chronic illness.

Pharmacological Interventions

Pharmacological treatment may be appropriate for patients suffering from depression associated with chronic illness. Antidepressants are fairly commonly prescribed under such circumstances, especially if the prognosis is poor.

Individual Therapy

Individual therapy is a common intervention for patients who have psychosocial complications due to chronic illness. But there are important differences between psychotherapy with medical patients and psychotherapy with patients who have primarily psychological complaints.

First, therapy with medical patients is more likely to be episodic than continuous. Chronic illness raises crises and issues intermittently that may require help. For example, problems with an adolescent daughter after her mother has been treated for breast cancer may not occur immediately but may develop over the subsequent months (Lichtman et al., 1984). Recurrence or worsening of a condition may present a crisis that needs to be addressed with a therapist, as for a cancer patient who has developed a new malignancy.

Second, collaboration with the patient's physician and family members is critical. The physician can inform the psychologist or other counselor of a patient's current physical status.

Third, therapy with medical patients more frequently requires respect for patients' defenses than does traditional psychotherapy. In traditional psychotherapy, one of the therapist's goals may be to challenge a patient's defenses that may interfere with an adequate understanding of his or her problems. However, in the case of chronically ill patients, the same defenses may serve a benign function in protecting them from the full realization of the ramifications of their disease.

Fourth and finally, the therapist working with a medical patient must have a comprehensive understanding of the patient's illness and its modes of treatment. Because many of the issues are centered around particular aspects of illness and treatment, the therapist who is uninformed about the illness will not be able to provide adequate help. Moreover, illness and treatments themselves produce psychological problems (for example, depression due to chemotherapy), and a therapist who is ignorant of this fact may make incorrect interpretations.

Psychotherapeutic Interventions

A number of psychotherapeutic interventions, often of short duration, have been shown to ameliorate distress in chronically ill patients. For example, in a culturally sensitive cognitive behavioral stress management intervention designed for Latino men under treatment for prostate cancer, the men experienced greater physical well-being, emotional well-being, and sexual functioning after the 10-week intervention compared to those in the control condition who went through a half-day stress management seminar (Penedo et al., 2007). The results are significant not only for showing the efficacy of the ten-week intervention, but also for illustrating the importance of culturally-sensitive interventions for maximum impact.

Much individual therapy is guided by CBT, often targeting specific problems, such as fatigue, mood-related disorders, functional impairments, or stress (Van Kessel et al., 2008). For example, an eight-week cognitive behavioral therapy intervention directed to reducing fatigue was effective with patients under treatment for multiple sclerosis. Relaxation therapy was also effective, although CBT was somewhat more so.

Even briefer therapies, such as those conducted over the telephone, have been shown to benefit patients,

enhancing a sense of personal control (Sandgren & McCaul, 2003). Although many interventions focus on coping skills, others use more novel techniques to improve a patient's emotional and behavioral responses to chronic illness. These include music, art, and dance therapies (see, for example, Pacchetti et al., 2000).

Patient Education

Patient education programs that include coping skills training improve functioning for chronic diseases, including end-stage renal disease, stroke, cardiovascular disease, and cancer. Such programs can increase knowledge about the disease, reduce anxiety, increase patients' feelings of purpose and meaning in life (Brantley, Mosley, Bruce, McKnight, & Jones, 1990; Johnson, 1982), reduce pain and depression (Lorig, Chastain, Ung, Shoor, & Holman, 1989), improve coping (Lacroix, Martin, Avendano, & Goldstein, 1991), promote adherence to treatment (Greenfield, Kaplan, Ware, Yano, & Frank, 1988), and increase confidence in the ability to manage pain and other side effects (Parker et al., 1988), relative to wait-list patients who have not yet participated in the program or to patients who do not participate (Helgeson, Cohen, Shulz, & Yasko, 2001).

The Internet poses exciting possibilities for providing interventions in a cost-effective manner. Information about illnesses can be presented in a clear and simple way, and even instruction in coping with common illness-related problems can be posted on websites for use by patients and their families (Budman, 2000). In one study, breast cancer patients who used the Internet for medical information experienced greater social support and less loneliness than those who did not use the Internet for information. Moreover, the time involved was less than an hour a week, suggesting that these psychological benefits may result from only a minimal time commitment (Fogel, Albert, Schnabel, Ditkoff, & Neugut, 2002). In addition to providing emotional support and information, the Internet can be used to implement specific interventions. For example, an Internet-based eight-week intervention directed to Type II diabetes patients was successful in increasing physical activity (McKay, Seeley, King, Glasgow, & Eakin, 2001).

In Chapter 7, we discussed the benefits of expressive writing for coping with stress. These interventions have been especially beneficial to chronically ill patients. A study of metastatic renal cell carcinoma patients, for example, found that those who wrote about their cancer (versus those who wrote about a neutral topic) had less sleep disturbance and better sleep quality and duration and fewer problems with activities of daily life (de Moor et al., 2002).

Relaxation, Stress Management, and Exercise

Relaxation training is a widely used intervention with the chronically ill. Along with other stress management techniques, it can reduce the likelihood that asthmatics will have an asthma attack (Lehrer, Feldman, Giardino, Song, & Schmaling, 2002), it can decrease anxiety and nausea from chemotherapy, decrease pain for cancer patients (Carey & Burish, 1988), and increase energy and vigor in multiple sclerosis patients (Sutherland, Andersen, & Morris, 2005). Combinations of relaxation training with stress management and blood pressure monitoring have proven useful in the treatment of essential hypertension (Agras, Taylor, Kraemer, Southam, & Schneider, 1987) and asthma (Smyth, Soefer, Hurewitz, & Stone, 1999).

In recent years, mindfulness-based stress reduction (MBSR) has been used to improve adjustment to medical illness (Brown & Ryan, 2003). Mindfulness meditation teaches people to strive for a state of mind in which one is highly aware and focused on the present moment, accepting and acknowledging it without becoming distracted or distressed by stress. Thus, the goal of MBSR is to help people approach stressful situations mindfully rather than reacting to them automatically (Bishop, 2002). The long-term efficacy of this approach is not yet known, but preliminary studies suggest that MBSR may be effective in reducing stress, anxiety, and distress (Bishop, 2002; Roth & Robbins, 2004). Acceptance and commitment therapy (ACT) has also been used with the chronically ill and helps patients to accept their illness experiences without avoidance or fruitless striving (Lundgren, Dahl, & Hayes, 2008).

Exercise interventions have been most commonly undertaken with MI patients. It is unclear whether exercise has a direct impact on mood in patients. However, physical fitness is reliably improved, and exercise can improve quality of life (Motl & McAuley, 2009).

Social Support Interventions

As we noted in Chapter 7, social support is an important resource for people suffering from chronic disease. Chronically ill patients who report good social relationships are more likely to be well adjusted to their illness.

The importance of social support to adjustment has been found for cancer patients (Neuling & Winefield, 1988), arthritis patients (Goodenow, Reisine, & Grady, 1990), patients suffering from end-stage renal disease (Siegel, Mesagno, Chen, & Christ, 1987), and patients with spinal cord injuries (Schulz & Decker, 1985), among others. Social support can also influence health outcomes favorably, promoting recovery or longevity (Christensen, Wiebe, Smith, & Turner, 1994; Grodner et al., 1996; Kaplan & Toshima, 1990; Wilcox, Kasl, & Berkman, 1994; see Chapter 7).

However, as noted, social support resources can be threatened by a chronic illness. Patients need to recognize the potential sources of support in their environment and be taught how to draw on these resources (Messeri, Silverstein, & Litwak, 1993). For example, patients might be urged to join community groups, interest groups, informal social groups, and self-help groups.

Family Support

Family support is especially important: It enhances the patient's physical and emotional functioning, and it promotes adherence to treatment (Martire, Lustig, Schulz, Miller, & Helgeson, 2004). Family members can remind the patient about activities that need to be undertaken and even participate in them, so that adherence is more likely. For example, the family may undertake a daily jog through the neighborhood just before breakfast or dinner.

Sometimes family members also need guidance in the well-intentioned actions they should nonetheless avoid because such actions actually make things worse (Dakof & Taylor, 1990; Martin, Davis, Baron, Suls, & Blanchard, 1994). Some family members think they should encourage a chronically ill patient to be relentlessly cheerful, which can have the unintended adverse effect of making the patient feel unable to share distress or concerns with others. At different times during the course of an illness, patients may be best served by different kinds of support. Tangible aid, such as being driven to and from medical appointments, may be important at some points in time. At other times, however, emotional support may be more important (Dakof & Taylor, 1990; Martin et al., 1994).

To separate supportive from potentially unsupportive behaviors, friends and relatives may themselves require interventions. In one study of wives of men who had heart attacks, the majority reported feeling poorly informed about myocardial infarction, having few opportunities to ask experts questions, and consequently experiencing considerable stress (Thompson & Cordle, 1988). A short intervention designed to acquaint family or friends with a disease could ameliorate this lack of information.

Support Groups

Social **support groups** represent a resource for the chronically ill. Such groups are available for many patients with chronic illnesses, including stroke patients, patients recovering from myocardial infarction, and cancer patients. Some of these groups are initiated by a therapist, and in some cases, they are patient-led.

Support groups discuss issues of mutual concern that arise as a consequence of illness. They often provide specific information about how others have dealt with the problems and give people an opportunity to share their emotional responses with others facing the same problems (Gottlieb, 1988). Social support groups can satisfy unmet needs for social support from family and caregivers, or they may act as an additional source of support provided by those going through the same event. Although social support groups traditionally meet on a face-to-face basis to exchange personal accounts and information, the Internet now provides manifold opportunities for giving and receiving social support and information (Box 11.6).

Social support groups appear to help several patient groups, including rheumatoid arthritis patients (Bradley et al., 1987), men with prostate cancer (Lepore, Helgeson, Eton, & Schulz, 2003), and MI patients (Dracup, 1985), when participants' adjustment is compared to nonparticipants' or to that of people who have not yet participated. Self-help groups may help victims especially cope with the stigma associated with certain disorders, such as cancer or epilepsy (Droge, Arntson, & Norton, 1986), and such groups may help patients develop the motivation and techniques to adhere to complicated treatment regimens (Storer, Frate, Johnson, & Greenberg, 1987).

Although widely heralded as a low-cost, convenient treatment option for people to deal with a wide variety of problems, self-help groups currently reach only a small proportion of chronically ill patients (Taylor, Falke, Shoptaw, & Lichtman, 1986). Moreover, they appear to appeal disproportionately to well-educated, middle-class White women. Not only is this the segment of the population that is already served by traditional treatment services, but these participants in self-help groups may actually be the same individuals who use helping services of all kinds (Taylor et al., 1986). The potential for self-help groups to be a general resource for the chronically ill, then, has yet to be fully realized.

Despite advances in care for the chronically ill and an expanded understanding of the psychosocial issues

Social support groups can satisfy unmet needs for social support from family and friends and can enable people to share their personal experiences with others like themselves.

Help on the Internet

Janet and Peter Birnheimer were thrilled at the arrival of their newborn but learned almost immediately that he had cystic fibrosis (CF). Shocked at this discovery—they had no idea that they both were carrying the recessive gene for CF—they tried to learn as much as they could about the disease. Their hometown physician was able to provide them with some information, but they realized from newspaper articles that there was breaking news as well. Moreover, they wanted help dealing with the coughing, wheezing, and other symptoms so they could provide their youngster with the best possible care.

The couple turned to the Internet, where they found a website for parents of children with cystic fibrosis. Online, they learned much more about the disease, found out where they could get articles providing additional information, chatted with other parents about the best ways to manage the symptoms, and shared the complex and painful feelings they had to manage every day (Baig, 1997, February 17).

As this account implies, the Internet is increasingly a source of information and social support to the chronically ill. Websites provide instant access to other people going through the same events. CF is not a common disorder, and so the Birnheimers found that the website was one of their best sources for new breakthroughs in understanding the causes and treatments of the disease as well as the best sources for advice from other parents on the psychosocial issues that arose.

Websites are only as good as the information they contain, of course, and there is always the risk of misinformation. However, some of the better known websites are scrupulously careful about the information they post. Among such services currently available is WebMD, devoted to providing consumer and health information on the Internet. Websites have created opportunities for bringing together people who were once isolated, so that they can solve their problems through shared knowledge.

that the chronically ill face, medical and psychosocial care for the chronically ill is still irregular, as the burden on caregivers clearly attests. Consequently, managed care may need to assume responsibility for broader based behavioral and psychological approaches to improving health among the chronically ill. Physicians and other health practitioners need better training in behav-ioral and psychosocial approaches to chronic disorders. Techniques for teaching self-management of chronic illness need to be refined, and educational interventions for communicating them to patients need to be undertaken; monitoring the success of programs like these will be important as well (Center for the Advancement of Health, 1999). ●

SUMMARY

1. At any given time, 50% of the population has a chronic condition that requires medical management. Quality-of-life measures pinpoint problems associated with diseases and treatments and help in policy decision making regarding the effectiveness and cost-effectiveness of interventions.

2. Chronically ill patients often experience denial, intermittent anxiety, and long-term depression. But too often these reactions, especially anxiety and depression, are underdiagnosed, confused with symptoms of disease or treatment, or presumed to be normal and so not appropriate for intervention.

3. Anxiety is reliably tied to illness events, such as awaiting test results or obtaining regular checkups. Depression increases with the severity of disease, pain, and disability.

4. Active coping and flexible coping efforts are more effective than avoidance, passive coping, or use of one predominant coping strategy.

5. Patients develop concepts of their illness, its cause, and its controllability that relate to their coping.

Perceived personal control over illness and/or treatment is associated with good adjustment.

6. Rehabilitation centers around physical problems, especially recovery of functioning and adherence to treatment; vocational retraining, job discrimination, financial loss, and loss of insurance; gaps and problems in social support; and personal losses, such as the threat that disease poses for long-term goals.

7. Most patients experience some benefits as well as negative effects from chronic illness. These positive outcomes may occur because patients compensate for losses in some areas of their lives with value placed on other aspects of life.

8. Interventions with the chronically ill include pharmacological interventions; CBT; brief psychotherapeutic interventions; relaxation, stress management, and exercise; social support interventions; family support; and support groups. Support groups appear to be an underused but potentially helpful resource for the chronically ill.

KEY TERMS

body image
denial
depression
dietitians
functional somatic syndromes

occupational therapists
patient education
physical rehabilitation
physical therapists
quality of life

self-concept
self-management
social workers
support groups

CHAPTER 12

Psychological Issues in Advancing and Terminal Illness

At the first assembly of freshman year in a suburban high school, the principal opened his remarks by telling the assembled students, "Look around you. Look to your left, look to your right, look in front of you, and look in back of you. Four years from now, one of you will be dead." Most of the students were stunned by this remark, but one boy in the back feigned a death rattle and slumped to the floor in a mock display of the principal's prophecy. He was the one. Two weeks after he got his driver's license, his car spun out of control at high speed and crashed into a stone wall.

The principal, of course, had not peered into the future but had simply drawn on the statistics showing that even adolescents die, especially from accidents. By the time most of us reach age 18, we will have known at least one person who has died, whether it be a high school classmate, a grandparent, or a family friend. Many of these causes of death are preventable. Many children die from accidents in the home. Adolescents, as well as children, die in car crashes often related to risky driving, drugs, alcohol, or a combination of factors. Even death in middle and old age is most commonly due to the cumulative effects of bad health habits, such as smoking, poor eating habits, lack of exercise, and accompanying obesity (Mokdad, Marks, Stroup, & Gerberding, 2004).

■ DEATH ACROSS THE LIFE SPAN

Comedian Woody Allen is said to have remarked on his 40th birthday, "I shall gain immortality not through my work but by not dying." Many of us would echo this desire to live forever, but life inevitably ends in death. A mere 100 years ago, people died primarily from infectious diseases, such as tuberculosis, influenza, or pneumonia. Now those illnesses are much less widespread because of substantial advances in public health and preventive medical technologies that were developed in the 20th century. Just since the 1960s, age-adjusted death rates have declined 43% (MacDorman & Mathews, 2009). On average, people in the United States can now expect to live 77.7 years (Centers for Disease Control and Prevention, 2009, April). When death does come, it will probably stem from a chronic illness, such as heart disease or cancer, rather than from an acute disorder, as Tables 12.1 and 12.2 indicate. This fact means that, instead of facing a rapid, unanticipated death, the average American may know what he or she will probably die of for 5, 10, or even more years.

TABLE 12.1 | Deaths: Leading Causes in the United States, 2006

Rank and Cause	Number of Deaths
1. Heart disease	631,636
2. Cancer	559,888
3. Stroke	137,119
4. Chronic respiratory diseases	124,583
5. Accidents (unintentional injuries)	121,599
6. Diabetes	72,449
7. Alzheimer's disease	72,432
8. Influenza/pneumonia	56,326
9. Nephritis*	45,344
10. Septicemia	34,234

*Includes nephrotic syndrome and nephrosis.
Source: Centers for Disease Control and Prevention, 2009.

Understanding the psychological issues associated with death and dying first requires a tour—a rather grim tour—of death itself. What is the most likely cause of death for a person of any given age, and what kind of death will it be?

Death in Infancy and Childhood

Although the United States is one of the most technologically developed countries in the world, our **infant mortality rate** is high (6.7 per 1,000) (Centers for Disease Control and Prevention, 2009, April), higher than in most Western European nations. Although these figures represent a substantial decline in infant mortality since 1980 (from 12.6 per 1,000) (National Center for Health Statistics, 2008) (Figure 12.1), African American infants are still more than twice as likely to die during the first year as White infants are (Centers for Disease Control and Prevention, 2009, April).

Causes of Death   To what do we attribute such upsetting statistics? The countries that have a lower infant mortality rate than the United States all have national medical programs that provide free or low-cost maternal care during pregnancy. We are one of the few developed nations without such a program. When infants are born prematurely or die at birth, the problems can frequently be traced to poor prenatal care for the mother.

Remarkably, as reproductive technology has improved, racial disparities in infant mortality rates have

TABLE 12.2 | Leading Causes of Mortality Among Adults, Worldwide, 2004

Mortality, Low-income Countries			Mortality, High-income Countries		
Rank	Cause	Deaths	Rank	Cause	Deaths
1	Lower respiratory infections	2,940,000	1	Coronary heart disease	1,330,000
2	Coronary heart disease	2,470,000	2	Cerebrovascular disease and stroke	760,000
3	Diarrheal disease	1,810,000	3	Trachea, bronchus, lung cancers	480,000
4	HIV/AIDS	1,510,000	4	Lower respiratory infections	310,000
5	Cerebrovascular disease and stroke	1,480,000	5	Chronic obstructive pulmonary disease	290,000
6	Chronic obstructive pulmonary disease	940,000	6	Alzheimer's and other dementias	280,000
7	Tuberculosis	910,000	7	Colon and rectum cancers	270,000
8	Neonatal infections	900,000	8	Diabetes mellitus	220,000
9	Malaria	860,000	9	Breast cancer	160,000
10	Prematurity and low birth weight	840,000	10	Stomach cancer	140,000

Source: World Health Organization, November 2008.

actually increased, reflecting continued inequities in access to and allocation of health care resources. The availability of health care to all Americans would ameliorate these inequities and have the beneficial effect of bringing down the overall infant mortality rate.

During the first year of life, the main causes of death are congenital abnormalities and **sudden infant death syndrome (SIDS)**. The causes of SIDS are not entirely known—the infant simply stops breathing—

but epidemiologic studies reveal that it is more likely to occur in lower-class urban environments, when the mother smoked during her pregnancy and when the baby is put to sleep on its stomach or side (Lipsitt, 2003). Mercifully, SIDS appears to be a gentle death for the child, although not for parents: The confusion, self-blame, and suspicion from others who do not understand this phenomenon can take an enormous psychological toll on the parents (Downey, Silver, & Wortman, 1990). News

FIGURE 12.1 | Life Expectancy and Infant Mortality in the United States, 1900–2007
(*Source:* National Center for Health Statistics, 2009)

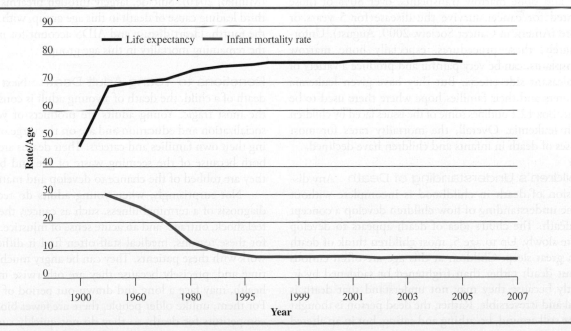

stories detailing how some infant deaths blamed on SIDS were, in fact, murders have not helped parents of SIDS babies cope either. SIDS may be confused with homicide, and vice versa, leading to legal and emotional complications (Nowack, 1992). For mothers of SIDS infants, adjustment seems to be better if they already have children, if they do not blame themselves for the death, and if they have had some contact with the infant before death (Graham, Thompson, Estrada, & Yonekura, 1987).

After the first year, the main cause of death among children under age 15 is accidents, which account for 40% of all deaths in this group. In early childhood, accidents are most frequently due to accidental poisoning, injuries, or falls in the home. In later years, automobile accidents take over as the chief cause of accidental death (Centers for Disease Control and Prevention, 2009, April). The good news is that both accidental deaths in the home and automobile deaths have declined in recent years, in part because of the increasing attention to these causes of childhood death and the preventive technologies, such as infant car seats, that have resulted.

Cancer, especially leukemia, is the second leading cause of death in youngsters age 1–15, and its incidence is rising. Leukemia is a form of cancer that strikes the bone marrow, producing an excessive number of white blood cells and leading to severe anemia and other complications. As recently as 30 years ago, a diagnosis of leukemia was a virtual death sentence for a child. Now, because of advances in treatment, including chemotherapy and bone marrow transplants, over 80% of those treated for cancer survive the disease for 5 years or more (American Cancer Society, 2009, August). Unfortunately, these procedures, especially bone marrow transplants, can be very painful and produce a variety of unpleasant side effects. But they have given leukemia sufferers and their families hope where there used to be none. Box 12.1 outlines some of the issues faced by children with leukemia. Overall, the mortality rates for most causes of death in infants and children have declined.

Children's Understanding of Death   Any discussion of death in childhood is incomplete without some understanding of how children develop a concept of death. The child's idea of death appears to develop quite slowly. Up to age 5, most children think of death as a great sleep. Children at this age are often curious about death rather than frightened or saddened by it, partly because they may not understand that death is final and irreversible. Rather, the dead person is thought to be still around, breathing and eating, but in an altered

state, like Snow White or Sleeping Beauty waiting for the prince (Bluebond-Langner, 1977).

Between ages 5 and 9, the idea that death is final may develop, although most children of this age do not have a biological understanding of death. For some of these children, death is personified into a shadowy figure, such as a ghost or the devil. They may, for example, believe that death occurs because a supernatural being comes to take the person away. The idea that death is universal and inevitable may not develop until age 9 or 10. At this point, the child typically has some understanding of the processes involved in death (such as burial and cremation), knows that the body decomposes, and realizes that the person who has died will not return (Bluebond-Langner, 1977; Kastenbaum, 1977).

Death in Adolescence and Young Adulthood

When asked their view of death, most young adults envision a trauma or fiery accident. This perception is realistic. Although the death rate in adolescence is low (about 0.79 per 1,000 for youths age 15–24), the major cause of death in this age group is unintentional injury, mainly involving automobiles (National Center for Health Statistics, 2007). Homicide is the second leading cause of death overall and the leading cause of death for young Black men. In fact, the homicide rate among young Black men age 15–24 is over six times that for young White men (Miniño, 2010). Suicide, largely through firearms, is the third leading cause of death in this age group, with cancer the fourth. Heart disease and AIDS account for most of the remaining mortality in this age group.

Reactions to Young Adult Death   Next to the death of a child, the death of a young adult is considered the most tragic. Young adults are products of years of socialization and education and are on the verge of starting their own families and careers. Their deaths are tragic both because of the seeming waste of life and because they are robbed of the chance to develop and mature.

Not surprisingly, when young adults do receive a diagnosis of a terminal illness, such as cancer, they may feel shock, outrage, and an acute sense of injustice. Partly for these reasons, medical staff often find it difficult to work with these patients. They can be angry much of the time and, precisely because they are otherwise in good health, may face a long and drawn-out period of dying. For them, unlike older people, there are fewer biological competitors for death, so they do not quickly succumb

BOX 12.1

Mainstreaming the Child with Leukemia

At one time, a diagnosis of leukemia inevitably meant death for a child. Now, however, many children who have had leukemia are living long, full lives, some with intermittent periods of disease and treatment, others with no sign of disease at all. Because so many children with leukemia have periods of remission (the symptom-free state), most are being mainstreamed back into their communities.

Although there are many advantages to main-streaming, there are some difficulties as well. Leukemic children may look different from other children. They may be thin, pale, and bald from treatments such as chemotherapy. They may have little energy for physical activities and may need to go to the hospital from time to time for treatments. Because leukemia is a form of cancer, it has the stigma of cancer associated with it, and its earlier association with death makes it upsetting to many people who do not understand it. Therefore, mainstreaming the leukemic child can require careful, sensitive preparation.

One large metropolitan children's hospital has developed several programs for such mainstreaming. The primary goal of the program is to work with the entire family (the ill child, parents, and siblings) and the child's total environment (home and school) to make the transition as smooth as possible. Several steps are undertaken while the child is in the acute phase of illness. The hospital provides a residential hotel for families of children undergoing radiation therapy so that the parents can be near the child throughout treatment. A community kitchen, dining room, and living room enable parents to meet and share information and concerns with each other.

Special recreational programs developed by trained patient activity specialists enable sick children to play and, at the same time, work out conflicts about illness and treatment. Doctor-patient games and body image games, for example, can reveal adjustment problems and can help the child make the transition back to normal life. Siblings who are having trouble adjusting to their brother's or sister's illness can also participate in the playrooms and work on their own issues and concerns.

Other interventions help the family understand the leukemic child's situation. Parents can participate in educational programs designed to allay fears, teach them how to provide daily home care, and help them help the child adjust to the disease.

Patient activity specialists also work with the schools to ease the child's transition back into the school environment. Following interviews with the child and family to identify potential problems and strains, the specialist meets with the principal, teachers, school nurse, and other staff both to educate them about the child's disease and needs and to help them make the child feel comfortable in the school setting. The specialist may also meet with the other children in the child's class to inform them about the disease and allay any fears. Alternatively, the specialist may help the child prepare a talk for the class about leukemia and its treatments. These steps help the peers of leukemic children relate to them normally.

Other interventions help children develop a positive self-image by exposing them to other children who have leukemia, as through a summer camp for leukemic and other children with cancer or blood disorders. If the counselors have themselves been leukemia patients, they act as living, positive role models for the younger children.

Programs for mainstreaming leukemic children are impressive examples of what can be done when a conscientious effort is made to address all of the chronically ill patient's social and psychological needs.

---

to complications, such as pneumonia or kidney failure. Of particular concern is the terminally ill parent of young children. These parents feel cheated of the chance to see their children grow up and develop and concerned over what will happen to their children without them.

Death in Middle Age

In middle age, death begins to assume more realistic and, in some cases, fearful proportions, both because it is more common and because people develop the chronic health problems that may ultimately kill them. The much popularized midlife crisis that may occur in the 40s or early 50s is believed to stem partly from the gradual realization of impending death. It may be touched off by the death of a parent, an acquaintance, or a friend or by clear bodily signs that one is aging (Kastenbaum, 1977). The fear of death may be symbolically acted out as a fear of loss of physical appearance, sexual prowess, or athletic ability. Or it may be focused on one's work: the

One of the chief causes of death among adolescents and young adults is vehicle accidents.

realization that one's work may be meaningless and that many youthful ambitions will never be realized. The abrupt life changes that are sometimes made in response to this crisis—such as a divorce, remarriage to a much younger person, or radical job change—may be viewed partly as an effort to postpone death (Gould, 1972).

Premature Death
The main cause of **premature death** in adulthood—that is, death that occurs before the projected age of 77—is sudden death due to heart attack or stroke. Members of a cancer conference some years ago were startled to hear the keynote speaker say that he wished everyone would die of a heart attack. What he meant is that, compared with a slow and painful death such as that caused by cancer, sudden death is quick and relatively painless.

When asked, most people reply that they would prefer a sudden, painless, and nonmutilating death. Although sudden death has the disadvantage of not allowing people to prepare their exit, in some ways it facilitates a more graceful departure, because the dying person does not have to cope with physical deterioration, pain, and loss of mental faculties. Sudden death is,

in some ways, kinder to family members as well. The family does not have to go through the emotional torment of witnessing the patient's worsening condition, and finances and other resources are not as severely taxed. A risk is that families may be poorly prepared financially to cope with the loss, or family members may be estranged, with reconciliation now impossible.

Overall, death rates in the middle-aged group have declined, due in large part to a 60% drop in cancers. This drop has been chiefly in lung cancers because of reduced smoking. Heart disease and stroke have also declined over the past decade (American Heart Association, 2003).

Death in Old Age

In olden times, as was the custom, an elderly woman went out of sight of others to become young again. She swam off a little way and discarded her aged skin, but on her return she was not recognized by her granddaughter, who became frightened and drove her away. The aged woman recovered her old skin from the water and resumed it. From then on, this power was lost to man; aging and death was inevitable. (Melanesian folk tale; Hinton, 1967, p. 36)

Dying is not easy at any time during the life cycle, but it may be easier in old age. The elderly are generally more prepared to face death than are the young. They may have thought about their death and have made some initial preparations. The elderly have seen friends and relatives die and often express readiness to die themselves. They may have come to terms with issues associated with death, such as loss of appearance and failure to meet all the goals they once had for themselves, and may have withdrawn from activities because of their now limited energy.

Typically, the elderly die of degenerative diseases, such as cancer, stroke, or heart failure, or simply from general physical decline that predisposes them to infectious disease or organ failure. The terminal phase of illness is generally shorter for them because there is often more than one biological competitor for death. As an age group, the elderly may have a greater chance to achieve death with dignity.

Health psychologists have begun to investigate the factors that predict mortality in the elderly. Why do some individuals live only into their 60s and others live into their 90s or longer? Obviously, new illnesses and the worsening of preexisting conditions account for many of these differences. But changes in psychosocial factors also appear to be important. Depression, self-reported poor mental health, and reduced satisfaction with life predict declines in health among the elderly (Myint et al., 2007; Rodin & McAvay, 1992; Zhang, Kahana, Kahana, Hu, & Pozuelo, 2009). By contrast, a sense of purpose is tied to a longer life (Boyle, Barnes, Buchman, & Bennett, 2009). Close family relationships appear to be protective of health, especially when a widowed parent has close relationships with adult children (Shipley, Der, Taylor, & Deary, 2007; Silverstein & Bengtson, 1991). On the other hand, fatigue, cognitive decline, and self-reports of poor health even in the absence of illness forecast functional decline and mortality (Avlund, Pedersen, & Schroll, 2003; Singh-Manoux et al., 2007). Clearly, psychosocial factors play an important role in health and illness throughout the life course.

In part because of such findings, health goals for the elderly now focus less on reducing mortality and more on improving quality of life. In the United States, people age 65 and up now experience less morbidity and fewer restricted-activity days than was true 15 years ago. However, the worldwide picture is quite different. People are living longer, averaging 64 years in third-world countries, but the prevalence of chronic diseases in those countries, especially those caused by smoking, bad diet, sedentary lifestyle, and alcohol abuse, means that many older people are living poor-quality lives.

As the emphasis on morbidity and the importance of enhancing quality of life takes precedence in health policy, we may see improvement in these figures. With the baby boom generation moving into old age over the next two decades, the need to reduce morbidity and improve quality of life still further will assume a special urgency so that the baby boomers do not completely consume health care resources.

One curious fact about the elderly is that women typically live longer than men—women to age 80 and men only to age 75 (Centers for Disease Control and Prevention, 2009, April). Box 12.2 explores some of the reasons for this difference in mortality rates between men and women. Table 12.3 provides a formula for roughly calculating personal longevity. A more recent website that offers projections about how likely you are to live is www.livingto100.com.

■ PSYCHOLOGICAL ISSUES IN ADVANCING ILLNESS

Although many people die suddenly, many people who are terminally ill know that they are going to die for some time before their death. As a consequence, a variety of medical and psychological issues arise for the patient.

Continued Treatment and Advancing Illness

Advancing and terminal illness frequently brings the need for continued treatments with debilitating and unpleasant side effects. For example, radiation therapy and chemotherapy for cancer may produce discomfort, nausea and vomiting, chronic diarrhea, hair loss, skin discoloration, fatigue, and loss of energy. The patient with advancing diabetes may require amputation of extremities, such as fingers or toes. The patient with advancing cancer may require removal of an organ to which the illness has now spread, such as a lung or part of the liver. The patient with degenerative kidney disease may be given a transplant, in the hope that it will forestall further deterioration.

Many patients find themselves repeated objects of surgical or chemical therapy in a desperate effort to save their lives; after several such efforts, the patient may resist any further intervention. Patients who have

BOX 12.2

Why Do Women Live Longer Than Men?

On average, women live nearly 5 years longer than men in the United States, a difference that also exists in most other industrialized countries. Only in underdeveloped countries, in which childbirth technology is poorly developed, or in countries where women are denied access to health care, do men live longer. What are the reasons that women typically live longer than men?

One theory maintains that women are biologically more fit than men. Although more male than female fetuses are conceived, more males are stillborn or miscarried than are females. This trend persists in infancy, with more male than female babies dying. In fact, the male death rate is higher at all ages. Thus, although more males than females are born, there will be more females than males left alive by the time young people reach their 20s. Exactly what biological mechanisms might make females more fit are still unknown. Some factors may be genetic; others may be hormonal. For example, women's buffered X chromosome may protect them against certain disorders to which men are more vulnerable. Males are more prone to infectious disease and parasites (Owens, 2002, September 20).

Another reason why men die in greater numbers at all ages than do women is that men engage in more risky behaviors (Williams, 2003). Chief among these is smoking, which accounts for as much as 40% of the mortality difference between men and women. Men are exposed to more occupational hazards and more men hold hazardous jobs, such as construction work, police work, or firefighting. Men's alcohol consumption is greater than women's, exposing them to liver damage and alcohol-related accidents, and they consume more drugs than do women. Men are more likely to participate in hazardous sports and to use firearms recreationally. Men's greater access to firearms, in turn, makes them more likely to

use guns to commit suicide—a method that is more effective than the methods typically favored by women (such as poison). Men also use automobiles and motorcycles more than women, contributing to their high death rate from accidents. Men's tendencies to cope with stress through fight (aggression) or flight (social withdrawal or withdrawal through drugs and alcohol) may thus also account for their shorter life span.

A third theory maintains that social support may be more protective for women than for men. On the one hand, being married benefits men more than women in terms of increased life span. In fact, marriage for women seems to serve little or no protective function (Kiecolt-Glaser & Newton, 2001). However, women report having more close friends and participating in more group activities, such as church, that may offer support. Social support keeps stress systems at low levels and so may prevent some of the wear and tear that men, especially unattached men, sustain (Taylor, Kemeny, Reed, Bower, & Gruenewald, 2000). Thus, women's tendencies to tend-and-befriend in response to stress may account for part of their longevity as well (Taylor, 2002).

Which of these theories is correct? The evidence suggests that all of them account for some of the sex difference in mortality. Whether the factors that have protected women from early mortality in the past will continue to do so is unknown. Changes in women's roles may erode their current advantage in life span (Rodin & Ickovics, 1990). Smoking, for example, which did not reach high levels in women for some decades after men had begun to smoke, is now taking its toll on women's health. The next decades will elucidate further whether the changes in men's and women's roles that expose them to similar activities and risks will eventually produce similar mortality rates.

---

undergone repeated surgery may feel that they are being disassembled bit by bit. Or patients who have had several rounds of cancer treatment may feel despair over the apparent uselessness of any new treatment. Each procedure raises anew the threat of death and underscores the fact that the disease has not been arrested, and in many cases, the sheer number of treatments can lead to discomfort, exhaustion, and depression.

Thus, there comes a time when the question of whether to continue treatments becomes an issue. In

some cases, refusal of treatment may indicate depression and feelings of hopelessness, but in many cases, the patient's decision may be supported by thoughtful choice. For example, a recent study of patients with end-stage renal disease who decided to discontinue kidney dialysis found that the decision was not influenced by a major depressive disorder or by ordinary suicidal thoughts, but rather represented a decision to forego aggressive painful therapy (Cohen, Dobscha, Hails, Pekow, & Chochinov, 2002).

TABLE 12.3 | How Long Will You Live?

This is a rough guide for calculating your personal longevity. The basic life expectancy for males in the United States is 74 and for females is 80 (National Vital Statistics System, 2001). Write down your basic life expectancy. If you are in your fifties or sixties, you should add 10 years to the basic figure because you have already proven yourself to be quite durable. If you are over age 60 and active, add another 2 years.

Basic Life Expectancy
Describe how each item below applies to you and add or subtract the appropriate number of years from your basic life expectancy.

1. Family history
   Add 5 years if 2 or more of your grandparents lived to 80 or beyond.   _5_
   Subtract 4 years if any parent, grandparent, sister, or brother died of a heart attack or stroke before 50;   _-2_
       subtract 2 years if anyone died from these diseases before 60.
   Subtract 3 years for each case of diabetes, thyroid disorders, breast cancer, cancer of the digestive system,   _-9_
   asthma, or chronic bronchitis among parents or grandparents.

2. Marital status
   If you are married and male, add 10 years; if married and female, add 4 years.   _____
   If you are over 25 and not married, subtract 1 year for every unwedded decade.   _____

3. Economic status
   Subtract 2 years if your family income is over $400,000 per year.   _____
   Subtract 3 years if you have been poor for the greater part of your life.   _____

4. Physique
   Subtract 1 year for every 10 pounds you are overweight.   _-1_
   For each inch your girth measurement exceeds your chest measurement deduct 2 years.   _____
   Add 3 years if you are over 40 and not overweight.   _____

5. Exercise
   Regular and moderate (jogging 3 times a week), add 3 years.   _____
   Regular and vigorous (long-distance running 3 times a week), add 5 years.   _____
   Subtract 3 years if your job is sedentary. Add 3 years if it is active.   _____

6. Alcohol*
   Add 2 years if you are a light drinker (1–3 drinks a day).   _____
   Subtract 5–10 years if you are a heavy drinker (more than 4 drinks a day).   _____
   Subtract 1 year if you are a teetotaler.   _____

7. Smoking
   Two or more packs of cigarettes per day, subtract 8 years.   _____
   One to two packs per day, subtract 4 years.   _____
   Less than one pack, subtract 2 years.   _____
   Subtract 2 years if you regularly smoke a pipe or cigars.   _____

8. Disposition
   Add 2 years if you are a reasoned, practical person.   _____
   Subtract 2 years if you are aggressive, intense, and competitive.   _____
   Add 1–5 years if you are basically happy and content with your life.   _____

9. Education
   Less than high school, subtract 2 years.   _____
   Four years of school beyond high school, add 1 year.   _____
   Five or more years beyond high school, add 3 years.   _____

10. Environment
    If you have lived most of your life in a rural environment, add 4 years.   _____
    Subtract 2 years if you have lived most of your life in an urban environment.   _____

11. Sleep
    More than 9 hours a day, subtract 5 years.   _____

12. Temperature
    Add 2 years if your home's thermostat is set at no more than 68°F.   _____

13. Health care
    Regular medical checkups and regular dental care, add 3 years.   _____
    Frequently ill, subtract 2 years.   _____

*It should be noted that these calculations for alcohol consumption are controversial and require additional evidence. It is not clear that moderate drinking is healthful relative to teetotaling, and indeed the reverse may be true.

Source: R. Schulz, *Psychology of Death, Dying, and Bereavement,* © 1978 by the McGraw-Hill Companies. Reprinted by permission of the McGraw-Hill Companies.

BOX 12.3

A Letter to My Physician Concerning My Decision About Physician Aid-in-Dying

Dear Dr. _____,

It is important to me to have excellent and compassionate medical care—to keep me healthy and alive and, at the end of my life, to alleviate suffering and ensure that I have a peaceful and dignified death. When there are measures available to extend my life, I would like to know their chances of success and how they will impact my quality of life.

I would like the reassurance:

• That if I am able to speak for myself, my requests will be honored; if I am not, the requests from my health care proxy and advance directives will be honored.

• That you will make an appropriate referral to hospice should I request it.

• That you will support my desire to die with dignity and in peace if the burdens of an incurable condition became too great.

I believe in physician aid-in-dying as one option at the end of life. If the end is inevitable, the quality of my life is more important than the quantity. My dignity, comfort and the burden I may be to those I love are critical considerations for me.

Thank you.

_____   _____

Signature   Date

_____

Source: From Compassion and Choices (formerly the Hemlock Society). For more information, visit www.compassionandchoices.org.

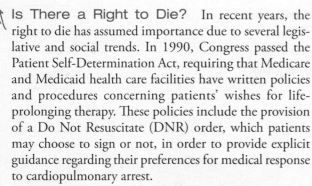

Is There a Right to Die? In recent years, the right to die has assumed importance due to several legislative and social trends. In 1990, Congress passed the Patient Self-Determination Act, requiring that Medicare and Medicaid health care facilities have written policies and procedures concerning patients' wishes for life-prolonging therapy. These policies include the provision of a Do Not Resuscitate (DNR) order, which patients may choose to sign or not, in order to provide explicit guidance regarding their preferences for medical response to cardiopulmonary arrest.

An important social trend affecting terminal care is the right-to-die movement, which maintains that dying should become more a matter of personal choice and personal control. Derek Humphry's book *Final Exit* virtually leaped off bookstore shelves when it appeared in 1991. A manual of how to commit suicide or assist in suicide for the dying, it was perceived to give back to dying people the means for achieving a dignified death at a time of one's choosing.

Receptivity to such ideas as suicide and assisted suicide for the terminally ill has increased in the American population. In a 1975 Gallup Poll, only 41% of respondents believed that someone in great pain with no hope of improvement had the moral right to commit suicide, but by 2007, 71% supported "euthanasia" (Carroll, 2007). Although some experts found that these preferences may change when people realize that they are facing death (Sharman, Garry, Jacobson, Loftus, & Ditto,

2008), declines in functioning appear to lead to reduced interest in life-sustaining treatments (Ditto et al., 2003) (see Box 12.3).

Moral and Legal Issues Increasingly, societies must struggle with the issue of **euthanasia,** that is, ending the life of a person who is suffering from a painful terminal illness. *Euthanasia* comes from the Greek word meaning "good death" (Pfeifer & Brigham, 1996). Terminally ill patients most commonly request euthanasia or assisted suicide when they are experiencing extreme distress and suffering, often due to inadequate relief from pain (Cherny, 1996).

In 1994, Oregon became the first state to pass a law permitting physician-assisted dying. Generally, at the patient's request, the physician provides a lethal dose of medication or sleeping pills that the patient can then ingest to end his or her life. Statistics show a steady increase in the number of people taking advantage of the law, with 60 Oregonians choosing assisted suicide in 2008. Many other patients obtain the drugs but do not use them (Oregon Department of Human Services, 2009). Although a 1997 Supreme Court ruling did not find physician-assisted dying to be a constitutional right, the Court nonetheless left legislation to individual states, and so the 1997 Oregon Death with Dignity Act became official, with the first physician-assisted death occurring in 1998 (Sears & Stanton, 2001).

BOX 12.4

Ready to Die: The Question of Assisted Suicide

Frans Swarttouw, former chairman of the Fokker aircraft company and one of the Netherlands' most colorful businessmen, bid an unusual farewell to his countrymen. Stricken with throat cancer, the executive, 64, who once characterized an entrepreneur as "a guy who works hard, drinks himself into the ground, and chases women," said he had stopped his painful therapy and opted out of a life-saving operation that would have left him an invalid. "I want to be able to draw the line myself," he said on TV. Three days later, he was put to death by a doctor. "His last evening at home was so cozy," his wife said. "Frans gave himself another quarter of an hour: 'One last gin and tonic and a cigarette, then we'll get down to work.'"

The touch of bravura was uniquely Swarttouw, but the candor about voluntary death was typically Dutch. While euthanasia and physician-assisted suicide remain taboo subjects in much of Europe and are contentious topics in the United States, they have been openly debated and researched for more than 30 years in Holland, which has a record of pragmatism in dealing with thorny social issues like drugs and abortion. Euthanasia is still, under Dutch law, a crime punishable by up to 12 years in prison. But in fact, the Netherlands has tolerated the practice for more than a decade, and the number of cases has risen dramatically over the past five years. Have the Dutch found a sensible and humane way of dealing with the unbearable pain and suffering that often comes at the end of life? Or is this a policy run amuck? (Branegan, 1997, p. 30)

The United States is only beginning to address these questions.

Source: Branegan, 1997, March 17. Reprinted by permission.

At one time, surveys suggested that 45% of oncologists (cancer specialists) supported the idea of physician-assisted suicide; but that figure has now dropped to 22.5%. Moreover, 35 states explicitly criminalize assisted suicide (www.euthanasia.com/bystate.html) (see Box 12.4). These changes may reflect Americans' increasingly critical stance toward the idea of assisted suicide, or they may stem from the fact that physicians now feel better able to handle the psychological issues that arise at the end of life.

More passive measures to terminate life have also received attention. A number of states have now enacted laws enabling people with terminal diseases to write a **living will,** requesting that extraordinary life-sustaining procedures not be used if they are unable to make this decision on their own. The will, which is signed in front of witnesses, is usually drawn up when the person is diagnosed as having a terminal illness. It provides instructions and legal protection for the physician, so that life-prolonging interventions, such as use of respirators, will not be indefinitely undertaken in a vain effort to keep the patient alive. This kind of document also helps to ensure that the patient's preferences, rather than a surrogate's (such as a relative), are respected (Ditto & Hawkins, 2005; Fagerlin, Ditto, Danks, Houts, & Smucker, 2001).

Unfortunately, research suggests that many physicians ignore the wishes of their dying patients and needlessly prolong pain and suffering. One study (Seneff, Wagner, Wagner, Zimmerman, & Knaus, 1995) found that although one-third of the patients had asked not to be revived with cardiopulmonary resuscitation, half the time this request was never indicated on their charts. Thus, at present, the living will and related tools are not completely successful in allowing patients to express their wishes and ensure that they are met. Box 12.5 presents a daughter's perspective on some of these issues with regard to her dying father.

The complex moral, legal, and ethical issues surrounding death are relatively new to our society, prompted in large part by substantial advances in health care technologies. Life-sustaining drugs, cardiopulmonary resuscitation, advanced cardiac life support, renal dialysis, nutritional support and hydration, mechanical ventilation, organ transplantation, antibiotics, and other interventions that prolong life—all were unheard of as recently as 30 years ago. However, our understanding of how to make appropriate use of these technologies has not kept up with their increasing sophistication. First, there is substantial inequity in access to life-sustaining technologies (Henifin, 1993). Those patients who are better off financially and who have better health insurance have greater access to and are more likely to receive life-sustaining technologies. Second, we do not yet have guidelines regarding cost-effectiveness and appropriateness of use. That is, life-sustaining technologies are often

BOX 12.5

Death: A Daughter's Perspective

My father sleeps, I sit writing . . . trying to get something on paper I know is there, but which is as elusive and slippery as the life that's ending before me.

My father has cancer. Cancer of the sinuses, and as the autopsy will show later, of the left occipital lobe, mastoid, cerebellum. . . .

I have not seen my father for nine months, when the lump was still a secret below his ear. A few months later I heard about it and headaches, and then from time to time all the diagnoses of arthritis, a cyst, sinusitis . . . even senility. Then finally—the lump now a painful burden to be carried—he was subjected to nine days of tests of bowels, bladder, blood. And on the last day a hollow needle was inserted into the growth; the cells gathered, magnified, interpreted, and pronounced cancer. Immediate surgery and/or cobalt treatment indicated. . . .

And after the trauma of no dentures, no hearing aid, and one unexpected cobalt treatment, triumphant that his mind functioned and his voice was firm, he stated unfalteringly: "Let me alone. No more treatments. I am 75. I have had an excellent life. It is time

for me to die in my own way." His decision was not to be met with approval. . . .

Death is not easy under any circumstances, but at least he did not suffer tubes and IVs and false hope, and we did not suffer the play-acting, the helpless agonies of watching a loved one suffer to no purpose, finally growing inured to it all or even becoming irritated with a dying vegetable that one cannot relate to any longer. In the end, I have learned, death is a very personal matter between parents and offspring, husbands and wives, loving neighbors and friends, and between God or symbols of belief and the dying ones and all who care about them.

There comes a point where it is no longer the business of the courts, the American Medical Association, the government. It is private business. And I write now publicly only because it needs to be said again, and my father would have agreed. . . .

Source: "Death Is a Personal Matter." Carol K. Littlebrant, originally published January 12, 1976, in *Newsweek* under the name of Carol K. Gross. Selected excerpts—by permission of the author.

extremely expensive, and guidelines must be developed as to when and with whom such interventions are appropriate (Kapp, 1993). Third, as touched on previously, most societies have yet to achieve consensus on the appropriate role that people may play in choosing the time and means of their deaths and the roles that health care practitioners may or may not play in assisting this process. These issues will assume increasing importance in the coming decades with the aging of the population.

Psychological and Social Issues Related to Dying

Changes in the Patient's Self-Concept
Just as chronically ill patients must engage in new health-related activities and continued monitoring of their physical condition, so must patients with advancing illness adjust their expectations and activities according to the stage of their disorder. The difference is that, for patients with progressive diseases such as cancer or severe diabetes, life is a constant process of readjusting expectations and activities to accommodate an ever-expanding patient role.

In recent years, grass roots movements expressing the rights to die and to physician-assisted suicide have gained strength in the United States.

Advancing illness can threaten the self-concept. As the disease progresses, patients are increasingly less able to present themselves effectively. It may become difficult for them to maintain control of biological and social functioning. They may be incontinent (unable to control urination or bowel movements); they may drool, have distorted facial expressions, or shake uncontrollably. None of this is attractive either to the patient or to others.

These patients may also be in intermittent pain, may suffer from uncontrollable retching or vomiting, and may experience a shocking deterioration in appearance due to weight loss, the stress of treatments, or the sheer drain of illness. Even more threatening to some patients is mental regression and the inability to concentrate. Cognitive decline accelerates in the years prior to death (Wilson, Beck, Bienias, & Bennett, 2007). Losses in cognitive function may also be due either to the progressive nature of disease or to the tranquilizing and disorienting effects of painkillers and other medications.

Issues of Social Interaction

The threats to the self-concept that stem from loss of mental and physical functioning spill over into threats to social interaction. Although terminally ill patients often want and need social contact, they may be afraid that their obvious mental and physical deterioration will upset visitors. Thus, patients may begin a process of social withdrawal, whereby they gradually restrict visits to only a few family members. Family and friends can help make this withdrawal less extreme: They can prepare visitors in advance for the patient's state so that the visitor's reaction can be controlled; they can also screen out some visitors who cannot keep their emotions in check.

Some disengagement from the social world is normal and may represent the grieving process through which the final loss of family and friends is anticipated. This period of anticipatory grieving may exacerbate communication difficulties because it is hard for the patient to express affection for others while simultaneously preparing to leave them.

In other cases, withdrawal may be caused by fear of depressing others and becoming an emotional burden. The patient may feel guilty for taking up so much of the family's time, energy, and money and may, therefore, withdraw so as not to be even more of a burden. In such cases, it is easy for misunderstandings to arise. The family may mistakenly believe that the patient wishes to be left alone and so may respect these wishes. Instead, family and friends may need to make a concerted effort to draw out the patient to forestall a potential severe depression, in part because depression appears to precipitate death (Herrmann et al., 1998; Wulsin, Vaillant, & Wells, 1999). Yet another cause of withdrawal may be the patient's bitterness over impending death and resentment of the living. In such cases, the family may need to understand that such bitterness is normal and that it usually passes.

Communication Issues

As long as a patient's prognosis is favorable, communication is usually open; however, as the prognosis worsens and treatment becomes more drastic, communication may start to break down. Medical staff may become evasive when questioned about the patient's status. Family members may be cheerfully optimistic with the patient but confused and frightened when they try to elicit information from medical staff. The potential for a breakdown in communication as illness advances can be traced to several factors.

First, death itself is still a taboo topic in our society. The issue is generally avoided in polite conversation; little research is conducted on death; and even when death strikes within a family, the survivors often try to bear their grief alone. The right thing to do, many people feel, is not to bring it up.

A second reason that communication may break down is because each person involved may believe that others do not want to talk about the death. Moreover, each of the participants may have personal reasons for not wanting to discuss death. Some patients do not want to hear the answers to their unasked questions because they know the answers and fear having to cope with the finality of having them confirmed. Family members may wish to avoid confronting any lingering guilt they have over whether they urged the patient to see a doctor soon enough or whether they did everything possible. Medical staff may fear having to cope with the reproaches of family members or the patient over whether enough was done.

The Issue of Nontraditional Treatment

As both health and communication deteriorate, some terminally ill patients turn away from traditional medical care. Many such patients fall victim to dubious remedies offered outside the formal health care system. Frantic family members, friends who are trying to be helpful, and patients themselves may scour fringe publications for seemingly effective remedies or cures; they may invest thousands of dollars in their generally unsuccessful search.

What prompts people to take these often uncomfortable, inconvenient, costly, and worthless measures? Some patients are so frantic at the prospect of death that they will use up both their own savings and those of the family in the hope of a miracle cure. In other cases, the turn to nontraditional medicine may be a symptom of a deteriorating relationship with the health care system and the desire for more humanistic care. This is not to suggest that a solid patient-practitioner relationship can prevent every patient from turning to quackery. However, when the patient is well informed and feels cared for by others, he or she is less likely to look for alternative remedies.

Strong criticism of nontraditional medicine frequently prompts strenuous objections coupled with loudly touted case histories of dramatic improvement due to some unlikely treatment. The criticism offered here should not be taken to mean that no patient ever

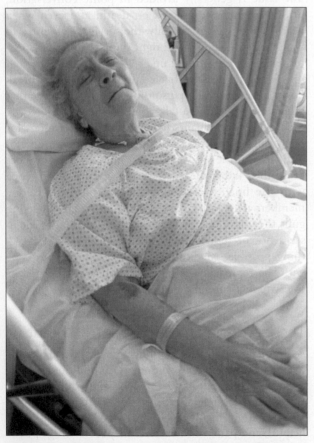

Many terminally ill patients who find themselves repeated objects of intervention become worn out and eventually refuse additional treatment.

benefits from nontraditional treatments or that some will not be found eventually to be effective treatments. Indeed, as Chapter 9 indicates, placebos alone effect miracle cures in some cases. However, these instances are relatively rare, and the small chance of being among them may not justify the great expense and hardship involved in undergoing these dubious therapies.

■ ARE THERE STAGES IN ADJUSTMENT TO DYING?

Do people pass through a predictable series of **stages of dying**?

Kübler-Ross's Five-Stage Theory

Elisabeth Kübler-Ross, a pioneer in the study of death and dying, suggested that people pass through five stages as they adjust to the prospect of death: denial, anger, bargaining, depression, and acceptance.

Denial   The first stage, denial, is thought to be a person's initial reaction on learning of the diagnosis of terminal illness. Denial is a defense mechanism by which people avoid the implications of an illness. They may act as if the illness were not severe, it will shortly go away, and it will have few long-term implications. In extreme cases, the patient may even deny that he or she has the illness, despite having been given clear information about the diagnosis (Ditto, Munro, et al., 2003). Denial, then, is the subconscious blocking out of the full realization of the reality and implications of the disorder.

The diagnosis of a terminal illness can come as a shock to a person. The immediate response may be that a mistake has been made, that the test results or X-rays have been mixed up with those of someone else, or that the diagnosis will be reversed. Shortly thereafter, everything suddenly seems to change. Plans—ranging from what to do tomorrow to what to do for the rest of one's life—may have to change. The initial diagnosis may be so disorienting that the person has difficulty gauging the degree of change that will be required. He or she may be as likely to wonder who will stop at the dry cleaner's tomorrow as to wonder about returning to school, having another child, or going on a long-planned trip.

It may be days or even weeks before these questions fall into place, arranging themselves in a proper hierarchy. The sheer quantity of issues to be considered may make the patient appear unresponsive, preoccupied by the wrong problems, and unable to understand the scope and limits of the treatments that will be required. The emotions most likely to accompany these initial feelings of disorientation are denial and anxiety.

For most people, this shocked denial that anything is wrong lasts only a few days. Denial early on in adjustment to life-threatening illness is both normal and useful because it can protect the patient from the full realization of impending death (Lazarus, 1983). Sometimes, denial lasts longer than a few days. When it does, it may require psychological intervention.

But is it not helpful to a patient to be able to deny death? Denial may give the appearance of being a useful psychological shelter from reality, but it is a primitive and ultimately unsuccessful defense (Weisman, 1972). It may mask anxiety without making it go away. The patient who is denying the implications of illness often appears rigidly overcontrolled, as if a crack in the defense would cause the entire facade to crumble. In fact, reality can break through for a few minutes or hours at a time, leaving the patient vulnerable and frightened. Long-term denial of one's illness, then, is a defensive pattern from which a patient should be coaxed through therapeutic intervention.

Anger   Denial usually abates because the illness itself creates circumstances that must be met. Decisions must be made regarding future treatments if any, where the patient will be cared for, and by whom. At this point, according to Kübler-Ross, the second stage, anger, may set in. The angry patient is asking, "Why me?" Considering all the other people who could have gotten the illness, all the people who had the same symptoms but got a favorable diagnosis, and all the people who are older, dumber, more bad-tempered, less useful, or just plain evil, why should the patient be the one who is dying? Kübler-Ross quotes one of her dying patients:

> I suppose most anybody in my position would look at somebody else and say, "Well, why couldn't it have been him?" and this has crossed my mind several times. An old man whom I have known ever since I was a little kid came down the street. He was eighty-two years old, and he is of no earthly use as far as we mortals can tell. He's rheumatic, he's a cripple, he's dirty, just not the type of person you would like to be. And the thought hit me strongly, now why couldn't it have been old George instead of me? (quoted in Kübler-Ross, 1969, p. 50)

The angry patient may show resentment toward anyone who is healthy, such as hospital staff, family members, or friends. Angry patients who cannot express their anger

directly by being irritable may do so indirectly by becoming embittered. Bitter patients show resentment through death jokes, cracks about their deteriorating appearance and capacities, or pointed remarks about all the exciting things that they will not be able to do because those events will happen after their death.

Anger is one of the harder responses for family and friends to deal with. They may feel they are being blamed by the patient for being well. The family may need to work together with a therapist to understand that the patient is not really angry with them but at fate; they need to see that this anger will be directed at anyone who is nearby, especially people with whom the patient feels no obligation to be polite and well behaved. Unfortunately, family members often fall into this category.

Bargaining   Bargaining is the third stage of Kübler-Ross's formulation. At this point, the patient abandons anger in favor of a different strategy: trading good behavior for good health. Bargaining frequently takes the form of a pact with God, in which the patient agrees to engage in good works or at least to abandon selfish ways in exchange for better health or more time. A sudden rush of charitable activity or uncharacteristically pleasant behavior may be a sign that the patient is trying to strike such a bargain.

Depression   Depression, the fourth stage in Kübler-Ross's model, may be viewed as coming to terms with lack of control. The patient acknowledges that little can now be done to stay the course of illness. This realization may be coincident with a worsening of symptoms, tangible evidence that the illness is not going to be cured. At this stage, patients may feel nauseated, breathless, and tired. They may find it hard to eat, to control elimination, to focus attention, and to escape pain or discomfort.

Kübler-Ross refers to the stage of depression as a time for "anticipatory grief," when patients mourn the prospect of their own deaths. This grieving process may occur in two stages, as the patient first comes to terms with the loss of past valued activities and friends and then begins to anticipate the future loss of activities and relationships. Depression, though far from pleasant, can be functional in that patients begin to prepare for the future. As a consequence, it may sometimes be wise not to intervene immediately with depression, but rather to let it run its course, at least for a brief time (Kübler-Ross, 1969).

The advice to let depression run its course obviously does not extend to clear cases of pathological depression, in which the patient is continually morose, unresponsive to friends and family, unable to eat, and basically uninterested in activity. In these cases, a therapist may have to intervene. In so doing, however, it is important that symptoms of depression be distinguished from symptoms of physical deterioration. In advanced illness, patients often have so little energy that they cannot discharge activities on their own. What such patients may need—rather than a therapist—is a quiet companion, someone to spoonfeed them, and someone to sponge them off from time to time.

Acceptance

The fifth stage in Kübler-Ross's theory is acceptance. At this point, the patient may be too weak to be angry and too accustomed to the idea of dying to be depressed. Instead, a tired, peaceful, though not necessarily pleasant calm may descend. Some patients use this time to make preparations, deciding how to divide up their remaining personal possessions and saying goodbye to old friends and family members. At one time, researchers speculated that "giving up" might actually influence time of death, but that does not appear to be the case (Skala & Freedland, 2004; Smith, 2006). Similarly, "holding on" to make it through a holiday or other major event does not appear to occur reliably either (Smith, 2004).

Evaluation of Kübler-Ross's Theory

How good an account of the process of dying is Kübler-Ross's stage theory? As a description of the reactions of dying patients, her work was invaluable. She has chronicled nearly the full array of reactions to death, as those who work with the dying will be quick to acknowledge. Her work is also of inestimable value in pointing out the counseling needs of the dying. Finally, along with other researchers, she has broken through the silence and taboos surrounding death, making it an object of both scientific study and sensitive concern.

As a stage theory, however, her work has some limitations. Patients do not go through five stages in a predetermined order. Some patients never go through a particular stage. Others will go through a stage more than once. All the feelings associated with the five stages may be experienced by some patients on an alternating basis. The resigned patient has moments of anger or depression. The angry patient may also experience denial. The depressed patient may still be hoping for a last-minute reprieve. In fairness to Kübler-Ross, it should be noted that she readily acknowledged that her "stages" can occur in varying, intermittent order. Unfortunately, this point

is sometimes missed by her audience. Nurses, physicians, social workers, and others who work with the dying may expect a dying person to go through these stages in order, and they may become upset when a patient does not "die right" (Liss-Levinson, 1982; Silver & Wortman, 1980).

Kübler-Ross's stage theory also does not fully acknowledge the importance of anxiety, which can be present throughout the dying process. Next to depression, anxiety is one of the most common responses (Hinton, 1967). What patients fear most is not being able to control pain; they may welcome or even seek death to avoid it (Hinton, 1967). Other symptoms, such as difficulty breathing or uncontrollable vomiting, likewise produce anxiety, which may exacerbate the patient's already deteriorating physical and mental condition.

Is Kübler-Ross's stage theory wrong and some other stage theory correct, or is it simply inappropriate to talk about stages of dying? The answer is that no stage model can be infallibly applied to the process of dying. Dying is a complex and individual process, subject to no rules and few regularities.

■ PSYCHOLOGICAL MANAGEMENT OF THE TERMINALLY ILL

Medical Staff and the Terminally Ill Patient

Approximately 41% of Americans who die each year die in hospitals (Flory et al., 2004). Unfortunately, death in the institutional environment can be depersonalized and fragmented. Wards may be understaffed, with the staff unable to provide the kind of emotional support the patient needs. Hospital regulations may restrict the number of visitors or the length of time that they can stay, thereby reducing the availability of support from family and friends. Pain is one of the chief symptoms in terminal illness, and in the busy hospital setting, the ability of patients to get the kind and amount of pain medication they need may be compromised. Moreover, as we saw in Chapter 10, prejudices against drug treatments for pain still exist, and so terminal patients run the risk of being undermedicated for their pain (Turk & Feldman, 1992a, 1992b). Death in an institution can be a long, lonely, mechanized, painful, and dehumanizing experience.

The Significance of Hospital Staff to the Patient   Physical dependence on hospital staff is great because the patient may need help for even the smallest activity, such as brushing teeth or turning over in bed. Patients are entirely dependent on medical staff for amelioration of their pain. And staff may be the only people to see a dying patient on a regular basis if he or she has no friends or family who can visit regularly.

Moreover, staff may be the only people who know the patient's actual physical state; hence, they are the patient's only source of realistic information. They may also know the patient's true feelings when others do not; often, patients put up a cheerful front for family and friends so as not to upset them. The patient, then, may welcome communication with staff because he or she can be fully candid with them. Finally, staff are important because they are privy to one of the patient's most personal and private acts, the act of dying.

Risks of Terminal Care for Staff   **Terminal care** is hard on hospital staff. It is the least interesting physical care because it is often **palliative care**—that is, care designed to make the patient feel comfortable—rather than **curative care**—that is, care designed to cure the patient's disease. Terminal care involves a lot of unpleasant custodial work, such as feeding, changing, and bathing the patient. Even more important is the emotional strain that terminal care places on staff. The staff may burn out from watching patient after patient die, despite their best efforts.

Staff may be tempted to withdraw into a crisply efficient manner rather than a warm and supportive one so as to minimize their personal pain. Physicians, in particular, want to reserve their time for patients who can most profit from it and, consequently, may spend little time with a terminally ill patient. Unfortunately, terminally ill patients may interpret such behavior as abandonment and take it very hard. Accordingly, a continued role for the physician in the patient's terminal care in the form of brief but frequent visits is desirable. The physician can interpret confusing physical changes and allay anxiety by providing information and a realistic timetable of events. The patient and the physician may also make decisions about subsequent medical interventions, such as the use of life support systems and the living will, as noted earlier.

A sometimes controversial issue regarding patient-staff interaction during the terminal phase of illness concerns what information patients should be given about their illness. At one time, it was widely believed that patients did not want to know if they were terminally ill, although research subsequently proved that belief groundless. Nonetheless, great disparities remain regarding preferences for information and beliefs about the amount of information that patients should have.

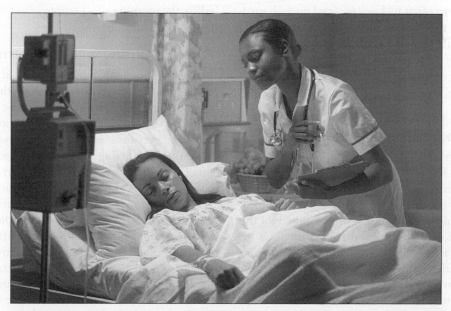

Medical staff can be very significant to a dying patient because they see the patient on a regular basis, provide realistic information, and are privy to the patient's last personal thoughts and wishes.

Achieving an Appropriate Death   Psychiatrist Avery Weisman (1972, 1977), a distinguished clinician who worked with dying patients for many years, outlined a useful set of goals for medical staff in their work with the dying:

- *Informed consent*—Patients should be told the nature of their condition and treatment and, to some extent, be involved in their own treatment.

- *Safe conduct*—The physician and other staff should act as helpful guides for the patient through this new and frightening stage of life.

- *Significant survival*—The physician and other medical staff should help the patient use his or her remaining time as well as possible.

- *Anticipatory grief*—Both the patient and his or her family members should be aided in working through their anticipatory sense of loss and depression.

- *Timely and appropriate death*—The patient should be allowed to die when and how he or she wants to, as much as possible. The patient should be allowed to achieve death with dignity.

These guidelines, established many years ago, still provide the goals and means for terminal care. Unfortunately, a "good death" is still not available to all. A survey of the survivors of 1,500 people who had died revealed that dying patients often had not received enough medication to ease their pain and had not experienced enough emotional support. Lack of open communication and lack of respect from medical staff were two other common complaints (Teno, Fisher, Hamel, Coppola, & Dawson, 2002).

Individual Counseling with the Terminally Ill

Many patients need the chance to talk with someone about how they feel about themselves, their lives, their families, and death, and they need an opportunity to regain a sense of control over their lives. Typically, medical staff cannot devote the kind of time required for this support. Accordingly, therapy for dying patients is becoming an increasingly available and utilized option.

Therapy with the dying is different from typical psychotherapy in several respects. First, for obvious reasons, it is likely to be short term. The format of therapy with the dying also varies from that of traditional psychotherapy. The nature and timing of visits must depend on the inclination and energy level of the patient,

rather than on a fixed schedule of appointments. The agenda should be set at least partly by the patient. And if an issue arises that the patient clearly does not wish to discuss, this wish should be respected.

Terminally ill patients may also need help in resolving unfinished business. Uncompleted activities may prey on the mind, and preparations may need to be made for survivors, especially dependent children. Through careful counseling, a therapist may help the patient come to terms with the need for these arrangements, as well as with the need to recognize that some things will remain undone (Abrams, 1966).

Some **thanatologists**—that is, those who study death and dying—have suggested that behavioral and cognitive-behavioral therapies can be constructively employed with dying patients (Sobel, 1981). For example, progressive muscle relaxation can ameliorate discomfort and instill a renewed sense of control. Positive self-talk, such as focusing on one's life achievements, can undermine the depression that often accompanies dying.

There are few guidelines available for **clinical thanatology**—that is, therapy with the dying. Nonetheless, such efforts can help dying people place their lives into perspective prior to death. Many people find meaning in **symbolic immortality,** a sense that one is leaving behind a legacy through one's children or one's work or that one is joining the afterlife and becoming one with God (Lifton, 1977). Thus, the last weeks of life can crystallize the meaning of a lifetime.

Family Therapy with the Terminally Ill

Dying does not happen in a vacuum but is often a family experience. As a consequence, family therapy can be an appropriate way to deal with the most common issues raised by terminal illness: communication, death-related plans and decisions, and the need to find meaning in life while making a loving and appropriate separation. Sometimes, the therapist will need to meet separately with family members as well as with the patient.

Family and patient may be mismatched in their adjustment to the illness. For example, family members may hold out hope, but the patient may be resigned to the prospect of death. Moreover, the needs of the living and the dying can be in conflict, with the living needing to maintain their resources and perform their daily activities at the same time that the patient needs a great deal of support. A therapist can help family members find a balance between their own needs and those of the patient.

Other conflicts may arise that require intervention. If a patient withdraws from some family members but not others, a therapist can anticipate the issues that may arise so that the patient's withdrawal is not misunderstood, becoming a basis for conflict. Both patients and family members may have difficulty saying what they mean to each other; therapists can interpret what patients and family members are trying to express. For many families, terminal illness can be a time of great closeness and sharing. It may be the only time when the family sets aside time to say what their lives within the family have meant.

The Management of Terminal Illness in Children

Working with terminally ill children is perhaps the most stressful of all terminal care. First, it is often the hardest kind of death to accept. Hospital staff typically serve only limited rotations in units with terminally ill children because they find the work so psychologically painful. Death in childhood can also be physically painful, which adds to the distress it causes. A common cause of childhood death is leukemia, which is not only painful in itself but is treated through a variety of stressful medical procedures, such as bone marrow transplants. Moreover, one must work not only with a confused and often frightened child but usually also with unhappy, frightened, and confused parents.

For these reasons, terminally ill children often receive even less straightforward information about their condition than do terminally ill adults. Their questions may go unanswered, or they and their parents may be led to falsely optimistic conclusions so that medical staff can avoid painful confrontations. To what extent is this a defensible policy? Precisely because they are children, it is easy to rationalize not giving children true information about their treatments and condition on the grounds that they will not understand it or that it will frighten them. However, it is clear that, just as is true for terminally ill adults, terminally ill children know more about their situation than they are given credit for (Spinetta, 1974, 1982). Children use cues from their treatments and from the people around them to infer what their condition must be. As their own physical condition deteriorates, they develop a conception of their own death and the realization that it may not be far off, as this exchange shows:

TOM: Jennifer died last night. I have the same thing. Don't I?

NURSE: But they are going to give you different medicines.

TOM: What happens when they run out? (Bluebond-Langner, 1977, p. 55)

It may be difficult to know what to tell a child. Unlike adults, children may not express their knowledge, concerns, or questions directly. They may communicate the knowledge that they will die only indirectly, as by wanting to have Christmas early so that they will be around for it. Or they may suddenly stop talking about their future plans:

> One child, who when first diagnosed said he wanted to be a doctor, became quite angry with his doctor when she tried to get him to submit to a procedure by explaining the procedure and telling him, "I thought you would understand, Sandy. You told me once you wanted to be a doctor." He screamed back at her, "I'm not going to be anything," and then threw an empty syringe at her. She said, "OK, Sandy." The nurse standing nearby said, "What are you going to be?" "A ghost," said Sandy, and turned over. (Bluebond-Langner, 1977, p. 59)

In some cases, death fantasies may be acted out by burying a doll or holding a funeral for a toy (Bluebond-Langner, 1977; Spinetta, 1974; Spinetta, Spinetta, Kung, & Schwartz, 1976). Parents who know that their child is aware of his or her likely death would do well to talk to their child about it. In one study, those who chose otherwise later regretted not having done so (Kreicbergs et al., 2004). Some of these problems may require counseling as well. Counseling with a terminally ill child can, in certain respects, proceed very much like counseling with a terminally ill adult. The therapist can take cues about what to say directly from the child, talking only when the child feels like talking and only about what the child wants to talk about.

In many cases, it is not just the terminally ill child who requires some kind of counseling but the family as well. Parents may blame themselves for the child's disease, and even in the best of cases, parents' fears may complicate the dying child's adjustment (DuHamel et al., 2004). The needs of other children may go relatively ignored, and those children may come to feel confused and resentful about their own position in the family. Parents may have needs for assistance in coping that are being ignored because of their child's needs (Meij et al., 2008). It may also be difficult for parents to get good information about the nature of their child's treatment and prognosis (Barbarin & Chesler, 1986). A therapist working with the family can ameliorate these difficulties.

ALTERNATIVES TO HOSPITAL CARE FOR THE TERMINALLY ILL

Hospital care for the terminally ill is palliative, emotionally wrenching, and demanding of personalized attention in ways that often go beyond the resources of the hospital. This has led to the development of treatment alternatives. As a result, two types of care have become increasingly popular: hospice care and home care.

Hospice Care

In recent decades, **hospice care** has emerged as a type of care for the dying. The idea behind hospice care is the acceptance of death in a positive manner, emphasizing the relief of suffering rather than the cure of illness. Hospice care is designed to provide palliative care and emotional support to dying patients and their family members.

In medieval Europe, a **hospice** was a place that provided care and comfort for travelers. In keeping with this original goal, hospice care is both a philosophy concerning a way of dying and a system of care for the terminally ill. Hospice care may be provided in the home, but it is also commonly provided in free-standing or hospital-affiliated units called hospices. Typically, painful or invasive therapies are discontinued. Instead, care is aimed toward managing symptoms, such as reducing pain and controlling nausea.

Most importantly, the patient's psychological comfort is stressed. Patients are encouraged to personalize their living areas as much as possible by bringing in their own familiar things. Thus, in institutional hospice care, each room may look very different, reflecting the personality and interests of its occupant. Patients also typically wear their own clothes and determine their own activities.

Hospice care is oriented toward improving a patient's social support system. Restrictions on visits from family or friends are removed as much as possible. Family may be encouraged to spend full days with the patient, to stay over in the hospice if possible, and to eat together with the patient. Staff are especially trained to interact with patients in a warm, emotionally caring

Hospice care, an alternative to hospital and home care for the terminally ill, is designed to provide personalized palliative treatment without the strains that home care can produce. This photograph shows a 73-year-old woman in a hospice, surrounded by photos of her family.

way. Usually, therapists are available—either on an individual basis or through family therapy—to deal with such problems as communication difficulties and depression. Some programs make discussion groups available to patients who wish to discuss their thoughts with others who are also facing death (Aiken & Marx, 1982; Young-Brockopp, 1982). Some hospices make use of volunteers who provide support. Examination of hospice records has revealed that patients who receive support from volunteers live significantly longer than those who do not (Herbst-Damm & Kulik, 2005). Yet, hospice care is currently underutilized by terminally ill patients (Gazelle, 2007).

When hospice care was first initiated, there was some concern that moving a patient to a facility that specialized in death—as hospices, in essence, do—would depress and upset both patients and family members. Such fears have largely proved groundless. Evaluations of hospice care suggest that it can provide palliative care on a par with that in hospitals—and more emotionally satisfying care for both patients and their families. However, there are sometimes problems attracting trained nursing and medical staff to such units, because palliative care is less technically challenging than other forms of medical care (Sorrentino, 1992).

Although hospices were originally developed to be facilities separate from hospitals, their success as a treatment model has led to their increasingly being incorporated into traditional hospitals. In addition, many hospice programs now involve home care, with residential hospice care as a backup option. Theoretically, this flexible program can meet all needs: Patients can remain home as long as the family members are able to manage it but receive professional care when the patients' needs exceed the families' abilities. Recent years have raised some cautions, however, as pressures on hospices to reduce costs have restricted even palliative care (Wright & Katz, 2007). This will be a trend to watch.

Home Care

Recent years have seen renewed interest in **home care** for dying patients. Home care appears to be the care of choice for most terminally ill patients (National Hospice and Palliative Care Organization, 2007). Because hospital costs have escalated so markedly, many people cannot afford hospitalization for terminal illness, particularly if dying is a long time coming. Also, some managed care programs do not fully cover hospital or residential hospice costs for some terminal illnesses.

Although home care would solve many logistical difficulties, the important question of quality of care arises. Can patients receive as competent care at home as in the hospital? Researchers believe that usually they can, provided that there is regular contact between medical personnel and family members and the family is adequately trained.

Psychological factors are increasingly raised as legitimate reasons for home care. In contrast to the mechanized and depersonalized environment of the hospital, the home environment is familiar and comfortable. The patient is surrounded by personal items and by loving family rather than by medical staff. The ability to make small decisions, such as what to wear or eat, can be maintained. The strongest psychological advantages of home care, then, are the opportunity to maintain a sense of control and the availability of social support.

Although home care is often easier on the patient psychologically, it can be very stressful for the family (Aneshensel, Pearlin, & Schuler, 1993). Even if the family is able to afford around-the-clock nursing, often at least one family member's energies must be devoted to the patient on an almost full-time basis. Given work schedules and other daily tasks, it may be difficult for any family member to do this. Such constant contact with the dying person is also stressful. Family members may be torn between wanting to keep the patient alive and wanting the patient's and their own suffering to end. Home care does give the family an opportunity to share their feelings and to be together at this important time. These benefits may well offset the stressors, and studies often find that families prefer home to hospital care.

■ PROBLEMS OF SURVIVORS

The death of a family member may be the most upsetting and dreaded event in a person's life. For many people, the death of a loved one is a more terrifying prospect than their own death or illness. Even when a death is anticipated and, on some level, actually wished for, it may be very hard for survivors to cope.

We have already discussed several methods of helping families prepare for death. But few such programs can really help the family prepare for life after the death. Nonetheless, it is often at this point that family members need the most help—and when they are less likely to get it.

The weeks just before the patient's death are often a period of frenzied activity. Visits to the hospital increase, preliminary legal or funeral preparations may be made,

Cultural Attitudes Toward Death

Each culture has its own way of coming to terms with death (Pickett, 1993; Stroebe, Gergen, Gergen, & Stroebe, 1992). Although in some cultures death is feared, in others it is seen as a normal part of life. Each culture, accordingly, has developed death-related ceremonies that reflect these cultural beliefs.

In traditional Japanese culture, death is regarded as a process of traveling from one world to another. When someone dies, that person goes to a purer country, a place often described as beautifully decorated with silver, gold, and other precious metals. The function of death rituals is to help the spirit make the journey. Thus, a series of rites and ceremonies takes place, aided by a minister, to achieve this end. The funeral events begin with a bedside service, in which the minister consoles the family. The next service is the *Yukan,* the bathing of the dead. An appreciation service follows the funeral, with food for all who have traveled long distances to attend. When the mourning period is over, a final party is given for friends and relatives as a way of bringing the mourners back into the community (Kübler-Ross, 1975).

The Andaman Islanders, in the Bay of Bengal, are one of many societies that respond to death with ritual weeping. Friends and relatives gather together with the mourners during the funeral to weep and show other signs of grief. This ritual of weeping is an expression of the bonds among individuals within the society and reaffirms these bonds when they are broken arbitrarily by death. Mourners are separated from the rest of society for a short time after the death; during this time, they become associated with the world of the dead. At the end of the mourning period, they are reunited with the rest of the community (Radcliffe-Brown, 1964).

In Hinduism, which is the main religion of India, death is not viewed as separate from life or as an ending. Rather, it is considered a continuous, integral part of life. Because Hindus believe in reincarnation, they believe that birth is followed by death and death by re-

birth; every moment one is born and dies again. Thus, death is like any transition in life. The Hindus teach that one should meet death with tranquillity and meditation. Death is regarded as the chief fact of life and a sign that all earthly desires are in vain. Only when an individual neither longs for nor fears death is that person capable of transcending both life and death and achieving nirvana—merging into unity with the Absolute. In so doing, the individual is freed from the fear of death, and death comes to be seen as a companion to life (Kübler-Ross, 1975).

What would people from another culture think about attitudes toward death in the United States if they were to witness our death practices? First, they would see that many deaths take place in the hospital without the presence of close relatives. Once death has occurred, the corpse is promptly removed without the help of the bereaved, who see it, if at all, only after morticians have made it acceptable for viewing. In some cases, the corpse is cremated shortly after death and is never again seen by the family. A paid organizer, often a director of a funeral home, takes over much of the direction of the viewing and burial rituals, deciding matters of protocol and the timing of services. In most subcultures within the United States, a time is set aside when the bereaved family accepts condolences from visiting sympathizers. A brief memorial service is then held, after which the bereaved and their friends may travel to the cemetery, where the corpse or ashes are buried. Typically, there are strong social pressures on the friends and relatives of the deceased to show little sign of emotion. The family is expected to establish this pattern, and other visitors are expected to follow suit. A friend or relative who is out of control emotionally will usually withdraw from the death ceremony or will be urged to do so by others. Following the ceremony, there may be a brief get-together at the home of the bereaved, after which the mourners return home (Huntington & Metcalf, 1979).

last-minute therapies may be initiated, or the patient may be moved to another facility. Family members are kept busy by the sheer amount of work that must be done. Even after the patient dies, there is typically a great deal of work. Although there are large cultural differences in reactions to death and the formalities that follow (Box 12.6), typically funeral arrangements must

be made, burial and tombstone details must be worked out, family members who have arrived for the services must be housed and fed, and well-intentioned friends who drop by to express their condolences must be talked to. Then, very abruptly, the activities cease. Visitors return home, the patient has been cremated or buried, and the survivor is left alone.

The Adult Survivor

During the period of terminal illness, the survivor's regular routine was probably replaced by illness-related activities. It may be hard to remember what one used to do before the illness began; even if one can remember, one may not feel much like doing it.

The survivor, then, is often left with lots of time and little to do but grieve. Moreover, the typical survivor is a widow in her 60s or older, who may have physical problems of her own. If she has lived in a traditional marriage, she may find herself with tasks, such as preparing her income tax return and making household repairs, that she has never had to do before. Survivors may be left with few resources to turn to. Increasingly, psychological researchers are turning their attention to the problems experienced by the bereaved (Stein, Folkman, Trabasso, & Richards, 1997; Weiss & Richards, 1997).

Grief, which is the psychological response to bereavement, is a feeling of hollowness, often marked by preoccupation with the image of the deceased person, expressions of hostility toward others, and guilt over the death. Bereaved people often show a restlessness and an inability to concentrate on activities, and they experience yearning for their loved one, as well as anger, depression, and other negative emotions, especially during the first 6 months (Maciejewski, Zhang, Block, & Prigerson, 2007). They may also experience adverse physical symptoms and health problems (Stroebe & Stroebe, 1987; Vahtera et al., 2006).

It may be difficult for outsiders to appreciate the degree of a survivor's grief. They may feel, especially if the death was a long time coming, that the survivor should be ready for it and thus show signs of recovery shortly after the death. Widows say that often, within a few weeks of their spouse's death, friends are urging them to pull out of their melancholy and get on with life. In some cases, the topic of remarriage is brought up within weeks after the death. However, normal grieving may go on for months, and a large percentage of widows and widowers are still deeply troubled by their spouse's death several years later (Silver & Wortman, 1980; Stroebe & Stroebe, 1987). Blaming health care providers for the death can complicate grief, but blaming the spouse's lifestyle reduces some of the symptoms of grieving (Carr, 2009).

Whether it is adaptive to grieve or to avoid prolonged grief is an important issue. In contrast to psychologists' usual caution that the avoidance of unpleasant emotion can be problematic, some evidence suggests that emotional avoidance (Bonanno, Keltner, Holen, & Horowitz, 1995) and positive appraisals (Stein et al., 1997) actually lead to better adjustment in the wake of a death. Bereaved adults who ruminate on their losses are less likely to have good social support, more likely to have higher levels of stress, and more likely to be depressed (Nolen-Hoeksema, McBride, & Larson, 1997).

The grief response appears to be more aggravated in men, in caregivers, and in those whose loss was sudden and unexpected (Aneshensel, Botticello, & Yamamoto-Mitani, 2004; Stroebe & Stroebe, 1987). Nonetheless, the majority of widows and widowers are resilient in response to their loss, especially if the partner's death had been long expected and they had had the opportunity to accept its inevitability (Bonanno et al., 2002). Although many women have short-term difficulties adjusting to widowhood (Vahtera et al., 2006), over the long term, the majority do well, with social support being a chief resource from which they draw (Wilcox et al., 2003). Among women who are depressed in widowhood, financial strain appears to be the biggest burden. For men, the strains associated with household management can lead to distress (Umberson, Wortman, & Kessler, 1992). Grief may be especially pronounced in mothers of children who have died (Li, Laursen, Precht, Olsen, & Mortensen, 2005). Grieving for a child may be complicated by depression (Meij et al., 2005).

As we will see in Chapter 14, the experience of bereavement can lead to adverse changes in immunologic functioning, increasing the risk of disease and even death (Janson, 1986; Osterweis, 1985; Stroebe & Stroebe, 1987). In addition, increases in alcohol and drug abuse and inability to work are common problems for survivors (Aiken & Marx, 1982). Programs designed to provide counseling to the bereaved can offset these adverse reactions (Aiken & Marx, 1982).

The Child Survivor

Explaining the death of a parent or sibling to a surviving child can be particularly difficult. As noted earlier, the child's understanding of death may be incomplete, and as a consequence, the child may keep expecting the dead person to return. Even if the child understands that the dead person is not going to return, he or she may not understand why. The child may believe either that the parent intended to leave or that the parent left because the child was "bad." It may take counseling to make the child see that this conclusion is not true.

Grief involves a feeling of hollowness, a preoccupation with the deceased person, and guilt over the death. Often, outsiders fail to appreciate the depth of a survivor's grief or the length of time it takes to get over the bereavement.

The death of a sibling raises particular complications, because many children have fervently wished, at one time or another, that a sibling were dead. When the sibling actually does die, the child may feel that he or she caused it. The likelihood that this problem will arise may be enhanced if the sibling was ill for some time before death. Very possibly, the surviving child did not get much attention during that time and may thus feel some temporary elation when the sibling is no longer around as a source of competition (Lindsay & McCarthy, 1974). As one child remarked on learning of his sibling's death, "Good. Now I can have all his toys" (Bluebond-Langner, 1977, p. 63). Such reactions are typically only temporary and may exacerbate the sorrow or guilt the child feels later on.

Consider this case:

Lars was seven when his sister died of leukemia. He was never told that she was sick and when she did die, he was sent away to a relative. After the funeral he returned home to find his sister gone and his parents in a state of grief. No explanation was offered and Lars was convinced he had done some thing that caused his sister's death. He carried this burden of guilt with him until he was fifteen. Academically, he had many problems. His math and reading remained at about the second-grade level. His parents were concerned and cooperative, but it was impossible for them to identify the problem. After leukemia was discussed in a health science class, Lars hesitantly told the teacher his story. Lars wanted to believe that he was not responsible for his sister's death, but he needed to hear it directly from his parents. A conference was set up, and with the support of his teacher, Lars told his parents his feelings of guilt. The parents were astonished. They had no idea their son felt any responsibility. Through many tears, they told him the entire story and tried to reassure him that in no way was he responsible. In fact, he had been a source of comfort and support to both his sister and his parents. (Spinetta, Spinetta, Kung, & Schwartz, 1976, p. 21)

In leading a child to cope with the death of a parent or a sibling, it is best not to wait until the death has actually occurred. Rather, the child should be prepared for the death, perhaps by drawing on the death of a pet or a flower to aid understanding (Bluebond-Langner, 1977). The child's questions about death should be answered as honestly as possible, but without unwanted detail. Providing only what is asked for when the timing is right is the best course.

Death Education

Some educators and researchers have maintained that one way to make surviving easier is to educate people about death earlier in their lives, before they have had much personal experience with it.

Because death has been a taboo topic, many people have misconceptions about it, including the idea that the dying wish to be left alone and not talk about their situation. Because of these concerns, some courses on dying, which may include volunteer work with dying patients, have been developed for college students. This approach is believed to eliminate myths and to promote realistic perceptions about what can be done to help the dying (Schulz, 1978). A potential problem with such courses is that they may attract the occasional suicidal student and provide unintended encouragement for self-destructive leanings. Accordingly, some instructors have recommended confronting such problems head-on, in the hopes that they can be forestalled.

Whether college students are the best and the only population that should receive death education is another concern. Unfortunately, organized means of educating people outside the university system are few, so college courses remain one of the more viable vehicles for death education. Yet a book about death and dying, *Tuesdays with Morrie* (Albom, 1997), was a best-seller for years, a fact that underscores how much people want to understand death. Moreover, causes of death, especially diseases with high mortality, dominate the news (Adelman & Verbrugge, 2000). At present, though, the news and a few books are nearly all there is to meet such needs. Through **death education,** it may be possible to develop realistic expectations, both about what modern medicine can achieve and about the kind of care the dying want and need. ●

SUMMARY

1. Causes of death vary over the life cycle. In infancy, congenital abnormalities and sudden infant death syndrome (SIDS) account for most deaths. From ages 1 to 15, the causes shift to accidents and childhood leukemia. In adolescence and young adulthood, death is often due to auto accidents, homicide, suicide, cancer, and AIDS. In adulthood, cancer and heart attacks are the most common causes of death. Death in old age is usually due to heart attacks, stroke, cancer, or physical degeneration.

2. Concepts of death change over the life cycle. In childhood, death is conceived of first as a great sleep and later as a ghostlike figure that takes a person away. Finally, death is seen as an irreversible biological stage. Many believe that middle age is the time when people first begin to come to terms with their own death.

3. Advancing disease raises many psychological issues, including treatment-related discomfort and decisions of whether to continue treatment. Increasingly, issues concerning the patient's directive to withhold extreme life-prolonging measures, assisted suicide, and euthanasia have been topics of concern in both medicine and law.

4. Patients' self-concepts must continually adapt in response to the progression of illness, change in appearance, energy level, control over physical processes, and degree of mental alertness. The patient may withdraw from family and friends as a result. Thus, issues of communication can be a focal point for intervention.

5. Kübler-Ross's theory of dying suggests that people go through stages, progressing through denial, anger, bargaining, depression, and finally acceptance. Research shows that patients do not necessarily go through these stages in sequence but that all these phenomena do describe reactions of dying people, to a degree.

6. Much of the responsibility for psychological management of terminal illness falls on medical staff. Medical staff can provide information, reassurance, and emotional support when others cannot.

7. Psychological counseling needs to be made available to terminally ill patients, because many people need a chance to develop a perspective on their lives. Developing methods for training therapists in clinical thanatology, then, is an educational priority. Family therapy may be needed to soothe the problems of the family and to help patient and family say goodbye to each other.

8. Counseling terminally ill children is especially important because both parents and children may be confused and frightened.

9. Hospice care and home care are alternatives to hospital care for the dying. Palliative and psychologically supportive care in the home or in a homelike environment can have beneficial psychological effects on dying patients and their survivors.

10. Grief is marked by a feeling of hollowness, preoccupation with an image of the deceased person, guilt over the death, expressions of hostility toward others, restlessness, and an inability to concentrate. Many people do not realize how long normal grieving takes.

KEY TERMS

clinical thanatology
curative care
death education
euthanasia
grief
home care

hospice
hospice care
infant mortality rate
living will
palliative care
premature death

stages of dying
sudden infant death syndrome (SIDS)
symbolic immortality
terminal care
thanatologists

CHAPTER 13

Heart Disease, Hypertension, Stroke, and Type II Diabetes

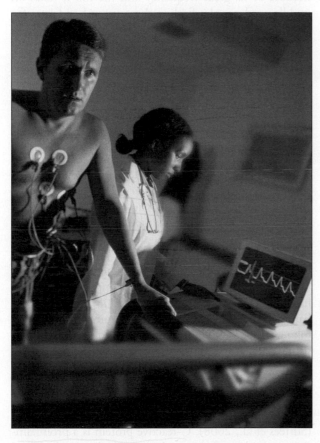

Andrea's father had a heart attack during her junior year in college. It was not entirely a surprise. He was overweight, suffered from hypertension, and had diabetes—all of which are risk factors for heart disease. Fortunately, the heart attack was a mild one, so, after a brief hospitalization, he returned home and began a program of cardiac rehabilitation.

Many aspects of his life required change. Although he had always had to watch his diet, dietary intervention now became especially important to his recovery. Previously, he had enjoyed watching sports from his armchair, but he now found that he had to take up physical exercise. And the cigarettes he had always enjoyed were out of the question. On weekends, Andrea called to make sure everything was okay.

First, her mother would get on the phone. "Your father is impossible, Andrea. He doesn't eat the things I fix for him, and he's not doing the exercise he's supposed to be doing. He stops after about 5 minutes. I think he's even sneaking a cigarette when he goes out to run errands."

Then Andrea's father would get on the phone. "Your mother is driving me crazy. It's like having a spy following me around all the time. I can't do anything without her getting on my case, constantly nagging me about my heart. My blood pressure's going up just having to deal with her."

Unfortunately, Andrea's parents' situation is not unusual. Adjustment to chronic disease is a difficult process, and one that often requires major changes in lifestyle that are very difficult to make.

In this chapter, we consider four major chronic disorders: heart disease, hypertension, stroke, and diabetes. All four involve the circulatory and/or metabolic system and often represent co-occurring disorders, especially in older adults. Moreover, due to their frequency, they affect large numbers of people. For example, 45% of American adults have hypertension, elevated cholesterol, or diabetes (Fryar, Hirsch, Eberhardt, Yoon, & Wright, 2010).

■ CORONARY HEART DISEASE

Coronary heart disease (CHD) is the number-one killer in the United States, accounting for more than one out of every five deaths (American Heart Association, 2009b). It was not a major cause of illness and death until the 20th century because, prior to that time, most people died of infectious diseases; most people did not live long enough to develop heart disease.

But CHD is also a disease of modernization, due at least in part to the alterations in diet and reductions in activity level that have accompanied modern life. Because of these factors, around the turn of the 20th century, the rate of CHD began to increase. Although it has recently begun to decline, it is estimated that in the United States, 1.2 million new cases are identified annually. One of the most significant aspects of CHD is that 32% of the deaths that occur each year are premature deaths; that is, they occur well before age 77 (American Heart Association, 2009b).

CHD is also a major chronic disease: Millions of Americans live with the diagnosis and symptoms. Because of its great frequency and the toll it takes on middle-aged people, finding the causes of and cure for heart disease has been a high priority of health research.

What Is CHD?

Coronary heart disease (CHD) is a general term that refers to illnesses caused by atherosclerosis, the narrowing of the coronary arteries, the vessels that supply the heart with blood (see Figure 13.1). As we saw in Chapter 2, when these vessels become narrowed or closed, the flow of oxygen and nourishment to the heart is partially or completely obstructed. Temporary shortages of oxygen and nourishment frequently cause pain, called angina pectoris, that radiates across the chest and arm. When severe deprivation occurs, a heart attack (myocardial infarction) can result.

Several factors are involved in the development of CHD (see Chapter 2). Research has implicated immune functioning (Kop & Gottdiener, 2005), especially inflammatory processes. A particular proinflammatory cytokine (IL-6) is thought to play a role in heart disease by stimulating processes that contribute to the buildup of atherosclerotic plaque (Suarez, 2003). Low-grade inflammation appears to underlie many, if not most, cases of cardiovascular disease. A strong predictor of heart disease is the level of C-reactive protein in the bloodstream (Surtees et al., 2008). C-reactive protein is a proinflammatory cytokine that is produced in the liver and released in the bloodstream in the presence of acute or chronic inflammation. Because inflammation can promote damage to the walls of the blood vessels, C-reactive protein is a prognostic sign that this damage may be occurring. A behavioral sign of inflammation activity is unexplained fatigue (Cho, Seeman, Bower, Kiefe, & Irwin, 2009).

Other risk factors for CHD include high blood pressure, diabetes, cigarette smoking, obesity, high serum cholesterol level, and low levels of physical activity (American Heart Association, 2004b). Exposure to air

FIGURE 13.1 | Atherosclerosis   The figure shows a normal artery with normal blood flow (figure A) and an artery containing plaque buildup (figure B).   (*Source:* National Heart, Lung, and Blood Institute, 2010a)

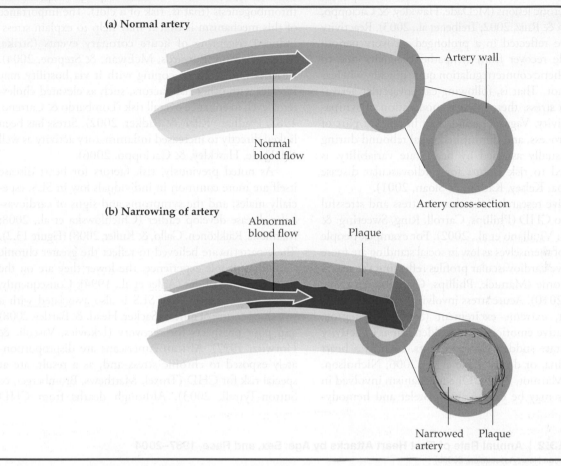

(a) Normal artery

Artery wall

Normal blood flow

Artery cross-section

(b) Narrowing of artery

Abnormal blood flow

Plaque

Narrowed   Plaque
artery

pollution is a recently identified contributing factor (K. A. Miller et al., 2007). Identifying patients with **metabolic syndrome** also helps predict heart attacks. Metabolic syndrome is diagnosed when a person has three or more of the following problems: obesity centered around the waist; high blood pressure; low levels of HDL, the so-called good cholesterol; difficulty metabolizing blood sugar, an indicator of risk for diabetes; and high levels of triglycerides, which are related to bad cholesterol. High cardiovascular reactivity may also be a component of this cluster (Waldstein & Burns, 2003). Routine screening for metabolic syndrome and inflammation (by assessing C-reactive protein) is recommended for most middle-aged adults.

Heart disease runs in families. A person may inherit a genetically-based predisposition to cardiovascular reactivity, which may emerge early in life (Yamada et al., 2002) and which is exacerbated by low socioeconomic status (SES) and a harsh (cold, nonnurturant, neglectful, and/or conflictual) family environment in childhood (Lehman, Taylor, Kiefe, & Seeman, 2005). Stress exposure and an inability to develop strong relationships may explain why these factors are related to early cardiovascular risk (Gallo & Matthews, 2006; Low, Salomon, & Matthews, 2009). Even in young adolescents, especially those low in SES, risk factors for heart disease begin to cluster by age 14 (Goodman, McEwen, Huang, Dolan, & Adler, 2005; Lawlor et al., 2005). However, all known risk factors together account for less than half of all newly diagnosed cases of CHD; accordingly, a number of risk factors remain to be identified.

The Role of Stress

Cardiovascular reactivity contributes to the development of CHD in part by damaging endothelial cells, which facilitates the deposit of lipids, increases inflammation, and ultimately contributes to the development of atherosclerotic lesions (McDade, Hawkley, & Cacioppo, 2006; Smith & Ruiz, 2002; Treiber et al., 2003). Reactivity may also be reflected in a prolonged recovery period; some people recover from sympathetic activity due to parasympathetic counterregulation quite quickly, whereas others do not. That is, following cardiovascular activation due to stress, there is vagal modulation of sympathetic reactivity. Vagal rebound is an important part of the stress process, and diminished vagal rebound during recovery, usually assessed by heart rate variability, is strongly tied to risk factors for cardiovascular disease (Mezzacappa, Kelsey, Katkin, & Sloan, 2001).

Extensive research links chronic stress and stressful life events to CHD (Phillips, Carroll, Ring, Sweeting, & West, 2005; Vitaliano et al., 2002). For example, people who think of themselves as low in social standing are more likely to have cardiovascular profiles reflecting the metabolic syndrome (Manuck, Phillips, Gianaros, Flory, & Muldoon, 2010). Acute stress involving emotional pressure, anger, extreme excitement (Strike & Steptoe, 2005), negative emotions, and sudden bursts of activity can precipitate sudden clinical events, such as a heart attack, angina, or death (Lane et al., 2006; Nicholson, Fuhrer, & Marmot, 2005). One mechanism involved in this process may be exaggerated platelet and hemodynamic reactivity associated with coronary artery disease, which may, in turn, contribute to plaque rupture and thrombogenesis (that is, risk of a clot). The importance of this mechanism is that it may help to explain stress-induced triggering of acute coronary events (Strike, Magid, Brydon, Edwards, McEwan, & Steptoe, 2004). Reactivity to stress or coping with it via hostility may interact with other risk factors, such as elevated cholesterol level, to enhance overall risk (Lombardo & Carreno, 1987; Pradhan, Rifai, & Ridker, 2002). Stress has been linked directly to increased inflammatory activity as well (McDade, Hawkley, & Cacioppo, 2006).

As noted previously, risk factors for heart disease itself are more common in individuals low in SES, especially males, and the symptoms and signs of cardiovascular disease develop earlier (Chichlowska et al., 2008; Matthews, Räikkönen, Gallo, & Kuller, 2008) (Figure 13.2). These patterns are believed to reflect the greater chronic stress that people experience, the lower they are on the socioeconomic ladder (Adler et al., 1994). Consequently, as one might expect, low SES is also associated with a worsened course of illness (Sacker, Head, & Bartley, 2008) and poor prospects for recovery (Ickovics, Viscoli, & Horwitz, 1997). African Americans are disproportionately exposed to chronic stress and, as a result, are at special risk for CHD (Troxel, Matthews, Bromberger, & Sutton-Tyrrell, 2003). Although deaths from CHD

FIGURE 13.2 | Annual Rate of First Heart Attacks by Age, Sex, and Race, 1987–2004
(*Source:* American Heart Association, 2009b)

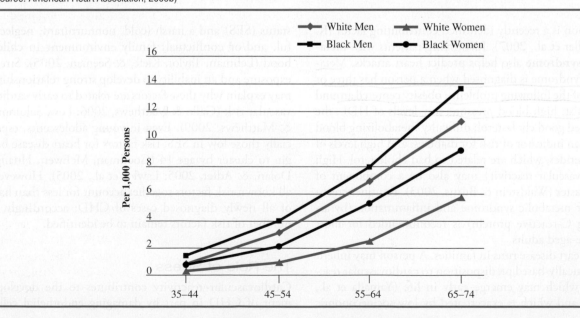

among both African Americans and Whites have decreased in recent years, the racial gap has actually increased (Zheng, Croft, Labarthe, Williams, & Mensah, 2001).

As already noted, CHD is a disease of modernization and industrialization. As we saw in Chapter 6, occupational stress has been related to its incidence (Repetti, 1993a). Research on CHD and the workplace reveals that several job factors are reliably related to increased risk: job strain, especially the combination of high work demands and low control; a discrepancy between educational level and occupation; low job security; little social support at work; high work pressure; and a vigilant coping strategy. Although men with low medical risk may not develop CHD in response to these factors, among men with higher initial risk, these job factors enhance risk of CHD (Siegrist, Peter, Runge, Cremer, & Seidel, 1990; see also Falk, Hanson, Isaacsson, & Ostergren, 1992).

More recently, research has suggested that an imbalance between control and demands in daily life more generally (not only at work) is a risk for atherosclerosis. That is, people whose lives are characterized by high levels of demands coupled with low levels of control both in and outside the workplace are at higher risk for atherosclerosis (Kamarck et al., 2004; Kamarck, Muldoon, Shiffman, & Sutton-Tyrrell, 2007).

Stress due to social instability may also be linked to higher rates of CHD. Migrants have a higher incidence of CHD than do geographically stable individuals, and acculturation to Western society is a risk factor for high blood pressure; distress associated with cultural change accounts for increases in risk factors for CHD (Steffen, Smith, Larson, & Butler, 2006). People who are occupationally, residentially, or socially mobile in a given culture have a higher frequency of CHD than do those who are less mobile (Kasl & Berkman, 1983). Generally, urban and industrialized countries have a higher incidence of CHD than do underdeveloped countries. Poor social support and social isolation are also associated with elevated risk for CHD (Grant, Hamer, & Steptoe, 2009; Kop et al., 2005).

Women and CHD

CHD is the leading killer of women in the United States and most other developed countries (Facts of Life, February 2002). Although the onset of CHD typically occurs about 10 years later in women than men, more women die of heart disease than men do. One in 10 women age 45–64 has some form of heart disease, a rate

that increases to 1 in 4 over the age of 65. In 2005, it accounted for 53% of all female deaths (American Heart Association, 2009b).

Because studies of risk factors, diagnosis, prognosis, and rehabilitation have focused heavily on men, less is known about patterns of women's heart disease (Burell & Granlund, 2002). This discrepancy may occur, in part, because premature death from cardiovascular disease does not occur as often for women as for men (Figure 13.3). Although heart disease typically occurs later for women, it is more dangerous when it does occur. Women have a 50% chance of dying from a first heart attack, compared to 30% for men. Of those who survive their heart attack, 38% will die within a year, compared to 25% of men. Forty-six percent of women are disabled by heart failure after a heart attack, compared to only 22% of men. And young women under the age of 50 who experience a heart attack may never have been diagnosed at all (Reitman, 2003, July 7).

Women seem to be protected at younger ages against coronary disease relative to men. One reason may be their higher levels of high-density lipoprotein (HDL), which appears to be linked to premenopausal women's higher levels of estrogen. Estrogen also diminishes sympathetic nervous system arousal, which may add to the protective effect against heart disease seen in women (Matthews & Rodin, 1992). In response to stress, premenopausal women show smaller increases in blood pressure, neuroendocrine, and some metabolic responses than do men and older women.

Women experience a higher risk of cardiovascular disease after menopause. They typically gain weight during menopause, and this weight gain may partly explain their enhanced risk; increases in blood pressure, cholesterol, and triglycerides may also contribute to their rising risk for CHD (Wing, Matthews, Kuller, Meilahn, & Plantinga, 1991). However, the belief that estrogen replacement therapy following menopause would keep rates of CHD among women low has proven to be groundless; the therapy may actually increase the risk for heart disease. Consequently, the relation of estrogen to heart disease remains unclear.

The fact that there is so little research on women and CHD means that less information about women's heart disease is in the media, leaving women misinformed about their health risks (Wilcox & Stefanick, 1999). Women are less likely to receive counseling about heart disease than men or to learn about the benefits of exercise, nutrition, and weight reduction in preventing heart disease (Stewart, Abbey, Shnek, Irvine, & Grace,

FIGURE 13.3 | Death Rates for Heart Disease, by Age, 2005   (*Source:* National Center for Health Statistics, 2008)

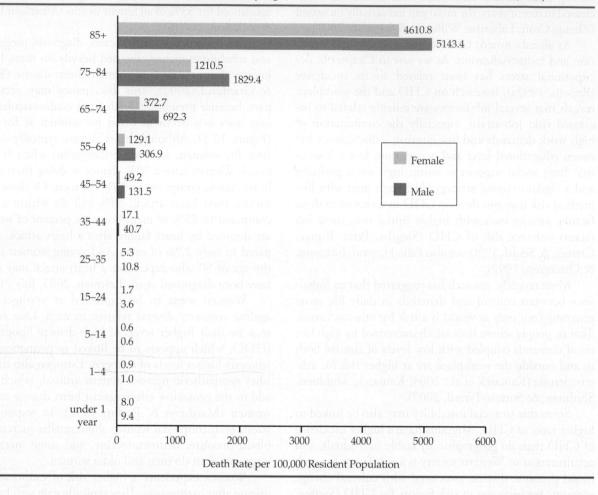

2004). They are also less likely to receive risk factor interventions for heart disease (Facts of Life, February 2002). They are significantly less likely than men to receive and use drugs for the treatment of heart disease including aspirin, beta blockers, and lipid-lowering agents (Vittinghoff et al., 2003), and they are significantly more likely not to be diagnosed or to be misdiagnosed (Chiaramonte & Friend, 2006).

What research there is suggests that CHD risk factors for women are relatively similar to those for men. As is true for men, women who are more physically active, who get regular exercise, and who have low body fat, low cholesterol and triglyceride levels (Lewis et al., 2009; Owens, Matthews, Wing, & Kuller, 1990) are less likely to develop heart disease. As is also true for men, social support, especially in the marriage, is associated with less advanced disease in women (Gallo, Troxel, Kuller,

et al., 2003). Hostility is associated with poor cardiovascular recovery from stress (Neumann, Waldstein, Sollers, Thayer, & Sorkin, 2004) and poor prognosis (Olson et al., 2005), as is pessimism (Matthews, Räikkönen, Sutton-Tyrrell, & Kuller, 2004). Anger and metabolic syndrome predict progression of atherosclerosis in women (Räikkönen et al., 2004). Among women, depression, especially when coupled with anxiety, and loneliness are risk factors for metabolic syndrome and for heart disease (Everson-Rose et al., 2009; Kinder, Carnethon, Palaniappan, King, & Fortmann, 2004; Rutledge et al., 2006; Rutledge et al., 2009; Thurston & Kubzansky, 2009).

Low SES is associated with greater early-stage atherosclerosis in women, as it is in men (Gallo, Matthews, Kuller, Sutton-Tyrrell, & Edmundowicz, 2001). Some of the same job-related factors that predict CHD in men

BOX 13.1

Can Male and Female Qualities Affect Your Health?

Researchers recently have begun to realize that there may be personality qualities associated with masculine or feminine construals of the world that may be differentially associated with health risks. Research has especially focused on *agency,* which is a focus on the self, versus *communion,* which is a focus on others, and on *unmitigated communion,* which is an extreme focus on others to the exclusion of the self. Men typically score higher than women do on measures of agency. Agency has been associated with good physical and mental health outcomes in several studies (Helgeson,

1993; Helgeson & Fritz, 1999; Helgeson & Lepore, 1997), and it is also associated with lower psychological distress.

Communion, a focus on other people in relationships, reflects a positive caring orientation to others, and it is typically higher in women than in men. It has few relations to mental and physical health outcomes. Unmitigated communion, however, exemplified in a self-sacrificing individual who fails to focus on her own needs, is reliably associated with poorer mental and physical health outcomes (Fritz, 2000; Helgeson & Fritz, 1999).

---

may do so for women as well (Lallukka et al., 2006). Employment as a clerical worker as opposed to a white-collar worker enhances risk for coronary artery disease in women (Gallo, Troxel, Matthews, et al., 2003). (See Box 13.1 for a discussion of other factors that may affect men's and women's heart disease rates.)

Much of what we have learned about women's heart disease has come from long-term clinical studies, such as the Nurses' Health Study. The Nurses' Health Study began in 1976 when more than 120,000 female nurses age 30–55 agreed to participate in a long-term study of medical history and lifestyle (Nurses' Health Study, 2004). Over the past 25 years, the expected incidence of heart disease in this sample has not appeared—in large part because more older women have stopped smoking and have changed their diets in healthy directions (Stoney, Owens, Guzick, & Matthews, 1997). Indeed, among women who adhered to recommended guidelines involving diet, exercise, and abstinence from smoking, there is a very low risk of CHD (Stampfer, Hu, Manson, Rimm, & Willett, 2000). As levels of obesity increase in this population, the incidence of heart disease may rise again (Hu et al., 2000), but at present, the study is testimony to the payoffs of good health habits.

Cardiovascular Reactivity, Personality, and CHD

Negative emotions, including anger and hostility, are implicated as risk factors for metabolic syndrome (Goldbacher & Matthews, 2007) and for CHD (Bleil, Gianaros, Jennings, Flory, & Manuck, 2008; Schum, Jorgensen, Verhaeghen, Sauro, & Thibodeau, 2003). Experiencing and expressing anger not only increases the risk of heart disease (Gallacher et al., 1999) but also predicts poor

likelihood of survival (Boyle et al., 2004) and acts as a potential trigger for heart attacks (Moller et al., 1999). As we will see, anger has also been implicated in hypertension and to a lesser degree in stroke and diabetes, suggesting that it may be a general risk factor for CHD, cardiovascular disease, and their complications. Hostility has been tied to higher levels of proinflammatory cytokines and to metabolic syndrome, which may explain its relation to CHD (Niaura et al., 2002).

A particular type of hostility is especially implicated—namely, cynical hostility, characterized by suspiciousness, resentment, frequent anger, antagonism, and distrust of others. People who have negative beliefs about others, such as the perception that other people are being antagonistic or threatening, are often highly verbally aggressive and exhibit subtly antagonistic behavior. People who are high in cynical hostility may have difficulty extracting social support from others, and they may fail to make effective use of available social support (Box 13.2). They also have more conflict with others, more negative affect, and more resulting sleep disturbance, which may further contribute to their heightened risk (Brissette & Cohen, 2002). Hostility combined with defensiveness may be particularly problematic for adverse cardiovascular changes (Helmers & Krantz, 1996).

Who's Hostile?

Overall, men show higher hostility, which may partially explain their heightened risk for CHD, relative to women (Matthews, Owens, Allen, & Stoney, 1992). Higher hostility is found among non-Whites and those of lower SES (Barefoot, 1992; Siegman, Townsend, Civelek, & Blumenthal, 2000). Hostility can be reliably measured at a young age and shows considerable stability among boys but not girls (Woodall & Matthews, 1993).

BOX 13.2

Hostility and Cardiovascular Disease

Research has implicated cynical hostility as a psychological culprit in the development of CVD. Many studies have employed measures of hostility to look at this association. Here are some sample statements of cynical hostility.

1. I don't matter much to other people.

2. People in charge often don't really know what they are doing.

3. Most people lie to get ahead in life.

4. People look at me like I'm incompetent.

5. Many of my friends irritate me with the things they do.

6. People who tell me what to do frequently know less than I do.

7. I trust no one; life is easier that way.

8. People who are happy most of the time rub me the wrong way.

9. I am often dissatisfied with others.

10. People often misinterpret my actions.

Developmental Antecedents Hostility reflects an oppositional orientation toward people that develops in childhood, stemming from feelings of insecurity about oneself and negative feelings toward others (Houston & Vavak, 1991). Certain child-rearing practices may foster hostility—specifically, parental interference, punitiveness, lack of acceptance, conflict, or abuse. Family environments that are nonsupportive, unaccepting, and filled with conflict promote the development of hostility in sons (Matthews, Woodall, Kenyon, & Jacob, 1996), and early hostility is related to early risk factors for later cardiovascular disease (Matthews, Woodall, & Allen, 1993). Hostility runs in families, and both genetic and environmental factors appear to be implicated (Weidner et al., 2000). Hyperactivity in childhood may also predict adult risk for cardiovascular disease (Keltikangas-Järvinen et al., 2006).

Expressing Versus Harboring Hostility Is hostility lethal as a psychological state or only in its expression? Research suggests that the expression of hostile emotions, such as anger and cynicism, may be more reliably associated with higher cardiovascular reactivity than is the state of anger or hostility (Siegman & Snow, 1997). For example, among men low in SES, the overt behavioral expression of anger is related to CHD incidence, but trait anger, or the experience of anger without expressing it, bears no relationship (Mendes de Leon, 1992). Although anger suppression and hostile attitudes have been related to atherosclerosis in women (Matthews, Owen, Kuller, Sutton-Tyrrell, & Jansen-McWilliams, 1998), the relation between hostile style and enhanced cardiovascular reactivity to stress is not as reliable for women as for men (Davidson, Hall, & MacGregor, 1996; Engebretson & Matthews, 1992).

Hostility and Social Relationships Hostile people have more interpersonal conflict in their lives and less social support, and this fallout may also contribute to their risk for disease. Their reactivity to stress seems especially to be engaged during these episodes of interpersonal conflict. For example, in one study, 60 couples participated in a discussion under conditions of high or low threat of evaluation by others while they were either agreeing or disagreeing with each other. Husbands who were high in hostility showed a greater blood pressure reactivity in response to stressful marital interaction in response to threat; the same relationship was not found for wives (Smith & Gallo, 1999; see also Newton & Sanford, 2003).

Hostile people may produce or seek out more stressful interpersonal encounters in their daily lives and, at the same time, undermine the effectiveness of their social support network (Allen, Markovitz, Jacobs, & Knox, 2001; Holt-Lunstad, Smith, & Uchino, 2008). Researchers are uncertain whether the enhanced CHD risk of hostile people is caused by the deficits in social support that hostility produces, by the hostile anger itself, or by the underlying cardiovascular reactivity that hostility may reflect. Hostile people may also ruminate on the causes of their anger and thereby turn acutely stressful events into chronic stress (Fernandez et al., 2010).

Hostility and Reactivity Some health psychologists now suspect that hostility is, at least in part, a social manifestation of cardiovascular reactivity. For example, cardiovascular reactivity in social situations explains the relation between hostility and the development of CHD (Guyll & Contrada, 1998). That is, when a hostile person is provoked in interpersonal situations, the hostility-hyperreactivity relation is seen (Suls & Wan, 1993).

Chronically hostile people show more pronounced physiological reactions in response to interpersonal stressors (Guyll & Contrada, 1998).

Hostile people exhibit a weak antagonistic response to sympathetic activity in response to stress, suggesting that their physiological reactivity not only is greater initially but also may last longer (Fukudo et al., 1992; Nelson et al., 2005). In response to provocation, hostile people have larger and longer-lasting blood pressure responses to anger-arousing situations (Fredrickson et al., 2000; Suarez et al., 1997). When coupled with anger and depression, hostility predicts high levels of C-reactive protein (Suarez, 2004).

The fact that hostility may reflect underlying tendencies toward cardiovascular reactivity in stressful circumstances does not undermine or deny the importance of childhood environment in the development of hostility or the significance of the social environment in eliciting it. For example, to the extent that hostility reflects a genetically based underlying physiological reactivity, parents and children predisposed to reactivity may create and respond to the family environment differently. For reactivity to assume the form of hostility, particular environmental circumstances—such as the parental child-rearing practices noted earlier or the interpersonal conflictive stressful circumstances that evoke hostile behavior—may need to be in place. Consequently, the reactivity-hostility relationship may be thought of as a biopsychosocial process.

Mechanisms Linking Reactivity and Psychological Factors   How might greater physiological and psychological reactivity in conflictive situations promote heart disease (Lovallo & Gerin, 2003)? In some people, stress causes vasorestriction in peripheral areas of the heart and at the same time accelerates heart rate. Thus, these individuals attempt to transfer more and more blood through ever-shrinking vessels. Presumably, this process produces wear and tear on the coronary arteries, which, in turn, produces atherosclerotic lesions. Blood pressure variability may have adverse effects on the endothelial tissue of the coronary arteries and may promote plaque formation (Sloan, Shapiro, Bagiella, Myers, & Gorman, 1999).

Catecholamines exert a direct chemical effect on blood vessels. The rise and fall of catecholamine levels, as may occur in chronic or recurrent exposure to stress, prompt continual changes in blood pressure that undermine the resilience of the vessels. Whether the effect of the catecholamines on the endothelial cells that main-

tain the integrity of the vessels is a mechanism that links psychosocial factors to CHD is not yet known (Harris & Matthews, 2004). Sympathetic activation also causes lipids to be shunted into the bloodstream, another possible contributor to atherosclerosis. Low levels of tonic vagal cardiac control impede recovery from stress and act as another mechanism increasing the risk of cardiovascular disease (Mezzacappa, Kelsey, Katkin, & Sloan, 2001). Hostility is also related to increased lipid profiles (Richards, Hof, & Alvarenga, 2000) and increased platelet activation in CHD patients, which can precipitate secondary heart disease events (Markovitz, 1998). Stress can contribute to increased migration and recruitment of immune cells to sites of infection and inflammation. This increase in leukocyte trafficking and consequent increase in inflammatory activity contributes to endothelial damage and the buildup of plaque (Redwine, Snow, Mills, & Irwin, 2003).

Hostile individuals may engage in high-risk health behaviors that enhance CHD risk. Higher hostility is associated with more caffeine consumption, higher weight, higher lipid levels, smoking, greater alcohol consumption, and hypertension (Greene, Houston, & Holleran, 1995; Lipkus, Barefoot, Williams, & Siegler, 1994; Siegler, Peterson, Barefoot, & Williams, 1992). Expressed hostility has also been related to higher total cholesterol and higher low-density lipoprotein (LDL) in both men and women (Dujovne & Houston, 1991). Further, hostile people are less likely to adhere to CHD interventions (Christensen, Wiebe, & Lawton, 1997). Hostility may be a step on the way to depression, to which we next turn (Stewart, Fitzgerald, & Kamarck, 2010).

Depression and CHD

There is also a well-established role for depression in the development, progression, and mortality from CHD, so much so that it is now generally recommended that patients at high risk be assessed and, if necessary, treated for depression (Carney et al., 2009; Dickens et al., 2008; Herbst, Pietrzak, Wagner, White, & Petry, 2007; Lett et al., 2007). As one newspaper headline put it, a life of quiet desperation is as dangerous as smoking. Depression is not a psychological by-product of other risk factors for CHD but an independent risk factor in its own right, and it appears to be environmentally rather than genetically based (Kronish, Rieckmann, Schwartz, Schwartz, & Davidson, 2009). The risk that depression poses with respect to heart disease is greater than that

Depression is a risk factor for CHD, even in monkeys.

posed by secondhand smoke. Even depressed monkeys have an elevated risk for CHD (Shively et al., 2008).

Research also supports a strong link between depressive symptoms and metabolic syndrome (Goldbacher, Bromberger, & Matthews, 2009), between depression and inflammation (Brummett et al., 2010; Elovainio, Aalto, et al., 2009), between depression and cardiovascular disease (Elovainio et al., 2005), between depression and the likelihood of a heart attack (Pratt et al., 1996), and between depression and heart failure among the elderly (S. A. Williams et al., 2002). This additional risk is not explained by health behaviors, social isolation, or work characteristics; and this relation is stronger in men than in women (Stansfeld, Fuhrer, Shipley, & Marmot, 2002). The exhaustion and depression characteristic of the phase just before an acute coronary event is thought by some to represent a reactivation of latent viruses and a concomitant inflammation of coronary vessels. These somatic, rather than emotional, markers of depression may be especially strongly related to adverse changes in cardiovascular risk factors (Bosch et al., 2009).

Assessing whether someone is depressed before surgery may represent valuable information. Symptoms of depression before coronary artery bypass graft surgery is an important predictor of long-term mortality (Burg, Benedetto, Rosenberg, & Soufer, 2003), and negative emotions before and after surgery predict long-term quality of life over time (Tully, Baker, Turnbull, Winefield, & Knight, 2009).

Depression may exert its adverse effects through several routes: elevated heart rate, low heart rate variability, low cardiovascular reactivity during stress, heightened inflammation, and delayed recovery following elevations in heart rate, as due to exercise, for example (Howren, Lamkin, & Suls, 2009; Hughes et al., 2008; Ohira et al., 2008; Salomon, Clift, Karlsdóttir, & Rottenberg, 2009; York et al., 2007).

Inflammatory processes appear to explain the relation of depression to heart failure as well (Pasic, Levy, & Sullivan, 2003). Depressive symptoms are also associated with indicators of metabolic syndrome, which may represent a related pathway to disease (McCaffrey, Niaura, Todaro, Swann, & Carmelli, 2003). In addition, heart rate turbulence may contribute to the poor survival of depressed patients following a heart attack (Carney et al., 2007).

Treatment of depression may improve the prospects of long-term recovery from heart attack. Depression is typically treated with serotonin reuptake inhibitors, such as Prozac, which help prevent serotonin from attaching to receptors (Bruce & Musselman, 2005). When the receptors in the bloodstream are blocked, it may reduce the formation of clots by preventing the aggregation of platelets in the arteries (Schins, Honig, Crijns, Baur, & Hamulyak, 2003). Essentially, antidepressants may act as blood thinners (Gupta, 2002, August 26). Moreover, a recent study found that treatment for depression reduced inflammation (Thornton, Andersen, Schuler, & Carson, 2009). Nonetheless, depression remains an underdiagnosed and untreated contributor to CHD morbidity and mortality (Grace et al., 2005).

Other Psychosocial Risk Factors and CHD

Vigilant coping—that is, chronically searching the environment for potential threats—has also been associated with risk factors for heart disease (Gump & Matthews, 1998). Anxiety has been implicated in a worsened course of illness and in sudden cardiac death, perhaps because anxiety may reduce vagal control of heart rate (Phillips et al., 2009; Székely et al., 2007). A composite of depression, anxiety, hostility, and anger may predict CHD better than each factor in isolation (Boyle, Michalek, & Suarez, 2006), suggesting that negative affectivity (see Chapter 7) is a broad general risk factor for CHD (Suls & Bunde, 2005). Tension and repressive coping have been found to predict CHD and mortality as well

(Denollet, Martens, Nyklícek, Conraads, & de Gelder, 2008; Eaker et al., 2005).

Helplessness, pessimism, and a tendency to ruminate over problems may also exacerbate CHD risk (Kubzansky, Davidson, & Rozanski, 2005; Gerin, Davidson, Christenfeld, Goyal, & Schwartz, 2006). The increasing evidence of comorbid psychiatric disorders among patients with CHD adds urgency to the task of exploring their role in the disease and its treatment (Bankier, Januzzi, & Littman, 2004; Martens, Smith, & Denollet, 2007).

Investigators have related vital exhaustion, a mental state characterized by extreme fatigue, feelings of being dejected or defeated, and enhanced irritability to cardiovascular disease (Cheung et al., 2009); vital exhaustion, in combination with other risk factors, predicts the likelihood of a heart attack (Bages, Appels, & Falger, 1999) and of a second heart attack after initial recovery (Kop, Appels, Mendes de Leon, de Swart, & Bar, 1994).

As we saw earlier, hostility can interfere with the ability to get social support. Social isolation in its own right confers increased risk for CHD, as does chronic interpersonal conflict (Smith & Ruiz, 2002). Unchecked inflammatory processes may account for these findings (Wirtz et al., 2003). The tendency to experience negative emotions and to inhibit their expression in interpersonal situations (sometimes referred to as Type D [distressed] personality; see Chapter 7) may be a particularly toxic combination with respect to CHD (Denollet, Pedersen, Vrints, & Conraads, 2006; Pelle et al., 2008; Williams, O'Carroll, & O'Connor, 2008). These effects may be explained by multiple factors, including poor regulation of the HPA axis (Molloy, Perkins-Porras, Strike, & Steptoe, 2008) and by poor health behaviors (Williams, O'Carroll, et al., 2008).

On the protective side, positive emotions, emotional vitality, and optimism appear to protect against depressive symptoms in heart disease (Kubzansky, Sparrow, Vokonas, & Kawachi, 2001), risk factors for CHD (e.g., Gallo, Espinosa de los Monteros, Ferent, Urbina, & Talavera, 2007), and the development of CHD itself (Bhattacharyya, Whitehead, Rakhit, & Steptoe, 2008; Kubzansky & Thurston, 2007).

Overall, there is still much to be learned about individual, environmental, and social factors that contribute to CHD, and especially how they differ between the sexes and races. We have considerable knowledge about White men, somewhat less about Black men, relatively little about women in general, and very little about Black women. These differences are a high priority for future research. (See Box 13.3 for a discussion of the role that the Internet is increasingly playing concerning information about cardiovascular diseases.)

Modification of CHD Risk-Related Behavior

In keeping with the general shift toward prevention, interventions have increasingly focused on those at risk for heart disease. These include preventive dietary interventions, programs to help people stop smoking, and exercise.

Interventions may be targeted to particular windows of vulnerability, during which time educational interventions to help people control their risk factors may be especially helpful. For example, women's risk for heart disease increases after menopause, so targeting diet and exercise interventions to this high-risk group is a promising strategy (Simkin-Silverman et al., 1995).

Modifying Hostility
As hostility is so clearly implicated in the development of risk for coronary heart disease, would modifying hostility reduce risk? Although a definitive answer is still under investigation, preliminary research suggests that the answer may be no. An intervention that targeted hostility found no effects on cardiovascular risk factors, suggesting that hostility may be a symptom of heart disease rather than a route to heart disease (Sloan et al., 2010).

Management of Heart Disease

Approximately 935,000 individuals suffer a heart attack each year in the United States. Of these, more than 400,000 die before reaching the hospital or while in the emergency room (American Heart Association, 2009b). Despite these dire statistics, hospital admissions for myocardial infarction have declined (Winslow, 2010, April 6), and quality of care given to patients suffering from acute myocardial infarction has improved steadily (Williams, Schmaltz, Morton, Koss, & Loeb, 2005), with the result that the number of heart attack deaths has been sharply lower in recent decades (Maugh, 2007, May 2).

The Role of Delay
One of the reasons for high rates of mortality and disability following heart attacks is that patients often delay several hours or even days before seeking treatment. Some patients are unable to face the fact that they have had a heart attack. Others interpret the symptoms as more mild disorders, such as gastric distress, and treat themselves. People who believe

BOX 13.3

Coronary Heart Disease and the Internet

The computer age has made it increasingly possible to improve the process of diagnosis and treatment of heart disease. Over many years, databases have been painstakingly constructed as physicians have provided details of thousands of cases of people with CHD. Duke University, for example, has a data bank that contains detailed information on thousands of heart attack patients, including age, family history, and enzyme levels, that, among other things, can be used to project the kind of treatment a patient should receive and generate a prediction of how that patient will respond (Ramos, 1996). From this database, practitioners and researchers get a much clearer picture of the factors that predict heart attacks and how risk factors can be identified early and treated most effectively.

In addition, computer data banks and the Internet also provide access to the most current information about advances in the diagnosis and treatment of CHD, greatly increasing the chances that every patient can receive the best possible treatment.

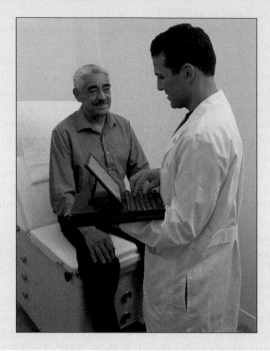

their symptoms are caused by stress and accompanying negative emotions delay longer (Perkins-Porras, Whitehead, Strike, & Steptoe, 2008). Depression seems to lead to delay as well (Bunde & Martin, 2006).

Older patients and African American heart attack victims appear to delay longer, as do patients who have consulted with a physician or engaged in self-treatment for their symptoms. Experiencing the attack during the daytime, as well as having a family member present, enhances delay, perhaps because the environment is more distracting under these circumstances. Surprisingly, too, a history of angina or diabetes actually increases, rather than decreases, delay (Dracup & Moser, 1991).

One of the psychosocial issues raised by heart attack, then, is how to improve treatment-seeking behavior and reduce the long delays that patients often demonstrate. At minimum, patients at high risk for an acute coronary event and their family members need to be trained in recognizing the signs of an impending or actual acute event.

Initial Treatment Depending on the clinical symptoms, the diagnosis of CHD may be managed in any of several ways. Many patients have coronary artery bypass graft (CABG) surgery to treat blockage of major

arteries. Patients who have received CABG surgery may suffer cognitive dysfunction that requires intervention (Phillips-Bute et al., 2006). During the acute phase following myocardial infarction (MI), the patient is typically hospitalized in a coronary care unit in which cardiac functioning is continually monitored. Many MI patients experience anxiety as they see their cardiac responses vividly illustrated on the machines before them and cope with the possibility of a recurrence. Anxiety, especially when coupled with perceptions of low control, predicts complications such as reinfarction and recurrent **ischemia** during the hospital phase. Sometimes, though, MI patients in the acute phase of the disease cope by using denial and thus may be relatively anxiety-free during this period. Depression, a diagnosis of posttraumatic stress disorder (PTSD), anger, and poor social support predict longer hospital stays (Contrada et al., 2008; Oxlad, Stubberfield, Stuklis, Edwards, & Wade, 2006).

Most heart attack patients return home after hospitalization. Therefore, a number of long- and short-term issues of rehabilitation arise. The process of adjusting emotionally to the experience of a heart attack begins almost immediately. Some heart attack patients experience cardiac arrest during their MI and have to be

BOX 13.4

Picturing the Heart

Do heart attack patients have knowledge about the damage that has been done to their hearts? And does that knowledge predict subsequent functioning? In an ingenious study, Elizabeth Broadbent, Keith Petrie, and colleagues (2004) examined whether myocardial infarction patients' drawings of their hearts predicted return to work, the amount of exercise they did, their distress about symptoms, and perceived recovery at 3 months.

Seventy-four middle-aged patients were asked to draw pictures of their hearts (Figure 13.4). Three months later, their functioning was assessed. Patients who drew damage to their hearts had recovered less 3 months later, believed their heart condition would last longer, and

had lower perceived control over their condition. They were also slower to return to work. Moreover, patients' drawings of the damage to their heart predicted recovery better than did medical indicators of damage.

In a subsequent study, Broadbent and colleagues (Broadbent, Ellis, Gamble, & Petrie, 2006) found that drawings of damage to the heart predicted long-term anxiety and more use of health services. Thus, a simple drawing of the heart may offer a good basis for doctors to assess patients' beliefs and follow-up problems when discussing their heart conditions.

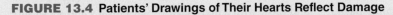

FIGURE 13.4 Patients' Drawings of Their Hearts Reflect Damage

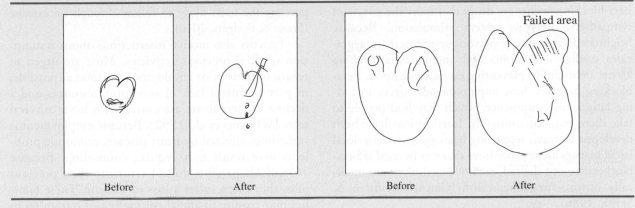

Before   After   Before   After

resuscitated through artificial means. Being a victim of cardiac arrest can produce a number of psychological difficulties, including nightmares, chronic anxiety, depression, and poor expectations of regaining health and vigor.

Cardiac Rehabilitation

Once the acute phase of illness has passed, a program of education and intervention begins, covering such topics as medical regimen, health risks, exercise, diet, work, and emotional stress. Most patients want and expect a shared or autonomous treatment decision-making role with their physician, but many patients do not experience this (Stewart et al., 2004). Because adherence to treatment regimens is so much better when patients are actively involved, providing more information to patients and involving them actively in the process is essential. Moreover, involvement in treatment may improve self-efficacy, which, in

turn, is tied to better coronary health (Sarkar, Ali, & Whooley, 2007).

Cardiac rehabilitation is defined as the active and progressive process by which people with heart disease attain their optimal physical, medical, psychological, social, emotional, vocational, and economic status. The goals of rehabilitation are to produce relief from symptoms, reduce the severity of the disease, limit further progression of disease, and promote psychological and social adjustment. Underlying the philosophy of cardiac rehabilitation is the belief that such efforts can stem advancing disease, reduce the likelihood of a repeat MI, and reduce the risk of sudden death.

Successful cardiac rehabilitation depends critically on the patient's active participation and commitment (see Box 13.4). An underlying goal of such programs is to restore a sense of mastery or self-efficacy; in its absence, adherence to rehabilitation and course of illness may be poor (Johnston, Johnston, Pollard, Kinmonth, & Mant, 2004; Sarkar, Ali, & Whooley, 2009).

The components of the typical cardiac rehabilitation program are very similar to the interventions used for people at risk for CHD and include training in smoking cessation, exercise therapy, psychological counseling, support groups, nutritional counseling, and education about coronary heart disease (Trockel, Burg, Jaffe, Barbour, & Taylor, 2008).

Treatment by Medication   Treatment for CHD begins immediately after diagnosis. Much of the drop in deaths from CHD can be attributed to the administration of clot-dissolving drugs and medical procedures such as angioplasty and coronary artery bypass surgery. During rehab, a regimen often includes self-administration of beta-adrenergic blocking agents on a regular basis. Beta-blocking agents are drugs that resist the effects of sympathetic nervous system stimulation. Because heightened sympathetic nervous system activity aggravates cardiac arrhythmia and angina, beta-blocking agents are useful in preventing excess stimulation. Beta-blockers, however, have unpleasant side effects, including fatigue and impotence, which may lead people to take them only intermittently. Interventions have been developed to teach recovering heart patients behavioral stress management procedures that can be used if beta-blockers are not desired, are not practical, or are medically unwise for some reason (Gatchel, Gaffney, & Smith, 1986).

Aspirin is commonly prescribed for people recovering from or at risk for heart attacks. Aspirin helps prevent blood clots by blocking one of the enzymes that cause platelets to aggregate. Men who take half an aspirin a day are at significantly reduced risk for fatal heart attacks (O'Neil, 2003, January 21) and women, too, appear to benefit from aspirin therapy. As with many drugs, however, adherence is problematic (Vittinghoff et al., 2003).

Drugs called statins are now frequently prescribed for patients following an acute coronary event, particularly if they have elevated lipids (Facts of Life, February 2007). Statins target LDL cholesterol (Cannon et al., 2004). So impressive have statins been that they are now recommended for patients and at-risk individuals as well to lower lipids before any diagnosis of heart disease is made. In fact, statin drugs have surpassed all other drug treatments for reducing the incidence of death, heart attack, and stroke. Not incidentally, statins appear to be protective against a wide range of diseases including multiple sclerosis, neurodegenerative disorders such as Alzheimer's disease, and some types of cancer (Topol, 2004).

Diet and Activity Level   Dietary restrictions may be imposed on the recovering MI patient in an attempt to lower cholesterol levels. Instructions to reduce smoking, lose weight, and control alcohol consumption are also frequently given. Most patients are put on an exercise program involving medically supervised walking, jogging, bicycling, or calisthenics at least three times a week for 30 to 45 minutes (DeBusk, Haskell, Miller, Berra, & Taylor, 1985). Exercise appears to improve not only cardiovascular functioning but also psychological recovery. However, adherence to exercise regimens is problematic, and therefore, building in relapse prevention is essential (Kugler, Dimsdale, Hartley, & Sherwood, 1990). Younger patients and those with a high sense of self-efficacy and social support are the most likely to follow through on exercise (Fraser & Rodgers, 2010).

Patients also receive instructions about resumption of their previous activities. Most are urged to return to their prior employment as soon as possible, in part because a lack of economic resources and a decline in income are associated with lower survival rates (Williams et al., 1992). Because employment is sometimes affected by heart disease, economic problems may result that require counseling. Because 20% of MI patients do not return to their previous jobs, they often suffer a loss of income. These families may require financial counseling or retraining to help them offset their losses. The problems experienced by one man in returning to work after a MI are described in Box 13.5. However, patients in high-stress jobs may be advised to cut back, to work part-time, or to take a position with fewer responsibilities. Unfortunately, adherence to work-related advice is not high, typically ranging from 50 to 80%, perhaps because it is perceived as lifestyle advice rather than medical advice.

Stress Management   Stress management is an important ingredient in cardiac rehabilitation as well, because stress can trigger fatal cardiac events (Donahue, Lampert, Dornelas, Clemow, & Burg, 2010; Jiang et al., 1996). Younger patients, female patients, and those with social support gaps, high social conflict, and negative coping styles appear to be most at risk for high stress levels following a diagnosis of coronary artery disease, and therefore might be especially targeted for stress management interventions (Brummett et al., 2004).

BOX 13.5

The Heart Patient Who Returns to Work

People who have gone through a heart attack often have difficulties when they try to return to work and experience psychological distress as a result (Brisson et al., 2005). They may be warned against certain activities, particularly those that are stress related or that may tax sympathetic nervous system activity. The following shows how one man attempted to cope with this advice, and the repercussions that followed.

> The physician instructed the patient that he could carry out all usual activities, except, "Avoid lifting." "Don't pick up heavy boxes at the office." In the first weeks of work return, he finds a sympathetic attitude among coworkers and pleasant relationships. As the occasion arises, he calls upon one or another to lift heavy boxes for him. Coworkers assist him, most willingly, in the first days after his return to work. Eventually, the tone in the office changes, and resentment stirs among those who are called upon to interrupt their own work and lift the occasional heavy boxes. The character of his informal associations alters, and he begins to have the feeling of becoming an outsider. Yet he has received doctor's orders on lifting, and he is unwilling to risk his health or his life by picking up boxes.

> Occasional mild chest pain and shortness of breath remind him that he is not the man he used to be. One day he asks a fellow worker to lift a box for him. The response comes, "Why don't you go ahead and drop dead, you lazy son-of-a-bitch!"

> The solutions are limited for this 55-year-old man. Transferring to another department is not possible, as the company is a small one. Leaving for another job is not possible for many reasons: limited employment opportunities in the marketplace during a recession; a record of years of personal attachment to the company; the strains of job hunting, relocating, and adjusting to a new work situation. Trying to win understanding and cooperation from fellow workers is a fruitless task, since the intermesh of personalities, resentments, and personal rivalries common to many offices continues to interfere.

> So picking up the heavy boxes seems the easiest solution—but for how long can he continue? What will be the eventual effects on his heart? Anxiety about health, death, and his family colors his life.

Source: Croog, 1983, pp. 300–301.

Yet, at present, stress management with coronary artery disease patients is hit-or-miss and often haphazard. Patients are urged to avoid stressful situations at work and at home, but these comments are often presented as vague treatment goals. Moreover, as many as 50% of patients say that they are unable to modify the stress in their lives.

These problems can be solved by employing methods such as those outlined in Chapter 6—namely, stress management programs. The patient is taught how to recognize stressful events, how to avoid those stressful activities when possible, and what to do about stress if it is unavoidable. Training in specific techniques, such as relaxation and mindfulness, improves the ability to manage stress (Cole, Pomerleau, & Harris, 1992).

Coping strategies may need to be targeted as well: Avoidant coping is associated with poor quality of life, whereas approach coping and optimism predict a higher quality of life (Echteld, van Elderen, & van der Kamp, 2003).

Recently, stress management interventions have targeted hostility. Declines in hostility in midlife are associated with lower risk (Siegler et al., 2003). Accordingly, one program found that eight weekly sessions designed to alter antagonism, cynicism, and anger were somewhat successful in reducing hostility levels (Gidron & Davidson, 1996; Gidron, Davidson, & Bata, 1999). Because anger is a risk factor both for heart disease initially and for a second heart attack (Mendes de Leon, Kop, de Swart, Bar, & Appels, 1996), interventions targeting anger have been implemented. However, as noted, modifying hostility may not modify cardiovascular risk factors (Sloan et al., 2010). Type D personality, which is characterized by chronic negative emotions, coupled with emotional inhibition, predicts poor quality of life as well (Pedersen & Denollet, 2003).

Targeting Depression Depression is a significant problem during cardiac rehabilitation, as it is throughout the management of CHD. The prevalence is high and it compromises treatment and adherence (Casey, Hughes, Waechter, Josephson, & Rosneck, 2008; Kaptein, de Jonge, van den Brink, & Korf, 2006). It is also one of the chief risk factors for rehospitalization following cardiac surgery (Tully, Baker, Turnbull, & Winefield, 2008) and may exert its adverse effects, at least in part, through poor heart rate recovery (Hughes et al., 2008). Depression and anxiety also compromise quality of life (Goyal, Idler, Krause, & Contrada, 2005). When depressed CHD patients are treated with cognitive-behavioral therapy to reduce depression, it can have beneficial effects on risk factors for advancing disease (Carney et al., 2000; Lett, Davidson, & Blumenthal, 2005). Even brief telephone counseling interventions appear to reduce psychological distress and improve self-perceived health (Bambauer et al., 2005).

Evaluation of Cardiac Rehabilitation   Cardiac rehabilitation is now a standard part of the aftercare of patients who have had heart attacks or who have been hospitalized for heart disease. Several hundred published studies have evaluated cardiovascular disease management programs, and most find that interventions that target weight, blood pressure, smoking, and, increasingly, quality of life are successful in reducing patients' standing on risk factors for heart disease and, in some cases, reducing the risk of death from cardiovascular disease (Center for the Advancement of Health, 2000b; Pischke, Scherwitz, Weidner, & Ornish, 2008). Although adherence is variable (Leung, Ceccato, Stewart, & Grace, 2007), evaluations show that the addition of psychosocial treatments to standard cardiac rehabilitation programs can reduce psychological distress and the likelihood that cardiac patients will experience cardiac symptoms, suffer a recurrence, or die following an acute cardiac event (Lisspers et al., 2005; Rozanski, 2005).

Problems of Social Support   As is true for other diseases, social support can help heart patients recover (Molloy, Perkins-Porras, et al., 2008). Heart patients without a spouse or a confidant have significantly elevated risks for adverse health events (Eaker, Sullivan, Kelly-Hayes, D'Agostino, & Benjamin, 2007). Lack of social support during hospitalization predicts depressive symptoms during recovery (Brummett et al., 1998). So important is social support for long-term prognosis (Burg et al., 2005) that it is now targeted for intervention during recovery (ENRICHD, 2001). Interventions to enhance social support or to help people experience social situations as supportive are now recommended (Barth, Schneider, & von Känel, 2010).

However, many factors may erode the potential for social support (Randall, Molloy, & Steptoe, 2009). Many patients live alone or have small social networks

(Rutledge et al., 2004). In the home setting, one of the MI patient's chief complaints is loss of independence. MI sharply reduces an individual's physical stamina, and many patients are surprised by the extent of their disability. Feelings of shame, helplessness, and low self-esteem may result. Further, conflict over changes in lifestyle can increase marital strife (Croog & Fitzgerald, 1978; Michela, 1987). The patient may find it difficult to adhere to dietary restrictions and exercise, whereas the spouse may be highly motivated to help the patient comply. Stressful interactions, such as the one that opened this chapter, can aggravate the patient's perceptions of dependence and exacerbate already existing depression.

Spouses of recovering heart attack patients tend to see the patient as dependent and irritable, whereas the recovering patient may regard the spouse as meddlesome and overprotective. An overly solicitous partner can actually aggregate symptoms, disability, and depression (Itkowitz, Kerns, & Otis, 2003). Unfortunately, to the extent that the spouse is successful in helping the patient cope and develop feelings of self-efficacy, the spouse's own distress may increase (Coyne & Smith, 1991). In addition, spouses of heart attack victims often show severe psychological responses to the MI, including depression, nightmares, and chronic anxiety over the patient's survival (Moser & Dracup, 2004). Although there is no evidence that a heart attack drives married couples apart, neither does it necessarily bring them closer together. It is a difficult situation for everyone involved. Marital counseling or family therapy may be needed to deal with marital strain.

Cardiac invalidism can be one consequence of MI: Patients and their spouses see the patient's abilities as lower than they actually are (Itkowitz et al., 2003). In a study designed to reduce this problem (Taylor, Bandura, Ewart, Miller, & DeBusk, 1985), wives of recovering MI patients were provided with information about their husbands' cardiovascular capabilities, observed their husbands' performance on a treadmill task, or took part in the treadmill activity personally. Wives who personally experienced the treadmill task increased their perceptions of their husbands' physical and cardiac efficiency after observing their husbands' treadmill attainments. Wives who were simply informed about their husbands' performance or who observed treadmill activity continued to regard their husbands as impaired.

Despite these problems, the family has an important role in follow-up care. Both patients and family members should be taught how to recognize the symptoms of an

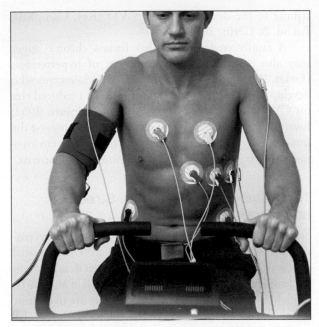

The treadmill test provides a useful indicator of the functional capacity of recovering myocardial infarction patients.

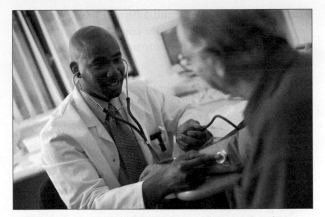

Hypertension is a symptomless disease. As a result, unless they obtain regular physical checkups or participate in hypertension screening programs, many adults are unaware that they have this disorder.

impending heart attack; how to differentiate them from more minor physical complaints, such as heartburn; and how to activate the emergency response system. In this way, delay behavior can be reduced and treatment can be improved in the event of a repeat event.

Family members of the MI patient should also be trained in **cardiopulmonary resuscitation (CPR).** Approximately 70% of sudden deaths from heart attacks occur in the home rather than the workplace, but relatively few programs have been initiated to train family members in CPR. More such training programs should be available for MI families (Dracup, Guzy, Taylor, & Barry, 1986; Nolan et al., 1999).

■ HYPERTENSION

Hypertension, also known as high blood pressure or **cardiovascular disease (CVD),** occurs when the supply of blood through the vessels is excessive. It can occur when cardiac output is too high, which puts pressure on the arterial walls as blood flow increases. It also occurs in response to peripheral resistance—that is, the resistance to blood flow in the small arteries of the body.

Hypertension is a serious medical problem. According to recent estimates, one in four U.S. adults has high blood pressure, but because there are no symptoms, nearly one-third of these people don't know they

have it (American Heart Association, 2004a). Moreover, hypertension is a risk factor for other disorders, such as heart disease and kidney failure (American Heart Association, 2001).

Untreated hypertension can also adversely affect cognitive functioning, producing problems in learning, memory, attention, abstract reasoning, mental flexibility, and other cognitive skills (Brown, Sollers, Thayer, Zonderman, & Waldstein, 2009). Even in healthy adults, elevated blood pressure appears to compromise cognitive functioning (Suhr, Stewart, & France, 2004). These problems appear to be particularly significant among young hypertensives (Waldstein et al., 1996). Given the risks and scope of hypertension, early diagnosis and treatment are essential.

How Is Hypertension Measured?

Hypertension is assessed by the levels of systolic and diastolic blood pressure as measured by a sphygmomanometer. As noted in Chapter 2, systolic blood pressure is the greatest force developed during contraction of the heart's ventricles. It is sensitive both to the volume of blood leaving the heart and to the arteries' ability to stretch to accommodate blood (their elasticity). Diastolic pressure is the pressure in the arteries when the heart is relaxed; it is related to resistance of the blood vessels to blood flow.

Of the two, systolic pressure has somewhat greater value in diagnosing hypertension. Mild hypertension is defined by a systolic pressure consistently between 140 and 159; moderate hypertension involves a pressure consistently between 160 and 179; and severe hypertension means a systolic pressure consistently above 180. Keeping systolic blood pressure under 120 is best.

What Causes Hypertension?

Approximately 5% of hypertension is caused by failure of the kidneys to regulate blood pressure. However, almost 90% of all hypertension is *essential*—that is, of unknown origin.

Some risk factors have been identified. Childhood temperament (emotional excitability) promotes central weight gain in adolescence (Pulkki-Råback et al., 2005), which, in turn, predicts CVD (Goldbacher, Matthews, & Salomon, 2005). Blood pressure reactivity in childhood and adolescence predicts later development of hypertension (Ingelfinger, 2004; Matthews, Salomon, Brady, & Allen, 2003). Prior to age 50, males are at greater risk for hypertension than are females; above age 55, however, both men and women in the United States face a 90% chance of developing hypertension; CVD risk factors are higher among minorities. This increased risk appears to be due in part to low socioeconomic status (Kivimäki et al., 2004; Marin, Chen, & Miller, 2008). Poor blood pressure recovery may play a role as well (Steptoe & Marmot, 2006).

Genetic factors play a role (see Smith et al., 1987): If one parent has high blood pressure, the offspring have a 45% chance of developing it; if two parents have high blood pressure, the probability increases to 95%. As is true for coronary heart disease more generally, the genetic factor in hypertension may be reactivity, a hereditary predisposition toward elevated sympathetic nervous system activity, especially in response to stressful events (DeQuattro & Lee, 1991; Everson, Lovallo, Sausen, & Wilson, 1992; Jeffery, 1991).

Emotional factors are also implicated in this constellation of risk. In particular, depression, hostility, and frequent experiences of intense arousal predict increases in blood pressure over time (Jonas & Lando, 2000; Matthews, Nelesen, & Dimsdale, 2005; Pollard & Schwartz, 2003). A tendency toward anger (Harburg, Julius, Kacirotti, Gleiberman, & Schork, 2003; Johnson, Schork, & Spielberger, 1987), cynical distrust (Williams, 1984), suppressed hostility (Zhang, Niaura, Todaro, et al., 2005), and excessive striving in the face of significant odds (James, Hartnett, & Kalsbeek, 1983) have all been implicated in the development of hypertension. Rumination following stressful events may prolong cardiovascular reactivity and con-

tribute to the development of CVD (Key, Campbell, Bacon, & Gerin, 2008).

A family environment that fosters chronic anger may also contribute to development of hypertension (Ewart, 1991). In contrast, children and adolescents who develop social competence skills may have a reduced risk for CVD (Chen, Matthews, Salomon, & Ewart, 2002; Ewart & Jorgensen, 2004). Such observations suggest the importance of intervening early in the family environment to prevent or modify its communication patterns.

The Relationship Between Stress and Hypertension

Stress has been suspected as a contributor to hypertension for many years (Henry & Cassel, 1969). Repeated exposures to stressful events contribute to development of chronically high blood pressure (Carroll et al., 2001). High blood pressure can result from exposure to chronic social conflict and from job strain—namely, the combination of high demands with little control (Pickering et al., 1996). Crowded, high-stress, and noisy locales produce higher rates of hypertension. Groups that have migrated from rural to urban areas have high rates of hypertension. In women, elevated blood pressure has been related to having extensive family responsibilities, and among women in white-collar occupations, the combined impact of family responsibilities and job strain has been tied to higher blood pressure (Brisson et al., 1999). At present, the suspicion is that hypertension results from high-stress reactivity, possibly genetically-based, in conjunction with high-stress exposure (Al'Absi

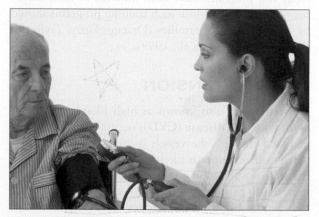

Many people have "white coat hypertension," that is, elevations in blood pressure during medical visits but not otherwise. White coat hypertension is sometimes misdiagnosed and medicated as hypertension.

& Wittmers, 2003; Schwartz, Meisenhelder, Ma, & Reed, 2003).

How Do We Study Stress and Hypertension?

One method brings people into the laboratory, often people at risk for or already diagnosed with hypertension, to see how they respond to physical or mental challenges that are stressful, such as difficult arithmetic tasks. Laboratory studies reliably show increased blood pressure responses, which predict symptoms in response to stress in daily life (Hilmert, Ode, Zielke, & Robinson, 2010). Another approach identifies stressful circumstances, such as high-pressure jobs, and examines the rates of hypertension and how blood pressure ebbs and flows in response to environmental demands (Steptoe, Roy, & Evans, 1996).

Building on this method, a third approach makes use of ambulatory monitoring to examine the relationship between lifestyle factors and blood pressure in natural settings, as people go through their daily lives. The person wears a blood pressure cuff, which assesses blood pressure at intervals throughout the day. This method has the advantage of charting the ebb and flow of blood pressure for each individual, and daily variation is considerable (Pickering, Schwartz, & James, 1995), especially among people who smoke, who drink heavily, who experience job strain, and who experience other stressful life conditions (Pickering et al., 1995). All three types of studies provide evidence that links increases or increased variability in blood pressure to stressful events.

The role of stress in the development and exacerbation of hypertension may be different for people at risk for hypertension than for those who are not, and it may change as hypertension progresses. People without pre-existing signs of hypertension exhibit large and reliable blood pressure responses to stressors, primarily when they must make an active behavioral response to that stress (Sherwood, Hinderliter, & Light, 1995). People with borderline hypertension show a similar pattern, although they also show exaggerated stress-induced cardiovascular responses to stress at a relatively young age (Matthews et al., 1993) and a stronger blood pressure response to laboratory stressors than do people with normal blood pressure (Tuomisto, 1997).

People already diagnosed with hypertension exhibit large blood pressure responses to a wide range of stressors, both passive stressors not requiring a behavioral response and active stressors that do require a behavioral response (Fredrickson & Matthews, 1990). The fact that diagnosed hypertensives show blood pressure responses to a wide array of stressors is consistent with the idea that excessive sympathetic nervous system activity—that is, reactivity in response to stress—may be significant in the development of hypertension.

Psychosocial Factors and Hypertension

Originally, hypertension was thought to be marked by personality factors, dominated by suppressed anger (Alexander, 1950; Dunbar, 1943). Although personality factors are now known to be insufficient to account for the development of hypertension, research continues to show that hostility and depression may play a role (Lin et al., 2008; Patten et al., 2009).

Research has focused heavily on the experience of anger and its expression. Originally, researchers thought that suppressed anger played a major role, but the importance of expressed anger is now recognized as well. Anger is fostered by experiences in young childhood that include stress exposure, violence exposure, and exposure to conflict in the family (Turner, Russell, Glover, & Hutto, 2007). Ruminating on the source of one's anger, whether one suppresses or expresses it, is associated with elevated blood pressure (Everson, Goldberg, Kaplan, Julkunen, & Salonen, 1998; Hogan & Linden, 2004; Schum, Jorgensen, Verhaeghen, Sauro, & Thibodeau, 2003). Hostility has also been tied to an abnormal cortisol response, specifically a failure to dip in the evening (Ranjit et al., 2009). Not surprisingly, the frequent experience of positive emotions may be protective against hypertension (Ostir, Berges, Markides, & Ottenbacher, 2006).

Social support is a resource for combating most health problems. However, hypertensives who are high in hostility can often drive those who might otherwise be supportive away (Vella, Kamarck, & Shiffman, 2008). Hostility may be associated with hypertension via its effects on interpersonal interaction—namely, by increasing the number of conflict-ridden or unpleasant interactions in daily life (Brondolo et al., 2003). Other negative emotions, including depression and anxiety, may be prospective risk factors for hypertension as well (Jonas & Lando, 2000; Rutledge & Hogan, 2002; Scherrer et al., 2003). Depression, hostility, and (lack of) social support are quite closely linked (Raynor, Pogue-Geile, Kamarck, McCaffery, & Manuck, 2002; Suarez, Kuhn, Schanberg, Williams, & Zimmermann, 1998).

In Chapter 7, we introduced the concept of Type D personality, which is characterized by chronic negative affect coupled with social inhibition. About a quarter of the general population may be characterized as having

Type D personality characteristics, and it is prognostic for cardiovascular disease as well (Hausteiner, Klupsch, Emeny, Baumert, & Ladwig, 2010).

Stress and Hypertension Among African Americans

Hypertension is a particular medical problem in African American communities. Its high prevalence in this population is tied to stress and low SES (Hong, Nelesen, Krohn, Mills, & Dimsdale, 2006; Lewis et al., 2006; Merritt, Bennett, Williams, Edwards, & Sollers, 2006). Hostility and anger may also contribute to this ethnic difference (Thomas, Nelesen, & Dimsdale, 2004). Genetic factors may be implicated as well. Racial differences in neuropeptide and cardiovascular responses to stressors also appear to influence the development of hypertension (Saab et al., 1997).

Low-income Blacks are likely to live in stressful neighborhoods, which are associated with the development of hypertension (Fleming, Baum, Davidson, Rectanus, & McArdle, 1987). Low-income Blacks report more psychological distress than do higher-income Whites and Blacks, and chronic life stress may interfere with sympathetic nervous system recovery in response to specific stressors (Pardine & Napoli, 1983). Exposure to discrimination and racism can contribute to high blood pressure among Blacks (Clark, 2006a, 2006b; Salomon & Jagusztyn, 2008), possibly by interfering with the normal decline at night (Brondolo et al., 2008). Dark-skinned African Americans appear to experience more frequent racial discrimination than their lighter-skinned counterparts, estimated in one study to be 11 times more common (Klonoff & Landrine, 2000).

African Americans have an elevated risk of obesity, which is tied to hypertension. Dietary factors, such as patterns of eating that develop in infancy (Myers, 1996), and salt intake may play a causal role. Cigarette smoking and low exercise are also implicated (Kershaw, Mezuk, Abdou, Rafferty, & Jackson, 2010). Compared to Whites, African Americans also show a lower nocturnal decrease in blood pressure (Ituarte, Kamarck, Thompson, & Bacanu, 1999); nondipping of blood pressure at night is a risk factor for hypertension (Räikkönen et al., 2004). Low SES, a stressful early environment, and hostility may explain this ethnic difference (Beatty & Matthews, 2009; Campbell, Key, Ireland, Bacon, & Ditto, 2008; Linden, Klassen, & Phillips, 2008; Stepnowsky, Neleson, De Jardin, & Dimsdale, 2004). Social support can ameliorate this risk (Rodriguez et al., 2008).

Cardiovascular reactivity among African Americans, especially older African Americans, may be part of a more general syndrome that implicates multiple risk factors for CVD, including greater heart rate reactivity, higher fasting insulin levels, lower high-density lipoprotein cholesterol levels, a higher waist-to-hip ratio, and greater body mass overall (Waldstein, Burns, Toth, & Poehlman, 1999). This clustering of metabolic factors, namely, metabolic syndrome, may predispose older African Americans to a higher risk for CVD and metabolic disorders, such as diabetes.

John Henryism

Because hypertension is a particular risk for Blacks, some research has examined a phenomenon known as **John Henryism.** John Henry, the "steel-driving" man, was an uneducated Black laborer who allegedly defeated a mechanical steam drill in a contest to see who could complete the most work in the shortest period of time. However, after winning the battle, John Henry reportedly dropped dead from exhaustion. S. A. James and colleagues (James, Hartnett, & Kalsbeek, 1983) coined the term "John Henryism," which refers to a personality predisposition to cope actively with psychosocial stressors. It becomes a lethal predisposition when active coping efforts are likely to be unsuccessful. The person scoring high on John Henryism would try harder and harder against ultimately insurmountable odds. Consequently, one would expect to find John Henryism to be especially lethal among the disadvantaged, especially low-income and poorly educated Blacks. Research tends to confirm these relations (James, Keenan, Strogatz, Browning, & Garrett, 1992). John Henryism also has a substantial genetic component (Wang, Trivedi, Treiber, & Snieder, 2005). The specific factors tying John Henryism to an increased risk for hypertension appear to be increased cardiovascular reactivity to stress and prolonged difficulty recovering from stress (Merritt, Bennett, Williams, Sollers, & Thayer, 2004).

Treatment of Hypertension

Hypertension has been controlled in a variety of ways. Commonly, patients are put on low-sodium diets, and reduction of alcohol intake is also recommended. Weight reduction in overweight patients is strongly urged, and exercise is recommended for all hypertensive patients.

Caffeine restriction is often included as part of the dietary treatment of hypertension, because caffeine, in conjunction with stress, elevates blood pressure responses among those at risk for or already diagnosed with hypertension (Lovallo et al., 2000).

Drug Treatments   Most commonly, hypertension is treated pharmacologically. Diuretics reduce blood volume by promoting the excretion of sodium. Another common treatment is beta-adrenergic blockers, which exert their antihypertensive effects by decreasing cardiac output and plasma renin activity. Central adrenergic inhibitors are also used to reduce blood pressure by decreasing the sympathetic outflow from the central nervous system. In addition, peripheral adrenergic inhibitors are used to deplete catecholamines from the brain and the adrenal medulla. Vasodilators, angiotensin-converting enzyme inhibitors, and calcium channel blockers have also been used in the treatment of hypertension.

Recently, drug treatments for hypertension have become controversial. Hypertension is only one of a cluster of factors that lead to the development of coronary heart disease. Certain of the drug treatments may have positive effects in reducing blood pressure but augment sympathetic activity overall, thereby aggravating rather than reducing the likelihood of CHD. Some drug treatments are more likely to enhance sympathetic nervous system activity than reduce it. The most effective treatment for lowering blood pressure with the fewest complications is the oldest traditional form of drug intervention, namely, diuretics (Altman, 2002, December 18).

Cognitive-Behavioral Treatments   A variety of cognitive-behavioral methods have been used to treat high blood pressure. Methods that draw on relaxation include biofeedback, progressive muscle relaxation, hypnosis, and meditation, all of which reduce blood pressure via the induction of a state of low arousal. Deep breathing and imagery are often added to accomplish this task. Evaluations of these treatments suggest modestly positive effects (Davison, Williams, Nezami, Bice, & DeQuattro, 1991; Jacob, Chesney, Williams, Ding, & Shapiro, 1991; Nakao et al., 1997), although hypertensive patients may not practice them as much as they should (Hoelscher, Lichstein, & Rosenthal, 1986). Giving patients feedback about exactly how poor their compliance efforts are can improve blood pressure control (Zuger, 1999, May 4). Self-reinforcement, self-calming talk, goal setting, and time management are also typically added to CBT interventions. Exercise also helps in blood pressure control (Brownley, West, Hinderliter, & Light, 1996).

Because obesity is implicated in the development of hypertension, interventions to promote weight loss may also reduce hypertension. However, the treatment of obesity itself remains difficult (see Chapter 4), and so a combination of diet, exercise, and behavioral strategies may be most desirable for maintaining weight loss (Jeffery, 1991).

The fact that anger has been linked to hypertension implies that teaching people how to manage their anger might be useful. In fact, studies suggest that training hypertensive patients how to manage confrontational scenes through such behavioral techniques as role-playing can produce better skills for managing such situations and can lower blood pressure reactivity (Davidson, MacGregor, Stuhr, & Gidron, 1999; Larkin & Zayfert, 1996).

Evaluation of Cognitive-Behavioral Interventions   How do CBT interventions fare comparatively in the treatment of hypertension? Of the nondrug approaches, weight reduction, physical exercise, and cognitive-behavioral therapy appear to be quite successful (Linden & Chambers, 1994). Although not all hypertensive patients benefit from such training, many do. Moreover, cognitive-behavioral methods have the advantage of being inexpensive as well as easy to implement: They can be used without supervision, and they have no side effects.

Cognitive-behavioral interventions may reduce the drug requirements for the treatment of hypertension (Shapiro, Hui, Oakley, Pasic, & Jamner, 1997), and accordingly be especially helpful to those people who do not tolerate the drugs well (Kristal-Boneh, Melamed, Bernheim, Peled, & Green, 1995). CBT appears to be especially successful with mild or borderline hypertensives and, with these groups, may actually substitute for drug control.

However, rates of adherence to cognitive-behavioral interventions are not particularly high. One reason is people's "commonsense" understanding of hypertension (Hekler et al., 2008). For example, some people take the concept of "hyper-tension" quite literally and assume that relaxing and reducing their level of stress is sufficient and that medication is not required (Frosch, Kimmel, & Volpp, 2008). At present, then, the combination of drugs and cognitive-behavioral treatments appears to be the best approach to the management of hypertension.

Problems in Treating Hypertension

The Hidden Disease   One of the biggest problems in the treatment of hypertension is that so many people who are hypertensive do not know that they are. Hypertension is largely a symptomless disease, so, rather than seeking treatment for hypertension, people are often diagnosed when they go in for a standard medical examination. Thus, many thousands of people who do not get regular physicals suffer from hypertension without realizing it. Untreated hypertension is related to a lower quality of life, compromised cognitive functioning, and fewer social activities, so, despite the fact that it is symptomless, it nonetheless has adverse effects on daily life (Saxby, Harrington, McKeith, Wesnes, & Ford, 2003).

National campaigns to educate the public about hypertension have had some success in getting people diagnosed (Horan & Roccella, 1988). Early detection is important because, as we have seen, more successful treatments may be available for borderline or mild hypertensives than for people with more serious forms of the disorder.

Work site–based screening programs have been successful in identifying people with hypertension (Alderman & Lamport, 1988). Increasingly, community interventions enable people to have their blood pressure checked by going to mobile units, churches or community centers, or even the local drugstore. The widespread availability of these screening programs has helped with early identification of people with hypertension.

Adherence   A second major problem for the management of hypertension is the high rate of nonadherence to therapy. This, too, is affected by the symptomless nature of the disease. Because hypertensive patients "feel fine," it can be difficult to get them to take medications on a regular basis. Many of us believe that when we are "cranked up," under stress, or annoyed, our blood pressure is high. In fact, the correlation between beliefs about level of blood pressure and actual blood pressure is low. Unfortunately, hypertensives tend to have such commonsense theories and may choose to medicate themselves on the basis of them (Meyer, Leventhal, & Gutmann, 1985).

What can be done to increase adherence? Clearly, one solution is to educate patients fully about the largely symptomless nature of the disease and the critical importance of treatment for controlling it (Zimmerman, Safer, Leventhal, & Baumann, 1986). It may be necessary to demonstrate to patients that their theories about their blood pressure are wrong (Baumann, Zimmerman, & Leventhal, 1989; Brondolo, Rosen, Kostis, & Schwartz, 1999). Enlisting the support of family members may help, as family social support predicts adherence (Triverdi, Ayotte, Edelman, & Bosworth, 2008).

Compliance with a hypertension regimen is influenced by factors that predict adherence more generally. Patients who expect greater control over health and hypertension, who have greater knowledge of the treatment regimen, and who have stronger social support are more likely to adhere to their hypertension regimen (Dunbar-Jacob, Dwyer, & Dunning, 1991; Stanton, 1987).

■ STROKE

Consider the following:

> Lee Phillips, 62, was shopping at a San Diego mall with her husband, Eric, when she felt an odd tugging on the right side of her face. Her mouth twisted into a lurid grimace. Suddenly she felt weak. "What kind of game are you playing?" asked Eric. "I'm not," Lee tried to respond—but her words came out in a jumble. "Let's go to the hospital," Eric urged her. All Lee wanted to do was go home and lie down. Fortunately, it turned out, her husband summoned an ambulance instead. Like 730,000 other Americans each year, Lee was suffering a stroke (Gorman, 1996, September 19).

Stroke, the third major cause of death in the United States, results from a disturbance in blood flow to the brain. Some strokes occur when blood flow to localized areas of the brain is interrupted, a condition that can be due to arteriosclerosis or hypertension. For example, when arteriosclerotic plaques damage the cerebral blood vessels, the damaged area may trap blood clots (thrombi) or produce circulating blood clots (emboli) that block the flow of blood (see Figure 13.5).

Stroke can also be caused by cerebral hemorrhage (bleeding caused by the rupture of a blood vessel in the brain). When blood leaks into the brain, large areas of nervous tissue may be compressed against the skull, producing widespread or fatal damage. Strokes caused approximately 1 of every 17 deaths in the United States in 2005 (American Heart Association, 2009b). The mortality rate is around 30% during the first month after a stroke (American Heart Association, 2007), and those who survive may suffer some degree of permanent physical impairment. In the United States, approximately 795,000 individuals experience a stroke every year (American Heart Association, 2009b), and currently, more than 5 million stroke survivors live with significant cognitive and emotional problems (American Heart Association, 2007). The warning signs of stroke are listed in Table 13.1.

A chief risk of stroke is that more will follow in its wake, ultimately leading to severe disability or death. Researchers have recently discovered that a simple intervention—aspirin—can greatly reduce this risk. Aspirin has immediate benefits for stroke patients by preventing coagulation. Following a stroke, even a few weeks' use of

FIGURE 13.5 | Stroke   Stroke is a condition that results from a disturbance in blood flow to the brain.   (*Source:* National Heart, Lung, and Blood Institute, 2010b)

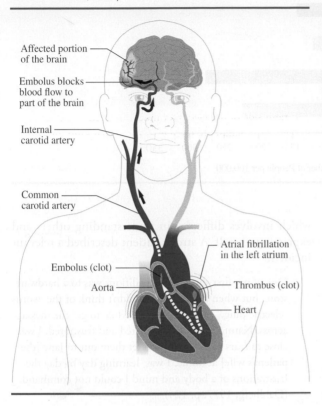

- Affected portion of the brain
- Embolus blocks blood flow to part of the brain
- Internal carotid artery
- Common carotid artery
- Embolus (clot)
- Aorta
- Atrial fibrillation in the left atrium
- Thrombus (clot)
- Heart

People who have had strokes often must relearn some aspects of cognitive functioning.

TABLE 13.1 | Stroke Warning Signs

The American Stroke Association says these are the warning signs of stroke:
- Sudden numbness or weakness of the face, arm, or leg, especially on one side of the body
- Sudden confusion, trouble speaking or understanding
- Sudden trouble seeing in one or both eyes
- Sudden trouble walking, dizziness, loss of balance or coordination
- Sudden, severe headache with no known cause

Source: American Heart Association, 2004a.

aspirin can reduce the risk of recurrent strokes by as much as a third (Chen et al., 2000). Statins appear to help, too.

Risk Factors for Stroke

Risk factors for stroke overlap heavily with those for heart disease. Some factors are hereditary, others result from lifestyle, and still others come from unknown

causes. Risk factors include high blood pressure, heart disease, cigarette smoking, a high red blood cell count, and transient ischemic attacks. Transient ischemic attacks are little strokes that produce temporary weakness, clumsiness, or loss of feeling in one side or limb; a temporary dimness or loss of vision, particularly in one eye; or a temporary loss of speech or difficulty in speaking or understanding speech (American Heart Association, 2000). Acute triggers for stroke include negative emotions, anger, and sudden change in posture in response to a startling event (Koton, Tanne, Bornstein, & Green, 2004). In addition, psychological distress is related to the likelihood of having a fatal stroke (May et al., 2002). Anger expression also appears to be related to stroke, as it is for coronary heart disease and hypertension; low levels of anger expression appear to be mildly protective (Eng, Fitzmaurice, Kubzansky, Rimm, & Kawachi, 2003).

The likelihood of a stroke increases with age, occurs more often in men than in women, and occurs more often in African Americans and among those who have diabetes. A prior stroke or a family history of stroke also increases the likelihood. Increasingly, health practitioners are recognizing the significance of psychosocial factors in stroke. Depression and anxiety are predictive of stroke (May et al., 2002) and appear to be especially strong predictors for White women and for African Americans (Jonas & Mussolino, 2000). The incidence of first stroke by gender and race is shown in Figure 13.6. The group at highest risk for stroke is Black men ages 45–64. During this period, strokes kill Black men at about three times the rate for White men (Villarosa, 2002, September 23).

As is true for heart disease, depression is a risk factor for stroke. In the case of stroke, cerebrovascular reactivity appears to be reduced in patients with depression,

FIGURE 13.6 | Stroke Incidence Rates for First-Ever Stroke, 2001   (*Source:* American Heart Association, 2009a)

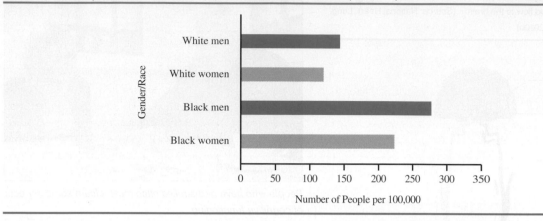

Number of People per 100,000

which may account for this relation (Neu, Schlattmann, Schilling, & Hartmann, 2004).

Consequences of Stroke

Stroke affects all aspects of one's life: personal, social, vocational, and physical. Although many victims have already reached retirement age, stroke can also affect younger people. Patients who are minimally impaired following a stroke may return to work after a few months, but many patients are unable to return to work even part-time. Stroke almost inevitably leads to increased dependence on others, at least for a while; as a consequence, family or other social relationships may be profoundly affected. Decline in cognitive functioning is a common consequence (Rafnsson, Deary, Smith, Whiteman, & Fowkes, 2007).

Motor Problems   Immediately after a stroke, motor difficulties are common. Because the right side of the brain controls movement in the left half of the body and the left side of the brain controls movement in the right half of the body, motor impairments occur on the side opposite to the side of the brain that was damaged in the stroke. It is usually difficult or impossible for the patient to move the arm and leg on the affected side; therefore, he or she usually requires help walking, dressing, and performing other physical activities. With physical therapy, some of these problems are greatly diminished (Gordon & Diller, 1983).

Cognitive Problems   The cognitive difficulties that the stroke victim faces depend on which side of the brain was damaged. Patients with left-brain damage may have communication disorders, such as aphasia,

which involves difficulty in understanding others and expressing oneself. A stroke patient described a relevant incident:

> One of my first shopping expeditions was to a hardware store, but when I got there I couldn't think of the words "electric plug," and it took me a while to get the message across. Naturally, I was humiliated and frustrated. I was close to tears at the store, and let them out to Jane [the patient's wife] at home. I was learning day by day the frustrations of a body and mind I could not command. (Dahlberg, 1977, p. 124)

Other problems of left-brain dysfunction include cognitive disturbances, an apparent reduction in intellect, and difficulty in learning new tasks. In particular, cognitive tasks that require the use of short-term memory seem to be particularly affected after a stroke that causes left-brain damage:

> Everyone repeats some stories, but within 15 minutes I told three stories that Jane had just heard—from me. Such experiences have not brought me humility, but I have lost some confidence, and I have developed patience with people. In the past, I have sometimes been arrogant. But since the stroke I have learned to say, "excuse me" and "I don't know." (Dahlberg, 1977, p. 126)

Patients with right-brain damage may be unable to process or make use of certain kinds of visual feedback. As a result, such a patient may shave only one side of his face or put makeup on only half her face. Or the patient may eat only the food on the right side of the plate and ignore the food on the left. Patients may have trouble reading a clock, dialing a phone, or making change. These patients also may have difficulty perceiving distances accurately and may bump into objects or walls.

In addition, patients with right-brain damage may feel that they are going crazy because they cannot understand the words they read or seem to be able to perceive only the last part of each word. They may also think they are hearing voices if a speaker is physically positioned on the impaired side and can thus be heard but not seen (Gordon & Diller, 1983). Although some stroke patients seem to have a good idea of how much damage has been done, a fact that is depressing in its own right, others are quite inaccurate in their assessment of how the stroke has changed their cognitive abilities, their memory, and their moods (Hibbard, Gordon, Stein, Grober, & Sliwinski, 1992). These misperceptions lead them to misjudge what they are capable of doing and to inaccurately assess how well they have done. A condition known as multi-infarct dementia, which results from the cumulative effects of small strokes, may produce Alzheimer's-like symptoms.

Emotional Problems   Emotional problems after a stroke are common. Patients with left-brain damage often react to their disorder with anxiety and depression; patients with right-brain damage more commonly seem indifferent to their situation. These differences in emotional response appear to be due to the nature of the neurological damage. Right-brain-damaged patients often have alexithymia, which involves difficulty in identifying and describing feelings (Spalletta et al., 2001).

Depression is a serious problem for stroke patients, and its degree depends on the site of the stroke and its severity. However, psychosocial factors also predict the degree of depression. Depression depends, in part, on the relationship the stroke patient has to the caregiver. Overprotection by a caregiver, a poor relation with a caregiver, and a caregiver who views the situation negatively all lead to depression on both sides. In addition, depression is aggravated if the person must live in worsened circumstances after the stroke, has a poor perception of the future, and perceives little meaning in life (S. C. Thompson et al., 1989). The consequences of stroke can be socially stigmatizing, and patients may find they are avoided or rejected by their colleagues and friends (Newman, 1984).

Positive emotions, not surprisingly, are associated with better recovery (Ostir, Berges, Ottenbacher, Clow, & Ottenbacher, 2008).

Types of Rehabilitative Interventions
Interventions with stroke patients have typically taken four approaches: psychotherapy, including treatment for depression; cognitive remedial training to restore intellectual functioning; movement therapies, which may include training in specific skills development; and the use of structured, stimulating environments to challenge the stroke patient's capabilities (Krantz & Deckel, 1983). Both individual counseling and group therapy are used with some stroke patients (Krantz & Deckel, 1983). Home visits from volunteers or counselors can provide help for the confused and frightened stroke patient who is too ill to go to a facility. Treatment for depression usually takes the form of antidepressants or therapy or both (Hibbard, Grober, Stein, & Gordon, 1992).

Movement-based therapies can help restore functioning following stroke. Although conventional physical therapy is not typically beneficial to stroke patients, a form of physical therapy called constraint-induced movement therapy, which is targeted to the upper extremities, is effective (Gauthier et al., 2008; Taub et al., 2006). Basically, it requires patients to use a more affected limb (such as the left arm) to the relative exclusion of a less affected limb (such as the right arm) for several hours each day. Patients so trained show improved functioning in the affected limbs (Taub et al., 2006).

Interventions designed to deal with cognitive problems after stroke have several goals (Gordon & Diller, 1983). First, patients must be made aware that they have problems. Often, the stroke patient thinks he or she is performing adequately when this is simply not so. A risk of making patients aware of these problems is the sense of discouragement or failure that may arise. Thus, it is important for patients to see that these deficits are correctable.

There are a variety of techniques to help right-brain-damaged stroke patients regain a full visual field (Gordon & Diller, 1983). One method involves spreading out an array of money before a patient and asking him or her to pick all of it up. The right-brain-damaged patient will pick up only the money on the right side, ignoring that on the left. When the patient is induced to turn his or her head toward the impaired side, he or she will see the remaining money and can then pick it up as well.

A scanning machine can improve this process further. Patients are first instructed to follow a moving stimulus with their eyes. When the stimulus moves to the left side of the stimulus array, it is out of sight of right-brain-damaged patients unless they turn their heads. Thus, patients quickly learn to turn their heads so they can pick up all information when the scanner moves into the left side of the visual field. Various tasks that require scanning, such as number canceling, are then introduced, so the patient can get practice using the entire visual field. Gradually, the patient is led to perform tasks without benefit of the artificial scanner. Through these kinds of retraining efforts, many stroke patients are able to regain many of their lost capabilities. Eventually, they can negotiate the world much as they did before the stroke (Gordon & Diller, 1983).

Cognitive remediation is a slow process, and skills retraining needs to proceed in an orderly fashion, beginning with easy problems and moving to more difficult ones. As each skill is acquired, practice is essential (Gordon & Hibbard, 1991).

A relatively recent approach to therapy with stroke patients, called neurorehabilitation, relies on the brain's ability to rebuild itself and learn new tasks. Essentially, the idea is to rewire the brain so that areas of the brain other than the one affected by the stroke can come to take on those functions, thus improving patients' ability to move, speak, and articulate.

Whereas it was once believed that stroke patients would achieve their maximum recovery within the first 6 months after stroke, it now appears that gains can occur over subsequent years (Allen, 2003, April 7).

Certain drugs such as antidepressants and cholesterol-lowering drugs appear to promote the growth of new neurons and may consequently be employed to treat stroke (Abbott, 2004, May 27).

■ TYPE II DIABETES

Type II diabetes is the third most common chronic illness in this country and one of the leading causes of death (Centers for Disease Control and Prevention, 2008b, July). Nearly 8% of the U.S. population has diabetes, and of the roughly 24 million individuals who have it, 5.7 million cases remain undiagnosed (Centers for Disease Control and Prevention, 2008b, July; University of Virginia Health Systems, 2007). People with diabetes are at high risk for hypertension and stroke as well (Roan, 2003, March 10). Diabetes costs the United States more than $174 billion a year in medical costs (American Diabetes Association, 2008). Diabetes is not just a problem in the U.S.; as Figure 13.7 shows, diabetes cases are projected to increase dramatically throughout the world.

FIGURE 13.7 | Diabetes Worldwide, Present and Projected (*Source:* World Health Organization, 2010)

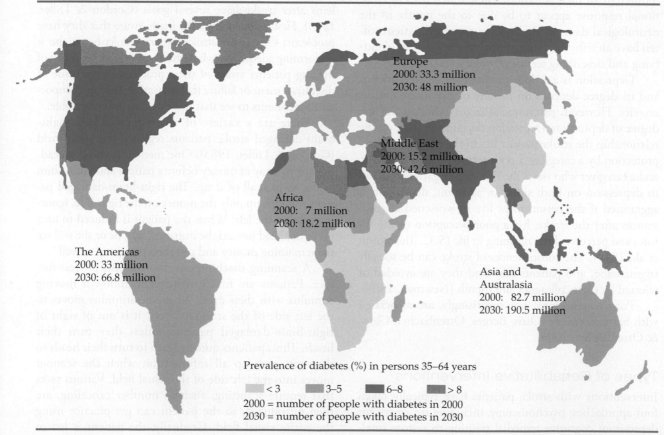

Europe
2000: 33.3 million
2030: 48 million

Middle East
2000: 15.2 million
2030: 42.6 million

Africa
2000: 7 million
2030: 18.2 million

The Americas
2000: 33 million
2030: 66.8 million

Asia and Australasia
2000: 82.7 million
2030: 190.5 million

Prevalence of diabetes (%) in persons 35–64 years

< 3   3–5   6–8   > 8

2000 = number of people with diabetes in 2000
2030 = number of people with diabetes in 2030

In the past 40 years in the U.S., the incidence of diabetes has increased sixfold, and each year, physicians diagnose nearly 1.6 million new cases (Centers for Disease Control and Prevention, 2008b, July). Altogether, diabetes contributed to 233,619 deaths in 2005 alone (Centers for Disease Control and Prevention, 2008b, July). Together with Type I diabetes, an autoimmune disorder covered in the next chapter, Type II diabetes is estimated to cause approximately 46,739 cases of kidney failure, 24,000 cases of blindness, and 71,000 amputations yearly. About 68% of deaths among people with diabetes are due to heart disease and stroke (Centers for Disease Control and Prevention, 2008b, July). At present, about

21.4 million Americans have Type II diabetes. The incidence of cases of Type II diabetes is increasing so rapidly that it is considered a pandemic (Taylor, 2004). The complications of diabetes are pictured in Figure 13.8.

Type II (or non-insulin-dependent) diabetes is typically a disorder of middle and old age. As obesity has become rampant, Type II diabetes, to which obesity is a major contributor, has become more prevalent, especially at earlier ages. Even children and adolescents are now Type II diabetics.

A good deal is known about the mechanisms that trigger Type II diabetes (Kiberstis, 2005). Glucose metabolism involves a delicate balance between insu-

FIGURE 13.8 | The Potential Health Complications of Diabetes Are Extensive, Life-Threatening, and Costly

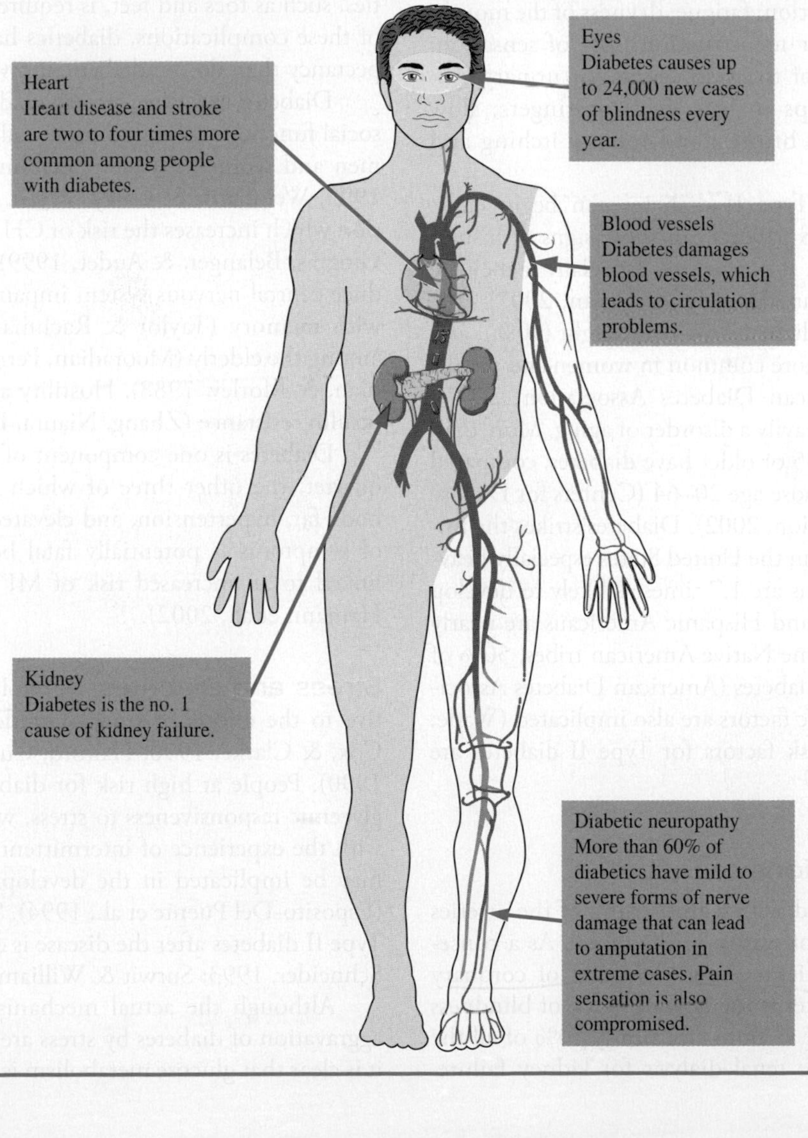

Heart
Heart disease and stroke are two to four times more common among people with diabetes.

Eyes
Diabetes causes up to 24,000 new cases of blindness every year.

Blood vessels
Diabetes damages blood vessels, which leads to circulation problems.

Kidney
Diabetes is the no. 1 cause of kidney failure.

Diabetic neuropathy
More than 60% of diabetics have mild to severe forms of nerve damage that can lead to amputation in extreme cases. Pain sensation is also compromised.

lin production and insulin responsiveness. As food is digested, carbohydrates are broken down into glucose. Glucose is absorbed from the intestines into the blood, where it travels to the liver and other organs. Rising levels of glucose in the blood trigger the pancreas to secrete insulin into the bloodstream. When this balance goes awry, it sets the stage for Type II diabetes. First, cells in muscle, fat, and the liver lose some of their ability to respond fully to insulin, a condition known as insulin resistance. In response to insulin resistance, the pancreas temporarily increases its production of insulin. At this point, insulin-producing cells may give out, with the result that insulin production falls, and the balance between insulin action and insulin secretion becomes disregulated, resulting in Type II diabetes (Alper, 2000). The symptoms include frequent urination; fatigue; dryness of the mouth; impotence; irregular menstruation; loss of sensation; frequent infection of the skin, gums, or urinary system; pain or cramps in legs, feet, or fingers; slow healing of cuts and bruises; and intense itching and drowsiness.

Precursors for Type II diabetes can begin early. Children of low-SES parents can show signs of insulin resistance by age 10, if not before, especially if they are also obese (Goodman, Daniels, & Dolan, 2007). The majority of Type II diabetics are overweight (90%), and Type II diabetes is more common in women and people of low SES (American Diabetes Association, 2007). Type II diabetes is heavily a disorder of aging. More than 17% of people age 65 or older have diabetes, compared with 1.2% among those age 20–64 (Centers for Disease Control and Prevention, 2002). Diabetes strikes the minority communities in the United States especially heavily. African Americans are 1.7 times as likely to develop diabetes as Whites, and Hispanic Americans are nearly twice as likely. In some Native American tribes, 50% of the population has diabetes (American Diabetes Association, 1999). Genetic factors are also implicated (Wade, 2007, April 27). Risk factors for Type II diabetes are listed in Table 13.2.

Health Implications of Diabetes

Diabetes is associated with a thickening of the arteries due to the buildup of wastes in the blood. As a consequence, diabetic patients show high rates of coronary heart disease. Diabetes is the leading cause of blindness among adults, and it accounts for nearly 50% of all the patients who require renal dialysis for kidney failure.

TABLE 13.2 | Risk Factors for Type II Diabetes

You are at risk if:
- You are overweight.
- You get little exercise.
- You have high blood pressure.
- You have a sibling or parent with diabetes.
- You had a baby weighing over 9 pounds at birth.
- You are a member of a high-risk ethnic group, which includes African Americans, Latinos, Native Americans, Asian Americans, and Pacifc Islanders.

Source: American Diabetes Association, 2007.

Diabetes can be associated with nervous system damage, including pain and loss of sensation. Foot ulcers may result, and in severe cases, amputation of the extremities, such as toes and feet, is required. As a consequence of these complications, diabetics have a shorter life expectancy than do nondiabetic individuals.

Diabetes may also exacerbate difficulties in psychosocial functioning, including sexual functioning in both men and women (Spector, Leiblum, Carey, & Rosen, 1993; Weinhardt & Carey, 1996), and risk for depression which increases the risk of CHD (Talbot, Nouwen, Gingras, Belanger, & Audet, 1999). Diabetes may produce central nervous system impairment that interferes with memory (Taylor & Rachman, 1988), especially among the elderly (Mooradian, Perryman, Fitten, Kavonian, & Morley, 1988). Hostility also appears to foster insulin resistance (Zhang, Niaura, Dyer, et al., 2005).

Diabetes is one component of the so-called deadly quartet, the other three of which are intra-abdominal body fat, hypertension, and elevated lipids. This cluster of symptoms is potentially fatal because it is strongly linked to an increased risk of MI and stroke (Weber-Hamann et al., 2002).

Stress and Diabetes   Type II diabetics are sensitive to the effects of stress (Gonder-Frederick, Carter, Cox, & Clarke, 1990; Halford, Cuddihy, & Mortimer, 1990). People at high risk for diabetes show abnormal glycemic responsiveness to stress, which, when coupled with the experience of intermittent or long-term stress, may be implicated in the development of the disease (Esposito-Del Puente et al., 1994). Stress also aggravates Type II diabetes after the disease is diagnosed (Surwit & Schneider, 1993; Surwit & Williams, 1996).

Although the actual mechanisms involved in the aggravation of diabetes by stress are still being explored, it is clear that glucose metabolism is influenced by stress.

As noted, glucose supplies cells with energy, and insulin is responsible for glucose storage. In the presence of stress hormones, such as cortisol, however, insulin is less effective in facilitating glucose storage. This process may result in increased insulin secretion. When insulin is high, systolic blood pressure and heart rate also tend to be elevated. When these processes are combined with overeating and inactivity, the results can lead to obesity, causing further insulin resistance and higher insulin secretion. Depression appears to be implicated in these pathways as well (Timonen et al., 2007).

Just as sympathetic nervous system reactivity is implicated in the development of CHD and hypertension, it is involved in the pathophysiology of Type II diabetes. In particular, a hyperresponsivity to epinephrine, higher levels of circulating catecholamines, and elevated levels of endogenous opioid-peptides are found in many diabetes patients. Thus, theoretically, as is the case with heart disease and hypertension patients, interventions to reduce sympathetic nervous system activity can be useful for modulating hyperglycemia.

Problems in Self-Management of Diabetes

The key to the successful control of diabetes is active self-management (Auerbach et al., 2001). Indeed, Type II diabetes can be completely prevented by changes in the lifestyle of high-risk individuals (Tuomilehto et al., 2001), and the trajectory of the disease in already diagnosed patients can be greatly improved by changes in lifestyle. The lifestyle factors most strongly implicated are exercise, weight loss among those who are overweight, stress management, and dietary control. However, adherence to lifestyle change is problematic, so a therapeutic approach is often undertaken. The ideal treatment is patient-centered and patient-directed, rather than physician-directed.

Managing Type II Diabetes   Type II diabetics are often unaware of the health risks they face. One survey found that only one-third of diagnosed diabetic patients realized that heart disease was among their most serious potential complications (*New York Times*, 2001, May 22). Clearly, education is an important component of intervention.

Dietary intervention involves reducing the sugar and carbohydrate intake of diabetic patients. Obesity especially seems to tax the insulin system, so patients are encouraged to achieve a normal weight. Exercise is espe-cially encouraged (Von Korff et al., 2005) because it helps use up glucose in the blood (Feinglos & Surwit, 1988) and helps reduce weight. Adherence is problematic for Type II diabetics. Poor adherence seems to be due more to transient situational factors, such as psychological stress and social pressure to eat (Goodall & Halford, 1991). People with good self-control skills do a better job of achieving glycemic control by virtue of their greater adherence to a treatment regimen (Peyrot, McMurry, & Kruger, 1999). The nature of the diabetes treatment regimen also contributes to poor rates of adherence. Specifically, the chief factors that require self-control—diet and exercise—are lifestyle factors, and, as we noted in Chapter 3, adherence to recommendations to alter lifestyle is often very low. Voluntarily restricting calories, avoiding desired foods, and engaging in an exercise program may seem like self-punishment, something that many patients are unwilling to do.

Improving Adherence   Nonadherence to treatment programs is influenced by knowledge and health beliefs. Many diabetic patients simply do not have enough information about glucose utilization and metabolic control of insulin. A patient may simply be told what to do without understanding the rationale for it. Patients who are threatened by their disease show poor metabolic control, and those who have strong feelings of self-efficacy achieve better control (Johnson, Tomer, Cunningham, & Henretta, 1990; Kavanaugh, Gooley, & Wilson, 1993).

Does social support improve adherence to a diabetes regimen? Generally, support improves adherence, but this generalization may not be so true for diabetes. Although social support can have beneficial effects on adjustment to the disease, active participation in a social network often leads diabetics to be exposed to norms about diet and temptations to eat that compromise diabetic functioning (Kaplan & Hartwell, 1987; Littlefield, Rodin, Murray, & Craven, 1990). Thus, the effects of social support on Type II diabetes adherence are mixed.

As is true with all chronic diseases, patients with diabetes must play an active role in their own care. Consequently, any intervention that focuses on improving a sense of self-efficacy and the ability to independently regulate one's behavior has the potential to improve adherence and glycemic control (Macrodimitris & Endler, 2001; Senecal, Nouwen, & White, 2000; Williams, McGregor, Zeldman, Freedman, & Deci, 2004). Because of the difficulties that diabetes poses, people may become depressed, particularly those who have one or more

Stress Management and the Control of Diabetes

Mrs. Goldberg had had Type II diabetes for some time. Her doctor had made the diagnosis 10 years earlier, just after her 40th birthday. She watched her diet, got sufficient exercise, and was able to control her blood glucose with oral medication. During the past several months, however, Mrs. Goldberg's diabetes control had begun to deteriorate. Despite the fact that she continued to follow her diet and exercise regimen, her blood glucose levels became elevated more frequently.

Mrs. Goldberg consulted her physician, who asked her if her lifestyle had changed in any way over the past several months. She told him that her boss had added several new responsibilities to her job and that they made her workday much more stressful. Things were so bad that she was having trouble sleeping at night and dreaded going to work in the morning. Mrs. Goldberg's physician told her that this additional stress might be responsible for her poor diabetes control.

Rather than initially changing her medications, he suggested that she first speak with her boss to see if some of the stress of her job might be relieved. Fortunately, her boss was understanding and allowed Mrs. Goldberg to share her responsibilities with another employee. Within several weeks, she no longer dreaded going to work, and her diabetes control improved significantly.

This case illustrates how a relatively simple change in a patient's environment may have a clinically significant impact on blood glucose control. It underscores the need for the physician to be aware of what is happening in the patient's life in order to determine requirements for treatment. Under the circumstances described, it would have been inappropriate to have altered this patient's medication.

Source: Feinglos & Surwit, 1988, p. 29.

coexisting chronic conditions, such as arthritis, stroke, or coronary artery disease.

Depression not only complicates prognosis but may also interfere with the active self-management role that diabetes patients must play (Katon et al., 2009). Depressed patients with Type II diabetes may especially need interventions that target a sense of self-efficacy in order to improve their adherence and ability to achieve control over their blood sugar levels (Cherrington, Wallston, & Rothman, 2010). Anger may undermine glycemic control as well (Yi, Yi, Vitaliano, & Weinger, 2008).

Interventions with Diabetics

A variety of cognitive-behavioral interventions have been undertaken with Type II diabetics to improve adherence to aspects of their regimen. Much nonadherence results from running out of medications or forgetting to take them, and so these are logical targets for intervention (Hill-Briggs et al., 2005). Some programs have focused on training patients to monitor blood sugar levels effectively (Wing, Epstein, et al., 1986). As a result of ties between stress and diabetes (Herschbach et al., 1997), behavioral investigators have examined the effect of stress management programs on diabetes control. An example of combating stress to control diabetes appears in Box 13.6. Even very brief interventions via telephone can improve functioning among Type II diabetics (Sacco, Malone, Morrison, Friedman, & Wells, 2009). Recently too, personal digital assistants that prompt people about aspects of their self-care have been used (Sevick et al., 2010).

Weight control improves glycemic control and reduces the need for medication, and so behavioral interventions that help diabetic patients lose weight hold promise (Wing, Epstein, et al., 1986). However, as with most weight-loss programs, following initial success, people often relapse to their poor habits and may gain back the weight (Wing, Blair, Marcus, Epstein, & Harvey, 1994).

Because the diabetes regimen is complex, involves lifestyle change, and implicates multiple risk factors, technical skills to manage the regimen as well as problem-solving skills and active coping methods are needed. Stress, depression, and low self-efficacy can undermine a commitment to behavior change (Kim, Bursac, DiLillo, White, & West, 2009). Thus, training in self-management and problem-solving skills is a vital part of many interventions with diabetes (Hill-Briggs, 2003). Building a sense of self-efficacy is important to this process (Dutton et al., 2009).

Many Type II diabetics fail to recognize that they have a chronic health condition that requires sustained commitment to medications and behavior change, and so ensuring that these patients have the correct beliefs about their illness is critical to adherence (Mann, Ponieman, Leventhal, & Halm, 2009; Searle et al., 2008). Because of problems involving adherence, a focus on maintenance and relapse prevention is also essential.

The fact that stress and social pressure to eat reduce adherence has led researchers to focus on social skills and problem-solving skills training in diabetes management (Glasgow, Toobert, Hampson, & Wilson, 1995). In addition, diabetic patients often need training in how to maintain the treatment regimen in the face of social circumstances that undermine it (Glasgow, Engel, & D'Lugoff, 1989; Goodall & Halford, 1991).

A complication of diabetes is that mental disorders may commonly predispose to or accompany it (Das-Munshi et al., 2007; Golden et al., 2007). Especially as symptoms increase and the disease intrudes increasingly on life activities, patients may become depressed (Sacco et al., 2005). Negative mood, including hostility, predicts subsequent glucose level and thus appears to enhance risk of progressing disease (Georgiades et al., 2009; Skaff et al., 2009; Surwit et al., 2009). Depression reduces self-efficacy, compromises adherence, and leads to poor glucose control and poor compliance with the diabetes treatment regimen (Sacco et al., 2007; Schweiger et al., 2008). Depression is also linked to an enhanced risk of CHD among women diagnosed with diabetes; thus, it represents a particularly problematic complication (Clouse et al., 2003). As a result, emotional distress often needs to be an object of treatment, as well as a symptom of the disease (Duangdao & Roesch, 2008). Unfortunately, a lack of distress can sometimes mean that patients are avoiding dealing with the illness, rather than adjusting to it (Thoolen, De Ridder, Bensing, Gorter, & Rutten, 2008).

Because diabetes is linked to other disorders, including cardiovascular disease, stroke, and heart attack, interventions that target multiple risk factors may be especially effective. One study that employed behavior modification and pharmacological therapy that targeted hyperglycemia, hypertension, elevated lipids, and CVD (treated by an aspirin) found substantial reduction not only in diabetes but in cardiovascular events as well (Goede et al., 2003).

Diabetes Prevention   Increasingly, health psychologists and policy makers are recognizing that diabetes is a major public health problem. Proactive responses to its increasing incidence are on the rise and include more active efforts to control obesity as the first defense against this common, costly, and rapidly growing disorder (Castro, Shaibi, & Boehm-Smith, 2009; Glasgow et al., 2002).

One investigation (Diabetes Prevention Program Research Group, 2002) identified 3,000 adults whose blood sugar levels were high but not yet high enough to be diagnosed with diabetes. These high-risk individuals were then assigned to one of three groups. One group received a placebo medication and lifestyle recommendations; the second group received lifestyle recommendations and a medication that lowers blood sugar; the third group received an intensive lifestyle intervention focused on weight loss, physical activity, and diet change. After only 4 years, the incidence of diabetes was decreased by 58% in the lifestyle intervention group and by 31% in the medication group when compared to the placebo group. The fact that only modest weight loss and small increases in physical activity were needed to achieve these results suggests that intervening with high-risk individuals to modify a lifestyle can be successful in reducing the incidence of diabetes. ●

SUMMARY

1. Coronary heart disease is the number one killer in the United States. It is a disease of lifestyle, and risk factors include cigarette smoking, obesity, elevated serum cholesterol, low levels of physical activity, chronic stress, and hostility.

2. Coronary proneness is associated with hostility, depression, and hyperreactivity to stressful situations, including a slow return to baseline. These exaggerated cardiovascular responses to stress may be partly genetically based, related to heightened neuroendocrine reactivity to environmental stressors.

3. Efforts to modify excessive reactivity to stress and hostility through training in relaxation and stress management show promise in reducing morbidity and mortality due to CHD.

4. Cardiac rehabilitation is designed to help diagnosed CHD patients obtain their optimal physical, medical, psychological, social, emotional, vocational, and economic status. Components of these programs typically include education in CHD, drug treatments, nutritional counseling, supervised exercise, stress management, and, under some circumstances, psychological counseling and/or social support group participation.

5. MI patients often have difficulty managing the stress reduction aspects of their regimens, and sometimes marital relations can be strained as a result of the changes forced on patient and spouse by the post-MI rehabilitative regimen.

6. Hypertension, or high blood pressure, affects one in four Americans. Most hypertension is of unknown origin, although risk factors include family history of hypertension. Low-SES Blacks are particularly vulnerable.

7. Hypertensives show heightened reactivity to stressful events. Hostility is also implicated.

8. Hypertension is typically treated by diuretics or beta-blocking drugs, which may have adverse side effects. Cognitive-behavioral treatments, including stress management, have been used to control the disorder and to reduce drug dosages.

9. The biggest problems related to the control of hypertension concern high rates of nondiagnosis and nonadherence to therapy. The fact that the disease is symptomless helps explain both problems. Low rates of adherence are also explained by the adverse side effects of drugs.

10. Stroke results from a disturbance in blood flow to the brain. It may disrupt all aspects of life. Motor difficulties, cognitive impairments, and depression are particular problems associated with stroke.

11. Interventions for stroke patients have typically involved psychotherapy, including treatment for depression; cognitive remedial training to restore intellectual functioning; skill building; and structured, stimulating environments to challenge the stroke patient's capabilities.

12. Type II diabetes is the third most common chronic disease in the United States. It typically develops after age 40.

13. The diabetes self-care regimen chiefly involves exercise, controlling diet, and stress reduction. Adherence to this regimen is poor.

14. Interventions can improve adherence, especially if the different components of the regimen are logically linked to each other in a programmatic effort toward effective self-care. Training in diabetes-specific social management skills and problem-solving skills are important, as is treatment for depression, if relevant.

KEY TERMS

cardiac invalidism
cardiac rehabilitation
cardiopulmonary resuscitation (CPR)

cardiovascular disease (CVD)
coronary heart disease (CHD)
hypertension
ischemia

John Henryism
metabolic syndrome
stroke
Type II diabetes

CHAPTER 14

Psychoneuroimmunology and Immune-Related Disorders

Mei-ling was facing the toughest semester she had ever had. Her father had lost his job, so in addition to trying to provide social support to her parents, she had been forced to take on a part-time job to help pay for her college expenses.

She had scheduled her courses for the first few hours of the morning so that by 1:30 she was able to get over to the accountant's office where she answered phones and billed clients until 6:00 at night. Then she headed back to the dorm to study long into the night. Her boyfriend, Mark, was complaining that he never saw her anymore. When he was free and wanted to go out to a movie or to a fraternity party, she was always studying, trying to make up for the time she lost while she was working. He hadn't actually said that he was going to start dating other women, but she suspected he might soon reach that point.

And now she faced exams. All of them promised to be challenging, and she would have to rearrange her work hours to accommodate the exam schedule. Her boss was annoyed enough at the fact that she sometimes had to reduce her hours to complete course requirements, and he was not going to appreciate the further complications in her schedule that the exams would create.

Mei-ling made it through her exams, but just barely. Following her last exam, in Spanish, she headed back to her room and collapsed into bed with a temperature of 102, where she stayed, nursing a respiratory flu, for the next 10 days.

In this chapter, we take up the question of immunity, the factors that influence it, and the situations that compromise it. Mei-ling's case is not unusual. Stress and problems in social support are among the conditions that compromise the ability of the body to mount resistance to potential infection.

For many years, the immune system was one of the most poorly understood systems of the human body. However, in recent decades, research advances in this area have been substantial, leading to the burgeoning field of psychoneuroimmunology. **Psychoneuroimmunology** refers to the interactions among behavioral, neuroendocrine, and immunological processes of adaptation (Ader, 1995).

■ PSYCHONEUROIMMUNOLOGY

The Immune System

As noted in Chapter 2, the immune system is the surveillance system of the body. It is implicated in infection, allergies, cancer, and autoimmune diseases, among other disorders. The primary function of the immune system is to distinguish between what is "self" and what is foreign and then to attack and rid the body of foreign invaders.

A Profile of the Immune System   To understand the relationship of psychosocial factors to the immune system, it is important to reiterate the distinction between natural and specific immunity. Natural immunity is involved in defense against pathogens. The cells involved in natural immunity provide defense not against a particular pathogen, but rather against many pathogens. Also, as noted in Chapter 2, the largest group of cells involved in natural immunity is granulocytes, which include neutrophils and macrophages; both are phagocytic cells that engulf target pathogens. Neutrophils and macrophages congregate at the site of an injury or infection and release toxic substances. Macrophages release cytokines that lead to inflammation and fever, among other side effects, and promote wound healing. Natural killer cells are also involved in natural immunity; they recognize "nonself" material (such as viral infections or cancer cells) and lyse (break up and disintegrate) those cells by releasing toxic substances. Natural killer cells are believed to be important in signaling potential malignancies and in limiting early phases of viral infections.

Specific immunity is slower and, as its name implies, more specific than natural immunity. The lymphocytes involved in specific immunity have receptor sites on their cell surfaces that fit with one, and only one, antigen, and thus, they respond to only one kind of invader. When they are activated, these antigen-specific cells divide and create a population of cells called the proliferative response.

Essentially, natural and specific immunity work together, such that natural immunity contains an infection or wound rapidly and early on following the invasion of a pathogen, whereas specific immunity involves a delay of up to several days before a full defense can be mounted. Figure 14.1 illustrates the interaction between lymphocytes and phagocytes.

Humoral and Cell-Mediated Immunity   As explained in Chapter 2, specific immunity is of two types—humoral and cell mediated. Humoral immunity is mediated by B lymphocytes, which provide protection against bacteria, neutralize toxins produced by bacteria, and prevent viral reinfection. Cell-mediated immunity, involving T lymphocytes from the thymus gland, operates at the cellular level. Cytotoxic (T_C) cells respond to

FIGURE 14.1 | Interaction Between Lymphocytes and Phagocytes   B lymphocytes release antibodies, which bind to pathogens and their products, aiding recognition by phagocytes. Cytokines released by T cells activate the phagocytes to destroy the material they have taken up. In turn, mononuclear phagocytes can present antigen to T cells, thereby activating them. (*Source:* Roitt, Brostoff, & Male, 1998)

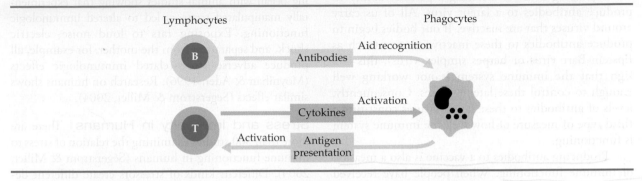

specific antigens and kill by producing toxic substances that destroy virally infected cells. Helper T (T$_H$) cells enhance the functioning of T$_C$ cells, B cells, and macrophages by producing lymphokines. Lymphokines also appear to serve a counterregulatory immune function that suppresses immune activity. Components of the immune system are pictured in Figure 14.2.

Assessing Immune Functioning

There are many potential indicators of immune functioning. Some approaches have been:

1. Assessing the functioning of immune cells
2. Assessing the production of antibodies to latent viruses

3. Assessing levels of immune system products, such as proinflammatory cytokines
4. Using indirect measures, such as wound healing or skin barrier functional recovery

Assessing the functioning of cells involves examining the activation, proliferation, transformation, and cytotoxicity of cells. One might assess the ability of lymphocytes to kill invading cells (lymphocyte cytotoxicity), the ability of lymphocytes to reproduce when artificially stimulated by a chemical (mitogen), and the ability of certain white blood cells to ingest foreign particles (phagocytotic activity). For example, in the mitogenic stimulation technique, it is assumed that the more

FIGURE 14.2 | Components of the Immune System   (*Source:* Roitt, Brostoff, & Male, 1998)

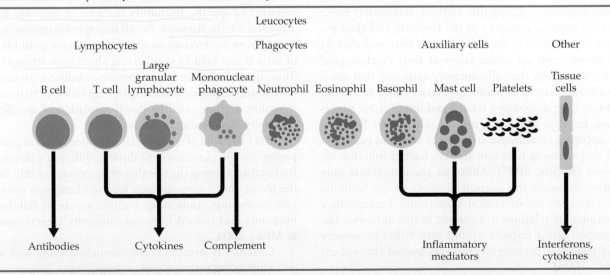

proliferation that occurs in response to the mitogen, the better the cells are functioning.

Another measure of how well the immune system is functioning involves assessing a person's ability to produce antibodies to a latent virus. All of us carry around viruses that are inactive. If our bodies begin to produce antibodies to these inactive viruses (such as Epstein-Barr virus or herpes simplex virus), this is a sign that the immune system is not working well enough to control these latent viruses. Consequently, levels of antibodies to these latent viruses constitute a third type of measure of how well the immune system is functioning.

Producing antibodies to a vaccine is also a measure of immune functioning. When people have received vaccination for particular disorders, the degree to which the body produces antibodies to the vaccine is a sign of good functioning. For example, people going through stress are less likely to show a strong response to vaccination (Marsland, Cohen, Rabin, & Manuck, 2001).

To assess immune functioning, researchers can also measure immune-related products in the blood, such as proinflammatory cytokines. These cytokines are indicative of inflammatory activity and may increase in response to stress. For example, one study (Moons, Eisenberger, & Taylor, 2010) found elevations in IL-6, a proinflammatory cytokine, following exposure to laboratory stressors, especially among people who responded to those stressors with fear.

Another way of studying the effects of stress and psychosocial resources on immune functioning is to examine wound healing or tape stripping. Wounds heal faster when the immune system is functioning more vigorously. Using this method, researchers make a small puncture, usually in the forearm, and then examine how quickly the wound heals over and shrinks in people who are under stress or not. Psychological distress impairs the inflammatory response that initiates wound repair (Broadbent, Petrie, Alley, & Booth, 2003). Tape stripping, a related and less invasive procedure, involves disrupting normal skin barrier function by applying an adhesive strip to the skin and pulling it off and assessing how quickly skin barrier function recovers (Robles, 2007). Although these methods only indirectly assess the relation of stress to the immune system, they are of critical importance because they demonstrate relations to a specific health outcome. For example, stress impairs wound repair due to surgery and thus may prolong the recovery period (Broadbent et al., 2003).

Stress and Immune Functioning

Many commonplace stressors can adversely affect the immune system. Research on stress and immune functioning began with animal studies showing that experimentally manipulated stressors led to altered immunologic functioning. Exposing rats to loud noise, electric shock, and separation from the mother, for example, all produce adverse stress-related immunologic effects (Moynihan & Ader, 1996). Research on humans shows similar effects (Segerstrom & Miller, 2004).

Stress and Immunity in Humans   There are more than 300 studies examining the relation of stress to immune functioning in humans (Segerstrom & Miller, 2004). Different kinds of stressors create different demands on the body, so they show different effects on the immune system. Human beings evolved so that, in response to sudden stress, changes in the immune system could take place quickly, leading to wound repair and infection prevention. Thus, short-term stressors (of a few minutes' duration) produce a fight-or-flight response and would be expected to elicit immune responses that anticipate risk of injury and possible entry of infectious agents into the bloodstream. Although short-term stressors now rarely involve wounds and the subsequent threat of infection, the system that evolved to deal with these threats is, nonetheless, mobilized in response to short-term stressors. So, for example, a short-term stressor, such as being called on in class or having to rapidly do arithmetic in one's head, leads to marked increases in both natural killer cells and large granular lymphocytes as well as enhanced response to vaccination (Edwards et al., 2008). In contrast, some measures of specific immunity decrease in response to acute short-term stressors. Recall that specific immunity is quite slow to develop, so specific immunity would be of little if any help in combatting short-term stressors. Thus, immediate short-term stressors produce a pattern of immune responses involving up-regulation of natural immunity accompanied by down-regulation of specific immunity (Segerstrom & Miller, 2004).

Brief stressors of several days' duration, such as preparing for an examination, show a different pattern. Rather than altering the number or percentage of cells in the blood, short-term stressors lead to changes in cytokine production, indicating a shift away from cellular immunity and toward humoral immunity (Segerstrom & Miller, 2004).

Chronically stressful events, including living with a disability, being unemployed, or engaging in long-term caregiving, are reliably tied to adverse effects on almost all functional measures of the immune system, involving both cellular and humoral down-regulation. These effects are stronger among people with preexisting vulnerabilities, such as old age or disease. Chronic inflammation, which may occur in response to chronically stressful conditions (Robles, Glaser, & Kiecolt-Glaser, 2005), contributes to a broad range of disorders, including heart disease (Miller & Blackwell, 2006) and declines in cognitive performance (Marsland, Petersen, et al., 2006).

Thus, different types of stressful events (short term versus a few days versus long term) make different demands on the body that are reflected in different patterns of immune activity, in ways consistent with evolutionary arguments.

The body's stress systems appear to partially regulate these effects. As we saw in Chapter 6, stress engages the sympathetic nervous system and the HPA axis, both of which also influence immune functioning. Sympathetic activation in response to stress has immediate effects of increasing immune activity, especially natural killer cell activity. Stress-related changes in hypothalamic adrenocortical functioning have immunosuppressive effects (Miller, Chen, & Zhou, 2007). That is, activation of the HPA axis leads to the release of glucocorticoids such as cortisol; cortisol reduces the number of white blood cells, affects the functioning of lymphocytes, and reduces the release of cytokines, which can reduce the ability of these substances to signal and communicate with other aspects of the immune system. Cortisol can also trigger apoptosis (cell death) of white blood cells. In addition, there may be downward modulation of the immune system by the cerebral cortex, possibly via the release of neuropeptides such as beta-endorphins (Levy, Fernstrom, et al., 1991; Morley, Kay, & Solomon, 1988).

Self-rated health, that enigmatic window that people seem to have into their own bodies that is independent of any diagnosable pathology, predicts levels of circulating cytokines. Possibly, levels of circulating cytokines are a source of people's perceptions of their own bodily states (Lekander, Elofsson, Neve, Hansson, & Undén, 2004).

Examples of Stress Studies Eleven astronauts who flew five different space shuttle flights ranging in length from 4 to 16 days were studied before launch and after landing (Mills, Meck, Waters, D'Aunno, & Ziegler, 2001). As expected, space flight was associated with a significant increase in the number of circulating white blood cells, and natural killer cells decreased. At landing,

catecholamines (epinephrine and norepinephrine) increased substantially, as did white blood cells. These effects were stronger for astronauts who had been in space approximately 1 week, but among those who had experienced long-term flight (about 2 weeks), the effects were attenuated. This evidence suggests that the stress of space flight and landing produces a sympathetic nervous system response that mediates redistribution of circulating leukocytes, but this response may be attenuated during longer missions. Perhaps the stress of landing is muted by the relief of coming home safely. Another study of astronauts found that space flight resulted in decreased T cell immunity and reactivation of the Epstein-Barr virus (a latent virus), consistent with the idea that the immune system was showing the effects of stress (Stowe, Pierson, & Barrett, 2001).

Many studies of stress involve the effects of natural disasters and other traumas on immune functioning. A study of community responses to Hurricane Andrew damage, for example, revealed substantial changes in the immune systems of those most directly affected, changes that appeared to be due primarily to sleep problems that occurred in the wake of the hurricane (Ironson et al., 1997). In a study with older adults, perceived stress was associated with a lower antibody response to influenza vaccine; however, people who had strong social support systems showed stronger antibody titres (Moynihan et al., 2004).

Stress involving threats to the self may be especially likely to produce changes in immune functioning. A study by Dickerson and colleagues (2004) had healthy participants write about neutral experiences or about traumatic experiences for which they blamed themselves. Those who wrote about traumas for which they blamed themselves showed an increase in shame and guilt, coupled with elevations in proinflammatory cytokine activity. These findings suggest that self-related emotions can cause changes in inflammatory processes (Gruenewald, Kemeny, Aziz, & Fahey, 2004).

Several studies have examined whether daily hassles are associated with immune functioning. One study focused especially on a group of people who were chronically low in NK cell activity. They found that the two factors that best predicted this group were age and severity of daily hassles. The authors concluded that people who perceived the events as especially serious were likely to exhibit chronically low NK cytotoxic activity (Levy et al., 1989). Living in a disadvantaged neighborhood, a source of both chronic and acute stress, has been related to higher levels of inflammatory activity, which also

BOX 14.1

Academic Stress and Immune Functioning

Students are a captive population who are often willing and able to participate in research; consequently, much of the groundbreaking work on stress and the immune system has involved coping with the stress of school. Students may take grim satisfaction from studies indicating that, indeed, examinations, public speaking, and other stressful events of academic life can lead to enhanced cardiovascular activity, changes in immunologic parameters, and even illness.

One study (Glaser, Kiecolt-Glaser, Stout, et al., 1985), for example, assessed immune parameters in a sample of 40 second-year medical students at 6 weeks before final exams and then again during finals. The students showed an increase in distress from the first to the second time period, and the percentages of total T and T_H lymphocytes were significantly lower during exams. There was also a decrease in NK cells and a significant depression in NK cell cytotoxic activity. Lymphocyte responsivity was lower during the exam period than at baseline, as was the quantity of interferon produced by stimulated leukocytes.

Several subsequent studies have confirmed these earlier observations (Cohen, Marshall, Cheng, Agarwal, & Wei, 2000; Glaser et al., 1999; Glaser et al., 1992; Tomei, Kiecolt-Glaser, Kennedy, & Glaser, 1990). Even children experience this effect. Boyce and colleagues (1993) conducted a study with children who had recently begun kindergarten and who experienced a mild earthquake about 6 weeks into the school year. Those who had shown significant alterations in immune functioning in response to beginning kindergarten were more likely to experience a respiratory infection, such as a cold, following the earthquake (Boyce et al., 1993), suggesting that the earlier compromise of their stress

Studies show that exams and other stressful aspects of academic life can adversely compromise immune functioning.

systems had left them vulnerable to an illness following the second stressor.

School-related stress, then, does appear to compromise immune functioning. Are these changes inevitable? If people take care of themselves, can they avoid adverse changes in immunity in response to stress? Students who are optimistic about their ability to manage school-related stress and who make active efforts to cope with it fare better both psychologically and immunologically than those who did not (Segerstrom, Taylor, Kemeny, & Fahey, 1998). Good coping, then, may help offset the adverse effects of stress on the immune system.

attests to the relationship between stress and immune functioning (Miller & Chen, 2007; Petersen et al., 2008).

Anticipatory stress can also compromise immune functioning. In a longitudinal study of patients vulnerable to genital herpes recurrences, M. E. Kemeny and her colleagues (1989) found that over a 6-month period the number of stressful events experienced was associated with a decreased percentage of T_H cells. More interesting is the fact that anticipated stressors, those that had not yet occurred but that were expected,

were also related to decreased percentage of T_H cells. Box 14.1 illustrates how academic stress affects immune functioning.

Interestingly, the effects of stress on immune functioning can be somewhat delayed. A study of antibody responses to the influenza vaccine suggested that psychological stress just before the vaccine was not related to the response, but in the 10 days following vaccination, stress had shaped long-term antibody responses. These effects may have been mediated by the effect of stress on sleep loss (Miller et al., 2004).

BOX 14.2

Autoimmune Disorders

In autoimmune diseases, the immune system attacks the body's own tissues, falsely identifying them as invaders (Medzhitov & Janeway, 2002). Autoimmune diseases include more than 80 conditions, and virtually every organ is potentially vulnerable. Some of the most common disorders include Type I diabetes; Graves' disease, involving excessive production of thyroid hormones; chronic active hepatitis, involving the chronic inflammation of the liver; lupus, which is chronic inflammation of the connective tissue and which can affect multiple organ systems; multiple sclerosis, which involves the destruction of the myelin sheath that surrounds nerves and which produces a range of neurological symptoms; and rheumatoid arthritis, in which the immune system attacks and inflames the tissue lining the joints. The conditions range from mildly annoying to severe, progressive, and fatal.

Nearly 80% of people who have these and other autoimmune disorders are women. Exactly why women are so vulnerable is not yet completely understood. One possibility is that hormonal changes relating to estrogen modulate the occurrence and severity of symptoms. Consistent with this point, many women first develop symptoms of an autoimmune disorder in their 20s, when estrogen levels are high. Another theory is that testosterone, a hormone that women have in

short supply, may help protect against autoimmune disorders (Angier, 2001, June 19). A third theory is that during pregnancy, mother and fetus exchange bodily cells, which can remain in the mother's body for years. Although these cells are very similar to the mother's own, they are not identical, and so, the theory suggests, the immune system may get confused and attack both the leftover fetal cells and the maternal cells that look similar.

Because autoimmune disorders are a related group of conditions, the likelihood of suffering from one and then contracting another is relatively high. Genetic factors are implicated in autoimmunity (Ueda et al., 2003); one family member may develop lupus, another rheumatoid arthritis, and a third Graves' disease. Efforts to understand autoimmune diseases have recently been given extra urgency by the fact that immune-related disorders are implicated in atherosclerosis and diabetes, which are common. For example, people with lupus are at risk for premature coronary artery atherosclerosis (Asanuma et al., 2003) and for accelerated atherosclerosis (Ham, 2003; Roman et al., 2003).

Autoimmune conditions appear to be on the rise, and consequently, understanding their causes and effective management will become a high priority for both scientists and health care practitioners.

Health Risks Is the immune modulation that is produced by psychological stressors sufficient to lead to actual effects on health? The answer seems to be yes. Research suggests that both children and adults under stress show increased vulnerability to infectious disease, including colds, flus, herpes virus infections (such as cold sores or genital lesions), chicken pox, mononucleosis, and Epstein-Barr virus (Cohen & Herbert, 1996; Cohen, Tyrrell, & Smith, 1993; Kiecolt-Glaser & Glaser, 1987). Among people who are already ill, such as those with a respiratory infection, stress predicts more severe illness and higher production of cytokines (Cohen, Doyle, & Skoner, 1999). Diseases whose onset and course are influenced by proinflammatory cytokines are also major health risks and include cardiovascular disease and arthritis (Kiecolt-Glaser, McGuire, Robles, & Glaser, 2002). Autoimmune disorders, which are described in Box 14.2, are also affected by stress.

Negative Affect and Immune Functioning

Stress may compromise immune functioning, in part, because it increases negative emotions such as depression or anxiety. Depression has been heavily studied as a culprit in the stress-immunity relationship (Cohen & Herbert, 1996; Robles et al., 2005). A review (Herbert & Cohen, 1993) found depression to be associated with several alterations in cellular immunity—specifically, lowered proliferative response of lymphocytes to mitogens, lowered NK cell activity, and alterations in numbers of white blood cells (see Miller, Cohen, & Herbert, 1999). These immune effects were stronger among older people and people who were hospitalized, suggesting that already vulnerable people are at special risk.

Moreover, there is a fairly straightforward relationship between depression and immunity such that the more depressed a person is, the more cellular immunity is likely to be compromised. Depressive symptoms can be associated with amplified and prolonged inflammatory responses as well, which may provide important links to disease (Robles et al., 2005). For example, depression has been tied to delayed wound healing (Bosch, Engeland, Cacioppo, & Marucha, 2007). The adverse effects of depression on immunity may also be mediated by the sleep disturbance that results from depression (Cover & Irwin, 1994).

By contrast, positive affect has been tied to more rapid recovery from a skin barrier disruption (Robles, Brooks, & Pressman, 2009).

Stress, Immune Functioning, and Interpersonal Relationships

Both human and animal research suggests the importance of personal relationships to immune functioning (Cohen & Herbert, 1996). One of the earliest investigations examined bereavement. In a prospective study, R. W. Bartrop and associates (1977) studied 26 bereaved individuals and 26 comparison subjects matched for age, sex, and race. A number of immunologic parameters were examined 3 weeks after bereavement and again 6 weeks later. At the second time point, the bereaved group showed less responsiveness to mitogenic challenge than did the comparison group. More recent research suggests that impaired immunity in response to bereavement is found largely among those people who become depressed in response to the bereavement (Zisook et al., 1994).

Loneliness also appears to adversely affect immune functioning. Lonely people have poorer health and show more immunocompromise on certain indicators than do people who are not lonely (Glaser, Kiecolt-Glaser, Speicher, & Holliday, 1985; Pressman et al., 2005). People with insecure attachments to others show lower NK cell cytotoxicity, suggesting potential health risks as well (Picardi et al., 2007).

Chronic interpersonal stress has been related to inflammatory activity over time; possibly this pathway underlies the relation of social stress to diseases that implicate inflammatory pathways, such as depression and atherosclerosis (Miller, Rohleder, & Cole, 2009). Social stress also desensitizes the regulation of lymphocytes by the HPA axis, which may also contribute to the health risks incurred by people who experience social stress (Cole, Mendoza, & Capitanio, 2009). Adolescents with high levels of interpersonal stress have elevated inflammation (Fuligni et al., 2009).

Marital Disruption and Conflict   Marital disruption and conflict have also been tied to adverse changes in immunity. In a study by J. K. Kiecolt-Glaser

and colleagues (1987), women who had been separated from their husbands for 1 year or less showed poorer functioning on some immune parameters than did their matched married counterparts. Among separated and divorced women, recent separation and continued attachment to or preoccupation with the ex-husband were associated with poorer immune functioning and with more depression and loneliness. Similar results have been found for men facing separation or divorce (Kiecolt-Glaser & Newton, 2001).

Not surprisingly, partner violence has been tied to adverse changes in immune functioning as well (Garcia-Linares, Sanchez-Lorente, Coe, & Martinez, 2004; Kiecolt-Glaser et al., 2005). Even short-term marital conflict can have a discernible effect on the immune system. J. K. Kiecolt-Glaser and colleagues (1993) assessed the relationship between marital conflict and immune functioning in 90 newlywed couples. The couples were asked to spend 30 minutes discussing their marital problems. Those who exhibited negative or hostile behaviors during the discussion also showed impairment on several functional immunologic tests. These results are especially noteworthy because marital adjustment among newlyweds is generally very high, and the couples had been initially selected because they had good physical and mental health. A subsequent study showed similar effects in couples who had been married, on average, 42 years, suggesting that even in long-term marriages, people are not protected against the adverse immunologic effects of marital conflict (Kiecolt-Glaser et al., 1997). Adverse effects of marital problems and conflict appear to fall more heavily on women than on men (see Kiecolt-Glaser & Newton, 2001, for a review). Positive behavior during marital conflict, however, can lead to steeper declines in stress hormones with concomitant beneficial effects on immunity (Graham et al., 2009; Robles, Shaffer, Malarkey, & Kiecolt-Glaser, 2006).

Caregiving   In Chapter 11, we saw how stressful caregiving can be for people who provide care for a friend or family member with a long-term illness, such as AIDS or Alzheimer's disease. Caregiving has been investigated for its impact on the immune system (Esterling, Kiecolt-Glaser, & Glaser, 1996; Kiecolt-Glaser, Glaser, Gravenstein, Malarkey, & Sheridan, 1996). In one study, caregivers for Alzheimer's patients were more depressed and showed lower life satisfaction than did a comparison sample. The caregivers had higher EBV antibody titres (an indication of poor immune control of latent virus reactivation) and lower percentages of

T cells and T_H cells. These differences did not appear to be related to nutrition, alcohol use, caffeine consumption, or sleep loss.

Other studies have found that the stress of caregiving has adverse effects on wound repair (Kiecolt-Glaser, Marucha, Malarkey, Mercado, & Glaser, 1995), on defects in NK cell function (Esterling et al., 1996), and on reactions to flu vaccine (Kiecolt-Glaser et al., 1996). Caregivers who experience emotional distress, such as anger or depression, may be at particular risk for adverse effects on the immune system (Scanlan, Vitaliano, Zhang, Savage, & Ochs, 2001). Effective coping can mitigate this distress (Engler et al., 2006).

Severe and long-term stressors, such as those that result from caregiving, may leave caregivers vulnerable to a range of health-related problems. Moreover, these immune alterations can persist well beyond the end of the stressful situation—that is, after caregiving activities have ceased (Esterling, Kiecolt-Glaser, Bodnar, & Glaser, 1994).

Protective Effects of Social Support

Emerging evidence points to a potentially important role for social support in buffering people against adverse immune change in response to stress. Studies with monkeys, for example, suggest that affiliating with fellow monkeys protects against decreases in lymphocyte response to mitogens that would normally be elicited by a chronic stressor (Cohen, Kaplan, Cunnick, Manuck, & Rabin, 1992). In a study of breast cancer patients, S. M. Levy and colleagues (1990) found that perceived social support buffered NK cell activity in response to stress. Specifically, the tendency to seek social support and the perception that one had good emotional support from one's spouse, from an intimate other, or from a physician were associated with high NK cell activity.

Coping and Coping Resources as Moderators of the Stress–Immune Functioning Relationship

In Chapter 7, we saw that the impact of stressful events on distress and adverse health outcomes can sometimes be muted by coping methods, such as problem solving, stress management, and relaxation. Research suggests that these resources may also moderate the relation between stress and immune functioning.

Optimism

S. C. Segerstrom and colleagues (1998) found that optimism and active coping strategies were protective against stress. In this study, 90 first-year law

students, tested at the beginning of law school and again halfway through the first semester, completed questionnaires measuring how they coped with the stress of law school, and they had blood drawn for an assessment of immune measures. The optimistic law students and students who used fewer avoidant coping methods showed less increase in distress across the quarter; pessimism, avoidance coping, and mood disturbance, in turn, predicted less NK cell cytotoxicity and fewer numbers of T cells, suggesting that optimism and coping can be important influences on stress-related distress and immune changes.

Personal Control/Benefit Finding

When people are exposed to stressors, such as noise, those who perceive that they can control the noise show little change in immune parameters. In contrast, those people exposed to stressors they perceive to be uncontrollable are more likely to show adverse effects (Sieber et al., 1992).

Similar findings have emerged with clinical populations suffering from immune-related disorders. For example, a study of female rheumatoid arthritis patients (Zautra, Okun, Roth, & Emmanual, 1989) found that those who perceived themselves as able to cope with stressful events and who felt satisfied with their ability to cope had higher levels of circulating B cells.

Finding benefits in stressful events may improve immune functioning or at least undercut the potential damage that stress may otherwise do. J. E. Bower and colleagues (2003) found that women who wrote about positive changes in important personal goals over a month-long period showed increases in natural killer cell cytotoxicity. Potentially, then, prioritizing goals and emphasizing relationships, personal growth, and meaning in life may have beneficial biological effects on immune functioning.

Other coping styles may also be related to the stress–immune functioning relationship (Cohen & Herbert, 1996). For example, exercise activates beta-endorphins, which may stimulate NK cell activity (Fiatarone et al., 1988); therefore, exercise may be an important buffer against stress-related immune changes.

Interventions to Improve Immune Functioning

Investigators have examined whether stress management interventions can mute the impact of stressful events on the immune system. In Chapter 7, we saw that emotional disclosure appears to enhance health and mood in individuals who have suffered a traumatic event. These results may be immunologically mediated. In one study (Pennebaker, Kiecolt-Glaser, & Glaser, 1988), 50 undergraduates wrote about either traumatic experiences or superficial topics for 20 minutes on each of 4 consecutive days. Those students who wrote about traumatic or upsetting events demonstrated a stronger response to mitogenic stimulation, compared with baseline, than did students who wrote about superficial topics.

Relaxation Relaxation may mute the effects of stress on the immune system. In a study with elderly adults (a group at risk for illness because of age-related declines in immune functioning generally), participants were assigned to relaxation training, social contact, or no intervention (Kiecolt-Glaser et al., 1985). Participants in the relaxation condition had significantly higher levels of NK cell activity after the intervention than at baseline and significantly lower antibody titres to herpes simplex virus 1, suggesting some enhancement of cellular immunity associated with the relaxation intervention.

Training in mindfulness meditation has produced demonstrable effects on immune functioning, specifically increasing antibody titres to influenza vaccine (Davidson et al., 2003). A study using tai chi chih (TCC) as an intervention for older adults reduced the intensity and severity of herpes zoster (shingles), suggesting that this may be a useful intervention as well (Irwin, Pike, Cole, & Oxman, 2003).

Overall, the evidence suggests that interventions can have significant effects on the immune system and even on health outcomes (Kiecolt-Glaser et al., 2002;

Training in relaxation may help people learn how to mute the adverse effects of stress on the immune system.

Miller & Cohen, 2001). Stress management interventions including relaxation show the most consistent benefits (Miller & Cohen, 2001).

Stress and the Developing Immune System

In addition to understanding the neuroendocrine regulation of immune functioning, the impact of stress on the developing immune system merits extensive investigation. The developing immune system may be especially vulnerable to effects of adverse psychological states such as stress, depression, or grief; moreover, these experiences may permanently affect the immune system in ways that persist into adulthood (Schleifer, Scott, Stein, & Keller, 1986).

■ HIV INFECTION AND AIDS

A Brief History of HIV Infection and AIDS

Acquired immune deficiency syndrome (AIDS) seems to have begun in central Africa, perhaps in the early 1970s. It spread rapidly throughout Zaire, Uganda, and other central African nations, largely because its causes were not understood. A high rate of extramarital sex, a lack of condom use, and a high rate of gonorrhea also facilitated the spread of the AIDS virus in the heterosexual population.

Medical clinics may have inadvertently promoted the spread of AIDS because, in attempting to vaccinate as many people as possible against common diseases in the area, needles were used over and over again, promoting the exchange of fluids. From Africa, the disease made its way slowly to Europe and to Haiti, and from Haiti into the United States, as Americans vacationing in Haiti may have brought the virus back. The current regional prevalence of HIV infection is shown in Figure 14.3.

Currently, an estimated 33 million people worldwide—30.8 million adults and 2.2 million children younger than 15—are living with HIV/AIDS, 15.5 million of whom are women. Approximately two-thirds of these people (22.5 million) live in Sub-Saharan Africa; another 14% (4 million) live in South and Southeast Asia (UNAIDS, 2008). The Centers for Disease Control and Prevention (CDC) estimates that approximately 1.1 million U.S. residents are living with HIV, at least 21% of whom are unaware of their infection (Centers for Disease Control and Prevention, August 2009b). Table 14.1 shows how HIV is transmitted.

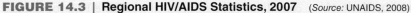

FIGURE 14.3 | Regional HIV/AIDS Statistics, 2007   (*Source:* UNAIDS, 2008)

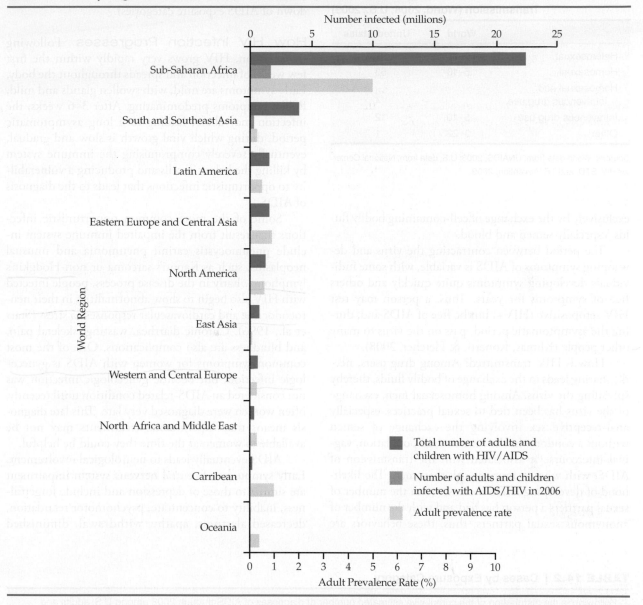

HIV researchers project an estimated 65 million deaths from AIDS by the year 2020—more than triple the number who died in the first 20 years of the epidemic—unless major efforts toward primary prevention or major developments in treatment take place (Altman, 2002, July 3). Currently AIDS is the fourth leading cause of death worldwide (World Health Organization, November 2008).

HIV Infection and AIDS in the United States

The first case of AIDS in the United States was diagnosed in 1981, but it now appears that there may have been isolated cases before that date. The viral agent is a retrovirus, the **human immunodeficiency virus (HIV),** and it attacks the helper T cells and macrophages of the immune system. The virus appears to be transmitted

TABLE 14.1 | How We Get AIDS: Cases by Mode of Transmission (World, 2008; U.S., 2009)

	World	United States
Heterosexual	70–75%	31%
Homosexual	5–10	53
Homosexual and intravenous drug use		4
Intravenous drug use	5–10	12
Other	3–22	1

Sources: World data from: UNAIDS, 2008; U.S. data from: National Center for HIV, STD, and TB Prevention, 2009.

exclusively by the exchange of cell-containing bodily fluids, especially semen and blood.

The period between contracting the virus and developing symptoms of AIDS is variable, with some individuals developing symptoms quite quickly and others free of symptoms for years. Thus, a person may test HIV-seropositive (HIV+) but be free of AIDS and, during the asymptomatic period, pass on the virus to many other people (Klimas, Koneru, & Fletcher, 2008).

How is HIV transmitted? Among drug users, needle sharing leads to the exchange of bodily fluids, thereby spreading the virus. Among homosexual men, exchange of the virus has been tied to sexual practices, especially anal-receptive sex involving the exchange of semen without a condom. In the heterosexual population, vaginal intercourse is associated with the transmission of AIDS, with women more at risk than men. The likelihood of developing AIDS increases with the number of sexual partners a person has had and with the number of anonymous sexual partners; thus, these behaviors are

considered to be risk-related (see Table 14.2 for a breakdown of AIDS exposure categories).

How HIV Infection Progresses Following transmission, HIV grows very rapidly within the first few weeks of infection and spreads throughout the body. Early symptoms are mild, with swollen glands and mild, flulike symptoms predominating. After 3–6 weeks, the infection may abate, leading to a long asymptomatic period, during which viral growth is slow and gradual, eventually severely compromising the immune system by killing the helper T cells and producing a vulnerability to opportunistic infections that leads to the diagnosis of AIDS.

Some of the more common opportunistic infections that result from the impaired immune system include pneumocystis carinii pneumonia and unusual neoplasms, such as Kaposi's sarcoma or non-Hodgkin's lymphoma. Early in the disease process, people infected with HIV also begin to show abnormalities in their neuroendocrine and cardiovascular responses to stress (Starr et al., 1996). Chronic diarrhea, wasting, skeletal pain, and blindness are also complications. One of the most common symptoms for women with AIDS is gynecologic infection, but because gynecologic infection was not considered an AIDS-related condition until recently, often women were diagnosed very late. This late diagnosis means that experimental treatments may not be available to women at the time they could be helpful.

AIDS eventually leads to neurological involvement. Early symptoms of central nervous system impairment are similar to those of depression and include forgetfulness, inability to concentrate, psychomotor retardation, decreased alertness, apathy, withdrawal, diminished

TABLE 14.2 | Cases by Exposure Category

Following is the distribution of the cumulative estimated number of diagnoses of AIDS through 2008 among U.S. adults and adolescents by exposure category. A breakdown by sex is provided where appropriate.

Exposure Category	Male	Female	Total
Male-to-male sexual contact	513,138	—	513,138
Injection drug use	183,052	84,339	267,391
Male-to-male sexual contact and injection drug use	74,155	—	74,155
Heterosexual contact*	68,546	120,039	188,585
Other**	13,083	7,426	20,509

*Heterosexual contact with a person known to have, or to be at high risk for, HIV infection.

**Includes hemophilia, blood transfusion, perinatal exposure, and risk not reported or not identified.

Source: National Center for HIV, STD, & TB Prevention, 2009.

interest in work, and loss of sexual desire. In more advanced stages, patients may experience confusion, disorientation, seizures, profound dementia, and coma.

The rate at which these changes take place can differ widely. Low-income Blacks and Hispanics who test positive for HIV go on to develop AIDS much faster than do Whites. Possible reasons include the greater prevalence of intravenous (IV) drug use and the higher levels of stress exposure. In addition, low-income Blacks and Hispanics do not get new medications as quickly as Whites do, so at any given time, they are less likely to have state-of-the-art treatment (Stolberg, 2002, May 2). Consequently, people from higher socioeconomic status (SES) groups have a much greater chance of survival over the long term.

Antiretroviral Therapy Highly active antiretroviral therapy (HAART) is a combination of antiretroviral medications that has dramatically improved the health of HIV individuals. So successful have these drug combinations been proven to be that, in some patients, HIV can no longer be discerned in the bloodstream. However, people on protease inhibitors must take these drugs faithfully, often several times a day, or the drugs will fail to work. Yet because the treatments are complex and can disrupt activities, adherence to the drug regimen is variable, posing a major problem for stemming the progress of the virus (Catz, Kelly, Bogart, Benotsch, & McAuliffe, 2000). Nonetheless, the drugs have made it possible for people with AIDS to live fairly normal lives. Unhappily, the number of new HIV infections that involve drug-resistant strains of the virus is increasing, meaning that some antiretroviral therapies will fail, as this problem increases (Little et al., 2002).

Who Gets AIDS? The CDC currently reports that the number of AIDS cases is growing faster among women, especially minority women, than any other group. In 1985 in the United States, women accounted for 7% of adults/adolescents living with AIDS—by 1999, the proportion had grown to 20%, and in 2007, the proportion was 26% (Centers for Disease control and Prevention, August 2009a). The epidemic has increased most dramatically among women of color. In the United States, African American and Hispanic women together represent less than one fourth of all U.S. women, yet they account for more than 80% of cases reported in women (Centers for Disease Control and Prevention, August 2009a). Worldwide, women working in the sex trade now represent a common source of the spread of infection (Morisky, Stein, Chiao, Ksobiech, & Malow, 2006). Child and adolescent runaways and homeless youths are especially vulnerable, as they may need to trade sex to get food and other essentials (Slesnick & Kang, 2008).

The Psychosocial Impact of HIV Infection

Thousands of people currently test positive for HIV but have not yet developed AIDS. Most health experts believe that the majority will eventually go on to develop AIDS. Thus, this group of people lives with a major health-threatening event (HIV+ status) coupled with substantial uncertainty and fear. How do these people cope?

Depression commonly accompanies an HIV diagnosis. Depression is most likely to occur among those with little social support, who engage in avoidant coping, and/or who have more severe HIV symptoms

The possibility that the AIDS virus may move into the adolescent population is substantial, but as yet there are few signs that adolescents have changed their sexual practices in response to the threat of AIDS.

(Heckman et al., 2004). Depression may result from a sense of being stigmatized as well, either by race, cultural background, or sexual preference (Chae & Yoshikawa, 2008; Hatzenbuehler, Nolen-Hoeksema, & Erickson, 2008). Thoughts of suicide are common especially among geographically isolated infected people (Heckman et al., 2002). Interventions that reduce depression are potentially valuable in the fight against AIDS because depression exacerbates many immune-related disorders (Motivala et al., 2003; Safren et al., 2010). Some people who test HIV-seropositive live in communities where many other people are seropositive or have AIDS as well, and so they continually experience bereavement. The bereavement itself can increase the likelihood that the disease will progress (Bower, Kemeny, Taylor, & Fahey, 1997), and so bereavement counseling can be important for reducing risk (Sikkema et al., 2006). The stigma associated with AIDS is a problem for many people and may act as a deterrent to those not yet tested (Herek, Capitanio, & Widaman, 2003; Lee et al., 2004).

Nonetheless, over the longer term, most people cope with AIDS fairly well. Most men who are seropositive and working continue to do so (Rabkin, McElhiney, Ferrando, Gorp, & Lin, 2004). The majority of people diagnosed with AIDS appear to make positive changes in their health behaviors almost immediately after diagnosis, including changing diet in a healthier direction, getting more exercise, quitting or reducing smoking, and reducing or eliminating drug use (Collins et al., 2001). Many of these changes improve psychological well-being, and they may affect the course of health as well.

Disclosure Not disclosing HIV status or simply lying about risk factors, such as the number of partners one has had, is a major barrier to controlling the spread of HIV infection (Kalichman, DiMarco, Austin, Luke, & DiFonzo, 2003). Moreover, those less likely to disclose their HIV+ status to sex partners also are less likely to use condoms during intercourse (DeRosa & Marks, 1998). Not having disclosed to a partner is associated with low self-efficacy, suggesting that self-efficacy interventions might well address the disclosure process (Kalichman & Nachimson, 1999). People with strong social support networks are more likely to disclose and are, in turn, more likely to receive social support (Kalichman, DiMarco, et al., 2003). Thus, disclosure appears to have psychosocial benefits. In addition, disclosure can have health benefits. In one study, those who had disclosed their HIV+ status to their friends had significantly

higher levels of CD4 and helper-cells than those who had not (Strachan, Bennett, Russo, & Roy-Byrne, 2007).

Whether to disclose HIV-seropositive status is influenced by cultural factors. For example, historically, family values have been an especially important influence on health among Latinos. In the case of HIV, however, there may be a desire to protect family members, which acts as a barrier to disclosure (Mason, Marks, Simoni, Ruiz, & Richardson, 1995; Szapocznik, 1995). Nondisclosure may mean that these young men are unable to get the social support they need from their families (Mason et al., 1995). In many countries, HIV remains a highly stigmatizing disease (Lee, Wu, Rotheram-Borus, Detels, Guan, & Li, 2004), which impedes disclosure as well.

Women and HIV The lives of HIV-infected women, particularly those with symptoms, are often chaotic and unstable. Many of these women have no partners, they may not hold jobs, and many depend on social services and Medicaid to survive. Some have problems with drugs, and many have experienced trauma from sexual or physical abuse (Simoni & Ng, 2002). To an outsider, being HIV+ would seem to be their biggest problem, but in fact, getting food and shelter for the family is often more salient (Updegraff, Taylor, Kemeny, & Wyatt, 2002). Low-income women who are HIV+ especially experience stress related to family issues (Schrimshaw, 2003), and the depression that can result can exacerbate the disease (Jones, Beach, Forehand, & Foster, 2003). Suicide attempts are not uncommon (Cooperman & Simoni, 2005).

Nonetheless, many women are able to find meaning in their lives, often prompted by the shock of testing positive. A study of low-income, HIV+ women (Updegraff et al., 2002) found that the majority reported positive changes in their lives, including the fact that the HIV diagnosis had gotten them off drugs, gotten them off the street, and enabled them to feel better about themselves (see also Littlewood, Vanable, Carey, & Blair, 2008).

Interventions to Reduce the Spread of HIV Infection

Interventions to reduce risk-related behavior loom large as the best way to control the spread of HIV infection. These interventions center around getting tested, refraining from high-risk sex, using a condom, and not

Prostitution is one source of the increasing numbers of women who are infected with HIV.

The overwhelming majority of early AIDS cases occurred among gay men. The gay community responded with dramatic and impressive efforts to reduce risk-related behaviors.

sharing needles. Given the diversity of groups at special risk for AIDS—adolescents, homosexuals, low-income women, minorities—intensive, community-based interventions aimed at particular at-risk populations are most likely to be effective. The CDC recommends that HIV testing be a standard part of medical care, as at least one quarter of people who are HIV positive do not know it. Unfortunately, this is more wish than reality. However, even brief educational or stages-of-change based interventions can increase the willingness to be tested (Carey, Coury-Doniger, Senn, Vanable, & Urban, 2008).

Education Most interventions begin by educating the target population about risky activity, providing information about HIV infection and modes of transmission. Studies suggest a high degree of "magical thinking" about HIV, with people overreacting to casual contact with HIV+ individuals but underreacting to their own

health risks resulting from casual sex and failure to use a condom. Beliefs that HIV infection is now a manageable disease and that people under treatment will not pass on an infection have contributed to a resurgence of new infections (Kalichman et al., 2007). These false beliefs need to be addressed in interventions (Kalichman, 2008).

On the whole, gay men are fairly well informed about AIDS, heterosexual adolescents are considerably less so, and some at-risk groups are very poorly informed. A study of urban female adolescents revealed that about half the participants underestimated the risks entailed in their sexual behavior (Kershaw, Ethier, Niccolai, Lewis, & Ickovics, 2003). Studies of single, pregnant, inner-city women likewise reveal poor knowledge about AIDS, little practice of safe sex, and little knowledge of their partner's current or past behavior and the ways in which it might place them at risk (Hobfoll, Jackson, Lavin, Britton, & Shepherd, 1993).

There may be particular teachable moments when AIDS education is vital. T. J. Mayne and colleagues (1998) found that men who had lost a partner were more likely to engage in unprotected anal intercourse in the following months. Men with a new primary partner are also more likely to practice risky behavior. Consequently, education at these time points may be especially valuable.

As more women have become infected with HIV, issues surrounding pregnancy have assumed concern. Many women lack knowledge regarding the transmission of HIV to infants, so their decision making with respect to pregnancy may be poorly informed. Only about 15–30% of infants born to HIV+ mothers will be sero-positive, and treatment can reduce that incidence to 4–8%. Providing education with respect to HIV and pregnancy, then, is an important educational priority as well.

How successful are educational interventions? Interventions designed to induce fear may not be very successful (Earl & Albarracin, 2007), but educational interventions may fare better. A review of 27 published studies that provided HIV counseling and testing information found that this type of education was an effective means of secondary prevention for HIV+ individuals, reducing behaviors that might infect others. However, it was not as effective as a primary prevention strategy for uninfected people (Weinhardt, Carey, Johnson, & Bickman, 1999; see also Albarracín et al., 2003).

Culturally sensitive interventions pitched to a specific target group may fare somewhat better. A study of African American, male, inner-city adolescents showed that providing information can be an effective agent of behavior change when knowledge is low (Jemmott, Jemmott, & Fong, 1992). The young men in this study were randomly assigned to an AIDS risk-reduction intervention aimed at increasing their knowledge about AIDS and risky sexual behavior or to a control group. The materials were developed so as to be especially interesting to inner-city, African American adolescents. This culturally sensitive intervention was successful over a 3-month period. The adolescents exposed to the intervention reported fewer instances of intercourse, fewer partners, greater use of condoms, and less anal intercourse, compared with adolescents not exposed to the intervention.

Health Beliefs and HIV Risk-Related Behavior   Knowledge, of course, provides only a beginning for interventions. One must also perceive oneself to be capable of controlling risk-related activity (Forsyth

& Carey, 1998). As is true for so many risk-related behaviors, perceptions of self-efficacy with respect to AIDS risk-related behavior is critical. Gay men who are higher in a sense of self-efficacy are more likely to use condoms, have fewer sex partners, and fewer anonymous sex partners (Aspinwall, Kemeny, Taylor, Schneider, & Dudley, 1991; Wulfert, Wan, & Backus, 1996). High self-efficacy also predicts condom use among African American adolescents (Jemmott, Jemmott, Spears, Hewitt, & Cruz-Collins, 1992), African American and Latina women (Nyamathi, Stein, & Brecht, 1995), and college students (O'Leary, Goodhardt, Jemmott, & Boccher-Lattimore, 1992; Wulfert & Wan, 1993; see also Forsyth & Carey, 1998).

The health belief model (see Chapter 3) has shown modest ability to predict the number of sex partners and number of anonymous sex partners of gay men (Aspinwall et al., 1991). It also predicts condom use among adolescents (Abraham, Sheeran, Spears, & Abrams, 1992). The theory of planned behavior (see Chapter 3) has been somewhat more informative, in part because social norms are so important to several of the populations at risk for AIDS, especially adolescents (Winslow, Franzini, & Hwang, 1992). J. B. Jemmott and colleagues (Jemmott, Jemmott, & Hacker, 1992), for example, studied inner-city, African American adolescents and found that those with more favorable attitudes toward condoms and those who perceived subjective norms to be supportive of condom use reported greater intentions to use condoms over the next few months. Fear of AIDS, perceived susceptibility, and believed behavioral control with respect to condom use also predict condom use.

Targeting Sexual Activity   Sexual activity is a very personal aspect of life, endowed with private meaning for each individual. Consequently, knowledge of how to practice safe sex and the belief that one is capable of doing so may not translate into behavior change if spontaneous sexuality is seen as an inherent part of one's identity. For example, for many gay men, being gay is associated with the belief that they should be free to do what they want sexually; consequently, modifying sexual activity represents a threat to identity and lifestyle. Not surprisingly, it has been difficult to modify HIV-related risk behaviors among gay men (Rosser et al., 2010).

Adolescents are another population that is difficult to reach. Adolescents often have very positive expectations about sex that influence how likely they are to have sex and unprotected sex (Guilamo-Ramos et al., 2007).

BOX 14.3

Safe Sex

THE MAGIC CONDOM

In a television program, a man and a woman are fondling each other, removing each other's clothes, and making steady progress toward the man's bed. As they approach it, she whispers, "Have you had a blood test?" He responds, "Last month. Negative. You?" She responds, "Negative, too. Do you have protection?" His response: "I'm covered." They fall to the bed and . . . (fade out).

This scene is Hollywood's idea of a safe-sex encounter. But where did the magic condom come from? Did he put it on in the taxi on the way back to his apartment? Did he put it on in the kitchen while he was pouring them each a glass of wine?

Hollywood's safe-sex encounters may be seamless, but in real life, safe sex is not. A first important step is getting people to recognize that safe sex is important— that is, that they are at risk for AIDS and other sexually transmitted diseases.

Inducing young people to take steps to practice safe sex is also problematic. Sexual counselors advocate asking prospective partners about their sexual histories, yet many young adults indicate that they would lie to a partner to minimize their HIV risk history (Cochran & Mays, 1990). Many adolescents don't use condoms because it is uncomfortable to insist on it in the passion of the moment. The very factors that the Hollywood encounter overlooked—namely, the interpersonal awkwardness and logistics of actually using condoms—act as barriers to their use.

Beliefs and behaviors related to sex can be very hard to modify. Complicating the picture still further, attitudes toward condom use can be quite negative and condom use can be highly variable (Kiene, Tennen, & Armeli, 2008). Consequently, these beliefs may need to be an intervention target (Charnigo, Crosby, & Troutman, 2010).

Past sexual practice is an important predictor of AIDS risk-related behavior (Guilamo-Ramos, Jaccard, Pena, & Goldberg, 2005). People who have had a large number of partners (especially anonymous partners), who have not used condoms in the past, and who meet their partners in bars or through the Internet tend to continue these behaviors and to expose themselves to risk, perhaps because those behaviors are well integrated into their sexual style (Horvath, Bowen, & Williams, 2006; van der Velde & van der Pligt, 1991) (Box 14.3).

Sexual encounters, particularly with a new partner, are often rushed, nonverbal, and passionate, conditions not very conducive to a rational discussion of safe-sex practices. To address these issues, health psychologists have developed interventions that involve practice in sexual negotiation skills. For example, in a cognitive-behavioral intervention (Kelly, Lawrence, Hood, & Brasfield, 1989), gay men were taught through modeling, role-playing, and feedback how to exercise self-control in sexual relationships and how to resist pressure to engage in high-risk sexual activity. With this training, the men became somewhat more skillful in handling sexual situations and were able to reduce their risky sexual behaviors and increase their use of condoms.

Sexual negotiation skills are especially important in interventions with high risk populations, such as minorities, women, and adolescents. One of the reasons that young women engage in unsafe sex is the coercive sexual behavior of their young male partners. Teaching sexual negotiation skills to both young men and women, and especially teaching young women how to resist coercion, is therefore important (Carey, 1999). Interventions need to be focused on building self-efficacy for practicing safe sex (Mausbach, Semple, Strathdee, Zians, & Patterson, 2007; O'Leary, Jemmott, & Jemmott, 2008).

For adolescents, risky sexual activity may be part of a more generally risky experimental lifestyle, involving cigarette smoking, illicit drug and alcohol use, and antisocial activities (Kalichman, Weinhardt, DiFonzo, Austin, & Luke, 2002). Unfortunately, these activities can increase temptations. One study found that simply imagining a new lover reduced perceptions of risk (Blanton & Gerrard, 1997; Corbin & Fromme, 2002). Moreover, attitudes toward condoms are not positive. Among adolescents, both gay and straight, the effort to modify AIDS risk-related behavior, then, needs to challenge peer norms about what constitutes erotic sex, eroticize safer sexual activity, and enhance a sense of personal efficacy about practicing safe sex (McKusick, Coates, Morin, Pollack, & Hoff, 1990). Interventions that directly address condom negotiation skills in a manner that is sensitive to these dynamics can be effective (Jemmott & Jones, 1993; Solomon & De Jong, 1989). In a major review of behavioral interventions conducted with adolescents, gay and bisexual men, inner-city women, college students, and mentally ill adults—all groups at significant risk for AIDS—interventions oriented toward reducing their sexual activity and enhancing their abilities to negotiate condom use with partners were beneficial for reducing risk-related behavior (Kalichman, Carey, & Johnson, 1996).

Cognitive-Behavioral Interventions
Cognitive-behavioral techniques show promise for maintaining adherence and reducing viral load (Safren et al., 2009). Social problem solving—that is, helping people recognize and control their moods and motivations in problem situations—can increase adherence (Johnson, Elliott, Neilands, Morin, & Chesney, 2006). Social support has been tied to adherence and lower viral load as well (Simoni, Frick, & Huang, 2006). Thus, addressing social support needs may have multiple positive repercussions. Even brief but intensive interventions addressing risk factors, motivation, self-efficacy, social support, and skills may have these beneficial effects (Kalichman et al., 2005; Naar-King et al., 2006).

CBT interventions can buffer the psychological and immunologic consequences of learning about HIV+ status, and improve surveillance of opportunistic infections, such as herpes (Safren et al., 2009). They also reliably promote better mental health and may exert modest effects on the course of disease (Carrico & Antoni, 2008; Crepaz et al., 2008). Many CBT interventions include a stress management component. Stress management interventions clearly improve quality of life and mental health (Brown & Vanable, 2008), but stress management may not affect immunologic functioning related to the course of illness (Scott-Sheldon, Kalichman, Carey, & Fielder, 2008).

Some programs have built in a motivational component to try to increase the motivation for at-risk groups to change their risk-related behavior. Recall that "motivation training" refers to inducing a state of readiness to change, as by helping individuals develop behavior-change goals, recognize the discrepancy between their goals and their current behavior, and develop a sense of self-efficacy that they can change. An empathetic, nonjudgmental style on the part of the therapist is thought to promote this motivational component. Research suggests that adding a motivational component to education and skills training can enhance the effectiveness of interventions designed to reduce HIV risk-related behavior (Kalichman et al., 2005).

CBT interventions may need to be directed not only to stress management, but also to health behaviors. Smoking, excessive alcohol use, and drug use commonly compromise health and adherence among people who are HIV seropositive (Webb, Vanable, Carey, & Blair, 2007).

Targeting Adherence
Because maintaining good health depends so critically on adhering to HAART, one would imagine that adherence levels are fairly high, and in fact, this is typically the case. However, stress can impede adherence (Mugavero et al., 2009), as can alcohol use (Parsons, Rosof, & Mustanski, 2008) and symptoms or worries related to HAART (Gonzalez et al., 2007). A subgroup of people who are HIV+ have difficulty getting HAART, and using it is a poor fit with their lifestyle. For homeless people, IV drug users, and alcoholics, there may be substantial barriers (Tucker, Orlando, Burnam, Sherbourne, Kung, & Gifford, 2004). For example, most of the drugs used to fight AIDS must be refrigerated, and homeless people, by definition, do not have refrigerators. Practical problems such as these account for some adherence problems.

Individual differences in psychosocial resources contribute to adherence as well (Gore-Felton & Koopman, 2008). Those who successfully adhere to HAART are more likely to have social support, low levels of depression, a positive state of mind (Gonzalez et al., 2004), and a sense of self-efficacy (Johnson et al., 2007). Those who fail to adhere appear to have greater negative mood, lower social support, more avoidant coping strategies, and more use of stimulants (Carrico et al., 2007; Weaver et al., 2005).

As is true for risk-related behavior, adherence to HAART is affected by motivational training. Having the right information, the motivation to adhere, and skills to do so significantly improves adherence to treatment (Starace, Massa, Amico, & Fisher, 2006). Interventions that enhance social support have also shown some success in improving adherence (Koenig et al., 2008).

Targeting IV Drug Use
Interventions with IV drug users need to be targeted toward both reducing contact with infected needles and changing sexual activity. Information about AIDS transmission, needle exchange programs, and instruction on how to sterilize needles can reduce risky injection practices among IV drug users (Des Jarlais & Semaan, 2008). Methadone maintenance treatments, coupled with HIV-related education, may help reduce the spread of AIDS by reducing the

frequency of injections and shared needle contacts, by reducing health risk behaviors, by increasing use of condoms, and by reducing the number of sexual partners (Margolin, Avants, Warburton, Hawkins, & Shi, 2003). However, the cognitive-behavioral intervention programs that work with other at-risk populations may not work as well with IV drug users because they may lack good impulse control.

HIV Prevention Programs

Prevention programs have now been developed for U.S. public schools to warn adolescents about the risks of unprotected sexual intercourse and to help instill safe-sex practices (DiClemente et al., 2008). Teenagers who are HIV+ sometimes pitch these programs, making the risk graphically clear to the audience. However, there is some evidence that adolescents try to distance themselves from peers who have HIV in an effort to control the threat that such an encounter produces, so interventions that stress information, motivation, and sexual negotiation skills, as opposed to peer-based interventions, may be more successful in changing adolescent behavior (Fisher, Fisher, Bryan, & Misovich, 2002). Research is still exploring which elements of school-based prevention programs are most successful.

When prominent public figures, such as Magic Johnson, make their HIV infection public, the desire for more information about AIDS and concern about AIDS increases (Zimet et al., 1993). This finding suggests that the effective timing and use of such announcements might be helpful in getting people tested and getting them to reduce their AIDS-related risk behaviors.

Interventions in schools have made use of HIV prevention videos that provide training in communication skills and condom use. Results suggest that this low-cost intervention can be an effective way of decreasing risky sexual behavior (Sanderson & Yopyk, 2007).

The stage model of behavior change may be helpful in guiding interventions to increase condom use. Some people have gaps in their knowledge about AIDS or about their own or their partners' behaviors that may put them at risk (Hobfoll et al., 1993). Therefore, they may profit from information-based interventions that move them from a precontemplation to a contemplation phase with regard to safe-sex practices. In contrast, moving from contemplation to preparation, or from preparation to action, may require specific training in condom negotiation skills (Catania, Kegeles, & Coates, 1990).

Efforts to prevent risk-related behavior may need to target not only high-risk sexual practices themselves but also other behaviors that facilitate high-risk sex (Locke & Newcomb, 2008). Chief among these are drug and alcohol use. That is, people who may be otherwise aware that they should not engage in risky sexual activities may be less inhibited about doing so when under the influence of drugs or alcohol (Norris et al., 2009). Debunking the myth that alcohol enhances sexual performance and pleasure may also contribute to reducing the behaviors that facilitate risky sex (Kalichman et al., 2002).

Interventions that address the norms surrounding sexual activity are needed as well. Any intervention that supports norms favoring more long-term relationships or decreasing the number of short-term sexual relationships an individual has is a reasonable approach to prevention (Tucker, Elliott, Wenzel, & Hambarsoomian, 2007).

Coping with HIV+ Status and AIDS

Coping with a life-threatening illness is always challenging and may be especially so for populations vulnerable to HIV infection. They are more likely to have a history of traumas and co-existing mental health problems, such as anxiety disorders, depression, and substance abuse disorders (Gaynes, Pence, Eron, & Miller, 2008; Whetten, Reif, Whetten, & Murphy-McMillan, 2008). Consequently, they may not have particularly good coping skills to draw on.

Moreover, people with HIV infection face particular challenges. Now that AIDS is a chronic rather than an acute disease, a number of psychosocial issues raised by chronic illness come to the fore. One such issue is employment. Research suggests that men with HIV who were working at the time of diagnosis continue to work but that those who are unemployed may not return to work. Interventions may be needed to help those who can return to work do so (Rabkin, McElhiney, Ferrando, Van Gorp, & Lin, 2004). People with AIDS must continually cope with the fear and prejudice that they encounter from the general community.

Coping Skills

Stress and its neuroendocrine consequences foster a more rapid course of illness in people with AIDS and lead to more opportunistic or more aggressive symptoms (Cole, 2008; Pereira et al., 2003). Thus, good coping skills are essential (Temoshok, Wald, Synowski, & Garzino-Demo, 2008). Coping effectiveness training appears to be helpful in managing the psychological distress that can be associated with

HIV+ status (Chesney, Chambers, Taylor, Johnson, & Folkman, 2003). In one study, a cognitive-behavioral stress management program designed to increase positive coping skills and the ability to enlist social support led to improved psychological well-being and quality of life among HIV+ individuals (Lutgendorf et al., 1998). Perceiving that one has control over a stressor is usually associated with better adjustment to that stressor, and this is also true of AIDS (Benight et al., 1997; Rotheram-Borus, Murphy, Reid, & Coleman, 1996).

Written disclosure is a successful coping intervention (see Chapter 7), and it appears to be so for people with HIV as well. A study by K. J. Petrie and associates (2004) found that writing about emotional topics led to higher CD4 lymphocyte counts, compared to writing about neutral topics, among HIV-infected patients.

Social Support Social support is very important to people with HIV infection or AIDS. Men with AIDS who have emotional, practical, and informational support are less depressed (Turner-Cobb et al., 2002), and men with strong partner support are less likely to practice risky sex (Darbes & Lewis, 2005). Informational support appears to be especially important in buffering the stress associated with AIDS-related symptoms (Hays, Turner, & Coates, 1992; Siegel, Karus, & Raveis, 1997), and support from family appears to be especially important for preventing depression (Schrimshaw, 2003).

The ability to talk to family members about HIV and AIDS is important, too. Unfortunately, although families have the potential to be especially helpful to men with AIDS, when men are depressed or have a large number of AIDS-related symptoms, they may not receive the support they need (Turner, Hays, & Coates, 1993). Augmenting natural social support and providing social support to people with AIDS should be an important mental health services priority.

The Internet represents an important resource for people with AIDS. Those who use the Internet in conjunction with managing their HIV+ status have more disease knowledge, have more active coping skills, engage in more information-seeking coping, and have more social support than those not using the Internet (Kalichman, Benotsch, et al., 2003). The Internet appears to be a promising resource in HIV/AIDS care in the future (Bowen, Williams, Daniel, & Clayton, 2008).

Psychosocial Factors That Affect the Course of HIV Infection

Psychosocial factors can influence the rate of immune system decline from AIDS (Ironson et al., 2005). Negative beliefs about the self and the future are associated with helper T cell (CD4) decline and onset of AIDS in people infected with HIV (Segerstrom, Taylor, Kemeny, Reed, & Visscher, 1996); negative expectations about the course of illness can lead to an accelerated course of disease (Ironson et al., 2005; Reed, Kemeny, Taylor, & Visscher, 1999; Reed, Kemeny, Taylor, Wang, & Visscher, 1994). Depression, stress, and trauma all adversely affect disease progression (Leserman, 2008).

On the positive side, optimism, active coping, extraversion, conscientiousness, and an openness to experience spirituality all predict slower disease progression (Ironson & Hayward, 2008; Ironson, O'Cleirigh, Weiss, Schneiderman, & Costa, 2008). The ability to find meaning in one's experiences slows declines in CD4 levels and has been related to less likelihood of AIDS-related mortality (Bower, Kemeny, Taylor, & Fahey, 1997). Optimists typically practice more health-promoting behaviors than pessimists, so one intervention (Mann, 2001) assigned HIV-infected women to write about positive events that would happen in the future or placed women in a no-writing control group. Among participants who were initially low in optimism, the writing intervention led to increased optimism, a self-reported increase in adherence to medication, and less distress from medication side effects. The results suggest that a future-oriented, positive writing intervention may be a useful technique for decreasing distress and increasing adherence, especially in pessimistic individuals. Optimism may also help people already infected with HIV better withstand additional stressors (Cruess, Antoni, Cruess, et al., 2000).

Psychological inhibition may promote a more rapid course of illness. In one investigation, HIV infection advanced more rapidly in men who concealed their homosexual identity relative to men who were openly gay (Cole, Kemeny, Taylor, Visscher, & Fahey, 1996). Psychological inhibition is known to lead to alterations in sympathetic nervous system activation and immune system function, which appears to largely account for these differences in physical health (Cole, Kemeny, Fahey, Zack, & Naliboff, 2003). This may also help explain the beneficial effects of disclosure of HIV status on CD4 levels.

Depression and death of a partner can have adverse effects on the immune systems of HIV+ men (Kemeny et al., 1994) and women (Ickovics et al., 2001). For example,

M. E. Kemeny and colleagues (1995) found that HIV+ men bereaved over the death of their partner showed a significant increase in immune activation and a significant decrease in proliferative response to mitogenic stimulation. Depression may also play a role in T cell declines. Kemeny and colleagues (1994) also found that HIV+ men who were depressed (but not due to bereavement) had significantly fewer helper/inducer T lymphocytes and more activated suppressor/cytotoxic T cells, as well as lower proliferative responses to mitogenic stimulation.

Positive affect lowers the risk of AIDS mortality (Moskowitz, 2003). In one intervention study, treating depression via cognitive-behavioral stress management (coupled with medication adherence training) was found not only to alleviate depressed mood but to enhance the effects of HAART on suppression of HIV viral load (Antoni et al., 2006). Antidepressants can help as well (Repetto & Petitto, 2008). Moreover, the successful management of depression may also affect the course of disease.

The research that ties psychosocial factors to the course of illness—such as beliefs about one's illness, coping strategies, and social support resources—is especially exciting. It not only clarifies the factors that may promote long-term survival in people with HIV infection but may also provide more general hypotheses for understanding how psychological and social factors affect the course of illness (S. E. Taylor et al., 2000).

■ CANCER

Cancer is a set of more than 100 diseases that have several factors in common. All cancers result from a dysfunction in DNA—that part of the cellular programming that controls cell growth and reproduction. Instead of ensuring the regular, slow production of new cells, this malfunctioning DNA causes excessively rapid cell growth and proliferation. Unlike other cells, cancerous cells provide no benefit to the body. They merely sap it of resources.

Cancer is second only to heart disease in causes of death in the United States and most developed countries (Figure 14.4). From 1900 until 1990, death rates from cancer progressively climbed. Since 1993, however, the

FIGURE 14.4 | Leading Sites of New Cancer Cases and Deaths, 2009 Estimates (*Source:* American Cancer Society, 2009)

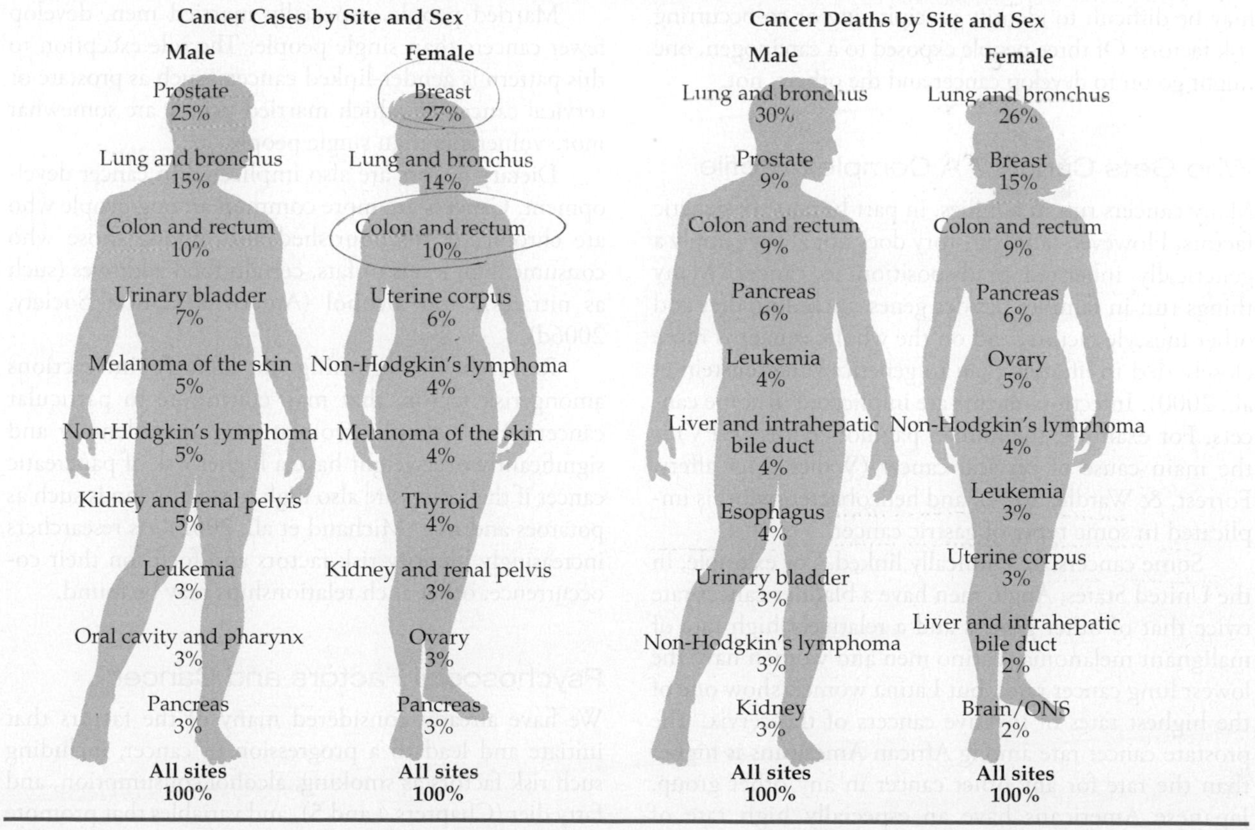

Cancer Cases by Site and Sex		Cancer Deaths by Site and Sex	
Male	**Female**	**Male**	**Female**
Prostate 25%	Breast 27%	Lung and bronchus 30%	Lung and bronchus 26%
Lung and bronchus 15%	Lung and bronchus 14%	Prostate 9%	Breast 15%
Colon and rectum 10%	Colon and rectum 10%	Colon and rectum 9%	Colon and rectum 9%
Urinary bladder 7%	Uterine corpus 6%	Pancreas 6%	Pancreas 6%
Melanoma of the skin 5%	Non-Hodgkin's lymphoma 4%	Leukemia 4%	Ovary 5%
Non-Hodgkin's lymphoma 5%	Melanoma of the skin 4%	Liver and intrahepatic bile duct 4%	Non-Hodgkin's lymphoma 4%
Kidney and renal pelvis 5%	Thyroid 4%	Esophagus 4%	Leukemia 3%
Leukemia 3%	Kidney and renal pelvis 3%	Urinary bladder 3%	Uterine corpus 3%
Oral cavity and pharynx 3%	Ovary 3%	Non-Hodgkin's lymphoma 3%	Liver and intrahepatic bile duct 2%
Pancreas 3%	Pancreas 3%	Kidney 3%	Brain/ONS 2%
All sites 100%	**All sites 100%**	**All sites 100%**	**All sites 100%**

U.S. cancer death rate has shown a steady drop (Centers for Disease Control and Prevention, June 2006). Most of the decline in death rates has occurred in lung, colorectal, breast, and prostate cancer, which account for almost half of all U.S. cancer deaths (American Cancer Society, 2009). The decline in smoking accounts for much of this change. The rest of the decline in cancer deaths can be attributed to improvements in treatment. Nonetheless, more than 562,340 people die of cancer each year in the United States (American Cancer Society, 2009).

Because psychosocial factors are implicated in the causes and course of cancer, the health psychologist has an important role in addressing issues involving the etiology and progression of cancer. Moreover, because cancer is a disease with which people often live for many years, interventions to reduce it and to improve coping with it are essential (Holland, 2002).

Why Is Cancer Hard to Study?

Cancer has been hard to study for a number of reasons. The causes, symptoms, and treatment for each cancer vary. Many cancers have long or irregular growth cycles. It may be difficult to identify precipitating or co-occurring risk factors: Of three people exposed to a carcinogen, one might go on to develop cancer and the others, not.

Who Gets Cancer? A Complex Profile

Many cancers run in families, in part because of genetic factors. However, family history does not always imply a genetically inherited predisposition to cancer. Many things run in families besides genes, including diet and other lifestyle factors, and on the whole, cancer is more closely tied to lifestyle than to genetics (Lichtenstein et al., 2000). Infectious agents are implicated in some cancers. For example, the human papillomavirus (HPV) is the main cause of cervical cancer (Waller, McCaffery, Forrest, & Wardle, 2004), and helicobacter pylori is implicated in some types of gastric cancer.

Some cancers are ethnically linked. For example, in the United States, Anglo men have a bladder cancer rate twice that of other groups and a relatively high rate of malignant melanoma. Latino men and women have the lowest lung cancer rates, but Latina women show one of the highest rates of invasive cancers of the cervix. The prostate cancer rate among African Americans is higher than the rate for any other cancer in any other group. Japanese Americans have an especially high rate of stomach cancer, whereas Chinese Americans have a high rate of liver cancer. Breast cancer is extremely common among northern European women and is relatively rare among Asians (National Cancer Institute, 2005).

Some cancers are culturally linked through lifestyle. For example, Japanese American women are more susceptible to breast cancer the longer they have lived in the United States and the more they have adopted the American culture (Wynder et al., 1963). This increase in vulnerability is believed to be linked to changes in diet. Most cancers are related to socioeconomic status, with low-SES individuals more at risk. Moreover, declines in mortality have been slower in minority populations than among Whites (Glanz, Croyle, Chollette, & Pinn, 2003).

The probability of developing some cancers changes with SES. For example, White women are more likely than African American women to develop breast cancer, but among African American women who have moved up the socioeconomic ladder, the breast cancer rate is the same as for White women at that economic level (Leffall, White, & Ewing, 1963). Figure 14.5 shows cancers of all types broken down by different ethnic groups in the United States, both by incidence and by mortality.

Married people, especially married men, develop fewer cancers than single people. The sole exception to this pattern is gender-linked cancers, such as prostate or cervical cancer, to which married people are somewhat more vulnerable than single people.

Dietary factors are also implicated in cancer development. Cancers are more common among people who are chronically malnourished and among those who consume high levels of fats, certain food additives (such as nitrates), and alcohol (American Cancer Society, 2006d).

Research is beginning to identify interactions among risk factors that may contribute to particular cancers. For example, women who are sedentary and significantly overweight have a higher risk of pancreatic cancer if their diets are also high in starchy foods such as potatoes and rice (Michaud et al., 2002). As researchers increasingly identify risk factors and focus on their co-occurrence, other such relationships may be found.

Psychosocial Factors and Cancer

We have already considered many of the factors that initiate and lead to a progression of cancer, including such risk factors as smoking, alcohol consumption, and fatty diet (Chapters 4 and 5), and variables that promote

FIGURE 14.5 | Average Annual Incidence and Mortality Rates of All Types of Cancer in the United States by Ethnicity (*Source:* American Cancer Society, 2009)

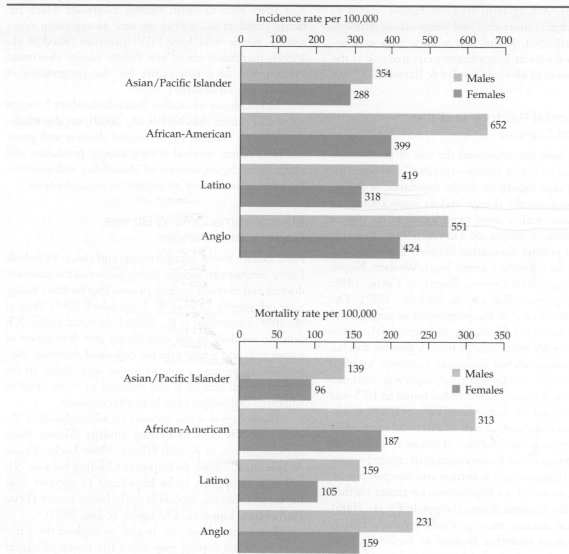

delay behavior and nonadherence (Chapters 8 and 9). In this chapter, we focus more heavily on the evidence regarding psychosocial factors in the initiation and progression of cancer.

For decades, there has been a stereotype of a cancer-prone personality as a person who is easygoing and acquiescent, repressing emotions that might interfere with smooth social and emotional functioning. As Woody Allen remarked in the film *Manhattan,* "I can't express anger. That's one of the problems I have. I grow a tumor instead." In fact, there is little evidence for such a stereotype.

Stress and Cancer   Does stress cause cancer? Although stress generally has not been linked to the onset of cancer (Nielsen & Grønbaek, 2006), a particular type of stress—lack or loss of social support—may affect the onset and course of cancer. The absence of close family ties in childhood may predict some cancers (Felitti et al., 1998; Grassi & Molinari, 1986; Shaffer, Duszynski, & Thomas, 1982). The absence of a current social support network has been tied to a worsening course of illness (Weihs, Enright, & Simmens, 2008). Experiencing major social stressors such as divorce, infidelity, marital quarreling, financial stress, and the like increases risk for cervical cancer (Coker, Bond, Madeleine, Luchok, & Pirisi, 2003). A long-term study of factors related to cancer incidence, mortality, and prognosis in Alameda County, California, found that women who were socially isolated were at a significantly elevated risk of dying from cancer of all sites (Kaplan & Reynolds, 1988).

Psychosocial Factors and the Course of Cancer

Researchers have also examined the role of psychosocial factors in the course of cancer—specifically, whether the cancer progresses rapidly or slowly. Avoidance, or the inability to confront the disease and its implications, has been associated with a more rapid course of the disease (Epping-Jordan, Compas, & Howell, 1994). Research has found a positive association between depression and cancer (see, for example, Carney, Jones, Woolson, Noyes, & Doebbeling, 2003; Dattore, Shontz, & Coyne, 1980; Persky, Kempthorne-Rawson, & Shekelle, 1987). Depression is implicated in the progression of cancer, both by itself (Brown, Levy, Rosberger, & Edgar, 2003) and in conjunction with other risk factors. A possible mechanism is through altered biological responses to stress (Giese-Davis et al., 2006). Moreover, depression can exacerbate other risk factors. Research has found an 18.5-fold increase in risk for smoking-related cancers among smokers who were depressed, as well as a 2.9-fold increase for non-smoking-associated cancers (Linkins & Comstock, 1990). Depression can be associated with elevated neuroendocrine responses such as cortisol and norepinephrine, which may, in turn, have implications for cancer via their impact on the immune system (Lutgendorf et al., 2005). Psychological distress more generally has been tied to colorectal cancer mortality (Kojima et al., 2005). Relationships between cancer development and use of denial or repressive coping strategies have been found as well (McKenna, Zevon, Corn, & Rounds, 1999).

Avoidant or passive coping is also a risk factor for psychological distress, depression, poor sleep, and other risk-related factors, which may represent additional routes by which these factors adversely influence course of disease (Hoyt, Thomas, Epstein, & Dirksen, 2009; Kim, Valdimarsdottir, & Bovbjerg, 2003). Repressive coping appears to be especially common in children with cancer, so this coping style warrants particular consideration in their care (Phipps, Steele, Hall, & Leigh, 2001).

Negative expectations regarding one's situation have been related to a more rapid course of illness in young cancer patients (Schulz, Bookwala, Knapp, Scheier, & Williamson, 1996). Inasmuch as negative expectations also affect time to death among diagnosed AIDS patients (Reed et al., 1994), as well as symptom onset among people who have HIV infection (Reed et al., 1999), pessimism about the future merits continued examination as a risk factor for the progression of immune-related disorders.

Although not all studies find relationships between stress and cancer (Michael et al., 2009), on the whole, the evidence relating psychological distress and pessimism to cancer survival is increasingly persuasive and underscores the importance of identifying and intervening early so as to mute its impact on survival course.

Mechanisms Linking Stress, Coping, and Cancer

How, exactly, might stressful events and cancer be linked? Likely mechanisms include dysregulation of the neuroendocrine and immune systems in ways that facilitate malignant cell growth (Antoni & Lutgendorf, 2007; Fang et al., 2008; Lutgendorf et al., 2008a). As noted earlier, NK cells are involved in the surveillance and destruction of tumor cells and virally infected cells, and therefore, they are believed to have a role in tumor surveillance in the body. NK cell activity is also believed to be involved in whether a carcinogen takes hold after exposure.

Psychological stress appears to adversely affect the ability of NK cells to destroy tumors (Glaser, Rice, Speicher, Stout, & Kiecolt-Glaser, 1986; Locke, Kraus, & Leserman, 1984), an important finding because NK cell activity appears to be important in survival rates for certain cancers, especially early breast cancer (Levy, Herberman, Lippman, D'Angelo, & Lee, 1991).

Researchers have also begun to explore the pathways by which coping may affect the course of cancer (Antoni, Lutgendorf, et al., 2006). Depression, anxiety, and repressive coping have been tied to autonomic, endocrine, and immunologic dysregulation (Giese-Davis et al., 2004; Lutgendorf, Lamkin, et al., 2008), and so alterations in biological stress regulatory pathways represent likely mechanisms for these relations as well (Antoni & Lutgendorf, 2007).

Adjusting to Cancer

The psychosocial toll of cancer is enormous. Two out of every three families will have a family member who develops cancer, and virtually every member of these families will be affected by the disease. This burden will fall disproportionately on minority and low-SES populations in the United States (Bach et al., 2002). However, more than one third of cancer victims live at least 5 years after their diagnosis, thus creating many issues of long-term adjustment. Many of the issues that we explored in Chapters 11 and 12 in the context of chronic, advancing, and terminal illness are especially relevant to the cancer experience. We highlight a few additional issues in this section.

Coping with Physical Limitations Physical difficulties usually stem from the pain and discomfort cancer can produce, particularly in the advancing and terminal phases of illness. Fatigue is an especially common and debilitating symptom (Curran, Beacham, & Andrykowski, 2004).

Cancer can lead to down-regulation of the immune system, which may enhance vulnerability to a variety of other disorders, including respiratory tract infections. These persistent health problems can compromise quality of life (Andersen, Kiecolt-Glaser, & Glaser, 1994). Fatigue due to illness and treatment is also one of the main complaints of cancer patients (Andrykowski, Curran, & Lightner, 1998).

Treatment-Related Problems Difficulties also arise as a consequence of treatment. Some cancers are treated surgically. Removal of organs can create problems in appearance, as for patients with head-and-neck cancer who may have a portion of this area removed (Vos, Garssen, Visser, Duivenvoorden, & de Haes, 2004). Body image concerns stem not only from concern about appearance following surgery but also from concerns about a sense of wholeness, bodily integrity, and the ability to function normally. Either concern can complicate reactions to treatment (Carver et al., 1998).

In some cases, organs that are vital to bodily functions must be taken over by a prosthesis. For example, a urinary ostomy patient must be fitted with an apparatus that makes it possible to excrete urine. A patient whose larynx has been removed must learn to speak with the help of a prosthetic speech device. Side effects due to surgery are also common. A colostomy (prosthetic replacement of the lower colon) produces a loss of bowel control. Men with prostate cancer often go through treatments that compromise sexual functioning (Steginga & Occhipinti, 2006).

Some cancer patients receive debilitating follow-up treatments. Patients undergoing chemotherapy may experience nausea and vomiting, and anticipatory nausea and vomiting that occurs before the chemotherapy session begins (Montgomery & Bovbjerg, 2003). As a result, symptoms of nausea, distress, and vomiting can continue to adversely affect quality of life among cancer patients long after the treatment has ended (Cameron et al., 2001). Because patients may expect to be nauseated, which itself can lead to nausea, these expectations should be a target for intervention (Colagiuri & Zachariae, 2010). Fortunately, in recent years, chemotherapies with less virulent side effects have been developed.

Patients and physicians do not always have the same priorities, especially with regard to treatments that have the potential to compromise quality of life. Therefore, it is especially essential that patients' input be solicited and taken into account (Elstein, Chapman, & Knight, 2005; Myers, 2005). Interventions to encourage shared decision making between patients and physicians may be needed (Revenson & Pranikoff, 2005; Siminoff & Step, 2005).

Psychosocial Issues and Cancer
Because of early identification techniques and promising treatments, many people who are diagnosed with cancer live long and fulfilling lives free of disease. Others may have recurrences but nonetheless maintain a high quality of life for 15–20 years. Still others live with active cancers over the long term, knowing that the disease will ultimately be fatal. All of these trajectories indicate that cancer is now a chronic disease, which poses long-term issues related to psychosocial adjustment.

Preparation for the aftermath of cancer and its treatment begins at the time of diagnosis. Assessment of psychosocial risk factors, such as a history of posttraumatic stress disorder (PTSD), depression, and stress, may be helpful for anticipating later needs (Golden-Kreutz et al., 2005).

Intermittent and long-term depression are among the most common difficulties experienced as a result of cancer (Stommel et al., 2004). Depression not only compromises quality of life in its own right but can have adverse effects on physical health outcomes as well (Andersen et al., 1994). Depression may initiate a process whereby people experience events as more stressful, which in turn feeds back into greater depression (Wu & Andersen, 2010). Adjustment problems appear to be greatest among women who have a history of life stressors or a lack of social support (Butler, Koopman, Classen, & Spiegel, 1999). Restriction of usual activities is a common outcome of the disease and its treatment, which can foster depression and other adverse psychosocial responses (Williamson, 2000). Passive coping style also predicts cancer-related distress (Kim, Valdimarsdottir, & Bovbjerg, 2003).

Issues Involving Social Support   Social support is important for cancer patients' recovery (Carpenter, Fowler, Maxwell, & Andersen, 2010), but, despite the fact that many cancer patients receive emotional support from their families and friends, social support can be problematic (Luszczynska, Boehmer, Knoll, Schulz, & Schwarzer, 2007). Effective support is important for several reasons. It may set the tone for future social encounters (Badr & Taylor, 2008), it improves psychological adjustment to cancer, and it can help patients deal with intrusive thoughts and ruminations about the cancer (Lewis et al., 2001). Support may improve immunologic responses to cancer as well. If there was any doubt of the importance of social support to cancer survival, one investigation (Lai et al., 1999) found that married patients with cancers have significantly better survival rates than single, separated, divorced, or widowed patients. Socially isolated cancer patients fare very poorly and have an elevated risk of mortality (Kroenke, Kubzansky, Schernhammer, Holmes, & Kawachi, 2006). How spouses provide support matters. Engaging in conversations with the patient about the cancer and finding constructive methods for solving problems can be beneficial (Hagedoorn et al., 2000); hiding one's concerns and overprotecting the patient are less beneficial. Interventions directed to these issues can significantly improve quality of life (Graves, 2003).

Problems concerning a cancer patient's children are relatively common. Young children may show fear or distress over the parent's prognosis (Compas et al., 1994), while older children may find new responsibilities thrust on them and in response may rebel. Problems with children may be especially severe if the cancer is one with a hereditary component, because the children may blame the parent for putting them at increased risk (Lichtman et al., 1984). Mothers with breast cancer have daughters who are now known to be vulnerable to cancer as well, and both mother and daughter may be distressed (Cohen & Pollack, 2005; Fletcher et al., 2006).

Marital and Sexual Relationships   A strong marital relationship is important because marital adjustment predicts psychological distress following cancer diagnosis (Banthia et al., 2003). Unfortunately, disturbances in marital relationships after a diagnosis of cancer

are not uncommon (Ybema, Kuijer, Buunk, DeJong, & Sanderman, 2001). When partners are unsupportive, the impact on cancer patients' quality of life may be long-term (Manne, Ostroff, Winkel, Grana, & Fox, 2005). Sexual functioning is particularly vulnerable. Body image concerns and concerns about a partner's reactions represent psychosocial vulnerabilities, especially when there has been disfiguring surgery, as in the case of breast cancer (Spencer et al., 1999). Breast-conserving techniques, such as lumpectomy, lead to better psychological, marital, sexual, and social adjustment than the more extensive mastectomy surgery (Moyer, 1997).

Sexual functioning can be directly affected by treatments, such as surgery or chemotherapy, and indirectly affected by anxiety or depression, which often reduce sexual desire (Andersen, Woods, & Copeland, 1997). Sexual functioning problems have also been particularly evident in patients with gynecologic cancers and prostate cancer and underscore the fact that different types of cancers create different kinds of problems (Moyer & Salovey, 1996).

Psychological Adjustment and Treatment

Psychological reactions to cancer can be poor when the treatments are severe (Jim, Andrykowski, Munster, & Jacobsen, 2007) or when the patient has a poor understanding of the disease and treatment, or both. Poor adjustment is also found when people have poor social support, pre-existing psychological conditions, and little ability to express or find positive emotions and experiences in their lives (Manne et al., 2008). Survivors of childhood leukemia, for example, sometimes show signs of PTSD, which may persist for years following treatment (Stuber, Christakis, Houskamp, & Kazak, 1996). Among adult patients, however, signs of PTSD appear to be relatively rare (Palmer, Kagee, Coyne, & DeMichele, 2004).

Identifying and attending to psychological distress in response to cancer is an important issue, not only for maintaining quality of life but also because psychological distress is related to prospects for long-term survival. Cancer survivors may have elevated cortisol levels and alterations in their HPA axis responses to stress due to fear of recurrence, stress associated with cancer treatment and the disease, or a combination (Porter et al., 2003). These hormones may, in turn, exert a regulatory effect on the immune system that may influence the likelihood of a recurrence.

Self-Presentation of Cancer Patients

Vocational disruption may occur for patients who have chronic discomfort from cancer or its treatments (Somerfield, Curbow, Wingard, Baker, & Fogarty, 1996), and job discrimination against cancer patients has been documented. Further, difficulties in managing social interactions can result from alterations in physical appearance, disrupting social and recreational activity. An ostomy patient—someone who has a surgically created opening that connects an internal organ (often the stomach) to the surface of the body—for example, described his fear of revolting others:

> When I smelled an odor on the bus or subway before the colostomy, I used to feel very annoyed. I'd think that the people were awful, that they didn't take a bath, or that they should have gone to the bathroom before traveling. I used to think that they might have odors from what they ate. I used to be terribly annoyed; to me it seemed that they were filthy, dirty. Of course, at the least opportunity I used to change my seat and if I couldn't, it used to go against my grain. So naturally, I believe that the young people feel the same way about me if I smell. (Goffman, 1963, p. 34)

Coping with Cancer

Certain coping strategies are helpful in dealing with the problems related to cancer. In a study of 603 cancer patients, C. Dunkel-Schetter and colleagues (1992) identified five patterns of coping:

1. Seeking or using social support
2. Focusing in on the positive
3. Distancing
4. Cognitive escape-avoidance
5. Behavioral escape-avoidance

Coping through social support, focusing on the positive, and distancing were all associated with less emotional distress from cancer. Patients high in optimism and in a sense of personal control also experience less psychological distress (Bárez, Blasco, Fernández-Castro, & Viladrich, 2009; Carver et al., 2005). A study of prostate cancer patients revealed that those who used problem-focused and emotion-focused coping were healthier both psychologically and physically, whereas those who used avoidance coping experienced more psychological distress and poorer health (Roesch et al., 2005; see also Yang, Brothers, & Andersen, 2008). When spouses cope with their partner's illness using these same avoidance strategies, a patient's distress may also be high (Ben-Zur, Gilbar, & Lev, 2001).

Despite documented psychosocial problems associated with cancer, many people clearly weather their cancer experiences quite well from a psychological standpoint, adjusting to major changes in their lives (Costanzo, Ryff, & Singer, 2009). With the exception of vulnerability to depression, the psychological distress experienced by cancer patients does not differ from that of people without cancer and is significantly less than that of people suffering from psychiatric disorders (van't Spijker et al., 1997). Overall, long-term distress in response to cancer appears to affect only about 15% of cancer patients (Henselmans et al., 2010).

Finding Meaning in Cancer

Some cancer patients report that their lives have been made better in important ways by the cancer experience, permitting them to experience growth (Taylor, 1983; Widows, Jacobsen, Booth-Jones, & Fields, 2005) and satisfaction in personal relationships that they might not otherwise have achieved (Fromm, Andrykowski, & Hunt, 1996; Katz, Flasher, Cacciapaglia, & Nelson, 2001; Taylor, 1983). The ability to find benefits in the cancer experience predicts lower levels of distress and depression years later (Carver & Antoni, 2004). Such growth experiences may mute neuroendocrine stress responses, which may, in turn, have a beneficial effect on the immune system (Cruess, Antoni, McGregor, et al., 2000).

People who experience a sense of personal control over their cancer, its treatments, or their daily activities cope more successfully with cancer (Newsom, Knapp, & Schulz, 1996; Taylor et al., 1991). Control over emotional reactions and physical symptoms appears to be especially important for psychosocial adjustment (Thompson et al., 1993). Optimism is also a valuable coping resource for dealing with cancer (McGregor et al., 2004).

Interventions

Prior to treatment, educational interventions are vital (Zimmermann, Heinrichs, & Baucom, 2007). During or following treatment, a number of interventions have been used. Cognitive-behavioral approaches to the management of cancer-related problems have focused on depression, stress, fatigue, pain, appetite control, and side effects associated with chemotherapy, radiation therapy, and other cancer treatments (Antoni et al., 2001; Curran, Beacham, & Andrykowski, 2004; Montgomery et al., 2009; Phillips et al., 2008). Interventions directed to these issues can significantly improve quality of life (Graves, 2003; Tatrow & Montgomery, 2006). In one study of a cognitive-behavioral stress management intervention with women newly diagnosed with breast cancer, the intervention reduced the prevalence of depression and increased the women's ability to find benefits in their experience, maintain a positive state of mind, maintain health behavior change, and experience improved social relationships (Antoni et al., 2001). This intervention also reduced cortisol levels in these women, which may have positive implications for the course of their cancer (Cruess, Antoni, McGregor, et al., 2000).

Mindfulness-based stress reduction interventions have promise as well. For example, a study of breast and prostate cancer patients employed a mindfulness intervention involving the active cultivation of conscious awareness through relaxation, meditation, and yoga, with daily practice. The intervention not only enhanced quality of life and decreased stress symptoms but also produced a shift in immune profile from one associated with depressive symptoms to a more normal profile (Carlson, Speca, Patel, & Goodey, 2003).

Recently, practitioners have recommended exercise as a general intervention to improve quality of life following cancer (Floyd & Moyer, 2010; Lynch, Cerin, Newman, & Owen, 2007). A review of 24 research studies found that physical exercise had a positive effect on quality of life following cancer diagnosis, including a heightened sense of self-efficacy, better physical functioning, and improved emotional well-being (McAuley, White, Rogers, Motl, & Courneya, 2010; Milne, Wallman, Gordon, & Courneya, 2008). Exercise adherence, though, can be a problem (Courneya et al., 2008). Interventions that draw on the theory of planned behavior or the stages of change model to promote exercise have shown some success (Park & Gaffey, 2007; Vallance, Courneya, Plotnikoff, & Mackey, 2008).

Pain is a relatively common problem among cancer patients, particularly those with advancing disease. Although painkillers remain the primary method of treating cancer-related pains, behavioral interventions increasingly are being adopted (Davis, Vasterling, Bransfield, & Burish, 1987). Relaxation therapy, hypnosis, cognitive-reappraisal techniques, visual imaging, self-hypnosis, and therapies that target illness cognitions have all proven to be at least somewhat useful in the management of pain due to cancer (Turk & Fernandez, 1990; Ward et al., 2008).

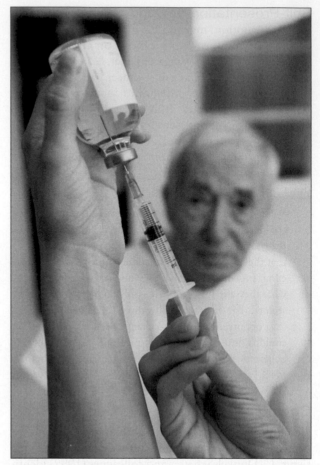

Many cancer patients who receive intravenously administered chemotherapy experience intense nausea and vomiting. Interventions using relaxation and guided imagery can substantially improve these problems.

Writing interventions involving expressive disclosure or writing about benefits derived from cancer have been tied to lower physical symptom reports and fewer medical appointments for cancer-related problems over a 3-month period (Low, Stanton, & Danoff-Burg, 2006). The opportunity to affirm important personal values and the use of emotional approach coping appear to account for these benefits (Creswell et al., 2007). Written emotional disclosure may especially help patients manage the negative feedback that they receive from family and friends when they try to express their emotions regarding cancer (Zakowski, Ramati, Morton, Johnson, & Flanigan, 2004). More generally, positive states of mind, whether induced by expressive writing or as a spontaneous reaction to the cancer experience, have been tied to both emotional and health-related benefits

(Aspinwall & Tedeschi, 2010), although not all researchers are persuaded (Coyne, Tennen, & Ranchor, 2010).

Psychotherapeutic Interventions   Psychotherapeutic interventions—including individual psychotherapy, group therapy, family therapy, and cancer support groups—attempt to meet the psychosocial and informational needs of cancer patients.

Individual Therapy   Patients seeking therapy after a diagnosis of cancer are most likely to experience the following:

- Significant anxiety, depression, or suicidal thoughts
- Central nervous system dysfunctions produced by the illness and treatment, such as the inability to concentrate
- Specific problems that have arisen as a consequence of the illness, its management, or family dynamics
- Previously existing psychological problems that have been exacerbated by the cancer
- Management of pain

Many of these interventions draw on CBT (Montgomery et al., 2009). Interventions may be most effective for patients with elevated distress (Schneider et al., 2010). Therapy with cancer patients often follows a crisis intervention format rather than an intensive psychotherapy model. That is, therapists working with cancer patients try to focus on the specific issues faced by the patient rather than undertaking a more general, probing, long-term analysis of the patient's psyche. The most common issues arising in individual therapy are fear of recurrence, pain, or death; fear of loss of organs as a consequence of additional surgeries; interference with valued activities; practical difficulties, such as job discrimination and problems with dating and social relationships; and communication problems with families. Psychotherapeutic interventions with children who have cancer involve many of the same guidelines and issues as in therapy with adult cancer patients.

Psychotherapeutic interventions are especially successful when they focus on helping a cancer patient make use of and build personal resources, such as optimism and control, as well as social resources, such as social support. These psychological resources are most important for mental and physical functioning over the long term (Helgeson, Snyder, & Seltman, 2004). Mindfulness interventions have also helped cancer patients decrease their level of stress and achieve a positive state of mind (Bränström, Kvillemo, Brandberg, & Moskowitz, 2010).

Family Therapy   Emotional support from family is highly desired by cancer patients, and it promotes good psychological adjustment (Helgeson & Cohen, 1996; Northouse, Templin, & Mood, 2001). Couples coping with cancer may benefit from couples intervention (Kershaw et al., 2008; Kim et al., 2008; Taylor et al., 2008). Patients who cope via emotional approach may especially benefit from this kind of intervention (Manne, Ostroff, & Winkel, 2007). Not all families are able to communicate freely with each other, though. When there is a mismatch in the social support wanted and received by cancer patients, psychological distress may increase (Reynolds & Perrin, 2004). Cancer patients' distress may also be hard for families to bear and may contribute to a loss of social support from the family (Alferi, Carver, Antoni, Weiss, & Duran, 2001). Family therapy provides an opportunity for family members to share their problems and difficulties in communicating. Couples therapy may be especially helpful to promote joint coping (Badr, Carmack, Kashy, Cristofanilli, & Revenson, 2010).

Group Interventions   As is true for other chronic illnesses, group interventions can be useful in providing information and counseling to cancer patients (Helgeson & Cohen, 1996). An intervention study that provided psychological counseling and educational information on a group level was successful with men with prostate cancer; men who began the intervention with lower prostate-specific self-efficacy and higher depression benefited the most from the intervention (Helgeson, Lepore, & Eton, 2006).

Support Groups   Self-help groups in which patients share emotional concerns are also available to many cancer patients (Helgeson & Cohen, 1996). Social support groups appear to be most helpful for women who have more problems, who lack support, or who have fewer personal resources, although they may provide few if any benefits for those who already have high levels of support (Cameron et al., 2005; Helgeson, Cohen, Schulz, & Yasko, 2000; Taylor, Lamdan, et al., 2003). A possible reason for the success of support groups is that the self-help format presents patients with an array of potential coping techniques from which they can draw the ones that fit in with their particular styles and problems

(Taylor et al., 1986). Spending time with well-adjusted people who have had the same disorder can satisfy patients' needs for information and emotional support (Stanton, Danoff-Burg, Cameron, Snider, & Kirk, 1999). Unhappily, though, only a small percent of people take advantage of support group opportunities (Sherman et al., 2008). The Internet also is now used extensively for social support from other cancer patients (Owen, Klapow, Roth, & Tucker, 2004). Social support groups may also contribute to longevity (Fawzy, Cousins, et al., 1990; Fawzy, Kemeny, et al., 1990; Levy, Herberman, Lee, Lippman, & d'Angelo, 1989; Spiegel, Bloom, Kraemer, & Gottheil, 1989).

In closing our discussion of cancer, we return to the issue of SES disparities and the fact that low-income people are at greater risk both for cancer initially and for a faster course of illness once detected. Clearly, more investigation into why SES is related to higher incidence and mortality is needed. In addition, the development of culturally appropriate interventions is needed to identify the needs of these underserved groups (Glanz, Croyle, Chollette, & Pinn, 2003).

■ ARTHRITIS

We learned in Chapter 2 about a set of diseases known as autoimmune diseases, in which the body falsely identifies its own tissue as foreign matter and attacks it. The most prevalent of these autoimmune diseases is arthritis, and it is also one of the most common causes of disability.

Arthritis has been with humankind since the beginning of recorded history. Ancient drawings of people with arthritic joints have been found in caves, and early Greek and Roman writers described the pain of arthritis (Johnson, 2003). *Arthritis* means "inflammation of a joint"; it refers to more than 100 diseases that attack the joints or other connective tissues. Forty-six million people in the United States are afflicted with arthritis severe enough to require medical care, a figure that is projected to rise to 67 million by 2030, due to the aging of the population (Centers for Disease Control and Prevention, October 2008). Although it is rarely fatal, arthritis ranks second only to heart disease as the most widespread chronic disease in the United States today. Arthritis costs the U.S. economy nearly $128 billion per year in medical care and indirect expenses such as lost wages and production (Centers for Disease Control and Prevention, June 2008b).

The severity of and prognosis for arthritis depend on the type; the disease ranges from a barely noticeable and occasional problem to a crippling, chronic condition. The two major forms of arthritis are rheumatoid arthritis and osteoarthritis.

Rheumatoid Arthritis

Rheumatoid arthritis (RA) affects 1.3 million Americans, mostly women (Centers for Disease Control and Prevention, January 2008a), and is the most crippling form of arthritis. The disease strikes primarily the 40–60 age group, although it can attack people of any age group, including children. It usually affects the small joints of the hands and feet, as well as the wrists, knees, ankles, and neck. In mild cases, only one or two joints are involved, but sometimes the disease becomes widespread. In severe cases, there may be inflammation of the heart muscle, blood vessels, and tissues just beneath the skin. Rheumatoid arthritis is brought on by an autoimmune process (Firestein, 2003): Agents of the immune system that are supposed to protect the body instead attack the thin membranes surrounding the joints.

Approximately 1.3 million people in the United States have rheumatoid arthritis, and it is especially common among older women.

This attack leads to inflammation, stiffness, and pain. If not controlled, the bone and surrounding muscle tissue of the joint may be destroyed. Almost half of RA patients recover completely, nearly half remain somewhat arthritic, and about 10% are severely disabled.

The main complications of RA are pain, limitations in activities, and the need to be dependent on others (van Lankveld et al., 1993). In addition, because RA primarily affects older people, its sufferers may have other chronic conditions as well, such as poor cognitive functioning and poor vision, which may interact with arthritis to produce high levels of disability (Shifren, Park, Bennett, & Morrell, 1999; Verbrugge, 1995). Not surprisingly, one of the most common complications of RA is depression (Dickens, McGowan, Clark-Carter, & Creed, 2002). Depression may feed back into the pain process, enhancing pain (Zautra & Smith, 2001), and may increase arthritis disease activity (Smith & Zautra, 2002). It may also lead to greater work disability (Löwe et al., 2004). A vicious spiral may be put into effect: As the disease progresses, psychological distress increases, and greater disability results (Zautra et al., 2007). Patients may come to doubt their abilities to manage vital life activities, which can contribute to depression, which, in turn, exacerbates physical impairment (Neugebauer, Katz, & Pasch, 2003). The couple's relationship may be affected, if spouses have unrealistic expectations or do not understand the cyclic nature of the disease (Sterba et al., 2008).

At one time, psychologists speculated that there might be a "rheumatoid arthritis personality." This personality type was said to be perfectionistic, depressed, and restricted in emotional expression, especially the expression of anger. Recent research now casts doubt on the accuracy of such a profile, at least as a cause of arthritis. However, cognitive distortions and feelings of helplessness can aggravate depression and other emotional responses to arthritis (Clemmey & Nicassio, 1997; Fifield et al., 2001). Gaps in social support may also be a consequence (Fyrand, Moum, Finset, & Glennas, 2002). Comorbid conditions—that is, other pain-related or psychiatric disorders—are the rule rather than the exception among people who have arthritis (Stang, Brandenburg, Lane, Merikangas, Von Korff, & Kessler, 2006), thereby complicating treatment.

Stress and RA   Stress may play a role both in the development of rheumatoid arthritis and in its aggravation. Disturbances in interpersonal relationships may contribute to the development of the disease (Anderson,

Bradley, Young, McDaniel, & Wise, 1985) and/or its course (Parrish, Zautra, & Davis, 2008). The depression felt by RA patients may also contribute to increased reactivity to stress and pain (Zautra & Smith, 2001).

The aggravation of RA by stress appears to be mediated by the immune system, inasmuch as people with RA show stronger immune responses to stress than do comparison groups (Harrington et al., 1993; Timko, Baumgartner, Moos, & Miller, 1993; Zautra & Smith, 2001). Unfavorable social reactions to people with rheumatoid arthritis may contribute to disability as well (McQuade, 2002).

Treatment of RA   Treatments to arrest or control the problems of rheumatoid arthritis include aspirin (which relieves both pain and inflammation), rest, and supervised exercise. Surgery is rarely needed, and hospitalization is necessary only in extreme cases or for extreme pain or flareups. Exercise is strongly recommended for RA patients so that they can gain more control over the affected joints (Waggoner & LeLieuvre, 1981). Unfortunately, adherence is often low. Self-management can be improved with strong support from a partner (Strating, van Schuur, & Suurmeijer, 2006).

Increasingly, psychologists have used cognitive-behavioral interventions in the treatment of RA (McCracken, 1991). In one study (O'Leary, Shoor, Lorig, & Holman, 1988), RA patients were randomized into a cognitive-behavioral treatment that taught skills in managing stress, pain, and symptoms of the disease, or they received an arthritis self-help book containing useful information about arthritis self-management. The cognitive-behavioral treatment was designed to increase perceptions of self-efficacy with respect to the disease. Patients in the cognitive-behavioral treatment experienced reduced pain and joint inflammation and improved psychosocial functioning. The degree to which people improved was correlated with the degree of self-efficacy enhancement, suggesting that self-efficacy to manage the disease was responsible for the positive effects. As one patient in such an intervention put it, "I went from thinking about arthritis as a terrible burden that had been thrust upon me to something I could control and manage. I redefined it for myself. It's no longer a tragedy, it's an inconvenience." As this comment also suggests, remaining optimistic and finding benefits in the RA experience can lead people to cope more actively with the disease, improving adjustment over time (Brenner, Melamed, & Panush, 1994), and lead to better relations with family and friends (Danoff-Burg &

Revenson, 2005). Nonetheless, as is true for all cognitive-behavioral interventions, relapse to old habits is likely. Therefore, relapse prevention strategies to preserve both behavioral changes and a sense of self-efficacy and optimism are an important part of these interventions (Keefe & Van Horn, 1993).

Overall, cognitive-behavioral interventions, including biofeedback, relaxation training, problem-solving skills, a focus on reducing negative expectations, and cognitive pain-coping skills training have been modestly successful in aiding pain management and reducing psychological distress for RA patients (Dixon, Keefe, Scipio, Perri, & Abernethy, 2007; Zautra et al., 2008), although interventions appear to be more effective for the patients who have had the illness for a shorter period of time (Astin, Beckner, Soeken, Hochberg, & Berman, 2002). Coordinating these cognitive-behavioral interventions with the use of drug therapies to control pain provides the most comprehensive approach at present (Zautra & Manne, 1992).

Recently, mindfulness interventions have been used with RA patients, and patients with depression appear to be especially benefitted (Zautra et al., 2008).

Juvenile RA   Another form of rheumatoid arthritis is juvenile RA. Its causes and symptoms are similar to those of the adult form, but the victims are children age 2–5. Among them, the disease flares up periodically until puberty. The disease is rare and affects girls four times as often as boys. With treatment, most children manage well and experience few adverse effects. However, one juvenile form of RA can be severely crippling and can lead to extensive psychological and physical problems for its sufferers, including missed school and nonparticipation in social activities (Billings, Moos, Miller, & Gottlieb, 1987). Social support from family members is important in helping the juvenile RA patient adjust to the disorder.

Osteoarthritis

Osteoarthritis affects an estimated 26.9 million Americans, mostly after age 45. Women are more commonly affected than men (Centers for Disease Control and Prevention, January 2008b). The disorder develops when the smooth lining of a joint, known as the articular cartilage, begins to crack or wear away because of overuse, injury, or other causes. Thus, the disease tends to affect the weight-bearing joints: the hips, knees, and spine. As the cartilage deteriorates, the joint may be-

come inflamed, stiff, and painful. The disease afflicts many elderly people and some athletes. As is true for other forms of arthritis, more serious and extensive symptoms require more aggressive treatment and lead to a poorer quality of life (Hampson, Glasgow, & Zeiss, 1994). Depression may result, and depressive symptoms may, in turn, elevate pain and distress (Zautra & Smith, 2001). Psychosocial interventions to reduce distress and improve coping have been shown to reduce pain significantly (Dixon et al., 2007). When these interventions target both catastrophizing pain as well as increasing a sense of self-efficacy, they may be especially effective (McKnight, Afram, Kashdan, Kasle, & Zautra, 2010).

With proper treatment, osteoarthritis can be managed through self-care. Treatment includes keeping one's weight down and taking aspirin. Exercise is recommended, although adherence to exercise recommendations is mixed; exercise can initially aggravate the discomfort associated with osteoarthritis, but over time, it can ameliorate pain and improve physical functioning (Focht, Ewing, Gauvin, & Rejeski, 2002), especially in younger patients (Focht, Gauvin, & Rejeski, 2004). Occasionally, use of potent pain relievers, anti-inflammatory drugs, or steroids is needed. Those who manage the pain of osteoarthritis through active coping efforts and spontaneous pain control efforts appear to cope better with the disease (Keefe et al., 1987).

Other Forms of Arthritis

Other common or significant forms of arthritis include fibromyalgia (which was discussed in Chapter 11), gout, and lupus. **Gout** affects about 1 million Americans, mostly men, and results from a buildup of uric acid crystals in the joints. It is usually treated by diet, fluid intake, and exercise, and leads to life-threatening consequences only if left untreated.

Lupus affects approximately 2 million Americans, most of them women. The disease acquired the name *lupus,* which means "wolf," because of the skin rash that can appear on the face. It leads to chronic inflammation, producing pain, heat, redness, and swelling, and can be life-threatening when it attacks the connective tissue of the body's internal organs. Depending on the severity of the disease, it may be managed by anti-inflammatory medications or immunosuppressive medications. Lupus is more common among Native Americans, African-Americans, and Asian Americans than among European Americans.

To summarize, arthritis is the second most prevalent chronic disease in the United States. Although it does not typically cause death, it causes substantial pain and discomfort, creating problems of management. The self-care regimen of arthritis patients centers largely around pain control, dietary control, stress management, and exercise; therefore, the health habits and issues of adherence that we have discussed throughout this book are clearly important in the effective management of arthritis.

■ TYPE I DIABETES

Type I diabetes is an autoimmune disorder characterized by the abrupt onset of symptoms, which result from lack of insulin production by the beta cells of the pancreas. The disorder may appear following viral infection and probably has a genetic contribution. Stress may precipitate Type I diabetes in individuals with a genetic risk (Lehman, Rodin, McEwen, & Brinton, 1991). In Type I diabetes, the immune system falsely identifies cells in the pancreas as invaders and, accordingly, destroys these cells, compromising or eliminating their ability to produce insulin. Type I diabetes usually develops relatively early in life, earlier for girls than for boys. There are two common time periods when the disorder arises: between the ages of 5 and 6 or, later, between 10 and 13.

The most common early symptoms are frequent urination, unusual thirst, excessive fluid consumption, weight loss, fatigue, weakness, irritability, nausea, uncontrollable craving for food (especially sweets), and fainting. These symptoms are due to the body's attempt to find sources of energy, which prompts it to feed off its own fats and proteins. By-products of these fats then build up in the body, producing symptoms; if the condition is untreated, a coma can result.

Type I diabetes is a serious, life-threatening illness accounting for about 10% of all diabetes. It is managed primarily through direct injections of insulin—hence the name insulin-dependent diabetes (American Diabetes Association, 1999). The Type I diabetic is especially vulnerable to hyperglycemia. When this occurs, the skin is flushed and dry, and the individual feels drowsy and has deep, labored breathing. Vomiting may occur, and the tongue is dry; feelings of hunger are rare, but thirst is common. Abdominal pain may occur, and a large amount of sugar is detectable in the urine. Hyperglycemia may require medical intervention because coma may result, requiring hospitalization.

Stress aggravates Type I diabetes. At least 14 studies have reported direct links between stress and poor diabetic control (see Brand, Johnson, & Johnson, 1986; Hanson & Pichert, 1986). This relationship is not caused by differences in adherence to medications (Hanson, Henggeler, & Burghen, 1987), coping efforts (Frenzel, McCaul, Glasgow, & Schafer, 1988), insulin regiment, diet, or exercise (Hanson & Pichert, 1986), although stress can also adversely affect adherence and diet as well (Balfour, White, Schiffrin, Dougherty, & Dufresne, 1993; Halford, Cuddihy, & Mortimer, 1990).

Managing Type I Diabetes   Because very tight control of glucose levels can make a big difference in the progression of this disease, patients with Type I diabetes need to monitor their glucose levels throughout each day and take immediate action when it is needed. However, promising new drug treatments suggest that Type I diabetes may become quite well controlled through regular drug treatments. Treating Type I diabetics with stem cells made from their own blood may also prove to be a promising treatment (Voltarelli et al., 2007). Nonetheless, at present, active involvement of the patient as a comanager in the disease treatment process is essential to success.

The treatment goal for diabetes is to keep blood sugar at normal levels. This regulation is typically accomplished through regular insulin injections, dietary control, weight control, and exercise. The number of calories taken in each day must be relatively constant. Food intake must be controlled by a meal plan and not by temptation or appetite. Insulin injections are most often recommended on a regular basis for Type I diabetes, whereas diet, weight control, and exercise figure prominently in the management of both types of diabetes. When blood glucose levels can be actively controlled through such methods, onset and progression of diabetes-related disorders, including eye disease, kidney disease, and nerve disorders, can be reduced by more than 50% (National Institute on Diabetes and Digestive and Kidney Disorders, 1999).

Adherence   Unfortunately, adherence to self-management programs appears to be low. For example, one set of investigations found that 80% of diabetic patients administered insulin incorrectly, 58% administered the wrong dosage, 77% tested their urine for sugar content inaccurately, 75% were not eating at sufficiently regular

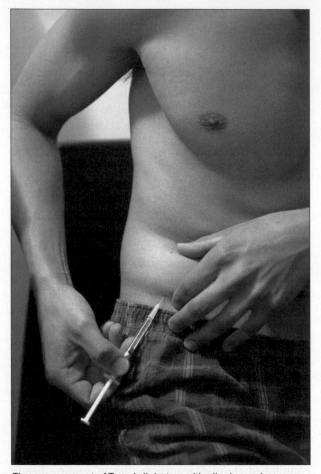

The management of Type I diabetes critically depends on proper monitoring of blood glucose level and regular injections of insulin, yet many adolescents and adults fail to adhere properly to the treatment regimen.

intervals, and 75% were not eating prescribed foods (Watkins, Roberts, Williams, Martin, & Coyle, 1967; Wing, Nowalk, Marcus, Koeske, & Finegold, 1986). Overall, only about 15% of patients appear to adhere to all their treatment recommendations.

Many of the severe complications of diabetes are not evident until 15–20 years after its onset. Therefore, complications do not frighten people into being adherent. They may feel no symptoms and, because the disease does not seem insistent on a day-to-day basis, fail to adhere to their treatment regimen. Many of the errors made by diabetics in adhering to their treatment regimen, then, are errors of omission rather than commission. That is, it is relatively unusual for diabetics to intentionally relapse but common for them to forget to

do particular behaviors they are supposed to perform regularly (Kirkley & Fisher, 1988).

One of the dilemmas involved in adequate adherence is that diabetic patients often fail to self-monitor their blood glucose level (Wysocki, Green, & Huxtable, 1989). Instead, like hypertensive patients, they rely on what their blood glucose level "feels like" (Hampson, Glasgow, & Toobert, 1990), and they rely strongly on their mood for making this judgment (Gonder-Frederick, Cox, Bobbitt, & Pennebaker, 1986). And, as is also the case in hypertension, even training in glucose level awareness fails to produce very accurate estimates of blood sugar levels (Diamond, Massey, & Covey, 1989). Depression, too, complicates glycemic control in Type I diabetic patients (Van Tilberg et al., 2001).

Patients do better managing the psychosocial aspects of their illness and their diabetes regimen when they use active coping strategies, as opposed to passive or avoidant ones (Luyckx, Vanhalst, Seiffge-Krenke, & Wheets, 2010). Adherence is also improved when patients and their physicians share treatment goals. One study that uncovered a high level of nonadherence to treatment among parents regulating their children's Type I diabetes found that parents and physicians had quite different goals. The parents' efforts to control diet were designed to avoid hypoglycemia, which is a short-term threat. In contrast, the physicians' goals were centered on the long-term threat of diabetes complications and the need to keep blood glucose levels steady. These differences in goals accounted for many of the departures from the prescribed regimen (Marteau, Johnston, Baum, & Bloch, 1987).

Effective diabetes management involves multiple aspects of behavior change, and complex regimens directed to multiple health habits are often difficult to implement. As a result, interventions with diabetics often pull together into a single treatment program all the self-regulation techniques that are required. Diabetics are trained in monitoring blood sugar accurately, using the information as a basis for making changes in behavior, reinforcing themselves for efforts to improve blood sugar control, managing stress, controlling diet, exercising, and developing social and problem-solving skills to deal with situational pressures to break with their treatment regimen (Schachinger et al., 2005). By seeing the relations among all the components in an organized program of self-regulation, adherence to the separate aspects of the regimen may be improved (Glasgow et al., 2002). Evidence suggests that intensive treatment interventions are more successful than less intensive programs in promoting long-term weight loss and maintaining adherence to treatment. Problem-solving skills aid in this process (Glasgow, Toobert, Barrera, & Strycker, 2004; Hill-Briggs et al., 2006).

Special Problems of Adolescent Diabetics

The management of diabetes is a particular problem with adolescents (Johnson, Freund, Silverstein, Hansen, & Malone, 1990). They are entangled in issues of independence and developing self-concept; diabetes and the restrictions that it imposes are inconsistent with these developmental tasks. Common stressors of adolescence aggravate metabolic control (Helgeson, Escobar, Siminerio, & Becker, 2010). Adolescents may see their parents' limitations on food as efforts to control them and may regard the need to monitor diet or to be conscientious about injections as rules and regulations imposed from the outside. Moreover, within the adolescent peer culture, those who are different are often stigmatized. Thus, the adolescent diabetic may neglect proper care to avoid rejection. Emotionally stable and conscientious adolescents are more likely to follow the complex regimen that diabetes requires than are those who do not have these qualities (Skinner, Hampson, & Fife-Schaw, 2002).

Relations with Family Problems in managing Type I diabetes among adolescents are not confined to the diabetic's own difficulties of accepting the limitations imposed by the disease. Other family members may also react in ways that undermine management efforts. Parents, for example, may treat their newly diagnosed adolescent diabetic as a child and restrict activities beyond what is necessary, infantilizing the adolescent and increasing dependence. Alternatively, the parents

may try to convince the child that he or she is normal, like everyone else, yet the adolescent quickly learns otherwise. Studies suggest that when parents are actively involved in diabetes management tasks, such as helping their adolescents monitor blood glucose levels, better metabolic control over the disease can be obtained (Pereira, Berg-Cross, Almeida, & Machado, 2008). However, when young adults with diabetes experience the help of others as efforts at social control, the efforts may be counter-productive (Thorpe, Lewis, & Sterba, 2008). Conflict with peers has also been found to undermine management of the disease as well as the depression that may sometimes accompany it (Helgeson, Lopez, & Kamarck, 2009). Indeed, depression itself is a common complicating condition in Type I diabetes tied to poor control and poor health outcome (Roy, Roy, & Affouf, 2007). Positive affect, by contrast, boosts the perception of competence on daily diabetes tasks and may foster better management (Frotenberry et al., 2009).

Increasingly, health psychologists have been involved in the development of interventions to improve adjustment and adherence to treatment regimens for Type I diabetes. The health psychologist can help with the delineation of problems in achieving control over diabetes (Glasgow & Anderson, 1995) and with the identification of complicating psychological and social factors not yet identified that may compromise the treatment of diabetes (Talbot, Nouwen, Gingras, Gosselin, & Audet, 1997).

The health psychologist, then, has an important role to play in the management of diabetes, by developing the best format for teaching the complex treatment regimen, ensuring adherence, developing effective means for coping with stress, and helping the diagnosed diabetic develop the self-regulatory skills needed to manage the multifactor treatment program that is required. ●

SUMMARY

1. The immune system is the surveillance system of the body; it guards against foreign invaders. It involves a number of complex processes, comprising humoral immunity and cell-mediated immunity.

2. Studies suggest that stressors, such as academic exams and stressful interpersonal relationships, can compromise immune functioning.

3. Negative emotions, such as depression or anxiety, may also compromise immune functioning. Coping methods may buffer the immune system against adverse changes due to stress.

4. Studies find that relaxation and stress management represent successful clinical efforts to augment immune system functioning in the face of stress.

5. Acquired immune deficiency syndrome (AIDS) was first identified in the United States in 1981. It results from the human immunodeficiency virus (HIV) and is marked by the presence of unusual opportunistic infectious diseases that result when the immune system, especially the helper T cells, has been compromised in its functioning.

6. Gay men and intravenous needle-sharing drug users have been the primary risk groups for AIDS in the United States. More recently, AIDS has spread rapidly in minority populations, especially minority women. Heterosexually active adolescents and young adults are also at risk.

7. Primary prevention, in the form of condom use and control of the number of partners, is a major avenue for controlling the spread of AIDS. Such interventions focus on providing knowledge, increasing perceived self-efficacy to engage in protective behavior, changing peer norms about sexual practices, and communicating sexual negotiation strategies.

8. Many people live with asymptomatic HIV-seropositivity for years. Exercise and active coping may help prolong this state. Drugs such as protease inhibitors now hold promise for enabling people with HIV and AIDS to live longer, healthier lives.

9. AIDS itself creates a variety of debilitating physical and psychosocial problems. The main psychosocial tasks faced by people diagnosed with AIDS are dealing psychologically with the likelihood of a shortened life, dealing with negative reactions from others, and developing strategies for maintaining physical and emotional health. A variety of coping interventions have been developed to aid in these tasks.

10. Cancer is a set of more than 100 diseases marked by malfunctioning DNA and rapid cell growth and proliferation. Research investigations have attempted to relate psychosocial factors to the onset and progression of cancer. Depression and avoidance coping may be implicated, especially in the progression of cancer, but as yet, the evidence is not definitive.

11. Cancer can produce a range of physical and psychosocial problems, including debilitating responses to chemotherapy, avoidance by the social network, vocational disruption, and adverse psychological responses such as depression. CBT and other psychotherapeutic interventions are used to manage these problems.

12. Arthritis, involving inflammation of the joints, affects about 46 million people in the United States. Rheumatoid arthritis is the most crippling form, but there are more than 100 disorders, including lupus and fibromyalgia, that account for this highly prevalent set of diseases. Stress appears to exacerbate the disease.

13. Interventions involving cognitive-behavioral techniques to help people manage pain effectively and increase perceptions of self-efficacy have proven helpful in alleviating some of the discomfort and psychosocial difficulties associated with arthritis.

14. Type I diabetes is an auto-immune disorder that often strikes in childhood or early adolescence. Its management involves integrating several different health habits, and unfortunately, especially with young Type I diabetes patients, adherence can be poor. Health psychologists can help in the design of interventions to improve the management of this disorder.

KEY TERMS

acquired immune deficiency syndrome (AIDS)
gout

human immunodeficiency virus (HIV)
lupus
osteoarthritis

psychoneuroimmunology
rheumatoid arthritis (RA)
Type I diabetes

Toward the Future

Health Psychology: Challenges for the Future

Sometimes when we focus on all the health-related issues that need to be solved, we forget how much progress in improving health outcomes has already been achieved. Consider the following trends:

- Life expectancy in the U.S. reached an all-time high of 77.9 years in 2007.

- Death rates dropped significantly for 8 of the 15 leading causes of death in the U.S. between 2006 and 2007.

- Fewer Americans died in traffic fatalities in 2008 than in any year since 1961.

- In 2007, 3 out of 10 children aged 5–17 did not miss a single day of school due to injury or illness within the preceding year.

- Worldwide, the proportion of undernourished children under 5 years of age dropped 7% between 1990 and 2005.

- From 2006–2008, the median percentage of U.S. schools that do not sell soda rose from 38% to 64%.

- The amount of trans fats in packaged food has declined by 50% since 2006.

- 71% of the U.S. population live under either a state or local ban on smoking in workplaces, and/or restaurants, and/or bars.

- Almost 62% of U.S. adults say they are in excellent health.

  Source: Beck, 2009, November 24.

Health psychology has contributed to many of these dramatic and impressive advances. In this last chapter, we highlight some of health psychology's research accomplishments and likely future directions of the field. In addition, we address some health-related trends that are not progressing as well as those just described, and how health psychology may contribute to amelioration of those issues.

■ HEALTH PROMOTION

In recent years, Americans have made substantial gains in altering their poor health habits. Many people have stopped smoking, and many have reduced their consumption of high-cholesterol and high-fat foods. Coronary heart disease and other chronic diseases have shown dramatic decreases as a result. Although alcohol consumption patterns remain largely unchanged, exercise has increased. Despite these advances, overweight and obesity are currently endemic and will shortly supplant smoking as the major avoidable contributor to mortality. Clearly, most people know that they need to practice good health behaviors, and many have tried to develop or change them on their own. Not everyone is successful, however. Thus, the potential for health psychology to make a contribution to health promotion remains.

Increasingly, we will see efforts to identify the most potent and effective elements of behavior-change programs in order to incorporate them into cost-effective, efficient interventions that reach the largest number of people. In particular, we can expect to see the design of interventions for mass consumption in the community, the workplace, the media (including the Internet), and the schools.

A Focus on Those at Risk

As medical research increasingly identifies genetic and behavioral risk factors for chronic illness, the at-risk role will be increasingly important. Individuals who are identified early as at risk for particular disorders need to learn how to cope with their risk status and how to change their modifiable risk-relevant behaviors. Health psychologists can aid substantially in both these tasks.

Studies of people who are at risk for particular disorders are very useful in identifying additional risk factors for various chronic disorders. Not everyone who is at risk for an illness will develop it, and by studying which people do and do not, researchers can identify the further precipitating or promoting factors of these illnesses.

Prevention

Preventing poor health habits from developing will continue to be a priority for health psychology. Adolescence is a window of vulnerability for most bad health habits, and so closing this window is of paramount importance. **Behavioral immunization** programs are already in existence for smoking, drug abuse, and, in some cases, diet and eating disorders. Programs that expose fifth and sixth graders to antismoking or antidrug material before they begin these habits are somewhat successful in keeping some adolescents from undertaking such habits. Behavioral immunization for other health habits—including safe sex and diet—also holds promise.

For some health habits, we may need to start even earlier and initiate behavioral pediatric programs to teach parents how to reduce the risks of accidents in the home, how to practice good safety habits in automobiles, and how to instill in their children good health habits such as exercise, proper diet, regular immunizations and medical checkups, and regular dental care.

A Focus on the Elderly

The rapid aging of the population means that within the next 10 years, we will have the largest elderly cohort ever seen in this and other countries (see Table 15.1). This cohort can be an ill one, marked by disease, disability, and depression (Kelley-Moore & Ferraro, 2005), or it can be a healthy, active one (Libow, 2005). Interventions should focus on helping the elderly achieve the highest level of functioning possible through programs that emphasize diet, exercise, control of alcohol consumption, and other health habits (Facts of Life, November 2006).

Refocusing Health Promotion Efforts

Some refocusing of health promotion efforts is in order. In the past, we have stressed mortality more than morbidity. Although the reduction of mortality, especially early mortality, is a priority, there will always be 10 major causes of death (Becker, 1993). Refocusing our effort toward morbidity is important for a number of reasons.

One obvious reason is cost. Chronic diseases are expensive to treat, particularly when those diseases persist for years, even decades (Yach, Leeder, Bell, & Kistnasamy, 2005). For example, conditions such as rheumatoid arthritis and osteoarthritis have little impact on mortality rates but have a major impact on the functioning and well-being of the population, particularly the elderly. Keeping people healthy for as long as possible will help reduce the burden of chronic illness costs. Moreover, maximizing the number of good years during which a person is free from the burdens of chronic illness produces a higher quality of life.

The health needs of the elderly will take on increasing importance with the aging of the population. Helping the elderly achieve a high level of functioning through interventions that emphasize diet, exercise, and other health habits is a high priority for the future.

Priorities for the future include developing interventions that can address more than one behavioral risk factor at a time, addressing the difficult issue of continued maintenance, and integrating individual-level interventions into the broader environmental and health policies that support and sustain individual efforts (Orleans, 2000).

Promoting Resilience

Future health promotion efforts should place greater weight on positive factors that may reduce morbidity or delay mortality. For example, although eliminating heart disease and cancer would lengthen lives by several years, marriage would add several years to a man's life. As W. J. McGuire (1984) suggested facetiously, health

TABLE 15.1 | Percent of Population Aged 65 and over

	1970	2010	2050 (Projected)
United States	9%	13%	21.6%
India	3.3	4.9	13.7
China	4.3	8.2	23.3
Japan	7	22.6	37.8
United Kingdom	13.0	16.6	22.9
Western Europe	13.1	18.4	28.9

Source: Financial Times, 2009, October 15.

psychologists could make a giant leap forward by going after this health-related factor and opening a marriage bureau. The point is well taken.

Health psychologists are only beginning to understand the positive experiences that keep some people from developing chronic disorders. Studying how people spontaneously reduce their levels of stress, for example, and how they seek out opportunities for rest, renewal, and relaxation may provide knowledge for effective interventions. Personal resources, such as optimism or a sense of control, have proven to be protective against chronic illness. Can these resources be taught? Recent research suggests that they can (see, for example, Mann, 2001). The coming decades will explore these and related possibilities.

Health Promotion as a Part of Medical Practice

A true philosophy of health promotion cannot be adequately implemented until a focus on health promotion becomes an integral part of medical practice (Institute of Medicine, 2009). Although some progress in this direction has been made, we are still far away from having a health care system that is oriented toward health promotion.

As noted in Chapter 3, there is as yet no formal diagnostic process for identifying and targeting preventive health behaviors on an individual basis. If the annual physical that many people obtain were to include a simple review of the particular health issues and habits that the individual should focus on, this step would, at the very least, alert each of us to the health goals we should consider and might prod us in the direction of taking necessary action.

Physicians are high in status and tend to be persuasive when other potential change agents are not. A 28-year-old man in a high-stress occupation might be urged by his health care practitioner to practice stress management and be given a self-help program for stopping smoking. A young woman who wolfs down a burrito between classes might be given information about the need for a healthy diet and simple steps she can undertake to improve her diet, such as having yogurt, fruit, or cereal instead. In the future, we may see practicing physicians integrate prevention into their daily practice with their healthy patients as well as their ill ones.

SES and Health Disparities

Individual health behavior changes alone may not substantially improve the health of the general population. What is needed is individual change coupled with social

change. Although the United States spends more on health care than any other country in the world (Figure 15.1), we have neither the longest life expectancy nor the lowest infant mortality rate. A ranking of nations by the

FIGURE 15.1 | Public and Private Expenditure on Health

(*Source:* Organisation for Economic Co-operation and Development, 2007)

- Public health expenditure
- Private health expenditure

U.S. Dollars per Capita.

Commonwealth Fund in terms of quality of health care in developed countries placed the United States 15th out of 19, that is, near the very bottom (Center for the Advancement of Health, February 2007). Our political and economic system has produced great disparities in the conditions under which people live, and many people live in intrinsically unhealthy environments (Taylor, Repetti, & Seeman, 1997).

Thus, efforts to postpone morbidity and disability into the last years of life will be unsuccessful without attention to our country's and the world's large socio-economic disparities in health and health care (Minkler, Fuller-Thomson, & Guralnik, 2006). The United States is only just beginning to move toward universal health care coverage, the last of the industrialized nations to do so (Oberlander, 2010; Quadagno, 2004). Forty-seven million people are without health insurance, and hundreds of millions more have difficulty paying their health care bills (Cohen & Bloom, 2010; U.S. Department of Commerce, 2009). The United States is also the only country where health care for most people is financed by for-profit, minimally regulated private insurance companies (Quadagno, 2004).

From birth throughout life, those born into the lower social classes experience more and more intense stressors of all kinds, which take a cumulative toll in terms of health (Steinbrook, 2004a). Lower income and educational and occupational attainment lead to exposure to a broad array of stressors including inadequate housing, violence, danger, lack of vital goods and services, inadequate medical facilities, poor sanitation, and exposure to environmental pollutants and numerous other hazards (Center for the Advancement of Health, April 2003; Grzywacz, Almeida, Neupert, & Ettner, 2004; Yali & Revenson, 2004). In contrast, people with higher income and educational attainment have many psychosocial resources and a lower risk of illnesses and disabilities across the life span. Despite advances in health care, these disparities have barely declined (Warren & Hernandez, 2007).

The effect of low socioeconomic status on health is true for both men and women (McDonough, Williams, House, & Duncan, 1999), at all age levels and across most countries of the world (Mackenbach et al., 2008). Among the many risk factors tied to low SES are alcohol consumption, high levels of lipids, obesity, tobacco use, and fewer psychosocial resources such as a sense of mastery, self-esteem, and social support. Each of these has an effect on health (House, 2001; Kubzansky et al., 1998). Low SES is linked to a higher incidence of chronic illness, a heightened risk of low-birth-weight babies and infant mortality, and a heightened risk of accidents among numerous other causes of death and disability (Center for the Advancement of Health, December 2002). In fact, the overwhelming majority of diseases and disorders show an SES gradient, with poor people experiencing greater risk (Minkler et al., 2006). Even in the case of diseases that lower- and upper-class individuals are equally likely to develop, such as breast cancer, mortality is earlier among the more disadvantaged (Leclere, Rogers, & Peters, 1998).

Interventions targeted specifically to low-SES individuals to modify risk factors associated with social class, such as smoking, drug use, alcohol consumption, and diet, as well as those targeted to more general risk factors such as poor education (Trumbetta, Seltzer, Gottesman, & McIntyre, 2010) need to assume very high priority (Droomers, Schrijvers, & Mackenbach, 2002).

Increasingly, health psychologists are documenting racial differences in health, and the picture is bleak. African Americans have poorer health at all ages (Klonoff, 2009), as well as higher levels of depression, hostility, anxiety, and other emotional risk factors for chronic disease (Eaton, Muntaner, Bovasso, & Smith, 2001). The life expectancy gap between African Americans and Whites remains high, at a more than 5-year difference (National Center for Health Statistics, 2009). African Americans also have a higher infant mortality rate than Whites and higher rates of most chronic diseases and disorders, with racial differences especially dramatic for hypertension, HIV, diabetes, and trauma

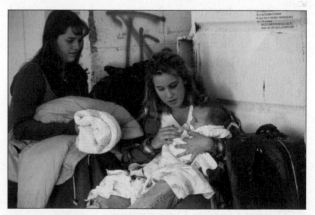

Stressful living situations with noise, crowding, and crime take a particular toll on vulnerable populations, such as children, the elderly, and the poor. Increasingly, research must focus on interventions to alleviate the impact of these conditions.

(Wong, Shapiro, Boscardin, & Ettner, 2002). Some of the racial differences in health stem from the fact that African Americans are, on average, lower in SES, so they are disproportionately subject to the stressors that accompany low SES. But some of the differences, as noted in Chapter 6, are due to the stresses of racism.

Disparities in health are not attributable solely to the social conditions in which people live. There are enormous SES and ethnic differences in the delivery of medical treatment as well (Garcia, Bernstein, & Bush, 2010; Institute of Medicine, 2009). More than 18% of the population has no health insurance, and this gap disproportionately affects the poor (National Center for Health Statistics, 2009). Although Medicaid, instituted in 1965, was designed to help the poor achieve high-quality health care, in many states, it has eroded to the point that families with poverty-level incomes are not eligible for benefits. Moreover, the costs of health care continue to increase. Between 2000 and 2006, health care expenditures per person increased by 45% (National Center for Health Statistics, 2009). We currently have essentially a two-tiered medical system: High-quality and high-technology care go to the well-to-do and not to the poor. Unless the health care available to the poorer segments of society begins to match that available to the wealthier segments, morbidity may not be significantly reduced by intervention efforts (House et al., 1990).

Gender and Health

Another significant gap in health care and research concerns gender (Matthews, Gump, Block, & Allen, 1997). As one critical article put it, "Women are studied for what distinguishes them from men—their breasts and genitals" (Meyerowitz & Hart, 1993). Thus, for example, breast, ovarian, and other cancers of the sex or reproductive organs have received substantial attention, but many disorders have not.

Weak justification for such discrimination has sometimes been based on the fact that women live, on average, 6.5 years longer than men. But women are sick more than men, and their advantage in mortality has been decreasing in recent years, a trend that appears to be due in part to women's use of cigarettes. Women are also less likely than men to have health insurance, and even if they do, their policies may fail to cover basic medical care, such as Pap smears for the detection of cervical cancer, a standard part of any gynecologic examination. More women are insured through their husbands' jobs than through their own jobs, but because of instability in marriage, coverage for women is irregular. These issues are especially problematic for African American women (Meyer & Pavalko, 1996).

Women are not included as research subjects in studies of many major diseases. It is essential to include women in medical studies for many reasons (Matthews, Shumaker, et al., 1997). First, women may have different risk factors for major diseases, or existing risk factors may be more or less virulent (Grady, 2004, April 14). For example, smoking may be two to three times more hazardous for women than for men (Taubes, 1993). Men and women differ in both their biochemistry and their physiological reactions to stress (Baum & Grunberg, 1991). Consequently, their symptoms, their age of onset for the same diseases, and their reactions to treatment and needed dosage levels of medications may all differ. For example, women's risk for coronary heart disease increases greatly following menopause.

Until recently, however, research unearthing these important relationships was not even conducted. Without a systematic investigation of women's health and their particular risk factors, as well as changes in both over the life span, women will simply be treated more poorly than men for the same diseases.

■ STRESS AND ITS MANAGEMENT

Substantial advances in stress research have been made in recent decades. Physiological, cognitive, motivational, and behavioral consequences of stress have been identified. Moreover, the biopsychosocial routes by which stress adversely affects bodily functions and increases the likelihood of illness are increasingly well understood.

Recent attention to stress and inflammatory processes represents a significant breakthrough of the past few years. Advances have been made in research on environmental and occupational stress. Stressors such as noise or crowding do not show consistently adverse effects but do appear to adversely affect vulnerable populations. Thus, the health needs of children, the elderly, and the poor have taken special priority in the study of stress and its reduction.

Occupational stress researchers have identified many of the job characteristics that are tied to stress, such as low control, high demands, and little opportunity for social support. As a consequence, promising workplace interventions have been developed to redesign jobs or reduce on-the-job stressors.

Nonetheless, the demographics of stress may be off-setting whatever concessions can or might be made in the workplace. The majority of American families find that both parents must work in order to make ends meet, yet, like all families, the two-career family must absorb an extra month a year of housework, home activities, and child care. Typically, this extra month a year is taken on by women (Hochschild, 1989). Moreover, increasing numbers of adult children have responsibility for their aging parents, and these responsibilities, too, more frequently fall to women than to men. These trends put the adult American female population under unprecedented stress, patterns that are increasing in other countries as well. Solutions to these dilemmas have yet to emerge.

Where Is Stress Research Headed?

Research should focus on those populations at particular risk for stress-related disorders in an attempt to reduce or offset their stressful circumstances. In theory, knowledge of how people adjust to stressful events can be translated into interventions to help those coping unsuccessfully to cope more successfully.

Many important advances in stress research will come from research on the neurophysiology of stress, particularly the links between stress and corticosteroid functioning, dispositional differences in sympathetic nervous system activity, factors influencing the release of endogenous opioid peptides, and links to the immune system, including inflammatory processes. Through these studies, we may increasingly understand the pathways by which stress exerts adverse effects on health.

One of the most significant advances in stress research is the discovery that social support can buffer stress. Fostering social support systems to offset social trends that isolate people, such as divorce and geographic mobility, should be a high priority for prevention. In addition, we should teach people how to provide support for others. We know that difficult and stressful relationships can adversely affect physical health and mental health and that positive social relations can protect against those outcomes. Moreover, providing social support, as well as receiving it, has health benefits.

Self-help groups, both real and virtual via the Internet, are possible ways of providing social support for those who otherwise might lack it. Through these formats, people can discuss a common problem and try to help each other work it out. Once oriented primarily around particular illnesses, such as cancer, or

particular health problems, such as obesity, these groups are becoming increasingly available for those going through divorce, the loss of a child, and other specific stressful events.

■ HEALTH SERVICES

Health care reform is one of the most urgent issues facing the United States (Obama, 2009). Our health care system is marked by at least three basic problems: Health care costs too much; the system is grossly inequitable, favoring the wealthy over the poor; and health care consumers use health care services inappropriately (Center for the Advancement of Health, October 2006).

Building Better Consumers

Decades of research have indicated that people who are ill and those who are treated for illness are frequently not the same individuals. For financial or cultural reasons, many ill people do not find their way into the health care delivery system, and about half to two-thirds of people who seek and receive treatment have complaints that are related to psychological distress. Creating responsible and informed health care consumers is thus a high priority.

Increasingly, patients need to be comanagers in their own care, monitoring their symptoms and treatments in partnership with physicians and other health care practitioners. It does little good to diagnose a disorder correctly and prescribe appropriate treatment if the patient cannot or will not follow through on treatment recommendations. Moreover, as good health behaviors are critical to the achievement of good health and to secondary prevention with the chronically ill, the fact that 97% of patients fail to adhere to lifestyle recommendations takes on added significance.

Trends within medical care suggest that the problem of patient-provider communication is likely to get worse, not better. Increasingly, patients are receiving their medical care through prepaid, colleague-centered services rather than through private, fee-for-service, client-centered practices. As noted in Chapters 8 and 9, these structural changes can improve the quality of medical care, but they may sacrifice the quality of communication.

The probability that communication suffers in these settings is heightened by the fact that the clientele served by prepaid plans is disproportionately poor, poorly educated, and non-English-speaking. Although the well-to-do can pay for emotionally satisfying care, the poor increasingly cannot. Health settings that rob patients of feelings of control can breed anger or depression, motivate people not to return for care, and possibly even contribute to a physiological state conducive to illness or its exacerbation. Thus, there is an expanding role for health psychologists in the development and design of health services.

Containing Costs of Health Care

The appropriate use of health services assumes increasing urgency in the context of current changes in its structure, technology, and costs. Medicine is high technology, and high technology is expensive (Callahan, 2003). Although policy makers often assume that patients are driving the development of this technology, in fact, this may not be the case. Most surveys suggest that patients want less, not more, expensive, high-tech treatment, especially in the terminal phase of illness (Schneiderman, Kronick, Kaplan, Anderson, & Langer, 1992). The increasing use of technology may have more to do with physicians' desire to provide state-of-the-art care.

Deficit financing of federal health care programs has added billions of dollars to the national debt, and the inability of the government to cover the uninsured, let alone fund Medicare and Medicaid, have contributed to the rapid rise in costs. These factors have prompted the scrutiny of health care by the government in recent years, and the widespread movement in the direction of managed care and a national health care policy represents efforts to address these issues.

■ MANAGEMENT OF SERIOUS ILLNESS

Because chronic illness has become our major health problem, its physical, vocational, social, and psychological consequences have been increasingly recognized. Although a number of specific programs have been initiated to deal with problems posed by chronic illness, these efforts are as yet not systematically coordinated or widely available to the majority of chronically ill patients.

Quality-of-Life Assessment

A chief goal for health psychologists in the coming years, then, should be to develop cost-effective interventions to improve quality of life. Initial assessment during the acute period is an important first step. Supplementing initial assessment with regular needs assessment over the

long term can help identify potential problems, such as anxiety or depression, before they fully disrupt the patient's life and bring additional costs to the health care system. Because psychosocial states such as depression and hostility affect both the development and the exacerbation of several chronic disorders, psychological interventions need to be directed to these important cofactors in illness. No intervention that fails to improve psychological functioning is likely to profoundly affect health or survival (Singer, 2000).

Pain Management

Among the advancements in the treatment of chronic disease is progress in pain management. Recent years have witnessed a shift away from dependence on expensive pharmacologic and invasive surgical pain control techniques to ones that favor cognitive-behavioral methods, such as relaxation. This change has brought about a shift in responsibility for pain control from practitioner to comanagement between patient and practitioner. The enhanced sense of control provided to the chronic pain patient is a treatment advance in its own right, as research on self-efficacy also underscores. The development of pain management programs has been valuable for consolidating what is known about pain control technology.

Health psychologists may need to become involved in the ongoing controversies that surround alternative medicine. Increasingly, both the worried well and those with chronic illnesses are treating themselves in nontraditional ways, through herbal medicine, homeopathy, and other untested regimens. What these sources of care do for those who make use of them may be heavily psychological. Health psychologists may need not only to evaluate these alternative medical practices but also to help develop interventions that will address the psychological needs currently met by these treatments.

Terminal Care

The past 20 years have witnessed substantial changes in attitudes toward terminal illness. Health psychology research has been both a cause and an effect of these changing attitudes, as clinical health psychologists have turned their attention to the needs of the terminally ill and the gaps in psychological care that still exist.

The appearance of AIDS has added weight to these issues. After more than a decade of watching thousands of America's talented gay men die in their youth, medical research has now uncovered the promise of longer-term survival in the form of protease inhibitors. However, the face of AIDS is changing, and it has spread heavily into the poor urban populations of the country, involving many Black and Hispanic men and women. Women are at special risk, and as a result, a growing population of infants is infected with HIV as well. Moreover, these people are less likely to have expensive protease inhibitors available, so their prospects for long-term survival may be low. AIDS is becoming a disease of families, and adequate attention needs to be paid to helping mothers, especially single mothers with HIV, manage their families while coping with their own deteriorating health and to helping the HIV-infected children who will survive their mothers.

With the prevalence of chronic disease increasing and the aging of the population occurring rapidly, ethical issues surrounding death and dying—including assisted suicide, living wills, the patient's right to die, family decision making on death and dying, and euthanasia—will increasingly assume importance. If a beginning resolution to these complex issues cannot be found by medical agencies and allied fields, including health psychology, then the solutions will undoubtedly be imposed externally by the courts.

The Aging of the Population

The substantial aging of the population poses a challenge for health psychologists (Yali & Revenson, 2004). What kinds of living situations will these increasing numbers of elderly people have, and what kinds of economic resources will they have available to them? How will these resources influence their health habits, their level of health, and their ability to seek treatment? How can we evaluate and monitor care in residential treatment settings, such as nursing homes, to guard against the risks of maltreatment?

As our population ages, we can expect to see a higher incidence of chronic but not life-threatening conditions, such as arthritis, osteoporosis, hearing losses, incontinence, and blindness. Some effort to control these disorders must necessarily focus on prevention. For example, the incidence of deafness is rising, attributable in part to the blasting rock music that teenagers in the 1950s and 1960s (who are now in their 50s, 60s, and 70s) listened to. Because rock music is not getting any quieter, and because adolescents now go to rock concerts and use headphones as well, prevention of deafness will take on increasing significance. This is just one example of the kinds of problems that are created for health psychologists as a result of the shift in age of the population as well as the shift in leisure-time activities (Figure 15.2).

FIGURE 15.2 | Population by Age Group

(*Source:* Population Division of the Department of Economic and Social Affairs of the United Nations Secretariat, 2002)

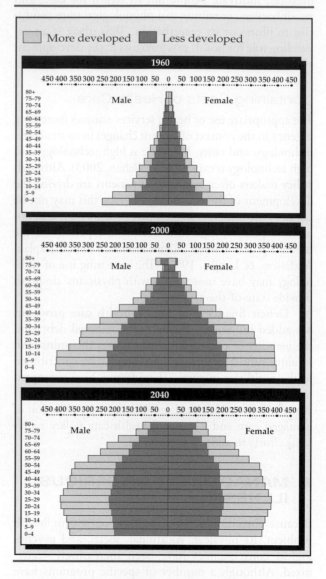

TRENDS IN HEALTH AND HEALTH PSYCHOLOGY

The Changing Nature of Medical Practice

Health psychology needs to be continually responsive to changes in health trends and medical practice (Nicassio, Meyerowitz, & Kerns, 2004). For example, as the population has aged, the significance of diseases of aging has increased, such as the morbidity and mortality due to prostate cancer.

The physical environment poses unprecedented challenges. For example, current levels of air pollution have chronic negative effects on lung development in children, leading to risks not only in childhood but in adulthood as well (Gauderman et al., 2004). Climate change affects patterns of illness. For example, tropical diseases such as malaria and diarrheal disorders are increasing in frequency and spreading north (Jack, 2007, April 25). The face of health psychology may change as patterns of infectious disease change. Although the past century has brought substantial control over infectious diseases, they remain a public health problem globally and are still responsible for 13 million U.S. deaths each year. Moreover, changes in society, technology, and microorganisms themselves are leading to the emergence of new diseases, the reemergence of diseases that were once controlled, and problems with drug-resistant strains of once-controlled disorders (Emerson & Purcell, 2004; Hien, de Jong, & Farrar, 2004; Musher & Musher, 2004).

How can health psychologists help? Getting people to use antibiotics correctly and not to overuse them may help deter the rise of drug-resistant strains (Cohen, 2000). Another example concerns the increasing availability of risk factor testing for identifying genes implicated in such diseases as Huntington's disease, breast cancer, and colon cancer. What will people's reactions to their genetic risks be (Cameron, Sherman, Marteau, & Brown, 2009)? How, then, should we disseminate the information to the public? How do we link that information to preventive behaviors that practitioners can teach to their patients (Hay et al., 2007)? And how do we ensure against discrimination on the bases of genetic information (Korobkin & Rajkumar, 2008)?

A handful of prescient health psychologists (see, for example, Croyle & Lerman, 1993) have begun to explore why some people fail to minimize their risk on learning that they may be vulnerable, as opposed to becoming more vigilant by taking effective preventive action or monitoring themselves more closely. But much of this work continues to be conducted in the laboratory on hypothetical risk factors, and more understanding of how people manage their actual risks is essential.

The Impact of Technology Technological advances in medicine have contributed greatly to the enormous costs of contemporary medicine (Fuchs, 2008). These complex aspects of medicine itself can also be daunting for many patients. Explaining the purposes of these technologies and using control-enhancing

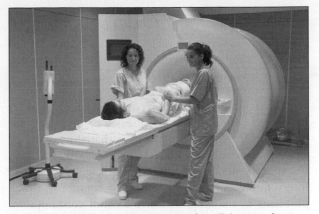

The technologically complex aspects of medicine are often intimidating to patients, but when the purpose of the technology is fully explained and patients are committed to its use, it helps reduce this anxiety.

interventions to enable people to feel like active participants in their treatment can help reduce fear.

The growth of medical technology also raises complex questions about how it should be used. For example, many types of transplants are now available, and yet they are disproportionally available to those who can pay. At the same time, there is a shortage of organ donations. Health psychologists have a potential role to play in designing communications to encourage people to donate organs (Siegel et al., 2008).

As medical care has grown more technologically complex, it has also, paradoxically, begun to incorporate psychological and spiritual approaches to healing, especially those that draw on Eastern healing traditions. Relaxation and other nontraditional treatment methods are a boon to HMOs because those methods are typically low cost and yet can be remarkably effective for treating stress-related disorders, including such severely problematic conditions as hypertension. Continued evaluation of the health benefits of such interventions as yoga and mindfulness meditation is important.

Comprehensive Intervention A trend within medicine that affects health psychology is the movement toward **comprehensive intervention models**. An example is pain management programs, in which all available treatments for pain have been brought together so that individual regimens can be developed for each patient. A second model is the hospice, in which palliative management technologies and psychotherapeutic technologies are available to the dying patient. Coordinated residential and outpatient rehabilitation programs for coronary heart disease patients, in which multiple health habits are dealt with simultaneously, constitute a third example. Similar interventions for other chronic diseases, such as cancer and AIDS, may be developed in the coming years.

Most comprehensive intervention models thus far have been geared to specific diseases or disorders, but increasingly, researchers are urging that this model be employed for concerted attacks on risk factors as well. The mass media, youth prevention projects, educational interventions, and social engineering solutions to such problems as smoking, excessive alcohol consumption, and drug abuse, for example, can supplement programs that currently focus primarily on health risks that are already in place. The coordination of public health management at the institutional and community levels, with individual health and illness management for those already ill, is represented in Figure 15.3.

Although comprehensive interventions for particular health problems may provide the best quality of care, they can also be expensive. Some hospitals have already dismantled their pain management centers, for example, for lack of funds. For comprehensive intervention models to continue to define the highest quality of care, attention must be paid to **cost effectiveness** as well as to **treatment effectiveness.**

Systematic Documentation of Cost Effectiveness and Treatment Effectiveness

An important professional goal of health psychology is the continued documentation of the treatment effectiveness of our interventions (Shadish, 2010). We know that our behavioral, cognitive, and psychotherapeutic technologies work, but we must communicate this success to others. This issue has taken on considerable significance as debate rages over whether and to what degree behavioral and psychological interventions should be covered in managed health care systems.

Cost containment pressures have prompted the development of interventions that are time limited, symptom focused, and offered on an outpatient basis

FIGURE 15.3 | Continuum of Care and Types and Levels of Intervention   (*Source:* Abrams et al., 1996)

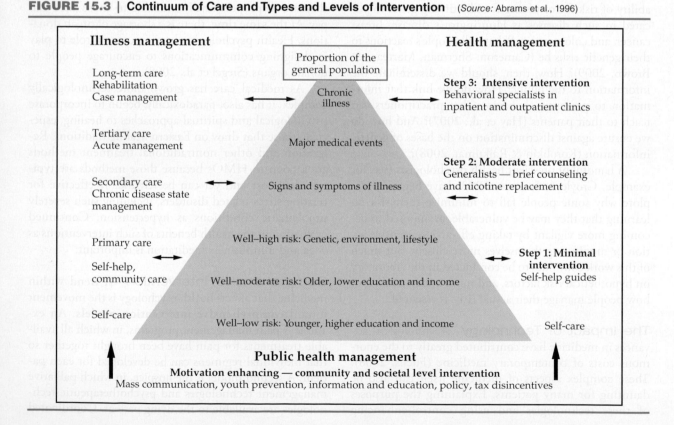

(Sanchez & Turner, 2003), a format that is not always conducive to change through behavioral intervention. Moreover, this trend has been accompanied by a shift in treatment decision-making power from behavioral health care providers to policy makers.

Subtly, the pressures of cost containment push health psychology in the direction of research that is designed to keep people out of the health care system altogether. On the clinical practice side, interventions include self-help groups, peer counseling, self-management programs, and other inexpensive ways to provide services to those who might otherwise not receive care. Writing about intensely traumatic or stressful events is also a low-cost, easily implemented intervention that has demonstrated beneficial effects (Ullrich & Lutgendorf, 2002). Another example is the stress reduction and pain amelioration benefits that can be achieved by simple, inexpensive techniques of relaxation and other cognitive-behavioral interventions (Blanchard et al., 1988). Table 15.2 shows the reduction in health care visits that can occur as a result of health psychology interventions.

A lack of empirical data regarding treatment outcomes and efficacy represents a striking gap in how behavioral scientists and practitioners present their interventions to policy makers (Keefe & Blumenthal, 2004). This gap occurs, in part, because behavioral scientists may fail to recognize or document the treatment implications of their work and because practitioners may lack the interest or expertise to conduct the formal scientific investigations that would make the scientific case for their interventions. Developing convincing

TABLE 15.2 | The Bottom Line

This chart shows the reduction in frequency of treatments as a result of various clinical behavioral medicine interventions.

Treatment	Frequency reduction
Total ambulatory care visits	−17%
Visits for minor illnesses	−35%
Pediatric acute illness visits	−25%
Office visits for acute asthma	−49%
Office visits by arthritis patients	−40%
Cesarean sections	−56%
Epidural anesthesia during labor and delivery	−85%
Average hospital length of stay for surgical patients (in days)	−1.5%

Source: American Psychological Society, 1996.

methods of measuring the success of psychosocial interventions is of paramount importance. Increasingly, too, health psychologists will need to identify the most critical components of their interventions that produce the greatest behavior change at the lowest cost (Napolitano et al., 2008).

The potential for health psychology to make contributions to medicine and medical practice has never been greater. **Evidence-based medicine** is now the criterion for adopting medical standards. Evidence-based medicine refers to the conscientious, explicit, judicious use of the best scientific evidence for making decisions about the care of individual patients (Davidson et al., 2003). This trend means that, with documentation of the success of health psychology interventions, the potential for empirical evidence to contribute to practice is enhanced.

Economic factors play a formidable role in the field of health psychology—one that has benefits and risks. On the one hand, the field cannot afford to pursue its scientific and clinical mission without regard to cost. On the other hand, cost containment issues can compromise scientific and intervention missions of the field by prematurely choking off areas of inquiry that do not immediately appear to be cost-effective. The relative lack of attention to issues of rehabilitation, in contrast to the heavy preponderance of research in primary prevention activities, can be regarded as one casualty of these pressures (see Figure 15.4).

The integration of health psychology into the medical curriculum, the development of departments of behavioral medicine within traditional medical schools, and the integration of behavioral medicine into health care institutions, such as hospitals and clinics—all are important ways of ensuring that advances in health psychology can have an impact on patient care and health care policy. In addition, tying health psychology research more closely to clinical interventions and to health policy increases the likelihood that health psychology's discoveries will have an impact (Nicassio, Meyerowitz, & Kerns, 2004). Making such discoveries known to the public will likewise increase their visibility (Nicassio et al., 2004).

International Health

The world's population has increased from 2.5 billion in 1950 to nearly 7 billion at the present time. Increasingly, the population has shifted away from Europe, North America, and Latin America toward Africa and Asia. Life expectancy has increased almost everywhere in

FIGURE 15.4 | National Health Care Expenditures: Selected Calendar Years, 1990-2013* *(Source:* Centers for
Medicare and Medicaid Services, 2004)

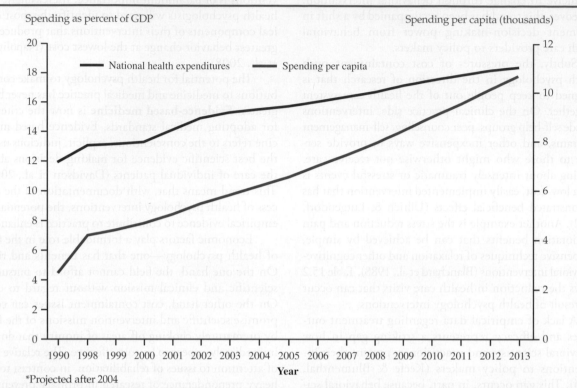

*Projected after 2004

the world, with particular improvements in developing countries. Significant challenges are created by these patterns, and increasingly, there is an important role for health psychologists in international health.

Disease prevalence varies greatly by country. Poverty, lack of education, and lack of health care resources contribute to a high incidence of acute infectious disease, for example. As smoking has declined in the United States, its incidence is rising in many developing countries. Whereas Americans are beginning to exercise more, countries that are becoming modernized are losing the exercise benefits that accompanied an active lifestyle. Many developing nations, such as China and India, are beginning to experience the burden of increases in chronic disease (Zhu, 2010; Reddy, Shah, Varghese, & Ramadoss, 2005; Yamada, 2008).

Health psychology can carry the hard-won lessons of the past few decades in the United States to countries in which exactly the same problems are now beginning to emerge (Anderson & Chu, 2007). Moreover, health psychologists and other behavioral scientists are more likely than people in traditional medical disciplines to

understand the significance of varying cultural norms and expectations, the way social institutions function, and the roles that culturally-specific attitudes and behaviors may play in health care practices and decisions. In the battle for a high level of international health care, then, the health psychologist appears to be well positioned to make a substantial and lasting contribution.

■ BECOMING A HEALTH PSYCHOLOGIST

If, after reading this textbook and taking a course in health psychology, you want to pursue a career in this field, what would you need to do?

Undergraduate Experience

As an undergraduate interested in continuing in health psychology, you would be wise to do several things. First, take all the health psychology courses that you can. Second, develop knowledge about the biological bases of behavior by taking courses in physiological psychology and neuroscience. Understanding the biological underpinnings of health psychology is important.

In addition, you should use your summers effectively. Find a psychologist who does research in health psychology, and see if you can get a research assistantship. Volunteer if you have to. You can look for summer employment opportunities in a medical school or hospital, which might give you patient contact or contact with medical care providers. Or you might try to find a managed care program that has internship opportunities. Even if you are involved only in paperwork, find out how the organization works. What kinds of patients does it see? In what areas are its costs higher than it would like, and how is the organization trying to reduce costs? Ask a lot of questions.

Graduate Experience

If you decide you want to go on in health psychology as a profession, you will need to acquire a Ph.D. At this point, you should decide whether your interests lie chiefly in research, in clinical practice (that is, direct contact with individual patients), or both.

If your interest is in research, what kind of research excites you the most? Is it the study of the biology of infection or transmission? Is it understanding how social support affects health? Is it research on increasing exercise or changing diet? The programs to which you apply may require you to choose a subfield within psychology. Your choices are likely to be physiological psychology, which focuses heavily on the biology and neurological aspects of health psychology; social psychology, which examines social and psychological processes in adopting preventive health behaviors, managing stress, and coping with chronic disease, among other issues; clinical psychology, in which interventions with patients will be one of your primary tasks; or developmental psychology, in which you will look especially at the health of children and the factors that affect it. A few health psychology programs around the country do not require you to declare a subspecialty when you apply, but many do.

During your 4 years in graduate school, if your interests are even partly in research, take courses in research methodology and statistics. You may take a course in epidemiology, as many health psychologists do, a course that would probably be taught in a school of public health. Most importantly, get practical experience. Work with a health psychologist on several research or clinical projects. Try to get into the field so that you gain experience not just in a university laboratory

but also in a hospital, a clinic, or another health care delivery situation.

In addition, look for opportunities to get practical, hands-on field experience. If you're interested in exercise, for example, go to a fitness center. If you want to understand how people cope with AIDS, volunteer at a local organization that assists people with AIDS. If you're interested in aging, go to senior citizen centers or other facilities for the elderly.

If you are interested in patient contact and apply to a clinical psychology program, you will be expected to take the standard clinical curriculum, which includes courses and practical experience addressing major mental disorders and community intervention and therapy. Your patient contact not only will involve people with medical problems but also will be heavily geared toward people with depression, anxiety, and other psychological disorders. Further, you will be expected to complete a year's internship in a field setting, so if your interests are in health, you should try for a field setting in a hospital, clinic, or health maintenance organization that gives you direct patient contact.

At the time of your dissertation, you will be expected to mount a major research project on your own. By this time, you will have a clear idea of what your interests are and can pursue a health-related project in-depth. This project will take you a year or more to complete.

On completion of your dissertation and receipt of your Ph.D., you have several options. If your plan is to go into clinical psychology, you may want to find a clinical setting in which you can get practical expertise in addition to that acquired during your internship. This training, coupled with your internship and coursework, should put you in a good position to get licensed in the state in which you choose to practice. You will have to take several hours of licensure exams, the exact form of which varies from state to state; on receipt of your license, you will be able to practice clinical psychology.

Postgraduate Work

Following graduate school, you can go on the job market, or you can get additional training in the form of postdoctoral research. Many health psychologists choose to acquire postdoctoral training because, at present, health psychology training is not uniform across universities. You may, for example, receive excellent instruction in stress and coping processes but be poorly informed about health habits. Or your program may provide you with lots of patient contact but very little in the way of training in neuroscience. You may decide that you want to concentrate on a particular disease, such as cancer or heart disease, but have insufficient knowledge about the risk factors and physiology of the illness for your research to be well informed. Identifying the gaps in your training reveals the type of postdoctoral training you should seek out.

Typically, postdoctoral training is undertaken at a laboratory different from the place at which you completed your Ph.D. and takes place under the guidance of a senior scientist whose work you admire. You may spend up to 3 years in this person's lab, after which you should be ready to go on the job market.

Employment

Table 15.3 shows where health psychologists typically work. About 45% of health psychologists go into academic settings or teach in medical schools (American Psychological Association, 1996; Williams & Kohout, 1999). In academic positions, health psychologists are responsible for educating undergraduate and graduate students, physicians, nurses, and other health care workers. Most health psychologists in academic settings also conduct research to uncover the factors associated with the maintenance of health and the onset of illness.

About 35% of health psychologists work with medical patients in a hospital or another treatment setting. About 28% are involved in private practice, in which they provide therapy and other mental health services to people with medically related problems. The short-term cognitive-behavioral interventions that work well in modifying health habits, controlling pain, managing side effects of treatments, and the like represent the kind of activities that health psychologists in these settings undertake. For example, a clinician might initiate individual psychotherapy to help a cancer patient recover from bouts of depression. Another clinician might work with family members to set up a self-care treatment regimen for an adolescent recently diagnosed with diabetes.

Increasingly, health psychologists are employed in the workplace or as consultants to the workplace. They advise employers attempting to set up new health care systems about what kind of system will provide the best

TABLE 15.3 | Where Do Health Psychologists Work?

Colleges and universities	24.9%
Medical schools	15.9
Other academic settings	3.0
Schools and other educational settings	1.0
Independent practice	27.4
Hospitals and clinics	17.4
Other	11.0

Source: American Psychological Society, 1996.

care for the least money. For example, they establish work-site interventions to teach employees how to manage stress, they set up exercise programs, or they establish work-site competitions to help overweight employees lose weight. Health psychologists consult with governmental agencies on how to reduce health care costs. They advise health care services about how to improve patient satisfaction or reduce inappropriate use of health services. In short, health psychologists deliver a wide range of services to an ever-growing and diverse group of employers, as Table 15.3 indicates.

The number of health psychologists in the United States and other countries is growing rapidly. Since the beginning of the field approximately 30 years ago, the number of health psychology training programs in the country has also grown exponentially. Health psychologists have proven vital to medical research and health services delivery in this country. The opportunities for the fledgling health psychologist are boundless, as Table 15.4 suggests. ●

TABLE 15.4 | What Do Health Psychologists Do?

Research	57.1%
Education	58.6
Health/mental health services	71.5
Educational services	20.9
Management/administration	20.4
Other	36.6

Source: American Psychological Association, 1996.

SUMMARY

1. Health psychology research and practice have identified the complexity of poor health habits and the ways to best modify them. Health promotion priorities for the future include modification of the most consequential risk factors, incorporation of the most potent and effective elements of behavior-change programs into cost-effective interventions, and the continuing search for the best venues for intervention.

2. Health psychology interventions will continue to focus on people at risk for particular disorders, on preventing poor health habits from developing, and on developing effective health promotion interventions with the elderly. Health promotion efforts must address not only mortality but also the reduction of morbidity and the importance of enhancing overall quality of life.

3. As medicine develops a health promotion orientation, the potential for collaborative interventions between health psychologists and medical practitioners through the media, the community, and the physician's office may come to be more fully realized.

4. An effective health promotion program must involve not only health behavior change but also social change that makes high-quality health care available to all elements of the population, especially those low in SES.

5. Research on stress will continue to focus on vulnerable populations and on trends in the economy and culture that increase the stress on particular subpopulations, such as children, women, the elderly, and the poor.

6. In the future, many important advances in stress research will come from research examining the biopsychosocial pathways by which stress adversely affects health.

7. The appropriate use of health services is an important target for the future, to reduce the improper use of services, initiation of malpractice litigation, and failure to adhere appropriately to medication and lifestyle recommendations.

8. The management of chronic and terminal illness will increasingly focus on quality of life and appropriate ways to measure it. Ethical issues involving assisted suicide, living wills, the patient's right to die, family decision making in death and dying, and euthanasia will continue to be prominent.

9. A target for future work is identification of the health and lifestyle issues that will be created by the aging of the population. Anticipating medical disorders and developing interventions to offset their potential adverse effects should be targets for research now.

10. Health psychology needs to be responsive to changes in medical practice, including changes in disease demographics (such as age). The changing face of medicine creates challenges for health psychologists, who must anticipate the impact of technologically complex interventions and help prepare patients for them.

11. Important goals for health psychology include systematic documentation of treatment effectiveness using the criteria of evidence-based medicine, systematic documentation of the cost effectiveness of interventions, and continued efforts to find ways to reduce health costs. In addition, there is an emerging and important role for health psychologists in the international health care arena.

12. Health psychology can be a rewarding career for anyone willing to gain the necessary education and research and field experience.

KEY TERMS

behavioral immunization
comprehensive intervention models

cost containment
cost effectiveness

evidence-based medicine
treatment effectiveness

GLOSSARY

abstinence violation effect   A feeling of loss of control that results when one has violated self-imposed rules, such as not to smoke or drink.

acquired immune deficiency syndrome (AIDS)   Progressive impairment of the immune system by the human immunodeficiency virus (HIV); a diagnosis of AIDS is made on the basis of the presence of one or more specific opportunistic infections.

acupuncture   A technique of healing and pain control, developed in China, in which long, thin needles are inserted into designated areas of the body to reduce discomfort in a target area.

acute disorders   Illnesses or other medical problems that occur over a short time, that are usually the result of an infectious process, and that are reversible.

acute pain   Short-term pain that usually results from a specific injury.

acute stress paradigm   A laboratory procedure whereby an individual goes through moderately stressful procedures (such as counting backwards rapidly by 7s), so that stress-related changes in emotions and physiological and/or neuroendocrine processes may be assessed.

addiction   The state of physical or psychological dependence on a substance that develops when that substance is used over a period of time.

adherence   The degree to which an individual follows a recommended health-related or illness-related recommendation.

adrenal glands   Two small glands, located on top of the kidneys, that are part of the endocrine system and secrete several hormones, including cortisol, epinephrine, and norepinephrine, that are involved in responses to stress.

aerobic exercise   High-intensity, long-duration, and high-endurance exercise, believed to contribute to cardiovascular fitness and other positive health outcomes. Examples are jogging, bicycling, running, and swimming.

aftereffects of stress   Performance and attentional decrements that occur after a stressful event has subsided; believed to be produced by the residual physiological, emotional, and cognitive draining in response to stressful events.

alcoholism   The state of physical addiction to alcohol that manifests through such symptoms as stereotyped drinking, drinking to maintain blood alcohol at a particular level, increasing frequency and severity of withdrawal, drinking early in the day and in the middle of the night, a sense of loss of control over drinking, and a subjective craving for alcohol.

allostatic load   The accumulating adverse effects of stress, in conjunction with preexisting risks, on biological stress regulatory systems.

angina pectoris   Chest pain that occurs because the muscle tissue of the heart is deprived of adequate oxygen or because removal of carbon dioxide and other wastes interferes with the flow of blood and oxygen to the heart.

anorexia nervosa   A condition produced by excessive dieting and exercise that yields body weight grossly below optimal level, most common among adolescent girls.

appraisal delay   The time between recognizing that a symptom exists and deciding that it is serious.

approach (confrontative, vigilant) coping style   The tendency to cope with stressful events by tackling them directly and attempting to develop solutions; may ultimately be an especially effective method of coping, although it may produce accompanying distress.

assertiveness training   Techniques that train people how to be appropriately assertive in social situations; often included as part of health behavior modification programs, on the assumption that some poor health habits, such as excessive alcohol consumption or smoking, develop in part to control difficulties in being appropriately assertive.

atherosclerosis   A major cause of heart disease; caused by the narrowing of the arterial walls due to the formation of plaques that reduce the flow of blood through the arteries and interfere with the passage of nutrients from the capillaries into the cells.

at risk   A state of vulnerability to a particular health problem by virtue of heredity, health practices, or family environment.

autoimmunity   A condition in which the body produces an immune response against its own tissue constituents.

avoidant (minimizing) coping style   The tendency to cope with threatening events by withdrawing, minimizing, or avoiding them; believed to be an effective short-term, though not an effective long-term, response to stress.

behavioral assignments   Home practice activities that clients perform on their own as part of an integrated therapeutic intervention for behavior modification.

behavioral delay   The time between deciding to seek treatment and actually doing so.

behavioral immunization   Programs designed to inoculate people against adverse health habits by exposing them to mild versions of persuasive communications that try to engage them in a poor health practice and giving them techniques that they can use to respond effectively to these efforts.

behavioral inoculation   Providing a person with a weak form of an argument, thus giving him or her the opportunity to develop counterarguments and successfully resist the message; similar to inoculation against disease.

biofeedback   A method whereby an individual is provided with ongoing, specific information or feedback about how a particular physiological process operates, so that he or she can learn how to modify that process.

biomedical model   The viewpoint that illness can be explained on the basis of aberrant somatic processes and that psychological and social processes are largely independent of the disease process; the dominant model in medical practice until recently.

biopsychosocial model   The view that biological, psychological, and social factors are all involved in any given state of health or illness.

blood pressure   The force that blood exerts against vessel walls.

body image   The perception and evaluation of one's body, one's physical functioning, and one's appearance.

buffering hypothesis   The hypothesis that coping resources are useful primarily under conditions of high stress and not necessarily under conditions of low stress.

bulimia   An eating syndrome characterized by alternating cycles of binge eating and purging through such techniques as vomiting and extreme dieting.

cardiac invalidism   A psychological state that can result after a myocardial infarction or diagnosis of coronary heart disease, consisting of the perception that a patient's abilities and capacities are lower than they actually are; both patients and their spouses are vulnerable to these misperceptions.

cardiac rehabilitation   An intervention program designed to help heart patients achieve their optimal physical, medical, psychological, social, emotional, vocational, and economic status after the diagnosis of heart disease or a heart attack.

cardiopulmonary resuscitation (CPR)   A method of reviving the functioning of heart and lungs after a loss of consciousness in which the patient's pulse has ceased or lungs have failed to function appropriately.

cardiovascular disease (CVD)   Chronically high blood pressure resulting from too much blood passing through too narrow vessels.

cardiovascular system   The transport system of the body responsible for carrying oxygen and nutrients to the body and carrying away carbon dioxide and other wastes to the kidneys for excretion; composed of the heart, blood vessels, and blood.

catecholamines   The neurotransmitters, epinephrine and norepinephrine, that promote sympathetic nervous system activity; released in substantial quantities during stressful times.

cell-mediated immunity   A slow-acting immunologic reaction involving T lymphocytes from the thymus gland; effective in defending against viral infections that have invaded the cells, and against fungi, parasites, foreign tissues, and cancer.

cerebellum   The part of the hindbrain responsible for the coordination of voluntary muscle movement, the maintenance of balance and equilibrium, and the maintenance of muscle tone and posture.

cerebral cortex   The main portion of the brain, responsible for intelligence, memory, and the detection and interpretation of sensation.

chronic benign pain   Pain that typically persists for 6 months or longer and is relatively intractable to treatment. The pain varies in severity and may involve any of a number of muscle groups. Chronic low back pain and myofascial pain syndrome are examples.

chronic illnesses   Illnesses that are long lasting and usually irreversible.

chronic pain   Pain that may begin after an injury but that does not respond to treatment and persists over time.

chronic progressive pain   Pain that persists longer than 6 months and increases in severity over time. Typically, it is associated with malignancies or degenerative disorders, such as skeletal metastatic disease or rheumatoid arthritis.

chronic strain   A stressful experience that is a usual but continually stressful aspect of life.

classical conditioning   The pairing of a stimulus with an unconditioned reflex, such that over time the new stimulus acquires a conditioned response, evoking the same behavior; the process by which an automatic response is conditioned to a new stimulus.

clinical thanatology   The clinical practice of counseling people who are dying on the basis of knowledge of reactions to dying.

cognitive-behavior therapy   The use of principles from learning theory to modify the cognitions and behaviors associated with a behavior to be modified; cognitive-behavioral approaches are used to modify poor health habits, such as smoking, poor diet, and alcoholism.

cognitive restructuring   A method of modifying internal monologues in stress-producing situations; clients are trained to monitor what they say to themselves in stress-provoking situations and then to modify their cognitions in adaptive ways.

colleague orientation   A physician orientation toward gaining the esteem and regard of one's colleagues; fostered by any health care provider arrangement that does not involve direct reimbursement to physicians by patients.

commonsense model of illness   A model maintaining that people hold implicit commonsense beliefs about their symptoms and illnesses that result in organized illness representations or schemas and that influence their treatment decisions and adherence.

comprehensive intervention models   Models that pool and coordinate the medical and psychological expertise in a well-defined area of medical practice so as to make all available technology and expertise available to a patient; the pain management program is one example of a comprehensive intervention model.

contingency contracting   A procedure in which an individual forms a contract with another person, such as a therapist, detailing what rewards or punishments are contingent on the performance or nonperformance of a target behavior.

control-enhancing interventions   Interventions with patients who are awaiting treatment for the purpose of enhancing their perceptions of control over those treatments.

controlled drinking   Training in discriminating blood alcohol level so as to control the extent of drinking; may also include coping skills for dealing with situations that are high risk for high alcohol consumption; see also **placebo drinking.**

conversion hysteria   The viewpoint, originally advanced by Freud, that specific unconscious conflicts can produce physical disturbances symbolic of the repressed conflict; no longer a dominant viewpoint in health psychology.

coping   The process of trying to manage demands that are appraised as taxing or exceeding one's resources.

coping outcomes   The beneficial effects that are thought to result from successful coping; these include reducing stress, adjusting more successfully to it, maintaining emotional equilibrium, having satisfying relationships with others, and maintaining a positive self-image.

coping style   An individual's preferred method of dealing with stressful situations.

coronary heart disease (CHD)   A general term referring to illnesses caused by atherosclerosis, which is the narrowing of the coronary arteries, the vessels that supply the heart with blood.

correlational research   Measuring two variables and determining whether they are associated with each other. Studies relating smoking to lung cancer are correlational, for example.

cost containment   The effort to reduce or hold down health care costs.

cost effectiveness   The formal evaluation of the effectiveness of an intervention relative to its cost and the cost of alternative interventions.

counterirritation   A pain control technique that involves inhibiting pain in one part of the body by stimulating or mildly irritating another area, sometimes adjacent to the area in which the pain is experienced.

craving   A strong desire to engage in a behavior or consume a substance, such as alcohol or tobacco, which appears, in part, to occur through the conditioning of physical dependence on environmental cues associated with the behavior.

creative nonadherence   The modification or supplementation of a prescribed treatment regimen on the basis of privately held theories about the disorder or its treatment.

curative care   Care designed to cure a patient's underlying disease.

daily hassles   Minor daily stressful events; believed to have a cumulative effect in increasing the likelihood of illness.

death education   Programs designed to inform people realistically about death and dying, the purpose of which is to reduce the terror connected with and avoidance of the topic.

delay behavior   The act of delaying seeking treatment for recognized symptoms.

denial   A defense mechanism involving the inability to recognize or deal with external threatening events; believed to be an early reaction to the diagnosis of a chronic or terminal illness.

depression   A neurotic or psychotic mood disorder marked especially by sadness, inactivity, difficulty with thinking and concentration, a significant increase or decrease in appetite and time spent sleeping, feelings of dejection and hopelessness, and sometimes suicidal thoughts or an attempt to commit suicide.

detoxification   The process of withdrawing from alcohol, usually conducted in a supervised, medically monitored setting.

diagnostic-related group (DRG)   A patient classification scheme that specifies the nature and length of treatment for particular disorders; used by some third-party reimbursement systems to determine the amount of reimbursement.

dieticians   Trained and licensed individuals who apply principles of nutrition and food management to meal planning for institutions such as hospitals or for individuals who need help planning and managing special diets.

direct effects hypothesis   The theory that coping resources, such as social support, have beneficial psychological and health effects under conditions of both high stress and low stress.

discriminative stimulus   An environmental stimulus that is capable of eliciting a particular behavior; for example, the sight of food may act as a discriminative stimulus for eating.

distraction   A pain control method that may involve either focusing on a stimulus irrelevant to the pain experience or reinterpreting the pain experience; redirecting attention to reduce pain.

double-blind experiment   An experimental procedure in which neither the researcher nor the patient knows whether the patient received the real treatment or the placebo until precoded records indicating which patient received which are consulted; designed to reduce the possibility that expectations for success will increase evidence for success.

emotion-focused coping   Efforts to regulate emotions associated with a stressful encounter; can be associated with distress.

emotional-approach coping   The process of clarifying, focusing on, and working through the emotions experienced in conjunction with a stressor; generally has positive effects on psychological functioning and health.

emotional support Indications from other people that one is loved, valued, and cared for; believed to be an important aspect of social support during times of stress.

endocrine system A bodily system of ductless glands that secrete hormones into the blood to stimulate target organs; interacts with nervous system functioning.

endogenous opioid-peptides Opiatelike substances produced by the body.

epidemiology The study of the frequency, distribution, and causes of infectious and noninfectious disease in a population, based on an investigation of the physical and social environment. Thus, for example, epidemiologists not only study who has what kind of cancer but also address questions such as why certain cancers are more prevalent in particular geographic areas than other cancers are.

etiology The origins and causes of illness.

euthanasia Ending the life of a person who has a painful terminal illness for the purpose of terminating the individual's suffering.

evidence-based medicine The conscientious, explicit, judicious use of the best scientific evidence for making decisions about the care of individual patients; the criterion for adopting medical standards.

experiment A type of research in which a researcher randomly assigns people to two or more conditions, varies the treatments that people in each condition are given, and then measures the effect on some response.

fear appeals Efforts to change attitudes by arousing fear to induce the motivation to change behavior; fear appeals are used to try to get people to change poor health habits.

fight-or-flight response A response to a threat in which the body is rapidly aroused and motivated via the sympathetic nervous system and the endocrine system to attack or flee a threatening stimulus; the response was first described by Walter Cannon in 1932.

functional somatic syndromes Syndromes marked by the symptoms, suffering, and disability they cause rather than by demonstrable tissue abnormality.

gate-control theory of pain A theory detailing how the experience of pain is reflected in sensory, psychological, and behavioral responses.

general adaptation syndrome Developed by Hans Selye, a profile of how organisms respond to stress; the general adaptation syndrome is characterized by three phases: a nonspecific mobilization phase, which promotes sympathetic nervous system activity; a resistance phase, during which the organism makes efforts to cope with the threat; and an exhaustion phase, which occurs if the organism fails to overcome the threat and depletes its physiological resources.

gout A form of arthritis produced by a buildup of uric acid in the body, producing crystals that become lodged in the joints; the most commonly affected area is the big toe.

grief A response to bereavement involving a feeling of hollowness and sometimes marked by preoccupation with the dead person, expressions of hostility toward others, and guilt over the death; may also involve restlessness, an inability to concentrate, and other adverse psychological and physical symptoms.

guided imagery A technique of relaxation and pain control in which a person conjures up a picture that is held in mind during a painful or stressful experience.

health The absence of disease or infirmity, coupled with a complete state of physical, mental, and social well-being; health psychologists recognize health to be a state that is actively achieved rather than the mere absence of illness.

health behaviors Behaviors undertaken by people to enhance or maintain their health, such as exercise or the consumption of a healthy diet.

health belief model A theory of health behaviors; the model predicts that whether a person practices a particular health habit can be understood by knowing the degree to which the person perceives a personal health threat and the perception that a particular health practice will be effective in reducing that threat.

health habit A health-related behavior that is firmly established and often performed automatically, such as buckling a seat belt or brushing one's teeth.

health locus of control The perception that one's health is under personal control; is controlled by powerful others, such as physicians; or is determined by external factors, including chance.

health maintenance organization (HMO) An organizational arrangement for receiving health care services, by which an individual pays a standard monthly rate and then uses services as needed at no additional or at greatly reduced cost.

health promotion A general philosophy maintaining that health is a personal and collective achievement; the process of enabling people to increase control over and improve their health. Health promotion may occur through individual efforts, through interaction with the medical system, and through a concerted health policy effort.

health psychology The subarea within psychology devoted to understanding psychological influences on health, illness, and responses to those states, as well as the psychological origins and impacts of health policy and health interventions.

holistic health A philosophy characterized by the belief that health is a positive state that is actively achieved; usually associated with certain nontraditional health practices.

home care   Care for dying patients in the home; the choice of care for the majority of terminally ill patients, though sometimes problematic for family members.

hospice   An institution for dying patients that encourages personalized, warm, palliative care.

hospice care   An alternative to hospital and home care, designed to provide warm, personal comfort for terminally ill patients; may be residential or home-based.

human immunodeficiency virus (HIV)   The virus that is implicated in the development of AIDS.

humoral immunity   A fast-acting immunologic reaction mediated by B lymphocytes that secrete antibodies into the bloodstream; effective in defending against bacterial infections and viral infections that have not yet invaded the cells.

hypertension   Excessively high blood pressure that occurs when the supply of blood through the blood vessels is excessive, putting pressure on the vessel walls; a risk factor for a variety of medical problems, including coronary heart disease.

hypnosis   A pain management technique involving relaxation, suggestion, distraction, and the focusing of attention.

hypothalamus   The part of the forebrain responsible for regulating water balance and controlling hunger and sexual desire; assists in cardiac functioning, blood pressure regulation, and respiration regulation; plays a major role in regulation of the endocrine system, which controls the release of hormones, including those related to stress.

illness delay   The time between recognizing that a symptom implies an illness and the decision to seek treatment.

illness representations   An organized set of beliefs about an illness or a type of illness, including its nature, cause, duration, and consequences.

immunity   The body's resistance to injury from invading organisms, acquired from the mother at birth, through disease, or through vaccinations and inoculations.

infant mortality rate   The number of infant deaths per thousand infants.

informational support   The provision of information to a person experiencing stress by friends, family, and other people in the individual's social network; believed to help reduce the distressing and health-compromising effects of stress.

invisible support   Support received from another person that is outside the recipient's awareness.

ischemia   A deficiency of blood to the heart due to obstruction or constriction of the coronary arteries; often associated with chest pain.

John Henryism   A personality predisposition to cope actively with psychosocial stressors; may become lethal when those active coping efforts are unsuccessful; the syndrome has been especially documented among lower-income Blacks at risk for or suffering from hypertension.

kidney dialysis   A procedure in which blood is filtered to remove toxic substances and excess fluid from the blood of patients whose kidneys do not function properly.

lay referral network   An informal network of family and friends who help an individual interpret and treat a disorder before the individual seeks formal medical treatment.

life-skills-training approach   A smoking prevention program characterized by the belief that training in self-esteem and coping skills will boost self-image to the point that smoking becomes unnecessary or inconsistent with lifestyle.

lifestyle rebalancing   Concerted lifestyle change in a healthy direction, usually including exercise, stress management, and a healthy diet; believed to contribute to relapse prevention after successful modification of a poor health habit, such as smoking or alcohol consumption.

living will   A will prepared by a person with a terminal illness, requesting that extraordinary life-sustaining procedures not be used in the event that the person's ability to make this decision is lost.

longitudinal research   The repeated observation and measurement of the same individuals over a period of time.

lupus   A chronic, inflammatory form of arthritis that may be managed by anti-inflammatory medications or immuno-suppressive medications, depending on its severity.

lymphatic system   The drainage system of the body; believed to be involved in immune functioning.

managed care   A health care arrangement in which an employer or employee pays a predetermined monthly fee to a health care or insurance agency that entitles the employee to use medical services at no additional (or a greatly reduced) cost.

matching hypothesis   The hypothesis that social support is helpful to an individual to the extent that the kind of support offered satisfies the individual's specific needs.

medical delay   A delay in treating symptoms, which results from problems within the medical system, such as faulty diagnoses or lost test results.

medical students' disease   The relabeling of symptoms of fatigue and exhaustion as a particular illness resulting from learning about that illness; called medical students' disease because overworked medical students are vulnerable to this labeling effect.

medulla   The part of the hindbrain that controls autonomic functions such as regulation of heart rate, blood pressure, and respiration.

metabolic syndrome   A pattern of risk factors for the chronic health problems of diabetes, heart disease, and hypertension, characterized by obesity, a high waist-to-hip ratio, and insulin resistance. Metabolic syndrome is exacerbated by inactivity, overeating, age, and hostility.

mind-body relationship The philosophical position regarding whether the mind and body operate indistinguishably as a single system or whether they act as two separate systems; the view guiding health psychology is that the mind and body are indistinguishable.

modeling Learning gained from observing another person performing a target behavior.

morbidity The number of cases of a disease that exist at a given point in time; it may be expressed as the number of new cases (incidence) or as the total number of existing cases (prevalence).

mortality The number of deaths due to particular causes.

myocardial infarction (MI) A heart attack produced when a clot has developed in a coronary vessel, blocking the flow of blood to the heart.

negative affectivity A personality variable marked by a pervasive negative mood, including anxiety, depression, and hostility; believed to be implicated in the experience of symptoms, the seeking of medical treatment, and possibly illness.

nervous system The system of the body responsible for the transmission of information from the brain to the rest of the body and from the rest of the body to the brain; it is composed of the central nervous system (the brain and the spinal cord) and the peripheral nervous system (which consists of the remainder of the nerves in the body).

neurotransmitters Chemicals that regulate nervous system functioning.

nociception The perception of pain.

nonadherence The failure to comply fully with treatment recommendations for modification of a health habit or an illness state.

nonspecific immune mechanisms A set of responses to infection or a disorder that is engaged by the presence of a biological invader.

nurse-practitioners Nurses who, in addition to their training in traditional nursing, receive special training in primary care so they may provide routine medical care for patients.

obesity An excessive accumulation of body fat, believed to contribute to a variety of health disorders, including cardiovascular disease.

occupational therapists Trained and licensed individuals who work with emotionally and/or physically disabled people to determine skill levels and to develop a rehabilitation program to build on and expand these skills.

operant conditioning The pairing of a voluntary, nonautomatic behavior with a new stimulus through reinforcement or punishment.

osteoarthritis A form of arthritis that results when the articular cartilage begins to crack or wear away because of overuse of a particular joint; may also result from injury or other causes; usually affects the weight-bearing joints and is common among athletes and the elderly.

pain behaviors Behaviors that result in response to pain, such as cutting back on work or taking drugs.

pain control The ability to reduce the experience of pain, report of pain, emotional concern over pain, inability to tolerate pain, or presence of pain-related behaviors.

pain management programs Coordinated, interdisciplinary efforts to modify chronic pain by bringing together neurological, cognitive, behavioral, and psychodynamic expertise concerning pain; such programs aim not only to make pain more manageable but also to modify the lifestyle that has evolved because of the pain.

pain-prone personality A constellation of personality traits that predisposes a person to experience chronic pain.

palliative care Care designed to make the patient comfortable, but not to cure or improve the patient's underlying disease; often part of terminal care.

parasympathetic nervous system The part of the nervous system responsible for vegetative functions, the conservation of energy, and the damping down of the effects of the sympathetic nervous system.

passive smoking See **secondhand smoke.**

patient education Programs designed to inform patients about their disorder and its treatment and to train them in methods for coping with a disorder and its corresponding limitations.

perceived stress The perception that an event is stressful independent of its objective characteristics.

person-environment fit The degree to which the needs and resources of a person and the needs and resources of an environment complement each other.

phagocytosis The process by which phagocytes ingest and attempt to eliminate a foreign invader.

physical dependence A state in which the body has adjusted to the use of a substance, incorporating it into the body's normal functioning.

physical rehabilitation A program of activities for chronically ill or disabled persons geared toward helping them use their bodies as much as possible, sense changes in the environment and in themselves so as to make appropriate physical accommodations, learn new physical and management skills if necessary, pursue a treatment regimen, and learn how to control the expenditure of energy.

physical therapists Trained and licensed individuals who help people with muscle, nerve, joint, or bone diseases to overcome their disabilities as much as possible.

physicians' assistants Graduates of 2-year programs who perform routine health care functions, teach patients about their treatment regimens, and record medical information.

pituitary gland   A gland located at the base of and controlled by the brain that secretes the hormones responsible for growth and organ development.

placebo   A medical treatment that produces an effect in a patient because of its therapeutic intent and not its nature.

placebo drinking   The consumption of nonalcoholic beverages in social situations in which others are drinking alcohol.

placebo effect   The medically beneficial impact of an inert treatment.

platelets   Small disks found in vertebrate blood that contribute to blood coagulation.

pons   The part of the hindbrain that links the hindbrain to the midbrain and helps control respiration.

post-traumatic stress disorder (PTSD)   A syndrome that results after exposure to a stressor of extreme magnitude, marked by emotional numbing, the reliving of aspects of the trauma, intense responses to other stressful events, and other symptoms, such as hyperalertness, sleep disturbance, guilt, or impaired memory or concentration.

preferred provider organization (PPO)   A network of affiliated practitioners that has agreed to charge preestablished rates for particular medical services.

premature death   Death that occurs before the projected age of 77.

primary appraisal   The perception of a new or changing environment as beneficial, neutral, or negative in its consequences; believed to be a first step in stress and coping.

primary prevention   Measures designed to combat risk factors for illness before an illness has a chance to develop.

private, fee-for-service care   The condition under which patients privately contract with physicians for services and pay them for services rendered.

problem drinking   Uncontrolled drinking that leads to social, psychological, and biomedical problems resulting from alcohol; the problem drinker may show some signs associated with alcoholism, but typically, problem drinking is considered to be a prealcoholic or a lesser alcoholic syndrome.

problem-focused coping   Attempts to do something constructive about the stressful situations that are harming, threatening, or challenging an individual.

prospective research   A research strategy in which people are followed forward in time to examine the relationship between one set of variables and later occurrences. For example, prospective research can enable researchers to identify risk factors for diseases that develop at a later time.

psychological control   The perception that one has at one's disposal a response that will reduce, minimize, eliminate, or offset the adverse effects of an unpleasant event, such as a medical procedure.

psychoneuroimmunology   Study of the interactions among behavioral, neuroendocrine, and immunological processes of adaptation.

psychosomatic medicine   A field within psychiatry, related to health psychology, that developed in the early 1900s to study and treat particular diseases believed to be caused by emotional conflicts, such as ulcers, hypertension, and asthma. The term is now used more broadly to mean an approach to health-related problems and diseases that examines psychological as well as somatic origins.

quality of life   The degree to which a person is able to maximize his or her physical, psychological, vocational, and social functioning; an important indicator of recovery from or adjustment to chronic illness.

randomized clinical trials   An experimental study of the effects of a variable (such as a drug or treatment) administered to human subjects who are randomly selected from a broad population and assigned on a random basis to either an experimental or a control group. The goal is to determine the clinical efficacy and pharmacologic effects of the drug or procedure.

reactivity   The predisposition to react physiologically to stress; believed to be genetically based in part; high reactivity is believed to be a risk factor for a range of stress-related diseases.

recurrent acute pain   Pain that involves a series of intermittent episodes of pain that are acute in character but chronic inasmuch as the condition persists for more than 6 months; migraine headaches, temporomandibular disorder (involving the jaw), and trigeminal neuralgia (involving spasms of the facial muscles) are examples.

relapse prevention   A set of techniques designed to keep people from relapsing to prior poor health habits after initial successful behavior modification; includes training in coping skills for high-risk-for-relapse situations and lifestyle rebalancing.

relaxation training   Procedures that help people relax; include progressive muscle relaxation and deep breathing; may also include guided imagery and forms of meditation or hypnosis.

renal system   Part of the metabolic system; responsible for the regulation of bodily fluids and the elimination of wastes; regulates bodily fluids by removing surplus water, surplus electrolytes, and waste products generated by the metabolism of food.

respiratory system   The system of the body responsible for taking in oxygen, excreting carbon dioxide, and regulating the relative composition of the blood.

retrospective research   A research strategy whereby people are studied for the relationship of past variables or conditions to current ones. Interviewing people with a particular disease and asking them about their childhood health behaviors or exposure to risks can identify conditions leading to an adult disease, for example.

rheumatoid arthritis   A crippling form of arthritis believed to result from an autoimmune process, usually attacking the small joints of the hands, feet, wrists, knees, ankles, and neck.

role conflict   Conflict that occurs when two or more social or occupational roles that an individual occupies produce conflicting standards for behavior.

secondary appraisal   The assessment of one's coping abilities and resources and the judgment as to whether they will be sufficient to meet the harm, threat, or challenge of a new or changing event.

secondary gains   Benefits of being treated for illness, including the ability to rest, to be freed from unpleasant tasks, and to be taken care of by others.

secondhand smoke   Smoke that is unintentionally inhaled by nonsmokers as a result of exposure to smokers; believed to cause health problems such as bronchitis, emphysema, and lung cancer.

self-affirmation   A process by which people focus on their personal values which bolsters the self-concept.

self-concept   An integrated set of beliefs about one's personal qualities and attributes.

self-control   A state in which an individual desiring to change behavior learns how to modify the antecedents and the consequences of that target behavior.

self-determination theory (SDT)   The theory that autonomous motivation and perceived competence are fundamental to behavior change.

self-efficacy   The perception that one is able to perform a particular action.

self-esteem   A global evaluation of one's qualities and attributes.

self-help aids   Materials that can be used by an individual on his or her own without the aid of a therapist to assist in the modification of a personal habit; often used to combat smoking and other health-related risk factors.

self-management   Involvement of the patient in all aspects of a chronic illness including medication management, changes in social and vocational roles, and coping.

self-monitoring   Assessing the frequency, antecedents, and consequences of a target behavior to be modified; also known as self-observation.

self-reinforcement   Systematically rewarding or punishing oneself to increase or decrease the occurrence of a target behavior.

self-talk   Internal monologues; people tell themselves things that may undermine or help them implement appropriate health habits, such as "I can stop smoking" (positive self-talk) or "I'll never be able to do this" (negative self-talk).

set point theory of weight   The concept that each individual has an ideal biological weight that cannot be greatly modified.

smoking prevention programs   Programs designed to keep people from beginning to smoke, as opposed to programs that attempt to induce people to stop once they have already become smokers.

social engineering   Social or lifestyle change through legislation; for example, water purification is done through social engineering rather than by individual efforts.

social influence intervention   A smoking prevention intervention that draws on the social learning principles of modeling and behavioral inoculation in inducing people not to smoke; youngsters are exposed to older peer models who deliver antismoking messages after exposure to simulated peer pressure to smoke.

social skills training   Techniques that teach people how to relax and interact comfortably in social situations; often a part of health behavior modification programs, on the assumption that maladaptive health behaviors, such as alcohol consumption or smoking, may develop in part to control social anxiety.

social support   Information from other people that one is loved and cared for, esteemed and valued, and part of a network of communication and mutual obligation.

social workers   Trained and licensed individuals who help patients and their families deal with problems by providing therapy, making referrals, and engaging in social planning; medical social workers help patients and their families ease transitions between illness and recovery states.

socialization   The process by which people learn the norms, rules, and beliefs associated with their family and society; parents and social institutions are usually the major agents of socialization.

somaticizers   People who express distress and conflict through bodily symptoms.

specific immune mechanisms   Responses designed to respond to specific invaders; includes cell-mediated and humoral immunity.

stages of dying   A theory, developed by Elisabeth Kübler-Ross, maintaining that people go through five temporal stages in adjusting to the prospect of death: denial, anger, bargaining, depression, and acceptance; believed to characterize some but not all dying people.

stimulus-control interventions   Interventions designed to modify behavior that involve the removal of discriminative stimuli that evoke a behavior targeted for change and the substitution of new discriminative stimuli that will evoke a desired behavior.

stress   Appraising events as harmful, threatening, or challenging, and assessing one's capacity to respond to those events; events that are perceived to tax or exceed one's resources are seen as stressful.

stress carriers   Individuals who create stress for others without necessarily increasing their own level of stress.

stress eating   Eating in response to stress; approximately half the population increases eating in response to stress.

stress management   A program for dealing with stress in which people learn how they appraise stressful events, develop skills for coping with stress, and practice putting these skills into effect.

stress moderators   Internal and external resources and vulnerabilities that modify how stress is experienced and its effects.

stressful life events   Events that force an individual to make changes in his or her life.

stressors   Events perceived to be stressful.

stroke   A condition that results from a disturbance in blood flow to the brain, often marked by resulting physical or cognitive impairments and, in the extreme, death.

sudden infant death syndrome (SIDS)   A common cause of death among infants, in which an infant simply stops breathing.

support groups   Groups of individuals who meet regularly and usually have a common problem or concern; support groups are believed to help people cope because they provide opportunities to share concerns and exchange information with similar others.

symbolic immortality   The sense that one is leaving a lasting impact on the world, as through one's children or one's work, or that one is joining the afterlife and becoming one with God.

sympathetic nervous system   The part of the nervous system that mobilizes the body for action.

systems theory   The view that all levels of an organization in any entity are linked to each other hierarchically and that change in any level will bring about change in other levels.

tangible assistance   The provision of material support by one person to another, such as services, financial assistance, or goods.

teachable moment   The idea that certain times are more effective for teaching particular health practices than others; pregnancy constitutes a teachable moment for getting women to stop smoking.

tend-and-befriend   A theory of responses to stress maintaining that in addition to fight-or-flight, humans respond to stress with social affiliation and nurturant behavior toward offspring; thought to depend on the stress hormone oxytocin; these responses may be especially true of women.

terminal care   Medical care of the terminally ill.

thalamus   The portion of the forebrain responsible for the recognition of sensory stimuli and the relay of sensory impulses to the cerebral cortex.

thanatologists   Those who study death and dying.

theory   A set of interrelated analytic statements that explain a set of phenomena, such as why people practice poor health behaviors.

theory of planned behavior   Derived from the theory of reasoned action, a theoretical viewpoint maintaining that a person's behavioral intentions and behaviors can be understood by knowing the person's attitudes toward the behavior, subjective norms regarding the behavior, and perceived behavioral control over that action.

time management   Skills for learning how to use one's time more effectively to accomplish one's goals.

tolerance   The process by which the body increasingly adapts to a substance, requiring larger and larger doses of it to obtain the same effects; a frequent characteristic of substance abuse, including alcohol and drug abuse.

transtheoretical model of behavior change   An analysis of the health behavior change process that draws on the stages and processes people go through in order to bring about successful long-term behavior change. The stages include precontemplation, contemplation, preparation, action, and maintenance. Successful attitude or behavior change at each stage depends on the appropriateness of the intervention. For example, attitude-change materials help move people from precontemplation to contemplation, whereas relapse prevention techniques help move people from action to maintenance.

treatment effectiveness   Formal documentation of the success of an intervention.

Type I diabetes   An autoimmune disorder characterized by lack of insulin production by the beta cells of the pancreas.

Type II diabetes   A metabolic disorder characterized by high blood glucose in the context of insulin resistance; often co-occurs with risk for heart disease.

wellness   An optimum state of health achieved through balance among physical, mental, and social well-being.

window of vulnerability   The fact that, at certain times, people are more vulnerable to particular health problems. For example, early adolescence constitutes a window of vulnerability for beginning smoking, drug use, and alcohol abuse.

withdrawal   Unpleasant physical and psychological symptoms that people experience when they stop using a substance on which they have become physically dependent; symptoms include anxiety, craving, hallucinations, nausea, headaches, and shaking.

worried well   Individuals free from illness who are nonetheless concerned about their physical state and frequently and inappropriately use medical services.

yo-yo dieting   The process of chronically alternating between dieting and regular eating, leading to successive weight gains and losses; over time, yo-yo dieters increase their chances of becoming obese by altering their underlying metabolism.

REFERENCES

Abbott, A. (2004, May 27). Striking back. *Nature, 429*, 338–339.

ABC News. (2004). Bitter medicine: Pills, profit, and the public health. Retrieved from http://abcnews.go.com/onair/ABCNEWSSpecials/pharmaceuticals_020529_pjr_feature.html

Abraham, C., & Graham-Rowe, E. (2009). Are worksite interventions effective in increasing physical activity? A systematic review and meta-analysis. *Health Psychology Review, 3*, 108–144.

Abraham, C., Sheeran, P., Spears, R., & Abrams, D. (1992). Health beliefs and promotion of HIV-preventive intentions among teenagers: A Scottish perspective. *Health Psychology, 11*, 363–370.

Abrams, D. B., Orleans, C. T., Niaura, R. S., Goldstein, M. G., Prochaska, J. O., & Velicer, W. (1996). Integrating individual and public health perspectives for treatment of tobacco dependence under managed health care: A combined stepped-care and matching model. *Annals of Behavioral Medicine, 18*, 290–304.

Abrams, R. D. (1966). The patient with cancer: His changing patterns of communication. *The New England Journal of Medicine, 274*, 317–322.

Accardi, M. C., & Milling, L. S. (2009). The effectiveness of hypnosis for reducing procedure-related pain in children and adolescents: A comprehensive methodological review. *Journal of Behavioral Medicine, 32*, 328–339.

Ackard, D. M., Fedio, G., Neumark-Sztainer, D., & Britt, H. R. (2008). Factors associated with disordered eating among sexually active adolescent males: Gender and number of sexual partners. *Psychosomatic Medicine, 70*, 232–238.

Adams, K. F., Schatzkin, A., Harris, T. B., Kipnis, V., Mouw, T., Ballard-Barbash, R., et al. (2006). Overweight, obesity, and mortality in a large prospective cohort of persons 50 to 71 years old. *The New England Journal of Medicine, 355*, 763–778.

Adams, M. A., Norman, G. J., Hovell, M. F., Sallis, J. F., & Patrick, K. (2009). Reconceptualizing decisional balance in an adolescent sun protection intervention: Mediating effects and theoretical interpretations. *Health Psychology, 28*, 217–225.

Adelman, R. C., & Verbrugge, L. M. (2000). Death makes news: The social impact of disease on newspaper coverage. *Journal of Health and Social Behavior, 41*, 347–367.

Ader, R. (1995). Historical perspectives on psychoneuroimmunology. In H. Friedman, T. W. Klein, & A. L. Friedman (Eds.), *Psychoneuroimmunology, stress, and infection* (pp. 1–24). Boca Raton, FL: CRC Press.

Adler, N., & Stewart, J. (Eds.). (2010). *The biology of disadvantage: Socioeconomic status and health* (Volume 1186). Malden, MA: Wiley-Blackwell.

Adler, N. E., Boyce, T., Chesney, M. A., Cohen, C., Folkman, S., Kahn, R. L., & Syme, L. S. (1994). Socioeconomic status and health: The challenge of the gradient. *American Psychologist, 49*, 15–24.

Adler, N. E., Boyce, W. T., Chesney, M. A., Folkman, S., & Syme, L. (1993). Socioeconomic inequalities in health: No easy solution. *Journal of the American Medical Association, 269*, 3140–3145.

Adler, S. (1991). Sudden unexpected nocturnal death syndrome among Hmong immigrants: Examining the role of the "nightmare." *The Journal of American Folklore, 104* (411), 54–71.

Affleck, G., Tennen, H., Pfeiffer, C., & Fifield, C. (1987). Appraisals of control and predictability in adapting to a chronic disease. *Journal of Personality and Social Psychology, 53*, 273–279.

Agras, W. S., Berkowitz, R. I., Arnow, B. A., Telch, C. F., Marnell, M., Henderson, J., et al. (1996). Maintenance following a very-low-calorie diet. *Journal of Consulting and Clinical Psychology, 64*, 610–613.

Agras, W. S., Kraemer, H. C., Berkowitz, R. I., Korner, A. F., & Hammer, L. D. (1987). Does a vigorous feeding style influence early development? *Journal of Pediatrics, 110*, 799–804.

Agras, W. S., Taylor, C. B., Kraemer, H. C., Southam, M. A., & Schneider, J. A. (1987). Relaxation training for essential hypertension at the worksite: II. The poorly controlled hypertensive. *Psychosomatic Medicine, 49*, 264–273.

Ahluwalia, J. S., Nollen, N., Kaur, H., James, A. S., Mayo, M. S., & Resnicow, K. (2007). Pathways to health: Cluster-randomized trial to increase fruit and vegetable consumption among smokers in public housing. *Health Psychology, 26*, 214–221.

Ai, A. L., Wink, P., Tice, T. N., Bolling, S. F., & Shearer, M. (2009). Prayer and reverence in naturalistic, aesthetic, and socio-moral contexts predicted fewer complications following coronary artery bypass. *Journal of Behavioral Medicine, 32*, 570–581.

Aiken, L. H., & Marx, M. M. (1982). Hospices: Perspectives on the public policy debate. *American Psychologist, 37*, 1271–1279.

Ajzen, I., & Fishbein, M. (1980). *Understanding attitudes and predicting social behavior.* Englewood Cliffs, NJ: Prentice-Hall.

Ajzen, I., & Madden, T. J. (1986). Prediction of goal-directed behavior: Attitudes, intentions, and perceived behavioral control. *Journal of Experimental Social Psychology, 22*, 453–474.

Akil, H., Mayer, D. J., & Liebeskind, J. C. (1972). Comparaison chez le Rat entre l'analgesie induite par stimulation de la substance grise periaqueducale et l'analgesie morphinique. *C. R. Academy of Science, 274*, 3603–3605.

Akil, H., Mayer, D. J., & Liebeskind, J. C. (1976). Antagonism of stimulation-produced analgesia by naloxone, a narcotic antagonist. *Science, 191*, 961–962.

Al'Absi, M., & Wittmers, L. E., Jr. (2003). Enhanced adrenocortical response to stress in hypertension-prone men and women. *Annals of Behavioral Medicine, 25*, 25–33.

Alati, R., O'Callaghan, M., Najman, J. M., Williams, G. M., Bor, W., & Lawlor, D. A. (2005). Asthma and internalizing behavior problems in adolescence: A longitudinal study. *Psychosomatic Medicine, 67*, 462–470.

Albarracín, D., Durantini, M. R., Earl, A., Gunnoe, J. B., & Leeper, J. (2008). Beyond the most willing audience: A meta-intervention to increase exposure to HIV-prevention programs by vulnerable populations. *Health Psychology, 27*, 638–644.

Albarracín, D., McNatt, P. S., Klein, C. T. F., Ho, R. M., Mitchell, A. L., & Kumkale, G. C. (2003). Persuasive communications to change actions: An analysis of behavioral and cognitive impact in HIV prevention. *Health Psychology, 22*, 166–177.

Albery, I. P., & Messer, D. (2005). Comparative optimism about health and nonhealth events in 8- and 9-year-old children. *Health Psychology, 24*(3), 316–320.

Albom, M. (1997). *Tuesdays with Morrie.* New York: Doubleday.

Alderman, M. H., & Lamport, B. (1988). Treatment of hypertension at the workplace: An opportunity to link service and research. *Health Psychology, 7* (Suppl.), 283–295.

Alexander, F. (1950). *Psychosomatic medicine.* New York: Norton.

Alferi, S. M., Carver, C. S., Antoni, M. H., Weiss, S., & Duran, R. E. (2001). An exploratory study of social support, distress, and life disruption among low-income Hispanic women under treatment for early stage breast cancer. *Health Psychology, 20*, 41–46.

Ali, J., & Avison, W. (1997). Employment transitions and psychological distress: The contrasting experiences of single and married mothers. *Journal of Health and Social Behavior, 38,* 345–362.

Allen, J., Markovitz, J., Jacobs, D. R., & Knox, S. S. (2001). Social support and health behavior in hostile black and white men and women. *Psychosomatic Medicine, 63,* 609–618.

Allen, J. E. (2003, April 7). Stroke therapy sets sights higher, farther. *Los Angeles Times,* pp. F1, F7.

Allen, K. (2003). Are pets a healthy pleasure? The influence of pets on blood pressure. *Current Directions in Psychological Science, 12,* 236–239.

Allen, K., Blascovich, J., & Mendes, W. B. (2002). Cardiovascular reactivity and the presence of pets, friends, and spouses: The truth about cats and dogs. *Psychosomatic Medicine, 64,* 727–739.

Allison, D. B., & Faith, M. S. (1996). Hypnosis as an adjunct to cognitive-behavioral psychotherapy for obesity: A meta-analytic reappraisal. *Journal of Consulting & Clinical Psychology, 64,* 513–516.

Almeida, N. D., Loucks, E. B., Kubzansky, L., Pruessner, J., Maselko, J., Meaney, M. J., et al. (2010). Quality of parental emotional care and calculated risk for coronary heart disease. *Psychosomatic Medicine, 72,* 148–155.

Alonso, C., & Coe, C. L. (2001). Disruptions of social relationships accentuate the association between emotional distress and menstrual pain in young women. *Health Psychology, 20,* 411–416.

Alper, J. (2000). New insights into Type II diabetes. *Science, 289,* 37–39.

Alpert, J. J. (1964). Broken appointments. *Pediatrics, 34,* 127–132.

Altman, L. K. (2002, July 3). U.N. forecasts big increase in AIDS death toll. *New York Times,* pp. A1, A6.

Altman, L. K. (2002, December 18). Older way to treat hypertension found best. *New York Times,* pp. A1, A27.

Alzheimer's Association. (2009). *2009 Alzheimer's disease facts and figures.* Retrieved October 7, 2009, from http://www.alz.org/national/documents/report_alzfactsfigures2009.pdf

Ambrosone, C. B., Flevdenheim, J. L., Graham, S., Marshall, J. R., Vena, J. E., Glasure, J. R., et al. (1996). Cigarette smoking, N-acetyltransferase 2, genetic polymorphisms, and breast cancer risk. *Journal of the American Medical Association, 276,* 1494–1501.

America, A., & Milling, L. S. (2008). The efficacy of vitamins for reducing or preventing depression symptoms in healthy individuals: Natural remedy or placebo? *Journal of Behavioral Medicine, 31,* 157–167.

American Association of Health Plans. (2001). *How to choose a health plan.* Retrieved from http://www.aahp.org

American Autoimmune Related Diseases Association. (2008). *Questions and answers.* Retrieved September 25, 2009, from http://www.aarda.org/q_and_a.php

American Cancer Society. (2001). *Tobacco use: Smoking cessation.* Atlanta: Author.

American Cancer Society. (2006). *Common questions about diet and cancer.* Retrieved June 14, 2007, from http://www.cancer.org/docroot/PED/content/PED_3_2X_Common_Questions_About_Diet_and_Cancer.asp

American Cancer Society. (2007). *Cancer facts & figures, 2007.* Retrieved September 25, 2009, from http://www.cancer.org/Research/CancerFactsFigures/cancer-facts-figures-2007

American Cancer Society. (2008). *Cancer prevalence: How many people have cancer?* Retrieved October 6, 2009 from http://www.cancer.org/cancer/cancerbasics/cancer-prevalence

American Cancer Society. (2009). *Cancer facts & figures, 2009.* Retrieved September 25, 2009, from http://www.cancer.org/downloads/STT/500809web.pdf

American Cancer Society. (2009, August). *Overview: Leukemia.* Retrieved September 28, 2009, from http://www.cancer.org/Cancer/Leukemia-AcuteLymphocyticALLinAdults/OverviewGuide/index

American Diabetes Association. (1999). *Diabetes facts and figures.* Alexandria, VA. Retrieved from http://www.diabetes.org/ada/facts.asp

American Diabetes Association. (2007). *Diabetes risk test.* Retrieved May 30, 2007, from http://www.diabetes.org/risk-test.jsp

American Diabetes Association. (2008). Economic costs of diabetes in the U.S. in 2007. *Diabetes Care, 31,* 596–615.

American Diabetes Association. (2009). *Diabetes statistics.* Retrieved October 6, 2009, from http://www.diabetes.org/diabetes-statistics.jsp

American Heart Association. (2000). *Heart and stroke a–z guide.* Dallas: Author.

American Heart Association. (2001). *2001 heart and stroke statistical update.* Dallas, Author.

American Heart Association. (2003). *Biostatistical fact sheet: Cigarette and tobacco smoke.* Dallas: Author. Retrieved from www.americanheart.org

American Heart Association. (2004a). *Heart disease and stroke statistics—2005 update.* Retrieved from http://www.americanheart.org/presenter.jhtml?identifier=1928

American Heart Association. (2004b). *Risk factors of cardiovascular disease.* Retrieved from http://www.americanheart.org/presenter.jhtml?identifier=3017033

American Heart Association. (2007). *Stroke Statistics.* Retrieved April 5, 2007, from http://www.americanheart.org/presenter.jhtml? identifier=4725

American Heart Association. (2009a). *Risk factors and coronary heart disease.* Retrieved September 28, 2009, from http://www.americanheart.org/presenter.jhtml? identifier=4726

American Heart Association. (2009b). Heart disease and stroke statistics 2009 update: A report from the American Heart Association statistics committee and stroke statistics subcommittee. *Circulation, 119, 21–181* Retrieved September 28, 2009, from http://circ.ahajournals.org/cgi/reprint/CIRCULATIONAHA.108.191261

American Hospital Association. (2009a). *Fast facts on US hospitals.* Retrieved October 13, 2009, from http://www.aha.org/aha/resource-center/Statistics-and-Studies/fast-facts.html

American Hospital Association. (2009b). Trendwatch Chartbook 2009: Trends Affecting Hospitals and Health Systems. Retrieved October 13, 2009 from http://www.aha.org/aha/research-and-trends/chartbook/index.html

American Obesity Association. (2005). *AOA fact sheets. Consumer protection: Weight management products and services.* Retrieved April 26, 2007, from http://www.obesity.org/subs/fastfacts/Obesity_Consumer_Protect.shtml

American Occupational Therapy Association, Inc. (2002). *Managing chronic pain.* Retrieved April 9, 2007, from http://www.aota.org/featured/area6/links/link02i.asp

American Psychiatric Association. (1980). *Diagnostic and statistical manual of mental disorders* (3rd ed.). Washington, DC: Author.

American Psychiatric Association. (2000). *Diagnostic and statistical manual of mental disorders* (4th ed., text revision). Washington, DC: Author.

American Psychological Association. (1996). *1993 APA directory survey, with new member updates for 1994 and 1995.* Washington, DC: American Psychological Association Research Office.

American Psychological Association. (2008). *Stress in America.* Washington, DC: American Psychological Association Research Office.

American Psychological Association Division 38. (2010). *About health psychology.* Retrieved March 23, 2010 from http://www.health-psych.org/AboutWhatWeDo.cfm

American Psychological Society. (1996). *APS observer: Special issue HCI report 4—Health living.* Washington, DC: Author.

American Society for Reproductive Medicine. (2004). *Frequently asked questions about infertility.* Retrieved from http://www.asrm.org/Patients/faqs.html

Amick, B. C., III, McDonough, P., Chang, H., Rodgers, W. H., Pieper, C. F., & Duncan, G. (2002). Relationship between all-cause mortality and cumulative working life course psychosocial and physical exposure in the United States labor market from 1968 to 1992. *Psychosomatic Medicine, 64,* 370–381.

Andersen, B. L., Cacioppo, J. T., & Roberts, D. C. (1995). Delay in seeking a cancer diagnosis: Delay stages and psychophysiological comparison processes. *British Journal of Social Psychology, 34,* 33–52.

Andersen, B. L., Kiecolt-Glaser, J., & Glaser, R. (1994). A biobehavioral model of cancer stress and disease course. *American Psychologist, 49,* 389–404.

Andersen, B. L., Woods, X. A., & Copeland, L. J. (1997). Sexual self-schema and sexual morbidity among gynecologic cancer survivors. *Journal of Consulting and Clinical Psychology, 65,* 1–9.

Andersen, M. R., Bowen, D. J., Morea, J., Stein, K. D., & Baker, F. (2009). Involvement in decision-making and breast cancer survivor quality of life. *Health Psychology, 28,* 29–37.

Anderson, C. B., Hughes, S. O., & Fuemmeler, B. F. (2009). Parent-child attitude congruence on type and intensity of physical activity: Testing multiple mediators of sedentary behavior in older children. *Health Psychology, 28,* 428–438.

Anderson, E. S., Winett, R. A., & Wojcik, J. R. (2000). Social-cognitive determinants of nutrition behavior among supermarket food shoppers: A structural equation analysis. *Health Psychology, 19,* 479–486.

Anderson, G. F., & Chu, E. (2007). Expanding priorities—Confronting chronic disease in countries with low income. *The New England Journal of Medicine, 356,* 209–211.

Anderson, K. O., Bradley, L. A., Young, L. D., McDaniel, L. K., & Wise, C. M. (1985). Rheumatoid arthritis: Review of psychological factors related to etiology, effects, and treatment. *Psychological Bulletin, 98,* 358–387.

Anderson, R. A., Baron, R. S., & Logan, H. (1991). Distraction, control, and dental stress. *Journal of Applied Social Psychology, 21,* 156–171.

Andrews, J. A., & Duncan, S. C. (1997). Examining the reciprocal relation between academic motivation and substance use: Effects of family relationships, self-esteem, and general deviance. *Journal of Behavioral Medicine, 20,* 523–549.

Andrews, J. A., Tildesley, E., Hops, H., & Li, F. (2002). The influence of peers on young adult substance use. *Health Psychology, 21,* 349–357.

Andrykowski, M. A., Curran, S. L., & Lightner, R. (1998). Off-treatment fatigue in breast cancer survivors: A controlled comparison. *Journal of Behavioral Medicine, 21,* 1–18.

Aneshensel, C. S., Botticello, A. L., & Yamamoto-Mitani, N. (2004). When caregiving ends: The course of depressive symptoms after bereavement. *Journal of Health and Social Behavior, 45,* 422–440.

Aneshensel, C. S., Pearlin, L. I., & Schuler, R. H. (1993). Stress, role captivity, and the cessation of caregiving. *Journal of Health and Social Behavior, 34,* 54–70.

Angel, R. J., Frisco, M., Angel, J. L., & Chiriboga, D. A. (2003). Financial strain and health among elderly Mexican-origin individuals. *Journal of Health and Social Behavior, 44,* 536–551.

Angier, N. (2001, June 19). Researchers piecing together autoimmune disease puzzle. *New York Times,* pp. D1, D8.

Anschutz, D. J., Van Strien, T., & Engels, R. C. M. (2008). Exposure to slim images in mass media: Television commercials as reminders of restriction in restrained eaters. *Health Psychology, 27,* 401–408.

Anstey, K. J., Jorm, A. F., Réglade-Meslin, C., Maller, J., Kumar, R., Von Sanden, C., et al. (2006). Weekly alcohol consumption, brain atrophy, and white matter hyperintensities in a community-based sample aged 60 to 64 years. *Psychosomatic Medicine, 68,* 778–785.

Anstey, K. J., & Luszcz, M. A. (2002). Mortality risk varies according to gender and change in depressive status in very old adults. *Psychosomatic Medicine, 64,* 880–888.

Antebi, A. (2007). Ageing: When less is more. *Nature, 447,* 536–537.

Antoni, M. H., Carrico, A. W., Durán, R. E., Spitzer, S., Penedo, F., Ironson, G., et al. (2006). Randomized clinical trial of cognitive behavioral stress management on human immunodeficiency virus viral load in gay men treated with highly active antiretroviral therapy. *Psychosomatic Medicine, 68,* 143–151.

Antoni, M. H., Lechner, S. C., Kazi, A., Wimberly, S. R., Sifre, T., Urcuyo, K. R., et al. (2006). How stress management improves quality of life after treatment for breast cancer. *Journal of Consulting and Clinical Psychology, 74,* 1143–1152.

Antoni, M. H., Lehman, J. M., Kilbourne, K. M., Boyers, A. E., Culver, J. L., Alferi, S. M., et al. (2001). Cognitive-behavioral stress management intervention decreases the prevalence of depression and enhances benefit finding among women under treatment of early-stage breast cancer. *Health Psychology, 20,* 20–32.

Antoni, M. H., & Lutgendorf, S. (2007). Psychosocial factors and disease progression in cancer. *Current Directions in Psychological Science, 16,* 42–46.

Antoni, M. H., Lutgendorf, S. K., Cole, S. W., Dhabhar, F. S., Sephton, S. E., McDonald, P. G., et al. (2006). The influence of bio-behavioural factors on tumor biology: Pathways and mechanisms. *Nature Reviews Cancer, 6,* 240–248.

Apanovitch, A. M., McCarthy, D., & Salovey, P. (2003). Using message framing to motivate HIV testing among low-income, ethnic minority women. *Health Psychology, 22,* 60–67.

Armitage, C. J. (2004). Evidence that implementation intentions reduce dietary fat intake: A randomized trial. *Health Psychology, 23,* 319–323.

Armitage, C. J. (2008). A volitional help sheet to encourage smoking cessation: A randomized exploratory trial. *Health Psychology, 27,* 557–566.

Armitage, C. J. (2009). Effectiveness of experimenter-provided and self-generated implementation intentions to reduce alcohol consumption in a sample of the general population: A randomized exploratory trial. *Health Psychology, 28,* 545–553.

Armitage, C. J., & Arden, M. A. (2008). How useful are the stages of change for targeting interventions? Randomized test of a brief intervention to reduce smoking. *Health Psychology, 27,* 789–798.

Arnow, B. A., Hunkeler, E. M., Blasey, C. M., Lee, J., Constantino, M. J., Fireman, B., et al. (2006). Comorbid depression, chronic pain, and disability in primary care. *Psychosomatic Medicine, 68,* 262–268.

Arnst, C. (2004, February 23). Let them eat cake—if they want to. *Business Week,* pp. 110–111.

Ary, D. V., Biglan, A., Glasgow, R., Zoref, L., Black, C., Ochs, L., et al. (1990). The efficacy of social-influence prevention programs versus "standard care": Are new initiatives needed? *Journal of Behavioral Medicine, 13,* 281–296.

Asanuma, Y., et al. (2003). Premature coronary artery atherosclerosis in systematic lupus erythematosus. *The New England Journal of Medicine, 349,* 2407–2415.

Aschbacher, K., Patterson, T. L., von Känel, R., Dimsdale, J. E., Mills, P. J., Adler, K. A., et al. (2005). Coping processes and hemostatic reactivity to acute stress in dementia caregivers. *Psychosomatic Medicine, 67,* 964–971.

Ashley, M. J., & Rankin, J. G. (1988). A public health approach to the prevention of alcohol-related problems. *Annual Review of Public Health, 9,* 233–271.

Aslaksen, P. M., & Flaten, M. A. (2008). The roles of physiological and subjective stress in the effectiveness of a placebo on experimentally induced pain. *Psychosomatic Medicine, 70,* 811–818.

Aspinwall, L. G. (2011). Future-oriented thinking, proactive coping, and the management of potential threats to health and well-being. In S. Folkman (Ed.), *The Oxford Handbook of Stress, Health, and Coping.* New York: Oxford University press.

Aspinwall, L. G., Kemeny, M. E., Taylor, S. E., Schneider, S. G., & Dudley, J. P. (1991). Psychosocial predictors of gay men's AIDS risk-reduction behavior. *Health Psychology, 10,* 432–444.

Aspinwall, L. G., Leaf, S. L., Dola, E. R., Kohlmann, W., & Leachman, S. A. (2008). CDKN2A/p16 genetic test reporting improves early detection intention and practices in high-risk melanoma families. *Cancer Epidemiology, Biomarkers & Prevention, 17,* 1510–1519.

Aspinwall, L. G., & MacNamara, A. (2005). Taking positive changes seriously: Toward a positive psychology of cancer survivorship and resilience. *Cancer, 104* (Suppl.), 2549–2556.

Aspinwall, L. G., & Taylor, S. E. (1997). A stitch in time: Self-regulation and proactive coping. *Psychological Bulletin, 121,* 417–436.

Aspinwall, L. G., & Tedeschi, R. G. (2010). The value of positive psychology for health psychology: Progress and pitfalls in examining the relation of positive phenomena to health psychology. *Annals of Behavioral Medicine, 39,* 4–15.

Astin, J. A., Beckner, W., Soeken, K., Hochberg, M. C., & Berman, B. (2002). Psychological interventions for rheumatoid arthritis: A meta-analysis of randomized controlled trials. *Arthritis and Rheumatism, 47,* 291–302.

Auerbach, S. M., Clore, J. N., Kiesler, D. J., Orr, T., Pegg, P. O., Quick, B. G., et al. (2001). Relation of diabetic patients' health-related control appraisals and physician-patient interpersonal impacts to patients' metabolic control and satisfaction with treatment. *Journal of Behavioral Medicine, 25,* 17–32.

Auerbach, S. M., Penberthy, A. R., & Kiesler, D. J. (2004). Opportunity for control, interpersonal impacts, and adjustment to a long-term invasive health care procedure. *Journal of Behavioral Medicine, 27,* 11–29.

Avlund, K., Osler, M., Damsgaard, M. T., Christensen, U., & Schroll, M. (2000). The relations between musculoskeletal diseases and mobility among old people: Are they influenced by socio-economic, psychosocial, and behavioral factors? *International Journal of Behavioral Medicine, 7,* 322–339.

Avlund, K., Pedersen, A. N., & Schroll, M. (2003). Functional decline from age 80 to 85: Influence of preceding changes in tiredness in daily activities. *Psychosomatic Medicine, 65,* 771–777.

Babyak, M., Blumenthal, J. A., Herman, S., Khatri, P., Doraiswamy, M., Moore, K., et al. (2000). Exercise treatment for major depression: Maintenance of therapeutic benefit at 10 months. *Psychosomatic Medicine, 62,* 633–638.

Bach, P. B., Schrag, D., Brawley, O. W., Galaznik, A., Yakrin, S., & Begg, C. B. (2002). Survival of blacks and whites after a cancer diagnosis. *The Journal of the American Association, 287,* 2106–2113.

Backhaus, J., Junganns, K., Born, J., Hohaus, K., Faasch, F., & Hohagen, F. (2006). Impaired declarative memory consolidation during sleep in patients with primary insomnia: Influences of sleep architecture and nocturnal cortisol release. *Biological Psychiatry, 60,* 1324–1330.

Bacon, C. G., Mittleman, M. A., Kawachi, I., Giovannucci, E., Glasser, D. B., & Rimm, E. B. (2006). A prospective study of risk factors for erectile dysfunction. *The Journal of Urology, 176,* 217–221.

Badr, H., Carmack, C. L., Kashy, D. A., Cristofanilli, M., & Revenson, T. A. (2010). Dyadic coping in metastatic breast cancer. *Health Psychology, 29,* 169–180.

Badr, H., & Taylor, C. L. C. (2008). Effects of relationship maintenance on psychological distress and dyadic adjustment among couples coping with lung cancer. *Health Psychology, 27,* 616–627.

Baer, J. S., Kivlahan, D. R., Fromme, K., & Marlatt, G. A. (1991). Secondary prevention of alcohol abuse with college students: A skills-training approach. In N. Heather, W. R. Miller, & J. Greeley (Eds.), *Self-control and the addictive behaviours* (pp. 339–356). New York: Maxwell-Macmillan.

Baer, J. S., Marlatt, G. A., Kivlahan, D. R., Fromme, K., Larimer, M. E., & Williams, E. (1992). An experimental test of three methods of alcohol risk

reduction with young adults. *Journal of Consulting and Clinical Psychology, 60,* 974–979.

Bages, N., Appels, A., & Falger, P. R. J. (1999). Vital exhaustion as a risk factor of myocardial infarction: A case-control study in Venezuela. *International Journal of Behavioral Medicine, 6,* 279–290.

Baig, E. (1997, February 17). The doctor is in cyberspace: Myriad sites offer feedback and support. *Business Week,* p. 102E8.

Bair, M. J., Robinson, R. L., Eckert, G. J., Stang, P. E., Croghan, T. W., & Kroenke, K. (2004). Impact of pain on depression treatment response in primary care. *Psychosomatic Medicine, 66,* 17–22.

Bair, M. J., Wu, J., Damush, T. M., Sutherland, J. M., & Kroenke, K. (2008). Association of depression and anxiety alone and in the combination with chronic musculoskeletal pain in primary care paitents. *Psychosomatic Medicine, 70,* 890–897.

Baker, C. K., Norris, F. H., Jones, E. C., & Murphy, A. D. (2009). Childhood trauma and adulthood physical health in Mexico. *Journal of Behavioral Medicine, 32,* 255–269.

Baker, C. W., Little, T. D., & Brownell, K. D. (2003). Predicting adolescent eating and activity behaviors: The role of social norms and personal agency. *Health Psychology, 22,* 189–198.

Baker, J. L., Olsen, L. W., & Sørensen, T. I. A. (2007). Childhood body-mass index and the risk of coronary heart disease in adulthood. *The New England Journal of Medicine, 357,* 2329–2337.

Baker, R. C., & Kirschenbaum, D. S. (1998). Weight control during the holidays: Highly consistent self-monitoring as a potentially useful coping mechanism. *Health Psychology, 17,* 367–370.

Baldwin, A. S., Rothman, A. J., Hertel, A. W., Linde, J. A., Jeffery, R. W., Finch, E. A., et al. (2006). Specifying the determinants of the initiation and maintenance of behavior change: An examination of self-efficacy, satisfaction, and smoking cessation. *Health Psychology, 25,* 626–634.

Bales, D. W., Spell, N., Cullen, D. J., Burdick, E., Laird, N., Peterson, L. A., et al. (1997). The cost of adverse drug events in hospitalized patients. *Journal of the American Medical Association, 277,* 307–311.

Balfour, L., White, D. R., Schiffrin, A., Dougherty, G., & Dufresne, J. (1993). Dietary disinhibition, perceived stress, and glucose control in young, Type I diabetic women. *Health Psychology, 12,* 33–38.

Bambauer, K. Z., Aupont, O., Stone, P. H., Locke, S. E., Mullan, M. G., Colagiovanni, J., et al. (2005). The effect of a telephone counseling intervention on self-rated health of cardiac patients. *Psychosomatic Medicine, 67,* 539–545.

Bandiera, F. C., Arheart, K. L., Caban-Martinez, A. J., Fleming, L. E., McCollister, K., Dietz, N. A., et al. (2010). Secondhand smoke exposure and depressive symptoms. *Psychosomatic Medicine, 72,* 68–72.

Bandura, A. (1969). *Principles of behavior modification.* New York: Holt, Rinehart & Winston.

Bandura, A. (1977). Self-efficacy: Toward a unifying theory of behavioral change. *Psychological Review, 84,* 191–215.

Bandura, A. (1991). Self-efficacy mechanism in physiological activation and health-promotion behavior. In J. Madden IV (Ed.), *Neurobiology of learning, emotion, and affect* (pp. 229–269). New York: Raven Press.

Bankier, B., Januzzi, J. L., & Littman, A. B. (2004). The high prevalence of multiple psychiatric disorders in stable outpatients with coronary heart disease. *Psychosomatic Medicine, 66,* 645–650.

Banks, S. M., Salovey, P., Greener, S., Rothman, A. J., Moyer, A., Beauvais, J., et al. (1995). The effects of message framing on mammography utilization. *Health Psychology, 14,* 178–184.

Banthia, R., Malcarne, V. L., Varni, J. W., Ko, C. M., Sadler, G. R., & Greenbergs, H. L. (2003). The effects of dyadic strength and coping styles on psychological distress in couples faced with prostate cancer. *Journal of Behavioral Medicine, 26,* 31–51.

Barbarin, O. A., & Chesler, M. (1986). The medical context of parental coping with childhood cancer. *American Journal of Community Psychology, 14,* 221–235.

Barefoot, J. C. (1992). Developments in the measurement of hostility. In H. S. Friedman (Ed.), *Hostility, coping, and health* (pp. 13–31). Washington, DC: American Psychological Association.

Barefoot, J. C., Maynard, K. E., Beckham, J. C., Brummett, B. H., Hooker, K., & Siegler, I. C. (1998). Trust, health, and longevity. *Journal of Behavioral Medicine, 21,* 517–526.

Bárez, M., Blasco, T., Fernández-Castro, J., & Viladrich, C. (2009). Perceived control and psychological distress in women with breast cancer: A longitudinal study. *Journal of Behavioral Medicine, 32,* 187–196.

Barnes, V. A., Davis, H. C., Murzynowski, J. B., & Treiber, F. A. (2004). Impact of meditation on resting and ambulatory blood pressure and heart rate in youth. *Psychosomatic Medicine, 66,* 909–914.

Barnett, R. C., & Marshall, N. L. (1993). Men, family-role quality, job-role quality, and physical health. *Health Psychology, 12,* 48–55.

Barnett, R. C., Raudenbush, S. W., Brennan, R. T., Pleck, J. H., & Marshall, N. L. (1995). Change in job and marital experiences and change in psychological distress: A longitudinal study of dual-earner couples. *Journal of Personality and Social Psychology, 69,* 839–850.

Bar-On, D. (1986). Professional models vs. patient models in rehabilitation after heart attack. *Human Relations, 39,* 917–932.

Bar-On, D. (1987). Causal attributions and the rehabilitation of myocardial infarction victims. *Journal of Social and Clinical Psychology, 5,* 114–122.

Bar-On, D., & Dreman, S. (1987). When spouses disagree: A predictor of cardiac rehabilitation. *Family Systems Medicine, 5,* 228–237.

Barth, J., Schneider, S., & von Känel, R. (2010). Lack of social support in the etiology and the prognosis of coronary heart disease: A systematic review and meta-analysis. *Psychosomatic Medicine, 72,* 229–238.

Bartholow, B. D., Sher, K. J., & Krull, J. L. (2003). Changes in heavy drinking over the third decade of life as a function of collegiate fraternity and sorority involvement: A prospective, multilevel analysis. *Health Psychology, 22,* 616–626.

Barton, B. K., & Schwebel, D. C. (2007). A contextual perspective on the etiology of children's unintentional injuries. *Health Psychology Review, 1,* 173–185.

Barton, J., Chassin, L., Presson, C. C., & Sherman, S. J. (1982). Social image factors as motivators of smoking initiation in early and middle adolescence. *Child Development, 53,* 1499–1511.

Bartrop, R. W., Lockhurst, E., Lazarus, L., Kiloh, L. G., & Penny, R. (1977). Depressed lymphocyte function after bereavement. *Lancet, 1,* 834–836.

Battle, E. K., & Brownell, K. D. (1996). Confronting a rising tide of eating disorders and obesity: Treatment vs. prevention and policy. *Addictive Behaviors, 21,* 755–765.

Baum, A. (1990). Stress, intrusive imagery, and chronic distress. *Health Psychology, 9,* 653–675.

Baum, A. (1994). Behavioral, biological, and environmental interactions in disease processes. In S. Blumenthal, K. Matthews, & S. Weiss (Eds.), *New research frontiers in behavioral medicine: Proceedings of the national conference* (pp. 61–70). Washington, DC: NIH Publications.

Baum, A., Friedman, A. L., & Zakowski, S. G. (1997). Stress and genetic testing for disease risk. *Health Psychology, 16,* 8–19.

Baum, A., & Grunberg, N. E. (1991). Gender, stress, and health. *Health Psychology, 10,* 80–85.

Baum, J. G., Clark, H. B., & Sandler, J. (1991). Preventing relapse in obesity through posttreatment maintenance systems: Comparing the relative efficacy of two levels of therapist support. *Journal of Behavioral Medicine, 14,* 287–302.

Bauman, K. E., Koch, G. G., & Fisher, L. A. (1989). Family cigarette smoking and test performance by adolescents. *Health Psychology, 8,* 97–105.

Baumann, L. J., Zimmerman, R. S., & Leventhal, H. (1989). An experiment in common sense: Education at blood pressure screening. *Patient Education Counseling, 14,* 53–67.

Beatty, D. L., & Matthews, K. A. (2009). Unfair treatment and trait anger in relation to nighttime ambulatory blood pressure in African American and White adolescents. *Psychosomatic Medicine, 71,* 813–820.

Beck, A. M., & Meyers, N. M. (1996). Health enhancement and companion animal ownership. *Annual Review of Public Health, 17,* 247–257.

Beck, L. (2007). Social status, social support, and stress: A comparative review of the health consequences of social control factors. *Health Psychology Review, 1,* 186–207.

Beck, M. (2009, November 24). 20 advances to be thankful for. *The Wall Street Journal,* p. D4.

Becker, M. H. (1993). A medical sociologist looks at health promotion. *Journal of Health and Social Behavior, 34,* 1–6.

Becker, M. H., & Janz, N. K. (1987). On the effectiveness and utility of health hazard/health risk appraisal in clinical and nonclinical settings. *Health Services Research, 22,* 537–551.

Becker, M. H., Kaback, M., Rosenstock, I., & Ruth, M. (1975). Some influences on public participation in a genetic screening program. *Journal of Community Health, 1,* 3–14.

Beckjord, E. B., Rutten, L. J. F., Arora, N. K., Moser, R. P., & Hesse, B. W. (2008). Information processing and negative affect: Evidence from the 2003 health information national trends survey. *Health Psychology, 27,* 249–257.

Beckman, H. B., & Frankel, R. M. (1984). The effect of physician behavior on the collection of data. *Annals of Internal Medicine, 101,* 692–696.

Beckner, V., Howard, I., Vella, L., & Mohr, D. C. (2010). Telephone-administered psychotherapy for depression in MS patients: Moderating role of social support. *Journal of Behavioral Medicine, 33,* 47–59.

Beecher, H. K. (1959). *Measurement of subjective responses.* New York: Oxford University Press.

Belisle, M., Roskies, E., & Levesque, J. M. (1987). Improving adherence to physical activity. *Health Psychology, 6,* 159–172.

Belloc, N. D., & Breslow, L. (1972). Relationship of physical health status and family practices. *Preventive Medicine, 1,* 409–421.

Belluck, P. (2005, March 17). Children's life expectancy being cut short by obesity. *New York Times,* p. A15.

Benight, C. C., Antoni, M. H., Kilbourn, K., Ironson, G., Kumar, M. A., Fletcher, M. A., et al. (1997). Coping self-efficacy buffers psychological and physiological disturbances in HIV-infected men following a natural disaster. *Health Psychology, 16,* 248–255.

Bennett, K. K., Compas, B. E., Beckjord, E., & Glinder, J. G. (2005). Self-blame among women with newly diagnosed breast cancer. *Journal of Behavioral Medicine, 28,* 313–323.

Bensley, L. S., & Wu, R. (1991). The role of psychological reactance in drinking following alcohol prevention messages. *Journal of Applied Social Psychology, 21,* 1111–1124.

Ben-Zur, H., Gilbar, O., & Lev, S. (2001). Coping with breast cancer: Patient, spouse, and dyad models. *Psychosomatic Medicine, 62,* 32–39.

Beran, T. M., Stanton, A. L., Kwan, L., Seldon, J., Bower, J. E., Vodermaier, A., et al. (2008). The trajectory of psychological impact in BRCA1/2 genetic testing: Does time heal? *Annals of Behavioral Medicine, 39,* 107–116.

Berkman, L. F. (1985). The relationship of social networks and social support to morbidity and mortality. In S. Cohen & S. L. Syme (Eds.), *Social support and health* (pp. 241–262). Orlando, FL: Academic Press.

Berkowitz, R. I., Agras, W. S., Korner, A. F., Kraemer, H. C., & Zeanah, C. H. (1985). Physical activity and adiposity: A longitudinal study from birth to childhood. *Journal of Pediatrics, 106,* 734–738.

Berlin, A. A., Kop, W. J., & Deuster, P. A. (2006). Depressive mood symptoms and fatigue after exercise withdrawal: The potential role of decreased fitness. *Psychosomatic Medicine, 68,* 224–230.

Berna, C., Leknes, S., Holmes, E. A., Edwards, R. R., Goodwin, G. M., & Tracey, I. (2010). Induction of depressed mood disrupts emotion regulation neurocircuitry and enhances pain unpleasantness. *Biological Psychiatry, 67,* 1083–1090.

Berntson, G. G., Norman, G. J., Hawkley, L. C., & Cacioppo, J. T. (2008). Spirituality and autonomic cardiac control. *Annals of Behavioral Medicine, 35,* 198–208.

Bhattacharyya, M. R., Whitehead, D. L., Rakhit, R., & Steptoe, A. (2008). Depressed mood, positive affect, and heart rate variability in patients with suspected coronary artery disease. *Psychosomatic Medicine, 70,* 1020–1027.

Bianco, A., & Schine, E. (1997, March 24). Doctors, Inc. *Business Week,* pp. 204–206, 208–210.

Biernat, M., Crosby, F. J., & Williams, J. C. (Eds.). (2004). The maternal wall: Research and policy perspective on discrimination against mothers. *Journal of Social Issues, 60.*

Biglan, A., McConnell, S., Severson, H. H., Bavry, J., & Ary, D. (1984). A situational analysis of adolescent smoking. *Journal of Behavioral Medicine, 7,* 109–114.

Billings, A. C., & Moos, R. H. (1984). Coping, stress, and social resources among adults with unipolar depression. *Journal of Personality and Social Psychology, 46,* 877–891.

Billings, A. C., Moos, R. H., Miller, J. J., III, & Gottlieb, J. E. (1987). Psychosocial adaptation in juvenile rheumatoid disease: A controlled evaluation. *Health Psychology, 6,* 343–359.

Bishop, S. R. (2002). What do we really know about mindfulness-based stress? *Psychosomatic Medicine, 64,* 71–84.

Bishop, S. R., & Warr, D. (2003). Coping, catastrophizing and chronic pain in breast cancer. *Journal of Behavioral Medicine, 26,* 265–281.

Bjorntorp, P. (1996). Behavior and metabolic disease. *International Journal of Behavioral Medicine, 3,* 285–302.

Blakeslee, S. (1998, October 13). Placebos prove so powerful even experts are surprised. *New York Times,* p. F2.

Blanchard, C. M., Fortier, M., Sweet, S., O'Sullivan, T., Hogg, W., Reid, R. D., et al. (2007). Explaining physical activity levels from a self-efficacy perspective: The physical activity counseling trial. *Annals of Behavioral Medicine, 34,* 323–328.

Blanchard, E. B., Andrasik, F., & Silver, B. V. (1980). Biofeedback and relaxation in the treatment of tension headaches: A reply to Belar. *Journal of Behavioral Medicine, 3,* 227–232.

Blanchard, E. B., McCoy, G. C., Wittrock, D., Musso, A., Gerardi, R. J., & Pangburn, L. (1988). A controlled comparison of thermal biofeedback and relaxation training in the treatment of essential hypertension: II. Effects on cardiovascular reactivity. *Health Psychology, 7,* 19–33.

Blanton, H., & Gerrard, M. (1997). Effect of sexual motivation on men's risk perception for sexually transmitted disease: There must be 50 ways to justify a lover. *Health Psychology, 16,* 374–379.

Bleil, M. E., Gianaros, P. J., Jennings, R., Flory, J. D., & Manuck, S. B. (2008). Trait negative affect: Toward an integrated model of understanding psychological risk for impairment in cardiac autonomic function. *Psychosomatic Medicine, 70,* 328–337.

Blinder, B. J., Cumella, E. J., & Sanathara, V. A. (2006). Psychiatric comorbidities of female inpatients with eating disorders. *Psychosomatic Medicine, 68,* 454–462.

Blissmer, B., & McAuley, E. (2002). Testing the requirements of stages of physical activity among adults: The comparative effectiveness of stage-matched, mismatched, standard care, and control interventions. *Annals of Behavioral Medicine, 24,* 181–189.

Blomhoff, S., Spetalen, S., Jacobsen, M. B., & Malt, U. F. (2001). Phobic anxiety changes the function of brain-gut axis in irritable bowel syndrome. *Psychosomatic Medicine, 63,* 959–965.

Bluebond-Langner, M. (1977). Meanings of death to children. In H. Feifel (Ed.), *New meanings of death* (pp. 47–66). New York: McGraw-Hill.

Blumenthal, J. A., & Emery, C. F. (1988). Rehabilitation of patients following myocardial infarction. *Journal of Consulting and Clinical Psychology, 56,* 374–381.

Bogart, L. M. (2001). Relationship of stereotypic beliefs about physicians to health-care relevant behaviors and cognitions among African American women. *Journal of Behavioral Medicine, 245,* 573–586.

Bogart, L. M., & Uyeda, K. (2009). Community-based participatory research: Partnering with communities for effective and sustainable behavioral health interventions. *Health Psychology, 28,* 391–393.

Bolger, N., & Amarel, D. (2007). Effects of social support visibility on adjustment to stress: Experimental evidence. *Journal of Personality and Social Psychology, 92,* 458–475.

Bolger, N., DeLongis, A., Kessler, R. C., & Schilling, E. A. (1989). Effects of daily stress on negative mood. *Journal of Personality and Social Psychology, 57,* 808–818.

Bolger, N., Zuckerman, A., & Kessler, R. C. (2000). Invisible support and adjustment to stress. *Journal of Personality and Social Psychology, 79,* 953–961.

Bolles, R. C., & Fanselow, M. S. (1982). Endorphins and behavior. *Annual Review of Psychology, 33,* 87–101.

Bombardier, C., Gorayeb, R., Jordan, J., Brooks, W. B., & Divine, G. (1991). The utility of the psychosomatic system checklist among hospitalized patients. *Journal of Behavioral Medicine, 14,* 369–382.

Bonanno, G. A., et al. (2002). Resilience to loss and chronic grief: A prospective study from preloss to 18-months postloss. *Journal of Personality and Social Psychology, 83,* 1150–1164.

Bonanno, G. A., Keltner, D., Holen, A., & Horowitz, M. J. (1995). When avoiding unpleasant emotions might not be such a bad thing: Verbal-autonomic response dissociation and midlife conjugal bereavement. *Journal of Personality and Social Psychology, 69,* 975–989.

Booth, A., & Amato, P. (1991). Divorce and psychological stress. *Journal of Health and Social Behavior, 32,* 396–407.

Bornschein, S., Hausteiner, C., Konrad, F., Förstl, H., & Zilker, T. (2006). Psychiatric morbidity and toxic burden in patients with environmental illness: A controlled study. *Psychosomatic Medicine, 68,* 104–109.

Boscarino, J. (2008). A prospective study of PTSD and early-age heart disease mortality among Vietnam veterans: Implications for surveillance and prevention. *Psychosomatic Medicine, 70,* 668–676.

Boscarino, J., & Chang, J. (1999). Higher abnormal leukocyte and lymphocyte counts 20 years after exposure to severe stress: Research and clinical implications. *Psychosomatic Medicine, 61,* 378–386.

Bosch, J. A., Engeland, C. G., Cacioppo, J. T., & Marucha, P. T. (2007). Depressive symptoms predict mucosal wound healing. *Psychosomatic Medicine, 69,* 597–605.

Bosch, N. M., Reise, H., Dietrich, A., Ormel, J., Verhulst, F. C., & Oldehinkel, A. J. (2009). Preadolescents' somatic and cognitive-affective depressive symptoms are differentially related to cardiac automatic function and cortisol: The TRAILS study. *Psychosomatic Medicine, 71,* 944–950.

Boskind-White, M., & White, W. C. (1983). *Bulimarexia: The binge/purge cycle.* New York: Norton.

Bosma, H., Marmot, M. G., Hemingway, H., Nicholson, A. C., Brunner, E., & Stanfeld, S. A. (1997). Low job control and risk of coronary heart disease in Whitehall II (prospective cohort) study. *British Medical Journal, 314,* 285.

Botvin, G. J., Dusenbury, L., Baker, E., James-Ortiz, S., Botvin, E. M., & Kerner, J. (1992). Smoking prevention among urban minority youth: Assessing effects on outcome and mediating variables. *Health Psychology, 11,* 290–299.

Bouchard, C. (2002). Genetic influences on body weight. In C. G. Fairburn & K. D. Brownell (Eds.), *Eating disorders and obesity: A comprehensive handbook* (pp. 16–21). New York: Guilford Press.

Bouchard, C., Tremblay, A., Despres, J. P., Nadeau, A., Lupien, P. J., Thierault, G., et al. (1990). The response to long-term overfeeding in identical twins. *The New England Journal of Medicine, 322,* 1477–1487.

Boudreaux, E. D., Baumann, B. M., Perry, J., Marks, D., Francies, S., Camargo, D., et al. (2008). Emergency department initiated treatments for tobacco: (EDITT): A pilot study. *Annals of Behavioral Medicine, 36,* 314–325.

Boutelle, K. N., Hannan, P., Fulkerson, J. A., Crow, S. J., & Stice, E. (2010). Obesity as a prospective predictor of depression In adolescent females. *Health Psychology, 29,* 293–298.

Boutelle, K. N., Kirschenbaum, D. S., Baker, R. C., & Mitchell, M. E. (1999). How can obese weight controllers minimize weight gain during the high risk holiday season? By self-monitoring very consistently. *Health Psychology, 18,* 364–368.

Bouton, M. E. (2000). A learning theory perspective on lapse, relapse, and the maintenance of behavior change. *Health Psychology, 19,* 57–63.

Bowen, A. M., Williams, M. L., Daniel, C. M., & Clayton, S. (2008). Internet based HIV prevention research targeting rural MSM: Feasibility, acceptability, and preliminary efficacy. *Journal of Behavioral Medicine, 31,* 463–477.

Bowen, D. J., Tomoyasu, N., Anderson, M., Carney, M., & Kristal, A. (1992). Effects of expectancies and personalized feedback on fat consumption, taste, and preference. *Journal of Applied Social Psychology, 22,* 1061–1079.

Bower, J. E., Kemeny, M. E., Taylor, S. E., & Fahey, J. L. (1997). Cognitive processing, discovery of meaning, CD 4 decline, and AIDS-related mortality among bereaved HIV-seropositive men. *Journal of Consulting and Clinical Psychology, 66,* 979–986.

Bower, J. E., Kemeny, M. E., Taylor, S. E., & Fahey, J. L. (2003). Finding meaning and its association with natural killer cell cytotoxicity among participants in bereavement-related disclosure intervention. *Annals of Behavioral Medicine, 25,* 146–155.

Boyce, W. T., Alkon, A., Tschann, J. M., Chesney, M. A., & Alpert, B. S. (1995). Dimensions of psychobiologic reactivity: Cardiovascular responses to laboratory stressors in preschool children. *Annals of Behavioral Medicine, 17,* 315–323.

Boyce, W. T., Chesney, M., Alkon, A., Tschann, J. M., Adams, S., Chesterman, B., et al. (1995). Psychobiologic reactivity to stress and childhood respiratory illness: Results of two prospective studies. *Psychosomatic Medicine, 57,* 411–422.

Boyce, W. T., Chesterman, E. A., Martin, N., Folkman, S., Cohen, F., & Wara, D. (1993). Immunologic changes occurring at kindergarten entry predict respiratory illnesses after the Loma Prieta earthquake. *Journal of Developmental and Behavioral Pediatrics, 14,* 296–303.

Boyle, P. A., Barnes, L. L., Buchman, A. S., & Bennett, D. A. (2009). Purpose in life is associated with mortality among community-dwelling older persons. *Psychosomatic Medicine, 71,* 574–579.

Boyle, S. H., Michalek, J. E., & Suarez, E. C. (2006). Covariation of psychological attributes and incident coronary heart disease in U.S. Air Force veterans of the Vietnam War. *Psychosomatic Medicine, 68,* 844–850.

Boyle, S. H., Williams, R. B., Mark, D. B., Brummett, B. H., Siegler, I. C., Helms, M. J., et al. (2004). Hostility as a predictor of survival in patients with coronary artery disease. *Psychosomatic Medicine, 66,* 629–632.

Bradley, L. A., Young, L. D., Anderson, K. O., Turner, R. A., Agudelo, C. A., McDaniel, L. K., et al. (1987). Effects of psychological therapy on pain behavior of rheumatoid arthritis patients: Treatment outcome and six-month followup. *Arthritis and Rheumatism, 30,* 1105–1114.

Bramwell, L. (1986). Wives' experiences in the support role after husbands' first myocardial infarction. *Heart and Lung, 15,* 578–584.

Brand, A. H., Johnson, J. H., & Johnson, S. B. (1986). Life stress and diabetic control in children and adolescents with insulin-dependent diabetes. *Journal of Pediatric Psychology, 11,* 481–495.

Branegan, J. (1997, March 17). I want to draw the line myself. *Time,* pp. 30–31.

Bränström, R., Kvillemo, P., Brandberg, Y., & Moskowitz, J. T. (2010). Self-report mindfulness as a mediator of psychological well-being in a stress reduction intervention for cancer patients—A randomized study. *Annals of Behavioral Medicine, 39,* 151–161.

Brantley, P. J., Dutton, G. R., Grothe, K. B., Bodenlos, J. S., Howe, J., & Jones, G. N. (2005). Minor life events as predictors of medical utilization in low income African American family practice patients. *Journal of Behavioral Medicine, 28,* 395–401.

Brantley, P. J., Mosley, T. H., Jr., Bruce, B. K., McKnight, G. T., & Jones, G. N. (1990). Efficacy of behavioral management and patient education on vascular access cleansing compliance in hemodialysis patients. *Health Psychology, 9,* 103–113.

Brennan, P. L., & Moos, R. H. (1990). Life stressors, social resources, and late-life problem drinking. *Psychology and Aging, 5,* 491–501.

Brennan, P. L., & Moos, R. H. (1995). Life context, coping responses, and adaptive outcomes: A stress and coping perspective on late-life problem drinking. In T. Beresford & E. Gomberg (Eds.), *Alcohol and aging* (pp. 230–248). New York: Oxford University Press.

Brenner, G. F., Melamed, B. G., & Panush, R. S. (1994). Optimism and coping as determinants of psychosocial adjustment to rheumatoid arthritis. *Journal of Clinical Psychology in Medical Settings, 1,* 115–134.

Breslau, N., & Davis, G. C. (1987). Posttraumatic stress disorder: The stressor criterion. *Journal of Nervous and Mental Disease, 175,* 255–264.

Breslow, L., & Enstrom, J. E. (1980). Persistence of health habits and their relationship to mortality. *Preventive Medicine, 9,* 469–483.

Brewer, N. T., Chapman, G. B., Gibbons, F. X., Gerrard, M., McCaul, K. D., & Weinstein, N. D. (2007). Meta-analysis of the relationship between risk perception and health behavior: The example of vaccination. *Health Psychology, 26,* 136–145.

Brewer, N. T., Weinstein, N. D., Cuite, C. L., & Herrington, J. E. (2004). Risk perceptions and their relation to risk behavior. *Annals of Behavioral Medicine, 27,* 125–130.

Dilcker, J. B., Rajan, B., Zalewski, M., Andersen, M. R., Ramey, M., & Peterson, A. V. (2009). Psychological and social risk factors in adolescent smoking transitions: A population-based longitudinal study. *Health Psychology, 28,* 439–447.

Brissette, I., & Cohen, S. (2002). The contribution of individual differences in hostility to the associations between daily interpersonal conflict, affect, and sleep. *Personality and Social Psychology Bulletin, 28,* 1265–1274.

Brissette, I., Scheier, M. F., & Carver, C. S. (2002). The role of optimism in social network development, coping, and psychological adjustment during a life transition. *Journal of Personality and Social Psychology, 82,* 102–111.

Brisson, C., LaFlamme, N., Moisan, J., Milot, A., Masse, B., & Vezina, M. (1999). Effect of family responsibilities and job strain on ambulatory blood pressure among white-collar women. *Psychosomatic Medicine, 61,* 205–213.

Brisson, C., Leblanc, R., Bourbonnais, R., Maunsell, E., Dagenais, G. R., Vézina, M., et al. (2005). Psychological distress in postmyocardial infarction patients who have returned to work. *Psychosomatic Medicine, 67,* 59–63.

Britton, A., & Marmot, M. (2004). Different measures of alcohol consumption and risk of coronary heart disease and all-cause mortality: 11-year follow-up of the Whitehall II Cohort Study. *Addiction, 99,* 109–116.

Broadbent, E., Ellis, C. J., Gamble, G., & Petrie, K. J. (2006). Changes in patient drawings of the heart identify slow recovery after myocardial infarction. *Psychosomatic Medicine, 68,* 910–913.

Broadbent, E., Niederhoffer, K., Hague, T., Corter, A., & Reynolds, L. (2009). Headache sufferers' drawings reflect distress, disability and illness perceptions. *Journal of Psychosomatic Research, 66,* 465–470.

Broadbent, E., Petrie, K. J., Alley, P. G., & Booth, R. J. (2003). Psychological stress impairs early wound repair following surgery. *Psychosomatic Medicine, 65,* 865–869.

Broadbent, E., Petrie, K. J., Ellis, C. J., Ying, J., & Gamble, G. (2004). A picture of health—myocardial infarction patients' drawings of their hearts and subsequent disability: A longitudinal study. *Journal of Psychosomatic Research, 57,* 583–587.

Broadbent, E., Stafford, R., & MacDonald, B. (2009). Acceptance of healthcare robots for the older population: Review and future directions. *International Journal of Social Robotics, 1,* 319–330.

Broadwell, S. D., & Light, K. C. (1999). Family support and cardiovascular responses in married couples during conflict and other interactions. *International Journal of Behavioral Medicine, 6,* 40–63.

Broderick, J. E., Junghaenel, D. U., & Schwartz, J. E. (2005). Written emotional expression produces health benefits in fibromyalgia patients. *Psychosomatic Medicine, 67,* 326–334.

Brody, J. E. (2002, January 22). Misunderstood opioids and needless pain. *New York Times,* p. D8.

Broman, C. L. (1993). Social relationships and health-related behavior. *Journal of Behavioral Medicine, 16,* 335–350.

Brondolo, E., Libby, D. J., Denton, E., Thompson, S., Beatty, D. L., Schwartz, J., et al. (2008). Racism and ambulatory blood pressure in a community sample. *Psychosomatic Medicine, 70,* 49–56.

Brondolo, E., Rieppi, R., Erickson, S. A., Bagiella, E., Shapiro, P. A., KcKinley, P., et al. (2003). Hostility, interpersonal interactions, and ambulatory blood pressure. *Psychosomatic Medicine, 65,* 1003–1011.

Brondolo, E., Rieppi, R., Kelly, K. P., & Gerin, W. (2003). Perceived racism and blood pressure: A review of the literature and conceptual and methodological critique. *Annals of Behavioral Medicine, 25,* 55–65.

Brondolo, E., Rosen, R. C., Kostis, J. B., & Schwartz, J. E. (1999). Relationship of physical symptoms and mood to perceived and actual blood pressure in hypertensive men: A repeated-measure design. *Psychosomatic Medicine, 61,* 311–318.

Brondolo, E., ver Halen, N. B., Pencille, M., Beatty, D., & Contrada, R. J. (2009). Coping with racism: A selective review of the literature and a theoretical and methodological critique. *Journal of Behavioral Medicine, 32,* 64–88.

Brosschot, J., Godaert, G., Benschop, R., Olff, M., Ballieux, R., & Heijnen, C. (1998). Experimental stress and immunological reactivity: A closer look at perceived uncontrollability. *Psychosomatic Medicine, 60,* 359–361.

Brown, G. W., & Harris, T. (1978). *Social origins of depression: A study of psychiatric disorder in women.* New York: Free Press.

Brown, J. D., & McGill, K. L. (1989). The cost of good fortune: When positive life events produce negative health consequences. *Journal of Personality and Social Psychology, 57,* 1103–1110.

Brown, J. D., & Siegel, J. M. (1988). Exercise as a buffer of life stress: A prospective study of adolescent health. *Health Psychology, 7,* 341–353.

Brown, J. L., Sheffield, D., Leary, M. R., & Robinson, M. E. (2003). Social support and experimental pain. *Psychosomatic Medicine, 65,* 276–283.

Brown, J. L., & Vanable, P. A. (2008). Cognitive-behavioral stress management interventions for persons living with HIV: A review and critique of the literature. *Annals of Behavioral Medicine, 35,* 26–40.

Brown, J. P., Sollers, J. J., Thayer, J. F., Zonderman, A. B., & Waldstein, S. R. (2009). Blood pressure reactivity and cognitive function in the Baltimore longitudinal study of aging. *Health Psychology, 28,* 641–646.

Brown, K. M., Middaugh, S. J., Haythornthwaite, J. A., & Bielory, L. (2001). The effects of stress, anxiety and outdoor temperature on the frequency and severity of Raynaud's attacks: The Raynaud treatment study. *Journal of Behavioral Medicine, 24,* 137–153.

Brown, K. W., Levy, A. R., Rosberger, Z., & Edgar, L. (2003). Psychological distress and cancer survival: A follow-up 10 years after diagnosis. *Psychosomatic Medicine, 65,* 636–643.

Brown, K. W., & Ryan, R. M. (2003). The benefits of being present: Mindfulness and its role in psychological well-being. *Journal of Personality and Social Psychology, 84,* 822–848.

Brown, S. L. (1997). Prevalence and effectiveness of self-regulatory techniques used to avoid drunk driving. *Journal of Behavioral Medicine, 20,* 55–66.

Brown, S. L., Nesse, R. M., Vinokur, A. D., & Smith, D. M. (2003). Providing social support may be more beneficial than receiving it: Results from a prospective study of mortality. *Psychological Science, 14,* 320–327.

Brownell, K. D. (1982). Obesity: Understanding and treating a serious, prevalent and refractory disorder. *Journal of Consulting and Clinical Psychology, 50,* 820–840.

Brownell, K. D., Cohen, R. Y., Stunkard, A. J., Felix, M. R. J., & Cooley, B. (1984). Weight loss competitions at the work site: Impact on weight, morale, and cost-effectiveness. *American Journal of Public Health, 74,* 1283–1285.

Brownell, K. D., & Felix, M. R. J. (1987). Competitions to facilitate health promotion: Review and conceptual analysis. *American Journal of Health Promotion, 2,* 28–36.

Brownell, K. D., & Frieden, T. R. (2009). Ounces of prevention – The public policy cases for taxes on sugared beverages. *The New England Journal of Medicine, 360,* 1805–1808.

Brownell, K. D., Greenwood, M. R. C., Stellar, E., & Shrager, E. E. (1986). The effects of repeated cycles of weight loss and regain in rats. *Physiology and Behavior, 38,* 459–464.

Brownell, K. D., & Kramer, F. M. (1989). Behavioral management of obesity. *Medical Clinics of North America, 73,* 185–201.

Brownell, K. D., Marlatt, G. A., Lichtenstein, E., & Wilson, G. T. (1986). Understanding and preventing relapse. *American Psychologist, 41,* 765–782.

Brownell, K. D., & Napolitano, M. A. (1995). Distorting reality for children: Body size proportions of Barbie and Ken dolls. *International Journal of Eating Disorders, 18,* 295–298.

Brownell, K. D., & Rodin, J. (1996). The dieting maelstrom: Is it possible and advisable to lose weight? *American Psychologist, 49,* 781–791.

Brownell, K. D., Steen, S. N., & Wilmore, J. H. (1987). Weight regulation practices in athletes: Analysis of metabolic and health effects. *Medicine and Science in Sports and Exercise, 19,* 546–556.

Brownell, K. D., & Stunkard, A. J. (1981). Couples training, pharmacotherapy and behavior therapy in the treatment of obesity. *Archives of General Psychiatry, 38,* 1224–1229.

Brownell, K. D., Stunkard, A. J., & McKeon, P. E. (1985). Weight reduction at the work site: A promise partially fulfilled. *American Journal of Psychiatry, 142,* 47–52.

Brownell, K. D., & Wadden, T. A. (1992). Etiology and treatment of obesity: Understanding a serious, prevalent, and refractory disorder. *Journal of Consulting and Clinical Psychology, 60,* 505–517.

Browning, C. R., & Cagney, K. A. (2003). Moving beyond poverty: Neighboring structure, social processes, and health. *Journal of Health and Social Behavior, 44,* 552–571.

Browning, L., Ryan, C. S., Greenberg, M. S., & Rolniak, S. (2006). Effects of cognitive adaptation on the expectation-burnout relationship among nurses. *Journal of Behavioral Medicine, 29,* 139–150.

Brownley, K. A., West, S. G., Hinderliter, A. L., & Light, K. C. (1996). Acute aerobic exercise reduces ambulatory blood pressure in borderline hypertensive men and women. *American Journal of Hypertension, 9,* 200–206.

Brubaker, R. G., & Wickersham, D. (1990). Encouraging the practice of testicular self-examination: A field application of the theory of reasoned action. *Health Psychology, 9,* 154–163.

Bruce, E. C., & Musselman, D. L. (2005). Depression, alterations in platelet function, and ischemic heat disease. *Psychosomatic Medicine, 67,* S34–S36.

Bruce, J. M., Hancock, L. M., Arnett, P., & Lynch, S. (2010). Treatment adherence in multiple sclerosis: Associations with emotional status, personality, and cognition. *Journal of Behavioral Medicine, 33,* 219–227.

Bruehl, S., al'Absi, M., France, C. R., France, J., Harju, A., Burns, J. W., et al. (2007). Anger management style and endogenous opioid function: Is gender a moderator? *Journal of Behavioral Medicine, 30,* 209–219.

Bruehl, S., Burns, J. W., Chung, O. Y., & Quartana, P. (2008). Anger management style and emotional reactivity to noxious stimuli among chronic pain patients and healthy controls: The role of endogenous opioids. *Health Psychology, 27,* 204–214.

Brummett, B. H., Babyak, M. A., Barefoot, J. C., Bosworth, H. B., Clapp-Channing, N. E., Siegler, I. C., et al. (1998). Social support and hostility as predictors of depressive symptoms in cardiac patients one month after hospitalization: A prospective study. *Psychosomatic Medicine, 60,* 707–713.

Brummet, B. H., Babyak, M. A., Mark, D. B., Clapp-Channing, N. E., Siegler, I. C., & Barefoot, J. C. (2004). Prospective study of perceived stress in cardiac patients. *Annals of Behavioral Medicine, 27,* 22–30.

Brummett, B. H., Babyak, M. A., Siegler, I. C., Vitaliano, P. P., Ballard, E. L., Gwyther, L. P., et al. (2006). Associations among perceptions of social support, negative affect, and quality of sleep in caregivers and noncaregivers. *Health Psychology, 25,* 220–225.

Brummett, B. H., Boyle, S. H., Ortel, T. L., Becker, R. C., Siegler, I. C., & Williams, R. B. (2010). Association of depressive symptoms, trait hostility, and gender with C-reactive and interleukin-6 responses after emotion recall. *Psychosomatic Medicine, 72,* 333–339.

Brummett, B. H., Siegler, I. C., Rohe, W. M., Barefoot, J. C., Vitaliano, P. P., Surwit, R. S., et al. (2005). Neighborhood characteristics moderate effects of caregiving on glucose functioning. *Psychosomatic Medicine, 67,* 752–758.

Bryan, A., Fisher, J. D., & Fisher, W. A. (2002). Tests of the mediational role of preparatory safer sexual behavior in the context of the theory or planned behavior. *Health Psychology, 21,* 71–80.

Bryant, R. A., & Guthrie, R. M. (2005). Maladaptive appraisals as a risk factor for posttraumatic stress: A study of trainee firefighters. *Psychological Science, 16,* 749–752.

Buchman, A. S., Boyle, P. A., Wilson, R. S., Tang, Y., & Bennett, D. A. (2007). Frailty is associated with incident Alzheimer's disease and cognitive decline in the elderly. *Psychosomatic Medicine, 69,* 483–489.

Buchman, A. S., Kopf, D., Westphal, S., Lederbogen, F., Banaschewski, T., Esser, G., et al. (2010). Impact of early parental child-rearing behavior on young adults' cardiometabolic risk profile: A prospective study. *Psychosomatic Medicine, 72,* 156–162.

Buchwald, D., Herrell, R., Ashton, S., Belcourt, M., Schmaling, K., Sullivan, P. et al. (2001). A twin study of chronic fatigue. *Psychosomatic Medicine, 63,* 936–943.

Budman, S. H. (2000). Behavioral health care dot-com and beyond: Computer-mediated communications in mental health and substance abuse treatment. *American Psychologist, 55,* 1290–1300.

Bukberg, J., Penman, D., & Holland, J. C. (1984). Depression in hospitalized cancer patients. *Psychosomatic Medicine, 46,* 199–212.

Bulik, C. M., Thornton, L., Pinheiro, A. P., Plotnicov, K., Klump, K. L., Brandt, H., et al. (2008). Suicide attempts in anorexia nervosa. *Psychosomatic Medicine, 70,* 378–383.

Buller, D. B., Buller, M. K., & Kane, I. (2005). Web-based strategies to disseminate a sun safety curriculum to public elementary schools and state-licensed child-care facilities. *Health Psychology, 24,* 470–476.

Bunde, J., & Martin, R. (2006). Depression and prehospital delay in the context of myocardial infarction. *Psychosomatic Medicine, 68,* 51–57.

Bureau of Labor Statistics. (2004). *Industry-occupation employment matrix.* Retrieved from http://data.bls.gov/oep/nioem/empiohm.jsp

Burell, G., & Granlund, B. (2002). Women's hearts need special treatment. *International Journal of Behavioral Medicine, 9,* 228–242.

Burg, M. M., Barefoot, J., Berkman, L., Catellier, D. J., Czajkowski, S., Saab, P., et al. (2005). Low perceived social support and post-myocardial infarction prognosis in the enhancing recovery in coronary heart disease clinical trial: The effects of treatment. *Psychosomatic Medicine, 67,* 879–888.

Burg, M. M., Benedetto, M. C., Rosenberg, R., & Soufer, R. (2003). Presurgical depression predicts medical mortality 6 months after coronary artery bypass graft surgery. *Psychosomatic Medicine, 65,* 111–118.

Burgard, S. A., & Ailshire, J. A. (2009). Putting work to bed: Stressful experiences on the job and sleep quality. *Journal of Health and Social Behavior, 50,* 476–492.

Burgard, S. A., Brand, J. E., & House, J. S. (2007). Toward a better estimation of the effect of job loss on health. *Journal of Health and Social Behavior, 48,* 369–384.

Burgess, C., Morris, T., & Pettingale, K. W. (1988). Psychological response to cancer diagnosis: II. Evidence for coping styles. *Journal of Psychosomatic Research, 32,* 263–272.

Burish, T. G., Carey, M. P., Wallston, K. A., Stein, M. J., Jamison, R. N., & Lyles, J. N. (1984). Health locus of control and chronic disease: An external orientation may be advantageous. *Journal of Social and Clinical Psychology, 2,* 326–332.

Burish, T. G., & Lyles, J. N. (1979). Effectiveness of relaxation training in reducing the aversiveness of chemotherapy in the treatment of cancer. *Journal of Behavior Therapy and Experimental Psychiatry, 10,* 357–361.

Burnam, M. A., Timbers, D. M., & Hough, R. L. (1984). Two measures of psychological distress among Mexican Americans, Mexicans and Anglos. *Journal of Health and Social Behavior, 25,* 24–33.

Burns, J. W. (2000). Repression predicts outcome following multidisciplinary treatment of chronic pain. *Health Psychology, 19,* 75–84.

Burns, J. W., Elfant, E., & Quartana, P. J. (2010). Supression of pain-related thoughts and feelings during pain-induction: Sex differences in delayed pain responses. *Journal of Behavioral Medicine, 33,* 200–208.

Burns, J. W., & Evon, D. (2007). Common and specific process factors in cardiac rehabilitation: Independent and interactive effects of the working alliance and self-efficacy. *Health Psychology, 26,* 684–692.

Burns, J. W., Holly, A., Quartana, P., Wolff, B., Gray, E., & Bruehl, S. (2008). Trait anger management style moderates effects of actual ("state") anger regulation on symptom-specific reactivity and recovery among chronic low back pain patients. *Psychosomatic Medicine, 70,* 898–905.

Burns, J. W., Quartana, P., & Bruehl, S. (2008). Anger inhibition and pain: Conceptualizations, evidence and new directions. *Journal of Behavioral Medicine, 31,* 259–279.

Burton, R. P. D. (1998). Global integrative meaning as a mediating factor in the relationship between social roles and psychological distress. *Journal of Health and Social Behavior, 39,* 201–215.

Bush, C., Ditto, B., & Feuerstein, M. (1985). A controlled evaluation of paraspinal EMG biofeedback in the treatment of chronic low back pain. *Health Psychology, 4,* 307–321.

Businelle, M. S., Kendzor, D. E., Reitzel, L. R., Costello, T. J., Cofta-Woerpel, L., Li, Y., et al. (2010). Mechanisms linking socioeconomic status to smoking cessation: A structural equation modeling approach. *Health Psychology, 29,* 262–273.

Buske-Kirschbaum, A., von Auer, K., Kreiger, S., Weis, S., Rauh, W., & Hellhammer, D. (2003). Blunted cortisol responses to psychosocial stress in asthmatic children: A general feature of atopic disease? *Psychosomatic Medicine, 65,* 806–810.

Butler, L. D., Koopman, C., Classen, C., & Spiegel, D. (1999). Traumatic stress, life events, and emotional support in women with metastatic breast cancer: Cancer-related traumatic stress symptoms associated with past and current stressors. *Health Psychology, 18,* 555–560.

Butler, L. D., Koopman, C., Neri, E., Giese-Davis, J., Palesh, O., Thorne-Yocam, K. A., et al. (2009). Effects of supportive-expressive group therapy on pain in women with metastatic breast cancer. *Health Psychology, 28,* 579–587.

Butler, R. N. (1978). The doctor and the aged patient. In W. Reichel (Ed.), *The geriatric patient* (pp. 199–206). New York: HP.

Buunk, B. P., Doosje, B. J., Jans, L. G. J. M., & Hopstaken, L. E. M. (1993). Perceived reciprocity, social support, and stress at work: The role of exchange and communal orientation. *Journal of Personality and Social Psychology, 65,* 801–811.

Cabizuca, M., Marques-Portella, C., Mendlowicz, M. V., Coutinho, E. S. F., & Figueira, I. (2009). Posttraumatic stress disorders in parents with children with chronic illness: A meta-analysis. *Health Psychology, 28,* 379–388.

Cacioppo, J. T., Hawkley, L. C., Crawford, L. E., Ernst, J. M., Burleson, M. H., Kowalewski, R. B., et al. (2002). Loneliness and health: Potential mechanisms. *Psychosomatic Medicine, 64,* 407–417.

Cafri, G., Thompson, J. K., Jacobsen, P. B., & Hillhouse, J. (2009). Investigating the role of appearance-based factors in predicting sunbathing and tanning salon use. *Journal of Behavioral Medicine, 32,* 532–544.

Calfas, K. J., et al. (1997). Mediators of change in physical activity following an intervention in primary care: PACE. *Preventive Medicine, 26,* 297–304.

California Environmental Protection Agency. (2005). *Proposed identification of environmental tobacco smoke as a toxic air contaminant, part B: Health effects.* Retrieved October 20, 2009, from http://www.oehha.org/air/environmental_tobacco/pdf/app3partb2005.pdf

Callahan, D. (2003). *What price better health? Hazards of the research imperative.* Berkeley: University of California Press.

Calle, E. E., Rodriguez, C., Walker-Thurmond, K., & Thun, M. J. (2003). Overweight, obesity, and mortality from cancer in a prospectively studied cohort in U.S. adults. *The New England Journal of Medicine, 348,* 1625–1638.

Cameron, C. L., Cella, D., Herndon, J. E., II, Kornblith, A. B., Zuckerman, E., Henderson, E., et al. (2001). Persistent symptoms among survivors of Hodgkin's disease: An explanatory model based on classical conditioning. *Health Psychology, 20,* 71–75.

Cameron, E. Z., Setsaas, T. H., & Linklater, W. L. (2009). Social bonds between unrelated females increase reproductive success in feral horses. *Proceedings of the National Academy of Sciences of the USA,* 106:13850–13853.

Cameron, L., Booth, R. J., Schlatter, M., Ziginskas, D., Harman, J. E., & Benson, S. R. C. (2005). Cognitive and affective determinants of decisions to attend a group psychosocial support program for women with breast cancer. *Psychosomatic Medicine, 67,* 584–589.

Cameron, L., Leventhal, E. A., & Leventhal, H. (1995). Seeking medical care in response to symptoms and life stress. *Psychosomatic Medicine, 57,* 1–11.

Cameron, L. D., Sherman, K. A., Marteau, T. M., & Brown, P. M. (2009). Impact of genetic risk information and type of disease on perceived risk, anticipated affect, and expected consequences of genetic tests. *Health Psychology, 28,* 307–316.

Campbell, M. K., James, A., Hudson, M. A., Carr, C., Jackson, E., Oates, V., et al. (2004). Improving multiple behaviors for colorectal cancer prevention among African American church members. *Health Psychology, 23,* 492–502.

Campbell, M. K., McLerran, D., Turner-McGrievy, G., Feng, Z., Havas, S., Sorensen, G., et al. (2008). Mediation of adult fruit and vegetable consumption in the national 5 a day for better health community studies. *Annals of Behavioral Medicine, 35,* 49–60.

Campbell, T. S., Key, B. L., Ireland, A. D., Bacon, S. L., & Ditto, B. (2008). Early socioeconomic status is associated with adult nighttime blood pressure dipping. *Psychosomatic Medicine, 70,* 276–281.

Cankaya, B., Chapman, B. P., Talbot, N. L., Moynihan, J., & Duberstein, P. R. (2009). History of sudden unexpected loss is associated with elevated interleukin-6 and decreased insulin-like growth factor-1 in women in an urban primary care setting. *Psychosomatic Medicine, 71,* 914–919.

Cannon, C. P., Braunwald, E., McCabe, C. H., Rader, D. J., Rouleau, J. L., Belder, R., et al. (2004). Intensive versus moderate lipid lowering with statins after acute coronary syndromes. *The New England Journal of Medicine, 350,* 1495–1504.

Cannon, W. B. (1932). *The wisdom of the body.* New York: Norton.

Carels, R. A., Darby, L., Cacciapaglia, H. M., Konrad, K., Coit, C., Harper, J., et al. (2007). Using motivational interviewing as a supplement to obesity treatment: A stepped-care approach. *Health Psychology, 26,* 369–374.

Carels, R. A., Wott, C. B., Young, K. M., Gumble, A., Darby, L. A., Oehlhof, M. W., et al. (2009). Successful weight loss with self-help: A stepped-care approach. *Journal of Behavioral Medicine, 32,* 503–509.

Carey, J. (2002, November 11). Waking up a sleeping anticancer gene. *Business Week,* p. 82.

Carey, M. P. (1999). Prevention of HIV infection through changes in sexual behavior. *American Journal of Health Promotion, 14,* 104–111.

Carey, M. P., & Burish, T. G. (1988). Etiology and treatment of the psychological side effects associated with cancer chemotherapy: A critical review and discussion. *Psychological Bulletin, 104,* 307–325.

Carey, M. P., Coury-Doniger, P., Senn, T. E., Vanable, P. A., & Urban, M. A. (2008). Improving HIV rapid testing rates among STD clinic patients: A randomized controlled trial. *Health Psychology, 27,* 833–838.

Carlson, L. E., Speca, M., Patel, K. D., & Goodey, E. (2003). Mindfulness-based stress reduction in relation to quality of life, mood, symptoms of stress, and immune parameters in breast and prostate cancer outpatients. *Psychosomatic Medicine, 65,* 571–581.

Carmack Taylor, C. L., Badr, H., Lee, J. H., Fossella, F., Pisters, K., Gritz, E. R., et al. (2008). Lung cancer patients and their spouses: Psychological and relationship functioning within 1 month of treatment initiation. *Annals of Behavioral Medicine, 36,* 129–140.

Carmin, C. N., Weigartz, P. S., Hoff, J. A., & Kondos, G. T. (2003). Cardiac anxiety in patients self-referred for electron beam tomography. *Journal of Behavioral Medicine, 26,* 67–80.

Carmody, J., & Baer, R. A. (2008). Relationships between mindfulness practice and levels of mindfulness, medical and psychological symptoms and well-being in a mindfulness-based stress reduction program. *Journals of Behavioral Medicine, 31,* 23–33.

Carmody, T. P., Matarazzo, J. D., & Istvan, J. A. (1987). Promoting adherence to heart-healthy diets: A review of the literature. *Journal of Compliance in Health Care, 2,* 105–124.

Carney, C. P., Jones, L., Woolson, R. F., Noyes, R., & Doebbeling, B. N. (2003). Relationship between depression and pancreatic cancer in the general population. *Psychosomatic Medicine, 65,* 884–888.

Carney, R. M., Freedland, K. E., Stein, P. K., Skala, J. A., Hoffman, P., & Jaffe, A. S. (2000). Change in heart rate and heart rate variability during treatment of depression in patients with coronary heart disease. *Psychosomatic Medicine, 62,* 639–647.

Carney, R. M., Freedland, K. E., Steinmeyer, B., Blumenthal, J. A., de Jonge, P., Davidson, K. W., et al. (2009). History of depression and survival after acute myocardial infarction. *Psychosomatic Medicine, 71,* 253–259.

Carney, R. M., Howells, W. B., Blumenthal, J. A., Freedland, K. E., Stein, P. K., Berkman, L. F., et al. (2007). Heart rate turbulence, depression, and survival after acute myocardial infarction. *Psychosomatic Medicine, 69,* 4–9.

Carpenter, K. M., Fowler, J. M., Maxwell, G. L., & Andersen, B. L. (2010). Direct and buffering effects of social support among gynecologic cancer survivors. *Annals of Behavioral Medicine, 39,* 79–90.

Carr, D. (2009). Who's to blame? Perceived responsibility for spousal death and psychological distress among older widowed persons. *Journal of Health and Social Behavior, 50,* 359–375.

Carr, D., & Friedman, M. A. (2005). Is obesity stigmatizing? Body weight, perceived discrimination, and psychological well-being in the United States. *Journal of Health and Social Behavior, 46,* 244–259.

Carrico, A. W., & Antoni, M. H. (2008). Effects of psychological interventions on neuroendocrine hormone regulation and immune status in HIV-positive persons: A review of randomized controlled trials. *Psychosomatic Medicine, 70,* 575–584.

Carrico, A. W., Johnson, M. O., Moskowitz, J. T., Neilands, T. B., Morin, S. F., Charlebois, E. D., et al. (2007). Affect regulation, stimulant use, and viral load among HIV-positive persons on anti-retroviral therapy. *Psychosomatic Medicine, 69,* 785–792.

Carroll, D., Smith, G. D., Shipley, M. J., Steptoe, A., Brunner, E. J., & Marmot, M. G. (2001). Blood pressure reactions to acute psychological stress and future blood pressure status: A 10-year follow-up of men in the Whitehall II study. *Psychosomatic Medicine, 63,* 737–743.

Carroll, J. (2007). Public divided over moral acceptability of doctor-assisted suicide. *Gallup News Services.* Retrieved September 25, 2009, from http://www.gallup.com/poll/27727/public-divided-over-moral-acceptability-doctorassisted-suicide.aspx

Carver, C. S. (1997). You want to measure coping but your protocol's too long: Consider the Brief COPE. *International Journal of Behavioral Medicine, 4,* 92–100.

Carver, C. S., & Antoni, M. H. (2004). Finding benefit in breast cancer during the year after diagnosis predicts better adjustment 5 to 8 years after diagnosis. *Health Psychology, 23,* 565–598.

Carver, C. S., Lehman, J. M., & Antoni, M. H. (2003). Dispositional pessimism predicts illness-related disruption of social and recreational activities among breast cancer patients. *Journal of Personality and Social Psychology, 84,* 813–821.

Carver, C. S., Pozo-Kaderman, C., Price, A. A., Noriega, V., Harris, S. D., Derhagopian, R. P., et al. (1998). Concern about aspects of body image and adjustment to early stage breast cancer. *Psychosomatic Medicine, 60,* 168–174.

Carver, C. S., Scheier, M. F., & Weintraub, J. K. (1989). Assessing coping strategies: A theoretically based approach. *Journal of Personality and Social Psychology, 56,* 267–283.

Carver, C. S., Smith, R. G., Antoni, M. H., Petronis, V. M., Weiss, S., & Derhagopian, R. P. (2005). Optimistic personality and psychosocial well-being during treatment predict psychosocial well-being among long-term survivors of breast cancer. *Health Psychology, 24,* 508–516.

Casey, E., Hughes, J. W., Waechter, D., Josephson, R., & Rosneck, J. (2008). Depression predicts failure to complete phase-II cardiac rehabilitation. *Journal of Behavioral Medicine, 31,* 421–431.

Cassileth, B. R., Lusk, E. J., Strouse, T. B., Miller, D. S., Brown, L. L., & Cross, P. A. (1985). A psychological analysis of cancer patients and their next-of-kin. *Cancer, 55,* 72–76.

Cassileth, B. R., Temoshok, L., Frederick, B. E., Walsh, W. P., Hurwitz, S., Guerry, D., et al. (1988). Patient and physician delay in melanoma diagnosis. *Journal of the American Academy of Dermatology, 18,* 591–598.

Castro, C. M., King, A. C., & Brassington, G. S. (2001). Telephone versus mail interventions for maintenance of physical activity in older adults. *Health Psychology, 20,* 438–444.

Castro, C. M., Wilcox, S., O'Sullivan, P., Bauman, K., & King, A. C. (2002). An exercise program for women who are caring for relatives with dementia. *Psychosomatic Medicine, 64,* 458–468.

Castro, F. G., Newcomb, M. D., McCreary, C., & Baezconde-Garbanati, L. (1989). Cigarette smokers do more than just smoke cigarettes. *Health Psychology, 8,* 107–129.

Castro, F. G., Shaibi, G. Q., & Boehm-Smith, E. (2009). Ecodevelopmental contexts for preventing type 2 diabetes in Latino and other racial/ethnic minority populations. *Journal of Behavioral Medicine, 32,* 89–105.

Catalano, R., Dooley, D., Wilson, C., & Hough, R. (1993). Job loss and alcohol abuse: A test using data from the epidemiologic catchment area. *Journal of Health and Social Behavior, 34,* 215–225.

Catalano, R., Hansen, H., & Hartig, T. (1999). The ecological effect of unemployment on the incidence of very low birthweight in Norway and Sweden. *Journal of Health and Social Behavior, 40,* 422–428.

Catania, J. A., Kegeles, S. M., & Coates, T. J. (1990). Towards an understanding of risk behavior: An AIDS risk reduction model (ARRM). *Health Education Quarterly, 17,* 53–72.

Catz, S. L., Kelly, J. A., Bogart, L. M., Benotsch, E. G., & McAuliffe, T. L. (2000). Patterns, correlates, and barriers to medication adherence among persons prescribed new treatments for HIV disease. *Health Psychology, 19,* 124–133.

Center for the Advancement of Health. (1999). *How managed care can help older persons live well with chronic conditions.* Washington, DC: Author.

Center for the Advancement of Health. (2000a). *Exercising your options: The benefits of physical activity.* Washington, DC: Author.

Center for the Advancement of Health. (2000b). *Selected evidence for behavioral approaches to chronic disease management in clinical settings. Cardiovascular disease.* Washington, DC: Author.

Center for the Advancement of Health. (2000c). *Selected evidence for behavioral approaches to chronic disease management in clinical settings: Chronic back pain.* Washington, DC: Author.

Center for the Advancement of Health. (2000d). *Selected evidence for behavioral approaches to chronic disease management in clinical settings: Depression.* Washington, DC: Author.

Center for the Advancement of Health. (2000e). *Selected evidence for behavioral approaches to chronic disease management in clinical settings: Diabetes.* Washington, DC: Author.

Center for the Advancement of Health. (2000f). *Selected evidence for behavioral risk reduction in clinical settings: Dietary practices.* Washington, DC: Author.

Center for the Advancement of Health. (2000g). *Selected evidence for behavioral risk reduction in clinical settings: Physical inactivity.* Washington, DC: Author.

Center for the Advancement of Health. (2000h). *Smoking.* Washington, DC: Author.

Center for the Advancement of Health. (2001). *Targeting the at-risk drinker with screening and advice.* Washington, DC: Author.

Center for the Advancement of Health. (2002, June). Point, click, heal. *Good Behavior!*

Center for the Advancement of Health. (2002, December). Life lessons: Studying education's effect on health. *Facts of Life, 7,* 1.

Center for the Advancement of Health. (2003, April). Lifestyle changes could prevent a third of world cancers. *Habit, 6.*

Center for the Advancement of Health. (2004, May). *Is our people healthy?* Washington, DC: Author.

Center for the Advancement of Health. (2005). *No killer apps in health information.* Washington, DC: Author.

Center for the Advancement of Health. (2006, March). A new vision of aging. *Good Behavior!*

Center for the Advancement of Health. (2006, October). November solutions. *Good Behavior!*

Center for the Advancement of Health. (2007, February). Lipstick-on-a-pig health reform. *Good Behavior!*

Center for the Advancement of Health. (2008). Larger patients: In search of fewer lectures, better health care. *The Prepared Patient, 1,* 1–2.

Center for the Advancement of Health. (2009). Taking charge of your health records. *The Prepared Patient, 2,* 1–2.

Centers for Disease Control and Prevention. (2002). Prevalence of diagnosed diabetes by age, United States, 1980–2002. *Diabetes Health Resource.*

Centers for Disease Control and Prevention. (2004a). *Facts about prevalence of arthritis—U.S. 2004.* Retrieved from http://www.cdc.gov/nccdphp/arthritis/

Centers for Disease Control and Prevention. (2004b). *Sudden infant death syndrome and vaccination.* Retrieved from: http://www.cdc.gov

Centers for Disease Control and Prevention. (2005, July). Annual smoking-attributable mortality, years of potential life lost, and productivity losses—United States, 1997–2001. *Morbidity and Mortality Weekly Report, 54*(25), 625–628. Retrieved October 26, 2006, from http://www.cdc.gov/mmwr/preview/mmwrhtml/mm5425a1.htm#tab

Centers for Disease Control and Prevention. (2006, May). *Healthy youth! Tobacco use.* Retrieved October 27, 2006, from http://www.cdc.gov/HealthyYouth/tobacco/facts.htm

Centers for Disease Control and Prevention. (2006, June). *National vital statistics report, deaths: Preliminary data for 2004.* Retrieved March 1, 2007, from http://www.cdc.gov/nchs/data/nvsr/nvsr54/nvsr54_19.pdf

Centers for Disease Control and Prevention. (2006, December). *Viral hepatitis.* Retrieved June 12, 2007, from http://www.cdc.gov/ncidod/diseases/hepatitis/index.htm

Centers for Disease Control and Prevention. (2008). Cigarette use among high school students—United States, 1991–2007. *Morbidity and Mortality Weekly Report, 57.* Retrieved October 19, 2009, from http://www.cdc.gov/mmwr/preview/mmwrhtml/mm5725a3.htm

Centers for Disease Control and Prevention. (2008a, January). *Arthritis types-overview.* Retrieved October 7, 2009, from http://www.cdc.gov/arthritis/arthritis/rheumatoid.htm

Centers for Disease Control and Prevention. (2008b, January). *Arthritis types-overview.* Retrieved October 7, 2009, from http://www.cdc.gov/arthritis/basics/osteoarthritis.htm

Centers for Disease Control and Prevention. (2008a, June). *Hepatitis C FAQs for the public.* Retrieved September 25, 2009, from http://www.cdc.gov/hepatitis/C/cFAQ.htm

Centers for Disease Control and Prevention. (2008b, June). *Quick stats on arthritis.* Retrieved October 8, 2009, from http://www.cdc.gov/arthritis/resources/quickstats.htm

Centers for Disease Control and Prevention. (2008a, July). *Hepatitis B FAQs for the public.* Retrieved September 25, 2009, from http://www.cdc.gov/hepatitis/B/bFAQ.htm

Centers for Disease Control and Prevention. (2008b, July). *2007 National Diabetes Fact Sheet.* Retrieved September 25, 2009, from http://www.cdc.gov/diabetes/pubs/estimates07.htm#1

Centers for Disease Control and Prevention. (2008, September). *Alcohol and public health.* Retrieved October 5, 2009, from http://www.cdc.gov/alcohol/index.htm

Centers for Disease Control and Prevention. (2008, October). *Arthritis data and statistics.* Retrieved October 7, 2009, from http://www.cdc.gov/arthritis/data_statistics/index.htm

Centers for Disease Control and Prevention. (2009a). *Obesity: Halting the epidemic by making health easier.* Retrieved September 28, 2009, from http://www.cdc.gov/nccdphp/publications/AAG/obesity.htm

Centers for Disease Control and Prevention. (2009b). *State indicator report on fruit and vegetables, 2009.* Retrieved September 30, 2009, from http://www.fruitsandveggiesmatter.gov/health_professionals/statereport.html

Centers for Disease Control and Prevention. (2009c). *Chronic diseases: The power to prevent, the call to control.* At a Glance 2009. Retrieved October 6, 2009, from http://www.cdc.gov/nccdphp/publications/AAG/chronic.htm

Centers for Disease Control and Prevention. (2009, February). *National poison prevention week.* Retrieved September 30, 2009, from http://www.cdc.gov/ncipc/duip/poisonweek.htm

Centers for Disease Control and Prevention. (2009, March). *Skin cancer prevention and education initiative.* Retrieved September 30, 2009, from http://www.cdc.gov/cancer/skin/pdf/sunsafety_v0908.pdf

Centers for Disease Control and Prevention. (2009, April). *National vital statistics report, deaths: Final data for 2006.* Retrieved September 25, 2009, from http://www.cdc.gov/nchs/data/nvsr/ nvsr57/nvsr57_14.pdf

Centers for Disease Control and Prevention. (2009, June). Estimates of health-care-associated infections. Retrieved February 2, 2011, from http://www.cdc.gov/hai

Centers for Disease Control and Prevention. (2009a, August). *10 leading causes of injury death by age group highlighting unintentional injury deaths, United States—2006.* Retrieved September 30, 2009, from http://www.cdc.gov/injury/Images/LC-Charts/10lc%20-Unintentional%20Injury%202006-7_6_09-a.pdf

Centers for Disease Control and Prevention. (2009b, August). *HIV/AIDS in the United States.* Retrieved October 8, 2009, from http://www.cdc.gov/hiv/resources/factsheets/us.htm

Centers for Disease Control and Prevention. (2009, September). *National child passenger safety week September 12–18, 2009.* Retrieved February 2, 2011, from http://www.cdc.gov/features/passengersafety/Child_Passenger_Safety/childseat-spot.html

Centers for Disease Control and Prevention. (2009, October). *Chronic Disease Overview.* Retrieved October 29, 2009, from http://www.cdc.gov/chronic-disease/overview/index.htm

Centers for Disease Control and Prevention. (2010). *Tobacco-related mortality.* Retrieved January 13, 2011, from http://www.cdc.gov/tobacco/data_statistics/fact_sheets/health_effects/tobacco_related_mortality/index.htm

Center for Drug Evaluation and Research. (2002). *Preventable adverse drug reactions: A focus on drug interactions.* Retrieved April 5, 2007, from http://www.fda.gov/cder/drug/drugReactions/

Centers for Medicare and Medicaid Services. (2004). *National health expenditures and selected economic indicators, levels and average annual percent change: Selected calendar years 1990–2013.* Retrieved from http://www.cms.hhs.gov/statistics/nhe/projections–2003/t1.asp

Centers for Medicare and Medicaid Services. (2008). *National health expenditures 2007 highlights.* Retrieved September 28, 2009, from http://www.cms.hhs.gov/NationalHealthExpendData/downloads/highlights.pdf

Cepeda-Benito, A. (1993). Meta-analytical review of the efficacy of nicotine chewing gum in smoking treatment programs. *Journal of Consulting and Clinical Psychology, 61,* 822–830.

Cerin, E., Vandelanotte, C., Leslie, E., & Merom, D. (2008). Recreational facilities and leisure-time physical activity: An analysis of moderators and self-efficacy as a mediator. *Health Psychology, 27,* S126–S135.

Cesana, G., Sega, R., Ferrario, M., Chiodini, P., Corrao, G., & Mancia, G. (2003). Job strain and blood pressure in employed men and women: A pooled analysis of four northern Italian population samples. *Psychosomatic Medicine, 65,* 558–563.

Chae, D. H., & Yoshikawa, H. (2008). Perceived group devaluation, depression, and HIV-risk behavior among Asian gay men. *Health Psychology, 27,* 140–148.

Champion, V. L. (1990). Breast self-examination in women 35 and older: A prospective study. *Journal of Behavioral Medicine, 13,* 523–538.

Champion, V. L., Skinner, C. S., Menon, U., Seshadri, R., Anzalone, D. C., & Rawl, S. M. (2002). Comparisons of tailored mammography interventions at two months postintervention. *Annals of Behavioral Medicine, 24,* 211–218.

Champion, V. L., & Springston, J. (1999). Mammography adherence and beliefs in a sample of low-income African American women. *International Journal of Behavioral Medicine, 6,* 228–240.

Chapman, C. R., & Gavrin, J. (1999). Suffering: The contributions of persisting pain. *Lancet, 353,* 2233–2237.

Charles, S. T., Gatz, M., Kato, K., & Pedersen, N. L. (2008). Physical health 25 years later: The predictive ability of neuroticism. *Health Psychology, 27,* 369–378.

Charnigo, R., Crosby, R. A., & Troutman, A. (2010). Psychological constructs associated with condom use among high-risk African American men newly diagnosed with a sexually transmitted disease. *Annals of Behavioral Medicine.*

Chassin, L., Presson, C. C., Sherman, S. J., & Kim, K. (2003). Historical changes in cigarette smoking and smoking-related beliefs after 2 decades in a Midwestern community. *Health Psychology, 22,* 347–353.

Chassin, L., Presson, C., Seo, D. C., Sherman, S. J., Macy, J., Wirth, R. J., et al. (2008). Multiple trajectories of cigarette smoking and the intergenerational transmission of smoking: A multigenerational, longitudinal study of a midwestern community sample. *Health Psychology, 27,* 819–828.

Chaves, I. F., & Barber, T. X. (1976). Hypnotism and surgical pain. In D. Mostofsky (Ed.), *Behavioral control and modification of physiological activity.* Englewood Cliffs, NJ: Prentice-Hall.

Chen, E., Bloomberg, G. R., Fisher, E. B., Jr., & Strunk, R. C. L. (2003). Predictors of repeat hospitalizations in children with asthma: The role of psychosocial and socioenvironmental factors. *Health Psychology, 22,* 12–18.

Chen, E., Fisher, E. B., Bacharier, L. B., & Strunk, R. C. (2003). Socioeconomic status, stress, and immune markers in adolescents with asthma. *Psychosomatic Medicine, 65,* 984–992.

Chen, E., Hermann, C., Rodgers, D., Oliver-Welker, T., & Strunk, R. C. (2006). Symptom perception in childhood asthma: The role of anxiety and asthma severity. *Health Psychology, 25,* 389–395.

Chen, E., Matthews, K. A., & Boyce, W. T. (2002). Socioeconomic differences in children's health: How and why do these relationships change with age? *Psychological Bulletin, 128,* 295–329.

Chen, E., Matthews, K. A., Salomon, K., & Ewart, C. K. (2002). Cardiovascular reactivity during social and nonsocial stressors: Do children's personal goals and expressive skills matter? *Health Psychology, 21,* 16–24.

Chen, Z., Sandercock, P., Pan, P., Counsell, C., Collins, R., Liu, L., et al. (2000). Indications of early aspirin use in acute ischemic stroke: A combined analysis of 40,000 randomized patients from the Chinese acute stroke trial and the international stroke trial. *Stroke, 31,* 1240–1249.

Cheng, C. (2003). Cognitive and motivational processes underlying coping flexibility: A dual-process model. *Journal of Personality and Social Psychology, 84,* 425–438.

Cheng, C., Hui, W., & Lam, S. (1999). Coping style of individuals with functional dyspepsia. *Psychosomatic Medicine, 61,* 789–795.

Cheng, C., Hui, W., & Lam, S. (2004). Psychosocial factors and perceived severity of functional dyspeptic symptoms: A psychosocial interactionist model. *Psychosomatic Medicine, 66,* 85–91.

Cherny, N. I. (1996). The problem of inadequately relieved suffering. *Journal of Social Issues, 52,* 13–30.

Cherrington, A., Wallston, K. A., & Rothman, R. L. (2010). Exploring the relationship between diabetes self-efficacy, depressive symptoms, and glycemic control among men and women with type 2 diabetes. *Journal of Behavioral Medicine, 33,* 81–89.

Chesney, M. A., Chambers, D. B., Taylor, J. M., Johnson, L. M., & Folkman, S. (2003). Coping effectiveness training for men living with HIV: Results from a randomized clinical trial testing a group-based intervention. *Psychosomatic Medicine, 65,* 1038–1046.

Cheung, N., Rogers, S., Mosley, T. H., Klein, R., Couper, D., & Wong, T. Y. (2009). Vital exhaustion and retinal microvascular changes in cardiovascular disease: Atherosclerosis risk in communities study. *Psychosomatic Medicine, 71,* 308–312.

Chiaramonte, G. R., & Friend, R. (2006). Medical students' and residents' gender bias in the diagnosis, treatment, and interpretation of coronary heart disease symptoms. *Health Psychology, 25,* 255–266.

Chichlowska, K. L., Rose, K. M., Diez-Roux, A. V., Golden, S. H., McNeill, A. M., & Heiss, G. (2008). Individual and neighborhood socioeconomic status characteristics and prevalence of metabolic syndrome: The atherosclerosis risk in communities (ARIC) study. *Psychosomatic Medicine, 70,* 986–992.

Chida, Y., & Steptoe, A. (2008). Positive psychological well-being and mortality: A quantitative review of prospective observational studies. *Psychosomatic Medicine, 70,* 741–756.

Chilcoat, H. D., & Breslau, N. (1996). Alcohol disorders in young adulthood: Effects of transitions into adult roles. *Journal of Health and Social Behavior, 37,* 339–349.

Chipperfield, J. G., & Perry, R. P. (2006). Primary and secondary-control strategies in later life: Predicting hospital outcomes in men and women. *Health Psychology, 25,* 226–236.

Cho, H. J., Hotopf, M., & Wessely, S. (2005). The placebo response in the treatment of chronic fatigue syndrome: A systematic review and meta-analysis. *Psychosomatic Medicine, 67,* 301–313.

Cho, H. J., Seeman, T. E., Bower, J. E., Kiefe, C. I., & Irwin, M. R. (2009). Prospective association between C-reactive protein and fatigue in the coronary artery risk development in young adults study. *Biological Psychiatry, 66,* 871–878.

Christakis, N. A., & Fowler, J. H. (2007). The spread of obesity in a large social network over 32 years. *The New England Journal of Medicine, 357,* 370–379.

Christakis, N. A., & Fowler, J. H. (2008). The collective dynamics of smoking in a large social network. *The New England Journal of Medicine, 358,* 2249–2258.

Christenfeld, N. (1997). Memory for pain and the delayed effects of distraction. *Health Psychology, 16,* 327–330.

Christensen, A. J., Edwards, D. L., Wiebe, J. S., Benotsch, E. G., McKelvey, L., Andrews, M., et al. (1996). Effect of verbal self-disclosure on natural killer cell activity: Moderating influence of cynical hostility. *Psychosomatic Medicine, 58,* 150–155.

Christensen, A. J., Ehlers, S. L., Raichle, K. A., Bertolatus, J. A., & Lawton, W. J. (2000). Predicting change in depression following renal transplantation: Effect of patient coping preferences. *Health Psychology, 19,* 348–353.

Christensen, A. J., Moran, P. J., Wiebe, J. S., Ehlers, S. L., & Lawton, W. J. (2002). Effect of a behavioral self-regulation intervention on patient adherence in hemodialysis. *Health Psychology, 21,* 393–397.

Christensen, A. J., Wiebe, J. S., & Lawton, W. J. (1997). Cynical hostility, powerful others, control expectancies and patient adherence in hemodialysis. *Psychosomatic Medicine, 59,* 307–312.

Christensen, A. J., Wiebe, J. S., Smith, T. W., & Turner, C. W. (1994). Predictors of survival among hemodialysis patients: Effect of perceived family support. *Health Psychology, 13,* 521–525.

Christie-Mizell, C. A., & Perlata, R. L. (2009). The gender gap in alcohol consumption during late adolescence and young adulthood: Gendered attitudes and adult roles. *Journal of Health and Social Behavior, 50,* 410–426.

Christman, N. J., McConnell, E. A., Pfeiffer, C., Webster, K. K., Schmitt, M., & Ries, J. (1988). Uncertainty, coping, and distress following myocardial infarction: Transition from hospital to home. *Research in Nursing and Health, 11,* 71–82.

Chuang, Y. C., Ennett, S. T., Bauman, K. E., & Foshee, V. A. (2005). Neighborhood influences on adolescent cigarette and alcohol use: Mediating effects through parents and peer behaviors. *Journal of Health and Social Behavior, 46,* 187–204.

Ciccone, D., Just, N., & Bandilla, E. (1999). A comparison of economic and social reward in patients with chronic nonmalignant back pain. *Psychosomatic Medicine, 61,* 552–563.

Cin, S. D., Worth, K. A., Gerrard, M., Gibbons, F. X., Stoolmiller, M., Wills, T. A., et al. (2009). Watching and drinking: Expectancies, prototypes, and friend's alcohol use mediate the effect of exposure to alcohol use in movies on adolescent drinking. *Health Psychology, 28,* 473–483.

Clark, M. (1977). The new war on pain. *Newsweek,* pp. 48–58.

Clark, M. A., Rakowski, W., & Bonacore, L. B. (2003). Repeat mammography: Prevalence estimates and considerations for assessment. *Annals of Behavioral Medicine, 26,* 201–211.

Clark, R. (2006a). Perceived racism and vascular reactivity in black college women: Moderating effects of seeking social support. *Health Psychology, 25,* 20–25.

Clark, R. (2006b). Interactive but not direct effects of perceived racism and trait anger predict resting systolic and diastolic blood pressure in black adolescents. *Health Psychology, 25,* 580–585.

Clarke, V. A., Lovegrove, H., Williams, A., & Macpherson, M. (2000). Unrealistic optimism and the health belief model. *Journal of Behavioral Medicine, 23,* 367–376.

Clarke, V. A., Williams, T., & Arthey, S. (1997). Skin type and optimistic bias in relation to the sun protection and suntanning behaviors of young adults. *Journal of Behavioral Medicine, 20,* 207–222.

Clemens, J. Q., Nadler, R. B., Schaeffer, A. J., Belani, J., Albaugh, J., & Bushman, W. (2000). Biofeedback, pelvic floor re-education, and bladder training for male chronic pelvic pain syndrome. *Urology, 56,* 951–955.

Clemmey, P. A., & Nicassio, P. M. (1997). Illness self-schemas in depressed and nondepressed rheumatoid arthritis patients. *Journal of Behavioral Medicine, 20,* 273–290.

Clouse, R. E., Lustman, P. J., Freedland, K. E., Griffith, L. S., McGill, J. B., & Carney, R. M. (2003). Depression and coronary heart disease in women with diabetes. *Psychosomatic Medicine, 65,* 376–383.

Cochran, S. D., & Mays, V. M. (1990). Sex, lies, and HIV. *The New England Journal of Medicine, 322,* 774–775.

Cohen, F., Kemeny, M. E., Zegans, L. S., Johnson, P., Kearney, K. A., & Stites, D. P. (2007). Immune function declines with unemployment and recovers after stressor termination. *Psychosomatic Medicine, 69,* 225–234.

Cohen, F., & Lazarus, R. (1979). Coping with the stresses of illness. In G. C. Stone, F. Cohen, & N. E. Adler (Eds.), *Health psychology: A handbook* (pp. 217–254). San Francisco: Jossey-Bass.

Cohen, L., Baile, W. F., Henninger, E., Agarwal, S. K., Kudelka, A. P., Lenzi, R., et al. (2003). Physiological and psychological effects of delivering medical news using a simulated physician-patient scenario. *Journal of Behavioral Medicine, 26,* 459–471.

Cohen, L., Cohen, R., Blount, R., Schaen, E., & Zaff, J. (1999). Comparative study of distraction versus topical anesthesia for pediatric pain management during immunizations. *Health Psychology, 18,* 591–598.

Cohen, L., Marshall, G. D., Jr., Cheng, L., Agarwal, S. K., & Wei, Q. (2000). DNA repair capacity in healthy medical students during and after exam stress. *Journal of Behavioral Medicine, 23,* 531–544.

Cohen, L. M., Dobscha, S. K., Hails, K. C., Pekow, P. S., & Chochinov, H. M. (2002). Depression and suicidal ideation in patients who discontinue the life-support treatment of dialysis. *Psychosomatic Medicine, 64,* 889–896.

Cohen, M., & Pollack, S. (2005). Mothers with breast cancer and their adult daughters: The relationship between mothers' reaction to breast cancer and their daughters' emotional and neuroimmune status. *Psychosomatic Medicine, 67,* 64–71.

Cohen, M. L. (2000). Changing patterns of infectious disease. *Nature, 406,* 762–767.

Cohen, R. A., & Bloom, B. (2010). Access to and utilization of medical care for young adults aged 20–29 years: United States, 2008. *NCHS Data Brief, 29,* 1–8.

Cohen, R. Y., Brownell, K. D., & Felix, M. R. J. (1990). Age and sex differences in health habits and beliefs of schoolchildren. *Health Psychology, 9,* 208–224.

Cohen, R. Y., Stunkard, A., & Felix, M. R. J. (1986). Measuring community change in disease prevention and health promotion. *Preventive Medicine, 15,* 411–421.

Cohen, S. (1978). Environmental load and allocation of attention. In A. Baum, J. E. Singer, & S. Valins (Eds.), *Advances in environmental psychology* (Vol. 2, pp. 1–29). Hillsdale, NJ: Erlbaum.

Cohen, S. (1980). Aftereffects of stress on human performance and social behavior: A review of research and theory. *Psychological Bulletin, 88,* 82–108.

Cohen, S., Alper, C. M., Doyle, W. J., Adler, N., Treanor, J. J., & Turner, R. B. (2008). Objective and subjective socioeconomic status and susceptibility to the common cold. *Health Psychology, 27,* 268–274.

Cohen, S., Alper, C. M., Doyle, W. J., Treanor, J. J., & Turner, R. B. (2006). Positive emotional style predicts resistance to illness after experimental exposure to rhinovirus or influenza a virus. *Psychosomatic Medicine, 68,* 809–815.

Cohen, S., Doyle, W., & Skoner, D. (1999). Psychological stress, cytokine production, and severity of upper respiratory illness. *Psychosomatic Medicine, 61,* 175–180.

Cohen, S., Doyle, W. J., Skoner, D. P., Rabin, B. S., & Gwaltney, J. M., Jr. (1997). Social ties and susceptibility to the common cold. *Journal of the American Medical Association, 277,* 1940–1944.

Cohen, S., Doyle, W. J., Turner, R. B., Alper, C. M., & Skoner, D. P. (2003). Emotional style and susceptibility to the common cold. *Psychosomatic Medicine, 65,* 652–657.

Cohen, S., Glass, D. C., & Phillip, S. (1978). Environment and health. In H. E. Freeman, S. Levine, & L. G. Reeder (Eds.), *Handbook of medical sociology* (pp. 134–149). Englewood Cliffs, NJ: Prentice-Hall.

Cohen, S., Hamrick, N., Rodriguez, M. S., Feldman, P. J., Rabin, B. S., & Manuck, S. R. (2002). Reactivity and vulnerability to stress-associated risk for upper respiratory illness. *Psychosomatic Medicine, 64,* 302–310.

Cohen, S., & Herbert, T. B. (1996). Health psychology: Psychological factors and physical disease from the perspective of human psychoneuroimmunology. *Annual Review of Psychology, 47,* 113–142.

Cohen, S., & Hoberman, H. M. (1983). Positive events and social supports as buffers of life change stress. *Journal of Applied Social Psychology, 13,* 99–125.

Cohen, S., Janicki-Deverts, D., & Miller, G. E. (2007). Psychological stress and disease. *Journal of the American Medical Association, 298,* 1685–1687.

Cohen, S., Kamarck, T., & Mermelstein, R. (1983). A global measure of perceived stress. *Journal of Health and Social Behavior, 24,* 385–396.

Cohen, S., Kaplan, J. R., Cunnick, J. E., Manuck, S. B., & Rabin, B. S. (1992). Chronic social stress, affiliation, and cellular immune response in nonhuman primates. *Psychological Science, 3,* 301–304.

Cohen, S., Kessler, R. C., & Gordon, L. U. (1995). Conceptualizing stress and its relation to disease. In S. Cohen, R. C. Kessler, & L. U. Gordon (Eds.), *Measuring stress: A guide for health and social scientists* (pp. 3–26). New York: Oxford University Press.

Cohen, S., & Lemay, E. P. (2007). Why would social networks be linked to affect and health practices? *Health Psychology, 26,* 410–417.

Cohen, S., Lichtenstein, E., Prochaska, J. O., Rossi, J. S., Gritz, E. R., Carr, C. R., et al. (1989). Debunking myths about self-quitting: Evidence from ten prospective studies of persons quitting smoking by themselves. *American Psychologist, 44,* 1355–1365.

Cohen, S., Line, S., Manuck, S. B., Rabin, B. S., Heise, E. R., & Kaplan, J. R. (1997). Chronic social stress, social status, and susceptibility to upper respiratory infection in nonhuman primates. *Psychosomatic Medicine, 59,* 213–221.

Cohen, S., & McKay, G. (1984). Social support, stress, and the buffering hypothesis: A theoretical analysis. In A. Baum, S. E. Taylor, & J. Singer (Eds.), *Handbook of psychology and health* (Vol. 4, pp. 253–268). Hillsdale, NJ: Erlbaum.

Cohen, S., & Pressman, S. D. (2006). Positive affect and health. *Current Directions in Psychological Science, 15,* 122–125.

Cohen, S., Sherrod, D. R., & Clark, M. S. (1986). Social skills and the stress-protective role of social support. *Journal of Personality and Social Psychology, 50,* 963–973.

Cohen, S., & Spacapan, S. (1978). The aftereffects of stress: An attentional interpretation. *Environmental Psychology and Nonverbal Behavior, 3,* 43–57.

Cohen, S., Tyrrell, D. A. J., & Smith, A. P. (1993). Negative life events, perceived stress, negative affect, and susceptibility to the common cold. *Journal of Personality and Social Psychology, 64,* 131–140.

Cohen, S., & Williamson, G. M. (1988). Perceived stress in a probability sample of the United States. In S. Spacapan & S. Oskamp (Eds.), *The social psychology of health* (pp. 31–67). Newbury Park, CA: Sage.

Cohen, S., & Williamson, G. M. (1991). Stress and infectious disease in humans. *Psychological Bulletin, 109,* 5–24.

Cohen, S., & Wills, T. A. (1985). Stress, social support, and the buffering hypothesis. *Psychological Bulletin, 98,* 310–357.

Coker, A. L., Bond, S., Madeleine, M. M., Luchok, K., & Pirisi, L. (2003). Psychological stress and cervical neoplasia risk. *Psychosomatic Medicine, 65,* 644–651.

Colagiuri, B., & Zachariae, R. (2010). Patient expectancy and post-chemotherapy nausea: A meta-analysis. *Annals of Behavioral Medicine.*

Cole, P. A., Pomerleau, C. S., & Harris, J. K. (1992). The effects of nonconcurrent and concurrent relaxation training on cardiovascular reactivity to a psychological stressor. *Journal of Behavioral Medicine, 15,* 407–427.

Cole, S. W. (2008). Psychosocial influences on HIV-1 disease progression: Neural, endocrine, and virologic mechanisms. *Psychosomatic Medicine, 70,* 562–568.

Cole, S. W., Kemeny, M. E., Fahey, J. L., Zack, J. A., & Naliboff, B. D. (2003). Psychological risk factors for HIV pathogenesis: Mediation by the autonomic nervous system. *Biological Psychiatry, 54,* 1444–1456.

Cole, S. W., Kemeny, M. E., Taylor, S. E., Visscher, B. R., & Fahey, J. L. (1996). Accelerated course of human immunodeficiency virus infection in gay men who conceal their homosexual identity. *Psychosomatic Medicine, 58,* 219–231.

Cole, S. W., Mendoza, S. P., & Capitanio, J. P. (2009). Social stress desensitizes lymphocytes to regulation by endogenous glucocorticoids: Insights from in vivo cell trafficking dynamics in rhesus macaques. *Psychosomatic Medicine, 71,* 591–597.

Collins, G. (1997, May 30). Trial near in new legal tack in tobacco war. *New York Times,* p. A10.

Collins, N. L., Dunkel-Schetter, C., Lobel, M., & Scrimshaw, S. C. M. (1993). Social support in pregnancy. Psychosocial correlates of birth outcomes and postpartum depression. *Journal of Personality and Social Psychology, 6,* 1243–1258.

Collins, R. L., Kanouse, D. E., Gifford, A. L., Senterfitt, J. W., Schuster, M. A., McCaffrey, D. F., et al. (2001). Changes in health-promoting behavior following diagnosis with HIV: Prevalence and correlates in a national probability sample. *Health Psychology, 20,* 351–360.

Collins, R. L., Taylor, S. E., & Skokan, L. A. (1990). A better world or a shattered vision? Changes in perspectives following victimization. *Social Cognition, 8,* 263–285.

Columbia Encyclopedia, 6th ed. (2004). *Alcoholics Anonymous.* Columbia University Press.

Compas, B. E., Barnez, G. A., Malcarne, V., & Worsham, N. (1991). Perceived control and coping with stress: A developmental perspective. *Journal of Social Issues, 47,* 23–34.

Compas, B. E., Worsham, N. L., Epping-Jordan, J. A. E., Grant, K. E., Mireault, G., Howell, D. C., et al. (1994). When mom or dad has cancer: Markers of psychological distress in cancer patients, spouses, and children. *Health Psychology, 13,* 507–515.

Compas, B. E., Worsham, N. L., Ey, S., & Howell, D. C. (1996). When mom or dad has cancer: II. Coping, cognitive appraisals, and psychological distress in children of cancer patients. *Health Psychology, 15,* 167–175.

Conis, E. (2003, August 4). Chips for some, tofu for others. *Los Angeles Times,* p. F8.

Conn, V. S., Valentine, J. C., & Cooper, H. M. (2002). Interventions to increase physical activity among aging adults: A meta-analysis. *Annals of Behavioral Medicine, 24,* 190–200.

Conrad, P. (2005). The shifting engines of medicalization. *Journal of Health and Social Behavior, 46,* 3–14.

Conroy, D. E., Hyde, A. L., Doerksen, S. E., & Riebeiro, N. F. (2010). Implicit attitudes and explicit motivation prospectively predict physical activity. *Annals of Behavioral Medicine, 39,* 112–118.

Contrada, R. J., Boulifard, D. A., Hekler, E. B., Idler, E. L., Spruill, T. M., Labouvie, E. W., et al. (2008). Psychosocial factors in heart surgery: Presurgical vulnerability and postsurgical recovery. *Health Psychology, 27,* 309–319.

Contrada, R. J., Goyal, T. M., Cather, C. C., Rafalson, L., Idler, E. L., & Krause, T. J. (2004). Psychosocial factors in outcomes of heart surgery: The impact of religious involvement and depressive symptoms. *Health Psychology, 23,* 227–238.

Cooper, J. K., Love, D. W., & Raffoul, P. R. (1982). Intentional prescription nonadherence (noncompliance) by the elderly. *Journal of the American Geriatric Society, 30,* 329–333.

Cooper, M. L., Wood, P. K., Orcutt, H. K., & Albino, A. (2003). Personality and the predisposition to engage in risky or problem behaviors during adolescence. *Journal of Personality and Social Psychology, 84,* 390–410.

Cooperman, N. A., & Simoni, J. M. (2005). Suicidal ideation and attempted suicide among women living with HIV/AIDS. *Journal of Behavioral Medicine, 28,* 149–156.

COPD International. (2008). *COPD.* Retrieved September 25, 2009, from http://www.copd-international.com/copd.htm

Corbin, W. R., & Fromme, K. (2002). Alcohol use and serial monogamy as risks for sexually transmitted diseases in young adults. *Health Psychology, 21,* 229–236.

Cordova, M. J., Cunningham, L. L. C., Carlson, C. R., & Andrykowski, M. A. (2001). Posttraumatic growth following breast cancer: A controlled comparison study. *Health Psychology, 20,* 176–185.

Corle, D. K., Sharbaugh, C., Mateski, D. J., Coyne, T., Paskett, E. D., Cahill, J., et al. (2001). Self-rated quality of life measures: Effect of change to a low-fat, high fiber, fruit and vegetable enriched diet. *Annals of Behavioral Medicine, 23,* 198–207.

Cornwell, E. Y., & Waite, L. J. (2009). Social disconnectedness, perceived isolation, and health among older adults. *Journal of Health and Social Behavior, 50,* 31–48.

Corral, I., & Landrine, H. (2008). Acculturation and ethnic-minority health behavior: A test of the operant model. *Health Psychology, 27,* 737–745.

Costanzo, E. S., Lutgendorf, S. K., Bradley, S. L., Rose, S. L., & Anderson, B. (2005). Cancer attributions, distress, and health practices among gynecologic cancer survivors. *Psychosomatic Medicine, 67,* 972–980.

Costanzo, E. S., Ryff, C. D., & Singer, B. H. (2009). Psychosocial adjustment among cancer survivors: Findings from a national survey of health and well-being. *Health Psychology, 28,* 147–156.

Costello, D. (2004, March 29). Insurers limit obesity surgery. *Los Angeles Times,* p. F1.

Costello, D. M., Dierker, L. C., Jones, B. L., & Rose, J. S. (2008). Trajectories of smoking from adolescence to early adulthood and their psychosocial risk factors. *Health Psychology, 27,* 811–818.

Courneya, K. S., & Friedenreich, C. M. (2001). Framework PEACE: An organizational model for examining physical exercise across the cancer experience. *Annals of Behavioral Medicine, 23,* 263–272.

Courneya, K. S., McKenzie, D. C., Reid, R. D., Mackey, J. R., Gelmon, K., Freidenreich, C. M., et al. (2008). Barriers to supervised exercise training in a randomized trial of breast cancer patients receiving chemotherapy. *Annals of Behavioral Medicine, 35,* 116–122.

Cousins, N. (1979). *Anatomy of an illness.* New York: Norton.

Coutu, M. F., Dupuis, G., D'Antono, B., & Rochon-Goyer, L. (2003). Illness representation and change in dietary habits in hypercholesterolemic patients. *Journal of Behavioral Medicine, 26,* 133–152.

Cover, H., & Irwin, M. (1994). Immaturity and depression: Insomnia, retardation, and reduction of natural killer cell activity. *Journal of Behavioral Medicine, 17,* 217–223.

Cowley, G. (2002, June 24). The disappearing minds. *Newsweek,* pp. 40–50.

Cox, C. R., Cooper, D. P., Vess, M., Arndt, J., Goldenberg, J. L., & Routledge, C. (2009). Bronze is beautiful but pale can be pretty: The effects of appearance standards and mortality salience on sun-tanning outcomes. *Health Psychology, 28,* 746–752.

Cox, D. J., Tisdelle, D. A., & Culbert, J. P. (1988). Increasing adherence to behavioral homework assignments. *Journal of Behavioral Medicine, 11,* 519–522.

Coyne, J. C., & Smith, D. A. F. (1991). Couples coping with a myocardial infarction: A contextual perspective on wives' distress. *Journal of Personality and Social Psychology, 61,* 404–412.

Coyne, J. C., Tennen, H., & Ranchor, A. V. (2010). Positive psychology in cancer care: A story line resistant to evidence. *Annals of Behavioral Medicine, 39,* 35–42.

Creed, F., Guthrie, E., Ratcliffe, J., Fernandes, L., Rigby, C., Tomenson, B., et al. (2005). Reported sexual abuse predicts impaired functioning but a good response to psychological treatments in patients with severe irritable bowel syndrome. *Psychosomatic Medicine, 67,* 490–499.

Crepaz, N., Passin, W. F., Herbst, J. H., Rama, S. M., Malow, R. M., Purcell, D. W., et al. (2008). Meta-analysis of cognitive behavioral interventions on HIV-positive persons' mental health and immune functioning. *Health Psychology, 27,* 4–14.

Creswell, J. D., Lam, S., Stanton, A. L., Taylor, S. E., Bower, J. E., & Sherman, D. K. (2007). Does self-affirmation, cognitive processing, or discovery of meaning explain cancer-related health benefits of expressive writing? *Personality and Social Psychology Bulletin, 33,* 238–250.

Creswell, J. D., Way, B. M., Eisenberger, N. I., & Lieberman, M. D. (2007). Neural correlates of dispositional mindfulness during affect labeling. *Psychosomatic Medicine, 69,* 560–565.

Creswell, J. D., Welch, W. T., Taylor, S. E., Sherman, D. K., Gruenewald, T., & Mann, T. (2005). Affirmation of personal values buffers neuroendocrine and psychological stress responses. *Psychological Science, 16,* 846–851.

Critser, G. (2003). *Fat land: How Americans became the fattest people in the world.* Boston: Houghton Mifflin.

Croog, S. H. (1983). Recovery and rehabilitation of heart patients: Psychosocial aspects. In D. S. Krantz & J. S. Singer (Eds.), *Handbook of psychology and health* (Vol. 3, pp. 295–334). Hillsdale, NJ: Erlbaum.

Croog, S. H., & Fitzgerald, E. F. (1978). Subjective stress and serious illness of a spouse: Wives of heart patients. *Journal of Health and Social Behavior, 9,* 166–178.

Crosnoe, R. (2002). Academic and health-related trajectories in adolescence: The intersection of gender and athletics. *Journal of Health and Social Behavior, 43,* 317–335.

Crosnoe, R., & Muller, C. (2004). Body mass index, academic achievement, and school context: Examining the educational experiences of adolescents at risk of obesity. *Journal of Health and Social Behavior, 45,* 393–407.

Cross, C. K., & Hirschfeld, M. A. (1986). Psychosocial factors and suicidal behavior. *Annals of the New York Academy of Sciences, 487,* 77–89.

Croyle, R. T., & Ditto, P. H. (1990). Illness cognition and behavior: An experimental approach. *Journal of Behavioral Medicine, 13,* 31–52.

Croyle, R. T., & Hunt, J. R. (1991). Coping with health threat: Social influence processes in reactions to medical test results. *Journal of Personality and Social Psychology, 60,* 382–389.

Croyle, R. T., & Lerman, C. (1993). Interest in genetic testing for colon cancer susceptibility: Cognitive and emotional correlates. *Preventive Medicine, 22,* 284–292.

Croyle, R. T., Loftus, E. F., Barger, S. D., Sun, Y. C., Hart, M., & Gettig, J. (2006). How well do people recall risk factor test results? Accuracy and bias among cholesterol screening participants. *Health Psychology, 25,* 425–432.

Croyle, R. T., Smith, K. R., Botkin, J. R., Baty, B., & Nash, J. (1997). Psychological responses to BRCA1 mutation testing: Preliminary findings. *Health Psychology, 16,* 63–72.

Croyle, R. T., Sun, Y. C., & Louie, D. H. (1993). Psychological minimization of cholesterol test results: Moderators of appraisal in college students and community residents. *Health Psychology, 12,* 503–507.

Cruess, D. G., Antoni, M., McGregor, B. A., Kilbourn, K. M., Boyers, A. E., Alferi, S. M., et al. (2000). Cognitive-behavioral stress management reduces serum cortisol by enhancing benefit finding among women being treated for early stage breast cancer. *Psychosomatic Medicine, 62,* 304–308.

Cruess, S., Antoni, M., Cruess, D., Fletcher, M., Ironson, G., Kumar, M., et al. (2000). Reduction in herpes simplex virus type 2 antibody titers after cognitive behavioral stress management and relationships with neuroendocrine function, relaxation skills, and social support in HIV-positive men. *Psychosomatic Medicine, 62,* 828–837.

Cuijpers, P., van Straten, A., & Andersson, G. (2008). Internet-administered cognitive behavior therapy for health problems: A systematic review. *Journal of Behavioral Medicine, 31,* 169–177.

Cullen, K. W., & Zakeri, I. (2004). Fruit, vegetables, milk, and sweetened beverages consumption and access to à la carte/snack bar meals at school. *American Journal of Public Health, 94,* 463–467.

Cunningham, J. A., Lin, E., Ross, H. E., & Walsh, G. W. (2000). Factors associated with untreated remissions from alcohol abuse or dependence. *Addictive Behaviors, 25,* 317–321.

Curbow, B., Bowie, J., Garza, M. A., McDonnell, K., Scott, L. B., Coyne, C. A., et al. (2004). Community-based cancer screening programs in older populations: Making progress but can we do better? *Preventive Medicine, 38,* 676–693.

Curran, S. L., Beacham, A. O., & Andrykowski, M. A. (2004). Ecological momentary assessment of fatigue following breast cancer treatment. *Journal of Behavioral Medicine, 27,* 425–444.

Currie, S. R., Wilson, K. G., & Curran, D. (2002). Clinical significance and predictors of treatment response to cognitive-behavior therapy for insomnia secondary to chronic pain. *Journal of Behavioral Medicine, 25,* 135–153.

Curry, S. J. (1993). Self-help interventions for smoking cessation. *Journal of Consulting and Clinical Psychology, 61,* 790–803.

Cushman, L. A. (1986). Secondary neuropsychiatric complications in stroke: Implications for acute care. *Archives of Physical Medicine and Rehabilitation, 69,* 877–879.

Cvengros, J. A., Christensen, A. J., Cunningham, C., Hillis, S. L., & Kaboli, P. J. (2009). Patient preference for and reports of provider behavior: Impact of symmetry on patient outcomes. *Health Psychology, 28,* 660–667.

Czaja, S. J., & Rubert, M. P. (2002). Telecommunications technology as an aid to family caregivers of persons with dementia. *Psychosomatic Medicine, 64,* 469–476.

Dahlberg, C. C. (1977, June). Stroke. *Psychology Today,* pp. 121–128.

Dahlquist, L. M., McKenna, K. D., Jones, K. K., Dillinger, L., Weiss, K. E., & Ackerman, C. S. (2007). Active and passive distraction using a head-mounted display helmet: Affects on cold pressor pain in children. *Health Psychology, 26,* 794–801.

Dahlquist, L. M., Pendley, J. S., Landthrip, D. S., Jones, C. L., & Steuber, C. P. (2002). Distraction intervention for preschoolers undergoing intramuscular injections and subcutaneous port access. *Health Psychology, 21,* 94–99.

Dakof, G. A., & Taylor, S. E. (1990). Victims' perceptions of social support: What is helpful from whom? *Journal of Personality and Social Psychology, 58,* 80–89.

Dallman, M. F., et al. (2003). Chronic stress and obesity: A new view of "comfort food." *Proceedings of the National Academy of Sciences, 100,* 11696–11701.

Daly, M., Delaney, L., Doran, P. P., Harmon, C., & MacLachlan, M. (2010). Naturalistic monitoring of the affect-heart rate relationship: A day reconstruction study. *Health Psychology, 29,* 186–195.

D'Amico, E. J., & Fromme, K. (1997). Health risk behaviors of adolescent and young adult siblings. *Health Psychology, 16,* 426–432.

Damush, T. M., Wu, J., Bair, M. J., Sutherland, J. M., & Kroenke, K. (2008). Self-management practices among primary care patients with musculoskeletal pain and depression. *Journal of Behavioral Medicine, 31,* 301–307.

Danoff, B., Kramer, S., Irwin, P., & Gottlieb, A. (1983). Assessment of the quality of life in long-term survivors after definitive radiotherapy. *American Journal of Clinical Oncology, 6,* 339–345.

Danoff-Burg, S., & Revenson, T. A. (2005). Benefit-finding among patients with rheumatoid arthritis: Positive effects on interpersonal relationships. *Journal of Behavioral Medicine, 28,* 91–103.

Dar, R., Leventhal, E. A., & Leventhal, H. (1993). Schematic processes in pain perception. *Cognitive Therapy and Research, 17,* 341–357.

Darbes, L. A., & Lewis, M. A. (2005). HIV-specific social support predicts less sexual risk behavior in gay male couples. *Health Psychology, 24,* 617–622.

Das-Munshi, J., Stewart, R., Ismail, K., Bebbington, P. E., Jenkins, R., & Prince, M. J. (2007). Diabetes, common mental disorders, and disability: Findings from the UK national psychiatric morbidity survey. *Psychosomatic Medicine, 69,* 543–550.

Dattore, P. I., Shontz, F. C., & Coyne, L. (1980). Premorbid personality differentiation of cancer and noncancer groups: A test of the hypothesis of cancer proneness. *Journal of Consulting and Clinical Psychology, 48,* 388–394.

Davidson, K. W., Goldstein, M., Kaplan, R. M., Kaufmann, P. G., Knatterud, G. L., Orleans, C. T., et al. (2003). Evidence-based behavioral medicine: What is it and how do we achieve it? *Annals of Behavioral Medicine, 26,* 161–171.

Davidson, K. W., Hall, P., & MacGregor, M. (1996). Gender differences in the relation between interview-derived hostility scores and resting blood pressure. *Journal of Behavioral Medicine, 19,* 185–202.

Davidson, K. W., MacGregor, M. W., Stuhr, J., & Gidron, Y. (1999). Increasing constructive anger verbal behavior decreases resting blood pressure: A secondary analysis of a randomized controlled hostility intervention. *International Journal of Behavioral Medicine, 6,* 268–278.

Davison, K. K., Schmalz, D. L., & Downs, D. S. (2010). Hop, skip...no! Explaining adolescent girls' disinclination for physical activity. *Annals of Behavioral Medicine.*

Davis, M., Matthews, K., & McGrath, C. (2000). Hostile attitudes predict elevated vascular resistance during interpersonal stress in men and women. *Psychosomatic Medicine, 62,* 17–25.

Davis, M. C., Matthews, K. A., Meilahn, E. N., & Kiss, J. E. (1995). Are job characteristics related to fibrinogen levels in middle-aged women? *Health Psychology, 14,* 310–318.

Davis, M. C., Twamley, E. W., Hamilton, N. A., & Swan, P. D. (1999). Body fat distribution and hemodynamic stress responses in premenopausal obese women: A preliminary study. *Health Psychology, 18,* 625–633.

Davis, M., Vasterling, J., Bransfield, D., & Burish, T. G. (1987). Behavioural interventions in coping with cancer-related pain. *British Journal of Guidance and Counselling, 15,* 17–28.

Davison, G. C., Williams, M. E., Nezami, E., Bice, T. L., & DeQuattro, V. L. (1991). Relaxation, reduction in angry articulated thoughts, and improvements in borderline hypertension and heart rate. *Journal of Behavioral Medicine, 14,* 453–468.

De Graaf, R., & Bijl, R. V. (2002). Determinants of mental distress in adults with a severe auditory impairment: Difference between prelingual and postlingual deafness. *Psychosomatic Medicine, 64,* 61–70.

De Jonge, P., Latour, C., & Huyse, F. J. (2003). Implementing psychiatric interventions on a medical ward: Effects on patients' quality of life and length of hospital stay. *Psychosomatic Medicine, 65,* 997–1002.

De Moor, C., Sterner, J., Hall, M., Warneke, C., Gilani, Z., Amato, R., et al. (2002). A pilot study of the side effects of expressive writing on psychological and behavioral adjustment in patients in a phase II trial of vaccine therapy for metastatic renal cell carcinoma. *Health Psychology, 21,* 615–619.

De Moor, J. S., De Moor, C. A., Basen-Engquist, K., Kudelka, A., Bevers, M. W., & Cohen, L. (2006). Optimism, distress, health-related quality of life, and change in cancer antigen 125 among patients with ovarian cancer undergoing chemotherapy. *Psychosomatic Medicine, 68,* 555–562.

De Peuter, S., Lemaigre, V., Van Diest, I., & Van den Bergh, O. (2008). Illness-specific catastrophic thinking and overperception in asthma. *Health Psychology, 27,* 93–99.

De Vente, W., Kamphuis, J. H., Emmelkamp, P. M. G., & Blonk, R. W. B. (2008). Individual and group cognitive-behavioral treatment for work-related stress complaints and sickness absence: A randomized controlled trial. *Journal of Occupational Health Psychology, 13,* 214–231.

De Wit, J. B. F., Das, E., & Vet, R. (2008). What works best: Objective statistics or a personal testimonial? An assessment of the persuasive effects of different types of message evidence on risk perception. *Health Psychology, 27,* 110–115.

Deary, I. J., Batty, G. D., Pattie, A., & Gale, C. R. (2008). More intelligent, more dependable children live longer: A 55-year longitudinal study of a representative sample of the Scottish nation. *Psychological Science, 19,* 874–880.

Deaton, A. V. (1985). Adaptive noncompliance in pediatric asthma: The parent as expert. *Journal of Pediatric Psychology, 10,* 1–14.

DeBusk, R. F., Haskell, W. L., Miller, N. H., Berra, K., & Taylor, C. B. (1985). Medically directed at-home rehabilitation soon after clinically uncomplicated acute myocardial infarction: A new model for patient care. *American Journal of Cardiology, 55,* 251–257.

Deci, E. L., & Ryan, R. M. (1985). *Intrinsic motivation and self-determination in human behavior.* New York: Plenum.

Dedert, E. A., Calhoun, P. S., Watkins, L. L., Sherwood, A., & Beckham, J. C. (2010). Posttraumatic stress disorder, cardiovascular, and metabolic disease: A review of the evidence. *Annals of Behavioral Medicine, 39,* 61–78.

DeLongis, A., Coyne, J. C., Dakof, G., Folkman, S., & Lazarus, R. S. (1982). Relationship of daily hassles, uplifts, and major life events to health status. *Health Psychology, 1,* 119–136.

Denollet, J., Martens, E. J., Nyklíček, I., Conraads, V. M., & de Gelder, B. (2008). Clinical events in coronary patients who report low distress: Adverse effect of repressive coping. *Health Psychology, 27,* 302–308.

Denollet, J., Pedersen, S. S., Vrints, C. J., & Conraads, V. M. (2006). Usefulness of type D personality in predicting five-year cardiac events above and beyond concurrent symptoms of stress in patients with coronary heart disease. *American Journal of Cardiology, 97,* 970–973.

Department for Professional Employees. (April, 2006). *Fact sheet 2006, professional women: Vital statistics.* Retrieved April 13, 2007, from http://www.dpeaflcio.org/programs/factsheets/fs_2006_Professional_Women.htm#_edn14

DeQuattro, V., & Lee, D. D. P. (1991). Blood pressure reactivity and sympathetic hyperactivity. *American Journal of Hypertension, 4,* 624S–628S.

DeRosa, C. J., & Marks, G. (1998). Preventative counseling of HIV-positive men and self-disclosure of serostatus to sex partners: New opportunities for prevention. *Health Psychology, 17,* 224–231.

Dersh, J., Polatin, P. B., & Gatchel, R. J. (2002). Chronic pain and psychopathology: Research findings and theoretical considerations. *Psychosomatic Medicine, 64,* 773–786.

Des Jarlais, D. C., & Semaan, S. (2008). HIV prevention for injecting drug users: The first 25 years and counting. *Psychosomatic Medicine, 70,* 606–611.

Detweiler, J. B., Bedell, B. T., Salovey, P., Pronin, E., & Rothman, A. J. (1999). Message framing and sunscreen use: Gain-framed messages motivate beach-goers. *Health Psychology, 18,* 189–196.

DeVellis, B. M., Blalock, S. J., & Sandler, R. S. (1990). Predicting participation in cancer screening: The role of perceived behavioral control. *Journal of Applied Social Psychology, 20,* 659–660.

Devine, C. M., Connors, M. M., Sobal, J., & Bisogni, C. A. (2003). Sandwiching it in: Spillover of work onto food choices and family roles in low- and moderate-income urban households. *Social Science and Medicine, 56,* 617–630.

Dew, M. A., Hoch, C. C., Buysse, D. J., Monk, T. H., Begley, A. E., Houck, P. R., et al. (2003). Healthy older adults' sleep predicts all-cause mortality at 4 to 19 years of follow-up. *Psychosomatic Medicine, 65,* 63–73.

Di Giorgio, A., Hudson, M., Jerjes, W., & Cleare, A. J. (2005). 24-hour pituitary and adrenal hormone profiles in chronic fatigue syndrome. *Psychosomatic Medicine, 67,* 433–440.

Diabetes Prevention Program Research Group. (2002). Reduction in the incidence of type 2 diabetes with lifestyle intervention or metformin. *The New England Journal of Medicine, 346,* 393–403.

Diamond, J., Massey, K. L., & Covey, D. (1989). Symptom awareness and blood glucose estimation in diabetic adults. *Health Psychology, 8,* 15–26.

Dias, J. A., Griffith, R. A., Ng, J. J., Reinert, S. E., Friedmann, P. D., & Moulton, A. W. (2002). Patients' use of the Internet for medical information. *Journal of General Internal Medicine, 17,* 180–185.

Dickens, C., McGowan, L., Clark-Carter, D., & Creed, F. (2002). Depression and rheumatoid arthritis: A systematic review of the literature with meta-analysis. *Psychosomatic Medicine, 64,* 52–60.

Dickens, C., McGowan, L., & Dale, S. (2003). Impact of depression on experimental pain perception: A systematic review of the literature with meta-analysis. *Psychosomatic Medicine, 65,* 369–375.

Dickens, C., McGowan, L., Percival, C., Tomenson, B., Cotter, L., Heagerty, A., et al. (2008). New onset depression following myocardial infarction predicts cardiac mortality. *Psychosomatic Medicine, 70,* 450–455.

Dickerson, S. S., Kemeny, M. E., Aziz, N., Kim, K. H., & Fahey, J. L. (2004). Immunological effects of induced shame and guilt. *Psychosomatic Medicine, 66,* 124–131.

DiClemente, R. J., Crittenden, C. P., Rose, E., Sales, J. M., Wingood, G. M., Crosby, R. A., et al. (2008). Psychosocial predictors of HIV-associated sexual behavior and the efficacy of prevention interventions in adolescents at-risk for HIV infection: What works and what doesn't work? *Psychosomatic Medicine, 70,* 598–605.

Diefenbach, M. A., Leventhal, E. A., Leventhal, H., & Patrick-Miller, L. (1996). Negative affect relates to cross-sectional but not longitudinal symptom reporting: Data from elderly adults. *Health Psychology, 15,* 282–288.

Diego, M. A., Jones, N. A., Field, T., Hernandez-Reif, M., Schanberg, S., Kuhn, C., et al. (2006). Maternal psychological distress, prenatal cortisol, and fetal weight. *Psychosomatic Medicine, 68,* 747–753.

Dientsbier, R. A. (1989). Arousal and physiological toughness: Implications for mental and physical health. *Psychological Review, 96,* 84–100.

Dietz, W. H. (2004). Overweight in childhood and adolescence. *The New England Journal of Medicine, 350,* 855–857.

Dietz, W. H., & Gortmaker, S. L. (2001). Preventing obesity in children and adolescents. *Annual Review of Public Health, 22,* 337–353.

Dillon, C. F., Gu, Q., Hoffman, H. J., & Ko, C. W. (2010). Vision, hearing, balance, and sensory impairment in Americans aged 70 years and over: United States, 1999–2006. *NCHS Data Brief, 31,* 1–8.

DiLorenzo, T. A., Schnur, J., Montgomery, G. H., Erblich, J., Winkel, G., & Bovbjerg, D. H. (2006). A model of disease-specific worry in heritable disease: The influence of family history, perceived risk and worry about other illnesses. *Journal of Behavioral Medicine, 29,* 37–49.

DiMatteo, M. R. (2004). Social support and patient adherence to medical treatment: A meta-analysis. *Health Psychology, 23,* 207–218.

DiMatteo, M. R., & DiNicola, D. D. (1982). *Achieving patient compliance: The psychology of the medical practitioner's role.* New York: Pergamon Press.

DiMatteo, M. R., Friedman, H. S., & Taranta, A. (1979). Sensitivity to bodily nonverbal communication as a factor in practitioner-patient rapport. *Journal of Nonverbal Behavior, 4,* 18–26.

DiMatteo, M. R., Giordani, P. J., Lepper, H. S., & Croghan, T. W. (2002). Patient adherence and medical treatment outcomes: A meta-analysis. *Medical Care, 40,* 794–811.

DiMatteo, M. R., Hays, R. D., & Prince, L. M. (1986). Relationship of physicians' nonverbal communication skill to patient satisfaction, appointment noncompliance, and physical workload. *Health Psychology, 5,* 581–594.

DiMatteo, M. R., Lepper, H. S., & Croghan, T. W. (2000). Depression is a risk factor for noncompliance with medical treatment. *Archives of Internal Medicine, 160,* 2101–2107.

DiMatteo, M. R., Sherbourne, C. D., Hays, R. D., Ordway, L., Kravitz, R. L., McGlynn, E. A., Kaplan, S., & Rogers, W. H. (1993). Physicians' characteristics influence patients' adherence to medical treatment: Results from the Medical Outcomes Study. *Health Psychology, 12,* 93–102.

Dirkzwager, A. J. E., van der Velden, P. G., Grievink, L., & Yzermans, C. J. (2007). Disaster-related posttraumatic stress disorder and physical health. *Psychosomatic Medicine, 69,* 435–440.

Dishman, R. K. (1982). Compliance/adherence in health-related exercise. *Health Psychology, 1,* 237–267.

Dishman, R. K., Hales, D. P., Pfeiffer, K. A., Felton, G., Saunders, R., Ward, D. S., et al. (2006). Physical self-concept and self-esteem mediate cross-sectional relations of physical activity and sport participation with depression symptoms among adolescent girls. *Health Psychology, 25,* 396–407.

Ditto, P. H., Druley, J. A., Moore, K. A., Danks, H. J., & Smucker, W. D. (1996). Fates worse than death: The role of valued life activities in health-state evaluations. *Health Psychology, 15,* 332–343.

Ditto, P. H., & Hawkins, N. A. (2005). Advance directives and cancer decision making near the end of life. *Health Psychology, 24*(Suppl.), S63–70.

Ditto, P. H., Munro, G. D., Apanovich, A. M., Scepansky, J. A., & Lockhart, L. K. (2003). Spontaneous skepticism: The interplay of motivation and expectation in response to favorable and unfavorable medical diagnoses. *Personality and Social Psychology Bulletin, 29,* 1120–1132.

Ditto, P. H., Smucker, W. D., Danks, J. H., Jacobson, J. A., Houts, R. M., Fagerlin, A., et al. (2003). Stability of older adults' preferences for life-sustaining medical treatment. *Health Psychology, 22,* 605–615.

Ditzen, B., Hoppmann, C., & Klumb, P. (2008). Positive couple interactions and daily cortisol: On the stress-protecting role of intimacy. *Psychosomatic Medicine, 70,* 883–889.

Ditzen, B., Neumann, I. D., Bodenmann, G., von Dawans, B., Turner, R. A., Ehlert, U., et al. (2007). Effects of different kinds of couple interaction on cortisol and heart rate responses to stress in women. *Psychoneuroendocrinology, 32,* 565–574.

Dixon, K. E., Keefe, F. J., Scipio, C. D., Perri, L. M., & Abernethy, A. P. (2007). Psychological interventions for arthritis pain management in adults: A meta-analysis. *Health Psychology, 26,* 241–250.

Dobbins, T. A., Simpson, J. M., Oldenburg, B., Owen, N., & Harris, D. (1998). Who comes to a workplace health risk assessment? *International Journal of Behavioral Medicine, 5,* 323–334.

Dobson, K. S. (Ed.) (2010). *Handbook of cognitive behavioral therapies.* New York: Guilford.

Doll, J., & Orth, B. (1993). The Fishbein and Ajzen theory of reasoned action applied to contraceptive behavior: Model variants and meaningfulness. *Journal of Applied Social Psychology, 23,* 395–341.

Dominguez, T. P., Dunkel-Schetter, C., Glynn, L. M., Hobel, C., & Sandman, C. A. (2008). Racial differences in birth outcomes: The role of general, pregnancy, and racism stress. *Health Psychology, 27,* 194–203.

Donahue, R. G., Lampert, R., Dornelas, E., Clemow, L., & Burg, M. M. (2010). Rationale and design of a randomized clinical trial comparing stress reduction treatment to usual cardiac care: The reducing variability to implantable cardioverter defibrillator shock-treated ventricular arrhythmias (RISTA) trial. *Psychosomatic Medicine, 72,* 172–177.

Donaldson, S. I., Graham, J. W., & Hansen, W. B. (1994). Testing the generalizability of intervening mechanism theories: Understanding the effects of adolescent drug use prevention interventions. *Journal of Behavioral Medicine, 17,* 195–216.

Donaldson, S. I., Graham, J. W., Piccinin, A. M., & Hansen, W. B. (1995). Resistance-skills training and onset of alcohol use: Evidence for beneficial and potentially harmful effects in public schools and in private Catholic schools. *Health Psychology, 14,* 291–300.

Donovan, J. E., & Jessor, R. (1985). Structure of problem behavior in adolescence and young adulthood. *Journal of Consulting and Clinical Psychology, 53,* 890–904.

Donovan, J. E., Jessor, R., & Costa, F. M. (1991). Adolescent health behavior and conventionality-unconventionality: An extension of problem-behavior theory. *Health Psychology, 10,* 52–61.

Dore, G. A., Elias, M. F., Robbins, M. A., Budge, M. M., & Elias, P. K. (2008). Relation between central adiposity and cognitive function in the Maine-Syracuse study: Attenuation by physical activity. *Annals of Behavioral Medicine, 35,* 341–350.

Dorgan, C., & Editue, A. (1995). *Statistical record of health and medicine: 1995.* Detroit: Orale Research.

Doshi, A., Patrick, K., Sallis, J. F., & Calfas, K. (2003). Evaluation of physical activity web sites for use of behavior change theories. *Annals of Behavioral Medicine, 25,* 105–111.

Dougall, A. L., Smith, A. W., Somers, T. J., Posluszny, D. M., Rubinstein, W. S., & Baum, A. (2009). Coping with genetic testing for breast cancer susceptibility. *Psychosomatic Medicine, 71,* 98–105.

Dowda, M., Dishman, R. K., Porter, D., Saunders, R. P., & Pate, R. R. (2009). Commercial facilities, social cognitive variables, and physical activity of 12th grade girls. *Annals of Behavioral Medicine, 37,* 70–87.

Downey, G., Silver, R. C., & Wortman, C. B. (1990). Reconsidering the attribution-adjustment relation following a major negative event: Coping with the loss of a child. *Journal of Personality and Social Psychology, 59,* 925–940.

Dracup, K. (1985). A controlled trial of couples' group counseling in cardiac rehabilitation. *Journal of Cardiopulmonary Rehabilitation, 5,* 436–442.

Dracup, K., Guzy, P. M., Taylor, S. E., & Barry, J. (1986). Cardiopulmonary resuscitation (CPR) training: Consequences for family members of high-risk cardiac patients. *Archives of Internal Medicine, 146,* 1757–1761.

Dracup, K., & Moser, D. (1991). Treatment-seeking behavior among those with signs and symptoms of acute myocardial infarction. *Heart and Lung, 20,* 570–575.

Drewnowski, A., Darmon, N., & Briend, A. (2004). Replacing fats and sweets with vegetables and fruits—a question of cost. *American Journal of Public Health, 94,* 1555–1559.

Droge, D., Arntson, P., & Norton, R. (1986). The social support function in epilepsy self-help groups. *Small Group Behavior, 17,* 139–163.

Droomers, M., Schrijivers, C. T. M., & Mackenbach, J. P. (2002). Why do lower educated people continue smoking? Explanations from the longitudinal GLOBE study. *Health Psychology, 21,* 263–272.

Drossman, D. A., Leserman, J., Li, Z., Keefe, F., Hu, Y. J. B., & Toomey, T. C. (2000). Effects of coping on health outcome among women with gastrointestinal disorders. *Psychosomatic Medicine, 62,* 309–317.

D'Souza, P. J., Lumley, M. A., Kraft, C. A., & Dooley, J. A. (2008). Relaxation training and written emotional disclosure for tension or migraine headaches: A randomized, controlled trial. *Annals of Behavioral Medicine, 36,* 21–32.

Duangdao, K. M., & Roesch, S. C. (2008). Coping with diabetes in adulthood: A meta-analysis. *Journal of Behavioral Medicine, 31,* 291–300.

Dube, S. R., Fairweather, D., Pearson, W. S., Felitti, V. J., Anda, R. F., & Croft, J. B. (2009). Cumulative childhood stress and autoimmune diseases in adults. *Psychosomatic Medicine, 71,* 243–250.

Duenwald, M. (2002, September 17). Students find another staple of campus life: Stress. *New York Times,* p. F5.

DuHamel, K. N., Manne, S., Nereo, N., Ostroff, J., Martini, R., Parsons, S., et al. (2004). Cognitive processing among mothers of children undergoing bone marrow/stem cell transplantation. *Psychosomatic Medicine, 66,* 92–103.

Duits, A. A., Boeke, S., Taams, M. A., Passchier, J., & Erdman, R. A. M. (1997). Prediction of quality of life after coronary artery bypass graft surgery: A review and evaluation of multiple, recent studies. *Psychosomatic Medicine, 59,* 257–268.

Dujovne, V. F., & Houston, B. K. (1991). Hostility-related variables and plasma lipid levels. *Journal of Behavioral Medicine, 14,* 555–565.

Dunbar, F. (1943). *Psychosomatic diagnosis.* New York: Hoeber.

Dunbar-Jacob, J., Dwyer, K., & Dunning, E. J. (1991). Compliance with antihypertensive regimen: A review of the research in the 1980s. *Annals of Behavioral Medicine, 13,* 31–39.

Duncan, S. C., Duncan, T. E., & Strycker, L. A. (2005). Sources and types of social support in youth physical activity. *Health Psychology, 24,* 3–10.

Duncan, S. C., Duncan, T. E., Strycker, L. A., & Chaumeton, N. R. (2002). Relations between youth antisocial and prosocial activities. *Journal of Behavioral Medicine, 25,* 425–438.

Dunkel-Schetter, C., Feinstein, L. G., Taylor, S. E., & Falke, R. L. (1992). Patterns of coping with cancer. *Health Psychology, 11,* 79–87.

Dunton, G. F., & Vaughan, E. (2008). Anticipated affective consequences of physical activity adoption and maintenance. *Health Psychology, 27,* 703–710.

DuPont, R. L. (1988). The counselor's dilemma: Treating chemical dependence at college. In T. M. Rivinus (Ed.), *Alcoholism/chemical dependency and the college student* (pp. 41–61). New York: Haworth Press.

Dutton, G. R., Tan, F., Provost, B. C., Sorenson, J. L., Allen, B., & Smith, D. (2009). Relationships between self-efficacy and physical activity among patients with type 2 diabetes. *Journal of Behavioral Medicine, 32,* 270–277.

Duxbury, M. L., Armstrong, G. D., Dren, D. J., & Henley, S. J. (1984). Head nurse leadership style with staff nurse burnout and job satisfaction in neonatal intensive care units. *Nursing Research, 33,* 97–101.

Eaker, E. D., Sullivan, L. M., Kelly-Hayes, M., D'Agostino, R. B., & Benjamin, E. J. (2005). Tension and anxiety and the prediction of the 10-year incidence of coronary heart disease, atrial fibrillation, and total mortality: The Framingham Offspring Study. *Psychosomatic Medicine, 67,* 692–696.

Eaker, E. D., Sullivan, L. M., Kelly-Hayes, M., D'Agostino, R. B., & Benjamin, E. J. (2007). Marital status, marital strain, and risk of coronary heart disease or total mortality: The Framingham offspring study. *Psychosomatic Medicine, 69,* 509–513.

Eakin, E. G., Bull, S. S., Riley, K. M., Reeves, M. M., McLaughlin, P., & Gutierrez, S. (2007). Resources for health: A primary-care-based diet and physical activity intervention targeting urban Latinos with multiple chronic conditions. *Health Psychology, 26,* 392–400.

Earl, A., & Albarracin, D. (2007). Nature, decay, and spiraling of the effects of fear-inducing arguments and HIV counseling and testing: A meta-analysis of the short- and long-term outcomes of HIV-prevention interventions. *Health Psychology, 26,* 496–506.

Eaton, W. W., Muntaner, C., Bovasso, G., & Smith, C. (2001). Socioeconomic status and depressive syndrome: The role of inter- and intra-generational mobility, government assistance, and work environment. *Journal of Health and Social Behavior, 42,* 277–294.

Echteld, M. A., van Elderen, T., & van der Kamp, L. J. (2003). Modeling predictors of quality of life after coronary angioplasty. *Annals of Behavioral Medicine, 26,* 49–60.

The Economist. (2005, October 1). *Molecular self-loathing,* pp. 75–76.

The Economist. (2007, July 1). *Killing Time,* p. 78.

Edwards, K. M., Burns, V. E., Adkins, A. E., Carroll, D., Drayson, M., & Ring, C. (2008). Meningococcal A vaccination response in enhanced by acute stress in men. *Psychosomatic Medicine, 70,* 147–151.

Edwards, R. R. (2008). The association of perceived discrimination with low back pain. *Journal of Behavioral Medicine, 31,* 379–389.

Edwards, R. R., Campbell, C., Jamison, R. N., & Wiech, K. (2009). The neurobiological underpinnings of coping with pain. *Current Directions in Psychological Science, 18,* 237–241.

Edwards, R. R., Smith, M. T., Klick, B., Magyar-Russell, G., Haythornthwaite, J. A., Holavanahalli, R., et al. (2007). Symptoms of depression and anxiety as unique predictors of pain-related outcomes following burn injury. *Annals of Behavioral Medicine, 34,* 313–322.

Edwards, R., Telfair, J., Cecil, H., & Lenoci, J. (2001). Self-efficacy as a predictor of adult adjustment to sickle cell disease: One-year outcomes. *Psychosomatic Medicine, 63,* 850–858.

Edwards, S., Hucklebridge, F., Clow, A., & Evans, P. (2003). Components of the diurnal cortisol cycle in relation to upper respiratory symptoms and perceived stress. *Psychosomatic Medicine, 65,* 320–327.

Egede, L. E. (2005). Effect of comorbid chronic diseases on prevalence and odds of depression in adults with diabetes. *Psychosomatic Medicine, 67,* 46–51.

Eifert, G. H., Hodson, S. E., Tracey, D. R., Seville, J. L., & Gunawardane, K. (1996). Heart-focused anxiety, illness beliefs, and behavioral impairment: Comparing healthy heart-anxious patients with cardiac and surgical inpatients. *Journal of Behavioral Medicine, 19,* 385–400.

Eisenberg, D., & Sieger, M. (2003, June 9). The doctor won't see you now. *Time,* pp. 46–60.

Eisenberg, D. M., Kessler, R. C., Foster, C., Norlock, F. E., Calkins, D. R., & Delbanco, T. L. (1993). Unconventional medicine in the United States: Prevalence, costs, and patterns of use. *The New England Journal of Medicine, 328,* 246–252.

Eiser, J. R., van der Plight, J., Raw, M., & Sutton, S. R. (1985). Trying to stop smoking: Effects of perceived addiction, attributions for failure, and expectancy of success. *Journal of Behavioral Medicine, 8,* 321–342.

Eiser, R., & Gentle, P. (1988). Health behavior as goal-directed action. *Journal of Behavioral Medicine, 11,* 523–536.

Eitle, D. J., & Eitle, T. M. (2004). School and county characteristics as predictors of school rates of drug, alcohol, and tobacco offenses. *Journal of Health and Social Behavior, 45,* 408–421.

Ekkekakis, P., Hall, E. E., VanLanduyt, L. M., & Petruzzello, S. J. (2000). Walking in (affective) circles: Can short walks enhance affect? *Journal of Behavioral Medicine, 23,* 245–275.

Ekstedt, M., Åkerstedt, T., & Söderström, M. (2004). Microarousals during sleep are associated with increased levels of lipids, cortisol, and blood pressure. *Psychosomatic Medicine, 66,* 925–931.

Elchisak, M. A. (2001). *Acamprosate (Campral): Medication for alcohol abuse and alcoholism treatment.* Retrieved from www.doctordeluca.com/Documents/AcamprosateSummary.htm

Elder, J. P., Ayala, G. X., Campbell, N. R., Slymen, D., Lopez-Madurga, E. T., Engelberg, M., et al. (2005). Interpersonal and print nutrition communication for Spanish-dominant Latino population: Secretos de la Buena vida. *Health Psychology, 24,* 49–57.

Ellington, L., & Wiebe, D. (1999). Neuroticism, symptom presentation, and medical decision making. *Health Psychology, 18,* 634–643.

Ellis, A. (1962). *Reason and emotion in psychotherapy.* New York: Lyle Stuart.

Elmore, J. G., & Gigerenzer, G. (2005). Benign breast disease—the risks of communicating risk. *The New England Journal of Medicine, 353,* 297–299.

Elovainio, M., Aalto, A. M., Kivimäki, M., Pirkola, S., Sundvall, J., Lönnqvist, J., et al. (2009). Depression and C-reactive protein: Population-based health 2000 study. *Psychosomatic Medicine, 71,* 423–430.

Elovainio, M., Ferrie, J. E., Gimeno, D., De Vogli, R., Shipley, M., Brunner, E. J., et al. (2009). Organizational justice and sleeping problems: The Whitehall II study. *Psychosomatic Medicine, 71,* 334–340.

Elovainio, M., Keltikangas-Järvinen, L., Kivimäki, M., Pulkki, L., Puttonen, S., Heponiemi, T., et al. (2005). Depressive symptoms and carotid artery intima-media thickness in young adults: The cardiovascular risk in young Finns study. *Psychosomatic Medicine, 67,* 561–567.

Elstein, A. S., Chapman, G. B., & Knight, S. J. (2005). Patients' values and clinical substituted judgments: The case of localized prostate cancer. *Health Psychology, 24,* S85–S92.

Emerson, S. U., & Purcell, R. H. (2004). Running like water—the omnipresence of hepatitis E. *The New England Journal of Medicine, 351,* 2367–2368.

Emery, C. F., Kiecolt-Glaser, J. K., Glaser, R., Malarkey, W. B., & Frid, D. J. (2005). Exercise accelerates wound healing among healthy older adults: A preliminary investigation. *Journal of Gerontology: Medical Sciences, 60A,* 1432–1436.

Emmons, C., Biernat, M., Teidje, L. B., Lang, E. L., & Wortman, C. B. (1990). Stress, support, and coping among women professionals with preschool children. In J. Eckenrode & S. Gore (Eds.), *Stress between work and family* (pp. 61–93). New York: Plenum Press.

Emmons, K. M., Hammond, S. K., Fava, J. L., Velicer, W. F., Evans, J. L., & Monroe, A. D. (2001). A randomized trial to reduce passive smoke exposure in low-income households with young children. *Pediatrics, 108,* 18–24.

Eng, P. M., Fitzmaurice, G., Kubzansky, L. D., Rimm, E. B., & Kawachi, I. (2003). Anger in expression and risk of stroke and coronary heart disease among male health professionals. *Psychosomatic Medicine, 65,* 100–110.

Engebretson, T. O., & Matthews, K. A. (1992). Dimensions of hostility in men, women, and boys: Relationships to personality and cardiovascular responses to stress. *Psychosomatic Medicine, 54,* 311–323.

Engler, P., Anderson, B., Herman, D., Bishop, D., Miller, I., Pirraglia, P., et al. (2006). Coping and burden among HIV caregivers. *Psychosomatic Medicine, 68,* 985–992.

Ennett, S. T., & Bauman, K. E. (1993). Peer group structure and adolescent cigarette smoking: A social network analysis. *Journal of Health and Social Behavior, 34,* 226–236.

ENRICHD. (2001). Enhancing recovery in coronary heart disease (ENRICHD) study intervention: rational and design. *Psychosomatic Medicine, 63,* 747–755.

Enright, M. F., Resnick, R., DeLeon, P. H., Sciara, A. D., & Tanney, F. (1990). The practice of psychology in hospital settings. *American Psychologist, 45,* 1059–1065.

Environmental Health Perspectives. (2004). Study finds that combined exposure to second-hand smoke and urban air pollutants during pregnancy adversely affects birth outcomes. Retrieved from http://ehp.niehs.nih.gov/press/012304.html

Epel, E. S., McEwen, B., Seeman, T., Matthews, K., Catellazzo, G., Brownell, K., et al. (2000). Stress and body shape: Stress-induced cortisol secretion is consistently greater among women with central fat. *Psychosomatic Medicine, 62,* 623–632.

Epilepsy Foundation. (2009). *About epilepsy.* Retrieved February 2, 2011, from http://www.epilepsyfoundation.org/about/

Epker, J., & Gatchel, R. J. (2000). Coping profile differences in the biopsychosocial functioning of patients with temporomandibular disorder. *Psychosomatic Medicine, 62,* 69–75.

Epping-Jordan, J., Williams, R., Pruitt, S., Patterson, T., Grant, I., Wahlgren, D., et al. (1998). Transition to chronic pain in men with low back pain: Predictive relationships among pain intensity, disability, and depressive symptoms. *Health Psychology, 17,* 421–427.

Epping-Jordan, J. A., Compas, B. E., & Howell, D. C. (1994). Predictors of cancer progression in young adult men and women: Avoidance, intrusive thoughts, and psychological symptoms. *Health Psychology, 13,* 539–547.

Epstein, F. M., Sloan, D. M., & Marx, B. P. (2005). Getting to the heart of the matter: Written disclosure, gender, and heart rate. *Psychosomatic Medicine, 67,* 413–419.

Epstein, L. H., Kilanowski, C. K., Consalvi, A. R., & Paluch, R. A. (1999). Reinforcing value of physical activity as a determinant of child activity level. *Health Psychology, 18,* 599–603.

Epstein, L. H., Paluch, R. A., Roemmich, J. N., & Beecher, M. D. (2007). Family-based obesity treatments, then and now: Twenty-five years of pediatric obesity treatment. *Health Psychology, 26,* 381–391.

Epstein, L. H., Saelens, B. E., Myers, M. D., & Vito, D. (1997). Effects of decreasing sedentary behaviors on activity choice in obese children. *Health Psychology, 16,* 107–113.

Epstein, L. H., Valoski, A. M., Vara, L. S., McCurley, J., Wisniewski, L., Kalarchian, M. A., et al. (1995). Effects of decreasing sedentary behavior and increasing activity on weight change in obese children. *Health Psychology, 14,* 109–115.

Epstein, L. H., Valoski, A., Wing, R. R., & McCurley, J. (1994). Ten-year outcomes of behavioral family-based treatment for childhood obesity. *Health Psychology, 13,* 373–383.

Epstein, R. M., Shields, C. G., Meldrum, S. C., Fiscella, K., Carroll, J., Carney, P. A., et al. (2006). Physicians' responses to patients' medically unexplained symptoms. *Psychosomatic Medicine, 68,* 269–276.

Epstein, S., & Katz, L. (1992). Coping ability, stress, productive load, and symptoms. *Journal of Personality and Social Psychology, 62,* 813–825.

Epton, T., & Harris, P. R. (2008). Self-affirmation promotes health behavior change. *Health Psychology, 27,* 746–752.

Escobar, J. I., & Gureje, O. (2007). Influence of cultural and social factors on the epidemiology of idiopathic somatic complaints and syndroms. *Psychosomatic Medicine, 69,* 841–845.

Esposito-Del Puente, A., Lillioja, S., Bogardus, C., McCubbin, J. A., Feinglos, M. N., Kuhn, C. M., et al. (1994). Glycemic response to stress is altered in euglycemic Pima Indians. *International Journal of Obesity, 18,* 766–770.

Estabrooks, P. A., Bradshaw, M., Dzewaltowski, D. A., & Smith-Ray, R. L. (2008). Determining the impact of walk Kansas: Applying a team-building approach to community physical activity promotion. *Annals of Behavioral Medicine, 36,* 1–12.

Estabrooks, P. A., Lee, R. E., & Gyurcsik, N. C. (2003). Resources for physical activity participation: Does availability and accessibility differ by neighborhood socioeconomic status? *Annals of Behavioral Medicine, 25,* 100–104.

Esterling, B. A., Kiecolt-Glaser, J. K., Bodnar, J. C., & Glaser, R. (1994). Chronic stress, social support, and persistent alterations in the natural killer cell response to cytokines in older adults. *Health Psychology, 13,* 291–298.

Esterling, B. A., Kiecolt-Glaser, J. K., & Glaser, R. (1996). Psychosocial modulation of cytokine-induced natural killer cell activity in older adults. *Psychosomatic Medicine, 58,* 264–272.

Evans, G. W., & Wener, R. E. (2006). Rail commuting duration and passenger stress. *Health Psychology, 25,* 408–412.

Evans, W. D., Powers, A., Hersey, J., & Renaud, J. (2006). The influence of social environment and social image on adolescent smoking. *Health Psychology, 25,* 26–33.

Everson, S. A., Goldberg, D. E., Kaplan, G. A., Julkunen, J., & Salonen, J. T. (1998). Anger expression and incident hypertension. *Psychosomatic Medicine, 60,* 730–735.

Everson, S. A., Lovallo, W. R., Sausen, K. P., & Wilson, M. F. (1992). Hemodynamic characteristics of young men at risk for hypertension at rest and during laboratory stressors. *Health Psychology, 11,* 24–31.

Everson-Rose, S. A., Lewis, T. T., Karavolos, K., Dugan, S. A., Wesley, D., & Powell, L. H. (2009). Depressive symptoms and increased visceral fat in middle-aged women. *Psychosomatic Medicine, 71,* 410–416.

Ewart, C. K. (1991). Familial transmission of essential hypertension: Genes, environments, and chronic anger. *Annals of Behavioral Medicine, 13,* 40–47.

Ewart, C. K., & Jorgensen, R. S. (2004). Agonistic interpersonal striving: Social-cognitive mechanism of cardiovascular risk in youth? *Health Psychology, 23,* 75–85.

Facebook. (2009). *Statistics.* Retrieved October 7, 2009, from http://www.facebook.com/press/info.php?statistics

Facts of Life. (2002, February). Women and heart disease: Looks different, kills just the same. Center for the Advancement of Health, *7*(2).

Facts of Life. (2002, July). Cover your hide: Too much sun can lead to skin cancer. Center for the Advancement of Health, *7*(7).

Facts of Life. (2002, November). Food for thought: Prevention of eating disorders in children. Center for the Advancement of Health, *7*(11).

Facts of Life. (2003, March). Talking the talk: Improving patient-provider communication. Center for the Advancement of Health, *8*(3).

Facts of Life. (2003, November). Health education: Schools learn the hard way. Center for the Advancement of Health, *8*(11).

Facts of Life. (2003, December). Potential health benefits of moderate drinking. Center for the Advancement of Health, *8*(12).

Facts of Life. (2004, March). Working out the problem of insufficient exercise. Center for the Advancement of Health, *9*(3).

Facts of Life. (2004, May). On the road to improving traffic safety. Center for the Advancement of Health, *9*(5).

Facts of Life. (2004, December). Weighing the data: Obesity affects elderly, too. Center for the Advancement of Health, *9*(12).

Facts of Life. (2005, February). Staying safe at home. Center for the Advancement of Health, *10*(2).

Facts of Life. (2005, July). Smoking cessation: Beyond the patch. Center for the Advancement of Health, *10*(7).

Facts of Life. (2005, September). The economics of obesity. Center for the Advancement of Health, *10*(9).

Facts of Life. (2006, February). Different risk: Race-based health care and medicine. Center for the Advancement of Health, *11*(2).

Facts of Life. (2006, March). Aging well: Preventing falls among older adults. Center for the Advancement of Health, *11*(3).

Facts of Life. (2006, May). Aging well: Why exercise is essential. Center for the Advancement of Health, *11*(5).

Facts of Life. (2006, June). Genes, screens and a healthy future. Center for the Advancement of Health, *11*(6).

Facts of Life. (2006, November). An aging marketplace. Center for the Advancement of Health, *11*(11).

Facts of Life. (2007, February). Statins: Still going strong. Center for the Advancement of Health, *12*(2).

Fagan, J., Galea, S., Ahern, J., Bonner, S., & Vlahov, D. (2003). Relationship of self-reported asthma severity and urgent health care utilization to psychological sequelae of the September 11, 2001 terrorist attacks on the World Trade Center among New York City area residents. *Psychosomatic Medicine, 65*, 993–996.

Fagerlin, A., Ditto, P. H., Danks, J. H., Houts, R. M., & Smucker, W. D. (2001). Projection in surrogate decisions about life-sustaining medical treatments. *Health Psychology, 20*, 166–175.

Falba, T. (2005). Health events and the smoking cessation of middle aged Americans. *Journal of Behavioral Medicine, 28*, 21–33.

Falk, A., Hanson, B. S., Isaacsson, C., & Ostergren, P. (1992). Job strain and mortality in elderly men: Social network support and influence as buffers. *American Journal of Public Health, 82*, 1136–1139.

Fang, C. Y., Miller, S. M., Bovbjerg, D. H., Bergman, C., Edelson, M. I., Rosenblum, N. G., et al. (2008). Perceived stress is associated with impaired T-cell response to HPV16 in women with cervical dysplasia. *Annals of Behavioral Medicine, 35*, 87–96.

Fawzy, F. I., Cousins, N., Fawzy, N. W., Kemeny, M. E., Elashoff, R., & Morton, D. (1990). A structured psychiatric intervention for cancer patients, I: Changes over time in methods of coping and affective disturbance. *Archives of General Psychiatry, 47*, 720–725.

Fawzy, F. I., Kemeny, M. E., Fawzy, M. W., Elashoff, R., Morton, D., Cousins, N., & Fahey, J. (1990). A structured psychiatric intervention for cancer patients, II: Changes over time in immunological measures. *Archives of General Psychiatry, 47*, 729–735.

Federspiel, J. F. (1983). *The ballad of Typhoid Mary.* New York: Dutton.

Feeny, N., Foa, E. B., Treadwell, K. R. H., & March, J. (2004). Posttraumatic stress disorder in youth: A critical review of the cognitive and behavioral treatment outcome literature. *Professional Psychology: Research and Practice, 35*, 466–476.

Feinglos, M. N., & Surwit, R. S. (1988). *Behavior and diabetes mellitus.* Kalamazoo, MI: Upjohn.

Feldman, P., Cohen, S., Doyle, W., Skoner, D., & Gwaltney, J. (1999). The impact of personality on the reporting of unfounded symptoms and illness. *Journal of Personality and Social Psychology, 77*, 370–378.

Feldman, P. J., Dunkel-Schetter, C., Sandman, C. A., & Wadhwa, P. D. (2000). Maternal social support predicts birth weight and fetal growth in human pregnancy. *Psychosomatic Medicine, 62*, 715–725.

Feldman, P. J., & Steptoe, A. (2004). How neighborhoods and physical functioning are related: The roles of neighborhood socioeconomic status, perceived neighborhood strain, and individual health risk factors. *Annals of Behavioral Medicine, 27*, 91–99.

Felitti, V. J., Anda, R. F., Nordenberg, D., Williamson, D. F., Apitz, A. M., Edwards, V., et al. (1998). Relationship of childhood abuse and household dysfunction to many of the leading causes of death in adults. *American Journal of Preventive Medicine, 14*, 245–258.

Ferguson, E., Williams, L., O'Connor, R. C., Howard, S., Hughes, B. M., Johnston, D. W., et al. (2009). A taxometric analysis of type-D personality. *Psychosomatic Medicine, 71*, 981–986.

Fernandez, A. B., Soufer, R., Collins, D., Soufer, A., Ranjbaran, H., & Burg, M. M. (2010). Tendency to angry rumination predicts stress-provoked endothelin-1 increase in patients with coronary artery disease. *Psychosomatic Medicine, 72*, 348–353.

Fernandez, E., & Turk, D. C. (1992). Sensory and affective components of pain: Separation and synthesis. *Psychological Bulletin, 112*, 205–217.

Fernández-Mendoza, J., Vela-Bueno, A., Vgontzas, A. N., Ramos-Platón, M. J., Olavarrieta-Bernardino, S., Bixler, E. O., et al. (2010). Cognitive-emotional hyperarousal as a premorbid characteristic of individuals vulnerable to insomnia. *Psychosomatic Medicine, 72*, 397–403.

Fiatarone, M. A., Morley, J. E., Bloom, E. T., Benton, D., Makinodan, T., & Solomon, G. F. (1988). Endogenous opioids and the exercise-induced augmentation of natural killer cell activity. *Journal of Laboratory and Clinical Medicine, 112*, 544–552.

Fichten, C. S., Libman, E., Creti, L., Balles, S., & Sabourin, S. (2004). Long sleepers sleep more and short sleepers sleep less: A comparison of older adults who sleep well. *Behavioral Sleep Medicine, 2*, 2–23.

Fielding, J. E. (1978). Successes of prevention. *Milbank Memorial Fund Quarterly, 56*, 274–302.

Fife, B. L., & Wright, E. R. (2000). The dimensionality of stigma: A comparison of its impact on the self of persons with HIV/AIDS and cancer. *Journal of Health and Social Behavior, 41*, 50–67.

Fifield, J., McQuinlan, J., Tennen, H., Sheehan, T. J., Reisine, S., Hesselbrock, V., et al. (2001). History of affective disorder and the temporal trajectory of fatigue in rheumatoid arthritis. *Annals of Behavioral Medicine, 23*, 34–41.

Filipkowski, K. B., Smyth, J. M., Rutchick, A. M., Santuzzi, A. M., Adya, M., Petrie, K. J., et al. (2009). Do healthy people worry? Modern health worries, subjective health complaints, perceived health, and health care utilization. *International Journal of Behavioral Medicine, 17*, 182–188.

Fillingham, R. B., & Maixner, W. (1996). The influence of resting blood pressure and gender on pain responses. *Psychosomatic Medicine, 58*, 326–332.

Finan, P. H., Zautra, A. J., & Davis, M. C. (2009). Daily affect relations in fibromyalgia patients reveal positive affective disturbance. *Psychosomatic Medicine, 71*, 474–482.

Financial Times. (2009, October 14). Ways to take stock of it all. *Financial Times*, p. 9.

Finch, E. A., Linde, J. A., Jeffery, R. W., Rothman, A. J., King, C. M., & Levy, R. L. (2005). The effects of outcome expectations and satisfaction on weight loss and maintenance: Correlational and experimental analyses—a randomized trial. *Health Psychology, 24*, 608–616.

Findley, J. C., Kerns, R., Weinberg, L. D., & Rosenberg, R. (1998). Self-efficacy as a psychological moderator of chronic fatigue syndrome. *Journal of Behavioral Medicine, 21*, 351–362.

Findley, T. (1953). The placebo and the physician. *Medical Clinics of North America, 37*, 1821–1826.

Fink, P., Toft, T., Hansen, M. S., Ornbol, E., & Olesen, F. (2007). Symptoms and syndromes of bodily distress: An exploratory study of 978 internal medical, neurological, and primary care patients. *Psychosomatic Medicine, 69*, 30–39.

Finney, J. W., & Moos, R. H. (1995). Entering treatment for alcohol abuse: A stress and coping method. *Addiction, 90*, 1223–1240.

Firestein, G. S. (2003). Evolving concepts of rheumatoid arthritis. *Nature, 423*, 356–361.

Fishbain, D., Cutler, R., Rosomoff, H., & Rosomoff, R. (1998). Do antidepressants have an analgesic effect in psychogenic pain and somatoform pain disorder? A meta-analysis. *Psychosomatic Medicine, 60*, 503–509.

Fishbein, M., & Ajzen, I. (1975). *Belief, attitude, intention, and behavior: An introduction to theory and research.* Reading, MA: Addison-Wesley.

Fisher, J. D., & Fisher, W. A. (1992). Changing AIDS-risk behavior. *Psychological Bulletin, 111*, 455–474.

Fisher, J. D., Fisher, W. A., Amico, K. R., & Harman, J. J. (2006). An information-motivation-behavioral skills model of adherence to antiretroviral therapy. *Health Psychology, 25*, 462–473.

Fisher, J. D., Fisher, W. A., Bryan, A. D., & Misovich, S. J. (2002). Information-motivation-behavioral skills model-based HIV risk behavior change intervention for inner-city high school youth. *Health Psychology, 21*, 177–186.

Fisher, L., Soubhi, H., Mansi, O., Paradis, G., Gauvin, L., & Potvin, L. (1998). Family process in health research: Extending a family typology to a new cultural context. *Health Psychology, 17*, 358–366.

Fisher, W. A., Fisher, J. D., & Harman, J. J. (2003). The information-motivation-behavioral skills model: A general social psychological approach to understanding and promoting health behavior. In J. Suls & K. Wallston (Eds.), *Social psychological foundations of health and illness* (pp. 82–105). Oxford, UK: Blackwell.

Fisher, W. A., Fisher, J. D., & Rye, B. J. (1995). Understanding and promoting AIDS-preventive behavior: Insights from the theory of reasoned action. *Health Psychology, 14*, 255–264.

Fitzgerald, S. T., Haythornthwaite, J. A., Suchday, S., & Ewart, C. K. (2003). Anger in young black and white workers: Effects of job control, dissatisfaction, and support. *Journal of Behavioral Medicine, 26*, 283–296.

Fjeldsoe, B. S., Miller, Y. D., & Marshall, A. L. (2010). MobileMums: A randomized controlled trial of an SMS-based physical activity intervention. *Annals of Behavioral Medicine, 39*, 101–111.

Flay, B. R., Koepke, D., Thomson, S. J., Santi, S., Best, J. A., & Brown, K. S. (1992). Six year follow-up of the first Waterloo school smoking prevention trial. *American Journal of Public Health, 68*, 458–478.

Flegal, K. M., Graubard, B, I., Williamson, D. F., & Gail, M. H. (2007). Cause-specific excess deaths associated with underweight, overweight, and obesity. *Journal of the American Medical Association, 298*, 2028–2037.

Fleming, R., Baum, A., Davidson, L. M., Rectanus, E., & McArdle, S. (1987). Chronic stress as a factor in physiologic reactivity to challenge. *Health Psychology, 6*, 221–237.

Fleming, R., Leventhal, H., Glynn, K., & Ershler, J. (1989). The role of cigarettes in the initiation and progression of early substance use. *Addictive Behaviors, 14*, 261–272.

Fletcher, K. E., Clemow, L., Peterson, B. A., Lemon, S. C., Estabrook, B., & Zapka, J. G. (2006). A path analysis of factors associated with distress among first-degree female relatives of women with breast cancer diagnosis. *Health Psychology, 25*, 413–425.

Flood, A. M., McDevitt-Murphy, M. E., Weathers, F. W., Eakin, D. E., & Benson, T. A. (2009). Substance use behaviors as a mediator between post-traumatic stress disorder and physical health in trauma-exposed college students. *Journal of Behavioral Medicine, 32*, 234–243.

Flor, H., Birbaumer, N., & Turk, D. C. (1990). The psychology of chronic pain. *Advances in Behavior Research and Therapy, 12*, 47–84.

Flores, G. (2006). Language barriers to health care in the United States. *The New England Journal of Medicine, 355*, 229–231.

Flory, J., Young-Xu, Y., Gurol, I., Levinsky, N., Ash, A., & Emanuel, E. (2004). Place of death: U.S. trends since 1980. *Health Affairs, 23*, 194–200.

Flory, J. D., & Manuck, S. B. (2009). Impulsiveness and cigarette smoking. *Psychosomatic Medicine, 71*, 431–437.

Floyd, A., & Moyer, A. (2010). Group versus individual exercise interventions for women with breast cancer: A meta-analysis. *Health Psychology Review, 4*, 22–41.

Focht, B. C., Ewing, V., Gauvin, L., & Rejeski, W. J. (2002). The unique and transient impact of exercise on pain perception in older, overweight, or obese adults with knee osteoarthritis. *Annals of Behavioral Medicine, 24*, 201–210.

Focht, B. C., Gauvin, L., & Rejeski, W. J. (2004). The contribution of daily experiences and acute exercise to fluctuations in daily feeling states among older, obese adults with knee osteoarthritis. *Journal of Behavioral Medicine, 27*, 101–121.

Fogel, J., Albert, S. M., Schnabel, F., Ditkoff, B. A., & Neuget, A. I. (2002). Internet use and support in women with breast cancer. *Health Psychology, 21*, 398–404.

Folkman, S., Chesney, M., McKusick, L., Ironson, G., Johnson, D. S., et al. (1991). Translating coping theory into intervention. In J. Eckenrode (Ed.), *The social context of coping* (pp. 239–259). New York: Plenum.

Folkman, S., & Lazarus, R. S. (1980). An analysis of coping in a middle-aged community sample. *Journal of Health and Social Behavior, 21*, 219–239.

Folkman, S., & Moskowitz, J. T. (2004). Coping: Pitfalls and promise. *Annual Review of Psychology, 55*, 745–774.

Folkman, S., Schaefer, C., & Lazarus, R. S. (1979). Cognitive processes as mediators of stress and coping. In V. Hamilton & D. M. Warburton (Eds.), *Human stress and cognition: An information processing approach* (pp. 265–298). London: Wiley.

Forsyth, A. D., & Carey, M. P. (1998). Measuring self-efficacy in the context of HIV risk reduction: Research challenges and recommendations. *Health Psychology, 6*, 559–568.

Foster, G. D., Wadden, T. A., & Vogt, R.A. (1997). Body image in obese women before, during, and after weight loss treatment. *Health Psychology, 16*, 226–229.

Foster, G. D., Wadden, T. A., Vogt, R. A., & Brewer, G. (1997). What is a reasonable weight loss? Patients' expectations and evaluations of obesity treatment outcomes. *Journal of Consulting and Clinical Psychology, 65*, 79–85.

Fox, R. C. (2005). Cultural competence and the culture of medicine. *The New England Journal of Medicine, 353*, 1316–1319.

Frances, R. J., Franklin, J., & Flavin, D. (1986). Suicide and alcoholism. *Annals of the New York Academy of Sciences, 487*, 316–326.

Francis, A., Fyer, M., & Clarkin, J. (1986). Personality and suicide. *Annals of the New York Academy of Sciences, 487*, 281–293.

Francis, L. A., & Birch, L. L. (2005). Maternal influences on daughters' restrained eating behavior. *Health Psychology, 24*, 548–554.

Frankenberg, E., & Jones, N. R. (2004). Self-rated health and mortality: Does the relationship extend to a low income setting? *Journal of Health and Social Behavior, 45*, 441–452.

Frankenhaeuser, M. (1991). The psychophysiology of workload, stress, and health: Comparison between the sexes. *Annals of Behavioral Medicine, 13*, 197–204.

Frankenhaeuser, M., Lundberg, U., Fredrikson, M., Melin, B., Tuomisto, M., Myrsten, A., et al. (1989). Stress on and off the job as related to sex and occupational status in white-collar workers. *Journal of Organizational Behavior, 10*, 321–346.

Franko, D. L., Mintz, L. B., Villapiano, M., Green, T. C., Mainelli, D., Folensbee, L., et al. (2005). Food, mood, and attitude: Reducing risk for eating disorders in college women. *Health Psychology, 24*, 567–578.

Franko, D. L., Thompson, D., Affenito, S. G., Barton, B. A., & Striegel-Moore, R. H. (2008). What mediates the relationship between family meals and adolescent health issues? *Health Psychology, 27*, S109–S117.

Fraser, S. N., & Rodgers, W. M. (2010). An examination of psychosocial correlates of exercise tolerance in cardiac rehabilitation participants. *Journal of Behavioral Medicine, 33*, 159–167.

Frayne, S. M., Seaver, M. R., Loveland, S., Christiansen, C. L., Spiro III, A., Parker, V. A., et al. (2004). Burden of medical illness in women with depression and posttraumatic stress disorder. *Archives of Internal Medicine, 164*, 1306–1312.

Fredrickson, B. L., Maynard, K. E., Helms, M. J., Haney, T. L., Siegler, I. C., & Barefoot, J. C. (2000). Hostility predicts magnitude and duration of blood pressure response to anger. *Journal of Behavioral Medicine, 23*, 229–243.

Fredrickson, B. L., Tugade, M. M., Waugh, C. E., & Larkin, G. R. (2003). What good are positive emotions in crises? A prospective study of resilience and emotions following the terrorist attacks on the United States on September 11th, 2001. *Journal of Personality and Social Psychology, 84,* 365–376.

Fredrickson, M., & Matthews, K. A. (1990). Cardiovascular responses to behavioral stress and hypertension: A meta-analytic review. *Annals of Behavioral Medicine, 12,* 30–39.

Freedman, V. A. (1993). Kin and nursing home lengths of stay: A backward recurrence time approach. *Journal of Health and Social Behavior, 34,* 138–152.

French, A. P., & Tupin, J. P. (1974). Therapeutic application of a simple relaxation method. *American Journal of Psychotherapy, 28,* 282–287.

French, J. R. P., Jr., & Caplan, R. D. (1973). Organizational stress and the individual strain. In A. J. Marrow (Ed.), *The failure of success.* New York: Amacon.

Frenzel, M. P., McCaul, K. D., Glasgow, R. E., & Schafer, L. C. (1988). The relationship of stress and coping to regimen adherence and glycemic control of diabetes. *Journal of Social and Clinical Psychology, 6,* 77–87.

Friedman, E. M., & Herd, P. (2010). Income, education and inflammation: Differential associations in a national probability sample (the MIDUS study). *Psychosomatic Medicine, 72,* 290–300.

Friedman, E. M., Love, G. D., Rosenkranz, M. A., Urry, H. L., Davidson, R. J., Singer, B. H., et al. (2007). Socioeconomic status predicts objective and subjective sleep quality in aging women. *Psychosomatic Medicine, 69,* 682–691.

Friedman, H. S., & Adler, N. E. (2007). The history and background of health psychology. In H. S. Friedman and R. C. Silver (Eds.), *Oxford Foundations of Health Psychology.* New York: Oxford University Press.

Friedman, H. S., & Booth-Kewley, S. (1987). The "disease-prone" personality: A meta-analytic view of the construct. *American Psychologist, 42,* 539–555.

Friedman, H. S., & Silver, R. C. (Eds.) (2007). *Foundations of health psychology.* Oxford: Oxford University Press.

Friedman, H. S., Tucker, J. S., Schwartz, J. E., Martin, L. R., Tomlinson-Keasey, C., Wingard, D. L., et al. (1995). Childhood conscientiousness and longevity: Health behaviors and cause of death. *Journal of Personality and Social Psychology, 68,* 696–703.

Friedman, H. S., Tucker, J. S., Tomlinson-Keasey, C., Schwartz, J. E., Wingard, D. L., et al. (1993). Does childhood personality predict longevity? *Journal of Personality and Social Psychology, 65,* 176–185.

Friedman, L. C., Romero, C., Elledge, R., Chang, J., Kalidas, M., Dulay, M. F., et al. (2007). Attribution of blame, self-forgiving attitude and psychological adjustment in women with breast cancer. *Journal of Behavioral Medicine, 30,* 351–357.

Freidson, E. (1961). *Patients' views of medical practice.* New York: Russell Sage.

Friman, P. C., Finney, J. W., Glasscock, S. G., Weigel, J. W., & Christopherson, E. R. (1986). Testicular self-examination: Validation of a training strategy for early cancer detection. *Journal of Applied Behavior Analysis, 19,* 87–92.

Fritz, H. L. (2000). Gender-linked personality traits predict mental health and functional status following a first coronary event. *Health Psychology, 19,* 420–428.

Fromm, K., Andrykowski, M. A., & Hunt, J. (1996). Positive and negative psychosocial sequelae of bone marrow transplantation: Implications for quality of life assessment. *Journal of Behavioral Medicine, 19,* 221–240.

Frosch, D. L., Kimmel, S., & Volpp, K. (2008). What role do lay beliefs about hypertension etiology play in perceptions of medication effectiveness? *Health Psychology, 27,* 320–326.

Frostholm, L., Fink, P., Christensen, K. S., Toft, T., Oernboel, E., Olesen, F., et al. (2005a). The patients' illness perceptions and the use of primary health care. *Psychosomatic Medicine, 67,* 997–1005.

Frostholm, L., Fink, P., Oernboel, E., Christensen, K. S., Toft, T., Olesen, F., et al. (2005b). The uncertain consultation and patient satisfaction: The impact of patients' illness perceptions and a randomized controlled trial on the training of physicians' communication skills. *Psychosomatic Medicine, 67,* 897–905.

Frotenberry, K. T., Butler, J. M., Butner, J., Berg, C. A., Upchurch, R., & Weibe, D. J. (2009). Perceived diabetes task competence mediates the relationship of both negative and positive affect with blood glucose in adolescents with type I diabetes. *Annals of Behavioral Medicine, 37,* 1–9.

Fryar, C. D., Hirsch, R., Eberhardt, M. S., Yoon, S. S., & Wright, J. D. (2010). Hypertension, high serum total cholesterol, and diabetes: Racial and ethnic prevalence differences in U.S. adults, 1999–2006. *NCHS Data Brief, 36,* 1–8.

Fuchs, V. R. (2008). Election 2008: Three "inconvenient truths" about health care. *The New England Journal of Medicine, 359,* 1749–1751.

Fuglestad, P. T., Rothman, A. J., & Jeffery, R. W. (2008). Getting there and hanging on: The effect of regulatory focus on performance in smoking and weight loss interventions. *Health Psychology, 27,* S260–S270.

Fukudo, S., Lane, J. D., Anderson, N. B., Kuhn, C. M., Schanberg, S. M., McCown, N., et al. (1992). Accentuated vagal antagonism of beta-adrenergic effects on ventricular repolarization: Evidence of weaker antagonism in hostile Type A men. *Circulation, 85,* 2045–2053.

Fuligni, A. J., Telzer, E. H., Bower, J., Cole, S. W., Kiang, L., & Irwin, M. R. (2009). A preliminary study of daily interpersonal stress and C-reactive protein levels among adolescents from Latin American and European backgrounds. *Psychosomatic Medicine, 71,* 329–333.

Fuller, R. K., & Hiller-Strumhofel, S. (1999). Alcoholism treatment in the United States. An overview. *Alcohol Research and Health. The Journal of the National Institute on Alcohol Abuse and Alcoholism, 23,* 69–77.

Fuller, T. D., Edwards, J. N., Sermsri, S., & Vorakitphokatorn, S. (1993). Gender and health: Some Asian evidence. *Journal of Health and Social Behavior, 34,* 252–271.

Fung, T. T., Willett, W. C., Stampfer, M. J., Manson, J. E., & Hu, F. B. (2001). Dietary patterns and the risk of coronary heart disease in women. *Archives of Internal Medicine, 161,* 1857–1862.

Fyrand, L., Moum, T., Finset, A., & Glennas, A. (2002). The impact of disability and disease duration on social support of women with rheumatoid arthritis. *Journal of Behavioral Medicine, 25,* 251–268.

Gaab, J., Hüster, D., Peisen, R., Engert, V., Schad, T., Schürmeyer, T. H., et al. (2002). Low-dose dexamethasone suppression test in chronic fatigue syndrome and health. *Psychosomatic Medicine, 64,* 311–318.

Gale, C. R., Batty, G. D., & Deary, I. J. (2008). Locus of control at age 10 years and health outcomes and behaviors at age 30 years: The 1970 British cohort study. *Psychosomatic Medicine, 70,* 397–403.

Galesic, M., Garcia-Retamero, R., & Gigerenzer, G. (2009). Using icon arrays to communicate medical risks: Overcoming low numeracy. *Health Psychology, 29,* 210–216.

Gall, T. L., Kristjansson, E., Charbonneau, C., Florack, P. (2009). A longitudinal study on the role of spirituality in response to the diagnosis and treatment of breast cancer. *Journal of Behavioral Medicine, 32,* 174–186.

Gallacher, J. E. J., Yarnell, J. W. G., Sweetnam, P. M., Elwood, P. C., & Stansfeld, S. A. (1999). Anger and incident heart disease in the Caerphilly study. *Psychosomatic Medicine, 61,* 446–453.

Gallagher, S., Phillips, A. C., Drayson, M. T., & Carroll, D. (2009). Caregiving for children with developmental disabilities is associated with a poor antibody response to influenza vaccination. *Psychosomatic Medicine, 71,* 341–344.

Gallo, L. C., Espinosa de los Monteros, K., Ferent, V., Urbina, J., & Talavera, G. (2007). Eduation, psychosocial resources, and metabolic syndrome variables in Latinas. *Annals of Behavioral Medicine, 34,* 14–25.

Gallo, L. C., & Matthews, K. A. (2006). Adolescents' attachment orientation influences ambulatory blood pressure responses to everyday social interactions. *Psychosomatic Medicine, 68,* 253–261.

Gallo, L. C., Matthews, K. A., Kuller, L. H., Sutton-Tyrell, K., & Edmundowicz, D. (2001). Educational attainment and coronary and aortic calcification in postmenopausal women. *Psychosomatic Medicine, 63,* 925–935.

Gallo, L. C., Troxel, W. M., Kuller, L. H., Sutton-Tyrell, K., Edmundowicz, D., & Matthews, K. A. (2003). Marital status, marital quality and atherosclerotic burden in postmenopausal women. *Psychosomatic Medicine, 65,* 952–962.

Gallo, L. C., Troxel, W. M., Matthews, K. A., Jansen-McWilliams, L., Kuller, L. H., & Sutton-Tyrell, K. (2003). Occupation and subclinical carotid artery disease in women: Are clerical workers at greater risk? *Health Psychology, 22,* 19–29.

Gallup Poll. (2009). *Religion.* Retrieved October 15, 2009, from http://www.gallup.com/poll/1690/Religion.aspx

Garcia, T. C., Bernstein, A. B., & Bush, M. A. (2010). Emergency department visitors and visits: Who used the emergency room in 2007? *NCHS Data Brief, 38,* 1–8.

Garcia-Linares, M. I., Sanchez-Lorente, S., Coe, C. L., & Martinez, M. (2004). Intimate male partner violence impairs immune control over herpes simplex virus type 1 in physically and psychologically abused women. *Psychosomatic Medicine, 66,* 965–972.

Garfinkel, P. E., & Garner, D. M. (1983). The multidetermined nature of anorexia nervosa. In P. L. Darby, P. E. Garfinkel, D. M. Garner, & D. V. Coscina (Eds.), *Anorexia nervosa: Recent developments in research.* New York: Liss.

Garner, D. M., & Wooley, S. C. (1991). Confronting the failure of behavioral and dietary treatments for obesity. *Clinical Psychology Review, 11,* 729–780.

Gatchel, R. J., Gaffney, F. A., & Smith, J. E. (1986). Comparative efficacy of behavioral stress management versus propranolol in reducing psychophysiological reactivity in postmyocardial infarction patients. *Journal of Behavioral Medicine, 9,* 503–513.

Gauchet, A., Tarquinio, C., & Fischer, G. (2007). Psychosocial predictors of medication adherence among persons living with HIV. *International Journal of Behavioral Medicine, 14,* 141–150.

Gauderman, W. J., Avol, E., Gilliland, F., Vora, H., Thomas, D., Berhane, K., et al. (2004). The effect of air pollution on lung development from 10 to 18 years of age. *The New England Journal of Medicine, 351,* 1057–1067.

Gaughan, M. (2006). The gender structure of adolescent peer influence on drinking. *Journal of Health and Social Behavior, 47,* 47–61.

Gauthier, L. V., Taub, E., Perkins, C., Ortmann, M., Mark, V. W., & Uswatte, G. (2008). Remodeling the brain: Plastic structural brain changes produced by different motor therapies after stroke. *Stroke, 39,* 1520–1525.

Gaynes, B. N., Pence, B. W., Eron, J. J., & Miller, W. C. (2008). Prevalence and comorbidity of psychiatric diagnoses based on reference standard in an HIV+ patient population. *Psychosomatic Medicine, 70,* 505–511.

Gazelle, G. (2007). Understanding hospice—An underutilized option for life's final chapter. *The New England Journal of Medicine, 357,* 321–324.

Geers, A. L., Wellman, J. A., Helfer, S. G., Fowler, S. L., & France, C. R. (2008). Dispositional optimism and thoughts of well-being determine sensitivity to an experimental pain task. *Annals of Behavioral Medicine, 36,* 304–313.

Geers, A. L., Wellman, J. A., Seligman, L. D., Wuyek, L. A., & Neff, L. A. (2010). Dispositional optimism, goals, and engagement in health treatment programs. *Journal of Behavioral Medicine, 33,* 123–134.

Gemming, M. G., Runyan, C. W., Hunter, W. W., & Campbell, B. J. (1984). A community health education approach to occupant protection. *Health Education Quarterly, 11,* 147–158.

George, L. K., Ellison, C. G., & Larson, D. B. (2002). Explaining the relationships between religious involvement and health. *Psychology Inquiry, 13,* 190–200.

Georgiades, A., Lane, J. D., Boyle, S. H., Brummett, B. H., Barefoot, J. C., Kuhn, C. M., et al. (2009). Hostility and fasting glucose in African American women. *Psychosomatic Medicine, 71,* 642–645.

Gerardo-Gettens, T., Miller, G. D., Horwitz, B. A., McDonald, R. B., Brownell, K. D., Greenwood, M. R. C., et al. (1991). Exercise decreases fat selection in female rats during weight cycling. *American Journal of Physiology, 260,* R518–R524.

Gerbert, B., Stone, G., Stulbarg, M., Gullion, D. S., & Greenfield, S. (1988). Agreement among physician assessment methods: Searching for the truth among fallible methods. *Medical Care, 26,* 519–535.

Gerend, M. A., & Shepherd, J. E. (2007). Using message framing to promote acceptance of the human papillomavirus vaccine. *Health Psychology, 26,* 745–752.

Gerend, M. A., Shepherd, J. E., & Monday, K. A. (2008). Behavioral frequency moderates the effects of message framing on HPV vaccine acceptability. *Annals of Behavioral Medicine, 35,* 221–229.

Gerin, W., Davidson, K. W., Christenfeld, N. J. S., Goyal, T., & Schwartz, J. E. (2006). The role of angry rumination and distraction in blood pressure recovery from emotional arousal. *Psychosomatic Medicine, 68,* 64–72.

Gerrard, M., Gibbons, F. X., Benthin, A. C., & Hessling, R. M. (1996). A longitudinal study of the reciprocal nature of risk behaviors and cognitions in adolescents: What you do shapes what you think, and vice versa. *Health Psychology, 15,* 344–354.

Gerrard, M., Gibbons, F. X., Lane, D. J., & Stock, M. L. (2005). Smoking cessation: Social comparison level predicts success for adult smokers. *Health Psychology, 24,* 623–629.

Gibbons, F. X., & Eggleston, T. J. (1996). Smoker networks and the "typical smoker": A prospective analysis of smoking cessation. *Health Psychology, 15,* 469–477.

Gibbons, F. X., & Gerrard, M. (1995). Predicting young adults' health risk behavior. *Journal of Personality and Social Psychology, 69,* 505–517.

Gibbons, F. X., Gerrard, M., Lane, D. J., Mahler, H. I. M., & Kulik, J. A. (2005). Using UV photography to reduce use of tanning booths: A test of cognitive mediation. *Health Psychology, 24,* 358–363.

Gidron, Y., & Davidson, K. (1996). Development and preliminary testing of a brief intervention for modifying CHD-predictive hostility components. *Journal of Behavioral Medicine, 19,* 203–220.

Gidron, Y., Davidson, K., & Bata, I. (1999). The short-term effects of a hostility-reduction intervention on male coronary heart disease patients. *Health Psychology, 18,* 416–420.

Giese-Davis, J., Sephton, S. E., Abercrombie, H. C., Durán, R. E. F., & Spiegel, D. (2004). Repression and high anxiety are associated with aberrant diurnal cortisol rhythms in women with metastatic breast cancer. *Health Psychology, 23,* 645–650.

Giese-Davis, J., Wilhelm, F. H., Conrad, A., Abercrombie, H. C., Sephton, S., Yutsis, M., et al. (2006). Depression and stress reactivity in metastatic breast cancer. *Psychosomatic Medicine, 68,* 675–683.

Gigerenzer, G., Gaissmaier, W., Kurz-Milcke, E., Schwartz, L. M., & Woloshin, S. (2007). Helping doctors and patients make sense of health statistics. *Psychological Science in the Public Interest, 8,* 53–96.

Gil, K. M., Carson, J. W., Porter, L. S., Scipio, C., Bediako, S. M., & Orringer, E. (2004). Daily mood and stress predict pain, health care use, and work activity in African American adults with sickle-cell disease. *Health Psychology, 23,* 267–274.

Gil, K. M., Wilson, J. J., Edens, J. L., Webster, D. A., Abrams, M. A., Orringer, E., et al. (1996). Effects of cognitive coping skills training on coping strategies and experimental pain sensitivity in African American adults with sickle cell disease. *Health Psychology, 15,* 3–10.

Gil, S., & Caspi, Y. (2006). Personality traits, coping style, and perceived threat as predictors of posttraumatic stress disorder after exposure to a terrorist attack: A prospective study. *Psychosomatic Medicine, 68,* 904–909.

Gilbertson, M. W., Paulus, L. A., Williston, S. K., Gurvits, T. V., Lasko, N. B., Pitman, R. K., et al. (2006). Neurocognitive function in monozygotic twins discordant for combat exposure: Relationship to posttraumatic stress disorders. *Journal of Abnormal Psychology, 115,* 484–495.

Gill, T. M., Baker, D. I., Gottschalk, M., Peduzzi, P. N., Allore, H., & Byers, A. (2002). A randomized trial of a prehabilitation program to prevent functional decline among frail community-living older persons. *The New England Journal of Medicine, 347,* 1068–1074.

Gilliam, W., Burns, J. W., Quartana, P., Matsuura, J., Nappi, C., & Wolff, B. (2010). Interactive effects of catastrophizing and suppression on responses to acute pain: A test of an appraisal x emotion regulation model. *Journal of Behavioral Medicine, 33,* 191–199.

Gillum, R. F., & Ingram, D. D. (2006). Frequency of attendance at religious services, hypertension, and blood pressure: The third national health and nutrition examination survey. *Psychosomatic Medicine, 68,* 382–385.

Girdler, S. S., Jamner, L. D., Jarvik, M., Soles, J. R., & Shapiro, D. (1997). Smoking status and nicotine administration differentially modify hemodynamic stress reactivity in men and women. *Psychosomatic Medicine, 59,* 294–306.

Girion, L. (2005, April 6). Obesity is costly to state, report says. *Los Angeles Times,* pp. C1, C5.

Glantz, S. A. (2004). Effect of public smoking ban in Helena, Montana: Author's reply. *British Medical Journal, 328,* 1380.

Glanz, K., Croyle, R. T., Chollette, V. Y., & Pinn, V. W. (2003). Cancer-related health disparities in women. *American Journal of Public Health, 93,* 292–298.

Glaros, A. G., & Burton, E. (2004). Parafunctional clenching, pain, and effort in temporomandibular disorders. *Journal of Behavioral Medicine, 27,* 91–100.

Glaser, R., Kiecolt-Glaser, J. K., Bonneau, R. H., Malarkey, W., Kennedy, S., & Hughes, J. (1992). Stress-induced modulation of the immune response to recombinant hepatitis B vaccine. *Psychosomatic Medicine, 54,* 22–29.

Glaser, R., Kiecolt-Glaser, J. K., Marucha, P. T., MacCallum, R. C., Laskowski, B. F., & Malarkey, W. B. (1999). Stress-related changes in proinflammatory cytokine production in wounds. *Archives of General Psychiatry, 56,* 450–456.

Glaser, R., Kiecolt-Glaser, J. K., Speicher, C. E., & Holliday, J. E. (1985). Stress, loneliness, and changes in herpesvirus latency. *Journal of Behavioral Medicine, 8,* 249–260.

Glaser, R., Kiecolt-Glaser, J. K., Stout, J. C., Tarr, K. L., Speicher, C. E., & Holliday, J. E. (1985). Stress-related impairments in cellular immunity. *Psychiatry Research, 16,* 233–239.

Glaser, R., Rice, J., Speicher, C. E., Stout, J. C., & Kiecolt-Glaser, J. K. (1986). Stress depresses interferon production by leukocytes concomitant with a decrease in natural killer cell activity. *Behavioral Neuroscience, 100,* 675–678.

Glasgow, M. S., Engel, B. T., & D'Lugoff, B. C. (1989). A controlled study of a standardized behavioral stepped treatment for hypertension. *Psychosomatic Medicine, 51,* 10–26.

Glasgow, R. E. (2008). What types of evidence are most needed to advance behavioral medicine? *Annals of Behavioral Medicine, 35,* 19–25.

Glasgow, R. E., & Anderson, B. J. (1995). Future directions for research on pediatric chronic disease management: Lessons from diabetes. *Journal of Pediatric Psychology, 20,* 389–402.

Glasgow, R. E., Estabrooks, P. A., Marcus, A. C., Smith, T. L., Gaglio, B., Levinson, A. H., et al. (2008). Evaluating initial reach and robustness of a particular randomized trial of smoking reduction. *Health Psychology, 27,* 780–788.

Glasgow, R. E., Funnell, M. M., Bonomi, A. E., Davis, C., Beckham, V., & Wagner, E. H. (2002). Self-management aspects of the improving chronic illness care breakthrough series: Implementation with diabetes and heart failure teams. *Annals of Behavioral Medicine, 24,* 80–87.

Glasgow, R. E., Toobert, D. J., Barrera Jr., M., & Strycker, L. A. (2004). Assessments of problem-solving: A key to successful diabetes self-management. *Journal of Behavioral Medicine, 27,* 477–490.

Glasgow, R. E., Toobert, D. J., Hampson, S. E., & Wilson, W. (1995). Behavioral research on diabetes at the Oregon Research Institute. *Annals of Behavioral Medicine, 17,* 32–40.

Glass, T. A., deLeon, C. M., Marottoli, R. A., & Berkman, L. F. (1999). Population based study of social and productive activities as predictors of survival among elderly Americans. *British Medical Journal, 319,* 478–483.

Glei, D. A., Goldman, N., Chuang, Y. L., & Weinstein, M. (2007). Do chronic stressors lead to physiological dysregulation? Testing the theory of allostatic load. *Psychosomatic Medicine, 69,* 769–776.

Glenn, B., & Burns, J. W. (2003). Pain self-management in the process and outcome of multidisciplinary treatment of chronic pain: Evaluation of a stage of change model. *Journal of Behavioral Medicine, 26,* 417–433.

Global Information Incorporated. (2007). *Pain management: World prescription drug markets.* Retrieved from http://www.theinfoshop.com/study/tv12667_pain_management.html

Glombiewski, J. A., Tersek, J., & Rief, W. (2008). Muscular reactivity and specificity in chronic back pain patients. *Psychosomatic Medicine, 70,* 125–131.

Gluck, M. E., Geliebter, A., Hung, J., & Yahav, E. (2004). Cortisol, hunger, and desire to binge eat following a cold stress test in obese women with binge eating disorder. *Psychosomatic Medicine, 66,* 876–881.

Glynn, L. M., Christenfeld, N., & Gerin, W. (1999). Gender, social support, and cardiovascular responses to stress. *Psychosomatic Medicine, 61,* 234–242.

Glynn, L. M., Dunkel-Schetter, C., Hobel, C. J., & Sandman, C. A. (2008). Pattern of perceived stress and anxiety in pregnancy predicts preterm birth. *Health Psychology, 27,* 43–51.

Goede, P., Vedel, P., Larsen, N., Jensen, G. V. H., Parving, H., & Pedersen, O. (2003). Multifactorial intervention and cardiovascular disease in patients with type 2 diabetes. *The New England Journal of Medicine, 348,* 383–393.

Goffman, E. (1961). *Asylums.* Garden City, NY: Doubleday.

Goffman, E. (1963). *Stigma: Notes on the management of spoiled identity.* Englewood Cliffs, NJ: Prentice-Hall.

Goldbacher, E. M., Bromberger, J., & Matthews, K. A. (2009). Lifetime history of major depression predicts the development of the metabolic syndrome in middle-aged women. *Psychosomatic Medicine, 71,* 266–272.

Goldbacher, E. M., & Matthews, K. A. (2007). Are psychological characteristics related to risk of the metabolic syndrome? A review of the literature. *Annals of Behavioral Medicine, 34,* 240–252.

Goldbacher, E. M., Matthews, K. A., & Salomon, K. (2005). Central adiposity is associated with cardiovascular reactivity to stress in adolescents. *Health Psychology, 24,* 375–384.

Goldberg, J. H., Halpern-Felsher, B. L., & Millstein, S. G. (2002). Beyond invulnerability: The importance of benefits in adolescents' decision to drink alcohol. *Health Psychology, 21,* 477–484.

Goldberg, R. J. (1981). Management of depression in the patient with advanced cancer. *Journal of the American Medical Association, 246,* 373–376.

Golden, J. S., & Johnston, G. D. (1970). Problems of distortion in doctor-patient communications. *Psychiatry in Medicine, 1,* 127–149.

Golden, S. H., Lee, H. B., Schreiner, P. J., Diez Roux, A., Fitzpatrick, A. L., Szklo, M., et al. (2007). Depression and type 2 diabetes mellitus: The multiethnic study of atherosclerosis. *Psychosomatic Medicine, 69,* 529–536.

Golden-Kreutz, D. M., Thornton, L. M., Gregorio, S. W., Frierson, G. M., Jim, H. S., Carpenter, K. M., et al. (2005). Traumatic stress, perceived global stress, and life events: Prospectively predicting quality of life in breast cancer patients. *Health Psychology, 24,* 288–296.

Goldring, A. B., Taylor, S. E., Kemeny, M. E., & Anton, P. A. (2002). Impact of health beliefs, quality of life and the physician-patient relationship on the treatment intentions of inflammatory bowel disease patients. *Health Psychology, 21*, 219–228.

Gollwitzer, P. M., & Sheeran, P. (2006). Implementation intentions and goal achievement: A meta-analysis of effects and processes. *Advances in Experimental Social Psychology, 38*, 69–119.

Gonder-Frederick, L. A., Carter, W. R., Cox, D. J., & Clarke, W. L. (1990). Environmental stress and blood glucose change in insulin-dependent diabetes mellitus. *Health Psychology, 9*, 503–515.

Gonder-Frederick, L. A., Cox, D. J., Bobbitt, S. A., & Pennebaker, J. W. (1986). Blood glucose symptom beliefs of diabetic patients: Accuracy and implications. *Health Psychology, 5*, 327–341.

Gonzalez, J. S., Penedo, F. J., Antoni, M. H., Durán, R. E., Fernandez, M. I., McPherson-Baker, S., et al. (2004). Social support, positive states of mind, and HIV treatment adherence in men and women living with HIV/AIDS. *Health Psychology, 23*, 413–418.

Gonzalez, J. S., Penedo, F. J., Llabre, M. M., Durán, R. E., Antoni, M. H., Schneiderman, N., et al. (2007). Physical symptoms, beliefs about medications, negative mood, and long-term HIV medication adherence. *Annals of Behavioral Medicine, 34*, 46–55.

Good, A., & Abraham, C. (2007). Measuring defensive responses to threatening messages: A meta-analysis of measures. *Health Psychology Review, 1*, 208–229.

Goodall, T. A., & Halford, W. K. (1991). Self-management of diabetes mellitus: A critical review. *Health Psychology, 10*, 1–8.

Goodenow, C., Reisine, S. T., & Grady, K. E. (1990). Quality of social support and associated social and psychological functioning in women with rheumatoid arthritis, *Health Psychology, 9*, 266–284.

Goodman, E., & Capitman, J. (2000). Depressive symptoms and cigarette smoking among teens. *Pediatrics, 106*, 748–755.

Goodman, E., Daniels, S. R., & Dolan, L. M. (2007). Socioeconomic disparities in insulin resistance: Results from the Princeton school district study. *Psychosomatic Medicine, 69*, 61–67.

Goodman, E., McEwen, B. S., Huang, B., Dolan, L. M., & Adler, N. E. (2005). Social inequalities in biomarkers of cardiovascular risk in adolescence. *Psychosomatic Medicine, 67*, 9–15.

Goodnough, A. (2009, December 17). A state's lower smoking rate draws attention. *The New York Times*, p. A29.

Goodwin, R. D., Cox, B. J., & Clara, I. (2006). Neuroticism and physical disorders among adults in the community: Results from the national comorbidity survey. *Journal of Behavioral Medicine, 29*, 229–238.

Goodwin, R. D., Fischer, M. E., & Goldberg, J. (2007). A twin study of posttraumatic stress disorder symptoms and asthma. *American Journal of Respiratory and Critical Care Medicine, 176*, 983–987.

Goodwin, R. D., Kroenke, K., Hoven, C. W., & Spitzer, R. L. (2003). Major depression, physical illness and suicidal ideation in primary care. *Psychosomatic Medicine, 65*, 501–505.

Goodwin, R. D., & Stein, M. B. (2002). Generalized anxiety disorder and peptic ulcer disease among adults in the United States. *Psychosomatic Medicine, 64*, 862–866.

Gordon, C. M., Carey, M. P., & Carey, K. B. (1997). Effects of a drinking event on behavioral skills and condom attitudes in men: Implications for HIV risk from a controlled experiment. *Health Psychology, 16*, 490–495.

Gordon, J. R., & Marlatt, G. A. (1981). Addictive behaviors. In J. L. Shelton & R. L. Levy (Eds.), *Behavioral assignments and treatment compliance* (pp. 167–186). Champaign, IL: Research Press.

Gordon, W. A., & Diller, L. (1983). Stroke: Coping with a cognitive deficit. In T. G. Burish & L. A. Bradley (Eds.), *Coping with chronic disease: Research and applications.* (pp. 113–135). New York: Academic Press.

Gordon, W. A., & Hibbard, M. R. (1991). The theory and practice of cognitive remediation. In J. S. Kreutzer & P. H. Wehman (Eds.), *Cognitive rehabilitation for persons with traumatic brain injury: A functional approach.* (pp. 13–22). Baltimore: Paul H. Brookes Publishing Co.

Gore-Felton, C., & Koopman, C. (2008). Behavioral mediation of the relationship between psychosocial factors and HIV disease progression. *Psychosomatic Medicine, 70*, 569–574.

Gorin, S. S. (2005). Correlates of colorectal cancer screening compliance among urban Hispanics. *Journal of Behavioral Medicine, 28*, 125–137.

Gorman, C. (1996, September 19). Damage control. *Time.*

Gorman, C. (1999, March 29). Get some sleep. *Time*, p. 225.

Gottlieb, B. H. (Ed.). (1988). *Marshalling social support: Formats, processes, and effects.* Newbury Park, CA: Sage.

Gottlieb, J., & Yi, D. (2003, April 28). Hepatitis B a deadly threat to U.S. Asians. *Los Angeles Times*, p. B6.

Gottlieb, N. H., & Green, L. W. (1984). Life events, social network, life-style, and health: An analysis of the 1979 national survey on personal health practices and consequences. *Health Education Quarterly, 11*, 91–105.

Gould, R. (1972). The phases of adult life: A study in developmental psychology. *American Journal of Psychiatry, 129*, 521–531.

Goyal, T. M., Idler, E. L., Krause, T. J., & Contrada, R. J. (2005). Quality of life following cardiac surgery: Impact of the severity and course of depressive symptoms. *Psychosomatic Medicine, 67*, 759–765.

Grace, S. L., Abbey, S. E., Pinto, R., Shnek, Z. M., Irvine, J., & Stewart, D. E. (2005). Longitudinal course of depressive symptomatology after a cardiac event: Effects of gender and cardiac rehabilitation. *Psychosomatic Medicine, 67*, 52–58.

Grady, D. (2002, May 23). Hormones may explain difficulty dieters have keeping weight off. *New York Times*, pp. A1, A24.

Grady, D. (2004, April 14). Lung cancer affects sexes differently. *New York Times*, p. A18.

Graham, J. E., Glaser, R., Loving, T. J., Malarkey, W. B., Stowell, J. R., & Kiecolt-Glaser, J. K. (2009). Cognitive word use during marital conflict and increases in proinflammatory cytokines. *Health Psychology, 28*, 621–630.

Graham, J. E., Lobel, M., Glass, P., & Lokshina, I. (2008). Effects of written anger expression in chronic pain patients: Making meaning from pain. *Journal of Behavioral Medicine, 31*, 201–212.

Graham, M. A., Thompson, S. C., Estrada, M., & Yonekura, M. L. (1987). Factors affecting psychological adjustment to a fetal death. *American Journal of Obstetrics and Gynecology, 157*, 254–257.

Gramling, S. E., Clawson, E. P., & McDonald, M. K. (1996). Perceptual and cognitive abnormality model of hypochondriasis: Amplification and physiological reactivity in women. *Psychosomatic Medicine, 58*, 423–431.

Grandner, M. A., & Kripke, D. F. (2004). Self-reported sleep complaints with long and short sleep: A nationally representative sample. *Psychosomatic Medicine, 66*, 239–241.

Granö, N., Vahtera, J., Virtanen, M., Keltikangas-Järvinen, L., & Kivimäki, M. (2008). Association of hostility with sleep duration and sleep disturbances in an employee population. *International Journal of Behavioral Medicine, 15*, 73–80.

Grant, B. F., Dawson, D. A., Stinson, F. S., Chou, S. P., Dufour, M. C., & Pickering, R. P. (2004). The 12-month prevalence and trends in DSM-IV alcohol abuse and dependence: United States, 1991–1992 and 2001–2002. *Drug and Alcohol Dependence, 74*, 223–234.

Grant, I., Adler, K. A., Patterson, T. L., Dimsdale, J. E., Ziegler, M. G., & Irwin, M. R. (2002). Health consequences of Alzheimer's caregiving transitions: Effects of placement and bereavement. *Psychosomatic Medicine, 64*, 477–486.

Grant, J. A., & Rainville, P. (2009). Pain sensitivity and analgesic effects of mindful states in zen mediators: A cross-sectional study. *Psychosomatic Medicine, 71*, 106–114.

Grant, N., Hamer, M., & Steptoe, A. (2009). Social isolation and stress-related cardiovascular, lipid, and cortisol responses. *Annals of Behavioral Medicine, 37,* 29–37.

Grassi, L., & Molinari, S. (1986). Intrafamilial dynamics and neoplasia: Prospects for a multidisciplinary analysis. *Rivista di Psichiatria, 21,* 329–341.

Graugaard, P., & Finset, A. (2000). Trait anxiety and reactions to patient-centered and doctor-centered styles of communication: An experimental study. *Psychosomatic Medicine, 62,* 33–39.

Graves, K. D. (2003). Social cognitive theory and cancer patients' quality of life: A meta-analysis of psychosocial intervention components. *Health Psychology, 22,* 210–219.

Green, J. H. (1978). *Basic clinical physiology* (3rd ed.). New York: Oxford University Press.

Green, C. A., Freeborn, D. K., & Polen, M. R. (2001). Gender and alcohol use: The roles of social support, chronic illness, and psychological well-being. *Journal of Behavioral Medicine, 24,* 383–399.

Greenberg, E. S., & Grunberg, L. (1995). Work alienation and problem alcohol behavior. *Journal of Health and Social Behavior, 36,* 83–102.

Greene, R. E., Houston, B. K., & Holleran, S. A. (1995). Aggressiveness, dominance, developmental factors, and serum cholesterol level in college males. *Journal of Behavioral Medicine, 18,* 569–580.

Greenfield, S., Kaplan, S. H., Ware, J. E., Jr., Yano, E. M., & Frank, H. J. L. (1988). Patients' participation in medical care: Effects on blood sugar control and quality of life in diabetes. *Journal of General Internal Medicine, 3,* 448–457.

Greer, J., & Halgin, R. (2006). Predictors of physician-patient agreement on symptom etiology in primary care. *Psychosomatic Medicine, 68,* 277–282.

Gregg, M. E. D., Matyas, T. A., & James, J. E. (2005). Association between hemodynamic profile during laboratory stress and ambulatory pulse pressure. *Journal of Behavioral Medicine, 28,* 573–579.

Grembowski, D., Patrick, D., Diehr, P., Durham, M., Beresford, S., Kay, E., et al. (1993). Self-efficacy and health behavior among older adults. *Journal of Health and Social Behavior, 34,* 89–104.

Griffin, M. J., & Chen, E. (2006). Perceived control and immune and pulmonary outcomes in children with asthma. *Psychosomatic Medicine, 68,* 493–499.

Grodner, S., Prewitt, L. M., Jaworski, B. A., Myers, R., Kaplan, R. M., & Ries, A. L. (1996). The impact of social support in pulmonary rehabilitation of patients with chronic obstructive pulmonary disease. *Annals of Behavioral Medicine, 18,* 139–145.

Gross, A. M., Eudy, C., & Drabman, R. S. (1982). Training parents to be physical therapists with their physically handicapped child. *Journal of Behavioral Medicine, 5,* 321–328.

Grossardt, B. R., Bower, J. H., Geda, Y. E., Colligan, R. C., & Rocca, W. A. (2009). Pessimistic, anxious, and depressive personality traits predict all-cause mortality: The mayo clinic cohort study of personality and aging. *Psychosomatic Medicine, 71,* 491–500.

Grossman, H. Y., Brink, S., & Hauser, S. T. (1987). Self-efficacy in adolescent girls and boys with insulin-dependent diabetes mellitus. *Diabetes Care, 10,* 324–329.

Groth-Marnat, G., & Fletcher, A. (2000). Influence of neuroticism, catastrophizing, pain, duration, and receipt of compensation on short-term response to nerve block treatment for chronic back pain. *Journal of Behavioral Medicine, 23,* 339–350.

Gruenewald, T. L., Kemeny, M. E., Aziz, N., & Fahey, J. L. (2004). Acute threat to the social self: Shame, social self-esteem, and cortisol activity. *Psychosomatic Medicine, 66,* 915–924.

Gruman, J. (2003). *Ship happens. Essays on good behavior.* Center for the Advancement of Health. Retrieved July 16, 2007, from http://www.cfah.org/about/essay/ship.cfm

Grunberg, N. E., & Acri, J. B. (1991). Conceptual and methodological considerations for tobacco addiction research. *British Journal of Addiction, 86,* 637–641.

Grunberg, N. E., & Straub, R. O. (1992). The role of gender and taste class in the effects of stress on eating. *Health Psychology, 11,* 97–100.

Grzywacz, J. G., Almeida, D. M., Neupert, S. D., & Ettner, S. L. (2004). Socioeconomic status and health: A micro-level analysis of exposure and vulnerability to daily stressors. *Journal of Health and Social Behavior, 45,* 1–16.

Guilamo-Ramos, V., Jaccard, J., Dittus, P., Bouris, A., Holloway, I., & Casillas, E. (2007). Adolescent expectancies, parent-adolescent communication and intentions to have sexual intercourse among inner-city, middle school youth. *Annals of Behavioral Medicine, 34,* 56–66.

Guilamo-Ramos, V., Jaccard, J., Pena, J., & Goldberg, V. (2005). Acculturation-related variables, sexual initiation, and subsequent sexual behavior among Puerto Rican, Mexican, and Cuban youth. *Health Psychology, 24,* 88–95.

Gump, B. B., & Matthews, K. A. (1998). Vigilance and cardiovascular reactivity to subsequent stressors in men: A preliminary study. *Health Psychology, 17,* 93–96.

Gump, B. B., & Matthews, K. A. (2000). Are vacations good for your health? The 9-year mortality experience after the multiple risk factor intervention trial. *Psychosomatic Medicine, 62,* 608–612.

Gunthert, K. C., Cohen, L. H., & Armeli, S. (1999). The role of neuroticism in daily stress and coping. *Journal of Personality and Social Psychology, 77,* 1087–1100.

Gupta, S. (2002, August 26). Don't ignore heart-attack blues. *Time,* p. 71.

Gupta, S. (2004, October 24). Click to get sick? *Time,* p. 102.

Gurevich, M., Devins, G. M., Wilson, C., McCready, D., Marmar, C. R., & Rodin, G. M. (2004). Stress responses syndromes in women undergoing mammography: A comparison of women with and without a history of breast cancer. *Psychosomatic Medicine, 66,* 104–112.

Guyll, M., & Contrada, R. J. (1998). Trait hostility and ambulatory cardiovascular activity: Responses to social interaction. *Health Psychology, 17,* 30–39.

Hackett, T. P., & Cassem, N. H. (1973). Psychological adaptation to convalescence in myocardial infarction patients. In J. P. Naughton, H. K. Hellerstein, & I. C. Mohler (Eds.), *Exercise testing and exercise training in coronary heart disease.* New York: Academic Press.

Haemmerli, K., Znoj, H., & Berger, T. (2010). Internet-based support for infertile patients: A randomized controlled study. *Journal of Behavioral Medicine, 33,* 135–146.

Haerens, L., Deforche, B., Maes, L., Brug, J., Vandelanotte, C., & De Bourdeaudhuij, I. (2007). A computer-tailored dietary fat intake intervention for adolescents: Results of a randomized controlled trial. *Annals of Behavioral Medicine, 34,* 253–262.

Hagedoorn, M., Kuijer, R. G., Buunk, B. P., DeJong, G., Wobbes, T., & Sanderman, R. (2000). Marital satisfaction in patients with cancer: Does support from intimate partners benefit those who need it the most? *Health Psychology, 19,* 274–282.

Hagedoorn, M., & Molleman, E. (2006). Facial disfigurement in patients with head and neck cancer: The role of social self-efficacy. *Health Psychology, 25,* 643–647.

Hagger, M. S., Wood, C., Stiff, C., & Chatzisarantis, N. L. D. (2009). The strength model of self-regulation failure and health-related behavior. *Health Psychology Review, 3,* 208–238.

Halberstam, M. J. (1971, February 14). The doctor's new dilemma: Will I be sued? *New York Times Magazine,* pp. 8–9, 33–39.

Halford, W. K., Cuddihy, S., & Mortimer, R. H. (1990). Psychological stress and blood glucose regulation in Type I diabetic patients. *Health Psychology, 9,* 516–528.

Hall, J. A., Epstein, A. M., DeCiantis, M. L., & McNeil, B. J. (1993). Physicians' liking for their patients: More evidence for the role of affect in medical care. *Health Psychology, 12,* 140–146.

Hall, J. A., Irish, J. T., Roter, D. L., Ehrlich, C. M., & Miller, L. H. (1994). Gender in medical encounters: An analysis of physician and patient communication in a primary care setting. *Health Psychology, 13,* 384–392.

Hall, K. S., Crowley, G. M., McConnell, E. S., Bosworth, H. B., Sloane, R., Ekelund, C. C., et al. (2010). Change in goal ratings as a mediating variable between self-efficacy and physical activity in older men. *Annals of Behavioral Medicine, 39,* 267–273.

Hall, M., Buysse, D. J., Nowell, P. D., Nofzinger, E. A., Houck, P., Reynolds, C. F., et al. (2000). Symptoms of stress and depression as correlates of sleep in primary insomnia. *Psychosomatic Medicine, 62,* 227–230.

Hall, M., Vasko, R., Buysse, D., Ombao, H., Chen, Q., Cashmere, J. D., et al. (2004). Acute stress affects heart rate variability during sleep. *Psychosomatic Medicine, 66,* 56–62.

Hall, P. A., Crossley, M., & D'Arcy, C. (2010). Executive function and survival in the context of chronic illness. *Annals of Behavioral Medicine, 39,* 119–127.

Hall, P. A., Dubin, J. A., Crossley, M., Holmqvist, M. E., & D'Arcy, C. (2009). Does executive function explain the IQ-mortality association? Evidence from the Canadian study on health and aging. *Psychosomatic Medicine, 71,* 196–204.

Hall, S., Weinman, J., & Marteau, T. M. (2004). The motivating impact of informing women smokers of a link between smoking and cervical cancer: The role of coherence. *Health Psychology, 23,* 419–424.

Halpern-Felsher, B. L., Millstein, S. G., Ellen, J. M., Adler, N. E., Tschann, J. M., & Biehl, M. (2001). The role of behavioral experience in judging risks. *Health Psychology, 20,* 120–126.

Ham, B. (Ed.). (2003). Health behavior information transfer. *Habit, 6.* Retrieved from http://www.cfah.org/habit/

Hamburg, D. A., & Adams, J. E. (1967). A perspective on coping behavior: Seeking and utilizing information in major transitions. *Archives of General Psychiatry, 19,* 277–284.

Hamer, M., & Steptoe, A. (2007). Association between physical fitness, parasympathetic control, and proinflammatory responses to mental stress. *Psychosomatic Medicine, 69,* 660–666.

Hamer, M., Williams, E., Vuonovirta, R., Giacobazzi, P., Gibson, E. L., & Steptoe, A. (2006). The effects of effort-reward imbalance on inflammatory and cardiovascular responses to mental stress. *Psychosomatic Medicine, 68,* 408–413.

Hamilton, J. G., Lobel, M., & Moyer, A. (2009). Emotional distress following genetic testing for hereditary breast and ovarian cancer: A meta-analytic review. *Health Psychology, 28,* 510–518.

Hamilton, M. K., Gelwick, B. P., & Meade, C. J. (1984). The definition and prevalence of bulimia. In R. C. Hawkins, W. J. Fremouw, & P. F. Clement (Eds.), *The binge-purge syndrome* (pp. 3–26). New York: Springer.

Hamilton, N. A., Catley, D., & Karlson, C. (2007). Sleep and the affective response to stress and pain. *Health Psychology, 26,* 288–295.

Hamilton, N. A., Karoly, P., & Zautra, A. J. (2005). Health goal cognition and adjustment in women with fibromyalgia. *Journal of Behavioral Medicine, 28,* 455–466.

Hamilton, V. L., Broman, C. L., Hoffman, W. S., & Renner, D. S. (1990). Hard times and vulnerable people: Initial effects of plant closing on autoworkers' mental health. *Journal of Health and Social Behavior, 31,* 123–140.

Hammen, C., Marks, T., Mayol, A., & DeMayo, R. (1985). Depressive self-schemas, life stress, and vulnerability to depression. *Journal of Abnormal Psychology, 94,* 308–319.

Hampson, S. E., Andrews, J. A., Barckley, M., Lichtenstein, E., & Lee, M. E. (2000). Conscientiousness, perceived risk, and risk-reduction behaviors: A preliminary study. *Health Psychology, 19,* 496–500.

Hampson, S. E., Glasgow, R. E., & Toobert, D. J. (1990). Personal models of diabetes and their relations to self-care activities. *Health Psychology, 9,* 632–646.

Hampson, S. E., Glasgow, R. E., & Zeiss, A. M. (1994). Personal models of osteoarthritis and their relation to self-management activities and quality of life. *Journal of Behavioral Medicine, 17,* 143–158.

Hamrick, N., Cohen, S., & Rodriguez, M. S. (2002). Being popular can be healthy or unhealthy: Stress, social network diversity, and incidence of upper respiratory infection. *Health Psychology, 21,* 294–298.

Han, S., & Shavitt, S. (1994). Persuasion and culture: Advertising appeals in individualistic and collectivistic societies. *Journal of Experimental Social Psychology, 30,* 326–350.

Hannerz, H., Albertsen, K., Nielsen, M. L., Tüchsen, F., & Burr, H. (2004). Occupational factors and 5-year weight change among men in a Danish national cohort. *Health Psychology, 23,* 283–288.

Hanson, C. L., Henggeler, S. W., & Burghen, G. A. (1987). Models of associations between psychosocial variables and health-outcome measures of adolescents with IDDM. *Diabetes Care, 10,* 752–758.

Hanson, C. L., & Pichert, J. W. (1986). Perceived stress and diabetes control in adolescents. *Health Psychology, 5,* 439–452.

Hanson, M. D., & Chen, E. (2007). Socioeconomic status and health behaviors in adolescence: A review of the literature. *Journal of Behavioral Medicine, 30,* 263–285.

Harburg, E., Julius, M., Kacirotti, N., Gleiberman, L., & Schork, M. A. (2003). Expressive/suppressive anger-coping responses, gender, and types of mortality: A 17-year follow-up (Tecumseh, Michigan, 1971–1988). *Psychosomatic Medicine, 65,* 588–597.

Harnish, J. D., Aseltine, R. H., & Gore, S. (2000). Resolution of stressful experiences as an indicator of coping effectiveness in young adults: An event history analysis. *Journal of Health and Social Behavior, 41,* 121–136.

Harrington, L., Affleck, G., Urrows, S., Tennen, H., Higgins, P., Zautra, A., et al. (1993). Temporal covariation of soluble interleukin-2 receptor levels, daily stress, and disease activity in rheumatoid arthritis. *Arthritis and Rheumatism, 36,* 199–207.

Harris, A. H. S., Thoresen, C. E., Humphreys, K., & Faul, J. (2005). Does writing affect asthma? A randomized trial. *Psychosomatic Medicine, 67,* 130–136.

Harris, J. L., Bargh, J. A., & Brownell, K. D. (2009). Priming effects of television food advertising on eating behavior. *Health Psychology, 28,* 404–413.

Harris, K. F., & Matthews, K. A. (2004). Interactions between autonomic nervous system activity and the endothelial function: A model for the development of cardiovascular disease. *Psychosomatic Medicine, 66,* 153–164.

Harris, P. R., Mayle, K., Mabbott, L., & Napper, L. (2007). Self-affirmation reduces smokers' defensiveness to graphic on-pack cigarette warning labels. *Health Psychology, 26,* 437–446.

Hartley, H. (1999). The influence of managed care on supply of certified nurse-midwives: An evaluation of the physician dominance thesis. *Journal of Health and Social Behavior, 40,* 87–101.

Harvey, A. G., Bryant, R. A., & Tarrier, N. (2003). Cognitive behaviour therapy for posttraumatic stress disorder. *Clinical Psychology Review, 23,* 501–522.

Haskard, K. B., Williams, S. L., DiMatteo, M. R., Rosenthal, R., White, M. K., & Goldstein, M. G. (2008). Physician and patient communication training in primary care: Effects on participation and satisfaction. *Health Psychology, 27,* 513–522.

Hatzenbuehler, M. L., Nolen-Hoeksema, S., & Erickson, S. J. (2008). Minority stress predictors of HIV risk behavior, substance use, and depressive symptoms: Results from a prospective study of bereaved gay men. *Health Psychology, 27,* 455–462.

Hauenstein, M. S., Schiller, M. R., & Hurley, R. S. (1987). Motivational techniques of dieticians counseling individuals with Type II diabetes. *Journal of the American Dietetic Association, 87,* 37–42.

Haug, M. R., & Folmar, S. J. (1986). Longevity, gender, and life quality. *Journal of Health and Social Behavior, 27,* 332–345.

Haug, M. R., & Ory, M. G. (1987). Issues in elderly patient-provider interactions. *Research on Aging, 9,* 3–44.

Häuser, W., Zimmer, C., Schiedermaier, P., & Grandt, D. (2004). Biopsychosocial predictors of health-related quality of life in patients with chronic hepatitis C. *Psychosomatic Medicine, 66,* 954–958.

Hausteiner, C., Klupsch, D., Emeny, R., Baumert, J., & Ladwig, K. H. (2010). Clustering of negative affectivity and social inhibition in the community: Prevalence of type D personality as a cardiovascular risk marker. *Psychosomatic Medicine, 72,* 163–171.

Hawkley, L. C., Burleson, M. H., Berntson, G. G., & Cacioppo, J. T. (2003). Loneliness in everyday life: Cardiovascular activity, psychosocial context, and health behaviors. *Journal of Personality and Social Psychology, 85,* 105–120.

Hawkley, L. C., Thisted, R. A., & Cacioppo, J. T. (2009). Loneliness predicts reduced physical activity: Cross-sectional & longitudinal analyses. *Health Psychology, 28,* 354–363.

Hay, J. L., Meischke, H. W., Bowen, D. J., Mayer, J., Shoveller, J., Press, N., et al. (2007). Anticipating dissemination of cancer genomics in public health: A theoretical approach to psychosocial and behavioral challenges. *Annals of Behavioral Medicine, 34,* 275–286.

Hayes-Bautista, D. E. (1976). Modifying the treatment: Patient compliance, patient control, and medical care. *Social Science and Medicine, 10,* 233–238.

Haynes, R. B., McKibbon, K. A., & Kanani, R. (1996). Systematic review of randomized controlled trials of the effects on patient adherence and outcomes of interventions to assist patients to follow prescriptions for medications. *The Cochrane Library, 2,* 1–26.

Haynes, S. G., Odenkirchen, J., & Heimendinger, J. (1990). Worksite health promotion for cancer control. *Seminars in Oncology, 17,* 463–484.

Hays, J., et al. (2003). Effects of estrogen plus progestin on health-related quality of life. *The New England Journal of Medicine, 348,* 1839–1854.

Hays, R. B., Turner, H., & Coates, T. J. (1992). Social support, AIDS-related symptoms, and depression among gay men. *Journal of Consulting and Clinical Psychology, 60,* 463–469.

Haythornthwaite, J., Lawrence, J., & Fauerbach, J. (2001). Brief cognitive interventions for burn pain. *Annals of Behavioral Medicine, 23,* 42–49.

Hazuda, H. P., Gerety, M. B., Lee, S., Mulrow, C. D., & Lichtenstein, M. J. (2002). Measuring subclinical disability in older Mexican Americans. *Psychosomatic Medicine, 64,* 520–30.

Health Promotion Advocates. (2008). *Annual costs of unhealthy lifestyle.* Retrieved August 24, 2009 from http://healthpromotionadvocates.org/resources/presentation.htm

Heaney, C. A., Israel, B. A., & House, J. A. (1994). Chronic job insecurity among automobile workers: Effects on job satisfaction and health. *Social Science and Medicine, 38,* 1431–1437.

Heatherton, T. F., Herman, C. P., & Polivy, J. (1991). Effects of physical threat and ego threat on eating behavior. *Journal of Personality and Social Psychology, 60,* 138–143.

Heatherton, T. F., Herman, C. P., & Polivy, J. (1992). Effects of distress on eating: The importance of ego-involvement. *Journal of Personality and Social Psychology, 62,* 801–803.

Heatherton, T. F., & Sargent, J. D. (2009). Does watching smoking in movies promote teenage smoking? *Current Directions in Psychological Science, 18,* 63–67.

Heckman, T. G. (2003). The chronic illness quality of life (CIQOL) model: Explaining life satisfaction in people living with HIV disease. *Health Psychology, 22,* 140–147.

Heckman, T. G., Anderson, E. S., Sikkema, K. J., Kochman, A., Kalichman, S. C., & Anderson, T. (2004). Emotional distress in nonmetropolitan persons living with HIV disease enrolled in a telephone-delivered, coping improvement group intervention. *Health Psychology, 23,* 94–100.

Heckman, T. G., Miller, J., Kochman, A., Kalichman, S. C., Carlson, B., & Silverthorn, M. (2002). Thoughts of suicide among HIV-infected rural persons enrolled in telephone-delivered mental health intervention. *Annals of Behavioral Medicine, 2002,* 141–148.

Heesch, K. C., Mâsse, L. C., Dunn, A. L., Frankowski, R. F., & Mullen, P. D. (2003). Does adherence to a lifestyle physical activity intervention predict changes in physical activity? *Journal of Behavioral Medicine, 26,* 333–348.

Heim, C., Nater, U. M., Maloney, E., Boneva, R., Jones, J. F., & Reeves, W. C. (2009). Childhood trauma and risk for chronic fatigue syndrome: Association with neuroendocrine dysfunction. *Archives of General Psychiatry, 66,* 72–80.

Heim, E., Valach, L., & Schaffner, L. (1997). Coping and psychosocial adaptation: Longitudinal effects over time and stages in breast cancer. *Psychosomatic Medicine, 59,* 408–418.

Heisler, M., Wagner, T. H., & Piette, J. D. (2005). Patient strategies to cope with high prescription medication costs: Who is cutting back on necessities, increasing debt, or underusing medications? *Journal of Behavioral Medicine, 28,* 43–51.

Hekler, E. B., Lambert, J., Leventhal, E., Leventhal, H., Jahn, E., & Contrada, R. J. (2008). Commonsense illness beliefs, adherence behaviors, and hypertension control among African Americans. *Journal of Behavioral Medicine, 31,* 391–400.

Helgeson, V. S. (1993). Implications of agency and communion for patient and spouse adjustment to a first coronary event. *Journal of Personality and Social Psychology, 64,* 807–816.

Helgeson, V. S. (2003). Cognitive adaptation, psychological adjustment and disease progression among angioplasty patients: 4 years later. *Health Psychology, 22,* 30–38.

Helgeson, V. S., & Cohen, S. (1996). Social support and adjustment to cancer: Reconciling descriptive, correlational, and intervention research. *Health Psychology, 15,* 135–148.

Helgeson, V. S., Cohen, S., Schulz, R., & Yasko, J. (2000). Group support interventions for women with breast cancer: Who benefits from what? *Health Psychology, 19,* 107–117.

Helgeson, V. S., Cohen, S., Schulz, R., & Yasko, J. (2001). Long-term effects of educational and peer discussion group interventions on adjustment to breast cancer. *Health Psychology, 20,* 387–392.

Helgeson, V. S., Escobar, O., Siminerio, L., & Becker, D. (2010). Relation of stressful life events to metabolic control among adolescents with diabetes: 5-year longitudinal study. *Health Psychology, 29,* 153–159.

Helgeson, V. S., & Fritz, H. L. (1999). Cognitive adaptation as a predictor of new coronary events after percutaneous transluminal coronary angioplasty. *Psychosomatic Medicine, 61,* 488–495.

Helgeson, V. S., & Lepore, S. J. (1997). Men's adjustment to prostate cancer: The role of agency and unmitigated agency. *Sex Roles, 37,* 251–267.

Helgeson, V. S., Lepore, S. J., & Eton, D. T. (2006). Moderators of the benefits of psychoeducational interventions for men with prostate cancer. *Health Psychology, 25,* 348–354.

Helgeson, V. S., Lopez, L. C., & Kamarck, T. (2009). Peer relationships and diabetes: Retrospective and ecological momentary assessment approaches. *Health Psychology, 28,* 273–282.

Helgeson, V. S., Snyder, P., & Seltman, H. (2004). Psychological and physical adjustment to breast cancer over 4 years: Identifying distinct trajectories of change. *Health Psychology, 23,* 3–15.

Hellsten, L., Nigg, C., Norman, G., Burbank, P., Braun, L., Breger, R., et al. (2008). Accumulation of behavioral validation evidence for physical activity state of change. *Health Psychology, 27,* S43–S53.

Helmers, K. F., & Krantz, D. S. (1996). Defensive hostility, gender and cardiovascular levels and responses to stress. *Annals of Behavioral Medicine, 18,* 246–254.

Hemmingsson, T., Kriebel, D., Melin, B., Allebeck, P., & Lundberg, I. (2008). How does IQ affect onset of smoking and cessation of smoking—Linking the Swedish 1969 conscription cohort to the Swedish survey of living conditions. *Psychosomatic Medicine, 70,* 805–810.

Henifin, M. S. (1993). New reproductive technologies: Equity and access to reproductive health care. *Journal of Social Issues, 49,* 62–74.

Henningsen, P., Zimmermann, T., & Sattel, H. (2003). Medically unexplained physical symptoms, anxiety, and depression: A meta-analytic review. *Psychosomatic Medicine, 65,* 528–533.

Henry, J. P., & Cassel, J. C. (1969). Psychosocial factors in essential hypertension: Recent epidemiologic and animal experimental evidence. *American Journal of Epidemiology, 90,* 171–200.

Henselmans, I., Helgeson, V. S., Seltman, H., de Vries, J., Sanderman, R., & Ranchor, A. V. (2010). Identification and prediction of distress trajectories in the first year after a breast cancer diagnosis. *Health Psychology, 29,* 160–168.

Henson, J. M., Carey, M. P., Carey, K. B., & Maisto, S. A. (2006). Associations among health behaviors and time perspective in young adults: Model testing with boot-strapping replication. *Journal of Behavioral Medicine, 29,* 127–137.

Herbert, A., Gerry, N. P., McQueen, M. B., Heid, I. M., Pfeufer, A., Illig, T., et al. (2006). A common genetic variant is associated with adult and childhood obesity. *Science, 312,* 279–283.

Herbert, T. B., & Cohen, S. (1993). Stress and immunity in humans: A meta-analytic review. *Psychosomatic Medicine, 5,* 364–379.

Herbst, S., Pietrzak, R. H., Wagner, J., White, W. B., & Petry, N. M. (2007). Lifetime major depression is associated with coronary heart disease in older adults: Results from the national epidemiologic survey on alcohol and related conditions. *Psychosomatic Medicine, 69,* 729–734.

Herbst-Damm, K. L., & Kulik, J. A. (2005). Volunteer support, marital status, and the survival times of terminally ill patients. *Health Psychology, 24,* 225–229.

Herek, G. M., Capitanio, J. P., & Widaman, K. F. (2003). Stigma, social risk, and health policy: Public attitudes toward HIV surveillance policies and the social construction of illness. *Health Psychology, 22,* 533–540.

Herman, S., Blumenthal, J. A., Babyak, M., Khatri, P., Craighead, W. E., Krishnan, K. R., et al. (2002). Exercise therapy for depression in middle-aged and older adults: Predictors of early dropout and treatment failure. *Health Psychology, 21,* 553–563.

Hermand, D., Mullet, E., & Lavieville, S. (1997). Perception of the combined effects of smoking and alcohol on health. *Journal of Health Psychology, 2,* 481–491.

Hermann, C., & Blanchard, E. B. (2002). Biofeedback in the treatment of headache and other childhood pain. *Applied Psychophysiology and Biofeedback, 27,* 143–162.

Hernandez, A., & Sachs-Ericsson, N. (2006). Ethnic differences in pain reports and the moderating role of depression in a community sample of Hispanic and Caucasian participants with serious health problems. *Psychosomatic Medicine, 68,* 121–128.

Herrmann, C., Brand-Driehorst, S., Kaminsky, B., Leibing, E., Staats, H., & Ruger, U. (1998). Diagnostic groups and depressed mood as predictors of 22-month mortality in medical inpatients. *Psychosomatic Medicine, 60,* 570–577.

Herschbach, P., Duran, G., Waadt, S., Zettler, A., Amm, C., Marten-Mittag, B., et al. (1997). Psychometric properties of the questionnaire on stress in patients with diabetes-revised (QSD-F). *Health Psychology, 16,* 171–174.

Hersey, J. C., Niederdeppe, J., Evans, W. D., Nonnemaker, J., Blahut, S., Holden, D., et al. (2005). The theory of "truth": How counterindustry media campaigns affect smoking behavior among teens. *Health Psychology, 24,* 22–31.

Hertel, A. W., Finch, E. A., Kelly, K. M., King, C., Lando, H., Linde, J. A., et al. (2008). The impact of expectations and satisfaction on the initiation and maintenance of smoking cessation: An experimental test. *Health Psychology, 27,* S197–S206.

Herzog, A. R., House, J. D., & Morgan, J. N. (1991). Relation of work and retirement to health and well-being in older age. *Psychology and Aging, 6,* 202–211.

Herzhog, T. A. (2008). Analyzing the transtheoretical model using the framework of Weinstein, Rothman, and Sutton (1998): The example of smoking cessation. *Health Psychology, 27,* 548–556.

Hewig, J., Cooper, S., Trippe, R. H., Hecht, H., Straube, T., & Miltner, W. H. R. (2008). Drive for thinness and attention toward specific body parts in a nonclinical sample. *Psychosomatic Medicine, 70,* 729–736.

Hibbard, M. R., Gordon, W. A., Stein, P. N., Grober, S., & Sliwinski, M. (1992). Awareness of disability in patients following stroke. *Rehabilitation Psychology, 37,* 103–120.

Hibbard, M. R., Grober, S. E., Stein, P. N., & Gordon, W. A. (1992). Post-stroke depression. In A. Freeman & F. M. Dattilio (Eds.), *Comprehensive casebook of cognitive therapy* (pp. 303–310). New York: Plenum.

Hien, T. T., de Jong, M., & Farrar, J. (2004). Avian influenza— A challenge to global health care structures. *The New England Journal of Medicine, 351,* 2363–2365.

Higgins-Biddle, J. C., Babor, T. F., Mullahy, J., Daniels, J., & McRee, B. (1997). Alcohol screening and brief intervention: Where research meets practice. *Connecticut Medicine, 61,* 565–575.

Hill, T. D., Ellison, C. G., Burdette, A. M., & Musick, M. A. (2007). Religious involvement and healthy lifestyles: Evidence from the survey of Texas adults. *Annals of Behavioral Medicine, 34,* 217–222.

Hill-Briggs, F. (2003). Problem solving in diabetes self-management: A model of chronic illness self-management behavior. *Annals of Behavior Medicine, 25,* 182–193.

Hill-Briggs, F., Gary, T. L., Bone, L. R., Hill, M. N., Levine, D. M., & Brancati, F. L. (2005). Medication adherence and diabetes control in urban African Americans with type 2 diabetes. *Health Psychology, 24,* 349–357.

Hill-Briggs, F., Gary, T. L., Yeh, H., Batts-Turner, M., Powe, N. R., Saudek, C. D., et al. (2006). Association of social problem solving with glycemic control in a sample of urban African Americans with type 2 diabetes. *Journal of Behavioral Medicine, 29,* 69–78.

Hillhouse, J. J., Stair, A. W., & Adler, C. M. (1996). Predictors of sunbathing and sunscreen use in college undergraduates. *Journal of Behavioral Medicine, 19,* 543–562.

Hilmert, C. J., Dunkel-Schetter, C., Dominguez, T. P., Abdou, C., Hobel, C. J., Glynn, L., et al. (2008). Stress and blood pressure during pregnancy: Racial differences and associations with birthweight. *Psychosomatic Medicine, 70,* 57–64.

Hilmert, C. J., Ode, S., Zielke, D. J., & Robinson, M. D. (2010). Blood pressure reactivity predicts somatic reactivity to stress in daily life. *Journal of Behavioral Medicine, 33,* 282–292.

Hinton, J. M. (1967). *Dying.* Baltimore, MD: Penguin.

Hintsanen, M., Elovainio, M., Puttonen, S., Kivimäki, M., Koskinen, T., Raitakari, O. T., et al. (2007). Effort-reward imbalance, heart rate, and heart-rate variability: The cardiovascular risk in young Finns study. *International Journal of Behavioral Medicine, 14,* 202–212.

Hintsanen, M., Kivimäki, M., Elovainio, M., Pulkki-Råback, L., Keskivaara, P., Juonala, M., et al. (2005). Job strain and early atherosclerosis: The cardiovascular risk in young Finns study. *Psychosomatic Medicine, 67,* 740–747.

Hirayama, T. (1981). Non-smoking wives of heavy smokers have a higher risk of lung cancer: A study from Japan. *British Medical Journal, 282,* 183–185.

Hobel, C. J., Dunkel-Schetter, C., & Roesch, S. (1998). Maternal stress as a signal to the fetus. *Prenatal and Neonatal Medicine, 3,* 116–120.

Hobfoll, S. E., Jackson, A. P., Lavin, J., Britton, P. J., & Shepherd, J. B. (1993). Safer sex knowledge, behavior, and attitudes of inner-city women. *Health Psychology, 12,* 481–488.

Hochbaum, G. (1958). *Public participation in medical screening programs* (DHEW Publication No. 572, Public Health Service). Washington, DC: U.S. Government Printing Office.

Hochschild, A. (1989). *The second shift: Working parents and the revolution at home.* New York: Viking Penguin.

Hodis, H. N., Mack, W. J., Azen, S. P., Lobo, P. A., Shoupe, D., Mahrer, P. R., et al. (2003). Hormone therapy and the progression of coronary-artery atherosclerosis in postmenopausal women. *The New England Journal of Medicine, 349,* 535–545.

Hoelscher, T. J., Lichstein, K. L., & Rosenthal, T. L. (1986). Home relaxation practice in hypertension treatment: Objective assessment and compliance induction. *Journal of Consulting and Clinical Psychology, 54,* 217–221.

Hoffman, B. M., Papas, R. K., Chatkoff, D. K., & Kerns, R. D. (2007). Meta-analysis of psychological interventions for chronic low back pain. *Health Psychology, 26,* 1–9.

Hogan, B. E., & Linden, W. (2004). Anger response style and blood pressure: At least don't ruminate about it! *Annals of Behavioral Medicine, 27,* 38–49.

Holahan, C. J., & Moos, R. H. (1990). Life stressors, resistance factors, and improved psychological functioning: An extension of the stress resistance paradigm. *Journal of Personality and Social Psychology, 58,* 909–917.

Holahan, C. J., & Moos, R. H. (1991). Life stressors, personal and social resources, and depression: A four-year structural model. *Journal of Abnormal Psychology, 100,* 31–38.

Holahan, C. J., Moos, R. H., Holahan, C. K., & Brennan, P. L. (1997). Social context, coping strategies, and depressive symptoms: An expanded model with cardiac patients. *Journal of Personality and Social Psychology, 72,* 918–928.

Holbrook, T. L., Hoyt, D. B., Stein, M. B., & Sieber, W. J. (2002). Gender differences in long-term post-traumatic stress disorder outcomes after major trauma: Women are at higher risk of adverse outcomes than men. *The Journal of Trauma, Injury, Infection, and Critical Care, 53,* 882–888.

Holland, J. C. (2002). History of psycho-oncology: Overcoming attitudinal and conceptual barriers. *Psychosomatic Medicine, 64,* 206–221.

Hollis, J. F., Carmody, T. P., Connor, S. L., Fey, S. G., & Matarazzo, J. D. (1986). The nutrition attitude survey: Associations with dietary habits, psychological and physical well-being, and coronary risk factors. *Health Psychology, 5,* 359–374.

Holman, E. A., Silver, R. C., & Waitzkin, H. (2000). Traumatic life events in primary care patients: A study in an ethnically diverse sample. *Archives of Family Medicine, 9,* 802–810.

Holmes, J., Powell-Griner, E., Lethbridge-Cejku, M., & Heyman, K. (2009). Aging differently: Physical limitations among adults aged 50 years and over: United States, 2001–2007. *NCHS Data Brief, 20,* 1–7.

Holmes, J. A., & Stevenson, C. A. Z. (1990). Differential effects of avoidant and attentional coping strategies on adaptation to chronic and recent-onset pain. *Health Psychology, 9,* 577–584.

Holmes, T. H., & Rahe, R. H. (1967). The social readjustment rating scale. *Journal of Psychosomatic Research, 11,* 213–218.

Holt, C. L., Clark, E. M., Kreuter, M. W., & Rubio, D. M. (2003). Spiritual health locus of control and breast cancer beliefs among urban African American women. *Health Psychology, 22,* 294–299.

Holt-Lunstad, J., Birmingham, W., & Jones, B. Q. (2008). Is there something unique about marriage? The relative impact of marital status, relationship quality, and network social support on ambulatory blood pressure and mental health. *Annals of Behavioral Medicine, 35,* 239–244.

Holt-Lunstad, J., Birmingham, W. A., & Light, K. C. (2008). Influence of a "warm touch" support enhancement intervention among married couples on ambulatory blood pressure, oxytocin, alpha amylase, and cortisol. *Psychosomatic Medicine, 70,* 976–985.

Holt-Lunstad, J., Smith, T. W., & Uchino, B. N. (2008). Can hostility interfere with the health benefits of giving and receiving social support? The impact of cynical hostility on cardiovascular reactivity during social support interactions among friends. *Annals of Behavioral Medicine, 35,* 319–330.

Honda, K., & Gorin, S. S. (2005). Modeling pathways to affective barriers on colorectal cancer screening among Japanese Americans. *Journal of Behavioral Medicine, 28,* 2005.

Hong, S., Nelesen, R. A., Krohn, P. L., Mills, P. J., & Dimsdale, J. E. (2006). The association of social status and blood pressure with markers of vascular inflammation. *Psychosomatic Medicine, 68,* 517–523.

Horan, M. J., & Roccella, E. J. (1988). Non-pharmacologic treatment of hypertension in the United States. *Health Psychology, 7* (Suppl.), 267–282.

Horgen, K. B., & Brownell, K. D. (2002). Comparison of price change and health message interventions in promoting healthy food choices. *Health Psychology, 21,* 505–512.

Horvath, K. J., Bowen, A. M., & Williams, M. L. (2006). Virtual and physical venues as contexts for HIV risk among rural men who have sex with men. *Health Psychology, 25,* 237–242.

Horwitz, A. V., Reinhard, S. C., & Howell-White, S. (1996). Caregiving as reciprocal exchange in families with seriously mentally ill members. *Journal of Health and Social Behavior, 37,* 149–162.

House, J. A. (1981). *Work stress and social support.* Reading, MA: Addison-Wesley.

House, J. S. (2001). Understanding social factors and inequalities in health: 20th century progress and 21st century prospects. *Journal of Health and Social Behavior, 43,* 125–142.

House, J. S., Kessler, R. C., Herzog, A. R., Mero, R. P., Kinney, A. M., & Breslow, M. J. (1990). Age, socioeconomic status, and health. *The Milbank Quarterly, 68,* 383–411.

House, J. S., Landis, K. R., & Umberson, D. (1988). Social relationships and health. *Science, 241,* 540–545.

House, J. S., & Smith, D. A. (1985). Evaluating the health effects of demanding work on and off the job. In T. F. Drury (Ed.), *Assessing physical fitness and physical activity in population-base surveys* (pp. 481–508). Hyattsville, MD: National Center for Health Statistics.

Houston, B. K., & Vavak, C. R. (1991). Cynical hostility: Developmental factors, psychosocial correlates, and health behaviors. *Health Psychology, 10,* 9–17.

Howren, M. B., Christensen, A. J., Karnell, L. H., & Funk, G. F. (2010). Health-related quality of life in head and neck cancer survivors: Impact of pretreatment depressive symptoms. *Health Psychology, 29,* 65–71.

Howren, M. B., Lamkin, D. M., & Suls, J. (2009). Associations of depression with C-reactive protein, IL-1, and IL-6: A meta-analysis. *Psychosomatic Medicine, 71,* 171–186.

Howren, B., Suls, J., & Martin, R. (2009). Depressive symptomatology, rather than neuroticism, predicts inflated physical symptom reports in community-residing women. *Psychosomatic Medicine, 71,* 951–957.

Hoyt, M. A., Thomas, K. S., Epstein, D. R., & Dirksen, S. R. (2009). Coping style and sleep quality in men with cancer. *Annals of Behavioral Medicine, 37,* 88–93.

Hu, F. B., Stampfer, M. J., Manson, J. E., Grodstein, F., Colditz, G. A., Speizer, F. E., et al. (2000). Trends in the incidence of coronary heart disease and changes in diet and lifestyle in women. *The New England Journal of Medicine, 343,* 530–537.

Hu, F. B., Willett, W. C., Li, T., Stampfer, M. J., Colditz, G. A., & Manson, J. E. (2004). Adiposity as compared with physical activity in predicting mortality among women. *The New England Journal of Medicine, 351,* 2694–2703.

Hu, L., Motl, R. W., McAuley, E., & Konopack, J. F. (2007). Effects of self-efficacy on physical activity enjoyment in college-aged women. *International Journal of Behavioral Medicine, 14,* 92–96.

Hudson, J. I., Hiripi, E., Pope, H. G., & Kessler, R. C. (2007). The prevalence and correlates of eating disorders in the national comorbidity survey replication. *Biological Psychiatry, 61,* 348–358.

Hughes, J. R. (1993). Pharmacotherapy for smoking cessation: Unvalidated assumptions, anomalies, and suggestions for future research. *Journal of Consulting and Clinical Psychology, 61,* 751–760.

Hughes, J. W., York, K. M., Li, Q., Freedland, K. E., Carney, R. M., & Sheps, D. S. (2008). Depressive symptoms predict heart rate recovery after exercise treadmill testing in patients with coronary artery disease: Results from the psychophysiological investigation of myocardial ischemia study. *Psychosomatic Medicine, 70,* 456–460.

Hughes, M. E., & Waite, L. J. (2002). Health in household context: Living arrangements and health in late middle age. *Journal of Health and Social Behavior, 43,* 1–21.

Huizink, A. C., Robles de Medina, P. G., Mulder, E. J. H., Visser, G. H. A., & Buitelaar, J. K. (2002). Coping in normal pregnancy. *Annals of Behavioral Medicine, 24,* 132–140.

Hulbert, A. (2006, July 16). Confidant crisis: Americans have fewer close friends than before. Is that a problem? *New York Times Magazine,* p. 15.

Humpel, N., Marshall, A. L., Leslie, E., Bauman, A., & Owen, N. (2004). Changes in neighborhood walking are related to changes in perceptions of environmental attributes. *Annals of Behavioral Medicine, 27,* 60–67.

Huntington, R., & Metcalf, P. (1979). *Celebrations of death: The anthropology of mortuary ritual.* New York: Cambridge University Press.

Huntington's Disease Society of America. (2009). *What is Huntington's disease?* Retrieved September 25, 2009, from http://www.hdsa.org/about/our-mission/what-is-hd.html

Hutchison, K. E., McGeary, J., Smolen, A., Bryan, A., & Swift, R. M. (2002). The DRD4 VNTR polymorphism moderates craving after alcohol consumption. *Health Psychology, 21,* 139–146.

Ickovics, J. R., Hamburger, M. E., Vlahov, D., Schoenbaum, E. E., Schuman, P., Boland, R. J., et al. (2001). Mortality, CD4 cell count decline, and depressive symptoms among HIV-seropositive women. *Journal of the American Medical Association, 285,* 1466–1474.

Ickovics, J. R., Viscoli, C. M., & Horwitz, R. I. (1997). Functional recovery after myocardial infarction in men: The independent effects of social class. *Annals of Behavioral Medicine, 127,* 518–525.

Ikeda, H., Stark, J., Fischer, H., Wagner, M., Drdla, R., Jäger, T., et al. (2006). Synaptic amplifier of inflammatory pain in the spinal dorsal horn. *Science, 312,* 1659–1662.

Ingelfinger, J. R. (2004). Pediatric antecedents of adult cardiovascular disease-awareness and intervention. *The New England Journal of Medicine, 350,* 2123–2126.

Ingersoll, K. S., & Cohen, J. (2008). The impact of medication regiment factors on adherence to chronic treatment: A review of literature. *Journal of Behavioral Medicine, 31,* 213–224.

Ingram, R. E., Atkinson, J. H., Slater, M. A., Saccuzzo, D. P., & Garfin, S. R. (1990). Negative and positive cognition in depressed and nondepressed chronic-pain patients. *Health Psychology, 9,* 300–314.

Institute for Clinical Systems Improvement (ICSI). (2004). *Preventive counseling and education—by topic: The percentage of patients with documentation in their medical records of counseling information given within specific topic areas within the last five years.* Bloomington, MN: Author.

Institute of Medicine. (1999). *To err is human: Building a safer health system.* Retrieved from http://www.iom.edu/report.asp?id=5575

Institute of Medicine. (2002). *Unequal treatment: Confronting racial and ethnic disparities in health care.* Washington, DC: National Academic Press.

Institute of Medicine. (2009). *Informing the Future: Critical Issues in Health,* 5th Edition. Washington, DC: The National Academies Press.

Interian, A., Gara, M. A., Díaz-Martínez, A. M., Warman, M. J., Escobar, J. I., Allen, L. A., et al. (2004). The value of pseudoneurological symptoms for assessing psychopathology in primary care. *Psychosomatic Medicine, 66,* 141–146.

Ironson, G., & Hayward, H. (2008). Do positive psychosocial factors predict disease progression in HIV-1? A review of the evidence. *Psychosomatic Medicine, 70,* 546–554.

Ironson, G., O'Cleirigh, C., Fletcher, M., Laurenceau, J. P., Balbin, E., Klimas, N., et al. (2005). Psychosocial factors predict CD4 and viral load change in men and women with human immunodeficiency virus in the era of highly active antiretroviral treatment. *Psychosomatic Medicine, 67,* 1013–1021.

Ironson, G., O'Cleirigh, C., Weiss, A., Schneiderman, N., & Costa, P. T. (2008). Personality and HIV disease progression: Role of NEO-PI-R openness, extraversion, and profiles of engagement. *Psychosomatic Medicine, 70,* 245–253.

Ironson, G., Wynings, C., Schneiderman, N., Baum, A., Rodriguez, M., Greenwood, D., et al. (1997). Posttraumatic stress symptoms, intrusive thoughts, loss, and immune function after Hurricane Andrew. *Psychosomatic Medicine, 59,* 128–141.

Irvin, J. E., Bowers, C. A., Dunn, M. E., & Wang, M. C. (1999). Efficacy of relapse prevention: A meta-analytic review. *Journal of Consulting and Clinical Psychology, 67,* 563–570.

Irvine, J., Baker, B., Smith, J., Janice, S., Paquette, M., Cairns, J., et al. (1999). Poor adherence to placebo or amiodarone therapy predicts mortality: Results from the CAMIAT study. *Psychosomatic Medicine, 61,* 566–575.

Irwin, M. R., Cole, J. C., & Nicassio, P. M. (2006). Comparative meta-analysis of behavioral interventions for insomnia and their efficacy in middle-aged adults and in older adults 55+ years of age. *Health Psychology, 25,* 3–14.

Irwin, M. R., Pike, J. L., Cole, J. C., & Oxman, M. N. (2003). Effects of a behavioral intervention, tai chi chih, on Varicella-Zoster virus specific immunity and health functioning in older adults. *Psychosomatic Medicine, 65,* 824–830.

Ishizawa, T., Yoshiuchi, K., Takimoto, Y., Yamamoto, Y., & Akabayashi, A. (2008). Heart rate and blood pressure variability and baroreflex sensitivity in patients with anorexia nervosa. *Psychosomatic Medicine, 70,* 695–700.

Itkowitz, N. I., Kerns, R. D., & Otis, J. D. (2003). Support and coronary heart disease: The importance of significant other responses. *Journal of Behavioral Medicine, 26,* 19–30.

Ituarte, P. H., Kamarck, T. W., Thompson, H. S., & Bacanu, S. (1999). Psychosocial mediators of racial differences in nighttime blood pressure dipping among normotensive adults. *Health Psychology, 18,* 393–402.

Jaccard, J., Dodge, T., & Guilamo-Ramos, V. (2005). Metacognition, risk behavior, and risk outcomes: The role of perceived intelligence and perceived knowledge. *Health Psychology, 24,* 161–170.

Jachuck, S. J., Brierley, H., Jachuck, S., & Willcox, P. M. (1982). The effect of hypotensive drugs on the quality of life. *Journal of the Royal College of General Practitioners, 32,* 103–105.

Jack, A. (2007, April 25). Climate change bites. *Financial Times,* p. 9.

Jackson, J. L., & Kroenke, K. (2008). Prevalence, impact, and prognosis of multisomatoform disorder in primary care: A 5-year follow-up study. *Psychosomatic Medicine, 70,* 430–434.

Jackson, J. L., Passamonti, M., & Kroenke, K. (2007). Outcome and impact of mental disorders in primary care at 5 years. *Psychosomatic Medicine, 69,* 270–276.

Jackson, K. M., & Aiken, L. S. (2000). A psychosocial model of sun protection and sunbathing in young women: The impact of health beliefs, attitudes, norms, and self-efficacy for sun protection. *Health Psychology, 19,* 469–478.

Jackson, K. M., & Aiken, L. S. (2006). Evaluation of a multicomponent appearance-based sun-protective intervention for young women: Uncovering the mechanisms of program efficacy. *Health Psychology, 25,* 34–46.

Jacob, R. G., Chesney, M. A., Williams, D. M., Ding, Y., & Shapiro, A. P. (1991). Relaxation therapy for hypertension: Design effects and treatment effects. *Annals of Behavioral Medicine, 13,* 5–17.

Jacobs, N., Rijsdijk, F., Derom, C., Vlietinck, R., Delespaul, P., Van Os, J., et al. (2006). Genes making one feel blue in the flow of daily life: A momentary assessment study of gene-stress interaction. *Psychosomatic Medicine, 68,* 201–206.

Jacobsen, P. B., Manne, S. L., Gorfinkle, K., Schorr, O., Rapkin, B., & Redd, W. H. (1990). Analysis of child and parent behavior during painful medical procedures. *Health Psychology, 9,* 559–576.

Jacobson, P. B., Wasserman, J., & Anderson, J. R. (1997). Historical overview of tobacco legislation and regulation. *Journal of Social Issues, 53,* 75–95.

Jacobson, M. F., & Brownell, K. D. (2000). Small taxes on soft drinks and snack foods to promote health. *American Journal of Public Health, 90,* 854–857.

Jacoby, D. B. (1986). Letter to the editor. *The New England Journal of Medicine, 315,* 399.

James, S. A., Hartnett, S. A., & Kalsbeek, W. D. (1983). John Henryism and blood pressure differences among Black men. *Journal of Behavioral Medicine, 6,* 259–278.

James, S. A., Keenan, N. L., Strogatz, D. S., Browning, S. R., & Garrett, J. M. (1992). Socioeconomic status, John Henryism, and blood pressure in Black adults: The Pitt County study. *American Journal of Epidemiology, 135,* 59–67.

Jameson, M. (2004, January 19). No standing pat. *Los Angeles Times,* p. F7.

Janicki-Deverts, D., Cohen, S., Adler, N. E., Schwartz, J. E., Matthews, K. A., & Seeman, T. E. (2007). Socioeconomic status is related to urinary catecholamines in the coronary artery risk development in young adults (CARDIA) study. *Psychosomatic Medicine, 69,* 514–520.

Janicki-Deverts, D., Cohen, S., Matthews, K. A., & Cullen, M. R. (2008). History of unemployment predicts future elevations in C-reactive protein among male participants in the coronary artery risk development in young adults (CARDIA) study. *Annals of Behavioral Medicine, 36,* 176–185.

Janis, I. L. (1958). *Psychological stress.* New York: Wiley.

Janson, M. A. H. (1986). A comprehensive bereavement program. *Quality Review Bulletin, 12,* 130–135.

Jay, S. M., Elliott, C. H., Woody, P. D., & Siegel, S. (1991). An investigation of cognitive-behavior therapy combined with oral Valium for children undergoing painful medical procedures. *Health Psychology, 10,* 317–322.

Jeffery, R. W. (1991). Weight management and hypertension. *Annals of Behavioral Medicine, 13,* 18–22.

Jeffery, R. W., French, S. A., & Rothman, A. J. (1999). Stage of change as a predictor of success in weight control in adult women. *Health Psychology, 18,* 543–546.

Jeffery, R. W., Hennrikus, D. J., Lando, H. A., Murray, D. M., & Liu, J. W. (2000). Reconciling conflicting findings regarding postcessation weight concerns and success in smoking cessation. *Health Psychology, 19,* 242–246.

Jeffery, R. W., Kelly, K. M., Rothman, A. J., Sherwood, N. E., & Boutelle, K. N. (2004). The weight loss experience: A descriptive analysis. *Annals of Behavioral Medicine, 27,* 100–106.

Jeffery, R. W., Pirie, P. L., Rosenthal, B. S., Gerber, W. M., & Murray, D. M. (1982). Nutritional education in supermarkets: An unsuccessful attempt to influence knowledge and produce sales. *Journal of Behavioral Medicine, 5,* 189–200.

Jeffery, R. W., & Wing, R. R. (1995). Long-term effects of interventions for weight loss using food provision and money incentives. *Journal of Consulting and Clinical Psychology, 63,* 793–796.

Jellinek, E. M. (1960). *The disease concept of alcoholism.* Highland Park, NJ: Hillhouse Press.

Jemmott, J. B., III, Croyle, R. T., & Ditto, P. H. (1988). Commonsense epidemiology: Self-based judgments from laypersons and physicians. *Health Psychology, 7,* 55–73.

Jemmott, J. B., III, Jemmott, L. S., & Fong, G. (1992). Reductions in HIV risk–associated sexual behaviors among Black male adolescents: Effects of an AIDS prevention intervention. *American Journal of Public Health, 82,* 372–377.

Jemmott, J. B., III, Jemmott, L. S., & Hacker, C. I. (1992). Predicting intentions to use condoms among African American adolescents: The theory of planned behavior as a model of HIV risk–associated behavior. *Ethnicity Discussions, 2,* 371–380.

Jemmott, J. B., III, Jemmott, L. S., Spears, H., Hewitt, N., & Cruz-Collins, M. (1992). Self-efficacy, hedonistic expectancies, and condom-use intentions among inner-city Black adolescent women: A social cognitive approach to AIDS risk behavior. *Journal of Adolescent Health, 13,* 512–519.

Jemmott, J. B., III, & Jones, J. M. (1993). Social psychology and AIDS among ethnic minorities: Risk behaviors and strategies for changing them. In J. Pryor & G. Reeder (Eds.), *The social psychology of HIV infection* (pp. 183–244). Hillsdale, NJ: Erlbaum.

Jensen, M., & Patterson, D. R. (2006). Hypnotic treatment of chronic pain. *Journal of Behavioral Medicine, 29,* 95–124.

Jiang, W., Babyak, M., Krantz, D. S., Waugh, R. A., Coleman, R. E., Hanson, M. M., et al. (1996). Mental stress-induced myocardial ischemia and cardiac events. *Journal of the American Medical Association, 275,* 1651–1656.

Jim, H. S., Andrykowski, M. A., Munster, P. N., & Jacobsen, P. B. (2007). Physical symptoms/side effects during breast cancer treatment predict posttreatment distress. *Annals of Behavioral Medicine, 34,* 200–208.

Jimerson, D. C., Mantzoros, C., Wolfe, B. E., & Metzger, E. D. (2000). Decreased serum leptin in bulimia nervosa. *The Journal of Clinical Endocrinology & Metabolism, 85,* 4511–4514.

Johansson, E., & Lindberg, P. (2000). Low back pain patients in primary care: Subgroups based on the multidimensional pain inventory. *International Journal of Behavioral Medicine, 7,* 340–352.

Johnsen, L., Spring, B., Pingitore, R., Sommerfeld, B. K., & MacKirnan, D. (2002). Smoking as subculture? Influence on Hispanic and non-Hispanic White women's attitudes toward smoking and obesity. *Health Psychology, 21,* 279–287.

Johnson, E. H., Schork, N. J., & Spielberger, C. D. (1987). Emotional and familial determinants of elevated blood pressure in Black and White adolescent females. *Journal of Psychosomatic Research, 31,* 731–741.

Johnson, J. (1982). The effects of a patient education course on persons with a chronic illness. *Cancer Nursing, 5,* 117–123.

Johnson, J. E. (1984). Psychological interventions and coping with surgery. In A. Baum, S. E. Taylor, & J. E. Singer (Eds.), *Handbook of psychology and health* (Vol. 4, pp. 167–188). Hillsdale, NJ: Erlbaum.

Johnson, J. E., Christman, N., & Stitt, C. (1985). Personal control interventions: Short- and long-term effects on surgical patients. *Research in Nursing and Health, 8,* 131–145.

Johnson, J. E., Cohen, P., Pine, D. S., Klein, D. F., Kasen, S., & Brook, J. S. (2000). Association between cigarette smoking and anxiety disorders during adolescence and early adulthood. *Journal of the American Medical Association, 284,* 2348–2351.

Johnson, J. E., Lauver, D. R., & Nail, L. M. (1989). Process of coping with radiation therapy. *Journal of Consulting and Clinical Psychology, 57,* 358–364.

Johnson, J. E., & Leventhal, H. (1974). Effects of accurate expectations and behavioral instructions on reactions during a noxious medical examination. *Journal of Personality and Social Psychology, 29,* 710–718.

Johnson, M. K. (2004). Further evidence on adolescent employment and substance use: Differences by race and ethnicity. *Journal of Health and Social Behavior, 45,* 187–197.

Johnson, M. O., Elliott, T. R., Neilands, T. B., Morin, S. F., & Chesney, M. A. (2006). A social problem-solving model of adherence to HIV medications. *Health Psychology, 25,* 355–363.

Johnson, M. O., Neilands, T. B., Dilworth, S. E., Morin, S. F., Remien, R. H., & Chesney, M. A. (2007). The role of self-efficacy in HIV treatment adherence: Validation of the HIV treatment adherence self-efficacy scale (HIV-ASES). *Journal of Behavioral Medicine, 30,* 359–370.

Johnson, R. J., McCaul, K. D., & Klein, W. M. P. (2002). Risk involvement and risk perception among adolescents and young adults. *Journal of Behavioral Medicine, 25,* 67–82.

Johnson, S. (2003). *Arthritis has plagued mankind throughout the ages.* DeWitt.

Johnson, S. B., Freund, A., Silverstein, J., Hansen, C. A., & Malone, J. (1990). Adherence-health status relationships in childhood diabetes. *Health Psychology, 9,* 606–631.

Johnson, S. B., Tomer, A., Cunningham, W. R., & Henretta, J. C. (1990). Adherence in childhood diabetes: Results of a confirmatory factor analysis. *Health Psychology, 9,* 493–501.

Johnston, D. W., Johnston, M., Pollard, B., Kinmonth, A. L., & Mant, D. (2004). Motivation is not enough: Prediction of risk behavior following diagnosis of coronary heart disease from the theory of planned behavior. *Health Psychology, 23,* 533–538.

Jokela, M., Elovainio, M., Singh-Manoux, A., & Kivimäki, M. (2009). IQ, socioeconomic status, and early death: The US national longitudinal survey of youth. *Psychosomatic Medicine, 71,* 322–328.

Jonas, B. S., & Lando, J. F. (2000). Negative affect as a prospective risk factor for hypertension. *Psychosomatic Medicine, 62,* 188–196.

Jonas, B. S., & Mussolino, M. E. (2000). Symptoms of depression as a prospective risk factor of stroke. *Psychosomatic Medicine, 62,* 463–471.

Jones, D. J., Beach, S. R. H., Forehand, R., & Foster, S. E. (2003). Self reported health in HIV-positive African American women: The role of family stress and depressive symptoms. *Journal of Behavioral Medicine, 26,* 577–599.

Jones, J. L., & Leary, M. R. (1994). Effects of appearance-based admonitions against sun exposure on tanning intentions in young adults. *Health Psychology, 13,* 86–90.

Jorgensen, R. S., Frankowski, J. J., & Carey, M. P. (1999). Sense of coherence, negative life events and appraisal of physical health among university students. *Personality and Individual Differences, 27,* 1079–1089.

Jun, H. J., Subramanian, S. V., Gortmaker, S., & Kawachi, I. (2004). A multi-level analysis of women's status and self-rated health in the United States. *Journal of the American Medical Women's Association, 59,* 172–180.

Jung, W., & Irwin, M. (1999). Reduction of natural killer cytotoxic activity in major depression: Interaction between depression and cigarette smoking. *Psychosomatic Medicine, 61,* 263–270.

Kabat-Zinn, J., & Chapman-Waldrop, A. (1988). Compliance with an outpatient stress reduction program: Rates and predictors of program completion. *Journal of Behavioral Medicine, 11,* 333–352.

Kagan, N. I. (1974). Teaching interpersonal relations for the practice of medicine. *Lakartidningen, 71,* 4758–4760.

Kahana, E., Lawrence, R. H., Kahana, B., Kercher, K., Wisniewski, A., Stoller, E., et al. (2002). Long-term impact of preventive proactivity on quality of life of the old-old. *Psychosomatic Medicine, 64,* 382–394.

Kahn, J. R., & Pearlin, L. I. (2006). Financial strain over the life course and health among older adults. *Journal of Health and Social Behavior, 47,* 17–31.

Kahn, R. L. (1981). *Work and health.* New York: Wiley.

Kahn, R. L., & Juster, F. T. (2002). Well-being: Concepts and measures. *Journal of Social Issues, 58,* 627–644.

Kalaydjian, A., & Merikangas, K. (2008). Physical and mental comorbidity of headache in a national representative sample of US adults. *Psychosomatic Medicine, 70,* 773–780.

Kalichman, S. C. (2008). Co-occurrence of treatment nonadherence and continued HIV transmission risk behavior: Implications for positive prevention interventions. *Psychosomatic Medicine, 70,* 593–597.

Kalichman, S. C., Benotsch, E. G., Weinhardt, L., Austin, J., Luke, W., & Cherry, C. (2003). Health related Internet use, coping, social support, and health indicators in people living with HIV/AIDS: Preliminary results from community survey. *Health Psychology, 22,* 111–116.

Kalichman, S. C., Cain, D., Weinhardt, L., Benotsch, E., Presser, K., Zweben, A., et al. (2005). Experimental components analysis of brief theory-based HIV/AIDS risk-reduction counseling for sexually transmitted infection patients. *Health Psychology, 24,* 198–208.

Kalichman, S. C., Carey, M. P., & Johnson, B. T. (1996). Prevention of sexually transmitted HIV infection: A meta-analytic review of the behavioral outcome literature. *Annals of Behavioral Medicine, 18,* 6–15.

Kalichman, S. C., Cherry, C., Cain, D., Weinhardt, L. S., Benotsch, E., Pope, H., et al. (2006). Health information on the Internet and people living with HIV/AIDS: Information evaluation and coping styles. *Health Psychology, 25,* 205–210.

Kalichman, S. C., & Coley, B. (1996). Context framing to enhance HIV-antibody-testing messages targeted to African American women. *Health Psychology, 14,* 247–254.

Kalichman, S. C., DiMarco, M., Austin, J., Luke, W., & DiFonzo, K. (2003). Stress, social support, and HIV-status disclosure to family and friends among HIV-positive men and women. *Journal of Behavioral Medicine, 26,* 315–332.

Kalichman, S. C., Eaton, L., Cain, D., Cherry, C., Fuhrel, A., Kaufman, et al. (2007). Changes in HIV treatment beliefs and sexual risk behaviors among gay and bisexual men, 1997–2005. *Health Psychology, 26,* 650–656.

Kalichman, S. C., & Nachimson, D. (1999). Self-efficacy and disclosure of HIV-positive serostatus to sex partners. *Health Psychology, 18,* 281–287.

Kalichman, S. C., Weinhardt, L., DiFonzo, K., Austin, J., & Luke, W. (2002). Sensation seeking and alcohol use as markers of sexual transmission risk behavior in HIV-positive men. *Annals of Behavioral Medicine, 24,* 229–235.

Kamarck, T. W., Muldoon, M. F., Shiffman, S. S., & Sutton-Tyrrell, K. (2007). Experiences of demand and control during daily life are predictors of carotid atherosclerotic progression among healthy men. *Health Psychology, 26,* 324–332.

Kamarck, T. W., Muldoon, M. F., Shiffman, S., Sutton-Tyrell, K., Gwaltney, C., & Janieki, D. L. (2004). Experiences of demand and control in daily life as correlates of subclinical carotid atherosclerosis in a healthy older sample. *Health Psychology, 23,* 24–32.

Kanaan, R. A. A., Lepine, J. P., & Wessely, S. C. (2007). The association or otherwise of the functional somatic syndromes. *Psychosomatic Medicine, 69,* 855–859.

Kanner, A. D., Coyne, J. C., Schaeffer, C., & Lazarus, R. S. (1981). Comparison of two modes of stress measurement: Daily hassles and uplifts versus major life events. *Journal of Behavioral Medicine, 4,* 1–39.

Kaplan, G. A., & Reynolds, P. (1988). Depression and cancer mortality and morbidity: Prospective evidence from the Alameda County Study. *Journal of Behavioral Medicine, 11,* 1–13.

Kaplan, R. M. (1990). Behavior as the central outcome in health care. *American Psychologist, 45,* 1211–1220.

Kaplan, R. M. (2000). Two pathways to prevention. *American Psychologist, 55,* 382–396.

Kaplan, R. M. (2003). The significance of quality of life in health care. *Quality of Life Research, 12* (Suppl. 1), 3–16.

Kaplan, R. M., & Hartwell, S. L. (1987). Differential effects of social support and social network on physiological and social outcomes in men and women with Type II diabetes mellitus. *Health Psychology, 6,* 387–398.

Kaplan, R. M., Orleans, C. T., Perkins, K. A., & Pierce, J. P. (1995). Marshaling the evidence for greater regulation and control of tobacco products: A call for action. *Annals of Behavioral Medicine, 17,* 3–14.

Kaplan, R. M., Ries, A. L., Prewitt, L. M., & Eakin, E. (1994). Self-efficacy expectations predict survival for patients with chronic obstructive pulmonary disease. *Health Psychology, 13,* 366–368.

Kaplan, R. M., & Simon, H. J. (1990). Compliance in medical care: Reconsideration of self-predictions. *Annals of Behavioral Medicine, 12,* 66–71.

Kaplan, R. M., & Toshima, M. T. (1990). The functional effects of social relationships on chronic illnesses and disability. In B. R. Sarason, I. G. Sarason, & G. R. Pierce (Eds.), *Social support: An interactional view* (pp. 427–453). New York: Wiley-Interscience.

Kapp, M. B. (1993). Life-sustaining technologies: Value issues. *Journal of Social Issues, 49,* 151–167.

Kaptein, K. I., de Jonge, P., van den Brink, R. H. S., & Korf, J. (2006). Course of depressive symptoms after myocardial infarction and cardiac prognosis: A latent class analysis. *Psychosomatic Medicine, 68,* 662–668.

Karasek, R., Baker, D., Marxer, F., Ahlbom, A., & Theorell, T. (1981). Job decision latitude, job demands, and cardiovascular disease: A prospective study of Swedish men. *American Journal of Public Health, 71,* 694–705.

Karlamangla, A. S., Singer, B. H., & Seeman, T. E. (2006). Reduction in allostatic load in older adults is associated with lower all-cause mortality risk: MacArthur studies of successful aging. *Psychosomatic Medicine, 68,* 500–507.

Karlin, W. A., Brondolo, E., & Schwartz, J. (2003). Workplace social support and ambulatory cardiovascular activity in New York City traffic agents. *Psychosomatic Medicine, 65,* 167–176.

Karoly, P., & Ruehlman, L. S. (1996). Motivational implications of pain: Chronicity, psychological distress, and work goal construal in a national sample of adults. *Health Psychology, 15,* 383–390.

Kasl, S. V., & Berkman, L. (1983). Health consequences of the experience of migration. *Annual Review of Public Health, 4,* 69–90.

Kassem, N. O., & Lee, J. W. (2004). Understanding soft drink consumption among male adolescents using the theory of planned behavior. *Journal of Behavioral Medicine, 27,* 273–296.

Kastenbaum, R. (1977). Death and development through the lifespan. In H. Feifel (Ed.), *New meanings of death* (pp. 17–46). New York: McGraw-Hill.

Katon, W. J., Richardson, L., Lozano, P., & McCauley, E. (2004). The relationship of asthma and anxiety disorder. *Psychosomatic Medicine, 66,* 349–355.

Katon, W., Russo, J., Lin, E. H. B., Heckbert, S. R., Karter, A. J., Williams, L. H., et al. (2009). Diabetes and poor disease contol: Is comorbid depression associated with poor medication adherence or lack of treatment intensification? *Psychosomatic Medicine, 71,* 965–972.

Katon, W., Von Korff, W., Lin, E., Lipscomb, P., Russo, J., Wagner, E., et al. (1990). Distressed high utilizers of medical care: DSM-III-R diagnosis and treatment needs. *General Hospital Psychiatry, 12,* 355–362.

Katz, R. C., Flasher, L., Cacciapaglia, H., & Nelson, S. (2001). The psychological impact of cancer and lupus: A cross validation study that extends the generality of "benefit finding" in patients with chronic disease. *Journal of Behavioral Medicine, 24,* 561–571.

Katz, R. C., & Jernigan, S. (1991). An empirically derived educational program for detecting and preventing skin cancer. *Journal of Behavioral Medicine, 14,* 421–428.

Katz, S. T., Ford, A. B., Moskowitz, R. W., Jackson, B. A., & Jaffee, M. W. (1983). Studies of illness in the aged: The index of ADL. *Journal of the American Medical Association, 185,* 914–919.

Kaufman, M. R. (1970). Practicing good manners and compassion. *Medical Insight, 2,* 56–61.

Kaugars, A. S., Klinnert, M. D., Robinson, J., & Ho, M. (2008). Reciprocal influences in children's and families' adaptation to early childhood wheezing. *Health Psychology, 27,* 258–267.

Kavanaugh, D. J., Gooley, S., & Wilson, P. H. (1993). Prediction of adherence and control in diabetes. *Journal of Behavioral Medicine, 16,* 509–522.

Kaysen, D., Pantalone, D. W., Chawla, N., Lindgren, K. P., Clum, G. A., Lee, C., et al. (2008). Posttraumatic stress disorder, alcohol use, and physical concerns. *Journal of Behavioral Medicine, 31,* 115–125.

Keane, T. M., & Wolfe, J. (1990). Comorbidity in post-traumatic stress disorder: An analysis of community and clinical studies. *Journal of Applied Social Psychology, 20,* 1776–1788.

Kearney, M. H., Rosal, M. C., Ockene, J. K., & Churchill, L. C. (2002). Influences on older women's adherence to a low-fat diet in the women's health initiative. *Psychosomatic Medicine, 64,* 450–457.

Keefe, F. J., & Blumenthal, J. A. (2004). Health psychology: What will the future bring? *Health Psychology, 23,* 156–157.

Keefe, F. J., Caldwell, D. S., Queen, K. T., Gil, K. M., Martinez, S., Crisson, J. E., et al. (1987). Pain coping strategies in osteoarthritis patients. *Journal of Consulting and Clinical Psychology, 55,* 208–212.

Keefe, F. J., Dunsmore, J., & Burnett, R. (1992). Behavioral and cognitive-behavioral approaches to chronic pain: Recent advances and future directions. *Journal of Consulting and Clinical Psychology, 60,* 528–536.

Keefe, F. J., Lumley, M. A., Buffington, A. L. H., Carson, J. W., Studts, J. L., Edwards, C. L., et al. (2002). Changing face of pain: Evolution of pain research in Psychosomatic Medicine. *Psychosomatic Medicine, 64,* 921–938.

Keefe, F. J., & Van Horn, Y. (1993). Cognitive-behavioral treatment of rheumatoid arthritis pain. *Arthritis Care and Research, 6,* 213–222.

Kehler, M. D., & Hadjistavropoulos, H. D. (2009). Is health anxiety a significant problem for individuals with multiple sclerosis? *Journal of Behavioral Medicine, 32,* 150–161.

Kelder, G. E., Jr., & Daynard, R. A. (1997). Judicial approaches to tobacco control: The third wave of tobacco litigation as a tobacco control mechanism. *Journal of Social Issues, 53,* 169–186.

Kellerman, J., Rigler, D., & Siegel, S. E. (1979). Psychological responses of children to isolation in a protected environment. *Journal of Behavioral Medicine, 2,* 263–274.

Kelley, J. M., Lembo, A. J., Ablon, S., Villanueva, J. J., Conboy, L. A., Levy, R., et al. (2009). Patient and practitioner influences on the placebo effect in irritable bowel syndrome. *Psychosomatic Medicine, 71,* 789–797.

Kelley-Moore, J. A., & Ferraro, K. F. (2005). A 3-D model of health decline: disease, disability, and depression among Black and White older adults. *Journal of Health and Social Behavior, 46,* 376–391.

Kelly, J. A., Lawrence, J. S., Hood, H. V., & Brasfield, T. L. (1989). Behavioral intention to reduce AIDS risk activities. *Journal of Consulting and Clinical Psychology, 57,* 60–67.

Keltikangas-Järvinen, L., Pulkki-Råback, L., Puttonen, S., Viikari, J., & Raitakari, O. T. (2006). Childhood hyperactivity as a predictor of carotid artery intima media thickness over a period of 21 years: The cardiovascular risk in young Finns study. *Psychosomatic Medicine, 68,* 509–516.

Kemeny, M. E. (2003). The psychobiology of stress. *Current Directions, 12,* 124–129.

Kemeny, M. E., Cohen, R., Zegans, L. S., & Conant, M. A. (1989). Psychological and immunological predictors of genital herpes recurrence. *Psychosomatic Medicine, 51,* 195–208.

Kemeny, M. E., Weiner, H., Duran, R., Taylor, S. E., Visscher, B., & Fahey, L. (1995). Immune system changes following the death of a partner in HIV positive gay men. *Psychosomatic Medicine, 57,* 549–554.

Kemeny, M. E., Weiner, H., Taylor, S. E., Schneider, S., Visscher, B., & Fahey, J. L. (1994). Repeated bereavement, depressed mood, and immune parameters in HIV seropositive and seronegative homosexual men. *Health Psychology, 13,* 14–24.

Kenchaiah, S., Evans, J. C., Levy, D., Wilson, P. W. F., Benjamin, E. J., Larson, M. G., et al. (2002). Self-appraised problem solving and pain-relevant social support as predictors of the experience of chronic pain. *Annals of Behavioral Medicine, 24,* 100–105.

Kendall, P. C., Williams, L., Pechacek, T. F., Graham, L. E., Shisslak, C., & Herzoff, N. (1979). Cognitive-behavioral and patient education interventions in cardiac catheterization procedures: The Palo Alto medical psychology project. *Journal of Consulting and Clinical Psychology, 47,* 49–58.

Kendler, K. S., Silberg, J. L., Neale, M. C., Kessler, R. C., Heath, A. C., & Eaves, L. J. (1992). Genetic and environmental factors in the aetiology of menstrual, premenstrual and neurotic symptoms: A population-based twin study. *Psychological Medicine, 22,* 85–100.

Kendzor, D. E., Businelle, M. S., Mazas, C. A., Cofta-Woerpel, L. M., Reitzel, L. R., Vidrine, J. I., et al. (2009). Pathways between socioeconomic status and modifiable risk factors among African American smokers. *Journal of Behavioral Medicine, 32,* 545–557.

Kerckhoff, A. C., & Back, K. W. (1968). *The June bug: A study of hysterical contagion.* New York: Appleton-Century-Crofts.

Kern, M. L., Friedman, H. S., Martin, L. R., Reynolds, C. A., & Luong, G. (2009). Conscientiousness, career success, and longevity: A lifespan analysis. *Annals of Behavioral Medicine, 37,* 154–163.

Kerns, R. D., Rosenberg, R., & Otis, J. D. (2002). Self-appraised problem solving and pain-relevant social support as predictors of the experience of chronic pain. *Annals of Behavioral Medicine, 24,* 100–105.

Kershaw, K. N., Mezuk, B., Abdou, C. M., Rafferty, J. A., & Jackson, J. S. (2010). Socioeconomic position, health behaviors, and C-reactive protein: A moderated-mediation analysis. *Health Psychology, 29,* 307–316.

Kershaw, T. S., Ethier, K. A., Niccolai, L. M., Lewis J. B., & Ickovics, J. R. (2003). Misperceived risk among female adolescents: Social and psychological factors associated with sexual risk accuracy. *Health Psychology, 22,* 523–532.

Kershaw, T. S., Mood, D. W., Newth, G., Ronis, D. L., Sandra, M. G., Vaishampayan, U., et al. (2008). Longitudinal analysis of a model to predict quality of life in prostate cancer patients and their spouses. *Annals of Behavioral Medicine, 36,* 117–128.

Kessler, R. C., Kendler, K. S., Heath, A. C., Neale, M. C., & Eaves, L. J. (1992). Social support, depressed mood, and adjustment to stress: A genetic epidemiological investigation. *Journal of Personality and Social Psychology, 62,* 257–272.

Kessler, R. C., Turner, J. B., & House, J. S. (1987). Intervening processes in the relationship between unemployment and health. *Psychological Medicine, 17,* 949–961.

Kessler, R. C., Turner, J. B., & House, J. S. (1988). Effects of unemployment on health in a community survey: Main, modifying, and mediating effects. *Journal of Social Issues, 44,* 69–85.

Kessler, R. C., & Wethington, E. (1991). The reliability of life event reports in a community survey. *Psychological Medicine, 21,* 723–738.

Key, B. L., Campbell, T. S., Bacon, S. L., & Gerin, W. (2008). The influence of trait and state rumination on cardiovascular recovery from a negative emotional stressor. *Journal of Behavioral Medicine, 31,* 237–248.

Key, T. J., Allen, N. E., Spencer, E. A., & Travis, R. C. (2002). The effects of diet on risk of cancer. *The Lancet, 360,* 861–868.

Khashan, A. S., McNamee, R., Abel, K. M., Pedersen, M. G., Webb, R. T., Kenney, L. C., et al. (2008). Reduced infant birthweight consequent upon maternal exposure to severe life events. *Psychosomatic Medicine, 70,* 688–694.

Kiberstis, P. A. (2005). A surfeit of suspects. *Science, 307,* 369.

Kiecolt-Glaser, J. K. (2010). Stress, food, and inflammation: Psychoneuroimmunology and nutrition at the cutting edge. *Psychosomatic Medicine, 72,* 365–369.

Kiecolt-Glaser, J. K., Christian, L., Preston, H., Houts, C. R., Malarkey, W. B., Emery, C. F., et al. (2010). Stress, inflammation, and yoga practice. *Psychosomatic Medicine, 72,* 113–121.

Kiecolt-Glaser, J. K., Fisher, L., Ogrocki, P., Stout, J. C., Speicher, C. E., & Glaser, R. (1987). Marital quality, marital disruption, and immune function. *Psychosomatic Medicine, 49,* 13–34.

Kiecolt-Glaser, J. K., & Glaser, R. (1987). Psychosocial influences on herpes virus latency. In E. Kurstak, Z. J. Lipowski, & P. V. Morozov (Eds.), *Viruses, immunity, and mental disorders* (pp. 403–412). New York: Plenum.

Kiecolt-Glaser, J. K., Glaser, R., Cacippo, J. T., MacCallum, R. C., Snydersmith, M., Kim, C., et al. (1997). Marital conflict in older adults: Endocrinological and immunological correlates. *Psychosomatic Medicine, 59,* 339–349.

Kiecolt-Glaser, J. K., Glaser, R., Gravenstein, S., Malarkey, W. B., & Sheridan, J. (1996). Chronic stress alters the immune response to influenza virus vaccine in older adults. *Proceedings of the National Academy of Science USA, 93,* 3043–3047.

Kiecolt-Glaser, J. K., Glaser, R., Williger, D., Stout, J., Messick, G., Sheppard, S., et al. (1985). Psychosocial enhancement of immunocompetence in a geriatric population. *Health Psychology, 4,* 25–41.

Kiecolt-Glaser, J. K., Loving, T. J., Stowell, J. R., Malarkey, W. B., Lemeshow, S., Dickinson, S. L., et al. (2005). Hostile marital interactions, proinflammatory cytokine production, and wound healing. *Archives of General Psychiatry, 62,* 1377–1384.

Kiecolt-Glaser, J. K., Malarkey, W. B., Chee, M. A., Newton, T., Cacippo, J. T., Mao, H. Y., et al. (1993). Negative behavior during marital conflict is associated with immunological down-regulation. *Psychosomatic Medicine, 55,* 395–409.

Kiecolt-Glaser, J. K., Marucha, P. T., Malarkey, W. B., Mercado, A. M., & Glaser, R. (1995). Slowing of wound healing by psychological stress. *Lancet, 346,* 1194–1196.

Kiecolt-Glaser, J. K., McGuire, L., Robles, T. F., & Glaser, R. (2002). Psychoneuroimmunology and psychosomatic medicine: Back to the future. *Psychosomatic Medicine, 64,* 15–28.

Kiecolt-Glaser, J. K., & Newton, T. L. (2001). Marriage and health: His and hers. *Psychological Bulletin, 127,* 472–503.

Kiefer, A., Lin, J., Blackburn, E., & Epel, E. (2008). Dietary restraint and telomere length in pre-and postmenopausal women. *Psychosomatic Medicine, 70,* 845–849.

Kiene, S. M., Tennen, H., & Armeli, S. (2008). Today I'll use a condom, but who knows about tomorrow: A daily process study of variability in predictors of condom use. *Health Psychology, 27,* 463–472.

Kim, J., Knight, B. G., & Flynn Longmire, C. V. (2007). The role of familism in stress and coping processes among African American and White dementia caregivers: Effects on mental and physical health. *Health Psychology, 26,* 564–576.

Kim, K. H., Bursac, Z., DiLillo, V., White, D. B., & West, D. S. (2009). Stress, race, and body weight. *Health Psychology, 28,* 131–135.

Kim, Y., Kashy, D. A., Wellisch, D. K., Spillers, R. L., Kaw, C. K., & Smith, T. G. (2008). Quality of life of couples dealing with cancer: Dyadic and individual adjustment among breast and prostate cancer survivors and their spousal caregivers. *Annals of Behavioral Medicine, 35,* 230–238.

Kim, Y., Schulz, R., & Carver, C. S. (2007). Benefit finding in the cancer caregiving experience. *Psychosomatic Medicine, 69,* 283–291.

Kim, Y., Valdimarsdottir, H. B., & Bovbjerg, D. H. (2003). Family histories of breast cancer, coping styles, and psychological adjustment. *Journal of Behavioral Medicine, 26,* 225–243.

Kimm, S. Y. S., Glynn, N. W., Kriska, A. M., Barton, B. A., Kronsberg, S. S., Daniels, S. R., et al. (2002). Decline in physical activity in Black girls and White girls during adolescence. *The New England Journal of Medicine, 347,* 709–715.

Kinder, L. S., Bradley, K. A., Katon, W. J., Ludman, E., McDonell, M. B., & Bryson, C. L. (2008). Depression, posttraumatic stress disorder, and mortality. *Psychosomatic Medicine, 70,* 20–26.

Kinder, L. S., Carnethon, M. R., Palaniappan, L. P., King, A. C., & Fortmann, S. P. (2004). Depression and the metabolic syndrome in young adults: Findings from the third national health and nutrition examination survey. *Psychosomatic Medicine, 66,* 316–322.

King, A. C., Ahn, D. F., Atienza, A. A., & Kraemer, H. C. (2008). Exploring refinements in targeted behavioral medicine intervention to advance public health. *Annals of Behavioral Medicine, 35,* 251–260.

King, A. C., Friedman, R., Marcus, B., Castro, C., Napolitano, M., Ahn, D., et al. (2007). Ongoing physical activity advice by humans versus computers: The community health advice by telephone (CHAT) trial. *Health Psychology, 26,* 718–727.

King, L. A., & Miner, K. N. (2000). Writing about the perceived benefits of traumatic events: Implications for physical health. *Personality and Social Psychology Bulletin, 26,* 220–230.

Kirby, E. D., Williams, V. P., Hocking, M. C., Lane, J. D., & Williams, R. B. (2006). Psychosocial benefits of three formats of a standardized behavioral stress management program. *Psychosomatic Medicine, 68,* 816–823.

Kirby, J. B. (2002). The influence of parental separation on smoking initiation in adolescents. *Journal of Health and Social Behavior, 43,* 56–71.

Kirby, J. B., & Kaneda, T. (2005). Neighborhood socioeconomic disadvantage and access to health care. *Journal of Health and Social Behavior, 46,* 15–31.

Kirkley, B. G., & Fisher, E. B., Jr. (1988). Relapse as a model of nonadherence to dietary treatment of diabetes. *Health Psychology, 7,* 221–230.

Kirkley, B. G., Schneider, J. A., Agras, W. J., & Bachman, J. A. (1985). Comparison of two group treatments for bulimia. *Journal of Consulting and Clinical Psychology, 53,* 43–48.

Kirmayer, L. J., & Young, A. (1998). Culture and somatization: Clinical, epidemiological, and ethnographic perspectives. *Psychosomatic Medicine, 60,* 420–430.

Kirschbaum, C., Klauer, T., Filipp, S., & Hellhammer, D. H. (1995). Sex-specific effects of social support on cortisol and subjective responses to acute psychological stress. *Psychosomatic Medicine, 57,* 23–31.

Kirscht, J. P. (1983). Preventive health behavior: A review of research and issues. *Health Psychology, 2,* 277–301.

Kitzmann, K. M., Dalton, W. T., Stanley, C. M., Beech, B. M., Reeves, T. P., Buscemi, J., et al. (2010). Lifestyle interventions for youth who are overweight: A meta-analytic review. *Health Psychology, 29,* 91–101.

Kivimäki, M., Head, J., Ferrie, J. E., Brunner, E., Marmot, M. G., Vahtera, J., et al. (2006). Why is evidence on job strain and coronary heart disease mixed? An illustration of measurement challenges in the Whitehall II study. *Psychosomatic Medicine, 68,* 398–401.

Kivimäki, M., Kinnunen, M., Pitkänen, T., Vahtera, J., Elovainio, M., & Pulkkinen, L. (2004). Contribution of early and adult factors to socioeconomic variation in blood pressure: Thirty-four-year follow-up study of school children. *Psychosomatic Medicine, 66,* 184–189.

Kivimäki, M., Vahtera, J., Elovainio, M., Lillrank, B., & Kevin, M. V. (2002). Death or illness of a family member, violence, interpersonal conflict, and financial difficulties as predictors of sickness absence: Longitudinal cohort study on psychological and behavioral links. *Psychosomatic Medicine, 64,* 817–825.

Kiviniemi, M. T., Voss-Humke, A. M., & Seifert, A. L. (2007). How do I feel about the behavior? The interplay of affective associations with behaviors and cognitive beliefs as influences on physical activity behavior. *Health Psychology, 26,* 152–158.

Kivlahan, D. R., Marlatt, G. A., Fromme, K., Coppel, D. B., & Williams, E. (1990). Secondary prevention with college drinkers: Evaluation of an alcohol skills training program. *Journal of Consulting and Clinical Psychology, 58,* 805–810.

Klebanov, P. K., & Jemmott, J. B., III. (1992). Effects of expectations and bodily sensations on self-reports of premenstrual symptoms. *Psychology of Women Quarterly, 16,* 289–310.

Klem, M., Wing, R R., McGuire, M. T., Seagle, H. M., & Hill, J. O. (1998). Psychological symptoms in individuals successful at long-term maintenance of weight loss. *Health Psychology, 17,* 336–345.

Klepp, K. I., Kelder, S. H., & Perry, C. L. (1995). Alcohol and marijuana use among adolescents: Long-term outcomes of the class of 1989 study. *Annals of Behavioral Medicine, 17,* 19–24.

Klesges, R. C., Eck, L. H., Hanson, C. L., Haddock, C. K., & Klesges, L. M. (1990). Effects of obesity, social interactions, and physical environment on physical activity in preschoolers. *Health Psychology, 9,* 435–449.

Klimas, N., Koneru, A. O., & Fletcher, M. A. (2008). Overview of HIV. *Psychosomatic Medicine, 70,* 523–530.

Klohn, L. S., & Rogers, R. W. (1991). Dimensions of the severity of a health threat: The persuasive effects of visibility, time of onset, and rate of onset on young women's intentions to prevent osteoporosis. *Health Psychology, 10,* 323–329.

Klonoff, E. A. (2009). Disparities in the provision of medical care: An outcome in search of an explanation. *Journal of Behavioral Medicine, 32,* 48–63.

Klonoff, E. A., & Landrine, H. (1992). Sex roles, occupational roles, and symptom-reporting: A test of competing hypotheses on sex differences. *Journal of Behavioral Medicine, 15,* 355–364.

Klonoff, E. A., & Landrine, H. (1999). Acculturation and cigarette smoking among African Americans: Replication and implications for prevention and cessation programs. *Journal of Behavioral Medicine, 22,* 195–204.

Klonoff, E. A., & Landrine, H. (2000). Is skin color a marker for racial discrimination? Explaining the skin color–hypertension relationship. *Journal of Behavioral Medicine, 23,* 329–338.

Klopfer, B. (1959). Psychological variables in human cancer. *Journal of Projective Techniques, 21,* 331–340.

Klumb, P., Hoppmann, C., & Staats, M. (2006). Work hours affect spouse's cortisol secretion—For better and for worse. *Psychosomatic Medicine, 68,* 742–746.

Klump, K. L., & Culbert, K. M. (2007). Molecular genetic studies of eating disorders. *Current Directions in Psychological Science, 16,* 37–41.

Köblitz, A. R., Magnan, R. E., McCaul, K. D., Dillard, A. J., O'Neill, H. K., & Crosby, R. (2009). Smoker's thoughts and worries: A study using ecological momentary assessment. *Health Psychology, 28,* 484–492.

Koenig, L. B., & Vaillant, G. E. (2009). A prospective study of church attendance and health over the lifespan. *Health Psychology, 28,* 117–124.

Koenig, L. J., Pals, S. L., Bush, T., Pratt-Palmore, M., Stratford, D., & Ellerbrock, T. V. (2008). Randomized controlled trial of an intervention to prevent adherence failure among HIV-infected patients initiating antiretroviral therapy. *Health Psychology, 27,* 159–169.

Kogon, M. M., Biswas, A., Pearl, D., Carlson, R. W., & Spiegel, D. (1997). Effect of medical and psychotherapeutic treatment on the survival of women with metastatic breast carcinoma. *Cancer, 80,* 225–230.

Kohler, C. L., Fish, L., & Greene, P. G. (2002). The relationship of perceived self-efficacy to quality of life in chronic obstructive pulmonary disease. *Health Psychology, 21,* 610–614.

Kojima, M., Wakai, K., Tokudome, S., Tamakoshi, K., Toyoshima, H., Watanabe, Y., et al. (2005). Perceived psychologic stress and colorectal cancer mortality: Findings from the Japan collaborative cohort study. *Psychosomatic Medicine, 67,* 72–77.

Koltun, A., & Stone, G. A. (1986). Past and current trends in patient noncompliance research: Focus on diseases, regimens-programs, and provider-disciplines. *Journal of Compliance in Health Care, 1,* 21–32.

Konopack, J. F., Marquez, D. X., Hu, L., Elavsky, S., McAuley, E., & Kramer, A. F. (2008). Correlates of functional fitness in older adults. *International Journal of Behavioral Medicine, 15,* 311–318.

Koo-Loeb, J. H., Costello, N., Light, K., & Girdler, S. S. (2000). Women with eating disorder tendencies display altered cardiovascular, neuroendocrine, and psychosocial profiles. *Psychosomatic Medicine, 62,* 539–548.

Kop, W. J., Appels, A. P. W. M., Mendes de Leon, C. F., de Swart, H. B., & Bar, F. W. (1994). Vital exhaustion predicts new cardiac events after successful coronary angioplasty. *Psychosomatic Medicine, 56,* 281–287.

Kop, W. J., Berman, D. S., Gransar, H., Wong, N. D., Miranda-Peats, R., White, M. D., et al. (2005). Social network and coronary artery calcification in asymptomatic individuals. *Psychosomatic Medicine, 67,* 343–352.

Kop, W. J., & Gottdiener, J. S. (2005). The role of immune system parameters in the relationship between depression and coronary artery disease. *Psychosomatic Medicine, 67,* S37–S41.

Kopelman, P. G. (2000). Obesity as a medical problem. *Nature, 404,* 635–643.

Koretz, G. (2003, November 10). Those heavy Americans. *Business Week,* p. 34.

Korobkin, R., & Rajkumar, R. (2008). The genetic information nondiscrimination act—A half-step toward risk sharing. *New England Journal of Medicine, 359,* 335–337.

Korstjens, E., May, A. M., van Weert, E., Mesters, I., Tan, F., Ros, W. J. G., et al. (2008). Quality of life after self-management cancer rehabilitation: A randomized controlled trial comparing physical and cognitive-behavioral training versus physical training. *Psychosomatic Medicine, 70,* 422–429.

Koton, S., Tanne, D., Bornstein, N. M., & Green, M. S. (2004). Triggering risk factors for ischemic stroke: A case-crossover study. *Neurology, 63,* 2006–2010.

Kouyanou, K., Pither, C., & Wessely, S. (1997). Iatrogenic factors and chronic pain. *Psychosomatic Medicine, 59,* 597–604.

Kowal, J., & Fortier, M. S. (2007). Physical activity behavior change in middle-aged and older women: The role of barriers and of environmental characteristics. *Journal of Behavioral Medicine, 30,* 232–242.

Kozak, B., Strelau, J., & Miles, J. N. V. (2005). Genetic determinants of individual differences in coping styles. *Anxiety, Stress and Coping: An International Journal, 18,* 1–15.

Krantz, D. S., & Deckel, A. W. (1983). Coping with coronary heart disease and stroke. In T. G. Burish & L. A. Bradley (Eds.), *Coping with chronic disease: Research and applications* (pp. 85–112). New York: Academic Press.

Krause, N., Ingersoll-Dayton, B., Liang, J., & Sugisawa, H. (1999). Religion, social support, and health among the Japanese elderly. *Journal of Health and Social Behavior, 40,* 405–421.

Krause, N., & Markides, K. S. (1985). Employment and psychological well-being in Mexican American women. *Journal of Health and Social Behavior, 26,* 15–26.

Kreicbergs, U., Valdimarsdóttir, U., Onelöv, E., Henter, J., & Steineck, G. (2004). Talking about death with children who have severe malignant disease. *The New England Journal of Medicine, 351,* 1175–1186.

Kreuter, M. W., Bull, F. C., Clark, E. M., & Oswald, D. L. (1999). Understanding how people process health information: A comparison of tailored and nontailored weight-loss materials. *Health Psychology, 18,* 487–494.

Kristal-Boneh, E., Melamed, S., Bernheim, J., Peled, I., & Green, M. S. (1995). Reduced ambulatory heart rate response to physical work and complaints of fatigue among hypertensive males treated with beta-blockers. *Journal of Behavioral Medicine, 18,* 113–126.

Kroeber, A. L. (1948). *Anthropology.* New York: Harcourt.

Kroenke, C. H., Kubzansky, L. D., Schernhammer, E. S., Holmes, M. D., & Kawachi, I. (2006). Social networks, social support, and survival after breast cancer diagnosis. *Journal of Clinical Oncology, 24,* 1105–1111.

Krohne, H. W., & Slangen, K. E. (2005). Influence of social support on adaptation to surgery. *Health Psychology, 24,* 101–105.

Kronish, I. M., Rieckmann, N., Schwartz, J. E., Schwartz, D. R., & Davidson, K. W. (2009). Is depression after an acute coronary syndrome simply a marker of known prognostic factors for mortality? *Psychosomatic Medicine, 71,* 697–703.

Kübler-Ross, E. (1969). *On death and dying.* New York: Macmillan.

Kübler-Ross, E. (1975). *Death: The final stage of growth.* Englewood Cliffs, NJ: Prentice-Hall.

Kubzansky, L. D., Berkman, L. F., Glass, T. A., & Seeman, T. E. (1998). Is educational attainment associated with shared determinants of health in the elderly? Findings from the MacArthur studies of successful aging. *Psychosomatic Medicine, 60,* 578–585.

Kubzansky, L. D., Davidson, K. W., & Rozanski, A. (2005). The clinical impact of negative psychological states: Expanding the spectrum of risk for coronary artery disease. *Psychosomatic Medicine, 67,* S10–S14.

Kubzansky, L. D., Koenen, K. C., Jones, C., & Eaton, W. W. (2009). A prospective study of posttraumatic stress disorder symptoms and coronary heart disease in women. *Health Psychology, 28,* 125–130.

Kubzansky, L. D., Martin, L. T., & Buka, S. L. (2009). Early manifestations of personality and adult health: A life course perspective. *Health Psychology, 28,* 364–372.

Kubzansky, L. D., Sparrow, D., Vokonas, P., & Kawachi, I. (2001). Is the glass half empty or half full? A prospective study of optimism and coronary heart disease in the normative aging study. *Psychosomatic Medicine, 63,* 910–916.

Kubzansky, L. D., & Thurston, R. C. (2007). Emotional vitality and incident coronary heart disease. *Archives of General Psychiatry, 64,* 1393–1401.

Kubzansky, L. D., Wright, R. J., Cohen, S., Weiss, S., Rosner, B., & Sparrow, D. (2002). Breathing easy: A prospective study of optimism and pulmonary function in the normative aging study. *Annals of Behavioral Medicine, 24,* 345–353.

Kugler, J., Dimsdale, J. E., Hartley, L. H., & Sherwood, J. (1990). Hospital supervised versus home exercise in cardiac rehabilitation: Effects on aerobic fitness, anxiety, and depression. *Archives of Physical Medicine and Rehabilitation, 71,* 322–325.

Kulik, J. A., & Carlino, P. (1987). The effect of verbal communication and treatment choice on medication compliance in a pediatric setting. *Journal of Behavioral Medicine, 10,* 367–376.

Kulik, J. A., & Mahler, H. I. M. (1987). Effects of preoperative roommate assignment on preoperative anxiety and recovery from coronary-bypass surgery. *Health Psychology, 6,* 525–543.

Kulik, J. A., & Mahler, H. I. M. (1989). Social support and recovery from surgery. *Health Psychology, 8,* 221–238.

Kulik, J. A., & Mahler, H. I. M. (1993). Emotional support as a moderator of adjustment and compliance after coronary artery bypass surgery: A longitudinal study. *Journal of Behavioral Medicine, 16,* 45–64.

Kulik, J. A., Moore, P. J., & Mahler, H. I. M. (1993). Stress and affiliation: Hospital roommate effects on preoperative anxiety and social interaction. *Health Psychology, 12,* 118–124.

Kullowatz, A., Rosenfield, D., Dahme, B., Magnussen, H., Kanniess, F., & Ritz, T. (2008). Stress effects on lung function in asthma are mediated by changes in airway inflammation. *Psychosomatic Medicine, 70,* 468–475.

Kumanyika, S. K., Van Horn, L., Bowen, D., Perri, M. G., Rolls, B. J., Czajkowski, S. M., et al. (2000). Maintenance of dietary behavior change. *Health Psychology, 19,* 42–56.

Kumari, M., Badrick, E., Chandola, T., Adler, N., Epel, E., Seeman, T., et al. (2010). Measures of social position and cortisol secretion in an aging population: Findings from the Whitehall II study. *Psychosomatic Medicine, 72,* 27–34.

Kundermann, B., Spernal, J., Huber, M. T., Krieg, J. C., & Lautenbacher, S. (2004). Sleep deprivation affects thermal pain thresholds but not somatosensory thresholds in healthy volunteers. *Psychosomatic Medicine, 66,* 932–937.

Kupper, N., Gidron, Y., Winter, J., & Denollet, J. (2009). Association between type D personality, depression, and oxidative stress in patients with chronic heart failure. *Psychosomatic Medicine, 71,* 973–980.

Kutner, N. G. (1987). Issues in the application of high cost medical technology: The case of organ transplantation. *Journal of Health and Social Behavior, 28,* 23–36.

Lacey, H. P., Fagerlin, A., Loewenstein, G., Smith, D. M., Riis, J., & Ubel, P. A. (2008). Are they really that happy? Exploring scale recalibration in estimates of well-being. *Health Psychology, 27,* 669–675.

Lacroix, J. M., Martin, B., Avendano, M., & Goldstein, R. (1991). Symptom schemata in chronic respiratory patients. *Health Psychology, 10,* 268–273.

Lai, H., Lai, S., Krongrad, A., Trapido, E., Page, J. B., & McCoy, C. B. (1999). The effect of marital status on survival in late-stage cancer patients: An analysis based on surveillance, epidemiology, and end results (SEER) data, in the United States. *International Journal of Behavioral Medicine, 6,* 150–176.

Lallukka, T., Martikainen, P., Reunanen, A., Roos, E., Sarlo-Lahteenkorva, S., & Lahelma, E. (2006). Associations between working conditions and angina pectoris symptoms among employed women. *Psychosomatic Medicine, 68,* 348–354.

Lam, T. H., Stewart, M., & Ho, L. M. (2001). Smoking and high-risk sexual behavior among young adults in Hong Kong. *Journal of Behavioral Medicine, 24,* 503–518.

Lamb, R., & Joshi, M. S. (1996). The stage model and processes of change in dietary fat reduction. *Journal of Human Nutrition and Dietetics, 9,* 43–53.

Lamprecht, F., & Sack, M. (2002). Posttraumatic stress disorder revisited. *Psychosomatic Medicine, 64,* 222–237.

Landsbergis, P. A., Schnall, P. L., Deitz, D., Friedman, R., & Pickering, T. (1992). The patterning of psychological attributes and distress by "job strain" and social support in a sample of working men. *Journal of Behavioral Medicine, 15,* 379–414.

Lane, R. D., Laukes, C., Marcus, F. I., Chesney, M. A., Sechrest, L., Gear, K., et al. (2006). Psychological stress preceding idiopathic ventricular fibrillation. *Psychosomatic Medicine, 67,* 359–365.

Lane, R. D., Waldstein, S. R., Chesney, M. A., Jennings, J. R., Lovallo, W. R., Kozel, P. J., et al. (2009a). The rebirth of neuroscience in psychosomatic medicine, part I: Historical context, methods, and relevant basic science. *Psychosomatic Medicine, 71,* 117–134.

Lane, R. D., Waldstein, S. R., Critchley, H. D., Derbyshire, S. W., Drossman, D. A., Wager, T. D., et al. (2009b). The rebirth of neuroscience in psychosomatic medicine, part II: Clinical applications and implications for research. *Psychosomatic Medicine, 71,* 135–151.

Lang, A. R., & Marlatt, G. A. (1982). Problem drinking: A social learning perspective. In R. J. Gatchel, A. Baum, & J. E. Singer (Eds.), *Handbook of psychology and health: Vol. 1. Clinical psychology and behavioral medicine: Overlapping disciplines* (pp. 121–169). Hillsdale, NJ: Erlbaum.

Lange, L. J., & Piette, J. D. (2006). Personal models for diabetes in context and patients' health status. *Journal of Behavioral Medicine, 29,* 239–253.

Langelaan, S., Bakker, A. B., Schaufeli, W. B., van Rhenen, W., & van Doornen, J. P. (2007). Is burnout related to allostatic load? *International Journal of Behavioral Medicine, 14,* 213–221.

Langens, T. A., & Schüler, J. (2007). Effects of written emotional expression: The role of positive expectancies. *Health Psychology, 26,* 174–182.

Langston, C. A. (1994). Capitalizing on and coping with daily-life events: Expressive responses to positive events. *Journal of Personality and Social Psychology, 67,* 1112–1125.

Lankford, T. R. (1979). *Integrated science for health students* (2nd ed.). Reston, VA: Reston.

Lantz, P. M., House, J. S., Mero, R. P., & Williams, D. R. (2005). Stress, life events, and socioeconomic disparities in health: Results from the Americans' changing lives study. *Journal of Health and Social Behavior, 46,* 274–288.

Lantz, P. M., Weigers, M. E., & House, J. S. (1997). Education and income differentials in breast and cervical cancer screening: Policy implications for rural women. *Medical Care, 35,* 219–236.

Larimer, M. E., Palmer, R. S., & Marlatt, G. A. (1999). Relapse prevention: An overview of Marlatt's cognitive-behavioral model. *Alcohol Research and Health, 23,* 151–160.

Larkin, K. T., & Zayfert, C. (1996). Anger management training with mild essential hypertensive patients. *Journal of Behavioral Medicine, 19,* 415–434.

Larsen, D. (1990, March 18). Future of fear. *Los Angeles Times,* pp. E1, E8.

Latimer, A. E., Williams-Piehota, P., Katulak, N. A., Cox, A., Mowad, L., Higgins, E. T., et al. (2008). Promoting fruit and vegetable intake through messages tailored to individual differences in regulatory focus. *Annals of Behavioral Medicine, 35,* 363–369.

Latkin, C. A., Williams, C. T., Wang, J., & Curry, A. D. (2005). Neighborhood social disorder as a determinant of drug injection behaviors: A structural equation modeling approach. *Health Psychology, 24,* 96–100.

Lau, R. R., Kane, R., Berry, S., Ware, J. E., Jr., & Roy, D. (1980). Channeling health: A review of televised health campaigns. *Health Education Quarterly, 7,* 56–89.

Laubmeier, K. K., Zakowski, S. G., & Blair, J. P. (2004). The role of spirituality in the psychological adjustment to cancer: A test of the transactional model of stress and coping. *International Journal of Behavioral Medicine, 11,* 48–55.

Lauver, D. R., Henriques, J. B., Settersten, L., & Bumann, M. C. (2003). Psychosocial variables, external barriers, and stage of mammography adoption. *Health Psychology, 22,* 649–653.

Laveist, T. A., & Nuru-Jeter, A. (2002). Is doctor-patient race concordance associated with greater satisfaction with care? *Journal of Health and Social Behavior, 43,* 296–306.

Lavoie, K. L., Bouchard, A., Joseph, M., Campbell, T. S., Favereau, H., & Bacon, S. L. (2008). Association of asthma self-efficacy to asthma control and quality of life. *Annals of Behavioral Medicine, 36,* 100–106.

Lawhon, D., Humfleet, G. L., Hall, S. M., Reus, V. I., & Muñoz, R. F. (2009). Longitudinal analysis of abstinence-specific social support and smoking cessation. *Health Psychology, 28,* 465–472.

Lawler, K. A., Younger, J. W., Piferi, R. L., Jobe, R. L., Edmondson, K. A., & Jones, W. H. (2005). The unique effects of forgiveness on health: An exploration of pathways. *Journal of Behavioral Medicine, 28,* 157–167.

Lawler, S. P., Winkler, E., Reeves, M. M., Owen, N., Graves, N., & Eakin, E. G. (2010). Multiple health behavior changes and co-variation in a telephone counseling trial. *Annals of Behavioral Medicine, 39,* 250–257.

Lawlor, D. A., O'Callaghan, M. J., Mamun, A. A., Williams, G. M., Bor, W., & Najman, J. M. (2005). Socioeconomic position, cognitive function, and clustering of cardiovascular risk factors in adolescence: Findings from the Mater University study of pregnancy and its outcomes. *Psychosomatic Medicine, 67,* 862–868.

Lawton, R., Conner, M., & McEachan, R. (2009). Desire or reason: Predicting health behaviors from affective and cognitive attitudes. *Health Psychology, 28,* 56–65.

Lawton, R., Conner, M., & Parker, D. (2007). Beyond cognition: Predicting health risk behaviors from instrumental and affective beliefs. *Health Psychology, 26,* 259–267.

Lazarus, R. S. (1983). The costs and benefits of denial. In S. Bresnitz (Ed.), *Denial of stress* (pp. 1–30). New York: International Universities Press.

Lazarus, R. S., & Folkman, S. (1984a). Coping and adaptation. In W. D. Gentry (Ed.), *The handbook of behavioral medicine* (pp. 282–325). New York: Guilford Press.

Lazarus, R. S., & Folkman, S. (1984b). *Stress, appraisal, and coping.* New York: Springer.

Lazarus, R. S., & Launier, R. (1978). Stress-related transactions between person and environment. In L. A. Pervin & M. Lewis (Eds.), *Internal and external determinants of behavior* (pp. 287–327). New York: Plenum.

Lecci, L., & Cohen, D. J. (2002). Perceptual consequences of an illness-concern induction and its relation to hypochondriacal tendencies. *Health Psychology, 21,* 147–156.

Leclere, F. B., Rogers, R. G., & Peters, K. (1998). Neighborhood social context and racial differences in women's heart disease mortality. *Journal of Health and Social Behavior, 39,* 91–107.

Lee, J. (2000, November). Easing the pain. *Money,* pp. 179–180.

Lee, M. B., Wu, Z., Rotheram-Borus, M., Detels, R., Guan, J., & Li, L. (2004). HIV-related stigma among market workers in China. *Health Psychology, 24,* 435–438.

Lee, S. S., & Ruvkun, G. (2002). Don't hold your breath. *Nature, 418,* 287–288.

Leffall, L. D., Jr., White, J. E., & Ewing, J. (1963). Cancer of the breast in Negroes. *Surgery, Gynecology, Obstetrics, 117,* 97–104.

Leger, D., Scheuermaier, K., Phillip, P., Paillard, M., & Guilleminault, C. (2001). SF–36: Evaluation of quality of life in severe and mild insomniacs compared with good sleepers. *Psychosomatic Medicine, 63,* 49–55.

Lehman, B. J., Taylor, S. E., Kiefe, C. I., & Seeman, T. E. (2005). Relation of childhood socioeconomic status and family environment to adult metabolic functioning in the CARDIA study. *Psychosomatic Medicine, 67,* 846–854.

Lehman, C. D., Rodin, J., McEwen, B., & Brinton, R. (1991). Impact of environmental stress on the expression of insulin-dependent diabetes mellitus. *Behavioral Neuroscience, 105,* 241–245.

Lehrer, P., Feldman, J., Giardino, N., Song, H. S., & Schmaling, K. (2002). Psychological aspects of asthma. *Journal of Consulting and Clinical Psychology, 70,* 691–711.

Leigh, H., & Reiser, M. F. (1986). Comparison of theoretically oriented and patient-oriented behavioral science courses. *Journal of Medical Education, 61,* 169–174.

Lekander, M., Elofsson, S., Neve, I., Hansson, L., & Undén, A. (2004). Self-rated health is related to levels of circulating cytokines. *Psychosomatic Medicine, 66,* 559–593.

Lemoine, J., & Mougne, C. (1983). Why has death stalked the refugees? *Natural History, 92,* 6–19.

Lemonick, M. D. (2004). The other lung disease. *Time.*

Lenert, L., & Skoczen, S. (2002). The Internet as a research tool: Worth the price of admission? *Annals of Behavioral Medicine, 24,* 251–256.

Lennon, M. C., & Rosenfield, S. (1992). Women and mental health: The interaction of job and family conditions. *Journal of Health and Social Behavior, 33,* 316–327.

Lepore, S. J., Helgeson, V. S., Eton, D. T., & Schulz, R. (2003). Improving quality of life in men with prostate cancer: A randomized controlled trial of group education interventions. *Health Psychology, 22,* 443–452.

Lepore, S. J., Ragan, J. D., & Jones, S. (2000). Talking facilitates cognitive-emotional processes of adaptation to an acute stressor. *Journal of Personality and Social Psychology, 78,* 499–508.

Lepore, S. J., & Smyth, J. (Eds.). (2002). *The writing cure: How expressive writing influences health and well-being.* Washington, DC: American Psychological Association.

Lerman, C., Caporaso, N. E., Audrain, J., Main, D., Bowman, E. D., Lockshin, B., et al. (1999). Evidence suggesting the role of specific genetic factors in cigarette smoking. *Health Psychology, 18,* 14–20.

Lerman, C., Gold, K., Audrain, J., Lin, T. H., Boyd, N. R., Orleans, C. T., et al. (1997). Incorporating biomarkers of exposure and genetic susceptibility into smoking cessation treatment: Effects on smoking-related cognitions, emotions, and behavior change. *Health Psychology, 16,* 87–99.

Lerman, C., Shields, P. G., Wileyto, E. P., Audrain, J., Hawk, L. H., Jr., Pinto, A., et al. (2003). Effects of dopamine transporter and receptor polymorphisms of smoking cessation in a bupropion clinical trial. *Health Psychology, 22,* 541–548.

Leserman, J. (2008). Role of depression, stress, and trauma in HIV disease progression. *Psychosomatic Medicine, 70,* 539–545.

Lett, H. S., Blumenthal, J. A., Babyak, M. A., Catellier, D. J., Carney, R. M., Berkman, L. F., et al. (2007). Social support and prognosis in patients at increased psychosocial risk recovering from myocardial infarction. *Health Psychology, 26,* 418–427.

Lett, H. S., Davidson, J., & Blumenthal, J. A. (2005). Nonpharmacologic treatments for depression in patients with coronary heart disease. *Psychosomatic Medicine, 67,* S58–S62.

Leung, Y. W., Ceccato, N., Stewart, D. E., & Grace, S. L. (2007). A prospective examination of patterns and correlates of exercise maintenance in coronary artery disease patients. *Journal of Behavioral Medicine, 30,* 411–421.

Leveille, S. G., Wagner, E. H., Davis, C., Grothaus, L., Wallace, J., LoGerfo, M., et al. (1998). Preventing disability and managing chronic illness in frail older adults: A randomized trial of community-based partnership with primary care. *Journal of the American Geriatrics Society, 46,* 191–198.

Levenkron, J. C., Greenland, P., & Bowlby, N. (1987). Using patient instructors to teach behavioral counseling skills. *Journal of Medical Education, 62,* 665–672.

Levenson, J. L., McClish, D. K., Dahman, B. A., Bovbjerg, V. E., Citero, V. D. A., Penberthy, L. T., et al. (2008). Depression and anxiety in adults with sickle cell disease: The PiSCES project. *Psychosomatic Medicine, 70,* 192–196.

Leventhal, E. A., Easterling, D., Leventhal, H., & Cameron, L. (1995). Conservation of energy, uncertainty reduction, and swift utilization of medical care among the elderly: Study II. *Medical Care, 33,* 988–1000.

Leventhal, E. A., Hansell, S., Diefenbach, M., Leventhal, H., & Glass, D. C. (1996). Negative affect and self-report of physical symptoms: Two longitudinal studies of older adults. *Health Psychology, 15,* 193–199.

Leventhal, E. A., Leventhal, H., Schacham, S., & Easterling, D. V. (1989). Active coping reduces reports of pain from childbirth. *Journal of Consulting and Clinical Psychology, 57,* 365–371.

Leventhal, H. (1970). Findings and theory in the study of fear communications. In L. Berkowitz (Ed.), *Advances in experimental social psychology* (Vol. 5, pp. 120–186). New York: Academic Press.

Leventhal, H., Diefenbach, M., & Leventhal, E. A. (1992). Illness cognition: Using common sense to understand treatment adherence and affect cognition interactions. *Cognitive Therapy and Research, 16,* 143–163.

Leventhal, H., Meyer, D., & Nerenz, D. (1980). The common sense representation of illness danger. In S. Rachman (Ed.), *Contributions to medical psychology* (Vol. II, pp. 7–30). New York: Pergamon Press.

Leventhal, H., & Nerenz, D. R. (1982). A model for stress research and some implications for the control of stress disorders. In D. Meichenbaum & M. Jaremko (Eds.), *Stress prevention and management: A cognitive behavioral approach.* New York: Plenum.

Leventhal, H., Nerenz, D., & Strauss, A. (1982). Self-regulation and the mechanisms for symptom appraisal. In D. Mechanic (Ed.), *Monograph series in psychosocial epidemiology, 3: Symptoms, illness behavior, and help-seeking* (pp. 55–86). New York: Neale Watson.

Leventhal, H., Prochaska, T. R., & Hirschman, R. S. (1985). Preventive health behavior across the life span. In J. C. Rosen & L. J. Solomon (Eds.), *Prevention in health psychology* (Vol. 8, pp. 190–235). Hanover, NH: University Press of New England.

Leventhal, H., Weinman, J., Leventhal, E. A., & Phillips, L. A. (2008). Health psychology: The search for pathways between behavior and health. *Annual Review of Psychology, 59,* 477–505.

Levine, J. A., Lanningham-Foster, L. M., McCrady, S. K., Krizan, A. C., Olson, L. R., Kane, P. H., et al. (2005). Interindividual variation in posture allocation: Possible role in human obesity. *Science, 30,* 584–586.

Levine, J. D., Gordon, N. C., & Fields, H. L. (1978). The mechanism of placebo analgesia. *Lancet, 2,* 654–657.

Levine, M. N., Guyatt, G. H., Gent, M., De Pauw, S., Goodyear, M. D., Hryniuk, W. M., et al. (1988). Quality of life in stage II breast cancer: An instrument for clinical trials. *Journal of Clinical Oncology, 6,* 1798–1810.

Levinson, R. M., McCollum, K. T., & Kutner, N. G. (1984). Gender homophily in preferences for physicians. *Sex Roles, 10,* 315–325.

Levitsky, L. L. (2004). Childhood immunizations and chronic illness. *The New England Journal of Medicine, 350,* 1380–1382.

Levy, B. R., Slade, M. D., Kunkel, S. R., & Kasl, S. V. (2002). Longevity increased by positive self-perceptions of aging. *Journal of Personality and Social Psychology, 83,* 261–270.

Levy, S. M., Fernstrom, J., Herberman, R. B., Whiteside, T., Lee, J., Ward, M., et al. (1991). Persistently low natural killer cell activity and circulating levels of plasma beta endorphin: Risk factors for infectious disease. *Life Sciences, 48,* 107–116.

Levy, S. M., Herberman, R. B., Lee, J. K., Lippman, M. E., & d'Angelo, T. (1989). Breast conservation versus mastectomy: Distress sequelae as a function of choice. *Journal of Clinical Oncology, 7,* 367–375.

Levy, S. M., Herberman, R. B., Lippman, M., D'Angelo, T., & Lee, J. (1991). Immunological and psychosocial predictors of disease recurrence in patients with early-stage breast cancer. *Behavioral Medicine, 17,* 67–75.

Levy, S. M., Herberman, R. B., Whiteside, T., Sanzo, K., Lee, J., & Kirkwood, J. (1990). Perceived social support and tumor estrogen/progesterone receptor status as predictors of natural killer cell activity in breast cancer patients. *Psychosomatic Medicine, 52,* 73–85.

Levy, S. M., Lee, J. K., Bagley, C., & Lippman, M. (1988). Survival hazards analysis in first recurrent breast cancer patients: Seven-year follow-up. *Psychosomatic Medicine, 50,* 520–528.

Lewin, K. (1946). Action research and minority problems. *Journal of Social Issues, 2,* 34–36.

Lewis, E., Mayer, J. A., Slymen, D., Belch, G., Engelberg, M., Walker, K., et al. (2005). Disseminating a sun safety program to zoological parks: The effects of tailoring. *Health Psychology, 24,* 456–462.

Lewis, J. A., Manne, S. L., DuHamel, K. N., Vickburgh, S. M. J., Bovbjerg, D. H., Currie, V., et al. (2001). Social support, intrusive thoughts, and quality of life in breast cancer survivors. *Journal of Behavioral Medicine, 24,* 231–245.

Lewis, J. W., Terman, S. W., Shavit, Y., Nelson, L. R., & Liebeskind, J. C. (1984). Neural, neurochemical, and hormonal bases of stress-induced analgesia. In L. Kruger & J. C. Liebeskind (Eds.), *Advances in pain research and therapy* (Vol. 6, pp. 277–288). New York: Raven Press.

Lewis, M. A., & Rook, K. S. (1999). Social control in personal relationships: Impact on health behaviors and psychological distress. *Health Psychology, 18,* 63–71.

Lewis, T. T., Everson-Rose, S. A., Karavolos, K., Janssen, I., Wesley, D., & Powell, L. H. (2009). Hostility is associated with visceral, but not with subcutaneous, fat in middle-aged African Amercian and White women. *Psychosomatic Medicine, 71,* 733–740.

Lewis, T. T., Everson-Rose, S. A., Powell, L. H., Matthews, K. A., Brown, C., Karavolos, K., et al. (2006). Chronic exposure to everyday discrimination and coronary artery calcification in African-American women: The SWAN heart study. *Psychosomatic Medicine, 68,* 362–368.

Li, J., Cowden, L. G., King, J. D., Briles, D. A., Schroeder, H. W., Stevens, A. B., et al. (2007). Effects of chronic stress and interleukin-10 gene polymorphism on antibody response to tetanus vaccine in family caregivers of patients with Alzheimer's disease. *Psychosomatic Medicine, 69,* 551–559.

Li, J., Laursen, T. M., Precht, D. H., Olsen, J., & Mortensen, P. B. (2005). Hospitalization for mental illness among parents after the death of a child. *The New England Journal of Medicine, 352,* 1190–1196.

Li, J., Vestergaard, M., Obel, C., Precht, D. H., Christensen, J., Lu, M., et al. (2009). Prenatal stress and cerebral palsy: A nationwide cohort study in Denmark. *Psychosomatic Medicine, 71,* 615–618.

Li, Y., & Ferraro, K. F. (2005). Volunteering and depression in later life: Social benefit or selection processes? *Journal of Health and Social Behavior, 46,* 68–84.

Liberman, A., & Chaiken, S. (1992). Defensive processing of personally relevant health messages. *Personality and Social Psychology Bulletin, 18,* 669–679.

Liberman, R. (1962). An analysis of the placebo phenomenon. *Journal of Chronic Diseases, 15,* 761–783.

Libow, L. S. (2005). Geriatrics in the United States—baby boomers' boon? *The New England Journal of Medicine, 352,* 750–752.

Lichtenstein, E., & Cohen, S. (1990). Prospective analysis of two modes of unaided smoking cessation. *Health Education Research, 5,* 63–72.

Lichtenstein, E., Glasgow, R. E., Lando, H. A., Ossip-Klein, D. J., & Boles, S. M. (1996). Telephone counseling for smoking cessation: Rationales and meta-analytic review of evidence. *Health Education Research: Theory and Practice, 11,* 243–257.

Lichtenstein, E., Zhu, S. H., & Tedeschi, G. J. (2010). Smoking cessation quitlines: An underrecognized intervention success story. *American Psychologist, 65,* 252–261.

Lichtenstein, P., Holm, N. V., Verkasalo, P. K., Iliadou, A., Kaprio, J., Koskenvuo, M., et al. (2000). Environmental and heritable factors in the causation of cancer: Analyses of cohorts of twins from Sweden, Denmark, and Finland. *The New England Journal of Medicine, 343,* 78–85.

Lichtman, R. R., Taylor, S. E., Wood, J. V., Bluming, A. Z., Dosik, G. M., & Leibowitz, R. L. (1984). Relations with children after breast cancer: The mother-daughter relationship at risk. *Journal of Psychosocial Oncology, 2,* 1–19.

Lieberman, M. D., Jarcho, J. M., Berman, S., Naliboff, B. D., Suyenobu, B. Y., Mandelkern, M., et al. (2004). The neural correlates of placebo effects: A disruption account. *NeuroImage, 22,* 447–455.

Lifton, R. J. (1977). The sense of immortality: On death and the continuity of life. In H. Feifel (Ed.), *New meanings of death.* New York: McGraw-Hill.

Lillis, J., Hayes, S. C., Bunting, K., & Masuda, A. (2009). Teaching acceptance and mindfulness to improve the lives of the obese: A preliminary test of a theoretical model. *Annals of Behavioral Medicine, 37,* 58–69.

Lin, T. K., Weng, C. Y., Wang, W. C., Chen, C. C., Lin, I. M., & Lin, C. L. (2008). Hostility trait and vascular dilatory functions in healthy Taiwanese. *Journal of Behavioral Medicine, 31,* 517–524.

Lindauer, R. T. L., van Meijel, E. P. M., Jalink, M., Olff, M., Carlier, I. V. E., & Gersons, B. P. R. (2006). Heart rate responsivity to script-driven imagery in posttraumatic stress disorder: Specificity of response and effects of psychotherapy. *Psychosomatic Medicine, 68,* 33–40.

Linden, W., & Chambers, L. (1994). Clinical effectiveness of non-drug treatment for hypertension: A meta-analysis. *Annals of Behavioral Medicine, 16,* 35–45.

Linden, W., Klassen, K., & Phillips, M. (2008). Can psychological factors account for a lack of nocturnal blood pressure dipping? *Annals of Behavioral Medicine, 36,* 253–258.

Lindsay, M., & McCarthy, D. (1974). Caring for the brothers and sisters of a dying child. In T. Burton (Ed.), *Care of the child facing death* (pp. 189–206). Boston: Routledge & Kegan Paul.

Lingsweiler, V. M., Crowther, J. H., & Stephens, M. A. P. (1987). Emotional reactivity and eating in binge eating and obesity. *Journal of Behavioral Medicine, 10,* 287–300.

Link, B. G., Phelan, J. C., Miech, R., & Westin, E. L. (2008). The resources that matter: Fundamental social causes of health disparities and the challenge of intelligence. *Journal of Health and Social Behavior, 49,* 72–91.

Linke, S., Murray, E., Butler, C., & Wallace, P. (2007). Internet-based interactive health intervention for the promotion of sensible drinking: Patterns of use and potential impact on members of the genereal public. *Journal of Medical Internet Research, 9,* e10.

Linkins, R. W., & Comstock, G. W. (1990). Depressed mood and development of cancer. *American Journal of Epidemiology, 134,* 962–972.

Linnan, L., Bowling, M., Childress, J., Lindsay, G., Blakey, C., Pronk, S., et al. (2008). Results of the 2004 national worksite health promotion survey. *American Journal of Public Health, 98,* 1503–1509.

Linnan, L. A., Emmons, K. M., Klar, N., Fava, J. L., LaForge, R. G., & Abrams, D. B. (2002). Challenges to improving the impact of worksite cancer prevention programs: Comparing reach, enrollment, and attrition using active versus passive recruitment strategies. *Annals of Behavioral Medicine, 24,* 157–166.

Linton, S. J., & Buer, N. (1995). Working despite pain: Factors associated with work attendance versus dysfunction. *International Journal of Behavioral Medicine, 2,* 252–262.

Liossi, C., White, P., & Hatira, P. (2006). Randomized clinical trial of local anesthetic versus a combination of local anesthetic with self-hypnosis in the management of pediatric procedure-related pain. *Health Psychology, 25,* 307–315.

Lipkus, I. M., Barefoot, J. C., Williams, R. B., & Siegler, I. C. (1994). Personality measures as predictors of smoking initiation and cessation in the UNC Alumni Heart Study. *Health Psychology, 13,* 149–155.

Lipkus, I. M., McBride, C. M., Pollak, K. I., Schwartz-Bloom, R. D., Tilson, E., & Bloom, P. N. (2004). A randomized trial comparing the effects of self-help materials and proactive telephone counseling on teen smoking cessation. *Health Psychology, 23,* 397–406.

Lippke, S., Ziegelmann, J. P., Schwarzer, R., & Velicer, W. F. (2009). Validity of stage assessment in the adoption and maintenance of physical activity and fruit and vegetable consumption. *Health Psychology, 28,* 183–193.

Lipsitt, L. P. (2003). Crib death: A biobehavioral phenomenon? *Current Directions in Psychological Science, 12,* 164–170.

Liss-Levinson, W. S. (1982). Reality perspectives for psychological services in a hospice program. *American Psychologist, 37,* 1266–1270.

Lisspers, J., Sundin, Ö., Öhman, A., Hofman-Bang, C., Rydén, L., & Nygren, Å. (2005). Long-term effects of lifestyle behavior change in coronary artery disease: Effects on recurrent coronary events after percutaneous coronary intervention. *Health Psychology, 24,* 41–48.

Litt, M. D., Kloppinger, A., & Judge, J. O. (2002). Initiation and maintenance of exercise behavior in older women: Predictors from the social learning model. *Journal of Behavioral Medicine, 25,* 83–97.

Little, S. J., Holte, S., Routy, J., Daar, E. S., Markowitz, M., Collier, A. C., et al. (2002). Antiretroviral drug resistance among patients recently infected with HIV. *The New England Journal of Medicine, 347,* 385–394.

Littlebrant, C. K. (1976, January 12). Death is a personal matter. *Newsweek.* Originally published under the name of Carol K. Gross.

Littlefield, C. H., Rodin, G. M., Murray, M. A., & Craven, J. L. (1990). Influence of functional impairment and social support on depressive symptoms in persons with diabetes. *Health Psychology, 9,* 737–749.

Littlewood, R. A., Vanable, P. A., Carey, M. P., & Blair, D. C. (2008). The association of benefit finding to psychosocial and health behavior adaptation among HIV+ men and women. *Journal of Behavioral Medicine, 31,* 145–155.

Liu, H., & Umberson, D. J. (2008). The times they are a changin': Marital status and health differentials from 1972 to 2003. *Journal of Health and Social Behavior, 49,* 239–253.

Lobel, M., Cannella, D. L., Graham, J. E., DeVincent, C., Schneider, J., & Meyer, B. A. (2008). Pregnancy-specific stress, prenatal health behaviors, and birth outcomes. *Health Psychology, 27,* 604–615.

Locke, R. G. (2010). *The prevalence and impact of gastroesophageal reflux disease.* Retrieved June 17, 2010, from http://www.aboutgerd.org/site/about-gerd/characteristics/prevalence

Locke, S. E., Kraus, L., & Leserman, J. (1984). Life change, stress, psychiatric symptoms, and natural killer cell activity. *Psychosomatic Medicine, 46,* 441–453.

Locke, T. F., & Newcomb, M. D. (2008). Correlates and predictors of HIV risk among inner-city African American female teenagers. *Health Psychology, 27,* 337–348.

Logsdon, R. G., Gibbons, L. E., McCurry, S. M., & Teri, L. (2002). Assessing quality of life in older adults with cognitive impairment. *Psychosomatic Medicine, 64,* 510–519.

Lombardi, V. C., Ruscetti, F. W., Das Gupta, J., Pfost, M. A., Hagen, K. S., Peterson, D. L., et al. (2009). Detection of an infectious retrovirus, XMRV, in blood cells of patients with chronic fatigue syndrome. *Science, 326,* 585–589.

Lombardo, T., & Carreno, L. (1987). Relationship of Type A behavior pattern in smokers to carbon monoxide exposure and smoking topography. *Health Psychology, 6,* 445–452.

Lopez, E. N., Drobes, D. J., Thompson, J. K., & Brandon, T. H. (2008). Effects of a body image challenge on smoking motivation among college females. *Health Psychology, 27,* S243–S251.

Lorig, K., Chastain, R. L., Ung, E., Shoor, S., & Holman, H. (1989). Development and evaluation of a scale to measure perceived self-efficacy in people with arthritis. *Arthritis and Rheumatism, 32,* 37–44.

Los Angeles Times. (1993, March 30). Three-hundred-sixty days in row not overwork.

Loscocco, K. A., & Spitze, G. (1990). Working conditions, social support, and the well-being of female and male factory workers. *Journal of Health and Social Behavior, 31,* 313–327.

Lovallo, W. R., Al'Absi, M., Pincomb, G. A., Passey, R. B., Sung, B., & Wilson, M. F. (2000). Caffeine, extended stress, and blood pressure in borderline hypertensive men. *International Journal of Behavioral Medicine, 7,* 183–188.

Lovallo, W. R., & Gerin, W. (2003). Psychophysical reactivity: Mechanisms and pathways to cardiovascular disease. *Psychosomatic Medicine, 65,* 36–45.

Love, R. R., Leventhal, H., Easterling, D. V., & Nerenz, D. R. (1989). Side effects and emotional distress during cancer chemotherapy. *Cancer, 63,* 604–612.

Low, C. A., Bower, J. E., Kwan, L., & Seldon, J. (2008). Benefit finding in response to BRCA1/2 testing. *Annals of Behavioral Medicine, 35,* 61–69.

Low, C. A., Salomon, K., & Matthews, K. A. (2009). Chronic life stress, cardiovascular reactivity, and subclinical cardiovascular disease in adolescents. *Psychosomatic Medicine, 71,* 927–931.

Low, C. A., Stanton, A. L., & Danoff-Burg, S. (2006). Expressive disclosure and benefit finding among breast cancer patients: Mechanisms for positive health effects. *Health Psychology, 25,* 181–189.

Löwe, B., Grafe, K., Kroenke, K., Zipfel, S., Quentier, A., Wild, B., et al. (2003). Predictors of psychiatric comorbidity in medical outpatients. *Psychosomatic Medicine, 65,* 764–770.

Löwe, B., Willand, L., Eich, W., Zipfel, S., Ho, A. D., Herzog, W., et al. (2004). Psychiatric comorbidity and work disability in patients with inflammatory rheumatic diseases. *Psychosomatic Medicine, 66,* 395–402.

Lowry, R., Galuska, D. A., Fulton, J. E., Wechsler, H., & Kann, L. (2002). Weight management goals and practices among U.S. high school students: Associations with physical activity, diet, and smoking. *Journal of Adolescent Health, 31,* 133–144.

Lozito, M. (2004). Chronic pain: The new workers' comp. *The Case Manager, 15,* 61–63.

Lubitz, J., Cai, L., Kramarow, E., & Lentzner, H. (2003). Health, life expectancy, and health care spending among the elderly. *The New England Journal of Medicine, 349,* 1048–1055.

Lucas, T., Michalopoulou, G., Falzarano, P., Menon, S., & Cunningham, W. (2008). Healthcare provider cultural competency: Development and initial validation of a patient report measure. *Health Psychology, 27,* 185–193.

Luckow, A., Reifman, A., & McIntosh, D. N. (1998, August). *Gender differences in coping: A meta-analysis.* Poster session presented at the 106th annual convention of the American Psychological Association, San Francisco.

Ludescher, B., Leitlein, G., Schaefer, J. E., Vanhoeffen, S., Baar, S., Machann, J., et al. (2009). Changes of body composition in bulimia nervosa: Increased visceral fat and adrenal gland size. *Psychosomatic Medicine, 71,* 93–97.

Ludwick-Rosenthal, R., & Neufeld, R. W. J. (1988). Stress management during noxious medical procedures: An evaluative review of outcome studies. *Psychological Bulletin, 104,* 326–342.

Ludwig, D. S., Pereira, M. A., Kroenke, C. H., Hilner, J. E., Van Horn, L., Slattery, M., et al. (1999). Dietary fiber, weight gain, and cardiovascular disease risk factors in young adults. *Journal of the American Medical Association, 282,* 1539–1546.

Luecken, L. J., Rodriguez, A. P., & Appelhans, B. M. (2005). Cardiovascular stress responses in young adulthood associated with family-of-origin relationship experiences. *Psychosomatic Medicine, 67,* 514–521.

Luecken, L. J., Suarez, E., Kuhn, C., Barefoot, J., Blumenthal, J., Siegler, I., et al. (1997). Stress in employed women: Impact of marital status and children at home on neurohormone output and home strain. *Psychosomatic Medicine, 59,* 352–359.

Lumley, M. A., Abeles, L. A., Melamed, B. G., Pistone, L. M., & Johnson, J. H. (1990). Coping outcomes in children undergoing stressful medical procedures: The role of child-environment variables. *Behavioral Assessment, 12,* 223–238.

Lundgren, T., Dahl, J., & Hayes, S. C. (2008). Evaluation of mediators of change in the treatment of epilepsy with acceptance and commitment therapy. *Journal of Behavioral Medicine, 31,* 225–235.

Lustman, P. J. (1988). Anxiety disorders in adults with diabetes mellitus. *Psychiatric Clinics of North America, 11,* 419–432.

Lustman, P. J., Griffith, L. S., & Clouse, R. E. (1988). Depression in adults with diabetes: Results of a 5-year follow-up study. *Diabetes Care, 11,* 605–612.

Luszczynska, A., Boehmer, S., Knoll, N., Schulz, U., & Schwarzer, R. (2007). Emotional support for men and women with cancer: Do patients receive what their partners provide? *International Journal of Behavioral Medicine, 14,* 156–163.

Luszczynska, A., Sobczyk, A., & Abraham, C. (2007). Planning to lose weight: Randomized controlled trial of an implementation intention prompt to enhance weight reduction among overweight and obese women. *Health Psychology, 26,* 507–512.

Lutgendorf, S. K., Anderson, B., Sorosky, J. I., Buller, R. E., & Lubaroff, D. M. (2000). Interleukin-6 and use of social support in gynecologic cancer patients. *International Journal of Behavioral Medicine, 7,* 127–142.

Lutgendorf, S. K., Antoni, M. H., Ironson, G., Starr, K., Costello, N., Zuckerman, M., et al. (1998). Changes in cognitive coping skills and social support during cognitive behavioral stress management intervention and distress outcomes in symptomatic human immunodeficiency virus (HIV)–seropositive gay men. *Psychosomatic Medicine, 60,* 204–214.

Lutgendorf, S. K., Degeest, K., Sung, C. Y., Arevalo, J. M., Penedo, F., Lucci, J., et al. (2008). Depression, social support, and beta-adrenergic transcription control in human ovarian cancer. *Brain, Behavior, and Immunity, 23,* 176–183.

Lutgendorf, S. K., Lamkin, D. M., Degeest, K., Anderson, B., Dao, M., McGinn, S., et al. (2008). Depressed and anxious mood and T-cell cytokine expressing populations in ovarian cancer patients. *Brain, Behavior, and Immunity, 22,* 890–900.

Lutgendorf, S. K., Lang, E. V., Berbaum, K. S., Russell, D., Berbaum, M. L., Logan, H., et al. (2007). Effects of age on responsiveness to adjunct hypnotic analgesia during invasive medical procedures. *Psychosomatic Medicine, 69,* 191–199.

Lutgendorf, S. K., Sood, A. K., Anderson, B., McGinns, S., Maiseri, H., Dao, M., et al. (2005). Social support, psychological distress, and natural killer cell activity in ovarian cancer. *Journal of Clinical Oncology, 23,* 7105–7113.

Luyckx, K., Vanhalst, J., Seiffge-Krenke, I., & Wheets, I. (2010). A typology of coping with Type 1 diabetes in emerging adulthood: Associations with demographic, psychological, and clinical parameters. *Journal of Behavioral Medicine, 33,* 228–238.

Lynch, B. M., Cerin, E., Newman, B., & Owen, N. (2007). Physical activity, activity change, and their correlates in a population-based sample of colorectal cancer survivors. *Annals of Behavioral Medicine, 34,* 135–143.

Lynch, D. J., Birk, T. J., Weaver, M. T., Gohara, A. F., Leighton, R. F., Repka, F. J., et al. (1992). Adherence to exercise interventions in the treatment of hypercholesterolemia. *Journal of Behavioral Medicine, 15,* 365–378.

MacDorman, M. F., & Mathews, T. J. (2009). Behind international rankings of infant mortality: How the United States compares with Europe. *NCHS Data Brief, 23,* 1–8.

Maciejewski, P. K., Zhang, B., Block, S. D., & Prigerson, H. G. (2007). An empirical examination of the stage theory of grief. *Journal of the American Medical Association, 297,* 716–723.

Mackenbach, J. P., Stribu, I., Roskam, A. J. R., Schaap, M. M., Menvielle, G., Leinsalu, M., et al. (2008). Socioeconomic inequalities in health in 22 European countries. *The New England Journal of Medicine, 358,* 2468–2481.

Macrodimitris, S. D., & Endler, N. S. (2001). Coping, control and adjustment in type 2 diabetes. *Health Psychology, 20,* 208–216.

Madden, T. J., Ellen, P. S., & Ajzen, I. (1992). A comparison of the theory of planned behavior and the theory of reasoned action. *Personality and Social Psychology Bulletin, 18,* 3–9.

Maddux, J. E., Roberts, M. C., Sledden, E. A., & Wright, L. (1986). Developmental issues in child health psychology. *American Psychologist, 41,* 25–34.

Madlensky, L., Natarajan, L., Flatt, S. W., Faerber, S., Newman, V. A., & Pierce, J. P. (2008). Timing of dietary change in response to a telephone counseling intervention: Evidence from the WHEL study. *Health Psychology, 27,* 539–547.

Maeland, J. G., & Havik, O. E. (1987). Psychological predictors for return to work after a myocardial infarction. *Journal of Psychosomatic Research, 31,* 471–481.

Maggi, S., Hertzman, C., & Vaillancourt, T. (2007). Changes in smoking behaviors from late childhood to adolescence: Insights from the Canadian National Longitudinal Survey of Children and Youth. *Health Psychology, 26,* 232–240.

Magnan, R. E., Köblitz, A. R., Zielke, D. J., & McCaul, K. D. (2009). The effects of warning smokers on perceived risk, worry, and motivation to quit. *Annals of Behavioral Medicine, 37,* 46–57.

Mahler, H. I. M., & Kulik, J. A. (1998). Effects of preparatory videotapes on self-efficacy beliefs and recovery from coronary bypass surgery. *Annals of Behavioral Medicine, 20,* 39–46.

Mahler, H. I. M., Kulik, J. A., Gerrard, M., & Gibbons, F. X. (2007). Long-term effects of appearance-based interventions on sun protection behaviors. *Health Psychology, 26,* 350–360.

Mahler, H. I. M., Kulick, J. A., Gibbons, F. X., Gerrard, M., & Harrell, J. (2003). Effects of appearance-based interventions on sun protection intentions and self-reported behaviors. *Health Psychology, 22,* 199–209.

Maier, K. J., Waldstein, S. R., & Synowski, S. J. (2003). Relation of cognitive appraisal to cardiovascular reactivity, affect, and task engagement. *Annals of Behavioral Medicine, 26,* 32–41.

Maisel, N. C., & Gable, S. L. (2009). The paradox of received social support: The importance of responsiveness. *Psychological Sciences, 20,* 928–932.

Maisto, S. A., Ewart, C. K., Connors, G. J., Funderburk, J. S., & Krenek, M. (2009). Use of the social competence interview and the anger transcendence challenge in individuals with alcohol use disorder. *Journal of Behavioral Medicine, 32,* 285–293.

Majer, M., Welberg, L. A. M., Capuron, L., Miller, A. H., Pagnoni, G., & Reeves, W. C. (2008). Neuropsychological performance in persons with chronic fatigue syndrome: Results from a population-based study. *Psychosomatic Medicine, 70,* 829–836.

Mallett, K., Price, J. H., Jurs, S. G., & Slenker, S. (1991). Relationships among burnout, death anxiety, and social support in hospice and critical care nurses. *Psychological Reports, 68,* 1347–1359.

Maloney, E. M., Boneva, R., Nater, U. M., & Reeves, W. C. (2009). Chronic fatigue syndrome and high allostatic load: Results from a population-based case-control study in Georgia. *Psychosomatic Medicine, 71,* 549–556.

Maly, R. C., Stein, J. A., Umezawa, Y., Leake, B., & Anglin, M. D. (2008). Racial/ethnic differences in breast cancer outcomes among older patients: Effects of physician communication and patient empowerment. *Health Psychology, 27,* 728–736.

Manber, R., Kuo, T. F., Cataldo, N., & Colrain, I. M. (2003). The effects of hormone replacement therapy on sleep-disordered breathing in postmenopausal women: A pilot study. *Journal of Sleep & Sleep Disorders Research, 26,* 163–168.

Mancini, A. D., & Bonanno, G. A. (2009). Predictors and parameters of resilience to loss: Toward an individual differences model. *Journal of Personality, 77,* 1805–1832.

Mancuso, R. A., Dunkel-Schetter, C., Rini, C. M., Roesch, S. C., & Hobel, C. J. (2004). Maternal prenatal anxiety and corticitropin-releasing hormone associated with timing of delivery. *Psychosomatic Medicine, 66,* 762–769.

Mann, D. M., Ponieman, D., Leventhal, H., & Halm, E. A. (2009). Predictors of adherence to diabetes medications: The role of disease and medication beliefs. *Journal of Behavioral Medicine, 32,* 278–284.

Mann, T. (2001). Effects of future writing and optimism on health behaviors in HIV-infected women. *Annals of Behavioral Medicine, 23,* 26–33.

Mann, T., Nolen-Hoeksema, S., Huang, K., Burgard, D., Wright, A., & Hanson, K. (1997). Are two interventions worse than none? Joint primary and secondary prevention of eating disorders in college females. *Health Psychology, 16,* 215–225.

Mann, T., Sherman, D., & Updegraff, J. (2005). Dispositional motivations and message framing: A test of the congruency hypothesis in college students. *Health Psychology, 23,* 330–334.

Mann, T., Tomiyama, A. J., Westling, E., Lew, A., Samuels, B., & Chatman, J. (2007). Medicare's search for effective obesity treatments: Diets are not the answer. *American Psychologist, 62,* 220–233.

Manne, S., Ostroff, J. S., & Winkel, G. (2007). Social-cognitive processes as moderators of a couple-focused group intervention for women with early stage breast cancer. *Health Psychology, 26,* 735–744.

Manne, S., Rini, C., Rubin, S., Rosenblum, N., Bergman, C., Edelson, M., et al. (2008). Long-term trajectories of psychological adaptation among women diagnosed with gynecological cancers. *Psychosomatic Medicine, 70,* 677–687.

Manne, S. L., Bakeman, R., Jacobsen, P. B., Gorfinkle, K., Bernstein, D., & Redd, W. H. (1992). Adult-child interaction during invasive medical procedures. *Health Psychology, 11,* 241–249.

Manne, S. L., Bakeman, R., Jacobsen, P. B., Gorfinkle, K., & Redd, W. H. (1994). An analysis of a behavioral intervention for children undergoing venipuncture. *Health Psychology, 13,* 556–566.

Manne, S. L., Coups, E. J., Markowitz, A., Meropol, N. J., Haller, D., Jacobsen, P. B., et al. (2009). A randomized trial of genetic versus tailored interventions to increase colorectal cancer screening among intermediate risk siblings. *Annals of Behavioral Medicine, 37,* 207–217.

Manne, S. L., Jacobsen, P. B., Gorfinkle, K., Gerstein, F., & Redd, W. H. (1993). Treatment adherence difficulties among children with cancer: The role of parenting style. *Journal of Pediatric Psychology, 18,* 47–62.

Manne, S. L., Markowitz, A., Winawer, S., Meropol, N. J., Haller, D., Rakowski, W., et al. (2002). Correlates of colorectal cancer screening compliance and stage of adoption among siblings of individuals with early onset colorectal cancer. *Health Psychology, 21,* 3–15.

Manne, S. L., Ostroff, J., Winkel, G., Goldstein, L., Fox, K., & Grana, G. (2004). Posttraumatic growth after breast cancer: Patient, partner, and couple perspectives. *Psychosomatic Medicine, 66,* 442–454.

Manne, S. L., Ostroff, J., Winkel, G., Grana, G., & Fox, K. (2005). Partner unsupportive responses, avoidant coping, and distress among women with early stage breast cancer: Patient and partner perspectives. *Health Psychology, 24,* 635–641.

Manne, S. L., Redd, W. H., Jacobsen, P. B., Gorfinkle, K., Schorr, O., & Rapkin, B. (1990). Behavioral intervention to reduce child and parent distress during venipuncture. *Journal of Consulting and Clinical Psychology, 58,* 565–572.

Manne, S. L., & Zautra, A. J. (1990). Couples coping with chronic illness: Women with rheumatoid arthritis and their healthy husbands. *Journal of Behavioral Medicine, 13,* 327–342.

Manning, B. K., Catley, D., Harris, K. J., Mayo, M. S., & Ahluwalia, J. S. (2005). Stress and quitting among African American smokers. *Journal of Behavioral Medicine, 28,* 325–333.

Manson, J. E., Colditz, G. A., Stampfer, M. J., Willett, W. C., Rosner, B., Monson, R. R., et al. (1990). A prospective study of obesity and risk of coronary heart disease in women. *The New England Journal of Medicine, 322,* 882–888.

Manson, J. E., Hsia, J., Johnson, K. C., Rossouw, J. E., Assaf, A. R., Lasser, N. L., et al. (2003). Estrogen plus progestin and the risk of coronary heart disease. *The New England Journal of Medicine, 349,* 523–534.

Manson, J. E., Willett, W. C., Stampfer, M. J., Loiditz, G. A., Hunter, D. J., Hankinson, S. E., et al. (1995). Body weight and mortality among women. *The New England Journal of Medicine, 333,* 677–685.

Manuck, S. B., Phillips, J. E., Gianaros, P. J., Flory, J. D., & Muldoon, M. F. (2010). Subjective socioeconomic status and presence of the metabolic syndrome in midlife community volunteers. *Psychosomatic Medicine, 72,* 35–45.

Marbach, J. J., Lennon, M. C., Link, B. G., & Dohrenwend, B. P. (1990). Losing face: Sources of stigma as perceived by chronic facial pain patients. *Journal of Behavioral Medicine, 13,* 583–604.

Marcus, A. C., & Siegel, J. M. (1982). Sex differences in the use of physician services: A preliminary test of the fixed role hypothesis. *Journal of Health and Social Behavior, 23,* 186–197.

Marcus, B. H., Dubbert, P. M., Forsyth, L. H., McKenzie, T. L., Stone, E. J., Dunn, A. L., et al. (2000). Physical activity behavior change: Issues in adoption and maintenance. *Health Psychology, 19,* 32–41.

Marcus, B. H., Napolitano, M. A., King, A. C., Lewis, B. A., Whiteley, J. A., Albrecht, A., et al. (2007). Telephone versus print delivery of an individualized motivationally tailored physical activity intervention: Project STRIDE. *Health Psychology, 26,* 401–409.

Marcus, B. H., & Owen, N. (1992). Motivational readiness, self-efficacy and decision-making for exercise. *Journal of Applied Social Psychology, 22,* 3–16.

Margolin, A., Avants, S. K., Warburton, L. A., Hawkins, K. A., & Shi, J. (2003). A randomized clinical trial of a manual-guided risk reduction intervention for HIV-positive injection drug users. *Health Psychology, 22,* 223–228.

Marin, T. J., Chen, E., & Miller, G. E. (2008). What do trajectories of childhood socioeconomic status tell us about markers of cardiovascular health in adolescence? *Psychosomatic Medicine, 70,* 152–159.

Marin, T. J., Chen, E., Munch, J. A., & Miller, G. E. (2009). Double-exposure to acute stress and chronic family stress is associated with immune changes in children with asthma. *Psychosomatic Medicine, 71,* 378–384.

Marin, T. J., Martin, T. M., Blackwell, E., Stetler, C., & Miller, G. E. (2007). Differentiating the impact of episodic and chronic stressors on hypothalamic-pituitary-adrenocortical axis regulation in young women. *Health Psychology, 26,* 447–455.

Markovitz, J. H. (1998). Hostility is associated with increased platelet activation in coronary heart disease. *Psychosomatic Medicine, 60,* 586–591.

Marks, M., Sliwinski, M., & Gordon, W. A. (1993). An examination of the needs of families with a brain injured child. *Journal of Neurorehabilitation, 3,* 1–12.

Marlatt, G. A. (1990). Cue exposure and relapse prevention in the treatment of addictive behaviors. *Addictive Behaviors, 15,* 395–399.

Marlatt, G. A., Baer, J. S., Kivlahan, D. R., Dimeff, L. A., Larimer, M. E., Quigley, L. A., et al. (1998). Screening and brief intervention for high-risk college student drinkers: Results from a 2-year follow-up assessment. *Journal of Consulting and Clinical Psychology, 66,* 604–615.

Marlatt, G. A., & George, W. H. (1988). Relapse prevention and the maintenance of optimal health. In S. Shumaker, E. Schron, & J. K. Ockene (Eds.), *The adoption and maintenance of behaviors for optimal health.* New York: Springer.

Marlatt, G. A., & Gordon, J. R. (1980). Determinants of relapse: Implications for the maintenance of behavior change. In P. O. Davidson & S. M. Davidson (Eds.), *Behavioral medicine: Changing health lifestyles.* New York: Brunner/Mazel.

Marlatt, G. A., & Gordon, J. R. (1985). *Relapse prevention: Maintenance strategies in the treatment of addictive behaviors.* New York: Guilford Press.

Marlatt, G. A., Larimer, M. E., Baer, J. S., & Quigley, L. A. (1993). Harm reduction for alcohol problems: Moving beyond the controlled drinking controversy. *Behavior Therapy, 24,* 461–504.

Marquez, D. X., & McAuley, E. (2006). Social cognitive correlates of leisure time physical activity among Latinos. *Journal of Behavioral Medicine, 29,* 281–289.

Marsh, B. (2002, September 10). A primer on fat, some of it good for you. *New York Times,* p. D7.

Marsh, H. W., Papaioannou, A., & Theodorakis, Y. (2006). Causal ordering of physical self-concept and exercise behavior: Reciprocal effects model and the influence of physical education teachers. *Health Psychology, 25,* 316–328.

Marshall, A. L., Bauman, A. E., Owen, N., Booth, M. L., Crawford, D., & Marcus, B. H. (2003). Population-based randomized controlled trial of a stage-targeted physical activity intervention. *Annals of Behavioral Medicine, 25,* 194–202.

Marshall, E. (1986). Involuntary smokers face health risks. *Science, 234,* 1066–1067.

Marshall, J., Burnett, W., & Brasure, J. (1983). On precipitating factors: Cancer as a cause of suicide. *Suicide and Life-Threatening Behavior, 13,* 15–27.

Marsland, A. L., Cohen, S., Rabin, B. S., & Manuck, S. B. (2001). Associations between stress, trait negative affect, acute immune reactivity, and antibody response to hepatitis B injection in healthy young adults. *Health Psychology, 20,* 4–11.

Marsland, A. L., Cohen, S., Rabin, B. S., & Manuck, S. B. (2006). Trait positive affect and antibody response to hepatitis B vaccination. *Brain, Behavior, and Immunity, 20,* 261–269.

Marsland, A. L., Petersen, K. L., Sathanoori, R., Muldoon, M. F., Neumann, S. A., Ryan, C., et al. (2006). Interleukin–6 covaries inversely with cognitive performance among middle-aged community volunteers. *Psychosomatic Medicine, 68,* 895–903.

Marteau, T. M., Johnston, M., Baum, J. D., & Bloch, S. (1987). Goals of treatment in diabetes: A comparison of doctors and parents of children with diabetes. *Journal of Behavioral Medicine, 10,* 33–48.

Marteau, T. M., & Weinman, J. (2006). Self-regulation and the behavioural response to DNA risk information: A theoretical analysis and framework for future research. *Social Science & Medicine, 62,* 1360–1368.

Martens, E. J., Smith, O. R. F., & Denollet, J. (2007). Psychological symptom clusters, psychiatric comorbidity and poor self-reported health status following myocardial infaction. *Annals of Behavioral Medicine, 34,* 87–94.

Martin, J., Sheeran, P., Slade, P., Wright, A., & Dibble, T. (2009). Implementation intention formation reduces consultations for emergency contraception and pregnancy testing among teenage women. *Health Psychology, 28,* 762–769.

Martin, J. K., Tuch, S. A., & Roman, P. M. (2003). Problem drinking patterns among African Americans: The impacts of reports of discrimination, perceptions of prejudice, and "risky" coping strategies. *Journal of Health and Social Behavior, 44,* 408–425.

Martin, L. R., Friedman, H. S., Tucker, J. S., Tomlinson-Keasey, C., Criqui, M. H., & Schwartz, J. E. (2002). Life course perspective on childhood cheerfulness and its relations to mortality risk. *Personality and Social Psychology Bulletin, 28,* 1155–1165.

Martin, R., Davis, G. M., Baron, R. S., Suls, J., & Blanchard, E. B. (1994). Specificity in social support: Perceptions of helpful and unhelpful provider behaviors among irritable bowel syndrome, headache, and cancer patients. *Health Psychology, 13,* 432–439.

Martin, R., & Lemos, K. (2002). From heart attacks to melanoma: Do common sense models of somatization influence symptom interpretation for female victims? *Health Psychology, 21,* 25–32.

Martinez, S. M., Ainsworth, B. E., & Elder, J. P. (2008). A review of physical activity measures used among US Latinos: Guidelines for developing culturally appropriate measures. *Annals of Behavioral Medicine, 36,* 195–207.

Martire, L. M., Lustig, A. P., Schulz, R., Miller, G. E., & Helgeson, V. S. (2004). Is it beneficial to involve a family member? A meta-analysis of psychosocial interventions for chronic illness. *Health Psychology, 23,* 599–611.

Martire, L. M., Stephens, M. A. P., Druley, J. A., & Wojno, W. C. (2002). Negative reactions to received spousal care: Predictors and consequences of miscarried support. *Health Psychology, 21,* 167–176.

Maselko, J., Kubzansky, L., Kawachi, I., Seeman, T., & Berkman, L. (2007). Religious service attendance and allostatic load among high-functioning elderly. *Psychosomatic Medicine, 69,* 464–472.

Maslach, C. (1979). The burn-out syndrome and patient care. In C. Garfield (Ed.), *The emotional realities of life-threatening illness* (pp. 111–120). St. Louis, MO: Mosby.

Maslach, C. (2003). Job burnout: New directions in research and intervention. *Current Directions, 12,* 189–192.

Mason, E. (1970). Obesity in pet dogs. *Veterinary Record, 86,* 612–616.

Mason, H. R. C., Marks, G., Simoni, J. M., Ruiz, M. S., & Richardson, J. L. (1995). Culturally sanctioned secrets? Latino men's nondisclosure of HIV infection to family, friends, and lovers. *Health Psychology, 14,* 6–12.

Masters, K. S., & Spielmans, G. I. (2007). Prayer and health: Review, meta-analysis, and research agenda. *Journal of Behavioral Medicine, 30,* 329–338.

Masuda, A., Munemoto, T., Yamanaka, T., Takei, M., & Tei, C. (2002). Psychological characteristics and immunological functions in patients with postinfectious chronic fatigue syndrome and noninfectious chronic fatigue syndrome. *Journal of Behavioral Medicine, 25,* 477–485.

Mata, J., Silva, M. N., Vieira, P. N., Carraca, E. V., Andrade, A. M., Coutinho, S. R., et al. (2009). Motivational "spill-over" during weight control: Increased self-determination and exercise intrinsic motivation predict eating self-regulation. *Health Psychology, 28,* 709–716.

Mather, A. A., Cox, B. J., Enns, M. W., & Sareen, J. (2008). Associations between body weight and personality disorders in a nationally representative sample. *Psychosomatic Medicine, 70,* 1012–1019.

Matt, G. E., Quintana, P. J. E., Hovell, M. F., Bernert, J. T., Song, S., Novianti, N., et al. (2004). Households contaminated by environmental tobacco smoke: Sources of infant exposures. *Tobacco Control, 13,* 29–37.

Matthews, J. R., Friman, P. C., Barone, V. J., Ross, L. V., & Christophersen, E. R. (1987). Decreasing dangerous infant behaviors through parent instruction. *Journal of Applied Behavior Analysis, 20,* 165–169.

Matthews, K. A., Gallo, L. C., & Taylor, S. E. (2010). Are psychosocial factors mediators of SES and health connections?: A progress report and blueprint for the future. In N. Adler and J. Stewart (Eds.), *The Biology of Disadvantage: Socioeconomic Status and Health* (Vol. 1186; pp. 146–173). Malden, MA: Wiley-Blackwell.

Matthews, K. A., Gump, B. B., Block, D. R., & Allen, M. T. (1997). Does background stress heighten or dampen children's cardiovascular responses to acute stress? *Psychosomatic Medicine, 59,* 488–496.

Matthews, K. A., Gump, B. B., & Owens, J. F. (2001). Chronic stress influences cardiovascular and neuroendocrine responses during acute stress and recovery, especially in men. *Health Psychology, 20,* 403–410.

Matthews, K. A., Owens, J. F., Allen, M. T., & Stoney, C. M. (1992). Do cardiovascular responses to laboratory stress relate to ambulatory blood pressure levels? Yes, in some of the people, some of the time. *Psychosomatic Medicine, 54,* 686–697.

Matthews, K. A., Owens, J. F., Kuller, L. H., Sutton-Tyrrell, K., & Jansen-McWilliams, L. (1998). Are hostility and anxiety associated with carotid atherosclerosis in healthy postmenopausal women? *Psychosomatic Medicine, 60,* 633–638.

Matthews, K. A., Räikkönen, K., Everson, S. A., Flory, J. D., Marco, C. A., Owens, J. F., et al. (2000). Do the daily experiences of healthy men and women vary according to occupational prestige and work strain? *Psychosomatic Medicine, 62,* 346–353.

Matthews, K. A., Räikkönen, K., Gallo, L., & Kuller, L. H. (2008). Association between socioeconomic status and metabolic syndrome in women: Testing the reserve capacity model. *Health Psychology, 27,* 576–583.

Matthews, K. A., Räikkönen, K., Sutton-Tyrrell, S., & Kuller, L. H. (2004). Optimistic attitudes protect against progression of carotid atherosclerosis in healthy middle-aged women. *Psychosomatic Medicine, 66,* 640–644.

Matthews, K. A., & Rodin, J. (1992). Pregnancy alters blood pressure responses to psychological and physical challenge. *Psychophysiology, 29,* 232–240.

Matthews, K. A., Salomon, K., Brady, S. S., & Allen, M. T. (2003). Cardiovascular reactivity to stress predicts future blood pressure in adolescence. *Psychosomatic Medicine, 65,* 410–415.

Matthews, K. A., Shumaker, S. A., Bowen, D. J., Langer, R. D., Hunt, J. R., Kaplan, R. M., et al. (1997). Women's health initiative: Why now? What is it? What's new? *American Psychologist, 52,* 101–116.

Matthews, K. A., Woodall, K. L., & Allen, M. T. (1993). Cardiovascular reactivity to stress predicts future blood pressure status. *Hypertension, 22,* 479–485.

Matthews, K. A., Woodall, K. L., Kenyon, K., & Jacob, T. (1996). Negative family environment as a predictor of boys' future status on measures of hostile attitudes, interview behavior, and anger expression. *Health Psychology, 15,* 30–37.

Matthews, S. A., & Yang, T. C. (2010). Exploring the role of the built and social neighborhood environment in moderating stress and health. *Annals of Behavioral Medicine, 39,* 170–183.

Matthews, S. C., Nelesen, R. A., & Dimsdale, J. E. (2005). Depressive symptoms are associated with increased systemic vascular resistance to stress. *Psychosomatic Medicine, 67,* 509–513.

Mattson, M. P. (2004). Pathways towards and away from Alzheimer's disease. *Nature, 430,* 631–639.

Maugh, T. H. (2007, May 2). Heart attack deaths down sharply. *Los Angeles Times,* p. A14.

Maugh, T. H. (2009, October 9). Virus is found in many people with chronic fatigue. *Los Angeles Times,* p. A18.

Mauksch, H. O. (1973). Ideology, interaction, and patient care in hospitals. *Social Science and Medicine, 7,* 817–830.

Mausbach, B. T., Dimsdale, J. E., Ziegler, M. G., Mills, P. J., Ancoli-Israel, S., Patterson, T. L., et al. (2005). Depressive symptoms predict norepinephrine response to a psychological stressor task in Alzheimer's caregivers. *Psychosomatic Medicine, 67,* 638–642.

Mausbach, B. T., Patterson, T. L., Rabinowitz, Y. G., Grant, I., & Schulz, R. (2007). Depression and distress predict time to cardiovascular disease in dementia caregivers. *Health Psychology, 26,* 539–544.

Mausbach, B. T., Semple, S. J., Strathdee, S. A., Zians, J., & Patterson, T. L. (2007). Efficacy of a behavioral intervention for increasing safer sex behaviors in HIV-negative, heterosexual methamphetamine users: Results from the fast-lane study. *Annals of Behavioral Medicine, 34,* 263–274.

Mausbach, B. T., von Känel, R., Aschbacher, K., Roepke, S. K., Dimsdale, J. E., Ziegler, M. G., et al. (2007). Spousal caregivers of patients with Alzheimer's disease show longitudinal increases in plasma level of tissue-type plasminogen activator antigen. *Psychosomatic Medicine, 69,* 816–822.

Mausbach, B. T., von Känel, R., Patterson, T. L., Dimsdale, J. E., Depp, C. A., Aschbacher, K., et al. (2008). The moderating effect of personal mastery and the relations between stress and plasminogen activator inhibitor-1 (PAI-1) antigen. *Health Psychology, 27,* S172–S179.

Maxwell, T. D., Gatchel, R. J., & Mayer, T. G. (1998). Cognitive predictors of depression in chronic low back pain: Toward an inclusive model. *Journal of Behavioral Medicine, 21,* 131–143.

May, M., McCarron, P., Stansfeld, S., Ben-Schlomo, Y., Gallacher, J., Yarnell, J., et al. (2002). Does psychological distress predict the risk of ischemic stroke and transient ischemic attack? *Stroke, 33,* 7–12.

Mayer, D. J., Price, D. D., Barber, J., & Rafii, A. (1976). Acupuncture analgesia: Evidence for activation of a pain inhibitor system as a mechanism of action. In J. J. Bonica & D. Albe-Fessard (Eds.), *Advances in pain research and therapy* (Vol. 1, pp. 751–754). New York: Raven Press.

Mayne, T. J., Acree, M., Chesney, M. A., & Folkman, S. (1998). HIV sexual risk behavior following bereavement in gay men. *Health Psychology, 17,* 403–411.

Mazor, K. M., Simon, S. R., Yood, R. A., Martinson, B. C., Gunter, M. J., Reed, G. W., et al. (2004). Health plan members' views about disclosure of medical errors. *Annals of Internal Medicine, 140,* 409–418.

McAuley, E. (1992). The role of efficacy cognitions in the prediction of exercise behavior in middle-aged adults. *Journal of Behavioral Medicine, 15,* 65–88.

McAuley, E., & Courneya, K. S. (1992). Self-efficacy relationships with affective and exertion responses to exercise. *Journal of Applied Social Psychology, 22,* 312–326.

McAuley, E., Doerksen, S. E., Morris, K. S., Motl, R. W., Hu, L., Wójcicki, T. R., et al. (2008). Pathways from physical activity to quality of life in older women. *Annals of Behavioral Medicine, 36,* 13–20.

McAuley, E., Morris, K. S., Motl, R. W., Hu, L., Konopack, J. F., & Elavsky, S. (2007). Long-term follow-up of physical activity behavior in older adults. *Health Psychology, 26,* 375–380.

McAuley, E., Talbot, H., & Martinez, S. (1999). Manipulating self-efficacy in the exercise environment in women: Influences on affective responses. *Health Psychology, 18,* 288–294.

McAuley, E., White, S. M., Rogers, L. Q., Motl, R. W., & Courneya, K. S. (2010). Physical activity and fatigue in breast cancer and multiple sclerosis: Psychosocial mechanisms. *Psychosomatic Medicine, 72,* 88–96.

McBride, C. M., Pollack, K. I., Lyna, P., Lipkus, I. M., Samsa, G. P., & Bepler, G. (2001). Reasons for quitting smoking among low-income African American smokers. *Health Psychology, 20,* 334–340.

McCaffery, J. M., Niaura, R., Todaro, J. F., Swan, G. E., & Carmelli, D. (2003). Depressive symptoms and metabolic risk in adult male twins enrolled in the national heart, lung and blood study. *Psychosomatic Medicine, 65,* 490–497.

McCaffery, J. M., Pogue-Geile, M. F., Muldoon, M. F., Debski, T. T., Wing, R. R., & Manuck, S. B. (2001). The nature of the association between diet and serum lipids in the community: A twin study. *Health Psychology, 20,* 341–350.

McCann, B. S., Bovbjerg, V. E., Curry, S. J., Retzlaff, B. M., Walden, C. E., & Knopp, R. H. (1996). Predicting participation in a dietary intervention to lower cholesterol among individuals with hyperlipidemia. *Health Psychology, 15,* 61–64.

McCarroll, J. E., Ursano, R. J., Fullerton, C. S., Liu, X., & Lundy, A. (2002). Somatic symptoms in Gulf War mortuary workers. *Psychosomatic Medicine, 64,* 29–33.

McCarthy, C. J. (1995). The relationship of cognitive appraisals and stress coping resources to emotion-eliciting events. *Dissertation Abstracts International: Section B: The Sciences & Engineering, 56,* 1746.

McCaul, K. D., Branstetter, A. D., Schroeder, D. M., & Glasgow, R. E. (1996). What is the relationship between breast cancer risk and mammography screening? A meta-analytic review. *Health Psychology, 15,* 423–429.

McCaul, K. D., Glasgow, R. E., & O'Neill, H. K. (1992). The problem of creating habits: Establishing health-protective dental behaviors. *Health Psychology, 11,* 101–110.

McCaul, K. D., Johnson, R. J., & Rothman, A. J. (2002). The effects of framing and action instructions on whether older adults obtain flu shots. *Health Psychology, 21,* 624–628.

McCaul, K. D., Monson, N., & Maki, R. H. (1992). Does distraction reduce pain-produced distress among college students? *Health Psychology, 11,* 210–217.

McClearn, G., Johansson, B., Berg, S., Pedersen, N., Ahern, F., Petrill, S. A., et al. (1997). Substantial genetic influence on cognitive abilities in twins 80 or more years old. *Science, 276,* 1560–1563.

McClelland, L. E., & McCubbin, J. A. (2008). Social influence and pain response in women and men. *Journal of Behavioral Medicine, 31,* 413–420.

McCracken, L. M. (1991). Cognitive-behavioral treatment of rheumatoid arthritis: A preliminary review of efficacy and methodology. *Annals of Behavioral Medicine, 13,* 57–65.

McCracken, L. M., & Vowles, K. E. (2008). A prospective analysis of acceptance of pain and values-based action in patients with chronic pain. *Health Psychology, 27,* 215–220.

McCullough, M. E., Friedman, H. S., Enders, C. K., & Martin, L. R. (2009). Does devoutness delay death? Psychological investment in religion and its association with longevity in the Terman sample. *Journal of Personality and Social Psychology, 97,* 866–882.

McCullough, M. E., & Laurenceau, J. (2004). Gender and the natural history of self-rated health: A 59-year longitudinal study. *Health Psychology, 23,* 651–655.

McDade, T. W., Hawkley, L. C., & Cacioppo, J. T. (2006). Psychosocial and behavioral predictors of inflammation in middle-aged and older adults: The Chicago health, aging, and social relations study. *Psychosomatic Medicine, 68,* 376–381.

McDade-Montez, E. A., Christensen, A. J., Cvengros, J. A., & Lawton, W. J. (2006). The role of depression symptoms in dialysis withdrawal. *Health Psychology, 25,* 198–204.

McDonagh, A., Friedman, M., McHugo, G., Ford, J., Sengupta, A., Mueser, K., et al. (2005). Randomized trial of cognitive-behavioral therapy for chronic posttraumatic stress disorder in adult female survivors of childhood sexual abuse. *Journal of Consulting and Clinical Psychology, 73,* 515–524.

McDonough, P., Williams, D. R., House, J. S., & Duncan, G. J. (1999). Gender and the socioeconomic gradient in mortality. *Journal of Health and Social Behavior, 40,* 17–31.

McEwen, B. S. (1998). Protective and damaging effects of stress mediators. *The New England Journal of Medicine, 338,* 171–179.

McEwen, B. S., & Stellar, E. (1993). Stress and the individual: Mechanisms leading to disease. *Archives of Internal Medicine, 153,* 2093–2101.

McFarland, C., & Alvaro, C. (2000). The impact of motivation on temporal comparisons: Coping with traumatic events by perceiving personal growth. *Journal of Personality and Social Psychology, 79,* 327–343.

McFarland, C., Ross, M., & DeCourville, N. (1989). Women's theories of menstruation and biases in recall of menstrual symptoms. *Journal of Personality and Social Psychology, 57,* 522–531.

McGinnis, M., Richmond, J. B., Brandt, E. N., Windom, R. E., & Mason, J. O. (1992). Health progress in the United States: Results of the 1990 objectives for the nation. *Journal of the American Medical Association, 268,* 2545–2552.

McGonagle, K. A., & Kessler, R. C. (1990). Chronic stress, acute stress, and depressive symptoms. *American Journal of Community Psychology, 18,* 681–706.

McGrady, A., Conran, P., Dickey, D., Garman, D., Farris, E., & Schumann-Brzezinski, C. (1992). The effects of biofeedback-assisted relaxation on cell-mediated immunity, cortisol, and white blood cell count in healthy adult subjects. *Journal of Behavioral Medicine, 15,* 343–354.

McGregor, B. A., Bowen, D. J., Ankerst, D. P., Andersen, M. R., Yasui, Y., & McTiernan, A. (2004). Optimism, perceived risk of breast cancer, and cancer worry among a community-based sample of women. *Health Psychology, 23,* 339–344.

McGregor, S. (2006). Roles, power, and subjective choice. *Patient Education and Counseling, 60,* 5–9.

McGuire, F. L. (1982). Treatment of the drinking driver. *Health Psychology, 1,* 137–152.

McGuire, L., Heffner, K., Glaser, R., Needleman, B., Malarkey, W., Dickinson, S., et al. (2006). Pain and wound healing in surgical patients. *Annals of Behavioral Medicine, 31,* 165–172.

McGuire, W. J. (1964). Inducing resistance to persuasion: Some contemporary approaches. In L. Berkowitz (Ed.), *Advances in experimental social psychology* (Vol. 1, pp. 192–231). New York: Academic Press.

McGuire, W. J. (1973). Persuasion, resistance and attitude change. In I. de Sola Pool, F. W. Frey, W. Schramm, N. Maccoby, & E. B. Parker (Eds.), *Handbook of communication* (pp. 216–252). Chicago: Rand-McNally.

McGuire, W. J. (1984). Public communication as a strategy for inducing health-promoting behavioral change. *Preventive Medicine, 13,* 299–319.

McIntosh, D. N., Silver, R. C., & Wortman, C. B. (1993). Religion's role in adjustment to a negative life event: Coping with the loss of a child. *Journal of Personality and Social Psychology, 65,* 812–821.

McKay, H. G., Seeley, J. R., King, D., Glasgow, R. E., & Eakin, E. G. (2001). The diabetes network Internet-based physical activity intervention. *Diabetes Care, 24,* 1328–1334.

McKenna, F. P., & Horswill, M. S. (2006). Risk taking from the participant's perspective: The case of driving and accident risk. *Health Psychology, 25,* 163–170.

McKenna, M. C., Zevon, M. A., Corn, B., & Rounds, J. (1999). Psychological factors and the development of breast cancer: A meta-analysis. *Health Psychology, 18,* 520–531.

McKnight, P. E., Afram, A., Kashdan, T. B., Kasle, S., & Zautra, A. (2010). Coping self-efficacy as a mediator between catastrophizing and physical functioning: Treatment target selection in an osteoarthritis sample. *Journal of Behavioral Medicine, 33,* 239–249.

McKusick, L., Coates, T. J., Morin, S. F., Pollack, L., & Hoff, C. (1990). Longitudinal predictors of reductions in unprotected anal intercourse among gay men in San Francisco: The AIDS Behavioral Research Project. *American Journal of Public Health, 80,* 978–983.

McNeil, D. G., Jr. (2002, May 17). With folk medicine on rise, health group is monitoring. *New York Times,* p. A9.

McPherson, M., Smith-Lovin, L., & Brashears, M. E. (2006). Social isolation in America: Changes in core discussion networks over two decades. *American Sociological Review, 71,* 353–375.

McQuade, D. V. (2002). Negative social perception of hypothetical workers with rheumatoid arthritis. *Journal of Behavioral Medicine, 25,* 205–217.

McQuillan, G. M., Kruszon-Moran, D., Denniston, M. M., & Hirsch, R. (2010). Viral Hepatitis. *NCHS Data Brief, 27,* 1–8.

McQuillen, A. D., Licht, M. H., & Licht, B. G. (2003). Contributions of disease severity and perceptions of primary and secondary control to the prediction of psychological adjustment to Parkinson's disease. *Health Psychology, 22,* 504–512.

McVea, K. L. S. P. (2006). Evidence for clinical smoking cessation for adolescents. *Health Psychology, 25,* 558–562.

Meagher, M., Arnau, R., & Rhudy, J. (2001). Pain and emotion: Effects of affective picture modulation. *Psychosomatic Medicine, 63,* 79–90.

Means-Christensen, A. J., Arnau, R. C., Tonidandel, A. M., Bramson, R., & Meagher, M. W. (2005). An efficient method of identifying major depression and panic disorder in primary care. *Journal of Behavioral Medicine, 28,* 565–572.

Meara, E., White, C., & Cutler, D. M. (2004). Trends in medical spending by age, 1963–2000. *Health Affairs, 23,* 176–183.

Mechanic, D. (1972). Social psychologic factors affecting the presentation of bodily complaints. *The New England Journal of Medicine, 286,* 1132–1139.

Mechanic, D. (1975). The organization of medical practice and practice orientation among physicians in prepaid and nonprepaid primary care settings. *Medical Care, 13,* 189–204.

Mechanic, D. (2004). The rise and fall of managed care. *Journal of Health and Social Behavior, 45* (Suppl.), 78–86.

Mechlin, M. B., Maixner, W., Light, K. C., Fisher, J. M., & Girdler, S. S. (2005). African Americans show alterations in endogenous pain regulatory mechanisms and reduced pain tolerance to experimental pain procedures. *Psychosomatic Medicine, 67,* 948–956.

Medzhitov, R., & Janeway Jr., C. A. (2002). Decoding the patterns of self and nonself by the innate immune system. *Science, 296,* 298–316.

Meechan, G., Collins, J., & Petrie, K. J. (2003). The relationship of symptoms and psychological factors to delay in seeking medical care for breast symptoms. *Preventive Medicine, 36,* 374–378.

Meichenbaum, D. H. (1975). A self-instructional approach to stress management: A proposal for stress inoculation training. In C. D. Spielberger & I. Sarason (Eds.), *Stress and anxiety* (Vol. 2, pp. 237–264). New York: Wiley.

Meichenbaum, D. H., & Jaremko, M. E. (Eds.). (1983). *Stress reduction and prevention.* New York: Plenum.

Meichenbaum, D. H., & Turk, D. (1982). Stress, coping, and disease: A cognitive-behavioral perspective. In R. W. J. Neufield (Ed.), *Psychological stress and psychopathology* (pp. 289–306). New York: McGraw-Hill.

Meisinger, C., Kandler, U., & Ladwig, K. H. (2009). Living alone is associated with an increased risk of type 2 diabetes mellitus in men but not in women from the general population: The MONICA/KORA Augsburg cohort study. *Psychosomatic Medicine, 71,* 784–788.

Melamed, B. G., & Brenner, G. F. (1990). Social support and chronic medical stress: An interaction-based approach. *Journal of Social and Clinical Psychology, 9,* 104–117.

Melamed, B. G., & Siegel, L. (1975). Reduction of anxiety in children facing hospitalization and surgery by use of filmed modeling. *Journal of Consulting and Clinical Psychology, 43,* 511–521.

Mello, M. M., Studdert, D. M., & Brennan, T. A. (2006). Obesity—The new frontier of public health law. *The New England Journal of Medicine, 354,* 2601–2610.

Mellon, S., Janisse, J., Gold, R., Cichon, M., Berry-Bobovski, L., Tainsky, M. A., et al. (2009). Predictors of decision making in families at risk for inherited breast/ovarian cancer. *Health Psychology, 28,* 38–47.

Melzack, R., & Wall, P. D. (1982). *The challenge of pain.* New York: Basic Books.

Menaghan, E., Kowaleski-Jones, L., & Mott, F. (1997). The intergenerational costs of parental social stressors: Academic and social difficulties in early adolescence for children of young mothers. *Journal of Health and Social Behavior, 38,* 72–86.

Mendes de Leon, C. F. (1992). Anger and impatience/irritability in patients of low socioeconomic status with acute coronary heart disease. *Journal of Behavioral Medicine, 15,* 273–284.

Mendes de Leon, C. F., Kop, W. J., de Swart, H. B., Bar, F. W., & Appels, A. P. W. M. (1996). Psychosocial characteristics and recurrent events after percutaneous transluminal coronary angioplasty. *American Journal of Cardiology, 77,* 252–255.

Menning, C. L. (2006). Nonresident fathers' involvement and adolescents' smoking. *Journal of Health and Social Behavior, 47,* 32–46.

Mercado, A. C., Carroll, L. J., Cassidy, J. D., & Cote, P. (2000). Coping with neck and low back pain in the general population. *Health Psychology, 19,* 333–338.

Mercken, L., Candel, M., Willems, P., & de Vries, H. (2009). Social influence and selection effects in the context of smoking behavior: Changes during early and mid adolescence. *Health Psychology, 28,* 73–82.

Mermelstein, R., Cohen, S., Lichtenstein, E., Baer, J. S., & Kamarck, T. (1986). Social support and smoking cessation and maintenance. *Journal of Consulting and Clinical Psychology, 54,* 447–453.

Merritt, M. M., Bennett, G. G., Williams, R. B., Edwards, C. L., & Sollers, J. J. (2006). Perceived racism and cardiovascular reactivity and recovery to personally relevant stress. *Health Psychology, 25,* 364–369.

Merritt, M. M., Bennett, G. G., Williams, R. B., Sollers, J. J., III, & Thayer, J. F. (2004). Low educational attainment, John Henryism and cardiovascular reactivity to and recovery from personally relevant stress. *Psychosomatic Medicine, 66,* 49–55.

Mertens, M. C., Roukema, J. A., Scholtes, V. P. W., & De Vries, J. (2010). Trait anxiety predicts unsuccessful surgery in gallstone disease. *Psychosomatic Medicine, 72,* 198–205.

Messeri, P., Silverstein, M., & Litwak, E. (1993). Choosing optimal support groups: A review and reformulation. *Journal of Health and Social Behavior, 34,* 122–137.

Messina, C. R., Lane, D. S., Glanz, K., West, D. S., Taylor, V., Frishman, W., et al. (2004). Relationship of social support and social burden to repeated breast cancer screening in the women's health initiative. *Health Psychology, 23,* 582–594.

Messina, C. R., Lane, D. S., & Grimson, R. (2002). Effectiveness of women's telephone counseling and physician education to improve mammography screening among women who underuse mammography. *Annals of Behavioral Medicine, 24,* 279–289.

Meyer, D., Leventhal, H., & Gutmann, M. (1985). Common-sense models of illness: The example of hypertension. *Health Psychology, 4,* 115–135.

Meyer, J. M., & Stunkard, A. J. (1994). Twin studies of human obesity. In C. Bouchard (Ed.), *The genetics of obesity* (pp. 63–78). Boca Raton, FL: CRC Press.

Meyer, M. H., & Pavalko, E. K. (1996). Family, work, and access to health insurance among mature women. *Journal of Health and Social Behavior, 37,* 311–325.

Meyerowitz, B. E. (1980). Psychosocial correlates of breast cancer and its treatments. *Psychological Bulletin, 87,* 108–131.

Meyerowitz, B. E. (1983). Postmastectomy coping strategies and quality of life. *Health Psychology, 2,* 117–132.

Meyerowitz, B. E., & Hart, S. (1993, April). *Women and cancer: Have assumptions about women limited our research agenda?* Paper presented at the Women's Psychological and Physical Health Conference, Lawrence, KS.

Mezick, E. J., Matthews, K. A., Hall, M., Strollo, P. J., Buysse, D. J., Kamarck, T. W., et al. (2008). Influence of race and socioeconomic status on sleep: Pittsburgh sleep SCORE project. *Psychosomatic Medicine, 70,* 410–416.

Mezzacappa, E. S., Kelsey, R. M., Katkin, E. S., & Sloan, R. P. (2001). Vagal rebound and recovery from psychological stress. *Psychosomatic Medicine, 63,* 650–657.

Michael, Y. L., Carlson, N. E., Chlebowski, R. T., Aickin, M., Weihs, K. L., Ockene, J. K., et al. (2009). Influence of stressors on breast cancer incidence in the women's health initiative. *Health Psychology, 28,* 137–146.

Michaud, D. S., Liu, S., Giovannucci, E., Willett, W. C., Colditz, G. A., & Fuchs, C. S. (2002). Dietary sugar, glycemic load, and pancreatic cancer risk in a prospective study. *Journal of the National Cancer Institute, 94,* 1293–1300.

Michela, J. L. (1987). Interpersonal and individual impacts of a husband's heart attack. In A. Baum & J. E. Singer (Eds.), *Handbook of psychology and health* (Vol. 5, pp. 255–301). Hillsdale, NJ: Erlbaum.

Michie, S., Abraham, C., Whittington, C., McAteer, J., & Gupta, S. (2009). Effective techniques in healthy eating and physical activity interventions: A meta-regression. *Health Psychology, 28,* 690–701.

Midei, A. J., & Matthews, K. A. (2009). Social relationships and negative emotional traits are associated with central adiposity and arterial stiffness in healthy adolescents. *Health Psychology, 28,* 347–353.

Midei, A. J., & Matthews, K. A., & Bromberger, J. T. (2010). Childhood abuse is associated with adiposity in midlife women: Possible pathways through trait anger and reproductive hormones. *Psychosomatic Medicine, 72,* 215–223.

Millar, M. G., & Millar, K. (1996). The effects of anxiety on response times to disease detection and health promotion behaviors. *Journal of Behavioral Medicine, 19,* 401–414.

Miller, G. E., & Blackwell, E. (2006). Turning up the heat: Inflammation as a mechanism linking chronic stress, depression, and heart disease. *Current Directions in Psychological Science, 15,* 269–272.

Miller, G. E., & Chen, E. (2007). Unfavorable socioeconomic conditions in early life presage expression of proinflammatory phenotype in adolescence. *Psychosomatic Medicine, 69,* 402–409.

Miller, G. E., Chen, E., & Zhou, E. S. (2007). If it goes up, must it come down? Chronic stress and the hypothalamic-pituitary-adrenocortical axis in humans. *Psychological Bulletin, 133,* 25–45.

Miller, G. E., & Cohen, S. (2001). Psychological interventions and the immune system: A meta-analytic review and critique. *Health Psychology, 20,* 47–63.

Miller, G. E., Cohen, S., & Herbert, T. B. (1999). Pathways linking major depression and immunity in ambulatory female patients. *Psychosomatic Medicine, 61,* 850–860.

Miller, G. E., Cohen, S., Pressman, S., Barkin, A., Rabin, B. S., & Treanor, J. J. (2004). Psychological stress and antibody response to influenza vaccination: When is the critical period for stress, and how does it get inside the body? *Psychosomatic Medicine, 66,* 215–223.

Miller, G. E., Cohen, S., & Ritchey, A. K. (2002). Chronic psychological stress and the regulation of pro-inflammatory cytokines: A glucocorticoid-resistance model. *Health Psychology, 21,* 531–541.

Miller, G. E., Rohleder, N., & Cole, S. W. (2009). Chronic interpersonal stress predicts activation of pro- and anti-inflammatory signaling pathways 6 months later. *Psychosomatic Medicine, 71,* 57–62.

Miller, K. A., Siscovick, D. S., Sheppard, L., Shepherd, K., Sullivan, J. H., Anderson, G. L., et al. (2007). Long-term exposure to air pollution and incidence of cardiovascular events in women. *The New England Journal of Medicine, 356,* 447–458.

Miller, M., Mangano, C. C., Beach, V., Kop, W. J., & Vogel, R. A. (2010). Divergent effects of joyful and anxiety-provoking music on endothelial vasoreactivity. *Psychosomatic Medicine, 72,* 354–356.

Miller, N. E. (1989). Placebo factors in types of treatment: Views of a psychologist. In M. Shepherd & N. Sartorius (Eds.), *Non-specific aspects of treatment* (pp. 39–56). Lewiston, NY: Hans Huber.

Miller, W. R., & Rose, G. S. (2009). Toward a theory of motivational interviewing. *American Psychologist, 64,* 527–537.

Mills, P. J., Meck, J. V., Waters, W. W., D'Aunno, D., & Ziegler, M. G. (2001). Peripheral leukocyte subpopulations and catecholamine levels in astronauts as a function of mission duration. *Psychosomatic Medicine, 63,* 886–890.

Mills, R. T., & Krantz, D. S. (1979). Information, choice, and reactions to stress: A field experiment in a blood bank with laboratory analogue. *Journal of Personality and Social Psychology, 4,* 608–620.

Milne, H. M., Wallman, K. E., Gordon, S., & Courneya, K. S. (2008). Impact of a combined resistance and aerobic exercise program on motivational variables in breast cancer survivors: A randomized controlled trial. *Annals of Behavioral Medicine, 36,* 158–166.

Ming, E. E., Adler, G. K., Kessler, R. C., Fogg, L. F., Matthews, K. A., Herd, J. A., et al. (2004). Cardiovascular reactivity to work stress predicts subsequent onset of hypertension: The air traffic controller health change study. *Psychosomatic Medicine, 66,* 459–465.

Miniño, A. M. (2010). Mortality among teenagers aged 12–19 years: United States, 1999–2006. *NCHS Data Brief, 37,* 1–8.

Minkler, M., Fuller-Thomson, E., & Guralnik, J. M. (2006). Gradient of disability across the socioeconomic spectrum in the United States. *The New England Journal of Medicine, 355,* 695–702.

Mintzer, J. E., Rubert, M. P., Loewenstein, D., Gamez, E., Millor, A., Quinteros, R., et al. (1992). Daughters caregiving for Hispanic and non-Hispanic Alzheimer patients: Does ethnicity make a difference? *Community Mental Health Journal, 28,* 293–303.

Mirowsky, J., & Ross, C. E. (2007). Creative work and health. *Journal of Health and Social Behavior, 48,* 385–403.

Mitchell, J. E., Agras, S., & Wonderlich, S. (2007). Treatment of bulimia nervosa: Where are we and where are we going? *International Journal of Eating Disorders, 40,* 95–101.

Mitchell, J. E., Laine, D. E., Morley, J. E., & Levine, A. S. (1986). Naloxone but not CCK–8 may attenuate binge-eating behavior in patients with the bulimia syndrome. *Biological Psychiatry, 21,* 1399–1406.

Mittag, W., & Schwarzer, R. (1993). Interaction of employment status and self-efficacy on alcohol consumption: A two-wave study on stressful life transitions. *Psychology and Health, 8,* 77–87.

Mittermaier, C., Dejaco, C., Waldhoer, T., Oefferlbauer-Ernst, A., Miehsler, W., Beier, M., et al. (2004). Impact of depressive mood on relapse in patients with inflammatory bowel disease: A prospective 18-month follow-up study. *Psychosomatic Medicine, 66,* 79–84.

Mohr, D., Bedantham, K., Neylan, T., Metzler, T. J., Best, S., & Marmar, C. R. (2003). The mediating effects of sleep in the relationship between traumatic stress and health symptoms in urban police officers. *Psychosomatic Medicine, 65,* 485–489.

Mohr, D. C., Goodkin, D. E., Nelson, S., Cox, D., & Weiner, M. (2002). Moderating effects of coping on the relationship between stress and the development of new brain lesions in multiple sclerosis. *Psychosomatic Medicine, 64,* 803–809.

Mohr, D., Hart, S. L., & Goldberg, A. (2003). Effects of treatment for depression on fatigue in multiple sclerosis. *Psychosomatic Medicine, 65,* 542–547.

Mohr, D. C., Hart, S., & Vella, L. (2007). Reduction in disability in a randomized controlled trial of telephone-administered cognitive-behavioral therapy. *Health Psychology, 26,* 554–563.

Mokdad, A. H., Marks, J. S., Stroup, D. F., & Gerberding, J. L. (2004). Actual cause of death in the United Stated, 2000. *Journal of the American Medical Society, 291,* 1238–1245.

Moller, J., Hallqvist, J., Diderichsen, F., Theorell, T., Reuterwall, C., & Ahlbom, A. (1999). Do episodes of anger trigger myocardial infarction? A case-crossover analysis in the Stockholm Heart Epidemiology Program (SHEEP). *Psychosomatic Medicine, 61,* 842–849.

Molloy, G. J., Johnston, M., Johnston, D. W., Pollard, B., Morrison, V., Bonetti, D., et al. (2008). Spousal caregiver confidence and recovery from ambulatory activity limitations in stroke survivors. *Health Psychology, 27,* 286–290.

Molloy, G. J., Perkins-Porras, L., Strike, P. C., & Steptoe, A. (2008). Type-D personality and cortisol in survivors of acute coronary syndrome. *Psychosomatic Medicine, 70,* 863–868.

Mommersteeg, P. M., Denollet, J., Kavelaars, A., Geuze, E., Vermetten, E., & Heijnen, C. J. (2010). Type D personality, temperament, and mental health in military personnel awaiting deployment. *International Journal of Behavioral Medicine.*

Mommersteeg, P. M. C., Keijsers, G. P. J., Heijnen, C. J., Verbraak, M. J. P. M., & van Doornen, L. J. P. (2006). Cortisol deviations in people with burnout before and after psychotherapy: A pilot study. *Health Psychology, 25,* 243–248.

Monson, C. M., Schnurr, P. P., Resnick, P. A., Friedman, M. J., Young-Xu, Y., & Stevens, S. P. (2006). Cognitive processing therapy for veterans with military-related posttraumatic stress disorder. *Journal of Consulting and Clinical Psychology, 74,* 898–907.

Montano, D. E., & Taplin, S. H. (1991). A test of an expanded theory of reasoned action to predict mammography participation. *Social Science and Medicine, 32,* 733–741.

Monteleone, P., Luisi, M., Colurcio, B., Casarosa, E., Ioime, R., Genazzani, A. R., et al. (2001). Plasma levels of neuroactive steroids are increased in untreated women with anorexia nervosa or bulimia nervosa. *Psychosomatic Medicine, 63,* 62–68.

Monteleone, P., Martiadis, V., Colurcio, B., & Maj, M. (2002). Leptin secretion is related to chronicity and severity of the illness in bulimia nervosa. *Psychosomatic Medicine, 64,* 874–879.

Montgomery, G. H., & Bovbjerg, D. H. (2004). Presurgery distress and specific response expectancies predict postsurgery outcomes in surgery patients confronting breast cancer. *Health Psychology, 23,* 381–387.

Montgomery, G. H., Kangas, M., David, D., Hallquist, M. N., Green, S., Bovbjerg, D. H., et al. (2009). Fatigue during breast cancer radiotherapy: An initial randomized study of cognitive-behavioral therapy plus hypnosis. *Health Psychology, 28,* 317–322.

Moody, L., McCormick, K., & Williams, A. (1990). Disease and symptom severity, functional status, and quality of life in chronic bronchitis and emphysema (CBE). *Journal of Behavioral Medicine, 13,* 297–306.

Moons, W. G., Eisenberger, N. I., & Taylor, S. E. (2010). Anger and fear responses to stress have different biological profiles. *Brain, Behavior, and Immunity, 24,* 215–219.

Mooradian, A. D., Perryman, K., Fitten, J., Kavonian, G. D., & Morley, J. E. (1988). Cortical function in elderly non-insulin dependent diabetic patients. *Archives of Internal Medicine, 148,* 2369–2372.

Moos, R. H. (1988). Life stressors and coping resources influence health and well-being. *Psychological Assessment, 4,* 133–158.

Moos, R. H., Brennan, P. L., & Moos, B. S. (1991). Short-term processes of remission and nonremission among later-life problem drinkers. *Alcoholism: Clinical and Experimental Review, 15,* 948–955.

Moos, R. H., & Schaefer, J. A. (1987). Evaluating health care work settings: A holistic conceptual framework. *Psychology and Health, 1,* 97–122.

Mora, P. A., Halm, E., Leventhal, H., & Ceric, F. (2007). Elucidating the relationship between negative affectivity and symptoms: The role of illness-specific affective responses. *Annals of Behavioral Medicine, 34,* 77–86.

Morell, V. (1993). Huntington's gene finally found. *Science, 260,* 28–30.

Morens, D. M., Folkers, G. K., & Fauci, A. S. (2004). The challenge of emerging and re-emerging infectious diseases. *Nature, 430,* 242–249.

Morgan, D. L. (1985). Nurses' perceptions of mental confusion in the elderly: Influence of resident and setting characteristics. *Journal of Health and Social Behavior, 26,* 102–112.

Morin, C. M., Rodrigue, S., & Ivers, H. (2003). Role of stress, arousal, and coping skills in primary insomnia. *Psychosomatic Medicine, 65,* 259–267.

Morisky, D. E., Stein, J. A., Chiao, C., Ksobiech, K., & Malow, R. (2006). Impact of a social influence intervention on condom use and sexually transmitted infections among establishment-based female sex workers in the Philippines: A multilevel analysis. *Health Psychology, 25,* 595–603.

Morley, J. E., Kay, N. E., & Solomon, G. P. (1988). Opioid peptides, stress, and immune function. In Y. Tache, J. E. Morley, & M. R. Brown (Eds.), *Neuropeptides and stress* (pp. 222–234). New York: Springer.

Morris, P. L. P., & Raphael, B. (1987). Depressive disorder associated with physical illness: The impact of stroke. *General Hospital Psychiatry, 9,* 324–330.

Morrongiello, B. A., Corbett, M., & Bellissimo, A. (2008). "Do as I say, not as I do": Family influences on children's safety and risk behaviors. *Health Psychology, 27,* 498–503.

Morton, G. J., Cummings, D. E., Baskin, D. G., Barsh, G. S., & Schwartz, M. W. (2006). Central nervous system control of food intake and body weight. *Nature, 443,* 289–295.

Moser, D. K., & Dracup, K. (2004). Role of spousal anxiety and depression in patients' psychosocial recovery after a cardiac event. *Psychosomatic Medicine, 66,* 527–532.

Moses, H. (Producer). (1984, February 18). Helen. In *60 Minutes.* New York: CBS.

Moskowitz, J. T. (2003). Positive affect predicts lower risk of AIDS mortality. *Psychosomatic Medicine, 65,* 620–626.

Moskowitz, J. T., Epel, E. S., & Acree, M. (2008). Positive affect uniquely predicts lower risk of mortality in people with diabetes. *Health Psychology, 27,* S73–S82.

Moss-Morris, R., Petrie, K. J., & Weinman, J. (1996). Functioning in chronic fatigue syndrome: Do illness perceptions play a regulatory role? *British Journal of Health Psychology, 1,* 15–25.

Moss-Morris, R., & Spence, M. (2006). To "lump" or to "split" the functional somatic syndromes: Can infectious and emotional risk factors differentiate between the onset of chronic fatigue syndrome and irritable bowel syndrome? *Psychosomatic Medicine, 68,* 463–469.

Mostofsky, D. I. (1998). Behavior modification and therapy in the management of epileptic disorders. In D. I. Mostofsky & Y. Loyning (Eds.), *The neurobehavioral treatment of epilepsy.* Hillsdale, NJ: Erlbaum.

Motivala, S. J., Hurwitz, B. E., Llabre, M. M., Klimas, N. G., Fletcher, M. A., Antoni, M. H., et al. (2003). Psychological distress is associated with decreased memory and helper T-cell and B-cell counts in pre-AIDS HIV seropositive men and women but only in those with low viral load. *Psychosomatic Medicine, 65,* 627–635.

Motivala, S. J., & Irwin, M. R. (2007). Sleep and immunity: Cytokine pathways linking sleep and health outcomes. *Current Directions in Psychological Science, 16,* 21–25.

Motivala, S. J., Tomiyama, A. J., Ziegler, M., Khandrika, S., & Irwin, M. R. (2009). Nocturnal levels of ghrelin and leptin and sleep in chronic insomnia. *Psychoneuroendocrinology, 34,* 540–545.

Motl, R. W., Dishman, R. K., Ward, D. S., Saunders, R. P., Dowda, M., Felton, G., et al. (2005). Comparison of barriers self-efficacy and perceived behavioral control for explaining physical activity across year 1 among adolescent girls. *Health Psychology, 24,* 106–111.

Motl, R. W., & McAuley, E. (2009). Pathways between physical activity and quality of life in adults with multiple sclerosis. *Health Psychology, 28,* 682–689.

Motl, R. W., & Snook, E. M. (2008). Physical activity, self-efficacy, and quality of life in multiple sclerosis. *Annals of Behavioral Medicine, 35,* 111–115.

Moyer, A. (1997). Psychosocial outcomes of breast-conserving surgery versus mastectomy: A meta-analytic review. *Health Psychology, 16,* 284–298.

Moyer, A., & Salovey, P. (1996). Psychosocial sequelae of breast cancer and its treatment. *Annals of Behavioral Medicine, 18,* 110–125.

Moynihan, J. A., & Ader, R. (1996). Psychoneuroimmunology: Animal models of disease. *Psychosomatic Medicine, 58,* 546–558.

Moynihan, J. A., Larson, M. R., Treanor, J., Duberstein, P. R., Power, A., Shore, B., et al. (2004). Psychosocial factors and the response to influenza vaccination in older adults. *Psychosomatic Medicine, 66,* 950–953.

Mugavero, M. J., Raper, J. L., Reif, S., Whetten, K., Leserman, J., Thielman, N. M., et al. (2009). Overload: Impact of incident stressful events on antiretroviral medication adherence and virologic failure in a longitudinal, multisite human immunodeficiency virus cohort study. *Psychosomatic Medicine, 71,* 920–926.

Muhonen, T., & Torkelson, E. (2003). The demand-control-support model and health among women and men in similar occupations. *Journal of Behavioral Medicine, 26,* 601–613.

Mullen, B., & Smyth, J. M. (2004). Immigrant suicide rates as a function of ethnophaulisms: Hate speech predicts death. *Psychosomatic Medicine, 66,* 343–348.

Mullen, B., & Suls, J. (1982). The effectiveness of attention and rejection as coping styles: A meta-analysis of temporal differences. *Journal of Psychosomatic Research, 26,* 43–49.

Mullen, P. D., & Green, L. W. (1985). Meta-analysis points way toward more effective medication teaching. *Promoting Health,* pp. 6–8.

Murphy, D. A., Stein, J. A., Schlenger, W., Maibach, E., & National Institute of Mental Health Multisite HIV Prevention Trial Group. (2001). Conceptualizing the multidimensional nature of self-efficacy: Assessment of situational context and level of behavioral challenge to maintain safer sex. *Health Psychology, 20,* 281–290.

Murphy, K. (2000, May 8). An "epidemic" of sleeplessness. *Business Week,* pp. 161–162.

Murphy, S. L. (2000). Deaths: Final data for 1998. *National Vital Statistics Reports* (NCHS), pp. 26, 73.

Murphy, T. J., Pagano, R. R., & Marlatt, G. A. (1986). Lifestyle modification with heavy alcohol drinkers: Effects of aerobic exercise and meditation. *Addictive Behaviors, 11,* 175–186.

Murray, D. M., Davis-Hearn, M., Goldman, A. I., Pirie, P., & Luepker, R. V. (1988). Four- and five-year follow-up results from four seventh-grade smoking prevention strategies. *Journal of Behavioral Medicine, 11,* 395–406.

Musher, D. M., & Musher, B. L. (2004). Contagious acute gastrointestinal infections. *The New England Journal of Medicine, 351,* 2417–2427.

Musick, M. A., House, J. S., & Williams, D. R. (2004). Attendance at religious services and mortality in a national sample. *Journal of Health and Social Behavior, 45,* 198–213.

Mutterperl, J. A., & Sanderson, C. A. (2002). Mind over matter: Internalization of the thinness norm as a moderator of responsiveness to norm misperception education in college women. *Health Psychology, 21,* 519–523.

Myers, H. F. (2009). Ethnicity and socio-economic status-related stresses in context: An intergrative review and conceptual model. *Journal of Behavioral Medicine, 32,* 9–19.

Myers, M. M. (1996). Enduring effects of infant feeding experiences on adult blood pressure. *Psychosomatic Medicine, 58,* 612–621.

Myers, R. E. (2005). Decision counseling in cancer prevention and control. *Health Psychology, 24,* S71–S77.

Myint, P. K., Luben, R. N., Surtees, P. G., Wainwright, N. W. J., Welch, A. A., Bingham, S. A., et al. (2007). Self-reported mental health-related quality of life and mortality in men and women in the European perspective investigation into cancer (EPIC-Norfolk): A prospective population study. *Psychosomatic Medicine, 69,* 410–414.

Naar-King, S., Wright, K., Parsons, J. T., Frey, M., Templin, T., & Ondersma, S. (2006). Transtheoretical model and condom use in HIV-positive youths. *Health Psychology, 25,* 648–652.

Nakao, M., Nomura, S., Shimosawa, T., Yoshiuchi, K., Kumano, H., Kuboki, T., et al. (1997). Clinical effects of blood pressure biofeedback treatment on hypertension by auto-shaping. *Psychosomatic Medicine, 59,* 331–338.

Naliboff, B. D., Mayer, M., Fass, R., Fitzgerald, L. Z., Chang, L., Bolus, R., et al. (2004). The effect of life stress on symptoms of heartburn. *Psychosomatic Medicine, 66,* 426–434.

Napolitano, M. A., Fotheringham, M., Tate, D., Sciamanna, C., Leslie, E., Owen, N., et al. (2003). Evaluation of an Internet-based physical activity intervention: A preliminary investigation. *Annals of Behavioral Medicine, 25,* 92–99.

Napolitano, M. A., Papandonatos, G. D., Lewis, B. A., Whiteley, J. A., Williams, D. M., King, A. C., et al. (2008). Mediators of physical activity behavior change: A multivariate approach. *Health Psychology, 28,* 409–418.

Nash, J. M. (2003, August 25). Obesity goes global. *Time,* pp. 53–54.

Nash, J. M., Williams, D. M., Nicholson, R., & Trask, P. C. (2006). The contribution of pain-related anxiety to disability from headache. *Journal of Behavioral Medicine, 29,* 61–67.

Nater, U. M., Lin, J. M., Maloney, E. M., Jones, J. F., Tian, H., Boneva, R. S., et al. (2009). Psychiatric comorbidity in persons with chronic fatigue syndrome identified from the Georgia population. *Psychosomatic Medicine, 71,* 557–565.

National Cancer Institute. (2005). *Cancer health disparities: Fact sheet.* Retrieved on March 1, 2007, from http://www.cancer.gov/cancertopics/factsheet/cancerhealthdisparities

National Cancer Institute Breast Cancer Screening Consortium. (1990). Screening mammography: A missing clinical opportunity? Results of the NCI Breast Cancer Screening Consortium and National Health Interview survey studies. *Journal of the American Medical Association, 264,* 54–58.

National Center for Complementary and Alternative Medicine. (2004). *Expanding horizons of health care: Strategic plan 2005–2009* (NIH Publication No. 04–5568).

National Center for Complementary and Alternative Medicine. (2009). *National health statistic report: Cost of complementary and alternative medicine (CAM) and frequency of visits to CAM practitioners: United States, 2007.* Retrieved September 28, 2009, from http://nccam.nih.gov/news/camstats/costs/nhsrn18.pdf

National Center for Health Statistics. (2007). *10 Leading Causes of Injury Deaths by Age Group Highlighting Unintentional Injury Deaths, United States — 2007.* Retrieved January 30, 2011, from http://www.cdc.gov/injury/wisqars/pdf/Unintentional_2007-a.pdf

National Center for Health Statistics. (2009). *Health, United States, 2008 with special feature on the health of young adults.* Retrieved September 29, 2009, from http://www.cdc.gov/nchs/data/hus/hus08.pdf

National Center for HIV, STD, & TB Prevention. (2009). *HIV: Basic statistics.* Retrieved October 20, 2009, from http://www.cdc.gov/hiv/topics/surveillance/basic.htm#hivaidsexposure

National Committee for Quality Assurance. (2001). *Health plan report card.* Retrieved from http://www.ncqa.org/index.asp

National Heart, Lung, and Blood Institute. (2004). *Body mass index table.* Retrieved from http://www.nhlbi.nih.gov/guidelines/obesity/bmi_tbl.htm

National Heart, Lung, and Blood Institute. (2008). *What is asthma?* Retrieved October 6, 2009, from http://www.nhlbi.nih.gov/health/dci/Diseases/Asthma/Asthma_WhatIs.html

National Heart, Lung, and Blood Institute. (2010a). *What is cholesterol?* Retrieved June 6, 2010, from http://nhlbi.nih.gov/health/dci/Disease/Atherosclerosis/Atherosclerosis_WhatIs.html

National Heart, Lung, and Blood Institute. (2010b). *What are the signs and symptoms of atrial fibrillation?* Retrieved June 6, 2010, from http://nhlbi.nih.gov/health/dci/images/atrial_fib_stroke.jpg

National Highway Traffic Safety Administration. (2008). *Traffic safety facts 2008 data: Alcohol-impaired driving.* Retrieved October 5, 2009, from: http://www-nrd.nhtsa.dot.gov/Pubs/811155.pdf

National Hospice and Palliative Care Organization. (2007). *Keys to quality care.* Retrieved June 13, 2007, from http://www.nhpco.org/i4a/pages/index.cfm?pageid=3303

National Institute of Neurological Disorders and Stroke. (2006). *Brain basics: Understanding sleep.* Retrieved April 25, 2007, from http://www.ninds.nih.gov/disorders/brain_basics/understanding_sleep.htm#sleep_disorders

National Institute of Neurological Disorders and Stroke. (2007). *Pain: Hope through research.* Retrieved April 14, 2007, from http://www.ninds.nih.gov/disorders/chronic_pain/detail_chronic_pain.htm

National Institute on Alcohol Abuse and Alcoholism. (2000a). *Alcohol alert: New advances in alcoholism treatment.* Retrieved from www.niaaa.nih.gov

National Institute on Alcohol Abuse and Alcoholism. (2000b). *10th special report to the U.S. Congress on alcohol and health.* Retrieved from http://silk.nih.gov/silk/niaaa1/publication/10report/10-order.htm

National Institute on Alcohol Abuse and Alcoholism. (2000c). *Estimated economic costs of alcohol abuse in the United States, 1992 and 1998.* Retrieved January 13, 2011, from http://www.niaaa.nih.gov/Resources/QuickFacts/EconomicData/Pages/cost8.aspx

National Institute on Alcohol Abuse and Alcoholism. (2004). *A snapshot of annual high-risk college drinking consequences.* Retrieved October 1, 2004, from http://www.collegedrinkingprevention.gov/facts/snapshot.aspx

National Institute on Alcohol Abuse and Alcoholism. (2009). *A snapshot of annual high-risk college drinking consequences.* Retrieved October 5, 2009, from http://www.collegedrinkingprevention.gov/StatsSummaries/snapshot.aspx

National Institute on Diabetes and Digestive and Kidney Disorders. (1999). *Diabetes control and complications trial.* (National Institutes of Health Publication No. 97–3874). Retrieved from http://www.niddk.nih.gov/health/diabetes/pubs/dcct1/dcct.htm

National Institute on Diabetes and Digestive and Kidney Disorders. (2007). *Kidney disease of diabetes.* USRDS 2007 Annual Report Data. Retrieved from http://niddk.nih.gov/kudiseases/ pubs/kdd/

National Institute on Drug Abuse. (2008). *Treatment statistics: June 2008.* Retrieved October 12, 2009, from http://www.nida.nih.gov/PDF/Info-Facts/TreatmentStats08.pdf

National Multiple Sclerosis Society. (2009). *What is multiple sclerosis?* Retrieved February 4, 2011, from http://www.nationalmssociety.org/about-multiple-sclerosis/what-we-know-about-ms/what-is-ms/index.aspx

National Safety Council. (2009). *Safe bicycling.* Retrieved September 30, 2009, from http://downloads.nsc.org/pdf/factsheets/Safe_Bicycling.pdf

Navarro, A. M. (1996). Cigarette smoking among adult Latinos: The California tobacco baseline survey. *Annals of Behavioral Medicine, 18,* 238–245.

Nealey-Moore, J. B., Smith, T. W., Uchino, B. N., Hawkins, M. W., & Olson-Cerny, C. (2007). Cardiovascular reactivity during positive and negative marital interactions. *Journal of Behavioral Medicine, 30,* 505–519.

Neighbors, C., Lewis, M. A., Bergstrom, R. L., & Larimer, M. E. (2006). Being controlled by normative influences: Self-determination as a moderator of a normative feedback alcohol intervention. *Health Psychology, 25,* 571–579.

Nelson, C., Franks, S., Brose, A., Raven, P., Williamson, J., Shi, X., McGill, J., et al. (2005). The influence of hostility and family history of cardiovascular disease on autonomic activation in response to controllable versus noncontrollable stress, anger imagery induction, and relaxation imagery. *Journal of Behavioral Medicine, 28,* 213–221.

Nemeroff, C. B., Bremner, J. D., Foa, E. B., Mayberg, H. S., North, C. S., & Stein, M. B. (2006). Posttraumatic stress disorder: A state-of-the-science review. *Journal of Psychiatric Research, 40,* 1–21.

Nes, L. S., Roach, A. R., & Segerstrom, S. C. (2009). Executive functions, self-regulation, and chronic pain: A review. *Annals of Behavioral Medicine, 37,* 173–183.

Nestle, M. (2003, February 7). The ironic politics of obesity. *Science, 299,* p. 781.

Nestle, M. (2006). Food marketing and childhood obesity—a matter of policy. *The New England Journal of Medicine, 354,* 2527–2529.

Neu, P., Schlattmann, P., Schilling, A., & Hartmann, A. (2004). Cerebrovascular reactivity in major depression: A pilot study. *Psychosomatic Medicine, 66,* 6–8.

Neu, S., & Kjellstrand, C. M. (1986). Stopping long-term dialysis: An empirical study of withdrawal of life-supporting treatment. *The New England Journal of Medicine, 314,* 14–19.

Neugebauer, A., Katz, P. P., & Pasch, L. A. (2003). Effect of valued activity disability, social comparisons, and satisfaction with ability on depressive symptoms in rheumatoid arthritis. *Health Psychology, 22,* 253–262.

Neuling, S. J., & Winefield, H. R. (1988). Social support and recovery after surgery for breast cancer: Frequency and correlates of supportive behaviors by family, friends, and surgeon. *Social Science and Medicine, 27,* 385–392.

Neumann, M., Bensing, J., Mercer, S., Ernstmann, N., Ommen, O., & Pfaff, H. (2009). Analyzing the "nature" and "specific effectiveness" of clinical empathy: A theoretical overview and contribution towards a theory-based research agenda. *Patient Education and Counseling, 74,* 339–346.

Neumann, S. A., Waldstein, S. R., Sollers, J. J., Thayer, J. F., & Sorkin, J. D. (2004). Hostility and distraction have differential influences on cardiovascular recovery from anger recall in women. *Health Psychology, 23,* 631–640.

Neumark-Sztainer, D., Wall, M. M., Story, M., & Perry, C. L. (2003). Correlates of unhealthy weight-control behaviors among adolescents: Implications for prevention programs. *Health Psychology, 22,* 88–98.

New York Presbyterian Hospital. (2007). *Chronic pain.* Retrieved May 16, 2007, from http://www.nyp.org/health/chronic-pain.html

New York Times. (2000a, September 12). Men, women, and battles of the bulges, p. D8.

New York Times. (2000b, October 3). Passing along the diet-and-binge habit, p. D8.

New York Times. (2001, May 22). Diabetics reminded of heart risk, p. D8.

New York Times. (2002, March 25). Drinking still on rise at women's colleges, p. A16.

Newcomb, M. D., Rabow, J., Monte, M., & Hernandez, A. C. R. (1991). Informal drunk driving intervention: Psychosocial correlates among young adult women and men. *Journal of Applied Social Psychology, 21,* 1988–2006.

Newman, S. (1984). The psychological consequences of cerebrovascular accident and head injury. In R. Fitzpatrick et al. (Eds.), *The experience of illness.* London, England: Tavistock.

Newsom, J. T., Knapp, J. E., & Schulz, R. (1996). Longitudinal analysis of specific domains of internal control and depressive symptoms in patients with recurrent cancer. *Health Psychology, 15,* 323–331.

Newsom, J. T., Mahan, T. L., Rook, K. S., & Krause, N. (2008). Stable negative social exchange and health. *Health Psychology, 27,* 78–86.

Newsom, J. T., & Schulz, R. (1998). Caregiving from the recipient's perspective: Negative reactions to being helped. *Health Psychology, 17,* 172–181.

Newton, T. L., & Sanford, J. M. (2003). Conflict structure moderates associations between cardiovascular reactivity and negative marital interaction. *Health Psychology, 22,* 270–278.

Neylan, T. C., Metzler, T. J., Best, S. R., Weiss, D. S., Fagan, J. A., Liberman, A., et al. (2002). Critical incident exposure and sleep quality in police officers. *Psychosomatic Medicine, 64,* 345–352.

Ng, D. M., & Jeffery, R. W. (2003). Relationships between perceived stress and health behaviors in a sample of working adults. *Health Psychology, 22,* 638–642.

Niaura, R., Todaro, J. F., Stroud, L., Spiro, A., III, Ward, K. D., & Weiss, S. (2002). Hostility, the metabolic syndrome and incident coronary heart disease. *Health Psychology, 21,* 588–593.

Nicassio, P. M., Meyerowitz, B. E., & Kerns, R. D. (2004). The future of health psychology interventions. *Health Psychology, 23,* 132–137.

Nicassio, P. M., Radojevic, V., Schoenfeld-Smith, K., & Dwyer, K. (1995). The contribution of family cohesion and the pain-coping process to depressive symptoms in fibromyalgia. *Annals of Behavioral Medicine, 17,* 349–356.

Nichol, K. L., Nordin, J., Mullooly, J., Lask, R., Fillbrandt, K., & Iwane, M. (2003). Influenza vaccination and reduction in hospitalizations for cardiac disease and stroke among the elderly. *The New England Journal of Medicine, 348,* 1322–1332.

Nicholson, A., Fuhrer, R., & Marmot, M. (2005). Psychological distress as a predictor of CHD events in men: The effect of persistence and components of risk. *Psychosomatic Medicine, 67,* 522–530.

Nicholson, A., Rose, R., & Bobak, M. (2010). Associations between different dimensions of religious involvement and self-rated health in diverse European populations. *Health Psychology, 29,* 227–235.

Nielsen, N. R., & Grønbaek, M. (2006). Stress and breast cancer: A systematic update on the current knowledge. *Nature Clinical Practice Oncology, 3,* 612–620.

Nielsen, S. J., & Popkin, B. M. (2003). Patterns and trends in food portion sizes, 1977–1998. *Journal of the American Medical Association, 289,* 450–453.

Niemcryk, S. J., Jenkins, S. D., Rose, R. M., & Hurst, M. W. (1987). The prospective impact of psychosocial variables on rates of illness and injury in professional employees. *Journal of Occupational Medicine, 29,* 645–652.

Niemi, M. L., Laaksonen, R., Kotila, M., & Waltimo, O. (1988). Quality of life 4 years after stroke. *Stroke, 19,* 1101–1107.

Nivison, M. E., & Endresen, I. M. (1993). An analysis of relationships among environmental noise, annoyance and sensitivity to noise, and the consequences for health and sleep. *Journal of Behavioral Medicine, 16,* 257–271.

Nobles, J., & Frankenberg, E. (2009). Mothers' community participation and child health. *Journal of Health and Social Behavior, 50,* 16–30.

Nolan, R. P., Wilson, E., Shuster, M., Rowe, B. H., Stewart, D., & Zambon, S. (1999). Readiness to perform cardiopulmonary resuscitation: An emerging strategy against sudden cardiac death. *Psychosomatic Medicine, 61,* 546–551.

Nolen-Hoeksema, S., McBride, A., & Larson, J. (1997). Rumination and psychological distress among bereaved partners. *Journal of Personality and Social Psychology, 72,* 855–862.

Nollen, N., Befort, C., Pulvers, K., James, A. S., Kaur, H., Mayo, M. S., et al. (2008). Demographic and psychosocial factors associated with increased fruit and vegetable consumption among smokers in public housing enrolled in a randomized trial. *Health Psychology, 27,* S252-S259.

Nordgren, L. F., van der Pligt, J., & van Harreveld, F. (2008). The instability of health cognitions: Visceral states influence self-efficacy and related health beliefs. *Health Psychology, 27,* 722–727.

Norman, C. D., Maley, O., Skinner, H. A., & Li, X. (2008). Using the Internet to assist smoking prevention and cessation in schools: A randomized, controlled trial. *Health Psychology, 27,* 799–810.

Norris, J., Stoner, S. A., Hessler, D. M., Zawacki, T. M., George, W. H., Morrison, D. M., et al. (2009). Cognitive mediation of alcohol's effects on women's in-the-moment sexual decision making. *Health Psychology, 28,* 20–28.

North, R. B., Kidd, D. H., Olin, J., Sieracki, J. M., Farrokhi, F., Petrucci, L., et al. (2005). Spinal cord stimulation for axial low back pain. *SPINE, 30,* 1412–1418.

Northouse, L., Templin, T., & Mood, D. (2001). Couples' adjustment to breast disease during the first year following diagnosis. *Journal of Behavioral Medicine, 24,* 115–136.

Norton, T. R., Manne, S. L., Rubin, S., Hernandez, E., Carlson, J., Bergman, C., et al. (2005). Ovarian cancer patients' psychological distress: The role of physical impairment, perceived unsupportive family and friend behaviors, perceived control, and self-esteem. *Health Psychology, 24,* 143–152.

Novak, M., Ahlgren, C., & Hammarstrom, A. (2007). Inequalities in smoking: Influence of social chain of risks from adolescence to young adulthood: A prospective population-based cohort study. *International Journal of Behavioral Medicine, 14,* 181–187.

Novak, S. P., & Clayton, R. R. (2001). The influence of school environment and self-regulation on transitions between stages of cigarette smoking: A multilevel analysis. *Health Psychology, 20,* 196–207.

Nowack, R. (1992). Final ethics: Dutch discover euthanasia abuse. *Journal of NIH Research, 4,* 31–32.

Noyes, R., Hartz, A. J., Doebbeling, C. C., Malis, R. W., Happel, R. L., Werner, L. A., et al. (2003). Illness fears in the general population. *Psychosomatic Medicine, 62,* 318–325.

Nurses' Health Study. (2004). *History.* Retrieved August 1, 2004, from http://www.channing.harvard.edu/nhs/history/index.shtml

Nyamathi, A., Stein, J. A., & Brecht, M. L. (1995). Psychosocial predictors of AIDS risk behavior and drug use behavior in homeless and drug addicted women of color. *Health Psychology, 14,* 265–273.

Nylén, L., Melin, B., & Laflamme, L. (2007). Interference between work and outside-work demands relative to health: Unwinding possibilities among full-time and part-time employees. *International Journal of Behavioral Medicine, 14,* 229–236.

Obama, Barack. (2009, September). *Remarks by the president to a joint session of Congress on health care.* Speech presented at the U.S. Capitol, Capitol Hill, Washington, D.C.

Oberlander, J. (2010). A vote for health care reform. *The New England Journal of Medicine, 362,* e44(1)–e44(3).

O'Brien, A., Fries, E., & Bowen, D. (2000). The effect of accuracy of perceptions of dietary-fat intake on perceived risk and intentions to change. *Journal of Behavioral Medicine, 23,* 465–473.

O'Byrne, K. K., Peterson, L., & Saldana, L. (1997). Survey of pediatric hospitals' preparation programs: Evidence of the impact of health psychology research. *Health Psychology, 16,* 147–154.

O'Carroll, R. E., Ayling, R., O'Reilly, S. M., & North, N. T. (2003). Alexithymia and sense of coherence in patients with total spinal cord transection. *Psychosomatic Medicine, 65,* 151–155.

O'Cleirigh, C., Ironson, G., Weiss, A., & Costa, P. T. (2007). Conscientiousness predicts disease progression (CD4 number and viral load) in people living with HIV. *Health Psychology, 26,* 473–480.

O'Connor, A. (2004, February 6). Study details 30-year increase in calorie consumption. *New York Times,* p. A19.

O'Connor, D. B., Conner, M., Jones, F., McMillan, B., & Ferguson, E. (2009). Exploring the benefits of conscientiousness: An investigation of the role of daily stressors and health benefits. *Annals of Behavioral Medicine, 37,* 184–196.

O'Connor, D. B., Jones, F., Ferguson, E., Conner, M., & McMillan, B. (2008). Effects of daily hassles and eating style on eating behavior. *Health Psychology, 27,* S20–S31.

O'Connor, P. J. (2006). Improving medication adherence: Challenges for physicians, payers, and policy makers. *Archives of Internal Medicine, 166,* 1802–1804.

Ockene, J. K., Emmons, K. M., Mermelstein, R. J., Perkins, K. A., Bonollo, D. S., Voorhees, C. C., et al. (2000). Relapse and maintenance issues for smoking cessation. *Health Psychology, 19,* 17–31.

O'Donnell, M. L., Creamer, M., Elliott, P., & Bryant, R. (2007). Tonic and phasic heart rate as predictors of posttraumatic stress disorder. *Psychosomatic Medicine, 69,* 256–261.

Odendaal, J. S. J., & Meintjes, R. A. (2002). Neurophysiological correlates of affiliative behaviour between humans and dogs. *The Veterinary Journal, 165,* 296–301.

Oenema, A., Brug, J., Dijkstra, A., de Weerdt, I., & de Vries, H. (2008). Efficacy and use of an Internet-delivered computer-tailored lifestyle intervention, targetting saturated fat intake, physical activity and smoking cessation: A randomized controlled trial. *Annals of Behavioral Medicine, 35,* 125–135.

Ogden, J. (2003). Some problems with social cognition models: A pragmatic and conceptual analysis. *Health Psychology, 22,* 424–428.

Ohira, T., Diez Roux, A. V., Prineas, R. J., Kizilbash, M. A., Carnethon, M. R., & Folsom, A. R. (2008). Associations of psychosocial factors with heart rate and its short-term variability: Multi-ethnic study of atherosclerosis. *Psychosomatic Medicine, 70,* 141–146.

Oken, D. (2000). Multiaxial diagnosis and the psychosomatic model of disease. *Psychosomatic Medicine, 62,* 171–175.

O'Leary, A., Goodhardt, F., Jemmott, L. S., & Boccher-Lattimore, D. (1992). Predictors of safer sex on the college campus: A social cognitive theory analysis. *Journal of American College Health, 40,* 254–263.

O'Leary, A., Jemmott, L. S., & Jemmott, J. B. (2008). Mediation analysis of an effective sexual risk-reduction intervention for women: The importance of self-efficacy. *Health Psychology, 27,* S180–S184.

O'Leary, A., Shoor, S., Lorig, K., & Holman, H. R. (1988). A cognitive-behavioral treatment for rheumatoid arthritis. *Health Psychology, 7,* 527–544.

Oleck, J. (2001, April 23). Dieting: More fun with a buddy? *Business Week,* p. 16.

Oliver, G., Wardle, J., & Gibson, E. L. (2000). Stress and food choice: A laboratory study. *Psychosomatic Medicine, 62,* 853–865.

Olson, M. B., Krantz, D. S., Kelsey, S. F., Pepine, C. J., Sopko, G., Handberg, E., et al. (2005). Hostility scores are associated with increased risk of cardiovascular events in women undergoing coronary angiography: A report from the NHLBI-sponsored WISE study. *Psychosomatic Medicine, 67,* 546–552.

O'Malley, P. M., & Johnston, L. D. (2002). Epidemiology of alcohol and other drug use among American college students. *Journal of Studies on Alcohol, 14,* 23–39.

O'Neil, J. (2003, January 21). When aspirin can't help a heart. *New York Times,* p. D6.

Ong, A. D., Bergeman, C. S., Bisconti, T. L., & Wallace, K. A. (2006). Psychological resilience, positive emotions, and successful adaptation to stress in later life. *Journal of Personality and Social Psychology, 91,* 730–749.

Orbell, S., & Hagger, M. (2006). "When no means no": Can reactance augment the theory of planned behavior? *Health Psychology, 25,* 586–594.

Orbell, S., & Kyriakaki, M. (2008). Temporal framing and persuasion to adopt preventive health behavior: Moderating effect of individual differences in consideration of future consequences on sunscreen use. *Health Psychology, 27,* 770–779.

Orbell, S., Lidierth, P., Henderson, C. J., Geeraert, N., Uller, C., Uskul, A. K., et al. (2009). Social-cognitive beliefs, alcohol, and tobacco use: A prospective community study of change following a ban on smoking in public places. *Health Psychology, 28,* 753–761.

Oregon Department of Human Services. (2009). *2008 summary of Oregon's Death with Dignity Act.* Retrieved October 12, 2009, from http://oregon.gov/DHS/ph/pas/docs/year11.pdf

Organisation for Economic Co-operation and Development. (2007). *OECD factbook 2007—economic, environmental and social statistics: Quality of life: Health.* Retrieved April 16, 2007, from http://oberon.sourceoecd.org/vl=3821204/cl=12/nw=1/rpsv/factbook/11-01-04-g01.htm

Orleans, C. T. (2000). Promoting the maintenance of health behavior change: Recommendations for the next generation of research and practice. *Health Psychology, 19,* 76–83.

Orr, S. T., Reiter, J. P., Blazer, D. G., & James, S. A. (2007). Maternal prenatal pregnancy-related anxiety and spontaneous preterm birth in Baltimore, Maryland. *Psychosomatic Medicine, 69,* 566–570.

Oslin, D. W., Sayers, S., Ross, J., Kane, V., Have, T. T., Conigliaro, J., et al. (2003). Disease management for depression and at-risk drinking via telephone in an older population of veterans. *Psychosomatic Medicine, 65,* 931–937.

Osman, A., Barrios, F., Gutierrez, P., Kopper, B., Merrifield, T., & Grittmann, L. (2000). The pain and catastrophizing scale: Further psychometric evaluation with adult samples. *Journal of Behavioral Medicine, 23,* 351–365.

Osman, A., Barrios, F. X., Gutierrez, P. M., Schwarting, B., Kopper, B. A., & Wang, M. C. (2005). Reliability and construct validity of the pain distress inventory. *Journal of Behavioral Medicine, 28,* 169–180.

Osman, A., Breitenstein, J. L., Barrios, F. X., Gutierrez, P. M., & Kopper, B. A. (2002). The Fear of Pain Questionnaire-III: Further reliability and validity with nonclinical samples. *Journal of Behavioral Medicine, 25,* 155–173.

Osterweis, M. (1985). Bereavement care: Special opportunities for hospice. In K. Gardner (Ed.), *Quality of care for the terminally ill: An examination of the issues* (pp. 131–135). Chicago: Joint Commission on Accreditation of Hospitals.

Ostir, G. V., Berges, I. M., Markides, K. S., & Ottenbacher, K. J. (2006). Hypertension in older adults and the role of positive emotions. *Psychosomatic Medicine, 68,* 727–733.

Ostir, G. V., Berges, I. M., Ottenbacher, M. E., Clow, A., & Ottenbacher, K. J. (2008). Associations between positive emotion and recovery of functional status following stroke. *Psychosomatic Medicine, 70,* 404–409.

Owen, J. E., Klapow, J. C., Roth, D. L., & Tucker, D. C. (2004). Use of the Internet for information and support: Disclosure among persons with breast and prostate cancer. *Journal of Behavioral Medicine, 27,* 491–505.

Owens, I. P. F. (2002, September 20). Sex differences in mortality rate. *Science's Compass, 2008–2009.*

Owens, J. F., Matthews, K. A., Wing, R. R., & Kuller, L. H. (1990). Physical activity and cardiovascular risk: A cross-sectional study of middle-aged premenopausal women. *Preventive Medicine, 19,* 147–157.

Oxlad, M., Stubberfield, J., Stuklis, R., Edwards, J., & Wade, T. D. (2006). Psychological risk factors for increased post-operative length of hospital stay following coronary artery bypass graft surgery. *Journal of Behavioral Medicine, 29,* 179–190.

Ozer, E. J., & Weiss, D. S. (2004). Who develops posttraumatic stress disorder? *Current Directions in Psychological Science, 13,* 169–172.

Pacchetti, C., Mancini, F., Aglieri, R., Fundaro, C., Martignoni, E., & Nappi, G. (2000). Active music therapy in Parkinson's disease: An integrative method for motor and emotional rehabilitation. *Psychosomatic Medicine, 62,* 386–393.

Paffenbarger, R. S., Jr., Hyde, R. T., Wing, A. L., & Hsieh, C. C. (1986). Physical activity, all-cause mortality, and longevity of college alumni. *The New England Journal of Medicine, 314,* 605–613.

Pagoto, S., McChargue, D., & Fuqua, R. W. (2003). Effects of a multicomponent intervention on motivation and sun protection behaviors among Midwestern beachgoers. *Health Psychology, 22,* 429–433.

Pahl, K., Brook, D. W., Morojele, N. K., & Brook, J. S. (2010). Nicotine dependence and problem behaviors among urban South African adolescents. *Journal of Behavioral Medicine, 33,* 101–109.

Painter, J. E., Borba, C. P. C., Hynes, M., Mays, D., & Glanz, K. (2008). The use of theory in health behavior research from 2000 to 2005: A systematic review. *Annals of Behavioral Medicine, 35,* 358–362.

Pakenham, K. I. (2005). Benefit finding in multiple sclerosis and associations with positive and negative outcomes. *Health Psychology, 24,* 123–132.

Palmer, S. C., Kagee, A., Coyne, J. C., & DeMichele, A. (2004). Experience of trauma, distress, and posttraumatic stress disorder among breast cancer patients. *Psychosomatic Medicine, 66,* 258–264.

Pampel, F. C. (2001). Cigarette diffusion and sex differences in smoking. *Journal of Health and Social Behavior, 42,* 388–404.

Pampel, F. C., & Rogers, R. G. (2004). Socioeconomic status, smoking, and health: A test of competing theories of cumulative advantage. *Journal of Health and Social Behavior, 45,* 306–321.

Pantin, H., Prado, G., Lopez, B., Huang, S., Tapia, M. I., Schwartz, S. J., et al. (2009). A randomized controlled trial of familias unidas for hispanic adolescents with behavior problems. *Psychosomatic Medicine, 71,* 987–995.

Papies, E. K., Stroebe, W., & Aarts, H. (2008). Understanding dieting: A social cognitive analysis of hedonic processes in self-regulation. *European Review of Social Psychology, 19,* 339–383.

Paquet, C., Dubé, L., Gauvin, L., Kestens, Y., & Daniel, M. (2010). Sense of mastery and metabolic risk: Moderating role of the local fast-food environment. *Psychosomatic Medicine, 72,* 324–331.

Pardine, P., & Napoli, A. (1983). Physiological reactivity and recent life-stress experience. *Journal of Consulting and Clinical Psychology, 51,* 467–469.

Parikh, R. K. (2009, September 29). Your X-ray shows…Oh, excuse me. *The New York Times,* p. D5.

Park, C. L., & Adler, N. E. (2003). Coping style as a predictor of health and well-being across the first year of medical school. *Health Psychology, 22,* 627–631.

Park, C. L., Edmondson, D., Hale-Smith, A., & Blank, T. O. (2009). Religiousness/spirituality and health behaviors in younger adult cancer survivors: Does faith promote a healthier lifestyle? *Journal of Behavioral Medicine, 32,* 582–591.

Park, C. L., & Gaffey, A. E. (2007). Relationships between psychosocial factors and health behavior change in cancer survivors: An integrative review. *Annals of Behavioral Medicine, 34,* 115–134.

Park, D. C. (2007). Eating disorders: A call to arms. *American Psychologist, 62,* 158.

Park, E. R., DePue, J. D., Goldstein, M. G., Niaura, R., Harlow, L. L., Willey, C., et al. (2003). Assessing the transtheoretical model of change constructs for physicians counseling smokers. *Annals of Behavioral Medicine, 25,* 120–126.

Parker, J. C., Frank, R. G., Beck, N. C., Smarr, K. L., Buescher, K. L., Phillips, L. R., et al. (1988). Pain management in rheumatoid arthritis patients: A cognitive-behavioral approach. *Arthritis and Rheumatism, 31,* 593–601.

Parker, P. A., & Kulik, J. A. (1995). Burnout, self- and supervisor-rated job performance, and absenteeism among nurses. *Journal of Behavioral Medicine, 18,* 581–600.

Parkinson's Disease Foundation. (2009). *Incidence and prevalence.* Retrieved September 25, 2009, from http://www.neurologychannel.com/parkinsonsdisease/ incidence-prevalence.shtml

Parrish, B. P., Zautra, A. J., & Davis, M. C. (2008). The role of positive and negative interpersonal events on daily fatigue in women with fibromyalgia, rheumatoid arthritis, and osteoarthritis. *Health Psychology, 27,* 694–702.

Parsons, J. T., Rosof, E., & Mustanski, B. (2008). The temporal relationship between alcohol consumption and HIV-medication adherence: A multilevel model of direct and moderating effects. *Health Psychology, 27,* 628–637.

Pasic, J., Levy, W. C., & Sullivan, M. D. (2003). Cytokines in depression and heart failure. *Psychosomatic Medicine, 65,* 181–193.

Patten, S. B., Williams, J. V. A., Lavorato, D. H., Campbell, N. R. C., Eliasziw, M., & Campbell, T. S. (2009). Major depression as a risk factor for high blood pressure: Epidemiologic evidence from a national longitudinal study. *Psychosomatic Medicine, 71,* 273–279.

Patterson, T. L., Sallis, J. F., Nader, P. R., Rupp, J. W., McKenzie, T. L., Roppe, B., et al. (1988). Direct observation of physical activity and dietary behaviors in a structured environment: Effects of a family-based health promotion program. *Journal of Behavioral Medicine, 11,* 447–458.

Pavalko, E. K., Elder, G. H., Jr., & Clipp, E. C. (1993). Worklives and longevity: Insights from a life course perspective. *Journal of Health and Social Behavior, 34,* 363–380.

Pavalko, E. K., & Woodbury, S. (2000). Social roles as process: Caregiving careers and women's health. *Journal of Health and Social Behavior, 41,* 91–105.

Paxton, R. J., Motl, R. W., Aylward, A., & Nigg, C. R. (2010). Physical activity and quality of life—the complementary influence of self-efficacy for physical activity and mental health difficulties. *International Journal of Behavioral Medicine, 17,* 255–263.

Pearlin, L. I., & Schooler, C. (1978). The structure of coping. *Journal of Health and Social Behavior, 19,* 2–21.

Pearson, H. (2004). Public health: The demon drink. *Nature, 428,* 598–600.

Pedersen, S. S., & Denollet, J. (2003). Type D personality, cardiac events, and impaired quality of life: A review. *European Journal of Cardiovascular Prevention and Rehabilitation, 10,* 241–248.

Peeters, A., Barendregt, J. J., Willekens, F., Mackenbach, J. P., Mamun, A. A., & Bonneux, L. (2003). Obesity in adulthood and its consequences for life expectancy: A life-table analysis. *Annals of Internal Medicine, 138,* 24–32.

Peirce, R. S., Frone, M. R., Russell, M., & Cooper, M. L. (1994). Relationship of financial strain and psychosocial resources to alcohol use and abuse: The mediating role of negative affect and drinking motives. *Journal of Health and Social Behavior, 35,* 291–308.

Pelle, A. J., Erdman, R. A. M., van Domburg, R. T., Spriering, M., Kazemier, M., & Pedersen, S. S. (2008). Type D patients report poorer health status prior to and after cardiac rehabilitation compared to non-type D patients. *Annals of Behavioral Medicine, 36,* 167–175.

Peltzer, K. (2010). Leisure time physical activity and sedentary behavior and substance use among in-school adolescents in eight African countries. *International Journal of Behavioral Medicine, 17,* 271–278.

Penedo, F. J., Traeger, L., Dahn, J., Molton, I., Gonzalez, J. S., Schneiderman, N., et al. (2007). Cognitive behavioral stress management intervention improved quality of life in Spanish monolingual Hispanic men treated for localized prostate cancer: Results of a randomized controlled trial. *International Journal of Behavioral Medicine, 14,* 164–172.

Penick, S. B., Filion, R., Fox, S., & Stunkard, A. J. (1971). Behavior modification in the treatment of obesity. *Psychosomatic Medicine, 33,* 49–55.

Penley, J. A., Tomaka, J., & Wiebe, J. S. (2002). The association of coping to physical and psychological health outcomes: A meta-analytic review. *Journal of Behavioral Medicine, 25,* 551–603.

Pennebaker, J. W. (1980). Perceptual and environmental determinants of coughing. *Basic and Applied Social Psychology, 1,* 83–91.

Pennebaker, J. W. (1983). Accuracy of symptom perception. In A. Baum, S. E. Taylor, & J. Singer (Eds.), *Handbook of psychology and health* (Vol. 4, pp. 189–218). Hillsdale, NJ: Erlbaum.

Pennebaker, J. W. (1997). Writing about emotional experiences as a therapeutic process. *Psychological Science, 8,* 162–166.

Pennebaker, J. W., & Beall, S. (1986). Confronting a traumatic event: Toward an understanding of inhibition and disease. *Journal of Abnormal Psychology, 95,* 274–281.

Pennebaker, J. W., Colder, M., & Sharp, L. K. (1990). Accelerating the coping process. *Journal of Personality and Social Psychology, 58,* 528–537.

Pennebaker, J. W., Hughes, C., & O'Heeron, R. C. (1987). The psychophysiology of confession: Linking inhibitory and psychosomatic processes. *Journal of Personality and Social Psychology, 52,* 781–793.

Pennebaker, J. W., Kiecolt-Glaser, J., & Glaser, R. (1988). Disclosure of traumas and immune function: Health implications for psychotherapy. *Journal of Consulting and Clinical Psychology, 56,* 239–245.

Penninx, B. W. J. H., van Tilburg, T., Boeke, A. J. P., Deeg, D. J. H., Kriegsman, D. M. W., & van Eijk, J. T. M. (1998). Effects of social support and personal coping resources on depressive symptoms: Different for various chronic diseases? *Health Psychology, 17,* 551–558.

Penwell, L. M., & Larkin, K. T. (2010). Social support and risk for cardiovascular disease and cancer: A qualitative review examining the role of inflammatory processes. *Health Psychology Review, 4,* 42–55.

Peralta-Ramírez, M. I., Jiménez-Alonso, J., Godoy-García, J. F., & Pérez-García, M. (2004). The effects of daily stress and stressful life events on the clinical symptomatology of patients with lupus erythematosus. *Psychosomatic Medicine, 66,* 788–794.

Pereira, A. C., Huddleston, D. E., Brickman, A. M., Sosunov, A. A., Hen, R., McKhann, G. M., et al. (2007). An in vivo correlate of exercise-induced neurogenesis in the adult dentrare gyrus. *Proceedings of the National Academy of Sciences, 104,* 5638–5643.

Pereira, D. B., Antoni, M. H., Danielson, A., Simon, T. Efantis-Potter, J., Carver, C. S., et al. (2003). Life stress and cervical squamous intraepithelial lesions in women with human papillomavirus and human immunodeficiency virus. *Psychosomatic Medicine, 65,* 427–434.

Pereira, M. G., Berg-Cross, L., Almeida, P., & Machado, J. C. (2008). Impact of family environment and support on adherence, metabolic control, and quality of life in adolescents with diabetes. *International Journal of Behavioral Medicine, 15,* 187–193.

Perez, M. A., Skinner, E. C., & Meyerowitz, B. E. (2002). Sexuality and intimacy following radical prostatectomy: Patient and partner. *Health Psychology, 21,* 288–293.

Pérez-Peña, R., & Glickson, G. (2003, November 29). As obesity rises, so do indignities in health care. *New York Times,* pp. A1, A13.

Perkins, K. A. (1985). The synergistic effect of smoking and serum cholesterol on coronary heart disease. *Health Psychology, 4,* 337–360.

Perkins, K. A., Rohay, J., Meilahn, E. N., Wing, R. R., Matthews, K. A., & Kuller, L. H. (1993). Diet, alcohol, and physical activity as a function of smoking status in middle-aged women. *Health Psychology, 12,* 410–415.

Perkins-Porras, L., Whitehead, D. L., Strike, P. C., & Steptoe, A. (2008). Causal beliefs, cardiac denial and pre-hospital delays following the onset of acute coronary syndromes. *Journal of Behavioral Medicine, 31,* 498–505.

Perlis, M., Aloia, M., Millikan, A., Boehmler, J., Smith, M., Greenblatt, D., et al. (2000). Behavioral treatment of insomnia: A clinical case series study. *Journal of Behavioral Medicine, 23,* 149–161.

Perlis, M. L., Sharpe, M., Smith, M. T., Greenblatt, D., & Giles, D. (2001). Behavioral treatment of insomnia: Treatment outcome and the relevance of medical and psychiatric morbidity. *Journal of Behavioral Medicine, 24,* 281–296.

Perna, F. M., & McDowell, S. L. (1995). Role of psychological stress in cortisol recovery from exhaustive exercise among elite athletes. *International Journal of Behavioral Medicine, 2,* 13–26.

Persky, I., Spring, B., Vander Wal, J. S., Pagoto, S., & Hedeker, D. (2005). Adherence across behavioral domains in treatment promoting smoking cessation plus weight control. *Health Psychology, 24,* 153–160.

Persky, V. W., Kempthorne-Rawson, J., & Shekelle, R. B. (1987). Personality and risk of cancer: 20-year follow-up of the Western Electric Study. *Psychosomatic Medicine, 49,* 435–449.

Pescosolido, B. A., Tuch, S. A., & Martin, J. K. (2001). The profession of medicine and the public: Examining Americans' changing confidence in physician authority from the beginning of the "health care crisis" to the era of health care reform. *Journal of Health and Social Behavior, 42,* 1–16.

Pesonen, A., Räikkönen, K., Paavonen, E. J., Heinonen, K., Komsi, N., Lahti, J., et al. (2009). Sleep duration and regularity are associated with behavioral problems in 8-year-old children. *International Journal of Behavioral Medicine, 17,* 298–305.

Peters, E., Slovic, P., Hibbard, J. H., & Tusler, M. (2006). Why worry? Worry, risk perceptions, and willingness to act to reduce medical errors. *Health Psychology, 25,* 144–152.

Peters, M., Godaert, G., Ballieux, R., Brosschot, J., Sweep, F., Swinkels, L., et al. (1999). Immune responses to experimental stress: Effects of mental effort and uncontrollability. *Psychosomatic Medicine, 61,* 513–524.

Petersen, K. L., Marsland, A. L., Flory, J., Votruba-Drzal, E., Muldoon, M. F., & Manuck, S. B. (2008). Community socioeconomic status is associated with circulating interleukin-6 and c-reactive protein. *Psychosomatic Medicine, 70,* 646–652.

Peterson, L., Farmer, J., & Kashani, J. H. (1990). Parental injury prevention endeavors: A function of health beliefs? *Health Psychology, 9,* 177–191.

Peterson, L., & Soldana, L. (1996). Accelerating children's risk for injury: Mothers' decisions regarding common safety rules. *Journal of Behavioral Medicine, 19,* 317–332.

Petrie, K. J., Booth, R. J., Pennebaker, J. W., Davison, K. P., & Thomas, M. G. (1995). Disclosure of trauma and immune response to a hepatitis B vaccination program. *Journal of Consulting and Clinical Psychology, 63,* 787–792.

Petrie, K. J., Buick, D. L., Weinman, J., & Booth, R. J. (1999). Positive effects of illness reported by myocardial infarction and breast cancer patients. *Journal of Psychosomatic Research, 47,* 537–543.

Petrie, K. J., Fontanilla, I., Thomas, M. G., Booth, R. J., & Pennebaker, J. W. (2004). Effect of written emotional expression on immune function in patients with human immunodeficiency virus infection: A randomized trial. *Psychosomatic Medicine, 66,* 272–275.

Petrie, K. J., & Weinman, J. A. (Eds.). (1997). *Perceptions of health and illness: Current research and applications.* Reading, England: Harwood Academic.

Petrie, K. J., & Wessely, S. (2002). Modern worries, new technology, and medicine. *British Journal of Medicine, 324,* 690–691.

Petrovic, P., Kalso, E., Peterson, K. M., & Ingvar, M. (2002). Placebo and opioid analgesia – Imaging a shared neuronal network. *Science, 295,* 1737–1740.

Petry, N. M., Barry, D., Pietrzak, R. H., & Wagner, J. A. (2008). Overweight and obesity are associated with psychiatric disorders: Results from the national epidemiologic survey on alcohol and related conditions. *Psychosomatic Medicine, 70,* 288–297.

Peyrot, M., McMurry, J. F., Jr., & Kruger, D. F. (1999). A biopsychosocial model of glycemic control in diabetes: Stress, coping and regimen adherence. *Journal of Health and Social Behavior, 40,* 141–158.

Pfeifer, J. E., & Brigham, J. C. (Eds.). (1996). Psychological perspectives on euthanasia. *Journal of Social Issues, 52* (entire issue).

Philips, H. C. (1983). Assessment of chronic headache behavior. In R. Meizack (Ed.), *Pain measurement and assessment* (pp. 97–104). New York: Raven Press.

Phillips, A. C., Batty, G. D., Gale, C. R., Deary, I. J., Osborn, D., MacIntyre, K., et al. (2009). Generalized anxiety disorder, major depressive disorder, and their comorbidity as predictors of all-cause and cardiovascular mortality: The Vietnam experience study. *Psychosomatic Medicine, 71,* 395–403.

Phillips, A. C., Carroll, D., Ring, C., Sweeting, H., & West, P. (2005). Life events and acute cardiovascular reactions to mental stress: A cohort study. *Psychosomatic Medicine, 67,* 384–392.

Phillips, K. M., Antoni, M. H., Lechner, S. C., Blomberg, B. B., Llabre, M. M., Avisar, E., et al. (2008). Stress management intervention reduces serum cortisol and increases relaxation during treatment for nonmetastatic breast cancer. *Psychosomatic Medicine, 70,* 1044–1049.

Phillips-Bute, B., Mathew, J. P., Blumenthal, J. A., Grocott, H. P., Laskowitz, D. T., Jones, R. H., et al. (2006). Association of neurocognitive function and quality of life 1 year after coronary artery bypass graft (CABG) surgery. *Psychosomatic Medicine, 68,* 369–375.

Phipps, S., & Steele, R. (2002). Repressive adaptive style in children with chronic illness. *Psychosomatic Medicine, 64,* 34–42.

Phipps, S., Steele, R. G., Hall, K., & Leigh, L. (2001). Repressive adaptation in children with cancer: A replication and extension. *Health Psychology, 20,* 445–451.

Piasecki, T. M. (2006). Relapse to smoking. *Clinical Psychology Review, 26,* 196–215.

Picardi, A., Battisti, F., Tarsitani, L., Baldassari, M., Copertaro, A., Mocchegiani, E., et al. (2007). Attachment security and immunity in healthy women. *Psychosomatic Medicine, 69,* 40–46.

Picciano, J. F., Roffman, R. A., Kalichman, S. C., & Walker, D. D. (2007). Lowering obstacles to HIV prevention services: Effects of a brief, telephone-based intervention using motivational enhancement therapy. *Annals of Behavioral Medicine, 34,* 177–187.

Pichon, L. C., Arredondo, E. M., Roesch, S., Sallis, J. F., Ayala, G. X., & Elder, J. P. (2007). The relation of acculturation to Latina's perceived neighborhood safety and physical activity: A structural equation analysis. *Annals of Behavioral Medicine, 34,* 295–303.

Pickering, T. G., Devereux, R. B., James, G. D., Gerin, W., Landsbergis, P., Schnall, P. L., et al. (1996). Environmental influences on blood pressure and the role of job strain. *Journal of Hypertension, 14* (Suppl.), S179–S185.

Pickering, T. G., Schwartz, J. E., & James, G. D. (1995). Ambulatory blood pressure monitoring for evaluating the relationships between lifestyle, hypertension, and cardiovascular risk. *Clinical and Experimental Pharmacology and Physiology, 22,* 226–231.

Pickett, M. (1993). Cultural awareness in the context of terminal illness. *Cancer Nursing, 16,* 102–106.

Pieper, S., & Brosschot, J. F. (2005). Prolonged stress-related cardiovascular activation: Is there any? *Annals of Behavioral Medicine, 30,* 91–103.

Pieper, S., Brosschot, J. F., van der Leeden, R., & Thayer, J. F. (2007). Cardiac effects of momentary assessed worry episodes and stressful events. *Psychosomatic Medicine, 69,* 901–909.

Pignone, M. P., Gaynes, B. N., Rushton, J. L., Burchell, C. M., Orleans, C. T., Mulrow, C. D., et al. (2002). Screening for depression in adults: A summary of the evidence for the U.S. preventive services task force. *Annals of Internal Medicine, 136,* 765–776.

Pike, J., Smith, T., Hauger, R., Nicassio, P., Patterson, T., McClintock, J., et al. (1997). Chronic life stress alters sympathetic, neuroendocrine, and immune responsivity to an acute psychological stressor in humans. *Psychosomatic Medicine, 59,* 447–457.

Pike, K. M., & Rodin, J. (1991). Mothers, daughters, and disordered eating. *Journal of Abnormal Psychology, 100,* 1–7.

Piliavin, J. A., & Siegl, E. (2007). Health benefits of volunteering in the Wisconsin longitudinal study. *Journal of Health and Social Behavior, 48,* 450–464.

Pischke, C. R., Scherwitz, L., Weidner, G., & Ornish, D. (2008). Long-term effects of lifestyle changes on well-being and cardiac variables among coronary heart disease patients. *Health Psychology, 27,* 584–592.

Pitman, D. L., Ottenweller, J. E., & Natelson, B. H. (1988). Plasma corticosterone levels during repeated presentation of two intensities of restraint stress: Chronic stress and habituation. *Physiology and Behavior, 43,* 47–55.

Plomin, R., Scheier, M. F., Bergeman, S. C., Pedersen, N. L., Nesselroade, J. R., & McClearn, G. E. (1992). Optimism, pessimism, and mental health: A twin/adoption study. *Personality and Individual Differences, 13,* 921–930.

Polivy, J., & Herman, C. P. (1985). Dieting and binging: A causal analysis. *American Psychologist, 40,* 193–201.

Polk, D. E., Cohen, S., Doyle, W. J., Skoner, D. P., & Kirschbaum, C. (2005). State and trait affect as predictors of salivary cortisol in healthy adults. *Psychoneuroendocrinology, 30,* 261–272.

Pollard, T. M., & Schwartz, J. E. (2003). Are changes in blood pressure and total cholesterol related to changes in mood? An 18-month study of men and women. *Health Psychology, 22,* 47–53.

Population Division of the Department of Economic and Social Affairs of the United Nations Secretariat. (2002). *World population prospects: The 2002 revision and world urbanization prospects: The 2001 revision.* Retrieved October 20, 2004, from http://esa.un.org/unpp

Porter, L. S., Mishel, M., Neelon, V., Belyea, M., Pisano, E., & Soo, M. S. (2003). Cortisol levels and responses to mammography screening in breast cancer survivors: A pilot study. *Psychosomatic Medicine, 65,* 842–848.

Powell, L. H., Shahabi, L., & Thoresen, C. E. (2003). Religion and spirituality: Linkages to physical health. *American Psychologist, 58,* 36–52.

Powell, L. H., William, R. L., Matthews, K. A., Meyer, P., Midgley, A. R., Baum, A., et al. (2002). Physiologic markers of chronic stress in premenopausal, middle-aged women. *Psychosomatic Medicine, 64,* 502–509.

Power, E., Van Jaarsveld, C. H. M., McCaffery, K., Miles, A., Atkin, W., & Wardle, J. (2008). Understanding intentions and action in colorectal cancer screening. *Annals of Behavioral Medicine, 35,* 285–294.

Power, M., Bullinger, M., Harper, A., & the World Health Organization Quality of Life Group. (1999). The World Health Organization WHOQOL–100: Tests of the universality of quality of life in 15 different cultural groups worldwide. *Health Psychology, 18,* 495–505.

Pradhan, A. D., Rifai, N., & Ridker, P. (2002). Soluble intercellular adhesion molecule–1, soluble vascular adhesion molecule–1, and the development of symptomatic peripheral arterial disease in men. *Circulation, 106,* 820–825.

Pratt, L. A., & Brody, D. J. (2010). Depression and smoking in the U.S. household population aged 20 and over, 2005–2008. *NCHS Data Brief, 34,* 1–8.

Pratt, L. A., Ford, D. E., Crum, R. M., Armenian, H. K., Gallo, J. J., & Eaton, W. W. (1996). Depression, psychotropic medication, and risk of myocardial infarction: Prospective data from the Baltimore ECA follow-up. *Circulation, 15,* 3123–3129.

Pressman, E., & Orr, W. C. (Eds.). (1997). *Understanding sleep: The evolution and treatment of sleep disorders.* Washington, DC: American Psychological Association.

Pressman, S. D., & Cohen, S. (2005). Does positive affect influence health? *Psychological Bulletin, 131,* 925–971.

Pressman, S. D., & Cohen, S. (2007). Use of social words in autobiographies and longevity. *Psychosomatic Medicine, 69,* 262–269.

Pressman, S. D., Cohen, S., Miller, G. E., Barkin, A., Rabin, B. S., & Treanor, J. J. (2005). Loneliness, social network size, and immune response to influenza vaccination in college freshmen. *Health Psychology, 24,* 297–306.

Pressman, S. D., Matthews, K. A., Cohen, S., Martire, L. M., Scheier, M., Baum, A., et al. (2009). Association of enjoyable leisure activities with psychological and physical well-being. *Psychosomatic Medicine, 71,* 725–732.

Presti, D. E., Ary, D. V., & Lichtenstein, E. (1992). The context of smoking initiation and maintenance: Findings from interviews with youths. *Journal of Substance Abuse, 4,* 35–45.

Prestwich, A., Perugini, M., & Hurling, R. (2010). Can implementation intentions and text messages promote brisk walking? A randomized trial. *Health Psychology, 29,* 40–49.

Prinstein, M. J., & La Greca, A. M. (2009). Childhood depressive symptoms and adolescent cigarette use: A six-year longitudinal study controlling for peer relations correlates. *Health Psychology, 28,* 283–291.

Prochaska, J. J., & Sallis, J. F. (2004). A randomized controlled trial of single versus multiple health behavior change: Promoting physical activity and nutrition among adolescents. *Health Psychology, 23,* 314–318.

Prochaska, J. J., Velicer, W. F., Prochaska, J. O., Delucchi, K., & Hall, S. M. (2006). Comparing intervention outcomes in smokers treated for single versus multiple behavioral risks. *Health Psychology, 25,* 380–388.

Prochaska, J. O. (1994). Strong and weak principles for progressing from pre-contemplation to action on the basis of 12 problem behaviors. *Health Psychology, 13,* 47–51.

Prochaska, J. O., & DiClemente, C. C. (1984). *The transtheoretical approach: Crossing traditional boundaries of therapy.* Chicago: Dow Jones/Irwin.

Prochaska, J. O., DiClemente, C. C., & Norcross, J. C. (1992). In search of how people change: Applications to addictive behaviors. *American Psychologist, 47,* 1102–1114.

Pruessner, J. C., Hellhammer, D. H., & Kirschbaum, C. (1999). Burnout, perceived stress, and cortisol responses to awakening. *Psychosomatic Medicine, 61,* 197–204.

Pruessner, M., Hellhammer, D. H., Pruessner, J. C., & Lupien, S. J. (2003). Self-reported depressive symptoms and stress levels in healthy young men: Associations with the cortisol response to awakening. *Psychosomatic Medicine, 65,* 92–99.

Ptacek, J. T., & McIntosh, E. G. (2009). Physician challenges in communicating bad news. *Journal of Behavioral Medicine, 32,* 380–387.

Puhl, R. M., Schwartz, M. B., & Brownell, K. D. (2005). Impact of perceived consensus on stereotypes about obese people: A new approach for reducing bias. *Health Psychology, 24,* 517–525.

Pulkki-Råback, L., Elovainio, M., Kivimäki, M., Raitakari, O. T., & Keltikangas-Järvinen, L. (2005). Temperament in childhood predicts body mass in adulthood: The cardiovascular risk in young Finns study. *Health Psychology, 24,* 307–315.

Quadagno, J. (2004). Why the United States has no national health insurance: Stakeholder mobilization against the welfare state, 1945–1996. *Journal of Health and Social Behavior, 45* (extra issue), 25–44.

Quartana, P. J., Bounds, S., Yoon, K. L., Goodin, B. R., & Burns, J. W. (2010). Anger suppression predicts pain, emotional, and cardiovascular responses to the cold pressor. *Annals of Behavioral Medicine, 39,* 211–221.

Quartana, P. J., Burns, J. W., & Lofland, K. R. (2007). Attentional strategy moderates effects of pain catastrophizing on symptom-specific physiological response in chronic low back pain patients. *Journal of Behavioral Medicine, 30,* 221–231.

Quick, J. C. (1999). Occupational health psychology: Historical roots and future directions. *Health Psychology, 18,* 82–88.

Quinlan, K. B., & McCaul, K. D. (2000). Matched and mismatched interventions with young adult smokers: Testing a stage theory. *Health Psychology, 19,* 165–171.

Quinn, J. M., Pascoe, A., Wood, W., & Neal, D. T. (2010). Can't control yourself? Monitor those bad habits. *Personality and Social Psychology Bulletin, 36,* 499–511.

Quittner, A. L., Espelage, D. L., Opipari, L. C., Carter, B., Eid, N., & Eigen, H. (1998). Role strain in couples with and without a child with a chronic illness: Associations with marital satisfaction, intimacy, and daily mood. *Health Psychology, 17,* 112–124.

Rabin, C., Ward, S., Leventhal, H., & Schmitz, M. (2001). Explaining retrospective reports of symptoms in patients undergoing chemotherapy: Anxiety, initial symptom experience and posttreatment symptoms. *Health Psychology, 20,* 91–98.

Rabius, V., McAlister, A. L., Geiger, A., Huang, P., & Todd, R. (2004). Telephone counseling increases cessation rates among young adult smokers. *Health Psychology, 23,* 539–541.

Rabkin, J. G., McElhiney, M., Ferrando, S. J., Van Gorp, W., & Lin, S. H. (2004). Predictors of employment of men with HIV/AIDS: A longitudinal study. *Psychosomatic Medicine, 66,* 72–78.

Rachman, S. J., & Phillips, C. (1978). *Psychology and medicine.* Baltimore, MD: Penguin.

Radcliffe-Brown, A. R. (1964). *The Andaman Islanders.* New York: Free Press.

Raeburn, P., Forster, D., Foust, D., & Brady, D. (2002, October 21). Why we're so fat. *Business Week,* pp. 112–114.

Rafnsson, S. B., Deary, I. J., Smith, F. B., Whiteman, M. C., & Fowkes, F. G. R. (2007). Cardiovascular disease and decline in cognitive function in an elderly community population: The Edinburgh artery study. *Psychosomatic Medicine, 69,* 425–434.

Rahe, R. H., Mahan, J. L., & Arthur, R. J. (1970). Prediction of near-future health change from subjects' preceding life changes. *Journal of Psychosomatic Research, 14,* 401–406.

Rahe, R. H., Taylor, C. B., Tolles, R. L., Newhall, L. M., Veach, T. L., & Bryson, S. (2002). A novel stress and coping workplace program reduces illness and healthcare utilization. *Psychosomatic Medicine, 64,* 278–286.

Räikkönen, K., Matthews, K. A., Flory, J. D., Owens, J. F., & Gump, B. B. (1999). Effects of optimism, pessimism, and trait anxiety on ambulatory blood pressure and mood during everyday life. *Journal of Personality and Social Psychology, 76,* 104–113.

Räikkönen, K., Matthews, K. A., Sutton-Tyrrell, K., & Kuller, L. H. (2004). Trait anger and the metabolic syndrome predict progression of carotid atherosclerosis in healthy middle-aged women. *Psychosomatic Medicine, 66,* 903–908.

Rains, J. C., Penzien, D. B., & Jamison, R. N. (1992). A structured approach to the management of chronic pain. In L. VandeCreek, S. Knapp, & T. L. Jackson (Eds.), *Innovations in clinical practice: A source book* (Vol. 11, pp. 521–539). Sarasota, FL: Professional Resource Press.

Rakoff, V. (1983). Multiple determinants of family dynamics in anorexia nervosa. In P. L. Darby, P. E. Garfinkel, D. M. Garner, & D. V. Coscina (Eds.), *Anorexia nervosa: Recent developments in research* (pp. 29–40). New York: Liss.

Ramirez-Maestre, C., Lopez-Martinez, A. E., & Zarazaga, R. E. (2004). Personality characteristics as differential variables of the pain experience. *Journal of Behavioral Medicine, 27,* 147–165.

Ramos, J. C. (1996). Doc in a box. *Time,* pp. 55–57.

Randall, G., Molloy, G. J., & Steptoe, A. (2009). The impact of an acute cardiac event on the partners of patients: A systematic review. *Health Psychology Review, 3,* 1–84.

Ranjit, N., Diez-Roux, A. V., Sanchez, B., Seeman, T., Shea, S., Shrager, S., et al. (2009). Association of salivary cortisol circadian pattern with cynical hostility: Multi-ethnic study of artherosclerosis. *Psychosomatic Medicine, 71,* 748–755.

Rapoff, M. A., & Christophersen, E. R. (1982). Improving compliance in pediatric practice. *Pediatric Clinics of North America, 29,* 339–357.

Raven, B. H., Freeman, H. E., & Haley, R. W. (1982). Social science perspectives in hospital infection control. In A. W. Johnson, O. Grusky, & B. Raven (Eds.), *Contemporary health services: Social science perspectives* (pp. 139–176). Boston: Auburn House.

Raynor, D. A., Pogue-Geile, M. F., Kamarck, T. W., McCaffery, J. M., & Manuck, S. B. (2002). Covariation of psychosocial characteristics associated with cardiovascular disease: Genetic and environmental influences. *Psychosomatic Medicine, 64,* 191–203.

Reaney, P. (1998, November 19). *Chinese tobacco deaths to soar to 3 million.* Reuters News Service, www.reuters.com

Rebuffe-Scrive, M., Walsh, U. A., McEwen, B., & Rodin, J. (1992). Effect of chronic stress and exogenous glucocorticoids on regional fat distribution and metabolism. *Physiology and Behavior, 52,* 583–590.

Reddy, K. S., Shah, B., Varghese, C., & Ramadoss, A. (2005). Responding to the threat of chronic diseases in India. *The Lancet, 366,* 1744–1749.

Redman, S., Webb, G. R., Hennrikus, D. J., Gordon, J. J., & Sanson-Fisher, R. W. (1991). The effects of gender on diagnosis of psychological disturbance. *Journal of Behavioral Medicine, 14,* 527–540.

Redwine, L., Dang, J., Hall, M., & Irwin, M. (2003). Disordered sleep, nocturnal cytokines, and immunity in alcoholics. *Psychosomatic Medicine, 65,* 75–85.

Redwine, L., Mills, P. J., Sada, M., Dimsdale, J., Patterson, T., & Grant, I. (2004). Differential immune cell chemotaxis responses to acute psychological stress in Alzheimer caregivers compared to non-caregiver controls. *Psychosomatic Medicine, 66,* 770–775.

Redwine, L., Snow, S., Mills, P., & Irwin, M. (2003). Acute psychological stress: Effects in chemotaxosis and cellular adhesion molecule expression. *Psychosomatic Medicine, 65,* 598–603.

Reed, G. M. (1989). *Stress, coping, and psychological adaptation in a sample of gay and bisexual men with AIDS.* Unpublished doctoral dissertation, University of California, Los Angeles.

Reed, G. M., Kemeny, M. E., Taylor, S. E., & Visscher, B. R. (1999). Negative HIV-specific expectancies and AIDS-related bereavement as predictors of symptom onset in asymptomatic HIV-positive gay men. *Health Psychology, 18,* 354–363.

Reed, G. M., Kemeny, M. E., Taylor, S. E., Wang, H. Y. J., & Visscher, B. R. (1994). Realistic acceptance as a predictor of decreased survival time in gay men with AIDS. *Health Psychology, 13,* 299–307.

Reif, J. S., Dunn, K., Ogilvie, G. K., & Harris, C. K. (1992). Passive smoking and canine lung cancer risk. *American Journal of Epidemiology, 135,* 234–239.

Reitman, V. (2003, March 24). Healing sound of a word: "Sorry." *Los Angeles Times,* pp. F1, F8.

Reitman, V. (2003, July 7). Heart attacks in young women. *Los Angeles Times,* pp. F1, F4.

Reitman, V. (2004, June 28). Ill effects of cutting back on medications. *Los Angeles Times,* p. F2.

Rejeski, W. J., Brawley, L. R., Ambrosius, W. T., Brubaker, P. H., Focht, B. C., Foy, C. G., & Fox, L. D. (2003). Older adults with chronic disease: Benefits of group-mediated counseling in the promotion of physically active lifestyles. *Health Psychology, 22,* 414–423.

Repetti, R. L. (1989). Effects of daily workload on subsequent behavior during marital interactions: The role of social withdrawal and spouse support. *Journal of Personality and Social Psychology, 57,* 651–659.

Repetti, R. L. (1993a). The effects of workload and the social environment at work on health. In L. Goldberger & S. Bresnitz (Eds.), *Handbook of stress* (pp. 368–385). New York: Free Press.

Repetti, R. L. (1993b). Short-term effects of occupational stressors on daily mood and health complaints. *Health Psychology, 12,* 125–131.

Repetti, R. L., & Pollina, S. L. (1994). *The effects of daily social and academic failure experiences on school-age children's subsequent interactions with parents.* Unpublished manuscript, University of California, Los Angeles.

Repetti, R. L., Taylor, S. E., & Seeman, T. E. (2002). Risky families: Family social environments and the mental and physical health of offspring. *Psychological Bulletin, 128,* 330–336.

Repetto, M. J., & Petitto, J. M. (2008). Psychopharmacology in HIV-infected patients. *Psychosomatic Medicine, 70,* 585–592.

Repetto, P. B., Caldwell, C. H., & Zimmerman, M. A. (2005). A longitudinal study of the relationship between depressive symptoms and cigarette use among African American adolescents. *Health Psychology, 24,* 209–219.

Resnick, B., Orwig, D., Yu-Yahiro, J., Hawkes, W., Shardell, M., Hebel, J. R., et al. (2007). Testing the effectiveness of the exercise plus program in older women post-hip fracture. *Annals of Behavioral Medicine, 34,* 67–76.

Resnicow, K., Davis, R., Zhang, N., Konkel, J., Strecher, V. J., Shaikh, A. R., et al. (2008). Tailoring a fruit and vegetable intervention on novel motivational constructs: Results of a randomized study. *Annals of Behavioral Medicine, 35,* 159–169.

Resnicow, K., DiIorio, C., Soet, J. E., Borrelli, B., Hecht, J., & Ernst, D. (2002). Motivational interviewing in health promotion: It sounds like something is changing. *Health Psychology, 21,* 444–451.

Resnicow, K., Reddy, S. P., James, S., Gabebodeen Omardien, R., Kambaran, N. S., Langner, R. G., et al. (2008). Comparison of two school-based smoking prevention programs among South African high school students: Results of a randomized trial. *Annals of Behavioral Medicine, 36,* 231–243.

Revenson, T. A., & Pranikoff, J. R. (2005). A contextual approach to treatment decision making among breast cancer survivors. *Health Psychology, 24* (Suppl.), S93–S98.

Reynolds, C. F., Serody, L., Okun, M. L., Hall, M., Houck, P. R., Patrick, S., et al. (2010). Protecting sleep, promoting health in later life: A randomized clinical trial. *Psychosomatic Medicine, 72,* 178–186.

Reynolds, D. V. (1969). Surgery in the rat during electrical analgesia induced by focal brain stimulation. *Science, 164,* 444–445.

Reynolds, J. S., & Perrin, N. A. (2004). Mismatches in social support and psychological adjustment to breast cancer. *Health Psychology, 23,* 425–430.

Reynolds, K. D., Buller, D. B., Yaroch, A. L., Maloy, J. A., & Cutter, G. R. (2006). Mediation of a middle school skin cancer prevention program. *Health Psychology, 25,* 616–625.

Rhee, H., Holditch-Davis, D., & Miles, M. S. (2005). Patterns of physical symptoms and relationships with psychosocial factors in adolescents. *Psychosomatic Medicine, 67,* 1006–1012.

Rhodes, N., Roskos-Ewoldsen, D. R., Edison, A., & Bradford, M. B. (2008). Attitude and norm accessibility affect processing of anti-smoking messages. *Health Psychology, 27,* S224–S232.

Rhodes, R. E., Naylor, P. J., & McKay, H. A. (2010). Pilot study of a family physical activity planning intervention among parents and their children. *Journal of Behavioral Medicine, 33,* 91–100.

Rhodes, R. E., & Plotnikoff, R. C. (2006). Understanding action control: Predicting physical activity intention-behavior profiles across 6 months in a Canadian sample. *Health Psychology, 25,* 292–299.

Rhodes, R. E., Plotnikoff, R. C., & Courneya, K. S. (2008). Predicting the physical activity intention-behavior profiles of adopters and maintainers using three social cognition models. *Annals of Behavioral Medicine, 36,* 244–252.

Richards, J. C., Hof, A., & Alvarenga, M. (2000). Serum lipids and their relationships with hostility and angry affect and behaviors in men. *Health Psychology, 19,* 393–398.

Richardson, J. L., Marks, G., Johnson, C. A., Graham, J. W., Chan, K. K., Selser, J. N., et al. (1987). Path model of multidimensional compliance with cancer therapy. *Health Psychology, 6,* 183–207.

Richardson, L. (2004, January 9). Obesity blamed as disability rates soar for those under 60. *Los Angeles Times,* p. A22.

Richman, L. S., Bennett, G. G., Pek, J., Siegler, I., & Williams, R. B. (2007). Discrimination, dispositions, and cardiovascular responses to stress. *Health Psychology, 26,* 675–683.

Richman, L. S., Kubzansky, L., Maselko, J., Kawachi, I., Choo, P., & Bauer, M. (2005). Positive emotion and health: Going beyond the negative. *Health Psychology, 24,* 422–429.

Rief, W., Hessel, A., & Braehler, E. (2001). Somatization symptoms and hypochondriacal features in the general population. *Psychosomatic Medicine, 63,* 595–602.

Rief, W., Martin, A., Klaiberg, A., & Brähler, E. (2005). Specific effects of depression, panic, and somatic symptoms on illness behavior. *Psychosomatic Medicine, 67,* 596–601.

Rietschlin, J. (1998). Voluntary association membership and psychological distress. *Journal of Health and Social Behavior, 39,* 348–355.

Rimes, K. A., Salkovskis, P. M., Jones, L., & Lucassen, A. M. (2006). Applying a cognitive-behavioral model of health anxiety in a cancer genetics service. *Health Psychology, 25,* 171–180.

Rini, C., Dunkel-Schetter, C., Wadhwa, P., & Sandman, C. (1999). Psychological adaptation and birth outcomes: The role of personal resources, stress, and socio-cultural context in pregnancy. *Health Psychology, 18,* 333–345.

Rini, C., Manne, S., DuHamel, K., Austin, J., Ostroff, J., Boulad, F., et al. (2008). Social support from family and friends as a buffer of low social support among mothers of critically ill children: A multilevel modeling approach. *Health Psychology, 27,* 593–603.

Rini, C., O'Neill, S., Valdimarsdottir, H., Goldsmith, R. E., Jandorf, L., Brown, K., et al. (2009). Cognitive and emotional factors predicting decisional conflict among high-risk breast cancer survivors who receive uninformative BRCA1/2 results. *Health Psychology, 28,* 569–578.

Ritz, T., & Steptoe, A. (2000). Emotion and pulmonary function in asthma: Reactivity in the field and relationship with laboratory induction of emotion. *Psychosomatic Medicine, 62,* 808–815.

Riva, R., Mork, P. J., Westgaard, R. H., Rø, M., & Lundberg, U. (2010). Fibromyalgia syndrome is associated with hypocortisolism. *International Journal of Behavioral Medicine, 17,* 223–233.

Roan, S. (2003, March 10). Diabetes study has wide reach. *Los Angeles Times,* p. F3.

Robbins, C. A., & Martin, S. S. (1993). Gender, styles of deviance, and drinking problems. *Journal of Health and Social Behavior, 34,* 302–321.

Roberts, A. H., Kewman, D. G., Mercier, L., & Hovell, M. (1993). The power of nonspecific effects in healing: Implications for psychosocial and biological treatments. *Clinical Psychology Review, 13,* 375–391.

Roberts, M. C., & Turner, D. S. (1984). Preventing death and injury in childhood: A synthesis of child safety seat efforts. *Health Education Quarterly, 11,* 181–193.

Robinson, R. G., & Price, T. R. (1982). Poststroke depressive disorders: A follow-up study of 103 patients. *Stroke, 13,* 635–640.

Robinson, T. N. (1999). Reducing children's television viewing to prevent obesity. *Journal of the American Medical Association, 282,* 1561–1567.

Robles, T. F. (2007). Stress, social support, and delayed skin barrier recovery. *Psychosomatic Medicine, 69,* 807–815.

Robles, T. F., Brooks, K. P., & Pressman, S. D. (2009). Trait positive affect buffers the effects of acute stress on skin barrier recovery. *Health Psychology, 28,* 373–378.

Robles, T. F., Glaser, R., & Kiecolt-Glaser, J. K. (2005). Out of balance: A new look at chronic stress, depression, and immunity. *Current Directions in Psychological Science, 14,* 111–115.

Robles, T. F., Shaffer, V. A., Malarkey, W. B., & Kiecolt-Glaser, J. K. (2006). Positive behaviors during marital conflict: Influences on stress hormones. *Journal of Social and Personal Relationships, 23,* 305–325.

Rodgers, A., Corbett, T., Bramley, D., Riddell, T., Wills, M., Lin, R. B., et al. (2005). Do u smoke after txt? Results of a randomized trial of smoking cessation using mobile phone text messaging. *Tobacco Control, 14,* 255–261.

Rodin, J., & Ickovics, J. R. (1990). Women's health: Review and research agenda as we approach the 21st century. *American Psychologist, 45,* 1018–1034.

Rodin, J., & McAvay, G. (1992). Determinants of change in perceived health in a longitudinal study of older adults. *Journal of Gerontology, 47,* P373–P384.

Rodin, J., & Plante, T. (1989). The psychological effects of exercise. In R. S. Williams & A. Wellece (Eds.), *Biological effects of physical activity* (pp. 127–137). Champaign, IL: Human Kinetics.

Rodriguez, C. J., Burg, M. M., Meng, J., Pickering, T. G., Jin, Z., Sacco, R. L., et al. (2008). Effect of social support on nocturnal blood pressure dipping. *Psychosomatic Medicine, 70,* 7–12.

Rodriguez, D., Moss, H. B., & Audrain-McGovern, J. (2005). Developmental heterogeneity in adolescent depressive symptoms: Associations with smoking behavior. *Psychosomatic Medicine, 67,* 200–210.

Rodriguez, D., Romer, D., & Audrain-McGovern, J. (2007). Beliefs about the risks of smoking mediate the relationship between exposure to smoking and smoking. *Psychosomatic Medicine, 69,* 106–113.

Roelofs, J., McCracken, L., Peters, M. L., Crombez, G., van Breukelen, G., & Vlaeyen, J. W. S. (2004). Psychometric evaluation of the pain anxiety symptoms scale (PASS) in chronic pain patients. *Journal of Behavioral Medicine, 27,* 167–183.

Roesch, S. C., Adams, L., Hines, A., Palmores, A., Vyas, P., Tran, C., et al. (2005). Coping with prostate cancer: A meta-analytic review. *Journal of Behavioral Medicine, 28,* 281–293.

Roitt, I., Brostoff, J., & Male, D. (1998). *Immunology* (5th ed.). London, England: Mosby International.

Rojo, L., Conesa, L., Bermudez, O., & Livianos, L. (2006). Influence of stress in the onset of eating disorders: Data from a two-stage epidemiologic controlled study. *Psychosomatic Medicine, 68,* 628–635.

Rokke, P. D., & Al Absi, M. (1992). Matching pain coping strategies to the individual: A prospective validation of the cognitive coping strategy inventory. *Journal of Behavioral Medicine, 15,* 611–626.

Rokke, P. D., Fleming-Ficek, S., Siemens, N. M., & Hegstad, H. J. (2004). Self-efficacy and choice of coping strategies for tolerating acute pain. *Journal of Behavioral Medicine, 27,* 343–360.

Rollman, B. L., & Shear, M. K. (2003). Depression and medical comorbidity: Red flags for current suicidal ideation in primary care. *Psychosomatic Medicine, 65,* 506–507.

Roman, M. J., Shanker, B. A., Davis, A., Lockshin, M. D., Sammaritano, L., Simantov, R., et al. (2003). Prevalence and correlates of accelerated atherosclerosis in systematic lupus erythematosus. *The New England Journal of Medicine, 349,* 2399–2406.

Romano, J. M., Jensen, M. P., Schmaling, K. B., Hops, H., & Buchwald, D. S. (2009). Illness behaviors in patients with unexplained chronic fatigue are associated with significant other responses. *Journal of Behavioral Medicine, 32,* 558–569.

Romero, C., Friedman, L. C., Kalidas, M., Elledge, R., Chang, J., & Liscum, K. R. (2006). Self-forgiveness, spirituality, and psychological adjustment in women with breast cancer. *Journal of Behavioral Medicine, 29,* 29–36.

Ronis, D. L. (1992). Conditional health threats: Health beliefs, decisions, and behaviors among adults. *Health Psychology, 11,* 127–134.

Rosal, M. C., Ockene, J. K., Yunsheng, M., Hebert, J. R., Ockene, I. S., Merriam, P., et al. (1998). Coronary artery smoking intervention study (CASIS): 5-year follow-up. *Health Psychology, 17,* 476–478.

Rose, J. S., Chassin, L., Presson, C. C., & Sherman, S. J. (1996). Prospective predictors of quit attempts and smoking cessation in young adults. *Health Psychology, 15,* 261–268.

Rosenberger, P. H., Kerns, R., Jokl, P., & Ickovics, J. R. (2009). Mood and attitude predict pain outcomes following arthroscopic knee surgery. *Annals of Behavioral Medicine, 37,* 70–76.

Rosenfield, S. (1992). The costs of sharing: Wives' employment and husbands' mental health. *Journal of Health and Social Behavior, 33,* 213–225.

Rosenstock, I. M. (1966). Why people use health services. *Milbank Memorial Fund Quarterly, 44,* 94ff.

Rosenstock, I. M. (1974). Historical origins of the health belief model. *Health Education Monographs, 2,* 328–335.

Ross, C. E., & Bird, C. E. (1994). Sex stratification and health lifestyle: Consequences for men's and women's perceived health. *Journal of Health and Social Behavior, 35,* 161–178.

Ross, C. E., & Mirowsky, J. (1988). Child care and emotional adjustment to wives' employment. *Journal of Health and Social Behavior, 29,* 127–138.

Ross, C. E., & Mirowsky, J. (2001). Neighborhood disadvantages, disorder, and health. *Journal of Health and Social Behavior, 42,* 258–276.

Rosser, B. R. S., Hatfield, L. A., Miner, M. H., Ghiselli, M. E., Lee, B. R., & Welles, S. L. (2010). Effects of a behavioral intervention to reduce serodiscordant unsafe sex among HIV positive men who have sex with men: The

Positive Connections randomized controlled trial study. *Journal of Behavioral Medicine, 33,* 147–158.

Rossy, L. A., Buckelew, S. P., Dorr, N., Hagglund, K. J., Thayer, J. F., McIntosh, M. J., et al. (1999). A meta-analysis of fibromyalgia treatment interventions. *Annals of Behavioral Medicine, 21,* 180–191.

Roth, B., & Robbins, D. (2004). Mindfulness-based stress reduction and health-related quality of life: Findings from a bilingual inner-city patient population. *Psychosomatic Medicine, 66,* 113–123.

Roth, G. S., Lane, M. A., Ingram, D. K., Mattison, J. A., Elahi, D., Tobin, J. D., et al. (2002). Biomarkers of caloric restriction may predict longevity in humans. *Science, 297,* p. 811.

Rotheram-Borus, M. J., Murphy, D. A., Reid, H. M., & Coleman, C. L. (1996). Correlates of emotional distress among HIV+ youths: Health status, stress, and personal resources. *Annals of Behavioral Medicine, 18,* 16–23.

Rothman, A. J. (2000). Toward a theory-based analysis of behavioral maintenance. *Health Psychology, 19,* 64–69.

Rothman, A. J., & Salovey, P. (1997). Shaping perceptions to motivate healthy behavior: The role of message framing. *Psychological Bulletin, 121,* 3–19.

Rowe, M. M. (1999). Teaching health-care providers coping: Results of a two-year study. *Journal of Behavioral Medicine, 22,* 511–527.

Roy, B., Diez-Roux, A. V., Seeman, T., Ranjit, N., Shea, S., & Cushman, M. (2010). Association of optimism and pessimism with inflammation and hemostasis in the multi-ethnic study of artherosclerosis (MESA). *Psychosomatic Medicine, 72,* 134–140.

Roy, M. S., Roy, A., & Affouf, M. (2007). Depression is a risk factor for poor glycemic control and retinopathy in African-Americans with type I diabetes. *Psychosomatic Medicine, 69,* 537–542.

Rozanski, A. (2005). Integrating psychological approaches into the behavioral management of cardiac patients. *Psychosomatic Medicine, 67,* S67–S73.

Rubin, G. J., Cleare, A., & Hotopf, M. (2004). Psychological factors in postoperative fatigue. *Psychosomatic Medicine, 66,* 959–964.

Ruble, D. N. (1972). Premenstrual symptoms: A reinterpretation. *Science, 197,* 291–292.

Ruchlin, H. (1997). Prevalence and correlates of breast and cervical cancer screening among older women. *Obstetrics and Gynecology, 90,* 16–21.

Rushing, B., Ritter, C., & Burton, R. P. D. (1992). Race differences in the effects of multiple roles on health: Longitudinal evidence from a national sample of older men. *Journal of Health and Social Behavior, 33,* 126–139.

Russek, L. G., & Schwartz, G. E. (1997). Feelings of parental caring can predict health status in midlife: A 35-year follow-up of the Harvard Mastery of Stress study. *Journal of Behavioral Medicine, 20,* 1–13.

Ruthig, J. C., & Chipperfield, J. G. (2007). Health incongruence in later life: Implications for subsequent well-being and health care. *Health Psychology, 26,* 753–761.

Rutledge, T., & Hogan, B. E. (2002). A quantitative review of prospective evidence linking psychological factors with hypertension development. *Psychosomatic Medicine, 64,* 758–766.

Rutledge, T., Linden, W., & Paul, D. (2000). Cardiovascular recovery from acute laboratory stress: Reliability and concurrent validity. *Psychosomatic Medicine, 62,* 648–654.

Rutledge, T., Linke, S. E., Krantz, D. S., Johnson, B. D., Bittner, V., Eastwood, J. A., et al. (2009). Comorbid depression and anxiety symptoms as predictors of cardiovascular events: Results from the NHLBI-sponsored women's ischemia syndrome evaluations (WISE) study. *Psychosomatic Medicine, 71,* 958–964.

Rutledge, T., Linke, S. E., Olson, M. B., Francis, J., Johnson, B. D., Bittner, V., et al. (2008). Social networks and incident stroke among women with suspected myocardial ischemia. *Psychosomatic Medicine, 70,* 282–287.

Rutledge, T., Matthews, K., Lui, L. Y., Stone, K. L., & Cauley, J. A. (2003). Social networks and marital status predict mortality in older women: Pro-

spective evidence from the Study of Osteoporotic Fractures (SOF). *Psychosomatic Medicine, 65,* 688–694.

Rutledge, T., Reis, S. E., Olson, M., Owens, J., Kelsey, S. F., Pepine, C. J., et al. (2004). Social networks are associated with lower mortality rates among women with suspected coronary disease: The national heart, lung, and blood institute-sponsored women's ischemia syndrome evaluation study. *Psychosomatic Medicine, 66,* 882–888.

Rutledge, T., Reis, S. E., Olson, M., Owens, J., Kelsey, S. F., Pepine, C. J., et al. (2006). Depression is associated with cardiac symptoms, mortality risk, and hospitalization among women with suspected coronary disease: The NHLBI-sponsored WISE study. *Psychosomatic Medicine, 68,* 217–223.

Rutledge, T., Stucky, E., Dollarhide, A., Shively, M., Jain, S., Wolfson, T., et al. (2009). A real-time assessment of work stress in physicians and nurses. *Health Psychology, 28,* 194–200.

Ryan, J., Zwerling, C., & Orav, E. J. (1992). Occupational risks associated with cigarette smoking: A prospective study. *American Journal of Public Health, 82,* 29–32.

Ryan, R. M., & Deci, E. L. (2000). Self-determination theory and the facilitation of intrinsic motivation, social development, and well-being. *American Psychologist, 55,* 68–78.

Ryff, C. D., Keyes, C. L. M., & Hughes, D. L. (2003). Status inequalities, perceived discrimination, and eudaimonic well-being: Do the challenges of minority life hone purpose and growth? *Journal of Health and Social Behavior, 44,* 275–291.

Ryff, C. D., & Singer, B. (1996). Psychological well-being: Meaning, measurement, and implications for psychotherapy research. *Psychotherapy and Psychosomatics, 65,* 14–23.

Ryff, C. D., & Singer, B. (2000). Interpersonal flourishing: A positive health agenda for the new millennium. *Personality and Social Psychology Review, 4,* 30–44.

Saab, P. G., Llabre, M. M., Schneiderman, N., Hurwitz, B. E., McDonald, P. G., Evans, J., et al. (1997). Influence of ethnicity and gender on cardiovascular responses to active coping and inhibitory-passive coping challenges. *Psychosomatic Medicine, 59,* 434–446.

Sacco, W. P., Malone, J. I., Morrison, A. D., Friedman, A., & Wells, K. (2009). Effect of a brief, regular telephone intervention by paraprofessionals for type 2 diabetes. *Journal of Behavioral Medicine, 32,* 349–359.

Sacco, W. P., Wells, K. J., Friedman, A., Matthew, R., Perez, S., & Vaughan, C. A. (2007). Adherence, body mass index, and depression in adults with type 2 diabetes: The mediational role of diabetes symptoms and self-efficacy. *Health Psychology, 26,* 693–700.

Sacco, W. P., Wells, K. J., Vaughan, C. A., Friedman, A., Perez, S., & Matthew, R. (2005). Depression in adults with type 2 diabetes: The role of adherence, body mass index, and self-efficacy. *Health Psychology, 24,* 630–634.

Sacker, A., Head, J., & Bartley, M. (2008). Impact of coronary heart disease on health functioning in an aging population: Are there differences according to socioeconomic position? *Psychosomatic Medicine, 70,* 133–140.

Sadava, S. W., & Pak, A. W. (1994). Problem drinking and close relationships during the third decade of life. *Psychology of Addictive Behaviors, 8,* 251–258.

Safer, M. A., Tharps, Q. J., Jackson, T. C., & Leventhal, H. (1979). Determinants of three stages of delay in seeking care at a medical care clinic. *Medical Care, 17,* 11–29.

Safren, S. A., O'Cleirigh, C., Tan, J. Y., Raminani, S. R., Reilly, L. C., Otto, M. W., et al. (2009). A randomized controlled trial of cognitive behavioral therapy for adherence and depression (CBT-AD) in HIV-infected individuals. *Health Psychology, 28,* 1–10.

Safren, S. A., Traeger, L., Skeer, M. R., O'Cleirigh, C., Meade, C. S., Covahey, C., et al. (2010). Testing a social-cognitive model of HIV transmission risk behaviors in HIV-infected MSM with and without depression. *Health Psychology, 29,* 215–221.

Sallis, J. F., King, A. C., Sirard, J. R., & Albright, C. L. (2007). Perceived environmental predictors of physical activity over 6 months in adults: Activity counseling trial. *Health Psychology, 26,* 701–709.

Sallis, J. F., Prochaska, J. J., Taylor, W. C., Hill, J. O., & Geraci, J. C. (1999). Correlates of physical activity in a national sample of girls and boys in grades 4 through 12. *Health Psychology, 18,* 410–415.

Salmon, J., Owen, N., Crawford, D., Bauman, A., & Sallis, J. F. (2003). Physical activity and sedentary behavior: A population-based study of barriers, enjoyment, and preference. *Health Psychology, 22,* 178–188.

Salmon, P., Humphris, G. M., Ring, A., Davies, J. C., & Dowrick, C. F. (2007). Primary care consultations about medically unexplained symptoms: Patient presentations and doctor responses that influence the probability of somatic intervention. *Psychosomatic Medicine, 69,* 571–577.

Salomon, K., Clift, A., Karlsdóttir, M., & Rottenberg, J. (2009). Major depressive disorder is associated with attenuated cardiovascular reactivity and impared recovery among those free of cardiovascular disease. *Health Psychology, 28,* 157–165.

Salomon, K., & Jagusztyn, N. E. (2008). Resting cardiovascular levels and reactivity to interpersonal incivility among Black, Latino/a, and White individuals: The moderating role of ethnic discrimination. *Health Psychology, 27,* 473–481.

Samwel, H. J. A., Kraaimaat, F. W., Crul, B. J. P., & Evers, A. W. M. (2007). The role of fear-avoidance and helplessness in explaining functional disability in chronic pain: A prospective study. *International Journal of Behavioral Medicine, 14,* 237–241.

Sanchez, L. M., & Turner, S. M. (2003). Practicing psychology in the era of managed care: Implications for practice and training. *American Psychologist, 58,* 116–129.

Sanderson, C. A., Darley, J. M., & Messinger, C. S. (2002). "I'm not as thin as you think I am": The development and consequences of feeling discrepant from the thinness norm. *Personality and Social Psychology Bulletin, 28,* 172–183.

Sanderson, C. A., & Yopyk, D. J. A. (2007). Improving condom use intentions and behavior by changing perceived partner norms: An evaluation of condom promotion videos for college students. *Health Psychology, 26,* 481–487.

Sandgren, A. K., & McCaul, K. D. (2003). Short-term effects of telephone therapy for breast cancer patients. *Health Psychology, 22,* 310–315.

Sarason, I. G., Johnson, J. H., & Siegel, J. M. (1978). Assessing the impact of life changes: Development of the Life Experiences Survey. *Journal of Consulting and Clinical Psychology, 46,* 932–946.

Sarason, I. G., Sarason, B. R., Pierce, G. R., Shearin, E. N., & Sayers, M. H. (1991). A social learning approach to increasing blood donations. *Journal of Applied Social Psychology, 21,* 896–918.

Sareen, J., Cox, B. J., Stein, M. B., Afifi, T. O., Fleet, C., & Asmundson, G. J. G. (2007). Physical and mental comorbidity, disability, and suicidal behavior associated with posttraumatic stress disorder in a large community sample. *Psychosomatic Medicine, 69,* 242–248.

Sargent, J. D., & Heatherton, T. F. (2009). Comparison of trends for adolescent smoking and smoking in movies, 1990–2007. *Journal of the American Medical Association, 301,* 2211–2213.

Sarkar, U., Ali, S., & Whooley, M. A. (2007). Self-efficacy and health status in patients with coronary heart disease: Findings from the heart and soul study. *Psychosomatic Medicine, 69,* 306–312.

Sarkar, U., Ali, S., & Whooley, M. A. (2009). Self-efficacy as a marker of cardiac function and predictor of heart failure hospitalization and mortality in patients with stable coronary heart disease: Findings from the heart and soul study. *Health Psychology, 28,* 166–173.

Sausen, K. P., Lovallo, W. R., Pincomb, G. A., & Wilson, M. F. (1992). Cardiovascular responses to occupational stress in male medical students: A paradigm for ambulatory monitoring studies. *Health Psychology, 11,* 55–60.

Sauter, S. L., Murphy, L. R., & Hurrell, J. J., Jr. (1990). Prevention of work-related psychological disorders: A national strategy proposed by the National Institute for Occupational Safety and Health (NIOSH). *American Psychologist, 45,* 1146–1158.

Saxbe, D. E., Repetti, R. L., & Nishina, A. (2008). Marital satisfaction, recovery from work, and diurnal cortisone among men and women. *Health Psychology, 27,* 15–25.

Saxby, B. K., Harrington, F., McKeith, I. G., Wesnes, K., & Ford, G. A. (2003). Effects of hypertension in attention, memory and executive function in older adults. *Health Psychology, 22,* 587–591.

Sayette, M. A., Loewenstein, G., Griffin, K. M., & Black, J. J. (2008). Exploring the cold-to-hot empathy gap in smokers. *Psychological Science, 19,* 926–932.

Sbarra, D. A. (2009). Marriage protects men from clinically meaningful elevations in C-reactive protein: Results from the national social life, health, and aging project (NSHAP). *Psychosomatic Medicine, 71,* 828–835.

Sbarra, D. A., & Nietert, P. J. (2009). Divorce and death: Forty years of the Charleston heart study. *Psychological Science, 20,* 107–113.

Scanlan, J. M., Vitaliano, P. P., Zhang, J., Savage, M., & Ochs, H. D. (2001). Lymphocyte proliferation is associated with gender, caregiving, and psychosocial variables in older adults. *Journal of Behavioral Medicine, 24,* 537–559.

Schachinger, H., Hegar, K., Hermanns, N., Straumann, M., Keller, U., Fehm-Wolfsdorf, G., et al. (2005). Randomized controlled clinical trial of blood glucose awareness training (BGAT III) in Switzerland and Germany. *Journal of Behavioral Medicine, 28,* 587–594.

Schanowitz, J. Y., & Nicassio, P. M. (2006). Predictors of positive psychosocial functioning of older adults in residential care facilities. *Journal of Behavioral Medicine, 29,* 191–201.

Schechtman, K. B., Ory, M. G., & the FICSIT group. (2001). The effects of exercise on the quality of life of frail older adults: A preplanned meta-analysis of the FICSIT trials. *Annals of Behavioral Medicine, 23,* 186–197.

Scheier, M. F., Carver, C. S., & Bridges, M. W. (1994). Distinguishing optimism from neuroticism (and trait anxiety, self-mastery, and self-esteem): A reevaluation of the Life Orientation Test. *Journal of Personality and Social Psychology, 67,* 1063–1078.

Scheier, M. F., Matthews, K. A., Owens, J., Magovern, G. J., Sr., Lefebvre, R. C., Abbott, R. A., et al. (1989). Dispositional optimism and recovery from coronary artery bypass surgery: The beneficial effects on physical and psychological well-being. *Journal of Personality and Social Psychology, 57,* 1024–1040.

Scheier, M. F., Weintraub, J. K., & Carver, C. S. (1986). Coping with stress: Divergent strategies of optimists and pessimists. *Journal of Personality and Social Psychology, 51,* 1257–1264.

Schernhammer, E. (2005). Taking their own lives—The high rate of physician suicide. *The New England Journal of Medicine, 352,* 2473–2476.

Scherrer, J. F., Xian, H., Bucholz, K. K., Eisen, S. E., Lyons, M. J., Goldberg, J., et al. (2003). A twin study of depression symptoms, hypertension, and heart disease in middle-aged men. *Psychosomatic Medicine, 65,* 548–557.

Scheufele, P. M. (2000). Effects of progressive relaxation and classical music on measurements of attention, relaxation, and stress responses. *Journal of Behavioral Medicine, 23,* 207–228.

Schieken, R. M. (1988). Preventive cardiology: An overview. *Journal of the American College of Cardiology, 12,* 1090–1091.

Schins, A., Honig, A., Crijns, H., Baur, L., & Hamulyak, K. (2003). Increased coronary events in depressed cardiovascular patients: 5HT2A receptor as missing link? *Psychosomatic Medicine, 65,* 729–737.

Schleifer, S. J., Scott, B., Stein, M., & Keller, S. E. (1986). Behavioral and developmental aspects of immunity. *Journal of the American Academy of Child Psychiatry, 26,* 751–763.

Schlotz, W., Hellhammer, J., Schulz, P., & Stone, A. A. (2004). Perceived work overload and chronic worrying predict weekend-weekday differences in the cortisol awakening response. *Psychosomatic Medicine, 66,* 207–214.

Schnall, E., Wassertheil-Smoller, S., Swencionis, C., Zemon, V., Tinker, L., O'Sullivan, M. J., et al. (2010). The relationship between religion and cardiovascular outcomes and all-cause mortality in the women's health initiative observational study. *Psychology and Health, 25,* 249–263.

Schneider, J. A., O'Leary, A., & Agras, W. S. (1987). The role of perceived self-efficacy in recovery from bulimia: A preliminary examination. *Behavioral Research and Therapy, 25,* 429–432.

Schneider, M. S., Friend, R., Whitaker, P., & Wadhwa, N. K. (1991). Fluid noncompliance and symptomatology in end-stage renal disease: Cognitive and emotional variables. *Health Psychology, 10,* 209–215.

Schneider, S., Moyer, A., Knapp-Oliver, S., Sohl, S., Cannella, D., & Targhetta, V. (2010). Pre-intervention distress moderated the efficacy of psychosocial treatment for cancer patients: A meta-analysis. *Journal of Behavioral Medicine, 33,* 1–14.

Schneiderman, L. J., Kronick, R., Kaplan, R. M., Anderson, J. P., & Langer, R. D. (1992). Effects of offering advance directives on medical treatments and costs. *Annals of Internal Medicine, 117,* 599–606.

Schnurr, P. P., Friedman, M. J., Engel, C. C., Foa, E. B., Shea, M. T., Chow, B. K., et al. (2007). Cognitive behavioral therapy for posttraumatic stress disorder in women: A randomized controlled trial. *Journal of the American Medical Association, 297,* 820–830.

Scholz, U., Keller, R., & Perren, S. (2009). Predicting behavioral intentions and physical exercise: A test of the health action process approach at the intrapersonal level. *Health Psychology, 28,* 702–708.

Schommer, N. C., Hellhammer, D. H., & Kirschbaum, C. (2003). Dissociation between reactivity of the hypothalamus-pituitary-adrenal axis and the sympathetic-adrenal-medullary system to repeated psychosocial stress. *Psychosomatic Medicine, 65,* 450–460.

Schreier, H. M. C., & Chen, E. (2010). Longitudinal relationships between family routines and biological profiles among youth with asthma. *Health Psychology, 29,* 82–90.

Schrimshaw, E. W. (2003). Relationship-specific unsupportive social interactions and depressive symptoms among women living with HIV/AIDS: Direct and moderating effects. *Journal of Behavioral Medicine, 26,* 297–313.

Schroeder, D. H., & Costa, P. T., Jr. (1984). Influence of life event stress on physical illness: Substantive effects or methodological flaws? *Journal of Personality and Social Psychology, 46,* 853–863.

Schulz, R. (1978). *The psychology of death, dying, and bereavement.* Reading, MA: Addison-Wesley.

Schulz, R., & Beach, S. R. (1999). Caregiving as a risk factor for mortality: The caregiver health effects study. *Journal of the American Medical Association, 282,* 2215–2219.

Schulz, R., Bookwala, J., Knapp, J. E., Scheier, M., & Williamson, G. (1996). Pessimism, age, and cancer mortality. *Psychology and Aging, 11,* 304–309.

Schulz, R., & Decker, S. (1985). Long-term adjustment to physical disability: The role of social support, perceived control, and self-blame. *Journal of Personality and Social Psychology, 48,* 1162–1172.

Schum, J. L., Jorgensen, R. S., Verhaeghen, P., Sauro, M., & Thibodeau, R. (2003). Trait anger, anger expression, and ambulatory blood pressure: A meta-analytic review. *Journal of Behavioral Medicine, 26,* 395–415.

Schwartz, C., Meisenhelder, J. B., Ma, Y., & Reed, G. (2003). Altruistic social interest behaviors are associated with better mental health. *Psychosomatic Medicine, 65,* 778–785

Schwartz, J. E., Neale, J., Marco, C., Shiffman, S. S., & Stone, A. A. (1999). Does trait coping exist? A momentary assessment approach to the evaluation of traits. *Journal of Personality and Social Psychology, 77,* 360–369.

Schwartz, M. B., & Brownell, K. D. (1995). Matching individuals to weight loss treatments: A survey of obesity experts. *Journal of Consulting and Clinical Psychology, 63,* 149–153.

Schwartz, M. D., Taylor, K. L., & Willard, K. S. (2003). Prospective association between distress and mammography utilization among women with a family history of breast cancer. *Journal of Behavioral Medicine, 26,* 105–117.

Schwartz, M. D., Valdimarsdottir, H. B., DeMarco, T. A., Peshkin, B. N., Lawrence, W., Rispoli, J., et al. (2009). Randomized trial of a decision aid for BRCA1/BRCA2 mutation carriers: Impact on measure of decision making and satisfaction. *Health Psychology, 28,* 11–19.

Schwarzer, R., Luszczynska, A., Ziegelmann, J. P., Scholz, U., & Lippke, S. (2008). Social-cognitive predictors of physical exercise adherence: Three longitudinal studies in rehabilitation. *Health Psychology, 27,* S54-S63.

Schwarzer, R., & Renner, B. (2000). Social-cognitive predictors of health behavior: Action self-efficacy and coping self-efficacy. *Health Psychology, 19,* 487–495.

Schweiger, U., Greggersen, W., Rudolf, S., Pusch, M., Menzel, T., Winn, S., et al. (2008). Disturbed glucose disposal in patients with major depression; Application of the glucose technique. *Psychosomatic Medicine, 70,* 170–176.

Scott, K. M., Von Koff, M., Alonso, J., Angermeyer, M. C., Benjet, C., Bruffaerts, R., et al. (2008). Childhood adversity, early-onset depressive/anxiety disorders, and adult-onset asthma. *Psychosomatic Medicine, 70,* 1035–1043.

Scott-Sheldon, L. A. J., Kalichman, S. C., Carey, M. P., & Fielder, R. L. (2008). Stress management interventions for HIV+ adults: A meta-analysis of randomized controlled trials, 1989–2006. *Health Psychology, 27,* 129–139.

Scrimshaw, S. M., Engle, P. L., & Zambrana, R. E. (1983, August). *Prenatal anxiety and birth outcome in U.S. Latinas: Implications for psychosocial interventions.* Paper presented at the annual meeting of the American Psychological Association, Anaheim, CA.

Searle, A., Wetherell, M. A., Campbell, R., Dayan, C., Weinman, J., & Vedhara, K. (2008). Do patient's beliefs about type 2 diabetes differ in accordance with complications: An investigation into diabetic foot ulceration and retinopathy. *International Journal of Behavioral Medicine, 15,* 173–179.

Sears, S. R., & Stanton, A. L. (2001). Physician-assisted dying: Review of issues and roles for health psychologists. *Health Psychology, 20,* 302–310.

Sears, S. R., Stanton, A. L., & Danoff-Burg, S. (2003). The yellow brick road and the emerald city: Benefit finding, positive reappraisal coping and posttraumatic growth in women with early-stage breast cancer. *Health Psychology, 22,* 487–497.

Seeman, M., Seeman, A. Z., & Budros, A. (1988). Powerlessness, work, and community: A longitudinal study of alienation and alcohol use. *Journal of Health and Social Behavior, 29,* 185–198.

Seeman, T. E., Berkman, L. F., Gulanski, B. I., Robbins, R. J., Greenspan, S. L., Charpentier, P. A., et al. (1995). Self-esteem and neuroendocrine response to challenge: MacArthur studies of successful aging. *Journal of Psychosomatic Research, 39,* 69–84.

Seeman, T. E., Dubin, L. F., & Seeman, M. (2003). Religiosity/spirituality and health: A critical review of the evidence for biological pathways. *American Psychologist, 58,* 53–63.

Seeman, T. E., Lusignolo, T. M., Albert, M., & Berkman, L. (2001). Social relationships, social support, and patterns of cognitive aging in healthy, high-functioning older adults: MacArthur studies of successful aging. *Health Psychology, 20,* 243–255.

Seeman, T. E., Singer, B., Horwitz, R., & McEwen, B. S. (1997). The price of adaptation—Allostatic load and its health consequences: MacArthur studies of successful aging. *Archives of Internal Medicine, 157,* 2259–2268.

Seeman, T. E., Singer, B. H., Ryff, C. D., Love, G. D., & Levy-Storms, L. (2002). Social relationships, gender, and allostatic load across two age cohorts. *Psychosomatic Medicine, 64,* 395–406.

Segan, C. J., Borland, R., & Greenwood, K. M. (2004). What is the right thing at the right time? Interactions between stages and processes of change among smokers who make a quit attempt. *Health Psychology, 23,* 86–93.

Segerstrom, S. C. (2001). Optimism, goal conflict, and stressor-related immune change. *Journal of Behavioral Medicine, 24,* 441–467.

Segerstrom, S. C. (2006a). How does optimism suppress immunity? Evaluation of three affective pathways. *Health Psychology, 25,* 653–657.

Segerstrom, S. C. (2006b). Optimism and resources: Effects on each other and on health over 10 years. *Journal of Research in Personality, 41,* 772–786.

Segerstrom, S. C., Castañeda, J. O., & Spencer, T. E. (2003). Optimism effects on cellular immunity: Testing the affective and persistence models. *Personality and Individual Differences, 35,* 1615–1624.

Segerstrom, S. C., & Miller, G. E. (2004). Psychological stress and the human immune system: A meta-analytic study of 30 years of inquiry. *Psychological Bulletin, 130,* 601–630.

Segerstrom, S. C., & Sephton, S. E. (2010). Optimistic expectancies and cell-mediated immunity: The role of positive affect. *Psychological Science, 21,* 448–455.

Segerstrom, S. C., Taylor, S. E., Kemeny, M. E., & Fahey, J. L. (1998). Optimism is associated with mood, coping, and immune change in response to stress. *Journal of Personality and Social Psychology, 74,* 1646–1655.

Segerstrom, S. C., Taylor, S. E., Kemeny, M. E., Reed, G. M., & Visscher, B. R. (1996). Causal attributions predict rate of immune decline in HIV-seropositive gay men. *Health Psychology, 15,* 485–493.

Seidman, D. F., Westmaas, J. L., Goldband, S., Rabius, V., Katkin, E. S., Pike, K. J., et al. (2010). Randomized controlled trial of an interactive Internet smoking cessation program with long-term follow-up. *Annals of Behavioral Medicine, 39,* 48–60.

Self, C. A., & Rogers, R. W. (1990). Coping with threats to health: Effects of persuasive appeals on depressed, normal, and antisocial personalities. *Journal of Behavioral Medicine, 13,* 343–358.

Selye, H. (1956). *The stress of life.* New York: McGraw-Hill.

Selye, H. (1976). *Stress in health and disease.* Woburn, MA: Butterworth.

Senecal, C., Nouwen, A., & White, D. (2000). Motivation and dietary self-care in adults with diabetes: Are self-efficacy and autonomous self-regulation complementary or competing constructs? *Health Psychology, 19,* 452–457.

Seneff, M. G., Wagner, D. P., Wagner, R. P., Zimmerman, J. E., & Knaus, W. A. (1995). Hospital and 1-year survival of patients admitted to intensive care units with acute exacerbation of chronic obstructive pulmonary disease. *Journal of the American Medical Association, 274,* 1852–1857.

Sengupta, M., Bercovitz, A., & Harris-Kojetin, L. D. (2010). Prevalence and management of pain, by race and dementia among nursing home residents: United States, 2004. *NCHS Data Brief, 30,* 1–8.

Serido, J., Almeida, D. M., & Wethington, E. (2004). Chronic stress and daily hassles: Unique and interactive relationships with psychological distress. *Journal of Health and Social Behavior, 45,* 17–33.

Severeijns, R., Vlaeyen, J. W. S., van den Hout, M. A., & Picavet, H. S. J. (2004). Pain catastrophizing is associated with health indices in musculoskeletal pain: A cross-sectional study in the Dutch community. *Health Psychology, 23,* 49–57

Sevick, M. A., Stone, R. A., Zickmund, S., Wang, Y., Korytkowski, M., & Burke, L. E. (2010). Factors associated with probability of personal digital assistant-based dietary self-monitoring in those with type 2 diabetes. *Journal of Behavioral Medicine, 33,* 315–325.

Shadel, W. G., & Mermelstein, R. J. (1996). Individual differences in self-concept among smokers attempting to quit: Validation and predictive utility of measures of the smoker self-concept and abstainer self-concept. *Annals of Behavioral Medicine, 18,* 151–156.

Shadel, W. G., Niaura, R., & Abrams, D. B. (2004). Who am I? The role of self-conflict in adolescents' responses to cigarette advertising. *Journal of Behavioral Medicine, 27,* 463–475.

Shadish, W. R. (2010). Introduction: The perils of science in the world of policy and practice. *Health Psychology, 29,* 105–106.

Shaffer, W. J., Duszynski, K. R., & Thomas, C. B. (1982). Family attitudes in youth as a possible precursor of cancer among physicians: A search for explanatory mechanisms. *Journal of Behavioral Medicine, 15,* 143–164.

Shai, I., Schwarfuchs, D., Henkin, Y., Shahar, D. R., Witkow, S., Greenberg, I., et al. (2008). Weight loss with a low-carbohydrate, Mediterranean, or low-fat diet. *The New England Journal of Medicine, 359,* 229–241.

Shapiro, A. K. (1960). A contribution to a history of the placebo effect. *Behavioral Science, 5,* 109–135.

Shapiro, A. K. (1964). Factors contributing to the placebo effect: Their implications for psychotherapy. *American Journal of Psychotherapy, 18,* 73–88.

Shapiro, D., Hui, K. K., Oakley, M. E., Pasic, J., & Jamner, L. D. (1997). Reduction in drug requirements for hypertension by means of a cognitive-behavioral intervention. *American Journal of Hypertension, 10,* 9–17.

Shapiro, D. E., Boggs, S. R., Melamed, B. G., & Graham-Pole, J. (1992). The effect of varied physician affect on recall, anxiety, and perceptions in women at risk for breast cancer: An analogue study. *Health Psychology, 11,* 61–66.

Sharman, S. J., Garry, M., Jacobson, J. A., Loftus, E. F., & Ditto, P. H. (2008). False memories for end-of-life decisions. *Health Psychology, 27,* 291–296.

Sharpe, T. R., Smith, M. C., & Barbre, A. R. (1985). Medicine use among the rural elderly. *Journal of Health and Social Behavior, 26,* 113–127.

Shattuck, F. C. (1907). The science and art of medicine in some of their aspects. *Boston Medical and Surgical Journal, 157,* 63–67.

Shaver, J. L. F., Johnston, S. K., Lentz, M. J., & Landis, C. A. (2002). Stress exposure, psychological distress, and physiological stress activation in midlife women with insomnia. *Psychosomatic Medicine, 64,* 793–802.

Sheahan, S. L., Coons, S. J., Robbins, C. A., Martin, S. S., Hendricks, J., & Latimer, M. (1995). Psychoactive medication, alcohol use, and falls among older adults. *Journal of Behavioral Medicine, 18,* 127–140.

Sheeran, P., Conner, M., & Norman, P. (2001). Can the theory of planned behavior explain patterns of health behavior change? *Health Psychology, 20,* 12–19.

Sheese, B. E., Brown, E. L., & Graziano, W. G. (2004). Emotional expression in cyberspace: Searching for moderators of the Pennebaker Disclosure Effect via e-mail. *Health Psychology, 23,* 457–464.

Sheffield, D., Biles, P., Orom, H., Maixner, W., & Sheps, D. (2000). Race and sex differences in cutaneous pain perception. *Psychosomatic Medicine, 62,* 517–523.

Shelby, R. A., Somers, T. J., Keefe, F. J., Silva, S. G., McKee, D. C., She, L., et al. (2009). Pain catastrophizing in patients with noncardiac chest pain: Relationships with pain, anxiety, and disability. *Psychosomatic Medicine, 71,* 861–868.

Shelton, J. L., & Levy, R. L. (1981). *Behavioral assignments and treatment compliance: A handbook of clinical strategies.* Champaign, IL: Research Press.

Sherbourne, C. D., Hays, R. D., Ordway, L., DiMatteo, M. R., & Kravitz, R. L. (1992). Antecedents of adherence to medical recommendations: Results from the medical outcomes study. *Journal of Behavioral Medicine, 15,* 447–468.

Sherman, A. C., Pennington, J., Simonton, S., Latif, U., Arent, L., & Farley, H. (2008). Determinants of participation in cancer support groups: The role of health beliefs. *International Journal of Behavioral Medicine, 15,* 92–100.

Sherman, A. C., Plante, T. G., Simonton, S., Latif, U., & Anaissie, E. J. (2009). A prospective study of religious coping among patients undergoing autologous stem cell transplantation. *Journal of Behavioral Medicine, 32,* 118–128.

Sherman, D. K., Bunyan, D. P., Creswell, J. D., & Jaremka, L. M. (2009). Psychological vulnerability and stress: The effects of self-affirmation on sympathetic nervous system responses to naturalistic stressors. *Health Psychology, 28,* 554–562.

Sherman, D. K., & Cohen, G. L. (2006). The psychology of self-defense: Self-affirmation theory. In M. P. Zanna (Ed.), *Advances in Experimental Social Psychology* (Vol. 38, pp. 183–242). San Diego, CA: Academic Press.

Sherman, J. J., LeResche, L., Hanson Huggins, K., Mancl, L. A., Sage, J. C., & Dworkin, S. F. (2004). The relationship of somatization and depression to experimental pain response in women with temporomandibular disorders. *Psychosomatic Medicine, 66,* 852–860.

Sherwood, A., Hinderliter, A. L., & Light, K. C. (1995). Physiological determinants of hyperreactivity to stress in borderline hypertension. *Hypertension, 25,* 384–390.

Shewchuk, R. M., Richards, J. S., & Elliott, T. R. (1998). Dynamic processes in health outcomes among caregivers of patients with spinal cord injuries. *Health Psychology, 17,* 125–129.

Shiffman, S., Fischer, L. A., Paty, J. A., Gnys, M., Hickcox, M., & Kassel, J. D. (1994). Drinking and smoking: A field study of their association. *Annals of Behavioral Medicine, 16,* 203–209.

Shiffman, S., Hickcox, M., Paty, J. A., Gnys, M., Kassel, J. D., & Richards, T. J. (1996). Progression from a smoking lapse to relapse: Prediction from abstinence violation effects, nicotine dependence, and lapse characteristics. *Journal of Consulting and Clinical Psychology, 64,* 993–1002.

Shiffman, S., Kassel, J. D., Paty, J., Gnys, M., & Zettler-Segal, M. (1994). Smoking typology profiles of clippers and regular smokers. *Journal of Substance Abuse, 6,* 21–35.

Shifren, K., Park, D. C., Bennett, J. M., & Morrell, R. W. (1999). Do cognitive processes predict mental health in individuals with rheumatoid arthritis? *Journal of Behavioral Medicine, 22,* 529–547.

Shiloh, S., Drori, E., Orr-Urtreger, A., & Friedman, E. (2009). Being 'at-risk' for developing cancer: Cognitive representations and psychological outcomes. *Journal of Behavioral Medicine, 32,* 197–208.

Shiloh, S., Gerad, L., & Goldman, B. (2006). Patients' information needs and decision-making processes: What can be learned from genetic counselees? *Health Psychology, 25,* 211–219.

Shiloh, S., & Ilan, S. (2005). To test or not to test? Moderators of the relationship between risk perceptions and interest in predictive genetic testing. *Journal of Behavioral Medicine, 28,* 467–479.

Shimazu, A., de Jonge, J., & Irimajiri, H. (2008). Lagged effects of active coping within the demand-control model: A three wave panel study among Japanese employees. *International Journal of Behavioral Medicine, 15,* 44–53.

Shimizu, M., & Pelham, B. W. (2004). The unconsciousness cost of good fortune: Implicit and explicit self-esteem, positive life events, and health. *Health Psychology, 23,* 101–105.

Shinn, M., Rosario, M., Morch, H., & Chestnut, D. E. (1984). Coping with job stress and burnout in the human services. *Journal of Personality and Social Psychology, 46,* 864–876.

Shipley, B. A., Der, G., Taylor, M. D., & Deary, I. J. (2007). Association between mortality and cognitive change over 7 years in a large representative sample of UK residents. *Psychosomatic Medicine, 69,* 640–650.

Shipley, B. A., Weiss, A., Der, G., Taylor, M. D., & Deary, I. J. (2007). Neuroticism, extraversion, and mortality in the UK health and lifestyle survey: A 21-year prospective cohort study. *Psychosomatic Medicine, 69,* 923–931.

Shively, C. A., Register, T. C., Adams, M. R., Golden, D. L., Willard, S. L., & Clarkson, T. B. (2008). Depressive behavior and coronary artery atherogenesis in adult female cynomolgus monkeys. *Psychosomatic Medicine, 70,* 637–645.

Shmueli, D., & Prochaska, J. J. (2009). Resisting tempting foods and smoking behavior: Implications from a self-control theory perspective. *Health Psychology, 28,* 300–306.

Shnayerson, M. (2002, September 30). The killer bug. *Fortune,* p. 149.

Sidney, S., Friedman, G. D., & Siegelaub, A. B. (1987). Thinness and mortality. *American Journal of Public Health, 77,* 317–322.

Sieber, W. J., Rodin, J., Larson, L., Ortega, S., Cummings, N., Levy, S., et al. (1992). Modulation of human natural killer cell activity by exposure to uncontrollable stress. *Brain, Behavior, and Immunity, 6,* 1–16.

Siegel, J. T., Alvaro, E. M., Crano, W. D., Lac, A., Ting, S., & Jones, S. P. (2008). A quasi-experimental investigation of message appeal variations on organ donor registration rates. *Health Psychology, 27,* 170–178.

Siegel, K., Karus, D., & Raveis, V. H. (1997). Correlates of change in depressive symptomatology among gay men with AIDS. *Health Psychology, 16,* 230–238.

Siegel, K., Mesagno, F. P., Chen, J. Y., & Christ, G. (1987, June). *Factors distinguishing homosexual males practicing safe and risky sex.* Paper presented at the Third International Conference on AIDS, Washington, DC.

Siegler, I. C., Costa, P. T., Brummett, B. H., Helms, M. J., Barefoot, J. C., Williams, R. B., et al. (2003). Patterns of change in hostility from college to midlife in the UNC alumni heart study predict high-risk status. *Psychosomatic Medicine, 65,* 738–745.

Siegler, I. C., Peterson, B. L., Barefoot, J. C., & Williams, R. B. (1992). Hostility during late adolescence predicts coronary risk factors at mid-life. *American Journal of Epidemiology, 136,* 146–154.

Siegman, A. W., & Snow, S. C. (1997). The outward expression of anger, the inward experience of anger, and CVR: The role of vocal expression. *Journal of Behavioral Medicine, 20,* 29–46.

Siegman, A. W., Townsend, S. T., Civelek, A. C., & Blumenthal, R. S. (2000). Antagonistic behavior, dominance, hostility, and coronary heart disease. *Psychosomatic Medicine, 62,* 248–257.

Siegrist, J., Peter, R., Runge, A., Cremer, P., & Seidel, D. (1990). Low status control, high effort at work, and ischemic heart disease: Prospective evidence from blue-collar men. *Social Science and Medicine, 31,* 1127–1134.

Sieverding, M., Matterne, U., & Ciccarello, L. (2010). What role do social norms play in the context of men's cancer screening intentions and behavior? Application of an extended theory of planned behavior. *Health Psychology, 29,* 72–81.

Sikkema, K. J., Hansen, N. B., Ghebremichael, M., Kochman, A., Tarakeshwar, N., Meade, C. S., et al. (2006). A randomized controlled trial of a coping group intervention for adults with HIV who are AIDS bereaved: Longitudinal effects on grief. *Health Psychology, 25,* 563–570.

Silver, E. J., Bauman, L. J., & Ireys, H. T. (1995). Relationships of self-esteem and efficacy to psychological distress in mothers of children with chronic physical illnesses. *Health Psychology, 14,* 333–340.

Silver, R. C., Holman, E. A., McIntosh, D. N., Poulin, M., & Gil-Rivas, V. (2002). Nationwide longitudinal study of psychological responses to September 11. *Journal of the American Medical Association, 288,* 1235–1244.

Silver, R. L., & Wortman, C. B. (1980). Coping with undesirable life events. In J. Garber & M. E. P. Seligman (Eds.), *Human helplessness: Theory and applications.* New York: Academic Press.

Silverstein, M., & Bengtson, V. L. (1991). Do close parent-child relations reduce the mortality risk of older parents? *Journal of Health and Social Behavior, 32,* 382–395.

Siminoff, L. A., & Step, M. M. (2005). A communication model of shared decision making: Accounting for cancer treatment decisions. *Health Psychology, 24*(Suppl.), S99–S105.

Simkin-Silverman, L., Wing, R. R., Hansen, D. H., Klem, M. L., Pasagian-Macaulay, A., Meilahn, E. N., et al. (1995). Prevention of cardiovascular risk factor elevations in healthy premenopausal women. *Preventive Medicine, 24*, 509–571.

Simkin-Silverman, L. R., Wing, R. R., Boraz, M. A., & Kuller, L. H. (2003). Lifestyle intervention can prevent weight gain during menopause: Results from a 5-year randomized clinical trial. *Annals of Behavioral Medicine, 26*, 212–220.

Simon, N. (2003). Can you hear me now? *Time.*

Simon, R. W. (1992). Parental role strains, salience of parental identity and gender differences in psychological distress. *Journal of Health and Social Behavior, 33*, 25–35.

Simon, R. W. (1998). Assessing sex differences in vulnerability among employed parents: The importance of marital status. *Journal of Health and Social Behavior, 39*, 38–54.

Simonelli, L. E., Fowler, J., Maxwell, G. L., & Andersen, B. L. (2008). Physical sequelae and depressive symptoms in gynecologic cancer survivors: Meaning in life as a mediator. *Annals of Behavioral Medicine, 35*, 275–284.

Simoni, J. M., Frick, P. A., & Huang, B. (2006). A longitudinal evaluation of a social support model of medication adherence among HIV-positive men and women on antiretroviral therapy. *Health Psychology, 25*, 74–81.

Simoni, J. M., & Ng, M. T. (2002). Abuse, health locus of control, and perceived health among HIV-positive women. *Health Psychology, 21*, 89–93.

Simons-Morton, B., Chen, R., Abroms, L., & Haynie, D. L. (2006). Latent growth curve analyses of peer and parent influences on smoking progression among early adolescents. *Health Psychology, 23*, 612–621.

Simrén, M., Ringstrom, G., Björnsson, E. S., & Abrahamsson, H. (2004). Treatment with hypnotherapy reduces the sensory and motor component of the gastrocolonic response in irritable bowel syndrome. *Psychosomatic Medicine, 66*, 233–238.

Singer, B. H. (Ed.). (2000). *Future directions for behavioral and social sciences research at the National Institutes of Health.* Washington, DC: National Academy of Sciences Press.

Singh-Manoux, A., Gueguen, A., Martikainen, P., Ferrie, J., Marmot, M., & Shipley, M. (2007). Self-rated health and mortality: Short- and long-term associations in the Whitehall II study. *Psychosomatic Medicine, 69*, 138–143.

Singh-Manoux, A., Richards, M., & Marmot, M. (2003). Leisure activities and cognitive function in middle age: Evidence from the Whitehall II study. *Journal of Epidemiology and Community Health, 57*, 907–913.

Sinha, R., Fisch, G., Teague, B., Tamborlane, W. V., Banyas, B., Allen, K., et al. (2002). Prevalence of impaired glucose tolerance among children and adolescents with marked obesity. *The New England Journal of Medicine, 346*, 802–810.

Sinyor, D., Amato, P., Kaloupek, D. G., Becker, R., Goldenberg, M., & Coopersmith, H. (1986). Post-stroke depression: Relationships to functional impairment, coping strategies, and rehabilitation outcomes. *Stroke, 17*, 1102–1107.

Skaff, M. M., Mullan, J. T., Almeida, D. M., Hoffman, L., Masharani, U., Mohr, D., et al. (2009). Daily negative mood affects fasting glucose in type 2 diabetes. *Health Psychology, 28*, 265–272.

Skala, J. A., & Freedland, K. E. (2004). Death takes a raincheck. *Psychosomatic Medicine, 66*, 382–386.

Skapinakis, P., Lewis, G., & Mavreas, V. (2004). Temporal relations between unexplained fatigue and depression: Longitudinal data from an international study in primary care. *Psychosomatic Medicine, 66*, 330–335.

Skinner, N., & Brewer, N. (2002). The dynamics of threat and challenge appraisals prior to stressful achievement events. *Journal of Personality and Social Psychology, 83*, 678–692.

Skinner, T. C., Hampson, S. E., & Fife-Schaw, C. (2002). Personality, personal model beliefs, and self-care in adolescents and young adults with type 1 diabetes. *Health Psychology, 21*, 61–70.

Slater, R., Cantarella, A., Gallella, S., Worley, A., Boyd, S., Meek, J., et al. (2006). Cortical pain responses in human infants. *Journal of Neuroscience, 26*, 3662–3666.

Sledjeski, E. M., Speisman, B., & Dierker, L. C. (2008). Does number of lifetime traumas explain the relationship between PTSD and chronic medical conditions? Answers from the national comorbidity survey-replication (NCS-R). *Journal of Behavioral Medicine, 31*, 341–349.

Slesnick, N., & Kang, M. J. (2008). The impact of an integrated treatment on HIV risk behavior among homeless youth: A randomized controlled trial. *Journal of Behavioral Medicine, 31*, 45–59.

Sloan, R. P., Shapiro, P. A., Bagiella, E., Myers, M. M., & Gorman, J. M. (1999). Cardiac autonomic control buffers blood pressure variability responses to challenge: A psychophysiologic model of coronary artery disease. *Psychosomatic Medicine, 61*, 58–68.

Sloan, R. P., Shapiro, P. A., Gorenstein, E. E., Tager, F. A., Monk, C. E., McKinley, P. S., et al. (2010). Cardiac autonomic control and treatment of hostility: A randomized controlled trial. *Psychosomatic Medicine, 72*, 1–8.

Smalec, J. L., & Klingle, R. S. (2000). Bulimia interventions via interpersonal influence: The role of threat and efficacy in persuading bulimics to seek help. *Journal of Behavioral Medicine, 23*, 37–57.

Smerecnik, C. M. R., Mesters, I., de Vries, N. K., & de Vries, H. (2009). Alerting the general population to genetic risks: The value of health messages communicating the existence of genetic risk factors for public health promotion. *Health Psychology, 28*, 734–745.

Smith, A. M., Loving, T. J., Crockett, E. E., & Campbell, L. (2009). What's closeness got to do with it? Men's and women's cortisol responses when providing and receiving support. *Psychosomatic Medicine, 71*, 843–851.

Smith, B. W., & Zautra, A. J. (2002). The role of personality in exposure and reactivity to interpersonal stress in relation to arthritis disease activity and negative effects in women. *Health Psychology, 21*, 81–88.

Smith, G. (2004). Asian-American deaths near the harvest moon festival. *Psychosomatic Medicine, 66*, 378–381.

Smith, G. (2006). The five elements and Chinese-American mortality. *Health Psychology, 25*, 124–129.

Smith, J. A., Lumley, M. A., & Longo, D. J. (2002). Contrasting emotional approach coping with passive coping for chronic myofascial pain. *Annals of Behavioral Medicine, 24*, 326–335.

Smith, L., Adler, N., & Tschann, J. (1999). Underreporting sensitive behaviors: The case of young women's willingness to report abortion. *Health Psychology, 18*, 37–43.

Smith, P., Frank, J., Bondy, S., & Mustard, C. (2008). Do changes in job control predict differences in health status? Results from a longitudinal national survey of Canadians. *Psychosomatic Medicine*, 85–91.

Smith, P. J., Blumenthal, J. A., Hoffman, B. M., Cooper, H., Strauman, T. A., Welsh-Bohmer, K., et al. (2010). Aerobic exercise and neurocognitive performance: A meta-analytic review of randomized controlled trials. *Psychosomatic Medicine, 72*, 239–252.

Smith, T. W., & Gallo, L. C. (1999). Hostility and cardiovascular reactivity during marital interaction. *Psychosomatic Medicine, 61*, 436–445.

Smith, T. W., Orleans, C. T., & Jenkins, C. D. (2004). Prevention and health promotion: Decades of progress, new challenges, and an emerging agenda. *Health Psychology, 23*, 126–131.

Smith, T. W., Peck, J. R., Milano, R. A., & Ward, J. R. (1988). Cognitive distortion in rheumatoid arthritis: Relation to depression and disability. *Journal of Consulting and Clinical Psychology, 56*, 412–416.

Smith, T. W., & Ruiz, J. M. (2002). Psychosocial influences on the development and course of coronary heart disease: Current status and implications for research and practice. *Journal of Consulting and Clinical Psychology, 70,* 548–568.

Smith, T. W., Ruiz, J. M., & Uchino, B. N. (2000). Vigilance, active coping, and cardiovascular reactivity during social interaction in young men. *Health Psychology, 19,* 382–392.

Smith, T. W., Ruiz, J. M., & Uchino, B. N. (2004). Mental activation of supportive ties, hostility, and cardiovascular reactivity to laboratory stress in young men and women. *Health Psychology, 23,* 476–485.

Smith, T. W., Turner, C. W., Ford, M. H., Hunt, S. C., Barlow, G. K., Stults, B. M., et al. (1987). Blood pressure reactivity in adult male twins. *Health Psychology, 6,* 209–220.

Smyth, J. M., Soefer, M. H., Hurewitz, A., & Stone, A. A. (1999). The effect of tape-recorded relaxation training on well-being, symptoms and peak expiratory flow rate in adult asthmatics: A pilot study. *Psychology and Health, 14,* 487–501.

Smyth, J. M., Stone, A. A., Hurewitz, A., & Kaell, A. (1999). Effects of writing about stressful experiences on symptom reduction in patients with asthma or rheumatoid arthritis. *Journal of the American Medical Association, 281,* 1304–1309.

Sobel, H. (1981). Toward a behavioral thanatology in clinical care. In H. Sobel (Ed.), *Behavioral therapy in terminal care: A humanistic approach* (pp. 3–38). Cambridge, MA: Ballinger.

Solano, L., Donati, V., Pecci, F., Persichetti, S., & Colaci, A. (2003). Postoperative course after papilloma resection: Effects of written disclosure of the experience in subjects with different alexithymia levels. *Psychosomatic Medicine, 65,* 477–484.

Solomon, L. J., Higgins, S. T., Heil, S. H., Badger, G. J., Monheon, J. A., & Bernstein, I. M. (2006). Psychological symptoms following smoking cessation in pregnant smokers. *Journal of Behavioral Medicine, 29,* 151–160.

Solomon, M. Z., & De Jong, W. (1989). Preventing AIDS and other STDs through condom promotion: A patient education intervention. *American Journal of Public Health, 79,* 453–458.

Solomon, Z., Mikulincer, M., & Avitzur, E. (1988). Coping, locus of control, social support, and combat-related posttraumatic stress disorder: A prospective study. *Journal of Personality and Social Psychology, 55,* 279–285.

Somerfield, M. R., Curbow, B., Wingard, J. R., Baker, F., & Fogarty, L. A. (1996). Coping with the physical and psychosocial sequelae of bone marrow transplantation among long-term survivors. *Journal of Behavioral Medicine, 19,* 163–184.

Sone, T., Nakaya, N., Ohmori, K., Shimazu, T., Higashiguchi, M., Kakizaki, M., et al. (2008). Sense of life worth (ikigai) and mortality in Japan: Ohsaki study. *Psychosomatic Medicine, 70,* 709–715.

Soreca, I., Rosano, C., Jennings, J. R., Sheu, L. K., Kuller, L. H., Matthews, K. A., et al. (2009). Gain in adiposity across 15 years is associated with reduced gray matter volume in healthy women. *Psychosomatic Medicine, 71,* 485–490.

Sorensen, G., Thompson, B., Basen-Engquist, K., Abrams, D., Kuniyuki, A., DiClemente, C., et al. (1998). Durability, dissemination, and institutionalization of worksite tobacco control programs: Results from the working well trial. *International Journal of Behavioral Medicine, 5,* 335–351.

Sorkin, D., Rook, K. S., & Lu, J. L. (2002). Loneliness, lack of emotional support, lack of companionship, and the likelihood of having a heart condition in an elderly sample. *Annals of Behavioral Medicine, 24,* 290–298.

Sorrentino, E. A. (1992). Hospice care: A unique clinical experience for MSN students. *American Journal of Hospice and Palliative Care, 9,* 29–33.

Spalletta, G., Pasini, A., Costa, A., De Angelis, D., Ramundo, N., Paolucci, S., et al. (2001). Alexithymic features in stroke: Effects of laterality and gender. *Psychosomatic Medicine, 63,* 944–950.

Speca, M., Carlson, L. E., Goodey, E., & Angen, M. (2000). A randomized, wait-list controlled clinical trial: The effect of a mindfulness meditation–based stress reduction program on mood and symptoms of stress in cancer outpatients. *Psychosomatic Medicine, 62,* 613–622.

Spector, I. P., Leiblum, S. R., Carey, M. P., & Rosen, R. C. (1993). Diabetes and female sexual function: A critical review. *Annals of Behavioral Medicine, 15,* 257–264.

Speisman, J., Lazarus, R. S., Mordkoff, A., & Davidson, L. (1964). Experimental reduction of stress based on ego defense theory. *Journal of Abnormal and Social Psychology, 68,* 367–380.

Spencer, S. M., Lehman, J. M., Wynings, C., Arena, P., Carver, C. S., Antoni, M. H., et al. (1999). Concerns about breast cancer and relations to psychosocial well-being in a multiethnic sample of early-stage patients. *Health Psychology, 18,* 159–168.

Spiegel, D., Bloom, J. R., Kraemer, H. C., & Gottheil, E. (1989). Effect of psychosocial treatment on survival of patients with metastatic breast cancer. *Lancet, 14,* 888–891.

Spiegel, K., Tasali, E., Penev, P., & Van Cauter, E. (2004). Brief communication: Sleep curtailment in healthy young men is associated with decreased leptin levels, elevated ghrelin levels, and increased hunger and appetite. *Annals of Internal Medicine, 141,* 846–850.

Spinetta, J. J. (1974). The dying child's awareness of death: A review. *Psychological Bulletin, 81,* 256–260.

Spinetta, J. J. (1982). Behavioral and psychological research in childhood cancer: An overview. *Cancer, 50 (Suppl.),* 1939–1943.

Spinetta, J. J., Spinetta, P. D., Kung, F., & Schwartz, D. B. (1976). *Emotional aspects of childhood cancer and leukemia: A handbook for parents.* San Diego, CA: Leukemia Society of America.

Spinney, L. (2006, June 15). Eat your cake and have it. *Nature,* pp. 807–809.

Spitzer, C., Barnow, S., Völzke, H., John, U., Freyberger, H. J., & Grabe, H. J. (2009). Trauma, posttraumatic stress disorder, and physical illness: Findings from the general population. *Psychosomatic Medicine, 71,* 1012–1017.

Spitzer, R. L., Yanovski, S., Wadden, T., Wing, R., Marcus, M. D., Stunkard, A., et al. (1993). Binge eating disorder: Its further validation in a multisite study. *International Journal of Eating Disorders, 13,* 137–153.

Spragins, E. (1996, June 24). Does your HMO stack up? *Newsweek,* pp. 56–61, 63.

Srinivasan, K., & Joseph, W. (2004). A study of lifetime prevalence of anxiety and depressive disorders in patients presenting with chest pain to emergency medicine. *General Hospital Psychiatry, 26,* 470–474.

Stadler, G., Oettingen, G., & Gollwitzer, P. M. (2010). Intervention effects of information and self-regulation on eating fruits and vegetables over two years. *Health Psychology, 29,* 274–283.

Stafford, L., Jackson, H. J., & Berk, M. (2008). Illness beliefs about heart disease and adherence to secondary prevention regimens. *Psychosomatic Medicine, 70,* 942–948.

Stall, R., & Biernacki, P. (1986). Spontaneous remission from the problematic use of substances: An inductive model derived from a comparative analysis of the alcohol, opiate, tobacco, and food/obesity literatures. *International Journal of the Addictions, 21,* 1–23.

Stampfer, M. J., Hu, F. B., Manson, J. E., Rimm, E. B., & Willett, W. C. (2000). Primary prevention of coronary heart disease in women through diet and lifestyle. *The New England Journal of Medicine, 343,* 16–22.

Stang, P. E., Brandenburg, N. A., Lane, M. C., Merikangas, K. R., Von Korff, M. R., & Kessler, R. C. (2006). Mental and physical comorbid conditions and days in role among persons with arthritis. *Psychosomatic Medicine, 68,* 152–158.

Stansfeld, S. A., Bosma, H., Hemingway, H., & Marmot, M. G. (1998). Psychosocial work characteristics and social support as predictors of SF-36 health functioning: The Whitehall II study. *Psychosomatic Medicine, 60,* 247–255.

Stansfeld, S. A., Fuhrer, R., Shipley, M. J., & Marmot, M. G. (2002). Psychological distress as a risk factor for coronary heart disease in the Whitehall II study. *International Journal of Epidemiology, 31,* 248–255.

Stanton, A. L. (1987). Determinants of adherence to medical regimens by hypertensive patients. *Journal of Behavioral Medicine, 10,* 377–394.

Stanton, A. L. (2010). Regulating emotions during stressful experiences: The adaptive utility of coping through emotional approach. In S. Folkman (Ed.), *Oxford Handbook of Stress, Health and Coping.* New York: Oxford University Press.

Stanton, A. L., Danoff-Burg, S., Cameron, C. L., Snider, P. R., & Kirk, S. B. (1999). Social comparison and adjustment to breast cancer: An experimental examination of upward affiliation and downward evaluation. *Health Psychology, 18,* 151–158.

Stanton, A. L., Danoff-Burg, S., Sworowski, L. A., Collins, C. A., Branstetter, A. D., Rodriguez-Hanley, A., et al. (2002). Randomized, controlled trial of written emotional expression and benefit finding in breast cancer patients. *Journal of Clinical Oncology, 20,* 4160–4168.

Stanton, A. L., Kirk, S. B., Cameron, C. L., & Danoff-Burg, S. (2000). Coping through emotional approach: Scale construction and validation. *Journal of Personality and Social Psychology, 78,* 1150–1169.

Stapleton, J., Turrisi, R., Hillhouse, J., Robinson, J. K., & Abar, B. (2010). A comparison of the efficacy of an appearance-focused skin cancer intervention within indoor tanner subgroups identified by latent profile analysis. *Journal of Behavioral Medicine, 33,* 181–190.

Starace, F., Massa, A., Amico, K. R., & Fisher, J. D. (2006). Adherence to antiretroviral therapy: An empirical test of the information-motivation-behavioral skills model. *Health Psychology, 25,* 153–162.

Starkman, M. N., Giordani, B., Berent, S., Schork, M. A., & Schteingart, D. E. (2001). Elevated cortisol levels in Cushing's disease are associated with cognitive decrements. *Psychosomatic Medicine, 63,* 985–993.

Starr, K. R., Antoni, M. H., Hurwitz, B. E., Rodriguez, M. S., Ironson, G., Fletcher, M. A., et al. (1996). Patterns of immune, neuroendocrine, and cardiovascular stress responses in asymptomatic HIV seropositive and seronegative men. *International Journal of Behavioral Medicine, 3,* 135–162.

Stathopoulou, G., Powers, M. B., Berry, A. C., Smits, J. A. J., & Otto, M. W. (2006). Exercise interventions for mental health: A quantitative and qualitative review. *Clinical Psychology: Science and Practice, 13,* 179–193.

Steele, C. (1988). The psychology of self-affirmation: Sustaining the integrity of the self. In L. Berkowitz (Ed.), *Advances in Experimental Social Psychology* (Vol. 21, pp. 261–302). San Diego, CA: Academic Press.

Steele, C., & Josephs, R. A. (1990). Alcohol myopia: Its prized and dangerous effects. *American Psychologist, 45,* 921–933.

Steen, S. N., Oppliger, R. A., & Brownell, K. D. (1988). Metabolic effects of repeated weight loss and regain in adolescent wrestlers. *Journal of the American Medical Association, 260,* 47–50.

Steenland, K., Hu, S., & Walker, J. (2004). All-cause and cause-specific mortality by socioeconomic status among employed persons in 27 US states, 1984–1997. *American Journal of Public Health, 94,* 1037–1042.

Steffen, P. R., Smith, T. B., Larson, M., & Butler, L. (2006). Acculturation to western society as a risk factor for high blood pressure: A meta-analytic review. *Psychosomatic Medicine, 68,* 386–397.

Steginga, S. K., & Occhipinti, S. (2006). Dispositional optimism as a predictor of men's decision-related distress after localized prostate cancer. *Health Psychology, 25,* 135–143.

Stein, J. (2010, January 14). U.S. obesity rates reach a resting point, but trend isn't yet reversed. *The Los Angeles Times,* p. A10.

Stein, M. B., Belik, S. L., Jacobi, F., & Sareen, J. (2008). Impairment associated with sleep problems in the community: Relationship to physical and mental health comorbidity. *Psychosomatic Medicine, 70,* 913–919.

Stein, N., Folkman, S., Trabasso, T., & Richards, T. A. (1997). Appraisal and goal processes as predictors of psychological well-being in bereaved caregivers. *Journal of Personality and Social Psychology, 72,* 872–884.

Stein, P. N., Gordon, W. A., Hibbard, M. R., & Sliwinski, M. J. (1992). An examination of depression in the spouses of stroke patients. *Rehabilitation Psychology, 37,* 121–130.

Steinbrook, R. (2004a). Disparities in health care—from politics to policy. *The New England Journal of Medicine, 350,* 1486–1488.

Steinbrook, R. (2004b). Surgery for severe obesity. *The New England Journal of Medicine, 350,* 1075–1079.

Steinbrook, R. (2006). Imposing personal responsibility for health. *The New England Journal of Medicine, 355,* 753–756.

Steinmetz, K. A., Kushi, L., Bostick, R., Folsom, A., & Potter, J. (1994). Vegetables, fruit, and colon cancer in the Iowa Women's Health Study. *American Journal of Epidemiology, 139,* 1–15.

Stephens, M. A. P., Druley, J. A., & Zautra, A. J. (2002). Older adults' recovery from surgery for osteoarthritis of the knee: Psychological resources and constraints as predictors of outcomes. *Health Psychology, 21,* 377–383.

Stepnowsky C. J., Jr., Nelesen, R. A., De Jardin, D., & Dimsdale, J. E. (2004). Socioeconomic status is associated with nocturnal blood pressure dipping. *Psychosomatic Medicine, 66,* 651–655.

Steptoe, A., Brydon, L., & Kunz-Ebrecht, S. (2005). Changes in financial strain over three years, ambulatory blood pressure, and cortisol responses to awakening. *Psychosomatic Medicine, 67,* 281–287.

Steptoe, A., Doherty, S., Kerry, S., Rink, E., & Hilton, S. (2000). Sociodemographic and psychological predictors of changes in dietary fat consumption in adults with high blood cholesterol following counseling in primary care. *Health Psychology, 19,* 411–419.

Steptoe, A., Kerry, S., Rink, E., & Hilton, S. (2001). The impact of behavioral counseling on stage of change in fat intake, physical activity, and cigarette smoking in adults at increased risk of coronary heart disease. *American Journal of Public Health, 91,* 265–269.

Steptoe, A., & Marmot, M. (2003). Burden of psychosocial adversity and vulnerability in middle age: Associations with biobehavioral risk factors and quality of life. *Psychosomatic Medicine, 65,* 1029–1037.

Steptoe, A., & Marmot, M. (2006). Psychosocial, hemostatic, and inflammatory correlates of delayed poststress blood pressure recovery. *Psychosomatic Medicine, 68,* 531–537.

Steptoe, A., Perkins-Porras, L., Rink, E., Hilton, S., & Cappuccio, F. P. (2004). Psychological and social predictors of changes in fruit and vegetable consumption over 12 months following behavioral and nutrition education counseling. *Health Psychology, 23,* 574–581.

Steptoe, A., Roy, M. P., & Evans, O. (1996). Psychosocial influences on ambulatory blood pressure over working and non-working days. *Journal of Psychophysiology, 10,* 218–227.

Steptoe, A., Siegrist, J., Kirschbaum, C., & Marmot, M. (2004). Effort-reward imbalance, overcommitment, and measures of cortisol and blood pressure over the working day. *Psychosomatic Medicine, 66,* 323–329.

Sterba, K. R., DeVellis, R. F., Lewis, M. A., DeVellis, B. M., Jordan, J. M., & Baucom, D. H. (2008). Effect of couple illness perception congruence on psychological adjustment in women with rheumatoid arthritis. *Health Psychology, 27,* 221–229.

Stern, M. J., Pascale, L., & Ackerman, A. (1977). Life adjustment postmyocardial infarction: Determining predictive variables. *Archives of Internal Medicine, 137,* 1680–1685.

Stetler, C. A., & Miller, G. E. (2008). Social integration of daily activities and cortisol secretion: A laboratory based manipulation. *Journal of Behavioral Medicine, 31,* 249–257.

Stevens, V., Peterson, R., & Maruta, T. (1988). Changes in perception of illness and psychosocial adjustment. *The Clinical Journal of Pain, 4,* 249–256.

Stewart, A. L., King, A. C., Killen, J. D., & Ritter, P. L. (1995). Does smoking cessation improve health-related quality-of-life? *Annals of Behavioral Medicine, 17,* 331–338.

Stewart, D. E., Abbey, S. E., Shnek, Z. M., Irvine, J., & Grace, S. L. (2004). Gender differences in health information needs and decisional preferences in patients recovering from an acute ischemic coronary event. *Psychosomatic Medicine, 66*, 42–48.

Stewart, J. C., Fitzgerald, G. J., & Kamarck, T. W. (2010). Hostility now, depression later? Longitudinal associations among emotional risk factors for coronary artery disease. *Annals of Behavioral Medicine 39*, 258–266.

Stewart, M. A., Brown, J. B., Weston, W. W., McWhinney, I. R., McWilliam, C. L., & Freeman, T. R. (2003). *Patient-centered medicine: Transforming the clinical method.* Oxon, UK: Radcliffe Medical Press Ltd.

Stewart-Williams, S. (2004). The placebo puzzle: Putting together the pieces. *Health Psychology, 23*, 198–206.

Stice, E., Presnell, K., & Spangler, D. (2002). Risk factors for binge eating onset in adolescent girls: A 2-year prospective investigation. *Health Psychology, 21*, 131–138.

Stilley, C. S., Bender, C. M., Dunbar-Jacob, J., Sereika, S., & Ryan, C. M. (2010). The impact of cognitive function on medication management: Three studies. *Health Psychology, 29*, 50–55.

Stilley, C. S., Sereika, S., Muldoon, M. F., Ryan, C. M., & Dunbar-Jacob, J. (2004). Psychological and cognitive function: Predictors of adherence with cholesterol lowering treatment. *Annals of Behavioral Medicine, 27*, 117–124.

Stolberg, S. G. (1999, April 25). Sham surgery returns as a research tool. *New York Times*, p. 3.

Stolberg, S. G. (2002, May 2). Racial disparity is found in AIDS clinical studies. *New York Times*, p. A24.

Stommel, M., Kurtz, M. E., Kurtz, J. C., Given, C. W., & Given, B. A. (2004). A longitudinal analysis of the course of depressive symptomatology in geriatric patients with cancer of the breast, colon, lung, or prostate. *Health Psychology, 23*, 564–573.

Stone, A. A., Kennedy-Moore, E., & Neale, J. M. (1995). Association between daily coping and end-of-day mood. *Health Psychology, 14*, 341–349.

Stone, A. A., Mezzacappa, E. S., Donatone, B. A., & Gonder, M. (1999). Psychosocial stress and social support are associated with prostate-specific antigen levels in men: Results from a community screening program. *Health Psychology, 18*, 482–486.

Stone, A. A., & Neale, J. M. (1984). A new measure of daily coping: Development and preliminary results. *Journal of Personality and Social Psychology, 46*, 892–906.

Stone, G. C., Cohen, F., & Adler, N. E. (Eds.) (1979). *Health Psychology—A handbook: Theories, applications, and challenges of a psychological approach to the health care system.* San Francisco: Jossey-Bass.

Stoney, C., Niaura, R., Bausserman, L., & Matacin, M. (1999). Lipid reactivity to stress: I. Comparison of chronic and acute stress responses in middle-aged airline pilots. *Health Psychology, 18*, 241–250.

Stoney, C. M., & Finney, M. L. (2000). Social support and stress: Influences on lipid reactivity. *International Journal of Behavioral Medicine, 7*, 111–126.

Stoney, C. M., Owens, J. F., Guzick, D. S., & Matthews, K. A. (1997). A natural experiment on the effects of ovarian hormones on cardiovascular risk factors and stress reactivity: Bilateral salpingo oophorectomy versus hysterectomy only. *Health Psychology, 16*, 349–358.

Storer, J. H., Frate, D. M., Johnson, S. A., & Greenberg, A. M. (1987). When the cure seems worse than the disease: Helping families adapt to hypertension treatment. *Family Relations, 36*, 311–315.

Stotts, A. L., DiClemente, C. C., Carbonari, J. P., & Mullen, P. D. (2000). Postpartum return to smoking: Staging a "suspended" behavior. *Health Psychology, 19*, 324–332.

Stowe, R. P., Pierson, D. L., & Barrett, A. D. T. (2001). Elevated stress hormone levels relate to Epstein-Barr virus reactivation in astronauts. *Psychosomatic Medicine, 63*, 891–895.

Strachan, E. D., Bennett, W. R. M., Russo, J., & Roy-Byrne, P. P. (2007). Disclosure of HIV status and sexual orientation independently predicts increased absolute CD4 cell counts over time for psychiatric patients. *Psychosomatic Medicine, 69*, 74–80.

Strating, M. M. H., van Schuur, W. H., & Suurmeijer, T. P. B. M. (2006). Contribution of partner support in self-management of rheumatoid arthritis patients. An application of the theory of planned behavior. *Journal of Behavioral Medicine, 29*, 51–60.

Straus, R. (1988). Interdisciplinary biobehavioral research on alcohol problems: A concept whose time has come. *Drugs and Society, 2*, 33–48.

Strecher, V. J., DeVellis, B. M., Becker, M. H., & Rosenstock, I. M. (1986). The role of self-efficacy in achieving health behavior change. *Health Education Quarterly, 13*, 73–92.

Streisand, B. (2006, October 9). Treating war's toll on the mind. *U.S. News & World Report*, pp. 55–62.

Striegel-Moore, R. H., & Bulik, C. M. (2007). Risk factors for eating disorders. *American Psychologist, 62*, 181–198.

Striegel-Moore, R. H., Silberstein, L. R., Frensch, P., & Rodin, J. (1989). A prospective study of disordered eating among college students. *International Journal of Eating Disorders, 8*, 499–511.

Strigo, I. A., Simmons, A. N., Matthews, S. C., Craig, A. D., & Paulus, M. P. (2008). Increased affective bias revealed using experimental graded heat stimuli in young depressed adults: Evidence of "emotional allodynia." *Psychosomatic Medicine, 70*, 338–344.

Strike, P. C., Magid, K., Brydon, L., Edwards, S., McEwan, J. R., & Steptoe, A. (2004). Exaggerated platelet and hemodynamic reactivity to mental stress in men with coronary artery disease. *Psychosomatic Medicine, 66*, 492–500.

Strike, P. C., & Steptoe, A. (2005). Behavioral and emotional triggers of acute coronary syndromes: A systematic review and critique. *Psychosomatic Medicine, 67*, 179–186.

Stroebe, M., Gergen, M. M., Gergen, K. J., & Stroebe, W. (1992). Broken hearts or broken bonds: Love and death in historical perspective. *American Psychologist, 47*, 1205–1212.

Stroebe, W., & Stroebe, M. S. (1987). *Bereavement and health: The psychological and physical consequences of partner loss.* New York: Cambridge University Press.

Strong, K., Mathers, C., Leeder, S., & Beaglehole, R. (2005). Preventing chronic diseases: How many lives can we save? *Lancet, 366*, 1578–1582.

Strube, M. J., Smith, J. A., Rothbaum, R., & Sotelo, A. (1991). Measurement of health care attitudes in cystic fibrosis patients and their parents. *Journal of Applied Social Psychology, 21*, 397–408.

Stuber, M. L., Christakis, D. A., Houskamp, B., & Kazak, A. E. (1996). Posttrauma symptoms in childhood leukemia survivors and their parents. *Psychosomatics, 57*, 254–261.

Stunkard, A. J. (1979). Behavioral medicine and beyond: The example of obesity. In O. F. Pomerleau & J. P. Brady (Eds.), *Behavioral medicine: Theory and practice* (pp. 279–298). Baltimore, MD: Williams & Wilkins.

Stunkard, A. J. (1988). Some perspectives on human obesity: Its causes. *Bulletin of the New York Academy of Medicine, 64*, 902–923.

Stunkard, A. J., Cohen, R. Y., & Felix, M. R. J. (1989). Weight loss competitions at the work site: How they work and how well. *Journal of Preventive Medicine, 18*, 460–474.

Sturges, J. W., & Rogers, R. W. (1996). Preventive health psychology from a developmental perspective: An extension of protection motivation theory. *Health Psychology, 15*, 158–166.

Suarez, E. C. (2003). Joint effect of hostility and severity of depressive symptoms on plasma interleukin–6 concentration. *Psychosomatic Medicine, 65*, 523–527.

Suarez, E. C. (2004). C-reactive protein is associated with psychological risk factors of cardiovascular disease in apparently healthy adults. *Psychosomatic Medicine, 66*, 684–691.

Suarez, E. C., Kuhn, C. M., Schanberg, S. M., Williams, R. B., & Zimmermann, E. (1998). Neuroendocrine, cardiovascular, and emotional responses of hostile men: The role of interpersonal challenge. *Psychosomatic Medicine, 60,* 78–88.

Suarez, E. C., Shiller, A. D., Kuhn, C. M., Schanberg, S., Williams, R. B., Jr., & Zimmermann, E. A. (1997). The relationship between hostility and B-adrenergic receptor physiology in healthy young males. *Psychosomatic Medicine, 59,* 481–487.

Suendermann, O., Ehlers, A., Boellinghaus, I., Gamer, M., & Glucksman, E. (2010). Early heart rate responses to standardized trauma-related pictures predict posttraumatic stress disorder: A prospective study. *Psychosomatic Medicine, 72,* 301–308.

Suglia, S. F., Ryan, L., Laden, F., Dockery, D. W., & Wright, R. J. (2008). Violence exposure, a chronic psychosocial stressor, and childhood lung function. *Psychosomatic Medicine, 70,* 160–169.

Suhr, J. A., Stewart, J. C., & France, C. R. (2004). The relationship between blood pressure and cognitive performance in the Third National Health and Nutrition Examination Survey (NHANES III). *Psychosomatic Medicine, 66,* 291–297.

Sullivan, H. W., & Rothman, A. J. (2008). When planning is needed: Implementation intentions and attainment of approach versus avoidance health goals. *Health Psychology, 27,* 438–444.

Suls, J., & Bunde, J. (2005). Anger, anxiety, and depression as risk factors for cardiovascular disease: The problems and implications of overlapping affective dispositions. *Psychological Bulletins, 131,* 260–300.

Suls, J., & Fletcher, B. (1985). The relative efficacy of avoidant and nonavoidant coping strategies: A meta-analysis. *Health Psychology, 4,* 249–288.

Suls, J., & Green, P. (2003). Pluralistic ignorance and college student perceptions of gender-specific alcohol norms. *Health Psychology, 22,* 479–486.

Suls, J., & Rothman, A. (2004). Evolution of the biopsychosocial model: Prospects and challenges for health psychology. *Health Psychology, 23,* 119–125.

Suls, J., & Wan, C. K. (1993). The relationship between trait hostility and cardiovascular reactivity: A quantitative review and analysis. *Psychophysiology, 30,* 1–12.

Suls, J., Wan, C. K., & Sanders, G. S. (1988). False consensus and false uniqueness in estimating the prevalence of health-protective behaviors. *Journal of Applied Social Psychology, 18,* 66–79.

Surtees, P. G., Wainwright, N. W. J., Boekholdt, S. M., Luben, R. N., Wareham, N. J., & Khaw, K. T. (2008). Major depression, C-reactive protein, and incident ischemic heart disease in healthy men and women. *Psychosomatic Medicine, 70,* 850–855.

Surtees, P. G., Wainwright, N. W. J., Luben, R., Khaw, K., & Day, N. E. (2006). Mastery, sense of coherence, and mortality: Evidence of independent associations from the EPIC-Norfolk prospective cohort study. *Health Psychology, 25,* 102–110.

Surwit, R. S., Feinglos, M. N., McCaskill, C. C., Clay, S. L., Babyak, M. A., Brownlow, et al. (1997). Metabolic and behavioral effects of a high-sucrose diet during weight loss. *American Journal of Clinical Nutrition, 65,* 908–915.

Surwit, R. S., Lane, J. D., Millington, D. S., Zhang, H., Feinglos, M. N., Minda, S., et al. (2009). Hostility and minimal model of glucose kinetics in African American women. *Psychosomatic Medicine, 71,* 646–651.

Surwit, R. S., & Schneider, M. S. (1993). Role of stress in the etiology and treatment of diabetes mellitus. *Psychosomatic Medicine, 55,* 380–393.

Surwit, R. S., & Williams, P. G. (1996). Animal models provide insight into psychosomatic factors in diabetes. *Psychosomatic Medicine, 58,* 582–589.

Sussman, S., Sun, P., & Dent, C. W. (2006). A meta-analysis of teen cigarette smoking cessation. *Health Psychology, 25,* 549–557.

Sutherland, G., Andersen, M. B., & Morris, T. (2005). Relaxation and health-related quality of life in multiple sclerosis: The example of autogenic training. *Journal of Behavioral Medicine, 28,* 249–256.

Sutton, S., McVey, D., & Glanz, A. (1999). A comparative test of the theory of reasoned action and the theory of planned behavior in the prediction of condom use intentions in a national sample of English young people. *Health Psychology, 18,* 72–81.

Sutton, S. R., & Eiser, J. R. (1984). The effect of fear-arousing communications on cigarette smoking: An expectancy-value approach. *Journal of Behavioral Medicine, 7,* 13–34.

Swaim, R. C., Oetting, E. R., & Casas, J. M. (1996). Cigarette use among migrant and nonmigrant Mexican American youth: A socialization latent-variable model. *Health Psychology, 15,* 269–281.

Swaveley, S. M., Silverman, W. H., & Falek, A. (1987). Psychological impact of the development of a presymptomatic test for Huntington's disease. *Health Psychology, 6,* 149–157.

Swindle, R. E., Jr., & Moos, R. H. (1992). Life domains in stressors, coping, and adjustment. In W. B. Walsh, R. Price, & K. B. Crak (Eds.), *Person environment psychology: Models and perspectives* (pp. 1–33). New York: Erlbaum.

Szapocznik, J. (1995). Research on disclosure of HIV status: Cultural evolution finds an ally in science. *Health Psychology, 14,* 4–5.

Székely, A., Balog, P., Benkö, E., Breuer, T., Székely, J., Kertai, M. D., et al. (2007). Anxiety predicts mortality and morbidity after coronary artery and valve surgery—A 4-year follow-up. *Psychosomatic Medicine, 69,* 625–631.

Talbot, F., Nouwen, A., Gingras, J., Belanger, A., & Audet, J. (1999). Relations of diabetes intrusiveness and personal control to symptoms of depression among adults with diabetes. *Health Psychology, 18,* 537–542.

Talbot, F., Nouwen, A., Gingras, J., Gosselin, M., & Audet, J. (1997). The assessment of diabetes-related cognitive and social factors: The multidimensional diabetes questionnaire. *Journal of Behavioral Medicine, 20,* 291–312.

Talbot, N. L., Chapman, B., Conwell, Y., McCollumn, K., Franus, N., Cotescu, S., et al. (2009). Childhood sexual abuse is associated with physical illness burden and functioning in psychiatric patients 50 years of age and older. *Psychosomatic Medicine, 71,* 417–422.

Tamres, L., Janicki, D., & Helgeson, V. S. (2002). Sex differences in coping behavior: A meta-analytic review. *Personality and Social Psychology Review, 6,* 2–30.

Tatrow, K., & Montgomery, G. H. (2006). Cognitive behavioral therapy techniques for distress and pain in breast cancer patients: A meta-analysis. *Journal of Behavioral Medicine, 29,* 17–27.

Taub, E., Uswatte, G., King, D. K., Morris, D., Crago, J. E., & Chatterjee, A. (2006). A placebo-controlled trial of constraint-induced movement therapy for upper extremity after stroke. *Stroke, 37,* 1045–1049.

Taubes, G. (1993). Claim of higher risk for women smokers attacked. *Science, 262,* 1375.

Taylor, C. B., Bandura, A., Ewart, C. K., Miller, N. H., & DeBusk, R. F. (1985). Exercise testing to enhance wives' confidence in their husbands' cardiac capability soon after clinically uncomplicated acute myocardial infarction. *American Journal of Cardiology, 55,* 635–638.

Taylor, C. B., & Curry, S. J. (2004). Implementation of evidence-based tobacco use cessation guidelines in managed care organizations. *Annals of Behavioral Medicine, 27,* 13–21.

Taylor, K. L., Lamdan, R. M., Siegel, J. E., Shelby, R., Moran-Klimi, K., & Hrywna, M. (2003). Psychological adjustment among African American patients: One-year follow-up results of a randomized psychoeducational group intervention. *Health Psychology, 22,* 316–323.

Taylor, L. A., & Rachman, S. J. (1988). The effects of blood sugar level changes on cognitive function, affective state, and somatic symptoms. *Journal of Behavioral Medicine, 11,* 279–292.

Taylor, M. D., Whiteman, M. C., Fowkes, G. R., Lee, A. J., Allerhand, M., & Deary, I. J. (2009). Five factor model personality traits and all-cause mortality in the Edinburgh artery study cohort. *Psychosomatic Medicine, 71,* 631–641.

Taylor, R. (2004). Causation of type 2 diabetes—The Gordian Knot unravels. *The New England Journal of Medicine, 350,* 639–641.

Taylor, R. R., Jason, L. A., & Jahn, S. C. (2003). Chronic fatigue and sociodemographic characteristics as predictors of psychiatric disorders in a community-based sample. *Psychosomatic Medicine, 65,* 896–901.

Taylor, S. E. (1983). Adjustment to threatening events: A theory of cognitive adaptation. *American Psychologist, 41,* 1161–1173.

Taylor, S. E. (1989). *Positive illusions: Creative self-deception and the healthy mind.* New York: Basic Books.

Taylor, S. E. (2002). *The tending instinct: How nurturing is essential to who we are and how we live.* New York: Holt.

Taylor, S. E. (2010). Social support: A review. In H. S. Friedman (Ed.), *Oxford Handbook of Health Psychology.* New York: Oxford University Press.

Taylor, S. E., & Aspinwall, L. G. (1990). Psychological aspects of chronic illness. In G. R. VandenBos & P. T. Costa, Jr. (Eds.), *Psychological aspects of serious illness.* Washington, DC: American Psychological Association.

Taylor, S. E., Eisenberger, N. I., Saxbe, D., Lehman, B. J., & Lieberman, M. D. (2006). Neural responses to emotional stimuli are associated with childhood family stress. *Biological Psychiatry, 60,* 296–301.

Taylor, S. E., Falke, R. L., Shoptaw, S. J., & Lichtman, R. R. (1986). Social support, support groups, and the cancer patient. *Journal of Consulting and Clinical Psychology, 54,* 608–615.

Taylor, S. E., Gonzaga, G. C., Klein, L. C., Hu, P., Greendale, G. A., & Seeman, T. E. (2006). Relation of oxytocin to psychological stress responses and hypothalamic-pituitary-adrenocortical axis activity in older women. *Psychosomatic Medicine, 68,* 238–245.

Taylor, S. E., Helgeson, V. S., Reed, G. M., & Skokan, L. A. (1991). Self-generated feelings of control and adjustment to physical illness. *Journal of Social Issues, 47,* 91–109.

Taylor, S. E., Kemeny, M. E., Reed, G. M., Bower, J. E., & Gruenewald, T. L. (2000). Psychological resources, positive illusions, and health. *American Psychologist, 55,* 99–109.

Taylor, S. E., Klein, L. C., Lewis, B. P., Gruenewald, T. L., Gurung, R. A. R., & Updegraff, J. A. (2000). Biobehavioral responses to stress in females: Tend-and-befriend, not fight-or-flight. *Psychological Review, 107,* 411–429.

Taylor, S. E., Lichtman, R. R., & Wood, J. V. (1984a). Attributions, beliefs about control, and adjustment to breast cancer. *Journal of Personality and Social Psychology, 46,* 489–502.

Taylor, S. E., Lichtman, R. R., & Wood, J. V. (1984b). Compliance with chemotherapy among breast cancer patients. *Health Psychology, 3,* 553–562.

Taylor, S. E., Repetti, R. L., & Seeman, T. (1997). Health psychology: What is an unhealthy environment and how does it get under the skin? *Annual Review of Psychology, 48,* 411–447.

Taylor, S. E., & Stanton, A. (2007). Coping resources, coping processes, and mental health. *Annual Review of Clinical Psychology, 3,* 129–153.

Taylor, S. E., & Thompson, S. C. (1982). Stalking the elusive "vividness" effect. *Psychological Review, 89,* 155–181.

Taylor, S. E., Wood, J. V., & Lichtman, R. R. (1983). *Life change following cancer.* Unpublished manuscript, University of California, Los Angeles.

Tegethoff, M., Greene, N., Olsen, J., Meyer, A. H., & Meinlschmidt, G. (2010). Maternal psychosocial adversity during pregnancy is associated with length of gestation and offspring size at birth: Evidence from a population-based cohort study. *Psychosomatic Medicine, 72,* 419–426.

Teh, C. F., Zaslavsky, A. M., Reynolds, C. F., & Cleary, P. D. (2010). Effect of depression treatment on chronic pain outcomes. *Psychosomatic Medicine, 72,* 61–67.

Teixeira, P. J., Going, S. B., Houtkooper, L. B., Cussler, E. C., Martin, C. J., Metcalfe, L. L., et al. (2002). Weight loss readiness in middle-aged women: Psychosocial predictors of success for behavioral weight reduction. *Journal of Behavioral Medicine, 25,* 499–523.

Telch, C. F., & Agras, W. S. (1996). Do emotional states influence binge eating in the obese? *International Journal of Eating Disorders, 20,* 271–279.

Temcheff, C. E., Serbin, L. A., Martin-Storey, A., Stack, D. M., Ledingham, J., & Schwartzman, A. E. (2010). Predicting adult physical health outcomes from childhood aggression, social withdrawal and likeability: A 30-year prospective, longitudinal study. *International Journal of Behavioral Medicine, 18,* 5–12.

Temoshok, L. R., Wald, R. L., Synowski, S., & Garzino-Demo, A. (2008). Coping as a multisystem construct associated with pathways mediating HIV-relevant immune function and disease progression. *Psychosomatic Medicine, 70,* 555–561.

Tempelaar, R., de Haes, J. C. J. M., de Ruiter, J. H., Bakker, D., van den Heuvel, W. J. A., & van Nieuwenhuijzen, M. G. (1989). The social experiences of cancer patients under treatment: A comparative study. *Social Science and Medicine, 29,* 635–642.

Tennen, H., Affleck, G., Urrows, S., Higgins, P., & Mendola, R. (1992). Perceiving control, construing benefits, and daily processes in rheumatoid arthritis. *Canadian Journal of Behavioral Science, 24,* 186–203.

Tennen, H., Affleck, G., & Zautra, A. (2006). Depression history and coping with chronic pain: A daily process analysis. *Health Psychology, 25,* 370–379.

Teno, J. M., Fisher, E. S., Hamel, M. B., Coppola, K., & Dawson, N. V. (2002). Medical care inconsistent with patients' treatment goals: Association with 1-year medicare resource use and survival. *Journal of the American Geriatrics Society, 50,* 496–500.

Terracciano, A., Löckenhoff, C. E., Zonderman, A. B., Ferrucci, L., & Costa, P. T. (2008). Personality predictors of longevity: Activity, emotional stability, and conscientiousness. *Psychosomatic Medicine, 70,* 621–627.

Terracciano, A., Sutin, A. R., McCrae, R. R., Deiana, B., Ferrucci, L., Schlessinger, D., et al. (2009). Facets of personality linked to underweight and overweight. *Psychosomatic Medicine, 71,* 682–689.

Teychenne, M., Ball, K., & Salmon, J. (2010). Sedentary behavior and depression among adults: A review. *International Journal of Behavioral Medicine, 17,* 246–254.

Theorell, T., Blomkvist, V., Lindh, G., & Evengard, B. (1999). Critical life events, infections, and symptoms during the year preceding chronic fatigue syndrome (CFS): An examination of CFS patients and subjects with a nonspecific life crisis. *Psychosomatic Medicine, 61,* 304–310.

Theorell, T., Emdad, R., Arnetz, B., & Weingarten, A. M. (2001). Employee effects of an educational program for managers at an insurance company. *Psychosomatic Medicine, 63,* 724–733.

Thoits, P. A. (1994). Stressors and problem-solving: The individual as psychological activist. *Journal of Health and Social Behavior, 35,* 143–159.

Thoits, P. A., Harvey, M. R., Hohmann, A. A., & Fletcher, B. (2000). Similar-other support for men undergoing coronary artery bypass surgery. *Health Psychology, 19,* 264–273.

Thomas, K. S., Bardwell, W. A., Ancoli-Israel, S., & Dimsdale, J. E. (2006). The toll of ethnic discrimination on sleep architecture and fatigue. *Health Psychology, 25,* 635–642.

Thomas, K. S., Nelesen, R. A., & Dimsdale, J. E. (2004). Relationships between hostility, anger expression, and blood pressure dipping in an ethnically diverse sample. *Psychosomatic Medicine, 66,* 298–304.

Thombre, A., Sherman, A. C., & Simonton, S. (2010). Posttraumatic growth among cancer patients in India. *Journal of Behavioral Medicine, 33,* 15–23.

Thompson, D. R., & Cordle, C. J. (1988). Support of wives of myocardial infarction patients. *Journal of Advanced Nursing, 13,* 223–228.

Thompson, R. F., & Glanzman, D. L. (1976). Neural and behavioral mechanism of habituation and sensitization. In T. J. Tighe & R. N. Leatron (Eds.), *Habituation* (pp. 49–94). Hillsdale, NJ: Erlbaum.

Thompson, S. C. (1981). Will it hurt less if I can control it? A complex answer to a simple question. *Psychological Bulletin, 90,* 89–101.

Thompson, S. C., Cheek, P. R., & Graham, M. A. (1988). The other side of perceived control: Disadvantages and negative effects. In S. Spacapan & S. Oskamp (Eds.), *The social psychology of health: The Claremont Applied Social Psychology Conference* (Vol. 2, pp. 69–94). Beverly Hills, CA: Sage.

Thompson, S. C., Nanni, C., & Levine, A. (1994). Primary versus secondary and central versus consequence-related control in HIV-positive men. *Journal of Personality and Social Psychology, 67,* 540–547.

Thompson, S. C., Nanni, C., & Schwankovsky, L. (1990). Patient-oriented interventions to improve communication in a medical office visit. *Health Psychology, 9,* 390–404.

Thompson, S. C., Sobolew-Shubin, A., Galbraith, M. E., Schwankovsky, L., & Cruzen, D. (1993). Maintaining perceptions of control: Finding perceived control in low-control circumstances. *Journal of Personality and Social Psychology, 64,* 293–304.

Thompson, S. C., Sobolew-Shubin, A., Graham, M. A., & Janigian, A. S. (1989). Psychosocial adjustment following a stroke. *Social Science and Medicine, 28,* 239–247.

Thompson, S. C., & Spacapan, S. (1991). Perceptions of control in vulnerable populations. *Journal of Social Issues, 47,* 1–22.

Thomsen, D. K., Mehlsen, M. Y., Olesen, F., Hokland, M., Viidik, A., Avlund, K., et al. (2004). Is there an association between rumination and self-reported physical health? A one-year follow-up in a young and an elderly sample. *Journal of Behavioral Medicine, 27,* 215–231.

Thoolen, B., De Ridder, D., Bensing, J., Gorter, K., & Rutten, G. (2008). No worries, no impact? A systematic review of emotional, cognitive, and behavioural responses to the diagnosis of type 2 diabetes. *Health Psychology Review, 2,* 65–93.

Thornton, B., Gibbons, F. X., & Gerrard, M. (2002). Risk perception and prototype perception: Independent processes predicting risk behaviors. *Personality and Social Psychology Bulletin, 28,* 986–999.

Thornton, L. M., Andersen, B. L., Schuler, T. A., & Carson, W. E. (2009). A psychological intervention reduces inflammatory markers by alleviating depressive symptoms: Secondary analysis of a randomized controlled trial. *Psychosomatic Medicine, 71,* 715–724.

Thorpe, C. T., Lewis, M. A., & Sterba, K. R. (2008). Reactions to health-related social control in young adults with type I diabetes. *Journal of Behavioral Medicine, 31,* 93–103.

Thorsteinsson, E. B., James, J. E., & Gregg, M. E. (1998). Effects of video-relayed social support on hemodynamic reactivity and salivary cortisol during laboratory-based behavioral challenge. *Health Psychology, 17,* 436–444.

Thurston, R. C., & Kubzansky, L. D. (2009). Women, loneliness, and incident coronary heart disease. *Psychosomatic Medicine, 71,* 836–842.

Tibben, A., Timman, R., Bannink, E. C., & Duivenvoorden, H. J. (1997). Three-year follow-up after presymptomatic testing for Huntington's disease in tested individuals and partners. *Health Psychology, 16,* 20–35.

Timberlake, D. S., Haberstick, B. C., Lessem, J. M., Smolen, A., Ehringer, M., Hewitt, J. K., et al. (2006). An association between the DAT1 polymorphism and smoking behavior in young adults from the National Longitudinal Study of Adolescent Health. *Health Psychology, 25,* 190–197.

Time. (1970, November 2). The malpractice mess, pp. 36, 39.

Time. (1996, October 7). Notebook: The bad news, p. 30.

Time. (2001, June 25). Notebook: Verbatim, p. 19.

Time. (2005, January 17). Numbers, p. 16.

Timko, C., Baumgartner, M., Moos, R. H., & Miller, J. J., III. (1993). Parental risk and resistance factors among children with juvenile rheumatic disease: A four-year predictive study. *Journal of Behavioral Medicine, 16,* 571–589.

Timko, C., Finney, J. W., Moos, R. H., & Moos, B. S. (1995). Short-term treatment careers and outcomes of previously untreated alcoholics. *Journal of Studies on Alcohol, 56,* 597–610.

Timko, C., Stovel, K. W., Moos, R. H., & Miller, J. J., III. (1992). A longitudinal study of risk and resistance factors among children with juvenile rheumatic disease. *Journal of Clinical Child Psychology, 21,* 132–142.

Timman, R., Roos, R., Maat-Kievit, A., & Tibben, A. (2004). Adverse effects of predictive testing for Huntington disease underestimated: Long-term effects 7–10 years after the test. *Health Psychology, 23,* 189–197.

Timonen, M., Salmenkaita, I., Jokelainen, J., Laakso, M., Härkönen, P., Koskela, P., et al. (2007). Insulin resistance and depressive symptoms in young adult males: Findings from Finnish military conscripts. *Psychosomatic Medicine, 69,* 723–728.

Tobe, S. W., Kiss, A., Sainsbury, S., Jesin, M., Geerts, R., & Baker, B. (2007). The impact of job strain and marital cohesion on ambulatory blood pressure during 1 year: The double exposure study. *American Journal of Hypertension, 20,* 148–153.

Tobe, S. W., Kiss, A., Szalai, J. P., Perkins, N., Tsigoulis, M., & Baker, B. (2005). Impact of job and marital strain on ambulatory blood pressure: Results from the double exposure study. *American Journal of Hypertension, 18,* 1046–1051.

Tobin, J. J., & Friedman, J. (1983). Spirits, shamans, and nightmare death: Survivor stress in a Hmong refugee. *American Journal of Orthopsychiatry, 53,* 439–448.

Tolmunen, T., Lehto, S. M., Heliste, M., Kurl, S., & Kauhanen, J. (2010). Alexithymia is associated with increased cardiovascular mortality in middle-aged Finnish men. *Psychosomatic Medicine, 72,* 187–191.

Tomei, L. D., Kiecolt-Glaser, J. K., Kennedy, S., & Glaser, R. (1990). Psychological stress and phorbol ester inhibition of radiation-induced apoptosis in human peripheral blood leukocytes. *Psychiatry Research, 33,* 59–71.

Tomfohr, L., Cooper, D. C., Mills, P. J., Nelesen, R. A., & Dimsdale, J. E. (2010). Everyday discrimination and nocturnal blood pressure dipping in Black and White Americans. *Psychosomatic Medicine, 72,* 266–272.

Tomiyama, A. J., Mann, T., Vinas, D., Hunger, J. M., DeJager, J., & Taylor, S. E. (2010). Low calorie dieting increases cortisol. *Psychosomatic Medicine, 72,* 357–364.

Topol, E. J. (2004). Intensive strain therapy—A sea change in cardiovascular prevention. *The New England Journal of Medicine, 350,* 1562–1564.

Toshima, M. T., Kaplan, R. M., & Ries, A. L. (1992). Self-efficacy expectancies in chronic obstructive pulmonary disease rehabilitation. In R. Schwarzer (Ed.), *Self-efficacy: Thought control of action* (pp. 325–354). London, England: Hemisphere.

Tovian, S. M. (2004). Health services and health care economics: The health psychology marketplace. *Health Psychology, 23,* 138–141.

Treiber, F. A., Kamarck, T., Schneiderman, N., Sheffield, D., Kapuku, G., & Taylor, T. (2003). Cardiovascular reactivity and development of preclinical and clinical disease states. *Psychosomatic Medicine, 65,* 46–62.

Treue, W. (1958). *Doctor at court* (trans. Frances Fawcett). London: Weidenfeld & Nicolson.

Triverdi, R. B., Ayotte, B., Edelman, D., & Bosworth, H. B. (2008). The association of emotional well-being and marital status with treatment adherence among patients with hypertension. *Journal of Behavioral Medicine, 31,* 489–497.

Trockel, M., Burg, M., Jaffe, A., Barbour, K., & Taylor, C. B. (2008). Smoking behavior postmyocardial infarction among ENRICHD trial participants: Cognitive behavior therapy intervention for depression and low perceived social support compared with care as usual. *Psychosomatic Medicine, 70,* 875–882.

Troisi, A., Di Lorenzo, G., Alcini, S., Croce, R., Nanni, C., Di Pasquale, C., et al. (2006). Body dissatisfaction in women with eating disorders: Relationship to early separation anxiety and insecure attachment. *Psychosomatic Medicine, 68,* 449–453.

Troxel, W. M., Matthews, K. A., Bromberger, J. T., & Sutton-Tyrrell, K. (2003). Chronic stress burden, discrimination, and subclinical carotid artery disease in African American and Caucasian women. *Health Psychology, 22,* 300–309.

Trumbetta, S. L., Seltzer, B. K., Gottesman, I. I., & McIntyre, K. M. (2010). Mortality predictors in a 60-year follow up of adolescent males: Exploring delinquency, socioeconomic status, IQ, high school drop-out status, and personality. *Psychosomatic Medicine, 72,* 46–52.

Tsenkova, V. K., Love, G. D., Singer, B. H., & Ryff, C. D. (2008). Coping and positive affect predict longitudinal change in glycosylated hemoglobin. *Health Psychology, 27,* 163–171.

Tucker, J. S., Elliott, M. N., Wenzel, S. L., & Hambarsoomian, K. (2007). Relationship commitment and its implications for unprotected sex among impoverished women living in shelters and low-income housing in Los Angeles county. *Health Psychology, 26,* 644–649.

Tucker, J. S., Friedman, H. S., Schwartz, J. E., Criqui, M. H., Tomlinson-Keasey, C., Wingard, D. L., et al. (1997). Parental divorce: Effects on individual behavior and longevity. *Journal of Personality and Social Psychology, 73,* 381–391.

Tucker, J. S., Orlando, M., Burnam, M. A., Sherbourne, C. D., Kung, F. Y., & Gifford, A. L. (2004). Psychosocial mediators of antiretroviral nonadherence in HIV-positive adults with substance use and mental health problems. *Health Psychology, 23,* 363–370.

Tugade, M. M., & Fredrickson, B. L. (2004). Resilient individuals use positive emotions to bounce back from negative emotional experiences. *Journal of Personality and Social Psychology, 86,* 320–333.

Tully, P. J., Baker, R. A., Turnbull, D., & Winefield, H. (2008). The role of depression and anxiety symptoms in hospital readmissions after cardiac surgery. *Journal of Behavioral Medicine, 31,* 281–290.

Tully, P. J., Baker, R. A., Turnbull, D., Winefield, H., & Knight, J. L. (2009). Negative emotions and quality of life six months after cardiac surgery: The dominant role of depression not anxiety symptoms. *Journal of Behavioral Medicine, 32,* 510–522.

Tuomilehto, J., Lindstrom, J., Eriksson, J. G., Valle, T. T., Hamalainen, H., Ilanne-Parikka, P., et al. (2001). Prevention of Type 2 diabetes mellitus by changes in lifestyle among subjects with impaired glucose tolerance. *The New England Journal of Medicine, 344,* 1343–1350.

Tuomisto, M. T. (1997). Intra-arterial blood pressure and heart rate reactivity to behavioral stress in normotensive, borderline, and mild hypertensive men. *Health Psychology, 16,* 554–565.

Turbin, M. S., Jessor, R., Costa, F. M., Dong, Q., Zhang, H., & Wang, C. (2006). Protective and risk factors in health-enhancing behavior among adolescents in China and the United States: Does social context matter? *Health Psychology, 25,* 445–454.

Turk, D. C., & Feldman, C. S. (1992a). Facilitating the use of noninvasive pain management strategies with the terminally ill. In D. C. Turk & C. S. Feldman (Eds.), *Non-invasive approaches to pain management in the terminally ill* (pp. 1–25). New York: Haworth Press.

Turk, D. C., & Feldman, C. S. (1992b). Noninvasive approaches to pain control in terminal illness: The contribution of psychological variables. In D. C. Turk & C. S. Feldman (Eds.), *Non-invasive approaches to pain management in the terminally ill* (pp. 193–214). New York: Haworth Press.

Turk, D. C., & Fernandez, E. (1990). On the putative uniqueness of cancer pain: Do psychological principles apply? *Behavioural Research and Therapy, 28,* 1–13.

Turk, D. C., Kerns, R. D., & Rosenberg, R. (1992). Effects of marital interaction on chronic pain and disability: Examining the downside of social support. *Rehabilitation Psychology, 37,* 259–274.

Turk, D. C., & Meichenbaum, D. (1991). Adherence to self-care regimens: The patient's perspective. In R. H. Rozensky, J. J. Sweet, & S. M. Tovian (Eds.), *Handbook of clinical psychology in medical settings* (pp. 249–266). New York: Plenum.

Turk, D. C., & Rudy, T. E. (1991). Neglected topics in the treatment of chronic pain patients—Relapse, noncompliance, and adherence enhancement. *Pain, 44,* 5–28.

Turk, D. C., Wack, J. T., & Kerns, R. D. (1995). An empirical examination of the "pain-behavior" construct. *Journal of Behavioral Medicine, 8,* 119–130.

Turner, H. A., Hays, R. B., & Coates, T. J. (1993). Determinants of social support among gay men: The context of AIDS. *Journal of Health and Social Behavior, 34,* 37–53.

Turner, L. R., & Mermelstein, R. J. (2005). Psychosocial characteristics associated with sun protection practices among parents of young children. *Journal of Behavioral Medicine, 28,* 77–90.

Turner, R. J., & Avison, W. R. (1992). Innovations in the measurement of life stress: Crisis theory and the significance of event resolution. *Journal of Health and Social Behavior, 33,* 36–50.

Turner, R. J., & Avison, W. R. (2003). Status variations in stress exposure: Implications for the interpretation of research on race, socioeconomic status, and gender. *Journal of Health and Social Behavior, 44,* 488–505.

Turner, R. J., & Lloyd, D. A. (1999). The stress process and the social distribution of depression. *Journal of Health and Social Behavior, 40,* 374–404.

Turner, R. J., & Noh, S. (1988). Physical disability and depression: A longitudinal analysis. *Journal of Health and Social Behavior, 29,* 23–37.

Turner, R. J., Russell, D., Glover, R., & Hutto, P. (2007). The social antecedents of anger proneness in young adulthood. *Journal of Health and Social Behavior, 48,* 68–83.

Turner-Cobb, J. M., Gore-Felton, C., Marouf, F., Koopman, C., Kim, P., Israelski, D., et al. (2002). Coping, social support, and attachment style as psychosocial correlates of adjustment in men and women with HIV/AIDS. *Journal of Behavioral Medicine, 25,* 337–353.

Turner-Cobb, J. M., Sephton, S. E., Koopman, C., Blake-Mortimer, J., & Spiegel, D. (2000). Social support and salivary cortisol in women with metastatic breast cancer. *Psychosomatic Medicine, 62,* 337–345.

Turner-Stokes, L., Erkeller-Yuksel, F., Miles, A., Pincus, T., Shipley, M., & Pearce, S. (2003). Outpatient cognitive behavioral pain management programs: A randomized comparison of a group-based multidisciplinary versus an individual therapy model. *Archives of Physical Medicine and Rehabilitation, 84,* 781–788.

Turrisi, R., Hillhouse, J., Gebert, C., & Grimes, J. (1999). Examination of cognitive variables relevant to sunscreen use. *Journal of Behavioral Medicine, 22,* 493–509.

Turrisi, R., Hillhouse, J., Robinson, J. K., & Stapleton, J. (2007). Mediating variables in a parent based intervention to reduce skin cancer risk in children. *Journal of Behavioral Medicine, 30,* 385–393.

Ueda, H., et al. (2003). Association of the T-cell regulatory gene CTLA–4 with susceptibility to autoimmune disease. *Nature, 423,* 506–511.

Ullrich, P. M., & Lutgendorf, S. K. (2002). Journaling about stressful events: Effects of cognitive processing and emotional expression. *Annals of Behavioral Medicine, 24,* 244–250.

Umberson, D. (1987). Family status and health behaviors: Social control as a dimension of social integration. *Journal of Health and Social Behavior, 28,* 306–319.

Umberson, D., Wortman, C. B., & Kessler, R. C. (1992). Widowhood and depression: Explaining long-term gender differences in vulnerability. *Journal of Health and Social Behavior, 33,* 10–24.

UNAIDS. (2008). *2008 report on the global AIDS epidemic.* Retrieved October 8, 2009, from http://viewer.zmags.com/publication/ad3eab7c#/ad3eab7c/1

Unger, J. B., Hamilton, J. E., & Sussman, S. (2004). A family member's job loss as a risk factor for smoking among adolescents. *Health Psychology, 23*(3), 308–313.

United Cerebral Palsy. (2009). *Cerebral palsy fact sheet.* Retrieved September 25, 2009, from http://www.ucp.org/uploads/ cp_fact_sheet.pdf

University of Virginia Health Systems. (2007). *Diabetes.* Retrieved December 14, 2009, from http://uvahealth.com/services/diabetes-and-metabolism/conditions-treatments/11902

Updegraff, J. A., Taylor, S. E., Kemeny, M. E., & Wyatt, G. E. (2002). Positive and negative effects of HIV infection in women with low socioeconomic resources. *Personality and Social Psychology Bulletin, 28,* 382–394.

U.S. Census Bureau. (2000). *Housing—Physical characteristics.* Retrieved October 18, 2006, http://factfinder.census.gov/servlet/ACSSAFFHousing?_event=&geo_id=01000US&_geoContext=01000US&_street=&_county=&_cityTown=&_state=&_zip=&_lang=en&_e=on&ActiveGeoDiv=&_useEV=&pctxt=fph&pgsl=010&_submenuId=housing_1&ds_name=null&_ci_nbr=null&qr_name=null&reg=null%3Anull&_keyword=&_industry=

U.S. Census Bureau. (2009). *Income, poverty, and health insurance coverage in the United States: 2008.* Retrieved October 5, 2009 from http://www.census.gov/prod/2009pubs/p60-236.pdf

U.S. Department of Agriculture. (2006). *Dietary guidelines for Americans.* Washington, DC: Author. Retrieved from http://warp.nal.usda.gov/fnic/dga

U.S. Department of Commerce. (2009). Current population reports: Consumer income. *Income, Poverty, and Health Insurance Coverage in the United States: 2008,* 20–25.

U.S. Department of Health and Human Services. (2007). *Prescription drug spending.*

U.S. Department of Health and Human Services. (2009). *2008 Physical Activity Guidelines for Americans.* Retrieved October 14, 2009, from http://www.health.gov/paguidelines/guidelines/default.aspx#toc

U.S. Department of Health, Education, and Welfare and U.S. Public Health Service. (1964). *Smoking and health: Report of the advisory committee to the surgeon general of the Public Health Service* (Publication No. PHS–1103). Washington, DC: U.S. Government Printing Office.

U.S. Department of Labor, Bureau of Labor Statistics. (2009). Occupational Outlook Handbook, 2008–09 Edition. Retrieved October 7, 2009, from http://www.bls.gov/oco

U.S. Preventive Services Task Force. (2009). Screening for breast cancer: U.S. preventive services task force recommendation statement. *Annals of Internal Medicine, 151,* 716–726.

Ussher, J. M., Perz, J., Hawkins, Y., & Brack, M. (2009). Evaluating the efficacy of psychosocial interventions for informal carers of cancer patients: A systematic review of the research literature. *Health Psychology Review, 3,* 85–107.

Uzark, K. C., Becker, M. H., Dielman, T. E., & Rocchini, A. P. (1987). Psychosocial predictors of compliance with a weight control intervention for obese children and adolescents. *Journal of Compliance in Health Care, 2,* 167–178.

Vahtera, J., Kivimäki, M., Väänänen, A., Linna, A., Pentti, J., Helenius, H., et al. (2006). Sex differences in health effects of family death or illness: Are women more vulnerable than men? *Psychosomatic Medicine, 68,* 283–291.

Valdimarsdottir, H. B., Zakowski, S. G., Gerin, W., Mamakos, J., Pickering, T., & Bovbjerg, D. H. (2002). Heightened psychobiological reactivity to laboratory stressors in healthy women at familial risk for breast cancer. *Journal of Behavioral Medicine, 25,* 51–65.

Valet, M., Gündel, H., Sprenger, T., Sorg, C., Mühlau, M., Zimmer, C., et al. (2009). Patients with pain disorder show gray-matter loss in pain-processing structures: A voxel-based morphometric study. *Psychosomatic Medicine, 71,* 49–56.

Vallance, J. K. H., Courneya, K. S., Plotnikoff, R. C., & Mackey, J. R. (2008). Analyzing theoretical mechanisms of physical activity behavior change in breast cancer survivors: Results from the activity promotion (ACTION) trial. *Annals of Behavioral Medicine, 35,* 150–158.

Valois, P., Desharnais, R., & Godin, G. (1988). A comparison of the Fishbein and Ajzen and the Triandis attitudinal models for the prediction of exercise intention and behavior. *Journal of Behavioral Medicine, 11,* 459–472.

Vamos, E. P., Mucsi, I., Keszei, A., Kopp, M. S., & Novak, M. (2009). Comorbid depression is associated with increased healthcare utilization and lost productivity in persons with diabetes: A large nationally representative Hungarian population survey. *Psychosomatic Medicine, 71,* 501–507.

Van De Ven, M. O. M., Engels, R. C. M., Otten, R., & Van Den Eijnden, R. J. J. (2007). A longitudinal test of the theory of planned behavior predicting smoking onset among asthmatic and non-asthmatic adolescents. *Journal of Behavioral Medicine, 30,* 435–445.

Van den Berg, J. F., Miedema, H. M. E., Tulen, J. H. M., Neven, A. K., Hofman, A., Witteman, J. C. M., et al. (2008). Long sleep duration is associated with serum cholesterol in the elderly: The Rotterdamn study. *Psychosomatic Medicine, 70,* 1005–1011.

Van den Berg, M., Timmermans, D. R. M., Knol, D. L., van Eijk, J. T. M., de Smit, D. J., van Vugt, J. M. G., et al. (2008). Understanding women's decision making concerning prenatal screening. *Health Psychology, 27,* 430–437.

Van den Putte, B., Yzer, M., Willemsen, M. C., & de Bruijn, G. J. (2009). The effects of smoking self-identity and quitting self-identity on attempts to quit smoking. *Health Psychology, 28,* 535–544.

Van der Ploeg, H. P., Streppel, K. R. M., van der Beek, A. J., van der Woude, L. H. V., van Harten, W. H., & van Mechelen, W. (2008). Underlying mechanisms of improving physical activity behavior after rehabilitation. *International Journal of Behavioral Medicine, 15,* 101–108.

Van der Velde, F. W., & Van der Pligt, J. (1991). AIDS-related health behavior: Coping, protection, motivation, and previous behavior. *Journal of Behavioral Medicine, 14,* 429–452.

Van der Zwaluw, C. S., Scholte, R. H. J., Vermulst, A. A., Buitelaar, J. K., Verkes, R. J., & Engels, R. C. M. E. (2008). Parental problem drinking, parenting, and adolescent alcohol use. *Journal of Behavioral Medicine, 31,* 189–200.

Van Jaarsveld, C. H. M., Fidler, J. A., Simon, A. E., & Wardle, J. (2007). Persistent impact of pubertal timing on trends in smoking, food choice, activity, and stress in adolescents. *Psychosomatic Medicine, 96,* 798–806.

Van Kessel, K., Moss-Morris, R., Willoughby, E., Chalder, T., Johnson, M. H., & Robinson, E. (2008). A randomized controlled trial of cognitive behavior therapy for multiple sclerosis fatigue. *Psychosomatic Medicine, 70,* 205–213.

Van Koningsbruggen, G. M., Das, E., & Roskos-Ewoldsen, D. R. (2009). How self-affirmation reduces defensive processing of threatening health information: Evidence at the implicit level. *Health Psychology, 28,* 563–568.

Van Lankveld, W., Naring, G., van der Staak, C., van't Pad Bosch, P., & van de Putte, L. (1993). Stress caused by rheumatoid arthritis: Relation among subjective stressors of the disease, disease status, and well-being. *Journal of Behavioral Medicine, 16,* 309–322.

Van Lieshout, R., Bienenstock, J., & MacQueen, G. M. (2009). A review of candidate pathways underlying the association between asthma and major depressive disorder. *Psychosomatic Medicine, 71,* 187–195.

Van Rood, Y. R., Bogaards, M., Goulmy, E., & van Houwelingen, H. C. (1993). The effects of stress and relaxation on the *in vitro* immune response in man: A meta-analytic study. *Journal of Behavioral Medicine, 16,* 163–182.

Van Ryn, M., & Fu, S. S. (2003). Paved with good intensions: Do public health and human service providers contribute to racial/ethnic disparities in health? *American Journal of Public Health, 93,* 248–255.

Van Stralen, M. M., De Vries, H., Mudde, A. N., Bolman, C., & Lechner, L. (2009). Determinants of initiation and maintenance of physical activity among older adults: A literature review. *Health Psychology Review, 3,* 147–207.

Van't Spijker, A., Trijsburg, R. W., & Duivenvoorden, H. J. (1997). Psychological sequelae of cancer diagnosis: A meta-analytic review of 58 studies after 1980. *Psychosomatic Medicine, 59,* 280–293.

Van Tilberg, M. A. L., McCaskill C. C., Lane, J. D., Edwards, C. L., Bethel, A., Feinglos, M. N., et al. (2001). Depressed mood is a factor in glycemic control in type 1 diabetes. *Psychosomatic Medicine, 65,* 551–555.

Van YPeren, N. W., Buunk, B. P., & Schaufelli, W. B. (1992). Communal orientation and the burnout syndrome among nurses. *Journal of Applied Social Psychology, 22,* 173–189.

Van Zundert, R. M. P., Ferguson, S. G., Shiffman, S., & Engels, R. C. M. (2010). Dynamic effects of self-efficacy on smoking lapses and relapse among adolescents. *Health Psychology, 29,* 246–254.

VanderPlate, C., Aral, S. O., & Magder, L. (1988). The relationship among genital herpes simplex virus, stress, and social support. *Health Psychology, 7,* 159–168.

Varni, J. W., Burwinkle, T. M., Rapoff, M. A., Kamps, J. L., & Olson, N. (2004). The PedsQL in pediatric asthma: Reliability and validity of the Pediatric Quality of Life Inventory Generic Core Scales and Asthma Module. *Journal of Behavioral Medicine, 27,* 297–318.

Vartanian, L. R., Herman, C. P., & Wansink, B. (2008). Are we aware of the external factors that influence our food intake? *Health Psychology, 27,* 533–538.

Vedhara, K., Brant, E., Adamopoulos, E., Byrne-Davis, L., Mackintosh, B., Hoppitt, L., et al. (2010). A preliminary investigation into whether attentional bias influences mood outcomes following emotional disclosure. *International Journal of Behavioral Medicine, 17,* 195–206.

Vella, E. J., Kamarck, T. W., & Shiffman, S. (2008). Hostility moderates the effects of social support and intimacy on blood pressure in daily social interactions. *Health Psychology, 27,* S155–S162.

Vendrig, A. (1999). Prognostic factors and treatment-related changes associated with return to working: The multimodal treatment of chronic back pain. *Journal of Behavioral Medicine, 22,* 217–232.

Verbrugge, L. M. (1983). Multiple roles and physical health of women and men. *Journal of Health and Social Behavior, 24,* 16–30.

Verbrugge, L. M. (1995). Women, men, and osteoarthritis. *Arthritis Care and Research, 8,* 212–220.

Verkuil, B., Brosschot, J. F., & Thayer, J. F. (2007). A sensitive body or a sensitive mind? Associations among somatic sensitization, cognitive sensitization, health worry, and subjective health complaints. *Journal of Psychosomatic Research, 63,* 673–681.

Vernon, S. W., Gritz, E. R., Peterson, S. K., Amos, C. I., Perz, C. A., Baile, W. F., et al. (1997). Correlates of psychologic distress in colorectal cancer patients undergoing genetic testing for hereditary colon cancer. *Health Psychology, 16,* 73–86.

Vickers, K. S., Patten, C. A., Lane, K., Clark, M. M., Croghan, I. T., Schroeder, D. R., et al. (2003). Depressed versus nondepressed young adult tobacco users: Differences in coping style, weight concerns, and exercise level. *Health Psychology, 22,* 498–503.

Villarosa, L. (2002, September 23). As Black men move into middle age, dangers rise. *New York Times,* pp. E1, E8.

Vila, G., Porche, L., & Mouren-Simeoni, M. (1999). An 18-month longitudinal study of posttraumatic disorders in children who were taken hostage in their school. *Psychosomatic Medicine, 61,* 746–754.

Vila, G., Zipper, E., Dabbas, M., Bertrand, C., Robert, J. J., Ricour, C., et al. (2004). Mental disorders in obese children and adolescents. *Psychosomatic Medicine, 66,* 387–394.

Visotsky, H. M., Hamburg, D. A., Goss, M. E., & Lebovitz, B. Z. (1961). Coping behavior under extreme stress. *Archives of General Psychiatry, 5,* 423–428.

Vitaliano, P. P., Maiuro, R. D., Russo, J., Katon, W., DeWolfe, D., & Hall, G. (1990). Coping profiles associated with psychiatric, physical health, work, and family problems. *Health Psychology, 9,* 348–376.

Vitaliano, P. P., Scanlan, J. M., Zhang, J., Savage, M. V., Hirsch, I. B., & Siegler, I. C. (2002). A path model of chronic stress, the metabolic syndrome, and coronary heart disease. *Psychosomatic Medicine, 64,* 418–435.

Vitiello, M. V. (2009). Recent advances in understanding sleep and sleep disturbances in older adults: Growing older does not mean sleeping poorly. *Current Directions in Psychological Science, 18,* 316–320.

Vittinghoff, E., Shlipak, M. G., Varosy, P. D., Furberg, C. D., Ireland, C. C., Khan, S. S., et al. (2003). Risk factors and secondary prevention in women with heart disease: The Heart and Estrogen/Progestin Replacement Study. *Annals of Internal Medicine, 138,* 81–89.

Vogt, F., Hall, S., Hankins, M., & Marteau, T. M. (2009). Evaluating three theory-based interventions to increase physicians recommendations of smoking cessation services. *Health Psychology, 28,* 174–182.

Voltarelli, J. C., Couri, C. E., Stracieri, A. B., Oliveira, M. C., Moraes, D. A., Pieroni, F., et al. (2007). Autologous nonmyeloablative hematopoietic stem cell transplantation in newly diagnosed type 1 diabetes mellitus. *Journal of the American Medical Association, 297,* 1568–1576.

Von Känel, R., Bellingrath, S., & Kudielka, B. M. (2009). Overcommitment but not effort–reward imbalance relates to stress-induced coagulation changes in teachers. *Annals of Behavioral Medicine, 37,* 20–28.

Von Kaenel, R., Dimsdale, J. E., Patterson, T. L., & Grant, I. (2003). Acute procoagulant stress response as a dynamic measure of allostatic load in Alzheimer caregivers. *Annals of Behavioral Medicine, 26,* 42–48.

Von Korff, M., Katon, W., Lin, E. H. B., Simon, G., Ludman, E., Ciechanowski, P., et al. (2005). Potentially modifiable factors associated with disability among people with diabetes. *Psychosomatic Medicine, 67,* 233–240.

Vos, P. J., Garssen, B., Visser, A. P., Duivenvoorden, H. J., & de Haes, C. J. M. (2004). Early stage breast cancer: Explaining level of psychosocial adjustment using structural equation modeling. *Journal of Behavioral Medicine, 27,* 557–580.

Voss, U., Kolling, T., & Heidenreich, T. (2006). Role of monitoring and blunting coping styles in primary insomnia. *Psychosomatic Medicine, 68,* 110–115.

Vowles, K. E., McCracken, L. M., & Eccleston, C. (2008). Patient functioning and catastrophizing in chronic pain: The mediating effects of acceptance. *Health Psychology, 27,* S136–S143.

Vowles, K. E., Zvolensky, M. J., Gross, R. T., & Sperry, J. A. (2004). Pain-related anxiety in the prediction of chronic low-back pain distress. *Journal of Behavioral Medicine, 27,* 77–89.

Wachholtz, A. B., & Pargament, K. I. (2008). Migranes and meditation: does spirituality matter? *Journal of Behavioral Medicine, 31,* 351–366.

Wade, N. (2007, April 27). Scientists identify 7 new diabetes genes: Findings yield clues to biology of disease, but not treatment. *New York Times,* p. A20.

Wade, T. D., Bulik, C. M., Sullivan, P. F., Neale, M. C., & Kendler, K. S. (2000). The relation between risk factors for binge eating and bulimia nervosa: A population-based female twin study. *Health Psychology, 19,* 115–123.

Wade, T. D., Tiggemann, M., Bulik, C. M., Fairburn, C. G., Wray, N. R., & Martin, N. G. (2008). Shared temperament risk factors for anorexia nervosa: A twin study. *Psychosomatic Medicine, 70,* 239–244.

Wager, T. D., Rilling, J. K., Smith, E. E., Sokolik, A., Casey, K. L., Davidson, R. J., et al. (2004). Placebo-induced changes in fMRI in the anticipation and experience of pain. *Science, 303,* 1162–1167.

Waggoner, C. D., & LeLieuvre, R. B. (1981). A method to increase compliance to exercise regimens in rheumatoid arthritis patients. *Journal of Behavioral Medicine, 4,* 191–202.

Wagner, P. J., & Curran, P. (1984). Health beliefs and physician identified "worried well." *Health Psychology, 3,* 459–474.

Waitzkin, H. (1985). Information giving in medical care. *Journal of Health and Social Behavior, 26,* 81–101.

Waldron, I., Weiss, C. C., & Hughes, M. E. (1998). Interacting effects of multiple roles on women's health. *Journal of Health and Social Behavior, 39,* 216–236.

Waldstein, S. R., & Burns, H. O. (2003). Interactive relation of insulin and gender to cardiovascular reactivity in healthy young adults. *Annals of Behavioral Medicine, 25,* 163–171.

Waldstein, S. R., Burns, H. O., Toth, M. J., & Poehlman, E. T. (1999). Cardiovascular reactivity and central adiposity in older African Americans. *Health Psychology, 18,* 221–228.

Waldstein, S. R., Jennings, J. R., Ryan, C. M., Muldoon, M. F., Shapiro, A. P., Polefrone, J. M., et al. (1996). Hypertension and neuropsychological performance in men: Interactive effects of age. *Health Psychology, 15,* 102–109.

Walker, L. S., Smith, C. A., Garber, J., & Claar, R. L. (2005). Testing a model of pain appraisal and coping in children with chronic abdominal pain. *Health Psychology, 24,* 364–374.

Wall Street Journal. (2005, August 9). Fatalities rise after repeal of helmet laws, p. D6.

Waller, J., McCaffery, K. J., Forrest, S., & Wardle, J. (2004). Human papillomavirus and cervical cancer: Issues for biobehavioral and psychosocial research. *Annals of Behavioral Medicine, 27,* 68–79.

Wallston, B. S., Alagna, S. W., DeVellis, B. M., & DeVellis, R. F. (1983). Social support and physical health. *Health Psychology, 2,* 367–391.

Wallston, K. A., Wallston, B. S., & DeVellis, R. (1978). Development of the Multidimensional Health Locus of Control (MHLC) Scale. *Health Education Monographs, 6,* 161–170.

Walsh, D. C., & Gordon, N. P. (1986). Legal approaches to smoking deterrence. *Annual Review of Public Health, 7,* 127–149.

Wanburg, K. W., & Horn, J. L. (1983). Assessment of alcohol use with multidimensional concepts and measures. *American Psychologist, 38,* 1055–1069.

Wang, J., & Etter, J. F. (2004). Administering an effective health intervention for smoking cessation online: The international users of Stop-Tabac. *Preventive Medicine, 39,* 962–968.

Wang, S. S., Houshyar, S., & Prinstein, M. J. (2006). Adolescent girls' and boys' weight-related health behaviors and cognitions: Associations with reputation- and preference-based peer status. *Health Psychology, 25,* 658–663.

Wang, X., Trivedi, R., Treiber, F., & Snieder, H. (2005). Genetic and environmental influences on anger expression, John Henryism, and stressful life events: The Georgia Cardiovascular Twin Study. *Psychosomatic Medicine, 67,* 16–23.

Ward, A., & Mann, T. (2000). Don't mind if I do: Disinhibited eating under cognitive load. *Journal of Personality and Social Psychology, 78,* 753–763.

Ward, S., Donovan, H., Gunnarsdottier, S., Serlin, R. C., Shapiro, G. R., & Hughes, S. (2008). A randomized trial of a representational intervention to decrease cancer pain (RIDcancerPAIN). *Health Psychology, 27,* 59–67.

Ward, S., & Leventhal, H. (1993). *Explaining retrospective reports of side effects: Anxiety, initial side effect experience, and post-treatment side effects.* Series paper from the School of Nursing, University of Wisconsin, Madison.

Ward, S. E., Leventhal, H., & Love, R. (1988). Repression revisited: Tactics used in coping with a severe health threat. *Personality and Social Psychology Bulletin, 14,* 735–746.

Wardle, J., Robb, K. A., Johnson, F., Griffith, J., Brunner, E., Power, C., et al. (2004). Socioeconomic variation in attitudes to eating and weight in female adolescents. *Health Psychology, 23,* 275–282.

Wardle, J., Williamson, S., McCaffery, K., Sutton, S., Taylor, T., Edwards, R., et al. (2003). Increasing attendance at colorectal cancer screening: Testing the efficacy of a mailed, psychoeducational intervention in a community sample of older adults. *Health Psychology, 22,* 99–105.

Wardle, J., Williamson, S., Sutton, S., Biran, A., McCaffery, K., Cuzik, J., et al. (2003). Psychological impact of colorectal cancer screening. *Health Psychology, 22,* 54–59.

Ware, J. E., Jr. (1994). Norm-based interpretation. *Medical Outcomes Trust Bulletin, 2,* 3.

Ware, J. E., Jr., Bayliss, M. S., Rogers, W. H., & Kosinski, M. (1996). Differences in four-year health outcomes for elderly and poor, chronically ill patients in HMO and fee-for-service systems: Results from the Medical Outcomes Study. *Journal of the American Medical Association, 276,* 1039–1047.

Ware, J. E., Jr., Davies-Avery, A., & Stewart, A. L. (1978). The measurement and meaning of patient satisfaction: A review of the literature. *Health and Medical Care Services Review, 1,* 1–15.

Warren, J. R., & Hernandez, E. M. (2007). Did socioeconomic inequalities in morbidity and mortality change in the United States over the course of the twentieth century? *Journal of Health and Social Behavior, 48,* 335–351.

Warren, M., Weitz, R., & Kulis, S. (1998). Physician satisfaction in a changing health care environment: The impact of challenges to professional autonomy, authority, and dominance. *Journal of Health and Social Behavior, 39,* 356–367.

Warziski, M. T., Sereika, S. M., Styn, M. A., Music, E., & Burke, L. E. (2008). Changes in self-efficacy and dietary adherence: The impact on weight loss in the PREFER study. *Journal of Behavioral Medicine, 31,* 81–92.

Watkins, J. D., Roberts, D. E., Williams, T. F., Martin, D. A., & Coyle, I. V. (1967). Observations of medication errors made by diabetic patients in the home. *Diabetes, 16,* 882–885.

Watson, D., & Clark, L. A. (1984). Negative affectivity: The disposition to experience aversive emotional states. *Psychological Bulletin, 96,* 465–490.

Watson, D., & Pennebaker, J. W. (1989). Health complaints, stress, and distress: Exploring the central role of negative affectivity. *Psychological Review, 96,* 234–264.

Weaver, K. E., Llabre, M. M., Durán, R. E., Antoni, M. H., Ironson, G., Penedo, F., et al. (2005). A stress coping model of medication adherence and viral load in HIV positive men and women on highly active antiretroviral therapy (HAART). *Health Psychology, 24,* 385–392.

Webb, M. S. (2008). Treating tobacco dependence among African Americans: A meta-analytic review. *Health Psychology, 27,* S271-S282.

Webb, M. S., de Ybarra, D. R., Baker, E. A., Reis, I. M., & Carey, M. P. (2010). Cognitive behavioral therapy to promote smoking cessation among African American smokers: A randomized clinical trial. *Journal of Consulting and Clinical Psychology, 78,* 24–33.

Webb, M. S., Hendricks, P. S., & Brandon, T. H. (2007). Expectancy priming of smoking cessation messages enhances the placebo effect of tailored interventions. *Health Psychology, 26,* 598–609.

Webb, M. S., Simmons, V. N., & Brandon, T. H. (2005). Tailored interventions for motivating smoking cessation: Using placebo tailoring to examine the influence of expectancies and personalization. *Health Psychology, 24,* 179–188.

Webb, M. S., Vanable, P. A., Carey, M. P., & Blair, D. C. (2007). Cigarette smoking among HIV+ men and women: Examining health, substance use, and psychological correlates across the smoking spectrum. *Journal of Behavioral Medicine, 30,* 371–383.

Weber-Hamann, B., Hentschel, F., Kniest, A., Deuschle, M., Colla, M., Lederbogen, F., et al. (2002). Hypercortisolemic depression is associated with increased intra-abdominal fat. *Psychosomatic Medicine, 64,* 274–277.

Wechsler, H., Lee, J. E., Kuo, M., Seibring, M., Nelson, T. F., & Lee, H. (2002). Trends in college binge drinking during a period of increased prevention efforts. *Journal of American College Health, 50,* 203–217.

Wechsler, H., Seibring, M., Liu, I. C., & Ahl, M. (2004). Colleges respond to student binge drinking: Reducing student demand or limiting access. *Journal of American College Health, 52,* 159–168.

Wegman, H. L., & Stetler, C. (2009). A meta-analytic review of the effects of childhood abuse on medical outcomes in adulthood. *Psychosomatic Medicine, 71,* 805–812.

Weidner, G., Archer, S., Healy, B., & Matarazzo, J. D. (1985). Family consumption of low fat foods: Stated preference versus actual consumption. *Journal of Applied Social Psychology, 15,* 773–779.

Weidner, G., Boughal, T., Connor, S. L., Pieper, C., & Mendell, N. R. (1997). Relationship of job strain to standard coronary risk factors and psychological characteristics in women and men of the family heart study. *Health Psychology, 16,* 239–247.

Weidner, G., Rice, T., Knox, S. S., Ellison, C., Province, M. A., Rao, D. C., et al. (2000). Familial resemblance for hostility: The National Heart, Lung, and Blood Institute Family Heart Study. *Psychosomatic Medicine, 62,* 197–204.

Weihs, K. L., Enright, T. M., & Simmens, S. J. (2008). Close relationships and emotional processing predict decreased mortality in women with breast cancer: Preliminary evidence. *Psychosomatic Medicine, 70,* 117–124.

Weinhardt, L. S., & Carey, M. P. (1996). Prevalence of erectile disorder among men with diabetes mellitus: Comprehensive review, methodological critique, and suggestions for future research. *Journal of Sex Research, 33,* 205–214.

Weinhardt, L. S., Carey, M. P., Carey, K. B., Maisto, S. A., & Gordon, C. M. (2001). The relation of alcohol use to sexual HIV risk behavior among adults with a severe and persistent mental illness. *Journal of Consulting and Clinical Psychology, 69,* 77–84.

Weinhardt, L. S., Carey, M. P., Johnson, B. T., & Bickman, N. L. (1999). Effects of HIV counseling and testing on sexual risk behavior: A meta-analytic review of published research, 1985–1997. *American Journal of Public Health, 89,* 1397–1405.

Weinman, J., Petrie, K. J., Moss-Morris, R., & Horne, R. (1996). The illness perception questionnaire: A new method for assessing the cognitive representation of illness. *Psychology and Health, 11,* 431–445.

Weinstein, N. D. (1993). Testing four competing theories of health-protective behavior. *Health Psychology, 12,* 324–333.

Weinstein, N. D., & Klein, W. M. (1995). Resistance of personal risk perceptions to debiasing interventions. *Health Psychology, 14,* 132–140.

Weinstein, N. D., Kwitel, A., McCaul, K. D., Magnan, R. E., Gerrard, M., & Gibbons, F. X. (2007). Risk perceptions: Assessment and relationship to influenza vaccination. *Health Psychology, 26,* 146–151.

Weinstein, N. D., Rothman, A. J., & Sutton, S. R. (1998). Stage theories of health behavior: Conceptual and methodological issues. *Health Psychology, 17,* 290–299.

Weintraub, A. (2004, January 26). "I can't sleep." *Business Week,* pp. 67–70, 72, 74.

Weisman, A. D. (1972). *On death and dying.* New York: Behavioral Publications.

Weisman, A. D. (1977). The psychiatrist and the inexorable. In H. Feifel (Ed.), *New meanings of death* (pp. 107–122). New York: McGraw-Hill.

Weisman, C. S., & Teitelbaum, M. A. (1985). Physician gender and the physician-patient relationship: Recent evidence and relevant questions. *Social Sciences and Medicine, 20,* 1119–1127.

Weiss, A., Gale, C. R., Batty, D., & Deary, I. J. (2009). Emotionally stable, intelligent men live longer: The Vietnam experience study cohort. *Psychosomatic Medicine, 71,* 385–394.

Weiss, R. S., & Richards, T. A. (1997). A scale for predicting quality of recovery following the death of a partner. *Journal of Personality and Social Psychology, 72,* 885–891.

Wells, S., Mullin, B., Norton, R., Langley, J., Connor, J., Lay-Yee, R., et al. (2004). Motorcycle rider conspicuity and crash related injury: Case control study. *British Medical Journal, 328,* 857–860.

Wenninger, K., Weiss, C., Wahn, U., & Staab, D. (2003). Body image in cystic fibrosis—Development of a brief diagnostic scale. *Journal of Behavioral Medicine, 26,* 81–94.

Westmaas, J. L., Wild, T. C., & Ferrence, R. (2002). Effects of gender in social control of smoking cessation. *Health Psychology, 21,* 368–376.

Whalen, C. K., Jamner, L. D., Henker, B., & Delfino, R. J. (2001). Smoking and moods in adolescents with depressive and aggressive dispositions: Evidence from surveys and electronic diaries. *Health Psychology, 20,* 99–111.

Whetten, K., Reif, S., Whetten, R., & Murphy-McMillan, L. K. (2008). Trauma, mental health, distrust, and stigma among HIV-positive persons: Implications for effective care. *Psychosomatic Medicine, 70,* 531–538.

Whisman, M. A., & Kwon, P. (1993). Life stress and dysphoria: The role of self-esteem and hopelessness. *Journal of Personality and Social Psychology, 65,* 1054–1060.

Whitbeck, L. B., Hoyt, D. R., McMorris, B. J., Chen, X., & Stubben, J. D. (2001). Perceived discrimination and early substance abuse among American Indian children. *Journal of Health and Social Behavior, 42,* 405–424.

Whitbeck, L. B., McMorris, B. J., Hoyt, D. R., Stubben, J. D., & LaFromboise, T. (2002). Perceived discrimination, traditional practices, and depressive symptoms among American Indians in the upper Midwest. *Journal of Health and Social Behavior, 43,* 400–418.

White, L. P., & Tursky, B. (1982). Where are we? Where are we going? In L. White & B. Tursky (Eds.), *Clinical biofeedback: Efficacy and mechanisms* (pp. 438–448). New York: Guilford Press.

Wholey, D. R., & Burns, L. R. (1991). Convenience and independence: Do physicians strike a balance in admitting decisions? *Journal of Health and Social Behavior, 32,* 254–272.

Wichstrom, L. (1994). Predictors of Norwegian adolescents' sunbathing and use of sunscreen. *Health Psychology, 13,* 412–420.

Wickrama, K. A. S., Conger, R. D., & Lorenz, F. O. (1995). Work, marriage, lifestyle, and changes in men's physical health. *Journal of Behavioral Medicine, 18,* 97–112.

Wickrama, K. A. S., Conger, R. D., Wallace, L. E., & Elder, G. H., Jr. (2003). Linking early social risks to impaired physical health during the transition to adulthood. *Journal of Health and Social Behavior, 44,* 61–74.

Widows, M., Jacobsen, P., Booth-Jones, M., & Fields, K. K. (2005). Predictors of posttraumatic growth following bone marrow transplantation for cancer. *Health Psychology, 24,* 266–273.

Widows, M., Jacobsen, P., & Fields, K. (2000). Relation of psychological vulnerability factors to posttraumatic stress disorder symptomatology in bone marrow transplant recipients. *Psychosomatic Medicine, 62,* 873–882.

Wijngaards-Meij, L., Stroebe, M., Schut, H., van den Bout, J., van der Heijden, P., et al. (2005). Couples at risk following the death of their child: Predictors of grief versus depression. *Journal of Consulting and Clinical Psychology, 73,* 617–623.

Wijngaards-Meij, L., Stroebe, M., Schut, H., Stroebe, W., van den Bout, J., van der Heijden, P. G., et al. (2008). Parents grieving the loss of their child: Interdependence in coping. *British Journal of Clinical Psychology, 47,* 31–42.

Wikman, A., Bhattacharyya, M., Perkins-Porras, L., & Steptoe, A. (2008). Persistence of posttraumatic stress symptoms 12 and 36 months after acute coronary syndrome. *Psychosomatic Medicine, 70,* 764–772.

Wilbert-Lampen, U., Leistner, D., Greven, S., Pohl, T., Sper, S., Völker, C., et al. (2008). Cardiovascular events during world cup soccer. *The New England Journal of Medicine, 358,* 475–483.

Wilcox, S., Evenson, K. R., Aragaki, A., Wassertheil-Smoller, S., Mouton, C. P., & Loevinger, B. L. (2003). The effects of widowhood on physical and mental health, health behaviors, and health outcomes: The women's health initiative. *Health Psychology, 22,* 513–522.

Wilcox, S., & Stefanick, M. L. (1999). Knowledge and perceived risk of major diseases in middle-aged and older women. *Health Psychology, 18,* 346–353.

Wilcox, V. L., Kasl, S. V., & Berkman, L. F. (1994). Social support and physical disability in older people after hospitalization: A prospective study. *Health Psychology, 13,* 170–179.

Wilfley, D. E., Tibbs, T. L., Epstein, L. H., Van Buren, D. J., Reach, K. P., Walker, M. S., et al. (2007). Lifestyle interventions in the treatment of childhood overweight: A meta-analytic review of randomized controlled trials. *Health Psychology, 26,* 521–532.

Wilkin, H. A., Valente, T. W., Murphy, S., Cody, M. J., Huang, G., & Beck, V. (2007). Does entertainment-education work with Latinos in the United States? Identification and the effects of a telenovela breast cancer storyline. *Journal of Health Communication, 12,* 455–469.

Willenbring, M. L., Levine, A. S., & Morley, J. E. (1986). Stress induced eating and food preference in humans: A pilot study. *International Journal of Eating Disorders, 5,* 855–864.

Williams, D. R. (2002). Racial/ethnic variations in women's health: The social embeddedness of health. *American Journal of Public Health, 92,* 588–597.

Williams, D. R. (2003). The health of men: Structured inequalities and opportunities. *American Journal of Public Health, 93,* 724–731.

Williams, D. R., & Mohammed, S. A. (2009). Discrimination and racial disparities in health: Evidence and needed research. *Journal of Behavioral Medicine, 32,* 20–47.

Williams, G. C., Cox, E. M., Hedberg, V. A., & Deci, E. L. (2000). Extrinsic life goals and health-related behaviors in adolescents. *Journal of Applied Social Psychology, 30,* 1756–1771.

Williams, G. C., Cox, E. M., Kouides, R., & Deci, E. L. (1999). Presenting the facts about smoking to adolescents: Effects of an autonomy-supporting style. *Archives of Pediatrics and Adolescent Medicine, 153,* 959–964.

Williams, G. C., Gagne, M., Ryan, R. M., & Deci, E. L. (2002). Supporting autonomy to motivate smoking cessation: A test of self-determination theory. *Health Psychology, 21,* 40–50.

Williams, G. C., Lynch, M., & Glasgow, R. E. (2007). Computer-assisted intervention improves patient-centered diabetes care by increasing autonomy support. *Health Psychology, 26,* 728–734.

Williams, G. C., McGregor, H. A., Sharp, D., Kouides, R. W., Levesque, C. S., Ryan, R. M., et al. (2006). A self-determination multiple risk intervention trial to improve smokers health. *Journal of General Internal Medicine, 21,* 1288–1294.

Williams, G. C., McGregor, H. A., Sharp, D., Levesque, C., Kouides, R. W., Ryan, R. M., et al. (2006). Testing a self-determination theory intervention for motivating tobacco cessation: Supporting autonomy and competence in a clinical trial. *Health Psychology, 25,* 91–101.

Williams, G. C., McGregor, H. A., Zeldman, A., Freedman, Z. R., & Deci, E. L. (2004). Testing a self-determination theory process model for promoting glycemic control through diabetes self-management. *Health Psychology, 23,* 58–66.

Williams, K. J., Suls, J., Alliger, G. M., Learner, S. M., & Wan, C. K. (1991). Multiple role juggling and daily mood states in working mothers: An experience sampling study. *Journal of Applied Psychology, 76,* 664–674.

Williams, L., O'Carroll, R. E., & O'Connor, R. C. (2008). Type D personality and cardiac output in response to stress. *Psychology and Health, 24,* 489–500.

Williams, L., O'Conner, R. C., Howard, S., Hughes, B. M., Johnston, D. W., Hay, J. L., et al. (2008). Type-D personality mechanisms of effect: The role of health-related behavior and social support. *Journal of Psychosomatic Research, 64,* 63–69.

Williams, P. D., Williams, A. R., Graff, J. C., Hanson, S., Stanton, A., Hafeman, C., et al. (2002). Interrelationships among variables affecting well siblings and mothers in families of children with chronic illness or disability. *Journal of Behavioral Medicine, 25,* 411–424.

Williams, P. G., Colder, C. R., Lane, J. D., McCaskill, C. C., Feinglos, M. N., & Surwit, R. S. (2002). Examination of the neuroticism-symptom reporting relationship in individuals with type-2 diabetes. *Personality and Social Psychology Bulletin, 28,* 1015–1025.

Williams, R. B. (1984). An untrusting heart. *The Sciences, 24,* 31–36.

Williams, R. B., Barefoot, J. C., Califf, R. M., Haney, T. L., Saunders, W. B., Pryor, D. B., et al. (1992). Prognostic importance of social and economic resources among medically treated patients with angiographically documented coronary artery disease. *Journal of the American Medical Association, 267,* 520–524.

Williams, S., & Kohout, J. L. (1999). Psychologists in medical schools in 1997. *American Psychologist, 54,* 272–276.

Williams, S. A., Kasil, S. V., Heiat, A., Abramson, J. L., Krumholtz, H. M., & Vaccarino, V. (2002). Depression and risk of heart failure among the elderly: A prospective community-based study. *Psychosomatic Medicine, 64,* 6–12.

Williams, S. C., Schmaltz, S. P., Morton, D. J., Koss, R. G., & Loeb, J. M. (2005). Quality of care in U.S. hospitals as reflected by standardized measures, 2002–2004. *The New England Journal of Medicine, 353,* 255–264.

Williamson, D. A., Anton, S. D., Han, H., Champagne, C. M., Allen, R., LeBlanc, E., et al. (2010). Early behavioral adherence predicts short and long-term weight loss in the POUNDS LOST study. *Journal of Behavioral Medicine, 33,* 305–314.

Williamson, G. M. (2000). Extending the activity restriction model of depressed affect: Evidence from a sample of breast cancer patients. *Health Psychology, 19,* 339–347.

Williamson, G. M., Shaffer, D. R., & Schulz, R. (1998). Activity restriction and prior relationship history as contributors to mental health outcomes among middle-aged and older spousal caregivers. *Health Psychology, 17,* 152–162.

Williamson, G. M., Walters, A. S., & Shaffer, D. R. (2002). Caregiver models of self and others, coping, and depression: Predictors of depression in children with chronic pain. *Health Psychology, 21,* 405–410.

Wills, T. A. (1984). Supportive functions of interpersonal relationships. In S. Cohen & L. Syme (Eds.), *Social support and health* (pp. 61–82). New York: Academic Press.

Wills, T. A., Sandy, J. M., & Yaeger, A. M. (2002). Stress and smoking in adolescence: A test of directional hypotheses. *Health Psychology, 21,* 122–130.

Wills, T. A., Sargent, J. D., Stoolmiller, M., Gibbons, F. X., Worth, K. A., & Cin, S. D. (2007). Movie exposure to smoking cues and adolescent smoking onset: A test for mediation through peer affiliation. *Health Psychology, 26,* 769–776.

Wills, T. A., & Vaughan, R. (1989). Social support and substance use in early adolescence. *Journal of Behavioral Medicine, 12,* 321–340.

Wilson, D. K., & Ampey-Thornhill, G. (2001). The role of gender and family support on dietary compliance in an African American adolescent hypertension prevention study. *Annals of Behavioral Medicine, 23,* 59–67.

Wilson, D. K., Kliewer, W., Teasley, N., Plybon, L., & Sica, D. A. (2002). Violence exposure, catecholamine excretion, and blood pressure nondipping status in African American male versus female adolescents. *Psychosomatic Medicine, 64,* 906–915.

Wilson, G. T. (1994). Behavioral treatment of childhood obesity: Theoretical and practical implications. *Health Psychology, 13,* 371–372.

Wilson, G. T., Grilo, C. M., & Vitousek, K. M. (2007). Psychological treatment of eating disorders. *American Psychologist, 62,* 199–216.

Wilson, K. G., Ainsworth, B. E., & Bowles, H. (2007). Body mass index and environmental supports for physical activity among active and inactive residents of a U.S. southeastern county. *Health Psychology, 26,* 701–717.

Wilson, R. (1963). The social structure of a general hospital. *Annals of the American Academy of Political and Social Science, 346,* 67–76.

Wilson, R. S., Beck, T. L., Bienias, J. L., & Bennett, D. A. (2007). Terminal cognitive decline: Accelerated loss of cognition in the last years of life. *Psychosomatic Medicine, 69,* 131–137.

Wilson, R. S., Krueger, K. R., Gu, L., Bienias, J. L., Mendes de Leon, C. F., & Evans, D. A. (2005). Neuroticism, extraversion, and mortality in a defined population of older persons. *Psychosomatic Medicine, 67,* 841–845.

Winett, R. A. (2003). Comments on "challenges to improving the impact of worksite cancer prevention programs": Paradigm lost? *Annals of Behavioral Medicine, 26,* 221.

Winett, R. A., Wagner, J. L., Moore, J. F., Walker, W. B., Hite, L. A., Leahy, M., et al. (1991). An experimental evaluation of a prototype public access nutrition information system for supermarkets. *Health Psychology, 10,* 75–78.

Wing, R. R. (2000). Cross-cutting themes in maintenance of behavior change. *Health Psychology, 19,* 84–88.

Wing, R. R., Blair, E., Marcus, M., Epstein, L. H., & Harvey, J. (1994). Year-long weight loss treatment for obese patients with Type II diabetes: Does including an intermittent very-low-calorie diet improve outcome? *American Journal of Medicine, 97,* 354–362.

Wing, R. R., Epstein, L. H., Nowalk, M. P., Scott, N., Koeske, R., & Hagg, S. (1986). Does self-monitoring of blood glucose levels improve dietary competence for obese patients with Type II diabetes? *American Journal of Medicine, 81,* 830–836.

Wing, R. R., Jeffery, R. W., Burton, L. R., Thorson, C., Nissinoff, K. S., & Baxter, J. E. (1996). Food provision versus structured meal plans in the behavioral treatment of obesity. *International Journal of Obesity, 20,* 56–62.

Wing, R. R., Matthews, K. A., Kuller, L. H., Meilahn, E. N., & Plantinga, P. L. (1991). Weight gain at the time of menopause. *Archives of Internal Medicine, 151,* 97–102.

Wing, R. R., Nowalk, L. H., Marcus, M. D., Koeske, R., & Finegold, D. (1986). Subclinical eating disorders and glycemic control in adolescents with Type I diabetes. *Diabetes Care, 9,* 162–167.

Winslow, R. (2010, April 6). Some success fighting heart disease. *The Wall Street Journal,* p. D1.

Winslow, R. W., Franzini, L. R., & Hwang, J. (1992). Perceived peer norms, casual sex, and AIDS risk prevention. *Journal of Applied Social Psychology, 22,* 1809–1827.

Wirtz, P. H., Ehlert, U., Emini, L., Rüdisüli, K., Groessbauer, S., Gaab, J., et al. (2006). Anticipatory cognitive stress appraisal and the acute procoagulant stress response in men. *Psychosomatic Medicine, 68,* 851–858.

Wirtz, P. H., Redwine, L. S., Ehlert, U., & von Känel, R. (2009). Independent association between lower level of social support and higher coagulation activity before and after acute psychosocial stress. *Psychosomatic Medicine, 71,* 30–37.

Wirtz, P. H., von Känel, R., Schnorpfeil, P., Ehlert, U., Frey, K., & Fischer, J. E. (2003). Reduced glucocorticoid sensitivity of monocyte interleukin–6 production in male industrial employees who are vitally exhausted. *Psychosomatic Medicine, 65,* 672–678.

Wisniewski, L., Epstein, L., Marcus, M. D., & Kaye, W. (1997). Differences in salivary habituation to palatable foods in bulimia nervosa patients and controls. *Psychosomatic Medicine, 59,* 427–433.

Witkiewitz, K., & Marlatt, G. A. (2004). Relapse prevention for alcohol and drug problems: That was Zen, this is Tao. *American Psychologist, 59,* 224–235.

Wolf, E. J., & Mori, D. L. (2009). Avoidant coping as a predictor of mortality in veterans with end-stage renal disease. *Health Psychology, 28,* 330–337.

Wolff, B., Burns, J. W., Quartana, P. J., Lofland, K., Bruehl, S., & Chung, O. Y. (2008). Pain catastrophizing, physiological indexes, and chronic pain severity: Tests of mediation and moderation models. *Journal of Behavioral Medicine, 31,* 105–114.

Wolff, N. J., Darlington, A. E., Hunfeld, J. A. M., Verhulst, F. C., Jaddoe, V. W. V., Moll, H. A., et al. (2009). The association of parent behaviors, chronic pain, and psychological problems with venipuncture distress in infants: The generation R study. *Health Psychology, 28,* 605–613.

Wolpe, J. (1958). *Psychotherapy by reciprocal inhibition.* Stanford, CA: Stanford University Press.

Wong, M., & Kaloupek, D. G. (1986). Coping with dental treatment: The potential impact of situational demands. *Journal of Behavioral Medicine, 9,* 579–598.

Wong, M. D., Shapiro, M. F., Boscardin, W. J., & Ettner, S. L. (2002). Contribution of major diseases to disparities in mortality. *The New England Journal of Medicine, 347,* 1585–1592.

Woodall, K. L., & Matthews, K. A. (1993). Changes in and stability of hostile characteristics: Results from a 4-year longitudinal study of children. *Journal of Personality and Social Psychology, 64,* 491–499.

World Health Organization. (1948). *Constitution of the World Health Organization.* Geneva, Switzerland: World Health Organization Basic Documents.

World Health Organization. (1996). *The global burden of disease: A comprehensive assessment of mortality and disability from diseases, injuries, and risk factors in 1990 and projected to 2020.* (C. J. L. Murray & A. D. Lopez, Eds.). Cambridge, MA: Harvard University Press.

World Health Organization. (2006). *Obesity and overweight.* Retrieved April 25, 2007, from http://www.who.int/mediacentre/factsheets/fs311/en/

World Health Organization. (2008). *Asthma fact sheet.* Retrieved September 25, 2009, from http://www.who.int/mediacentre/ factsheet/fs307/en/index.html

World Health Organization. (2008, November). *The top 10 causes of death.* Retrieved October 7, 2009, from http://www.who.int/mediacentre/factsheets/fs310_2008.pdf

World Health Organization. (2009). *Global status report on road safety: Time for action.* Retrieved September 30, 2009, from http://whqlibdoc.who.int/publications/2009/9789241563840_eng.pdf

World Health Organization. (2010). *Diabetes programme.* Retrieved July 22, 2010, from http://www.who.int/diabetes/actionnow/en/mapdiabprev.pdf

Worthington, E. L., Witvliet, C. V. O., Pietrini, P., & Miller, A. J. (2007). Forgiveness, health, and well-being: A review of evidence for emotional versus decisional forgiveness, dispositional forgivingness, and reduced unforgiving. *Journal of Behavioral Medicine, 30,* 291–302.

Wright, A. A., & Katz, I. T. (2007). Letting go of the rope—aggressive treatment, hospice care, and open access. *New England Journal of Medicine, 357,* 324–327.

Wroe, A. L. (2001). Intentional and unintentional nonadherence: A study of decision making. *Journal of Behavioral Medicine, 25,* 355–372.

Wrosch, C., Miller, G. E., Lupien, S., & Pruessner, J. C. (2008). Diurnal cortisol secretion and 2-year changes in older adults' physical symptoms: The moderating roles of negative affect and sleep. *Health Psychology, 27,* 685–693.

Wrosch, C., Miller, G. E., & Schulz, R. (2009). Cortisol secretion and functional disabilities in old age: Importance of using adaptive control strategies. *Psychosomatic Medicine, 71,* 996–1003.

Wrosch, C., Schulz, R., & Heckhausen, J. (2002). Health stresses and depressive symptomatology in the elderly: The importance of health engagement control strategies. *Health Psychology, 21,* 340–348.

Wrosch, C., Schulz, R., Miller, G. E., Lupien, S., & Dunne, E. (2007). Physical health problems, depressive mood, and cortisol secretion in old age: Buffer effects of health engagement control strategies. *Health Psychology, 26,* 341–349.

Wu, S. M., & Andersen, B. L. (2010). Stress generation over the course of breast cancer survivorship. *Journal of Behavioral Medicine, 33,* 250–257.

Wulfert, E., & Wan, C. K. (1993). Condom use: A self-efficacy model. *Health Psychology, 12,* 346–353.

Wulfert, E., Wan, C. K., & Backus, C. A. (1996). Gay men's safer sex behavior: An integration of three models. *Journal of Behavioral Medicine, 19,* 345–366.

Wulsin, L. R., Vaillant, G. E., & Wells, V. E. (1999). A systematic review of the mortality of depression. *Psychosomatic Medicine, 61,* 6–17.

Wynder, E. L., Kajitani, T., Kuno, I. J., Lucas, J. C., Jr., DePalo, A., & Farrow, J. (1963). A comparison of survival rates between American and Japanese patients with breast cancer. *Surgery, Gynecology, Obstetrics, 117,* 196–200.

Wysocki, T., Green, L., & Huxtable, K. (1989). Blood glucose monitoring by diabetic adolescents: Compliance and metabolic control. *Health Psychology, 8,* 267–284.

Xu, J., & Roberts, R. E. (2010). The power of positive emotions: It's a matter of life or death—Subjective well-being and longevity over 28 years in a general population. *Health Psychology, 29,* 9–19.

Yach, D., Leeder, S. R., Bell, J., & Kistnasamy, B. (2005). Global chronic diseases. *Science, 307,* 317.

Yali, A. M., & Revenson, T. A. (2004). How changes in population demographics will impact health psychology: Incorporating a broader notion of cultural competence into the field. *Health Psychology, 23,* 147–155.

Yamada, T. (2008). In search of new ideas for global health. *New England Journal of Medicine, 358,* 1324–1325.

Yamada, Y., Izawa, H., Ichihara, S., Takatsu, F., Ishihara, H., Hirayama, H., et al. (2002). Prediction of the risk of myocardial infarction from polymorphisms in candidate genes. *The New England Journal of Medicine, 347,* 1916–1923.

Yang, H. C., Brothers, B. M., & Andersen, B. L. (2008). Stress and quality of life in breast cancer recurrence: Moderation or mediation of coping? *Annals of Behavioral Medicine, 35,* 188–197.

Yarnold, P., Michelson, E., Thompson, D., & Adams, S. (1998). Predicting patient satisfaction: A study of two emergency departments. *Journal of Behavioral Medicine, 21,* 545–563.

Yazdanbakhsh, M., Kremsner, P. G., & van Ree, R. (2002). Allergy, parasites, and the hygiene hypothesis. *Science, 296,* 490–494.

Ybema, J. F., Kuijer, R. G., Buunk, B. P., DeJong, G. M., & Sanderman, R. (2001). Depression and perceptions of inequity among couples facing cancer. *Personality and Social Psychology Bulletin, 27,* 3–13.

Yi, J. P., Yi, J. C., Vitaliano, P. P., & Weinger, K. (2008). How does anger coping style affect glycemic control in diabetes patients? *International Journal of Behavioral Medicine, 15,* 167–172.

Yong, H. H., & Borland, R. (2008). Functional beliefs about smoking and quitting activity among adult smokers in four countries: Findings from the international tobacco control four-country survey. *Health Psychology, 27,* S216-S223.

York, K. M., Hassan, M., Li, Q., Li, H., Fillingim, R. B., & Sheps, D. S. (2007). Coronary artery disease and depression: Patients with more depressive symptoms have lower cardiovascular reactivity during laboratory-induced mental stress. *Psychosomatic Medicine, 69,* 521–528.

Young, D. R., He, X., Genkinger, J., Sapun, M., Mabry, I., & Jehn, M. (2004). Health status among urban African American women: Associations among well-being, perceived stress, and demographic factors. *Journal of Behavioral Medicine, 27,* 63–76.

Young-Brockopp, D. (1982). Cancer patients' perceptions of five psychosocial needs. *Oncology Nursing Forum, 9,* 31–35.

Zabinski, M. F., Calfas, K. J., Gehrman, C. A., Wilfley, D. E., & Sallis, J. F. (2001). Effects of a physical activity intervention on body image in university seniors: Project GRAD. *Annals of Behavioral Medicine, 23,* 247–252.

Zakowski, S. G., Hall, M. H., Klein, L. C., & Baum, A. (2001). Appraised control, coping, and stress in a community sample: A test of the goodness-of-fit hypothesis. *Annals of Behavioral Medicine, 23,* 158–165.

Zakowski, S. G., Ramati, A., Morton, C., Johnson, P., & Flanigan, R. (2004). Written emotional disclosure buffers the effects of social constraints on distress among cancer patients. *Health Psychology, 23,* 555–563.

Zanstra, Y. J., Schellekens, J. M. H., Schaap, C., & Kooistra, L. (2006). Vagal and sympathetic activity burnouts during a mentally demanding workday. *Psychosomatic Medicine, 68,* 583–590.

Zastowny, T. R., Kirschenbaum, D. S., & Meng, A. L. (1986). Coping skills training for children: Effects on distress before, during, and after hospitalization for surgery. *Health Psychology, 5,* 231–247.

Zautra, A. J. (2009). Resilience: One part recovery, two parts sustainability. *Journal of Personality, 77,* 1935–1943.

Zautra, A. J., Davis, M. C., Reich, J. W., Nicassario, P., Tennen, H., Finan, P., et al. (2008). Comparison of cognitive behavioral and mindfulness mediation interventions on adaptation to rheumatoid arthritis for patients with and without history of recurrent depression. *Journal of Consulting and Clinical Psychology, 76,* 408–421.

Zautra, A. J., Fasman, R., Reich, J. W., Harakas, P., Johnson, L. M., Olmsted, M. E., et al. (2005). Fibromyalgia: Evidence for deficits in positive affect regulation. *Psychosomatic Medicine, 67,* 147–155.

Zautra, A. J., Hall, J. S., & Murray, K. E. (2008). Resilience: A new integrative approach to health and mental health research. *Health Psychology Review, 2,* 41–64.

Zautra, A. J., & Manne, S. L. (1992). Coping with rheumatoid arthritis: A review of a decade of research. *Annals of Behavioral Medicine, 14,* 31–39.

Zautra, A. J., Maxwell, B. M., & Reich, J. W. (1989). Relation among physical impairment, distress, and well-being in older adults. *Journal of Behavioral Medicine, 12,* 543–557.

Zautra, A. J., Okun, M. A., Roth, S. H., & Emmanual, J. (1989). Life stress and lymphocyte alterations among patients with rheumatoid arthritis. *Health Psychology, 8,* 1–14.

Zautra, A. J., Parrish, B. P., Van Puymbroeck, C. M., Tennen, H., Davis, M. C., Reich, J. W., et al. (2007). Depression history, stress, and pain in rheumatoid arthritis patients. *Journal of Behavioral Medicine, 30,* 187–197.

Zautra, A. J., & Smith, B. W. (2001). Depression and reactivity to stress in older women with rheumatoid arthritis and osteoarthritis. *Psychosomatic Medicine, 63,* 687–696.

Zelinski, E. M., Crimmins, E., Reynolds, S., & Seeman, T. (1998). Do medical conditions affect cognition in older adults? *Health Psychology, 17,* 504–512.

Zhang, J., Kahana, B., Kahana, E., Hu, B., & Pozuelo, L. (2009). Joint modeling of longitudinal changes in depressive symptoms and mortality in a sample of community-dwelling elderly people. *Psychosomatic Medicine, 71,* 704–714.

Zhang, J., Niaura, R., Dyer, J. R., Shen, B., Todaro, J. F., McCaffery, J. M., et al. (2005). Hostility and urine norepinephrine interact to predict insulin resistance: The VA normative aging study. *Psychosomatic Medicine, 68,* 718–726.

Zhang, J., Niaura, R., Todaro, J. F., McCaffery, J. M., Shen, B., Spiro, A., III, et al. (2005). Suppressed hostility predicted hypertension incidence among middle-aged men: The normative aging study. *Journal of Behavioral Medicine, 28,* 443–454.

Zheng, Z. J., Croft, J. B., Labarthe, D., Williams, J. E., & Mensah, G. A. (2001). Racial disparity in coronary heart disease mortality in the United States: Has the gap narrowed? *Circulation 2001, 104,* 787.

Zhu, C. (2010). Science-based health care. *Science, 327,* 1429.

Zhu, S. H., Sun, J., Hawkins, S., Pierce, J., & Cummins, S. (2003). A population study of low-rate smokers: Quitting history and instability over time. *Health Psychology, 22,* 245–252.

Ziegelstein, R. C., Kim, S. Y., Kao, D., Fauerbach, J. A., Thombs, B. D., McCann, U., et al. (2005). Can doctors and nurses recognize depression in patients hospitalized with an acute myocardial infarction in the absence of formal screening? *Psychosomatic Medicine, 67,* 393–397.

Zillman, D., de Wied, M., King-Jablonski, C., & Jenzowsky, S. (1996). Drama-induced affect and pain sensitivity. *Psychosomatic Medicine, 58,* 333–341.

Zimbardo, P. G. (1969). The human choice: Individuation, reason, and order versus deindividuation, impulse, and chaos. In W. J. Arnold & D. Levine (Eds.), *Nebraska symposium on motivation.* Lincoln: University of Nebraska Press.

Zimet, G. D., Lazebnik, R., DiClemente, R. J., Anglin, T. M., Williams, P., & Ellick, E. M. (1993). The relationship of Magic Johnson's announcement of HIV infection to the AIDS attitudes of junior high school students. *Journal of Sex Research, 30,* 129–134.

Zimmer, C. (2001). Do chronic diseases have an infectious root? *Science, 293,* 1974–1977.

Zimmerman, R. (2005, March 15). Nonconventional therapies gain broader acceptance. *Wall Street Journal,* p. 24.

Zimmerman, R. S., Safer, M. A., Leventhal, H., & Baumann, L. J. (1986). The effects of health information in a worksite hypertension screening program. *Health Education Quarterly, 13,* 261–280.

Zimmermann, T., Heinrichs, N., & Baucom, D. H. (2007). "Does one size fit all?" Moderators in psychosocial interventions for breast cancer patients: A meta-analysis. *Annals of Behavioral Medicine, 34,* 225–239.

Zisook, S., Shuchter, S. R., Irwin, M., Darko, D. F., Sledge, P., & Resovsky, K. (1994). Bereavement, depression, and immune function. *Psychiatry Research, 52,* 1–10.

Zoccola, P. M., Dickerson, S. S., & Lam, S. (2009). Rumination predicts longer sleep onset latency after an acute psychosocial stressor. *Psychosomatic Medicine, 71,* 771–775.

Zola, I. K. (1966). Culture and symptoms—An analysis of patients' presenting complaints. *American Sociological Review, 31,* 615–630.

Zucker, R. A., & Gomberg, E. S. L. (1986). Etiology of alcoholism reconsidered: The case for a biopsychosocial process. *American Psychologist, 41,* 783–793.

Zuger, A. (1999, May 4). A simpler, cheaper plan for fighting high blood pressure. *New York Times,* p. D12.

CREDITS

Text and Line Art Credits

Chapter 1 **Table 1.1** From World Health Organization, *The Global Burden of Disease: A Comprehensive Assessment of Mortality and Disability from Diseases, Injuries, and Risk Factors in 1990 and Projected to 2020*, edited by C.J.L. Murray and A.D. Lopcz (Cambridge, Mass: Harvard University Press, 1996). Reprinted with the permission of the Global Burden of Disease Unit, Harvard Center for Population and Development Studies.

Chapter 3 **Figure 3.6** From Prohaska et al., In search of how people change: Applications to addictive behavior from American Psychologist 47 (1992): 1102–1114. Used by permission.

Chapter 5 **Table 5.1** From Wechsler et al., Trends in college binge drinking during a period of increased prevention efforts from Journal of American College Health 50 (2002), published by Heldref Publications, 1319 Eighteenth Street, N.W., Washington, DC 20036-1802. Copyright © 2002. **Table 5.2** From Wechsler et al., Trends in college binge drinking during a period of increased prevention efforts from Journal of American College Health 50 (2002), published by Heldref Publications, 1319 Eighteenth Street, N.W., Washington, DC 20036-1802. Copyright © 2002.

Chapter 7 **Box 7.1** From M.F. Scheier and C.S. Carver, Optimism, coping and health: Assessment and implications of generalized outcome expectancies from Health Psychology 4: 219–247. Reprinted with the permission of Lawrence Erlbaum Associates/Routledge and M.F. Scheier. **Box 7.3** From C.S. Carver, You want to measure coping but your protocol's too long: Consider the Brief COPE from International Journal of Behavioral Medicine 4: 92–100. Used by permission of the author.

Chapter 8 **Figure 8.1** From B.L. Anderson, J.T. Cacioppo, and D.C. Roberts, Delay in seeking a cancer diagnosis: Delay stages with psychophysiological comparison processes from British Journal of Social Psychology (1995: 35, figure 1). Copyright © by The British Psychological Society. Used by permission.

Chapter 10 **Figure 10.1** From R. Melzack, The McGill Pain Questionnaire: Major properties and scoring methods from Pain 1, no. 3 (September 1975): 277–299. Copyright © 1971, 1975. Reprinted with permission from Dr. R. Melzack.

Chapter 11 **Figure 11.2** From K. Petrie, D.L. Buick, J. Weinman, and R.J. Booth, Positive effects of illness reported by myocardial infarction and breast cancer patients from Journal of Psychosomatic Medicine (1999: figure 1). Copyright © 2009. Reprinted with permission from Elsevier.

Chapter 12 **Figure 12.4** From Compassion & Choices (formerly The Hemlock Society). For more information, visit www.compassionandchoices.org **Table 12.3** From R. Schultz, *Psychology of Death, Dying, and Bereavement*. Copyright © 1978 by The McGraw-Hill Companies. Reprinted with the permission of The McGraw-Hill Companies. **Box 12.5** Carol K. Littlebrandt, selected excerpts from "Death is a Personal Matter" from Newsweek (January 16, 1976). Originally published under the name Carol K. Gross. Reprinted with the permission of the author.

Chapter 14 **Figure 14.1** From Roitt, Brostoff, and Male, *Immunology, Fifth Edition* (London: Mosby International, 1998). Reprinted with the permission of the authors and Elsevier. **Figure 14.2** From Roitt, Brostoff, and Male, *Immunology, Fifth Edition* (London: Mosby International, 1998). Reprinted with the permission of the authors and Elsevier.

Chapter 15 **Figure 15.1** From Organization for Economic Co-operation and Development (2007). Reprinted by permission. **Figure 15.2** From Population Division of the Department of Economic and Social Affairs of the United Nations Secretariat, *World Population Prospects: The 2002 Revision and World Urbanization Prospects: The 2001 Revision*, http://esa.un.org/unpp (October 20, 2004). Used with permission. **Figure 15.3** From D.B. Abrams et al., Integrating individual and public health perspectives for treatment of tobacco dependence under managed health care: A combined stepped-care and matching model from Annals of Behavioral Medicine 18 (1996). Reprinted by permission of Routledge via Copyright Clearance Center.

Photo Credits:

Part Openers: 1: © David Young-Wolff/Photo Edit; 2: © Stockbyte/PunchStock RF; 3: © Stockbyte/Getty RF; 4: © Keith Brofsky/Getty RF; 5: © Bob Daemmrich/Photo Edit; 6: © David Young-Wolff/Photo Edit

Chapter 1 Opener: © McGraw-Hill Higher Education Companies, Inc./Ken Karp, photographer; p. 5: Courtesy National Library of Medicine Prints and Photographs; p. 11: © Brand X Pictures/PunchStock RF

Chapter 2 Opener: © David Young-Wolff/Photo Edit

Chapter 3 Opener: © BananaStock/PunchStock RF; p. 48: © Myrleen Ferguson Cate/Photo Edit; p. 49: © BananaStock/PunchStock RF; p. 51. © Marcy Maloy/Getty RF; p. 53: © A. Ramey/Photo Edit; p. 68: © Getty RF; p. 71: © Tony Freeman/Photo Edit; p. 73: © Michael A. Dwyer/Stock Boston

Chapter 4 Opener: © RubberBall Productions/Getty RF; p. 80: © Corbis RF; p. 85: © Ryan McVay/Getty RF; p. 86: © Dynamic Graphics/Jupiter Images RF; p. 87: © The McGraw-Hill Companies, Inc./Barry Barker, photographer; p. 89 (grain): © Comstock/PunchStock RF; p. 89 (dairy): © Mitch Hrdlicka/PhotoDisc/Getty RF; p. 89 (vegetables): © Lex van Lieshout/Image shop/Alamy RF; p. 89 (meat): © IT Stock/PunchStock RF; p. 89 (oil): © Duncan Smith/Getty RF; p. 89 (fruits): © Lex van Lieshout/Image shop/Alamy RF; p. 95: © Ryan McVay/Getty RF; p. 96: © Michael Weisbrot/The Image Works; p. 98: © Image Source/Corbis RF; p. 101: © AP Photo/Natacha Pisarenko; p. 104: © AP Photo; p. 109: © Mary Kate Denny/Photo Edit

Chapter 5 Opener: © Scott T. Baxter/Getty RF; p. 116: © Redlink/Corbis RF; p. 120: © PunchStock/Image Source RF; p. 124: © Corbis RF; p. 129: Courtesy State of Health Products, www.buttout.com 888-428-8868; p. 134: © D. Falconer/PhotoDisc/Getty RF

Chapter 6 Opener: © Grant V. Faint/Getty RF; p. 146: © Corbis RF; p. 149 (left): © Corbis/PictureQuest RF; p. 149 (right): © PhotoDisc/PunchStock RF; p. 151: © AP Photo/Victor R. Caivano; p. 153: © Corbis/